APPLIED ETHICS IN AMERICAN SOCIETY

APPLIED ETHICS IN AMERICAN SOCIETY

Diane Michelfelder Wilcox

California Polytechnic State University

William H. Wilcox

California Polytechnic State University

Under the general editorship of
Robert C. Solomon
The University of Texas - Austin

Harcourt Brace College Publishers

Fort Worth   Philadelphia   San Diego   New York   Orlando   Austin   San Antonio
Toronto   Montreal   London   Sydney   Tokyo

Publisher Christopher P. Klein
Senior Acquisitions Editor David Tatom
Developmental Editor Susan Petty
Project Editor steve Norder
Production Manager Lois West
Art Director Sue Hart

Requests for permission to make copies of any part of the work should be mailed to: Permissions Department, Harcourt Brace & Company, 6277 Sea Harbor Drive, Orlando, FL 32887-6777.

Address for Editorial Correspondence
Harcourt Brace College Publishers, 301 Commerce Street, Suite 3700, Fort Worth, TX 76102

Address for Orders
Harcourt Brace & Company, 6277 Sea Harbor Drive, Orlando, FL 32887
1-800-782-4479, or 1-800-433-0001 (in Florida)

Harcourt Brace College Publishers may provide complimentary instructional aids and supplements of supplement packages to those adopters qualified under our adoption policy. Please contact your sales representative for more information. If as an adopter or potential user you receive supplements you do not need, please return them to your sales representative or send them to:

Attn: Returns Department
Troy Warehouse
465 South Lincoln Drive
Troy, MO 63379

ISBN: 0-15-502859-6

Library of Congress Catalogue Number: 96-078327

Printed in the United States of America

6 7 8 9 0 1 2 3 4 5   039   10 9 8 7 6 5 4 3 2 1

This book is dedicated to our parents.

PREFACE

This book is primarily intended for undergraduates taking philosophy courses that address contemporary moral problems such as abortion, euthanasia, affirmative action and discrimination, welfare, and the like. These issues, as well as those of capital punishment, freedom of expression, sexual harassment, gay rights, animals and the environment, and privacy, are the ones represented in this book. In the 1990s such issues frequently find themselves in American newspaper headlines, court cases, and political campaigns. While vigorous debate on these issues is a feature of contemporary public culture, our predominant focus is on the philosophical contributions to these debates as they go on within American society today.

It has now been about twenty-five years since professional philosophers in the English speaking world have begun to address social issues in a serious way. We hope that this book will be seen to include some of the best work from that period. While we include some of the essays that have come to be regarded as classics in applied ethics (most dating from the early 1970s), we have made a conscious attempt to include a substantial amount of more recent material, mostly from the last decade.

The primary goal in selecting readings has been to include writings of high philosophical quality, but this goal has been balanced by a desire to represent diversity in positions defended and philosophical approaches taken. In addition, we have been guided by our experience in teaching undergraduates to include discussions of positions and lines of argument that we know students can find attractive. Reaching these goals has resulted in a book that provides students with a more thorough discussion of each issue represented than would be found in many recent applied ethics textbooks. Teachers are also provided with a book that contains not only essays with which they have been long familiar, but also more recent contributions to the philosophical discussion.

Our experience has taught us that it is not a challenge to get students engaged with issues in applied ethics. One of the pleasures of teaching applied ethics courses is that students generally enter them already interested in the issues at stake and frequently hold opinions about them as well. The challenges lie in developing the interest with which they enter the classroom. Students who already have their minds made up about a particular issue often need to be helped toward a greater appreciation of that issue's complexity, with an accompanying appreciation of the fact that perhaps not everyone who disagrees with them is a complete idiot. Other students often need help in understanding that the complexity of a matter need not prevent one from forming a well-reasoned opinion on it. Still other students wonder if competing opinions in matters of ethics can be rationally compared and evaluated. Our hope is that this book will help convince students that intellectually serious and respectable cases can be made for different positions on these issues without leading them into a facile subjectivism according to which any position is as reasonable as any other.

We have also tried to be responsive to students' needs in developing the chapter introductions; these aim to assist students by situating each topic addressed within the context of an overview of their philosophical and often their social context. Introductions for each reading selection highlight the main points or lines of argument and thus help lead students into the readings themselves. Suggestions for further readings at the end of each chapter will be useful for students who wish to pursue a topic further, either for a class assignment or for their own interests. Since many of our readings are best approached with at least some understanding of ethical theory, we have included readings on this topic in a separate chapter.

In working on this book, we did not work alone; and we would like to acknowledge those whose assistance contributed to and improved the final results. For their many perceptive suggestions and comments we would like to thank our reviewers: Michael Anker, Contra Costa College, California; James Broyles, Washington State University; Richard Combes, University of South Carolina, Spartanburg; Joan Whitman Hoff, Lock Haven University, Pennsylvania; Joan McGregor, Arizona State University; Mario Morelli, Western Illinois University; Evelyn Pluhar, Penn State, Fayette; Kevin Possin, Winona State University, Minnesota; Susan Rouse, Kennesaw State College, Georgia; Robert Schwager, State University of New York, Cortland; and Daniel Shapiro, Bowling Green State University, Ohio. This book also benefited from the conscientious efforts of two skilled student assistants, Barbara Cail and Juan Hernandez. Janice Stone and others in the Interlibrary Loan department of the Robert E. Kennedy Library at California Polytechnic State University were unfailingly helpful. Patricia Lindsey, as always, provided consideration and support. We are also grateful to Cindy Hoag for suggesting this project to us. Finally, we would like to express our appreciation to Claire Brantley, steve Norder, Susan Petty, and David Tatom, our editors at Harcourt Brace College Publishers, for their encouragement, expertise, and patience, which remained intact despite what must have seemed at times to them to be our best intention to try it.

CONTENTS

APPLIED ETHICS IN AMERICAN SOCIETY

Chapter 1

MORAL THEORY

In a sense, whenever anyone faced with a moral dilemma takes up that dilemma in a thoughtful and deliberative manner, that person can be said to be engaging in "applied ethics." The moral dilemmas that each of us faces throughout our lives can, however, roughly be divided into two types. Some moral problems can be of deep concern to the individual involved but of no or very little concern to society as a whole. For example, if you found an envelope on the sidewalk containing a number of hundred dollar bills, you, but not society as a whole, would find yourself faced with a moral problem. Other moral decisions that you as an individual might need to make, however, are related to issues that are debated, sometimes hotly so, by society as a whole. Whether or not to have an abortion, for example, is a moral difficulty that is at the same time both a personal moral dilemma and the subject matter of great moral controversy within American society.

In this book, our focus will be on moral problems of this second kind and on the solutions proposed to them by the authors who are represented here. Because these solutions often unfold from the perspective of a particular moral theory, understanding these solutions often involves an understanding of moral theory. Just as one can draw at least a rough distinction between the "pure" (or theoretical) sciences such as physics and the applied sciences such as civil engineering, it is possible to draw a rough distinction between moral theory and applied ethics itself.

The applied sciences are not independent of scientific theory; for instance, someone who knew nothing about physics could not be a successful engineer. Because of this dependence, physics courses are almost certainly prerequisites for courses in engineering, so an engineering textbook would not need to begin with a discussion of physics. Similarly, applied ethics is not completely independent of ethical theory, but a course in ethical theory is rarely a prerequisite for a course in applied ethics. In fact, since courses focusing on moral problems are widely thought to be more accessible than courses on moral theory, applied ethics courses are usually treated as being more introductory than theory courses. Since we are not going to assume that users of this textbook will have any background in moral theory, it is worth beginning with some attention to this field. This will help make it easier to understand many of the essays in the other chapters in this book and might confront at the outset concerns some readers might have about the enterprise of trying to decide what is right and wrong.

Issues in moral theory are frequently divided among two areas, metaethics and normative moral theory. Philosophers would disagree about how exactly these two areas should be understood, but the following characterizations would be fairly typical ways of trying to describe them.

Metaethics focuses on moral judgments and statements—judgments and statements about what is right and wrong, good and bad—and tries to understand the nature of these judgments and statements. The following set of questions constitutes an example of a metaethical inquiry: When people claim that it is wrong to lie, what are they doing? Are they describing their attitude toward lying, for example, claiming they disapprove of it? Are they expressing an attitude; are they for instance doing something that amounts to a linguistic version of sneering? Are they describing lying? Could what they say be objectively true? Or is it *just* their opinion?

Normative moral theory raises questions at a very general level about how we should live, what sorts of people we should try to be, what makes an act right or wrong, and what makes something good or bad. Examples of issues in normative moral theory can be found in the following questions: Do the ends always justify the means? In other words, is any act—no matter how brutal—potentially permissible, or even required, to bring about a worthy goal? Are some types of acts always wrong? What is it to have a good character?

It will be seen that many of the essays on the applied issues found in this book presuppose some familiarity with some basic ideas in normative moral theory. The readings in this chapter represent some of the major approaches to the questions of normative moral theory, and they should help readers to understand the later essays. None of the readings in this chapter deals directly with metaethical issues. We believe, though, that many who first approach applied ethics do so with perhaps unrecognized metaethical assumptions and concerns, which if not confronted might prevent full engagement with the issues at stake. Hence, most of this introduction will be devoted to addressing some of these assumptions and concerns.

METAETHICS

The authors of most of the essays found in this book offer arguments for some moral conclusion. Some try to provide us with reasons for thinking that some course of action really is morally required, permitted, or forbidden; some try to convince us that one public policy would be better than another; and some try to argue that we really should change the ways in which we live. The authors of these essays invite their readers to become involved in rational reflection and debate about these matters. To mention several topics that arise in this book, the essays invite us to think seriously about whether it is wrong to abort a human fetus, whether the death penalty should be abolished, and whether it matters if a species becomes extinct if its extinction would in no way harm human beings.

Some people hold metaethical positions that would challenge the possibility of rationally reflecting and arguing about moral matters, because they believe that in some sense any moral position is as "good" as any other. They believe there is something intellectually flimsy about moral inquiry, especially, perhaps, when compared with inquiries in fields such as physics or mathematics where there are provable right answers. Such views need to be taken seriously, not only because they appear to be widely held, but also because they directly challenge the very possibility of doing what this book attempts to do and of courses this book is intended to serve.

Most of the topics discussed in this book are ones about which most of us are likely to have an opinion. We are likely to have some opinion, for example, about the death penalty, about abortion, or about affirmative action. The question that needs to be addressed is this: Is *opinion* all there is to it? Are ethical positions *just* a matter of opinion? Some would maintain that each of us has his or her opinion and that anyone's opinion is as good as anyone else's. One often hears in response to a claim that some course of action would be right or wrong the retort, "That's *just* your opinion." Someone responding in this way intends to cast some type of doubt on the moral belief that has been expressed. Had the speaker said, "That's just *your* opinion," doubt would have been expressed about the rationality or expertise of the opinion's source. Usually, however, the doubt concerns the nature of the opinion and not just its source. The worry is that it is a *moral* opinion and hence could never be more than just opinion. Can there be more to moral belief than *mere* opinion? Is it possible to say that some opinions are rationally more defensible than others? Is it possible, perhaps, even rationally to persuade one another that some of our opinions should be changed? If not, then the authors whose essays appear in this book would seem to be wasting their time. Those who maintain that moral beliefs are merely opinion would seem to challenge the very possibility of the type of activity these authors want to pursue. We need therefore to take this type of challenge seriously.

Some of those who challenge the possibility of engaging in moral inquiry and debate in an intellectually serious way maintain that morality is purely subjective.[1] What exactly it would mean to claim that morality is subjective (or for that matter that it is objective) is unclear, and we will not attempt to provide any exact account of objectivity and subjectivity here. There does, however, seem to be at least some intuitive distinction between matters that are subjective and matters that are objective, and we will simply rely on that intuitive understanding.

So at an intuitive level, how do subjective and objective matters differ? Ice cream flavor preferences seem to provide a good example of a matter that is perfectly subjective. Objectively, vanilla is not better than chocolate, nor is chocolate better than vanilla. It is literally just a matter of taste. However, some things do seem objective. If I believe that George Bush is still president, then I am just wrong. I do not have the objective facts right. The question about morality might be: Are moral opinions more like a preference for vanilla ice cream or more like a belief about who is president? If morality were like ice cream flavors, then a book such as this might well be a waste of time. We do not want to argue here that there is no important sense in which morality might correctly be regarded as being subjective. We do want to suggest, however, that at least the most common reasons given by students for thinking morality is subjective are not sufficient for concluding that it is as much a waste of time to think and argue seriously about moral issues as it would be to do so about the relative merits of ice cream flavors.

What reasons might there be for thinking morality is subjective? Many who maintain that morality is subjective point to the apparent fact that there is no way to *prove* which moral beliefs are true. However, the mere fact that we cannot prove what the answer is to some question does not by itself show that there is no (objective) answer. It is easy to come up with questions to which we think there are objective answers even though no one will ever be in a position to prove what those answers are. To take an example, there is probably no way to prove exactly how much Julius Caesar weighed to the nearest milligram exactly 38 hours after his birth, but surely there is some objective answer to the question about his weight at that time. To take a slightly less silly example of a question that was widely debated in 1995, there may never be a way to *prove* whether or not O. J. Simpson is a murderer, but this certainly does not show that objectively he neither is nor is not.

Perhaps the most influential consideration leading many to believe that morality is subjective is the pervasiveness of moral controversy. Subjectivists often maintain that there is much more disagreement about moral matters than one should expect were there objective answers to moral questions. As a result, subjectivists sometimes advance what might be called the argument from disagreement. Roughly, the argument maintains that there is a tremendous amount of disagreement when it comes to moral matters, much more disagreement than there is about nonmoral matters. The best explanation of such disagreement, it is claimed, is that there are no objective answers to moral questions. If there were such answers, we would discover what many of them are and there would be less disagreement.

Sometimes those using the argument from disagreement invite us to reflect on moral controversies of the sort considered in this book. For instance, they point out that more than twenty years after abortions have been legally available in the United States, the population remains deeply divided about the rightness or wrongness of abortions. How do we account for the apparently intractable nature of moral disputes such as this one? If there were an objectively correct position concerning the morality of abortion, subjectivists maintain, one would think that after more than two decades of extensive debate there would be more agreement about what that position is. Instead, there appears to be as much disagreement as ever. Subjectivists then often proceed to contrast the pervasiveness of controversy in the moral realm with the ease with which agreement is reached on nonmoral matters. For example, nearly everyone would agree that the average elephant is larger than the average mouse. How are we to explain our ability to reach agreement about nonmoral matters and our inability to reach agreement about moral matters? The subjectivist will suggest that this difference is best explained by the existence of objectively correct positions regarding nonmoral matters and the nonexistence of such objectively correct beliefs concerning moral matters.

Subjectivists using the argument from disagreement usually unfairly exaggerate the degree of moral disagreement and understate the degree of nonmoral disagreement. It should be obvious that the version of the argument found in the preceding paragraph was unfair in its choice of examples of moral and nonmoral matters. A bias was created by the choice of a difficult moral issue and an enormously simple nonmoral issue. It would be possible to pick examples that would bias the matter in the opposite direction. Suppose, for instance, someone were to argue that the fact we can all agree that it would be wrong for a teacher to shoot a student to illustrate a point in an ethics class but cannot agree about whether or not O. J. Simpson has killed, shows that positions on moral matters can be objectively correct but positions on nonmoral matters cannot. Few would accept such an argument because it would be obvious that the examples are not typical of moral and nonmoral issues.

If we do not choose examples with an eye toward confusing matters, it should be apparent that in both the moral and nonmoral spheres there is a good bit of both agreement and disagreement. While it is obvious that we disagree with one another widely about moral matters, it is easy to overlook the fact that this disagreement takes place against a shared background of enormous moral agreement as well. For example, nearly everyone can agree that it would be wrong for affluent American parents to regard their children as a source of food. Few of us, perhaps, have thought about the fact that we hold this moral belief, and there is good reason for the fact that we have not. Since we all agree, the issue simply does not arise. We tend to notice our moral beliefs only where there is uncertainty or controversy. As a result, it is easy to believe that disagreement and controversy are a more pervasive aspect of the moral realm than of the nonmoral realm. A balanced view, however, makes it unclear whether the two realms differ in the degree to which agreement and disagreement are to be found.

Even though many people are ready to announce a belief in moral subjectivity when they are being "philosophical," many of the same people behave as if they believe that morality can be objective. Many of the ways in which we experience morality in our lives seem to presuppose a belief in at least the possibility of some moral positions being objectively better than others. Consider, for example, the following ways in which our moral experience seems to suggest at least some degree of belief in moral objectivity. Most of us have changed our minds about some moral matters during our lives. When this occurs, it does not seem as if a mere change in our moral beliefs has occurred; rather it seems as if our moral beliefs have improved. Our previous moral beliefs seem to be in some way inferior to the new ones we have adopted. This view of the change seems to presuppose the possibility of some moral views being really better than others; in other words, it seems to presuppose the possibility of moral objectivity. Another example of an activity that seems to presuppose moral objectivity arises when we face what we regard as a moral dilemma. We must choose what to do and are uncertain about what would be right. On occasion such decisions can lead to serious soul searching and sleepless nights. The worry about reaching the right decision seems again to presuppose some degree of belief in the possibility of some decisions really being right, and again this seems to be a presupposition of some form of moral objectivity.

The considerations we have raised concerning the objectivity of morality suggest two things. First, some of the most common reasons offered for the view that morality is purely subjective are not conclusive, at least not without further development. Second, the way in which many of us lead and experience our own moral lives suggests at least some belief in moral objectivity. These considerations should be sufficient for the limited purpose of this discussion, which is to argue that there could be enough objectivity in ethics to make it possible to debate moral issues in an intellectually serious and responsible manner, as the authors of the essays in this book attempt to do.

As noted earlier, many people are ready to claim a theoretical adherence to moral subjectivism even though their moral lives and experiences suggest an adherence to moral objectivism—or at least to the possibility of moral objectivism. It may be worth considering why there should be such a common discrepancy between theory and practice. To put the matter slightly differently, why do so many people claim to believe morality is purely subjective when they act as if it is not? It could be the result of having the "who's to say" thought. The "who's to say" thought arises in two ways. The first occurs when you notice that others, even others you respect, have moral beliefs different from your own. This might lead you to wonder, "Who am I to say they are wrong or to tell them how they should live?" Or some busybody comes along to tell you that you are immoral, and you react by thinking or saying, "Who are you to tell me how I should live my life?" These are both common experiences, and they might lead us to conclude that no one is to say that others are wrong because, in fact, since morality is purely subjective, no one really is wrong.

While there is probably something important and insightful about the "who's to say" thought, it is doubtful that it should be thought to lead to at least a strong version of moral subjectivism. One way of seeing this is to note that those in the grip of the "who's to say" thought probably believe that people *should not* be making (or perhaps expressing) certain judgments about others—that there is, in some situations anyway, something *wrong* with saying someone's behavior is immoral. To believe this, however, is to have a moral thought, and this moral thought would be as subjective as any other if morality is purely subjective. Suppose the busybody in the example in the preceding paragraph continues to criticize you even after you have asked who he or she is to criticize. You might want to complain that since the busybody has no standing to criticize, he or she should stop. If morality is purely subjective, however, a legitimate response to this complaint would be that your belief that criticism is unwarranted is just your subjective opinion.

There is an interpretation of the "who's to say" thought different from subjectivism, one that is more compatible with the belief that people should be hesitant about judging others. This alternative interpretation, sometimes called "moral fallibilism," holds that a reluctance to say who is right and who is wrong at least sometimes reasonably arises from an acknowledgment of the difficulty of some moral issues and the recognition that one's own moral views might be mistaken. The belief that one is fallible is merely the belief that one can make mistakes, so the belief that one is morally fallible is the belief that one is capable of making mistakes about moral matters.

Sometimes, the "who's to say" thought is a symptom of the belief that people should be more tolerant of those whose moral views differ from their own—that people should not try to impose their own moral ideals on others. Those who interpret the "who's to say" thought as support for subjectivism hope to argue that since morality is purely subjective, people should not try to impose their moral beliefs on others. There are at least two problems with this line of thought, however. First, the conclusion that one *should not* impose one's moral views on others seems itself to be a moral conclusion, and given subjectivism, it too could be nothing more than just someone's subjective opinion, no better or worse than the subjective opinion that one should impose one's ideals on others. The second problem is that nearly everyone would agree that there should be limits to moral tolerance. Few would want to tolerate, for instance, parents who believe that incest with their juvenile children is permissible. It is difficult for the subjectivist to explain why morally one should not tolerate some practices.

Moral fallibilism might be able to explain more adequately both why some differences should be tolerated and why there should be a limit to toleration. Insofar as we believe that it is possible to make mistakes about our moral beliefs, the more likely we think it is that we have made a mistake, the less likely we would be to impose our possibly mistaken beliefs on others. Furthermore, the more people who seem to be reasonable and of good will who disagree with us, the less confident we are likely to be in our own moral beliefs. Even fallibilists are going to be confident of some of their beliefs, however. For example, most of us would be confident that it is wrong to engage in incest with one's juvenile children. Part of our confidence might arise from the fact that we do not often (if ever) run into people who disagree and who seem both otherwise reasonable and of good will. When we are quite confident of our opinion concerning some moral matter, and when we believe that matter is of great moral importance, the more likely it is that we should believe that those who wish to act contrary to that opinion should not be tolerated.

Moral fallibilism might account better than subjectivism for what is intuitively attractive about the "who's to say" thought. Furthermore, moral fallibilism is incompatible with at least the most straightforward forms of moral subjectivism. The key belief of the fallibilist is that his or her moral beliefs might be mistaken, but if moral beliefs are nothing but subjective matters of opinion, then it would seem to be impossible to be mistaken. To believe that one's own moral beliefs could be mistaken is to believe that some moral beliefs can truly be better than others, and this latter belief seems to require room for at least some objectivity in morality.

In this section, our purpose has been very limited. It has not been to argue that morality is not subjective, but rather to argue that at least a case can be made for moral objectivity. The issues involved in the debate between those who maintain that morality is objective and those who claim it is not are enormously complex, and we do not intend this discussion to make a contribution to this debate. Our goal has been a more modest one of trying to convince those nonspecialists who come to moral philosophy with a strong suspicion that morality is subjective, and who consequently might be tempted to dismiss the possibility of serious and fruitful moral discussion, that the attempt to answer moral questions is not obviously futile.

NORMATIVE MORAL THEORY

The readings in this chapter represent four different approaches to normative moral theory—the attempt to answer at a very general level questions about how we should live and what sorts of people we should be. The first two readings, those from John Stuart Mill and Immanuel Kant, represent apparently conflicting approaches to these questions known as consequentialism and deontology respectively, approaches that have dominated Western philosophical ethics for the last two centuries. Philippa Foot's essay advocates a return to an approach known as virtue ethics that had been more characteristic of normative moral theory in ancient ethics, and Susan Sherwin explains both feminine and feminist reactions to traditional moral theory.

Consequentialists and deontologists differ over the role the future should play in determining how we should act. At least roughly, consequentialists maintain that the rightness or wrongness of what we do depends entirely on the goodness or badness of the consequences of what we do—on the goodness or badness of the future effects of our actions. Deontologists, on the other hand, deny that the future effects of our behavior are the only morally relevant features of our actions. Instead, they maintain that we have duties to perform or not to perform certain acts and that what we have a duty to do is not completely determined by the consequences of what we do. Utilitarianism is the most influential consequentialist moral theory, and as developed by Mill, it maintains that the aim of our acts should be to increase the amount of happiness in the world as a whole. Kant, on the other hand, maintains that the rightness of an act is not determined by its goal or its consequences but rather by the fact that the act is motivated by the recognition of its being required by duty. While the reading from Kant focuses primarily on the behavior of individuals, John Rawls in his contribution to the chapter uses a basically Kantian outlook to describe what he believes would be a just society.

Both consequentialist and deontological approaches to moral theory have been under attack over the last couple of decades. Those who advocate an ethical approach based on the ideas of virtues and vices believe that both utilitarians and Kantians focus too much on what a moral agent does, consequently neglecting questions about what type of character a moral agent should have. Another challenge to both utilitarianism and Kantianism has been sparked by feminist concerns that these approaches to moral theory have in some way ignored moral outlooks that are characteristic of the lives of women or do not adequately address the needs of women. The essays by Foot and Sherwin address these challenges to consequentialism and deontology.

NOTE

1. A slightly different challenge is provided by moral relativism. Relativists do not deny that there can be right (or true) answers to moral questions, but do deny that there are universal right answers. They hold instead that the right answer varies from group to group, or in some cases individual to individual. Much of our discussion of moral subjectivism could be applied to moral relativism as well.

What Utilitarianism Is
John Stuart Mill

John Stuart Mill (1806-1873) was an important nineteenth century British philosopher who is best known for his work in moral and political philosophy, but who also made significant contributions to other areas of philosophy, notably logic and epistemology. In these selections from his work *Utilitarianism*, Mill attempts to explain what the moral theory of utilitarianism is and to answer some of the most common objections to it.

Utilitarianism is a consequentialist moral theory maintaining that the rightness of acts depends entirely on the ways in which they affect happiness. According to Mill, an act is right to the degree to which it promotes happiness, where the promotion of happiness includes decreasing unhappiness. Furthermore, Mill accepts a hedonistic account of happiness according to which happiness consists simply of pleasure and the absence of pain. Among the objections that Mill attempts to counter in this selection is the belief that the pursuit of mere pleasure is degrading for human beings. Mill responds that the people raising such an objection fail to consider that human beings are capable of deriving pleasure from intellectual and moral activities. These "higher" pleasures, Mill maintains, are qualitatively better than pleasures of the body and a happy human life must contain them.

Mill also stresses that utilitarians are not guided by the pursuit of their own personal happiness but by the happiness of everyone that is affected by their behavior. Utilitarianism requires in this sense strict impartiality. When faced between options that will bring some happiness to oneself or some greater happiness to another, the impartiality of utilitarianism would require the choice of the other's happiness. Many complain that this impartial aspect of utilitarianism is too demanding for actual human beings, since it demands from them much more than they are willing to give. Mill attempts to respond by maintaining that the objection ignores a distinction between a standard that explains what behavior is morally required and what would be an appropriate motive for behaving morally. This complaint about the demandingness of utilitarianism, and attempts to answer it roughly along the lines suggested by Mill, continue to play a major role in discussions of utilitarianism taking place in contemporary moral philosophy. Many of the other objections to utilitarianism discussed by Mill in the remainder of this piece also are still debated by moral philosophers.

The creed which accepts as the foundation of morals "utility" or the "greatest happiness principle" holds that actions are right in proportion as they tend to promote happiness; wrong as they tend to produce the reverse of happiness. By happiness is intended pleasure and the absence of pain; by unhappiness, pain and the privation of pleasure. To give a clear view of the moral standard set up by the theory, much more requires to be said; in particular, what things

---

From *Utilitarianism*, by John Stuart Mill (1861).

it includes in the ideas of pain and pleasure, and to what extent this is left an open question. But these supplementary explanations do not affect the theory of life on which this theory of morality is grounded—namely, that pleasure and freedom from pain are the only things desirable as ends; and that all desirable things (which are as numerous in the utilitarian as in any other scheme) are desirable either for pleasure inherent in themselves or as means to the promotion of pleasure and the prevention of pain.

Now such a theory of life excites in many minds, and among them in some of the most estimable in feeling and purpose, inveterate dislike. To suppose that life has (as they express it) no higher end than pleasure—no better and nobler object of desire and pursuit—they designate as utterly mean and groveling, as a doctrine worthy only of swine, to whom the followers of Epicurus were, at a very early period, contemptuously likened; and modern holders of the doctrine are occasionally made the subject of equally polite comparisons by its German, French, and English assailants.

When thus attacked, the Epicureans have always answered that it is not they, but their accusers, who represent human nature in a degrading light, since the accusation supposes human beings to be capable of no pleasures except those of which swine are capable. If this supposition were true, the charge could not be gainsaid, but would then be no longer an imputation; for if the sources of pleasure were precisely the same to human beings and to swine, the rule of life which is good enough for the one would be good enough for the other. The comparison of the Epicurean life to that of beasts is felt as degrading, precisely because a beast's pleasures do not satisfy a human being's conceptions of happiness. Human beings have faculties more elevated than the animal appetites and, when once made conscious of them, do not regard anything as happiness which does not include their gratification. I do not indeed, consider the Epicureans to have been by any means faultless in drawing out their scheme of consequences from the utilitarian principle. To do this in any sufficient manner, many Stoic, as well as Christian, elements require to be included. But there is no known Epicurean theory of life which does not assign to the pleasures of the intellect, of the feelings and imagination, and of the moral sentiments a much higher value as pleasures than to those of mere sensation. It must be admitted, however, that utilitarian writers in general have placed the superiority of mental over bodily pleasures chiefly in the greater permanency, safety, uncostliness, etc., of the former—that is, in their circumstantial advantages rather than in their intrinsic nature. And on all these points utilitarians have fully proved their case; but they might have taken the other and, as it may be called, higher ground with entire consistency. It is quiet compatible with the principle of utility to recognize the fact that some kinds of pleasure are more desirable and more valuable than others. It would be absurd that, while in estimating all other things quality is considered as well as quantity, the estimation of pleasure should be supposed to depend on quantity alone.

If I am asked what I mean by difference of quality in pleasures, or what makes one pleasure more valuable than another, merely as a pleasure, except its being greater in amount, there is but one possible answer. Of two pleasures, if there be one to which all or almost all who have experience of both give a decided preference, irrespective of any feeling of moral obligation to prefer it, that is the more desirable pleasure. If one of the two is, by those who are competently acquainted with both, placed so far above the other that they prefer it, even though knowing it to be attended with a greater amount of discontent, and would not resign it for any quantity of the other pleasure which their nature is capable of, we are justified in ascribing to the preferred enjoyment a superiority in quality so far outweighing quantity as to render it, in comparison, of small account.

Now it is an unquestionable fact that those who are equally acquainted with and equally capable of appreciating and enjoying both do give a most marked preference to the manner of existence which employs their higher faculties. Few human creatures would consent to be changed into any of the lower animals for a promise of the fullest allowance of a beast's pleasures; no intelligent human being would consent to be a fool, no instructed person would be an ignoramus, no person of feeling and conscience would be selfish and base, even though they should be persuaded that the fool, the dunce, or the rascal is better satisfied with his lot than they are with theirs. They would not resign what they possess more than he for the most complete satisfaction of all the desires which they have in common with him. If they ever fancy they would, it is only in cases of unhappiness so extreme that to escape from it they would exchange their lot for almost any other, however undesirable in their own eyes. A being of higher faculties requires more to make him happy, is capable probably of more acute suffering, and certainly accessible to it at more points than one of an inferior type; but in spite of these liabilities, he can never really wish to sink into what he feels to be a lower grade of existence. We may give what explanation we please of this unwillingness; we may attribute it to pride, a name which is given indiscriminately to some of the most and to some of the least estimable feelings of which mankind are capable; we may refer it to the love of liberty and personal independence, an appeal to which was with the Stoics one of the most effective means for the inculcation of it; to the love of power or to the love of excitement, both of which do really enter into and contribute to it; but its most appropriate appellation is a sense of dignity, which all human beings possess in one form or other, and in some, though by no means in exact, proportion to their higher faculties, and which is so essential a part of the happiness of those in whom it is strong that nothing which conflicts with it could be otherwise than momentarily an object of desire to them. Whoever supposes that this preference takes place at a sacrifice of happiness—that the superior being, in anything like equal circumstances, is not happier than the inferior—confounds the two very different ideas of happiness and content. It is indisputable that the being whose capacities of enjoyment are low has the greatest chance of having them fully satisfied; and a highly endowed being will always feel that any happiness which he can look for, as the world is constituted, is imperfect.

But he can learn to bear its imperfections if they are at all bearable; and they will not make him envy the being who is indeed unconscious of the imperfections, but only because he feels not at all the good which those imperfections qualify. It is better to be a human being dissatisfied than a pig satisfied; better to be Socrates dissatisfied than a fool satisfied. And if the fool, or the pig, are of a different opinion, it is because they only know their own side of the question. The other party to the comparison knows both sides.

It may be objected that many who are capable of the higher pleasures occasionally, under the influence of temptation, postpone them to the lower. But this is quite compatible with a full appreciation of the intrinsic superiority of the higher. Men often, from infirmity of character, make their election for the nearer good, though they know it to be the less valuable; and this no less when the choice is between two bodily pleasures than when it is between bodily and mental. They pursue sensual indulgences to the injury of health, though perfectly aware that health is the greater good. It may be further objected that many who begin with youthful enthusiasm for everything noble, as they advance in years, sink into indolence and selfishness. But I do not believe that those who undergo this very common change voluntarily choose the lower description of pleasures in preference to the higher. I believe that, before they devote themselves exclusively to the one, they have already become incapable of the other. Capacity for the nobler feelings is in most natures a very tender plant, easily killed, not only by hostile influences, but by mere want of sustenance; and in the majority of young persons it speedily dies away if the occupations to which their position in life has devoted them, and the society into which it has thrown them, are not favorable to keeping that higher capacity in exercise. Men lose their high aspirations as they lose their intellectual tastes, because they have not time or opportunity for indulging them; and they addict themselves to inferior pleasures, not because they deliberately prefer them, but because they are either the only ones to which they have access or the only ones which they are any longer capable of enjoying. It may be questioned whether anyone who has remained equally susceptible to both classes of pleasures ever knowingly and calmly preferred the lower, though many, in all ages, have broken down in an ineffectual attempt to combine both.

From this verdict of the only competent judges, I apprehend there can be no appeal. On a question which is the best worth having of two pleasures, or which of two modes of existence is the most grateful to the feelings, apart from its moral attributes and from its consequences, the judgment of these who are qualified by knowledge of both, or, if they differ, that of the majority among them, must be admitted as final. And there needs be the less hesitation to accept this judgment respecting the quality of pleasures, since there is no other tribunal to be referred to even on the question of quantity. What means are there of determining which is the acutest of two pains, or the intensest of two pleasurable sensations, except the general suffrage of those who are familiar with both? Neither pains nor pleasures are homogeneous, and pain is always heterogeneous with pleasure. What is there to decide whether a particular pleasure is worth purchasing at the cost of a particular pain, except the feelings and judgment of the experienced? When, therefore, those feelings and judgment declare the pleasures derived from the higher faculties to be preferable *in kind,* apart from the question of intensity, to those of which the animal nature, disjoined from the higher faculties, is susceptible, they are entitled on this subject to the same regard.

I have dwelt on this point as being part of a perfectly just conception of utility or happiness considered as the directive rule of human conduct. But it is by no means an indispensable condition to the acceptance of the utilitarian standard; for that standard is not the agent's own greatest happiness, but the greatest amount of happiness altogether; and if it may possibly be doubted whether a noble character is always the happier for its nobleness, there can be no doubt that it makes other people happier, and that the world in general is immensely a gainer by it. Utilitarianism, therefore, could only attain its end by the general cultivation of nobleness of character, even if each individual were only benefitted by the nobleness of others, and his own, so far as happiness is concerned, were a sheer deduction from the benefit. But the bare enunciation of such an absurdity as this last renders refutation superfluous.

According to the greatest happiness principle, as above explained, the ultimate end, with reference to and for the sake of which all other things are desirable—whether we are considering our own good or that of other people—is an existence exempt as far as possible from pain, and as rich as possible in enjoyments, both in point of quantity and quality; the test of quality and the rule for measuring it against quantity being the preference felt by those who, in their opportunities of experience, to which must be added their habits of self-consciousness and self-observation, are best furnished with the means of comparison. This, being according to the utilitarian opinion the end of human action, is necessarily also the standard of morality, which may accordingly be defined "the rules and precepts for human conduct," by the observance of which an existence such as has been described might be, to the greatest extent possible, secured to all mankind; and not to them only, but, so far as the nature of things admits, to the whole sentient creation. . . .

Unquestionably it is possible to do without happiness; it is done involuntarily by nineteen-twentieths of mankind, even in those parts of our present world which are least deep in barbarism; and it often has to be done voluntarily by the hero or the martyr, for the sake of something which he prizes more than his individual happiness. But this something, what is it, unless the happiness of others or some of the requisites of happiness? It is noble to be capable of resigning entirely one's own portion of happiness, or chances of it; but, after all, this self-sacrifice must be for some end; it is not its own end; and if we are told that its end is not happiness but virtue, which is better than happiness, I ask, would the sacrifice be made if the hero or martyr did not believe that it would earn for others immunity from similar sacrifices? Would it be made if he thought that his renunciation of happiness for himself would produce no fruit for any of his fellow creatures, but to make their lot like his and place them also in the condition of persons who have renounced happiness? All honor to those who can abnegate for themselves the personal enjoyment of life when by such renunciation they contribute worthily to increase the amount of happiness in the world; but he who does it or professes to do it for any other purpose is no more deserving of admiration than the ascetic mounted on his pillar. He may be an inspiriting proof of what men *can* do, but assuredly not an example of what they *should.*

Though it is only in a very imperfect state of the world's arrangements that anyone can best serve the happiness of others by the absolute sacrifice of his own, yet, so long as the world is in that imperfect state, I fully acknowledge that the readiness to make such a sacrifice is the highest virtue which can be found in man. I will add that in this condition of the world, paradoxical as the assertion may be, the conscious ability to do without happiness gives the best prospect of realizing such happiness as is attainable. For nothing except that consciousness can raise a person above the chances of life by making him feel that, let fate and fortune do their worst, they have not power to subdue him; which, once felt, frees him from excess of anxiety concerning the evils of life and enables him, like many a Stoic in the worst times of the Roman Empire, to cultivate in tranquillity the sources of satisfaction accessible to him, without concerning himself about the uncertainty of their duration any more than about their inevitable end.

Meanwhile, let utilitarians never cease to claim the morality of self-devotion as a possession which belongs by as good a right to them as either to the stoic or to the Transcendentalist. The utilitarian morality does recognize in human beings the power of sacrificing their own greatest good for the good of others. It only refuses to admit that the sacrifice is itself a good. A sacrifice which does not increase or tend to increase the sum total of happiness, it considers as wasted. The only self-renunciation which it applauds is devotion to the happiness, or to some of the means of happiness, of others, either of mankind collectively or of individuals within the limits imposed by the collective interests of mankind.

I must again repeat what the assailants of utilitarianism seldom have the justice to acknowledge, that the happiness which forms the utilitarian standard of what is right in conduct is not the agent's own happiness but that of all concerned. As between his own happiness and that of others, utilitarianism requires him to be as strictly impartial as a disinterested and benevolent spectator. In the golden rule of Jesus of Nazareth, we read the complete spirit of the ethics of utility. "To do as you would be done by," and "to love your neighbor as yourself," constitute the ideal perfection of utilitarian morality. As the means of making the nearest approach to this ideal, utility would enjoin, first, that laws and social arrangements should place the happiness or (as, speaking practically, it may be called) the interest of every individual as nearly as possible in harmony with the interest of the whole; and, secondly, that education and opinion, which have so vast a power over human character, should so use that power as to establish in the mind of every individual an indissoluble association between his own happiness and the good of the whole, especially between his own happiness and the practice of such modes of conduct, negative and positive, as regard for the universal happiness prescribes; so that not only he may be unable to conceive the possibility of happiness to himself, consistently with conduct opposed to the general good, but also that a direct impulse to promote the general good may be in every individual one of the habitual motives of action, and the sentiments connected therewith may fill a large and prominent place in every human being's sentient existence. If the impugners of the utilitarian morality represented it to their own minds in this its true character, I know not what recommendation possessed by any other morality they could possibly affirm to be wanting to it; what more beautiful or more exalted developments of human nature any other ethical system can be supposed to foster, or what springs of action, not accessible to the utilitarian, such systems rely on for giving effect to their mandates.

The objectors to utilitarianism cannot always be charged with representing it in a discreditable light. On the contrary, those among them who entertain anything like a just idea of its disinterested character sometimes find fault with its standard as being too high for humanity. They say it is exacting too much to require that people shall always act from the inducement of promoting the general interest of society. But this is to mistake the very meaning of a standard of morals and confound the rule of action with the motive of it. It is the business of ethics to tell us what are our duties, or by what test we may know them; but no system of ethics requires that the sole motive of all we do shall be a feeling of duty; on the contrary, ninety-nine hundredths of all our actions are done from other motives, and rightly so done if the rule of duty does not condemn them. It is the more unjust to utilitarianism that this particular misapprehension should be made a ground of objection to it, inasmuch as utilitarian moralists have gone beyond almost all others in affirming that the motive has nothing to do with the morality of the action, though much with the worth of the agent. He who saves a fellow creature from drowning does what is morally right, whether his motive be duty or the hope of being paid for his trouble; he who betrays the friend that trusts him is guilty of a crime, even if his object be to serve another friend to whom he is under greater obligations.[1] But to speak only of actions done from the motive of duty, and in direct obedience to principle: it is a misapprehension of the utilitarian mode of thought to conceive it as implying that people would fix their minds upon so wide a generality as the world, or society at large. The great majority of good actions are intended not for the benefit of the world, but for that of individuals, of which the good of the world is made up; and the thoughts of the most virtuous man need not on these occasions travel beyond the particular persons concerned, except so far as is necessary to assure himself that in benefiting them he is not violating the rights, that is, the legitimate and authorized expectations, of anyone else. The multiplication of happiness is, according to the utilitarian ethics, the object of virtue: the occasions on which any person (except one in a thousand) has it in his power to do this on an extended scale—in other words, to be a public benefactor—are but exceptional; and on these occasions alone is he called on to consider public utility; in every other case, private utility, the interest or happiness of some few persons, is all he has to attend to. Those alone the influence of whose actions extends to society in general need concern themselves habitually about so large an object. In the case of abstinences indeed—of things which people forbear to do from moral considerations, though the consequences in the particular case might be beneficial—it would be unworthy of an intelligent agent not to be consciously aware that the action is of a class which, if practiced generally, would be generally injurious, and that this is the ground of the obligation to abstain from it. The amount of regard for the public interest implied in this recognition is no greater than is demanded by every system of morals, for they all enjoin to abstain from whatever is manifestly pernicious to society. . . .

It may not be superfluous to notice a few more of the common misapprehensions of utilitarian ethics, even those which are so obvious and gross that it might appear impossible for any person of candor and intelligence to fall into them; since persons, even of considerable mental endowment often give themselves so little trouble to understand the bearings of any opinion against which they entertain a prejudice, and men are in general so little conscious of this voluntary ignorance as a defect that the vulgarest misunderstandings of ethical doctrines are continually met with in the deliberate writings of persons of the greatest pretensions both to high principle and to philosophy. We not uncommonly hear the doctrine of utility inveighed against a *godless* doctrine. If it be necessary to say anything at all against so mere an assumption, we may say that the question depends upon what idea we have formed of the moral character of the Deity. If it be a true belief that God desires, above all things, the happiness of his creatures, and that this was his purpose in their creation, utility is not only not a godless doctrine, but more profoundly religious than any other. If it be meant that utilitarianism does not recognize the revealed will of God as the supreme law of morals, I answer that a utilitarian who believes in the perfect goodness and wisdom of *God* necessarily believes that whatever God has thought fit to reveal on the subject of morals must fulfill the requirements of utility in a supreme degree. But others besides utilitarians have been of opinion that the Christian revelation was intended, and is fitted, to inform the hearts and minds of mankind with a spirit which should enable them to find for themselves what is right, and incline them to do it when found, rather than to tell them, except in a very general way, what it is; and that we need a doctrine of ethics, carefully followed out, to *interpret* to us the will of God. Whether this opinion is correct or not, it is superfluous here to discuss; since whatever aid religion, either natural or revealed, can afford to ethical investigation is as open to the utilitarian moralist as to any other. He can use it as the testimony of God to the usefulness or hurtfulness of any given course of action by as good a right as others can use it for the indication of a transcendental law having no connection with usefulness or with happiness.

Again, utility is often summarily stigmatized as an immoral doctrine by giving it the name of "expediency," and taking advantage of the popular use of that term to contrast it with principle. But the expedient, in the sense in which it is opposed to the right, generally means that which is expedient for the particular interest of the agent himself: as when a minister sacrifices the interests of his country to keep himself in place. When it means anything better than this, it means that which is expedient for some immediate object, some temporary purpose, but which violates a rule whose observance is expedient in a much higher degree. The expedient, in this sense, instead of being the same thing with the useful, is a branch of the hurtful. Thus it would often be expedient, for the purpose of getting over some momentary embarrassment, or attaining some object immediately useful to ourselves or others, to tell a lie. But inasmuch as the cultivation in ourselves of a sensitive feeling on the subject of veracity is one of the most useful, and the enfeeblement of that feeling one of the most hurtful, things to which our conduct can be instrumental; and inasmuch as any, even unintentional, deviation from truth does that much toward weakening the trustworthiness of human assertion, which is not only the principal support of all present social well-being, but the insufficiency of which does more than any one thing that can be named to keep back civilization, virtue, everything on which human happiness on the largest scale depends—we feel that the violation, for a present advantage, of a rule of such transcendent expediency is not expedient, and that he who, for the sake of convenience to himself or to some other individual, does what depends on him to deprive mankind of the good, and inflict upon them the evil, involved in the greater or less reliance which they can place in each other's words, acts the part of one of their worst enemies. Yet that even this rule, sacred as it is, admits of possible exceptions is acknowledged by all moralists; the chief of which is when the withholding of some fact (as of information from a malefactor, or of bad news from a person dangerously ill) would save an individual (especially an individual other than oneself) from great and unmerited evil, and when the withholding can only be effected by denial. But in order that the exception may not extend itself beyond the need, and may have the least possible effect in weakening reliance on veracity, it ought to be recognized and, if possible, its limits defined; and, if the principle of utility is good for anything, it must be good for weighing these conflicting utilities against one another and marking out the region within which one or the other preponderates.

Again, defenders of utility often find themselves called upon to reply to such objections as this—that there is not time, previous to action, for calculating and weighing the effects of any line of conduct on the general happiness. This is exactly as if anyone were to say that it is impossible to guide our conduct by Christianity because there is not time, on every occasion on which anything has to be done, to read through the Old and New Testaments. The answer to the objection is that there has been ample time, namely, the whole past duration of the human species. During all that time mankind have been learning by experience the tendencies of actions; on which experience all the prudence as well as all the morality of life are dependent. People talk as if the commencement of this course of experience had hitherto been put off, and as if, at the moment when some man feels tempted to meddle with the property or life of another, he had to begin considering for the first time whether murder and theft are injurious to human happiness. Even then I do not think that he would find the question very puzzling; but, at all events, the matter is now done to his hand. It is truly a whimsical supposition that, if mankind were agreed in considering utility to be the test of morality, they would remain without any agreement as to what *is* useful, and would take no measures for having their notions on the subject taught to the young and enforced by law and opinion. There is no difficulty in proving any ethical standard whatever to work ill if we suppose universal idiocy to be conjoined with it; but on any hypothesis short of that, mankind must by this time have acquired positive beliefs as to the effects of some actions on their happiness; and the beliefs which have thus come down are the rules of morality for the multitude, and for the philosopher until he has succeeded in finding better. That philosophers might easily do this, even now, on many subjects; that the received code of ethics is by no means of divine right; and that mankind have still much to learn as to the effects of actions on the general happiness, I admit or rather earnestly maintain. The corollaries from the principle of utility, like the precepts of every practical art, admit of indefinite improvement, and, in a progressive state of the human mind, their improvement is perpetually going on. But to consider the rules of morality as improvable is one thing; to pass over the intermediate generalization entirely and endeavor to test each individual action directly by the first principle is another. It is a strange notion that the acknowledgment of a first principle is inconsistent with the admission of secondary ones. To inform a traveler respecting the place of his ultimate destination is not to forbid the use of landmarks and direction-posts on the way. The proposition that happiness is the end and aim of morality does not mean that no road ought to be laid down to that goal, or that persons going thither should not be advised to take one direction rather than another. Men really ought to leave off talking a kind of nonsense on this subject, which they would neither talk nor listen to on other matters of practical concernment. Nobody argues that the art of navigation is not founded on astronomy because sailors cannot wait to calculate the Nautical Almanac. Being rational creatures, they go to sea with it ready calculated; and all rational creatures go out upon the sea of life with their minds made up on the common questions of right and wrong, as well as on many of the far more difficult questions of wise and foolish. And this, as long as foresight is a human quality, it is to be presumed they will continue to do. Whatever we adopt as the fundamental principle of morality, we require subordinate principles to apply it by; the impossibility of doing without them, being common to all systems, can afford no argument against any one in particular; but gravely to argue as if no such secondary principles could be had, and as if mankind had remained till now, and always must remain, without drawing any general conclusions from the experience of human life is as high a pitch, I think, as absurdity has ever reached in philosophical controversy.

The remainder of the stock arguments against utilitarianism mostly consist in laying to its charge the common infirmities of human nature, and the general difficulties which embarrass conscientious persons in shaping their course through life. We are told that a utilitarian will be apt to make his own particular case an exception to moral rules, and, when under temptation, will see a utility in the breach of a rule, greater than he will see in its observance. But is utility the only creed which is able to furnish us with excuses for evil-doing and means of cheating our own conscience? They are afforded in abundance by all doctrines which recognize as a fact in morals the existence of conflicting considerations, which all doctrines do that have been believed by sane persons. It is not the fault of any creed, but of the complicated nature of human affairs, that rules of conduct cannot be so framed as to require no exceptions, and that hardly any kind of action can safely be laid down as either always obligatory or always condemnable. There is no ethical creed which does not temper the rigidity of its laws by giving a certain latitude, under the moral responsibility of the agent, for accommodation to peculiarities of circumstances; and under every creed, at the opening thus made, self-deception and dishonest casuistry get in. There exists no moral system under which there do not arise unequivocal cases of conflicting obligation. These are the real difficulties, the knotty points both in the theory of ethics and in the conscientious guidance of personal conduct. They are overcome practically, with greater or with less success, according to the intellect and virtue of the individual; but it can hardly be pretended that anyone will be the less qualified for dealing with them, from possessing an ultimate standard to which conflicting rights and duties can be referred. If utility is the ultimate source of moral obligations, utility may be invoked to decide between them when their demands are incompatible. Though the application of the standard may be difficult, it is better than none at all; while in other systems, the moral laws all claiming independent authority, there is no common umpire entitled to interfere between them; their claims to precedence one over another rest on little better than sophistry, and, unless determined, as they generally are, by the unacknowledged influence of consideration of utility, afford a free scope for the action of personal desires and partialities. We must remember that only in these cases of conflict between secondary principles is it requisite that first principles should be appealed to. There is no case of moral obligation in which some secondary principle is not involved; and if only one, there can seldom be any real doubt which one it is, in the mind of any person by whom the principle itself is recognized.

NOTE

1. An opponent, whose intellectual and moral fairness it is a pleasure to acknowledge (the Rev. J. Llewellyn Davies), has objected to this passage, saying, "Surely

the rightness or wrongness of saving a man from drowning does depend very much upon the motive with which it is done. Suppose that a tyrant, when his enemy jumped into the sea to escape from him, saved him from drowning simply in order that he might inflict upon him more exquisite tortures, would it tend to clearness to speak of that rescue as 'a morally right action'? Or suppose again, according to one of the stock illustrations of ethical inquiries, that a man betrayed a trust received from a friend, because the discharge of it would fatally injure that friend himself or someone belonging to him, would utilitarianism compel one to call the betrayal 'a crime' as much as if it had been done from the meanest motive?"

I submit that he who saves another from drowning in order to kill him by torture afterwards does not differ only in motive from him who does the same thing from duty or benevolence; the act itself is different. The rescue of the man is, in the case supposed, only the necessary first step of an act far more atrocious than leaving him to drown would have been. Had Mr. Davies said, "The rightness or wrongness of saving a man from drowning does depend very much"—not upon the motive, but—"upon the *intention*," no utilitarian would have differed from him. Mr. Davies, by an oversight too common not to be quite venial, has in this case confounded the very different ideas of Motive and Intention. There is no point which utilitarian thinkers (and Bentham pre-eminently) have taken more pains to illustrate than this. The morality of the action depends entirely upon the intention—that is, upon what the agent *wills to do*. But the motive, that is, the feeling which makes him will so to do, if it makes no difference in the act, makes none in the morality: though it makes a great difference in our moral estimation of the agent, especially if it indicates a good or a bad habitual *disposition*—a bent of character from which useful, or from which hurtful actions are likely to arise.

Selections from *Groundwork of the Metaphysic of Morals*
Immanuel Kant

Immanuel Kant (1724–1804) is regarded by nearly all academic philosophers as one of the most important Western philosophers, having reshaped the way in which issues in epistemology, metaphysics, and ethics are conceived. Reprinted here are portions of his most widely read work in moral philosophy. In these portions, he first argues that the good will is the only thing that is good without qualification, where a person with a good will is one who acts because of the recognition that an act is demanded by duty rather than acting because of his or her inclinations. Furthermore, Kant maintains that our duties must consist of a categorical imperative rather than hypothetical imperatives. Hypothetical imperatives portray acts as being necessary for the pursuit of some further end, whereas a categorical imperative portrays an act as being demanded by rationality regardless of what ends one might have. While Kant's terminology can be difficult to understand, the view that morality must consist of categorical imperatives is roughly a restatement of the ordinary view that morality binds us even if it requires us to do something we would prefer not to do.

In the final sections, Kant gives two of his formulations of the categorical imperative. The first requires that we act only on maxims that we can will to be universal laws. As rational beings, Kant believes that we do things for reasons, and a maxim is a principle that specifies our reasons for doing what we do. The first formulation of the categorical imperative requires that we follow only those principles that we would be willing to have universally followed—that is, followed by everyone whenever the principles apply. In part, Kant is demanding that we not be hypocrites, people with one set of principles by which to judge our own behavior and another set of principles by which to judge the behavior of others. Instead, the categorical imperative demands that we be principled people who live by principles we are willing to have impartially applied to everyone. It should be noted that while Kant's view is similar to the ordinary thought that one should not do something unless one is willing to have everyone do it, Kant's categorical imperative is not actually applied to acts but rather to the principles underlying our acts.

The second formulation of the categorical imperative included in this selection requires us to treat humanity as an end in itself and never merely as a means. It is fairly easy to see some acts that would be prohibited by this principle; one should not use a human being as a thing to be manipulated purely for one's own purposes. It is somewhat less clear, though, what sort of behavior is required. Kant believed that treating human beings as ends in themselves is related to acting only on maxims that one could will to be universal laws. Treating people as ends in themselves is at least partly a matter of treating them according to principles that would be rationally acceptable to them as well as to oneself. When one party's behavior toward another is allowed by principles that both parties could rationally accept, then neither is being treated as a mere means.

[*THE GOOD WILL*]

It is impossible to conceive anything at all in the world, or even out of it, which can be taken as good without qualification, except a *good will.* Intelligence, wit, judgement, and any other *talents* of the mind we may care to name, or courage, resolution, and constancy of purpose, as qualities of *temperament,* are without doubt good and desirable in many respects; but they can also be extremely bad and hurtful when the will is not good which has to make use of these gifts of nature, and which for this reason has the term *'character'* applied to its peculiar quality. It is exactly the same with *gifts of fortune.* Power, wealth, honour, even health and that complete well-being and contentment with one's state which goes by the name of *'happiness'*, produce boldness, and as a consequence often over-boldness as well, unless a good will is present by which their influence on the mind—and so too the whole principle of action—may be corrected and adjusted to universal ends; not to mention that a rational and impartial spectator can never feel approval in contemplating the uninterrupted prosperity of a being graced by no touch of a pure and good will, and that consequently a good will seems to constitute the indispensable condition of our very worthiness to be happy.

Some qualities are even helpful to this good will itself and can make its task very much easier. They have none the less no inner unconditioned worth, but rather presuppose a good will which sets a limit to the esteem in which they are rightly held and does not permit us to regard them as absolutely good. Moderation in affections and passions, self-control, and sober reflection are not only good in many respects: they may even seem to constitute part of the *inner* worth of a person. Yet they are far from being properly described as good without qualification (however unconditionally they have been commended by the ancients). For without the principles of a good will they may become exceedingly bad; and the very coolness of a scoundrel makes him, not merely more dangerous, but also immediately more abominable in our eyes than we should have taken him to be without it.

[*THE GOOD WILL AND ITS RESULTS*]

A good will is not good because of what it effects or accomplishes—because of its fitness for attaining some proposed end: it is good through its willing alone—that is, good in itself. Considered in itself it is to be esteemed beyond comparison as far higher than anything it could ever bring about merely in order to favour some inclination or, if you like, the sum total of inclinations. Even if, by some special disfavour of destiny or by the niggardly endowment of step-motherly nature, this will is entirely lacking in power to carry out its intentions; if by its utmost effort it still accomplishes nothing, and only good

From *Groundwork of the Metaphysic of Morals,* by Immanuel Kant, translated by H. J. Paton (New York: Harper & Row, 1964).

will is left (not, admittedly, as a mere wish, but as the straining of every means so far as they are in our control); even then it would still shine like a jewel for its own sake as something which has its full value in itself. Its usefulness or fruitlessness can neither add to, nor subtract from, this value. Its usefulness would be merely, as it were, the setting which enables us to handle it better in our ordinary dealings or to attract the attention of those not yet sufficiently expert, but not to commend it to experts or to determine its value.

[*THE FUNCTION OF REASON*]

Yet in this Idea of the absolute value of a mere will, all useful results being left out of account in its assessment, there is something so strange that, in spite of all the agreement it receives even from ordinary reason, there must arise the suspicion that perhaps its secret basis is merely some high-flown fantasticality, and that we may have misunderstood the purpose of nature in attaching reason to our will as its governor. We will therefore submit our Idea to an examination from this point of view.

In the natural constitution of an organic being—that is, of one contrived for the purpose of life—let us take it as a principle that in it no organ is to be found for any end unless it is also the most appropriate to that end and the best fitted for it. Suppose now that for a being possessed of reason and a will the real purpose of nature were his *preservation,* his *welfare,* or in a word his *happiness.* In that case nature would have hit on a very bad arrangement by choosing reason in the creature to carry out this purpose. For all the actions he has to perform with this end in view, and the whole rule of his behavior, would have been mapped out for him far more accurately by instinct; and the end in question could have been maintained far more surely by instinct than it ever can be by reason. If reason should have been imparted to this favoured creature as well, it would have had to serve him only for contemplating the happy disposition of his nature, for admiring it, for enjoying it, and for being grateful to its beneficent Cause—not for subjecting his power of appetition to such feeble and defective guidance or for meddling incompetently with the purposes of nature. In a word, nature would have prevented reason from striking out into a *practical use* and from presuming, with its feeble vision, to think out for itself a plan for happiness and for the means to its attainment. Nature would herself have taken over the choice, not only of ends, but also of means, and would with wise precaution have entrusted both to instinct alone.

In actual fact too we find that the more a cultivated reason concerns itself with the aim of enjoying life and happiness, the farther does man get away from true contentment. This is why there arises in many, and that too in those who have made most trial of this use of reason, if they are only candid enough to admit it, a certain degree of *misology*—that is, a hatred of reason; for when they balance all the advantage they draw, I will not sat from thinking out all the arts of ordinary indulgence, but even from science (which in the last resort seems to them to be also an indulgence of the mind), they discover that they have in fact only brought more trouble on their heads than they have gained in the way of happiness. On this account they come to envy, rather than to despise, the more common run of men, who are closer to the guidance of mere natural instinct, and who do not allow their reason to have much influence on their conduct. So far we must admit that the judgement of those who seek to moderate—and even to reduce below zero—the conceited glorification of such advantages as reason is supposed to provide in the way of happiness and contentment with life is in no way soured or ungrateful to the goodness with which the world is governed. These judgements rather have as their hidden ground the Idea of another and much more worthy purpose of existence, for which, and not for happiness, reason is quite properly designed, and to which, therefore, as a supreme condition the private purposes of man must for the most part be subordinated.

For since reason is not sufficiently serviceable for guiding the will safely as regards its objects and the satisfaction of all our needs (which it in part even multiplies)—a purpose for which an implanted natural instinct would have led us much more surely; and since none the less reason has been imparted to us as a practical power—that is, as one which is to have influence on the *will*; its true function must be to produce a *will* which is *good*, not as a *means* to some further end, but *in itself*; and for this function reason was absolutely necessary in a world where nature, in distributing her aptitudes, has everywhere else gone to work in a purposive manner. Such a will need not on this account be the sole and complete good, but it must be the highest good and the condition of all the rest, even of all our demands for happiness. In that case we can easily reconcile with the wisdom of nature our observation that the cultivation of reason which is required for the first and unconditioned purpose may in many ways, at least in this life, restrict the attainment of the second purpose—namely, happiness—which is always conditioned; and indeed that it can even reduce happiness to less than zero without nature proceeding contrary to its purpose; for reason, which recognizes as its highest practical function the establishment of a good will, in attaining this end is capable only of its own peculiar kind of contentment—contentment in fulfilling a purpose which in turn is determined by reason alone, even if this fulfillment should often involve interference with the purposes of inclination.

[*THE GOOD WILL AND DUTY*]

We have now to elucidate the concept of a will estimable in itself and good apart from any further end. This concept, which is already present in a sound natural understanding and requires not so much to be taught as merely to be clarified, always holds the highest place in estimating the total worth of our actions and constitutes the condition of all the rest. We will therefore take up the concept of *duty*, which includes that of a good will, exposed, however, to certain subjective limitations and obstacles. These, so far from hiding a good will or disguising it, rather bring it out by contrast and make it shine forth more brightly.

[*THE MOTIVE OF DUTY*]

I will here pass over all actions already recognized as contrary to duty, however useful they may be with a view to this or that end; for about these the question does not even arise whether they could have been done *for the sake of duty* inasmuch as they are directly opposed to it. I will also set aside actions which in fact accord with duty, yet for which men have *no immediate inclination,* but perform them because impelled to do so by some other inclination. For there it is easy to decide whether the action which accords with duty has been done *from duty* or from some purpose of self-interest. This distinction is far more difficult to perceive when the action accords with duty and the subject has in addition an *immediate* inclination to the action. For example, it certainly accords with duty that a grocer should not overcharge his inexperienced customer; and where there is much competition a sensible shopkeeper refrains from so doing and keeps to a fixed and general price for everybody so that a child can buy from him just as well as anyone else. Thus people are served *honestly*; but this is not nearly enough to justify us in believing that the shopkeeper has acted in this way from duty or from principles of fair dealing; his interests required him to do so. We cannot assume him to have in addition an immediate inclination towards his customers, leading him, as it were out of love, to give no man preference over another in the matter of price. Thus the action was done neither from duty nor from immediate inclination, but solely from purposes of self-interest.

On the other hand, to preserve one's life is a duty, and besides this every one has also an immediate inclination to do so. But on account of this the often anxious precautions taken by the greater part of mankind for this purpose have no inner worth, and the maxim of their action is without moral content. They do protect their lives *in conformity with duty,* but not *from the motive of duty.* When on the contrary, disappointments and hopeless misery have quite taken away the taste for life; when a wretched man, strong in soul and more angered at his fate than faint-hearted or cast down, longs for death and still preserves his life without loving it—not from inclination or fear but from duty; then indeed his maxim has a moral content.

To help others where one can is a duty, and besides this there are many spirits of so sympathetic a temper that, without any further motive of vanity or self-interest, they find an inner pleasure in spreading happiness around them and can take delight in the contentment of others as their own work. Yet I maintain that in such a case an action of this kind, however right and however amiable it may be, has still no genuinely moral worth. It stands on the same footing as other inclinations—for example, the inclination for honour, which if fortunate enough to hit on something beneficial and right and consequently honourable, deserves praise and encouragement, but not esteem; for its maxim lacks moral content, namely, the performance of such actions, not from inclination, but *from duty*. Suppose then that the mind of this friend of man were overclouded by sorrows of his own which extinguished all sympathy with the fate of others, but that he still has power to help those in distress, though no longer stirred by the need of others because sufficiently occupied with his own; and suppose that, when no longer moved by any inclination, he tears himself out of this deadly insensibility and does the action without any inclination for the sake of duty alone; then for the first time his action has its genuine moral worth. Still further: if nature had implanted little sympathy in this or that man's heart; if (being in other respects an honest fellow) he were cold in temperament and indifferent to the sufferings of others—perhaps because, being endowed with the special gift of patience and robust endurance in his own sufferings, he assumed the like in others or even demanded it; if such a man (who would in truth not be the worst product of nature) were not exactly fashioned by her to be a philanthropist, would he not still find in himself a source from which he might draw a worth far higher than any that a good-natured temperament can have? Assuredly he would. It is precisely in this that the worth of character begins to show—a moral worth and beyond all comparison the highest—namely, that he does good, not from inclination, but from duty.

To assure one's own happiness is a duty (at least indirectly); for discontent with one's state, in a press of cares and amidst unsatisfied wants, might easily become a great *temptation to the transgression of duty*. But here also, apart from regard to duty, all men have already of themselves the strongest and deepest inclination towards happiness, because precisely in this Idea of happiness all inclinations are combined into a sum total. The prescription for happiness is, however, often so constituted as greatly to interfere with some inclinations, and yet men cannot form under the name of 'happiness' any determinate and assured conception of the satisfaction of all inclinations as a sum. Hence it is not to be wondered at that a single inclination which is determinate as to what it promises and as to the time of its satisfaction may outweigh a wavering Idea; and that a man, for example, a sufferer from gout, may choose to enjoy what he fancies and put up with what he can—on the ground that on balance he has here at least not killed the enjoyment of the present moment because of some possibly groundless expectations of the good fortune supposed to attach to soundness of health. But in this case also, when the universal inclination towards happiness has failed to determine his will, when good health, at least for him, has not entered into his calculations as so necessary, what remains over, here as in other cases, is a law—the law of furthering his happiness, not from inclination, but from duty; and in this for the first time his conduct has a real moral worth.

It is doubtless in this sense that we should understand too the passages from Scripture in which we are commanded to love our neighbor and even our enemy. For love out of inclination cannot be commanded; but kindness done from duty—although no inclination impels us, and even although natural and unconquerable disinclination stands in our way—is *practical,* and not *patho-logical,* love, residing in the will and not in the propensions of feeling, in principles of action and not of melting compassion; and it is this practical love alone which can be an object of command.

[*THE FORMAL PRINCIPLE OF DUTY*]

Our second proposition is this: An action done from duty has its moral worth, *not in the purpose* to be attained by it, but in the maxim in accordance with which it is decided upon; it depends therefore, not on the realization of the object of the action, but solely on the *principle* of *volition* in accordance with which, irrespective of all objects of the faculty of desire, the action has been performed. That the purposes we may have in our actions, and also their effects considered as ends and motives of the will, can give to actions no unconditioned and moral worth is clear from what has gone before. Where then can this worth be found if we are not to find it in the will's relation to the effect hoped for from the action? It can be found nowhere but *in the principle of the will,* irrespective of the ends which can be brought about by such an action; for between its *a priori* principle, which is formal, and its *a posteriori* motive, which is material, the will stands, so to speak, at a parting of the ways; and since it must be determined by some principle, it will have to be determined by the formal principle of volition when an action is done from duty, where as we have seen, every material principle is taken away from it.

[*REVERENCE FOR THE LAW*]

Our third proposition, as an inference from the two preceding, I would express thus: *Duty is the necessity to act out of reverence for the law.* For an object as the effect of my proposed action I can have an *inclination,* but *never reverence,* precisely because it is merely the effect, and not the activity, of a will. Similarly for inclination as such, whether my own or that of another, I cannot have reverence: I can at most in the first case approve, and in the second case sometimes even love—that is, regard it as favourable to my own advantage. Only something which is conjoined with my will solely as a ground and never as an effect—something which does not serve my inclination, but outweighs it or at least leaves it entirely out of account in my choice—and therefore only bare law for its own sake, can be an object of reverence and therewith a command. Now an action done from duty has to set aside altogether the influence of inclination, and along with inclination every object of the will; so there is nothing left able to determine the will except objectively the *law* and subjectively *pure reverence* for this practical law, and therefore the maxim[1] of obeying this law even to the detriment of all my inclinations.

Thus the moral worth of an action does not depend on the result expected from it, and so too does not depend on any principle of action that needs to borrow its motive from this expected result. For all these results (agreeable states and even the promotion of happiness in others) could have been brought about by other causes as well, and consequently their production did not require the will of a rational being, in which, however, the highest and unconditioned good can alone be found. Therefore nothing but the *idea of the law* in itself, *which admittedly is present only in a rational being*—so far as it, and not an expected result, is the ground determining the will—can constitute that pre-eminent good which we call moral, a good which is already present in the person acting on this idea and has not to be awaited merely from the result.[2]

[*THE CATEGORICAL IMPERATIVE*]

But what kind of law can this be the thought of which, even without regard to the results expected from it, has to determine the will if this is to be called good absolutely and without qualification? Since I have robbed the will of every inducement that might arise for it as a consequence of obeying any particular law, nothing is left but the conformity of actions to universal law as such, and this alone must serve the will as its principle. That is to say, I ought never to act except in such a way *that I can also will that my maxim should become a universal law.* Here bare conformity to universal law as such (without having as its base any law prescribing particular actions) is what serves the will as its principle, and must so serve it if duty is not to be everywhere an empty delusion and a chimerical concept. The ordinary reason of mankind also agrees with this completely in its practical judgements and always has the aforesaid principle before its eyes.

Take this question, for example. May I not, when I am hard pressed, make a promise with the intention of not keeping it? Here I readily distinguish the two senses which the question can have—Is it prudent, or is it right, to make a false promise? The first no doubt can often be the case. I do indeed see that it is not enough for me to extricate myself from present embarrassment by this subterfuge: I have to consider whether from this lie there may not subsequently accrue to me much greater inconvenience than that from which I now escape, and also—since, with all my supposed *astuteness*, to foresee the consequences is not so easy that I can be sure there is no chance, once confidence in me is lost, of this proving far more disadvantageous than all the ills I now think to avoid—whether it may not be a *more prudent* action to proceed here on a general maxim and make it my habit not to give a promise except with the intention of keeping it. Yet it becomes clear to me at once that such a maxim is always founded solely on fear of consequences. To tell the truth for the sake of duty is something entirely different from doing so out of concern for inconvenient results; for in the first case the concept of the action already contains in itself a law for me, while in the second case I have first of all to look around elsewhere in order to see what effects may be bound up with it for me. When I deviate from the principle of duty, this is quite certainly bad; but if I desert my prudential maxim, this can often be greatly to my advantage, though it is admittedly safer to stick to it. Suppose I seek, however, to learn in the quickest way and yet unerringly how to solve the problem 'Does a lying promise accord with duty?' I have then to ask myself 'Should I really be content that my maxim (the maxim of getting out of a difficulty by a false promise) should hold as a universal law (one valid both for myself and others)? And could I really say to myself that every one may make a false promise if he finds himself in a difficulty from which he can extricate himself in no other way?' I then become aware at once that I can indeed will to lie, but I can by no means will a universal law of lying; for by such a law there could properly be no promises at all, since it would be futile to profess a will for future action to others who would not believe my profession or who, if they did so over-hastily, would pay me back in like coin; and consequently my maxim, as soon as it was made a universal law, would be bound to annul itself.

Thus I need no far-reaching ingenuity to find out what I have to do in order to possess a good will. Inexperienced in the course of world affairs and incapable of being prepared for all the chances that happen in it, I ask myself only 'Can you also will that your maxim should become a universal law?' Where you cannot, it is to be rejected, and that not because of a prospective loss to you or even to others, but because it cannot fit as a principle into a possible enactment of universal law. For such an enactment reason compels my immediate reverence, into whose grounds (which the philosopher may investigate) I have as yet no *insight*, although I do at least understand this much: reverence is the assessment of a worth which far outweighs all the worth of what is commended by inclination, and the necessity for me to act out of *pure* reverence for the practical law is what constitutes duty, to which every other motive must give way because it is the condition of a will good *in itself,* whose value is above all else. . . .

[CLASSIFICATION OF IMPERATIVES]

All *imperatives* command either *hypothetically* or *categorically.* Hypothetical imperatives declare a possible action to be practically necessary as a means to the attainment of something else that one wills (or that one may will). A categorical imperative would be one which represented an action as objectively necessary in itself apart from its relation to a further end.

Every practical law represents a possible action as good and therefore as necessary for a subject whose actions are determined by reason. Hence all imperatives are formulae for determining an action which is necessary in accordance with the principle of a will in some sense good. If the action would be good solely as a means *to something else,* the imperative is *hypothetical*; if the action is represented as good *in itself* and therefore as necessary, in virtue of its principle, for a will which of itself accords with reason, then the imperative is *categorical.*

An imperative therefore tells me which of my possible actions would be good; and it formulates a practical rule for a will that does not perform an action straight away because the action is good—whether because the subject does not always know that it is good or because, even if he did know this, he might still act on maxims contrary to the objective principles of practical reason.

A hypothetical imperative thus says only that an action is good for some purpose or other, either *possible* or *actual*. In the first case it is a *problematic* practical principle; in the second case an *assertoric* practical principle. A categorical imperative, which declares an action to be objectively necessary in itself without reference to some purpose—that is, even without any further end—ranks as an *apodeictic* practical principle. . . .

[*THE FORMULA OF UNIVERSAL LAW*]

In this task we wish first to enquire whether perhaps the mere concept of a categorical imperative may not also provide us with the formula containing the only proposition that can be a categorical imperative; for even when we know the purport of such an absolute command, the question of its possibility will still require a special and troublesome effort, which we postpone to the final chapter.

When I conceive a *hypothetical* imperative in general, I do not know beforehand what it will contain—until its condition is given. But if I conceive a *categorical* imperative, I know at once what it contains. For since besides the law this imperative contains only the necessity that our maxim[3] should conform to this law, while the law, as we have seen, contains no condition to limit it, there remains nothing over to which the maxim has to conform except the universality of a law as such; and it is this conformity alone that the imperative properly asserts to be necessary.

There is therefore only a single categorical imperative and it is this: '*Act only on that maxim through which you can at the same time will that it should become a universal law*'.

Now if all imperatives of duty can be derived from this one imperative as their principle, then even although we leave it unsettled whether what we call duty may not be an empty concept, we shall still be able to show at least what we understand by it and what the concept means.

[*THE FORMULA OF THE LAW OF NATURE*]

Since the universality of the law governing the production of effects constitutes what is properly called *nature* in its most general sense (nature as regards its form)—that is, the existence of things so far as determined by universal laws—the universal imperative of duty may also run as follows: '*Act as if the maxim of your action were to become through your will a universal law of nature*.'

[ILLUSTRATIONS]

We will now enumerate a few duties, following their customary division into duties towards self and duties towards others and into perfect and imperfect duties.[4]

1. A man feels sick of life as the result of a series of misfortunes that has mounted to the point of despair, but he is still so far in possession of his reason as to ask himself whether taking his own life may not be contrary to his duty to himself. He now applies the test 'Can the maxim of my action really become a universal law of nature?' His maxim is 'From self-love I make it my principle to shorten my life if its continuance threatens more evil than it promises pleasure.' The only further question to ask is whether this principle of self-love can become a universal law of nature. It is then seen at once that a system of nature by whose law the very same feeling whose function (*Bestimmung*) is to stimulate the furtherance of life should actually destroy life would contradict itself and consequently could not subsist as a system of nature. Hence this maxim cannot possibly hold as a universal law of nature and is therefore entirely opposed to the supreme principle of all duty.

2. Another finds himself driven to borrowing money because of need. He well knows that he will not be able to pay it back; but he sees too that he will get no loan unless he gives a firm promise to pay it back within a fixed time. He is inclined to make such a promise; but he has still enough conscience to ask 'Is it not unlawful and contrary to duty to get out of difficulties in this way?' Supposing, however, he did resolve to do so, the maxim of his action would run thus: 'Whenever I believe myself short of money, I will borrow money and promise to pay it back, though I know that this will never be done'. Now this principle of self-love or personal advantage is perhaps quite compatible with my own entire future welfare; only there remains the question 'Is it right?' I therefore transform the demand of self-love into a universal law and frame my question thus: 'How would things stand if my maxim became a universal law?' I then see straight away that this maxim can never rank as a universal law of nature and be self-consistent, but must necessarily contradict itself. For the universality of a law that every one believing himself to be in need can make any promise he pleases with the intention not to keep it would make promising, and the very purpose of promising, itself impossible, since no one would believe he was being promised anything, but would laugh at utterances of this kind as empty shams.

3. A third finds in himself a talent whose cultivation would make him a useful man for all sorts of purposes. But he sees himself in comfortable circumstances, and he prefers to give himself up to pleasure rather than to bother about increasing and improving his fortunate natural aptitudes. Yet he asks himself further 'Does my maxim of neglecting my natural gifts, besides agreeing in itself with my tendency to indulgence, agree also with what is called duty?' He then sees that a system of nature could indeed always subsist under such a universal law, although (like the South Sea Islanders) every man should let his talents rust and should be bent on devoting his life solely to idleness,

indulgence, procreation, and, in a word, to enjoyment. Only he cannot possibly *will* that this should become a universal law of nature or should be implanted in us as such a law by a natural instinct. For as a rational being he necessarily wills that all his powers should be developed, since they serve him, and are given him, for all sorts of possible ends.

4. Yet a *fourth* is himself flourishing, but he sees others who have to struggle with great hardships (and whom he could easily help); and he thinks 'What does it matter to me? Let every one be as happy as Heaven wills or as he can make himself; I won't deprive him of anything; I won't even envy him; only I have no wish to contribute anything to his well-being or to his support in distress!' Now admittedly if such an attitude were a universal law of nature, mankind could get on perfectly well—better no doubt than if everybody prates about sympathy and goodwill, and even takes pains, on occasion, to practise them, but on the other hand cheats where he can, traffics in human rights, or violates them in other ways. But although it is possible that a universal law of nature could subsist in harmony with this maxim, yet it is impossible to *will* that such a principle should hold everywhere as a law of nature. For a will which decided in this way would be in conflict with itself, since many a situation might arise in which the man needed love and sympathy from others, and in which, by such a law of nature sprung from his own will, he would rob himself of all hope of the help he wants for himself.

[*THE CANON OF MORAL JUDGEMENT*]

These are some of the many actual duties—or at least of what we take to be such—whose derivation from the single principle cited above leaps to the eye. We must *be able to will* that a maxim of our action should become a universal law—this is the general canon for all moral judgement of action. Some actions are so constituted that their maxim cannot even be *conceived* as a universal law of nature without contradiction, let alone be *willed* as what *ought* to become one. In the case of others we do not find this inner impossibility, but it is still impossible to *will* that their maxim should be raised to the universality of a law of nature, because such a will would contradict itself. It is easily seen that the first kind of action is opposed to strict or narrow (rigorous) duty, the second only to wider (meritorious) duty; and thus that by these examples all duties—so far as the type of obligation is concerned (not the object of dutiful action)—are fully set out in their dependence on our single principle. . . .

[*THE FORMULA OF THE END IN ITSELF*]

The will is conceived as a power of determining oneself to action *in accordance with the idea of certain laws*. And such a power can be found only in rational beings. Now what serves the will as a subjective ground of its self-determination is an *end*; and this, if it is given by reason alone, must be equally valid for all rational beings. What, on the other hand, contains merely the ground of the possibility of an action whose effect is an end is called a *means*. The subjective ground of a desire is an *impulsion (Triebfeder)*; the objective ground of a volition is a *motive (Bewegungsgrund)*. Hence the difference between subjective ends, which are based on impulsions, and objective ends, which depend on motives valid for every rational being. Practical principles are *formal* if they abstract from all subjective ends; they are *material*, on the other hand, if they are based on such ends and consequently on certain impulsions. Ends that a rational being adopts arbitrarily as *effects* of his action (material ends) are in every case only relative; for it is solely their relation to special characteristics in the subject's power of appetition which gives them their value. Hence this value can provide no universal principles, no principles valid and necessary for all rational beings and also for every volition— that is, no practical laws. Consequently all these relative ends can be the ground only of hypothetical imperatives.

Suppose, however, there were something *whose existence* has *in itself* an absolute value, something which as *an end in itself* could be a ground of determinate laws; then in it, and in it alone, would there be the ground of a possible categorical imperative—that is, of a practical law.

Now I say that man, and in general every rational being, *exists* as an end in himself, *not merely as a means* for arbitrary use by this or that will: he must in all his actions, whether they are directed to himself or to other rational beings, always be viewed *at the same time as an end*. All the objects of inclination have only a conditioned value; for if there were not these inclinations and the needs grounded on them, their object would be valueless. Inclinations themselves, as sources of needs, are so far from having an absolute value to make them desirable for their own sake that it must rather be the universal wish of every rational being to be wholly free from them. Thus the value of all objects that can *be produced* by our action is always conditioned. Beings whose existence depends, not on our will, but on nature, have none the less, if they are non-rational beings, only a relative value as means and are consequently called *things*. Rational beings, on the other hand, are called *persons* because their nature already marks them out as ends in themselves— that is, as something which ought not to be used merely as a means—and consequently imposes to that extent a limit on all arbitrary treatment of them (and is an object of reverence). Persons, therefore, are not merely subjective ends whose existence as an object of our actions has a value *for us*: they are *objective ends*—that is, things whose existence is in itself an end, and indeed an end such that in its place we can put no other end to which they should serve *simply* as means; for unless this is so, nothing at all of *absolute* value would be found anywhere. But if all value were conditioned—that is, contingent—then no supreme principle could be found for reason at all.

If then there is to be a supreme practical principle and—so far as the human will is concerned—a categorical imperative, it must be such that from the idea of something which is necessarily an end for every one because it is an *end in itself* it forms an *objective* principle of the will and consequently can serve as a practical law. The ground of this principle is: *Rational nature exists as an end in itself.* This is the way in which a man necessarily conceives his own existence: It is therefore so far a *subjective* principle of human actions. But it is also the way in which every other rational being conceives his existence on the same rational ground which is valid also for me, hence it is at the same time an *objective* principle, from which, as a supreme practical ground, it must be possible to derive all laws for the will. The practical imperative will therefore be as follows: *Act in such a way that you always treat humanity, whether in your own person or in the person of any other, never simply as a means, but always at the same time as an end.* We will now consider whether this can be carried out in practice.

[*ILLUSTRATIONS*]

Let us keep to our previous examples.

First, as regards the concept of necessary duty to oneself, the man who contemplates suicide will ask 'Can my action be compatible with the Idea of humanity *as an end in itself?*' If he does away with himself in order to escape from a painful situation, he is making use of a person merely as *a means* to maintain a tolerable state of affairs till the end of his life. But man is not a thing—not something to be used *merely* as a means: he must always in all his actions be regarded as an end in himself. Hence I cannot dispose of man in my person by maiming, spoiling, or killing. (A more precise determination of this principle in order to avoid all misunderstanding—for example, about having limbs amputated to save myself or about exposing my life to danger in order to preserve it, and so on—I must here forego: This question belongs to morals proper.)

Secondly, so far as necessary or strict duty to others is concerned, the man who has a mind to make a false promise to others will see at once that he is intending to make use of another man *merely as a means* to an end he does not share. For the man whom I seek to use for my own purposes by such a promise cannot possibly agree with my way of behaving to him, and so cannot himself share the end of the action. This incompatibility with the principle of duty to others leaps to the eye more obviously when we bring in examples of attempts on the freedom and property of others. For then it is manifest that a violator of the rights of man intends to use the person of others merely as a means without taking into consideration that, as rational beings, they ought always at the same time to be rated as ends—that is, only as beings who must themselves be able to share in the end of the very same action.[5]

Thirdly, in regard to contingent (meritorious) duty to oneself, it is not enough that an action should refrain from conflicting with humanity in our own person as an end in itself: it must also *harmonize with this end.* Now there are in humanity capacities for greater perfection which form part of nature's purpose for humanity in our person. To neglect these can admittedly be compatible with the *maintenance* of humanity as an end in itself, but not with the *promotion* of this end.

Fourthly, as regards meritorious duties to others, the natural end which all men seek is their own happiness. Now humanity could no doubt subsist if everybody contributed nothing to the happiness of others but at the same time refrained from deliberately impairing their happiness. This is, however, merely to agree negatively and not positively with *humanity as an end in itself* unless every one endeavours also, so far as in him lies, to further the ends of others. For the ends of a subject who is an end in himself must, if this conception is to have its *full* effect in me, be also, as far as possible, *my* ends.

NOTES

1. A *maxim* is the subjective principle of a volition: an objective principle (that is, one which would also serve subjectively as a practical principle for all rational beings if reason has full control over the faculty of desire) is a practical *law.*

2. It might be urged against me that I have merely tried, under cover of the word '*reverence*', to take refuge in an obscure feeling instead of giving a clearly articulated answer to the question by means of a concept of reason. Yet although reverence is a feeling, it is not a feeling *received* through outside influence, but one *self-produced* by a rational concept, and therefore specifically distinct from feelings of the first kind, all of which can be reduced to inclination or fear. What I recognize immediately as law for me, I recognize with reverence, which means merely consciousness of the *subordination* of my will to a law without the mediation of external influences on my senses. Immediate determination of the will by the law and consciousness of this determination is called '*reverence*', so that reverence is regarded as the *effect* of the law on the subject and not as the *cause* of the law. Reverence is properly awareness of a value which demolishes my self-love. Hence there is something which is regarded neither as an object of inclination nor as an object of fear, though it has at the same time some analogy with both. The *object* of reverence is the *law* alone—that law which we impose *on ourselves* but yet as necessary in itself. Considered as a law, we are subject to it without any consultation of self-love; considered as self-imposed it is a consequence of our will. In the first respect it is analogous to fear, in the second to inclination. All reverence for a person is properly only reverence for the law (of honesty and so on) of which that person gives us an example. Because we regard the development of our talents as a duty, we see too in a man of talent a sort of *example of the law* (the law of becoming like him by practice), and this is what constitutes our reverence for him. All moral *interest,* so-called, consists solely in *reverence* for the law.

3. A *maxim* is a subjective principle of action and must be distinguished from an *objective principle*—namely, a practical law. The former contains a practical rule determined by reason in accordance with the conditions of the subject (often his ignorance or again his inclinations): it is thus a principle on which the subject *acts.* A law, on the other hand, is an objective principle valid for every rational being; and it is a principle on which he *ought to act*—that is, an imperative.

4. It should be noted that I reserve my division of duties entirely for a future *Metaphysic of Morals* and that my present division is therefore put forward as arbitrary (merely for the purpose of arranging my examples). Further, I understand here by a perfect duty one which allows no exception in the interests of inclination, and so I recognize among *perfect duties,* not only outer ones, but also inner. This is contrary to the accepted usage of the schools, but I do not intend to justify it here, since for my purpose it is all one whether this point is conceded or not.

5. Let no one think that here the trivial *'quod tibi non vis fieri, etc.'* can serve as a standard or principle. For it is merely derivative from our principle, although subject to various qualifications: it cannot be a universal law since it contains the ground neither of duties to oneself nor of duties of kindness to others (for many a man would readily agree that others should not help him if only he could be dispensed from affording help to them), nor finally of strict duties towards others; for on this basis the criminal would be able to dispute with the judges who punish him, and so on.

The Kantian Interpretation of a Theory of Justice

John Rawls

John Rawls, Professor of Philosophy Emeritus at Harvard University, is at least one of the most important political philosophers of the twentieth century. His work *A Theory of Justice* (1971), from which the following readings have been selected, provided an entirely new way of thinking about social justice and changed the ways in which moral and political philosophy was done, at least in the English speaking world. More recently Rawls has revised and clarified his vision of social justice in *Political Liberalism* (1993).

Rawls develops what is sometimes known as a contractarian theory, since it is a development of the social contract tradition of political theory. However, Rawls does not believe that the basic principles of justice depend in any way on the actual contracts or agreements that people make. Instead, he uses a thought experiment to ask what people would agree to under certain morally ideal conditions. The correct principles of justice by which to assess the justice of society's basic institutions, he maintains, are those that would be agreed upon by people who are behind what Rawls calls the "Veil of Ignorance." Behind this veil, people are ignorant of all the specific facts about themselves and are aware only of general facts about the world. For example, a person behind the veil of ignorance would not know his or her age, sex, skills, limitations, or even his or her conception of what constitutes a valuable life. Nonetheless, such a person would know what human beings and human institutions are like in general. In such a position, people are expected to choose principles of justice with an eye toward making their own lives as good as possible. However, they know too little about themselves as individuals to tailor the principles to give advantage to people with their particular tastes and talents. As a result, people behind the veil of ignorance are forced by their lack of knowledge to adopt an impartial standpoint. In the final section of these selections, Rawls argues that his theory can be understood as a Kantian theory, because the principles selected from behind the veil of ignorance constitute an expression of people's nature as free and equal rational beings.

THE MAIN IDEA OF THE THEORY OF JUSTICE

My aim is to present a conception of justice which generalizes and carries to a higher level of abstraction the familiar theory of the social contract as found, say, in Locke, Rousseau, and Kant.[1] In order to do this we are not to think of the original contract as one to enter a particular society or to set up a particular form of government. Rather, the guiding idea is that the principles of justice for the basic structure of society are the object of the original agreement. They are the principles that free and rational persons concerned to

From *A Theory of Justice*, by John Rawls (Cambridge, MA: Harvard University Press, 1971).

further their own interests would accept in an initial position of equality as defining the fundamental terms of their association. These principles are to regulate all further agreements; they specify the kinds of social cooperation that can be entered into and the forms of government that can be established. This way of regarding the principles of justice I shall call justice as fairness.

Thus we are to imagine that those who engage in social cooperation choose together, in one joint act, the principles which are to assign basic rights and duties and to determine the division of social benefits. Men are to decide in advance how they are to regulate their claims against one another and what is to be the foundation charter of their society. Just as each person must decide by rational reflection what constitutes his good, that is, the system of ends which it is rational for him to pursue, so a group of persons must decide once and for all what is to count among them as just and unjust. The choice which rational men would make in this hypothetical situation of equal liberty, assuming for the present that this choice problem has a solution, determines the principles of justice.

In justice as fairness the original position of equality corresponds to the state of nature in the traditional theory of the social contract. This original position is not, of course, thought of as an actual historical state of affairs, much less as a primitive condition of culture. It is understood as a purely hypothetical situation characterized so as to lead to a certain conception of justice.[2] Among the essential features of this situation is that no one knows his place in society, his class position or social status, nor does any one know his fortune in the distribution of natural assets and abilities, his intelligence, strength, and the like. I shall even assume that the parties do not know their conceptions of the good or their special psychological propensities. The principles of justice are chosen behind a veil of ignorance. This ensures that no one is advantaged or disadvantaged in the choice of principles by the outcome of natural chance or the contingency of social circumstances. Since all are similarly situated and no one is able to design principles to favor his particular condition, the principles of justice are the result of a fair agreement or bargain. For given the circumstances of the original position, the symmetry of everyone's relations to each other, this initial situation is fair between individuals as moral persons, that is, as rational beings with their own ends and capable, I shall assume, of a sense of justice. The original position is, one might say, the appropriate initial status quo, and thus the fundamental agreements reached in it are fair. This explains the propriety of the name "justice as fairness": it conveys the idea that the principles of justice are agreed to in an initial situation that is fair. The name does not mean that the concepts of justice and fairness are the same, any more than the phrase "poetry as metaphor" means that the concepts of poetry and metaphor are the same.

Justice as fairness begins, as I have said, with one of the most general of all choices which persons might make together, namely, with the choice of the first principles of a conception of justice which is to regulate all subsequent criticism and reform of institutions. Then, having chosen a conception of justice, we can suppose that they are to choose a constitution and a legislature to enact laws, and so on, all in accordance with the principles of justice initially agreed upon. Our social situation is just if it is such that by this sequence of hypothetical agreements we would have contracted into the general system of rules which defines it. Moreover, assuming that the original position does determine a set of principles (that is, that a particular conception of justice would be chosen), it will then be true that whenever social institutions satisfy these principles those engaged in them can say to one another that they are cooperating on terms to which they would agree if they were free and equal persons whose relations with respect to one another were fair. They could all view their arrangements as meeting the stipulations which they would acknowledge in an initial situation that embodies widely accepted and reasonable constraints on the choice of principles. The general recognition of this fact would provide the basis for a public acceptance of the corresponding principles of justice. No society can, of course, be a scheme of cooperation which men enter voluntarily in a literal sense; each person finds himself placed at birth in some particular position in some particular society, and the nature of this position materially affects his life prospects. Yet a society satisfying the principles of justice as fairness comes as close as a society can to being a voluntary scheme, for it meets the principles which free and equal persons would assent to under circumstances that are fair. In this sense its members are autonomous and the obligations they recognize self-imposed.

One feature of justice as fairness is to think of the parties in the initial situation as rational and mutually disinterested. This does not mean that the parties are egoists, that is, individuals with only certain kinds of interests, say in wealth, prestige, and domination. But they are conceived as not taking an interest in one another's interests. They are to presume that even their spiritual aims may be opposed, in the way that the aims of those of different religions may be opposed. Moreover, the concept of rationality must be interpreted as far as possible in the narrow sense, standard in economic theory, of taking the most effective means to given ends. I shall modify this concept to some extent, as explained later, but one must try to avoid introducing into it any controversial ethical elements. The initial situation must be characterized by stipulations that are widely accepted.

In working out the conception of justice as fairness one main task clearly is to determine which principles of justice would be chosen in the original position. To do this we must describe this situation in some detail and formulate with care the problem of choice which it presents. These matters I shall take up in the immediately succeeding chapters. It may be observed, however, that once the principles of justice are thought of as arising from an original agreement in a situation of equality, it is an open question whether the principle of utility would be acknowledged. Offhand it hardly seems likely that persons who view themselves as equals, entitled to press their claims upon one another, would agree to a principle which may require lesser life prospects for some simply for the sake of a greater sum of advantages enjoyed by others. Since each desires to protect his interests, his capacity to advance his conception of the good, no one has a reason to acquiesce in an enduring loss for himself in order to bring about a greater net balance of satisfaction. In the absence of strong and lasting benevolent impulses, a rational man would not accept a basic structure merely because it maximized the algebraic sum of advantages irrespective of its permanent effects on his own basic rights and interests. Thus it seems that the principle of utility is incompatible with the conception of social cooperation among equals for mutual advantage. It appears to be inconsistent with the idea of reciprocity implicit in the notion of a well-ordered society. Or, at any rate, so I shall argue.

I shall maintain instead that the persons in the initial situation would choose two rather different principles: the first requires equality in the assignment of basic rights and duties, while the second holds that social and economic inequalities, for example inequalities of wealth and authority, are just only if they result in compensating benefits for everyone, and in particular for the least advantaged members of society. These principles rule out justifying institutions on the grounds that the hardships of some are offset by a greater good in the aggregate. It may be expedient but it is not just that some should have less in order that others may prosper. But there is no injustice in the greater benefits earned by a few provided that the situation of persons not so fortunate is thereby improved. The intuitive idea is that since everyone's well-being depends upon a scheme of cooperation without which no one could have a satisfactory life, the division of advantages should be such as to draw forth the willing cooperation of everyone taking part in it, including those less well situated. Yet this can be expected only if reasonable terms are proposed. The two principles mentioned seem to be a fair agreement on the basis of which those better endowed, or more fortunate in their social position, neither of which we can be said to deserve, could expect the willing cooperation of others when some workable scheme is a necessary condition of the welfare of all.[3] Once we decide to look for a conception of justice that nullifies the accidents of natural endowment and the contingencies of social circumstance as counters in quest for political and economic advantage, we are led to these principles. They express the result of leaving aside those aspects of the social world that seem arbitrary from a moral point of view.

The problem of the choice of principles, however, is extremely difficult. I do not expect the answer I shall suggest to be convincing to everyone. It is, therefore, worth noting from the outset that justice as fairness, like other contract views, consists of two parts: (1) an interpretation of the initial situation and of the problem of choice posed there, and (2) a set of principles which, it is argued, would be agreed to. One may accept the first part of the theory (or some variant thereof), but not the other, and conversely. The concept of the initial contractual situation may seem reasonable although the particular principles proposed are rejected. To be sure, I want to maintain that the most appropriate conception of this situation does lead to principles of justice contrary to utilitarianism and perfectionism, and therefore that the contract doctrine provides an alternative to these views. Still, one may dispute this contention even though one grants that the contractarian method is a useful way of studying ethical theories and of setting forth their underlying assumptions.

Justice as fairness is an example of what I have called a contract theory. Now there may be an objection to the term "contract" and related expressions, but I think it will serve reasonably well. Many words have misleading connotations which at first are likely to confuse. The terms "utility" and "utilitarianism" are surely no exception. They too have unfortunate suggestions which hostile critics have been willing to exploit; yet they are clear enough for those prepared to study utilitarian doctrine. The same should be true of the term "contract" applied to moral theories. As I have mentioned, to understand it one has to keep in mind that it implies a certain level of abstraction. In particular, the content of the relevant agreement is not to enter a given society or to adopt a given form of government, but to accept certain moral principles. Moreover, the undertakings referred to are purely hypothetical: a contract view holds that certain principles would be accepted in a well-defined initial situation.

The merit of the contract terminology is that it conveys the idea that principles of justice may be conceived as principles that would be chosen by rational persons, and that in this way conceptions of justice may be explained and justified. The theory of justice is a part, perhaps the most significant part, of the theory of rational choice. Furthermore, principles of justice deal with conflicting claims upon the advantages won by social cooperation; they apply to the relations among several persons or groups. The word "contract" suggests this plurality as well as the condition that the appropriate division of advantages must be in accordance with principles acceptable to all parties. The condition of publicity for principles of justice is also connoted by the contract phraseology. Thus, if these principles are the outcome of an agreement, citizens have a knowledge of the principles that others follow. It is characteristic of contract theories to stress the public nature of political principles. Finally there is the long tradition of the contract doctrine. Expressing the tie with this line of thought helps to define ideas and accords with natural piety. There are then several advantages in the use of the term "contract." With due precautions taken, it should not be misleading.

A final remark. Justice as fairness is not a complete contract theory. For it is clear that the contractarian idea can be extended to the choice of more or less an entire ethical system, that is, to a system including principles for all the virtues and not only for justice. Now for the most part I shall consider only principles of justice and others closely related to them; I make no attempt to discuss the virtues in a systematic way. Obviously if justice as fairness succeeds reasonably well, a next step would be to study the more general view suggested by the name "rightness as fairness." But even this wider theory fails to embrace all moral relationships, since it would seem to include only our relations with other persons and to leave out of account how we are to conduct ourselves toward animals and the rest of nature. I do not contend that the contract notion offers a way to approach these questions which are certainly of the first importance; and I shall have to put them aside. We must recognize the limited scope of justice as fairness and of the general type of view that it exemplifies. How far its conclusions must be revised once these other matters are understood cannot be decided in advance. . . .

TWO PRINCIPLES OF JUSTICE

I shall now state in a provisional form the two principles of justice that I believe would be chosen in the original position. In this section I wish to make only the most general comments, and therefore the first formulation of these principles is tentative. As we go on I shall run through several formulations and approximate step by step the final statement to be given much later. I believe that doing this allows the exposition to proceed in a natural way.

The first statement of the two principles reads as follows.

> First: each person is to have an equal right to the most extensive basic liberty compatible with a similar liberty for others.
>
> Second: social and economic inequalities are to be arranged so that they are both (a) reasonably expected to be to everyone's advantage, and (b) attached to positions and offices open to all. . . .

By way of general comment, these principles primarily apply, as I have said, to the basic structure of society. They are to govern the assignment of rights and duties and to regulate the distribution of social and economic advantages. As their formulation suggests, these principles presuppose that the social structure can be divided into two more or less distinct parts, the first principle applying to the one, the second to the other. They distinguish between those aspects of the social system that define and secure the equal liberties of citizenship and those that specify and establish social and economic inequalities. The basic liberties of citizens are, roughly speaking, political liberty (the right to vote and to be eligible for public office) together with freedom of speech and assembly; liberty of conscience and freedom of thought; freedom of the person along with the right to hold (personal) property; and freedom from arbitrary arrest and seizure as defined by the concept of the rule of law. These liberties are all required to be equal by the first principle, since citizens of a just society are to have the same basic rights.

The second principle applies, in the first approximation, to the distribution of income and wealth and to the design of organizations that make use of differences in authority and responsibility, or chains of command. While the distribution of wealth and income need not be equal, it must be to everyone's advantage, and at the same time, positions of authority and offices of command must be accessible to all. One applies the second principle by holding positions open, and then, subject to this constraint, arranges social and economic inequalities so that everyone benefits.

These principles are to be arranged in a serial order with the first principle prior to the second. This ordering means that a departure from the institutions of equal liberty required by the first principle cannot be justified by, or compensated for, by greater social and economic advantages. The distribution of wealth and income, and the hierarchies of authority, must be consistent with both the liberties of equal citizenship and equality of opportunity.

It is clear that these principles are rather specific in their content, and their acceptance rests on certain assumptions that I must eventually try to explain and justify. A theory of justice depends upon a theory of society in ways that will become evident as we proceed. For the present, it should be observed that the two principles (and this holds for all formulations) are a special case of a more general conception of justice that can be expressed as follows.

> All social values—liberty and opportunity, income and wealth, and the bases
> of self-respect—are to be distributed equally unless an unequal distribution
> of any, or all, of these values is to everyone's advantage.

Injustice, then, is simply inequalities that are not to the benefit of all. Of course, this conception is extremely vague and requires interpretation. . . .

THE KANTIAN INTERPRETATION
OF JUSTICE AS FAIRNESS

For the most part I have considered the content of the principle of equal liberty and the meaning of the priority of the rights that it defines. It seems appropriate at this point to note that there is a Kantian interpretation of the conception of justice from which this principle derives. This interpretation is based upon Kant's notion of autonomy. It is a mistake, I believe, to emphasize the place of generality and universality in Kant's ethics. That moral principles are general and universal is hardly new with him; and as we have seen these conditions do not in any case take us very far. It is impossible to construct a moral theory on so slender a basis, and therefore to limit the discussion of Kant's doctrine to these notions is to reduce it to triviality. The real force of his view lies elsewhere.[4]

For one thing, he begins with the idea that moral principles are the object of rational choice. They define the moral law that men can rationally will to govern their conduct in an ethical commonwealth. Moral philosophy becomes the study of the conception and outcome of a suitably defined rational decision. This idea has immediate consequences. For once we think of moral principles as legislation for a kingdom of ends, it is clear that these principles must not only be acceptable to all but public as well. Finally Kant supposes that this moral legislation is to be agreed to under conditions that characterize men as free and equal rational beings. The description of the original position is an attempt to interpret this conception. I do not wish to argue here for this interpretation on the basis of Kant's text. Certainly some will want to read him differently. Perhaps the remarks to follow are best taken as suggestions for relating justice as fairness to the high point of the contractarian tradition in Kant and Rousseau.

Kant held, I believe, that a person is acting autonomously when the principles of his action are chosen by him as the most adequate possible expression of his nature as a free and equal rational being. The principles he acts upon are not adopted because of his social position or natural endowments, or in view of the particular kind of society in which he lives or the specific things that he happens to want. To act on such principles is to act heteronomously. Now the veil of ignorance deprives the persons in the original position of the knowledge that would enable them to choose heteronomous principles. The parties arrive at their choice together as free and equal rational persons knowing only that those circumstances obtain which give rise to the need for principles of justice.

To be sure, the argument for these principles does add in various ways to Kant's conception. For example, it adds the feature that the principles chosen are to apply to the basic structure of society; and premises characterizing this structure are used in deriving the principles of justice. But I believe that this and other additions are natural enough and remain fairly close to Kant's doctrine, at least when all of his ethical writings are viewed together. Assuming, then, that the reasoning in favor of the principles of justice is correct, we can say that when persons act on these principles they are acting in accordance with principles that they would choose as rational and independent persons in an original position of equality. The principles of their actions do not depend upon social or natural contingencies, nor do they reflect the bias of the particulars of their plan of life or the aspirations that motivate them. By acting from these principles persons express their nature as free and equal rational beings subject to the general conditions of human life. For to express one's nature as a being of a particular kind is to act on the principles that would be chosen if this nature were the decisive determining element. Of course, the choice of the parties in the original position is subject to the restrictions of that situation. But when we knowingly act on the principles of justice in the ordinary course of events, we deliberately assume the limitations of the original position. One reason for doing this, for persons who can do so and want to, is to give expression to one's nature.

The principles of justice are also categorical imperatives in Kant's sense. For by a categorical imperative Kant understands a principle of conduct that applies to a person in virtue of his nature as a free and equal rational being. The validity of the principle does not presuppose that one has a particular desire or aim. Whereas a hypothetical imperative by contrast does assume this: it directs us to take certain steps as effective means to achieve a specific end. Whether the desire is for a particular thing, or whether it is for something more general, such as certain kinds of agreeable feelings or pleasures, the corresponding imperative is hypothetical. Its applicability depends upon one's having an aim which one need not have as a condition of being a rational human individual. The argument for the two principles of justice does not assume that the parties have particular ends, but only that they desire certain primary goods. These are things that it is rational to want whatever else one wants. Thus given human nature, wanting them is part of being rational; and while each is presumed to have some conception of the good, nothing is known about his final ends. The preference for primary goods is derived, then, from only the most general assumptions about rationality and the conditions of human life. To act from the principles of justice is to act from categorical imperatives in the sense that they apply to us whatever in particular our aims are. This simply reflects the fact that no such contingencies appear as premises in their derivation.

We may note also that the motivational assumption of mutual disinterest accords with Kant's notion of autonomy, and gives another reason for this condition. So far this assumption has been used to characterize the circumstances of justice and to provide a clear conception to guide the reasoning of the parties. We have also seen that the concept of benevolence, being a second-order notion, would not work out well. Now we can add that the assumption of mutual disinterest is to allow for freedom in the choice of a system of final ends.[5] Liberty in adopting a conception of the good is limited only by principles that are deduced from a doctrine which imposes no prior constraints on these conceptions. Presuming mutual disinterest in the original position carries out this idea. We postulate that the parties have opposing claims in a suitably general sense. If their ends were restricted in some specific way, this would appear at the outset as an arbitrary restriction on freedom. Moreover, if the parties were conceived as altruists, or as pursuing certain kinds of pleasures, then the principles chosen would apply, as far as the argument would have shown, only to persons whose freedom was restricted to choices compatible with altruism or hedonism. As the argument now runs, the principles of justice cover all persons with rational plans of life, whatever their content, and these principles represent the appropriate restrictions on freedom. Thus it is possible to say that the constraints on conceptions of the good are the result of an interpretation of the contractual situation that puts no prior limitations on what men may desire. There are a variety of reasons, then, for the motivational premise of mutual disinterest. This premise is not only a matter of realism about the circumstances of justice or a way to make the theory manageable. It also connects up with the Kantian idea of autonomy.

There is, however, a difficulty that should be clarified. It is well expressed by Sidgwick.[6] He remarks that nothing in Kant's ethics is more striking than the idea that a man realizes his true self when he acts from the moral law, whereas if he permits his actions to be determined by sensuous desires or contingent aims, he becomes subject to the law of nature. Yet in Sidgwick's opinion this idea comes to naught. It seems to him that on Kant's view the lives of the saint and the scoundrel are equally the outcome of a free choice (on the part of the noumenal self) and equally the subject of causal laws (as a phenomenal self). Kant never explains why the scoundrel does not express in a bad life his characteristic and freely chosen selfhood in the same way that a saint expresses his characteristic and freely chosen selfhood in a good one. Sidgwick's objection is decisive, I think, as long as one assumes, as Kant's exposition may seem to allow, both that the noumenal self can choose any consistent set of principles and that acting from such principles, whatever they are, is sufficient to express one's choice as that of a free and equal rational being. Kant's reply must be that though acting on any consistent set of principles could be the outcome of a decision on the part of the noumenal self, not all such action by the phenomenal self expresses this decision as that of a free and equal rational being. Thus if a person realizes his true self by expressing it in his actions, and if he desires above all else to realize this self, then he will choose to act from principles that manifest his nature as a free and equal rational being. The missing part of the argument concerns the concept of expression. Kant did not show that acting from the moral law expresses our nature in identifiable ways that acting from contrary principles does not.

This defect is made good, I believe, by the conception of the original position. The essential point is that we need an argument showing which principles, if any, free and equal rational persons would choose and these principles must be applicable in practice. A definite answer to this question is required to meet Sidgwick's objection. My suggestion is that we think of the original position as the point of view from which noumenal selves see the world. The parties qua noumenal selves have complete freedom to choose whatever principles they wish; but they also have a desire to express their nature as rational and equal members of the intelligible realm with precisely this liberty to choose, that is, as beings who can look at the world in this way and express this perspective in their life as members of society. They must decide, then, which principles when consciously followed and acted upon in everyday life will best manifest this freedom in their community, most fully reveal their independence from natural contingencies and social accident. Now if the argument of the contract doctrine is correct, these principles are indeed those defining the moral law, or more exactly, the principles of justice for institutions and individuals. The description of the original position interprets the point of view of noumenal selves, of what it means to be a free and equal rational being. Our nature as such beings is displayed when we act from the principles we would choose when this nature is reflected in the conditions determining the choice. Thus men exhibit their freedom, their independence from the contingencies of nature and society, by acting in ways they would acknowledge in the original position.

Properly understood, then, the desire to act justly derives in part from the desire to express most fully what we are or can be, namely free and equal rational beings with a liberty to choose. It is for this reason, I believe, that Kant speaks of the failure to act on the moral law as giving rise to shame and not to feelings of guilt. And this is appropriate, since for him acting unjustly is acting in a manner that fails to express our nature as a free and equal rational being. Such actions therefore strike at our self-respect, our sense of our own worth, and the experience of this loss is shame. We have acted as though we belonged to a lower order, as though we were a creature whose first principles are decided by natural contingencies. Those who think of Kant's moral doctrine as one of law and guilt badly misunderstand him. Kant's main aim is to deepen and to justify Rousseau's idea that liberty is acting in accordance with a law that we give to ourselves. And this leads not to a morality of austere command but to an ethic of mutual respect and self-esteem.[7]

The original position may be viewed, then, as a procedural interpretation of Kant's conception of autonomy and the categorical imperative. The principles regulative of the kingdom of ends are those that would be chosen in this position, and the description of this situation enables us to explain the sense in which acting from these principles expresses our nature as free and equal rational persons. No longer are these notions purely transcendent and lacking explicable connections with human conduct, for the procedural conception of the original position allows us to make these ties. It is true that I have departed from Kant's views in several respects. I shall not discuss these matters here; but two points should be noted. The person's choice as a noumenal self I have assumed to be a collective one. The force of the self's being equal is that the principles chosen must be acceptable to other selves. Since all are similarly free and rational, each must have an equal say in adopting the public principles of the ethical commonwealth. This means that as noumenal selves, everyone is to consent to these principles. Unless the scoundrel's principles would be chosen, they cannot express this free choice, however much a single self might be of a mind to opt for them. Later I shall try to define a clear sense in which this unanimous agreement is best expressive of the nature of even a single self. It in no way overrides a person's interests as the collective nature of the choice might seem to imply. But I leave this aside for the present.

Secondly, I have assumed all along that the parties know that they are subject to the conditions of human life. Being in the circumstances of justice, they are situated in the world with other men who likewise face limitations of moderate scarcity and competing claims. Human freedom is to be regulated by principles chosen in the light of these natural restrictions. Thus justice as fairness is a theory of human justice and among its premises are the elementary facts about persons and their place in nature. The freedom of pure intelligences not subject to these constraints, and the freedom of God, are outside the scope of the theory. It might appear that Kant meant his doctrine to apply to all rational beings as such and therefore to God and the angels as well. Men's social situation in the world may seem to have no role in his theory in determining the first principles of justice. I do not believe that Kant held this view, but I cannot discuss this question here. It suffices to say that if I am mistaken, the Kantian interpretation of justice as fairness is less faithful to Kant's intentions than I am presently inclined to suppose.

NOTES

1. As the text suggests, I shall regard Locke's *Second Treatise of Government,* Rousseau's *The Social Contract,* and Kant's ethical works beginning with *The Foundations of the Metaphysics of Morals* as definitive of the contract tradition. For all of its greatness, Hobbes's *Leviathan* raises special problems. A general historical survey is provided by J. W. Gough, *The Social Contract,* 2nd ed. (Oxford, The Clarendon Press, 1957), and Otto Gierke, *Natural Law and the Theory of Society,* trans. with an introduction by Ernest Barker (Cambridge, The University Press, 1934). A presentation of the contract view as primarily an ethical theory is to be found in G. R. Grice, *The Grounds of Moral Judgment* (Cambridge, The University Press, 1967).

2. Kant is clear that the original agreement is hypothetical. See *The Metaphysics of Morals,* pt. I (*Rechtslehre*), especially §§47, 52; and pt. II of the essay "Concerning the Common Saying: This May Be True in Theory but It Does Not Apply in Practice," in *Kant's Political Writings,* ed. Hans Reiss and trans. by H. B. Nisbet (Cambridge, The University Press, 1970), pp. 73–87. See Georges Vlachos, *La Pensée politique de Kant* (Paris, Presses Universitaires de France, 1962), pp. 326–335; and J. G. Murphy, *Kant: The Philosophy of Right* (London, Macmillan, 1970), pp. 109–112, 133–136, for a further discussion.

3. For the formulation of this intuitive idea I am indebted to Allan Gibbard.

4. To be avoided at all costs is the idea that Kant's doctrine simply provides the general, or formal, elements for a utilitarian (or indeed for any other) theory. See, for example, R. M. Hare, *Freedom and Reason* (Oxford, The Clarendon Press, 1963), pp. 123f. One must not lose sight of the full scope of his view, one must take the later works into consideration. Unfortunately, there is no commentary on Kant's moral theory as a whole; perhaps it would prove impossible to write. But the standard works of H. J. Paton, *The Categorical Imperative* (Chicago, University of Chicago Press, 1948), and L. W. Beck, *A Commentary on Kant's Critique of Practical Reason* (Chicago, University of Chicago Press, 1960), and others need to be further complemented by studies of the other writings. See here M. J. Gregor's *Laws of Freedom* (Oxford, Basil Blackwell, 1963), an account of *The Metaphysics of Morals,* and J. G. Murphy's brief *Kant: The Philosophy of Right* (London, Macmillan, 1970). Beyond this, *The Critique of Judgment, Religion within the Limits of Reason,* and the political writings cannot be neglected without distorting his doctrine. For the last, see *Kant's Political Writings,* ed. Hans Reiss and trans. H. B. Nisbet (Cambridge, The University Press, 1970).

5. For this point I am indebted to Charles Fried.

6. See *The Methods of Ethics,* 7th ed. (London, Macmillan, 1907), Appendix, "The Kantian Conception of Free Will" (reprinted from *Mind,* vol. 13, 1888), pp. 511–516, esp. p. 516.

7. See B. A. O. Williams, "The Idea of Equality," in *Philosophy, Politics and Society,* Second Series, ed. Peter Laslett and W. G. Runciman (Oxford, Basil Blackwell, 1962), pp. 115f. For confirmation of this interpretation, see Kant's remarks on moral education in *The Critique of Practical Reason,* pt. II. See also Beck, *A Commentary on Kant's Critique of Practical Reason,* pp. 233–236.

Virtues and Vices
Philippa Foot

Philippa Foot, who until her retirement was professor of philosophy at the University of California at Los Angeles and is now senior research fellow at Sommerville College, Oxford, has been an important contributor to discussions in both moral theory and applied ethics for many years. She was one of the first to argue that moral philosophy in the second half of the twentieth century had unfortunately neglected a traditional moral concern with the virtues. The essay reprinted here, one of her contributions to the renewed discussion of the virtues for which she is partly responsible, attempts to achieve a better understanding of what virtues are. She argues that virtues are states of character that are generally beneficial both to those who possess them and to others; in fact, they might be understood as causal dispositions to produce good actions. Furthermore, they tend to oppose motivations to do wrong that are common to human nature. Her account of what a virtue is might also, she believes, help us to understand a notorious claim that Kant is sometimes interpreted as making. According to that interpretation, Kant maintains that an act of duty can have moral worth only if it is done reluctantly against the agent's inclination. She argues that with a proper understanding of the virtues, one can appreciate the moral importance of both doing duty reluctantly and doing it happily.

I

For many years the subject of the virtues and vices was strangely neglected by moralists working within the school of analytic philosophy. The tacitly accepted opinion was that a study of the topic would form no part of the fundamental work of ethics; and since this opinion was apparently shared by philosophers such as Hume, Kant, Mill, G. E. Moore, W. D. Ross, and H. A. Prichard, from whom contemporary moral philosophy has mostly been derived, perhaps the neglect was not so surprising after all. However that may be, things have recently been changing. . . .

In spite of this recent work, it is best when considering the virtues and vices to go back to Aristotle and Aquinas. I myself have found Plato less helpful, because the individual virtues and vices are not so clearly or consistently distinguished in his work. It is certain, in any case, that the most systematic account is found in Aristotle, and in the blending of Aristotelian and Christian philosophy found in St. Thomas. By and large Aquinas followed Aristotle—sometimes even heroically—where Aristotle gave an opinion, and where St. Thomas is on his own, as in developing the doctrine of the theological virtues of faith, hope and charity, and in his theocentric doctrine of happiness,

From *Virtues and Vices and Other Essays in Moral Philosophy*, by Philippa Foot (Berkeley, CA: University of California Press, 1978), pp. 1–18.

he still uses an Aristotelian framework where he can: as for instance in speaking of happiness as man's last end. However, there are different emphases and new elements in Aquinas's ethics: often he works things out in far more detail than Aristotle did, and it is possible to learn a great deal from Aquinas that one could not have got from Aristotle. It is my opinion that the *Summa Theologica* is one of the best sources we have for moral philosophy, and moreover that St. Thomas's ethical writings are as useful to the atheist as to the Catholic or other Christian believer. . . .

I will come back to Aristotle and Aquinas, and shall indeed refer to them frequently in this paper. But I want to start by making some remarks, admittedly fragmentary, about the concept of a moral virtue as we understand the idea.

First of all it seems clear that virtues are, in some general way, beneficial. Human beings do not get on well without them. Nobody can get on well if he lacks courage, and does not have some measure of temperance and wisdom, while communities where justice and charity are lacking are apt to be wretched places to live, as Russia was under the Stalinist terror, or Sicily under the Mafia. But now we must ask to whom the benefit goes, whether to the man who has the virtue or rather to those who have to do with him? In the case of some of the virtues the answer seems clear. Courage, temperance and wisdom benefit both the man who has these dispositions and other people as well; and moral failings such as pride, vanity, worldliness, and avarice harm both their possessor and others, though chiefly perhaps the former. But what about the virtues of charity and justice? These are directly concerned with the welfare of others, and with what is owed to them; and since each may require sacrifice of interest on the part of the virtuous man both may seem to be deleterious to their possessor and beneficial to others. Whether in fact it is so has, of course, been a matter of controversy since Plato's time or earlier. It is a reasonable opinion that on the whole a man is better off for being charitable and just, but this is not to say that circumstances may not arise in which he will have to sacrifice everything for charity or justice. . . .

Let us say then, leaving unsolved problems behind us, that virtues are in general beneficial characteristics, and indeed ones that a human being needs to have, for his own sake and that of his fellows. This will not, however, take us far towards a definition of a virtue, since there are many other qualities of a man that may be similarly beneficial, as for instance bodily characteristics such as health and physical strength, and mental powers such as those of memory and concentration. What is it, we must ask, that differentiates virtues from such things?

As a first approximation to an answer we might say that while health and strength are excellences of the body, and memory and concentration of the mind, it is the will that is good in a man of virtue. But this suggestion is worth only as much as the explanation that follows it. What might we mean by saying that virtue belongs to the will?

In the first place we observe that it is primarily by his intentions that a man's moral dispositions are judged. If he does something unintentionally this is usually irrelevant to our estimate of his virtue. But of course this thesis must be qualified, because failures in performance rather than intention may show a lack of virtue. This will be so when, for instance, one man brings harm to another without realizing he is doing it, but where his ignorance is itself culpable. Sometimes in such cases there will be a previous act or omission to which we can point as the source of the ignorance. Charity requires that we take care to find out how to render assistance where we are likely to be called on to do so, and thus, for example, it is contrary to charity to fail to find out about elementary first aid. But in an interesting class of cases in which it seems again to be performance rather than intention that counts in judging a man's virtue there is no possibility of shifting the judgement to previous intentions. For sometimes one man succeeds where another fails not because there is some specific difference in their previous conduct but rather because his heart lies in a different place; and the disposition of the heart is part of virtue.

Thus it seems right to attribute a kind of moral failing to some deeply discouraging and debilitating people who say, without lying, that they mean to be helpful; and on the other side to see virtue *par excellence* in one who is prompt and resourceful in doing good. In his novel *A Single Pebble* John Hersey describes such a man, speaking of a rescue in a swift flowing river:

> It was the head tracker's marvellous swift response that captured my admiration at first, his split second solicitousness when he heard a cry of pain, his finding in mid-air, as it were, the only way to save the injured boy. But there was more to it than that. His action, which could not have been mulled over in his mind, showed a deep, instinctive love of life, a compassion, an optimism, which made me feel very good . . .

What this suggests is that a man's virtue may be judged by his innermost desires as well as by his intentions; and this fits with our idea that a virtue such as generosity lies as much in someone's attitudes as in his actions. Pleasure in the good fortune of others is, one thinks, the sign of a generous spirit; and small reactions of pleasure and displeasure often the surest signs of a man's moral disposition.

None of this shows that it is wrong to think of virtues as belonging to the will; what it does show is that 'will' must here be understood in its widest sense, to cover what is wished for as well as what is sought. . . .

II

I shall now turn to another thesis about the virtues, which I might express by saying that they are *corrective*, each one standing at a point at which there is some temptation to be resisted or deficiency of motivation to be made good. As Aristotle put it, virtues are about what is difficult for men, and I want to see in what sense this is true, and then to consider a problem in Kant's moral philosophy in the light of what has been said.

Let us first think about courage and temperance. Aristotle and Aquinas contrasted these virtues with justice in the following respect. Justice was concerned with operations, and courage and temperance with passions. . . . It is obviously true that courage and temperance have to do with particular springs of action as justice does not. Almost any desire can lead a man to act unjustly, not even excluding the desire to help a friend or to save a life, whereas a cowardly act must be motivated by fear or a desire for safety, and an act of intemperance by a desire for pleasure, perhaps even for a particular range of pleasures such as those of eating or drinking or sex. And now, going back to the idea of virtues as correctives, one may say that it is only because fear and the desire for pleasure often operate as temptations that courage and temperance exist as virtues at all. As things are we often want to run away not only where that is the right thing to do but also where we should stand firm; and we want pleasure not only where we should seek pleasure but also where we should not. If human nature had been different there would have been no need of a corrective disposition in either place, as fear and pleasure would have been good guides to conduct throughout life. . . .

As with courage and temperance so with many other virtues: there is, for instance, a virtue of industriousness only because idleness is a temptation; and of humility only because men tend to think too well of themselves. Hope is a virtue because despair too is a temptation; it might have been that no one cried that all was lost except where he could really see it to be so, and in this case there would have been no virtue of hope.

With virtues such as justice and charity it is a little different, because they correspond not to any particular desire or tendency that has to be kept in check but rather to a deficiency of motivation; and it is this that they must make good. If people were as much attached to the good of others as they are to their own good there would no more be a general virtue of benevolence than there is a general virtue of self-love. And if people cared about the rights of others as they care about their own rights no virtue of justice would be needed to look after the matter, and rules about such things as contracts and promises would only need to be made public, like the rules of a game that everyone was eager to play.

On this view of the virtues and vices everything is seen to depend on what human nature is like, and the traditional catalogue of the two kinds of dispositions is not hard to understand. Nevertheless it may be defective, and anyone who accepts the thesis that I am putting forward will feel free to ask himself where the temptations and deficiencies that need correcting are really to be found. It is possible, for example, that the theory of human nature lying behind the traditional list of the virtues and vices puts too much emphasis on hedonistic and sensual impulses, and does not sufficiently take account of less straightforward inclinations such as the desire to be put upon and dissatisfied, or the unwillingness to accept good things as they come along.

It should now be clear why I said that virtues should be seen as correctives; and part of what is meant by saying that virtue is about things that are difficult for men should also have appeared. The further application of this idea is, however, controversial, and the following difficulty presents itself: that we both are and are not inclined to think that the harder a man finds it to act virtuously the more virtue he shows if he does act well. For on the one hand great virtue is needed where it is particularly hard to act virtuously; yet on the other it could be argued that difficulty in acting virtuously shows that the agent is imperfect in virtue: according to Aristotle, to take pleasure in virtuous action is the mark of true virtue, with the self-mastery of the one who finds virtue difficult only a second best. How then is this conflict to be decided? Who shows most charity, the one who finds it easy to make the good of others his object, or the one who finds it hard?

What is certain is that the thought that virtues are corrective does not constrain us to relate virtue to difficulty in each individual man. Since men in general find it hard to face great dangers or evils, and even small ones, we may count as courageous those few who without blindness or indifference are nevertheless fearless even in terrible circumstances. And when someone has a natural charity or generosity it is at least part of the virtue that he has; if natural virtue cannot be the whole of virtue this is because a kindly or fearless disposition could be disastrous without justice and wisdom, and because these virtues have to be learned, not because natural virtue is too easily acquired. I have argued that the virtues can be seen as correctives in relation to human nature in general but not that each virtue must present a difficulty to each and every man.

Nevertheless many people feel strongly inclined to say that it is for moral effort that moral praise is to be bestowed, and that in proportion as a man finds it easy to be virtuous so much the less is he to be morally admired for his good actions. The dilemma can be resolved only when we stop talking about difficulties standing in the way of virtuous action as if they were of only one kind. The fact is that some kinds of difficulties do indeed provide an occasion for much virtue, but that others rather show that virtue is incomplete.

To illustrate this point I shall first consider an example of honest action. We may suppose for instance that a man has an opportunity to steal, in circumstances where stealing is not morally permissible, but that he refrains. And now let us ask our old question. For one man it is hard to refrain from stealing and for another man it is not: which shows the greater virtue in acting as he should? It is not difficult to see in this case that it makes all the difference whether the difficulty comes from circumstances, as that a man is poor, or that his theft is unlikely to be detected, or whether it comes from something that belongs to his own character. The fact that a man is *tempted* to steal is something about him that shows a certain lack of honesty: of the thoroughly honest man we say that it 'never entered his head', meaning that it was never a real possibility for him. But the fact that he is poor is something that makes the occasion more *tempting*, and difficulties of this kind make honest action all the more virtuous.

A similar distinction can be made between different obstacles standing in the way of charitable action. Some circumstances, as that great sacrifice is needed, or that the one to be helped is a rival, give an occasion on which a man's charity is severely tested. Yet in given circumstances of this kind it is the man who acts easily rather than the one who finds it hard who shows the most charity. Charity is a virtue of attachment, and that sympathy for others which makes it easier to help them is part of the virtue itself. . . .

Both the distinction between different kinds of obstacles to virtuous action and the general idea that virtues are correctives will be useful in resolving a difficulty in Kant's moral philosophy closely related to the issues discussed in the preceding paragraphs. In a passage in the first section of the *Groundwork of the Metaphysics of Morals* Kant notoriously tied himself into a knot in trying to give an account of those actions which have as he put it 'positive moral worth'. Arguing that only actions done out of a sense of duty have this worth he contrasts a philanthropist who 'takes pleasure in spreading happiness around him' with one who acts out of respect for duty, saying that the actions of the latter but not the former have moral worth. Much scorn has been poured on Kant for this curious doctrine, and indeed it does seem that something has gone wrong, but perhaps we are not in a position to scoff unless we can give our own account of the idea on which Kant is working. After all it does seem that he is right in saying that some actions are in accordance with duty, and even required by duty, without being the subjects of moral praise, like those of the honest trader who deals honestly in a situation in which it is in his interest to do so.

It was this kind of example that drove Kant to his strange conclusion. He added another example, however, in discussing acts of self-preservation; these he said, while they normally have no positive moral worth, may have it when a man preserves his life not from inclination but without inclination and from a sense of duty. Is he not right in saying that acts of self-preservation normally have no moral significance but that they may have it, and how do we ourselves explain this fact?

To anyone who approaches this topic from a consideration of the virtues the solution readily suggests itself. Some actions are in accordance with virtue without requiring virtue for their performance, whereas others are both in accordance with virtue and such as to show possession of a virtue. So Kant's trader was dealing honestly in a situation in which the virtue of honesty is not required for honest dealing, and it is for this reason that his action did not have 'positive moral worth'. Similarly, the care that one ordinarily takes for one's life, as for instance on some ordinary morning in eating one's breakfast and keeping out of the way of a car on the road, is something for which no virtue is required. As we said earlier there is no general virtue of self-love as there is a virtue of benevolence or charity, because men are generally attached sufficiently to their own good. Nevertheless in special circumstances virtues such as temperance, courage, fortitude, and hope may be needed if someone is to preserve his life. . . . And it is this that explains why there may be a moral aspect to suicide which does not depend on possible injury to other people. It is not that suicide is 'always wrong', whatever that would mean, but that suicide is *sometimes* contrary to virtues such as courage and hope.

Let us now return to Kant's philanthropists, with the thought that it is action that is in accordance with virtue and also displays a virtue that has moral worth. We see at once that Kant's difficulties are avoided, and the happy philanthropist reinstated in the position which belongs to him. For charity is, as we said, a virtue of attachment as well as action, and the sympathy that makes it easier to act with charity is part of the virtue. The man who acts charitably out of a sense of duty is not to be undervalued, but it is the other who most shows virtue and therefore to the other that most moral worth is attributed. Only a detail of Kant's presentation of the case of the dutiful philanthropist tells on the other side. For what he actually said was that this man felt no sympathy and took no pleasure in the good of others because 'his mind was clouded by some sorrow of his own', and this is the kind of circumstance that increases the virtue that is needed if a man is to act well.

III

It was suggested above that an action with 'positive moral worth', or as we might say a positively good action, was to be seen as one which was in accordance with virtue, by which I mean contrary to no virtue, and moreover one for which a virtue was required. Nothing has so far been said about another case, excluded by the formula, in which it might seem that an act displaying one virtue was nevertheless contrary to another. In giving this last description I am thinking not of two virtues with competing claims, as if what were required by justice could nevertheless be demanded by charity, or something of that kind, but rather of the possibility that a virtue such as courage or temperance or industry which overcomes a special temptation, might be displayed in an act of folly or villainy. Is this something that we must allow for, or is it only good or innocent actions which can be acts of these virtues? Aquinas, in his definition of virtue, said that virtues can produce only good actions and that they are dispositions 'of which no one can make bad use', except when they are treated as objects, as in being the subject of hatred or pride. The common opinion nowadays is, however, quite different. . . . Most people take it for granted that the virtues of courage and temperance may aid a bad man in his evil work. . . .

There are, however, reasons for thinking that the matter is not so simple as this. . . . Is there not more difficulty than might appear in the idea of an act of injustice which is nevertheless an act of courage? Suppose for instance that a sordid murder were in question, say a murder done for gain or to get an inconvenient person out of the way, but that this murder had to be done in alarming circumstances or in the face of real danger; should we be happy to say that such an action was an act of courage or a courageous act? Did the murderer, who certainly acted boldly, or with intrepidity, if he did the murder, also act courageously? Some people insist that they are ready to say this, but

I have noticed that they like to move over to a murder for the sake of conscience, or to some other act done in the course of a villainous enterprise but whose immediate end is innocent or positively good. On their hypothesis, which is that bad acts can easily be seen as courageous acts or acts of courage, my original example should be just as good.

What are we to say about this difficult matter? There is no doubt that the murderer who murdered for gain was *not a coward*: he did not have a second moral defect which another villain might have had. There is no difficulty about this because it is clear that one defect may neutralise another. As Aquinas remarked, it is better for a blind horse if it is slow. It does not follow, however, that an act of villainy can be courageous; we are inclined to say that it 'took courage', and yet it seems wrong to think of courage as equally connected with good actions and bad.

One way out of this difficulty might be to say that the man who is ready to pursue bad ends does indeed have courage, and shows courage in his action, but that in him courage is not a virtue. Later I shall consider some cases in which this might be the right thing to say, but in this instance it does not seem to be. For unless the murderer consistently pursues bad ends his courage will often result in good; it may enable him to do many innocent or positively good things for himself or for his family and friends. On the strength of an individual bad action we can hardly say that in him courage is not a virtue. Nevertheless there is something to be said even about the individual action to distinguish it from one that would readily be called an act of courage or a courageous act. Perhaps the following analogy may help us to see what it is. We might think of words such as 'courage' as naming characteristics of human beings in respect of a certain power, as words such as 'poison' and 'solvent' and 'corrosive' so name the properties of physical things. The power to which virtue-words are so related is the power of producing good action, and good desires. But just as poisons, solvents and corrosives do not always operate characteristically, so it could be with virtues. If P (say arsenic) is a poison it does not follow that P acts as a poison wherever it is found. It is quite natural to say on occasion 'P does not act as a poison here' though P is a poison and it is P that is acting here. Similarly courage is not operating as a virtue when the murderer turns his courage, which is a virtue, to bad ends. Not surprisingly the resistance that some of us registered was not to the expression 'the courage of the murderer' or to the assertion that what he did 'took courage' but rather to the description of that action as an act of courage or a courageous act. It is not that the action *could* not be so described, but that the fact that courage does not here have its characteristic operation is a reason for finding the description strange.

In this example we were considering an action in which courage was not operating as a virtue, without suggesting that in that agent it generally failed to do so. But the latter is also a possibility. If someone is both wicked and foolhardy this may be the case with courage, and it is even easier to find examples of a general connexion with evil rather than good in the case of some other virtues. Suppose, for instance, that we think of someone who is over-industrious, or too ready to refuse pleasure, and this is characteristic of him rather than something we find on one particular occasion. In this case the virtue of industry, or the virtue of temperance, has a systematic connexion with defective action rather than good action; and it might be said in either case that the virtue did not operate as a virtue in this man. Just as we might say in a certain setting 'P is not a poison here' though P is a poison and P is here, so we might say that industriousness, or temperance, is not a virtue in some. Similarly in a man habitually given to wishful thinking, who clings to false hopes, hope does not operate as a virtue and we may say that it is not a virtue in him.

The thought developed in the last paragraph, to the effect that not every man who has a virtue has something that is a virtue in him, may help to explain a certain discomfort that one may feel when discussing the virtues. It is not easy to put one's finger on what is wrong, but it has something to do with a disparity between the moral ideals that may seem to be implied in our talk about the virtues, and the moral judgements that we actually make. Someone reading the foregoing pages might, for instance, think that the author of this paper always admired most those people who had all the virtues, being wise and temperate as well as courageous, charitable, and just. And indeed it is sometimes so. There are some people who do possess all these virtues and who are loved and admired by all the world, as Pope John XXIII was loved and admired. Yet the fact is that many of us look up to some people whose chaotic lives contain rather little of wisdom or temperance, rather than to some others who possess these virtues. And while it may be that this is just romantic nonsense I suspect that it is not. For while wisdom always operates as a virtue, its close relation prudence does not, and it is prudence rather than wisdom that inspires many a careful life. Prudence is not a virtue in everyone, any more than industriousness is, for in some it is rather an over-anxious concern for safety and propriety, and a determination to keep away from people or situations which are apt to bring trouble with them; and by such defensiveness much good is lost. It is the same with temperance. Intemperance can be an appalling thing, as it was with Henry VIII of whom Wolsey remarked that

> rather than he will either miss or want any part of his will or appetite, he will put the loss of one half of his realm in danger.

Nevertheless in some people temperance is not a virtue, but is rather connected with timidity or with a grudging attitude to the acceptance of good things. Of course what is best is to live boldly yet without imprudence or intemperance, but the fact is that rather few can manage that.

Ethics, "Feminine" Ethics, and Feminist Ethics
Susan Sherwin

Susan Sherwin is a professor of philosophy at Dalhousie University and the author of a number of publications that address issues in applied ethics from a feminist point of view. Sherwin begins by describing three standard models of ethical theory—Kantianism, utilitarianism, and contractarianism. Despite the significant differences among these theories, Sherwin alleges that from the point of view of women's experience they share similar problems. First, the three theories present the same picture of the ideal moral agent: one who reasons rationally, impartially, and autonomously in making moral decisions. Secondly, they share a picture of the purpose of morality itself as a vehicle for making essentially self-interested persons act for the common good. Sherwin contends that both pictures are foreign to women's experiences of moral reasoning, in which neither abstracting oneself from the problem at hand or from the web of social relationships in which one is already situated is seen as desirable.

Sherwin next turns to an alternative model of ethical theory, largely developed by women philosophers, which she calls "feminine" ethics and which is also known as the ethics of care. While the emphasis of this perspective on the contextuality of moral reasoning and the moral significance of care-giving, an activity in which most women are deeply involved, represents to Sherwin an improvement over standard moral theory, the label she gives to it indicates its primary disadvantage. Her concern is that by focusing their moral activities on caring for others, women can reinforce the social conditions that cause them to be oppressed.

In the final part of this essay, Sherwin presents a defense of feminist ethics. While feminist ethics challenges traditional ethics in some of the same ways as "feminine" ethics, anyone using feminist ethics as a framework for deliberation would be interested in both care and justice, and would be concerned to make decisions that would help to end the oppression of women. For these reasons, Sherwin believes feminist ethics offers a better alternative to both standard ethical theory and the ethics of care.

TRADITIONAL ETHICS

Several different traditions are followed by the philosophers who currently work in ethics. Because I mean to distinguish my own position of feminist ethics from the major competitors in traditional, mainstream (malestream)[1] ethics, I shall briefly review the positions adopted by most philosophers working in the field of nonfeminist ethics and try to explain why I reject these alternatives. To explain my departure from the leading traditions, I focus on the elements that I find problematic within each theory. . . .

From *No Longer Patient: Feminist Ethics and Health Care*, by Susan Sherwin (Philadelphia: Temple University Press, 1992), pp. 35-57.

Most modern, Western theorists pursue one of three distinct approaches, which are known by philosophers as deontological ethics, consequentialism and social contract theory.[2] Deontologists believe that ethics is a matter of determining which actions are required or prohibited as a matter of moral duty. These actions are right (or wrong) because they are required (or proscribed) by a moral law or set of rules that is binding on persons, independent of their specific interests. Immanuel Kant is the most influential of the deontologists, and although his most important work in ethics was published more than two hundred years ago (*Groundwork of the Metaphysic of Morals* [1785]), his general approach is still widely followed today.

Kant proposed that the right-making characteristic of an action is defined by the logical nature of the principle it embodies. He believed that moral duties are identified by rational, free persons through the purely abstract process of reason. Kant argued that the moral law must be above personal considerations, that is, independent of the feelings of those involved in particular applications. The moral evaluation he called for explicitly disallows consideration of the specific circumstances of the agent or of other parties affected. Rather, moral conclusions must be reached through reasoning that has been abstracted from the circumstances of application, whereby agents decide if the maxims under which they would act could be willed to be universally binding. (For example, the maxim to tell the truth can be willed to be universal without contradiction, but the maxim to lie to take advantage of others' good faith cannot.) Kant was well aware that the specific consequences of performing an action prescribed by such a principle might be undesirable in a particular circumstance, but he believed that morality consists in following the moral law and not in pursuing the consequences we prefer. . . .

Deontological theories pay scant attention to the specific details of individuals' moral experiences and relationships. They admit that special obligations arise from specific relationships—for example, to friends and family—but little discussion is devoted to exploring the range or force of such duties. Almost all the theoretical work is concentrated on exploring the nature of general, rather than specific, obligations. As Cheshire Calhoun argues, such neglect creates two ideological views about the moral life that amount to an inherent gender bias: most moral theorists imply (1) that it is self-evident that special obligations are less important than the general, impersonal duties that theorists chiefly emphasize, and (2) that general, rather than special, obligations are experienced most frequently in the moral lives of persons. The moral lives of women are often taken up with the details of special obligations, yet these concerns are discounted. . . .

[Secondly,] deontological ethics [does] not express any interest in accommodating feminist concerns about the effects of oppressive practices on subordinate groups as part of their moral evaluations of such practices. . . . Kant [does not] provide grounds for directing our attention to the specific experiences and interests of members of oppressed groups. Hence feminists cannot find space within . . . deontological ethics to address the specific harms of the patterns of dominance they seek to change.

Moreover, feminists must object to the formulation of Kant's ethics, because like many other moral theorists, Kant assumed that only men would fully qualify as moral agents. He believed that women—together with children and idiots—were unable (or unwilling) to engage in a process that required them to ignore personal sentiments in their moral decision-making. Because of this "deficiency," he considered women inferior moral agents, unfit for public life. Rather than accept Kant's view of women as deficient moral agents, feminists generally judge his determination to discount the role of sentiment to be a mark of inadequacy in the theory itself. . . .

Consequentialists have an entirely different vision of morality from Kant's: they believe that the moral worth of an action is measured in terms of the worth of the consequences of the action. Consequentialists determine a measure against which states of affairs can be evaluated and hold that an action is right if it maximizes what is desirable in its outcome, in comparison with the results of all alternatives. The most familiar form of consequentialism is utilitarianism, in which consequences are evaluated in terms of the aggregate effects of an action on the welfare or happiness of persons (or sentient beings). Like other consequentialists, utilitarians deny that rules should be followed if they result in less desirable outcomes, even if those rules appear rational in the abstract. Unlike Kantians, consequentialists believe that the particular feelings and attitudes both of agents and of those affected by the actions in question should be considered when determining the moral value of actions; in this sense, their analysis focuses on concrete experience.

Those who promote consequentialism in its traditional formulations still operate on an abstract plane, however, because ultimately, rightness of an action is calculated by appeal to the total amount of happiness and suffering created by an act, without regard to whose happiness or suffering is at issue. For example, if a utilitarian can produce the greatest amount of happiness by performing an action that will benefit her enemies rather than her children, she is obligated to do that. Although the individual agent would find it preferable to benefit her loved ones rather than her enemies, and although her own pain at the outcome is an element to be considered in the calculation, the theory says that what is important is the total amount of happiness that will be produced by the act. There is no assurance that this requirement will allow her to act on behalf of those she loves, rather than on behalf of those she fears or loathes. . . .

Like Kantianism, then, consequentialism has usually been understood to demand a level of impartiality on the part of agents, which many people find psychologically unacceptable and morally repugnant. The details of the emotional lives and the relationships of the particular persons affected are rendered irrelevant from the moral point of view, except insofar as these details contribute to overall measures of happiness or suffering. All persons are essentially interchangeable for the purposes of both moral theories. Specifically, no special role is directly assigned to a person's status in dominance/subordination relationships. In both Kantian deontology and consequentialism, moral agents are asked to distance themselves from their personal experience and concerns. Kant directs agents to think in terms of universal laws, without regard to the circumstances from which actions arise; consequentialists direct them to weigh their own interests equally with those of everyone else, and on most accounts there is no moral evaluation of the worth of the interests themselves. Both theories deny giving special weight to the details of individuals' actual positions in dominance hierarchies. This abstract neutrality is objectionable from the perspective of feminist ethics, which demands explicit focus on the social and political contexts of individuals in its moral deliberations.

Contractarianism, or social contract theory, is the third form of moral theory widely embraced in contemporary Anglo-American philosophy. It combines elements of both Kantian theory and consequentialism; moreover, it shares with feminism a commitment to placing the discussion of moral judgments within an explicitly social context (although for contractarians, this context is likely to be an artificial one). Nevertheless, most contractarians differ from feminists in their assumptions about human nature. Most believe persons are inherently independent and self-interested, and they see the task of morality as that of ensuring cooperation among essentially competitive individuals. They appeal to the notion of a hypothetical agreement—what they commonly call "the social contract"—which would be the logical outcome of reasoned negotiation that would be conducted among separate, self-interested beings. The contract is the means by which these hypothetical selves acknowledge the mutual advantage of restraining aggressive (non-moral) behavior against one another; without this agreement, their relationships presumably would be characterized by aggression and coercion (a life that is "solitary, poor, nasty, brutish, and short," as Thomas Hobbes so vividly put it). Because most contractarians assume that other people pose a serious threat to one's self-interest, morality is presented as the rational option by which to limit the dangers of social life.

Like Kant, most contractarians propose that only the abstract features common to all persons can have moral significance in determining the terms of the contract; hence they usually limit their assumptions about human beings to the characteristics that are assumed to define moral agency, those of rationality, autonomy, and self-interest. They share with consequentialists the belief that the role of morality is to help facilitate humanly desired ends. The ideal moral community that contractarians invite us to imagine is described as being composed of equal, rational, autonomous, independent persons. Generally, social contract theorists do not address the moral status of persons who do not meet these ideal standards, nor do they investigate the nature of the moral relationships that exist among persons of unequal power. Attention to the particular details of the lives of the contractors (for example, family life, status in the hierarchical pecking order, specific skills and talents, or disabilities) is generally thought to compromise, rather than enhance, the legitimacy of the contract.[3] But these kinds of details are important. Contracts made under the "veil of ignorance" tend to perpetuate, rather than correct, the structures that maintain oppressive practices. . . . By refusing to distinguish between various differences among people, most contractarians proceed as if traits such as gender and race can be treated as being on a par with eye colour; they fail to identify the mechanisms that must be put in place in a currently oppressive society to achieve the quality they presume. Therefore, most feminists find none of the existing social contract theories adequate to address their political concerns.

Because all three moral theories are extraordinarily abstract, most people who appeal to them to inform actual moral decision-making have found the theories woefully inadequate for the practical tasks of moral life. Moral behavior arises in the context of particular lives that are embedded in particular sorts of relationships. Therefore, ethics should attend to the nature of the relationships that hold among those who are involved in situations requiring moral deliberation. As we have seen, none of the leading formulations of traditional theories allows sufficient room for such considerations.

"FEMININE" ETHICS

Many women have found the approaches discussed above (as well as most of the other proposals for ethics that have been presented throughout the history of Western thought) to be alienating and unsatisfactory. . . . They have identified a number of objections to traditional ethical theory as it is usually conceived. Their concerns can be categorized into two distinct groups. The first set, which I label "Feminine" ethics, consists of observations of how the traditional approaches to ethics fail to fit the moral experiences and intuitions of women. It includes suggestions for how ethics must be modified if it is to be of value to women. The other set of concerns, addressed in the next section, is what I consider to be feminist ethics proper; it applies a specifically political perspective and offers suggestions for how ethics must be revised if it is to get at the patterns of dominance and oppression as they affect women. . . .

For years, feminists fought against men's claim that women pursue morality differently from men. They sought to establish an equality of moral ability between men and women; this equality was deemed necessary if women were to achieve equal political rights with men. Hence, many important reformist thinkers and activists, including prominent figures of the Anglo-American feminist movement, argued that women have, at least in principle, the same moral capacities as men. Others, however, including leading feminists of the European community, accepted the claim that there is a gender difference in male and female moral thinking; they sought to have the feminine approach to moral thought recognized as a legitimate and important element, which needs to be added to discussions in the public sphere. These theorists argued that rather than disqualifying women from public life, women's distinctive moral perspective makes it urgent that they be included in public debates so that their voices can be heard. Recently, many feminists on both sides of the Atlantic have embraced this notion of women's different approach to moral reasoning.

Carol Gilligan has provided us with an important empirical study that seems to identify a gender difference in moral thinking. She found that when women are presented with moral conflicts, they tend to focus on details about the relationships that hold between the individuals concerned, and they seek out innovative solutions that protect the interests of all participants; that is, they strive to find options that avoid bringing harm to anyone. Men, in contrast, tend to try to identify the appropriate rules that govern the sort of situation described; they select the course of action most compatible with the dominant rule, even if someone's interests may be sacrificed to considerations of justice. Gilligan named the former an ethic of responsibility or care and the latter an ethic of justice. The empirical gender correlations are not perfect, because women sometimes opt for a justice solution and men sometimes choose in accordance with an ethic of care; but statistically, she found that girls and women are likely to choose responses that are sensitive to considerations of responsibility, whereas boys and men are likely to reflect considerations of justice in their analysis. On Gilligan's view, the ideal for all moral agents would be an ethics that includes elements of both approaches.

Thus, it appears that Gilligan supports the assumption . . . that women focus on the particular, expressing their concern for the feelings and special relationships of the persons involved in moral dilemmas, but unlike Kant and his followers she does not disallow such responses from the realm of the moral. Instead, she expands the definition of moral considerations, so that traditionally feminine thinking is recognized as morally relevant, rather than deficient. Gilligan thereby includes women's characteristic moral experiences and approach to moral decision-making in the field of legitimate moral thinking. . . .

Interestingly, Gilligan also found that most men reflect a fear of intimacy; they identify separation as the desirable norm and view interactions as anomalous and threatening. It appears, then, that men have constructed ethics in their own psychological image. The ethical theories in the tradition of mainstream philosophy seem to have been principally designed to protect the rights of independent beings in the "disturbing" circumstances of human interaction.

Ethical models based on the image of ahistorical, self-sufficient, atom-like individuals are simply not credible to most women. Because women are usually charged with the responsibility of caring for children, the elderly, and the ill as well as the responsibility of physically and emotionally nurturing men, both at work and at home, most women experience the world as a complex web of interdependent relationships, where responsible caring for others is implicit in their moral lives. The abstract reasoning of morality that centers on the rights of independent agents is inadequate for the moral reality in which they live. Most women find that a different model for ethics is necessary; the traditional ones are not persuasive.

Nel Noddings has taken Gilligan's move a step further; she, too, accepts that caring is morally significant, but she goes so far as to argue that it is the only legitimate moral consideration. In *Caring* (1984) she argues that everyone (men and women alike) ought to pursue a feminine ethic of caring and abandon the insensitive demands of the abstract moral rules of justice. She focuses on "how to meet the other morally" and defines the proper locus of ethical thought as the quality of relationships, rather than a quality of judgments or acts. An agent's moral obligation, in Noddings's view, is to meet others as "one-caring" and to maintain conditions that permit caring to flourish. These others, for their part, have a responsibility to exhibit reciprocity or, at least, to acknowledge the caring. Ethical behaviour, for Noddings, involves putting oneself at the service of others, seeing the world from their perspective, and acting "as though in my own behalf, but in behalf of the other" (Noddings 1984, 33).

Other women engaged in moral theory have spoken of the ethics associated with the characteristically feminine activity of mothering. Most notably, Sara Ruddick has proposed that maternal thinking, the moral perspective appropriate to the demands of mothering, is a distinctive way of knowing and caring that has implications for such important social issues as pacifism and antimilitarism. She believes that women are particularly skilled at such thinking, whether or not they are mothers, because they have been raised to be mothers.

Virginia Held shares Ruddick's concern with the ethics of mothering and urges us to explore the relationships between mothering persons and their children as an alternative model for moral thought (in contrast to the contractarian model of anonymous, isolated individuals). Held objects to the emphasis in mainstream ethics on relationships among rational, self-interested, independent beings; she suggests that "instead of importing into the household principles derived from the market place, perhaps we should export to the wider society the relations suitable from mothering persons and children." Like several other female theorists, she proposes developing an ethics rooted in characteristically female activities to replace the traditional approaches that seem tied to men's stereotypical development and interests. . . .

It seems, then, that the traditional approaches to ethics are not adequate for addressing all of women's moral intuitions or concerns. . . . Hence many women have begun to spell out the elements of moral reasoning that must be included in any moral theory that might be useful to them. The general consensus of female theorists is that such theories should involve models of human interaction that parallel the rich complexity of actual human relationships and should recognize the moral significance of the actual ties that bind people in their various relationships.

FEMINIST ETHICS

Feminist ethics is different from feminine ethics. It derives from the explicitly political perspective of feminism, wherein the oppression of women is seen to be morally and politically unacceptable. Hence, it involves more than recognition of women's actual experiences and moral practices; it incorporates a critique of the specific practices that constitute their oppression. Nevertheless, it is not altogether separate from what I have termed "feminine ethics."

In my view, feminist ethics must recognize the moral perspective of women; insofar as that includes the perspective described as an ethics of care, we should expand our moral agenda accordingly. Feminists have reason, however, to be cautious about the place of caring in their approach to ethics; it is necessary to be wary of the implications of gender traits within a sexist culture. Because gender differences are central to the structures that support dominance relations, it is likely that women's proficiency at caring is somehow related to women's subordinate status.

Within dominance relations, those who are assigned the subordinate positions, that is, those with less power, have special reason to be sensitive to the emotional pulse of others, to see things in relational terms, and to be pleasing and compliant. Thus the nurturing and caring at which women excel are, among other things, the survival skills of an oppressed group that lives in the close contact with its oppressors. This could help explain . . . evidence . . . which shows that the orientation and associated worldview that are ascribed to women in Gilligan's study of American women are similar to the orientation and worldview held by contemporary African and Afro-Americans of both genders. The dichotomy of values that Gilligan identifies between men and women is paralleled by a dichotomy between Europeans and formerly colonized peoples. Whatever positive value these common traits may hold, the virtues to which women have been shown to aspire seem to be virtues of subordination. Further, the African data reveal that the perspective that Gilligan associates with men is actually held only by some men, specifically those of European descent. . . .

Another danger inherent in proposals for feminine ethics is that caring about the welfare of others often leads women to direct all their energies toward meeting the needs of others; it may even lead them to protect the men who oppress them. Hence, feminists caution against valorising the traits that help perpetuate women's subordinate status. . . . Within the existing patterns of sexism, there is a clear danger that women will understand the prescriptions of feminine ethics to be directing them to pursue the virtues of caring, while men continue to focus on abstractions that protect their rights and autonomy. Although Gilligan sees the two perspectives of moral reasoning as complementary, not competitive, and believes that both elements must be incorporated into any adequate moral view, it is easy to read her evidence as entrenching the gender differences she uncovers. In a society where the feminine is devalued and equated with inferiority, it is not easy to perceive men embracing a moral approach described as feminine. Because the world is still filled with vulnerable, dependent persons who need care, if men do not assume the responsibilities of caring, then the burden for doing so remains on women.

Nonetheless, despite its politically suspect origins, caring is often a morally admirable way of relating to others. Feminists join with feminine ethicists in rejecting the picture that malestream ethicists offer of a world organized around purely self-interested agents—a world many women judge to be an emotionally and morally barren place that we would all do well to avoid. Feminists perceive that the caring that women do is morally valuable, but most feminists believe that women need to distinguish between circumstances in which care is appropriately offered and those in which it is better withheld. Therefore, an important task of feminist ethics is to establish moral criteria by which we can determine when caring should be offered and when it should be withheld. Feminist analyses of power structures suggest that specific instances of moral caring should be evaluated in the context of the social and political relations that each instance supports or challenges. In feminist ethics, evaluating the moral worth of specific acts and patterns of caring involves making political judgments.

Feminist ethics also takes from feminine ethics its recognition that personal feelings, such as empathy, loyalty, or guilt, can play an ethically significant role in moral deliberations. I think, however, that the proponents of abstraction are right to insist that there are limits to the place of caring in ethics. We should guard against allowing preferences, especially those tied to feelings of personal animosity, from being granted full range in ethical matters. For example, it would not be appropriate to decide to withdraw life support from a patient because she has been aggressive, complaining, and uncooperative, and hence her caregivers do not like her. Although there is something morally abhorrent about the obligation to make moral decisions without regard for the effects on loved ones, there is also great danger in believing we are only responsible for the interests of those for whom we feel affection. Morality must include respect for sentiments, but it cannot give full authority to particular sentiments without considering both their source and their effects. Because feminism arises from moral objections to oppression, it must maintain a commitment to the pursuit of social justice; that commitment is not always compatible with preferences derived from existing relationships and attitudes. Hence we must recognize that feminist ethics involves a commitment to considerations of justice, as well as to those of caring.

Feminist ethics takes its inspiration for other important features from what I have characterized as feminine ethics. It can agree with Gilligan that the morally relevant features of any decision making situation include the agents' responsibilities to specific persons, including themselves. It also shares with feminine ethics a recognition of the significance of rooting ethical discussion in specific contexts and thus rejecting traditional ethical theory's commitment to purely abstract reasoning. Like feminine ethics, feminist ethics directs us to consider the details of experience when evaluating practices. For example, when one is asked to decide about a morally uncertain policy such as euthanasia, it is important to remember the terror and pain of any of our own friends and relatives who were denied that option and also the constraints we may have observed in specific individuals' ability to make such decisions once their illnesses took over their lives. We cannot adequately develop moral attitudes toward a controversial practice such as euthanasia if we restrict our reasoning to abstract rules about the duty to respect life or about the importance of autonomy.

In addition, feminist ethics shares with feminine ethics a rejection of the paradigm of moral subjects as autonomous, rational, independent, and virtually indistinguishable from one another. . . . We must reconceive the concept of the individual, which has been taken as the central concept of ethical theory in Western thought. . . . We value persons as unique individuals whose lives are of concern to us, and in that respect, the individual person is still an important element of ethical thought. We cannot speak of the individual as the central unit of analysis, however, without considering that persons only exist in complex, social relationships. Unless we recognize that a person's desires, needs, and beliefs are formed only within human society, we may mistakenly imagine ourselves and our interests to be independent from others and their interests.

Individual persons learn moral values, judgments, and behaviours within human communities that teach them how to interpret the events and sensations that they experience. People do not approach a social contract with no moral history, as most contractarians would have it; nor do they privately deliberate about moral laws as purely rational beings, as Kant presumes. Further, they can only follow the utilitarian injunction to value the happiness of others if they experience themselves as members of a community where people are mutually caring about one another's well-being. Because persons do not exist in abstraction, apart from their social circumstances, moral directives to disregard the details of personal life under some imaginary "veil of ignorance" are pernicious for ethical and political analysis. These injunctions trivialize many of the most important moral facts. . . .

Most important, feminist ethics is characterized by its commitment to the feminist agenda of eliminating the subordination of women—and of other oppressed persons—in all of its manifestations. The principal insight of feminist ethics is that oppression, however it is practised, is morally wrong. Therefore, moral considerations demand that we uncover and examine the moral injustice of actual oppression in its many guises. When pressed, other sorts of moral theorists will acknowledge that oppressive practices are wrong, but such general declarations are morally inadequate in the face of insidious, systematic oppression. If we want moral change and not mere moral platitudes, then the particular practices that constitute oppression of one group by another must be identified and subjected to explicit moral condemnation; feminists demand the elimination of each oppressive practice. . . .

In pursuing feminist ethics, we must continually raise the question, what does it mean for women? When, for example, feminists consider medical research, confidentiality, or the new reproductive technologies, they need to ask not only most of the standard moral questions but also the general questions of how the issue under consideration relates to the oppression of women and what the implications of a proposed policy would be for the political status of women. Unless such questions are explicitly asked, the role of practices in the oppression of women (or others) is unlikely to be apparent, and offensive practices may well be morally defended. According to feminist ethics, other moral questions and judgments come into play only if we can assure ourselves that the act or practice in question is not itself one of a set of interlocking practices that maintains oppressive structures.

In practice, the constraints imposed by feminist ethics mean that, for instance, we cannot discuss abortion purely in terms of the rights of fetuses, without noticing that fetuses are universally housed in women's bodies. . . . Any morally adequate discussion of such practices must come to terms with the fact that the resulting social policy will have profound implications on the lives of women. Feminist ethics demands that the effects of any decision on women's lives be a feature of moral discussion and decision-making. In its appeal to contextual features, feminist ethics resists the model of traditional ethics, wherein the principal task is to define a totalizing or universal theory that prescribes rules for all possible worlds. Feminist ethics focuses instead on the need to develop a moral analysis that fits the actual world in which we live, without worrying about the implications of these considerations in some radically different set of circumstances.

NOTES

1. Apparently, this handy feminist term originated with O'Brien in her influential book *The Politics of Reproduction* (1981). It has been widely adopted by feminist critics in many disciplines, and it is hard to imagine how we ever got along without it.
2. Because my thinking is most influenced by work in the Anglo-American tradition, the sort of philosophy most commonly pursued in North American institutions, my discussion is limited to the leading ethical traditions within that paradigm. Continental and non-Western styles of philosophy propose different ethical models from those explored here, but they are beyond the scope of this review.
3. E.g., see Rawls, *A Theory of Justice* (1971). He argues that one can arrive at a just contract only if one does not know the special, distinguishing features of one's life, and hence each contractor must carefully consider the possibility of occupying each position that will exist within the society.

SUGGESTIONS FOR FURTHER READING

Aristotle. *Nicomachean Ethics.* Terence Irwin, trans. (Indianapolis: Hackett, 1985).

A particularly useful translation for nonspecialists of this classic treatment of the virtues.

Baier, Annette C. "What Do Women Want in a Moral Theory?" *Nous* 19 (1985), 53–63.

A thoughtful proposal to take the concept of trust as the key concept in any moral theory that would successfully accommodate the perspective of women.

Gilligan, Carol. *In a Different Voice.* (Cambridge, MA: Harvard University Press, 1982).

This seminal work maintains that traditional moral theory has neglected a way of perceiving morality that is more characteristic of the experience of women.

Herman, Barbara. *The Practice of Judgment.* (Cambridge, MA: Harvard University Press, 1993).

This is a collection of essays by a prominent contemporary Kantian moral philosopher in which she both interprets and extends Kant's ethical theory.

Jaggar, Alison M. "Feminist Ethics: Some Issues for the Nineties," *Journal of Social Philosophy* 20 (Spring–Fall 1989), 91–107.

Jaggar's aim in this widely-anthologized essay is to provide "minimum conditions of adequacy" that any feminist ethics needs to meet and to identify five debates within this approach.

MacIntyre, Alasdair. *After Virtue.* (Notre Dame, IN: University of Notre Dame Press, 1981).

One of the most important critiques in recent years of standard, rule-based ethical theories. MacIntyre suggests that such theories have deep problems of justification, and argues that the best ethical view so far is represented by the Aristotelian tradition of the virtues.

Rachels, James. *The Elements of Moral Philosophy*, 2nd ed. (New York: McGraw-Hill, Inc., 1993).

This is an excellent, evenhanded introduction to moral philosophy covering topics both in metaethics and normative moral theory.

Smart, J. J. C. and Bernard Williams. *Utilitarianism: For and Against.* (Cambridge, England: Cambridge University Press, 1973).

After two decades, this work is still one of the best exchanges on the merits and potential problems confronting utilitarianism.

Chapter 2

ABORTION

For more than twenty years, especially since the 1973 Supreme Court decision of *Roe v. Wade* establishing a legal right to at least some abortions, our society has been involved in vigorous debate (increasingly accompanied by violence) about abortion. Much of the history of this debate is discussed in this chapter's first reading by Mary Anne Warren. The issues of abortion include questions about both personal and political morality. The former concern the choice of an abortion by an individual. Is such a choice morally permissible, and if so, under what circumstances? A significant portion of America's population believes that at least most abortions are a serious moral wrong, perhaps even a matter of murder, but another significant portion of the population believes that at least many abortions are not wrong at all or not so wrong that a woman should not be able to choose to have one. The question of political morality arises in part because of the extent of the controversy. Given pervasive disagreement within the populace, how should the government respond to abortion, especially in a democracy presumably dedicated to governing according to the will of the people? Should abortions ever be legally prohibited? If so, under what circumstances should they be so?

The personal and political issues are not identical, and it should not be assumed that they must be answered in the same way. Some believe that even though abortions are morally wrong, they should not be legally prohibited in part because of the degree and seriousness of the disagreement over their moral status. It may also be consistent to argue that even though abortions are morally permissible, the nature of the controversy concerning them supports their legal prohibition. In this introduction, we shall first look at the issue of personal morality and then turn to the issue of political morality.

THE ISSUE OF PERSONAL MORALITY

At least four arguments are frequently heard in everyday discussions about the permissibility of abortion. While these arguments have been thoroughly developed and elaborated in the academic literature, it is worth beginning by considering very brief versions of the arguments to see what further questions need to be addressed in an attempt to elaborate and fully defend them.[1]

The Conservative Argument

Following what has become common practice, we shall refer to the position according to which all (or nearly all) abortions are morally wrong as being the conservative position. At least in broad outline, conservatives frequently argue in the following manner:

1. It is wrong to kill innocent human beings.
2. A human fetus is an innocent human being.
3. Therefore, it is wrong to kill a human fetus.

Each of the premises, 1. and 2., needs to be qualified, explained, and defended. While no one doubts that it is *typically* wrong to kill innocent human beings, it is widely believed that there are exceptions. For example, while waging a just war, the killing of some innocent civilians, for instance when bombing, may be unavoidable. If the first premise is to be used to show that abortion is wrong, it is necessary to consider the exceptions to the general wrongness of killing and ask whether any of these exceptions occur during pregnancies. It is often held, for example, that it is permissible to kill someone who innocently endangers your life if doing so is the only way to prevent that danger. (Such a person is called an "innocent threat.") A pregnancy that endangers a woman's life may well invoke that exception.

Much of the debate about the morality of abortion has centered on the second premise of the conservative argument. As Mary Anne Warren points out in her essay "On the Moral and Legal Status of Abortion" the claim that a human fetus is a human being can be understood in two ways. On one understanding, according to which the premise states that a fetus is genetically human, the claim would be accepted by everyone. However, if the concept of a human being is understood in this sense, few would think it always wrong to destroy human beings. There seems little wrong with wiping up and destroying blood that drips from a cut, for example, even though it too is genetically human. So the advocates of the conservative position must mean that a fetus is a human in some moral sense, that a fetus is the sort of being that deserves full moral standing and respect. In the literature on abortion, those deserving of such moral standing are called "persons." The claim that a fetus is a person in this sense is controversial and needs defense. One common way of addressing the question, "Is a fetus a person?" is to assume that most adult human beings are persons and try to decide what features possessed by most adult humans make them deserving of full moral standing. Mary Anne Warren argues that when we do this, we should conclude that fetuses are not persons, indeed are less personlike, she says in a somewhat notorious claim, than a fish.

Not all who believe abortion is immoral try to base their position on the claim that a fetus is a person. Don Marquis argues in his contribution to the chapter that abortions can be shown to be seriously immoral without having to assume that a fetus is a person.

The Liberal Argument

Those who believe that abortion is always (or nearly always) morally permissible (so-called "liberals") often base their position on an appeal to women's right to choose what happens to their bodies. In rough outline, such an argument might go as follows:

1. One has the right to choose what happens to one's own body.
2. The fetus is an object within a woman's body.
3. Therefore, a woman has the right to remove a fetus from her body.

As was the case for the conservative argument, both premises of the liberal argument need elaboration if they are to be accepted. The right to choose what to do with one's body, for example, is limited by the rights of others. Without your permission, for example, I have no right to stick my hand into your wallet. So again we are led to ask questions about the moral status of a fetus. Is it a being capable of having rights that would limit a woman's right to choose? Even if it is, further issues need to be addressed. Given that a fetus is dependent on someone else's body for continued existence, it may not have a right to such support even if it has rights generally. Its rights, after all, would also be limited by the rights of others including the rights of the woman carrying it. So if the fetus has rights, it would appear that pregnancy may be a situation in which rights conflict. If so, we would need to ask how it is generally decided what has precedence when rights conflict and try to apply those general lessons to pregnancy. Considerations such as these lead many conservatives to our next argument, the consent argument.

The Consent Argument

The consent argument maintains that in at least most pregnancies, a woman's right to choose what happens to her body does not extend to a right to abort. This line of argument might be outlined as follows:

1. Rights can be waived through voluntary action.
2. By engaging in intercourse, a woman waives part of her right to choose what happens to her body.
3. She tacitly consents to the use of her body by any resulting fetus.
4. Therefore, she has no right to remove it.

The first thing to notice about the consent argument is that it is limited in scope. Since it is based on the idea that rights can be waived by *voluntary* action, it clearly would not apply to cases in which conception results from rape, nor would it seem to apply to cases in which people are nonnegligently uninformed or misinformed about the relationship between sexuality and pregnancy, as might be the case, for instance, with schoolchildren. It is also less than clear how the argument applies to couples who take efforts to prevent pregnancy.

A more central worry about the argument questions the claim that voluntary sexual activity constitutes a waiver of part of a woman's right to control her body on the grounds that it constitutes (tacit) consent to a fetus's dependence on her body. Why should consensual sexual activity be thought to constitute consent to pregnancy? Perhaps, the idea is that one knows that pregnancy is a possible result of sexual activity and that when one chooses to be sexually active knowing that pregnancy may result one must accept any pregnancy that does result. In other words, when one does something knowing the possible results, one accepts and consents to those results. Put this bluntly, the principles of the argument clearly should not be accepted. When I drive late at night, I know that it is possible that my car will be hit by a drunk driver, but it would be absurd to suppose that my late night driving constitutes consent to being hit. Whatever principles of tacit consent underlie the consent argument must be more subtle than one claiming that we consent to any outcome that we foresee might result from our behavior. While he does not appeal to the idea of tacit consent, the argument in Tom L. Huffman's selection might be considered an elaboration of the basic approach of the consent argument.

Before one endorses the consent argument, it would be worth questioning the attitudes that might be at the base of its appeal. The appeal of the consent argument might be thought to depend on a punitive attitude toward sexuality, and especially toward female sexuality. It seems to portray pregnancy as a form of punishment for women who are sexually active, implying that such sexual activity is wrong and hence deserving of punishment. We once had a student who in discussions of abortion repeatedly and approvingly paraphrased the consent argument as, "If you're going to play, you have to be willing to pay." While it might be possible to interpret the consent argument differently from this student, the ease with which it lends itself to his interpretation should lead us to ask whether its appeal is based on unhealthy attitudes toward both sexuality (especially female sexuality) and pregnancy.

The Potentiality Argument

Some who oppose abortion point to a fetus's potential to be a human being to support their position. Someone might appeal to this potential even if he or she believes the fetus is already an actual human being out of despair of convincing others of this position. A simple version of the potentiality argument might be formulated as follows:

1. It is wrong to kill potential human beings.
2. A human fetus is a potential human being.
3. Therefore, it is wrong to kill a human fetus.

The first premise requires defense. Even granting that it is wrong to kill human beings, why should it also be thought wrong to kill something that merely has the potential to become a human being? In response to this question defenders of the potentiality argument might try two basic approaches. The first, roughly consequentialist, approach maintains that human beings possess value and that abortions are wrong because they prevent some realization of that value. The second approach would be to argue that something with the potential to be a human being deserves at least some of the moral respect and protection of human beings.

Both approaches would need a good bit of development to be made plausible. For example, the belief that it is wrong to prevent the further realization of the value of human life would seem to imply that both contraception and sexual abstinence are wrong as well. These implications would be unwelcome to many who oppose abortion.

It is difficult to assess the claim that having the potential to be something deserving of moral respect and protection also creates desert for some of that same respect and protection. On the one hand, merely being potentially something does not provide one with all of the rights one would have when that potential is realized. On the other hand, it does seem as if potential is sometimes sufficient for moral respect. Consider, for example, someone who has won a presidential election but has not yet begun to serve. A president-elect is potentially a president in ways not altogether dissimilar to those in which a fetus is potentially a human being. A president-elect does not have all of the rights of a president, but surely a president-elect is deserving of at least as much of whatever moral respect someone has by virtue of being president. The assassination of a president-elect, for instance, would not be much less shocking from the moral point of view than the assassination of a president. Should we believe that there is a similar rough moral equivalence between abortion and killing an actual human being? One possible difference between a president-elect and a human fetus is that the former's moral standing may be based not on his or her *potential* to be president but rather on what he or she has *actually* accomplished—being elected by a majority of voters. If this is the case, the respect due a president-elect does not aid the cause of the advocate of the potentiality argument, who needs to maintain that a fetus is due moral concern, not because of what it is already, but because of what it will be.

A Note on Approaches to the Issue not Based on Rights

The arguments we have so far considered have construed the issue of abortion as one about potentially conflicting rights. Both consequentialists and those who wish to develop a moral theory more reflective of what they believe to be the perspective of women would be likely to challenge this understanding of the issue. At least in principle, consequentialists who are concerned with promoting the social good should be neither in favor of nor opposed to abortion. Instead, they should hold that the permissibility of abortion depends on the answers to empirical questions about how abortions affect the social good. The final three essays in this chapter by Catriona Mackenzie, Paul Gomberg, and Celia Wolf-Devine aim at providing an approach to the issue of abortion that would be more responsive to the experiences of women than is the traditional focus on rights. These authors differ, however, over what such an approach would be like.

THE ISSUE OF POLITICAL MORALITY

How should government in a secular democracy respond to the issue of abortion? Given the controversial nature of the issue, if abortions are either legally permitted or legally prohibited, a significant portion of the population will believe something morally outrageous has been done. We shall briefly consider two arguments, both of which begin by noting how great the controversy surrounding abortion is. One argument uses this controversy to support the view that abortions should be legally permitted, the other uses the controversy to support the legal prohibition of abortion.

The Argument from Controversy to Political Neutrality

The argument that favors abortion's legal availability might be put in the following way:

> Currently in America there is unresolvable controversy about the moral status of abortion. The role of government in a liberal democracy is not to enforce one side of a controversial moral issue, but rather to provide a stable environment in which people are free to pursue a life compatible with their own moral ideals. The current laws allowing abortion force no one to have an abortion, but a prohibition would force those who would choose abortion not to do so. A government that should remain neutral on matters of great moral controversy must leave the resolution of the issue up to the conscience of individuals. Only the current laws do so.

Obviously, this argument depends on a view about the proper role of government in a democracy. One way of putting that view would be to say that a democratic government properly expresses the will of the people. When the populace is as deeply divided as ours is about abortion, however, there is no such thing as the will of the people, so government must remain neutral and not take sides in areas of extreme moral controversy.

While the idea that government should not allow a portion of the population to impose its moral ideals on another portion has appeal, there are worries one might naturally have about the argument as it stands. The primary worry is that we can all easily think of examples in which our government did take sides on a controversial moral issue, and in which we believe it did so properly. The abolition of slavery is an obvious example. Few would accept an argument that allowing slavery forces no one to own slaves but only allows individuals to decide for themselves whether or not to own slaves and hence that slavery ought to be a legal option. Other examples in which we might think government appropriately took sides would be extending the vote to women or civil rights legislation and court decisions.

Can one both endorse the argument under consideration and approve of the government's taking sides in those cases that we think it did so properly? To do so, one needs to say there is a difference between those controversial moral issues about which government can legitimately take sides and those about which it would be wrong for government to do so. With this in mind, one *might* argue that prohibiting slavery and extending the vote to women were not merely matters of taking a side in a dispute over moral ideals, but were more significantly measures taken to protect fundamental human rights that were being violated in a systematic and discriminatory manner. However, if we hold that government can legitimately take sides to prevent discriminatory violations of fundamental rights, it becomes unclear what our government should do about abortion. Those who oppose abortion, after all, believe that abortion constitutes a violation of the right to life that discriminates against the unborn. Those who favor the legal availability of abortion believe that prohibition would discriminate against autonomy rights of women. It, therefore, remains uncertain what government should do in the light of this moral controversy.

The Argument from the Least Moral Risk

The argument from the least moral risk suggests that in light of uncertainty about the moral status of fetuses, abortion should be legally prohibited. The reasoning might be represented in the following way:

> There is widespread controversy about the morality of abortion. A sizable number of people believes abortion constitutes the killing of innocent human beings, in other words murder. Another sizable number believes that any restriction on abortion would constitute a serious violation of women's rights to control their bodies, which is perhaps a special case of a right to liberty. Therefore, both a policy of restricting abortion and a policy of allowing abortion potentially violate important rights. Given the degree of controversy, there is little hope of determining which right is actually at stake. Even though either violating the right to life or violating the right to control one's body would be a serious moral wrong, one should place oneself at the least moral risk. That is, when facing a choice between options, both of which may be wrong, but one (if wrong) would be less wrong than the other (if wrong), one should choose the course of action that risks doing the lesser wrong. Murder is worse than violating someone's right to liberty (including the right to choose what happens to one's body). Government should opt for the policy that threatens the less important right to liberty rather than the policy that threatens the right to life and should, therefore, prohibit abortion.

While this argument may seem initially appealing, as formulated above, it takes a much too simple approach to the evaluation of risk. When choosing among risky options, it is not enough to determine what and how great the *possible* risks are, it is also necessary to know, if possible, what the *probabilities* of those risks are. (If you have a choice between two actions, one of which might cost you $10 and the other of which might cost you $100, you should not automatically opt for the former. If the former will definitely cost you $10 and the latter has only a one in 1,000 chance of costing you $100, the latter is a much more reasonable option.) The argument from the least moral risk as it has been formulated here ignores the probabilities of the risks of either allowing or prohibiting abortions.

In response to the argument, it can be argued that the probability of abortion's being murder is controversial precisely because of the controversy about the moral status of fetuses. At any rate, the probability is certainly less than one. On the other hand, if abortions are prohibited, some women who would choose them will definitely be prevented from doing so. Hence, if a policy of prohibiting abortion is adopted, the probability that women's right to choose what happens to their bodies will be violated is one. As a result, it is at best unclear which option poses the least risk.

This response, however, may itself misrepresent the probability of women's rights to liberty being violated by a prohibition of abortion. We do not, after all, have an unqualified right to choose what to do with our own bodies. In most circumstances, it is wrong to use one's body to kill, and infringing someone's liberty to kill is not a moral wrong. While it is true that the probability that prohibiting abortion will restrict women's liberty is one, there is controversy about whether choosing abortion is something one has a right to do. Many think such a choice is a choice to kill. If so, restricting that liberty may not be a wrongful restriction on liberty; so the probability that restricting abortion constitutes a *wrongful* restriction of liberty is less than one. Again, we are led back to questions about the moral status of fetuses in order to assess the argument from the least moral risk, questions the argument has been put forth to bypass.

NOTE

1. As far as we know, the first person involved in the contemporary abortion debate to formulate some of the following arguments in a short syllogistic form was Peter Singer in his *Practical Ethics* (Cambridge: Cambridge University Press, 1979). In the following pages, we use his formulations of the conservative and potentiality arguments as well as his formulation of the principle concerning choice in the liberal argument.

The Abortion Struggle in America
Mary Anne Warren

Mary Anne Warren is a philosophy professor at San Francisco State University. Her publications include a number of articles in applied ethics. In this essay, Warren first traces the history of the social and legal status of abortion in the United States from roughly 1800 to the 1989 Supreme Court case of *Webster v. Reproductive Health Services*. She then considers some of implications of the *Webster* decision

---

On 3 July, the Supreme Court issued its decision in the case of *Webster v. Reproductive Health Services*. By a five-to-four vote, the Court stopped short of explicitly modifying or overturning *Roe v. Wade,* the 1973 case which established the constitutional right to abortion. At the same time, it extended the power of state and local governments to regulate abortion in two important areas: the use of public funds, facilities, or employees for abortion or abortion counselling, and so-called viability testing after the 20th week of pregnancy. The case represents the first significant erosion of the constitutional right to abortion, and is perhaps the first time that the Court has substantially diminished a fundamental constitutional right established by its own previous rulings.

In what follows, I will say more about the *Webster* decision, and its legal, practical, and political implications. But first I want to situate the case in a larger context, by making some observations about the history of anti-abortion legislation in this country, and the more recent anti-abortion movement.

THE FIRST AMERICAN ANTI-ABORTION CAMPAIGN

Before 1800, no American state had legislation dealing specifically with abortion.[1] The legal status of abortion was governed by British common law, as interpreted by the American courts. Common law had long distinguished between the destruction of a 'quickened' foetus—which was considered a crime—and the termination of pregnancy prior to quickening—which was not. Quickening was defined as the time when the woman first felt the foetus move, usually four or five months into the pregnancy. Even in the case of postquickening abortion, the woman herself was immune from prosecution under the common law.

By most accounts, the prohibition of (early) abortion was largely the result of a campaign led by the organized American medical profession. The 'regular' physicians opposed abortion as contrary to the Hippocratic Oath, which they accepted as the ethical foundation of the medical profession. They

From *Bioethics* 3 (October 1989), 320–332.

also had more pragmatic reasons for urging that abortion be outlawed. The campaign against abortion was useful in building support for licensing laws, which eventually gave the organized medical profession extensive power to determine who may or may not market health care services. Moreover, it enabled the regulars to enlist state power against many of their professional rivals, including midwives, herbalists, and vendors of home remedies, who often provided abortifacient medications.

The anti-abortion physicians were joined by a few conservative Protestant churches. However, most Protestant denominations took no public stand on the abortion issue. The American Catholic Church did not enter the debate, although in 1869 the Pope issued an almost categorical condemnation of abortion. Indeed, anti-Catholic sentiment contributed to the anti-abortion crusade. 'Nativists' feared that middle-class Protestant white women were not reproducing fast enough to offset new immigration and (what they took to be) higher birth rates among Catholics, blacks, and other ethnic minority groups. Birth rates had indeed declined during the nineteenth century, particularly among middle class women—a decline evidently made possible by the wide-spread availability of abortion. Most nineteenth century feminists condemned abortion in the strongest terms, advocating sexual abstinence as a better method of family planning. Nevertheless, anti-feminist as well as anti-Catholic, racist, and xenophobic sentiments were enlisted in the campaign against legal abortion.

The earliest anti-abortion statutes were passed in the decades prior to the Civil War. These were apparently motivated in large part by a concern for women's safety. Often, provisions banning abortifacients were included in statutes dealing with the regulation of poisonous substances. These early anti-abortion laws generally retained both the quickening and the woman's traditional immunity from prosecution. After the Civil War, however, states generally adopted stricter anti-abortion laws. The quickening distinction was eliminated, and criminal penalties were imposed upon both those who had abortions and those who provided them. Anti-obscenity laws were used to prohibit the overt or disguised advertising of abortion or abortifacients. By 1900, the criminal status of abortion was firmly established in the law of every American state, where it remained for another two thirds of a century.

THE ERA OF PROHIBITION

Of course, American women did not stop having abortions during the years when they were illegal. The prohibition fell hardest upon poor women, who could not pay sympathetic physicians or other trained medical practitioners for clandestine but reasonably competent abortions. For them, the alternative to having a child they could not support was usually a dangerous 'back alley' abortion, or even more dangerous self-abortion. Because the knowledge of herbal and other pharmaceutical means of abortion had already been suppressed, illegal abortions were usually done by surgical means—often under appalling conditions and by persons without medical training or knowledge.

Estimates of the number of illegal abortions in each of the years prior to 1973 range from a few hundred thousand to over a million. Each year thousands of women died from botched abortions, and many more were left infertile. Yet abortion was a subject rarely discussed in public, until the second wave of feminist activism made it a women's right issue in the 1960s. In most states, abortion laws were indifferently enforced, and prosecutions infrequent. Illegal abortion was quietly tolerated, while women who could afford it traveled to other countries or (after 1969) states in which abortion was legal.

By 1973, social and political foundations had been laid for the reform or repeal of criminal abortion laws. Women had entered the work force in record numbers, and the dual responsibilities of paid and domestic work made the capacity to control their own reproductive lives an even more vital necessity. Despite new and newly available methods of contraception, access to abortion remained important as a backup method of birth control. Many women who had been radicalized by the civil rights and anti-war movements found it intolerable that laws passed at a time when women still did not have the vote should be used to deny them the control of their own bodies. While some women were forced to bear children against their will, in much of the country poor women and women of colour were often involuntarily sterilized. Feminist groups united behind the call for 'Free abortion on demand and no forced sterilization'. There was, as yet, no organized anti-abortion movement.

Although American physicians were not known for their radical feminism, their attitudes towards abortion were different from those of their predecessors a century earlier. The American Medical Association's campaign to enact medical licensing laws had long since succeeded, and abortion providers were no longer a threat to the hegemony of the medical profession. Many physicians were disturbed by what they saw of the carnage resulting from illegal abortion. A number of prominent medical associations endorsed the adoption of less restrictive abortion laws.

ROE v. WADE AND ITS PREDECESSORS

Beginning in the 1920s, a series of Supreme and lower court decisions began to delineate a fundamental constitutional right to privacy. Although the word 'privacy' does not appear in the Constitution, various portions of the Bill of Rights and the Fourteenth Amendment were held to establish a constitutional protection from unwarranted government intrusion upon the personal and private lives of individuals. The right to privacy applies particularly, but not exclusively, to activities that occur in the home and/or in the context of marital or family life. Justice Louis Brandeis described this 'right to be let alone' as 'the most comprehensive of rights and the right most valued by civilized men.'[2] This right is not absolute. The Court has often noted that activities such as rape, incest, and drug use do not enjoy constitutional protection, even when they occur in the person's own home. However, to pass constitutional muster a law that significantly intrudes upon personal privacy must be based upon a legitimate and compelling state interest.

In the 1965 case of *Griswold v. Connecticut,* the Court struck down a law that prohibited the use of contraceptives.[3] This decision dealt only with the privacy rights of married persons. However, in 1972 the Court ruled that unmarried persons have the same right to use contraceptives. In *Elsenstadt v. Baird,* the Court held that,

> If the right of privacy means anything, it is the right of the *individual,* married or single, to be free from unwarranted governmental intrusion into matters so fundamentally affecting a person as the decision whether to bear or beget children.[4]

Several American courts had already taken the further step of applying the constitutional right to privacy to the choice of abortion. In 1969, the California Supreme Court and the U.S. District Court in Washington D.C. rejected anti-abortion statutes on grounds of unconstitutional vagueness and violation of the right to privacy.

Roe v. Wade was a case brought on behalf of a then-anonymous Texas woman, challenging the constitutionality of a Texas statute that prohibited abortion, except when necessary to save the woman's life. Speaking for the majority, Justice Blackmun wrote that, 'the constitutional right to privacy is broad enough to encompass a woman's decision whether or not to terminate a pregnancy.'[5] Whereas the state of Texas argued that a human being begins to exist at conception, the Court found that both the Constitution and the common law tradition presuppose that a legal person begins to exist only at birth. Consequently, a state may not endorse one particular 'theory of life' in order to justify the prohibition of all or most abortions, or the imposition of regulations that unduly burden a woman's right to terminate a pregnancy.

At the same time, the Court held that states have legitimate interests in regulating abortion in order to safeguard women's health, and to protect potential human life. Both these state interests were said to increase in strength as pregnancy progresses. The first interest becomes compelling in the second trimester, justifying somewhat stricter regulation of second-trimester abortions to ensure that they are medically safe. However, the state may not regulate either first- or second-trimester abortion in ways that unduly burden women's right to choose. The state's interest in protecting potential human life becomes compelling in the third trimester, when the foetus is apt to be viable, i.e., capable of surviving outside the womb. Thus, states are free to prohibit third-trimester abortion, except where it is necessary to protect the woman's life or health.

The decision in *Roe v. Wade* was not, as its critics claim, an unprecedented seizure of power by the Supreme Court. There were clear and well established legal precedents for the Court's ruling. It was, in important respects, a judicially conservative decision. Although the Court employed the concept of viability, rather than that of quickening, to identify a point in the pregnancy beyond which abortion may legally be prohibited, the practical effect was to make American abortion law more similar to what it had been before the nineteenth-century anti-abortion crusade.

THE SECOND ANTI-ABORTION CRUSADE

Thus, it could hardly have been predicted that *Roe v. Wade* would mark the beginning of an intensified political and ideological struggle between pro-choice and anti-abortion forces. The underlying causes of the second American anti-abortion movement are still somewhat difficult to understand. It is, to be sure, part of a conservative backlash against the feminist movement and perceived changes in sex roles and sexual morality. Why this backlash should have made the elimination of legal abortion its primary focus is somewhat less clear. However, the outlines of what has happened are clear enough.

After 1973, opposition to abortion became a rallying cry for a variety of right-wing organisations. The Catholic Church became politically active in the 'pro-life' movement, as did many fundamentalist Protestant churches. Many congregations were urged to support the anti-abortion cause, and to vote against politicians who failed to condemn abortion. Anti-abortion groups appeared that were allegedly secular, but that accepted financial support from these conservative churches. Fundamentalists and evangelical preachers made effective use of broadcast media and computerized mailing systems to raise funds for anti-abortion campaigns and increase membership. Conservative politicians courted support from such groups by denouncing legal abortion.

By 1980, ultra-conservative groups like the Moral Majority had gained enough wealth and influence to make what may have been a vital contribution to the nomination and election of Ronald Reagan, and other right-wing Republicans. The repeal of *Roe v. Wade* became part of the Reagan social agenda, along with the elimination of funding for family planning agencies here and in the Third World, cuts in medical and social welfare programs, school prayer, stricter enforcement of drug laws, and other policies which were promoted as 'pro-family.' During the early 1980s, the Administration attempted to shepherd a 'human life' statute or constitutional amendment through the Congress. These efforts to overturn *Roe v. Wade* by legislative action failed. More successful—as is now evident—was the Administration's strategy of appointing to the federal judiciary (including the Supreme Court) individuals with a firm commitment to the elimination of legal abortion.

WEBSTER v. REPRODUCTIVE HEALTH SERVICES

The case is a constitutional challenge to a Missouri statute passed in 1986. Four specific provisions of the law were challenged by a group of Missouri health care providers, and struck down by the U.S. Court of Appeals of the Eighth Circuit. These are:

1. the preamble to the statute, which states the 'finding' of the Missouri legislature that, 'the life of each human being begins at conception,'

and that, 'unborn children have protectable interests in life, health, and well-being';

2. the prohibition of the use of public funds, facilities, or employees for performing abortions which are not necessary to save the woman's life;

3. the prohibition of the use of public funds, facilities or employees for 'encouraging or counselling' women on the subject of abortion; and

4. the viability testing requirement, which mandates that before an abortion is done after 20 weeks, certain tests (e.g., amniocentesis and ultrasonography) be performed in order to ascertain whether the foetus might be viable.

All of these contested provisions of the Missouri statute were upheld. The Court reinstated the preamble, while declining to rule on its constitutionality, on the grounds that it had not specifically been used to restrict the actions of the appellees. The prohibition on the use of public funds, facilities or employees for abortions was found to be constitutional, since, 'Nothing in the Constitution requires the State to enter or remain in the abortion business or entitles private physicians and their patients to access to public facilities for the performance of abortions.'[6] The prohibition of abortion counselling by public employees or in public facilities was upheld, but as a funding provision only. (The contested portions of the statute were found to involve no direct constraint upon speech, because the specific provision of the Missouri law which directly constrained the speech of public employees had been invalidated by the Court of Appeals, and Missouri had chosen not to appeal that specific provision.)

Finally, the viability testing requirement was upheld, but by a more divided majority. While all five found the testing requirement constitutional they disagreed about the implications of that finding for the future of *Roe v. Wade.* The plurality (Rehnquist, White, and Kennedy) expressed the opinion that the testing requirement is in direct conflict with the trimester analysis of *Roe v. Wade,* and that this part of that decision should therefore be abandoned. In their view,

> There is no reason why the State's compelling interest in protecting potential human life should not extend throughout pregnancy rather than coming into existence only at the point of viability.[7] . . .

LEGAL IMPLICATIONS OF *WEBSTER*

The majority opinion is, of course, the only one that carries immediate legal force. The majority decision in *Webster* ostensibly leaves *Roe v. Wade* intact—though with several new cracks in its foundation. Yet the opinion of the plurality will not be without influence. It is, as Blackmun notes, 'filled with winks, and nods, and knowing glances to those who would do away with Roe entirely.'[8] Already, a stampede has begun in the state legislatures to introduce anti-abortion legislation designed to fit into the new legal spaces created by *Webster*, and/or to provide further test cases. About 27 states—most of them in the central and southern U.S.—now appear likely to enact new restrictions. In a few states, there are privacy provisions in the state constitution that apply to abortion, a pro-choice house in the legislature, or a governor likely to veto any anti-abortion legislation. In others, legislative and gubernatorial activism seem likely to lead to the passage of restrictions considerably more severe than those upheld in *Webster.*

One immediate result of *Webster* is that, in Missouri and states that have or will soon have similar laws, second-trimester abortions will become more expensive and much more difficult to obtain. The Truman Medical Center in Kansas City, where most post-16-week abortions in Missouri have been performed, stopped doing abortions the day of the *Webster* decision. For, although it is a privately owned and operated hospital, it occupies land leased from a subsidiary of the state government, and is therefore defined by the terms of the Missouri statute as a publicly supported facility. First-trimester abortions continue to be fairly widely available in private clinics in Missouri and elsewhere. However, there is no certainty that this will continue to be true after the next round of Court decisions. . . .

The outright reversal of *Roe v. Wade* now seems unlikely—until such time as one or more additional conservative Justices join the Court. However, that time may not be long in coming. Three of the four Justices who strongly support *Roe v. Wade* (Blackmun, Brennan and Marshall) are now in their eighties. President Bush is as committed to the abolition of legal abortion as was President Reagan, and his appointees will share that goal. In the end, it may not matter whether *Roe v. Wade* is ever formally reversed. It may instead be gradually undermined, until it becomes, in the words of Laurence Tribe, 'a derelict on the waters of the law.'[9]

THE COMING POLITICAL STRUGGLE IN THE STATES

The *Webster* decision has shifted the focus of the abortion struggle from the courts to the state legislators. A majority of legislators in a majority of states are avowedly anti-abortion. Thus, if *Roe v. Wade* continues to fall by stages, abortion law in much of the country could eventually be returned to something like the pre-*Roe* era. But that will not happen without a political struggle of monumental proportions. Polls taken both before and after the *Webster* decision indicate that a substantial majority of Americans (about 70 percent) favours keeping abortion legal. . . .

Yet it is obvious that the anti-abortion forces are in many ways better equipped to bring political influence to bear upon legislators and other public officials. They are much better funded, and can command large numbers of dedicated volunteers. For many years, anti-abortion activists have enjoyed disproportionate media attention. This year has been no exception. The frequent bombings and arson attacks against abortion clinics of a few years ago have been replaced in the news reports by the exploits of Operation Rescue. Each week, this well-organized group targets clinics around the country and tries to close them by obstructing the entrances and harassing those who try to enter or leave.

The new political struggle over abortion will be more divisive than any since the Vietnam War. New political alliances will be made and old ones broken. Whereas at the federal level the Republican Party is anti-abortion and the Democratic Party is pro-choice, at the state level the issue cuts across party lines in complex ways. The young, affluent and well-educated Americans whose votes the Republicans have sought in the last few elections tend to be pro-choice, while the working class, black and other minority voters who have traditionally voted Democratic are thought to be more anti-abortion. Some commentators have suggested that it will now become easier to reach compromise solutions respecting abortion, since neither party's interests will be served by making every election a referendum on this one issue. Unfortunately, the compromises seem likely to consist in further curtailments of the rights of certain particularly vulnerable groups—e.g., pregnant teenagers, poor women, and women who need second-trimester abortions.

CONCLUSION

The constitutional right to abortion survives, but it is no longer secure. For the time being, first-trimester abortions will remain generally available—that is, for those who can pay and who have alternatives to state-supported medical facilities. . . . It is evident [though] that the halcyon era during which *Roe v. Wade* has provided a bulwark against government infringements of the right to abortion is ending. The newly-expanded limits to the state's power to regulate abortion will be repeatedly tested—soon, in all probability, before a Supreme Court with an even more conservative membership. Thus the right to abortion will increasingly depend upon political action at the state and local levels, where pro-choice activists will have to scramble to catch up with the more powerful anti-abortion groups. . . .

In short, the future of legal abortion in America is radically uncertain. As Justice Blackmun wrote in his dissenting opinion:

> For today, at least, the law of abortion stands undisturbed. For today, the women of this nation still retain the liberty to control their destinies. But the signs are evident and very ominous, and a chill wind blows.[10]

NOTES

1. Perhaps the best historical study of the nineteenth-century anti-abortion campaign is James C. Mohr's *Abortion in America: The Origins and Evolution of National Policy, 1800–1900* (Oxford University Press, 1978). Many of the historical comments that follow are documented in this source.

2. Justice Louis Brandeis, dissenting opinion in *Olmstead v. United States*, 277 U.S. 438 (1928).

3. *Griswold v. Connecticut*, 381 U.S. 479 (1965).

4. Justice William Brennan, majority opinion in *Eisenstadt v. Baird*, 405 U.S. 438 (1972).

5. Justice Henry Blackmun, majority opinion in *Roe v. Wade*, 410 U.S. 113 (1973).

6. Chief Justice Rehnquist, majority opinion in *Webster v. Reproductive Health Services* (*Daily Appellate Report*, 6 July, 1989, p. 8725).

7. *Ibid.*

8. Blackmun, dissenting opinion in *Webster*, p. 8737.

9. Professor Laurence Tribe of the Harvard Law School, quoted in *U.S. News & World Report*, 17 July, 1989, p. 20.

10. Blackmun, p. 8740.

On the Moral and
Legal Status of Abortion
Mary Anne Warren

Mary Anne Warren, who was introduced in the previous reading, argues in this classic article on abortion that a human fetus has insufficient moral standing to support the belief that abortion is a serious moral wrong. She proposes that the claim that a human fetus is a human being can be understood in two ways. It can be understood in one sense as meaning that the fetus, as a member of the species *Homo sapiens*, is genetically human. However, it can also be understood as meaning that the fetus, as a member of the moral community, is human in a moral sense. While it is not controversial that a fetus is genetically human, this fact does not show that it is wrong to destroy a fetus. Advocates of the conservative position must therefore claim that a fetus is a human in some moral sense, that a fetus is the sort of being that deserves full moral standing and respect. In the literature on abortion, those deserving such moral standing are called "persons." Warren claims that fetuses are not persons. She further argues that a fetus's potential to be a person does not support the position that it would be a serious moral wrong to destroy it. Thus, Warren concludes, any legal restrictions on abortion at any stage of pregnancy would be morally unjustified.

––––––

We will be concerned with both the moral status of abortion, which for our purposes we may define as the act which a woman performs in voluntarily terminating, or allowing another person to terminate, her pregnancy, and the legal status which is appropriate for this act. I will argue that, while it is not possible to produce a satisfactory defense of a woman's right to obtain an abortion without showing that a fetus is not a human being, in the morally relevant sense of that term, we ought not to conclude that the difficulties involved in determining whether or not a fetus is human make it impossible to produce any satisfactory solution to the problem of the moral status of abortion. For it is possible to show that, on the basis of intuitions which we may expect even the opponents of abortion to share, a fetus is not a person, and hence not the sort of entity to which it is proper to ascribe full moral rights.

Of course, while some philosophers would deny the possibility of any such proof,[1] others will deny that there is any need for it, since the moral permissibility of abortion appears to them to be too obvious to require proof. But the inadequacy of this attitude should be evident from the fact that both the friends and the foes of abortion consider their position to be morally self-evident. Because pro-abortionists have never adequately come to grips with the conceptual issues surrounding abortion, most if not all, of the arguments which they advance in opposition to laws restricting access to abortion fail to

From *The Monist* 57 (1973), 43–61.

refute or even weaken the traditional antiabortion argument, i.e., that a fetus is a human being, and therefore abortion is murder. . . .

However we wish to construe the right to abortion, we cannot hope to convince those who consider abortion a form of murder of the existence of any such right unless we are able to produce a clear and convincing refutation of the traditional antiabortion argument, and this has not, to my knowledge, been done. With respect to the two most vital issues which that argument involves, i.e., the humanity of the fetus and its implication for the moral status of abortion, confusion has prevailed on both sides of the dispute.

Thus, both proabortionists and antiabortionists have tended to abstract the question of whether abortion is wrong to that of whether it is wrong to destroy a fetus, just as though the rights of another person were not necessarily involved. This mistaken abstraction has led to the almost universal assumption that if a fetus is a human being, with a right to life, then it follows immediately that abortion is wrong (except perhaps when necessary to save the woman's life), and that it ought to be prohibited. It has also been generally assumed that unless the question about the status of the fetus is answered, the moral status of abortion cannot possibly be determined. . . .

John Noonan is correct in saying that "the fundamental question in the long history of abortion is, How do you determine the humanity of a being?"[2] He summarizes his own antiabortion argument, which is a version of the official position of the Catholic Church, as follows:

> . . . it is wrong to kill humans, however poor, weak, defenseless, and lacking in opportunity to develop their potential they may be. It is therefore morally wrong to kill Biafrans. Similarly, it is morally wrong to kill embryos.[3]

Noonan bases his claim that fetuses are human upon what he calls the theologians' criterion of humanity: that whoever is conceived of human beings is human. But although he argues at length for the appropriateness of this criterion, he never questions the assumption that if a fetus is human then abortion is wrong for exactly the same reason that murder is wrong.

Judith Thomson is, in fact, the only writer I am aware of who has seriously questioned this assumption; she has argued that, even if we grant the antiabortionist his claim that a fetus is a human being, with the same right to life as any other human being, we can still demonstrate that, in at least some and perhaps most cases, a woman is under no moral obligation to complete an unwanted pregnancy.[4] Her argument is worth examining, since if it holds up it may enable us to establish the moral permissibility of abortion without becoming involved in problems about what entitles an entity to be considered human, and accorded full moral rights. . . .

I

[Professor Thomson's] argument is based upon a clever, but I think faulty, analogy. She asks us to picture ourselves waking up one day, in bed with a famous violinist. Imagine that you have been kidnapped, and your bloodstream hooked up to that of the violinist who happens to have an ailment which will certainly kill him unless he is permitted to share your kidneys for a period of nine months. No one else can save him, since you alone have the right type of blood. He will be unconscious all that time, and you will have to stay in bed with him, but after the nine months are over he may be unplugged, completely cured, that is provided that you have cooperated.

Now then, she continues, what are your obligations in this situation? The antiabortionist, if he is consistent, will have to say that you are obligated to stay in bed with the violinist: for all people have a right to life, and violinists are people, and therefore it would be murder for you to disconnect yourself from him and let him die (p. 49). But this is outrageous, and so there must be something wrong with the same argument when it is applied to abortion. It would certainly be commendable of you to agree to save the violinist, but it is absurd to suggest that your refusal to do so would be murder. His right to life does not obligate you to do whatever is required to keep him alive; nor does it justify anyone else in forcing you to do so. A law which required you to stay in bed with the violinist would clearly be an unjust law, since it is no proper function of the law to force unwilling people to make huge sacrifices for the sake of other people toward whom they have no such prior obligation.

Thomson concludes that, if this analogy is an apt one, then we can grant the antiabortionist his claim that a fetus is a human being, and still hold that it is at least sometimes the case that a pregnant woman has the right to refuse to be a Good Samaritan towards the fetus, i.e., to obtain an abortion. For there is a great gap between the claim that x has a right to life, and the claim that y is obligated to do whatever is necessary to keep x alive, let alone that he ought to be forced to do so. It is y's duty to keep x alive only if he has somehow contracted a *special* obligation to do so; and a woman who is unwillingly pregnant, e.g., who was raped, has done nothing which obligates her to make the enormous sacrifice which is necessary to preserve the conceptus.

This argument is initially quite plausible, and in the extreme case of pregnancy due to rape it is probably conclusive. Difficulties arise, however, when we try to specify more exactly the range of cases in which abortion is clearly justifiable even on the assumption that the fetus is human. Professor Thomson considers it a virtue of her argument that it does not enable us to conclude that abortion is *always* permissible. It would, she says, be "indecent" for a woman in her seventh month to obtain an abortion just to avoid having to postpone a trip to Europe. On the other hand, her argument enables us to see that "a sick and desperately frightened schoolgirl pregnant due to rape may *of course* choose abortion, and that any law which rules this out is an insane law" (p. 65). So far, so good; but what are we to say about the woman who becomes pregnant not through rape but as a result of her own carelessness, or because of contraceptive failure, or who gets pregnant intentionally and then changes her mind about wanting a child? With respect to such cases, the violinist analogy is of much less use to the defender of the woman's right to obtain an abortion.

Indeed, the choice of a pregnancy due to rape, as an example of a case in which abortion is permissible even if a fetus is considered a human being, is extremely significant; for it is only in the case of pregnancy due to rape that the woman's situation is adequately analogous to the violinist case for our intuitions about the latter to transfer convincingly. The crucial difference between a pregnancy due to rape and the *normal* case of an unwanted pregnancy is that in the normal case we cannot claim that the woman is in no way responsible for her predicament; she could have remained chaste, or taken her pills more faithfully, or abstained on dangerous days, and so on. If, on the other hand, you are kidnapped by strangers, and hooked up to a strange violinist, then you are free of any shred of responsibility for the situation, on the basis of which it could be argued that you are obligated to keep the violinist alive. Only when her pregnancy is due to rape is a woman clearly just as nonresponsible.[5]

Consequently, there is room for the antiabortionist to argue that in the normal case of unwanted pregnancy a woman has, by her own actions, assumed responsibility for the fetus. . . . Perhaps we can make this point more clear by altering the violinist story just enough to make it more analogous to a normal unwanted pregnancy and less to a pregnancy due to rape, and then seeing whether it is still obvious that you are not obligated to stay in bed with the fellow.

Suppose, then, that violinists are peculiarly prone to the sort of illness the only cure for which is the use of someone else's bloodstream for nine months, and that because of this there has been formed a society of music lovers who agree that whenever a violinist is stricken they will draw lots and the loser will, by some means, be made the one and only person capable of saving him. Now then, would you be obligated to cooperate in curing the violinist if you had voluntarily joined this society, knowing the possible consequences, and then your name had been drawn and you had been kidnapped? Admittedly, you did not promise ahead of time that you would, but you did deliberately place yourself in a position in which it might happen that a human life would be lost if you did not. Surely this is at lease a prima facie reason for supposing that you have an obligation to stay in bed with the violinist. Suppose that you had gotten your name drawn deliberately; surely *that* would be quite a strong reason for thinking that you had such an obligation. . . .

Whether or not this intuition is entirely correct, it brings us back once again to the conclusion that once we allow the assumption that a fetus has full moral rights it becomes an extremely complex and difficult question whether and when abortion is justifiable. Thus the Thomson analogy cannot help us produce a clear and persuasive proof of the moral permissibility of abortion. Nor will the opponents of the restrictive laws thank us for anything less; for their conviction (for the most part) is that abortion is obviously *not* a morally serious and extremely unfortunate, even though sometimes justified act, comparable to killing in self-defense or to letting the violinist die, but rather is closer to being a morally neutral act, like cutting one's hair.

The basis of this conviction, I believe, is the realization that a fetus is not a person, and thus does not have a full-fledged right to life. Perhaps the reason why this claim has been so inadequately defended is that it seems self-evident to those who accept it. And so it is, insofar as it follows from what I take to be perfectly obvious claims about the nature of personhood, and about the proper grounds for ascribing moral rights, claims which ought, indeed, to be obvious to both the friends and foes of abortion. Nevertheless, it is worth examining these claims, and showing how they demonstrate the moral innocuousness of abortion, since this apparently has not been adequately done before.

II

The question which we must answer in order to produce a satisfactory solution to the problem of the moral status of abortion is this: How are we to define the moral community, the set of beings with full and equal moral rights, such that we can decide whether a human fetus is a member of this community or not? What sort of entity, exactly, has the inalienable rights to life, liberty, and the pursuit of happiness? Jefferson attributed these rights to all *men*, and it may or may not be fair to suggest that he intended to attribute them *only* to men. Perhaps he ought to have attributed them to all human beings. If so, then we arrive, first, at Noonan's problem of defining what makes a being human, and, second, at the equally vital question which Noonan does not consider, namely, What reason is there for identifying the moral community with the set of all human beings, in whatever way we have chosen to define that term?

1. On the Definition of 'Human'

One reason why this vital second question is so frequently overlooked in the debate over the moral status of abortion is that the term 'human' has two distinct, but not often distinguished, senses. This fact results in a slide of meaning, which serves to conceal the fallaciousness of the traditional argument that since (1) it is wrong to kill innocent human beings, and (2) fetuses are innocent human beings, then (3) it is wrong to kill fetuses. For if 'human' is used in the same sense in both (1) and (2) then, whichever of the two senses is meant, one of these premises is question-begging. And if it is used in two different senses then of course the conclusion doesn't follow.

Thus, (1) is a self-evident moral truth,[6] and avoids begging the question about abortion, only if 'human being' is used to mean something like "a full-fledged member of the moral community." (It may or may not also be meant to refer exclusively to members of the species *Homo sapiens*.) We may call this the *moral* sense of 'human'. It is not to be confused with what we will call the *genetic* sense, i.e., the sense in which *any* member of the species is a human being, and no member of any other species could be. If (1) is acceptable only if the moral sense is intended, (2) is non-question-begging only if what is intended is the genetic sense.

In "Deciding Who is Human," Noonan argues for the classification of fetuses with human beings by pointing to the presence of the full genetic code, and the potential capacity for rational thought (p. 135). It is clear that what he needs to show, for his version of the traditional argument to be valid, is that fetuses are human in the moral sense, the sense in which it is analytically true that all human beings have full moral rights. But, in the absence of any argument showing that whatever is genetically human is also morally human, and he gives none, nothing more than genetic humanity can be demonstrated by the presence of the human genetic code. And, as we will see, the *potential* capacity for rational thought can at most show that an entity has the potential for *becoming* human in the moral sense.

2. Defining the Moral Community

Can it be established that genetic humanity is sufficient for moral humanity? I think that there are very good reasons for not defining the moral community in this way. I would like to suggest an alternative way of defining the moral community, which I will argue for only to the extent of explaining why it is, or should be, self-evident. The suggestion is simply that the moral community consists of all and only *people*, rather than all and only human beings;[7] and probably the best way of demonstrating its self-evidence is by considering the concept of personhood, to see what sorts of entity are and are not persons, and what the decision that a being is or is not a person implies about its moral rights.

What characteristics entitle an entity to be considered a person? This is obviously not the place to attempt a complete analysis of the concept of personhood, but we do not need such a fully adequate analysis just to determine whether and why a fetus is or isn't a person. All we need is a rough and approximate list of the most basic criteria of personhood, and some idea of which, or how many, of these an entity must satisfy in order to properly be considered a person.

In searching for such criteria, it is useful to look beyond the set of people with whom we are acquainted, and ask how we would decide whether a totally alien being was a person or not. (For we have no right to assume that genetic humanity is necessary for personhood.) Imagine a space traveler who lands on an unknown planet and encounters a race of beings utterly unlike any he has ever seen or heard of. If he wants to be sure of behaving morally toward these beings, he has to somehow decide whether they are people, and hence have full moral rights, or whether they are the sort of thing which he need not feel guilty about treating as, for example, a source of food.

How should he go about making this decision? If he has some anthropological background, he might look for such things as religion, art, and the manufacturing of tools, weapons, or shelters, since these factors have been used to distinguish our human from our prehuman ancestors, in what seems to be closer to the moral than the genetic sense of 'human'. And no doubt he would be right to consider the presence of such factors as good evidence that the alien beings were people, and morally human. It would, however, be overly anthropocentric of him to take the absence of these things as adequate evidence that they were not, since we can imagine people who have progressed beyond, or evolved without ever developing, these cultural characteristics.

I suggest that the traits which are most central to the concept of personhood, or humanity in the moral sense, are, very roughly, the following:

1. consciousness (of objects and events external and/or internal to the being), and in particular the capacity to feel pain;
2. reasoning (the *developed* capacity to solve new and relatively complex problems);
3. self-motivated activity (activity which is relatively independent of either genetic or direct external control);
4. the capacity to communicate, by whatever means, messages of an indefinite variety of types, that is, not just with an indefinite number of possible contents, but on indefinitely many possible topics;
5. the presence of self-concepts, and self-awareness, either individual or racial, or both.

Admittedly, there are apt to be a great many problems involved in formulating precise definitions of these criteria, let alone in developing universally valid behavioral criteria for deciding when they apply. But I will assume that both we and our explorer know approximately what (1)-(5) mean, and that he is also able to determine whether or not they apply. How, then, should he use his findings to decide whether or not the alien beings are people? We needn't suppose that an entity must have *all* of these attributes to be properly considered a person; (1) and (2) alone may well be sufficient for personhood, and quite probably (1)-(3) are sufficient. Neither do we need to insist that any one of these criteria is *necessary* for personhood, although once again (1) and (2) look like fairly good candidates for necessary conditions, as does (3), if 'activity' is construed so as to include the activity of reasoning.

All we need to claim, to demonstrate that a fetus is not a person, is that any being which satisfied *none* of (1)-(5) is certainly not a person. I consider this claim to be so obvious that I think anyone who denied it, and claimed that a being which satisfied none of (1)-(5) was a person all the same, would thereby demonstrate that he had no notion at all of what a person is—perhaps because he had confused the concept of a person with that of genetic humanity. If the opponents of abortion were to deny the appropriateness of these five criteria, I do not know what further arguments would convince them. We would probably have to admit that our conceptual schemes were indeed irreconcilably different, and that our dispute could not be settled objectively.

I do not expect this to happen, however, since I think that the concept of a person is one which is very nearly universal (to people), and that it is common to both proabortionists and antiabortionists, even though neither group has fully realized the relevance of this concept to the resolution of their dispute. Furthermore, I think that on reflection even the antiabortionists ought to agree not only that (1)-(5) are central to the concept of personhood, but also that it is a part of this concept that all and only people have full moral rights. The concept of a person is in part a moral concept; once we have admitted that x is a person we have recognized, even if we have not agreed to respect, x's right to be treated as a member of the moral community. It is true that the claim that x is a *human being* is more commonly voiced as part of an appeal to treat x decently than is the claim that x is a person, but this is either because 'human being' is here used in the sense which implies personhood, or because the genetic and moral senses of 'human' have been confused.

Now if (1)-(5) are indeed the primary criteria of personhood, then it is clear that genetic humanity is neither necessary nor sufficient for establishing that an entity is a person. Some human beings are not people, and there may well be people who are not human beings. A man or woman whose consciousness has been permanently obliterated but who remains alive is a human being which is no longer a person; defective human beings, with no appreciable mental capacity, are not and presumably never will be people; and a fetus is a human being which is not yet a person, and which therefore cannot coherently be said to have full moral rights. Citizens of the next century should be prepared to recognize highly advanced, self-aware robots or computers, should such be developed, and intelligent inhabitants of other worlds, should such be found, as people in the fullest sense, and to respect their moral rights. But to ascribe full moral rights to an entity which is not a person is as absurd as to ascribe moral obligations and responsibilities to such an entity.

3. Fetal Development and the Right to Life

Two problems arise in the application of these suggestions for the definition of the moral community to the determination of the precise moral status of a human fetus. Given that the paradigm example of a person is a normal adult human being, then (1) How like this paradigm, in particular how far advanced since conception, does a human being need to be before it begins to have a right to life by virtue, not of being fully a person as of yet, but of being *like* a person? and (2) To what extent, if any, does the fact that a fetus has the *potential* for becoming a person endow it with some of the same rights? Each of these questions requires some comment.

In answering the first question, we need not attempt a detailed consideration of the moral rights of organisms which are not developed enough, aware enough, intelligent enough, etc., to be considered people, but which resemble people in some respects. It does seem reasonable to suggest that the more like a person, in the relevant respects, a being is, the stronger is the case for regarding it as having a right to life, and indeed the stronger its right to life is. Thus we ought to take seriously the suggestion that, insofar as "the human individual develops biologically in a continuous fashion . . . the rights of a human person might develop in the same way."[8] But we must keep in mind that the attributes which are relevant in determining whether or not an entity is enough like a person to be regarded as having some of the same moral rights are no different from those which are relevant to determining whether or not it is fully a person—i.e., are no different from (1)-(5)—and that being genetically human, or having recognizably human facial and other physical features, or detectable brain activity, or the capacity to survive outside the uterus, are simply not among these relevant attributes.

Thus it is clear that even though a seven- or eight-month fetus has features which make it apt to arouse in us almost the same powerful protective instinct as is commonly aroused by a small infant, nevertheless it is not significantly more personlike than is a very small embryo. It is *somewhat* more personlike; it can apparently feel and respond to pain, and it may even have a rudimentary form of consciousness, insofar as its brain is quite active. Nevertheless, it seems safe to say that it is not fully conscious, in the way that an infant of a few months is, and that it cannot reason, or communicate messages of indefinitely many sorts, does not engage in self-motivated activity, and has no self-awareness. Thus, in the *relevant* respects, a fetus, even a fully developed one, is considerably less personlike than is the average mature mammal, indeed the average fish. And I think that a rational person must conclude that if the right to life of a fetus is to be based upon its resemblance to a person, then it cannot be said to have any more right to life than, let us say, a newborn guppy (which also seems to be capable of feeling pain), and that a right of that magnitude could never override a woman's right to obtain an abortion, at any state of her pregnancy. . . .

Thus, since the fact that even a fully developed fetus is not personlike enough to have any significant right to life on the basis of its personlikeness shows that no legal restrictions upon the stage of pregnancy in which an abortion may be performed can be justified on the grounds that we should protect the rights of the older fetus; and since there is no other apparent justification for such restrictions, we may conclude that they are entirely unjustified. Whether or not it would be *indecent* (whatever that means) for a woman in her seventh month to obtain an abortion just to avoid having to postpone a trip to Europe, it would not, in itself, be *immoral,* and therefore it ought to be permitted.

4. Potential Personhood and the Right to Life

We have seen that a fetus does not resemble a person in any way which can support the claim that it has even some of the same rights. But what about its *potential*, the fact that if nurtured and allowed to develop naturally it will very probably become a person? Doesn't that alone give it at least some right to life? It is hard to deny that the fact that an entity is a potential person is a strong prima facie reason for not destroying it; but we need not conclude from this that a potential person has a right to life, by virtue of that potential. It may be that our feeling that it is better, other things being equal, not to destroy a potential person is better explained by the fact that potential people are still (felt to be) an invaluable resource, not to be lightly squandered. Surely, if every speck of dust were a potential person, we would be much less apt to conclude that every potential person has a right to become actual.

Still, we do not need to insist that a potential person has no right to life whatever. There may well be something immoral, and not just imprudent, about wantonly destroying potential people, when doing so isn't necessary to protect anyone's rights. But even if a potential person does have some prima facie right to life, such a right could not possibly outweigh the right of a woman to obtain an abortion, since the rights of any actual person invariably outweigh those of any potential person, whenever the two conflict. Since this may not be immediately obvious in the case of a human fetus, let us look at another case.

Suppose that our space explorer falls into the hands of an alien culture, whose scientists decide to create a few hundred thousand or more human beings, by breaking his body into its component cells, and using these to create fully developed human beings, with, of course, his genetic code. We may imagine that each of these newly created men will have all of the original man's abilities, skills, knowledge, and so on, and also have an individual self-concept, in short that each of them will be a bona fide (though hardly unique) person. Imagine that the whole project will take only seconds, and that its chances of success are extremely high, and that our explorer knows all of this, and also knows that these people will be treated *fairly*. I maintain that in such a situation he would have every right to escape if he could, and thus to deprive all of these potential people of their potential lives; for his right to life outweighs all of theirs together, in spite of the fact that they are all genetically human, all innocent, and all have a very high probability of becoming people very soon, if only he refrains from acting.

Indeed, I think he would have a right to escape even if it were not his life which the alien scientists planned to take, but only a year of his freedom, or, indeed, only a day. Nor would he be obligated to stay if he had gotten captured (thus bringing all these people-potentials into existence) because of his own carelessness, or even if he had done so deliberately, knowing the consequences. Regardless of how he got captured, he is not morally obligated to remain in captivity for *any* period of time for the sake of permitting any number of potential people to come into actuality, so great is the margin by which one actual person's right to liberty outweighs whatever right to life even a hundred thousand potential people have. And it seems reasonable to conclude that the rights of a woman will outweigh by a similar margin whatever right to life a fetus may have by virtue of its potential personhood.

Thus, neither a fetus's resemblance to a person, nor its potential for becoming a person provides any basis whatever for the claim that it has any significant right to life. Consequently, a woman's right to protect her health, happiness, freedom, and even her life,[9] by terminating an unwanted pregnancy, will always override whatever right to life it may be appropriate to ascribe to a fetus, even a fully developed one. And thus, in the absence of any overwhelming social need for every possible child, the laws which restrict the right to obtain an abortion, or limit the period of pregnancy during which an abortion may be performed, are a wholly unjustified violation of woman's most basic moral and constitutional rights.

NOTES

1. For example, Roger Wertheimer, who in "Understanding the Abortion Argument" (*Philosophy and Public Affairs*, 1, No. 1 [Fall, 1971], 67-95), argues that the problem of the moral status of abortion is insoluble, in that the dispute over the status of the fetus is not a question of fact at all, but only a question of how one responds to the facts.
2. John Noonan, "Abortion and the Catholic Church: A Summary History," *Natural Law Forum*, 12 (1967), 125.
3. John Noonan, "Deciding Who is Human," *Natural Law Forum,* 13 (1968), 134.
4. Judith Thomson, "A Defense of Abortion," *Philosophy and Public Affairs*, 1, No. 1 (Fall, 1971), 47-66.
5. We may safely ignore the fact that she might have avoided getting raped, e.g., by carrying a gun, since by similar means you might likewise have avoided getting kidnapped, and in neither case does the victim's failure to take all possible precautions against a highly unlikely event (as opposed to reasonable precautions against a rather likely event) mean that he is morally responsible for what happens.
6. Of course, the principle that it is (always) wrong to kill innocent human beings is in need of many other modifications, e.g., that it may be permissible to do so to save a greater number of other innocent human beings, but we may safely ignore these complications here.
7. From here on, we will use 'human' to mean genetically human, since the moral sense seems closely connected to, and perhaps derived from, the assumption that genetic humanity is sufficient for membership in the moral community.
8. Thomas L. Hayes, "A Biological View," *Commonweal*, 85 (March 17, 1967), 677-78; quoted by Daniel Callahan, in *Abortion, Law, Choice, and Morality* (London: Macmillan & Co., 1970).
9. That is, insofar as the death rate, for the woman, is higher for childbirth than for early abortion.

Why Abortion Is Immoral
Don Marquis

Don Marquis, a philosophy professor at the University of Kansas, argues that at least nearly all abortions are seriously immoral. Unlike some who claim that abortion is wrong, Marquis does not want his position to depend on any view about whether or not a human fetus is a person. Instead, he begins by asking why it would be wrong (in almost all circumstances) to kill an adult human being, and answers that such killing is wrong because it deprives its victim of his or her future. It follows, he argues, that it is usually seriously wrong to deprive a being of a future of the sort that adult humans have—what he calls "a future-like-ours." However, a human fetus, if allowed to develop, will also have such a future. If it is wrong to deprive a being of a future like ours, then it is wrong to destroy a human fetus, since it too has a future like ours. Finally, Marquis attempts to meet the objection that his position would also imply that contraception is seriously immoral. He responds to this objection by arguing that before conception there is no nonarbitrarily identifiable being with a future of which it could be deprived by contraception.

The view that abortion is, with rare exceptions, seriously immoral has received little support in the recent philosophical literature. No doubt most philosophers affiliated with secular institutions of higher education believe that the anti-abortion position is either a symptom of irrational religious dogma or a conclusion generated by seriously confused philosophical argument. The purpose of this essay is to undermine this general belief. This essay sets out an argument that purports to show, as well as any argument in ethics can show, that abortion is, except possibly in rare cases, seriously immoral, that it is in the same moral category as killing an innocent adult human being.

The argument is based on a major assumption. Many of the most insightful and careful writers on the ethics of abortion—such as Joel Feinberg, Michael Tooley, Mary Anne Warren, H. Tristram Engelhardt, Jr., L. W. Sumner, John T. Noonan, Jr., and Philip Devine[1]—believe that whether or not abortion is morally permissible stands or falls on whether or not a fetus is the sort of being whose life it is seriously wrong to end. The argument of this essay will assume, but not argue, that they are correct.

Also, this essay will neglect issues of great importance to a complete ethics of abortion. Some anti-abortionists will allow that certain abortions, such as abortion before implantation or abortion when the life of a woman is threatened by a pregnancy or abortion after rape, may be morally permissible. This essay will not explore the casuistry of these hard cases. The purpose of

From *Journal of Philosophy* 86 (1989), 183-202.

this essay is to develop a general argument for the claim that the overwhelming majority of deliberate abortions are seriously immoral.

I

A sketch of standard anti-abortion and pro-choice arguments exhibits how those arguments possess certain symmetries that explain why partisans of those positions are so convinced of the correctness of their own positions, why they are not successful at convincing their opponents, and why, to others, this issue seems to be unresolvable. An analysis of the nature of this standoff suggests a strategy for surmounting it.

Consider the way a typical anti-abortionist argues. She will argue or assert that life is present from the moment of conception or that fetuses look like babies or that fetuses possess a characteristic such as a genetic code that is both necessary and sufficient for being human. Anti-abortionists seem to believe that (1) the truth of all of these claims is quite obvious, and (2) establishing any of these claims is sufficient to show that abortion is morally akin to murder.

A standard pro-choice strategy exhibits similarities. The pro-choicer will argue or assert that fetuses are not persons or that fetuses are not rational agents or that fetuses are not social beings. Pro-choicers seem to believe that (1) the truth of any of these claims is quite obvious, and (2) establishing any of these claims is sufficient to show that an abortion is not a wrongful killing.

In fact, both the pro-choice and the anti-abortion claims do seem to be true, although the "it looks like a baby" claim is more difficult to establish the earlier the pregnancy. We seem to have a standoff. How can it be resolved?

As everyone who has taken a bit of logic knows, if any of these arguments concerning abortion is a good argument, it requires not only some claim characterizing fetuses, but also some general moral principle that ties a characteristic of fetuses to having or not having the right to life or to some other moral characteristic that will generate the obligation or the lack of obligation not to end the life of a fetus. Accordingly, the arguments of the anti-abortionist and the pro-choicer need a bit of filling in to be regarded as adequate.

Note what each partisan will say. The anti-abortionist will claim that her position is supported by such generally accepted moral principles as "It is always prima facie seriously wrong to take a human life" or "It is always prima facie seriously wrong to end the life of a baby." Since these are generally accepted moral principles, her position is certainly not obviously wrong. The pro-choicer will claim that her position is supported by such plausible moral principles as "Being a person is what gives an individual intrinsic moral worth" or "It is only seriously prima facie wrong to take the life of a member of the human community." Since these are generally accepted moral principles, the pro-choice position is certainly not obviously wrong. Unfortunately, we have again arrived at a standoff.

Now, how might one deal with this standoff? The standard approach is to try to show how the moral principles of one's opponent lose their plausibility under analysis. It is easy to see how this is possible. On the one hand, the anti-abortionist will defend a moral principle concerning the wrongness of killing which tends to be broad in scope in order that even fetuses at an early stage of pregnancy will fall under it. The problem with broad principles is that they often embrace too much. In this particular instance, the principle "It is always prima facie wrong to take a human life" seems to entail that it is wrong to end the existence of a living human cancer-cell culture, on the grounds that the culture is both living and human. Therefore, it seems that the anti-abortionist's favored principle is too broad.

On the other hand, the pro-choicer wants to find a moral principle concerning the wrongness of killing which tends to be narrow in scope in order that fetuses will *not* fall under it. The problem with narrow principles is that they often do not embrace enough. Hence, the needed principles such as "It is prima facie seriously wrong to kill only persons" or "It is prima facie wrong to kill only rational agents" do not explain why it is wrong to kill infants or young children or the severely retarded or even perhaps the severely mentally ill. Therefore, we seem again to have a standoff. The anti-abortionist charges, not unreasonably, that pro-choice principles concerning killing are too narrow to be acceptable; the pro-choicer charges, not unreasonably, that anti-abortionist principles concerning killing are too broad to be acceptable. . . .

Passions in the abortion debate run high. There are both plausibilities and difficulties with the standard positions. Accordingly, it is hardly surprising that partisans of either side embrace with fervor the moral generalizations that support the conclusions they preanalytically favor, and reject with disdain the moral generalizations of their opponents as being subject to inescapable difficulties. It is easy to believe that the counterexamples to one's own moral principles are merely temporary difficulties that will dissolve in the wake of further philosophical research. . . . This might suggest to an impartial observer (if there are any) that the abortion issue is unresolvable.

There is a way out of this apparent dialectical quandary. The moral generalizations of both sides are not quite correct. The generalizations hold for the most part, for the usual cases. This suggests that they are all *accidental* generalizations, that the moral claims made by those on both sides of the dispute do not touch on the *essence* of the matter.

This use of the distinction between essence and accident is not meant to invoke obscure metaphysical categories. Rather, it is intended to reflect the rather atheoretical nature of the abortion discussion. If the generalization a partisan in the abortion dispute adopts were derived from the reason why ending the life of a human being is wrong, then there could not be exceptions to that generalization unless some special case obtains in which there are even more powerful countervailing reasons. Such generalizations would not be merely accidental generalizations; they would point to, or be based upon, the essence of the wrongness of killing, what it is that makes killing wrong. All this suggests that a necessary condition of resolving the abortion controversy is a more theoretical account of the wrongness of killing. After all, if we merely believe, but do not understand, why killing adult human beings such as ourselves is wrong, how could we conceivably show that abortion is either immoral or permissible?

II

In order to develop such an account, we can start from the following unproblematic assumption concerning our own case: it is wrong to kill *us*. Why is it wrong? Some answers can be easily eliminated. It might be said that what makes killing us wrong is that a killing brutalizes the one who kills. But the brutalization consists of being inured to the performance of an act that is hideously immoral; hence, the brutalization does not explain the immorality. It might be said that what makes killing us wrong is the great loss others would experience due to our absence. Although such hubris is understandable, such an explanation does not account for the wrongness of killing hermits, or those whose lives are relatively independent and whose friends find it easy to make new friends.

A more obvious answer is better. What primarily makes killing wrong is neither its effect on the murderer nor its effect on the victim's friends and relatives, but its effect on the victim. The loss of one's life is one of the greatest losses one can suffer. The loss of one's life deprives one of all the experiences, activities, projects, and enjoyments that would otherwise have constituted one's future. Therefore, killing someone is wrong, primarily because the killing inflicts (one of) the greatest possible losses on the victim. To describe this as the loss of life can be misleading, however. The change in my biological state does not by itself make killing me wrong. The effect of the loss of my biological life is the loss to me of all those activities, projects, experiences, and enjoyments which would otherwise have constituted my future personal life. These activities, projects, experiences, and enjoyments are either valuable for their own sakes or are means to something else that is valuable for its own sake. Some parts of my future are not valued by me now, but will come to be valued by me as I grow older and as my values and capacities change. When I am killed, I am deprived both of what I now value which would have been part of my future personal life, but also what I would come to value. Therefore, when I die, I am deprived of all of the value of my future. Inflicting this loss on me is ultimately what makes killing me wrong. This being the case, it would seem that what makes killing *any* adult human being prima facie seriously wrong is the loss of his or her future.[2]

How should this rudimentary theory of the wrongness of killing be evaluated? ... This analysis rests on the intuition that what makes killing a particular human or animal wrong is what it does to that particular human or animal. What makes killing wrong is some natural effect or other of the killing. ...

The claim that what makes killing wrong is the loss of the victim's future is directly supported by two considerations. In the first place, this theory explains why we regard killing as one of the worst of crimes. Killing is especially wrong, because it deprives the victim of more than perhaps any other crime. In the second place, people with AIDS or cancer who know they are dying believe, of course, that dying is a very bad thing for them. They believe that the loss of a future to them that they would otherwise have experienced is what makes their premature death a very bad thing for them. A better theory of the wrongness of killing would require a different natural property associated with killing which better fits with the attitudes of the dying. What could it be?

The view that what makes killing wrong is the loss to the victim of the value of the victim's future gains additional support when some of its implications are examined. In the first place, it is incompatible with the view that it is wrong to kill only beings who are biologically human. It is possible that there exists a different species from another planet whose members have a future like ours. Since having a future like that is what makes killing someone wrong, this theory entails that it would be wrong to kill members of such a species. Hence, this theory is opposed to the claim that only life that is biologically human has great moral worth, a claim which many anti-abortionists have seemed to adopt. This opposition, which this theory has in common with personhood theories, seems to be a merit of the theory.

In the second place, the claim that the loss of one's future is the wrong-making feature of one's being killed entails the possibility that the futures of some actual nonhuman mammals on our own planet are sufficiently like ours that it is seriously wrong to kill them also. Whether some animals do have the same right to life as human beings depends on adding to the account of the wrongness of killing some additional account of just what it is about my future or the futures of other adult human beings which makes it wrong to kill us. No such additional account will be offered in this essay. Undoubtedly, the provision of such an account would be a very difficult matter. Undoubtedly, any such account would be quite controversial. Hence, it surely should not reflect badly on this sketch of an elementary theory of the wrongness of killing that it is indeterminate with respect to some very difficult issues regarding animal rights.

In the third place, the claim that the loss of one's future is the wrong-making feature of one's being killed does not entail, as sanctity of human life theories do, that active euthanasia is wrong. Persons who are severely and incurably ill, who face a future of pain and despair, and who wish to die will not have suffered a loss if they are killed. It is, strictly speaking, the value of a human's future which makes killing wrong in this theory. This being so, killing does not necessarily wrong some persons who are sick and dying. Of course, there may be other reasons for a prohibition of active euthanasia, but that is another matter. Sanctity-of-human-life theories seem to hold that active euthanasia is seriously wrong even in an individual case where there seems to be good reason for it independently of public policy considerations. This consequence is most implausible, and it is a plus for the claim that the loss of a future of value is what makes killing wrong that it does not share this consequence.

In the fourth place, the account of the wrongness of killing defended in this essay does straightforwardly entail that it is prima facie seriously wrong to kill children and infants, for we do presume that they have futures of value. Since we do believe that it is wrong to kill defenseless little babies, it is important that a theory of the wrongness of killing easily account for this. Personhood theories of the wrongness of killing, on the other hand, cannot straightforwardly account for the wrongness of killing infants and young children.[3] Hence, such theories must add special ad hoc accounts of the wrongness of killing the young. The plausibility of such ad hoc theories seems to be a function of how desperately one wants such theories to work. The claim that the primary wrong-making feature of a killing is the loss to the victim of the value of its future accounts for the wrongness of killing young children and infants directly; it makes the wrongness of such acts as obvious as we actually think it is. This is a further merit of this theory. Accordingly, it seems that this value of a future-like-ours theory of the wrongness of killing shares strengths of both sanctity-of-life and personhood accounts while avoiding weaknesses of both. In addition, it meshes with a central intuition concerning what makes killing wrong.

The claim that the primary wrong-making feature of a killing is the loss to the victim of the value of its future has obvious consequences for the ethics of abortion. The future of a standard fetus includes a set of experiences, projects, activities, and such which are identical with the futures of adult human beings and are identical with the futures of young children. Since the reason that is sufficient to explain why it is wrong to kill human beings after the time of birth is a reason that also applies to fetuses, it follows that abortion is prima facie seriously morally wrong.

This argument does not rely on the invalid inference that, since it is wrong to kill persons, it is wrong to kill potential persons also. The category that is morally central to this analysis is the category of having a valuable future like ours; it is not the category of personhood. The argument to the conclusion that abortion is prima facie seriously morally wrong proceeded independently of the notion of person or potential person or any equivalent. . . .

The structure of this anti-abortion argument can be both illuminated and defended by comparing it to what appears to be the best argument for the wrongness of the wanton infliction of pain on animals. This latter argument is based on the assumption that it is prima facie wrong to inflict pain on me (or you, reader). What is the natural property associated with the infliction of pain which makes such infliction wrong? The obvious answer seems to be that the infliction of pain causes suffering and that suffering is a misfortune. The suffering caused by the infliction of pain is what makes the wanton infliction of pain on me wrong. The wanton infliction of pain on other adult humans causes suffering. The wanton infliction of pain on animals causes suffering. Since causing suffering is what makes the wanton infliction of pain wrong and since the wanton infliction of pain on animals causes suffering, it follows that the wanton infliction of pain on animals is wrong.

This argument for the wrongness of the wanton infliction of pain on animals shares a number of structural features with the argument for the serious prima facie wrongness of abortion. Both arguments start with an obvious assumption concerning what is wrong to do to me (or you, reader). Both then look for the characteristic or the consequence of the wrong action which makes the action wrong. Both recognize that the wrong-making feature of these immoral actions is a property of actions sometimes directed at individuals other than postnatal human beings. If the structure of the argument for the wrongness of the wanton infliction of pain on animals is sound, then the structure of the argument for the prima facie serious wrongness of abortion is also sound, for the structure of the two arguments is the same. The structure common to both is the key to the explanation of how the wrongness of abortion can be demonstrated without recourse to the category of person. In neither argument is that category crucial. . . .

Of course, this value of a future-like-ours argument, if sound, shows only that abortion is prima facie wrong, not that it is wrong in any and all circumstances. Since the loss of the future to a standard fetus, if killed, is, however, at least as great a loss as the loss of the future to a standard adult human being who is killed, abortion, like ordinary killing, could be justified only by the most compelling reasons. The loss of one's life is almost the greatest misfortune that can happen to one. Presumably abortion could be justified in some circumstances, only if the loss consequent on failing to abort would be at least as great. Accordingly, morally permissible abortions will be rare indeed unless, perhaps, they occur so early in pregnancy that a fetus is not yet definitely an individual. Hence, this argument should be taken as showing that abortion is presumptively very seriously wrong, where the presumption is very strong—as strong as the presumption that killing another adult human being is wrong.

III

How complete an account of the wrongness of killing does the value of a future-like-ours account have to be in order that the wrongness of abortion is a consequence? This account does not have to be an account of the necessary conditions for the wrongness of killing. Some persons in nursing homes may lack valuable human futures, yet it may be wrong to kill them for other reasons. Furthermore, this account does not obviously have to be the sole reason killing is wrong where the victim did have a valuable future. This analysis claims only that, for any killing where the victim did have a valuable future like ours, having that future by itself is sufficient to create the strong presumption that the killing is seriously wrong.

One way to overturn the value of a future-like-ours argument would be to find some account of the wrongness of killing which is at least as intelligible and which has different implications for the ethics of abortion. Two rival accounts possess at least some degree of plausibility. One account is based on the obvious fact that people value the experience of living and wish for that valuable experience to continue. Therefore, it might be said, what makes killing wrong is the discontinuation of that experience for the victim. Let us call this the *discontinuation account.*[4] Another rival account is based upon the obvious fact that people strongly desire to continue to live. This suggests that what makes killing us so wrong is that it interferes with the fulfillment of a strong and fundamental desire, the fulfillment of which is necessary for the fulfillment of any other desires we might have. Let us call this the *desire account.*[5]

Consider first the desire account as a rival account of the ethics of killing which would provide the basis for rejecting the anti-abortion position. Such an account will have to be stronger than the value of a future-like-ours account of the wrongness of abortion if it is to do the job expected of it. To entail the wrongness of abortion, the value of a future-like-ours account has only to provide a sufficient, but not a necessary, condition for the wrongness of killing. The desire account, on the other hand, must provide us also with a necessary condition for the wrongness of killing in order to generate a pro-choice conclusion on abortion. The reason for this is that presumably the argument from the desire account moves from the claim that what makes killing wrong is interference with a very strong desire to the claim that abortion is not wrong because the fetus lacks a strong desire to live. Obviously, this inference fails if someone's having the desire to live is not a necessary condition of its being wrong to kill that individual.

One problem with the desire account is that we do regard it as seriously wrong to kill persons who have little desire to live or who have no desire to live or, indeed, have a desire not to live. We believe it is seriously wrong to kill the unconscious, the sleeping, those who are tired of life, and those who are suicidal. The value-of-a-human-future account renders standard morality intelligible in these cases; these cases appear to be incompatible with the desire account.

The desire account is subject to a deeper difficulty. We desire life, because we value the goods of this life. The goodness of life is not secondary to our desire for it. If this were not so, the pain of one's own premature death could be done away with merely by an appropriate alteration in the configuration of one's desires. This is absurd. Hence, it would seem that it is the loss of the goods of one's future, not the interference with the fulfillment of a strong desire to live, which accounts ultimately for the wrongness of killing. . . .

The discontinuation account looks more promising as an account of the wrongness of killing. It seems just as intelligible as the value of a future-like-ours account, but it does not justify an anti-abortion position. Obviously, if it is the continuation of one's activities, experiences, and projects, the loss of which makes killing wrong, then it is not wrong to kill fetuses for that reason, for fetuses do not have experiences, activities, and projects to be continued or discontinued. Accordingly, the discontinuation account does not have the anti-abortion consequences that the value of a future-like-ours account has. Yet, it seems as intelligible as the value of a future-like-ours account, for when we think of what would be wrong with our being killed, it does seem as if it is the discontinuation of what makes our lives worthwhile which makes killing us wrong.

Is the discontinuation account just as good an account as the value of a future-like-ours account? The discontinuation account will not be adequate at all, if it does not refer to the *value* of the experience that may be discontinued. One does not want the discontinuation account to make it wrong to kill a patient who begs for death and who is in severe pain that cannot be re-lieved short of killing. (I leave open the question of whether it is wrong for other reasons.) Accordingly, the discontinuation account must be more than a bare discontinuation account. It must make some reference to the positive value of the patient's experiences. But, by the same token, the value of a future-like-ours account cannot be a bare future account either. Just having a future surely does not itself rule out killing the above patient. This account must make some reference to the value of the patient's future experiences and projects also. Hence, both accounts involve the value of experiences, projects, and activities. So far we still have symmetry between the accounts.

The symmetry fades, however, when we focus on the time period of the value of the experiences, etc., which has moral consequences. Although both accounts leave open the possibility that the patient in our example may be killed, this possibility is left open only in virtue of the utterly bleak future for the patient. It makes no difference whether the patient's immediate past con-tains intolerable pain, or consists in being in a coma (which we can imagine is a situation of indifference), or consists in a life of value. If the patient's future is a future of value, we want our account to make it wrong to kill the patient. If the patient's future is intolerable, whatever his or her immediate past, we want our account to allow killing the patient. Obviously, then, it is the value of that patient's future which is doing the work in rendering the morality of killing the patient intelligible.

This being the case, it seems clear that whether one has immediate past experiences or not does no work in the explanation of what makes killing wrong. The addition the discontinuation account makes to the value of a hu-man future account is otiose. Its addition to the value-of-a-future account plays no role at all in rendering intelligible the wrongness of killing. Therefore, it can be discarded with the discontinuation account of which it is a part.

IV

The analysis of the previous section suggests that alternative general accounts of the wrongness of killing are either inadequate or unsuccessful in getting around the anti-abortion consequences of the value of a future-like-ours argument. A different strategy for avoiding these anti-abortion consequences involves limiting the scope of the value of a future argument. More precisely, the strategy involves arguing that fetuses lack a property that is essential for the value-of-a-future argument (or for any anti-abortion argument) to apply to them.

One move of this sort is based upon the claim that a necessary condition of one's future being valuable is that one values it. Value implies a valuer. Given this one might argue that, since fetuses cannot value their futures, their futures are not valuable to them. Hence, it does not seriously wrong them deliberately to end their lives.

This move fails, however, because of some ambiguities. Let us assume that something cannot be of value unless it is valued by someone. This does not entail that my life is of no value unless it is valued by me. I may think, in a period of despair, that my future is of no worth whatsoever, but I may be wrong because others rightly see value—even great value—in it. Furthermore, my future can be valuable to me even if I do not value it. This is the case when a young person attempts suicide, but is rescued and goes on to significant human achievements. Such young people's futures are ultimately valuable to them, even though such futures do not seem to be valuable to them at the moment of attempted suicide. A fetus's future can be valuable to it in the same way. Accordingly, this attempt to limit the anti-abortion argument fails. . . .

V

In this essay, it has been argued that the correct ethic of the wrongness of killing can be extended to fetal life and used to show that there is a strong presumption that any abortion is morally impermissible. If the ethic of killing adopted here entails, however, that contraception is also seriously immoral, then there would appear to be a difficulty with the analysis of this essay.

But this analysis does not entail that contraception is wrong. Of course, contraception prevents the actualization of a possible future of value. Hence, it follows from the claim that futures of value should be maximized that contraception is prima facie immoral. This obligation to maximize does not exist, however; furthermore, nothing in the ethics of killing in this paper entails that it does. The ethics of killing in this essay would entail that contraception is wrong only if something were denied a human future of value by contraception. Nothing at all is denied such a future by contraception, however.

Candidates for a subject of harm by contraception fall into four categories: (1) some sperm or other, (2) some ovum or other, (3) a sperm and an ovum separately, and (4) a sperm and an ovum together. Assigning the harm to some sperm is utterly arbitrary, for no reason can be given for making a sperm the subject of harm rather than an ovum. Assigning the harm to some ovum is utterly arbitrary, for no reason can be given for making an ovum the subject of harm rather than a sperm. One might attempt to avoid these problems by insisting that contraception deprives both the sperm and the ovum separately of a valuable future like ours. On this alternative, too many futures are lost. Contraception was supposed to be wrong, because it deprived us of one future of value, not two. One might attempt to avoid this problem by holding that contraception deprives the combination of sperm and ovum of a valuable future like ours. But here the definite article misleads. At the time of contraception, there are hundreds of millions of sperm, one (released) ovum and millions of possible combinations of all of these. There is no actual combination at all. Is the subject of the loss to be a merely possible combination? Which one? This alternative does not yield an actual subject of harm either. Accordingly, the immorality of contraception is not entailed by the loss of a future-like-ours argument simply because there is no nonarbitrarily identifiable subject of the loss in the case of contraception.

VI

The purpose of this essay has been to set out an argument for the serious presumptive wrongness of abortion subject to the assumption that the moral permissibility of abortion stands or falls on the moral status of the fetus. Since a fetus possesses a property, the possession of which in adult human beings is sufficient to make killing an adult human being wrong, abortion is wrong. This way of dealing with the problem of abortion seems superior to other approaches to the ethics of abortion, because it rests on an ethics of killing which is close to self-evident, because the crucial morally relevant property clearly applies to fetuses, and because the argument avoids the usual equivocations on 'human life', 'human being', or 'person'. The argument rests neither on religious claims nor on Papal dogma. It is not subject to the objection of "speciesism." Its soundness is compatible with the moral permissibility of euthanasia and contraception. It deals with our intuitions concerning young children.

Finally, this analysis can be viewed as resolving a standard problem—indeed, *the* standard problem—concerning the ethics of abortion. Clearly, it is wrong to kill adult human beings. Clearly, it is not wrong to end the life of some arbitrarily chosen single human cell. Fetuses seem to be like arbitrarily chosen human cells in some respects and like adult humans in other respects. The problem of the ethics of abortion is the problem of determining the fetal property that settles this moral controversy. The thesis of this essay is that the problem of the ethics of abortion, so understood, is solvable.

NOTES

1. Feinberg, "Abortion," in *Matters of Life and Death: New Introductory Essays in Moral Philosophy*, Tom Regan, ed. (New York: Random House, 1986), pp. 256-293; Tooley, "Abortion and Infanticide," *Philosophy and Public Affairs*, II, 1

(1972):37–65, Tooley, *Abortion and Infanticide* (New York: Oxford, 1984); Warren, "On the Moral and Legal Status of Abortion," *The Monist*, I.VII, 1 (1973):43–61; Engelhardt, "The Ontology of Abortion," *Ethics*, I.XXXIV, 3 (1974):217–234; Sumner, *Abortion and Moral Theory* (Princeton: University Press, 1981); Noonan, "An Almost Absolute Value in History," in *The Morality of Abortion: Legal and Historical Perspectives*, Noonan, ed. (Cambridge: Harvard, 1970); and Devine, *The Ethics of Homicide* (Ithaca: Cornell, 1978).

2. I have been most influenced on this matter by Jonathan Glover, *Causing Death and Saving Lives* (New York: Penguin, 1977), ch. 3; and Robert Young, "What Is So Wrong with Killing People?" *Philosophy*, I.IV, 210 (1979):515–528.

3. Feinberg, Tooley, Warren, and Engelhardt have all dealt with this problem.

4. I am indebted to Jack Bricke for raising this objection.

5. Presumably a preference utilitarian would press such an objection. Tooley once suggested that his account has such a theoretical underpinning. See his "Abortion and Infanticide," pp. 44/5.

Abortion, Moral Responsibility, and Self-Defense

Tom L. Huffman

Tom L. Huffman, who teaches at Westmar University, responds in this essay to a common defense of the permissibility of abortion even under the assumption that a human fetus is a person with a right to life. According to that defense, even though a fetus has a right to life, abortion is permissible because the fetus depends on the use of a woman's body in a way to which it has no right. The specific version of this defense of abortion to which Huffman is responding bases the right to abortion on a right to defend oneself against threats to one's health and well-being. At least in many cases of pregnancy, according to this defense, a fetus does constitute such a threat. In what might be considered a version of the consent argument, Huffman argues that the right to self-defense does not apply to at least some risks that one has literally created. This loss of the right to self-defense is present in at least many pregnancies resulting from voluntary sexual activity. Huffman is aware that his argument can strike many as sexist since it seems to focus on the moral responsibility of women for pregnancy, and he argues that there are nonsexist reasons for such a focus.

———

Resolving the abortion debate requires answering both a metaphysical and a moral question. The metaphysical question ponders whether the fetus is a person, where "person" is interpreted to mean "a being with a right to life." The moral question concerns which moral principle(s) are best-suited to the abortion debate.

We used to think that resolving the personhood issue was decisive. Judith Thomson's landmark article seems to demonstrate the inadequacy of this approach.[1] Even if we assume the fetus has a right to life from the moment of conception, applying widely-accepted norms distinguishing the obligatory from the supererogatory show, at best, that refraining from abortion in the typical case[2] would be a *nice* thing to do, but is hardly demanded by minimal moral standards. Thus, even if the fetus is a person from the moment of conception, the conservative position requires further justification.

It is also doubtful whether the fetus's lack of personhood would count decisively in favor of the liberal view on abortion. Wondering whether a woman may have an abortion *may* be approached from the perspective of whether doing so violates a right to life, but it need not. Innumerable explanations for the wrongness of acts exist beyond the violation of someone's rights. Burning books, harming the environment, causing animals needless pain, and drug abuse are all examples of morally suspect behavior whose wrongness is not easily

From *Public Affairs Quarterly* 7 (October 1993), 287–302.

explained on the rights-violation model. Perhaps abortion is like this. The fetus has no right to life, but, nonetheless, perhaps killing it is wrong for independent reasons.

In any case, once we recognize that the fetus's personhood alone can neither sanction nor forbid abortion, we need to determine the appropriate moral principle whose application does much of the spade work in resolving this notoriously intractable moral dispute.

Several principles are good candidates. . . . What currently interests me, though, is the principle of self-defense. Perhaps applying the standards that determine when one may use deadly force in self-defense is a valuable tactic in addressing the abortion debate. I shall *not* argue that relying on the concept of self-defense is sufficient or even wise.[3] The metaphysical status of the fetus must still be addressed. But even after we address this question, we still need to invoke a moral principle appropriate to the debate and the principle of self-defense is but one plausible candidate. I shall also *not* attempt a general resolution of the moral permissibility of abortion. I merely hope to outline just what the principle of self-defense tells us about abortion just in case this admittedly controversial metaphysical assumption is true. So doing illuminates the often mentioned, but rarely carefully considered, question of what is required of women who wish to avoid moral responsibility for an unwanted pregnancy they intend to abort. . . .

I

In a widely-anthologized article, Jane English presents a moderate theory of abortion rights that relies partly upon the concept of the justified use of deadly force in self-defense.[4] English claims that it is permissible to kill a person in self-defense when two conditions obtain. First, the threat must be sufficiently serious. "Sufficiently serious" is defined as "an attack whose outcome would be [at least] as serious as rape, a severe beating or the loss of a finger."[5] English also points out that one may kill to avoid serious *psychological* harm as when one is threatened with a loss of long-term life prospects. In short, one may kill to avoid serious physical or psychological harm; or, as she puts it: "you may create an injury somewhat, but not enormously, greater than the injury to be avoided."[6]

Second, the use of deadly force in self-defense is justified only when it presents the *minimum* amount of force required to neutralize the attack. If one may avoid harm (however serious) simply by running away or incapacitating the attacker, then deadly force is unwarranted.

An important element in this analysis is that we need not concern ourselves with the attacker's *innocence*. Since the justification for self-defense lies in the legitimate interest one has in protecting one's own welfare and not in the need to punish wrong-doing, one's right to defend one's self is unaffected by an attacker's degree of culpability.

English's argument requires two steps. First, we are asked to accept her analysis of self-defense; and, second, we must determine whether this theory of self-defense justifies a moderate view of abortion. In the latter respect, English thinks that unwanted pregnancies often, though not always, present a threat to a woman that meets the first criterion for the justified use of deadly force. In those cases in which carrying a fetus to term do not present a serious physical or psychological threat, abortion would not be justified. She also claims that, unfortunately, the very nature of unwanted pregnancy is such that the *only* relief from it entails the death of the fetus. Because of this, the second criterion requiring minimum use of force is automatically met—no other effective means of protection are available.

English's analysis is defective in both respects. Both her account of self-defense and application of it to abortion are incomplete. Whether one may justifiably use deadly force in self-defense depends, in addition to the two conditions already mentioned, at least in part upon one's responsibility for the threat. This is illustrated by English's own thought experiment in which innocent persons are hypnotized by a mad scientist to ambush passers-by. She writes:

> Suppose a mad scientist, for instance, hypnotized innocent people to jump out of the bushes and attack innocent passers-by with knives. If you are so attacked, we agree you have a right to kill the attacker in self defense, if killing him is the only way to protect your life or save yourself from serious injury. It does not seem to matter here that the attacker is not malicious but himself an innocent pawn, for your killing of him is not done in a spirit of retribution but only in self-defense.[7]

Clearly, the passers-by have a right to kill their attackers in self-defense, but if the hypnotized attackers turned on the mad scientist, would he have this same right? Since he is exclusively responsible for the threat facing him, his right to kill his (blameless) attackers to save himself is doubtful.

Of course, the addition of this third requirement affects how we view an appeal to self-defense as a rationale for abortion. A woman's right to have an abortion will, at least partly, depend upon whether she is responsible for the pregnancy. Certainly victims of rape are not responsible for their pregnancy, but what of cases in which the pregnancy results from a failure of responsible birth control? It is tempting to point out that in the latter case a woman still *could* have avoided the pregnancy by remaining chaste. However, a woman *could* avoid a rape by staying indoors and remaining heavily armed. The question, then as to whether one is responsible for what occurs in one's life depends, not just upon whether one is able to avoid the situation (one can almost always do that), but whether one could be reasonably expected to have refrained from the behavior that is responsible for the situation. It is not reasonable to expect women to avoid going outdoors; hence, they are not responsible for rape simply because they do so. . . .

II

With respect to abortion, when will an appeal to self-defense be justified? First, we must know, and we surely do not, whether it is seriously wrong to kill a fetus. If killing a fetus is a prima facie wrong, much like killing an ordinary adult human is a prima facie wrong, then using the concept of self-defense to determine whether the killing is justified is a promising approach.[8]

Second, does the continuation of the pregnancy present the required degree of threat? No doubt in many, though not all, cases it does. In this respect, at least, English is probably right in thinking that an appeal to self-defense justifies a moderate stance towards abortion rights.

Third, is the death of the fetus the least drastic means of achieving the intended goal? This is a difficult question in light of the availability of adoption. In the majority of cases, abortion is chosen as a means of avoiding psychological and financial harm only, and we must consider whether choosing adoption over abortion saves the woman from the sort of harm envisaged without as a result inflicting similar psychological harms in the process. Neither adoption nor abortion should be an easy choice for a woman. Both involve a certain measure of trauma, and on the assumption that killing a fetus requires some very serious justification, abortion is permissible only if adoption would psychologically damage a woman to a degree similar to that which would warrant the use of deadly force in self-defense. . . . I suspect the amount of trauma adoption causes women varies considerably across individuals, which leads me to believe that empirical studies, and not philosophical analysis, offer the most promising approach to this question. . . .

Finally, when is a woman morally responsible for her pregnancy? Answering this question requires a more general account of moral responsibility which can then be applied to the specific case of pregnancy.

It is important to note that this issue has traditionally concerned only a *woman's* responsibility. Why this is so is not immediately clear since, at least in cases of voluntary intercourse, a man is equally responsible for a resulting pregnancy as is a woman. The traditional analysis appears to reveal a sexist bias. However, there are very good reasons why we ought to restrict our discussion of the responsibility for unwanted pregnancies in cases of *consensual* sex, reasons that have to do not with a sexist bias, but with a real concern for women's interests.

When asked to consider a man's responsibility for an unwanted pregnancy in the context of *abortion rights*, women face a very real dilemma. On the one hand, emphasizing a man's role in the matter is important not only as a recognition of biological facts, but as an explanation for why women are entitled to men's support throughout the process. On the other hand, to recognize that men bear some moral responsibility for an unwanted pregnancy seems not to be in the woman's interest, because to the extent we focus upon male *responsibility*, we are led to consider male *choice* as well. If women wish to retain the lone right to decide when, if, and in what manner pregnancies shall be terminated, then, *solely with respect to this decision*, we ought to focus only upon the woman's responsibility for the pregnancy. Of course, male responsibility is relevant with respect to offering a woman support (emotional and financial) for termination if she chooses it. However, the choice is ultimately hers alone. I propose, then, that with respect to this discussion only, we view male responsibility as a mere epiphenomenon—real enough, but playing no important role.

Thomson offers the following account of moral responsibility:

> Again, suppose it were like this: people-seeds drift about in the air like pollen, and if you open your windows, one may drift in and take root in your carpets or upholstery. . . . Someone may argue you are responsible for its rooting (despite the fact that you took measures to avoid it], that it does have a right to your house, because after all you *could* have lived out your life with bare floors and furniture, or with sealed windows and doors.[9] . . .

In [this] thought experiment, one opens a window voluntarily and yet Thomson maintains that one is not responsible for maintaining the lives of the people-seeds. Although Thomson does not say, her example seems to endorse the principle that one ought not be held responsible for supporting another against one's will if one's behavior that leads to the dependence is morally permissible. After all, we all have a right to leave our windows open if we like. . . .

I am not required to offer my carpet to people-seeds even though I voluntarily let them in, because I did not create them in the first place. In other words, their being in need of aid is not my fault. Even had I never existed, presumably people-seeds would have floated about looking for other places to roost and I am not obliged to offer *my* home as a roosting place unless I am responsible for their initial dependence.

How do we determine whether and how much one is responsible for another's dependence? The most obvious requirement involves a competent understanding of the primary morally relevant consequences of one's actions. If one has no idea that one's action will lead to someone's death either because of ignorance or incompetence, and it would be unreasonable to expect one to know this, then one cannot be held responsible for the consequences of what one does. For obvious reasons, we ordinarily do not hold children or mental incompetents responsible for what they do, so a 13 year-old girl or victim of serious retardation would not be responsible for her pregnancy regardless of any other considerations.

Moral responsibility requires that other conditions are met as well. For instance, it is important that the activity itself is permissible. We can establish this by asking the question, "Is it reasonable to expect a person to refrain from behavior with an outcome requiring the use of deadly force in self-defense?" This third requirement is important because, without it, we would be forced to conclude that a woman is morally responsible for a pregnancy due to rape. She is not responsible since it would be unreasonable (in most cases) to ask her to refrain from the activity leading up to the attack.

So, one is morally responsible for the existence of a threat defense from which requires using deadly force if the threat is created by one's own voluntary actions, one has a competent understanding of this, and one could be reasonably expected to have refrained from the activity that creates the threat.

When is a woman morally responsible for her pregnancy? If a woman engages in involuntary sex (rape), then she is certainly not responsible. However, what if she engages in voluntary sex, but uses birth control and thus does not intend—does not voluntarily wish—pregnancy?

There are, of course, many methods of birth control and the extent to which using one frees one from responsibility of an unwanted pregnancy depends in large part upon the effectiveness of the method employed. Given its notoriously low success rate, one may not, for instance, employ the "rhythm" method as one's sole means of protection and expect that one has, as a result, been freed of any moral responsibility should pregnancy occur. This matter, as John Noonan has observed in a similar context, is largely a question of probabilities. My responsibility for another's death is greatly attenuated if my action that caused the death was such that the *probability* that a lethal effect would result is extremely low.[10] How low is low enough? It is hard to say with any precision, but consider the following scenario.

Consider what would we think of a group of raucous youths who insisted upon running up and down an oceanside pier where several toddlers were playing when the youths are informed that their antics was endangering the children as one might be forced off the pier into the ocean below? It would not quite do if the youths justified their behavior on the grounds that there was merely a "one in a hundred" chance of their causing such a disaster. Nor, I suspect, would even a risk of one in a thousand be enough to free them from responsibility should the worst happen. Obviously, as we start to think of one in a million, or one in ten million, the sense that the youths would be responsible for such a tragedy begins to fade.

Of course, when considering such matters, we need take into account not only the probability that a death would occur. We need also take note of the nature of the risky behavior. All else being equal, causing someone's death (as imagined above) while pursuing idle recreation is worse than had the death been caused during the pursuit of an activity more central to one's fundamental needs. In fact, if the youths were engaged in an activity required for their very *survival*, then we would likely not hold them blameworthy for any resulting deaths even as the probability of a lethal outcome approached 1.0.

So, assuming that one is competent and informed, one's moral responsibility for the outcome of one's behavior is determined by the probability that the outcome will actually occur as a result of the behavior and whether, due to the necessity of the behavior itself, we could reasonably expect one to refrain from it.

Are there other relevant variables? It seems so. Consider the following example: a woman leisurely strolls through the most dangerous part of town at 3.00 AM wearing a very short skirt and a half-buttoned blouse. After only a very short while she is attacked and raped. If we assume that she is competent and informed and that the outcome of her behavior is quite predictable *and* that her leisurely walk is motivated solely out of a desire for recreation, then she is responsible for what occurs to her, and, hence may not use deadly force in self-defense even if there is no other way to deter her assailant and regardless of the seriousness of the threat. Surely something is *very* wrong with this analysis.

The mistake involves a subtle distinction between a threat for which one bears contributory responsibility on the one hand and a threat that one literally *creates* on the other hand.[11]

In the former sort of case, the careless walker pictured above being a good example, we often judge that one is blameworthy for a threat in the sense that the behavior leading to it is unwise and foolishly risky. We would not, however, go so far as to suggest that engaging in foolish behavior that precipitates an attack requires one to submit to the attack. This is like the people-seed case. Perhaps it is *unwise* to leave one's window open under those circumstances, but if one does then one need not submit to the people-seed infestation.

In contrast, . . . we feel that if one is literally responsible for the very existence of the threat with which one is faced, . . . then one can hardly kill another to defend one's self when the threat the other poses is the direct and sole responsibility of, indeed created by, the person being threatened.

A woman has a right to defend herself against attack even when her behavior is foolish and even provocative. A rapist is, after all, responsible for *his* actions and can always refuse the temptation without risking any harm to himself. A robber has no right to defend himself against the store clerk he intends to rob at gun point because the clerk plays no role whatever in creating the dangerous situation confronting them both.

What does this discussion bode for the abortion debate? It all depends how we view the sense in which it is meaningful to say that a woman is responsible for her pregnancy. Is she responsible in the contributory sense that the late-night walker negligently contributes to circumstances that lead to her being attacked; or, is she responsible in the full sense in which she literally creates the threat that faces her by engaging in consensual intercourse? Surely, she is responsible in the latter sense. She is responsible for the very *existence* of the threat she now faces if she knowingly and voluntarily engages in procreative sex with a man. The fetus certainly plays no contributory role at all in placing itself in a position of dependency, and the man's responsibility, although quite real, is not relevant to a woman's right to defend her interests through lethal means.

What does this tell us about the extent to which (if any) practicing birth control frees one from being morally responsible for an unwanted pregnancy? First, given the seriousness of the possible outcome—the death of a being with a right to life—the method must be *extremely* effective, perhaps more effective than any method (short of outright sterilization) medical science has produced or is likely to produce in the future. This conclusion, however, is moderated somewhat by the fact that engaging in satisfying sexual relations is undoubtedly necessary for a reasonably fulfilled life. There is, of course, no precise method by which these competing variables can be weighed, but at an absolute minimum, the use of birth control would be morally exculpatory only if the method employed were among the most effective means currently available—perhaps a combination of oral contraception and a barrier method— and the sexual activity itself were not of a promiscuous or gratuitously repetitive nature. . . .

III

There is one final concern that speaks directly to the principle of self-defense. If we assume that a fetus is a person from the moment of conception, then may we not consider *its* right of self-defense against the threat of abortion? It seems so. If it is proper to consider a woman's right to employ a physician in self-defense against an unwanted fetus, then it is equally proper to consider an interested third-party exercising the fetus's right of self-defense in its behalf against a woman who intends to abort. The fetus is, to use Tom Regan's phrase, a "moral patient" who has a right to life but must rely upon others to protect it against those who would threaten its interests.

In fact, the principle of self-defense seems to argue much more strongly in favor of the fetus's welfare than it does for the woman's. Recall the three criteria by which one determines whether using deadly force in self-defense is permissible—moral responsibility for the threat, seriousness of the threat, and availability of non-lethal means of avoiding or neutralizing the threat. The fetus is not responsible in any sense for the threat which confronts it. Also, the harm the fetus faces is always lethal. Finally, there is never any less serious means for securing its welfare short of compelling a woman to continue the pregnancy, at least until viability.

The upshot is that relying upon self-defense as a moral principle designed to resolve the abortion debate seems to argue more strongly for the fetus's welfare and against a woman's right to abort than has been previously supposed.

I conclude, therefore, that if one assumes that a fetus has a right to life from conception then, in the typical case, abortion is probably not justified on the self-defense model. I draw this conclusion, not because the threat of unwanted pregnancies is not sufficiently serious (it often is) or because there is an effective non-lethal option (it is unclear whether it is reasonable to ask women to choose adoption). Rather, in the typical case, except perhaps if one uses an *extremely* effective means of birth control and engages in sexual intercourse no more than is required for minimal personal satisfaction, a woman is responsible for her pregnancy and hence for the creation of a being whose continued existence requires her cooperation for at least nine months.

Even more fundamentally, if we consider the principle of self-defense seriously, we cannot escape the conclusion that, all things considered, it argues for the fetus's welfare and *against* abortion. This conclusion illustrates an interesting phenomenon. Since self-defense has been employed in the literature to argue *for* a woman's right to an abortion, it is clear that abstract moral principles are often unreliable allies in the service of specific moral claims.

NOTES

1. Judith Jarvis Thomson, "A Defense of Abortion," *Philosophy and Public Affairs*, vol. (1971), pp. 47–66.
2. By the "typical case" I mean an unwanted pregnancy that was not deliberately assumed, nor life-threatening, and whose termination is sought in the first few months of pregnancy.
3. For example, Nancy Davis ["Abortion and Self-Defense," *Philosophy and Public Affairs*, vol.13 (1984), pp. 175–207] argues that self-defense is *not* an appropriate principle to employ in the abortion debate, largely because the presence of third-party intervention makes an analogy between abortion and self-defense a poor one. Although I deem this claim mistaken, I shall not argue the point here. I wish merely to show what follows if we assume for the sake of the argument that the principle of self-defense is appropriate.
4. "Abortion and the Concept of a Person," originally published in the *Canadian Journal of Philosophy*, vol. 5 (1975), pp. 233–43. All quotes from *The Problem of Abortion*, edited by Joel Feinberg (Belmont, CA: Wadsworth, 1984), pp. 151–160.
5. Feinberg, p. 155.
6. *Ibid.,* p. 155.
7. *Ibid.,* p. 155.
8. For the record, I do not believe that a fetus has a right to life from the moment of conception, but gains this right gradually. For this reason, it would not be appropriate to invoke self-defense as a justification for abortion until the third trimester, but this is another paper.
9. Thomson, p. 182.
10. John Noonan, "An Almost Absolute Value in History," from *The Morality of Abortion: Legal and Historical Perspectives* (Cambridge, MA: Harvard University Press, 1970).
11. Of course, the *degree* of contribution is relevant here. There is a wide range of possibilities all the way from a nearly imperceptible contribution to the contribution of a full partner. This range is exemplified by the discussion of probabilities and the various rates of success possessed by birth control methods. The important point here, though, is that, all else being equal, women don't merely contribute to the flourishing of a fetus, they literally create it.

Abortion and Embodiment
Catriona Mackenzie

Catriona Mackenzie is a lecturer in the philosophy department of Macquarie University in Australia. In this essay, she presents a feminist view of abortion that, contrary to many feminist and non-feminist positions alike, does not take the central issue of abortion to be about the conflicting rights of women and fetuses. Instead, she believes that reflection on the morality of abortion needs to take into account the experience of pregnancy itself. According to Mackenzie, this experience "defies a sharp opposition between self and other, between the inside and the outside of the body." She suggests that the decision concerning abortion should be viewed as a decision about whether a part of oneself is to become a being to which one has parental responsibility, and that the freedom to make such a decision is necessary for women's personal autonomy. Such autonomy, Mackenzie claims, deserves recognition as the central moral issue of the problem of abortion itself.

I. INTRODUCTION

Feminist perspectives on abortion focus on a fact the moral implications of which are either overlooked or considered unimportant by most other disputants in the debate. This is the fact that a foetus is not a free-floating entity about whom questions of potentiality and personhood arise as though in a vacuum. Rather a foetus is a being whose existence and welfare are biologically and morally inseparable from the woman in whose body it develops. From a feminist perspective the central moral subjects of the abortion question are thus not only, or not primarily, foetuses but women.

Within an influential strand of the feminist philosophical literature it has been usual to understand the moral dilemmas arising from this unique relationship between a foetus and a woman in terms of a conflict of rights and to defend a woman's right to abortion via the notion of bodily autonomy. In its crudest form, the alleged conflict is between a) the 'right to life' of the foetus, a right based on the presumption that it is a being deserving of some moral consideration, and b) the right of the woman to bodily autonomy, that is, her right to decide what happens in and to her body. In attempting to resolve this conflict in women's favour feminist defenders of abortion have taken two main lines of argument.

The first, articulated best by Mary Anne Warren, argues that in abortion decisions the woman's right to bodily autonomy must always prevail over any rights which may be claimed on behalf of the foetus.[1] This is because the only beings with full moral standing are persons. Not only are foetuses not persons, they are not even personlike enough to warrant our regarding them

From *Australasian Journal of Philosophy* 70 (1992), 136-155.

as if they were persons. Indeed, Warren claims that an eight-month foetus is no more personlike than the average fish. On this view then, the 'right to life' of the foetus, to the extent that it has such a right, cannot possibly outweigh the right of a person to one of the fundamental rights of persons—the right to bodily autonomy. In fact, Warren claims that having an abortion is morally equivalent to cutting one's hair.

The second line of argument is best represented by Judith Jarvis Thomson and, following her, Christine Overall.[2] Their claim involves a sophisticated re-interpretation of the claim that even if a foetus does have a right to life, the woman's right to bodily autonomy overrides that right. By trying to show that even if the foetus is a being with moral standing it has no automatic right to occupancy of a woman's womb, their argument seeks to undermine the basic premise of the conservative position on abortion—namely the premise that if foetuses are persons, that is, beings with full moral rights, then abortion is necessarily wrong.

My aim in this article is to defend a feminist perspective on abortion by showing that questions of women's autonomy lie at the heart of the abortion issue. I shall argue, however, that the conflict-of-rights framework and rights-based models of bodily autonomy are liable seriously to misrepresent both the nature of abortion decisions and the reasons why the availability of abortion is essential to women's autonomy. My dissatisfaction with this kind of approach centres on four related concerns. Firstly, a conflict-of-rights approach fails adequately to address the issue of responsibility in pregnancy and abortion. Hence it mischaracterises both the nature of the moral relationship between woman and foetus and the kind of autonomy that is exercised in pregnancy and abortion. Secondly, it tends to oversimplify our conception of the status of the foetus. Thirdly, it leads to a misconstrual of the notion of bodily autonomy because it is inattentive to the kind of reflective bodily perspective that arises from a phenomenological account of pregnant embodiment. Finally, defending abortion solely on the grounds of women's right to bodily autonomy logically requires that the right to abortion cannot entail a right to secure the death of the foetus but only a right to foetal evacuation.

I shall argue that a strong feminist case for abortion needs to construe a woman's right to obtain an abortion as the right of an autonomous moral agent to be able to make a decision about whether she wishes to take responsibility for the future well-being of a being dependent upon her. In choosing an abortion in other words, a woman is not merely choosing not to allow the foetus occupancy of her uterus. Nor is she merely choosing not to undertake responsibility for a particular future child. Rather, as Steven Ross has pointed out, she is choosing that there be *no being at all* in relation to whom she is in a situation of such responsibility.[3] To require that a woman has no right to secure the death of the foetus, at least in the early stages of pregnancy, thus violates her autonomy.

Now against this claim it could be argued that here the woman is not only making decisions about her own life but about that of another. What entitles her to make such a decision? The next three sections of the article attempt to answer this question. In the second section I make some suggestions as to how we should understand the notions of responsibility and autonomy in pregnancy, while the third section assesses the moral status of the foetus both from the point of view of its intrinsic moral properties and from the point of view of its relationship with the woman in whose body it develops. Building on the previous two sections, the final section draws on a phenomenological account of pregnancy in order to explain the connection between autonomy, bodily autonomy and pregnant embodiment. My criticisms of the rights-based accounts of bodily autonomy emerge from this discussion.

II. RESPONSIBILITY AND AUTONOMY

Appeals to responsibility in the context of the abortion debate usually trade on the asymmetry between the situation of men and women with regard to pregnancy. The asymmetry is that while it is always possible for men to evade or even remain blissfully unaware of the consequences of their actions where those actions result in pregnancy, the same is not true for women. Further it is women alone who are physically able to sustain the foetus. Thus women come to be held 'responsible' for what was after all a joint action. Given this context it is hardly surprising that feminist defences of abortion often attempt to shift discussions of the abortion issue away from the question of responsibility. Thorny as it may be however, one of my central claims is that the issue of responsibility is crucial for an understanding of women's moral autonomy with respect to pregnancy and abortion. In this section I attempt to outline an adequate feminist approach to the question of responsibility in pregnancy and abortion.

A number of different aspects of responsibility are often conflated in the abortion debate. To disentangle these I want firstly to distinguish *causal responsibility* from *moral responsibility*. By causal responsibility I mean simply responsibility for the direct causal consequences of one's actions in cases where those consequences can be said to be reasonably foreseeable and where a person's actions were freely chosen. In this sense a woman can be said to be responsible for the existence of the foetus in much the same way as she can be said to be responsible for getting drunk, in that it is her actions, in this case along with those of another, which have brought about this outcome.[4] Although conservatives do not usually make an explicit distinction between causal and moral responsibility, the conservative claim seems to be that in the case of pregnancy, because the outcome here is to have brought into existence a being with full moral standing, then a woman's *causal responsibility* necessarily entails a moral responsibility towards maintaining the existence of the foetus.[5] . . .

What needs to be pointed out is that the conservative account of moral responsibility is premised on a set of assumptions which are fundamentally oppressive to women. For it is significant that in this whole debate about responsibility there seem to be only two possible ways for women to get pregnant. Either they are raped, in which case they have no causal responsibility for the existence of the foetus—although according to some conservatives they nevertheless have a moral responsibility towards it. Or else they are not raped, in which case they are held to be fully responsible, in both a causal and moral sense. In neither case however is men's moral responsibility ever seriously discussed, despite their obvious causal involvement in the pregnancy. The consequence of this blindness is that moral responsibility in pregnancy gets construed extremely narrowly, as just responsibility towards the foetus, and in a way that seems to commit women to maternity.

The challenge then seems to be to envision a notion of moral responsibility in pregnancy that acknowledges the moral complexities of the situation, and of the decision facing a woman who is weighing up the choices of abortion or maternity, but that does not imply that the only possible morally responsible course of action is to choose maternity. My starting point here is to accept, without argument at this stage, both that the foetus does have some moral significance and that this is in part why causal responsibility does entail some kind of moral responsibility. Having conceded that much to the conservatives I want to disentangle two aspects of moral responsibility which are confused in conservative arguments.

The first aspect, which I call *decision responsibility*, emerges as a strong theme in Carol Gilligan's interviews with women making the abortion decision.[6] Gilligan's women reveal that in their thinking about abortion, acceptance of causal responsibility means assuming a moral responsibility to make a decision or a series of decisions about your future relationship with the being whose existence you have directly brought about. The decision process is focused on questions such as whether you are in a position adequately to care for it, both now when it is in the foetal stage and, more importantly, when it is an independent being; how and whether it can be integrated into your life and the lives of others, for example other children, whose lives will also be significantly affected by your decision; whether you feel yourself able, or prepared, to provide the physical and emotional care and nurture needed in order for both foetus and child to flourish. What emerges from these discussions of responsibility is that the assumption of moral responsibility in pregnancy cannot be construed just in terms of responsibility towards the foetus but has a wider focus—on the self, on relations with significant others, on a person's other commitments and projects. When responsibility is construed in such a way it is clear that exercising moral responsibility in no way entails a commitment to maternity and that the choice of abortion is in many cases the morally responsible decision.

The second aspect of moral responsibility in pregnancy, which I call *parental responsibility*, is the one which a person assumes when a commitment has been made to maternity.[7] What this kind of assumption of responsibility involves is a responsibility not just to maintaining the existence of the foetus, nor even just a commitment to providing the care and nurture needed for it to flourish, but a commitment to bringing into existence a future child. Often, though not necessarily, it also involves a commitment to long-term care and nurture of that future child. My claim is that the decision to abort is a decision, for whatever reason, that one is not prepared to bring such a child into existence.

It should be pointed out here that with respect to all aspects of responsibility the situation of men and women—in pregnancy at least—is asymmetrical. The asymmetry is that while men and women are equally responsible for pregnancy in the causal sense, causal responsibility and decision responsibility are in effect completely separable for men, but inseparable for women. This is because a woman's bodily connection with the foetus makes causal responsibility and hence decision responsibility inescapable for her.[8] On the other hand men's bodily alienation from the consequences of their actions and from the physical, psychic and emotional experience of pregnancy means that they may be in a position where they are either unaware of their causal responsibility for the existence of the foetus or *choose* not to acknowledge their causal responsibility or assume decision responsibility.

A sensitivity to this difference illuminates two important points. Firstly, if causal and decision responsibility are inseparable for women, then pregnancy cannot be thought of simply as a merely 'natural' event which just *happens* to women and in relation to which they are passive. Although pregnancy certainly involves biological processes which are beyond the woman's control, these processes are always mediated by the cultural meanings of pregnancy, by the woman's personal and social context, and by the way she constitutes herself in response to these factors through the decisions she makes. In other words, pregnancy is never simply a biological process, it is always an active process of shaping for oneself a bodily and a moral perspective.[9] For this reason, the moral issues associated with pregnancy and abortion cannot be viewed in abstraction from the first-person perspective of the woman concerned.

Secondly, because of the particularity of the woman's situation in pregnancy, in cases of conflict over abortion ultimately it should be up to the woman to decide whether or not she will choose abortion.[10] To say this does not imply, however, that in situations where men are aware of and do acknowledge causal responsibility, they should have no say in an abortion decision. In such circumstances, because the decision made will obviously affect their autonomy, they should also be party to, and involved in, both decision responsibility and, where appropriate, parental responsibility. Indeed after birth they may assume most, or even all, parental responsibility. Nevertheless prior to birth the impact upon their autonomy of any decision is very different from its impact on the autonomy of the woman. This is why in cases of conflict the woman's decision should prevail. . . .

While this analysis of responsibility still leaves unanswered questions about the intrinsic moral status of the foetus, it does tend to suggest that, at least in part, its moral status is dependent on the relational properties it has with others and that the abortion issue cannot adequately be broached if we focus on intrinsic properties alone. This relational aspect of the foetus' moral standing is best captured through the notion of moral guardianship. I want to suggest that although a foetus cannot be a bearer of full moral rights because, as I shall argue in the next section, it lacks the requisite intrinsic properties (namely personhood), nevertheless in a context in which some one or more members of the moral community have decided to take parental responsibility for its future well-being, it has moral significance by virtue of its relations with her or them. We might say that in such a case it has *de facto* significance through her or them, until such a point when it can be considered a full moral being in its own right. This significance does not guarantee the foetus a 'right to life' which overrides all other possible competing claims, but rather provides some grounds for the foetus' claims to nurture and care, that is, guardianship, from the woman who bears it and protection from harm from others.

In this context it should he noted that once again the situation of men and women with regard to moral guardianship is inescapably asymmetrical in pregnancy. A man, no matter how well-intentioned, cannot act as the primary guardian of an *in utero* foetus. The reason for this asymmetry is not hard to discern, namely the physical inseparability of the foetus from the woman, but its moral implications are often overlooked. The main implications are firstly that, as I argued earlier, in cases of conflict it should be the woman who has the right to decide the fate of the foetus. Secondly, this asymmetry makes it clear that, as Warren has argued, the event of birth is morally significant. Its significance lies in the fact that at birth the infant becomes a member of the human moral community in its own right because its relationship with its mother and other human beings changes significantly. Not only is its body now separate from that of its mother, but it no longer needs to stand in a relation of moral and physical dependence on her in particular. Any responsible human adult will now be able to provide it with the care, nurture and moral protection required for it to flourish.

Having assessed the relational moral status of the foetus I want now to justify my earlier claim that causal responsibility for the existence of the foetus entails decision responsibility because the foetus is a morally significant being. A useful starting point for this discussion is Warren's account of foetal status.

III. FOETAL STATUS AND POTENTIALITY

If, following Warren, we distinguish between 'human beings' and 'persons' and argue that only persons can be members of the moral community, then it seems clear that the foetus is not a bearer of moral rights in the same sense that a person is and so does not have the same 'right to life' as a person.[11] Nevertheless, as Warren herself argues with respect to infants, it does not follow from the fact that, because anyone who is a person is entitled to strong moral protections, that it is wrong to extend moral protections to beings that are not persons.[12] The more personlike the being, the more it should be treated as a person. The question arises therefore of how far advanced since conception a human being needs to be before it begins to have a right to life by virtue of being like a person, that is, at what stage should we start treating a foetus as if it were a person? On this point Warren in her earlier paper claims that the foetus of seven or eight months is no more personlike, or even less personlike, than the average fish and thus should not be treated as a person. For although, like the fish, the late term foetus is sentient, sentience is not sufficient for personhood. *Contra* Thomson, she thus concludes that 'whether or not it would be indecent (whatever that means) for a woman in her seventh month to obtain an abortion just to avoid having to postpone a trip to Europe, it would not, in itself, be immoral, and therefore it ought to be permitted.[13]

Warren's comparison between foetuses and fish occurs in the context of a discussion of the nature of personhood. The intention of the comparison is to show that, while the foetus is indeed a member of the human species, as far as personhood and hence claims to rights are concerned the foetus is morally on a par with a fish. With respect to driving home the distinction between human beings and persons I do not dispute the effectiveness of Warren's comparison. However I want to suggest that the metaphor is problematic for two reasons. Firstly, it invites us to ignore the fact that, contingent though it may be, personhood is constituted by a complex of properties which supervene on a specific physical constitution.[14] Yet despite its contingency, or perhaps because of it, I believe that this fact is morally significant. Secondly, although the foetus/fish metaphor should not be read as providing a model of the relationship between a woman and a foetus, it has the serious, if unintended, effect of downplaying the moral significance and particularly of this relationship. In particular, it has the effect of de-emphasising both the woman's role as moral guardian and her parental responsibility for the present and future well-being of the foetus. The force of the feminist defence of abortion must lie in its highlighting of the moral particularity of the relationship between a woman and a foetus.

On the question of foetal status and potentiality my claim is that foetuses are morally significant beings by virtue of the fact that they are potential persons. This makes them morally different in kind from fish. However, I think it is plausible to suggest that the moral value of the foetus' potential personhood is not static, but changes during the course of a normal pregnancy. This is because potential for personhood is not the only thing that bestows moral status on the being with that potentiality. Rather, the moral value of a being's potential personhood is related to the physical or biological basis of the potentiality, in particular it is grounded in the degree of complexity and development of this physical basis. Thus the more physically complex and developed the being is, the more value we attribute to its potential for personhood. . . .

What is appealing about the general suggestion is that it enables us to agree with Warren's criteria of personhood while nevertheless resisting the counter intuitive implications of these criteria, *viz.*, that a being has no intrinsic moral significance unless it is a person and that there is no important moral difference between a conceptus and a late term foetus. For now it can be argued that the intrinsic moral status of the foetus changes in direct relation to its changing physical basis. Thus, at least in terms of its intrinsic properties, an early stage foetus does not have great value. With respect to a highly developed foetus, although it is not a being with full moral rights, its gradually increasing moral significance warrants our treating it, in most circumstances at least, as if it were such a being.

Combining this view with the guardianship view outlined earlier we get the idea that the moral position of the foetus changes over the course of pregnancy. At the early stages its moral standing is defined in relational terms, because it is a being with moral significance for the woman in whose body it develops and who acts as its moral guardian. As the foetus develops physically however its intrinsic moral significance increases. Its moral standing is less and less dependent on its relational properties with the woman in whose body it develops and more and more tied to its own intrinsic value. This does not mean, however, that the foetus is ever the moral equivalent of the woman. Hence in cases where the foetus' continued existence severely threatens the woman's physical or mental survival, her interests should always prevail up until the moment of birth. It does however suggest that late term abortion is morally different from early abortion and that they cannot be justified on the same grounds.

On the question of guardianship, I suggested above that the rationale behind Warren's defence of abortion (namely that the foetus is not a person), particularly in the context of the foetus/fish comparison, has the effect of downplaying the moral significance of the woman's parental responsibility for the present and future well-being of the foetus. This effect is reinforced by Warren's claim, which she justifies on the grounds of a woman's right to bodily autonomy, that a decision to abort is morally permissible up until the moment of birth. For now it looks as though the foetus is a potential threat to the woman's bodily autonomy up until the moment of birth, rather than a being in relation to whom the woman has a unique bodily and moral connection. In the next section I shall argue that this view is based on a flawed conception of bodily autonomy. Here I simply want to point out that in pregnancy the assumption of parental responsibility necessarily involves a certain commitment of one's body. In other words, the decision to continue a pregnancy (and presumably by seven months some prior decision has been made) is a decision to assume responsibility (even if only for nine months) for the well-being of the foetus and this entails providing bodily nurture for it, perhaps even at some bodily risk to yourself. Now obviously there are limits to this risk. I am not suggesting that women have responsibility to the foetus whatever the risk. As I have already indicated, I am also not suggesting that parties other than the woman, for example the medical establishment, or the state-legal apparatus, have a right to determine the limits of that risk. Like many other feminists, including Warren, I am alarmed by the recent move-ments advocating both so-called 'foetal rights' and the introduction of charges of 'foetal abuse' against women who do not do what is required to nurture the foetus in the uterus. Further the whole question of what is 'required' for adequate nurture is open to much interpretation against women's autonomy as persons. Nevertheless, I think that my accounts of potentiality, guardianship and responsibility explain why there is a genuine moral requirement upon a woman to protect and nurture a foetus once she has assumed parental re-sponsibility for its future well-being, without that requirement involving any infringement of her autonomy. In this context it should be noted that Warren's downplaying of the question of responsibility also fails to stress men's obliga-tions with respect to a pregnancy.

IV. PREGNANT EMBODIMENT AND BODILY AUTONOMY

I have argued so far that, at least in the early stages of its development, the moral standing of a foetus is dependent upon its relationship with the woman who bears it and who acts as its moral guardian. In terms of its own intrinsic properties its moral standing is not particularly significant. This is a necessary condition for the permissibility of abortion, but it is not sufficient. For it fails to explain why the availability of abortion is necessary for the moral au-tonomy of women and hence why a restriction on its accessibility violates their autonomy. In this section I attempt to explain and justify this claim. From my discussion it will also become clear why, in order to secure women's autonomy, abortion must be understood as foetal death rather than foetal evacuation.

What has emerged so far is that in order to understand the kind of au-tonomy that is exercised by women in pregnancy and abortion we must be attentive to the moral particularity of pregnancy. As we have seen there are a number of different factors which make pregnancy morally unique. To begin with, pregnancy is not simply a biological event with respect to which women are passive. Rather it is an active process and a social process which places women in a situation of moral responsibility—which I earlier called decision responsibility. This responsibility is due in part to the foetus' potential moral significance, but it is also due to the fact that the decision to commit or not to commit oneself to the existence of such a future person has far-reaching impli-cations for the woman's own life as well as, possibly, for the lives of others—for example, the 'father' of the possible future child, other children, relatives, friends and so on. But pregnancy is also morally unique because the physical connection between the woman and the foetus, and the physical processes which occur during pregnancy, give rise to a unique bodily perspective.

In what follows I shall draw on a phenomenological account of pregnant embodiment in order to give an account of the kind of reflective bodily perspective that emerges out of the experience of pregnancy. I shall also suggest that the experience of moral responsibility in pregnancy, which I have detailed above, is mediated by this reflective bodily perspective, which both structures and points to the moral particularity of the relationship between woman and foetus—especially to the fact that this relationship and the responsibilities it entails cannot be conceived of as extrinsic to the woman's subjectivity. I want to make it clear that this phenomenological description is not a description of the subjective feelings of individual women, but is rather a normative and reflective apprehension of the way in which conscious experience is structured by our (bodily) situations, perspectives and modes of perception. The phenomenological experience I describe is therefore not meant to be an empirical description of the way in which all women experience or feel about their pregnancies, since women's individual bodily perspectives, feelings and experiences depend upon a wide range of factors, including the cultural, social and historical context in which they live their lives.[15]

My suggestion is that although in some ways (for example, biologically) it makes sense to speak of the foetus as a separate being from the woman, in other ways (for example in terms of talking of a conflict of rights), it makes no sense at all—especially in the early stages of pregnancy.[16] Phenomenologically, the experience of pregnancy, particularly in the early stages, is unique in the sense that it defies a sharp opposition between self and other, between the inside and the outside of the body. From the perspective of the woman, there *is* no clear-cut boundary between herself and the foetus, between her body boundaries and the body boundaries of the foetus. The foetus, to the extent that it is experienced as part of the woman's body, is also experienced as part of her self, but as a part that is also other than herself. On the one hand it is another being, but it is another being growing inside her body, a being whose separateness is not fully realised as such by her. This is the case even with an unwanted pregnancy. The uniqueness and intimacy of this kind of relationship, one where the distinction between self and other is blurred, suggests that the welfare of the foetus, at least early on, is not easily separable from that of the woman. The foetus is not simply an entity extrinsic to her which happens to be developing inside her body and which she desires either to remove or to allow to develop. It is a being, both inseparable and yet separate from her, both part of and yet soon to be independent from her, whose existence calls into question her own present and future identity.

The changing phenomenology of pregnancy also concurs with the account I have given of foetal status. For it seems to me that one of the main reasons for the experience I have described is that in early pregnancy, although the woman's body is undergoing massive changes, the foetus itself is not very physically developed. The foetus' separateness is thus neither physically well established nor is it felt as such by the woman. What happens as pregnancy continues is that, as the foetus develops physically, a triple process occurs. Firstly, from the perspective of the woman, the foetus becomes more and more physically differentiated from her as her own body boundaries alter. Secondly, this gradual physical differentiation (which becomes very pronounced as soon as the foetus starts moving around—perhaps explaining why 'quickening' used to be considered morally significant) is paralleled by and gives rise to a gradual psychic differentiation, in the experience of the woman, between herself and the foetus. In other words, as the foetus' body develops it seems to become less and less a part of the woman and of her body although, as psychoanalysis reminds us, the psychic experiences of unity and differentiation continue to resonate for both mother and child right through infancy and early childhood. Thirdly, physical and psychic differentiation are usually accompanied by an increasing emotional attachment of the woman to the foetus, an attachment which is based both in her physical connection with the foetus and in an anticipation of her future relationship with a separate being who is also intimately related to her.

From the reflective perspective of the woman the foetus thus has a double and ambivalent status. On the one hand, it is experienced as interior to her own subjectivity, and this sense of interiority is grounded in the bodily connection between the woman and the foetus. On the other hand, this experience of interiority and connection is interrupted by an awareness that, if the pregnancy continues, this being which is now a part of her will become a separate being for whose welfare she is morally responsible. But this awareness itself arises in part from the woman's bodily experiences—for example, from the changes to her body shape and from feelings of the strangeness of her body to her—which remind her of the other being which is growing within her. I think it is this double character of the foetus' bodily and moral relationship to the woman that explains both why questions of responsibility are central to the experience of pregnancy and why the right of determination over the fate of the foetus is essential for a woman's autonomy.[17] . . .

To think that the question of autonomy in abortion is just a question about preserving the integrity of one's body boundaries, and to see the foetus merely as an occupant of the woman's uterus, is to divorce women's bodies from their subjectivities. Ironically it comes close to regarding women's bodies simply as foetal containers—the very charge which many feminists have levelled against the 'foetal rights' movement. If, however, we see our subjectivities as constituted through the constitution of our bodily perspectives so that, following Merleau-Ponty, we see the body as our point of view upon the world, then my body is no more my property than I myself am my own property.[18] Rather my body is my mode of being-in-the-world. Consequently changes to my body or to my perceptions of my body-image must affect my relation to the world. The experience of pregnant embodiment, that is, the gradual differentiation and development from within her own body of another being which is now a part of herself, thus affects a woman's mode of being-in-the-world both physically and morally and, as a consequence, re-shapes her sense of self. She is now no longer just herself but herself and another, but this other is not yet separate from herself. It is because of this psychic and bodily connectedness between the woman and the foetus that in pregnancy questions about the fate of the foetus cannot be separated out from the issue of a woman's right to self-determination. . . .

NOTES

1. My argument in this part of the article refers to Mary Anne Warren's paper 'On the Moral and Legal Status of Abortion' in R. Wasserstrom (ed.) *Today's Moral Problems* (London: Macmillan, 1975). In a very recent paper, to which I refer in more detail later, Warren's characterisation of the foetus is markedly different although her basic position on a woman's right to bodily autonomy remains unaltered. See 'The Moral Significance of Birth,' *Hypatia* 4 (1989) pp. 46–65. This paper is a modified version of an earlier paper with the same title which appeared in *Bioethics News*, Publication of the Centre for Human Bioethics, Monash University, vol. 7, no. 2, January 1988.

2. Judith Jarvis Thomson, 'A Defense of Abortion,' *Philosophy and Public Affairs*, 1 (1971) pp. 47–66; Christine Overall, *Ethics and Human Reproduction* (Boston: Allen & Unwin, 1987) chs. 3, 4.

3. Steven Ross, 'Abortion and the Death of the Foetus,' *Philosophy and Public Affairs* 11 (1982) pp. 232–245.

4. I discuss the question of men's responsibility below. Given this account of causal responsibility, a woman is, of course, not causally responsible in the case of rape. In cases where a woman cannot and cannot reasonably be expected to foresee the consequences of her actions (e.g. if she is a minor or mentally disabled), or if her actions were performed under duress (the distinction between rape and consent is not as hard and fast as many would think), or if she cannot be said to be acting autonomously (e.g. in a case of drug addiction or alcoholism or some other dependency), I would argue that, although a woman may have some causal responsibility for the outcome of her actions, she cannot be considered to be morally responsible for this outcome.

5. Somewhat surprisingly, some feminists have argued for a similar view. See Hilde and James Lindemann Nelson, 'Cutting Motherhood in Two: Some Suspicions Concerning Surrogacy,' *Hypatia* 4 (1989) pp. 85–94.

6. Carol Gilligan, *In A Different Voice* (Cambridge, MA: Harvard University Press, 1982). It should be noted here that the kinds of moral reflection in which these women engage is in part made possible by the fact that these women do have reproductive choice.

7. As I have indicated, decision responsibility is a process, not a single decision. Thus a woman may change her mind a number of times before finally assuming parental responsibility. She may also change her mind after having assumed it. For reasons which I explain below I think there is a significant *moral* difference between such a change of mind in the first trimester or early in the second trimester and a change of mind during the latter half of pregnancy—except of course where such a change is made for medical reasons or because of foetal deformity discoverable only by amniocentesis during the second trimester. It does not follow from this however that women should be *legally* prevented from obtaining abortions for other reasons later in pregnancy. I discuss the distinction between moral and legal responsibility below.

8. I discuss the nature of this bodily connection in detail in section IV.

9. I develop this point in more detail in section IV.

10. I have in mind here recent cases in the UK and Australia where men have attempted to obtain court orders, on the grounds of paternal right, to prevent women from obtaining an abortion. My analysis of the asymmetry in the positions of men

and women with respect to responsibility in pregnancy should make it clear why feminists have been so outraged by the men's presumption in these cases that they should be able to overrule the decisions of the women concerned.

11. Warren, 'On the Moral and Legal Status of Abortion.' *op. cit.* Warren supports this distinction by outlining five criteria for personhood, specifying that a person need not satisfy all these criteria but that a being which satisfied none of them could not be considered a person. The five criteria are:

    1. Consciousness (of objects and events external and/or internal to the being), and in particular the capacity to feel pain;
    2. Reasoning (the *developed* capacity to solve new and relatively complex problems);
    3. Self-motivated activity (activity which is relatively independent of either genetic or direct external control);
    4. The capacity to communicate, by whatever means, messages of an indefinite variety of types, that is, not just with an indefinite number of possible contents, but on indefinitely many possible topics;
    5. The presence of self-concepts, and self-awareness, either individual or racial, or both.

12. Warren, 'The Moral Significance of Birth,' *op. cit.* I follow Warren here in using the term 'person' because I think that in the context of abortion the distinction between 'human beings' and 'persons' is an important distinction to maintain. However I am not happy with the legalistic and individualist connotations of the term which tend to downplay the intersubjective processes of development by means of which infants become self-conscious subjects.

13. Warren, 'On the Moral and Legal Status of Abortion, *op. cit.*, p. 133.

14. In stressing the connection between the development of subjectivity and physical development I am not denying the significance of the social relationships in the context of which these developments must occur.

15. My account here builds on psychoanalytic insights into the mother-child relation, on some of the descriptions of pregnancy and maternity in the work of Julia Kristeva, on Iris Young's phenomenology of pregnant embodiment, and on my own *a posteriori* reconstructions. See Julia Kristeva, 'Motherhood According to Giovanni Bellini' in *Desire in Language* (Oxford: Blackwell, 1980) and 'Stabat Mater' in T. Moi (ed.), *The Kristeva Reader* (Oxford: Blackwell, 1986); Iris Marion Young, 'Pregnant Embodiment: Subjectivity and Alienation,' *The Journal of Medicine and Philosophy* 9 (1984) pp. 45–62.

16. The rights-based model has also been criticised on different but related grounds by other feminists. See Janet Farrell Smith, 'Rights-conflict, Pregnancy and Abortion' in Carol Gould (ed.), *Beyond Domination* (Totowa, NJ: Rowman & Allanheld, 1984) pp. 265–273.

17. At this point I would like to respond to an objection which is often made against the view I have proposed here. It could be argued that the woman's experience of the foetus as part of herself and as interior to her subjectivity is simply mistaken. So why should any moral weight be given to this experience? How is it different, for example, from the experience of a slave-owner who regards his/her slaves as a part of him/herself and thinks that because of this he/she has a right to determine their fate? My response to this suggestion is that these cases are completely disanalogous, and for two reasons. Firstly, I have argued that a necessary condition for the permissibility of abortion is that the foetus, especially in

the early stages of pregnancy, has little moral value in and of itself, although it may have a great deal of value for the woman in whose body it develops. This is not a merely arbitrary claim, like the claim of the slave-owner who may think that his/her slaves have little moral value in and of themselves. Rather it is justified by the fact that the foetus simply does not yet have the capacities which ground the moral worth of persons, and by the fact that the foetus' possible potential for personhood has little significance until those capacities are close to being actualised.

But, secondly, this objection ignores what I have been insisting on throughout this article, namely that the relationship of the woman to the foetus is morally unique. It is not a relationship of domination and subordination and inhuman ownership, as in the case of the slave-owner. Rather, it is a relationship in which one human being grows and develops inside the body of another, and in which the moral significance of the foetus is in part bound up with its significance for the woman. The moral particularity of this situation, in other words, is grounded in the nature of the bodily connection between woman and foetus. The woman's sense of the foetus as a part of herself is thus not arbitrary. It arises, as I have tried to show, from her own reflective bodily perspective and from the kind of moral reflection to which pregnancy gives rise.

Certainly it is possible to think up all kinds of examples in which the relationship between the woman and the foetus might have been different—as in Thomson's examples. But my point is that these examples cannot give us an adequate understanding of the moral complexities of the issues raised by pregnancy and abortion precisely because they overlook the context out of which these complexities arise, namely the bodily and moral connection between the woman and the foetus.

18. I am drawing here on Maurice Merleau-Ponty's discussion of the body in *The Phenomenology of Perception* (1945), translated by Colin Smith (London: Routledge, 1962).

Abortion and the Morality of Nurturance

Paul Gomberg

Paul Gomberg, a professor of philosophy at Chicago State University, argues that for the last twenty years the abortion debate has mistakenly focused on questions concerning the morality of killing. Instead, he suggests that the debate should be understood to be about the morality of nurturance, the central component of which is a parental duty to nurture offspring. Gomberg believes that the morality of nurturance comes into play only at that point at which a woman "accepts" her pregnancy, or perhaps at that point at which she should accept the pregnancy. The latter formulation is suggested by Gomberg's belief that the abortion debate is at least in part a debate about whether, and if so when, women have a duty to accept their pregnancies. According to Gomberg, the belief that women do have such a duty depends on holding a traditional (and in his eyes objectionable) conception of the appropriate social role of women, according to which they should primarily aim at being mothers. Unless nurturing attitudes are cultivated equally among men and women, he believes a satisfactory solution to the problem of abortion cannot be found.

I

The moral problem of abortion seemed simple to describe, if not resolve. There was consensus that at least some methods of birth control—avoiding or preventing the development of a conceptus—were not wrong. There was consensus that it was wrong to kill another person like ourselves. The problem seemed to be this: when in the development toward adult life does it become wrong to prevent or terminate that development? The conservatives said, 'from conception.' Liberals said that it became wrong after viability, or after birth, or after early infancy. Some moderate liberals have argued that there is an intermediate stage where stopping the development of a fetus is wrong—but not the same as killing a person—because of the fetus's similarity to or potential to become a person. While all agree on the moral principle that it is wrong to kill another person, there has been little progress toward agreement on how this principle applies to the fetus.[1]

The present paper explores a different approach. Perhaps the abortion controversy derives less from disagreement about how to apply the principle prohibiting the killing of another person and more from the part of our morality that concerns parental duties of nurturance to the young: what are our duties to our offspring? when do those duties take hold?[2]

From *Canadian Journal of Philosophy* 21:4 (December 1991), 513-524.

The proposal that the abortion controversy is a dispute about the morality of nurturance brings a number of issues into focus: it gives a better articulation of the objection to abortion than the claim that abortion is murder; it allows us to understand why many believe that later abortions are morally more problematic than earlier ones; it puts the issue of abortion in the context of the morality that governs family life; and, most important, it allows us to understand why there is, on the one hand, a connection between conservatism on abortion and traditional women's roles and, on the other, a connection between liberalism and affirmation of equality between men and women.

II. THE MORALITY OF NURTURANCE

The central norm of the morality of nurturance is that it is the duty of parents to nurture their offspring, to provide them with sustenance and guidance until they reach self-sufficiency.[3] Evidence that we accept this norm is found in laws requiring child support and punishing child neglect and in our moral condemnation of those who abandon or neglect, and particularly those who abuse their children. The norm applies in the first instance to biological parents and to others only by special arrangement. I am concerned with this norm as an important component of the morality of our culture, although I suspect that *some* principle regarding care of the young is part of the moral norms of every human society.

It may seem that the application of this principle to the fetus raises essentially the same problems as applying the principle prohibiting the killing of another person: in one case we must decide when something is a person, in the other when something is 'one's offspring.' But while the problems are parallel in many ways, they are different. The paradigm of someone protected by the principle prohibiting the killing of another is an adult with developed capabilities. The paradigm of one protected by the morality of nurturance is precisely the undeveloped, vulnerable, and dependent being biologically related to us. One reason that our babies have a moral claim on our care is precisely that they are not developed beings.

There are other significant differences between the two principles. It is during the transition from infancy to adulthood that we come to regard someone as a person, but, as I will argue in this section, it is *during pregnancy* that we come to regard something as our baby to be protected and nurtured. And, as we shall see in the next section, while both the concept of a person and that of an offspring are ones that we come to apply as a being acquires more and more characteristics paradigmatic of the concept, in borderline cases our conception of women's roles may be decisive in determining when we should regard something as our offspring.

Duties of nurturance, at least as they are understood in our society, apply paradigmatically to newborns.[4] By a natural extension of principles specifying our nurturing duties toward children, we condemn abuse of the fetus with drugs or alcohol. (Of course, moral condemnation of *addicts* may be pointless and inappropriate.) Well before birth we come to believe we are bound by a responsibility to care for the fetus and its future. We may feel obligated to give up cigarettes, alcohol, prescription drugs, and aspirin and to maintain a well balanced diet including adequate vitamins. We may take walks or swim. (These changes usually apply more particularly to the mother; others may apply equally to both parents.) We may take out insurance, stop picking up hitchhikers, sell the motorcycle, and try to drive more carefully. We may find a new place to live, paying particular attention to the schools in the neighborhood. If a rift has developed with the family of one of the parents, there may be an effort to repair it. We do these things because we believe ourselves responsible to a developing life; we are coming to regard the fetus as our offspring and ourselves as parents.

Neither our sense of responsibility toward the fetus nor a corresponding loving attitude springs suddenly into existence. As Rawls has stressed, there is a connection between the development of natural attitudes and of moral responsibilities: the attitudes entail moral commitments and among the commitments are to have certain attitudes.[5] It is our responsibility to love this child because without this love she cannot be properly nurtured.

As soon as we accept our pregnancy, we cultivate feelings which will allow this child to develop. We may personify the fetus, giving the fetus a name, not the name it will bear as a separate person, but a whimsical fetal name. The parents stroke the abdomen of the expectant mother, talking to and about the fetus. As the fetus grows, the personification of the fetus becomes more intense: we may scold it for taking up too much room, moving about and kicking, or getting the hiccups.[6]

I have described here how the morality of nurturance takes hold when we accept our pregnancy. But when a woman becomes aware that she is pregnant, she may not accept her pregnancy. She may, in fact, regard the thing developing inside her as alien.[7] Accordingly, she may seek to terminate the pregnancy if she can find a way to do so. It is true that in accepting a pregnancy, we begin to accept responsibility to nurture that fetus, to regard it as an offspring, and to develop the corresponding attitudes. But are we morally required to accept the pregnancy? I will turn to this question shortly.

III. NURTURANCE, ABORTION, AND WOMEN'S ROLES

Once it is accepted that a fetus is an offspring protected by the central norm of the morality of nurturance, it is easy to derive a condemnation of abortion. Recall the widely displayed photograph of the feet of an eight week fetus held in the fingers of an adult hand. We are supposed to respond, 'It's a miniature *baby!*' To destroy that is to destroy what we should nurture. By showing us an enlarged picture of tiny feet, appeals such as this try to convince us that the fetus is already an offspring.

The suggestion of this paper is that the morality of nurturance is central to the abortion debate. If this suggestion is correct, then the arguments of

Warren, Tooley, and many others that the fetus lacks those characteristics that make one a full-fledged person, a member of the moral community, may be correct, but fail to respond to objections to abortion derived from the morality of nurturance. *Of course* the fetus is not a full-fledged person; it is, after all, a baby, or becoming one, and in need of our care if it is to become a full-fledged person. The duties of nurturance are strongest precisely when the one to be nurtured lacks developed human capacities.

But Warren, Tooley, and the others were in fact only responding to the way the issue was defined by the conservatives on abortion. It was Noonan and others who argued that abortion is the taking of a human life comparable with the life of the mother. If this were true, then legal penalties for abortion should be comparable to those for any other murder. Few opponents of legal abortion are willing to accept the full consequences of the view that abortion is murder.[8]

If the morality of nurturance is the hidden issue in the abortion debate, then the condemnation of abortion is not condemnation of it as murder, a term whose paradigmatic application is to the morality between adults. As a violation of nurturing duties, abortion is less and more than murder. It is more than murder just as stuffing a newborn baby into a garbage can shocks us in a special way: we wonder what kind of monster could kill its own child.[9] What shocks us about infanticide is that it violates the morality of nurturance. Yet abortion and infanticide both are significantly less than murder. We are appalled by infanticide, but many human societies have tolerated it at the same time as they condemned murder.[10] The suggestion of this paper is that we accept Tooley's claim that abortion and infanticide are akin but recognize that there are serious objections to both based on duties of nurturance. If this is correct, the concession that abortion is not murder does not end the argument about tolerating it. If the morality of nurturance can generate a condemnation of infanticide or abandonment of an infant, then it may also generate a condemnation of abortion.

So the condemnation of abortion within the morality of nurturance is not the same as the condemnation of murder, but carries comparable emotional and moral weight. Earlier I said that once we accept a pregnancy, the morality of nurturance begins to take hold: we come to regard the fetus as an offspring and come to believe ourselves responsible for its care. I earlier set aside the question whether we are morally required to accept our pregnancies. Now we must deal with that question.

The morality of nurturance requires us to care for our offspring, but when does something become 'our offspring'? Just as we gradually acquire the characteristics of personhood, so also, at an earlier stage of our development, the ovum, zygote, blastocyst, embryo, and fetus gradually acquire the characteristics of an offspring. By the time a pregnancy has reached the ninth month, the fetus is an offspring of its parents. The facts speak too clearly for there to be room for dispute. We have duties to nurture the nine month fetus. But earlier in the pregnancy there is room for argument. Just as, in the case of personhood, any decision that 'now this is a person' seems arbitrary, so also any judgment that 'now this is your baby and you must care for it' also will seem arbitrary. So, at least in the case of the early fetus, the morality of nurturance cannot tell us that now something is our offspring and that a pregnancy must be accepted.

Because the fetus gradually becomes more and more like a baby, most of us believe that later abortions are morally and emotionally more problematic. Even if there is no precise point at which it is clear that the morality of nurturance must apply to the fetus, it is clear that the longer we wait to abort, the more like a baby is the thing we destroy. Conversely, for most of us early abortions seem consistent with the morality of nurturance. But not everyone would agree. For some people there are *other* considerations that lead them to apply the morality of nurturance to the early fetus. These people believe that all pregnancies must be accepted.

It is part of a traditional conception of a woman's role that a sexually active woman should bear and nurture children. On this conception a pregnancy is a fulfillment of one's role. Combining this traditional conception of a woman's role with the morality of nurturance generates a condemnation of abortion: it is our duty to accept our pregnancies and to nurture developing human life. The traditional morality of a woman's role leads us to apply the morality of nurturance to the early fetus (and even to earlier forms). It thus leads us to classify the early fetus as an offspring and hence generates the condemnation of even early abortions as akin to infanticide.[11]

IV. EXPLAINING THE ABORTION CONTROVERSY

The greatest advantage of interpreting the abortion controversy as a dispute centering on the morality of nurturance is that it allows us to understand what issues separate conservatives and liberals. The morality of nurturance generates a condemnation of all abortions when combined with a traditional conception of women's roles. This suggests that there are two foci of the dispute about abortion: (1) what does the morality of nurturance require of us, and (2) what is the proper role of women? These are in fact two major issues that separate conservatives and liberals.

If the abortion controversy really centers on the morality of nurturance, then one would expect that conservatives would see themselves as defenders of children and would perceive liberals as failing to appreciate our nurturing duties toward children. This is precisely what we find. Kristin Luker's study of activists is a rich source of data on (and useful interpretations of) the outlooks of both conservatives and liberals.[12]

We can draw the following (oversimplified) portrait of the conservative attitude toward duties of nurturance: duties of nurturance represent the highest expression of human morality, making women (the defenders of nurturance) morally superior to men (163). Children need to be looked upon more positively, the responsibilities of raising children being a full-time job (170, 161).

Liberals tend to value money and material possessions too highly, with the consequence that they view children as an obstacle to good things that money can buy (168). Money is not important to proper nurturance, and those who think that the rearing of children requires that they be provided with expensive possessions are misguided (206–7). The unconditioned love of parent for child 'where none of us has a price tag' is the highest expression of human morality, and those who value children for their potential for achievement and would abort embryos that are defective have a bad morality (207–8). (The conservative activists Luker interviewed were for the most part of very modest means and generally less affluent than the liberal activists.)

Conservatives regard the nurturing role as the *main life role* of sexually active people, particularly women. 'Women who choose to be in the public world of work should eschew the role of wife and mother, or, if they marry should be prepared to put the public world of work second to their role as wife and mother' (169). 'To try to balance a number of competing commitments—especially when parenthood gets shuffled into second or fourth place— is . . . morally wrong' (170). Hence, given only the qualification of sexual activity, those who oppose abortion express an ideal of life, particularly for women, where nurturing is the responsibility that takes priority over every other responsibility. If a woman fulfills her highest role in life by being a mother, then if she discovers she is pregnant, she should continue the pregnancy, not end it. So we can see how the anti-abortion position can be derived from a conception that the woman's role is to be a mother and uphold the morality of nurturance.

Those who uphold abortion rights might reply in two ways. First, they might deny the moral ideal of a woman's role as being to have and nurture children above all other duties. Second, they might reply, within the morality of nurturance, that nurturing the children one already has or preparing oneself to nurture children properly in the future may require, when other contraceptive means fail, availing oneself of abortion. Both replies are found both in the philosophical literature and in Luker's survey of activists.

Martha Bolton objects to the conservative conception of women's roles:

> I think it is also central to the life of a morally responsible person that he/
> she develop abilities which make him/her a useful, productive, contributing
> member of the community. Doing so often requires large commitments of a
> person's time, thought, and other personal resources; such commitments are
> liable to conflict with the activity of nurturing a fetus and raising a child.[13]

Bolton's view is echoed among abortion rights activists. According to Luker, they argue that '*control* over reproduction is essential for women to be able to live up to their full human potential.' Women's reproductive and family roles are 'potential barriers to full equality' (176; cf. 92). Hence, there are weighty moral reasons why the nurturing role cannot have absolute predominance, and abortion must be allowed where other means of birth control fail.

The second argument, within the morality of nurturance, that responsible parents must sometimes abort, is also made by both philosophers and activists. Bolton points out that development of the fetus and care of it may be in conflict with a woman's other commitments and may undermine her ability to fulfil responsibilities to others who are dependent on her.[14] From the context it is clear that commitments to living children are among those she has in mind. The people Luker interviewed gave a slightly different argument: that commitment to any children one might bear requires that we have the emotional and financial resources to give them the best possible life, and that this in turn requires control of fertility and, where other methods might fail, the availability of abortion (181-2). This argument is in direct conflict with the conservatives' views that it is natural to be a parent (and hence we need no special preparation for it) and that material things are not very significant for proper nurturance.[15]

V. CONCLUSION

The purpose of most papers on abortion is to make practical recommendations about the legality of abortions. My purpose has been different, one step removed: to argue that the arguments, in the philosophical literature, for the past twenty years have focused on the wrong set of issues, trying to judge the morality of abortion by moral concepts more appropriate to relations between adults.

Nevertheless, the proposal that conservatives have misarticulated their objection to abortion, that, at worst, abortion violates the morality of nurturance rather than the prohibition on killing a person, has practical consequences. Early abortions seem consistent with the morality of nurturance unless we take the conservative view of women's roles. Conservative objections to early abortions derive from the norm, based on traditional women's roles, that sexually active women should accept their pregnancies and regard the early fetus as a baby. Hence, it seems, our view of the morality of abortion depends in part on our view of women's roles.

If objections to abortion are based on the morality of nurturance, there is a second issue: what is the connection between abortion and our concern for children? Is there any justice to the conservatives' claims that liberalism about abortion is linked to indifference to children or excessive valuation of material things?

Let us deal first with the relation between abortion and the welfare of children. In our society we condemn infanticide rather strongly, and legally it is homicide. Yet even infanticide, where it has been practiced, has often coexisted with nurturing attitudes toward children. So it is doubtful that the conservatives can argue that widespread practice of abortion will undermine nurturing attitudes generally.

Still, our psychology sets limits to our morality. Wherever infanticide is practiced it seems to create emotional and moral difficulties, presumably because nurturing attitudes and morality take hold before birth.[16] This means that cavalier attitudes toward abortions and the insistence that late abortions are innocuous might undermine the morality of nurturance if these attitudes were widely held. I have in mind here Warren's remarks that abortion ought to be regarded as morally innocuous, like cutting one's hair, and that there is no moral wrong in aborting a seven month fetus to avoid postponing a trip to Europe. If such attitudes were widespread, would we develop a proper sense of our duties of nurturance toward our children? It is hard to be unaware that one is considering aborting what one might raise to an adult.[17]

The conservatives also claim that the liberals incorrectly identify proper nurturance with material wealth. This claim may contain a grain of truth, but no more. Generally, the conservatives show a pollyannish disregard for the difficulties many face in trying to provide proper nurturance for children. In our society, the conflict between what a woman must do to function adequately and the responsibilities of a pregnancy carried to term are real.

The issue of women's roles is much clearer. Women's labor in capitalist society has been demeaned: jobs stereotyped as women's jobs have received low pay and low status. Women are demeaned by sexist epithets; in the workplace they are routinely called 'honey' and referred to by their bosses as 'my girl.' The demeaning of women is linked ideologically to their role as mothers and childbearers: it is implied that women are good for this role and little else and that the things women can do have little value. Thus the conservatives' claim that women are morally superior is hypocritical, for they accept these traditional roles and their demeaned status. If the conservatives believed their own claim that women are morally superior because they are more committed to nurturance, then they would attempt to cultivate nurturing attitudes equally among men.

The liberals are right that equality between men and women requires that women be able to control their reproduction. Of all the moral issues implied in the abortion controversy the issue of equality of men and women is the clearest and the most favorable to the liberals. But even here I would add a qualification. The conservatives argue that if women as much as men pursue high status and success in our present business and academic environments, we will all be worse off, for the competitive environments of these worlds subordinate commitment to people to pursuit of status and success (Luker, 163). Even if this is, as I believe, one of their stronger arguments, the solution is not to advocate that women be confined to a demeaned status as servants of men and nannies to children. The conservatives glorify servility by calling it morality.

Let me suggest a twofold solution. First, instead of allowing the communism of the family to be undermined by the competitiveness of the capitalist order, the egalitarianism and commitment to others that characterize family relations at their best should be spread to the larger world. Second, nurturing attitudes can represent morality rather than servility in a world where they are cultivated equally among all adults; the duties of nurturance must fall equally on men. But where much of our social life is governed by market imperatives, it becomes impossible to share nurturing equally among men and women. This suggests that a satisfactory solution to the problems surrounding the abortion issue will require changing the economic structures of our society. The moral problems of abortion are really social problems of capitalist society.

NOTES

1. The conservative position on abortion is stated by John T. Noonan, Jr., 'An Almost Absolute Value in History,' in Noonan, ed., *The Morality of Abortion* (Cambridge, MA: Harvard University Press 1970) 1–59. The last several pages are frequently reprinted. A more developed argument for the conservative view is given by Baruch Brody, *Abortion and the Sanctity of Human Life* (Cambridge, MA: MIT Press 1975). A widely discussed presentation of an extremely liberal position (defending the innocuousness of infanticide) is Michael Tooley, 'Abortion and Infanticide,' *Philosophy and Public Affairs* 2 (1972) 37–65. Tooley amplifies his argument in *Abortion and Infanticide* (Oxford: Clarendon Press 1983). Mary Anne Warren defends a similar position, but tries to back off on the issue of infanticide, in 'On the Moral and Legal Status of Abortion,' *The Monist* 57 (1973) 43–61. Martha Brandt Bolton, 'Responsible Women and Abortion Decisions,' in Onora O'Neill and William Ruddick, eds., *Having Children* (New York: Oxford University Press 1979) puts the issue of abortion in the context of the array of moral responsibilities that may be part of a woman's life. The papers by Noonan, Warren, and Bolton are reprinted in Ronald Munson, ed., *Intervention and Reflection,* 3rd ed. (Belmont, CA: Wadsworth Publishing 1988).

   I use the terms 'conservative' and 'liberal' for what are sometimes called the 'pro-life' and 'pro-choice' positions because I believe that the latter terms are politically more loaded and less accurate. As I will argue, the former terms capture the essence of much of the political difference between the two camps.

2. Carol Gilligan, *In a Different Voice* (Cambridge, MA: Harvard University Press 1982) suggests that women's orientations toward moral problems are often different from those of men. She does not suggest what is proposed here: that both men and women have within their repertoires of moral competence both the morality of relations between adults and the morality of nurturance. Also the morality of nurturance is not the same as what she calls ethic of care, which is a fully developed orientation toward moral problems. Still, this work is relevant to the discussion at hand. For the morality of relations between adults is the morality that governs the relations between agents in the world of business and commerce in capitalist societies, a domain of social life traditionally dominated by men. The morality of nurturance, in contrast, is an important component of the morality that governs family relations, where women have traditionally concentrated their concerns.

3. The suggestion of this paper is that this norm is part of the morality of our culture. I doubt that the morality of nurturance is derivable from principles governing moral relations between adults, the principle prohibiting killing of another person being paradigmatic of morality between adults. Hence I doubt

the significance of both the attempts to derive a prohibition on abortion from potential to become an adult like ourselves, and the vindications of abortion which rely on criticisms of such arguments. For the latter see Tooley, *Abortion and Infanticide,* 178-83. Since the purpose of the present paper is only to understand the abortion debate, I adopt, methodologically, a moral intuitionism which articulates the moral imperatives commonly accepted in our culture.

4. I would speculate that our abhorrence of infanticide is related to the development of the technology of birth control. Societies that have had to limit population but have not had contraceptive technologies (all human societies throughout most of human prehistory) almost certainly had to practice infanticide. However emotionally difficult such a practice may have been, it was probably not severely condemned morally. The present controversy over abortion is probably partly due to the availability of pre-conceptive means of population control.

5. John Rawls, *A Theory of Justice* (Cambridge, MA: Harvard University Press 1971), 453-512 ('The Sense of Justice'), esp. 485-90.

6. For a published description of the personification of the fetus in late pregnancy see Barbara Katz Rothman, *Recreating Motherhood* (New York: Norton 1989), 97-105.

7. The idea that accepting a pregnancy is a crucial stage was suggested to me by a discussion with Charlotte Jackson. Laura Coleman pointed out to me that one can carry to term and never accept the pregnancy or develop a nurturing attitude. See Sandy Robey, 'Weighing the Mother Load,' *The Chicago Tribune,* May 14, 1989, Sect. 6, 1 for an account of a decision to accept a pregnancy. In that case, however, it seemed that nurturing attitudes were already at work in that decision. This suggests that the physical development of the fetus, combined with our awareness of what it will become, can cause us to accept a pregnancy.

8. But see Brody (63) for an attempt to explain why we might treat this particular instance of murder differently. I assume here that the conservatives are wrong, that abortion is not murder and that Warren and Tooley are correct. Otherwise there is no need for an alternative conception of the objection to abortion.

9. Of course, someone who does this is not necessarily a monster, but someone who, for whatever reason, did not develop a nurturing attitude toward this baby.

10. Infanticide is a common form of birth control when there are few other ways to limit births. See, for example, Marvin Harris, *Cultural Anthropology* (New York: Harper and Row 1983), 56-7. Killing of children may be murder *and* a violation of the morality of nurturance.

11. This conception of women's roles *by itself* is enough to generate a condemnation of abortion, but not as akin to infanticide. That is, this conception of women's roles does not by itself explain the focus on the fetus by the opponents of abortion.

    If I am right about the importance of the conceptions of women's roles in the abortion dispute, then the issue of abortion was raised in a more forthright way in the nineteenth century when, according to Linda Gordon, the criminalization of abortion was justified on the grounds that 'abortion was a sign of women's selfishness in evading their prescribed destiny as mothers.' See Linda Gordon, review of Barbara Katz Rothman, *Recreating Motherhood, New York Times Book Review,* April 16, 1989.

12. *Abortion and the Politics of Motherhood* (Berkeley: University of California Press 1984). Page references to Luker's study are in the text.

13. Bolton in Munson, 99.

14. *Ibid.*

15. Many complexities of Luker's study are omitted or inadequately covered here. She gives a sensitive account of how the conservatives' views on abortion are tied to their conceptions of sexuality, spirituality, birth control, relations between husbands and wives, and human relationships generally. Most important, she shows how the dispute about abortion is an attempt by women whose lives exemplify different conceptions of women's roles to defend the dignity and value of their lives.

16. On the difficulty of infanticide see Robert F. Spencer, *The North Alaskan Eskimo: A Study in Ecology and Society, Smithsonian Institution Bureau of American Ethnology Bulletin* 171 (Washington, DC: US Government Printing Office 1959), 94, also 87-8, 92-3. On secrecy about infanticide, a secrecy that seems to indicate shame, see Richard Lee, *The Kung San* (Cambridge: Cambridge University Press 1979), 451-2.

17. Two friends have reported to me that they have raised children that they considered aborting. They were explaining why they could not take abortion lightly. See also Robey (cited in n. 7).

Abortion and the "Feminine Voice"
Celia Wolf-Devine

Celia Wolf-Devine is a professor of philosophy at Stonehill College. Wolf-Devine recognizes that following the work of Harvard psychologist Carol Gilligan, many feminists have attempted to develop an approach to moral theory that speaks in a "feminine voice": that is, which emphasizes the values of care, connectedness, non-violence, non-exploitation, and respect for the balance of nature. (The morality of nurturance discussed in the previous reading might be an example of this approach.) The procedure of abortion, as Wolf-Devine sees it, emphasizes the opposite of each of these values. Abortion thus turns out to be a "masculine" response to the matter of pregnancy. Because many feminists who adopt an ethics of care also believe that women should have a legal right to abortion, Wolf-Devine believes their thinking on abortion is inconsistent with their acceptance of feminine moral theory. An ethics that speaks in a "feminine voice" would on her account lead to opposition to abortion, not to its support.

———

A growing number of feminists now seek to articulate the "feminine voice," to draw attention to women's special strengths, and to correct the systematic devaluation of these by our male-dominated society. . . Virtually all of those feminists who are trying to reassert the value of the feminine voice, also express the sort of unqualified support for free access to abortion which has come to be regarded as a central tenet of feminist "orthodoxy." What I wish to argue in this paper is that: (1) abortion is, by their own accounts, clearly a masculine response to the problems posed by an unwanted pregnancy, and is thus highly problematic for those who seek to articulate and defend the "feminine voice" as the proper mode of moral response, and that (2) on the contrary the "feminine voice" as it has been articulated generates a strong presumption against abortion as a way of responding to an unwanted pregnancy.[1]

These conclusions, I believe, can be argued without relying on a precise determination of the moral status of the fetus. A case at least can be made that the fetus is a person since it is biologically a member of the human species and will, in time, develop normal human abilities. Whether the burden of proof rests on those who defend the personhood of the fetus, or on those who deny it, is a matter of moral methodology, and for that reason will depend in part on whether one adopts a masculine or feminine approach to moral issues.

———

From *Public Affairs Quarterly* 3 (July 1989), 81–97.

MASCULINE VOICE/FEMININE VOICE

Moral Reasoning

According to [Carol] Gilligan, [in her book *In a Different Voice*,] girls, being brought up by mothers, identify with them, while males must define themselves through separation from their mothers. As a result, girls have "a basis for empathy built into their primary definition of self in a way that boys do not."[2] Thus while masculinity is defined by separation and threatened by intimacy, femininity is defined through attachment and threatened by separation; girls come to understand themselves as imbedded within a network of personal relationships.

A second difference concerns attitudes toward general rules and principles. Boys tend to play in larger groups than girls, and become "increasingly fascinated with the legal elaboration of rules, and the development of fair procedures for adjudicating conflicts."[3] We thus find men conceiving of morality largely in terms of adjudicating fairly between the conflicting rights of self-assertive individuals.

Girls play in smaller groups, and accord a greater importance to relationships than to following rules. They are especially sensitive to the needs of the particular other, instead of emphasizing impartiality, which is more characteristic of the masculine perspective. They think of morality more in terms of having responsibilities for taking care of others, and place a high priority upon preserving the network of relationships which makes this possible. While the masculine justice perspective requires detachment, the feminine care perspective sees detachment and separation as themselves the moral problem.[4]

The feminine voice in ethics attends to the particular other, thinks in terms of responsibilities to care for others, is sensitive to our interconnectedness, and strives to preserve relationships. It contrasts with the masculine voice, which speaks in terms of justice and rights, stresses consistency and principles, and emphasizes the autonomy of the individual and impartiality in one's dealings with others. . . .

Our Relationship with Nature

Many feminists hold that mind-body dualism which sees mind as transcendent to and superior to the body, leads to the devaluation of both women and nature. For the transcendent mind is conceived as masculine, and women, the body and nature assigned an inferior and subservient status.[5] As Rosemary Radford Reuther puts it:

> The woman, the body and the world are the lower half of a dualism that must be declared posterior to, created by, subject to, and ultimately alien to the nature of (male) consciousness in whose image man made his God.[6]

Women are to be subject to men, and nature may be used by man in any way he chooses. Thus the male ideology of transcendent dualism sanctions unlimited technological manipulation of nature; nature is an alien object to be conquered.

Carolyn Merchant, in her book *The Death of Nature: Women, Ecology and the Scientific Revolution*,[7] focuses on the Cartesian version of dualism as particularly disastrous to our relationship with nature, and finds the roots of our present ecological crisis to lie in the 17th century scientific revolution—itself based on Cartesian dualism and the mechanization of nature. According to Merchant, both feminism and the ecology movement are egalitarian movements which have a vision of our interconnectedness with each other and with nature.

Feminists who stress the deep affinities between feminism and the ecology movement are often called "ecofeminists." Stephanie Leland, radical feminist and co-editor of a recent collection of ecofeminist writings, has explained that:

> Ecology is universally defined as the study of the balance and interrelationship of all life on earth. The motivating force behind feminism is the expression of the feminine principle. As the essential impulse of the feminine principle is the striving towards balance and interrelationship, it follows that feminism and ecology are inextricably connected.[8]

The masculine urge is, she says, to "separate, discriminate and control," while the feminine impulse is "towards belonging, relationship and letting be."[9] The urge to discriminate leads, she thinks, to the need to dominate "in order to feel secure in the choice of a particular set of differences."[10] The feminine attitude springs from a more holistic view of the human person and sees us as imbedded in nature rather than standing over and above it. It entails a more egalitarian attitude, regarding the needs of other creatures as important and deserving of consideration. It seeks to "let be" rather than to control, and maintains a pervasive awareness of the interconnectedness of all things and the need to preserve this if all are to flourish.

Interconnectedness, which we found to be an important theme in feminist ethics, thus reappears in the writings of the ecofeminists as one of the central aspects of the feminine attitude toward nature.

Paradigms of Social Life

Feminists' descriptions of characteristically masculine and feminine paradigms of social life center around two different focuses. Those influenced by Gilligan tend to stress the contrast between individualism (which they take to be characteristic of the masculine "justice tradition") and the view of society as "a web of relationships sustained by a process of communication"[11] (which they take to characterize the feminine "care perspective"). According to them, the masculine paradigm sees society as a collection of self-assertive individuals seeking rules which will allow them to pursue their own goals without interfering with each other. . . . The feminine care perspective guides us to think about societal problems in a different way. We are already imbedded in a network of relationships, and must never exploit or hurt the other. We must strive to preserve those relationships as much as possible without sacrificing the integrity of the self.

The ecofeminists, pacifist feminists, and those whose starting point is a rejection of dualism, tend to focus more on the contrast between viewing social relationships in terms of hierarchy, power, and domination (the masculine paradigm) and viewing them in a more egalitarian and nonviolent manner (the feminine one). Feminists taking this position range from the moderate ones who believe that masculine social thought tends to be more hierarchical than feminine thought, to the extreme radicals who believe males are irredeemably aggressive and dominating, and prone to violence in order to preserve their domination.

The more moderate characterization of masculine social thought would claim that men tend to prefer a clear structure of authority; they want to know who is in control and have a clear set of procedures or rules for resolving difficult cases. The more extreme view, common among ecofeminists and a large number of radical feminists, is that males seek to establish and maintain patriarchy (systematic domination by males) and use violence to maintain their control. These feminists thus see an affinity between feminism (which combats male violence against women) and the pacifist movement (which does so on a more global scale). Mary Daly, for example, holds that "the rulers of patriarchy—males with power—wage an unceasing war against life itself. . . . female energy is essentially biophilic."[12] Another radical feminist, Sally Miller Gearhart, says that men possess the qualities of objectification, violence, and competitiveness, while women possess empathy, nurturance, and cooperation.[13] Thus the feminine virtues must prevail if we are to survive at all, and the entire hierarchical power structure must be replaced by "horizontal patterns of relationship."[14]

Women are thus viewed by the pacifist feminists as attuned in some special way to the values and attitudes underlying a pacifist commitment. Sara Ruddick, for example, believes that maternal practice, because it involves "preservative love" and nurtures growth, involves the kinds of virtues which, when put to work in the public domain, lead us in the direction of pacifism.[15]

ABORTION

A person who had characteristically masculine traits, attitudes and values as defined above would very naturally choose abortion, and justify it ethically in the same way in which most feminists do. Conversely, a person manifesting feminine traits, attitudes and values would not make such a choice, or justify it in that way.

According to the ecofeminists, the masculine principle is insensitive to the interconnectedness of all life; it strives to discriminate, separate and control. It does not respect the natural cycles of nature, but objectifies it, and imposes its will upon it through unrestrained technological manipulation. Such a way of thinking would naturally lead to abortion. If the woman does not

want to be pregnant, she has recourse to an operation involving highly sophisticated technology in order to defend her control of her body. This fits
the characterization of the masculine principle perfectly.

Abortion is a separation—a severing of a life-preserving connection between the woman and the fetus. It thus fails to respect the interconnectedness
of all life. Nor does it respect the natural cycles of nature. The mother and the
developing child together form a delicately balanced ecosystem with the
woman's entire hormonal system geared towards sustaining the pregnancy.[16]
The abortionist forces the cervical muscles (which have become thick and
hard in order to hold in the developing fetus) open and disrupts her hormonal system by removing it.

Abortion has something further in common with the behavior ecofeminists
and pacifist feminists take to be characteristically masculine; it shows a willingness to use violence in order to maintain control. The fetus is destroyed by
being pulled apart by suction, cut in pieces. or poisoned. It is not merely
killed inadvertently as fish might be by toxic wastes, but it is deliberately
targeted for destruction. Clearly this is not the expression of a "biophilic"
attitude. This point was recently brought home to me by a Quaker woman
who had reached the conclusion that the abortion she had had was contrary
to her pacifist principles. She said, "We must seek peaceableness both within
and without."

In terms of social thought, again, it is the masculine models which are
most frequently employed in thinking about abortion. If masculine thought is
naturally hierarchical and oriented toward power and control, then the interests of the fetus (who has no power) would naturally be suppressed in favor
of the interests of the mother. But to the extent that feminist social thought is
egalitarian, the question must be raised of why the mother's interests should
prevail over the child's.

Feminist thought about abortion has, in addition, been deeply pervaded
by the individualism which they so ardently criticize. The woman is supposed
to have the sole authority to decide the outcome of the pregnancy. But what
of her interconnectedness with the child and with others? Both she and the
unborn child already exist within a network of relationships ranging from the
closest ones—the father, grandparents, siblings, uncles and aunts, and so on—
to ones with the broader society—including the mother's friends, employer,
employees, potential adoptive parents, taxpayers who may be asked to fund
the abortion or subsidize the child, and all the numerous other people affected by her choice. To dismiss this already existing network of relationships
as irrelevant to the mother's decision is to manifest the sort of social atomism
which feminist thinkers condemn as characteristically masculine.

Those feminists who are seeking to articulate the feminine voice in ethics also face a *prima facie* inconsistency between an ethics of care and abortion. Quite simply, abortion is a failure to care for one living being who exists
in a particularly intimate relationship to oneself. If empathy, nurturance, and
taking responsibility for caring for others are characteristic of the feminine

voice, then abortion does not appear to be a feminine response to an unwanted pregnancy. If, as Gilligan says, "an ethic of care rests on the premise of nonviolence—that no one should be hurt,"[17] then surely the feminine response to an unwanted pregnancy would be to try to find a solution which does not involve injury to anyone including the unborn.

"Rights" have been invoked in the abortion controversy in a bewildering variety of ways, ranging from the "right to life" to the "right to control one's body." But clearly those who defend unrestricted access to abortion in terms of such things as the woman's right to privacy or her right to control her body are speaking the language of an ethics of justice rather than an ethics of care. For example, Judith Jarvis Thomson's widely read article "A Defense of Abortion"[18] treats the moral issue involved in abortion as a conflict between the rights of the fetus and the mother's rights over her own body. Mary Anne Warren also sees the issue in terms of a conflict of rights, but since the fetus does not meet her criteria for being a person, she weighs the woman's rights to "freedom, happiness and self-determination" against the rights of other people in the society who would like to see the fetus preserved for whatever reason.[19] And, insofar as she appeals to consciousness, reasoning, self-motivated activity, the capacity to communicate, and the presence of self-concepts and self-awareness as criteria of personhood, she relies on the kind of opposition between mind and nature criticized by many feminists as masculine. In particular, she is committed to what Jaggar calls "normative dualism"—the view that what is especially valuable about humans is their mental capacity for rational thought.

It is rather striking that feminists defending abortion lapse so quickly into speaking in the masculine voice. Is it because they feel they must do so in order to be heard in our male dominated society, or is it because no persuasive defense of abortion can be constructed from within the ethics of care tradition? We now consider several possible "feminine voice" defenses of abortion.

POSSIBLE RESPONSES AND REPLIES

... One line of thought is suggested by Gilligan, who holds that at the highest level of moral development, we must balance our responsibility to care for others against our need to care for ourselves. Perhaps we could, then, see the woman who has an abortion as still being caring and nurturing in that she is acting out of a legitimate care for herself. This is an implausible view of the actual feelings of women who undergo abortions. They may believe they are "doing something for themselves" in the sense of doing what they must do to safeguard their legitimate interests. But the operation is more naturally regarded as a violation of oneself than as a nurturing of oneself. This has been noted, even by feminists who support permissive abortion laws. For example, Caroline Whitbeck speaks of "the unappealing prospect of having someone scraping away at one's core,"[20] and Adrienne Rich says that "Abortion is violence: a deep, desperate violence inflicted by a woman upon, first of all, herself."[21]

We here come up against the problem that a directive to care, to nurture, to take responsibility for others, and so on, provides a moral orientation, but leaves unanswered many important questions and hence provides little guidance in problem situations. What do we do when caring for one person involves being uncaring toward another? How widely we must extend our circle of care? Are some kinds of not caring worse than others? Is it caring to give someone what they want even though it may be bad for them?

Thinking in terms of preserving relationships suggests another possible "feminine" defense of abortion—namely that the woman is striving to preserve her interconnectedness with her family, husband, or boyfriend. Or perhaps she is concerned to strengthen her relationship with her other children by having enough time and resources to devote to their care. To simply tell a woman to preserve *all* her existing relationships is not the answer. Besides the fact that it may not be possible (women *do* sometimes have to sever relationships), it is not clear that it would be desirable even if it were possible. Attempting to preserve our existing relationships has conservative tendencies in several unfortunate ways. It fails to invite us to reflect critically on whether those relationships are good, healthy or worthy of preservation.[22] It also puts the unborn at a particular disadvantage, since the mother's relationship with him or her is just beginning, while her relationships with others have had time to develop. And not only the unborn, but any needy stranger who shows up at our door can be excluded on the grounds that caring for them would disrupt our existing pattern of relationships. Thus the care perspective could degenerate into a rationalization for a purely tribal morality; I take care of myself and my friends.

But how are decisions about severing relationships to be made? One possibility is suggested by Gilligan in a recent article. She looks at the network of connections within which the woman who is considering abortion finds herself entangled, and says "to ask what actions constitute care or are more caring directs attention to the parameters of connection and the *costs of detachment* . . . (emphasis added)"[23] Thus, the woman considering abortion should reflect upon the comparative costs of severing various relationships. This method of decision, however, makes her vulnerable to emotional and psychological pressure from others, by encouraging her to sever whichever connection is easiest to break (the squeaky wheel principle).[24]

But perhaps we can lay out some guidelines (or, at least, rules of thumb) for making these difficult decisions. One way we might reason, from the point of view of the feminine voice, is that since preserving interconnectedness is good, we should prefer a short term estrangement to an irremediable severing of relationship. And we should choose an action which *may* cause an irremediable break in relationship over one which is certain to cause such a break. By either of these criteria, abortion is clearly to be avoided.[25]

Another consideration suggested by Gilligan's work is that since avoiding hurt to others (or non-violence) is integral to an ethics of care, severing a relationship where the other person will be only slightly hurt would be preferable to severing one where deep or lasting injury will be inflicted by our action. But on this criterion, again, it would seem she should avoid abortion, since loss of life is clearly a graver harm than emotional distress. . . .

It seems that the only way open to the person who seeks to defend abortion from the point of view of the feminine voice is to deny that a relationship (or at least any morally significant relationship) exists between the embryo/fetus and the mother. The question of how to tell when a relationship (or a morally significant relationship) exists is a deep and important one, which has, as yet, received insufficient attention from those who are trying to articulate the feminine voice in moral reasoning. The whole ecofeminist position relies on the assumption that our relationship with nature and with other species is a real and morally significant one. They, thus, have no basis at all for excluding the unborn from moral consideration.

There are those, however, who wish to define morally significant relationships more narrowly—thus effectively limiting our obligation to extend care. While many philosophers within the "justice tradition" (for example, Kant) have seen moral significance only where there is some impact upon rational beings, Nel Noddings, coming from the "care perspective" tries to limit our obligation to extend care in terms of the possibility of "completion" or "reciprocity" in a caring relationship.[26] Since she takes the mother-child relationship to be paradigmatic of caring, it comes as something of a surprise that she regards abortion as a permissible response to an unwanted pregnancy.[27]

There are, on Noddings' view, two different ways in which we may be bound, as caring persons, to extend our care to one for whom we do not already have the sort of feelings of love and affection which would lead us to do the caring action naturally. One is by virtue of being connected with our "inner circle" of caring (which is formed by natural relations of love and friendship) through "chains" of "personal or formal relations."[28] As an example of a person appropriately linked to the inner circle, she cites her daughter's fiancé. It would certainly *seem* that the embryo in one's womb would belong to one's "inner circle" (via natural caring), or at least be connected to it by a "formal relation" (that is, that of parenthood). But Noddings does not concede this. . . .

Noddings also claims that we sometimes are obligated to care for "the proximate stranger". She says:

> We cannot refuse obligation in human affairs by merely refusing to enter relation; we are, by virtue of our mutual humanity, already and perpetually in potential relation.[29]

Why, then, are we not obligated to extend care to the unborn? She gives two criteria for when we have an obligation to extend care: there must be "the existence of or potential for present relation" and the "dynamic potential for growth in relation, including the potential for increased reciprocity . . ." Animals are, she believes, excluded by this second criterion since their response is nearly static (unlike a human infant).

She regards the embryo/fetus as not having the potential for present relationships of caring and reciprocity, and thus as having no claim upon our care. As the fetus matures, he or she develops increasing potential for caring relationships, and thus our obligation increases also. There are problems with her position, however.

First of all, the only relationships which can be relevant to *my* obligation to extend care, for Noddings, must be relationships with *me*. Whatever the criteria for having a relationship are, it must be that at a given time, an entity either has a relationship with me or it does not. If it does not, it may either have no potential for a morally significant relationship with me (for example, my word processor), or it may have such potential in several ways: (1) The relationship may become actual at the will of one or both parties (for example, the stranger sitting next to me on the bus). (2) The relationship may become actual only after a change in relative spatial locations which will take time, and thus can occur only in the future (for example, walking several blocks to meet a new neighbor, or traveling to Tibet to meet a specific Tibetan). Or (3) The relationship may become actual only after some internal change occurs within the other (for example by waiting for a sleeping drug to wear off, for a deep but reversible coma to pass, or for the embryo to mature more fully) and thus can also happen only in the future.

In all three of these cases there is present now in the other the potential for relations of a caring and reciprocal sort. In cases (1) and (2) this is uncontroversial, but (3) requires some defense in the case of the unborn. The human embryo differs now from a rabbit embryo in that it possesses potential for these kinds of relationships although neither of them is presently able to enter into relationships of any sort.[30] That potential becomes actualized only over time, but it can become actualized only because it is there to be actualized (as it is not in the rabbit embryo).[31] Noddings fails to give any reason why the necessity for some internal change to occur in the other before relation can become actual has such moral importance that we are entitled to kill the other in case (3), but not in the others, especially since my refraining from killing it is a sufficient condition for the actualization of the embryo's potential for caring relationships. Her criterion as it stands would also seem to imply that we may kill persons in deep but predictably reversible comas.

Whichever strand of Noddings' thought we choose, then, it is hard to see how the unborn can be excluded from being ones for whom we ought to care. If we focus on the narrow, tribal morality of "inner circles" and "chains," then an objective connection exists tying the unborn to the mother and other relatives. If we are to be open to the needy stranger because of the real potential for relationship and reciprocity, then we should be open to the unborn because he or she also has the real and present potential for a relationship of reciprocity and mutuality which comes with species membership. . . .

Some feminists will say: yes, feminine virtues are a good thing for any person to have, and yes, abortion is a characteristically masculine way of dealing with an unwanted pregnancy, but in the current state of things we live in a male dominated society, and we must be willing to use now weapons which, ideally, in a good, matriarchal society, we would not use.[32] But there are no indications that an ideal utopian society is just around the corner; thus we are condemned to a constant violation of our own deepest commitments. If the traits, values and attitudes characteristic of the "feminine voice" are asserted to be good ones, we ought to act according to them. And such values and attitudes simply do not lend support to either the choice of abortion as a way of dealing with an unwanted pregnancy in individual cases, or to the political demand for unrestricted[33] access to abortion which has become so entrenched in the feminist movement. Quite the contrary.

NOTES

1. A strong presumption against abortion is not, of course, the same thing as an absolute ban on all abortions. I do not attempt here to resolve the really hard cases; it is not clear that the feminine voice (at least as it has been articulated so far) is sufficiently fine-grained to tell us exactly where to draw the line in such cases.
2. See Carol Gilligan, *In a Different Voice,* (Cambridge, MA: Harvard University Press, 1982), p. 8.
3. *Ibid.,* p. 10.
4. See Gilligan, "Moral Orientation and Moral Development" in *Women and Moral Theory,* p. 31.
5. See, e.g. Rosemary Radford Reuther, *New Woman, New Earth,* Elizabeth Dodson Gray, *Why the Green Nigger,* and Brian Easla, *Science and Sexual Oppression,* (London: Weidenfeld & Nicolson, 1981).
6. Reuther, *op cit,* p. 195.
7. Carolyn Merchant, *The Death of Nature: Women, Ecology and the Scientific Revolution* (San Francisco: Harper & Row, 1980).
8. Stephanie Leland and Leonie Caldecott, (eds.) *Reclaim the Earth: Women Speak out for Life on Earth* (London: The Women's Press, 1983), p. 72. For an overview of ecofeminist thought which focuses on the role of mind/body dualism, see Val Plumwood, "Ecofeminism: An Overview". *Australasian Journal of Philosophy,* Supplement to Vol. 64, (June, 1986), pp. 120–138.
9. Leland and Caldecott, *op. cit.,* p. 71.
10. *Ibid.,* p. 69.
11. Introduction to *Women and Moral Theory,* by Kittay and Meyers, p. 7.
12. Cited by Barbara Zanotti, "Patriarchy: A State of War", in *Reweaving the Web of Life,* Pam McAllister, (ed.), (Philadelphia: New Society Publishers. 1982), p. 17.
13. See, e.g., Sally Miller Gearhart, "The Future—if there is one—is Female" in *Reweaving the Web of Life,* p. 266.
14. *Ibid.,* p. 272.
15. See Sara Ruddick, "Remarks on the Sexual Politics of Reason".
16. I owe the idea of regarding mother and child as an ecosystem to a conversation with Leonie Caldecott, co-editor of *Reclaim the Earth.*

17. Gilligan. *op. cit.,* p. 174.

18. Judith Jarvis Thomson, "A Defense of Abortion," *Philosophy and Public Affairs,* vol. 1, (1971), pp. 47–66.

19. Mary Anne Warren, "On the Moral and Legal Status of Abortion", *The Monist,* vol. 57 (January, 1973), reprinted in Wasserstrom, *Today's Moral Problems,* (New York: Macmillan, 1985), p. 448.

20. Carolyn Whitbeck, "Women as People: Pregnancy and Personhood," in *Abortion and the Status of the Fetus,* W.B. Bondeson, et al. (ed.), (Boston: D. Reidel Publishing Co., 1983), p. 252.

21. Rich, *op. cit.,* p. 269.

22. Joan Tronto makes this point in "Beyond Gender Differences to a Theory of Care", *Signs,* vol. 22 (Summer, 1987), p. 666.

23. Carol Gilligan, "Moral Orientation and Moral Development" in *Women and Moral Theory,* p. 24.

24. This was evident in the reasoning of the women in Gilligan's case studies, many of whom had abortions in order to please or placate other significant persons in their lives.

25. Some post-abortion counsellors find the sense of irremediable break in relationship to be one of the most painful aspects of the post-abortion experience, and try to urge the woman to imaginatively re-create a relationship with the baby in order to be better able to complete the necessary grieving process. Conversation with Teresa Patterson, post-abortion counselor at Crisis Pregnancy Center in Walnut Creek, California.

26. It would seem that in using the term "obligation", Noddings is blurring the distinction between the masculine and feminine voice, since obligations imply rights. When she speaks of obligations to extend care, however, these are not absolute, but relative to the individual's choice of being a caring person as an ethical ideal. They are binding on us only as a result of our own prior choice, and our care is not something the other can claim as a matter of justice.

27. Noddings' discussion of abortion occurs on pp. 87–90 of *Caring: A Feminine Approach to Ethics.* (Berkeley: University of California Press, 1984). All quotes are from these pages unless otherwise noted.

28. *Ibid.,* p. 47.

29. I realize that Noddings would not be happy with the extent to which I lean on her use of the term "criteria", since she prefers to argue by autobiographical example. However, since moral intuitions about abortion vary so widely, this sort of argument is not effective here.

30. I omit here consideration of such difficult cases as severe genetic retardation.

31. The notion of potentiality I am relying on here is roughly an Aristotelean one.

32. For example, Annette Baier regards trust as the central concept in a feminine ethics, but speaks of "the principled betrayal of the exploiter's trust" (Baier, "What Do Women Want in a Moral Theory", p. 62.)

33. Restrictions can take many forms, including laws against abortion, mandatory counselling which includes information about the facts of fetal development and encourages the woman to choose other options, obligatory waiting periods, legal requirements to notify (and/or obtain the consent of) the father, or in the case of a minor girl's parents, etc. To defend the appropriateness of any particular sort of restrictions goes beyond the scope of this paper.

SUGGESTIONS FOR FURTHER READING

Cudd, Ann E. "Sensationalized Philosophy: A Reply to Marquis's 'Why Abortion Is Immoral,'" *Journal of Philosophy* 87 (1990), 262-264.

Cudd argues that Marquis shows at most that an abortion is like killing one of us, but this is not enough to show it is immoral because there are many cases of justified killing, such as self defense.

English, Jane. "Abortion and the Concept of a Person," *Canadian Journal of Philosophy* 5 (1975), 233-243.

In this classic essay, English argues for a moderate position according to which even if a fetus is a person, abortions are sometimes permissible, and even if a fetus is not a person, some abortions are wrong.

Gatens-Robinson, Eugenie. "A Defense of Women's Choice: Abortion and the Ethics of Care," *The Southern Journal of Philosophy* 30 (Fall 1992), 39-66.

Like Catriona Mackenzie, Gatens-Robinson rejects the idea that the problem of abortion is best conceived in terms of competing rights; unlike Mackenzie, she turns to the ethics of care to defend the morality of abortion.

Hursthouse, Rosalind. "Virtue Theory and Abortion," *Philosophy & Public Affairs* 20 (Summer 1991), 223-246.

This paper is both a very good introduction to virtue theory and a thoughtful application of it to the issue of abortion.

Kamm, Frances. *Creation and Abortion: A Study in Moral and Legal Philosophy.* (Oxford, England: Oxford University Press, 1992).

Kamm's book is the most philosophically sophisticated discussion of the issue of abortion as presenting a conflict of rights.

McInerney, Peter K. "Does a Fetus Have a Future-Like-Ours?" *Journal of Philosophy* 87 (1990), 264-268.

In this brief essay McInerney responds to the article by Don Marquis included in this chapter. He argues that even if Marquis is right about what makes killing wrong, his position does not show that abortions are seriously immoral.

Norcross, Alastair. "Killing, Abortion, and Contraception: A Reply to Marquis," *Journal of Philosophy* 87 (1990), 268-277.

Norcross argues that if the argument developed by Marquis reprinted in this volume succeeds, it would apply to contraception as well as abortion. Hence, it does not succeed.

Pojman, Louis P. and Francis J. Beckwith (eds.). *The Abortion Controversy.* (Boston: Jones & Bartlett, 1994).

This is an excellent, thorough anthology.

Sher, George. "Subsidized Abortion: Moral Rights and Moral Compromise," *Philosophy & Public Affairs* 10 (1981), 361-372.

Sher addresses two questions concerning society's role in the abortion debate: 1) Should the government provide funding for abortions for the poor, and 2) with the sides so deeply divided, how might society reach a moral compromise in this debate?

Thomson, Judith Jarvis. "A Defense of Abortion," *Philosophy & Public Affairs* 1 (1971), 47–66.

This essay by Thomson is probably the single most frequently discussed piece on abortion. She argues that women have a right to abortion even if fetuses have a right to life.

Tooley, Michael. "Abortion and Infanticide," *Philosophy & Public Affairs* 2 (1972), 37–65.

In this influential essay, Tooley defends the position that neither fetuses nor infants have a right to life.

Chapter 3

EUTHANASIA

Improvements in the medical profession's ability to prevent disease and to preserve life in the face of conditions that would have been almost certainly fatal even a century ago, combined with better nutrition for a large part of the world's population, have led to a significant increase in the average life span of human beings. One consequence of this increase is that at least in an affluent society one is more likely to die from a slow-acting degenerative disease than to die comparatively quickly from traumatic injury or infection. When faced with the prospect of a condition that is debilitating and/or inevitably fatal, many people would prefer to die earlier rather than later. This preference may lead them to request euthanasia.

Euthanasia, as we shall understand it, is a matter of intentionally bringing about a person's death through either action or inaction when an earlier death can reasonably be judged to be more beneficial for a person than continued life. (For the moment, we leave aside difficult questions about how such judgments could be made, including the question about who, if anyone, has a right to make them.) Those who believe it is never reasonable to judge that an earlier death is more beneficial than continued life should hold that euthanasia, as we understand it, is impossible.

In discussing euthanasia it is useful to make several distinctions. The distinction between *active* and *passive* euthanasia is commonly drawn to mark different ways in which the manner of death can be sought. A classic example of active euthanasia would be injecting a patient facing a terminal and painful disease with a lethal drug. Passive euthanasia is generally understood to be a matter of either withholding potentially life-continuing treatment or withdrawing such treatment after it has begun. Even though this distinction is generally thought to be roughly equivalent to the distinction between killing someone and allowing someone to die, it does not fit the latter distinction exactly. For instance, disconnecting someone from a respirator is typically classified as passive euthanasia even though this can easily seem to be a case of killing someone rather than allowing that person to die. (Consider, for example, a diver who disconnects another diver's air supply leading to that diver's death by drowning. An attempted defense against a charge of murder on the grounds that the disconnection from the air supply was merely a matter of allowing someone to die rather than a matter of killing could not be taken seriously.) Another way of trying to understand the difference between active and passive euthanasia would be in terms of what causes death in each case. When treatment is withheld or withdrawn from a patient, the patient's underlying medical condition is the cause of death, while in active euthanasia a new lethal condition is introduced, such as an injected drug. Even though it is difficult to draw the distinction between active and passive euthanasia sharply, it seems to many that there is an important difference between merely withholding or withdrawing life-sustaining treatment from a terminally ill patient and injecting such a patient with a lethal drug. It is very commonly held that the former is often permissible and even morally required, while the latter is seldom or never justified.

Forms of euthanasia are also classified on the basis of the patient's expressed preferences. *Voluntary* euthanasia occurs with a patient's consent, *involuntary* euthanasia occurs either when death is sought against a patient's expressed preference or when consent is not sought from a patient able to make a choice, and *nonvoluntary* euthanasia involves patients who are unable either to consent or to express a preference for continued treatment. Examples of the latter arise in the case of infants and the case of comatose patients who did not express a preference about their treatment while still able to do so.

Combining the differences between voluntary, involuntary, and nonvoluntary euthanasia with the distinction between active and passive yields six forms of euthanasia to be considered. Since involuntary euthanasia on its face seems much like murder, it is seldom discussed, but it is hard to believe that cases of involuntary passive euthanasia are not fairly common. (Such cases might, for instance, involve a physician's failure to inform a patient of possible forms of treatment that could extend life without curing the underlying disease because the physician believes it would not be reasonable to choose such treatment in the patient's particular situation.) Most discussions of euthanasia focus on active voluntary and passive nonvoluntary euthanasia.

RECENT HISTORY OF EUTHANASIA

Acceptance of euthanasia by both the law and the general population has increased significantly over the past two decades. In an early influential case, the Supreme Court of New Jersey ruled in 1976 that it was permissible to remove Karen Ann Quinlan, a patient diagnosed as being in a persistent vegetative state with no hope of recovering consciousness, from a respirator that was sustaining her life. Such permission was sought by Quinlan's parents. Quinlan was "weaned" from the respirator and survived without it until 1985 even though she never in fact recovered consciousness. In the 1980s, courts and the American Medical Association accepted removal of equipment providing nutrition and water in those cases in which it would be permissible to remove a respirator. Both of these types of cases would generally be classified as examples of passive euthanasia.

In 1990, Dr. Jack Kevorkian first used his "suicide machine" in the state of Michigan to assist patients in bringing about their own deaths. Since then, he has assisted the suicides of a number of people, for which criminal charges have been brought against him. In 1992, a referendum allowing active euthanasia was narrowly defeated in the state of California, but a similar referendum passed in the state of Oregon in 1994. The status of the latter law is currently in doubt since a federal judge ruled in July 1995 that it unconstitutionally discriminates against terminal patients. However, the recent reaction of the federal judiciary to euthanasia has been far from consistent. In March 1996, the U.S. 9th Circuit Court of Appeals ruled 8 to 3 that a Washington state law making it a felony for a physician to assist the suicide of terminally ill patients was unconstitutional. It is almost certain that this ruling will be reviewed by the Supreme Court.

These developments over the last two decades clearly demonstrate a growing legal and social acceptance of more aggressive forms of euthanasia in the United States. At this point, there is nearly universal support for passive euthanasia in the United States, but there is still considerable opposition to active euthanasia. Elsewhere, the trend toward a greater acceptance of euthanasia is even stronger. Active euthanasia has been legally tolerated in the Netherlands since 1972. Some see increasing the availability of euthanasia as a further expansion in human freedom. Just as we may be thought to have the right to live as we see fit (within limits), some advocates of euthanasia maintain that we have a right to choose the time and manner of our deaths (again, perhaps within limits). Opponents of euthanasia see its increasing acceptance as an assault on the dignity of human life. We shall now turn to some of the reasons given to support and oppose euthanasia. Our focus will be on active euthanasia, since most current opposition to euthanasia is specifically aimed at this form.

BENEVOLENCE AS A GROUND FOR ACTIVE EUTHANASIA

The most straightforward argument for euthanasia appeals to benevolence (or kindness). If a person's life has been reduced to such a state that its continuation is an evil, then the best thing for the person would be to die. In bringing about that death earlier, one is creating a benefit for the person. Presumably the basis for sometimes withdrawing or withholding treatment from a terminal patient is that the treatment would prolong life beyond the point at which that life is beneficial. Hence shortening life by foregoing treatment benefits the patient by reducing the amount of suffering he or she experiences before death. In other words kindness, the desire to reduce the degree to which a person suffers pain and loss of dignity, is one primary motive for passive euthanasia. The proponents of active euthanasia insist that this same motive gives greater support to active than to passive euthanasia. If one merely suspends treatment, a period of time—probably filled with suffering—will be required for the untreated condition to bring about death. If one wishes to end suffering, then such steps as lethal injections will achieve that goal more quickly and effectively.

Those who accept passive but not active euthanasia might respond to this line of argument by agreeing that even though a person's death may be desirable under certain conditions, it is nonetheless wrong to kill an innocent person even when the person's death is desirable. The most one can ethically do is to suspend treatment and allow the patient to die. Some would then argue that the distinction between killing someone and allowing someone to die is of such moral significance that the latter can be justified in cases of euthanasia but the former cannot. In his contribution to this chapter, James Rachels argues against the doctrine that the mere difference between killing and letting die has moral significance. If he is right, then killing would be justified under exactly the same circumstances that it would be justifiable to allow someone to die.

It is not obvious how to assess the difference between killing and letting die within the euthanasia context. Those who believe that killing is automatically morally worse than letting die also tend to believe that it is always morally worse to harm someone than to merely allow the same degree of harm to occur. Hence the difference between killing and letting die is just a special and very significant instance of the more general distinction between harming and allowing a harm to occur. However, we began this introduction by stating that euthanasia is a matter of bringing about a person's death when death can reasonably be judged to be beneficial. If so, killing in the case of euthanasia is a matter of benefiting someone rather than a case of harming someone. The difference between active and passive euthanasia, then, if it is understood in part as a difference between killing and letting die, is a difference between benefiting someone (by killing) and allowing a benefit to occur (by letting die). The person who now maintains that only passive euthanasia is permissible because it is always morally worse to kill than to let die seems to imply that at least in the case of euthanasia it is always morally worse to benefit a person than to allow the same benefit to occur, even when allowing the benefit to occur lessens it. On its face, this seems to be a strange thought; we do not in general think it is worse to benefit someone than to stand by and allow that benefit to occur.

Another way to confront the argument from benevolence is to argue that it is always wrong to bring about an innocent person's death *intentionally* either directly (by killing) or indirectly (by allowing to die). In fact, according to this view, no form of euthanasia, active or passive, is justified. Someone with this view could argue that some practices which are typically classified as forms of passive euthanasia should not be thought to be euthanasia at all, because if the acts are morally appropriate, then the patient's death is not in fact intended.

Often this line of argument appeals to a moral principle known as the *doctrine of double effect* according to which it is always wrong to bring about some evil either as one's end (i.e., one's goal) or as a means to one's end, even though it can be permissible knowingly to bring about that same evil as a side effect of pursuing one's end. Imagine a terminal patient who is suffering in a way that can be eliminated only by such high doses of medication that the medicine itself may hasten the patient's death. According to the doctrine of double effect it would be wrong to kill the patient, for instance by administering a lethal injection, as a means to the goal of ending the patient's suffering, because the death of an innocent person is an evil that one must not seek intentionally either as an end or as a means to an end. However, one could administer high doses of pain medication knowing that this might lead to death as long as one's goal is not the patient's death but rather the relief of suffering.

Some may think that making a distinction between the case of administering a lethal drug in pursuit of a patient's death and administering pain medication knowing it will very likely have as a side effect the patient's death is simply a matter of splitting hairs with no practical implications. However, practical implications could arise in cases where the administered drug does not result in death. If death is sought, then one would presumably try again. However, if death was merely a foreseen, unintended consequence of relieving pain and if the patient's pain is relieved by what turns out not to be a lethal dose of medication, one would not increase the dose to bring about death. The appeal of the doctrine of double effect may rest on the idea that there are some evils so great that one should never intentionally attempt to cause them. Even if the claim that there are such evils is true, however, for it to support a blanket rejection of euthanasia, it must be assumed or shown that the death of an innocent person is such an evil. Advocates of euthanasia deny that death is always an evil, or they at least maintain that situations can arise when death is less of an evil than continued life.

AUTONOMY AS A GROUND FOR ACTIVE EUTHANASIA

As we have seen, those arguing for active euthanasia on grounds of benevolence need to depend on the controversial claim that death can be beneficial. Those who argue on grounds of autonomy need not depend on this claim, though they need not deny it either. Rather the argument from autonomy maintains that human beings have a right to live as they see fit, at least to the extent that they do not harm others. Many would maintain that this right to determine the shape of one's own life should also include the right to determine the time and manner of one's own death—at least under certain conditions. So it might be claimed that one has the right to commit suicide, at least when doing so does not prevent one from meeting obligations one might have to others. If this is granted, then why should it not also be granted that voluntary active euthanasia should be allowed? If I have a right to bring about my own death, it might be asked, why should I not also have a right to enlist a physician as my agent to bring about that death? I have a right to paint my house, but if I am too lazy or unskilled to do so, I can also hire a professional to do it for me. If I have a right to bring about my own death, but I am unable to kill myself, what reason could there be to deny me professional assistance in achieving that end to which I have a right?

In response to this line of argument, many question the very intelligibility of a right to die. For instance, it is sometimes suggested that the moral purpose of the recognition of rights is to promote and protect the value of human freedom, but in choosing to die one would be giving up the ability to make free choices in the future. Since death deprives one of freedom and since the purpose of rights is to promote freedom, it is argued that the supposition that we have a right to die is just as absurd as the supposition that we have a right to enter into slavery. In both cases a right is asserted that actually undermines the purpose of rights in general. In his essay, David Velleman argues against the existence of a right to die on the grounds that recognizing such a right ends up harming even those who would be benefitted by death.

It can also be argued that the fact our rights are limited by our obligations undermines the claim that euthanasia is permissible. For instance, my right to drive my car where I wish is limited by my obligation to others in such a way that I have no right to drive it over my neighbor's garden. Many believe that we have a strong, general obligation not to take innocent human life and that this obligation extends to one's own life. Someone arguing in this manner would deny that we have a right to commit suicide as is suggested by those who appeal to autonomy to support euthanasia. But even if we grant that suicide can be permissible, active euthanasia is a matter of taking the innocent life of another, and again it can be argued, this is morally forbidden, except perhaps in cases of self-defense. What reason is there to believe that it is nearly always wrong to kill innocent human beings? One answer to this question is that such a belief serves our collective interest, and that answer leads to one of the most common and, perhaps, persuasive arguments against active euthanasia—namely, that permitting it may lead to extremely undesirable consequences.

ARGUMENTS AGAINST ACTIVE EUTHANASIA THAT APPEAL TO THE CONSEQUENCES

In our introduction to the topic of abortion, we mentioned that it is important to distinguish between issues concerning the moral permissibility of abortion and issues about what its legal status should be. The same distinction is important in the debate about euthanasia. It is possible to believe that active euthanasia is morally wrong but still believe that it should be legally available to at least some who would choose it. For example, someone may believe that active voluntary euthanasia is morally akin to suicide and that while suicide is morally wrong, no legal steps should be taken to prevent people from choosing to commit suicide.

A position taken much more frequently in the euthanasia debate is that even if voluntary active euthanasia is sometimes morally permissible, it should not be legally permitted because its legalization would probably cause more harm than good. One worry that is raised is that the legalization of voluntary euthanasia could lead to the practice of euthanasia that is less than fully voluntary. For example, in a time of rising medical costs and increased reliance on HMO delivery of medicine, it is imaginable that a patient with a very bad prognosis but who nonetheless wants to pursue aggressive treatment could be subtly influenced to opt for euthanasia instead by a physician wanting to cut costs. One way of doing this, perhaps, would be to treat the patient's pain inadequately. The argument that legalizing morally permissible forms of euthanasia would lead to morally impermissible forms of euthanasia is an example of a type of argument known as slippery slope arguments. Just as one might be unable to stop with a single step down a slippery slope, many worry that a policy that permits arguably permissible cases of killing will almost inevitably lead to impermissible cases of killing.

Another worry frequently raised about the consequences of legalizing euthanasia concerns the attitudes of members of society generally, and of medical care professionals specifically, toward life and death. Each of us is safer because there is a very strong socially inculcated inhibition against killing. Arguably, the more cases in which it is thought permissible to kill, the weaker that inhibition will be, leading to more unjustifiable killing in society. Also, health care professionals, especially physicians, often see themselves as champions of life; their job is, in part, to preserve life. Some argue that allowing physicians to kill will weaken their commitment to life, hence reducing the health care profession's effectiveness in pursuing the preservation of life. Edmund Pellegrino, a physician who is a contributor to this chapter, bases part of his opposition to euthanasia on worries about how it would affect the relationship between physicians and patients.

These concerns about legalized voluntary euthanasia leading to euthanasia that is less than fully voluntary and negatively affecting attitudes toward life and death are just two examples of the worries raised by those who oppose euthanasia on consequentialist grounds. Further examples are thoroughly discussed in the readings for this chapter. Those who wish to defend active euthanasia against these worries often claim that carefully crafted regulations concerning the conditions under which euthanasia would be allowed and procedures that must be followed before euthanasia is used should prevent at least many of the abuses that worry its opponents.

Suppose it is admitted that the legalization of active euthanasia would indeed risk all of the bad consequences that opponents to euthanasia mention. Merely admitting that some undertaking could have bad consequences is not sufficient to conclude that one should not go forward with it. At least two other factors need to be considered. First, one must take into account the possible good consequences, and second, the probabilities of the good and bad consequences need to be considered as well. Both Dan Brock and Joel Feinberg discuss these matters in their contributions to this chapter. Were active euthanasia legalized, the primary good consequence likely to be realized would be a reduction in suffering, and the probability of this occurring would seem to be quite high—indeed it seems virtually certain. As a result, it might be thought that the opponents of active euthanasia would need to argue that there is a fairly high probability that the bad consequences they fear would actually occur. In fact, some who argue against euthanasia on grounds of possible bad consequences maintain that they do not need to show that it is likely that those consequences would occur. Instead, they argue that the burden of proof is on those who propose the legalization of euthanasia to show that the bad consequences will not occur. Roughly, the argument maintains that legalizing euthanasia would constitute a radical change in our current system of medical care. Furthermore, our current system—though imperfect—works fairly well, and the proposed change could possibly bring about very bad consequences. The principle upon which the argument turns is that those who propose a radical change in a system that works fairly well have the burden of proof to show that those changes will not bring about disastrous bad consequences. Since the burden of proof is on those who support euthanasia, those who oppose it do not have to show that the bad consequences are very likely to occur; it is sufficient to show only that they may occur.

In response to this burden of proof argument, defenders of the legalization of euthanasia might question the principle on which it rests, or they might question the claim that legalizing euthanasia would be such a radical change or the claim that our medical system works well enough to bring the principle into play. Given the growing acceptance of euthanasia over the past two decades, one might well believe that at this point the legalization of active euthanasia would not be nearly the radical change in medicine that it would have been just a few years ago. One might well question whether our medical system, which may be very successful in preventing illness and healing, works all that well in addressing the needs of those facing near and inevitable death. Given such considerations, it is probably far from clear that the mere possibility of euthanasia's having bad consequences is sufficient to place the burden of carrying forth the argument entirely on the shoulders of those in favor of legalization.

Active and Passive Euthanasia
James Rachels

James Rachels, University Professor of Philosophy at the University of Alabama at Birmingham, is the author of many influential articles and books in both applied ethics and ethical theory, including *The Elements of Moral Philosophy* (1986). In this widely reprinted essay, Rachels defends active euthanasia against those who accept passive but not active euthanasia. He first argues that active euthanasia prevents more suffering than passive euthanasia and hence is more humane. Rachels also claims that the position allowing only passive euthanasia leads to clinical decisions concerning life and death being made on grounds that are entirely irrelevant to those decisions. He next considers opposition to active euthanasia based on the belief that it is morally worse to kill someone than to let someone die, arguing that the distinction between killing and letting die has no moral significance. Finally, he confronts the argument that physicians do nothing to bring about their patients' deaths when employing passive euthanasia but that active euthanasia requires them to do something and hence to kill. In response to this claim, Rachels argues that suspending treatment for the sake of euthanasia is in fact to do something—namely to suspend treatment.

The distinction between active and passive euthanasia is thought to be crucial for medical ethics. The idea is that it is permissible, at least in some cases, to withhold treatment and allow a patient to die, but it is never permissible to take any direct action designed to kill the patient. This doctrine seems to be accepted by most doctors, and it is endorsed in a statement adopted by the House of Delegates of the American Medical Association on December 4, 1973:

> The intentional termination of the life of one human being by another—mercy killing—is contrary to that for which the medical profession stands and is contrary to the policy of the American Medical Association.
>
> The cessation of the employment of extraordinary means to prolong the life of the body when there is irrefutable evidence that biological death is imminent is the decision of the patient and/or his immediate family. The advice and judgment of the physician should be freely available to the patient and/or his immediate family.

However, a strong case can be made against this doctrine. In what follows I will set out some of the relevant arguments, and urge doctors to reconsider their views on this matter.

To begin with a familiar type of situation, a patient who is dying of incurable cancer of the throat is in terrible pain, which can no longer be

From *The New England Journal of Medicine* 292 (1975), 78-80.

satisfactorily alleviated. He is certain to die within a few days, even if present treatment is continued, but he does not want to go on living for those days since the pain is unbearable. So he asks the doctor for an end to it, and his family joins in the request.

Suppose the doctor agrees to withhold treatment, as the conventional doctrine says he may. The justification for his doing so is that the patient is in terrible agony, and since he is going to die anyway, it would be wrong to prolong his suffering needlessly. But now notice this. If one simply withholds treatment, it may take the patient longer to die, and so he may suffer more than he would if more direct action were taken and a lethal injection given. This fact provides strong reason for thinking that, once the initial decision not to prolong his agony has been made, active euthanasia is actually preferable to passive euthanasia, rather than the reverse. To say otherwise is to endorse the option that leads to more suffering rather than less, and is contrary to the humanitarian impulse that prompts the decision not to prolong his life in the first place.

Part of my point is that the process of being "allowed to die" can be relatively slow and painful, whereas being given a lethal injection is relatively quick and painless. Let me give a different sort of example. In the United States about one in 600 babies is born with Down's syndrome. Most of these babies are otherwise healthy—that is, with only the usual pediatric care, they will proceed to an otherwise normal infancy. Some, however, are born with congenital defects such as intestinal obstructions that require operations if they are to live. Sometimes, the parents and the doctor will decide not to operate, and let the infant die. Anthony Shaw describes what happens then:

> . . . When surgery is denied [the doctor] must try to keep the infant from suffering while natural forces sap the baby's life away. As a surgeon whose natural inclination is to use the scalpel to fight off death, standing by and watching a salvageable baby die is the most emotionally exhausting experience I know. It is easy at a conference, in a theoretical discussion, to decide that such infants should be allowed to die. It is altogether different to stand by in the nursery and watch as dehydration and infection wither a tiny being over hours and days. This is a terrible ordeal for me and the hospital staff— much more so than for the parents who never set foot in the nursery.[1]

I can understand why some people are opposed to all euthanasia, and insist that such infants must be allowed to live. I think I can also understand why other people favor destroying these babies quickly and painlessly. But why should anyone favor letting "dehydration and infection wither a tiny being over hours and days?" The doctrine that says that a baby may be allowed to dehydrate and wither, but may not be given an injection that would end its life without suffering, seems so patently cruel as to require no further refutation. The strong language is not intended to offend, but only to put the point in the clearest possible way.

My second argument is that the conventional doctrine leads to decisions concerning life and death made on irrelevant grounds.

Consider again the case of the infants with Down's syndrome who need operations for congenital defects unrelated to the syndrome to live. Sometimes, there is no operation, and the baby dies, but when there is no such defect, the baby lives on. Now, an operation such as that to remove an intestinal obstruction is not prohibitively difficult. The reason why such operations are not performed in these cases is, clearly, that the child has Down's Syndrome and the parents and doctor judge that because of that fact it is better for the child to die.

But notice that this situation is absurd, no matter what view one takes of the lives and potentials of such babies. If the life of such an infant is worth preserving, what does it matter if it needs a simple operation? Or, if one thinks it better that such a baby should not live on, what difference does it make that it happens to have an unobstructed intestinal tract? In either case, the matter of life and death is being decided on irrelevant grounds. It is the Down's syndrome, and not the intestines, that is the issue. The matter should be decided, if at all, on that basis, and not be allowed to depend on the essentially irrelevant question of whether the intestinal tract is blocked.

What makes this situation possible, of course, is the idea that when there is an intestinal blockage, one can "let the baby die," but when there is no such defect there is nothing that can be done, for one must not "kill" it. The fact that this idea leads to such results as deciding life or death on irrelevant grounds is another good reason why the doctrine should be rejected.

One reason why so many people think that there is an important moral difference between active and passive euthanasia is that they think killing someone is morally worse than letting someone die. But is it? Is killing, in itself, worse than letting die? To investigate this issue, two cases may be considered that are exactly alike except that one involves killing whereas the other involves letting someone die. Then, it can be asked whether this difference makes any difference to the moral assessments. It is important that the cases be exactly alike, except for this one difference, since otherwise one cannot be confident that it is this difference and not some other that accounts for any variation in the assessments of the two cases. So, let us consider this pair of cases:

In the first, Smith stands to gain a large inheritance if anything should happen to his six-year-old cousin. One evening while the child is taking his bath, Smith sneaks into the bathroom and drowns the child, and then arranges things so that it will look like an accident.

In the second, Jones also stands to gain if anything should happen to his six-year-old cousin. Like Smith, Jones sneaks in planning to drown the child in his bath. However, just as he enters the bathroom Jones sees the child slip and hit his head, and fall face down in the water. Jones is delighted; he stands by, ready to push the child's head back under if it is necessary, but it is not necessary. With only a little thrashing about, the child drowns all by himself, "accidentally," as Jones watches and does nothing.

Now Smith killed the child, whereas Jones "merely" let the child die. That is the only difference between them. Did either man behave better, from a moral point of view? If the difference between killing and letting die were in itself a morally important matter, one should say that Jones's behavior was less reprehensible than Smith's. But does one really want to say that? I think not. In the first place, both men acted from the same motive, personal gain, and both had exactly the same end in view when they acted. It may be inferred from Smith's conduct that he is a bad man, although that judgment may be withdrawn or modified if certain further facts are learned about him— for example, that he is mentally deranged. But would not the very same thing be inferred about Jones from his conduct? And would not the same further considerations also be relevant to any modification of this judgment? More- over, suppose Jones pleaded, in his own defense, "After all, I didn't do anything except just stand there and watch the child drown. I didn't kill him; I only let him die." Again, if letting die were in itself less bad than killing, this defense should have at least some weight. But it does not. Such a "defense" can only be regarded as a grotesque perversion of moral reasoning. Morally speaking, it is no defense at all.

Now, it may be pointed out, quite properly, that the cases of euthanasia with which doctors are concerned are not like this at all. They do not involve personal gain or the destruction of normal healthy children. Doctors are con- cerned only with cases in which the patient's life is of no further use to him, or in which the patient's life has become or will soon become a terrible burden. However, the point is the same in these cases: the bare difference between killing and letting die does not, in itself, make a moral difference. If a doctor lets a patient die, for humane reasons, he is in the same moral posi- tion as if he had given the patient a lethal injection for humane reasons. If his decision was wrong—if, for example, the patient's illness was in fact curable— the decision would be equally regrettable no matter which method was used to carry it out. And if the doctor's decision was the right one, the method used is not in itself important.

The AMA policy statement isolates the crucial issue very well; the crucial issue is "the intentional termination of the life of one human being by another." But after identifying this issue, and forbidding "mercy killing," the statement goes on to deny that the cessation of treatment is the intentional termination of a life. This is where the mistake comes in, for what is the cessation of treatment, in these circumstances, if it is not "the intentional termination of the life of one human being by another?" Of course it is exactly that, and if it were not, there would be no point to it.

Many people will find this judgment hard to accept. One reason, I think, is that it is very easy to conflate the question of whether killing is, in itself, worse than letting die, with the very different question of whether most ac- tual cases of killing are more reprehensible than most actual cases of letting die. Most actual cases of killing are clearly terrible (think, for example, of all the murders reported in the newspapers), and one hears of such cases every day. On the other hand, one hardly ever hears of a case of letting die, except for the actions of doctors who are motivated by humanitarian reasons. So one learns to think of killing in a much worse light than of letting die. But this does not mean that there is something about killing that makes it in itself worse than letting die, for it is not the bare difference between killing and letting die that makes the difference in these cases. Rather, the other factors—the murderer's motive of personal gain, for example, contrasted with the doctor's humanitarian motivation—account for different reactions to the different cases.

I have argued that killing is not in itself any worse than letting die; if my contention is right, it follows that active euthanasia is not any worse than passive euthanasia. What arguments can be given on the other side? The most common, I believe, is the following:

"The important difference between active and passive euthanasia is that, in passive euthanasia, the doctor does not do anything to bring about the patient's death. The doctor does nothing, and the patient dies of whatever ills already afflict him. In active euthanasia, however, the doctor does something to bring about the patient's death: he kills him. The doctor who gives the patient with cancer a lethal injection has himself caused his patient's death; whereas if he merely ceases treatment, the cancer is the cause of the death."

A number of points need to be made here. The first is that it is not exactly correct to say that in passive euthanasia the doctor does nothing, for he does do one thing that is very important: he lets the patient die. "Letting someone die" is certainly different, in some respects, from other types of action—mainly in that it is a kind of action that one may perform by way of not performing certain other actions. For example, one may let a patient die by way of not giving medication, just as one may insult someone by way of not shaking his hand. But for any purpose of moral assessment, it is a type of action nonetheless. The decision to let a patient die is subject to moral appraisal in the same way that a decision to kill him would be subject to moral appraisal: it may be assessed as wise or unwise, compassionate or sadistic, right or wrong. If a doctor deliberately let a patient die who was suffering from a routinely curable illness, the doctor would certainly be to blame for what he had done, just as he would be to blame if he had needlessly killed the patient. Charges against him would then be appropriate. If so, it would be no defense at all for him to insist that he didn't "do anything." He would have done something very serious indeed, for he let his patient die.

Fixing the cause of death may be very important from a legal point of view, for it may determine whether criminal charges are brought against the doctor. But I do not think that this notion can be used to show a moral difference between active and passive euthanasia. The reason why it is considered bad to be the cause of someone's death is that death is regarded as a great evil—and so it is. However, if it has been decided that euthanasia—even passive euthanasia—is desirable in a given case, it has also been decided that in this instance death is no greater an evil than the patient's continued existence. And if this is true, the usual reason for not wanting to be the cause of someone's death simply does not apply.

Finally, doctors may think that all of this is only of academic interest—the sort of thing that philosophers may worry about but that has no practical bearing on their own work. After all, doctors must be concerned about the legal consequences of what they do, and active euthanasia is clearly forbidden by the law. But even so, doctors should also be concerned with the fact that the law is forcing upon them a moral doctrine that may well be indefensible, and has a considerable effect on their practices. Of course, most doctors are not now in the position of being coerced in this matter, for they do not regard themselves as merely going along with what the law requires. Rather, in statements such as the AMA policy statement that I have quoted, they are endorsing this doctrine as a central point of medical ethics. In that statement, active euthanasia is condemned not merely as illegal but as "contrary to that for which the medical profession stands," whereas passive euthanasia is approved. However, the preceding considerations suggest that there is really no moral difference between the two, considered in themselves (there may be important moral differences in some cases in their *consequences,* but, as I pointed out, these differences may make active euthanasia, and not passive euthanasia, the morally preferable option). So, whereas doctors may have to discriminate between active and passive euthanasia to satisfy the law, they should not do any more than that. In particular, they should not give the distinction any added authority and weight by writing it into official statements of medical ethics.

NOTE

1. Shaw A. 'Doctor, Do We Have a Choice?' *The New York Times Magazine,* January 30, 1972, p. 54

Doctors Must Not Kill
Edmund D. Pellegrino

Edmund D. Pellegrino is Director of the Center for Advanced Study of Ethics at Georgetown University and has published widely in medical ethics and the philosophy of medicine. Pellegrino, a medical doctor, argues against the moral permissibility and legalization of active euthanasia, concluding as his title suggests that the role of physicians requires them not to intentionally seek the death of patients. He first addresses the reasons most often given for euthanasia by its advocates, including claims that active euthanasia is required by benevolence or for the sake of personal autonomy, and argues that these reasons are not sufficient. Pellegrino also believes that active euthanasia is incompatible with the nature of the medical profession because it would distort the healing relationship he believes to be essential to medicine. Like others, Pellegrino is also concerned about the potentially bad social consequences of permitting active euthanasia. Even if legalized voluntary euthanasia were closely regulated, eventually less than voluntary euthanasia would be very likely to be common. Pellegrino concludes his paper by suggesting what responsibilities are born by physicians opposed to euthanasia. Among those responsibilities, he believes, is a duty to become more efficient at treating the pain, suffering, and loss of dignity that often accompany terminal illness so that there will be less demand for euthanasia.

INTRODUCTION

Is it ever morally licit for physicians intentionally to kill a patient to relieve suffering even with the patient's request? Should the longheld proscription against active euthanasia be relaxed legally and ethically, as it has been in the Netherlands? Are physicians who oppose active euthanasia being unfaithful to their traditional duty of compassion? These questions are being debated in the United States and in several Western European countries. They are highlighted by the legal, ethical, and social tolerance for euthanasia in Holland and the growing public and professional sentiment elsewhere that favors the termination of life by physicians. How the medical profession, society, and the public answer these questions promises to have a profound effect on the moral quality of the physician-patient relationship and of the whole of society.

In this article, I shall argue that physicians should not kill, directly or indirectly, even out of compassion, for three reasons. First, the moral arguments favoring euthanasia are logically inadequate. Second, killing by physicians seriously distorts the healing relationship. And third, the grave social consequences of such killing are morally prohibitive.

Euthanasia literally means "good" or "gentle" death. No one can reasonably oppose a "good" death. But some construals of euthanasia are morally defensible;

From *The Journal of Clinical Ethics* 3 (1992), 95–102.

others are not.[1] It is crucial, therefore, to define the sense in which I shall use the term. I shall argue against what is called "active" euthanasia—the intentional killing of a patient by a physician, with the patient's consent (voluntary euthanasia), or without consent when consent is impossible (nonvoluntary euthanasia), or when consent is possible but not sought (involuntary euthanasia). To include in this definition such qualifiers as "good" or "gentle," and to evade the use of the term "killing," is to beg the central moral question.

What is called "passive" euthanasia—allowing a patient with an incurable disease to die either by withholding or withdrawing life-sustaining support—will not be my concern in this essay. Nor will "mercy killing," which includes killing by family, friends, or someone designated by society to play this role. My focus is specifically on killing by physicians, for this is what many seek to legitimate today.

The line of argument I oppose can be summarized as follows. Active euthanasia is a beneficent and compassionate act because it relieves human suffering. Moreover, human beings should, on the principle of autonomy, have the right to end their lives when they wish to terminate their sufferings. Physicians, as agents of the patient's welfare, should assist either by directly killing the patient or by assisting the patient in suicide. Since physicians are best qualified to assist in dying, they should participate if the patient's "right to die" is to be actualized. Physicians already participate in passive euthanasia. Since there is no moral difference between killing and letting die, the opposition to active euthanasia is logically untenable.[2] In addition, the abuses envisioned in slippery-slope arguments can be prevented by legal guidelines and criteria, like those currently used in Holland.[3] No physician who is morally opposed need participate. Medical ethics should be updated to take account of the changed religious, moral, and political milieu. Because of all these arguments, the proscriptions in law and ethics against physician killing must be relaxed.

I recognize the appeal of this line of argument in a pluralistic, democratic, and secular society. Nothing that follows is meant to impugn the sincerity or motives of the proponents of euthanasia. Their desire to spare human suffering is commendable. It is the *means* they use to this end that are morally unacceptable.

I will make my case without invoking what, for many, are still the two most powerful arguments against euthanasia: (1) the Jewish and Christian belief that humans are stewards and not the absolute masters of the gift of life, and (2) the Christian belief that even human suffering may have meaning. David Thomasma and I have enlarged on this perspective in a forthcoming volume.[4] The religious viewpoint is unpalatable to contemporary mores, but it still hovers in attenuated form over the debate and is not lightly dismissed. However, since these arguments involve faith commitments, they are rejected by those without a faith commitment. For this reason, I shall confine my argument solely to the philosophical objections. Even without recourse to religious beliefs, active euthanasia is morally untenable.

ADEQUACY OF THE ARGUMENTS

The burden of proof weighs heavily on those who would abolish a moral proscription so deeply rooted in public and professional morals and in so many cultural traditions. However, a review of the major arguments advanced in favor of euthanasia does not sustain the necessary burden of proof.

The Distinction Between Killing and Letting Die

Advocates of euthanasia reason that there is no moral distinction between killing the patient and letting the patient die by deliberate withdrawal or withholding of life support or lifesaving treatment. This argument ignores the fact that in euthanasia, the physician is the immediate cause of a death that she fully intends. This act differs from withholding or withdrawing treatment. When treatment is discontinued, it is the disease that kills the patient. In so-called passive euthanasia, we remove our intervention for good reasons (for example, it is no longer effective or beneficial and its burdens are disproportionate). To continue treatment would be unethical, since futile, burdensome, and expensive treatments would be forced on the patient in violation of the canons of good medicine and of the patient's best interests. Adherence to these canons is a primary professional obligation. The physician also violates this moral canon if she continues with unnecessary, burdensome, or futile treatment.

James Rachels, who makes the most extended case against the distinction between killing and letting die, admits that the general sentiment that favors such distinction has some weight. He argues that such intuitions should be distrusted, however, because the well-off members of society have more to fear from relaxing the prohibition against active euthanasia than letting people die.[5] This is an unconvincing argument that begs the question of interest.

When the patient is "overmastered by the disease," to use the Hippocratic phraseology, we have a moral obligation to stop treatment, since our interventions serve no beneficial purpose.[6] When we do so, the natural course of the disease supervenes. The disease, not the physician, kills the patient.

Proponents of euthanasia also argue that there is no distinction between euthanasia and giving a patient morphine to relieve pain that could end in death from respiratory depression. This is a specious argument, because under these circumstances the primary intention is not to kill the patient as in active euthanasia, but to relieve pain; if death occurs, it is the result of a side effect of a powerful drug. Physicians use hazardous drugs and perform many operations in precarious cases where the intent is to help. The risk of dangerous side effects is tolerable, if benefits can be achieved in no other way. The use of morphine would be euthanasia only if the dose were deliberately calculated to cause respiratory depression. Rather, the effort is to titrate the dose, so as to achieve the beneficial and avoid the harmful effect. This titration is not controllable by formula. It may be in error, but the risks of side effects are outweighed by the proportionate potential for pain relief.

Euthanasia and Patient Autonomy

A second argument for euthanasia justifies it on grounds of respect for the moral right of autonomy and the dignity of the person. The logic of this assertion is suspect. When a patient opts for euthanasia, he uses his freedom to give up his freedom. In the name of autonomy, the patient chooses to eradicate life and consciousness, the indispensable conditions for the operation of autonomy. He loses control over a whole set of options, all of which cannot be foreseen and many of which would be of importance if life—the basis of freedom—had hot been forgone. Moreover, if suffering is so intense that it limits all other options, and euthanasia is the only choice, then that choice is really not free. Seriously ill persons suffer commonly from alienation, guilt, and feelings of unworthiness. They often perceive themselves, and are perceived by others, as economic, social, and emotional burdens. They are exquisitely susceptible to even the most subtle suggestion by physician, nurse, or family member that reinforces their guilt, shame, or sense of unworthiness. It takes as much courage to resist these subliminal confirmations of alienation as to withstand the physical ravages of the disease. Much of the suffering of dying patients comes from being subtly treated as nonpersons. The decision to seek euthanasia is often an indictment against those who treat or care for the patient. If the emotional impediments to freedom and autonomy are removed, and pain is properly relieved, there is evidence that many would not choose euthanasia.[7]

Euthanasia is too often an act of desperation that physician, family, and friends can forestall. To do so, they must provide the understanding, support, and sharing that will assure the sick person that she is still very much a member of the human community going through an experience everyone will eventually share.

Beneficence

The most powerful argument for euthanasia is based upon compassion, mercy, and beneficence. These are obligations intrinsic to medicine as a healing art. Even those who see meaning in suffering urge comfort and relief of pain for the dying. Compassion and mercy would seem to override all other considerations.

The duty of beneficence indeed obliges the physician to help the patient to a good and gentle death. It is also compassionate and morally commendable to help a person to die well. A good death completes life with a finale befitting our true dignity as thinking, conscious, and social beings. The aim of medicine should be to facilitate a death that is as pain-free as possible but that is also a human experience. We can justify euthanasia for our pets precisely because they cannot possibly understand suffering or dying. They cannot die in a "human" way. But humans can grow morally even with negative experiences. A good death contributes something valuable to the whole human community. It enables us to assess our human relationships and to come to grips with the important and ultimate questions of human destiny, which believers and nonbelievers alike must confront. A good death is the last act of a drama, which euthanasia artificially terminates before the drama is really completed.

Some might object that all of this can be achieved in preparation for euthanasia and, even more effectively, before suffering makes rational thought difficult. But is this really so? How much of the quality of our deaths is dependent on living through the experience as it presents itself? To cut off this experience abruptly is to abort what might be the most important experience of our lives and a contribution to the lives of family, friends, and those who attend us. Often we see ourselves most clearly at the hour of our death. We see what we have made of ourselves. Critical times force us to reveal and confront the inner self. Artifices and circumlocution are no longer acceptable. Euthanasia deprives us of these last insights into who and what we have been, and it closes the door on the final accounting we may want to make.

Finally, there is the illusion that a life that is free of all anxiety, suffering, or misfortune is the "good" life. But, such a life is devoid of opportunity for expression of some of our most characteristically human feelings—mercy, compassion, understanding, empathy, love, and giving of ourselves to others. To be sure, dying persons can teach us good and bad lessons. A "good" death helps all of us to become more humane—something we lose easily in the sanitized, atomistic, hedonistic world in which we live. Miguel de Unamuno may not have been entirely wrong when he wrote: "Suffering is the substance of life and the root of personality. Only suffering makes us persons."[8] This is not an argument for letting patients suffer, but it does suggest that inevitable suffering may serve some purposes that are not immediately apparent. The lives of many of the handicapped, the retarded, and the aged teach us much about courage and personal growth and give some substance to Unamuno's observation. . . .

The Necessity of Euthanasia

From the medical point of view, even if euthanasia were morally licit, does it follow that it is necessary? The motivation for euthanasia arises principally from two worries: fear of intolerable pain, suffering, and anguish, and fear of becoming a victim of overzealous physicians and dehumanizing medical technologies. These are legitimate worries, but both are well within the power of medicine to remedy without resort to euthanasia. Improved measures for relief of pain and anxiety are already available. It still remains for physicians to use them effectively.[9] We must be unequivocal about physicians' duty to do so. The current trend to active euthanasia only underscores the moral obligations of physicians to practice competent analgesia, to understand why the patient requests death, and to deal with and remove those reasons in a program of palliative care.[10]

Hospice programs or palliative care offer comprehensive alternatives to euthanasia that are more respectful of beneficence and autonomy than killing. They relieve pain and anxiety, prepare the patient for the experience of dying, anticipate the need and value of advance directives, and establish understanding between patient and physician about which life-support measures are acceptable to the patient and which are not. These programs enlist the help of family and friends to make dying a communal experience, in which the dying person contributes something positive to those around her as well as to her own growth as a person. The physician's obligation to act beneficently and to show respect for the patient's dignity is better served by these measures than by killing the patient.

Plebiscite Ethics

Another line of argument relies on the fact that "polls" show that a majority of people favor legalizing euthanasia. . . .

From the ethical point of view, arguments based on the results of polls assume that a plebiscite, a majority opinion, or even true consensus can establish what is right and good. Equally specious is the argument that if a practice exists widely, it should become law so it can be regulated. Or, that what becomes legal is therefore moral. And what is no longer secret gains moral credibility by being exposed to the "light of day."

These arguments are seriously flawed. There have been too many instances in human history—past and present—of immoral laws (segregation, slavery, suppression of the rights of women and children, and so forth). There have also been morally distorted societies in which popular approval and law condoned serious violations of human rights (Nazi Germany, Stalinist Russia, and Fascist Spain and Italy, for example). Something more philosophically cogent than public opinion, national sentiment, or law is needed to make a cogent case for the moral acceptability of euthanasia.

DISTORTION OF THE
HEALING RELATIONSHIP

Even if euthanasia did not have the deficiencies in moral reasoning I have outlined, it would be morally dubious in the light of the "internal morality" of medicine itself. By internal morality, I mean the moral obligations that devolve upon physicians by virtue of the nature of medical activity.[11] On this score, I am in agreement with Leon Kass[12] that euthanasia is a serious violation of the moral nature and purposes of medicine.

I have discussed my own philosophy of medicine elsewhere and will only summarize a few points here. Medicine is a healing relationship. Its long-term goal is restoration or cultivation of health; its more proximate goal is healing and helping a particular patient in a particular clinical situation. Medicine restores health when this is possible, and enables the patient to cope with disability and death when cure is not possible. The aims of medicine are positive, even when death is inevitable. Healing can occur even when cure is impossible. The patient can become "whole" again if the health-care professional helps him to live with a disability, to face dying, and to live as human a life as circumstances will allow.

Medicine is also ineradicably grounded in trust.[13] The physician invokes trust when she offers to help. The patient is forced to trust, because he is vulnerable and lacks the power to cure himself without help. The patient is dependent upon the physician's good will and character. The physician—to be faithful to the trust built into the relationship with the patient—must seek to heal, and not to remove the need for healing by killing the patient. When euthanasia is a possible option, this trust relationship is seriously distorted. Healing now includes killing. The already awesome powers of the doctor are expanded enormously. When cure is impossible, healing is displaced by killing. How can patients trust that the doctor will pursue every effective and beneficent measure when she can relieve herself of a difficult challenge by influencing the patient to choose death?

Uncertainty and mistrust are already too much a part of the healing relationship. Euthanasia magnifies these ordinary and natural anxieties. How will the patient know whether the physician is trying to heal or relinquishing the effort to cure or contain illness because she favors euthanasia, devalues the quality of the patient's life, or wants to conserve society's resources? The physician can easily divert attention from a good death by subtly leading the patient to believe that euthanasia is the only good or gentle death.

This is not a blanket indictment of the character of physicians. But the doctor is an ordinary human being called to perform extraordinary tasks. Her character is rarely faultless. We cannot simply say the "good" doctor would never abuse the privilege of euthanasia. Whose agent is the doctor when treatment becomes marginal and costs escalate? Will the physician's notion of benevolence to society become malevolent for the older patient? How can the aged be secure in the hands of younger physicians whose notion of a "quality" life may not include the gentler pleasures of aging that Cicero praised in the *De Senectute*? Can patients trust physicians when physicians arrogate to themselves the role of rationers of society's resources or are made to assume this role by societal policy? We already hear much talk of the social burdens imposed by chronically ill, handicapped, terminal adults and children and the necessity of rationing with the physician as gatekeeper.[14]

Moreover, there are clinical imponderables that can undermine the physician's judgment. To define a pain as intolerable, to distinguish gradations of suffering, and to prognosticate accurately are difficult enough in themselves. These difficulties are easily compounded when the patient pleads for release or the physician is frustrated, emotionally spent, or inclined to impose his or her values on the patient. When the proscription against killing is eroded, trust in the doctor cannot survive. This is already apparent in Holland, that great social laboratory for euthanasia. According to some observers, older and handicapped people are fearful of entering Dutch hospitals and nursing homes.[15] Older Dutch physicians have confided to some of us their personal fears of being admitted to their own hospitals. There is anecdotal evidence of physicians falsifying data to justify euthanasia, making egregious mistakes in diagnosis and prognosis, entering into collusion with families, and ordering involuntary euthanasia.[16] These anecdotal impressions must be better documented. Further study of the Dutch experience is therefore crucial for any society contemplating euthanasia as public policy. Present evidence indicates that the slippery slope—conceptual and actual—is no ethical myth but a reality in Holland.[17] When the physician who traditionally had only the power to heal and to help can now also kill, the medical fiduciary relationship—one of the oldest in human history—cannot survive.

There is also the serious effect on the physician's own psyche of premeditated, socially sanctioned killing. To some degree, physicians are desensitized to loss of life by their experiences with the anatomy lab, autopsy operating rooms, and the performance of painful procedures. To carry out their duties, doctors must steel themselves against suffering and death to avoid being emotionally paralyzed in the actions they must take daily. Euthanasia reinforces this objectification of death and dying, and further desensitizes to killing. A "gentle" death, as Van der Veer wants to call it, is still a premeditated, efficiently executed death of a living human being.[18] . . .

The medical profession is a moral community.[19] Its members have a collective moral responsibility to patients and society. For this reason, the whole profession must oppose the legalization of euthanasia as detrimental to the welfare of patients and the integrity of society. Individual physicians cannot abstain on grounds that they oppose euthanasia but believe in free choice. The social nature of the acts of dying and killing do not permit anyone to choose such a socially destructive option. This is why the American Medical Association and British Medical Association have recently reaffirmed the proscription against doctors killing patients under any circumstance.[20]

THE SOCIAL IMPACT OF EUTHANASIA

Much as libertarians would like to see euthanasia as an individual decision protected by an absolute privacy right, it is an event inescapably fraught with social significance. A society that sanctions killing must abandon the long-standing tradition of "state's interest" in human life.[21] This devalues all life but especially the lives of certain citizens—the chronically ill, the aged, and the handicapped. Those who do not take the easy exit that legalized euthanasia offers become selfish overconsumers of their neighbors' resources. The vaunted autonomy of the choice for euthanasia withers in the face of the subtle coercion of a social policy that suggests the incurably ill are a social, economic, and emotional burden. Few of us would not feel the pressure to do the "noble" thing and ask for euthanasia, especially if the physician is gently urging us to do so.

The social sanction of euthanasia presumes a responsibility to monitor the killing process to keep it within agreed upon constraints. Killing then becomes bureaucratized and standardized. But even with standardization of criteria, it is impossible to contain euthanasia within specified boundaries. Laws will not prevent abuses, despite the hopes of those who favor legalization in the United States. The Dutch experience shows that even when euthanasia is not legal but is tolerated, expansion of its boundaries—from voluntary to involuntary, from adults to children, from terminally ill to chronically ill, from intolerable suffering to dissatisfaction with the quality of life, from consent to contrived consent—is inevitable.[22] The ethical proscription against killing by doctors is a social sea wall. Once it is breached, it is impossible to avoid inundation. . . .

Another imminent social danger is the real possibility that euthanasia will converge with the current trend toward rationing of health-care resources. It is a short way from the need to contain costs to covertly or overtly planned euthanasia for those members of our society who present the greatest economic burdens. At the beginning, some might suggest rationing needed care to retarded or handicapped infants, very old people, or those with fatal, incurable diseases like Alzheimer's. Once euthanasia, in any of its forms, is legalized, the temptation to encourage its use, tacitly or overtly, to alleviate one of our most socially vexing problems—the increasing scarcity of health-care dollars—will be strong. This could be the first slip on the slippery slope, which leads inexorably from voluntary to nonvoluntary euthanasia. This is evident already in the recent Dutch government report on euthanasia in the Netherlands.[23] . . .

Rachels chooses to rely on the "good sense of judges and juries" and the medical profession to prevent abuses. In any case, he argues, the good results will outweigh whatever abuses might occur.[24] But experience in Holland and in the current debate in the United States suggests that this may not be the case at all. Rachels is right when he says that the slippery slope is the "outstanding argument" against legalized euthanasia, and he is seriously wrong when he disposes of its reality so cavalierly.

The arguments for making assisted suicide a moral option, moral duty, or legal choice are equally indefensible.[25] The arguments adduced here against euthanasia apply as well to assisted suicide. Physicians are *de facto* moral accomplices in what happens to their patients. Even when they are moved by compassion, as was Dr. Timothy Quill (the physician who recently revealed his role in a euthanasia case in the *New England Journal of Medicine*), physicians cannot morally justify cooperation in terminating the patient's life.[26] They cannot excuse themselves by a professional "Pontius Pilate Act" if they provide the lethal drugs and the directions for their effective use. This is indefensible moral cooperation, in that it shares the patient's intent to commit suicide. Further, the doctor's cooperation is essential for the patient to achieve his or her purpose. . . .

The proponents of euthanasia are right—legalization is impossible without cooperation of the medical profession. And for all the reasons I have given, physicians cannot cooperate in the killing of their patients directly or indirectly.

OBLIGATIONS OF PHYSICIANS
WHO REJECT EUTHANASIA

What are the moral obligations of physicians who reject all forms of euthanasia? To begin with, we must accept responsibility for confronting the reality of pain and suffering—the fear and emotional traumata of the fatally ill and dying person and the legitimate desire for a good death. We must counter the destructive force of euthanasia with a constructive effort. If, as I have argued, killing is not a good death, what can we—indeed, what must we—as physicians do to help the patient achieve as good a death as possible without killing him? First of all, physicians must recognize that the request for euthanasia is a plea for help and an attempt to regain some measure of control over one's life that fatal illness seems to take away so forcibly. Why does this particular patient want to be killed? Is it pain, suffering, loss of dignity, depression? Is it a challenge to see whether the physician, family, and friends really do care? Is it a test to see if the family really regards the patient as a burden? Is it fear of bankrupting the family, fear of being kept alive artificially to no purpose, or a response to the doctor's attitude of futility or disinterest? There are many reasons for the request to be killed and many remedies once we know the reason.

We must assure patients that they can control the starting and stopping of life-sustaining measures by advance directives when they lose their competence to do so as the disease progresses. Physicians should dispose of their own anxiety about making patients into addicts. Pain relief competently applied is a moral obligation, as are all other supportive measures. Addiction in the last weeks of life and even death as an unintended side effect of analgesia are morally defensible. Physicians unable or unwilling to make the investment of time and emotion required for comprehensive palliative care should not care for patients who need such care. They would be better placed in specialties that do not often confront terminal illness.

The advocates of legalized euthanasia are right when they insist that the physician is crucial to any effective social policy permitting patients to be killed on request. Doctors do have the necessary knowledge. They do control the prescription of the necessary lethal agents. They do know when the patient's diagnosis and prognosis portend a painful and inevitable death. These very facts impose an enormous moral responsibility on the profession to resist becoming moral accomplices or society's designated killers.

If euthanasia is legalized, the medical profession will bear a large burden of the blame if it does not educate the public to the dangers and if it fails to refuse to participate. The profession must also work to alleviate the societal conditions that foster euthanasia—the attitude of hopelessness and futility before death and dying, the financial pressures that all too forcibly convince the patient that he is a burden, and the illusion that life must be perfect and that any chance illness is an affront to human dignity. The profession as a whole must make it morally mandatory to make competent use of all measures that relieve pain and suffering.

There is much that physicians, individually and as a profession, can—and must—do short of killing patients to eliminate the problem of suffering. Legalization of euthanasia poses a far deeper moral challenge than the profession may appreciate. It challenges us to define what it really means to be a physician.

All morally responsible, compassionate, and merciful physicians share the same goal when confronted with a suffering, dying, terminally ill human being. They all strive to assist the suffering person to achieve a gentle and good death. They all share the "objective to do good," . . . What we do not share is the definition of "the good to be done." A good death does not, I have argued, include killing the patient, nor can one be a good physician and do so.

NOTES

1. D. C. Thomasma and G. C. Graber, *Euthanasia: Toward an Ethical Social Policy* (New York: Continuum, 1991), 1-11.

2. J. Rachels, *The End of Life* (New York: Oxford, 1986), 106-28.

3. M. A. M. de Wachter, "Active Euthanasia in the Netherlands" [Special Communication], *Journal of the American Medical Association* 23 (1989): 3316-19.

4. E. D. Pellegrino and D. C. Thomasma, *Helping and Healing: Religious Commitment and Health Care* (New York: Continuum, in press).

5. J. Rachels, "Killing and Starving to Death," *Philosophy* 54 (April 1979): 159-71.

6. *Hippocrates,* vol. 2, trans. W. H. S. Jones, Loeb Classical Library Series (Cambridge, MA: Harvard, 1981): 193-203.

7. N. Coyle, "The Last Four Weeks of Life," *American Journal of Nursing* 90 (December 1990): 75-78.

8. M. de Unamuno, "The Tragic Sense of Life," in *Men and Notions,* trans. A. Kerrigan, Bollingen Series 85, no. 4 (Princeton, NJ: Princeton University Press, 1972), 224.

9. Agency for Health Care Policy and Research, *Clinical Practical Guideline: Acute Pain Management: Operative or Medical Procedures and Trauma* (Washington, DC: US Department of Health and Human Services, 1992).

10. J. Lynn, "The Health Care Professional's Role When Active Euthanasia Is Sought," *Journal of Palliative Care* 4, nos. 1-2 (1988): 100-2.

11. E. D. Pellegrino, "The Healing Relationship: The Architectonics of Clinical Medicine," in *The Clinical Encounter: The Moral Fabric of the Patient-Physician Relationship,* Philosophy and Medicine Series 4, ed. Earl Shelp (Dordrecht, Holland: D. Reidel Publishing, 1983), 153-72.

12. L. Kass, "Neither for Love Nor Money: Why Doctors Must Not Kill," *Public Interest* 94 (Winter 1989): 25-46.

13. E. D. Pellegrino, "Trust and Distrust in Professional Ethics," in *Ethics, Trust, and the Professions: Philosophical and Cultural Aspects,* ed. E. D. Pellegrino, R. M. Veatch, and J. P. Langan (Washington, DC: Georgetown University Press, 1991), 68-89.

14. E. D. Pellegrino, "Rationing Health Care: The Ethics of Medical Gatekeeping," *Journal of Contemporary Health Law and Policy* 2 (Spring 1986): 23-45.

15. R. Fenigson, "A Case Against Dutch Euthanasia," *Hastings Center Report* 19, no. 1 (1989): 522-30; R. Fenigson, "Euthanasia in the Netherlands," *Issues in Law and Medicine* 6, no. 3 (1990): 229-45.

16. H. Ten Have, "Euthanasia in the Netherlands: The Legal Context and the Cases," *HEC Forum* 1. no. 1 (1989): 41–45.

17. I. Van der Sluis, "The Practice of Euthanasia in the Netherlands," *Issues in Law and Medicine* 4, no. 4 (1989): 455–65; B. Bostrom, "Euthanasia in the Netherlands, A Model for the United States?" *Issues in Law and Medicine* 4, no. 4 (1989): 467–86; C. F. Gomez, *Regulating Death: Euthanasia and the Case of the Netherlands* (New York: Free Press/Macmillan, 1991).

18. C. Van der Meer, "Euthanasia: A Definition and Ethical Conditions," *Journal of Palliative Care* 4, nos. 1–2 (1988), 103–6.

19. E. D. Pellegrino, "The Medical Profession as a Moral Community," *Bulletin of the New York Academy of Medicine* 66A, no. 3 (1990): 221–32.

20. *Euthanasia: Report Council on Ethical and Judicial Affairs of the American Medical Association* (Chicago: AMA, 1989); *Euthanasia: Report Working Part to Review the British Medical Association Guidance in Euthanasia* (London: BMA, May 1988), 69.

21. H. Tristram Engelhardt, Jr., "Fashioning an Ethic for Life and Death in a Post-Modern Society," *Hastings Center Report,* Special Supplement: *Mercy, Murder and Morality: Perspectives in Euthanasia,* 19, no. 1 (1989): 13–15.

22. R. Fenigson, "A Case Against Dutch Euthanasia."

23. P. J. Van Der Maas, J. J. M. van Delden, L. Pijnenborg, and C. W. N. Looman, "Euthanasia and Other Medical Decisions Concerning the End of Life," *Lancet* 338 (14 September 1991): 669–74.

24. J. Rachels, *The End of Life,* 187.

25. S. H. Wanzer, D. D. Federman, St. Edelstein, *et al.,* "The Physician's Responsibility Toward Hopelessly Ill Patients, A Second Look," *New England Journal of Medicine* 320 (1989): 884–89; C. K. Cassel and D. E. Meier, "Morals and Moralism in the Debate Over Euthanasia and Assisted Suicide," *New England Journal of Medicine* 323 (1990): 750–52.

26. T. E. Quill, "Death and Dignity: A Case of Individualized Decision-Making," *New England Journal of Medicine* 324 (1991): 691–94.

Voluntary Active Euthanasia
Dan W. Brock

Dan Brock is a philosophy professor and the director of the Center for Biomedical Ethics at Brown University. Brock's primary purpose in this essay is to clarify the considerations and issues underlying the debate about active euthanasia, since he believes those issues to be more complex than those engaged in the debate have realized. With reservations, Brock concludes that the considerations in favor of the moral permissibility and legalization of voluntary active euthanasia are stronger than those against. Active euthanasia is primarily supported, he believes, by the values of individual well-being and self-determination (or autonomy). The former gives us reason to end life when it becomes a burden rather than a benefit, and the latter gives us reason to respect an individual's choice about the manner and time in which he or she dies. Opponents of active euthanasia do not deny these values but rather claim that other moral considerations leading to the rejection of active euthanasia are weightier. In response to the claim that physicians must not intentionally kill, Brock suggests that this consideration would equally condemn passive euthanasia and hence is not a suitable basis for argument by those who accept passive but reject active euthanasia. He finally considers the possible good and bad consequences of permitting active euthanasia, concluding with his belief—about which he does not feel certain—that the good consequences would outweigh the bad.

Since the case of Karen Quinlan first seized public attention fifteen years ago, no issue in biomedical ethics has been more prominent than the debate about forgoing life-sustaining treatment. Controversy continues regarding some aspects of that debate, such as forgoing life-sustaining nutrition and hydration, and relevant law varies some from state to state. Nevertheless, I believe it is possible to identify an emerging consensus that competent patients, or the surrogates of incompetent patients, should be permitted to weigh the benefits and burdens of alternative treatments, including the alternative of no treatment, according to the patient's values, and either to refuse any treatment or to select from among available alternative treatments. This consensus is reflected in bioethics scholarship, in reports of prestigious bodies such as the President's Commission for the Study of Ethical Problems in Medicine, The Hastings Center, and the American Medical Association, in a large body of judicial decisions in courts around the country, and finally in the beliefs and practices of health care professionals who care for dying patients.[1]

More recently, significant public and professional attention has shifted from life-sustaining treatment to euthanasia—more specifically, voluntary active euthanasia—and to physician-assisted suicide. Several factors have contributed

From *The Hastings Center Report* 22 (March–April 1992), 10–22.

to the increased interest in euthanasia. In the Netherlands, it has been openly practiced by physicians for several years with the acceptance of the country's highest court.[2] In 1988 there was an unsuccessful attempt to get the question of whether it should be made legally permissible on the ballot in California. In November 1991 voters in the state of Washington defeated a widely publicized referendum proposal to legalize both voluntary active euthanasia and physician-assisted suicide. Finally, some cases of this kind, such as "It's Over, Debbie," described in the *Journal of the American Medical Association,* the "suicide machine" of Dr. Jack Kevorkian, and the cancer patient "Diane" of Dr. Timothy Quill, have captured wide public and professional attention.[3] Unfortunately, the first two of these cases were sufficiently problematic that even most supporters of euthanasia or assisted suicide did not defend the physicians' actions in them. As a result, the subsequent debate they spawned has often shed more heat than light. My aim is to increase the light, and perhaps as well to reduce the heat, on this important subject by formulating and evaluating the central ethical arguments for and against voluntary active euthanasia and physician-assisted suicide. My evaluation of the arguments leads me, with reservations to be noted, to support permitting both practices. My primary aim, however, is not to argue for euthanasia, but to identify confusion in some common arguments, and problematic assumptions and claims that need more defense of data in others. The issues are considerably more complex than either supporters or opponents often make out; my hope is to advance the debate by focusing attention on what I believe the real issues under discussion should be.

In the recent bioethics literature some have endorsed physician-assisted suicide but not euthanasia.[4] Are they sufficiently different that the moral arguments for one often do not apply to the other? A paradigm case of physician-assisted suicide is a patient's ending his or her life with a lethal dose of a medication requested of and provided by a physician for that purpose. A paradigm case of voluntary active euthanasia is a physician's administering the lethal dose, often because the patient is unable to do so. The only difference that need exist between the two is the person who actually administers the lethal dose—the physician or the patient. In each, the physician plays an active and necessary causal role.

In physician-assisted suicide the patient acts last (for example, Janet Adkins herself pushed the button after Dr. Kevorkian hooked her up to his suicide machine), whereas in euthanasia the physician acts last by performing the physical equivalent of pushing the button. In both cases, however, the choice rests fully with the patient. In both the patient acts last in the sense of retaining the right to change his or her mind until the point at which the lethal process becomes irreversible. How could there be a substantial moral difference between the two based only on this small difference in the part played by the physician in the causal process resulting in death? Of course, it might be held that the moral difference is clear and important—in euthanasia the physician kills the patient whereas in physician-assisted suicide the patient kills him- or herself. But this is misleading at best. In assisted suicide the physician and patient together kill the patient. To see this, suppose a physician supplied a lethal dose to a patient with the knowledge and intent that the patient will wrongfully administer it to another. We would have no difficulty in morality or the law recognizing this as a case of joint action to kill for which both are responsible.

If there is no significant intrinsic moral difference between the two, it is also difficult to see why public or legal policy should permit one but not the other; worries about abuse or about giving anyone dominion over the lives of others apply equally to either. As a result, I will take the arguments evaluated below to apply to both and will focus on euthanasia.

My concern here will be with *voluntary* euthanasia only—that is, with the case in which a clearly competent patient makes a fully voluntary and persistent request for aid in dying. Involuntary euthanasia, in which a competent patient explicitly refuses or opposes receiving euthanasia, and nonvoluntary euthanasia, in which a patient is incompetent and unable to express his or her wishes about euthanasia, will be considered here only as potential unwanted side-effects of permitting voluntary euthanasia. I emphasize as well that I am concerned with *active* euthanasia, not withholding or withdrawing life-sustaining treatment, which some commentators characterize as "passive euthanasia." Finally, I will be concerned with euthanasia where the motive of those who perform it is to respect the wishes of the patient and to provide the patient with a "good death," though one important issue is whether a change in legal policy could restrict the performance of euthanasia to only those cases.

THE CENTRAL ETHICAL ARGUMENT
FOR VOLUNTARY ACTIVE EUTHANASIA

The central ethical argument for euthanasia is familiar. It is that the very same two fundamental ethical values supporting the consensus on patient's rights to decide about life-sustaining treatment also support the ethical permissibility of euthanasia. These values are individual self-determination or autonomy and individual well-being. By self-determination as it bears on euthanasia, I mean people's interest in making important decisions about their lives for themselves according to their own values or conceptions of a good life, and in being left free to act on those decisions. Self-determination is valuable because it permits people to form and live in accordance with their own conception of a good life, at least within the bounds of justice and consistent with others doing so as well. In exercising self-determination people take responsibility for their lives and for the kinds of persons they become. A central aspect of human dignity lies in people's capacity to direct their lives in this way. The value of exercising self-determination presupposes some minimum of decision-making capacities or competence, which thus limits the scope of euthanasia supported by self-determination; it cannot justifiably be administered, for example, in cases of serious dementia or treatable clinical depression.

Does the value of individual self-determination extend to the time and manner of one's death? Most people are very concerned about the nature of the last stage of their lives. This reflects not just a fear of experiencing substantial suffering when dying, but also a desire to retain dignity and control during this last period of life. Death is today increasingly preceded by a long period of significant physical and mental decline, due in part to the technological interventions of modern medicine. Many people adjust to these disabilities and find meaning and value in new activities and ways. Others find the impairments and burdens in the last stage of their lives at some point sufficiently great to make life no longer worth living. For many patients near death, maintaining the quality of one's life, avoiding great suffering, maintaining one's dignity, and insuring that others remember us as we wish them to become of paramount importance and outweigh merely extending one's life. But there is no single, objectively correct answer for everyone as to when, if at all, one's life becomes all things considered a burden and unwanted. If self-determination is a fundamental value, then the great variability among people on this question makes it especially important that individuals control the manner, circumstances, and timing of their dying and death.

The other main value that supports euthanasia is individual well-being. It might seem that individual well-being conflicts with a person's self-determination when the person requests euthanasia. Life itself is commonly taken to be a central good for persons, often valued for its own sake, as well as necessary for pursuit of all other goods within a life. But when a competent patient decides to forgo all further life-sustaining treatment then the patient, either explicitly or implicitly, commonly decides that the best life possible for him or her with treatment is of sufficiently poor quality that it is worse than no further life at all. Life is no longer considered a benefit by the patient, but has now become a burden. The same judgment underlies a request for euthanasia: continued life is seen by the patient as no longer a benefit, but now a burden. Especially in the often severely compromised and debilitated states of many critically ill or dying patients, there is no objective standard, but only the competent patient's judgment of whether continued life is no longer a benefit.

Of course, sometimes there are conditions, such as clinical depression, that call into question whether the patient has made a competent choice, either to forgo life-sustaining treatment or to seek euthanasia, and then the patient's choice need not be evidence that continued life is no longer a benefit for him or her. Just as with decisions about treatment, a determination of incompetence can warrant not honoring the patient's choice; in the case of treatment, we then transfer decisional authority to a surrogate, though in the case of voluntary active euthanasia a determination that the patient is incompetent means that choice is not possible.

The value or right of self-determination does not entitle patients to compel physicians to act contrary to their own moral or professional values.

Physicians are moral and professional agents whose own self-determination or integrity should be respected as well. If performing euthanasia became legally permissible, but conflicted with a particular physician's reasonable understanding of his or her moral or professional responsibilities, the care of a patient who requested euthanasia should be transferred to another.

Most opponents do not deny that there are some cases in which the values of patient self-determination and well-being support euthanasia. Instead, they commonly offer two kinds of arguments against it that on their view outweigh or override this support. The first kind of argument is that in any individual case where considerations of the patient's self-determination and well-being do support euthanasia, it is nevertheless always ethically wrong or impermissible. The second kind of argument grants that in some individual cases euthanasia may *not* be ethically wrong, but maintains nonetheless that public and legal policy should never permit it. The first kind of argument focuses on features of any individual case of euthanasia, while the second kind focuses on social or legal policy. In the next section I consider the first kind of argument.

EUTHANASIA IS THE DELIBERATE KILLING OF AN INNOCENT PERSON

The claim that any individual instance of euthanasia is a case of deliberate killing of an innocent person is, with only minor qualifications, correct. If the deliberate killing of an innocent person is wrong, euthanasia would be nearly always impermissible.

In the context of medicine, the ethical prohibition against deliberately killing the innocent derives some of its plausibility from the belief that nothing in the currently accepted practice of medicine is deliberate killing. The belief that doctors do not in fact kill requires the corollary belief that forgoing life-sustaining treatment, whether by not starting or by stopping treatment, is allowing to die, not killing. Common though this view is, I shall argue that it is confused and mistaken.

Why is the common view mistaken? Consider the case of a patient terminally ill with ALS disease. She is completely respirator dependent with no hope of ever being weaned. She is unquestionably competent but finds her condition intolerable and persistently requests to be removed from the respirator and allowed to die. Most people and physicians would agree that the patient's physician should respect the patient's wishes and remove her from the respirator, though this will certainly cause the patient's death. The common understanding is that the physician thereby allows the patient to die. But is that correct?

Suppose the patient has a greedy and hostile son who mistakenly believes that his mother will never decide to stop her life-sustaining treatment and that even if she did her physician would not remove her from the respirator. Afraid that his inheritance will be dissipated by a long and expensive hospitalization, he enters his mother's room while she is sedated, extubates her, and she dies. Shortly thereafter the medical staff discovers what he has done and confronts the son. He replies, "I didn't kill her, I merely allowed her to die. It was her ALS disease that caused her death." I think this would rightly be dismissed as transparent sophistry—the son went into his mother's room and deliberately killed her. But, of course, the son performed just the same physical actions, did just the same thing, that the physician would have done. If that is so, then doesn't the physician also kill the patient when he extubates her?

I underline immediately that there are important ethical differences between what the physician and the greedy son do. First, the physician acts with the patient's consent whereas the son does not. Second, the physician acts with a good motive—to respect the patient's wishes and self-determination—whereas the son acts with a bad motive—to protect his own inheritance. Third, the physician acts in a social role through which he is legally authorized to carry out the patient's wishes regarding treatment whereas the son has no such authorization. These and perhaps other ethically important differences show that what the physician did was morally justified whereas what the son did was morally wrong. What they do *not* show, however, is that the son killed while the physician allowed to die. One can either kill or allow to die with or without consent, with a good or bad motive, within or outside of a social role that authorizes one to do so. . . .

Suppose that killing is worse than allowing to die and that withdrawing life support is not killing, although euthanasia is. Euthanasia still need not for that reason be morally wrong. To see this, we need to determine the basic principle for the moral evaluation of killing persons. What is it that makes paradigm cases of wrongful killing wrongful? One very plausible answer is that killing denies the victim something that he or she values greatly—continued life or a future. Moreover, since continued life is necessary for pursuing any of a person's plans and purposes, killing brings the frustration of all of these plans and desires as well. In a nutshell, wrongful killing deprives a person of a valued future, and of all the person wanted and planned to do in that future.

A natural expression of this account of the wrongness of killing is that people have a moral right not to be killed.[5] But in this account of the wrongness of killing, the right not to be killed, like other rights, should be waivable when the person makes a competent decision that continued life is no longer wanted or a good, but is instead worse than no further life at all. In this view, euthanasia is properly understood as a case of a person having waived his or her right not to be killed.

This rights view of the wrongness of killing is not, of course, universally shared. Many people's moral views about killing have their origins in religious views that human life comes from God and cannot be justifiably destroyed or taken away, either by the person whose life it is or by another. But in a pluralistic society like our own with a strong commitment to freedom of religion, public policy should not be grounded in religious beliefs which many in that society reject. I turn now to the general evaluation of public policy on euthanasia.

WOULD THE BAD CONSEQUENCES OF EUTHANASIA OUTWEIGH THE GOOD?

The argument against euthanasia at the policy level is stronger than at the level of individual cases, though even here I believe the case is ultimately unpersuasive, or at best indecisive. The policy level is the place where the main issues lie, however, and where moral considerations that might override arguments in favor of euthanasia will be found, if they are found anywhere. It is important to note two kinds of disagreement about the consequences for public policy of permitting euthanasia. First, there is empirical or factual disagreement about what the consequences would be. This disagreement is greatly exacerbated by the lack of firm data on the issue. Second, since on any reasonable assessment there would be both good and bad consequences, there are moral disagreements about the relative importance of different effects. In addition to these two sources of disagreement, there is also no single, well-specified policy proposal for legalizing euthanasia on which policy assessments can focus. But without such specification, and especially without explicit procedures for protecting against well-intentioned misuse and ill-intentioned abuse, the consequences for policy are largely speculative. Despite these difficulties, a preliminary account of the main likely good and bad consequences is possible. This should help clarify where better data or more moral analysis and argument are needed, as well as where policy safeguards must be developed.

Potential Good Consequences of Permitting Euthanasia

What are the likely good consequences? First, if euthanasia were permitted it would be possible to respect the self-determination of competent patients who want it, but now cannot get it because of its illegality. We simply do not know how many such patients and people there are. Even with better data on the number of persons who want euthanasia but cannot get it, significant moral disagreement would remain about how much weight should be given to any instance of failure to respect a person's self-determination in this way.

One important factor substantially affecting the number of persons who would seek euthanasia is the extent to which an alternative is available. The widespread acceptance in the law, social policy, and medical practice of the right of a competent patient to forgo life-sustaining treatment suggests that the number of competent persons in the United States who would want euthanasia if it were permitted is probably relatively small.

A second good consequence of making euthanasia legally permissible benefits a much larger group. Polls have shown that a majority of the American public believes that people should have a right to obtain euthanasia if they want it.[6] No doubt the vast majority of those who support this right to euthanasia will never in fact come to want euthanasia for themselves. Nevertheless, making it legally permissible would reassure many people that if they ever do want euthanasia they would be able to obtain it. This reassurance would supplement the broader control over the process of dying given by the right to decide about life-sustaining treatment. Having fire insurance on one's house benefits all who have it, not just those whose houses actually burn down, by reassuring them that in the unlikely event of their house burning down, they will receive the money needed to rebuild it. Likewise, the legalization of euthanasia can be thought of as a kind of insurance policy against being forced to endure a protracted dying process that one has come to find burdensome and unwanted, especially when there is no life-sustaining treatment to forgo. The strong concern about losing control of their care expressed by many people who face serious illness likely to end in death suggests that they give substantial importance to the legalization of euthanasia as a means of maintaining this control.

A third good consequence of the legalization of euthanasia concerns patients whose dying is filled with severe and unrelievable pain or suffering. When there is a life-sustaining treatment that, if forgone, will lead relatively quickly to death, then doing so can bring an end to these patients' suffering without recourse to euthanasia. For patients receiving no such treatment, however, euthanasia may be the only release from their otherwise prolonged suffering and agony. This argument from mercy has always been the strongest argument for euthanasia in those cases to which it applies.[7]

The importance of relieving pain and suffering is less controversial than is the frequency with which patients are forced to undergo untreatable agony that only euthanasia could relieve. If we focus first on suffering caused by physical pain, it is crucial to distinguish pain that *could* be adequately relieved with modern methods of pain control, though it in fact is not, from pain that is relievable only by death.[8] For a variety of reasons, including some physicians' fear of hastening the patient's death, as well as the lack of a publicly accessible means for assessing the amount of the patient's pain, many patients suffer pain that could be, but is not relieved.

Specialists in pain control, as for example the pain of terminally ill cancer patients, argue that there are very few patients whose pain could not be adequately controlled, though sometimes at the cost of so sedating them that they are effectively unable to interact with other people or their environment. Thus, the argument from mercy in cases of physical pain can probably be met in a large majority of cases by providing adequate measures of pain relief. This should be a high priority, whatever our legal policy on euthanasia—the relief of pain and suffering has long been, quite properly, one of the central goals of medicine. Those cases in which pain could be effectively relieved, but in fact is not, should only count significantly in favor of legalizing euthanasia if all reasonable efforts to change pain management techniques have been tried and have failed.

Dying patients often undergo substantial psychological suffering that is not fully or even principally the result of physical pain.[9] The knowledge about how to relieve this suffering is much more limited than in the case of relieving pain, and efforts to do so are probably more often unsuccessful. If the argument from mercy is extended to patients experiencing great and unrelievable psychological suffering, the numbers of patients to which it applies are much greater.

One last good consequence of legalizing euthanasia is that once death has been accepted, it is often more humane to end life quickly and peacefully, when that is what the patient wants. Such a death will often be seen as better than a more prolonged one. People who suffer a sudden and unexpected death, for example by dying quickly or in their sleep from a heart attack or stroke, are often considered lucky to have died in this way. We care about how we die in part because we care about how others remember us, and we hope they will remember us as we were in "good times" with them and not as we might be when disease has robbed us of our dignity as human beings. As with much in the treatment and care of the dying, people's concerns differ in this respect, but for at least some people, euthanasia will be a more humane death than what they have often experienced with other loved ones and might otherwise expect for themselves.

Some opponents of euthanasia challenge how much importance should be given to any of these good consequences of permitting it, or even whether some would be good consequences at all. But more frequently, opponents cite a number of bad consequences that permitting euthanasia would or could produce, and it is to their assessment that I now turn.

Potential Bad Consequences of Permitting Euthanasia

Some of the arguments against permitting euthanasia are aimed specifically against physicians, while others are aimed against anyone being permitted to perform it. I shall first consider one argument of the former sort. Permitting physicians to perform euthanasia, it is said, would be incompatible with their fundamental moral and professional commitment as healers to care for patients and to protect life. Moreover, if euthanasia by physicians became common, patients would come to fear that a medication was intended not to treat or care, but instead to kill, and would thus lose trust in their physicians. . . .

If permitting physicians to kill would undermine the very "moral center" of medicine, then almost certainly physicians should not be permitted to perform euthanasia. But how persuasive is this claim? Patients should not fear, as a consequence of permitting *voluntary* active euthanasia, that their physicians will substitute a lethal injection for what patients want and believe is part of their care. If active euthanasia is restricted to cases in which it is truly voluntary, then no patient should fear getting it unless she or he has voluntarily requested it. Patients' trust of their physicians could be increased, not eroded, by knowledge that physicians will provide aid in dying when patients seek it.

Might [those opposed to euthanasia] nevertheless be correct in their claim that the moral center of medicine would collapse if physicians were to become killers? This question raises what at the deepest level should be the guiding aims of medicine, a question that obviously cannot be fully explored here. But I do want to say enough to indicate the direction that I believe an appropriate response to this challenge should take. In spelling out above what I called the positive argument for voluntary active euthanasia, I suggested that two principal values—respecting patients' self-determination and promoting their well-being—underlie the consensus that competent patients, or the surrogates of incompetent patients, are entitled to refuse any life-sustaining treatment and to choose from among available alternative treatments. It is the commitment to these two values in guiding physicians' actions as healers, comforters, and protectors of their patients' lives that should be at the "moral center" of medicine, and these two values support physicians' administering euthanasia when their patients make competent requests for it.

What should not be at that moral center is a commitment to preserving patients' lives as such, without regard to whether those patients want their lives preserved or judge their preservation a benefit to them. . . .

A second bad consequence that some foresee is that permitting euthanasia would weaken society's commitment to provide optimal care for dying patients. We live at a time in which the control of health care costs has become, and is likely to continue to be, the dominant focus of health care policy. If euthanasia is seen as a cheaper alternative to adequate care and treatment, then we might become less scrupulous about providing sometimes costly support and other services to dying patients. . . .

This second worry is difficult to assess because there is little firm evidence about the likelihood of the feared erosion in the care of dying patients. There are at least two reasons, however, for skepticism about this argument. The first is that the same worry could have been directed at recognizing patients' or surrogates' rights to forgo life-sustaining treatment, yet there is no persuasive evidence that recognizing the right to refuse treatment has caused a serious erosion in the quality of care of dying patients. The second reason for skepticism about this worry is that only a very small proportion of deaths would occur from euthanasia if it were permitted. In the Netherlands, where euthanasia under specified circumstances is permitted by the courts, though not authorized by statute, the best estimate of the proportion of overall deaths that result from it is about 2 percent.[10] Thus, the vast majority of critically ill and dying patients will not request it, and so will still have to be cared for by physicians, families, and others. Permitting euthanasia should not diminish people's commitment and concern to maintain and improve the care of these patients.

The [third] potential bad consequence of permitting euthanasia has been developed by David Velleman and turns on the subtle point that making a new option or choice available to people can sometimes make them worse off, even if once they have the choice they go on to choose what is best for them.[11] Ordinarily, people's continued existence is viewed by them as given, a fixed condition with which they must cope. Making euthanasia available to people as an option denies them the alternative of staying alive by default. If people are offered the option of euthanasia, their continued existence is not a choice for which they can be held responsible and which they can be asked by others to justify. We care, and are right to care, about being able to justify ourselves to others. To the extent that our society is unsympathetic to justifying a severely dependent or impaired existence, a heavy psychological burden of proof may be placed on patients who think their terminal illness or chronic infirmity is not a sufficient reason for dying. Even if they otherwise view their life as worth living, the opinion of others around them that it is not can threaten their reason for living and make euthanasia a rational choice. Thus the existence of the option becomes a subtle pressure to request it.

This argument correctly identifies the reason why offering some patients the option of euthanasia would not benefit them. Velleman takes it not as a reason for opposing all euthanasia, but for restricting it to circumstances where there are "unmistakable and overpowering reasons for persons to want the option of euthanasia," and for denying the option in all other cases. But there are at least three reasons why such restriction may not be warranted. First, polls and other evidence support that most Americans believe euthanasia should be permitted (though the recent defeat of the referendum to permit it in the state of Washington raises some doubt about this support). Thus, many more people seem to want the choice than would be made worse off by getting it. Second, if giving people the option of ending their life really makes them worse off, then we should not only prohibit euthanasia, but also take back from people the right they now have to decide about life-sustaining treatment. The feared harmful effect should already have occurred from securing people's right to refuse life-sustaining treatment, yet there is no evidence of any such widespread harm or any broad public desire to rescind that right. Third, since there is a wide range of conditions in which reasonable people can and do disagree about whether they would want continued life, it is not possible to restrict the permissibility of euthanasia as narrowly as Velleman suggests without thereby denying it to most persons who would want it; to permit it only in cases in which virtually everyone would want it would be to deny it to most who would want it.

A [fourth] potential bad consequence of making euthanasia legally permissible is that it might weaken the general legal prohibition of homicide. This prohibition is so fundamental to civilized society, it is argued, that we should do nothing that erodes it. If most cases of stopping life support are killing, as I have already argued, then the court cases permitting such killing have already in effect weakened this prohibition. However, neither the courts nor most people have seen these cases as killing and so as challenging the prohibition of homicide. The courts have usually grounded patients' or their surrogates' rights to refuse life-sustaining treatment in rights to privacy, liberty, self-determination, or bodily integrity, not in exceptions to homicide laws.

Legal permission for physicians or others to perform euthanasia could not be grounded in patients' rights to decide about medical treatment. Permitting euthanasia would require qualifying, at least in effect, the legal prohibition against homicide, a prohibition that in general does not allow the consent of the victim to justify or excuse the act. Nevertheless, the very same fundamental basis of the right to decide about life-sustaining treatment—respecting a person's self-determination—does support euthanasia as well. Individual self-determination has long been a well-entrenched and fundamental value in the law, and so extending it to euthanasia would not require appeal to novel legal values or principles. That suicide or attempted suicide is no longer a criminal offense in virtually all states indicates an acceptance of individual self-determination in the taking of one's own life analogous to that required for voluntary active euthanasia. The legal prohibition (in most states) of assisting in suicide and the refusal in the law to accept the consent of the victim as a possible justification of homicide are both arguably a result of difficulties in the legal process of establishing the consent of the victim after the fact. If procedures can be designed that clearly establish the voluntariness of the person's request of euthanasia, it would under those procedures represent a carefully circumscribed qualification on the legal prohibition of homicide. Nevertheless, some remaining worries about this weakening can be captured in the final potential bad consequence, to which I will now turn.

This final potential bad consequence is the central concern of many opponents of euthanasia and, I believe, is the most serious objection to a legal policy permitting it. According to this "slippery slope" worry, although active euthanasia may be morally permissible in cases in which it is unequivocally voluntary and the patient finds his or her condition unbearable, a legal policy permitting euthanasia would inevitably lead to active euthanasia being performed in many other cases in which it would be morally wrong. To prevent those other wrongful cases of euthanasia we should not permit even morally justified performance of it.

Slippery slope arguments of this form are problematic and difficult to evaluate.[12] From one perspective, they are the last refuge of conservative defenders of the status quo. When all the opponent's objections to the wrongness of euthanasia itself have been met, the opponent then shifts ground and acknowledges both that it is not in itself wrong and that a legal policy which resulted only in its being performed would not be bad. Nevertheless, the opponent maintains, it should still not be permitted because doing so would result in its being performed in other cases in which it is not voluntary and would be wrong. In this argument's most extreme form, permitting euthanasia is the first and fateful step down the slippery slope to Nazism. Once on the slope we will be unable to get off.

Now it cannot be denied that it is *possible* that permitting euthanasia could have these fateful consequences, but that cannot be enough to warrant prohibiting it if it is otherwise justified. A similar *possible* slippery slope worry could have been raised to securing competent patients' rights to decide about life support, but recent history shows such a worry would have been un-founded. It must be relevant how likely it is that we will end with horren-dous consequences and an unjustified practice of euthanasia. How *likely* and *widespread* would the abuses and unwarranted extensions of permitting it be? By abuses, I mean the performance of euthanasia that fails to satisfy the conditions required for voluntary active euthanasia, for example, if the patient has been subtly pressured to accept it. By unwarranted extensions of policy, I mean later changes in legal policy to permit not just voluntary euthanasia, but also euthanasia in cases in which, for example, it need not be fully voluntary. Opponents of voluntary euthanasia on slippery slope grounds have not pro-vided the data or evidence neccessary to turn their speculative concerns into well-grounded likelihoods.

It is at least clear, however, that both the character and likelihood of abuses of a legal policy permitting euthanasia depend in significant part on the procedures put in place to protect against them. I will not try to detail fully what such procedures might be, but will just give some examples of what they might include:

1. The patient should be provided with all relevant information about his or her medical condition, current prognosis, available alternative treatments, and the prognosis of each.
2. Procedures should ensure that the patient's request for euthanasia is stable or enduring (a brief waiting period could be required) and fully voluntary (an advocate for the patient might be appointed to ensure this).
3. All reasonable alternatives must have been explored for improving the patient's quality of life and relieving any pain or suffering.
4. A psychiatric evaluation should ensure that the patient's request is not the result of a treatable psychological impairment such as de-pression.[13]

These examples of procedural safeguards are all designed to ensure that the patient's choice is fully informed, voluntary, and competent, and so a true exercise of self-determination. Other proposals for euthanasia would restrict its permissibility further—for example, to the terminally ill—a restriction that cannot be supported by self-determination. Such additional restrictions might, however, be justified by concern for limiting potential harms from abuse. At the same time, it is important not to impose procedural or substantive safe-guards so restrictive as to make euthanasia impermissible or practically infea-sible in a wide range of justified cases.

These examples of procedural safeguards make clear that it is possible to substantially reduce, though not to eliminate, the potential for abuse of a policy permitting voluntary active euthanasia. Any legalization of the practice should be accompanied by a well-considered set of procedural safeguards together with an ongoing evaluation of its use. Introducing euthanasia into only a few states could be a form of carefully limited and controlled social experiment that would give us evidence about the benefits and harms of the practice. Even then firm and uncontroversial data may remain exclusive, as the continuing controversy over what has taken place in the Netherlands in recent years indicates.[14]

The Slip into Nonvoluntary Active Euthanasia

While I believe slippery slope worries can largely be limited by making necessary distinctions both in principle and in practice, one slippery slope concern is legitimate. There is reason to expect that legalization of voluntary active euthanasia might soon be followed by strong pressure to legalize some nonvoluntary euthanasia of incompetent patients unable to express their own wishes. Respecting a person's self-determination and recognizing that continued life is not always of value to a person can support not only voluntary active euthanasia, but some nonvoluntary euthanasia as well. These are the same values that ground competent patients' right to refuse life-sustaining treatment. Recent history here is instructive. In the medical ethics literature, in the courts since Quinlan, and in norms of medical practice, that right has been extended to incompetent patients and exercised by a surrogate who is to decide as the patient would have decided in the circumstances if competent.[15] It has been held unreasonable to continue life-sustaining treatment that the patient would not have wanted just because the patient now lacks the capacity to tell us that. Life-sustaining treatment for incompetent patients is today frequently forgone on the basis of a surrogate's decision, or less frequently on the basis of an advance directive executed by the patient while still competent. The very same logic that has extended the right to refuse life-sustaining treatment from a competent patient to the surrogate of an incompetent patient (acting with or without a formal advance directive from the patient) may well extend the scope of active euthanasia. The argument will be, Why continue to force unwanted life on patients just because they have now lost the capacity to request euthanasia from us?

A related phenomenon may reinforce this slippery slope concern. In the Netherlands, what the courts have sanctioned has been clearly restricted to voluntary euthanasia. In itself, this serves as some evidence that permitting it need *not* lead to permitting the nonvoluntary variety. There is some indication, however, that for many Dutch physicians euthanasia is no longer viewed as a special action, set apart from their usual practice and restricted only to competent persons.[16] Instead, it is seen as one end of a spectrum of caring for dying patients. When viewed in this way it will be difficult to deny euthanasia to a patient for whom it is seen as the best or most appropriate form of care simply because that patient is now incompetent and cannot request it.

Even if voluntary active euthanasia should slip into nonvoluntary active euthanasia, with surrogates acting for incompetent patients, the ethical evaluation is more complex than many opponents of euthanasia allow. Just as in the case of surrogates' decisions to forgo life-sustaining treatment for incompetent patients, so also surrogates' decisions to request euthanasia for incompetent persons would often accurately reflect what the incompetent person would have wanted and would deny the person nothing that he or she would have considered worth having. Making nonvoluntary active euthanasia legally permissible, however, would greatly enlarge the number of patients on whom it might be performed and substantially enlarge the potential for misuse and abuse. As noted above, frail and debilitated elderly people, often demented or otherwise incompetent and thereby unable to defend and assert their own interests, may be especially vulnerable to unwanted euthanasia.

For some people, this risk is more than sufficient reason to oppose the legalization of voluntary euthanasia. But while we should in general be cautious about inferring much from the experience in the Netherlands to what our own experience in the United States might be, there may be one important lesson that we can learn from them. One commentator has noted that in the Netherlands families of incompetent patients have less authority than do families in the United States to act as surrogates for incompetent patients in making decisions to forgo life-sustaining treatment.[17] From the Dutch perspective, it may be we in the United States who are *already* on the slippery slope in having given surrogates broad authority to forgo life-sustaining treatment for incompetent persons. In this view, the more important moral divide, and the more important with regard to potential for abuse, is not between forgoing life-sustaining treatment and euthanasia, but instead between voluntary and nonvoluntary performance of either. If this is correct, then the more important issue is ensuring the appropriate principles and procedural safeguards for the exercise of decision-making authority by surrogates for incompetent persons in *all* decisions at the end of life. This may be the correct response to slippery slope worries about euthanasia.

I have cited both good and bad consequences that have been thought likely from a policy change permitting voluntary active euthanasia, and have tried to evaluate their likelihood and relative importance. Nevertheless, as I noted earlier, reasonable disagreement remains both about the consequences of permitting euthanasia and about which of these consequences are more important. The depth and strength of public and professional debate about whether, all things considered, permitting euthanasia would be desirable or undesirable reflects these disagreements. While my own view is that the balance of considerations supports permitting the practice, my principal purpose here has been to clarify the main issues. . . .

NOTES

1. President's Commission for the Study of Ethical Problems in Medicine and Biomedical and Behavioral Research, *Deciding to Forego Life-Sustaining Treatment* (Washington, D.C.: U.S. Government Printing Office, 1983); The Hastings Center, *Guidelines on the Termination of Life-Sustaining Treatment and Care of the*

Dying (Bloomington: Indiana University Press, 1987); *Current Opinions of the Council on Ethical and Judicial Affairs of the American Medical Association— 1989: Withholding or Withdrawing Life-Prolonging Treatment* (Chicago: American Medical Association, 1989); George Annas and Leonard Glantz, "The Right of Elderly Patients to Refuse Life-Sustaining Treatment," *Millbank Memorial Quarterly* 64, suppl. 2 (1986): 95–162; Robert F. Weir, *Abating Treatment with Critically Ill Patients* (New York: Oxford University Press, 1989); Sidney J. Wanzer et al. "The Physician's Responsibility toward Hopelessly Ill Patients," *NEJM* 310 (1984): 955–59.

2. M. A. M. de Wachter, "Active Euthanasia in the Netherlands," *JAMA* 262, no. 23 (1989): 3315–19.

3. Anonymous, "It's Over, Debbie," *JAMA* 259 (1988): 272; Timothy E. Quill, "Death and Dignity," *NEJM* 322 (1990): 1881–83.

4. Wanzer et al., "The Physician's Responsibility toward Hopelessly Ill Patients: A Second Look," *NEJM* 320 (1989): 844–49.

5. Dan W. Brock, "Moral Rights and Permissible Killing," in *Ethical Issues Relating to Life and Death,* ed. John Ladd (New York: Oxford University Press, 1979), pp. 94–117.

6. P. Painton and E. Taylor, "Love or Let Die," *Time,* 19 March 1990, pp. 62–71; *Boston Globe*/Harvard University Poll, *Boston Globe,* 3 November 1991.

7. James Rachels, *The End of Life* (Oxford: Oxford University Press, 1986).

8. Marcia Angell, "The Quality of Mercy," *NEJM* 306 (1982): 98–99; M. Donovan, P. Dillon, and L. Mcguire, "Incidence and Characteristics of Pain in a Sample of Medical-Surgical Inpatients," *Pain* 30 (1987): 69–78.

9. Eric Cassell, *The Nature of Suffering and the Goals of Medicine* (New York: Oxford University Press, 1991).

10. Paul J. Van der Maas et al., "Euthanasia and Other Medical Decisions Concerning the End of Life," *Lancet* 338 (1991): 669–74.

11. My formulation of this argument derives from David Velleman's statement of it in his commentary on an earlier version of this paper delivered at the American Philosophical Association Central Division meetings; a similar point was made to me by Elisha Milgram in discussion on another occasion. For more general development of the point see Thomas Schelling, *The Strategy of Conflict* (Cambridge, Mass.: Harvard University Press, 1960); and Gerald Dworkin, "Is More Choice Better Than Less?" in *The Theory and Practice of Autonomy* (Cambridge: Cambridge University Press, 1988).

12. Frederick Schauer, "Slippery Slopes," *Harvard Law Review* 99 (1985): 361–83; Wibren van der Burg, "The Slippery Slope Argument," *Ethics* 102 (October 1991): 42–65.

13. There is evidence that physicians commonly fail to diagnose depression. See Robert I. Misbin, "Physicians Aid in Dying," *NEJM* 325 (1991): 1304–7.

14. Richard Fenigsen, "A Case against Dutch Euthanasia," Special Supplement, *Hastings Center Report* 19, no. 1 (1989): 22–30.

15. Allen C. Buchanan and Dan W. Brock, *Deciding for Others: The Ethics of Surrogate Decisionmaking* (Cambridge: Cambridge University Press, 1989).

16. Van der Maas et al., "Euthanasia and Other Medical Decisions."

17. Margaret P. Battin, "Seven Caveats Concerning the Discussion of Euthanasia in Holland," *American Philosophical Association Newsletter on Philosophy and Medicine* 89, no. 2 (1990).

Living With Euthanasia:
A Futuristic Scenario
Albert R. Jonsen

Albert R. Jonsen is a professor in the Department of Medical History and Ethics at the University of Washington School of Medicine. In this essay, Jonsen imagines that he is in the future five years after active voluntary euthanasia has been made legal in the fictitious state of Redwood. In his assessment of those years, Jonsen supposes that the worst of the bad consequences that opponents of active euthanasia fear would not have been realized. Nonetheless, Jonsen finds enough worrisome about the practices that would have occurred that he still opposes euthanasia, though with a fair amount of ambivalence.

Five years ago, in 1992, the State of Redwood made legal by public initiative a practice called "aid-in dying". This practice allows a physician to end painlessly and humanely the life of a patient who made a competent request for such a service. I was then, as now, Professor of Ethics in Medicine at the State University of Redwood College of Medicine. Now, in 1997, the editors of this Journal have asked me to reflect on the experience of the last five years. I am less pleased to do so. The editors also asked me to express my conclusions about that experience. I am less pleased to do so, since I find myself still rather ambiguous. Still, I shall venture some ideas that may explain my ambiguity.

The 1992 vote on Initiative 6 was close: 53% in favor, 47% against, after a vigorous campaign that ended with a very large voter turnout. (Ironically, Washington State, Redwood's neighbor, defeated a similar proposition by the same margin!) To be precise, the ballot asked whether the Natural Death Act of the State of Redwood should be amended to allow "a competent patient to request of a physician "aid-in-dying". Aid-in-dying was defined as an act that would bring about the swift and painless death of the patient in a humane manner. Only a patient capable of a competent, voluntary request could receive this service from the physician at the time the request was made. At the same time, the ballot provided for two other revisions of the Natural Death Act. First, persistent vegetative state was to be added as a "terminal condition" for which life support could be terminated and, second, nutrition and hydration were added to the life-supporting technologies that could be discontinued under the provisions of the Directive to Physicians.

The latter two provisions were not contested by the majority of those who debated the initiative. The provision that permitted aid-in-dying, however,

From *The Journal of Medicine and Philosophy* 18 (1993), 241–51.

generated heated debate. Proponents argued that it was the logical extension of our endorsement of the principle of autonomy; opponents suggested that it would be the first slip on the slippery slope that would lead to involuntary euthanasia. Their reason for claiming this was the absence, in their view, of sufficient safeguards to detect and prevent abuses, principal among which were mentioned the possibility of coercion of the ill and elderly to end burdensome and costly lives, the overly hasty choice of death by distressed persons and, in the absence of any reporting requirement, the covert euthanasia of some who had not requested it. The debate was not on an equal footing. The proponents argued for the principle of autonomy and the elimination of pain, suffering and diminished quality of life that those who chose aid-in-dying selected for themselves. The opponents did not rest their argument so much on principle, but on the expected undesirable consequences that might come, should the principle of autonomy be dimmed in actual practice. This argument, of course, rests on unverifiable predictions about the future.

Physicians were deeply divided over the initiative. Polls showed an almost 50/50 split in opinion, although the official position of the Redwood Medical Association was negative, by an almost unanimous vote in its annual meeting. Many physicians felt that euthanasia was, as I wrote in an article around that time, "beyond the doctor's reference", (Jonsen, 1988, pp. 195–198) but many also felt that respect for their patient's autonomy and elimination of pain and suffering were within the range of a physician's duty. Some physicians openly stated that they had helped patients die; many others, while not speaking out, suggested that the practice was more widespread than commonly believed. They stated that legalization would merely remove the stigma from a practice that some physicians and patients already believed ethical and that, in fact, was more than occasionally practiced in privacy.

Since I was Professor of Medical Ethics at the Redwood State University College of Medicine, I was inevitably drawn into the debate. I did take the negative side in the debate, attempting to state in dignified academic tones the argument about the absence of safeguards and the potential for abuse. It was clear at the time that the philosophical arguments pro and con active euthanasia were of little concern in the public debate. Analyses of the conceptual differences between omission and commission, withdrawing and withholding, double effect, etc. were not welcome fodder for sound bites, talk shows and editorials. Rather, anecdotes about miserable deaths offered by one side clashed with predictions of dire consequences from the other. Thus, I rarely uttered a philosophical word, nor was I often asked a philosophical question. In all, despite the absence of depth, the public discussion was serious and honest, raising the sensitivity of the public to the questions of how one lives and dies in the world of modern health care.

We are now five years away from those debates. Aid-in-dying has been legal in the State of Redwood for half a decade. I should have reached a conclusion about the ethics of aid-in-dying on the basis of those five years of experience. Unfortunately, the issue remains for me profoundly ambiguous. I can say that I still lean to the negative, but my reasons for so doing are not quite as clear to me as once they were. I must admit that the philosophical arguments that were once so convincing to me are now less convincing. For some years prior to the advent of legalized euthanasia, good philosophers had reexamined those old arguments and given them a thorough shaking out. They may not be entirely threadbare, but they cover the conceptual anatomy less satisfactorily than they once did.

For example, many ethicists had long taken seriously the ancient moral distinction between direct and indirect killing and between commission and omission. Those distinctions were the basis for another common distinction between active and passive euthanasia, a distinction that physicians generally took for granted and that had found its way into contemporary professional codes of medical ethics. Those distinctions began to come under serious fire with James Rachels' well known article, "Active and Passive Euthanasia", which appeared in the *New England Journal of Medicine* in 1975 (Rachels, 1975, pp. 78–80). Subsequently, many philosophical studies showed up the frailties of the arguments that underlie those distinctions. Assuredly, as in almost all philosophical debates, the criticisms were met by countercriticisms, but in general, it was my impression that the philosophical soundness of the old arguments was weakened, although not destroyed. The President's Commission for the Study of Ethical Problems in Medicine cogently summarized the philosophical balance sheet on the old arguments in its influential 1982 Report, *Deciding To Forego Life Sustaining Treatment* (President's Commission, 1982). So, by 1992, it was not as easy as it had been to muster solid philosophical arguments against active euthanasia. Some of those who had followed this intellectual evolution, as I had, found it rather embarrassing to depend too heavily on those old arguments and thus turned to the more pragmatic argument about untoward social consequences of legal toleration of active euthanasia.

Whatever the state of philosophical argument, we have had legal euthanasia in the State of Redwood for five years. That may have come about because the philosophical debate had become murkier or (as I suspect) the philosophical points were ignored by a populace whose values had changed and who had become aware of the unpleasantness of dying a technological death. What has been our experience during these five years? It is hard to describe it very concretely, since the law covered the decision about aid-in-dying with the shroud (if I may be permitted a grim metaphor) of privacy. The decision is communicated by a patient to a doctor and no reporting is legally required. Even the legal statement of cause of death can be written in general, vague terms, such as "cardiorespiratory arrest". Thus, we have no statistics about how many persons have sought and received aid-in-dying; we have only a few reports about the exact conditions in which the decision and action were taken. Several social scientists and some pollsters have attempted to gain such information, but it is still very fragmentary. We guess, however, that over the last five years some 3,000 of the 175,000 reported deaths in the State of

Redwood were due to a "euthanasia decision". Since that designation includes all decisions in which death followed a patient request, it mixes "passive euthanasia"—the withdrawing or withholding of life-supporting measures—with "active euthanasia", or aid-in-dying. The actual number of deaths due to the latter cause is much smaller: probably only 600 or so. [Curiously, these numbers are quite close to those reported some years ago after the Netherlands undertook a more liberal policy on active euthanasia (Van der Maas, 1991, pp. 669–672).]

We know very little about the circumstances of most of these deaths. In the several surveys that have been published, the cases hold few surprises. In most of them, the typical patient is in the final stages of a lethal disease, has undergone long but progressively less helpful treatments, is suffering from considerable pain and discomfort (our law sets no standard about the degree or treatability of pain) and makes an explicit request for quick and painless death. These cases, as might be expected in voluntary reports, conform roughly to the expectations of the law. The primary conditions are "terminal condition" and "competent request". If there were to be any debate about the reported cases, it would be over the accuracy of the terminal nature of the patient's condition. However, since this is most often a guess rather than a prognosis and honest physicians can honestly differ, not much can be made over this matter. There are in the published literature a few cases which are borderline: a patient with myasthenia gravis far progressed but probably with some years to live, who feared loss of competence, a patient in "early" stages of Alzheimer's disease, who also had serious cancer. But these borderline cases are few. In general, what we know by small studies and anecdote, shows a picture of conformity with the law. What happens beyond our ken, in the absence of any reporting requirement, is, quite simply, beyond our ken. We might suspect that abuse has occurred in which either voluntariness or terminality were egregiously misinterpreted, but we have little evidence. I will describe below our one notable exception.

We do, of course, have the occasional widely publicized story. These usually have to do with disagreement between a patient who has requested aid-in-dying and members of the family who disagree with that choice. The law requires no notification or consultation with family members: the decision is the patient's alone to make. However, physicians do report that they have found themselves in the midst of family disputes (much as they did a decade ago about termination of life support). Several of my colleagues tell me that they have had to withdraw from cases in which they would have been willing to comply with a patient's request but did not wish to become embroiled in debate. One physician told me that she did so with particular regret because the relationship with that patient had been long and deep.

A good number of physicians have declined to avail themselves of the privilege accorded them by the law. Polls tell us that somewhere between 35 to 55 percent say that they would not accede to a request for aid-in-dying. Most of these refuse on personal moral grounds. Among those who have no moral objection, the most common reasons are that the request comes from the family rather than the patient or that the patient's condition cannot honestly be judged terminal. Some physicians note that they feel obliged to inform patients early in their relationship that they will not participate on moral grounds. Some find this embarrassing and difficult. Several of my colleagues have found themselves embarrassed when late in the relationship patients who were seriously ill asked them to assist in dying. Their refusal to do so was tantamount to a termination of the relationship.

A few physicians have become known as particularly ready to assist in aid-in-dying. In particular, several retired physicians, including two anesthesiologists, have made it known that they are willing to assist, but only at the request of an attending physician. The fee charged is about $500, approximately the fee for endoscopy (most private insurers reimburse at about that level but Medicare does not have a procedure code for aid-in-dying). But the numbers of procedures do not add up to a profitable practice and we have not seen the emergence of a new specialty of thanatology, as opponents of legalization had predicted. However, concern has been expressed that physicians are not particularly skilled at the procedures required to effect the death of the patient "painlessly and humanely". This is not taught in medical school at present though several continuing education seminars have been offered. There are still no "standards of practice". Hospital pharmacy and therapeutics committees have debated about what drugs are most effective and in what combinations and dosages. We have heard several reports of bungled procedures in which death was prolonged. In one case, a patient was severely brain damaged, but did not die for several months after a failed aid-in-dying attempt. The physician was sued by the family, but acquitted because there were no clear standards of practice that were violated.

One other legal case has stirred widespread concern. The son of a man who had requested and received aid-in-dying charged that his father had been neither competent nor terminal at the time the service was provided. His father was suffering from cancer and had told the family that he did not want his life prolonged and would even prefer to have it ended. While his cancer was in remission, he suffered a stroke, rendering him mentally incapacitated. His physician of long standing, Dr. Brian Belagier, administered a dose of a lethal drug, causing the patient's death. The son informed the District Attorney who brought homicide charges noting that the two essential conditions for legal aid-in-dying were not respected, namely competent request and terminal condition. The jury acquitted Dr. Belagier. The case revived the vigorous debate that has surrounded the passage of the legislation: opponents claiming that it represented the slippery slope; proponents claiming that it represented humane care and respect for autonomy, even though the exact provisions of the law were not fulfilled.

The case, however, reflects a larger issue. We have seen, in the last five years, a growing sympathy to enlarge the terms of the law. Indeed, another initiative petition is being readied which would allow for an advance directive for aid-in-dying. Some persons have felt that, should they have an early diagnosis of a deteriorating condition that would compromise mental status, such as Alzheimer's disease, they should be allowed to give an advance directive covering aid-in-dying as well as abatement of life support. Other commentators have noted that many persons who have serious diseases that have not reached the terminal stage are deprived of their right to avoid the indignity of that terminal stage. Thus, some persons with multiple sclerosis or muscular dystrophy have complained that they would prefer to have aid-in-dying before they are so sick that the requisite "terminal condition" can be diagnosed. Finally, the condition of certain patients, such as those severely damaged by trauma or congenital conditions, calls for some alleviation. They have never had the opportunity to make a request for aid-in-dying, but they should have the right to that service when it is reasonable. In particular, several neonatologists have argued in this vein: one published a widely discussed article in our leading metropolitan newspaper. She hinted that she had acted upon her beliefs in a number of cases; a flurry of letters to the editors predominantly sympathized with her argument. These advocates refer to the now commonly accepted notion that the non or never competent still have fundamental rights. This has been recognized in important judicial decisions with regard to foregoing life support; it should be recognized, say the proponents, with regard to aid-in-dying. Dr. Belagier's trial might have provided an opportunity to test this notion, but since he was acquitted, the argument was not urged in the appellate court. It appears to some, myself included, that the push onto the "slippery slope" has begun in the minds of the people of Redwood.

Unquestionably, the aid-in-dying legislation has brought peaceful surcease to some suffering patients. Many anecdotes told by physicians and families bear witness. At the same time, we do not know how often the conditions of competent request and terminal condition are respected. We do not know how many cases like that of Dr. Belagier have occurred. We do not know with any accuracy how many persons want the right to have their lives ended after they have lost competence or before they become terminal. We do believe that the original emphasis on autonomy, that was persuasive enough to win an election, has shifted. It was, when first proposed, quite clearly the central, indeed, the only, principle to which proponents referred: competent persons have the moral right to decide crucial questions about their life and death and they should be granted the legal right to implement these decisions. Like other appeals to autonomy in our culture this one, especially when many persons saw the life prolonging capabilities of modern medicine as leading to a kind of captivity, had powerful voter appeal. Five years later, the autonomy principle is being expanded in theory and possibly in practice. One expansion moves from active current request by a presently competent person to a request for euthanasia to be carried out in the future. Another expansion moves from the actuality of voluntary choice to the assumption of voluntary choice on the part of those who, in the eyes of others, would have chosen euthanasia, had they been able to do so.

It is worth noting that, in the history of the debates over active euthanasia, the earliest arguments concentrated on bringing merciful death to those
who were suffering great pain. It was an act of beneficence or mercy, whence
the common term "mercy killing". The voluntary choice of the patient was
mentioned, but does not hold a central or even necessary place in the arguments. In these earlier discussions, it was not unusual for the proponent to
slip easily from advocating euthanasia for those requesting it to advocating it
for those whose lives were, in the eyes of others, terrible. For example, a
physician of our state, known to many as a compassionate and honest man,
wrote in 1944, "To end a life that is useless, helpless and hopeless seems
merciful. . . the useless, helpless and hopeless are of many kinds. They either
always have been or have become unfit in the struggle of life . . . idiots and
the insane, imbeciles and morons, psychopaths, both mild and severe, criminals and delinquents, monsters and defectives, incurables and the worn out
senile" (Hinman, 1944, pp. 640–643). Even Joseph Fletcher, who centered his
moral philosophy on the freedom of individuals, advocated not only voluntary
euthanasia, but seemed to tolerate what he described as a "partly eugenic
position", namely, involuntary euthanasia for "monstrosities at birth and mental defectives" (Fletcher, 1952, p. 206). Arguments based on beneficence were
vulnerable to a strong counterargument, namely, that the opinion that some
persons might hold about "the useless, helpless and hopeless," might be seriously discriminatory. As my co-authors and I wrote years ago, "the 'angel of
mercy' can become the fanatic, bringing the 'comfort' of death to some who
do not so clearly request it, then to others who 'would really be better off
dead', finally to whole classes of 'undesirable persons'". (Jonsen, Siegler, Winslade,
1982, p. 127)

The more contemporary emphasis on the principle of autonomy avoids
this problem. It puts the evaluation of quality of life into the hands of the one
who requests that his or her life be ended. Others are only the implementers,
not the evaluators. Thus, in principle, the "slippery slope" is avoided: the level
ground of autonomy, persons making competent judgments in their own behalf, is the basis for legalization of euthanasia or, more accurately, assisted
suicide. However appealing this argument might be to philosophers and to
the public, it has become less sharp in the years since legalization. The principle of beneficence, with its vagueness about what might constitute benefit,
about who defines benefit and about who the beneficiaries should be, has
crept back in, even though autonomy remains the maxim propounded in essays and debates. The slippage from autonomy back into beneficence is not
much noticed.

Finally, the adoption of our statute about "aid-in-dying" was hailed by many
as a major humanitarian advance. In an era when technological medicine, so
beneficial in many respects, can save lives and doom them to great suffering
for the remainder of their time, those who face such dreadful and diminished
lives should have the power to demand that medicine, which has caused
them, also end them. So said the proponents and they illustrated their claim

by two typical vignettes: the patient trapped in the coils of medical machinery and the patient agonized by intractable pain. It is true, of course, that modern medicine does save lives that it cannot otherwise help. Still, life is prolonged today by the drugs that cured a pneumonia in a 50 year old or leukemia in a twelve year old. It is prolonged by nutrition, by immunization, by clean water and safer work places. The old very often become old without being subjected to intensive care and they deteriorate in body and mind despite what medicine can do. Many persons die miserably outside and apart from the world of health care. Many of these will not have the opportunity to request aid-in-dying, and many, even if they had it, might not choose to do so. Many of the proponents of a humane "death with dignity" seem to suggest that active euthanasia will abolish the terminal indignity of death itself. Unfortunately, it does not and even with this "humane" legislation, we must struggle with the ineradicable human problem of finitude.

Only a few weeks after the passage of Proposition 6, my elderly uncle, a retired physician, died. I was moved to reflect on his death in view of our recent controversies. I wrote,

> A proud, fastidious and philosophical man, he had been reduced in several weeks to incoherence, incomprehension and incontinence. Not in great pain, he was clearly uncomfortable and restless... He was at home, in his own bed, with his cherished wife at his side. Yet his last days were agony to us and apparently to him. When I whispered to him, 'we are not holding you back', he murmured, 'you are, you are. Why are you holding me?' Inevitably, I had to reflect, would it not be better for all to end this now? An injection, a potion could cut short this undesired misery... I meditated upon death and again found myself in the camp of the opposed (to active euthanasia). I suspect my late uncle would be there as well, even though he was the sufferer of terminal indignity. My meditation ushered in that conclusion because I believe that if we abolish terminal misery from our experience, we will foolishly hide an essential measure of our humanity.
>
> Active euthanasia for the voluntary and competent patient seems so plausible and liberal. Yet it suggests a technological solution to a perennial human problem. We can efficiently abolish not death but dying, the process that leads to death. We can hide the misery but not the ultimate fact itself. If we can ethically and legally do that for the requesting person, why not for each and every sufferer of terminal misery? The possibility of swift and painless death will inevitably become the necessity. The privilege granted to the competent will be seen as a right of which others less fortunate than the competent should not be deprived. In the end, banishing the misery of dying may not be the undiluted benefit that it appears to be from a distance (Jonsen, 1991, pp. 192–193).

Thus, having lived for five years in a state where the Hippocratic prohibition against "administering a poison to anyone even when asked to do so" has been modernized, I cannot say I have seen another holocaust. I cannot deny that some suffering persons have been granted much desired relief by an eased death. I am aware that on some occasions a liberal interpretation of the law has been tolerated. Still, I sense a reversion to the attitudes and sympathies that surrounded the notion of "mercy killing" and led to its profound ambiguity. It is this ambiguity that leads to my inability to formulate a definitive conclusion about the legalization of aid-in-dying. Its consequences as public policy have not to date been horrifying; but I continue to worry that it is a public policy filled with potential for such consequences. Aid-in-dying is the law in our state, but whether it is right and good I am still unsure.

REFERENCES

Fletcher, Joseph: 1952, *Morals and Medicine,* Boston, Beacon Press.

Hinman, F.: 1944, 'Euthanasia', *Journal of Neuromuscular Diseases,* 99, 640-644.

Jonsen, A., Siegler, M., Winslade, W.: 1982, *Clinical Ethics,* 1st Edition, Macmillan, New York.

Jonsen, A. R.: 1988, 'Beyond the doctor's reference', *Western Journal of Medicine,* 149, 195-198.

Jonsen, A. R.: 1992, 'Death, politics and philosophy', *Western Journal of Medicine,* 157, 192-193.

President's Commission for the Study of Ethical Problems in Medicine and in Biomedical and Behavioral Research: 1982, *Deciding To Forego Life Supporting Treatment,* U.S. Government Printing Office, Washington, D.C.

Rachels, James: 1975, 'Active and passive euthanasia', *New England Journal of Medicine,* 292, 78-80.

Van der Maas, P. et al.: 1991, 'Euthanasia and other medical decisions concerning the end of life', *Lancet* 338, 669-672.

Overlooking the Merits of the Individual Case: An Unpromising Approach to the Right to Die
Joel Feinberg

Until his retirement, Joel Feinberg was Regents Professor of Law and Philosophy at the University of Arizona. During his career he has been the author of many influential essays and books in social and legal philosophy, including his four-volume work, *The Moral Limits of the Criminal Law*. In the essay reprinted here, Feinberg responds to the commonly held position that even though individual cases of active euthanasia would be morally justified, the practice should not be made legal because of the potential bad consequences of such legalization. Among the bad consequences, it is usually claimed, would be instances of euthanasia that are not justified—in other words cases of unjustified killings that would not otherwise occur. Feinberg admits that this form of argument, which supports prohibiting *sometimes* permissible behavior because of the fear that without prohibition the behavior will occur when it is morally wrong, is reasonable in some contexts, but he argues against its use in the context of euthanasia. Both the choice of a policy permitting euthanasia and the choice of a policy prohibiting it carry with them dangers. If euthanasia is permitted, there may be some unjustified deaths, and if it is prohibited, some suffering will be prolonged unjustifiably. Those who accept the moral permissibility of some instances of euthanasia but reject its legalization must believe that the former danger is morally more compelling, a position that Feinberg rejects in this essay.

I

There are many standard situations in life in which authorities are expected to make decisions based on the merits of the individual cases they are evaluating. In most of these situations we expect the decision-makers rigorously to exclude consideration of any grounds other than the merits of the case before them. We are not accustomed, for example, to having referees at athletic contests declare that even though the victory in the 100 meter dash would be awarded to Angelo if the referee considered the case entirely on its merits, he proposes instead to appeal to other relevant criteria independent of the merits of the case, and judge "all things considered" that *Mario* has won the race. . . . Nevertheless, the deliberate overruling of strictly internal considerations for the sake of normally irrelevant external ones is a common practice in many legal and moral arguments. The controversy over the legalization of voluntary euthanasia is a good example.

From *Ratio Juris* 4 (1991), 131-151.

In his influential 1958 article the American legal scholar Yale Kamisar (1969) concedes that when judged entirely on their merits there are instances of mercy killings by doctors or others that have full moral justification. I think Professor Kamisar would agree that in cases of the kind he has in mind, the patient has a *moral right* to end his life, or lacking the ability for self-remedy, to have it ended for him by those who are willing and in a better position to do so. . . .

Nevertheless, Kamisar opposes the legalization of euthanasia, resolutely arguing against proposals to transform the moral right to die into a legal right to die by giving it legal recognition and enforcement. The reasons for his opposition have nothing further to do with the merits of the cases he considers, rather with the dangerous social consequences of giving any acts of killing legal certification. It would be better, he claims, to leave the law of homicide unchanged, bring murder charges against the family members, friends, and doctors who violate it, and then leave the fate of the mercy killers in the hands of sympathetic prosecutors, judges, and juries who will either refuse to indict, or else grant acquittals, suspended sentences, or reprieves, out of their recognition of the moral innocence of the criminal act. In that way, the "law on the books" will continue to testify to the community's profound and universal respect for human life, and serve to deter those who would kill for any reason, while "the law in action" would enable the bolder mercy killers to go unpunished for the crimes they undoubtedly committed, though from the highest and purest motives.

And what are the considerations powerful enough to outweigh the merits of individual cases of morally justified euthanasia? Kamisar lists them for us: Weighed against the moral quality of some individual cases considered solely on their merits are the inevitable occurrences of mistakes and abuses in *other* cases. In effect, then, what Kamisar tells the suffering patient whose moral right to die is beyond question is: "If we change the law to permit *your* worthy case, then we will be legalizing other less worthy cases—patients who have been misdiagnosed, patients who might otherwise recover, patients who don't really want to accelerate their deaths despite earlier death requests made hypothetically, patients who are being manipulated by family members who see their life savings dwindle as the medical costs rise, and other instances of 'mistake' and 'abuse'." What the blanket prohibition of homicide tells the responsible patient whose moral right to die is undoubted is that *he* may not do something that would be harmless or beneficial on balance because *others* cannot be trusted to do the same thing without causing grievous harm (unnecessary death).

Much the same kind of argument, it might be noted, was made in support of a blanket prohibition of alcoholic beverages in the United States in the 1920s. It is not an implausible argument on its face. Compulsive consumers of alcoholic beverages cause an enormous amount of harm to themselves and to others, including (among many other examples) over fifty percent of the fatalities in motor car accidents. Many millions of us, on the other hand, are unaddicted social drinkers who imbibe for occasional relaxation and pleasure, and never to excess. We are responsible in the way we drink wine (say) with dinner, and we might well insist on our moral right to drink as we please. But the very law that permits that innocent activity in our case permits the not-so-innocent drinking of others who are certain to cause widespread death, mutilation, and heartbreak. Is it really asking too much of us to forego our nightly highballs so that others might be prevented from wreaking their havoc on the highways and their destruction of families elsewhere? Perhaps it is an unfair sacrifice to force on us, the argument concludes, but on balance, more harm by far is prevented by a blanket prohibition than by blanket permission, and if error in this difficult calculation is inevitable, it is better that we err on the safe side.

If there is a crucial disanalogy between this argument for the prohibition of wine and spirits and the argument of Professor Kamisar for the continued prohibition of voluntary euthanasia, it is that the alcohol example is addressed to persons like us who are reluctant to give up some innocent pleasures, whereas the euthanasia argument is addressed to those like Matthew Donnelly and the parents of Nancy Beth Cruzan, who are bent on escaping intolerable pain, in Donnelly's case, or pointless psychological suffering in the Cruzan case, and who might well wonder what it is in their horrible circumstances that can be described as erring on "the safe side."

Matthew Donnelly's experiences in his final days were "sadly typical" of a class of cancer victims, and seem to match closely the sort of case Kamisar had in mind when, with admirable candor, he conceded that some patients might have a moral right to die. As Rachels (1986, 32) describes it:

> Skin cancer had riddled [his] tortured body [...] A physicist, he had done research for the past thirty years on the use of X-rays. He had lost part of his jaw, his upper lip, his nose, and his left hand. Growths had been removed from his right arm and two fingers from his right hand. He was left blind, slowly deteriorating, and in agony of body and soul. The pain was constant; at its worst, he could be seen lying in bed with teeth clenched and beads of perspiration standing out on his forehead. Nothing could be done except continued surgery and analgesia. The physicians estimated that he had about a year to live.

The "law on the books" commanded Donnelly not merely to sacrifice some harmless pleasures so that less responsible persons might not abuse theirs, as in the alcoholic prohibition example. Rather, it commanded him to forego his clear moral claim to a release from a full year's intolerable suffering. The argument that would overturn the merits of the individual case in the euthanasia example is to that extent at least, much weaker than its counterpart in the alcohol prohibition example. We have more reason, I think, to ban drinking wine with dinner than we do for prohibiting euthanasia in cases like that of Matthew Donnelly.[1]

The urgency of Donnelly's pain was missing in the case of Nancy Beth Cruzan, who was permanently incapable of experiencing pain—or anything else, for that matter. . . . As a consequence of a car accident, she suffered virtual destruction of her cerebral cortex, leaving her irreversibly in a "persistent vegetative state," without cognitive function, permanently comatose, which is to say forever without consciousness. . . . Common sense would maintain that Miss Cruzan is dead already and has been ever since the time when her coma became irreversible some eight years ago. Legally, however, this judgment of common sense has no bearing on Miss Cruzan's current status. Despite the fact that her "cerebral cortical atrophy is irreversible, permanent, progressive, and ongoing,"[2] the brain stem continues to function, permitting various motor reflexes, maintaining body temperature, heartbeat and breathing. She is unable to swallow food or water, so her body is kept going by surgically implanted gastrostomy feeding and hydrating tube. Her parents, after six years of constant visits to the bedside of their unconscious daughter's body, sought a court order directing withdrawal of the feeding and watering tube. The Supreme Court of Missouri declined to issue this order. The parents then appealed to the United States Supreme Court, and their case became something of a *cause célèbre* in 1990.

If we assume that Nancy Cruzan, when alive, preferred that her body not be kept alive if she were ever to be in such circumstances, then the merit of her parents' case is clear. All of the judges agreed that American constitutional law gives every competent adult the right to refuse medical treatment, and that the feeding and hydrating techniques that were keeping Nancy Cruzan's body alive did constitute medical treatment. The issues become cloudy only when the court considers the factual question of what Nancy's preferences actually were or would have been as to the continuance of this medical treatment. What little evidence was available to the court, the verbal testimony of a close teenage friend, suggested that Nancy had a deep aversion to her body being kept alive in a persistent vegetative state. . . . The situation in the Cruzan case, as the Supreme Court saw it, involved a conflict between the state's "interest in preserving human life" and Nancy Cruzan's constitutional right to have her preference for discontinuance of medical treatment in such circumstances honored.

The main problem, of course, is that there is only scanty evidence of what Nancy's preference actually was. So, given the state interest in preserving life (as we shall see, a very strange notion indeed as interpreted in this case), the state has the right to require especially convincing evidence of the preference for death. And so Missouri required not just a preponderance of the evidence, or a probability barely greater than half, but rather that "evidence of the incompetent's wishes as to the withdrawal of treatment be *proved by clear and convincing evidence*."[3] The main issue before the United States Supreme Court was whether the Missouri Supreme Court had a right to substitute this higher standard of evidence, and the highest court ruled that it did have that right.

What the Court did, in effect, was to go beyond the probable facts that constituted the merits of the Cruzan case to an external value judgment that would determine, from the outside as it were, what the facts of the case were. That value judgment is the same as the one underlying Kamisar's argument in euthanasia cases involving conscious suffering patients, namely that the Court's [skewed] allocation of the risk of error in our inferences to Nancy's preference is justified because it is more important *not* to terminate life support for someone who would wish it continued than to honor the wishes of someone [like Matthew Donnelly] who would not wish it continued. Like Professor Kamisar, the majority of the Supreme Court is determined that if it must err, it err on the "safe side." But the comparative value judgment that they bring in from the outside to give shape to the facts of the case, distorts those facts and, as I shall argue, misrepresents the case's actual merits.

II

Before returning to the subject of euthanasia, ii will be useful to consider one of the patterns of argument in other contexts that purports, often quite plausibly, to justify deciding cases on grounds other than what we can call their "internal merits." Consider for example the argument from abusable discretion. Suppose a legislature must decide what kind of night-time traffic signal, if any, to install at an intersection that has been the site of many nocturnal accidents. The least expensive solution would be to leave drivers free to decide whether lighting and traffic conditions require a complete stop, or only a slow-down and careful perusal of the traffic in both directions. The two rival proposals are that the ordinary three-color alternating stoplight continue to operate all night long and the counterproposal that from midnight until 6:00 in the morning the three-color alternating signal be converted into a yellow blinker, which is only a cautionary warning signal not requiring a stop. Imagine that studies of accident rates at similar intersections elsewhere show that there are twenty deaths a year at intersections that have all-night yellow blinkers, and only ten deaths at the intersections that have ordinary three-color alternations day and night. The argument for the all-night operation of the standard three-color light then is that it will probably cut in half the death rate from accidents at that corner. The argument on the other side is that ninety-nine percent of the drivers can be trusted to exercise careful discretion at this and other intersections especially at night when traffic is very sparse, and there are no obstructions to vision. It is not fair to this vast majority, so the argument goes, to inconvenience them by requiring them to stop, in total indifference to the merits of their own cases, just in order to deprive the tiny minority of untrustworthy drivers of a discretion they might abuse. . . .

An argument of similar form was frequently used by moderate drinkers in defense of their violations of the 1920's alcohol prohibition law, a law they often conceded to be supported by good reasons. The prohibitory law appeared to have a morally legitimate aim, namely reduction of the great harms caused by drunkards. But for people who had enjoyed their moderate drinking habits for decades and *knew* that they could be trusted to drink wine for dinner, or a highball at a party, without harmful consequences to others, it was natural to proceed in violation of a law they thought legitimate (for others) and to do so with clear consciences. This created a "market of innocents" and a business incentive for gangsters to sell in that market, with all the violent crime that led to the discrediting and eventually to the downfall, of Prohibition.

A law that grants terminal patients, their loved ones, or their physicians the legal authority to terminate lives, thereby confers discretion on those parties to decide their cases on the merits. If the situation is analogous to that in the traffic signal example, there will be some rare cases in which that discretion is abused. But the analogy is highly tenuous. What would count as "abuse" in the euthanasia case? What would be analogous to drunken or reckless driving in the other case? Again there is a danger of begging a central question in one kind of reply. One might say that the abuser of discretion is precisely he who uses it to choose death and not life, this being the kind of moral abuse that consists in giving priority to unworthy values like freedom from pain and personal autonomy. Whether in fact those values or the respect for human life are the most worthy ones is of course precisely the question at issue. . . .

In summary, we have found in everyday reasoning that there are some prohibitory rules that are defended with argument even though their defenders acknowledge that their applications in some individual cases are harmful. Deliberately overlooking these bad results in some individual cases is said to be a price worth paying to secure the greater benefits of the absolute prohibition. Some of these everyday arguments can be quite rational and convincing. It *can* be a rational social policy to withhold from trustworthy individuals discretion to make their own decisions on the ground that the less trustworthy individuals who would also be given that discretion by the same general rule might abuse it with socially harmful results. This form of argument can be rational to the extent that techniques to separate those who can be trusted with discretion from those who cannot, say by licensing procedures, are difficult and impractical.

The important point for our present purposes is that even though they all can be convincing in some everyday contexts, none of these forms of argument are plausible models for the categorical restriction of voluntary euthanasia. The least implausible model is that presupposed in Professor Kamisar's forceful argument for absolute prohibition. There may be no moral defect, Kamisar admits, in a given terminal patient's death request, when considered on the merits alone, and no reason internal to his case, for denying him the discretion to decide on his own whether his own life should continue. But if we grant discretion generally to all patients in similar circumstances, then some mistakes and abuses are bound to occur, and that would be an evil greater than the evil of denying the majority of patients the discretion their personal autonomy seems to require. So goes the argument from abusable discretion as applied to voluntary euthanasia. What separates the supporters from the critics of this argument is not a disagreement over the requirements of logic or over the empirical facts. It is a disagreement in value judgments—assessments of comparative costs or evils. Is it a greater evil that ten terminal patients suffering intolerable anguish be required to extend their hopeless existence against their clearly documented will than that one patient through medical mistake or the coercive influence of impatient relatives die unnecessarily? The controversy over legalized voluntary euthanasia hinges on questions of this form.

III

There is a comparative value judgment embedded in the Anglo-American criminal law, and traced by at least one writer to an Italian proverb (see Stevenson 1948, 1249, and cf. Reiman and van den Haag 1990), which had wide currency in the eighteenth century, and has been treated almost as a truism in Western nations ever since. In the pithy formulation of Sir William Blackstone, the maxim says that "It is better that ten guilty persons escape than that one innocent party suffer" (Blackstone 1844, 4:358). This use of numbers, of course, is a mere rhetorical device designed to make its message memorable. We cannot say with any degree of confidence that punishing the innocent is not only more unjust but exactly ten times more unjust than acquitting the guilty or that we are made to feel exactly ten times worse by the one kind of injustice than by the other. In fact, "we possess neither moral intuitions nor moral theories which could establish such a specific ratio" (Reiman and van den Haag 1990, 227). The core message in the famous slogan then is simply that it tends to be more unjust (even) to punish the innocent than to acquit the guilty. This maxim of justice should probably be treated like other moral precepts, as deliberately but usefully vague.

Still there are two ways in which numbers might get involved when this ethical maxim is actually invoked in a real life context. The first of these is well illustrated in the following series of examples:

> One of two identical twins is witnessed committing cold-blooded murder. It is impossible for anyone but the twins to tell themselves apart, and each claims that he was elsewhere when the murder was committed. You must choose between executing both or acquitting both. Since you would choose the latter (wouldn't you?), you regard it as *worse* to punish an innocent person than to let a guilty one escape punishment. The example-giver might then increase the size of the suspect family. Two of three identical triplets are witnessed committing cold-blooded murder (etc.). You must choose between executing all three or acquitting all three. Since you would still choose the latter (wouldn't you?), this implies even more strongly that you regard it as worse to punish an innocent person than to let a guilty one escape punishment. (Reiman and van den Haag 1990, 228)

In principle, we could increase the size of the murderous group to ten or more, although we should soon have to find some non-genetic explanation for the indistinguishable features of the suspects.

Part of what these hypothetical examples show is that our so-called "intuitions," which are so strong in the simple case of the identical twins, tend to weaken as the group of indistinguishable murder suspects grows larger. Part of the reason this is so, no doubt, is that we can no longer keep out of consideration the rights of unknown potential *victims* of this group of murderous rogues, and that weakens the focus of the example. No longer are we dealing with a comparison of two abstractions—ten acquittals of guilty persons versus one conviction of an innocent person. Now we have to add into our judgments a larger indeterminate number of potential innocent victims, and that so complicates the task for our intuitions that they can no longer give clear verdicts about the simple abstract moral problem with which we began. But we do learn something else of a useful nature from these examples, namely that occasions for the making of comparative numerical judgments between evils (types of injustice) can and do arise, within limits, in ordinary life.

The second way in which numbers may become involved in our judgments of comparative evils occurs at the level of policy creation. When we want to decide which is the worse evil, the enforced deprivation of a moderate "social drinker's" glass of wine with dinner or the continuance of the drunkard's heavy and dangerous drinking opportunities, for the purpose of legislating wisely in this area of drug abuse, then we need to have some accurate even though approximate sense of the relative numbers in the two groups. Once we get the numbers, our original question now assumes the more complex traditional formulation: Which is the worse evil, x million unrestrained drunkards or the prohibition of the harmless drinking of y million "social drinkers"?

We have done enough, however, to set the stage for a consideration of the "abusable discretion" argument against legalized voluntary euthanasia. The question before us has at least two parts, one involving numbers and one involving values (or evils). Which is the greater evil, we might ask, a rule which permits authorities to end the lives each year of $X,000$ suffering or comatose terminal patients at the cost of Y number of fatal mistakes, *or* a rule that categorically forbids the $X,000$ instances of voluntary euthanasia, thus preventing the Y number of mistaken killings? The evil caused by the first (permissive) rule is suffered by the Y number of patients who because of diagnostic error, unanticipated development of new cures, or psychological pressures, die needlessly or against their real wills. The evil caused by the second (prohibitory) rule is at the expense of terminal patients who are suffering pain, severe discomfort, and the anguish of hopelessness, and those who are irreversibly comatose but whose voluntary preferences for death in these circumstances are known or inferrable, and their friends and close relations. The prohibitory rule secures its benefits at the cost of pointless, emotionally wrenching and expensive maintenance of cortically dead bodies, and the continuance in pain and suffering of $X,000$ terminal patients. Is it possible to defend some rough rule of thumb like the Blackstone formula in the quite different context of guilt and punishment? Can we even hope to agree that *X* lives delivered from irreversible coma or intolerable pain is a greater good than the prevention of *Y* deaths through mistakes? Or, put negatively, that *Y* lives pointlessly ended is a greater evil than *X* lives pointlessly preserved in coma or pain? . . .

Professor Kamisar in his famous article apparently estimates that the number of victims of mistaken and unnecessary killing, if voluntary euthanasia were legalized, would be quite substantial. But his arguments for this estimate of numbers are not convincing, perhaps because he thinks that even small numbers of mistakes and abuses would be sufficient to discredit the euthanasia proposal, given the nature of the evil in those instances when compared with evils to those whose requests to die are turned down when euthanasia is kept illegal. In Blackstonian terms, I think that Kamisar believes that one life needlessly ended is a worse evil than ten lives needlessly and painfully extended.

Why does Kamisar think that under a system of voluntary euthanasia there would inevitably be, in his word, "appreciable" (Kamisar 1969, 105) mistakes and abuse? Mistakes, he thinks, would arise primarily from mistaken diagnoses and prognoses, and the chance of last minute medical discoveries. Exactly how frequently doctors diagnose curable illnesses to be fatal ones, and thus withhold treatments that would have been lifesaving, I cannot say. But any sensible scheme of euthanasia would require multiple medical consultations and other necessary ways of making sure, and despite the inevitability of some mistakes there are many more cases, like those of Matthew Donnelly and Nancy Beth Cruzan, that are perfectly clear. Why isn't the incorrect judgment in clearly incurable cases that those cases might be misdiagnosed just as morally telling a mistake as the rarer misdiagnoses given so much emphasis by Kamisar?

As for last minute medical discoveries, surely they cannot be the source of "appreciable" numbers of unnecessary killings. There is always a substantial delay between the discovery of a new medicine or a new surgical technique and its availability, and I suppose that awareness of the new possibility during that interval might in some cases revive hope and lead to postponement of mercy killing. In those cases the patient (or her guardian or proxy) and the physicians might keep the flickering hope alive as long as possible. In that way a sensible euthanasia scheme could accommodate the possibility of last minute discoveries. But equally certainly there are other cases that are incorrigibly hopeless, or such that the slenderness of the chance of a last minute discovery may not be worth the continued pain involved in the waiting. And in other cases there can be no chance whatever of a last minute cure, since the last minute has already come and gone. Once a cerebral cortex has been destroyed, for example, there can be nothing, short of a literal miracle, that can restore the existence of the comatose person. One can quibble about numbers and probabilities, and even concede that the number of otherwise terminal patients who turn out to be salvageable because of last minute discoveries is more than "tiny." The essential point from the moral point of view is that suspension of mercy killing for the vast majority of those who need and want it would be at least as serious a mistake as killing those who might have been saved, for all we can know, by a last minute discovery. Glanville Williams puts the point well: "Because of this risk for this tiny fraction of the total number of patients, patients who are dying in pain must be left to do so, year after year, against their entreaty to have it ended" (Williams 1969, 142).

Our traditional criminal law, Kamisar notes, does permit intentional killing in some circumstances, when it appears necessary for example to the defense of a threatened person or third parties. And of course, mistakes in judging this "necessity" in individual cases are inevitable. Reasonable mistakes in self-defense or defense of others, Kamisar explains, "are the inevitable by-products of efforts to save one or more human lives" (Kamisar 1969, 104). But can we not, in a perfectly parallel way, consider reasonable mistakes in a legalized voluntary euthanasia scheme to be "the inevitable by-products" of efforts to deliver human beings, at their own requests, from intolerable suffering, or from elaborate and expensive prolongations of a body's functioning in the permanent absence of any person to animate that body? Kamisar's answer is revealing: Only the saving of human lives, he thinks, is a value great enough to justify the taking of a human life. "The need the euthanasiast advances[...]is a good deal less compelling. It is only to ease pain" (Kamisar 1969, 104).

This view of the matter, which would have astonished Matthew Donnelly and the parents of Nancy Cruzan, is readily expressible in a Blackstonian formula without any numbers in its comparative judgment. In respect to guilt and innocence, Voltaire had written of "the great principle that it is better to run the risk to sparing the guilty than to condemn the innocent (Voltaire 1962, 20). Here there is no mention of numbers, no comparison of ten guilty men with one innocent person, as in Blackstone's more rhetorical formula. Perhaps Voltaire intended (or should have intended) a *ceteris paribus* clause— numbers and other possibly relevant matters being equal—to disconnect and isolate the point he was making, while acknowledging that in real life applications, matters are much more complex than his "great principle" would otherwise suggest, that numbers do count, and so do such externalities as the risk of further harm caused by the guilty who are "spared." Using Voltaire's maxim as a model for imitation we can attribute to Kamisar the view that it is better to run the risk that a patient, or her relatives and loved ones, will be made to suffer needlessly than to run the risk that a patient who requests euthanasia is not truly "terminal" or that his consent is not truly voluntary. Numbers aside, the maxim now says, when we compare one instance of needlessly taken life with one instance of needlessly extended life, considered in this abstract way, other things being equal, the former is always and necessarily a greater evil than the latter. That is, it is always a greater evil to let someone die by mistake than to keep a person alive by mistake. This non-numerical formulation of Kamisar's view makes it into a more modest and therefore a more plausible claim. Nevertheless, in the concluding section of this paper, after some efforts at clarification, I shall find reasons for doubting it.

IV

It should be clear then that two kinds of mistake are possible in the voluntary euthanasia situation, that both have their costs and projected frequencies. One creates the danger that curable patients will needlessly be killed or killed without their real consent; the other creates the danger that incurable terminal patients will have their sufferings pointlessly prolonged. It is the task of rule-makers to adopt the policy that will prevent the more serious mistakes, both in number and degree of evil, even at the cost of incurring inevitably the kind of mistake that exposes a smaller number to evils of lesser degree.

It will be my conclusion that one cannot say that one of the two kinds of mistake is in itself, isolated from other factors, always more serious than the other, and that *ceteris paribus* (degree of risk, numbers of affected people in each class, etc., being equal) that one kind of value, life, always is a weightier consideration than the other—cessation of suffering. Ordinarily we cannot get a pure *ceteris paribus* case, for there are always many variables in the euthanasia situation. In real life we compare real people who are always concrete and particular, and not mere abstract subjects for certain properties that interest us, and anyway no two have exactly the same properties. When we compare Matthew Donnelly or Nancy Beth Cruzan, say, with another specific person who *can* be saved, though knowing it not, he demands euthanasia *now*, we must consider properties other than the minimal characteristics that define the classes we are comparing. We must consider how severe is the suffering, thus how great an evil it is in itself, how old the patients are, how complex, expensive, and likely to succeed any future discovered treatment would have to be, and so on. Suppose we consider Donnelly who, let us imagine, is being asked to forego euthanasia because the rule permitting it will also enable a second patient to forego the soon-to-be-discovered last minute treatment that can cure him. In a concrete example like this, we would have a hard time ignoring such traits as the comparative ages, the life expectancies with and without treatment, the degree of vigorous activity that in the best outcome will be possible. We do not in this case deal with people as if they were personifications of abstractions like Suffering and Potential Salvageability. The degrees of comparative value and evil in our options will always be more complicated than that, since every patient must have some specific age, physical condition, and general prospect. Can we in good conscience impose another year of unremitting pain on Donnelly in order to protect a general rule that would permit a seventy-year-old Alzheimer Disease patient to be ready for a last minute cure, when he will have a two year life expectancy and an enfeebled bodily condition even if the possible last minute "cure" eventuates?

My thesis is that in the abstract, or as close as we can get to it, neither kind of consideration is weightier than the other. Hence, neither type of mistake is more serious than the other. In the comparison of actual concrete cases, sometimes one kind of mistake is more serious, sometimes the other. Kamisar, on the other hand, makes a categorical difference between the two types of mistakes, so that the one category in its entirety must always have priority. Considered "in themselves," in abstraction, *ceteris paribus,* we should always prefer the value in one category (life) over that in the other (surcease of hopeless suffering). On my view, in contrast, if we are forced to play the "whole category" game at all, we must conclude that the two categories of mistakes are of equal seriousness.

I am satisfied to let the Donnelly and Cruzan cases speak for themselves as examples of values that *can,* in a fully concrete context, outweigh life. That will enable me in the space that is left to deflate the value of "life preservation" as interpreted by various opponents of legalized voluntary euthanasia, especially the present United States Supreme Court. In this concluding section then, I shall concentrate, as it happens, on the recent pronouncements of the court about the value of life in the case of Nancy Beth Cruzan.

Why is it that the enemies of voluntary euthanasia attribute so great a value to "life as such" that it is supposed to outweigh even the evil of suffering whenever they conflict? Justice Rehnquist in his majority opinion in the Cruzan case admits that United States constitutional law[4] grants a right to all competent adults to refuse medical treatment if they wish. But this private "interest" in liberty must be balanced, Rehnquist declares, against relevant state interests. Chief among the latter is the state's interest in "the protection and preservation of human life." I am not sure how to explain this sense of "interest," but it would not be far off the mark to substitute for it "legitimate governmental function." Sometimes the state interest in the protection and preservation of human life overrides the liberty-interest of an individual in making his own decisions whether or not to accept a given medical treatment. Rehnquist's example of this is a Massachusetts case in 1905 in which the court favored the state's interest in preventing epidemic disease over an individual's liberty interest in declining an unwanted smallpox vaccination.[5] So even though "the forcible injection of medication into a nonconsenting person's body represents a substantial interference with that person's liberty,"[6] the state must give due weight to its function as protector of human life, even to the point sometimes of nullifying a citizen's constitutional right to liberty.

It is easy enough to understand why a court would legally compel a vaccination to help prevent the spread of a lethal disease, but how does this example serve to explain the state's interest in keeping Nancy Cruzan's mutilated body alive long after Nancy's person has vanished forever from it? Preservation of the functioning body of a departed person does no one any good. Not Nancy, because she will never know the difference, being permanently and irreversibly unconscious. Not the state of Missouri which must pay the costs of approximately $100,000 a year and rising. Not Nancy's parents for whom the unnatural preservation of the body of their beloved daughter is a ghoulish torture.

There remains of course the interest of Nancy as she was before she suffered her accident. Let us suppose for a moment that it was her firm and informed preference to be let die in case she should ever be rendered irreversibly comatose in an accident. This in fact was what she did prefer, according to the testimony of her friend and former roommate. If that is true, then keeping Nancy's body going while she is comatose is not in the interest of Nancy as she was before her accident. . . .

Now consider the other possibility, that Nancy did *not* have an informed preference for the continuance of medical sustenance after the onset of permanent coma. On this assumption either she was indifferent, never having even considered the matter perhaps, or she had a firm and informed preference that her living body be sustained. If she was indifferent, then it cannot be the case that her pre-accident interest would be set back by discontinuing her support. But if she preferred continuance, then it would appear that discontinuance would violate her pre-accident interest. But what kind of interest could it be that would be based on such a preference? It could not be an interest in having *her life* continued, for *ex hypothesi* nothing that happens will ever make any difference to her. If she were asked whether she would prefer death or permanent unconsciousness, she could not possibly express a rational choice, because from her own subjective point of view, there is not one iota of difference between death and permanent unconsciousness. From the perspective of the person whose life is at issue there is only a choice between permanent unconsciousness on the one hand and permanent unconsciousness on the other. On either alternative, there is no possibility of strivings, aversions, projects, goals, attachments, plans, actions, perceptions—the necessary components of a *human* life, as opposed to the "life," if we may use the word in that way, of a mere biological organism. . . .

Two types of mistake might be made in the treatment of patients in a persistent vegetative state like Nancy Cruzan, one of them very infrequent, the other very insignificant whenever it does occur. The infrequent mistake would be misdiagnosis—the expectation that the coma is irreversible when in fact it is not. In this age of high tech x-ray instruments, however, a cerebral cortex can be known to be both functionally incapacitated and progressively deteriorating, so that only a negligently superficial examination could lead to the mistaken prognosis. Physicians being human, of course, are fallible, and there will always be the possibility of error, but mistakes of this kind will not occur in significant numbers.

The other kind of mistake would be one of misattribution to the patient of a preference about the disposition of her living body. If she wants discontinuance of nutrition and care and doesn't get it, then that is a serious error, if not for her interests, for the interests of her parents, close relations, and friends, not to mention the bill-paying taxpayers. If, however, she prefers to have her body preserved in the manner of transferred property, just as if it were some handsome machine or art object, at the state's expense, and this genuine preference is misinterpreted or otherwise not honored, then *that* mistake is not a serious one. In short the risk of mistaken killing in cases of this kind is not in itself a very grave danger, partly because the purely medical mistake that could lead to the killing would not be made in significant numbers, and the mistaken attribution to the patient of a prior preference for death would not in itself be a very great evil.

The majority of the United States Supreme Court, however, found the danger of a mistaken withdrawal of life-sustaining treatment from Miss Cruzan a more serious evil than the danger of a mistake in the opposite direction, mainly because death is irrevocable and mistaken killings are therefore uncorrectible. The official summary of the Court's decision encapsulates the argument exactly:

> The clear and convincing evidence standard [. . .] serves as a social judgement about how the risk of error should be distributed between the litigants. Missouri may place the increased risk of erroneous decision on those seeking to terminate life-saving treatment. An erroneous decision not to terminate results in the maintenance of the *status quo* with at least the potential that a wrong decision will eventually be corrected or its impact mitigated by an event such as an advance in medical science or the patient's unexpected death. However, an erroneous decision to withdraw such treatment is not subject of correction.[7]

To this argument from the irrevocability of mistaken decisions to kill, Justice Brennan in his dissenting opinion makes the clear and obvious rejoinder: "From the point of view of the patient, an erroneous decision *in either direction* is irrevocable."[8] She is non-existent in either case, but her remains are on display permanently in the one case, but decently removed from view on the other.

> An erroneous decision to terminate artificial nutrition and hydration, to be sure, will lead to failure of that last remnant of physiological life, the brainstem, and result in complete brain death. An erroneous decision *not* to terminate the life-support however, robs a patient of the very qualities protected by the right to avoid unwanted medical treatment. His own degraded existence is perpetuated; his family's suffering is protracted; the memory he leaves behind becomes more and more distorted.[9]

And all of this, we might add, quite irrevocably.

The minority opinion of Justice Brennan correctly points out that there is no state interest in the preservation of merely biological life without consciousness, and hence that there can be no more a legitimate governmental function to maintain such "life" than there is to preserve some giant plant or vegetable. A life "completely abstracted from the interest of the person living that life"[10] can have no special value the state is committed to protect—nothing like the public health that can be threatened by an epidemic disease.

Of course Matthew Donnelly in *his* last days was in no way like a vegetable. Vegetables do not suffer pain and despair. But given the incurability of his condition, Donnelly's life was even less worth preserving, against his manifest will, than Nancy Cruzan's against the presumed preference she might have had before her accident. There is no point at all in keeping Nancy Cruzan's body alive, but no more possibility of harm to Nancy in doing so. The case for granting Donnelly his passionately requested relief, however, is stronger than that. We owe deliverance to the likes of Donnelly and we cruelly wrong him by withholding it from him. Letting him suffer unnecessarily for a full year is not to err on the "safe side." In life's difficult closing games there is often no safe side to err on; delay and inaction can be as serious a mistake as hasty or premature action. In that case we had better do whatever we can to let suffering patients determine their own course.

V

In summary, we have seen that most of the arguments against the legalization of voluntary euthanasia (or in favour of creating legal impediments to it) are indirect arguments. They don't argue that individual cases judged internally, that is on their own merits, do not warrant euthanasia. Indeed, some of these arguments candidly concede that judged on the merits, many individual cases do deserve euthanasia. Rather, these arguments favour deliberately overlooking the merits of individual cases, and cite extraneous considerations in favour of a blanket prohibition. The most plausible of these arguments is the argument from abusable discretion, which maintains that if legally competent individuals are granted the discretion to decide on their own whether in certain circumstances to continue or to terminate life-sustaining treatment, the inevitability of honest mistakes and not-so-honest abuses will create evils that outweigh the evils of sustaining the comatose and the pain-wracked against their presumed wills. Convincing as the argument from abusable discretion may be in some contexts, e.g., traffic control, it fails in its application to the euthanasia situation, because it cannot be shown that the likely number of mistakenly killed individuals would constitute a greater evil than the likely number of mistakenly sustained individuals. The philosophical problem of voluntary euthanasia is in large part a matter of comparing real risks. The enemy of voluntary euthanasia errs in minimizing the evils of human suffering and overrating the value of merely biological life in the absence of a human person, or in the presence of a human person whose sufferings are too severe for him to have a human life, even though his heart beats on.

NOTES

1. Rachels (1986, 32) writes that "Mr. Donelly begged his brother to shoot him, and he did."
2. *Nancy Beth Cruzan, By Her Parents and Co-Guardian, Lester L. Cruzan et ux, Petitioners v. Director, Missouri Department of Health,* 110 S Ct. 1028 (1990).
3. *Cruzan By Cruzan v. Harmon* 760 S.W. 2d, 408 (Mo banc 1488) at 415.

4. The primary source is the "Due Process" clause of the Fourteenth Amendment: "Nor shall any state deprive any person of life, liberty, or property, without due process of law." The key word in the application of this clause to medical treatment is "liberty."
5. Rehnquist cites *Jacobson v. Massachusetts,* 197 U.S. 11, 24–30 (1905).
6. Quoted by Rehnquist from *Washington v. Harper,* U.S. (1990).
7. *Cruzan v. Director, Missouri Department of Health,* at 2944.
8. *Ibid,* at 2873.
9. *Ibid.*
10. *Ibid,* at 2870.

REFERENCES

Black, Charles L., Jr. 1974. *Capital Punishment: The Inevitability of Caprice and Mistake.* New York: W. W. Norton.

Blackstone, William, 1844. *Commentaries on the Laws of England,* 21st ed. 4 vols. London: Sweet, Maxwell, Stevens & Norton.

Kamisar, Yale. 1969. "Euthanasia Legislation: Some Non-Religious Objections." In *Euthanasia and the Right to Death,* Ed. A. B. Downing. London: Peter Owen.

Poe, Edgar Allan, 1985a. "The Black Cat." In E. A. Poe, *Selected Writings.* Ed. D. Galloway, 320–29. Harmondsworth: Penguin.

_____. 1985b. "A Cask of Amontillado." In E. A. Poe, *Selected Writings.* Ed. D. Galloway, 360–66. Harmondsworth: Penguin.

Rachels, James. 1986. *The End of Life.* Oxford: Oxford University Press.

Reiman, Jeffrey, and Ernest van den Haag. 1990. "On the Common Saying that It Is Better that Ten Guilty Persons Escape than that One Innocent Suffer," *Social Philosophy and Policy* 7:226–48.

Stevenson, B., ed. 1948. *The Macmillan Book of Proverbs.* New York: Macmillan.

Voltaire, Jean François Marie Arouet de. 1962. "Zadig or Fate." In J. F. M. Arouet de Voltaire, *Candide and Other Stories.* London: Dent.

Williams, Glanville. 1969. "Euthanasia Legislation: A Rejoinder to the Non-Religious Objections." In *Euthanasia and the Right to Death.* Ed. A. B. Downing. London: Peter Owen.

Against the Right
to Die

J. David Velleman

In this essay J. David Velleman, who is a philosophy professor at the University of
Michigan, argues against the position that there should be a legally recognized right to
die that would allow some people, for instance terminal patients, to demand euthanasia.
Even though he believes that active euthanasia is sometimes morally justified and even
that people can be in a condition in which they would be morally entitled to
euthanasia, he does not think a right to die that would compel physicians to administer
euthanasia in those cases should be recognized. His subtle argument depends on the
claim that people are sometimes better off when they do not have the option of
choosing something that would be beneficial to them were it chosen and that they are
morally entitled to choose, and he believes the option to choose one's own death
through euthanasia is such a case. Having this option, he argues, can harm a person by
making it no longer possible to remain alive simply by default. Instead, one's continued
life is something that must be chosen and hence is something for which one can be
held responsible. For several reasons, Velleman argues that this responsibility can be
harmful. Velleman is uncertain about what the policy implications of his position should
be for the legal status of euthanasia. One possibility would be to permit euthanasia
when a physician has agreed to perform it, but Velleman worries that even this would,
in effect, give patients a harmful amount of control. He believes it may be better to
leave the laws against euthanasia as they are but not enforce them, at least not in a
vigorous manner.

In this paper[1] I offer an argument against establishing a right to die, but I do
not consider how my argument fares against countervailing considerations,
and so I do not draw any final conclusion on the subject. The argument laid
out in this paper has certainly inhibited me from favoring a right to die, and
it has also led me to recoil from many of the arguments offered for such a
right. But I am very far from an all-things-considered judgment.

My argument is addressed to a question of public policy—namely, whether
the law or the canons of medical practice should include a rule requiring,
under specified circumstances, that caregivers honor a patient's request to be
allowed or perhaps even helped to die. This question is distinct from the
question whether anyone is ever morally entitled to be allowed or helped to
die. I believe that the answer to the latter question is yes, but I doubt whether
our moral obligation to facilitate some people's deaths is best discharged
through the establishment of an institutional right to die.

From *The Journal of Medicine and Philosophy* 17 (1992), 665–681.

I

A moral entitlement to be allowed or helped to die is less likely to flow from principles of autonomy or respect, in my opinion, than from principles of simple benevolence. I strongly believe that a person's life can sometimes be made worse by being prolonged, and that a swift and painless death can then be a benefit (Velleman, 1991). I also believe that the harm of continuing to live can sometimes be sufficiently grave that causing or even allowing someone to undergo it would be morally wrong; or, conversely, that the benefit of death can sometimes be sufficiently important that providing it is morally obligatory. I therefore believe that someone can be morally entitled to be helped or allowed to die.

Furthermore, I believe that the proper goal of medical science is, not to prolong human life *per se,* but rather to make human life better—often by prolonging it, of course, but also by relieving pain, restoring function, or facilitating natural processes. And I know of no cogent reason why facilitating the process of death, when death would be a benefit, is a less appropriate activity for medical practitioners than that of facilitating the process of birth. I therefore believe, not only that a patient can have a moral right to passive or even active euthanasia, but also that his physician may be the appropriate person to provide it.

II

How can I think that death is sometimes a benefit to which a person can be morally entitled, and still argue against establishing a right to receive it? My answer, in its most general form, is that not all benefits—not even all morally significant benefits—can or should be secured by institutional rights.

Here a further clarification of 'the right to die' is in order. At present, there are institutional barriers that prevent or at least inhibit physicians from facilitating the deaths of patients to whom death would be a benefit. Since these institutional barriers hinder the provision of what I regard as a morally significant benefit, I am in favor of finding some way to remove them. And one might think that the removal of institutional barriers to morally justified euthanasia could in itself be described as the establishment of an institutional right to die.

Yet what 'the right to die' usually denotes, and what I have accepted it as denoting for the purposes of this paper, is not the mere absence of institutional barriers to justified euthanasia but the presence of an explicitly formulated, positive right to euthanasia, a right vested in patients by law or other institutional rules. Establishing a right to die, in this sense, is only one way of removing the barriers to justified euthanasia, and it is a rather extreme way of removing them. All that need be entailed in removing the barriers to justified euthanasia, strictly speaking, is a permission for caregivers to practice it, with the patient's consent; whereas the right to die would entail not just a permission but a positive obligation to practice euthanasia (or to give way to someone willing to practice it) at the patient's request.

Of course, merely permitting voluntary euthanasia might not guarantee that the benefit of death was provided in every case in which it was morally urgent. Patients' informed and earnest requests to die may well be the most reliable indicator of when death would be beneficial. Hence merely permitting rather than requiring caregivers to honor such requests would entail allowing for a gap between the need for euthanasia and the supply. What's more, a mere permission would fail to embody any moral rights of self-determination that patients may have in respect to their own deaths, since merely permitting voluntary euthanasia would still leave the ultimate decision in the hands of the caregiver rather than the patient.

But placing the decision in the hands of the patient is precisely what I am going to argue against. What is problematic about the right to die, in my opinion, is precisely that feature by virtue of which it exceeds a mere permission for caregivers to practice voluntary euthanasia—namely, that it gives the option of euthanasia directly to patients.

III

Yet how can I oppose giving the option of euthanasia to patients? One way, of course, would be to argue that giving this option to patients, even under carefully defined conditions, would commit us to assisting in some deaths that would not in fact be beneficial (Kamisar, 1970). But the argument that interests me does not depend on this strategy. My worry about the right to die is not that some patients might mistakenly choose to die when they would be better off living.

In order to demonstrate that I am not primarily worried about mistaken requests to die, I shall assume, from this point forward, that patients are infallible, and that euthanasia would therefore be chosen only by those for whom it would be a benefit. Even so, I believe, the establishment of a right to die would harm many patients, by increasing their autonomy in a sense that is not only un-Kantian but also very undesirable.

This belief is sometimes expressed in public debate, although it is rarely developed in any detail. Here, for example, is Yale Kamisar arguing against "Euthanasia Legislation":

> Is this the kind of choice... that we want to offer a gravely ill person? Will we not sweep up, in the process, some who are not really tired of life, but think others are tired of them; some who do not really want to die, but who feel they should not live on, because to do so when there looms the legal alternative of euthanasia is to do a selfish or a cowardly act? Will not some feel an obligation to have themselves "eliminated"... (Kamisar, 1970)?

Note that these considerations do not, strictly speaking, militate against euthanasia itself. Rather, they militate against a particular decision procedure for euthanasia—namely, the procedure of placing the choice of euthanasia in the patient's hands. What Kamisar is questioning in this particular passage is, not the practice of helping some patients to die, but rather the practice of asking them to choose whether to die. The feature of legalized euthanasia that troubles him is precisely its being an option offered to patients—the very feature for which it's touted, by its proponents, as an enhancement of the patients' autonomy. Kamisar's remarks thus betray the suspicion that this particular enhancement of one's autonomy is not to be welcomed.

But what exactly is the point of Kamisar's rhetorical questions? The whole purpose of giving people choices, surely, is to allow those choices to be determined by their reasons and preferences rather than ours. Kamisar may think that finding one's life tiresome is a good reason for dying whereas thinking that others find one tiresome is not. But if others honestly think otherwise, why should we stand in their way? Whose life is it, anyway?

IV

A theoretical framework for addressing this question can be found in Thomas Schelling's book *The Strategy of Conflict* (1960), and in Gerald Dworkin's paper 'Is more choice better than less?' (1982). These authors have shown that our intuitions about the value of options are often mistaken, and their work can help us to understand the point of arguments like Kamisar's.

We are inclined to think that, unless we are likely to make mistakes about whether to exercise an option (as I am assuming we are not), the value of having the option is as high as the value of exercising it and no lower than zero. Exercising an option can of course be worse than nothing, if it causes harm. But if we are not prone to mistakes, then we will not exercise a harmful option; and we tend to think that simply *having* the unexercised option cannot be harmful. And insofar as exercising an option would make us better off than we are, having the option must have made us better off than we were before we had it—or so we tend to think.

What Schelling showed, however, is that having an option can be harmful even if we do not exercise it and—more surprisingly—even if we exercise it and gain by doing so. Schelling's examples of this phenomenon were drawn primarily from the world of negotiation, where the only way to force one's opponent to settle for less may be by proving that one doesn't have the option of giving him more. Schelling pointed out that in such circumstances, a lack of options can be an advantage. The union leader who cannot persuade his members to approve a pay-cut, or the ambassador who cannot contact his head-of-state for a change of brief, negotiates from a position of strength; whereas the negotiator for whom all concessions are possible deals from weakness. If the rank-and-file give their leader the option of offering a pay-cut, then he may find that he has to exercise that option in order to get a contract, whereas he might have gotten a contract without a pay-cut if he had not had the option of offering one. The union leader will then have to decide whether to take the option and reach an agreement or to leave the option and call a strike. But no matter which of these outcomes would make him better off, choosing it will still leave him worse off than he would have been if he had never had the option at all.

Dworkin has expanded on Schelling's point by exploring other respects in which options can be undesirable. Just as options can subject one to pressure from an opponent in negotiation, for example, they can subject one to pressure from other sources as well. The night cashier in a convenience store doesn't want the option of opening the safe—and not because he fears that he'd make mistakes about when to open it. It is precisely because the cashier would know when he'd better open the safe that his having the option would make him an attractive target for robbers; and it's because having the option would make him a target for robbers that he'd be better off without it. The cashier who finds himself opening the safe at gunpoint can consistently think that he's doing what's best while wishing that he'd never been given the option of doing it.

Options can be undesirable, then, because they subject one to various kinds of pressure; but they can be undesirable for other reasons, too. Offering someone an alternative to the status quo makes two outcomes possible for him, but neither of them is the outcome that was possible before. He can now choose the status quo or choose the alternative; but he can no longer *have* the status quo without *choosing* it. And having the status quo by default may have been what was best for him, even though choosing the status quo is now worst. If I invite you to a dinner party, I leave you the possibilities of choosing to come or choosing to stay away; but I deprive you of something that you otherwise would have had—namely, the possibility of being absent from my table by default, as you are on all other evenings. Surely, preferring to accept an invitation is consistent with wishing you had never received it. These attitudes are consistent because refusing to attend a party is a different outcome from *not* attending without having to refuse; and even if the former of these outcomes is worse than attending, the latter may still have been better. Having choices can thus deprive one of desirable outcomes whose desirability depends on their being unchosen.

The offer of an option can also be undesirable because of what it expresses. To offer a student the option of receiving remedial instruction after class is to imply that he is not keeping up. If the student needs help but doesn't know it, the offer may clue him in. But even if the student does not need any help, to begin with, the offer may so undermine his confidence that he will need help before long. In the latter case, the student may ultimately benefit from accepting the offer, even though he would have been better off not receiving it al all.

Note that in each of these cases, a person can be harmed by having a choice even if he chooses what's best for him. Once the option of offering a concession has undermined one's bargaining position, once the option of opening the safe has made one the target of a robbery, once the invitation to a party has eliminated the possibility of absence by default, once the offer of remedial instruction has implied that one needs it—in short, once one has been offered a problematic choice—one's situation has already been altered for the worse, and choosing what's best cannot remedy the harm that one has already suffered. Indeed, choosing what's best in these cases is simply a way of cutting one's losses. . . .

V

Of course, the options that I have discussed can also be unproblematic for many people in many circumstances. Sometimes one has good reason to welcome a dinner invitation or an offer of remedial instruction. Similarly, some patients will welcome the option of euthanasia, and rightly so. The problem is how to offer the option only to those patients who will have reason to welcome it. Arguments like Kamisar's are best understood, I think, as warning that the option of euthanasia may unavoidably be offered to some who will be harmed simply by having the option, even if they go on to choose what is best.

I think that the option of euthanasia may harm some patients in all of the ways canvassed above; but I will focus my attention on only a few of those ways. The most important way in which the option of euthanasia may harm patients, I think, is that it will deny them the possibility of staying alive by default.

Once a person is given the choice between life and death, he will rightly be perceived as the agent of his own survival. Whereas his existence is ordinarily viewed as a given for him—as a fixed condition with which he must cope—formally offering him the option of euthanasia will cause his existence thereafter to be viewed as his doing.

The problem with this perception is that if others regard you as choosing a state of affairs, they will hold you responsible for it; and if they hold you responsible for a state of affairs, they can ask you to justify it. Hence if people ever come to regard you as existing by choice, they may expect you to justify your continued existence. If your daily arrival in the office is interpreted as meaning that you have once again declined to kill yourself, you may feel obliged to arrive with an answer to the question 'Why not?'.

I think that our perception of one another's existence as a given is so deeply ingrained that we can hardly imagine what life would be like without it. When someone shows impatience or displeasure with us, we jokingly say 'Well, excuse me for living!'. But imagine that it were no joke; imagine that living were something for which one might reasonably be thought to need an excuse. The burden of justifying one's existence might make existence unbearable—and hence unjustifiable.

VI

I assume that people care, and are right to care, about whether they can justify their choices to others. Of course, this concern can easily seem like slavishness or neurotic insecurity; but it should not be dismissed too lightly. Our ability to justify our choices to the people around us is what enables us to sustain the role of rational agent in our dealings with them; and it is therefore essential to our remaining, in their eyes, an eligible partner in cooperation and conversation, or an appropriate object of sympathy and respect.

Retaining one's status as a person among others is especially important to those who are ill or infirm. I imagine that when illness or infirmity denies one the rewards of independent activity, then the rewards of personal intercourse may be all that make life worth living. To the ill or infirm, then, the ability to sustain the role of rational person may rightly seem essential to retaining what remains of value in life. Being unable to account for one's choices may seem to entail the risk of being perceived as unreasonable—as not worth reasoning with—and consequently being cut off from meaningful intercourse with others, which is life's only remaining consolation.

Forcing a patient to take responsibility for his continued existence may therefore be tantamount to confronting him with the following prospect: unless he can explain, to the satisfaction of others, why he chooses to exist, his only remaining reasons for existence may vanish.

VII

Unfortunately, our culture is extremely hostile to any attempt at justifying an existence of passivity and dependence. The burden of proof will lie heavily on the patient who thinks that his terminal illness or chronic disability is not a sufficient reason for dying.

What is worse, the people with whom a patient wants to maintain intercourse, and to whom he therefore wants to justify his choices, are often in a position to incur severe financial and emotional costs from any prolongation of his life. Many of the reasons in favor of his death are therefore likely to be exquisitely salient in their minds. I believe that some of these people may actively pressure the patient to exercise the option of dying. (Students who hear me say this usually object that no one would ever do such a thing. My reply is that no one would ever do such a thing as abuse his own children or parents—except that many people do.)

In practice, however, friends and relatives of a patient will not have to utter a word of encouragement, much less exert any overt pressure, once the option of euthanasia is offered. For in the discussion of a subject so hedged by taboos and inhibitions, the patient will have to make some assumptions about what they think and how they feel, irrespective of what they say (See, Schelling, 1984). And the rational assumption for him to make will be that they are especially sensible of the considerations in favor of his exercising the option.

Thus, even if a patient antecedently believes that his life is worth living, he may have good reason to assume that many of the people around him do not, and that his efforts to convince them will be frustrated by prevailing opinions about lives like his, or by the biases inherent in their perspective. Indeed, he can reasonably assume that the offer of euthanasia is itself an expression of the attitudes that are likely to frustrate his efforts to justify declining it. He can therefore assume that his refusal to take the option of euthanasia will threaten his standing as a rational person in the eyes of friends and family, thereby threatening the very things that make his life worthwhile. This patient may rationally judge that he's better off taking the option of euthanasia, even though he would have been best off not having the option at all.

Establishing a right to die in our culture may thus be like establishing a right to duel in a culture obsessed with personal honor. If someone defended the right to duel by arguing that a duel is a private transaction between consenting adults, he would have missed the point of laws against duelling. What makes it rational for someone to throw down or pick up a gauntlet may be the social costs of choosing not to, costs that result from failing to duel only if one fails to duel by choice. Such costs disappear if the choice of duelling can be removed. By eliminating the option of duelling (if we can), we eliminate the reasons that make it rational for people to duel in most cases. To restore the option of duelling would be to give people reasons for duelling that they didn't previously have. Similarly, I believe, to offer the option of dying may be to give people new reasons for dying.

VIII

Do not attempt to refute this argument against the right to die by labelling it paternalistic. The argument is not paternalistic—at least, not in any derogatory sense of the word. Paternalism, in the derogatory sense, is the policy of saving people from self-inflicted harms, by denying them options that they might exercise unwisely. Such a policy is distasteful because it expresses a lack of respect for others' ability to make their own decisions.

But my argument is not paternalistic in this sense. My reason for withholding the option of euthanasia is not that others cannot be trusted to exercise it wisely. On the contrary, I have assumed from the outset that patients will be infallible in their deliberations. What I have argued is—not that people to whom we offer the option of euthanasia might harm themselves—but rather that in offering them this option, *we* will do them harm. My argument is therefore based on a simple policy of non-malfeasance rather than on the policy of paternalism. I am arguing that we must not harm others by giving them choices, not that we must withhold the choices from them lest they harm themselves.

IX

I have been assuming, in deference to existentialists, that a right to die would not alter the options available to a patient but would, at most, alter the social perception of his options. What would follow, however, if we assumed that death was not ordinarily a genuine option? In that case, offering someone the choice of euthanasia would not only cause his existence to be perceived as his responsibility; it would actually cause his existence to *be* his responsibility for the first time. And this new responsibility might entail new and potentially burdensome obligations.

That options can be undesirable because they entail obligations is a familiar principle in one area of everyday life—namely, the practice of offering, accepting, and declining gifts and favors. When we decline a gift or a favor that someone has spontaneously offered, we deny him an option, the option of providing us with a particular benefit. And our reason for declining is often that he could not have the option of providing the benefit without being obligated to exercise that option. Indeed, we sometimes feel obligated, on our part, to decline a benefit precisely in order to prevent someone from being obligated, on his part, to provide it.[2] We thus recognize that giving or leaving someone the option of providing a benefit to us may be a way of harming him, by burdening him with an obligation.

When we decline a gift or favor, our would-be benefactor sometimes protests in language similar to that used by proponents of the right to die. 'I know what I'm doing' he says, 'and no one is twisting my arm. It's my money [or whatever], and I *want* you to have it'. If he's unaware of the lurking allusion, he might even put it like this: 'Whose money is it, anyway?'

Well, it *is* his money (or whatever); and we do believe that he's entitled to dispose of his money as he likes. Yet his right of personal autonomy in disposing of his money doesn't always require that we let him dispose of it on us. We are entitled—and, as I have suggested, sometimes obligated—to restrict his freedom in spending his money for our benefit, insofar as that freedom may entail burdensome obligations.

The language in which favors are declined is equally interesting as that in which they are offered. What we often say when declining a favor is, 'I can't let you do that for me: it would be too much to ask'. The phrase 'too much to ask' is interesting because it is used only when we haven't in fact asked for anything. Precisely because the favor in question would be too much to ask, we haven't asked for it, and now our prospective benefactor is offering it spontaneously. Why, then, do we give our reason for not soliciting the favor as a reason for declining when it's offered unsolicited?

The answer, I think, is that we recognize how little distance there is between permitting someone to do us a favor and asking him to do it. Because leaving someone the option of doing us a favor can place him under an obligation to do it, it has all the consequences of asking for the favor. To say 'I'm leaving you the option of helping me but I'm not *asking* you to help' is to draw a distinction without a difference, since options can be just as burdensome as requests.

X

Clearly, a patient's decision to die will sometimes be a gift or a favor bestowed on loved ones whose financial or emotional resources are being drained by his condition. And clearly, death is the sort of gift that one might well want to decline, by denying others the option of giving it. Yet institutional rules guaranteeing the option of euthanasia would in effect guarantee the option of giving this gift, and they would thereby prevent the prospective beneficiaries from declining it. Establishing a right to die would thus be tantamount to adopting the public policy that death is never too much to ask.

I don't pretend to understand fully the ethics of gifts and favors. It's one of those subjects that gets neglected in philosophical ethics, perhaps because it has more to do with the supererogatory that the obligatory. One question that puzzles me is whether we are permitted to restrict people's freedom to benefit us in ways that require no active participation on our part. Someone cannot successfully give us a gift, in most cases, unless we cooperate by taking it into our possession; and denying someone the option of giving us a gift usually consists in refusing to do our part in the transaction. But what about cases in which someone can do us a good turn without any cooperation from us? To what extent are we entitled to decline the favor by means of restrictions on his behavior rather than omissions in ours?

Another question, of course, is whether we wouldn't, in fact, play some part in the deaths of patients who received socially sanctioned euthanasia. Would a medically assisted or supervised death be a gift that we truly took no part in accepting? What if 'we'—the intended beneficiary of the gift—were society as a whole, the body that established the right to die and trained physicians in its implementation? Surely, establishing the right to die is tantamount to saying, to those who might contemplate dying for the social good, that such favors will never be refused.

These considerations, inconclusive though they are, show how the theoretical framework developed by Schelling and Dworkin might support remarks like Kamisar's about patients' "obligation to have themselves 'eliminated'". The worry that a right to die would become an obligation to die is of a piece with other worries about euthanasia, not in itself, but as a problematic option for the patient.

XI

As I have said, I favor euthanasia in some cases. And of course, I believe that euthanasia must not be administered to competent patients without their consent. To that extent, I think that the option of dying will have to be presented to some patients, so that they can receive the benefit of a good death.

On the basis of the foregoing arguments, however, I doubt whether policymakers can formulate a general definition that distinguishes the circumstances in which the option of dying would be beneficial from those in which it would be harmful. The factors that make an option problematic are too subtle and too various to be defined in a statute or regulation. How will the option of euthanasia be perceived by the patient and his loved ones? How will it affect the relations among them? Is he likely to fear being spurned for declining the option? Would he exercise the option merely as a favor to them? And are they genuinely willing to accept that favor? Sensitivity to these and related questions could never be incorporated into an institutional rule defining conditions under which the option must be offered.

Insofar as I am swayed by the foregoing arguments, then, I am inclined to think that society should at most permit, and never require, health professionals to offer the option of euthanasia or to grant patients' requests for it. We can probably define some conditions under which the option should never be offered; but we are not in a position to define conditions under which it should always be offered; and so we can at most define a legal permission rather than a legal requirement to offer it. The resulting rule would leave caregivers free to withhold the option whenever they see fit, even if it is explicitly and spontaneously requested. And so long as caregivers are permitted to withhold the option of euthanasia, patients will not have a right to die.

XII

Let me offer one further reflection. The foregoing arguments make me worry even about an explicitly formulated permission for the practice of euthanasia, since an explicit law or regulation to this effect would already invite patients, and hence potentially pressure them, to request that the permission be exercised in their case. I feel most comfortable with a policy of permitting euthanasia by default—that is, by a tacit failure to enforce the institutional rules that currently serve as barriers to justified euthanasia, or a gradual elimination of those rules without fanfare. The best public policy on euthanasia, I sometimes think, is no policy at all.

This suggestion will surely strike some readers as scandalous, because of the trust that it would place in the individual judgment of physicians and patients. But I suspect that to place one's life in the hands of another person, in the way that one does today when placing oneself in the care of a physician, may simply be to enter a relationship in which such trust is essential, because it cannot be replaced or even underwritten by institutional guarantees. Although I do not share the conventional view that advances in medical technology have outrun our moral understanding of how they should be applied, I am indeed tempted to think they have outrun the capacity of institutional rules to regulate their application. I am therefore tempted to think that public policy regulating the relation between physician and patient should be weak and vague by design; and that insofar as the aim of medical ethics is to strengthen or sharpen such policy, medical ethics itself is a bad idea.

NOTES

1. This paper began as a comment on a paper by Dan Brock, presented at the Central Division of the APA in 1991. See *The Hastings Center Report* 1992, 22,

March/April, 10–22. For comments on the ideas presented here, I am indebted to Brock, Elizabeth Anderson, David Hills, Yale Kamisar, and Patricia White.

2. Of course, there are many other reasons for declining gifts and favors, such as pride, embarrassment, or a desire not to be in someone else's debt. My point is simply that there are cases in which these reasons are absent and a very different reason is present—namely, our desire not to burden someone else with obligations.

REFERENCES

Ackerman, Felicia: 1990, 'No, thanks, I don't want to die with dignity', *Providence Journal-Bulletin,* April 19, 1990.

Camus, Albert: 1956, 'The myth of Sisyphus', in *The Myth of Sisyphus and Other Essays,* tr. by Justin O'Brien, Vintage Books, New York.

Dworkin, Gerald: 1982, 'Is more choice better than less?', *Midwest Studies in Philosophy* 7, pp. 47–61.

Kamisar, Yale: 1970, 'Euthanasia legislation: Some non-religious objections', in A. B. Downing (ed.), *Euthanasia and the Right to Die*, Humanities Press, New York, pp. 85–133.

Schelling, Thomas: 1960, *The Strategy of Conflict,* Harvard University Press, Cambridge, Massachusetts.

Schelling, Thomas: 1984, 'Strategic relationships in dying', in *Choice and Consequence,* Harvard University Press, Cambridge, Massachusetts.

Velleman, J. David: 1991, 'Well-being and time', *Pacific Philosophical Quarterly* 72, pp. 48–77.

SUGGESTIONS FOR FURTHER READING

Battin, Margaret P. "Seven Caveats Concerning the Discussion of Euthanasia in Holland," *American Philosophical Association Newsletter on Philosophy and Medicine* 89 (Autumn 1990), 78–80.

In this essay and the next entry, Battin argues that bioethicists need to be careful about trying to draw conclusions from the practice of active euthanasia in Holland.

Battin, Margaret P. "Seven (More) Caveats Concerning the Discussion of Euthanasia in Holland," *American Philosophical Association Newsletter on Philosophy and Medicine* 92 (Spring 1993), 76–80.

Gunderson, Martin and David J. Mayo. "Altruism and Physician Assisted Death," *The Journal of Medicine and Philosophy* 18 (1993), 281–295.

The authors maintain that the primary argument for supporting active euthanasia is autonomy, and that arguments based on autonomy should support voluntary active euthanasia in cases in which the patient's condition is not terminal and cases in which a patient wishes euthanasia for altruistic reasons (e.g., to spare loved ones from a financial burden), as well as for self-interested ones.

Kass, Leon R. "Is There a Right to Die?" *The Hastings Center Report* 23 (January/February 1993), 34–43.

A vigorous argument against the views that there is a moral right to die and that there should be a legally recognized right to die.

Potts, Stephen G. "Looking for the Exit Door: Killing and Caring in Modern Medicine," *Houston Law Review* 25 (1988), 493–515.

Potts argues that given the possible bad consequences of legalizing active euthanasia, the burden of proof is on those who support legalization.

Rachels, James. *The End of Life: Euthanasia and Morality.* (Oxford, England: Oxford University Press, 1986).

A more thorough and recent defense of euthanasia by Rachels than the essay reprinted in this chapter.

Sullivan, Thomas D. "Active and Passive Euthanasia: An Impertinent Distinction?" *Human Life Review* 3 (1977), 40–46.

An attempt to respond to James Rachels's defense of active euthanasia.

Chapter 4

THE DEATH PENALTY

Over the past few decades, the death penalty has been abolished in many countries around the world, especially in Western democracies. In 1972, it appeared as if the United States would be a part of this trend when the Supreme Court ruled in *Furman v. Georgia* that the death penalty was unconstitutional because it was administered in an arbitrary and capricious manner. States in which there was strong support for capital punishment immediately began to draft legislation regulating the administration of the death penalty in order to reduce the arbitrariness of its application, and in 1976 the Supreme Court ruled in *Gregg v. Georgia* that the death penalty was constitutional for the crime of murder. Since 1976, public support for the death penalty has apparently grown, most states now have reinstituted the death penalty, and the number of executions grows from year to year.

The intentional killing of a human being is nearly always considered to be a great wrong. While most believe that there are exceptions to the wrongness of killing, such as self-defense, those exceptions are thought to be rare. Should the execution of murderers be considered to be among those exceptions? Dramatically opposed answers are given to this question. Those who wish to abolish the death penalty (often referred to as "abolitionists") sometimes claim that the state itself descends to the same moral level as murderers when it intentionally kills as a form of punishment. They claim that the murder of murderers is still, after all, murder and hence wrong. Some of those wishing to retain the death penalty (so-called "retentionists") argue that justice demands that murderers be executed. In this chapter, the abolitionist perspective is represented by Hugh Adam Bedau, while Ernest van den Haag defends the retentionist perspective. In between these positions would be one that holds that capital punishment is morally permissible but not morally required.

While the debate concerning the permissibility of capital punishment has captured much of the attention directed towards criminal justice, it is important to note that legal punishment in general is in need of justification. A concern that capital punishment may not be justifiable should be seen, at least initially, as just a special case of the more general concern that punishment of any sort may not be justifiable. All forms of punishment involve treating people in ways that at least under normal circumstances would be wrong. Fines coercively deprive people of their property; prisons deprive people of their liberty. At least typically, it is seriously wrong to take people's property and liberty. Why does punishment constitute an exception to this wrongness? Furthermore, those who are punished usually suffer because of the punishment; indeed, suffering seems to be the aim of punishment, not merely an unavoidable though regrettable consequence of it. The very point of punishment would appear to be to make the offender suffer. How can the intentional infliction of suffering be justified? Such questions lead to attempts to provide a general justification of punishment. Presumably, one's view about capital punishment specifically should be informed by one's view about what, if anything, justifies punishment generally.

The two primary traditions in the quest for a general justification of legal punishment are utilitarianism and retributivism. They differ in part in the temporal direction to which they look for justification. For utilitarians, punishment is justified to the extent to which it leads to a better future, a future with greater net utility. Retributivists, on the other hand, see the idea of desert as being key to understanding justified punishment. Those who are guilty of certain moral wrongs deserve punishment according to this tradition, so punishment is justified by what has already occurred; the offender did something deserving of punishment. We shall now look a bit more carefully at each tradition.

UTILITARIANISM

A utilitarian's initial thought about punishment would probably be that it involves the infliction of suffering on those who are punished. Since, according to utilitarianism, all suffering is intrinsically evil, punishment starts off with a strike against it since it involves an intrinsic evil. As a result, utilitarians, unlike retributivists, should not be committed to having a system that punishes offenders at all. A society should get into the business of punishing only if it is a cost-effective method of social control. Since a practice of punishing inflicts pain, it has a utilitarian cost that can be justified only if it brings about benefits that outweigh those costs *and* only if there is no less costly way of achieving those benefits. In other words, if utilitarians are to approve of punishment at all, their reasons should be similar to the reasons many of us might have for approving dentistry, a practice that in itself is unpleasant but a necessary evil in that the unpleasantness of its practice can prevent even greater unpleasantness. If the goals of dentistry could be achieved in some less unpleasant manner, by taking a daily pill perhaps, then dentistry would not be justifiable on utilitarian grounds. Similarly, if the benefits sought by punishment could be achieved in some other manner involving less suffering, then a system inflicting punishment would not be justifiable on utilitarian grounds. Indeed, some have thought that legal offenders should be seen as being in need of treatment of some sort rather than punishment. Few utilitarians, at this point however, seem to support eliminating our system of punishment entirely.

For utilitarians the primary benefit sought through a system of punishment would be reducing crime and hence the pain suffered because of crime. Punishment could reduce crime both by deterring people from potential criminal acts with the threat of punishment and by incapacitation, making those prone to commit crime incapable of doing so. Two types of deterrence might be thought to be achievable through punishment—specific and general deterrence. Specific deterrence is achieved when an offender is punished and is dissuaded from further offenses by a fear of additional punishment. General deterrence is achieved when the example of an offender's punishment dissuades others from committing criminal offenses, or when the mere threat of punishment, even if it is never used, leads people not to offend. Punishment can also incapacitate. For example, someone who is in prison is unable to commit at least some crimes that would be possible were he or she not incarcerated. It is often argued that the death penalty is a uniquely effective means of incapacitation.

It would appear, then, that the primary benefit of punishment for a utilitarian is less crime, and the primary cost would be the unhappiness of those who are punished. However, these are but some of the benefits and costs. It is worth considering what factors utilitarians would need to consider in determining whether some specific punishment would be appropriate for some specific crime. To simplify, let us imagine a utilitarian is considering punishing a particular act, say some form of physical assault, with a specific penalty. (This is a simplification in many ways. For example, a thorough utilitarian should consider a range of possible penalties, not as we are imagining a particular penalty or none at all.) To determine whether or not the act should be so punished, a utilitarian needs to consider two possible futures that are identical except for the respect that in one the act is punished and in the other it is not, and ask in which of those futures will there be greater net utility. So we need to consider what utility and disutility will be created by the punishment, and what utility and disutility would exist only if the act is not punished. Let us suppose we have already considered the way in which utility will be affected and proceed to consider some of the ways in which the two possible futures might differ in the pain and unhappiness they may contain.

First, let us consider some of the additional pains that will exist in the world in which assault is not punished. Under the assumption that punishment would deter some assaults and prevent others because the potential offenders have been incapacitated, a world that does not punish for assault will contain more assaults and, hence more pain of being a victim of assault. Furthermore, the victims' families and friends will suffer. In addition, when assault is more prevalent, people will feel insecure and frightened. What are some of the additional pains created by punishing those who assault? Most obviously, those who assault and who are caught and convicted will suffer from the punishment itself, and their families and friends will probably suffer as well. But even those who are not caught and convicted are likely to suffer because they fear being caught and punished. (Consider, for example, the temporary panic many of us suffer when we inadvertently run a red light and anxiously look around to see whether a police car is in sight.) Some who never commit assault will suffer because they are successfully deterred from acts they wish to engage in. Put simply, they will suffer from the frustration of wanting to assault but having to repress the desire because of the fear of punishment.

Obviously, this discussion of some of the ways the world in which assault is not punished will differ from the world in which it is punished in the pains that each will include is highly incomplete. Furthermore, the pains we have mentioned were also carefully selected to highlight a feature of the utilitarian approach to punishment that many find troubling. This feature might be explained partially by pointing out that for utilitarians, pains differ in moral quality only by virtue of their quantity. All pains are intrinsically bad for utilitarians, but some pains are intrinsically worse than others—the greater pains are always worse. Many feel that some pains are morally worse than others for reasons other than how severe those pains are. One of our students once looked at a similar list of the ways in which these two worlds might differ in the pains they include, and her response was straightforward and thoughtful. She said, "I look at such things as the apprehension felt by those who assault before they are caught and the frustration felt by those who want to assault but are deterred by a threat of punishment. Then I look at the pain of those who have been assaulted and the frustration of those too afraid of being assaulted to go out at night. When I compare these and look at the former, I think: So what? Who cares?"

Her point, which may be felt intuitively by many, is that the utilitarian approach seems to leave something out. For utilitarians pain is pain, all pain is intrinsically bad, and its badness does not depend on who feels it. However, for many, there appears to be a difference between the pain of the innocent and the pain of the guilty; the former seems worse and not merely because it is a greater pain. Some pains seem to be deserved and hence less bad, while some seem undeserved and hence worse. These differences seem to be left out of the utilitarian account.

This particular worry about utilitarianism is a special case of a more general objection some have raised. Utilitarianism is in the first instance concerned entirely with how much utility there is and not with how that utility is distributed. For utilitarians, patterns of distribution matter only to the extent to which they affect the aggregate net utility. Many, however, believe that justice requires us to be sensitive to issues of distribution for their own sake. Some, for example, would believe that distributions of wealth can become unjust simply by virtue of becoming too unequal, and even more people would think that a distribution of pain could become unjust by virtue of falling more heavily on the innocent than the guilty.

These considerations are not meant to suggest that a utilitarian approach would lead to the "wrong" result—that, for, instance, utilitarians would be likely to decriminalize physical assault. There is little doubt that when all the pleasures and pains are calculated there will be utilitarian reasons to try to control the use of physical violence. However, some believe that while utilitarians would arrive at the correct conclusion in this case, they would do so while omitting a morally relevant consideration—the difference between innocent and guilty suffering. Of course, utilitarians might respond that an act should be regarded as creating guilt only because it is the sort of act that is likely to cause significant net pain. So these intuitions about who is guilty and deserving of punishment and who is innocent are baseless unless they can be seen to rest ultimately on utilitarian considerations. We shall not pursue further this utilitarian attempt to allay the concern about utilitarianism's apparent lack of recognition of the moral significance of the difference between guilt and innocence.

RETRIBUTIVISM

What appears to be left out of consideration by a utilitarian approach to punishment, namely the moral significance of the difference between guilt and innocence, is precisely what is stressed by retributivism. Retributivists see punishment as an appropriate response, even a response demanded by justice, to certain forms of moral guilt. Those who behave in ways that are wrong deserve to be punished, and such desert is the sole legitimate justification for punishment. Classical retributivism has three elements:

1. Only the guilty should be punished.
2. The guilty should always be punished.
3. The severity of the punishment should be proportionate to the degree of guilt.

Since retributivism is a theory of just punishment, the idea of guilt it uses is not simply a matter of legal guilt but one of moral guilt. (Presumably, it would not be just to punish someone who disobeys a seriously immoral law.) Consequently, retributivists must appeal to some other moral theory to determine when exactly punishment is due. In other words, retributivism differs from a utilitarian theory of punishment; the latter is simply an application of a more general moral theory to the specific topic of punishment. Retributivism is specifically a theory of punishment that conditions justified punishment on moral guilt. The notion of moral guilt, however, is not itself explained by retributivism. Many retributivists are Kantians, and indeed Immanuel Kant held a firm retributivist position about punishment, but one could hold other background moral theories and be a retributivist. It is worth asking, though the matter will not be pursued here, whether it would be possible to hold utilitarianism as a background moral theory and be a retributivist concerning punishment.

The first two elements of the retributivist position are two aspects of a single idea, the idea that justice demands that people be treated as they deserve to be treated. Retributivists believe punishing those who are innocent would be a serious injustice, because it would be a matter of intentionally inflicting pain on those who are undeserving of it. However, most retributivists believe that a failure to punish those who are guilty would be an equally serious injustice, and it would be unjust for the same reason, namely that it fails to treat people according to their deserts. Those who have acted in a guilty manner deserve punishment for their behavior, and justice demands that they be responded to in the way they deserve.

The third element of retributivism is sometimes put by saying that the punishment should fit the crime. This claim is obviously a metaphor. Punishments are not like shoes that come with size numbers marked on them, nor is it obvious how crimes should be "sized," so a full understanding of retributivism requires an explanation of this metaphor. We shall return to this matter below when discussing how retributivists might view capital punishment.

Many Kantians believe that retributivism, unlike utilitarianism, treats even criminal offenders as ends in themselves rather than as mere means, because retributivists respond both to the innocent and guilty alike in ways that are determined by features of those guilty and innocent individuals. In order to treat a person as he or she deserves, one's focus must be on that person to determine the appropriate treatment. Furthermore, the thought that the punishment should "fit" the crime requires that one tailor one's treatment of the person punished to that person's specific acts. Compare this way of determining appropriate punishment with the way in which one would choose punishment if the goal is general deterrence. If this is our goal, the severity of punishment should depend in part on the nature of those whom we wish to deter. If the targeted group is easily frightened by the threat of punishment, then a fairly light punishment might be in order, but if it is not so easily frightened, then a more severe punishment would be necessary. Kantians would think such considerations concerning the degree of punishment improper, because the person being punished is used as a mere means to bring about the goal of general deterrence. Even those who are guilty, Kantians would believe, must be treated with respect, a part of which is to treat them in a way that responds to features of themselves. An example of how an offender of a capital crime could be treated with such respect is described by Bruce N. Waller in one of this chapter's selections. Waller believes it would be in greater accordance with the value of dignity to give such offenders the means to carry out their own deaths rather than to subject them to the psychologically grueling process of execution.

UTILITARIANISM AND CAPITAL PUNISHMENT

It follows from our earlier general discussion of the utilitarian theory of punishment that utilitarians should advocate the death penalty only if it is the least costly way of bringing about benefits sufficient to outweigh the disutility created by the penalty itself. To determine conclusively, then, whether utilitarians should accept the death penalty, we would need a good bit of empirical knowledge about what the consequences are of using the death penalty and about the consequences of not using it. Unfortunately, at this point those consequences are not fully known, but a couple of points can, perhaps, be made.

Often it is asked whether capital punishment is more beneficial than other forms of punishment, for example life in prison. Many argue, plausibly enough, that the death penalty is uniquely effective as a means of incapacitation. Even in prison, for example, people might have the opportunity to murder fellow inmates or prison personnel, but those who have been executed have no such opportunity. However, much of the argument concerning the death penalty from a consequentialist point of view centers on the issue of the penalty's effectiveness as a general deterrent. At this point, it is probably safe to say that it has not been shown conclusively whether or not the death penalty is more effective than such penalties as life in prison without the possibility of parole.

Assume for the sake of argument, however, that it could be shown that life in prison is as effective a general deterrent as capital punishment. What would follow? Frequently, it seems to be assumed that if it can be shown that the death penalty is no more effective as a deterrent than life in prison, then utilitarians must disapprove of the death penalty. It is not clear, however, why this is so. Presumably, utilitarians would prefer the penalty which causes the least unhappiness (assuming that each penalty will prevent the same amount of unhappiness and cause the same amount of happiness), and it seems far from obvious that the death penalty necessarily creates greater unhappiness than many years in prison. Whether or not it does depends, of course, on the way in which the death penalty is carried out—for instance on the method of execution—and on the conditions of imprisonment. Even from a utilitarian point of view, then, the question of the death penalty's permissibility does not turn entirely on its effectiveness as a deterrent.

RETRIBUTIVISM AND CAPITAL PUNISHMENT

Frequently one hears people claim that because of the nature of their crime, murderers deserve to die. Obviously, those who feel this way are attracted to retributivism. Their argument might be expressed by saying that a punishment must fit the crime and that only the death penalty fits the crime of murder. As mentioned earlier, however, this idea of punishment "fitting" a crime is at best metaphorical, so to evaluate the claim that only the death penalty fits murder we need a better understanding of what is meant by "fit."

One interpretation of the claim is a view called *lex talionis,* sometimes understood as requiring "an eye for an eye." The most straightforward understanding of *lex talionis* would be that justice requires that exactly the same thing be done to an offender as punishment that he or she did as the offense.

If the third element of retributivism is understood in this manner, then it would follow that murderers must be executed. However, we need to ask whether this understanding is acceptable, and there are at least two reasons for suspecting that retributivism would be unacceptable if so understood. The first is that there are many cases in which it would be literally impossible to do to the offender the same thing he or she did in offending. Obvious examples of such impossibility involve adult child molesters, mass murderers, and homeless home burglars.

Even when it would be possible to do to the offender what he or she has done, there would be cases where many people would find it morally unacceptable to do so. There are acts so morally repugnant that many would believe they simply should not be done, even as a form of retributive punishment. After all, punishment is done by the state as a representative of the people, and there may be acts we do not wish the state to do in our name. Examples would include what would be required by *lex talionis* for those who rape or torture, not to mention what would be required for the likes of Jeffrey Dahmer. It is easy to believe that a decent society would not have an official state rapist, torturer, or cannibal to carry out lawful retributivist sentences. Some argue that the death penalty should be included among those penalties that would not be used by a morally decent society.

A view sometimes called "proportional retributivism" is a second way of understanding the claim that the punishment should fit the crime, and it is not subject to the same objections as *lex talionis*. Proportional retributivism requires that the severity of punishment be proportionate to the seriousness of the crime. In other words, the more serious (or worse) an offender's offense is, the more severe the penalty should be. Unless the idea of proportionality is restricted in some further manner, this form of retributivism does not require that any particular penalties be a society's most and least severe. Suppose, for the sake of argument, that murder is the most serious offense and jaywalking is the least serious offense. A society where jaywalkers are fined $1 and murderers are imprisoned for life would be compatible with proportional retributivism, but so would a society in which jaywalkers are jailed for eight hours and murderers are executed. Proportional retributivism may or may not be an acceptable theory of punishment, but accepting it would not commit one to capital punishment.

In his contribution to this chapter, Igor Primoratz suggests a third understanding of the retributivist demand that the punishment fit the crime. This understanding, he argues, does imply that justice requires that murderers be executed. According to his way of understanding retributivism, a just punishment is one that deprives the criminal of the same amount of value that the criminal takes from his or her victim with the crime. For most crimes some loss of property and liberty will be equivalent to the loss of value suffered by the victim of crimes, but no loss of liberty and property can be equivalent to what a murder victim loses according to Primoratz. The victim of murder does not lose some set amount of value but rather loses all possibility of any further realization or experience of value. Given this, Primoratz argues a just punishment for murder must deprive the murderer of all possibility of the realization and experience of value. *If* Primoratz is right about what is required for just punishment and about what loss is suffered by murder victims, then he would seem to be right in supposing that only the death penalty fits the crime of murder. One worry concerning Primoratz's approach to just punishment is that it requires consideration of the amount of loss suffered by the victims of crime to determine an appropriate punishment. There has been a move away from a focus on crime victims in American criminal jurisprudence because such a focus sometimes results in putting victims on trial in criminal proceedings. This result was once common in the defense of those charged with sex crimes. It may be worth considering whether Primoratz's approach could have a similar result.

CAPITAL PUNISHMENT, RACE, AND WEALTH

Even if one decides that in principle the death penalty is a morally appropriate punishment, there remain concerns about how in practice it is administered. There is considerable evidence that in the United States, the use of the death penalty is heavily affected by considerations of race, ethnicity, and wealth. As Anthony Amsterdam points out in one of this chapter's reading selections, whites who are convicted of murder are much less likely to be sentenced to death than members of certain minorities, especially African Americans, and murderers of whites are more likely to receive a death sentence than murderers of nonwhites. Furthermore, those who are affluent are much less likely to face the prospect of a death sentence than those who are not, at least in large part because affluence pays for much better legal representation. Some argue that if the death penalty cannot be applied in an equitable fashion, it must not be applied at all. If so, our own society must find a way to rid itself of the apparent bias in its application of the death penalty or must abolish the penalty altogether. Those who argue in this manner maintain that it is unjust that the death penalty not be applied to all who equally deserve it, and if it cannot be so applied it must not be used at all.

In response to this line of argument, some would agree that a system in which the death penalty is not used equitably is indeed unjust but that those who conclude that the death penalty should be abolished mislocate the injustice. The injustice, they respond, is not that some murderers are executed but rather that some murderers equally deserving of execution are not. The injustice requires more executions for its righting, not fewer.

Suppose, however, that it would be impossible to construct a system that would equitably award a death sentence to all who deserve it. What should be done in that case? Either the death penalty could be abolished, creating a criminal justice system that comes closer to punishing all who are equally deserving in an equal way, or it could be retained where offenders who deserve the same punishment will be punished differently. Some would argue that the latter possibility is preferable. If one believes that all people who commit a particular crime, say murder, deserve the death penalty, then if the death penalty is abolished no murderer gets what he or she deserves, but if the death penalty is retained, even though it is not applied equally, at least some people will receive the punishment they deserve. Since it is better that some receive the treatment they deserve than that none do, if we are in the unfortunate and admittedly unjust situation where our biases bring about an inequitable use of the death penalty, it is less unjust to retain than to abolish it.

In support of the claim that in systems where the death penalty is applied inequitably—the injustice is not to those who receive the death penalty—one might consider more everyday penalties, for instance speeding tickets. It is clear that on any given day only a very small percentage of drivers who speed are penalized for their misdeeds. Indeed, whenever our classes are polled about the matter, we discover that there are many people who routinely drive over the speed limit but who have never received a ticket. Given this inequitable distribution of speeding tickets, do those who receive tickets have a valid claim of justice that their tickets be voided? Could they reasonably argue that since they acted no differently from the many who received no ticket, they should not be ticketed as well? In answer to these questions, many probably would without hesitation reply that there is nothing unjust about the tickets. Those who received them sped knowing that it was in violation of the traffic code and hence deserve their penalty. The fact that others did not receive the penalty does nothing to detract from the deservingness of those who were ticketed.

Intuitively, the response that the ticketed drivers have no complaint seems attractive, but it may be that this attractiveness is based on background beliefs about why some people get tickets and others do not. We are likely to believe that it is largely a matter of luck and perhaps slightly a matter of the police-spotting skill of drivers. If this is the explanation of why only some get tickets, it seems right to suggest the only injustice is that those lucky, skilled drivers who deserve tickets fail to get them.

But suppose the explanation is different. Suppose it turned out that police officers routinely look the other way when members of some races speed and routinely ticket drivers of other races even if they only barely exceed the speed limit. In this case, it is no longer so obvious that those who are ticketed have no complaint based on justice. The complaint might be that speeding tickets are not really being used to control traffic, at least not entirely, but are also being used to harass and express disdain for members of certain races. It could further be argued that if police officers, who are officials of society, express such disdain, then the society as a whole has acted unjustly. It may be that such a complaint would be reasonable even if those who use the law to so harass and express disdain are not conscious of what they do. If the line of argument just expressed is correct, it is worth considering what is done and expressed by a legal system that inequitably executes members of groups within society.

How to Argue About
the Death Penalty

Hugo Adam Bedau

Hugo Adam Bedau, the Austin B. Fletcher Professor of Philosophy at Tufts University, has been one of the most prominent philosophical voices opposed to the death penalty for many years. While his opposition to capital punishment is evident in the essay below, his initial purpose is to explain what he takes the issue concerning its permissibility to turn on. Frequently discussions among those who disagree about the matter focus on questions about empirical facts that are in dispute, for example questions about whether the death penalty is a more effective deterrent than other possible penalties and about the likelihood of innocent persons being executed. The factual issues felt by most to be relevant to the death penalty debate have not been answered conclusively, but Bedau points out that even if they had been those answers by themselves would not determine what should be done about the death penalty. Normative considerations must also play a role in arguments for public policy, and Bedau devotes most of this essay to an attempt to describe the normative considerations most relevant to the death penalty.

The normative considerations bearing on the death penalty are of two sorts. The first consists of social *goals* that might be sought through our penal system. The most important of such goals, Bedau believes, are utilitarian—reduction of crime in the least costly manner. The second type of normative considerations consists of *moral principles* that place limits on the permissible means by which legitimate social goals may be pursued. Bedau describes seven principles of this sort and comments on their implications on the issue of the death penalty. He concludes by suggesting that the "preponderance of reasons" favor the abolition of the death penalty, especially when three additional considerations are taken into account: 1) it is preferable to limit government power over individual lives; 2) public policy should be oriented toward the future; and 3) a retributivist attitude toward murder seems less attractive when it is seen how far from the ideal Kantian agent death-row inhabitants actually are.

I

Argument over the death penalty—especially in the United States during the past generation—has been concentrated in large part on trying to answer various disputed *questions of fact.* Among them two have been salient: is the death penalty a better deterrent to crime (especially murder) than the alternative of imprisonment? Is the death penalty administered in a discriminatory way—in particular, are black or other nonwhite offenders (or offenders whose victims are white) more likely to be tried, convicted, sentenced to death, and executed than whites (or than offenders whose victims are nonwhite)? Other

From *Israel Law Review* 25 (1991), 466–480.

questions of fact have also been explored, including these two: what is the risk that an innocent person could actually be executed for a crime he did not commit? What is the risk that a person convicted of a capital felony but not executed will commit another capital felony?

Varying degrees of effort have been expended in trying to answer these questions. Although I think the available answers are capable of further re-finement, I also think anyone who studies the evidence today must conclude that the best current answers to these four questions are as follows: (1) There is little or no evidence that the death penalty is a better deterrent to murder than is imprisonment: on the contrary, most evidence shows that these two punishments are about equally (in)effective as deterrents to murder. Further-more, as long as the death penalty continues to be used with relative rarity, there is no prospect of gaining more decisive evidence on the question.[1] (2) There is evidence that the death penalty has been and continues to be admin-istered, whether intentionally or not, in a manner that produces arbitrary and racially discriminatory results in sentencing. At the very least, this is true in those jurisdictions where the question has been investigated in recent years.[2] (3) It is impossible to calculate the risk that an innocent person will be ex-ecuted—but the risk is not zero, as the record of convicted, sentenced, and executed innocents shows.[3] (4) Recidivism data show that some convicted murderers have killed again, either in prison or after release, so there is a risk that others will do so as well.[4]

Let us assume that my summary of the results of research on these four questions is correct, and that further research will not significantly change these answers. The first thing to notice is that even if everyone accepted these answers, this would not by itself settle the dispute over whether to keep, expand, reduce, or abolish the death penalty. Agreement on these em-pirical claims about the administration and effects of the death penalty in our society does not entail a decision to support or oppose the death penalty. This would still be true even if we agreed on *all* the answers to the factual questions that can be asked about the death penalty.

There are two reasons for this. The facts as they currently stand and as seen from the abolitionist perspective do not point strongly and overwhelm-ingly to the futility of the death penalty or to the harm it does—at least, as long as the death penalty continues to be used only in the limited and re-stricted form of the past decade (i.e., confined to the crime of murder, with trial courts empowered to exercise "guided discretion" in sentencing, at which defence counsel may introduce anything as mitigating evidence, and with automatic review of both conviction and sentence by state and federal appel-late courts).[5] Nor do the facts show that the alternative of life imprisonment is on balance a noticeably superior punishment. The evidence of racial dis-crimination in the administration of the death penalty, while incontestable, may be no worse than racial discrimination where lesser crimes and punish-ments are concerned. No one who has studied the data thinks that racial discrimination in the administration of justice for murder reaches the level of discrimination that a generation ago affected the administration of justice in the South for rape.[6] Besides, it is always possible to argue that such discrimination is diminishing, or will diminish over time, and that in any case since the fault lies not in the capital statutes themselves—they are color-blind on their face—the remedy does not lie in repealing them. Nor is it clear that a life sentence in prison without the possibility of release is an enormous improvement from the offender's point of view over death.

But the marginal impact of the empirical evidence is not the major factor in explaining why settling disputes over matters of fact does not and cannot settle the larger controversy over the death penalty itself. As a matter of sheer logic, it is not possible to deduce a policy conclusion (such as the desirability of abolishing the death penalty) from any set of factual premises however general and well supported. Any argument intended to recommend continuing or reforming current policy on the death penalty must include among its premises one or more normative propositions. Unless disputants over the death penalty can agree about these normative propositions, their argument on the empirical facts will never suffice to resolve their dispute.

II

Accordingly, the course of wisdom for those interested in arguing about the death penalty is to focus attention on the normative propositions crucial to the dispute, in the hope that some headway may be made in narrowing disagreement over their number, content, and weight. . . .

These norms can be divided into two groups: those that express relevant and desirable *social goals or purposes,* and those that express relevant and respectable *moral principles.* Punishment is thus a practice or institution defined through various policies—such as the death penalty for murder—intended to be the means or instrument whereby certain social goals are achieved within the constraints imposed by acknowledged moral principles.[7]

Reduction of crime, or at least prevention of increase in crime, is an example of such a goal. This goal influences the choice of punishments because of their (hypothesized, verified) impact on the crime rate. No one, except for purists of a retributive stripe, would dissent from the view that this goal is relevant to the death penalty controversy. . . .

Similarly, that no one should be convicted and sentenced to death without a fair trial (i.e., in violation of "due process of law") is a principle of law and morality generally respected. Its general acceptance explains the considerable reformation in the laws governing the death penalty in the United States that have been introduced since 1972 in response to the Supreme Court's decisions in *Furman v. Georgia.*[8] The Court argued in *Furman* that capital trials and death sentencing were in practice unfair (in constitutional jargon, they were in violation of the Eighth and Fourteenth Amendments, which bar "cruel and unusual punishments" and require "equal protection of the laws", respectively). State legislatures and thoughtful observers agreed. Here again the only questions concern how important it is to comply with this principle (for some it is decisive) and the extent to which the death penalty currently violates it (I have remarked on this point above, too).

The chief use of a moral principle in the present setting is to constrain the methods used in pursuit of policy (as when respect for "due process" rules out curbstone justice as a tactic in crime-fighting). However, identifying the relevant goals, acknowledging the force of the relevant principles, and agreeing on the relevant general facts, will still not suffice to resolve the dispute. Disagreement over the relative importance of achieving a given goal or disagreement over the relative weight of a given principle is likely to show up in disagreement over the justification of the death penalty itself.

If this is a correct sketch of the structural character of debate and disagreement over the death penalty, then (as I noted earlier) the best hope for progress may lie in looking more carefully at the nonfactual normative ingredients so far isolated in the dispute. Ideally, we would identify and evaluate the policy goals relevant to punishment generally, as well as the moral principles that constrain the structure and content of the penalty schedule. We would also settle the proper relative weights to attach to these goals and constraints, if not in general then at least for their application in the present context. Then, with whatever relevant general facts are at our disposal, we would be in a position to draw the appropriate inferences and resolve the entire dispute, confident that we have examined and duly weighed everything that reason and morality can bring to bear on the problem.

As an abstract matter, therefore, the question is whether the set of relevant policies and principles, taken in conjunction with the relevant facts, favours reduction (even complete abolition) of the death penalty, or whether it favours retention (or even extension) of the death penalty. Lurking in the background, of course, is the troubling possibility, here as elsewhere, that the relevant norms and facts underdetermine the resolution of the dispute. But let us not worry about sharks on dry land, not yet.

III

Where choice of punishments is concerned, the relevant social goals, I suggest, are few. Two in particular generally commend themselves:

G1. Punishment ought to contribute to the reduction of crime: accordingly, the punishment for a crime ought not to be so idle a threat or so slight a deprivation that it has little or no deterrent or incapacitative effects; and it certainly ought not to contribute to the increase of crime.

G2. Punishments ought to be "economical"—they ought not to waste valuable social resources in futile or unnecessarily costly endeavours.

The instrumental character of these purposes and goals is evident. They reflect the fact that society does not institute and maintain the practice of punishment for its own sake, as though it were a good in itself. Rather, punishment is and is seen to be a means to an end or ends. The justification of a society's punitive policies and practices, therefore, must involve two steps: first, it must be assumed or argued that these ends are desirable; second, it must be shown that the practice of punishment is a necessary means to these ends. What is true of the justification of punishment generally is true *a fortiori* of justifying the death penalty.

Endorsement of these two policy goals tends to encourage support for the death penalty. Opponents of capital punishment need not reject these goals, however, and its defenders cannot argue that accepting these goals vindicates their preferred policy. Traditionally, it is true, the death penalty has often been supported on the ground that it provides the best social defence and is extremely cheap to administer. But since the time of Beccaria and Bentham these empirical claims have been challenged,[9] and rightly so. If support for the death penalty today in a country such as the United States were thought to rest on the high priority of achieving these goals, then there is much (some would say compelling) evidence to undermine this support. The most that can be said solely by reference to these goals is that recognition of their importance can always be counted on to kindle interest in capital punishment, and to that extent force its opponents on the defensive.

Whether punishment is intended to serve only the two goals so far identified is disputable. An argument can be made that there are two or three further goals, as follows:

G3. Punishment ought to rectify the harm and injustice caused by crime.
G4. Punishment ought to serve as a recognized channel for the release of public indignation and anger at the offender over crime.
G5. Punishment ought to make convicted offenders into better persons rather than leave them as they are or make them worse.

Obviously, anyone who accepts the fifth goal must reject the death penalty. I shall not try here to argue the merits of this goal, either in itself or relative to the other goals of punishment. Whatever its merits, this goal is less widely sought than the others, and for that reason alone is less useful in trying to develop rational agreement over the death penalty. Its persuasive power for those not already persuaded against the death penalty on other grounds is likely to be slight to zero. Although I am unwilling to strike it from the list of goals that punishment in general is and ought to be practices to achieve, I am unwilling to stress its pre-eminence in the present context.

The third proposed goal of punishment is open to the objection that rectification of injustice is not really a goal of punishment, even if it is a desirable goal wherever injustice is discovered. Indeed, it is widely believed that rectification is not a goal of punishment but of noncriminal tort judgments. That point to one side, imprisonment as typically practiced in the United States rectifies nothing. Since mere incarceration by itself does not provide any direct and unique benefit to the victims of crime or to society generally, there is no way it can rectify the unjust harms that crime causes. Nonetheless, this goal is at least indirectly important for the death penalty controversy. To the extent that one believes punishments ought to serve this goal, and that there is no possible way to rectify the crime of murder, one may come to believe the fourth goal is of even greater importance than would otherwise be the case. Indeed, striving to achieve this fourth goal and embracing the death penalty as a consequence is quite parallel to striving to achieve the fifth goal and consequently embracing abolition.

Does this fourth goal have a greater claim on our support than I have allowed is true of the fifth goal, so obviously incompatible with it? Many would say that it does. Some, such as Walter Berns,[10] would even argue that it is this goal, not any of the others, that is the paramount purpose of the practice of punishment under law. Whatever else punishment does, its threat and infliction are to be seen as the expression of legitimate social indignation at deliberate harm to the innocent. Preserving a socially acceptable vehicle for the expression of anger at offenders is absolutely crucial to the health of a just society.

There are in principle three ways to respond to this claim insofar as it is part of an argument for capital punishment. One is to reject it out of hand as a false proposition from start to finish. A second is to concede that the goal of providing a visible and acceptable channel for the emotion of anger is legitimate, but to argue that this goal can justify the death penalty only in a very small number of rare cases (the occasional Adolf Eichmann for example), or only if its importance is vastly exaggerated. A third is to concede both the legitimacy and relative importance of this goal, but to point out that its pursuit, like that of all other goals, is nonetheless constrained by moral principles (yet to be examined), and that once these principles are properly employed, the death penalty ceases to be a permissible method of achieving this goal. I think both the second and third objections are sound, and a few further words here about each are appropriate.

First of all, resentment or indignation is not the same as anger, since the former feeling or emotion can be aroused only through the perceived violation of some moral principle, whereas the latter does not have this constraint. But the question whether the feeling aroused by awareness of a horrible murder really is indignation rather than only anger just is the question whether the principles of justice have been severely violated or not. Knowing that the accused offender has no legal excuse or justification for his criminal conduct is not yet knowing enough to warrant the inference that he and his conduct are appropriate objects of our unqualified moral hostility. More about the context of the offence and its causation must be supplied; it may well be that in ordinary criminal cases one rarely or never knows enough to reach such a condemnatory judgment with confidence. Even were this not so, one has no reason to suppose that justified anger at offenders is of overriding importance, and that all countervailing considerations must yield to its claims. For one thing, the righteous anger needed for that role is simply not available in a pluralistic secular society; even if it were, we have been assured from biblical times that it passes all too easily into self-righteous and hypocritical repression by some sinners of others.

Quite apart from such objections, there is a certain anomaly, even irony, in the defence of the death penalty by appeal to this goal. On the one hand, we are told that a publicly recognized ritual for extermination of convicted murderers is a necessary vent for otherwise unchanneled disruptive public emotions. On the other hand our society scrupulously rejects time-honoured methods of execution that truly do express hatred and anger at offenders— beheading, crucifixion, dismemberment are unheard of today, and even hanging and the electric chair are disappearing. Execution by lethal injection, increasingly the popular option, hardly seems appropriate as the outlet of choice for such allegedly volatile energies. And is it not bizarre that this technique, invented to facilitate life-saving surgery, now turns out to be the preferred channel for the expression of moral indignation?

IV

If the purpose or goals of punishment lend a utilitarian quality to the practice of punishment, the moral principles relevant to the death penalty operate as deontological constraints on the pursuit of these goals. Stating all and only the principles relevant to the death penalty controversy is not easy, and the list that follows is no more than the latest approximation to the task.[11] With some overlap here and there, these principles are seven:

P1. No one's life may be deliberately and intentionally taken by another unless there is no feasible alternative to protect the latter's own life.

P2. The more severe a penalty is, the more important it is that it be imposed only on those who truly deserve it.

P3. The more severe a penalty is, the weightier the justification required to warrant its imposition on anyone.

P4. Whatever the criminal offence, the accused or convicted offender does not forfeit his rights and dignity as a person.

P5. There is an upper limit to the severity—cruelty, destructiveness, finality—of permissible punishments, regardless of the offence.

P6. Fairness requires that punishments should be graded in their severity according to the gravity of the offence.

P7. If human lives are to be risked, the risk should fall more heavily on wrong-doers (the guilty) than on the others (the innocent).

I cannot argue here for all these principles, but they really need no argument from me. Each is recognized implicitly or explicitly in our practice; each can be seen to constrain our conduct as individuals and as officers in democratic institutions. Outright repudiation or cynical disregard of any of these principles would disqualify one from engaging in serious discourse and debate over punishment in a liberal society. All can be seen as corollaries or theorems of the general principle that life, limb, and security of person—of all persons—are of paramount value. Thus, only minimal interference (in the jargon of the law, "the least restrictive means") is warranted with anyone's life, limb, and security in order to protect the rights of others.

How do these principles direct or advise us in regard to the permissibility or desirability of the death penalty? The first thing to note is that evidently none directly rules it out. I know of no moral principle that is both sufficiently precise and sufficiently well established for us to point to it and say "the practice of capital punishment is flatly contradictory to the requirements of this moral principle". (Of course, we might invent a principle that will have this consequence, but that is hardly to the point.) This should not be surprising; few if any of the critics or the defenders of the death penalty have supposed otherwise. Second, several of these principles do reflect the heavy burden that properly falls on anyone who advocates that certain human beings be deliberately killed by others, even though those to be killed are not at the time a danger to anyone. For example, whereas the first principle may justify lethal force in self-defense and other circumstances, it directly counsels against the death penalty in *all* cases without exception. The second and third principles emphasize the importance of "due process" and "equal protection" as the finality and incompensability of punishments increase. The fourth principle draws attention to the nature and value of persons, even those convicted of terrible crimes. The fifth reminds us that even if crimes have no upper limit in their wantonness, cruelty, destructiveness, and horror, punishments under law in a civilized society may not imitate crimes in this regard. Punishment does operate under limits, and these limits are not arbitrary.

The final two principles, however, seem to be exceptions to the generalization that the principles as a group tend to favour punishments other than death. The sixth principle entails that if murder is the greatest crime, then it must receive the severest punishment. This does not, of course, *require* a society to invoke the death penalty for murder—unless one accepts *lex talionis* ("a life for a life, an eye for an eye") in a singularly literal-minded manner. But *lex talionis* is not a sound principle on which to construct the penalty schedule generally, and so appealing to that interpretation of the sixth principle here simply begs the question. Nevertheless, the principle that punishments should be graded to fit the crime does encourage consideration of the death penalty, especially if it seems there is no other way to punish murder with utmost permissible severity.

Rather of more interest is the seventh principle. Some, primarily Ernest van den Haag,[12] make it the cornerstone of their defence of the death penalty. They argue that it is better to execute all convicted murderers, lest on some future occasion some of them murder again, than it is to execute none of them in order to avert the risk of executing the few who may be innocent. For, so the argument goes, a policy of complete abolition would result in thousands of convicted killers (only a few of whom are innocent) being held behind bars. This cohort constitutes a permanent risk to the safety of many millions of innocent citizens. The sole gain to counterbalance this risk is the guarantee that no lives—innocent or guilty—will be lost through legal executions. The practice of executions thus is argued to protect far more innocent citizens than the same practice puts in jeopardy.

This argument is far less conclusive than it may, at first, seem. Even if we grant it full weight, it is simply unreasonable to use it (or any other argument) as a way of dismissing the relevance of principles that counsel a different result, or as a tactic to imply the subordinate importance of all other relevant principles. Used in this objectionable manner, what I have called the seventh principle has been transformed. It has become a disguised version of the first policy goal (viz., Reduce crime!) and in effect elevates that goal to pre-eminence over every competing and constraining consideration. It has also ceased to be a constraint on policy. Second, the argument fosters the illusion that we can, in fact, reasonably estimate, if not actually calculate, the number of lives risked by a policy of abolition vs. a policy of capital punishment. This is false; we do not and cannot reasonably hope to know what the risk is of convicting the innocent,[13] even if we could estimate the risk of recidivist murder. We therefore cannot really compare the two risks with any precision. Finally, the argument gains whatever strength it appears to have by tacitly ignoring the following dilemma: If the argument is to be taken seriously, then death must be understood to be the mandatory penalty for everyone convicted of murder (never mind other crimes). But such a policy flies in the face of two centuries of political reality, which unquestionably demonstrates the impossibility of enforcing truly mandatory death penalties for murder or any other crime. The only feasible policy alternative is some version of a discretionary death penalty. But every version of this policy actually tried has proved vulnerable to criticism on grounds of inequality in its administration, as critic after critic has shown.[14]

The upshot is that society today runs both the risk of executing the innocent and the risk of recidivist murder, although it is necessary to run only one of these risks. At the same time it is politically impossible to avoid running *some* risk of recidivist murder.

V

What has our examination of the relevant goals and principles shown about the possibility of resolving the death penalty controversy on purely rational grounds? First, the death penalty is primarily a means to one or more ends (goals), but it is not the only and probably not the best means to those ends. Second, several principles familiar to us in many areas of punitive policy favour (although they do not demand) abolition of the death penalty. Third, there is no principle that constitutes a conclusive reason favouring either side in the dispute—except, of course, for conclusive reasons (like the fifth goal, or the sixth principle interpreted as *lex talionis*) that either one side or the other simply need not accept. This, too, should not be surprising. If a reason existed so conclusive that both sides had to accept it, one must wonder why its discovery continues to elude us. Finally, the several goals and principles of punishment that have been identified have no obvious rank order or relative weighting. As they stand, these goals and principles do indeed underdetermine the policy dispute over capital punishment. Perhaps such a ranking of principles could be provided by one or another general socio-ethical theory. But the lack of general acceptance for any such theory does not bode well for rational resolution of the controversy along these lines.

Despite the absence of any conclusive reasons or decisive ranking of principles, we may take refuge (as I have done elsewhere[15]) in the thought that a preponderance of reasons does favour one side rather than the other. Such a preponderance emerges, however, only when the relevant goals and principles of punishment are seen in a certain light, or from a particular angle of vision. This perhaps amounts to one rather than another weighting of goals and principles but without reliance upon any manifest theory. One relies instead on other considerations. I shall mention three whose importance may be decisive.

The first and by far the most important is the role and function of *power* in the hands of government. It is preferable, *ceteris paribus,* that such power over individuals shrink rather than expand. Where such power must be used, it is better to use it for constructive rather than destructive purposes—enhancing the autonomy and liberty of those persons directly affected by it. The death penalty is government power used in a dramatically destructive manner upon individuals in the absence of any compelling social necessity. No wonder it is the ultimate symbol of such power.

A second consideration that shapes my interpretation of the goals and principles of evaluation is an orientation to the *future* rather than to the past. We cannot do anything to benefit the dead victims of crime. (How many of those who oppose the death penalty would continue to do so if, *mirabile dictu,* executing the murderer brought the victim back to life?) But we can—or at least we can try to do something for the living: we can protect the innocent, console those in despair, and try to prevent future crimes. None of these constructive tasks presuppose or involve the expressive, vindictive, and retributive roles of punishment. The more we stress these roles to the neglect of all else, the more we orient our punitive policies toward the past—toward trying to use government power over the lives of a few as a socially approved instrument of moral bookkeeping.

Finally, the death penalty projects a false and misleading picture of man and society. Its professed message for those who support it is this: justice requires killing the convicted murderer. So we focus on the death that all murderers supposedly deserve, and overlook our inability to give a rational account of why so few actually get what they allegedly deserve. Hence the lesson taught by the practice of capital punishment is not what its retributivist defenders infer from their theory. Far from being a symbol of justice it is a symbol of brutality and stupidity. Perhaps if we lived in a world of autonomous Kantian moral agents, where even the criminals freely and rationally express their will in the intention to kill others without their consent or desert, then death for the convicted murderer might be just (as even Karl Marx was inclined to concede[16]). But a closer look at the convicts who actually are on our death rows shows that these killers are a far cry from the rational agents of Kant's metaphysical imagination. We fool ourselves if we think a system of ideal retributive justice designed for such persons is the appropriate model for the penal system in our society.

Have I implicitly conceded that argument over the death penalty is irrational? If I am right, that the death penalty controversy does not really turn on controversial social goals or controversial moral principles, any more than it does on disputed general facts, but instead turns on how all three are to be balanced or weighed, does it follow that reason alone cannot resolve the controversy, because reason alone cannot determine which weighting or balancing is the correct one? Or can reason resolve this problem, perhaps by appeal to further theory, theory that would deepen our appreciation of what truly underlies a commitment to liberal institutions and a belief in the possibilities for autonomy of all persons?[17] I think it can—but this is the right place to end this discussion, because we have reached the launching platform for another one.

NOTES

1. Lawrence R. Klein et al., "The Deterrent Effects of Capital Punishment: An Assessment of the Estimates", in Alfred Blumstein et al., eds., *Deterrence and Incapacitation: Estimating the Effects of Criminal Sanctions on Crime Rates* (Washington, D.C., National Academy of Sciences, 1978) 336-60.

2. David C. Baldus, George C. Woodworth, and Charles A. Pulaski, Jr., *Equal Justice and the Death Penalty: A Legal and Empirical Analysis* (Boston, Northeastern U. P., 1990).

3. H. A. Bedau and Michael l. Radelet, "Miscarriages of Justice in Potentially Capital Cases" (1987) 40 Stan. L. R. 21-180.

4. H. A. Bedau, ed., *The Death Penalty in America* (New York, Oxford U. P., 3rd ed., 1982) 173-80.

5. *Gregg v. Georgia,* 428 U.S. 153 (1976); *Proffitt v. Florida,* 428 U.S. 242 (1976); *Jurek v. Texas,* 428 U.S. 262 (1976).

6. Marvin E. Wolfgang and Marc Riedel, "Rape, Racial Discrimination, and the Death Penalty", in H. A. Bedau and Chester M. Pierce, eds., *Capital Punishment in the United States* (New York, AMS Press, 1976) 99-121.

7. *Cf.* Ronald Dworkin, *Taking Rights Seriously* (Cambridge, Mass., Harvard U.P., 1977) 22-23, 169-71.

8. *Furman v. Georgia,* 408 U.S. 238 (1972).

9. See H. A. Bedau, "Bentham's Utilitarian Critique of the Death Penalty" (1983) 74 J. Crim. L. & Criminology 1033-66, reprinted in H. A. Bedau, *Death is Different: Studies in the Morality, Law, and Politics of Capital Punishment* (Boston, Northeastern U. P., 1987) 64-91.

10. Walter Berns, *For Capital Punishment: Crime and the Morality of the Death Penalty* (New York, Basic Books, 1979).

11. H. A. Bedau, "Capital Punishment", in Tom Regan, ed., *Matters of Life and Death* (New York, Random House, 1980) 159-60; reprinted in Bedau, *Death is Different, supra* n. 9, at 24.

12. Ernest van den Haag, "The Ultimate Punishment: A Defense" (1986) 99 Harv. I R. 1662-69, at 1665 ff.

13. See Bedau and Radelet, *supra* n. 3, at 78-81, 83-85.

14. Vivian Berger, "Justice Delayed or Justice Denied?—A Comment on Recent Proposals to Reform Habeas Corpus" (1990) 90 Colum. L. R. 1665-1714; Anthony G. Amsterdam, "The Supreme Court and Capital Punishment" (1987) 14 Human rights 1, at 14-18; Ronald J. Tabak, "The Death of Fairness: The Arbitrary and Capricious Imposition of the Death Penalty in the 1980s" (1984) 14 N.Y.U.R.L. & Soc. Change 797-848; H. A. Bedau, "*Gregg v. Georgia* and the 'New' Death Penalty" (1985) 4 Crim. Justice Ethics 2, at 3-17; Robert Weisberg, "Deregulating Death" in S. Ct. R. 1983 (1984) 305-95; and Baldus et al., *supra* n. 2.

15. Bedau, *Death is Different, supra* n. 9, at 45.

16. Karl Marx, "Capital Punishment" (1853), reprinted in Lewis Feuer, ed., *Basic Writings on Politics and Philosophy: Karl Marx and Frederick Engels* (New York, Doubleday Anchor, 1959) 485-86.

17. Bedau, *Death is Different, supra* n. 9, at 123-28.

The Ultimate Punishment:
A Defense

Ernest van den Haag

Ernest van den Haag, formerly the John M. Olin Professor of Jurisprudence and Public Policy at Fordham University, has been a prominent supporter of the death penalty for many years. He is probably most known for a line of reasoning known as the "Best Bet Argument," alluded to in Part III of this reading and considered in the essay by Bedau. The Best Bet Argument is addressed to those who believe that the death penalty would be justified if and only if it more effectively deters potential murderers than other penalties. Someone holding this position may not know what policy to adopt because it is not conclusively known whether or not the death penalty is more effective as a deterrent. Van den Haag has argued that, given the assumption that the death penalty's justification depends on its deterrent value and in light of uncertainty about this, the death penalty should be retained. If the death penalty is retained and if it is not a more effective deterrent, then, again given our assumption, some murderers will be *unjustifiably* executed. On the other hand, if the death penalty is abolished and if it would have deterred additional murders had it been retained, then some murder victims lives will be *unjustifiably* lost. Given our uncertainty about the capacity of the death penalty to deter more effectively than other penalties, both retaining and abolishing the death penalty have as a risk unjustifiable killings. So the adoption of either policy is a matter of gambling with lives. However, retaining the death penalty gambles with the lives of convicted murderers, and abolishing the death penalty gambles with the lives of innocent people at risk of being murdered. If gambling with lives is unavoidable, van den Haag argues, it is better to gamble with the lives of murderers than with the lives of innocent people, so the death penalty should be retained. The burden of proof, then, is on those who wish to abolish the death penalty to show that it would not deter more effectively than other penalties.

While repeating his belief that it is more important to save the lives of the innocent than the lives of murderers, in this essay van den Haag is primarily concerned with answering several other objections frequently offered against the death penalty. For example, he argues that the death penalty is justified even if it is applied in a discriminatory manner, and even though some innocent people will *infrequently* be wrongly convicted and executed.

In an average year about 20,000 homicides occur in the United States. Fewer than 300 convicted murderers are sentenced to death. But because no more than thirty murderers have been executed in any recent year, most convicts sentenced to death are likely to die of old age.[1] Nonetheless, the death penalty

---

From *Harvard Law Review* 99 (1986), 1662-1669.

looms large in discussions: it raises important moral questions independent of the number of executions.

The death penalty is our harshest punishment.[2] It is irrevocable: it ends the existence of those punished, instead of temporarily imprisoning them. Further, although not intended to cause physical pain, execution is the only corporal punishment still applied to adults.[3] These singular characteristics contribute to the perennial, impassioned controversy about capital punishment.

I. DISTRIBUTION

Consideration of the justice, morality, or usefulness, of capital punishment is often conflated with objections to its alleged discriminatory or capricious distribution among the guilty. Wrongly so. If capital punishment is immoral *in se,* no distribution among the guilty could make it moral. If capital punishment is moral, no distribution would make it immoral. Improper distribution cannot affect the quality of what is distributed, be it punishments or rewards. Discriminatory or capricious distribution thus could not justify abolition of the death penalty. Further, maldistribution inheres no more in capital punishment than in any other punishment.

Maldistribution between the guilty and the innocent is, by definition, unjust. But the injustice does not lie in the nature of the punishment. Because of the finality of the death penalty, the most grievous maldistribution occurs when it is imposed upon the innocent. However, the frequent allegations of discrimination and capriciousness refer to maldistribution among the guilty and not to the punishment of the innocent.

Maldistribution on any punishment among those who deserve it is irrelevant to its justice or morality. Even if poor or black convicts guilty of capital offenses suffer capital punishment, and other convicts equally guilty of the same crimes do not, a more equal distribution, however desirable, would merely be more equal. It would not be more just to the convicts under sentence of death.

Punishments are imposed on persons, not on racial or economic groups. Guilt is personal. The only relevant question is: does the person to be executed deserve the punishment? Whether or not others who deserved the same punishment, whatever their economic or racial group, have avoided execution is irrelevant. If they have, the guilt of the executed convicts would not be diminished, nor would their punishment be less deserved. To put the issue starkly, if the death penalty were imposed on guilty blacks, but not on guilty whites, or, if it were imposed by a lottery among the guilty, this irrationally discriminatory or capricious distribution would neither make the penalty unjust, nor cause anyone to be unjustly punished, despite the undue impunity bestowed on others.

Equality, in short, seems morally less important than justice. And justice is independent of distributional inequalities. The ideal of equal justice demands that justice be equally distributed, not that it be replaced by equality. Justice requires that as many of the guilty as possible be punished, regardless of whether others have avoided punishment. To let these others escape the deserved punishment does not do justice to them, or to society. But it is not unjust to those who could not escape. Some inequality is unavoidable as a practical matter in any system. But, *ultra posse nemo obligatur.* (Nobody is bound beyond ability.) Unequal justice is the best we can do and better than injustice, equal or unequal, which would occur if, for the sake of equality, we allowed anyone to avoid the punishment due.

II. MISCARRIAGES OF JUSTICE

In a recent survey Professors Hugo Adam Bedau and Michael Radelet found that 7000 persons were executed in the United States between 1900 and 1985 and that 25 were innocent of capital crimes.[4] Among the innocent they list Sacco and Vanzetti as well as Ethel and Julius Rosenberg. Although their data may be questionable, I do not doubt that, over a long enough period, miscarriages of justice will occur even in capital cases.

Despite precautions, nearly all human activities, such as trucking, lighting, or construction, cost the lives of some innocent bystanders. We do not give up these activities, because the advantages, moral or material, outweigh the unintended losses.[5] Analogously, for those who think the death penalty just, miscarriages of justice are offset by the moral benefits and the usefulness of doing justice. For those who think the death penalty unjust even when it does not miscarry, miscarriages can hardly be decisive.

III. DETERRENCE

Despite much recent work, there has been no conclusive statistical demonstration that the death penalty is a better deterrent than are alternative punishments.[6] However, deterrence is less than decisive for either side. Most abolitionists acknowledge that they would continue to favor abolition even if the death penalty were shown to deter more murders than alternatives could deter. Abolitionists appear to value the life of a convicted murderer or, at least, his non-execution, more highly than they value the lives of the innocent victims who might be spared by deterring prospective murderers.

Deterrence is not altogether decisive for me either. I would favor retention of the death penalty as retribution even if it were shown that the threat of execution could not deter prospective murderers not already deterred by the threat of imprisonment.[7] Still, I believe the death penalty, because of its finality, is more feared than imprisonment, and deters some prospective murderers not deterred by the threat of imprisonment. Sparing the lives of even a few prospective victims by deterring their murderers is more important than preserving the lives of convicted murderers because of the possibility, or even the probability, that executing them would not deter others. Whereas the lives of the victims who might be saved are valuable, that of the murderer has only negative value, because of his crime. Surely the criminal law is meant to protect the lives of potential victims in preference to those of actual murderers. I share the view of Sir James Fitzjames Stephen: "Some men, probably, abstain from murder because they fear that, if they committed murder, they would be hanged. Hundreds of thousands abstain from it because they regard it with horror. One great reason why they regard it with horror is that murderers are hanged."[8]

IV. INCIDENTAL ISSUES: COST, RELATIVE SUFFERING, BRUTALIZATION

Many nondecisive issues are associated with capital punishment. Some believe that the monetary cost of appealing a capital sentence is excessive.[9] Yet most comparisons of the cost of life imprisonment with the cost of execution, apart from their dubious relevance, are flawed at least by the implied assumption that life prisoners will generate no judicial costs during their imprisonment. At any rate, the actual monetary costs are trumped by the importance of doing justice.

Others insist that a person sentenced to death suffers more than his victim suffered, and that this (excess) suffering is undue according to the *lex talionis* (rule of retaliation).[10] We cannot know whether the murderer on death row suffers more than his victim suffered; however, unlike the murderer, the victim deserved none of the suffering inflicted. Further, the limitations of the *lex talionis* were meant to restrain private vengeance, not the social retribution that has taken its place. Punishment—regardless of the motivation—is not intended to revenge, offset, or compensate for the victim's suffering, or to be measured by it. Punishment is to vindicate the law and the social order undermined by the crime. This is why a kidnapper's penal confinement is not limited to the period for which he imprisoned his victim; nor is a burglar's confinement meant merely to offset the suffering or the harm he caused his victim; nor is it meant only to offset the advantage he gained.[11]

Another argument heard at least since Beccaria[12] is that, by killing a murderer, we encourage, endorse, or legitimize unlawful killing. Yet, although all punishments are meant to be unpleasant, it is seldom argued that they legitimize the unlawful imposition of identical unpleasantness. Imprisonment is not thought to legitimize kidnapping; neither are fines thought to legitimize robbery. The difference between murder and execution, or between kidnapping and imprisonment, is that the first is unlawful and undeserved, the second a lawful and deserved punishment for an unlawful act. The physical similarities of the punishment to the crime are irrelevant. The relevant difference is not physical, but social.[13]

V. JUSTICE, EXCESS, DEGRADATION

We threaten punishments in order to deter crime. We impose them not only to make the threats credible but also as retribution (justice) for the crimes that were not deterred. Threats and punishments are necessary to deter and deterrence is a sufficient practical justification for them. Retribution is an independent moral justification.[14] Although penalties can be unwise, repulsive, or inappropriate, and those punished can be pitiable, in a sense the infliction of legal punishment on a guilty person cannot be unjust. By committing the crime, the criminal volunteered to assume the risk of receiving a legal punishment that he could have avoided by not committing the crime. The punishment he suffers is the punishment he voluntarily risked suffering and, therefore, it is no more unjust to him than any other event for which one knowingly volunteers to assume the risk. Thus, the death penalty cannot be unjust to the guilty criminal.

There remain, however, two moral objections. The penalty may be regarded as always excessive as retribution and always morally degrading. To regard the death penalty as always excessive, one must believe that no crime—no matter how heinous—could possibly justify capital punishment. Such a belief can be neither corroborated nor refuted; it is an article of faith.

One may believe that everybody, the murderer no less than the victim, has an imprescriptible right to life. I share Jeremy Bentham's view that any such "natural and imprescriptible rights" are "nonsense upon stilts."[15]

Justice Brennan has insisted that the death penalty is "uncivilized," "inhuman," inconsistent with "human dignity" and with "the sanctity of life,"[16] that it "treats members of the human race as nonhumans, as objects to be toyed with and discarded,"[17] that it is "uniquely degrading to human dignity"[18] and "by its very nature, [involves] a denial of the executed person's humanity."[19] Justice Brennan does not say why he thinks execution "uncivilized." Hitherto most civilizations have had the death penalty, although it has been discarded in Western Europe, where it is currently unfashionable probably because of its abuse by totalitarian regimes.

By "degrading," Justice Brennan seems to mean that execution degrades the executed convicts. Yet philosophers, such as Immanuel Kant and G. F. W. Hegel, have insisted that, when deserved, execution, far from degrading the executed convict, affirms his humanity by affirming his rationality and his responsibility for his actions. They thought that execution, when deserved, is required for the sake of the convict's dignity. (Does not life imprisonment violate human dignity more than execution, by keeping alive a prisoner deprived of all autonomy?)[20]

Common sense indicates that it cannot be death—our common fate— that is inhuman. Therefore, Justice Brennan must mean that death degrades when it comes not as a natural or accidental event, but as a deliberate social imposition. The murderer learns through his punishment that his fellow men have found him unworthy of living; that because he has murdered, he is being expelled from the community of the living. The social recognition of his self-degradation is the punitive essence of execution. To believe, as Justice Brennan appears to, that the degradation is inflicted by the execution reverses the direction of causality.

Execution of those who have committed heinous murders may deter only one murder per year. If it does, it seems quite warranted. It is also the only fitting retribution for murder I can think of.

NOTES

1. Death row as a semipermanent residence is cruel, because convicts are denied the normal amenities of prison life. Thus unless death row residents are integrated into the prison population, the continuing accumulation of convicts on death row should lead us to accelerate either the rate of executions or the rate of commutations. I find little objection to integration.

2. Some writers, for example, Cesare Bonesana, Marchese di Beccaria, have thought that life imprisonment is more severe. *See* C. Beccaria, *Dei Delitti E Delle Pene* 62–70 (1764). More recently, Jacques Barzun has expressed this view. *See* Barzun, "In Favor of Capital Punishment," in *The Death Penalty in America* 154 (H. Bedau ed. 1964). However, the overwhelming majority of both abolitionists and of convicts under death sentence prefer life imprisonment to execution.

3. For a discussion of the sources of opposition to corporal punishment, see E. van den Haag, *Punishing Criminals* 196–206 (1975).

4. Bedau & Radelet, "Miscarriages of Justice in Potentially Capital Cases" (1st draft, Oct. 1985) (on file at Harvard Law School Library).

5. An excessive number of trucking accidents or of miscarriages of justice could offset the benefits gained by trucking or the practice of doing justice. We are, however, far from this situation.

6. For a sample of conflicting views on the subject, see Baldus & Cole, "A Comparison of the Work of Thorsten Sellin and Isaac Ehrlich on the Deterrent Effect of Capital Punishment," 85 *Yale L. J.* 170 (1975); Bowers & Pierce, "Deterrence or Brutalization: What Is the Effect of Executions?," 26 *Crime & Delinq.* 453 (1980); Bowers & Pierce, "The Illusion of Deterrence in Isaac Ehrlich's Research on Capital Punishment," 85 *Yale L. J.* 187 (1975); Ehrlich, "Fear of Deterrence: A Critical Evaluation of the 'Report of the Panel on Research on Deterrent and Incapacitative Effects,'" 6 *J. Legal Stud.* 293 (1977); Ehrlich, "The Deterrent Effect of Capital Punishment: A Question of Life and Death," 65 *Am. Econ. Rev.* 397, 415–16 (1975); Ehrlich & Gibbons, "On the Measurement of the Deterrent Effect of Capital Punishment and the Theory of Deterrence," 6 *J. Legal Stud.* 35 (1977).

7. If executions were shown to increase the murder rate in the long run, I would favor abolition. Sparing the innocent victims who would be spared, *ex hypothesi*, by the nonexecution of murderers would be more important to me than the execution, however just, of murderers. But although there is a lively discussion of the subject, no serious evidence exists to support the hypothesis that executions produce a higher murder rate. *Cf.* Phillips, "The Deterrent Effect of Capital Punishment: New Evidence on an Old Controversy," 86 *Am. J. Soc.* 139 (1980) (arguing that murder rates drop immediately after executions of criminals).

8. H. Gross, *A Theory of Criminal Justice* 489 (1979) (attributing this passage to Sir James Fitzjames Stephen).

9. *Cf.* Kaplan, "Administering Capital Punishment," 36 *U. Fla. L. Rev.* 177, 178, 190–91 (1984) (noting the high cost of appealing a capital sentence).

10. For an example of this view, see A. Camus, *Reflections on the Guillotine* 24–30 (1959). On the limitations allegedly imposed by the *lex talionis,* see Reiman, "Justice, Civilization, and the Death Penalty: Answering van den Haag, 14 *Phil. & Pub. Aff.* 115, 119–34 (1985).

11. Thus restitution (a civil liability) cannot satisfy the punitive purpose of penal sanctions, whether the purpose be retributive or deterrent.

12. *See supra* note 2.

13. Some abolitionists challenge: if the death penalty is just and serves as a deterrent, why not televise executions? The answer is simple. The death even of a murderer, however well-deserved, should not serve as public entertainment. It so served in earlier centuries. But in this respect our sensibility has changed for the better, I believe. Further, television unavoidably would trivialize executions, wedged in, as they would be, between game shows, situation comedies and the like. Finally, because televised executions would focus on the physical aspects of the punishment, rather than the nature of the crime and the suffering of the victim, a televised execution would present the murderer as the victim of the state. Far from communicating the moral significance of the execution, television would shift the focus to the pitiable fear of the murderer. We no longer place in cages those sentenced to imprisonment to expose them to public view. Why should we so expose those sentenced to execution?

14. *See* van den Haag, "Punishment as a Device for Controlling the Crime Rate," 33 *Rutgers L. Rev.* 706, 719 (1981) (explaining why the desire for retribution, although independent, would have to be satisfied even if deterrence were the only purpose of punishment.)

15. *The Works of Jeremy Bentham* 105 (J. Bowring ed. 1972). However, I would be more polite about prescriptible natural rights, which Bentham described as "simple nonsense." *Id.* (It does not matter whether natural rights are called "moral or "human" rights as they currently are by most writers.)

16. *The Death Penalty in America* 256–63 (H. Bedau ed., 3rd ed. 1982) (quoting Furman v. Georgia, 408 U.S. 238, 286, 305 (1972) (Brennan, J., concurring).

17. *Id.* at 272–73; *see also* Gregg v. Georgia, 428 U.S. 153, 230 (1976) (Brennan, J., dissenting).

18. Furman v. Georgia, 408 U.S. 238, 291 (1972) (Brennan, J., concurring).

19. *Id.* 290.

20. *See* Barzun, *supra* note 2, *passim.*

A Case for Capital Punishment
W. E. Cooper and John King-Farlow

W. E. Cooper and John King-Farlow are philosophy professors at the University of Alberta, Canada. In this essay, they develop an argument for the death penalty that is based neither on retributivist nor on utilitarian grounds. Instead, they argue that the justification for capital punishment they imagine, "capital punishment with linkage" (or 'CPL' for short), would be accepted by rational contractors in a Rawlsian Original Position. Roughly, such contractors would choose principles governing the justice of society's basic institutions in ignorance of their position in society (see the essay by John Rawls in Chapter 1).

CPL is based on the widely shared intuition that if there is no way to save all, it is better to save the lives of innocent persons than it is to save the lives of murderers. Traditionally, defenders of the death penalty use this intuition to argue that the death penalty's effectiveness as a deterrent or as incapacitation justifies its use. Cooper and King-Farlow, however, argue that there may be other ways in which the use of the death penalty could save innocent lives. If it is assumed that it is economically less expensive to execute murderers than it is to imprison them for life, then the money saved by executing murderers could be used to save the lives of innocent persons. Under these conditions CPL would hold that the death penalty is justified. While the assumption that the death penalty is less expensive than life imprisonment seems to be false in the United States at the current time, it could be argued that this additional expense arises from the way in which the death penalty is administered rather than from the nature of the penalty itself. If so, CPL may imply that we should retain the death penalty and try to reduce significantly the cost of its administration.

We shall argue that there is adequate moral justification for capital punishment with linkage, that is, with linkage to keeping non-murderers from dying. We present the argument with two aims in mind. The first is to question the conventional wisdom, seldom challenged even by proponents of capital punishment, that being an abolitionist is closely connected to having a civilized respect for human life. This conventional wisdom, we hope to show, is somewhat off the mark. To this end we exhibit structural similarities between so-called lifeboat dilemmas and the public's relationship to a murderer. In a lifeboat dilemma one must choose between saving this life or that, since the lifeboat will not hold both persons. Now if this life were an innocent's and that one a murderer's, a choice to save the latter would not be met with accusations of callousness towards human life. We hope to project everyone's intuitions about this case onto the more baffling case of a society's relationship to the murderers and dying innocents in its midst. . . .

From *Journal of Social Philosophy* 20 (1989), 64–76.

Those whose lives are to be saved on the present proposal are not those who, were it not for the alleged deterrent effect of capital punishment, would be killed. If those lives are saved, so much the better; but our case for CPL simply bypasses the oft-heard objection that executing murderers is unjustified because it does not deter. The demand for deterrence often follows from a more general demand, which is reasonable enough, that murderers ought not to be executed unless doing so promotes some considerable social good; our view is sufficiently consequentialist to conform to this demand. But we question the normal quick inference from *no deterrence* to *no good achieved* and thence to *no capital punishment.* This is an utterly fallacious process unless every aspect of the political system is assumed to be fixed, except for the penalty for murder; only then is it quite plausible to suppose that the case for capital punishment will be tied to its deterrence value, since there is not much else in the way of social good that one might hope for in capital punishment, given the restrictive assumption. But we want to challenge the restriction.

Linkage will forge a moral permission to execute murderers when the cost of keeping them alive could be diverted to the saving of innocent lives. The cost in the broadest relevant sense is the total social cost, including taxpayers' costs for the incarceration of murderers, unavailability of murderers' organs for life-saving transplants, and so on. Organ-cost represents perhaps the closest similarity to lifeboat dilemmas, since often enough the executed murderer's organs might be the only ones available to save an innocent life, whereas it is tempting to say that taxpayers could always pay more, and citizens generally could do more, in order both to keep murderers alive and also save innocent lives that are currently lost. We reject this temptation for reasons to come, but in order to address it squarely we frame the case for CPL in terms of taxpayers' costs, and with this frame of reference it will be shown that there are sufficient similarities to a lifeboat dilemma, sufficient to incline the intellect towards acceptance of CPL. The empirical jumping-off place then is the hypothesis, which we regard as probably true, that it costs more, costs us taxpayers more, to keep murderers alive than to execute them, and enough more in fact that the remainder—that is, the cost of keeping the murderer alive less the cost of execution—could be used in order to save the life or lives of some innocent person or persons. (Frequently cited reckonings calculate the cost of incarcerating murderers at $30,000 to $50,000 per annum, but no exact or even approximate figure is essential to our argument, though it would indeed be essential to the practical implementation of CPL.) We acknowledge the high cost of a capital trial, of the appeals process, and of the special methods of custody for murderers awaiting execution. Such considerations amount to a small question mark for the hypothesis. But as first premises go it has the virtue of being an hypothesis rather than an item of faith, and an attractively testable hypothesis to boot comparing favorably for instance with the intractable claim that the death penalty deters. Moreover the hypothesis can always be strengthened, without sacrificing this attractiveness, by taking into account broader ranges of costs of keeping murderers alive, such as organ-cost.

Our empirical hypothesis is at least potentially a more secure beginning of a case for capital punishment than the moral principle lex talionis, understood as the principle that a criminal ought to be paid back in kind (an eye for an eye, a tooth for a tooth, etc.), with the implication that execution is the uniquely fitting punishment for murder: that murder merits this penalty and that the murderer deserves it. We reject this principle, noting its absurd or monstrous implications (a rape for a rape, torture for the torturer, etc.) and observing that there is no moral consensus on its validity. We distinguish it from the different and weaker principle, which we hold to be valid, that severity of a punishment should be proportional to the gravity of the offense. Though this principle of proportionality is open to question, one pays a high price to deny it, for it is manifestly a principle of common sense and one to which legislators and judges have attached great weight in arriving at schedules of punishment for violations of law. We shall interpret the principle as being consistent with the proposition that, in the spirit of Aristotle's golden mean, there is a range of punishments satisfying the requirement of proportionality. A punishment of hand-slapping for murder falls outside of the appropriate range by way of its deficiency, as does death by torture due to its excessive severity. Punishments of life imprisonment and imprisonment for lesser but lengthy periods fall within the appropriate range. Capital punishment, on the other hand, falls into a zone of indeterminacy between the range of appropriate punishment for murder and excess. Accordingly, we recommend the following principle as a tool for resolving this kind of indeterminacy: Unless there is a good reason for choosing a more rather than a less severe punishment for a crime, the less severe punishment is to be preferred. We shall argue that the saving of innocent lives constitutes such a good reason for capital punishment, nudging it from the zone of indeterminacy into the range of appropriate punishment. Our employment of the Good Reasons Principle is limited to the zone of indeterminacy and is not intended to replace the considered judgments which lead us to classify punishments as appropriate, deficient or excessive. . . .

Though we reject unqualifiedly consequentialist or retributivist justifications of capital punishment, we hold that retributivist and consequentialist points of view should have weight in an adequate justification, and that Rawls was on the right track in "Two Concepts of Rules" when he urged consequentialist reasoning at the level of justifying a practice of punishment and retributivist reasoning at the level of justifying punishment of a particular action which violates the laws of that practice: "...utilitarian arguments are appropriate with regard to questions about practices, while retributive arguments fit the application of particular rules to particular cases."[1] Thus the murderer really does deserve to die if CPL is in place, but the notion of desert here is parasitic upon the existence of a rule which expresses CPL, and the rule if justified by consequentialist arguments to the effect that the interests of society are best promoted by the inclusion of that rule. So the retributivist point of view of judge, jury and ordinary citizen is appropriate at one level, and the consequentialist point of view of the legislator is appropriate at another and more fundamental level.

> One can say, then, that the judge and the legislator stand in different positions and look in different directions: one to the past, the other to the future. The justification of what the judge does, *qua* judge, sounds like the retributive view; the justification of what the (ideal) legislator does, *qua* legislator, sounds like the utilitarian view. Thus both views have a point (this is as it should be since intelligent and sensitive persons have been on both sides of the argument); and one's initial confusion disappears once one sees that these views apply to persons holding different offices with different duties; and situated differently with respect to the system of rules that make up the criminal law.[2]

We follow Rawls further by invoking his *A Theory of Justice* in supposing that the consequentialist reasoning which justifies the practice of CPL should be constrained by considerations of fairness, such as those which structure his contractarian Original Position, a choice-situation in which all members of a society attempt to agree on principles that will regulate the basic structure of their society.[3] It will be recalled that these parties are conceived as free, equal, and rational, and as separated by a veil of ignorance from information that would permit them unfairly to tailor principles to their selfish advantage. We hope to show that fair reasoning of this sort can naturally be extended in justification of CPL. It is important to note that we accept the constraints of fairness on consequentialist reasoning, following the Rawls of *A Theory of Justice* in this regard and not the Rawls of "Two Concepts of Rules," where constraints on consequentialist reasoning at the level of the legislator are not developed.

We begin by asking whether a murderer has a right to life which blocks every justification for capital punishment. In this connection there is a useful thought-experiment that we borrow from Hugo Bedau, an opponent of capital punishment.[4] Bedau helpfully imagines a fanciful world in which the execution of a murderer would invariably bring the victim back to life, whole and restored. In such a world, he says, it is hard to see how anyone could oppose the death penalty on moral grounds. The implication for our world, he concludes, is that responsible opposition to the death penalty cannot be both moral and unconditional, but rather it must be conceded that there are conditions under which that opposition should cease. Thus far we adopt Bedau's reasoning as part of our argument, but we part ways now because he supposes that conditions of the appropriate sort do not obtain in our world; we affirm that they do. CPL will not bring the dead back to life, but it will bring life to the dying. Once Bedau's point has eliminated unconditional opposition to the death penalty, the condition we propose, that CPL will bring life to the dying, should recommend itself strongly. In order to arrive at this condition more clearly and certainly, we must first introduce and discuss what we will call *Capital Dilemmas*. In a Capital Dilemma either the life of some murderer or that of some innocent can be saved by a society's collective act, without violating anyone's rights; but it is impossible that both lives should be saved without violating someone's rights. CPL is a resolution of the dilemma in favor of the innocent, and we want to show how such dilemmas might arise and thereby suggest that we are confronted by them implicitly. That is, the circumstances that generate them are likely to be circumstances that would obtain if we were to attempt to save innocent lives that are now lost, when the attempt is made within constraints imposed by citizens' rights.

Consider a society which has been exposed to a conscientious political action and public education campaign, designed to encourage political changes, donations, voluntary activity, etc. towards facilitating life-saving research, rescue operations, provision of organ transplants, reduction of military spending, increased taxes, and so on. Assume that this publicity squeeze is not completely successful, and that a successful campaign would require unfair coercive or manipulative tactics, from which the public has a right to be free. (We assume that this right and others are products of the fair agreement in Rawls's original position.) The campaign's lack of success, then, entails that there is at least one person, whom we may call Smith, whose life could be saved if there were further donations. By hypothesis, however, no further donations will be forthcoming without violating citizens' rights, and there is no law in effect, or able to generate majority support, which would justify increased revenue in order to save Smith. But now let us suppose that murderer Olson is serving life in prison, and that CPL would divert resources sufficient to supply Smith with food, or a kidney dialysis machine, or a kidney, whatever else he needs in order to survive. In such a circumstance we think it fair to ask the reader to think of society as a jailer, with Olson on his left and Smith on his right, feeding expensive food to Olson as Smith starves to death, in circumstances which make it impossible to keep both from dying. The fact that we are not really so close to Smith and his death is of questionable significance, but if the suggested image is too dramatic, take up the bare thought that there is an apparent Capital Dilemma here. Yet by our practice we resolve the dilemma between the murderer Olson and innocent Smith by keeping Olson alive. Is it morally necessary that we resolve the dilemma in this way? Otherwise put: Is there something morally objectionable about CPL as a resolution of Capital Dilemmas, something more objectionable than public apathy and passiveness towards the deaths of innocents? Or should we be bound rather by a practice of punishment which includes something like the following rule: Execution should be an optional punishment for murderers, applicable when it is demonstrable by processes of reasoning accessible to the public that an innocent life could be saved by doing so, and that alternative means of doing so are not at hand, or would require infringement of the rights of citizens.

We turn now to a contractarian justification of resolving Capital Dilemmas in favor of innocents. We want to show that, when geared to problems about punishment, Rawls's Original Position of self-interested, rational, free, and equal contractors would lead to a choice of CPL. It can be assumed that Rawls's two principles have been agreed upon: Equal and maximally extensive liberties are to be guaranteed by the first of these, the liberty principle, and the discussion of capital punishment will occur in connection with the interpretation of this principle for a society like ours, in which there are all kinds and degrees of crime. It can be assumed further that a schedule of penalties is to be drafted according to various relevant principles (such as the principle that punishment should be proportional to the gravity of the offense) and in the light of relevant information (e.g., about rates of crime). One relevant bit of information about their society has to do with the probability of Capital Dilemmas. They will know whether they inherit circumstances sufficiently grim that innocent people die for want of funds used to maintain murderers. If so, they will be moved to bring capital punishment from the zone of indeterminacy to the range of appropriate punishment for murder, moved by what they can view as good reasons for imposing a more rather than a less severe penalty. Entertaining the proposal for capital punishment with linkage, each participant would reason that he has an equal chance of being an Olson or a Smith—and perhaps a greater than equal chance of being a Smith, should it be the case that many lives can be saved by Olson's execution. So they would best protect their own interests by opting for capital punishment with linkage, and they would interpret the liberty principle so that it does not guarantee a right not to be executed for murder. In sum, there is a plausible contractarian justification for resolving Capital Dilemmas by CPL.

The justification can be advanced further by considering now some important objections to the argument so far.

Objection 1. "In Rawls's ideal society there is no crime, and there would be social programs to prevent avoidable loss of human life."

Reply. Rawls does describe a well-ordered society in which all citizens act justly, but he also recognizes the need to apply his ideal to societies in which there is not strict compliance with demands of justice. This is the domain of what he calls partial compliance theory, and it is in this domain that we are operating in advocating CPL. . . .

Objection 3. "CPL uses the murderer as a means to an end, and therefore does not treat him with the respect due to persons.

Reply. The contractarian argument for CPL is one that the murderer himself, *qua* moral agent, would choose. If the original position is the fair position for deciding moral issues of this sort, there is a strong counter to the argument that the executed murderer is being treated as a mere means to an end of social welfare; for he is being treated with the respect owed to him as a being capable of a sense of justice. He is represented in a position appropriate to moral choice, under conditions, such as lack of knowledge that he is a murderer, which ensure fairness. And under these conditions he would choose CPL. He has nothing to lose by doing so, since his chances of being a saved Smith or an executed Olson are at least equal in virtue of the linkage requirement, and his chances are greater if the cost of saving Smiths is low compared to the cost of keeping Olsons alive. And as a participant in the original position he has no reason to favor Olson. It is agreed that criminals forfeit some greater or lesser extent of liberty, and he accepts a schedule of punishments in which Olson's murders demand the greatest severity. Linkage is the added consideration which inclines him to accept execution as this most severe punishment.

Objection 4. "Since no legal system is infallible, CPL risks the irremediable and unacceptable injustice of executing people who are not guilty."

Reply. Reasoning like that in the reply to Objection 3 is available in response to the problem of mistakenly executing an innocent person. The fair position for deliberation about capital punishment is one in which knowledge of whether one is innocent or guilty is bracketed. In this position the better argument favors capital punishment. Needless to say, part of that better argument will include insistence on a very reliable judicial system, and perhaps as well certain restrictions on categories of murder for which CPL is an option. But this is no different from their demanding safe roads if automobiles are to be permitted, given the loss of life attendant to their use.

It is none the less a large and terrible fact that an innocent person can die on CPL. But innocent persons die as an upshot of our present penal practice, as our argument has emphasized. The absolute certainty of saving such lives on CPL justifies, we have argued, risking the possibility of condemning an innocent person. We should replace pre-occupation with this possibility, and moral sentimentality about the lives of murderers, by a keener recognition of the suffering and loss of life which we might prevent by a political change that would do an injustice to no one.

Objection 5. "Murderers have a natural right to life. Since this natural right is violated by execution, CPL is unacceptable."

Reply. No appeal to Olson's natural right to life establishes anything on its own, since that right is possessed equally by the innocent Smith, and any feature of Olson that this doctrine might identify, such as his possessing a soul or his being blessed with grace by God, is equally a feature of Smith. If the objection is to be understood as emphasizing the wrong of violating Olson's right by executing him, and this is understood as different from letting Smith die because there is allegedly no violation in the latter case, see Objection 8 below. . . .

Objection 7. "By your reasoning the execution of pick-pockets could be justified, just in case the money saved by execution rather than incarceration were targeted for life-saving projects."

Reply. We have assumed all along a principle of proportionality which would rule out execution of pick-pockets as excessive for their crime. Part of the Rawlsian justification-procedure assumed here is reflective equilibrium, after all, which requires that choices made in the original position should be compatible with our considered judgments. This assumption would be arbitrary if we were presenting a simply utilitarian or simply rights-based justification of CPL. But ours is a mixed account, reflecting our belief that there are diverse sources of moral value which resist the philosophical demand for unity.

Objection 8. "Capital punishment is barbaric."

Reply. The objector may be granted the premise that the traditional methods of execution, such as the guillotine and the noose, have been more or less barbaric; but it would be wrong to conclude from this that capital punishment is so. This is to transfer the deficiency of a means to an end to the end itself, a fallacy too obvious to dwell upon.

Less obvious is the quiet barbarism lurking behind this objection. Quiet barbarism lets innocents die in order to avoid dirty hands, and perhaps also in order to experience the questionable moral frisson of keeping clean hands. The barbarism of this position is its failure to adopt the point of view of the legislator, and of focusing instead on what is done to the murderer. When a more balanced focus is attained by putting the weight of the legislator's point of view into the scales of judgment, it will be judged that it is a mistake to be preoccupied with the moral frisson of opposing the death penalty. Criticisms of capital punishment are not of course going to reduce to questions about technique, but if these questions can be isolated, it may be easier to accept the view of moral progress implied by our account, which would measure it in terms of our willingness to act on behalf of innocents, when they are in Capital Dilemmas with murderers. There may indeed be a moral cost to even relatively painless and dignified methods of execution, such as shooting, a cost alluded to in the suggestion that we do something barbaric to the murderer. But the capital dilemma requires a comparison of that cost to the loss of an innocent life. In that perspective the executioner and those whose public policy permits CPL can properly be viewed as expressing the will to live of the innocent who would otherwise die.

A companion-piece to the fallacy about barbaric means is the thought that capital punishment barbarizes us, a thought which makes a forceful appeal to our desire to be morally progressive, by associating capital punishment with disrespect for human life. But our proposal reveals the lack of depth in this association. How can we show respect for life by choosing, in Capital Dilemmas, to keep murderers alive rather than innocents? Far from barbarizing us, CPL would be apt to civilize us by broadening our awareness and engaging our concern about the plight of innocents who currently lack the public attention and public funds lavished on murderers.

Objection 9. "The wrongfulness of capital punishment lies in the difference between actually killing someone and letting someone die."

Reply. If there seems to be some vestigial force in the pair of thoughts about barbarism, perhaps this illusion can be located in a scruple about the action of executing Olson: the thought that there is something *active* about taking his life which is *toto caelo* different from the passivity involved in letting Smith die. On the strength of this thought, it can be supposed that the murderer is protected from Capital Dilemmas, and a society's resolution of such dilemmas by capital punishment with linkage, by the difference between actively killing and passively letting die. We grant that the distinction between killing and letting die is important within the sphere of private morality, where there is a strong prohibition on killing and robbery, and a relatively weak duty of aid to those in distress; no legal penalty attaches to not contributing to charities that relieve poverty, for instance, but there are penalties for taking someone's property or killing him. There is a moral as well as a legal asymmetry here, despite similarities in the upshot of the active deed and the passive omission—i.e., someone dies or loses his property. The asymmetry is presumably to be explained by the moral significance of the distinction between action and omission: killing and letting die, robbing and not providing, and so forth. The moral force of this distinction, then, is something to be weighed against whatever good might be done by a vigilante's action of killing a murderer in order to keep others from dying.

Whatever the weight of this distinction in private morality, its weight in public morality is less. Paradigmatic of public morality is the domain of legislation, where the legislator cannot excuse herself for the deaths of people in unsafe mines by noting that she did not kill them; she is responsible for drafting legislation that will not let people die like that. By the same token, the legislator cannot be accused of killing, or even having killed, those whom she drafts to fight a war, even if these deaths are the upshot of her legislation. The distinction between killing and letting die does not have its full force when the agent occupies a public role which makes moral demands on her of a consequentialist sort. By contrast, the demands on someone who does not occupy such public roles are predominantly concerned with respecting rights. One must not kill the miner, but one does not have the legislator's responsibility to ensure that he does not die because of unsafe working conditions. . . .

Objection 10. "CPL would pander to feelings of vengeance that should be restrained."

Reply. Political will for the linkage law would no doubt be fueled in good part by widespread feelings of vengeance towards murderers, and perhaps in greater part than by appreciation of the moral force of the argument in favor of CPL. In a certain sense we do not think this is to be deplored, however, since the voters will be availing themselves of one legitimate way of resolving a moral dilemma of the sort which the proposed law confronts them with. If they were in the proverbial life-boat and could save only a loved one or a stranger, they would be justified in acting on their sentiment, saving the loved one. If they could save only a stranger or a despised one, they would be justified in acting on their sentiment, and saving the stranger. A voter may be sentimentally disposed to save the lives of murderers, perhaps because of an aversion to capital punishment or because he has murderous friends; or he may be sentimentally disposed to save the lives of innocent strangers instead. We do not morally judge either sentiment at this political level of the argument. In a different context we might want to express admiration for the humane attitude of one who votes against the law, and deplore the mean vengeance that might motivate one who votes for the law. But at this political level we simply anticipate counting the votes and finding that a majority favors capital punishment with linkage. In short, we believe the linkage proposal could successfully harness the force of vengeance in order to bolster inadequate dispositions towards altruistic conduct; it could do so without violating Olson's rights, and in such a way as to further goals of justice. Moreover, assuming that the community's experience of a linkage law would have the civilizing effect predicted above, it can be hypothesized that public support for the law would come to draw less on vengeful motives, and more and more on reasons such as those that are decisive for the participants in the original position. . . .

In conclusion we want to emphasize that our argument has never relied on the thought that a murderer's life is worth less than an innocent's, or that he loses his right to life by murdering. We are simply not taking a stand on such thoughts here. Rather, we have argued that the murderer loses the various significant protections of his right to life which are enjoyed by ordinary citizens, losses which are reflected in what we have argued is a just punishment, CPL. The extent of the loss of protections puts him in a Capital Dilemma with a dying innocent, whose life is as precious as the murderer's, and who has the same right to life. As a society confronted by this dilemma we are justified in favoring the innocent, by passing CPL legislation.

NOTES

1. John Rawls, "Two Concepts of Rules," *The Philosophical Review* 64 (1955), 3–32.
2. Rawls, "Two Concepts of Rules," 3–32.
3. John Rawls, *A Theory of Justice* (1971: Harvard University Press).
4. Hugo Adam Bedau, "Capital Punishment and Social Defense," *Matters of Life and Death: New Introductory Essays in Moral Philosophy,* ed. Tom Regan (1980: Random House).

Race and the Death Penalty
Anthony G. Amsterdam

In this essay Anthony Amsterdam, the Judge Edward Weinfeld Professor of Law at New York University's School of Law, looks at racism within the criminal justice system in the United States. His specific focus is on the Supreme Court's decision in *McCleskey v. Kemp* (1986), in which the majority of the justices voted not to overturn a death sentence against Warren McCleskey, a black man convicted of killing a white man. The Court maintained that although convincing statistical evidence exists to show that race plays a large role in determining when death sentences are imposed, McCleskey had no proof that a specific racial bias against him played a role in his particular sentencing, and thus no basis to challenge his sentence on the grounds of racial discrimination. The proof that racial bias existed in the system as a whole was, in the eyes of the Court, insufficient. Amsterdam believes that this decision in effect licenses racism in the criminal justice system and is not, as a result, a justifiable decision.

There are times when even truths we hold self-evident require affirmation. For those who have invested our careers and our hopes in the criminal justice system, this is one of those times. Insofar as the basic principles that give value to our lives are in the keeping of the law and can be vindicated or betrayed by the decisions of any court, they have been sold down the river by a decision of the Supreme Court of the United States less than a year old.

I do not choose by accident a metaphor of slavery. For the decision I am referring to is the criminal justice system's *Dred Scott* case. It is the case of Warren McCleskey, a black man sentenced to die for the murder of a white man in Georgia. The Supreme Court held that McCleskey can be constitutionally put to death despite overwhelming unrebutted and unexplained statistical evidence that the death penalty is being imposed by Georgia juries in a pattern which reflects the race of convicted murderers and their victims and cannot be accounted for by any factor other than race.

This is not just a case about capital punishment. The Supreme Court's decision, which amounts to an open license to discriminate against people of color in capital sentencing, was placed upon grounds that implicate the entire criminal justice system. Worse still, the Court's reasoning makes us all accomplices in its toleration of a racially discriminatory administration of criminal justice.

Let us look at the *McCleskey* case. His crime was an ugly one: He robbed a furniture store at gunpoint, and he or one of his accomplices killed a police officer who responded to the scene. McCleskey may have been the triggerman. Whether or not he was, he was guilty of murder under Georgia law.

From *Criminal Justice Ethics* 7 (1988), pp. 2, 84–86.

But his case in the Supreme Court was not concerned with guilt. It was concerned with why McCleskey had been sentenced to death instead of life imprisonment for his crime. It was concerned with why, out of seventeen defendants charged with the killings of police officers in Fulton County, Georgia, between 1973 and 1980, only Warren McCleskey—a black defendant charged with killing a white officer—had been chosen for a death sentence. In the only other one of these seventeen cases in which the predominantly white prosecutor's office in Atlanta had pushed for the death penalty, a black defendant convicted of killing a black police officer had been sentenced to life instead.

It was facts of that sort that led the NAACP Legal Defense Fund to become involved in McCleskey's case. They were not unfamiliar facts to any of the lawyers who, like myself, had worked for the Legal Defense Fund for many years, defending Blacks charged with serious crimes throughout the South. We knew that in the United States black defendants convicted of murder or rape in cases involving white victims have always been sentenced to death and executed far out of proportion to their numbers, and under factual circumstances that would have produced a sentence of imprisonment—often a relatively light sentence of imprisonment—in identical cases with black victims or white defendants or both.

Back in the mid-sixties the Legal Defense Fund had presented to courts evidence of extensive statistical studies conducted by Dr. Marvin Wolfgang, one of the deans of American criminology, showing that the grossly disproportionate number of death sentences which were then being handed out to black defendants convicted of the rape of white victims could not be explained by any factor other than race. Prosecutors took the position then that these studies were insufficiently detailed to rule out the influence of every possible nonracial factor, and it was largely for that reason that the courts rejected our claims that our black death-sentenced clients had been denied the Equal protection of the Laws. Fortunately, in 1972 we had won a Supreme Court decision that saved the lives of all those clients and outlawed virtually every death-penalty statute in the United States on procedural grounds; and when the States enacted new death-penalty laws between 1973 and 1976, only three of them reinstated capital punishment for rape. Now that it no longer mattered much, the prosecutors could afford to take another tack. When we argued against the new capital murder statutes on the ground that the Wolfgang studies had shown the susceptibility of capital sentencing laws to racially discriminatory application, the Government of the United States came into the Supreme Court against us saying, Oh, yes, Wolfgang was "a careful and comprehensive study, and we do not question its conclusion that during the twenty years between [1945 and 1965]..., in southern states, there was discrimination in rape cases." However, said the Government, this "research does not provide support for a conclusion that racial discrimination continues,... or that it applies to murder cases."

So we were well prepared for this sort of selective agnosticism when we went to court in the *McCleskey* case. The evidence that we presented in support of McCleskey's claim of racial discrimination left nothing out. Our centerpiece was a pair of studies conducted by Professor David Baldus, of the University of Iowa, and his colleagues, which examined 2,484 cases of murder and non-negligent manslaughter that occurred in Georgia between 1973, the date when its present capital murder statute was enacted, and 1979, the year after McCleskey's own death sentence was imposed. The Baldus team got its data on these cases principally from official state records, supplied by the Georgia Supreme Court and the Georgia Board of Pardons and Paroles.

Through a highly refined protocol, the team collected information regarding more than five hundred factors in each case—information relating to the demographic and individual characteristics of the defendant and the victim, the circumstances of the crime and the strength of the evidence of guilt, and the aggravating and mitigating features of each case: both the features specified by Georgia law to be considered in capital sentencing and every factor recognized in the legal and criminological literature as theoretically or actually likely to affect the choice of life or death. Using the most reliable and advanced techniques of social-science research, Baldus processed the data through a wide array of sophisticated statistical procedures, including multiple-regression analyses based upon alternative models that considered and controlled for as few as 10 or as many as 230 sentencing factors in each analysis. When our evidentiary case was presented in court, Baldus reanalyzed the data several more times to take account of every additional factor, combination of factors, or model for analysis of factors suggested by the State of Georgia's expert witnesses, its lawyers, and the federal trial judge. The Baldus study has since been uniformly praised by social scientists as the best study of any aspect of criminal sentencing ever conducted.

What did it show? That death sentences were being imposed in Georgia murder cases in a clear, consistent pattern that reflected the race of the victim and the race of the defendant and could not be explained by any non-racial factor. For example:

1. Although less than 40 percent of Georgia homicide cases involve white victims, in 87 percent of the cases in which a death sentence is imposed, the victim is white. White-victim cases are almost eleven times more likely to produce a death sentence than are black-victim cases.
2. When the race of the defendant is considered too, the following figures emerge: 22 percent of black defendants who kill white victims are sentenced to death; 8 percent of white defendants who kill white victims are sentenced to death; 1 percent of black defendants who kill black victims are sentenced to death; 3 percent of white defendants who kill black victims are sentenced to death. It should be noted that out of the roughly 2,500 Georgia homicide cases found, only 64 involved killings of black victims by white defendants, so the 3 percent death-sentencing rate in this category represents a total of two death sentences over a six-year period. Plainly, the reason why

racial discrimination against black defendants does not appear even more glaringly evident is that most black murderers kill black victims; almost no identified white murderers kill black victims, and virtually nobody is sentenced to death for killing a mere black victim.

3. No non-racial factor explains these racial patterns. Under multiple regression analysis, the model with the maximum explanatory power shows that after controlling for legitimate non-racial factors, murderers of white victims are still being sentenced to death 4.3 times more often than murderers of black victims. Multiple regression analysis also shows that the race of the victim is as good a basis for predicting whether or not a murderer will be sentenced to death as are the aggravating circumstances which the Georgia statute explicitly says should be considered in favor of a death sentence, such as whether the defendant has a prior murder conviction, or whether he is the primary actor in the present murder.

4. Across the whole universe of cases, approximately 5 percent of Georgia killings result in a death sentence. Yet when more than 230 non-racial variables are controlled for, the death-sentencing rate is 6 percentage points higher in white-victim cases than in black-victim cases. What this means is that in predicting whether any particular person will get the death penalty in Georgia, it is less important to know whether or not he committed a homicide in the first place than to know whether, if he did, he killed a white victim or a black one.

5. However, the effects of race are not uniform across the entire range of homicide cases. As might be expected, in the least aggravated sorts of cases, almost no one gets a death sentence; in the really gruesome cases, a high percentage of both black and white murderers get death sentences; so it is in the mid-range of cases—cases like McCleskey's—that race has its greatest impact. The Baldus study found that in these mid-range cases the death-sentencing rate for killers of white victims is 34 percent as compared to 14 percent for killers of black victims. In other words, out of every thirty-four murderers sentenced to death for killing a white victim, twenty of them would not have gotten death sentences if their victims had been black.

The bottom line is this: Georgia has executed eleven murderers since it passed its present statute in 1973. Nine of the eleven were black. Ten of the eleven had white victims. Can there be the slightest doubt that this revolting record is the product of some sort of racial bias rather than a pure fluke?

A narrow majority of the Supreme Court pretended to have such doubts and rejected McCleskey's Equal-Protection challenge to his death sentence. It did not question the quality or the validity of the Baldus study, or any of the findings that have been described here. It admitted that the manifest racial discrepancies in death sentencing were unexplained by any non-racial variable, and that Baldus's data pointed to a "likelihood" or a "risk" that race was at work in the capital sentencing process. It essentially conceded that if a similar statistical showing of racial bias had been made in an employment-discrimination case or in a jury-selection case, the courts would have been required to find a violation of the Equal Protection Clause of the Fourteenth Amendment. But, the Court said, racial discrimination in capital sentencing cannot be proved by a pattern of sentencing results: a death-sentenced defendant like McCleskey must present proof that the particular jury or the individual prosecutor, or some other decision-maker in his own case, was personally motivated by racial considerations to bring about his death. Since such proof is never possible to obtain, racial discrimination in capital sentencing is never possible to prove.

The Court gave four basic reasons for this result. First, since capital sentencing decisions are made by a host of different juries and prosecutors, and are supposed to be based upon "innumerable factors that vary according to the characteristics of the individual defendant and the facts of the particular capital offense," even sentencing patterns that are explicable by race and inexplicable except by race do not necessarily show that any single decision-maker in the system is acting out of a subjective purpose to discriminate. Second, capital punishment laws are important for the protection of society; the "[i]mplementation of these laws necessarily requires discretionary judgments"; and, "[b]ecause discretion is essential to the criminal justice process, we [sh]ould demand exceptionally clear proof before we... infer that the discretion has been abused." Third, this same respect for discretionary judgments makes it imprudent to require juries and prosecutors to explain their decisions, so it is better to ignore the inference of racial discrimination that flows logically from their behavior than to call upon them to justify such behavior upon non-racial grounds.

Fourth, more is involved than capital punishment. "McCleskey's claim... throws into serious question the principles that underlie our entire criminal justice system." This is so because "the Baldus study indicates a discrepancy that appears to correlate with race," and "[a]pparent disparities in sentencing are an inevitable part of our criminal justice system." "Thus," says the Court, "if we accepted McCleskey's claim that racial bias has impermissibly tainted the capital sentencing decision, we could soon be faced with similar claims as to other types of penalty. Moreover, the claim that... sentence rests on the irrelevant factor of race easily could be extended to apply to claims based on unexplained discrepancies that correlate to membership in other minority groups, and even to gender"—and even to claims based upon "the defendant's facial characteristics, or the physical attractiveness of the... victim." In other words, if we forbid racial discrimination in meting out sentences of life or death, we may have to face claims of discrimination against blacks, or against women, or perhaps against ugly people, wherever the facts warrant such claims, in the length of prison sentences, in the length of jail sentences, in the giving of suspended sentences, in the making of pretrial release decisions, in the invocation of recidivist sentencing enhancements, in the prosecutor's decisions whether to file charges, and how heavily to load up the charges, against black defendants as compared with white defendants or against ugly defendants as compared with ravishingly beautiful defendants; and of course the whole criminal justice system will then fall down flat and leave us in a state of anarchy. In thirty years of reading purportedly serious judicial opinions, I have never seen one that came so close to Thomas De Quincy's famous justification for punishing the crime of murder: "If once a man indulges himself in murder, very soon he comes to think little of robbing; and from robbing he next comes to drinking and Sabbath-breaking, and from that to incivility and procrastination."

Notice that the Court's version of this slippery-slope argument merely makes explicit what is implied throughout its opinion in the *McCleskey* case. Its decision is not limited to capital sentencing but purports to rest on principles which apply to the whole criminal justice system. Every part of that system from arrest to sentencing and parole, in relation to every crime from murder to Sabbath-breaking, involves a multitude of separate decision-makers making individualized decisions based upon "innumerable [case-specific] factors." All of these decisions are important for the protection of society from crime. All are conceived as "necessarily requir[ing] discretionary judgments." In making these discretionary judgments, prosecutors and judges as well as jurors have traditionally been immunized from inquiry into their motives. If this kind of discretion implies the power to treat black people differently from white people and to escape the responsibility for explaining why one is making life-and-death decisions in an apparently discriminatory manner, it implies a tolerance for racial discrimination throughout the length and breadth of the administration of criminal justice. What the Supreme Court has held, plainly, is that the very nature of the criminal justice system requires that its workings be excluded from the ordinary rules of law and even logic that guarantee equal protection to racial minorities in our society.

And it is here, I suggest, that any self-respecting criminal justice professional is obliged to speak out against this Supreme Court's conception of the criminal justice system. We must reaffirm that there can be no justice in a system which treats people of color differently from white people, or treats crimes against people of color differently from crimes against white people.

We must reaffirm that racism is itself a crime, and that the toleration of racism cannot be justified by the supposed interest of society in fighting crime. We must pledge that when anyone—even a majority of the Supreme Court—tells us that a power to discriminate on grounds of race is necessary to protect society from crime, we will recognize that we are probably being sold another shipment of propaganda to justify repression. Let us therefore never fail to ask the question whether righteous rhetoric about protecting society from crime really refers to protecting only white people. And when the answer, as in the McCleskey case, is that protecting only white people is being described as "protecting society from crime," let us say that we are not so stupid as to buy this version of the Big Lie, nor so uncaring as to let it go unchallenged.

Let us reaffirm that neither the toleration of racism by the Supreme Court nor the pervasiveness of racism in the criminal justice system can make it right, and that these things only make it worse. Let us reaffirm that racism exists, and is against the fundamental law of this Nation, whenever people of different races are treated differently by any public agency or institution as a consequence of their race and with no legitimate non-racial reason for the different treatment. Let us dedicate ourselves to eradicating racism, and declaring it unlawful, not simply in the superficial, short-lived situation where we can point to one or another specific decision-maker and show that his decisions were the product of conscious bigotry, but also in the far more basic, more intractable, and more destructive situation where hundreds upon hundreds of different public decision-makers, acting like Georgia's prosecutors and judges and juries—without collusion and in many cases without consciousness of their own racial biases—combine to produce a pattern that bespeaks the profound prejudice of an entire population.

Also, let us vow that we will never claim—or stand by unprotestingly while others claim for us—that, because our work is righteous and important, it should be above the law. Of course, controlling crime is vital work; that is why we give the agencies of criminal justice drastic and unique coercive powers, including the powers of imprisonment and death. And of course discretion in the execution of such powers is essential. But it is precisely because the powers that the system regulates are so awesome, and because the discretion of its actors is so broad, that it cannot be relieved of accountability for the exercise of that discretion. Nor can it be exempted from the scrutiny that courts of law are bound to give to documented charges of discrimination on the ground of race by any agency of government. Let us declare flatly that we neither seek nor will accept any such exemption, and that we find it demeaning to be told by the Supreme Court that the system of justice to which we have devoted our professional lives cannot do its job without a special dispensation from the safeguards that assure to people of every race the equal protection of the law.

This is a stigma criminal justice practitioners do not deserve. Service in the criminal justice system should be a cause not for shame but for pride. Nowhere is it possible to dedicate one's labors to the welfare of one's fellow human beings with a greater sense that one is needed and that the quality of what one does can make a difference. But to feel this pride, and to deserve it, we must consecrate ourselves to the protection of all people, not a privileged few. We must be servants of humanity, not of caste. Whether or not the Supreme Court demands this of us, we must demand it of ourselves and of our coworkers in the system. For this is the faith to which we are sworn by our common calling: that doing justice is never simply someone else's job; correcting injustice is never simply someone else's responsibility.

A Life for a Life
Igor Primoratz

Igor Primoratz, a philosopher at the Hebrew University in Jerusalem, is the author of *Justifying Legal Punishment*, from which the following excerpts have been taken. Primoratz argues that the retributive requirement that punishment be proportionate to the crime implies that only the death penalty is appropriate for murderers. Since the victim of murder literally cannot ever again experience or realize value, a proportionate punishment must inflict the same loss of capacity on the murderer, and Primoratz argues, only death can do this. Only in the case of murder, according to Primoratz, does the retributivist demand for proportionate punishment require *lex talionis* for its fulfillment.

Much of the remainder of this selection from Primoratz's book consists of an attempt to respond to several arguments frequently made against the death penalty. First, he argues that murderers have no right to life which can be violated by execution. Partly because of this, those who argue that it is inconsistent for a state to condemn murderers and then "murder murderers" beg the question, since executions could count as murder only if they are examples of wrongful killing. He also points out that many considerations offered against the death penalty really constitute objections to our methods of applying it rather than to the penalty itself. Finally, he suggests that abolitionists would be able to make a better case if they were able to show that the death penalty should be considered to be an excessively cruel punishment.

According to the retributive theory, consequences of punishment, however important from the practical point of view, are irrelevant when it comes to its justification; *the* moral consideration is its justice. Punishment is morally justified insofar as it is meted out as retribution for the offense committed. When someone has committed an offense, he deserves to be punished: it is just, and consequently justified, that he be punished. The offense is the sole ground of the state's right and duty to punish. It is also the measure of legitimate punishment: the two ought to be proportionate. So the issue of capital punishment within the retributive approach comes down to the question, Is this punishment ever proportionate retribution for the offense committed, and thus deserved, just, and justified?

The classic representatives of retributivism believed that it was, and that it was the only proportionate and hence appropriate punishment, if the offense was *murder*—that is, criminal homicide perpetrated voluntarily and intentionally or in wanton disregard of human life. In other cases, the demand for proportionality between offense and punishment can be satisfied by fines

From *Justifying Legal Punishment*, by Igor Primoratz (Atlantic Highlands, New Jersey: Humanities Press International, 1989), pp. 158–186.

or prison terms. The crime of murder, however, is an exception in this respect, and calls for the literal interpretation of the *lex talionis*. The uniqueness of this crime has to do with the uniqueness of the value which has been deliberately or recklessly destroyed. We come across this idea as early as the original formulation of the retributive view—the biblical teaching on punishment: "You shall accept no ransom for the life of a murderer who is guilty of death; but he shall be put to death."[1] The rationale of this command—one that clearly distinguishes the biblical conception of the criminal law from contemporaneous criminal law systems in the Middle East—is that man was not only created *by* God, like every other creature, but also, alone among all the creatures, *in the image of God:*

> That man was made in the image of God... is expressive of the peculiar and supreme worth of man. Of all creatures, Genesis 1 relates, he alone possesses this attribute, bringing him into closer relation to God than all the rest and conferring upon him the highest value. . . . This view of the uniqueness and supremacy of human life. . . places life beyond the reach of other values. The idea that life may be measured in terms of money or other property . . . is excluded. Compensation of any kind is ruled out. The guilt of the murderer is infinite because the murdered life is invaluable; the kinsmen of the slain man are not competent to say when he has been paid for. An absolute wrong has been committed, a sin against God which is not subject to human discussion. . . . Because human life is invaluable, to take it entails the death penalty.[2]

This view that the value of human life is not commensurable with other values, and that consequently there is only one truly equivalent punishment for murder, namely death, does not necessarily presuppose a theistic outlook. It can be claimed that, simply because we have to be alive if we are to experience and realize any other value at all, there is nothing equivalent 'to the murderous destruction of a human life except the destruction of the life of the murderer. Any other retribution, no matter how severe, would still be less than what is proportionate, deserved, and just. As long as the murderer is alive, no matter how bad the conditions of his life may be, there are always at least *some* values he can experience and realize. This provides a plausible interpretation of what the classical representatives of retributivism as a philosophical theory of punishment, such as Kant and Hegel, had to say on the subject.[3]

It seems to me that this is essentially correct. With respect to the larger question of the justification of punishment in general, it is the retributive theory that gives the right answer. Accordingly, capital punishment ought to be retained where it obtains, and reintroduced in those jurisdictions that have abolished it, although we have no reason to believe that, as a means of deterrence, it is any better than a very long prison term. It ought to be retained, or reintroduced, for one simple reason: that justice be done in cases of murder, that murderers be punished according to their deserts.

There are a number of arguments that have been advanced against this rationale of capital punishment.

Two of these arguments have to do, in different ways, with the idea of the right to life. The first is the famous argument of Beccaria that the state cannot have the right to take away the life of its citizen, because its rights in relation to him are based on the social contract, and it cannot be assumed that he has transferred his right to life to the state and consented to be executed.

> What manner of right can men attribute to themselves to slaughter their fellow beings? Certainly not that from which sovereignty and the laws derive. These are nothing but the sum of the least portions of the private liberty of each person; they represent the general will, which is the aggregate of particular wills. Was there ever a man who can have wished to leave to other men the choice of killing him? Is it conceivable that the least sacrifice of each person's liberty should include sacrifice of the greatest of all goods, life? And if that were the case, how could such a principle be reconciled with the other, that man is not entitled to take his own life? He must be, if he can surrender that right to others or to society as a whole.[4] . . .

Both steps in his argument are wrong, and for the same reason. The act of consenting to be executed if one commits murder is presented as a kind of suicide. . . . By consenting to be executed if I murder someone, I do not commit a kind of suicide—I do not "sacrifice the greatest of all goods" I have, my own life. My consent could be described in these terms if it were unconditional, if it implied that others were entitled to do with my life whatever they chose, quite independently of my own choices and actions. In order to show that capital punishment is legitimate from the standpoint of the contract theory of political obligation, however, we need not assume that citizens have agreed to *that*. All that is needed is the assumption of a conditional consent—consent to be executed *if* one commits murder; and it is, of course, up to everyone to choose whether to commit such a crime or not. To agree to this, obviously, is not the same as to sacrifice one's life, to commit a suicide of sorts. And it is not so unreasonable to assume that citizens have agreed to this if, against the background of the social contract theory, we grant, first, that the laws, including criminal laws, ought to be just, and second, that the only proportionate and hence just punishment for murder is capital punishment.[5]

The second abolitionist argument makes use of the idea of a right to life in a more straightforward manner: it simply says that capital punishment is illegitimate because it violates the right to life, which is a fundamental, absolute, sacred right belonging to each and every human being, and therefore ought to be respected even in a murderer.[6]

If any rights are fundamental, the right to life is certainly one of them; but to claim that it is absolute, inviolable under any circumstances and for any reason, is a different matter. If an abolitionist wants to argue his case by asserting an absolute right to life, she will also have to deny moral legitimacy to taking human life in war, revolution, and self-defense. This kind of pacifism is a consistent but farfetched and hence implausible position.

I do not believe that the right to life (nor, for that matter, any other right) is absolute. I have no general theory of rights to fall back upon here; instead, let me pose a question. Would we take seriously the claim to an absolute, sacred, inviolable right to life—coming from the mouth of a *confessed murderer*? I submit that we would not, for the obvious reason that it is being put forward by the person who confessedly denied another human being this very right. But if the murderer cannot plausibly claim such a right for himself, neither can *anyone else* do that in his behalf. This suggests that there is an element of reciprocity in our general rights, such as the right to life or property. I can convincingly claim these rights only so long as I acknowledge and respect the same rights of others. If I violate the rights of others, I thereby lose the same rights. If I am a murderer, I have no *right* to live.

Some opponents of capital punishment claim that a criminal law system which includes this punishment is contradictory, in that it prohibits murder and at the same time provides for its perpetration: "It is one and the same legal regulation which prohibits the individual from murdering, while allowing the state to murder. . . . this is obviously a terrible irony, an abnormal and immoral logic, against which everything in us revolts."[7]

This seems to be one of the more popular arguments against the death penalty, but it is not a good one. If it were valid, it would prove too much. Exactly the same might be claimed of other kinds of punishment: of prison terms, that they are "contradictory" to the legal protection of liberty; of fines, that they are "contradictory" to the legal protection of property. Fortunately enough, it is not valid, for it begs the question at issue. In order to be able to talk of the state as "murdering" the person it executes, and to claim that there is "an abnormal and immoral logic" at work here, which thrives on a "contradiction," one has to use the word "murder" in the very same sense—that is, in the usual sense, which implies the idea of the *wrongful* taking the life of another—both when speaking of what the murderer has done to the victim and of what the state is doing to him by way of punishment. But this is precisely the question at issue: whether capital punishment *is* "murder," whether it is wrongful or morally justified and right.

The next two arguments attack the retributive rationale of capital punishment by questioning the claim that it is only this punishment that satisfies the demand for proportion between offense and punishment in the case of murder. The first points out that any two human lives are different in many important respects, such as age, health, physical and mental capability, so that it does not make much sense to consider them equally valuable. What if the murdered person was very old, practically at the very end of her natural life, while the murderer is young, with most of his life still ahead of him, for instance? Or if the victim was gravely and incurably ill, and thus doomed to live her life in suffering and hopelessness, without being able to experience almost anything that makes a human life worth living, while the murderer is in every respect capable of experiencing and enjoying things life has to offer? Or the other way round? Would not the death penalty in such cases amount either to taking a more valuable life as a punishment for destroying a less valuable one, or *vice versa?* Would it not be either too much, or too little, and in both cases disproportionate, and thus unjust and wrong, from the stand-point of the retributive theory itself?[8]

Any plausibility this argument might appear to have is the result of a conflation of differences between, and value of, human lives. No doubt, any two human lives are *different* in innumerable ways, but this does not entail that they are not *equally valuable.* I have no worked-out general theory of equality to refer to here, but I do not think that one is necessary in order to do away with this argument. The modern humanistic and democratic tradition in ethical, social, and political thought is based on the idea that all human beings are equal. This finds its legal expression in the principle of equality of people under the law. If we are not willing to give up this principle, we have to stick to the assumption that, all differences notwithstanding, any two hu-man lives, *qua* human lives, are equally valuable. If, on the other hand, we allow that, on the basis of such criteria as age, health, or mental or physical ability, it can be claimed that the life of one person is more or less valuable than the life of another, and we admit such claims in the sphere of law, in-cluding criminal law, we shall thereby give up the principle of equality of people under the law. In all consistency, we shall not be able to demand that property, physical and personal integrity, and all other rights and interests of individuals be given equal consideration in courts of law either—that is, we shall have to accept systematic discrimination between individuals on the basis of the same criteria across the whole field. I do not think anyone would seriously contemplate an overhaul of the whole legal system along these lines.

The second argument having to do with the issue of proportionality be-tween murder and capital punishment draws our attention to the fact that the law normally provides for a certain period of time to elapse between the passing of a death sentence and its execution. It is a period of several weeks or months; in some cases it extends to years. This period is bound to be one of constant mental anguish for the condemned. And thus, all things consid-ered, what is inflicted on him is disproportionately hard and hence unjust. It would be proportionate and just only in the case of "a criminal who had warned his victim of the date at which he would inflict a horrible death on him and who, from that moment onward, had confined him at his mercy for months."[9]

The first thing to note about this argument is that it does not support a full-fledged abolitionist stand; if it were valid, it would not show that capital punishment is *never* proportionate and just, but only that it is *very rarely* so. Consequently, the conclusion would not be that it ought to be abolished out-right, but only that it ought to be restricted to those cases that would satisfy the condition cited above. Such cases do happen, though, to be sure, not very often; the murder of Aldo Moro, for instance, was of this kind. But this is not the main point. The main point is that the argument actually does not hit at capital punishment itself, although it is presented with that aim in view. It hits at something else: a particular way of carrying out this punishment, which is widely adopted in our time. Some hundred years ago and more, in the Wild West, they frequently hanged the man convicted to die almost immediately after pronouncing the sentence. I am not arguing here that we should follow this example today; I mention this piece of historical fact only in order to show that the interval between sentencing someone to death and carrying out the sentence is not a *part* of capital punishment itself. However unpalatable we might find those Wild West hangings, whatever objections we might want to voice against the speed with which they followed the sentencing, surely we shall not deny them the *description* of "executions." So the implication of the argument is not that we ought to do away with capital punishment altogether, nor that we ought to restrict it to those cases of murder where the murderer had warned the victim weeks or months in advance of what he was going to do to her, but that we ought to reexamine the procedure of carrying out this kind of punishment. We ought to weigh the reasons for having this interval between the sentencing and executing, against the moral and human significance of the repercussions such an interval inevitably carries with it.

These reasons, in part, have to do with the possibility of miscarriages of justice and the need to rectify them. Thus we come to the argument against capital punishment which, historically, has been the most effective of all: many advances of the abolitionist movement have been connected with discoveries of cases of judicial errors. Judges and jurors are only human, and consequently some of their beliefs and decisions are bound to be mistaken. Some of their mistakes can be corrected upon discovery; but precisely those with most disastrous repercussions—those which result in innocent people being executed—can never be rectified. In all other cases of mistaken sentencing we can revoke the punishment, either completely or in part, or at least extend compensation. In addition, by exonerating the accused we give moral satisfaction. None of this is possible after an innocent person has been executed; capital punishment is essentially different from all other penalties by being completely irrevocable and irreparable.[10] Therefore, it ought to be abolished.

A part of my reply to this argument goes along the same lines as what I had to say on the previous one. It is not so far-reaching as abolitionists assume; for it would be quite implausible, even fanciful, to claim that there have *never* been cases of murder which left no room whatever for reasonable doubt as to the guilt and full responsibility of the accused. Such cases may not be more frequent than those others, but they do happen. Why not retain the death penalty at least for them?

Actually, this argument, just as the preceding one, does not speak out against capital punishment itself, but against the existing procedures for trying capital cases. Miscarriages of justice result in innocent people being sentenced to death and executed, even in the criminal-law systems in which greatest care is taken to ensure that it never comes to that. But this does not stem from the intrinsic nature of the institution of capital punishment; it results from deficiencies, limitations, and imperfections of the criminal law procedures in which this punishment is meted out. Errors of justice do not demonstrate the need to do away with capital punishment; they simply make it incumbent on us to do everything possible to improve even further procedures of meting it out.

To be sure, this conclusion will not find favor with a diehard abolitionist. "I shall ask for the abolition of Capital Punishment until I have the infallibility of human judgement demonstrated to me," that is, as long as there is even the slightest possibility that innocent people may be executed because of judicial errors, Lafayette said in his day.[11] Many an opponent of this kind of punishment will say the same today. The demand to do away with capital punishment altogether, so as to eliminate even the smallest chance of that ever happening—the chance which, admittedly, would remain even after everything humanly possible has been done to perfect the procedure, although then it would be very slight indeed—is actually a demand to give a privileged position to murderers as against all other offenders, big and small. For if we acted on this demand, we would bring about a situation in which proportionate penalties would be meted out for all offenses, *except* for murder. Murderers would not be receiving the only punishment truly proportionate to their crimes, the punishment of death, but some other, lighter, and thus disproportionate penalty. All other offenders would be punished according to their deserts; only murderers would be receiving less than *they* deserve. In all other cases justice would be done in full; only in cases of the gravest of offenses, the crime of murder, justice would not be carried out in full measure. It is a great and tragic miscarriage of justice when an innocent person is mistakenly sentenced to death and executed, but systematically giving murderers advantage over all other offenders would also be a grave injustice. Is the fact that, as long as capital punishment is retained, there is a possibility that over a number of years, or even decades, an injustice of the first kind may be committed, unintentionally and unconsciously, reason enough to abolish it altogether, and thus end up with a system of punishments in which injustices of the second kind are perpetrated daily, consciously, and inevitably?[12]

There is still another abolitionist argument that actually does not hit out against capital punishment itself, but against something else. Figures are sometimes quoted which show that this punishment is much more often meted out to the uneducated and poor than to the educated, rich, and influential people; in the United States, much more often to blacks than to whites. These figures are adduced as a proof of the inherent injustice of this kind of punishment. On account of them, it is claimed that capital punishment is not a way of doing justice by meting out deserved punishment to murderers, but rather a means of social discrimination and perpetuation of social injustice. I shall not question these findings, which are quite convincing, and anyway, there is no need to do that in order to defend the institution of capital punishment. For there seems to be a certain amount of discrimination and injustice not only in sentencing people to death and executing them, but also in meting out other penalties. The social structure of the death rows in American prisons, for instance, does not seem to be basically different from the general social structure of American penitentiaries. If this argument were valid, it would call not only for abolition of the penalty of death, but for doing away with other penalties as well.

> But it is not valid; as Burton Leiser has pointed out, . . . this is not an argument, either against the death penalty or against any other form of punishment. It is an argument against the unjust and inequitable distribution of penalties. If the trials of wealthy men are less likely to result in convictions than those of poor men, then something must be done to reform the procedure in criminal courts. If those who have money and standing in the community are less likely to be charged with serious offenses than their less affluent fellow citizens, then there should be a major overhaul of the entire system of criminal justice . . . But the maldistribution of penalties is no argument against any particular form of penalty.[13]

There is, finally, the argument that the moral illegitimacy of capital punishment is obvious from the widespread contempt for those who carry it out: "Logically, if the Death Penalty *were* morally justified, the executioner's calling would be considered an honourable one. The fact that even its keenest supporters shrink from such a man with loathing and exclude him from their circle, is in itself an indication that Capital Punishment stands morally condemned."[14]

This is also a poor argument, for several reasons. The contempt for the executioner and the accompanying social ostracism is by no means a universal phenomenon in history; on the contrary, it is a comparatively modern one. In earlier ages, the person who carried out capital punishment—whether the professional executioner or, before this became an occupation in its own right, the judge, or some other high-ranking official, sometimes even the ruler himself, or a relative of the murdered person—was always regarded with respect.[15] Quite apart from this, the so-called common moral consciousness, to which the argument appeals is not to be seen as some kind of supreme tribunal in moral matters. Among reasons of general nature for this is that it would be an unreliable, inconsistent, confused, and confusing tribunal. On the one hand, when viewed historically, it hardly seems a very good guide to the moral status of various occupations, for in earlier ages it used to condemn very resolutely and strongly the merchant, the banker, the actor, which no one would think of disparaging today, abolitionists included. On the other hand, it has proved itself quite inconsistent on the issue of the moral basis of punishment in general, voicing incompatible views, now retributive, now utilitarian. It is not at all surprising that both advocates and opponents of capital punishment have claimed its support for their views.[16] But if it supports both sides in this more restricted dispute as well, then it actually supports neither.

There is still another facet of this illogical, irrational streak inherent to the common moral consciousness that comes to the fore in connection with this dispute. If the contempt for the executioner is really rooted in the belief that what he carries out is morally reprehensible, then it is surely heaped upon the wrong person. For he merely carries out decisions on which he has no say whatsoever. Those who are responsible are, in the first instance, the judge and members of the jury. They, on their part, act as they do against the background of criminal laws for which responsibility lies at a further remove still—with the legislators. These, again, legislate in the name of the people, if the political system is a representative one. But for some reason the common moral consciousness has never evinced contempt of any of these.

RETRIBUTIVISM WITHOUT CAPITAL PUNISHMENT?

Everything I have said in the preceding section has had a pronounced defensive ring to it. I have attempted to show that none of the standard arguments against the death penalty, which would be relevant within the retributive approach to punishment in general, are really convincing. But I shall end on a conciliatory note. I can envisage a way for a retributivist to take an abolitionist stand, without thereby being inconsistent. Let me explain this in just a few words.

The Eighth Amendment to the Constitution of the United States says that "excessive bail shall not be required, nor excessive fines imposed, nor cruel and unusual punishments inflicted."[17] I do not find the idea of a "usual" or "unusual" punishment very helpful. But I do think that punishments ought not to be *cruel*. They ought not to be cruel in the relative sense, by being considerably more severe than what is proportionate to the offense committed, what is deserved and just; but they also ought not to be cruel in an absolute sense—that is, severe beyond a certain threshold.

Admittedly, it would be very difficult to determine that threshold precisely, but it is not necessary for my purpose here. It will be enough to provide a paradigmatic case of something that is surely beyond that threshold: torture. I do not believe that a torturer has a *right* not to be tortured. If we could bring ourselves to torture him, as a punishment for what he has done to the victim, I do not think that it could be plausibly claimed that what we were doing to him was something undeserved and unjust. But I also do not think that we should try to bring ourselves to do that, in pursuit of proportion between offense and punishment and in striving to execute justice. Justice is one of the most important moral principles—perhaps the most important one—but it is not *absolute*. On the other hand, I feel that torture is something *absolutely wrong* from the moral point of view: something indecent and inhuman, something immensely and unredeemably degrading both to the man tortured and to the torturer himself, something that is morally "beyond the pale." So to sentence a torturer to be tortured would not mean to give him a punishment which is undeserved and unjust, and hence cruel in the relative sense of the word; but it *would* mean to punish him in a way that is cruel in this second, absolute sense. On account of this, I would say that, when punishing a torturer, we ought to desist from giving him the full measure of what he has deserved by his deed, that we ought to settle for less than what in his case would be the full measure of justice. One of the moral principles limiting the striving to do justice is this prohibition of cruelty in the absolute sense of the word. We ought not to execute justice to the full, if that means that we shall have to be cruel.

I do not feel about executing a person in a swift and relatively painless manner the same way I feel about torturing him. But a person, or a society, could come to feel the same way about both. A person or a society that adhered to the retributive view of punishment, but at the same time felt this way about executing a human being, could decide that capital punishment is cruel and therefore unacceptable without being in any way inconsistent.

NOTES

1. Numbers 35:31 (R.S.V.)
2. M. Greenberg, "Some Postulates of Biblical Criminal Law," in J. Goldin (ed.) *The Jewish Expression* (New York: Bantam, 1970), pp. 25–26. (Post-biblical Jewish law evolved toward the virtual abolition of the death penalty, but that is of no concern here.)
3. "There is no *parallel* between death and even the most miserable life, so that there is no equality of crime and retribution [in the case of murder] unless the perpetrator is judicially put to death" (I. Kant, "The Metaphysics of Morals," *Kant's Political Writings,* ed. H. Reiss, trans. H.B. Nisbet [Cambridge: Cambridge University Press, 1970], p. 156). "Since life is the full compass of a man's existence, the punishment [for murder] cannot simply consist in a 'value', for none is great enough, but can consist only in taking away a second life" (G.W.F. Hegel, *Philosophy of Right,* trans. T.M. Knox [Oxford: Oxford University Press, 1965], p. 247).
4. C. Beccaria, *On Crimes and Punishments,* trans. H. Paolucci (Indianapolis: Bobbs-Merrill, 1977), p. 45.
5. For critical comments on my analysis and refutation of Beccaria's argument, developed in the paper on "Kant und Beccaria," *Kant-Studien* 69 (1978) and summarized here in the briefest way possible, see M.A. Cattaneo, *Beccaria e Kant. Il valore dell'uomo nel diritto penale* (Sassari: Università di Sassari, 1981), pp. 20–30.
6. For an example of this view, see L.N. Tolstoy, *Smertnaya kazn i hristianstvo* (Berlin: I.P. Ladizhnikov, n.d.), pp. 40–41.
7. S.V. Vulović, *Problem smrtne kazne* (Belgrade: Geca Kon, 1925), pp. 23–24.
8. Cf. W. Blackstone, *Commentaries on the Laws of England,* 4th ed., ed. J. DeWitt Andrews (Chicago: Callaghan & Co., 1899), p. 1224.
9. A. Camus, "Reflections on the Guillotine," *Resistance, Rebellion and Death,* trans. J. O'Brien (London: Hamish Hamilton, 1961), p. 143.
10. For an interesting critical discussion of this point, see M. Davis, "Is the Death Penalty Irrevocable?," *Social Theory and Practice* 10 (1984).
11. Quoted in E.R. Calvert, *Capital Punishment in the Twentieth Century* (London: G.P. Putnam's Sons, 1927), p. 132.

12. For a criticism of this argument, see L. Sebba, "On Capital Punishment—A Comment," *Israel Law Review* 17 (1982), pp. 392–395.

13. B.M. Leiser, *Liberty, Justice and Morals: Contemporary Value Conflicts* (New York: Macmillan, 1973), p. 225.

14. E.R. Calvert, *Capital Punishment,* p. 172.

15. For a good review of the relevant historical data, see A.F. Kistyakovsky, *Izsledovanie o smertnoy kazni,* 2d ed. (St. Petersburg: L.F. Panteleev, 1896), pp. 260–267.

16. Cf. I. Kant, "Metaphysics of Morals," p. 157, and C. Beccaria, *Crimes and Punishments,* p. 50.

17. On the question whether the death penalty is cruel and unusual within the meaning of the Eighth Amendment, see M.J. Radin, "The Jurisprudence of Death: Evolving Standards for the Cruel and Unusual Clause," *University of Pennsylvania Law Review* 126 (1978); H.A. Bedau, "Thinking of the Death Penalty as a Cruel and Unusual Punishment," *U.C. Davis Law Review* 18 (1985).

From Hemlock to Lethal Injection: The Case For Self-Execution

Bruce N. Waller

Bruce N. Waller is a philosophy professor at Youngstown State University. In this essay, he argues that those who advocate the death penalty have good reason to consider allowing condemned prisoners to kill themselves, perhaps by providing them with a cyanide pill that they would be free to use within some one-week period. Even those who currently accept the death penalty usually reject torture, and according to Waller, our methods of execution—which tend to exacerbate and stress the helplessness of the condemned—constitute a form of psychological torture. Waller believes that at least some of this psychological torture would be eliminated were self-execution allowed. Furthermore, self-execution would respect the dignity of condemned prisoners by treating them more fully as beings capable of exercising choice rather than as mere things. Finally, Waller considers some potential social benefits of self-execution and tries to answer objections to the procedure.

On the day of his execution Socrates passed a pleasant afternoon talking with his friends, then calmly and deliberately grasped the cup of hemlock and drank the bitter poison. Not quite 24 hundred years later, the condemned prisoner Gary Gilmore secretly consumed an overdose of sedatives in an effort to end his life. A group of emergency medical workers desperately administered treatment, and in a hospital emergency room he was snatched back from death. A few weeks later, on the scheduled day and at the appointed hour, he was bound to a chair—his request to stand during his execution having been denied—and a firing squad killed him. Two years later in Florida, a terrified John Spenkelink—his head shaved, heavy straps around his arms and legs, a hood over his head—was electrocuted. In a Texas prison the curtains of the witness room parted to reveal a man bound to a small litter: to insure easy intravenous insertion of the needle, he had been so completely immobilized that (witnesses reported) only his eyes could move. At the exact moment scheduled for his execution the lethal barbiturate dose was injected. He died swiftly and, we are assured, painlessly.

The above stories are true; the next is fiction. In Larry McMurtry's *Lonesome Dove* the charming but irresponsible Jake Spoon falls in with horse thieves and murderers, and is apprehended by old friends who resolve to hang all of the felons. When it is Jake's turn, the friends talk with him briefly, and he bids them—considering the circumstances—a rather fond farewell. Then Jake does not wait for someone to strike his horse and thus perform the execution; instead:

From *The International Journal of Applied Philosophy* 4 (1989), 53-58.

. . . Jake Spoon had quickly spurred his pacing horse high back in the flanks with both spurs. The rope squeaked against the bark of the limb. Augustus stepped over and caught the swinging body and held it still.

"I swear," Pea Eye said. "He didn't wait for you, Gus."

"Nope, he died fine," Augustus said. "Go dig him a grave, will you, Pea?"[1]

Socrates was of noble and courageous character, and would have faced death calmly in almost any circumstances; however, there is no doubt that being strapped into a chair or litter—helplessly awaiting the executioner's scheduled moment—would have made his final moments less dignified. Jake Spoon, in contrast, was shallow and arrogant; but by exercising some control of his own execution, he managed to extract an element of dignity from his death. Being condemned to death by society is a terrible thing; being trussed up, placed on display, and then efficiently slaughtered at precisely the appointed minute is to be demeaned and degraded—and, I shall argue, tortured.

In all the intense current debate on capital punishment (and methods of execution) self-execution has hardly been mentioned. (The only lengthy discussion of the notion that I have found in the current literature is satirical.[2]) But if there is genuine concern for more humane execution procedures, then self-execution merits serious consideration. What is here proposed is allowing condemned prisoners the choice of killing themselves, rather than requiring them to wait for a precise style of execution to be imposed upon them at an exactly prescribed moment. After appeals have ended and execution is inevitable, condemned prisoners should be given a period (perhaps one week) when they would have access to some efficient means of killing themselves (a cyanide pill, for example). The condemned could then cause his/her own death at any point during that period, and could exercise considerable control over the process (could administer the death potion at dawn or at dusk, in solitude or with friends, with elaborate ritual or swift secrecy). The condemned would not, of course, be required to carry out the execution: the option of a state executioner would remain (perhaps with the condemned setting the time for the execution at any time during the one week period, including—as would happen if the prisoner did nothing—at the very end).

Offering the condemned prisoner the alternative of self-execution is more humane. Self-execution is more humane in two important ways. First, it is less painful. Second, it shows greater respect for the humanity of the prisoner.

Consider first the question of reducing pain. We are sickened by the hideous tortures to which the condemned were once subjected, and even adamant advocates of capital punishment now oppose the use of torture. But torture can be psychological as well as physical, and agony amounting to psychological torture is the likely result of current methods of capital punishment. Obviously fear of death can not be eliminated from capital punishment. But the question here is not how to eliminate all unpleasantness from capital punishment; rather, the issue is whether allowing self-execution might significantly abate the psychological torture that is a common ingredient of contemporary executions. Allowing self-execution would substantially reduce one of the key factors which exacerbates that fear: the utter helplessness of the condemned.

One of the most horrible aspects of capital punishment must be the utter and abject helplessness of the condemned: death will be imposed at an exactly scheduled moment, in a precise manner—and there is absolutely nothing you can do to alter that process in even the smallest detail. To that horror one can add the hideous final moments of being strapped to a stretcher or a chair, completely immobilized—and the result is psychological torture comparable in misery to the appalling practices of centuries past. . . . The terror of being restrained in such a manner that one cannot turn one's head, cannot move a hand or foot—while awaiting the executioner—is the terror of ultimate helplessness.

If self-execution is allowed, then the condemned no longer experiences such utter helplessness. He or she could control the time of execution, and even the actual administering of the death potion. Knowledge that at any point one can to some degree "control one's fate" and effect the execution will reduce the helplessness and hence the suffering, even if the prisoner does not actually carry out the self-execution. When the condemned does take the lethal potion, the necessity for the cruel and degrading procedures of total physical constraint would be eliminated.

Allowing self-execution would not only mitigate the agonies of helplessness; it would also help preserve and respect the human dignity of the condemned. In the current debate on capital punishment—and on punishment generally—much has been made of "respecting the dignity" of the person punished. Many advocates of punishment and of capital punishment insist that only through retributive punishment can the humanity of the prisoner be respected.[3] But if we are serious about respecting the person of the condemned, then part of that respect must involve respecting so far as possible the choice-making capacity of the individual, which is the crux of whatever is distinctive in human beings. When the exact time and method of execution are strictly prescribed, the prisoner is rendered utterly incapable of having any effect on that matter of supreme importance; when the prisoner is shackled in totally constraining bonds during the time leading up to execution, then everything possible has been done to reduce the prisoner to a mere object, deprived of all the decision-making capacities of a human being. If it is important to respect the dignity of the condemned, then that entails as much respect as possible for the source of that dignity the human reasoning, choosing, decision-making power of the human individual.[4] . . .

In addition to significant gains for the dignity and humanity of the prisoner, a self-execution procedure offers substantial societal advantages. First, it would reduce—though not eliminate—the violence inherent in capital punishment. It is quite possible that imposing violent death on condemned prisoners has a brutalizing effect on society and encourages some members of that society to also engage in acts of violence. If instead the prisoner is allowed self-execution, the violence might be lessened. (One incidental point concerning such societal brutalization: If the condemned were allowed a week in which to carry out the execution, then perhaps society might be spared the hideous spectacle of crowds gathering at the gates of the prison to cheer the hour of execution.)

Also, self-execution should somewhat lessen the brutalization of those who work in the state punishment system. Guarding prisoners will have some unavoidably brutalizing aspects; guarding condemned prisoners, those problems must be exacerbated. But if no one were routinely required to shackle prisoners to a chair, throw the switch or pull the trigger, then at least some of the worst elements might be mitigated.

Self-execution has another advantage, though this one is relative: it is an advantage for a democratic society, a disadvantage for totalitarian systems. An execution process that demonstrates the absolute power of the state to execute, and to execute at the exact moment and manner of its choice a condemned prisoner who is bound and helpless, is not the most effective means of symbolizing values of democracy, individualism, and freedom. A totalitarian society might well oppose any compromise of its symbolic and actual demonstration of absolute power over the condemned individual, but a democratic society should be eager to soften the totalitarian symbolism inherent in current methods and procedures of execution. There are probably limits to that: it is not easy to make the state's power of destroying individual life seem compatible with individualist, democratic values. However, self-execution certainly seems closer to matching such values than does the frightening display of absolute power over the individual exhibited by current methods, in which the condemned is tightly shackled and then killed at the exact instant and in the precise manner chosen by the State.

When we look closely and seriously at self-execution, its advantages loom large. However, there are some possible objections. Some may suggest that allowing self-execution gives the prisoner the right to "determine his own sentence," and thus is unacceptable. I'm not sure that allowing the prisoner to determine his own sentence is always such a bad thing, but that is another matter. In any case, allowing self-execution does not do that—or at least it does not do so in a way that differs significantly from ways that are currently approved. After all, there are many states in which the condemned chooses the method of execution: lethal injection or electrocution, or firing squad or hanging, for example.[5] This would be a similar sort of choice: lethal injection or electrocution or self-administered cyanide. In none of these cases does the condemned choose his own sentence, which is in each instance a death sentence; rather, the prisoner only chooses the means by which the sentence will be executed.

More significantly, some will worry that allowing self-execution is a state endorsement of suicide. The example of Socrates undercuts that objection. Certainly Socrates drank the hemlock without being force fed, and thus carried out his own execution. But that is no more a case of suicide than is—to use an apocryphal illustration from childhood pirate lore—the step one takes off the end of the plank and into the ocean, thus avoiding the pirate cutlass. Under sentence of death with only the choice of means of dying—and no way to avoid death in the immediate future—one does not voluntarily choose to terminate one's own life, and surely that must be an element of suicide.

In fact, the sort of self-execution here proposed is so far from being suicide that it completely avoids the major suicide-related arguments that arise in the capital punishment debate. Opponents of capital punishment argue that some who wish to commit suicide, but lack the courage to carry out the process, may be tempted to commit a capital crime and thus have the state become the agent for their "suicide." . . . Presumably the individual who desires the assistance of the state in affecting his or her death would choose to wait for the executioner, rather than carrying out self-execution (self-destruction being precisely the act which, by hypothesis, the individual in question cannot bring himself to do); so allowing self-execution would certainly not make capital punishment any more attractive for such individuals.

The most serious objection to self-execution is likely to be made by opponents of capital punishment. Most abolitionists opposed execution by lethal injection, on the grounds that it would make capital punishment too "sanitized," too easy. Along similar lines, it might seem that allowing self-execution would render capital punishment easier and more socially acceptable. That is a legitimate concern; however, I think that the effect is likely to be the opposite, for several reasons.

First, self-execution does not trivialize execution in the manner in which lethal injection threatens to do. Death by lethal injection suggests a neat, clean, sanitized process, in which the condemned is a passive victim killed with the highest level of technical efficiency. It is a process that demeans and trivializes—dehumanizes—the object of execution. In contrast, self-execution would involve the condemned as a central and decisive figure, a full human being with full participation in the act of execution. In contrast to lethal injection—with its efficient, systematic, uniform procedures which trivialize the condemned—self-execution would allow the condemned some control over the process, and thus would accentuate the terrible uniqueness of each such execution as well as the uniqueness of each condemned prisoner.

The second reason why self-execution is likely to work against (rather than facilitating) capital punishment is closely connected with the first. By allowing self-execution, each condemned prisoner will be able to retain more human dignity and choice-making capacity and individuality. One way to tolerate capital punishment is through conceiving of the victims as subhuman, as outside the human community. This illusion is easy to sustain when the condemned is trussed up like an animal for slaughter, bound and gagged and efficiently killed by a technically proficient executioner. If the condemned carries out his/her own execution, with some choice of moment and setting and circumstances, then the human character of the condemned is evident and undeniable.

If our goal is to efficiently slaughter something that appears to be (and in some cases has been reduced by terror to) a subhuman, then self-execution should not be considered. On the other hand, if we wish, as even the sternest retributivists claim to desire, to treat the condemned prisoner as a unique, choice-making, responsible human being, then self-execution comes nearer to doing so than does any other means of capital punishment.

NOTES

1. Larry McMurtry, *Lonesome Dove* (New York: Simon and Schuster, 1985), p. 641. (Page reference to Pocket Books edition.)
2. See Rufus King, "Some Reflections on Do-It-Yourself Capital Punishment," *American Bar Association Journal* 47, no. 7 (July 1961).
3. Prominent examples are Herbert Morris, "Persons and Punishment," *The Monist*, 52, no. 4 (October 1968): 475-501; and Andrew Oldenquist, "An Explanation of Retribution," *The Journal of Philosophy* 85, no. 9 (September 1988): 464-478.
4. Note that this must involve genuine choices—such as the time and process of execution—and certainly not forced participation. Being compelled to place the hood over one's own head would not enhance dignity. Like being forced to dig one's own grave, it would instead be a dignity reducing demonstration of the helplessness of the condemned and the power of the executioner.
5. Several states allow such choices; for example, in Montana and Washington the condemned can choose between hanging and lethal barbiturate injection, and in North Carolina between lethal gas and lethal injection.

SUGGESTIONS FOR FURTHER READING

Bedau, Hugo Adam, ed. *The Death Penalty,* 3rd ed. (New York: Oxford University Press, 1982).

This is an excellent anthology.

Morris, Herbert. "Persons and Punishment," *The Monist* 52 (1968), 475-501.

This is a classic defense of a retributivist theory of punishment, especially against views that would shift the responsibility for crime away from criminals and toward external conditions that may have influenced them.

Nathanson, Stephen. "Does It Matter if the Death Penalty Is Arbitrarily Administered?" *Philosophy & Public Affairs* 14 (1985), 149-164.

Nathanson argues forcefully that the question raised by his title should be answered positively and that the arbitrary nature in which the death penalty is administered provides strong reason against its use.

Nussbaum, Martha C. "Equity and Mercy," *Philosophy & Public Affairs* 22 (1993), 83-125.

Nussbaum suggests that the criminal law should give more attention to the idea of mercy that contrasts with the concerns for retributivism.

Reiman, Jeffrey H. "Justice, Civilization, and the Death Penalty: Answering van den Haag," *Philosophy & Public Affairs* 14 (1985), 115-148.

Reiman argues against Ernest van den Haag's view that the death penalty is likely to be a more effective deterrent than other penalties. Furthermore, Reiman believes that the respect shown for human life by abolishing the death penalty could have good social effects.

Reiman, Jeffrey, and Ernest van den Haag. "On the Common Saying that It Is Better that Ten Guilty Persons Escape Than that One Innocent Suffer: *Pro* and *Con*," *Social Philosophy & Policy* 7 (1990), 226-248.

A spirited debate between Reiman, who has long opposed the death penalty, and van den Haag.

Chapter 5

Distributive Justice: Welfare and World Hunger

Distributive justice, or as it is sometimes called, economic justice, is concerned with issues about how the world's resources should be divided. It should be obvious that the current distribution of the world's resources results in human lives that differ greatly in their quality. Many, though a minority of the world's population, have lives containing anywhere from moderate to extravagant luxury while many others must endure extreme poverty or are even unable to sustain life because of the lack of basic nutrition, housing, or health care. Not only is there great inequality among the resources possessed and used by individuals, there is a similar inequality among societies or nations. The United States, for example, is so affluent that many who are impoverished by its national standards have lives much less impoverished than the poor (or even the majority) of some other nations.

One primary issue of distributive justice addresses this distribution of resources, asking whether those who are well off are morally required to give up some (or perhaps even all) of their luxuries to help those who are living in poverty or who will die without such assistance.

Two more specific issues, each of which corresponds to a part of this chapter, underlie the issue concerning a just distribution of resources. The first focuses on a single society and asks how resources should be divided among members of that particular society. Welfare programs are a response to this question, and their justification would have to be based on the idea that those individuals who are best off should give assistance to those individuals who are worst off, at least under certain conditions.

As mentioned above, just as there are both wealthy and poor individuals within particular societies (or nations), there are both wealthy and poor societies, and the second question focuses on the relations among different societies. The problem of "world hunger" concerns the fact that within affluent societies the average person lives a life containing considerable luxury, while within those societies that are worst off the average person may barely be able to meet his or her basic biological needs. Does any reasonable principle of justice demand that members of affluent societies give up some of their luxuries to help people in other societies who are barely able to sustain life?

The relationship between questions concerning the distribution of resources within a society and questions concerning the distribution of resources among societies also raises interesting issues. For example, assume for the sake of argument that those who are well off do have some duty to help those who are not. Would such a duty apply only to those who are not well off in one's own society, or would it also apply to members of other societies as well? Suppose one could help either some members of one's own society or members of another but not both. How should one choose? Should one choose to help the people who are worst off regardless of where they reside? Or should some preference be given to members of one's own society?

This chapter concentrates on three aspects of distributive justice. The first two articles (as well as much of the selection from the work of John Rawls reprinted in Chapter 1) ask at an abstract level what duties, if any, the better off have to help those who are worse off. Then essays by Trudy Govier and Nancy Fraser focus on "welfare" programs aimed at reducing domestic poverty. The final three essays confront the fact that frequently people face starvation in parts of the world and ask whether those societies with more food than is necessary to sustain life should help.

IS THERE ANY DUTY TO GIVE TO THOSE IN NEED?

The discussions concerning domestic poverty and world poverty differ in that the former discussion tends to focus on the legitimacy of government-run social welfare programs, while the latter tends to focus on individuals, asking whether relatively affluent individuals have a duty to help those who are poor in other societies. The discussions do not have to differ in this way. After all, it can be asked whether individuals have a duty to help their neighbors, and questions can certainly be raised about government-run foreign aid programs. Perhaps, though, it should not be surprising that the discussion of domestic poverty should focus on government programs. There are at least two reasons why the focus on government action should be expected. First, pervasive empirical controversy currently exists about how the state could act in a way that actually would be effective in combating poverty. Much of the current debate about our own welfare programs is centered on this sort of empirical matter. Second, it should not be surprising that the focus has been on government action, since most people would agree that it is at least a good thing for individuals to help those less fortunate than themselves. (Such behavior displays the virtue of charity, or kindness, after all.) The controversy arises only when it is asked whether people should be forced to help, and since government programs are funded by nonvoluntary taxation they do force people to help.

Libertarianism, a position advocated in the essay by John Hospers, maintains that all government social welfare programs—at least all such programs supported by taxes—are morally illegitimate. As the name of their position suggests, libertarians celebrate the moral importance of individual liberty and typically see government as the greatest potential threat to that liberty, because government is essentially a coercive institution. According to libertarians, people should be free to live their lives as they see fit, free from both private and governmental interference as long as their behavior does not interfere with the liberty of others. Hospers further explains the libertarian position by claiming that individuals have three rights—a right to life, a right to liberty, and a right to property—and it is always illegitimate to violate these rights regardless of whether the violation is done by individuals or by government.

Given the moral importance of individual liberty, libertarians believe the sole legitimate function of government is to protect individual rights. It is legitimate, for instance, for government to use its police powers to prevent violations of the rights to life, liberty, and property. Any further use of governmental power, however, is illegitimate. For example, social welfare programs that redistribute resources from those who are better off to those who are worse off would themselves violate citizens' right to property since those programs are supported by taxes citizens are forced to pay. It is important to note that libertarians do not limit their opposition to social welfare programs intended to help those who are economically disadvantaged, such as Aid to Families with Dependent Children (AFDC) and food stamps. While such programs are the ones that often come first to mind when the word 'welfare' is used, the libertarian opposition extends to public education, mandatory social security programs, farm subsidies, and national parks. All are supported by nonvoluntary taxation and go beyond the legitimate governmental role of protecting individual rights.

It is worth noting that at least some libertarians would not regard the current distribution of resources in the United States as being just. In light of the injustice of the current distribution, some coercive redistribution might be required to return the distribution to a just condition. For libertarians, the justice of some particular distribution of resources depends entirely on how that distribution was brought about. In other words, one must look at the actual history leading up to a particular distribution of resources to determine whether or not that distribution is just. If it was brought about in a just way, by uncoerced voluntary behavior, then the distribution is just; otherwise it is not. To use a simple example: Suppose we possess a car; our possessing that car is part of the current distribution of resources. Is that portion of the distribution just? Surely, that depends on how it actually came about that the car is in our possession. If we purchased it or were given it by its previous owner, then our possession of it is just, but not if we stole it. In the latter case, libertarians would believe that the police powers of the state could legitimately be used to return the car to its rightful owner. This would be an example of a legitimate redistribution of resources for the purpose of putting right a current injustice in the distribution.

It is clear that from a libertarian point of view much injustice exists in the history leading to the current distribution of resources in the United States. Two obvious and extreme examples would include the institution of slavery and the taking of land from Native Americans. At least some libertarians would believe that our government could engage in coercive redistribution to make up for wrongs such as these. It would be worth considering whether anything like our current welfare programs could be justified along such grounds.

Some might object to the libertarian position that no one should be required to assist others by maintaining that the libertarian list of rights is too short. Why not think that everyone has a right to an education or to a decent standard of living? Libertarians, however, claim that all rights are "negative" rather than "positive." Negative rights are rights *not* to have things done to one, while positive rights are rights to have things done for one. For example, the right to life could be understood as either a negative or a positive right. If the right to life is merely a negative right, then the only way to violate that right would be to kill its bearer. Those who believe that the right to life is best understood as a positive right would believe that a person's right to life can be violated not only by killing but also by some failures to provide people with what they need to sustain life.

By maintaining that there are no positive rights, libertarians are claiming that in the absence of voluntarily undertaken special relations, for example contractual or parental relations, no one has a moral claim on the assistance of others—at least no moral claim that may be coercively enforced. Libertarians, at least for the most part, do not deny that it is virtuous to help those who are less fortunate, but they emphasize that such assistance must be left up to the individual to choose to give. In fact, some libertarians would argue that the belief that someone has a moral claim on the assistance of others is morally similar to an endorsement of (partial) slavery, as it implies that the person with such a right may legitimately force others to use their labor for his or her benefit.

To consider whether it is reasonable to believe that people can have a moral claim to the assistance of others, it might be useful to consider real cases in which people failed to assist. One such case that is still widely remembered occurred in New York in 1964. Kitty Genovese was attacked and stabbed to death outside her apartment building. The murder took more than thirty minutes, with the murderer twice leaving the scene and returning. During this time thirty-eight people watched and listened from their apartments located on floors over the area in which she was being murdered, without doing anything to help. No one even picked up a telephone to make an anonymous call to the police, which would have possibly saved Kitty Genovese's life. When this case is presented to our students, nearly all agree that those who watched the murder without assisting did something that was very wrong. What they "did," however, was nothing; they failed to assist someone in need. If one agrees with this judgment, one must hold that it is sometimes possible to do something very wrong by not assisting people one is in a position to assist.

How might libertarians respond to this example? A very straightforward response would be to deny that there was anything wrong with the failure to assist Genovese. After all, they might claim, the witnesses did nothing to harm her; it was only the murderer who harmed her. Another perhaps more plausible response would be to admit that while the witnesses did in fact do something wrong, the wrongness of what they did was not a violation of any right possessed by Genovese; as a result, coercion to prevent them from acting as they did would not be justified. Their failure to act was more akin to being uncharitable or unkind than to the violation of a right, and libertarians might argue, while such gross unkindness may be wrong, coercion to prevent it is unwarranted.

The libertarian view would seem to find some support in the Anglo-American legal tradition, which until very recently has included no legal duty to assist others. Recently a very few states have enacted such a duty, but the citizens who watched the murder of Kitty Genovese acted within the law, and their behavior would still be lawful today in the state of New York. However, reluctance to create a duty to assist in cases like that of Kitty Genovese may be based on some reason other than a belief that coercion to bring about such assistance is unjustified. For example, it may be thought that even though coercion to force people to make a phone call in such cases would be justified, if the state were given the power to use coercion for such purposes, that power would very likely be abused and lead to unjustified uses of coercion. It is worth considering whether it would be acceptable to use some, perhaps small, amount of state coercion, if one were convinced that the power to use such coercion could not be abused and that such coercion would lead to there being significantly fewer cases like the one we have been discussing.

Libertarians frequently attempt to base their moral position on facts about human nature, claiming for instance that the liberty they champion is necessary for a fulfilling human life. In another of this chapter's reading selections, Thomas Nagel argues that an appropriate understanding of our nature leads to an egalitarian position that almost certainly requires government to take an active role in assisting those who are worst off. Nagel, who works within the Kantian tradition, believes that egalitarianism is more consistent with one aspect of our nature—that aspect capable of perceiving the world impartially. When we do view the world from an impartial (or impersonal) point of view, Nagel believes we recognize that those who are worse off than we have a valid claim to our assistance. These claims must compete in our moral lives with our more personal aims which would be well served by a libertarian understanding of liberty which includes freedom from duties to help others. Presumably, then, Nagel would believe that libertarians base their view on only one aspect of human nature and that their political ideals are not compatible with a complete understanding of what we are like.

SHOULD ASSISTANCE BE CONDITIONAL?

For the sake of argument, let us assume at least the possibility that the libertarian position is incorrect. If it is, then one legitimate function of government would be to use its tax revenues to help its citizens. In the United States, programs to help citizens include not only such programs as AFDC and food stamps, both aimed at relieving poverty, but also such programs as disaster relief and public education, both of which can benefit citizens from all economic classes. All of the programs just mentioned can reasonably be construed as forms of social welfare. Unless one is opposed to all such programs, it would seem to be arbitrary to rule out the legitimacy of only those programs that focus on poverty.

If programs to assist the poor are assumed to be legitimate, then we need to consider what forms those programs should take and what the conditions for eligibility for assistance should be. It is precisely this type of question that concerns Trudy Govier in her essay "The Right to Eat and the Duty to Work." Part of her examination of the issue focuses on the choice between welfare systems that would give all members of society an unconditional right to the resources necessary to meet their basic needs and systems that would make such resources conditional on the recipients' willingness to work for those resources. The latter sort of systems would be what has come to be known in recent years as systems of "workfare."

Clearly it is a bad thing that people are unable to provide food and shelter for themselves and their children. If we have decided that society has a responsibility to help people when they reach such a condition, why should that assistance be made conditional on anything other than their need? Why, in particular should it be made conditional on a willingness to work for that assistance? Those who advocate workfare would argue that there are both consequentialist considerations and considerations of justice or fairness in favor of requiring a willingness to work.

Some argue in a consequentialist vein that unless eligibility for public assistance required recipients either to work for that assistance or at least to be willing to do so, life on public assistance would be too attractive to too many people. The number of people receiving assistance would grow and this would have bad economic effects on society. The requirement that recipients should be willing to work, then, serves as a disincentive to receiving assistance.

Nonconsequentialists concerned about fairness might maintain that those unwilling to work for assistance do not deserve it. They are unfairly taking advantage of the efforts of the laboring members of society. That labor is the cost required to produce society's resources, and those unwilling to work for resources are unwilling to bear their fair share of the cost.

While questions could be raised about the logical strength of these arguments, one might also wonder if these arguments appeal to some for reasons unrelated to whatever logical strength they might possess. At least in much of our society there is a strong stigma attached to being a recipient of such programs as AFDC and food stamps, and it is suspected that there are many people taking advantage of these programs receiving aid either that they do not need or do not deserve. This suspicion has created anger and resentment among large numbers of people in our own society, fueling at least some of the demand to replace welfare with workfare. Such anger and resentment seem to be focused almost entirely on social welfare programs that are aimed at relieving poverty and are not much in evidence concerning other social welfare programs.

Consider, for example, public higher education. It can be viewed as a coercive redistributive social welfare program that forces some members of society to subsidize the lives of other members. At the state university where we teach, the cost of each student's education is heavily subsidized by the state. Currently, the fees paid by students for their education cover less than 20 percent of the actual cost of that education. The other 80 percent is covered by revenues coming largely from the state's tax revenues. The value of that subsidy for each month of study is greater than the funds that would be received from AFDC by a single parent with two children to provide for the biological needs of those children.

Unfortunately, from personal experience we can attest that some students are in effect "welfare cheats," because they do not use their educational subsidies as they were intended to be used. Some cut many of their classes, even though their space in each and every class is paid for by taxpayers. Some take many more years than necessary to finish, in part because they do not want a very demanding class schedule. Perhaps worse, some never graduate; in fact, some spend a couple of years partying at taxpayers' expense before becoming academically ineligible to continue.

The same anger and resentment that is commonly expressed toward the possibility that some recipients of such benefits as AFDC and food stamps abuse their benefits is rarely directed at college students who do not make good use of their state subsidy. It is worth asking why. Nancy Fraser in her contribution to this chapter suggests that the difference in attitudes is at least partly attributable to bias against women. She believes that beneficiaries of AFDC and other social welfare programs that have primarily served women are viewed as recipients of charity, whereas beneficiaries of programs that have either traditionally served primarily men, or at least where women have not made up the bulk of the recipients, tend to be viewed as having a right to those benefits. Since the latter are thought to deserve their benefits, there is less worry and suspicion that they are in some way taking advantage of taxpayers. It is possible that racial and class biases could also play a role. One difference between, say, AFDC and a state university education is that all classes are eligible for the latter benefit, whereas poverty is required for the former.

Unless there were some such bias at work, it would be difficult to see why there should not be more resentment of the state university student who does not study in order to party than of an AFDC recipient who does not work in order to preserve health care benefits for his or her children. Such a student could come from a very affluent family. Indeed, such a student could personally possess enormous inherited wealth and still receive state funds that would come in part from the taxes paid by a person working two minimum wage jobs in order to make ends meet. Fraser's claim that, for at least many of us, our attitudes toward different social welfare programs are based on bias seems plausible when such examples are confronted. If so, it would be valuable to reexamine those attitudes and try to develop a set of consistent attitudes that could be supported by unbiased principles.

WORLD HUNGER

No doubt many who will read this have been horrified by the images on television news programs of emaciated people in refugee camps seeking relief from famine and/or war. What, if anything, are those of us with relatively comfortable and even luxurious lives required to do to help relieve or prevent such suffering? Many of the considerations bearing on the issue of welfare bear on the issue of world hunger as well. In both cases, for example, a libertarian position would seem to imply that there is no duty to aid. If the issues concerning world hunger and welfare differ in principle, it must be because our moral duties to people depend on what side of our national borders they happen to be. While the selections in this chapter do not really focus on the issue of whether or not there is such a dependence, it would be worthwhile keeping that issue in mind while reading.

Peter Singer believes that members of affluent nations have a duty to make fairly radical changes in their ways of life so that the resources currently used to provide their luxuries can be used instead to prevent starvation around the world. One version of the principle used by Singer to argue for this conclusion is that if one can prevent something bad from happening without giving up anything of comparable moral importance, one has an obligation to do so. This principle would imply that we should give up our own luxuries to prevent the death from starvation of others. For Singer, national borders should not be regarded as having moral significance; one ought to address the greater need wherever it is. If one should focus on meeting the needs of those in some foreign nations rather than meeting the needs of those in our own affluent nation, it is because the need is greater elsewhere than at home. Even most of those who are regarded as living in poverty in the United States have their basic needs more fully met than the poor in many other nations.

Garrett Hardin seems to share with Singer a basic consequentialist orientation to moral questions, but his analysis of world hunger leads him to regard national borders as having moral significance and looking specifically at the United States to disapprove of using our resources to help the hungry in other nations. He believes that reducing starvation in other nations will allow the populations in those nations to grow, eventually leading to a situation where the populations will have so far outstripped the ability of their nations' land to support them that there will be much greater death from starvation. Hardin uses the image of lifeboats as a metaphor for nations and suggests that by helping other nations, we endanger our own nation by reducing the surplus that might allow it to meet some future emergency. Because of considerations such as these, Hardin concludes that attempts to feed the hungry in other nations will very likely have bad consequences both for the nations that receive the aid and those that give it.

It might be worth considering whether Hardin is right to see the sides of the lifeboats (to continue with his metaphor) as being the same as national borders. Why not, for instance, see the entire world as a single lifeboat? Why not lifeboats smaller than nations? Hardin may indeed prefer the image of smaller lifeboats since much of his reasoning might seem to imply that helping the poor within our own society is as dangerous as helping the hungry in other nations. His worries about "the tragedy of the commons" may be as applicable to some forms of welfare as it is to world hunger. We should at least ask ourselves what Hardin's position would imply for welfare as we consider his arguments.

Our final reading on world hunger, by Robert N. Van Wyk, looks at this problem from a Kantian perspective. In Van Wyk's view, members of affluent nations have a duty to contribute to famine relief and to help in other ways to alleviate suffering in less affluent nations, though not a duty to sacrifice as much to help as Singer's position implies. It is interesting that many libertarians who, as we have seen reject the idea of positive rights, believe that their position follows from a Kantian demand that people be treated as ends in themselves and not as mere means. Van Wyk argues that this Kantian moral demand requires us to accept some positive rights. It would be worth considering which position yields a more plausible interpretation of the Kantian ideal of treating humans as ends in themselves.

What Libertarianism Is
John Hospers

John Hospers, who has been an active participant in debates in moral and political philosophy for many years, is Professor Emeritus of Philosophy at the University of Southern California. Here, Hospers tries to explain and defend libertarianism, a view according to which each person is the "owner" of his or her own life, and according to which no one is the owner of another's life. It follows from the latter claim, according to Hospers, that in the absence of special contractual relationships no one has legitimate moral claim to the labor or the products of the labor of others. Furthermore, libertarianism implies that governments have only a very narrow legitimate role to play. The sole legitimate function of government is to protect individuals' rights to life, liberty, and property. Hospers further explains how these rights should be understood.

The political philosophy that is called libertarianism (from the Latin *libertas,* liberty) is the doctrine that every person is the owner of his own life, and that no one is the owner of anyone else's life; and that consequently every human being has the right to act in accordance with his own choices, unless those actions infringe on the equal liberty of other human beings to act in accordance with *their* choices.

There are several other ways of stating the same libertarian thesis:

1. *No one is anyone else's master, and no one is anyone else's slave.* Since I am the one to decide how my life is to be conducted, just as you decide about yours, I have no right (even if I had the power) to make you my slave and be your master, nor have you the right to become the master by enslaving me. Slavery is *forced* servitude, and since no one owns the life of anyone else, no one has the right to enslave another. Political theories past and present have traditionally been concerned with who should be the master (usually the king, the dictator, or government bureaucracy) and who should be the slaves, and what the extent of the slavery should be. Libertarianism holds that no one has the right to use force to enslave the life of another, or any portion or aspect of that life.

2. *Other men's lives are not yours to dispose of.* I enjoy seeing operas; but operas are expensive to produce. Opera-lovers often say, "The state (or the city, etc.) should subsidize opera, so that we can all see it. Also it would be for people's betterment, cultural benefit, etc." But what they are advocating is nothing more or less than legalized plunder.

From *The Libertarian Alternative: Essays in Social and Political Philosophy*, ed. Tibor R. Machan (Chicago: Nelson-Hall, 1974), pp. 3–20.

They can't pay for the productions themselves, and yet they want to see opera, which involves a large number of people and their labor; so what they are saying in effect is, "Get the money through legalized force. Take a little bit more out of every worker's paycheck every week to pay for the operas we want to see." But I have no right to take by force from the workers' pockets to pay for what I want.

Perhaps it would be better if he *did* go to see opera—then I should try to convince him to go voluntarily. But to take the money from him forcibly, because in my opinion it would be good for *him,* is still seizure of his earnings, which is plunder.

Besides, if I have the right to force him to help pay for my pet projects, hasn't he equally the right to force me to help pay for his? Perhaps he in turn wants the government to subsidize rock-and-roll, or his new car, or a house in the country? If I have the right to milk him, why hasn't he the right to milk me? If I can be a moral cannibal, why can't he too?

We should beware of the inventors of utopias. They would remake the world according to their vision—with the lives and fruits of the labor of *other* human beings. Is it someone's utopian vision that others should build pyramids to beautify the landscape? Very well, then other men should provide the labor; and if he is in a position of political power, and he can't get men to do it voluntarily, then he must *compel* them to "cooperate"—i.e. he must enslave them.

A hundred men might gain great pleasure from beating up or killing just one insignificant human being; but other men's lives are not theirs to dispose of. "In order to achieve the worthy goals of the next five year plan, we must forcibly collectivize the peasants . . ."; but other men's lives are not theirs to dispose of. Do you want to occupy, rent-free, the mansion that another man has worked for twenty years to buy? But other men's lives are not yours to dispose of. Do you want operas so badly that everyone is forced to work harder to pay for their subsidization through taxes? But other men's lives are not yours to dispose of. Do you want to have free medical care at the expense of other people, whether they wish to provide it or not? But this would require them to work longer for you whether they want to or not, and other men's lives are not yours to dispose of.

The freedom to engage in any type of enterprise, to produce, to own and control property, to buy and sell on the free market, is derived from the rights to life, liberty, and property . . . which are stated in the Declaration of Independence. . . . [but] when a government guarantees a "right" to an education or parity on farm products or a guaranteed annual income, it is staking a claim on the property of one group of citizens for the sake of another group. In short, it is violating one of the fundamental rights it was instituted to protect.[1]

3. *No human being should be a nonvoluntary mortgage on the life of another.* I cannot claim your life, your work, or the products of your effort as mine. The fruit of one man's labor should not be fair game for every freeloader who comes along and demands it as his own. The orchard that has been carefully grown, nurtured, and harvested by its owner should not be ripe for the plucking for any bypasser who has a yen for the ripe fruit. The wealth that some men have produced should not be fair game for looting by government, to be used for whatever purposes its representatives determine, no matter what their motives in so doing may be. The theft of your money by a robber is not justified by the fact that he used it to help his injured mother.

It will already be evident that libertarian doctrine is embedded in a view of the rights of man. Each human being has the right to live his life as he chooses, compatibly with the equal right of all other human beings to live their lives as they choose.

All man's rights are implicit in the above statement. Each man has the right to life: any attempt by others to take it away from him, or even to injure him, violates this right, through the use of coercion against him. Each man has the right to liberty: to conduct his life in accordance with the alternatives open to him without coercive action by others. And every man has the right to property: to work to sustain his life (and the lives of whichever others he chooses to sustain, such as his family) and to retain the fruits of his labor.

People often defend the rights of life and liberty but denigrate property rights, and yet the right to property is as basic as the other two; indeed, without property rights no other rights are possible. Depriving you of property is depriving you of the means by which you live.

. . . All that which an individual possesses by right (including his life and property) are morally his to use, dispose of and even destroy, as he sees fit. If I own my life, then it follows that I am free to associate with whom I please and not to associate with whom I please. If I own my knowledge and services it follows that I may ask any compensation I wish for providing them for another, or I may abstain from providing them at all, if I so choose. If I own my house, it follows that I may decorate it as I please and live in it with whom I please. If I control my own business, it follows that I may charge what I please for my products or services, hire whom I please and not hire whom I please. All that which I own in fact, I may dispose of as I choose to in reality. For anyone to attempt to limit my freedom to do so is to violate my rights.

Where do my rights end? Where yours begin. I may do anything I wish with my own life, liberty and property without your consent; but I may do nothing with your life, liberty and property without your consent. If we recognize the principle of man's rights, it follows that the individual is sovereign of the domain of his own life and property, and is sovereign of no other domain. To attempt to interfere forcibly with another's use, disposal or destruction of his own property is to initiate force against him and to violate his rights.

I have no right to decide how *you* should spend your time or your money. I can make that decision for myself, but not for you, my neighbor. I may deplore your choice of life-style, and I may talk with you about it provided you are willing to listen to me. But I have no right to use force to change it. Nor have I the right to decide how you should spend the money you have earned. I may appeal to you to give it to the Red Cross, and you may prefer to go to prizefights. But that is your decision, and however much I may chafe about it I do not have the right to interfere forcibly with it, for example by robbing you in order to use the money in accordance with *my* choices. (If I have the right to rob you, have you also the right to rob me?)

When I claim a right, I carve out a niche, as it were, in my life, saying in effect, "This activity I must be able to perform without interference from others. For you and everyone else, this is off limits." And so I put up a "no trespassing" sign, which marks off the area of my right. Each individual's right is his "no trespassing" sign in relation to me and others. I may not encroach upon his domain any more than he upon mine, without my consent. Every right entails a duty, true—but the duty is only that of *forbearance*—that is, of *refraining* from violating the other person's right. If you have a right to life, I have no right to take your life; if you have a right to the products of your labor (property), I have no right to take it from you without your consent. The non-violation of these rights will not guarantee you protection against natural catastrophes such as floods and earthquakes, but it will protect you against the aggressive activities *of other men.* And rights, after all, have to do with one's relations to other human beings, not with one's relations to physical nature. . . .

The *right to property* is the most misunderstood and unappreciated of human rights, and it is one most constantly violated by governments. "Property" of course does not mean only real estate; it includes anything you can call your own—your clothing, your car, your jewelry, your books and papers.

The right of property is not the right to just *take* it from others. For this would interfere with *their* property rights. It is rather the right to work for it, to obtain non-coercively, the money or services which you can present in voluntary exchange.

The right to property is consistently underplayed by intellectuals today, sometimes even frowned upon, as if we should feel guilty for upholding such a right in view of all the poverty in the world. But the right to property is absolutely basic. It is your hedge against the future. It is your assurance that what you have worked to earn will still be there, and be yours, when you wish or need to use it, especially when you are too old to work any longer.

Government has always been the chief enemy of the right to property. The officials of government, wishing to increase their power, and finding an increase of wealth an effective way to bring this about, seize some or all of what a person has earned—and since government has a monopoly of physical force within the geographical area of the nation, it has the power (but not the right) to do this. When this happens, of course, every citizen of that country is insecure: he knows that no matter how hard he works the government can swoop down on him at any time and confiscate his earnings and possessions. A person sees his life savings wiped out in a moment when the tax-collectors descend to deprive him of the fruits of his work; or, an industry which has been fifty years in the making and cost millions of dollars and millions of hours of time and planning, is nationalized overnight. Or the government, via inflation, cheapens the currency, so that hard-won dollars aren't worth anything any more. The effect of such actions, of course, is that people lose hope and incentive: if no matter how hard they work the government agents can take it all away, why bother to work at all, for more than today's needs? Depriving people of property is *depriving them of the means by which they live*—the freedom of the individual citizen to do what he wishes with his own life and to plan for the future. Indeed, only if property rights are respected is there any point to planning for the future and working to achieve one's goals. *Property rights are what makes long-range planning possible*— the kind of planning which is a distinctively human endeavor, as opposed to the day-by-day activity of the lion who hunts, who depends on the supply of game tomorrow but has no real insurance against starvation in a day or a week. Without the right to property, the right to life itself amounts to little: how can you sustain your life if you cannot plan ahead? And how can you plan ahead if the fruits of your labor can at any moment be confiscated by government? . . .

"But why not say that everybody owns everything? That we *all* own everything there is?"

To some this may have a pleasant ring—but let us try to analyze what it means. If everybody owns everything, then everyone has an equal right to go everywhere, do what he pleases, take what he likes, destroy if he wishes, grow crops or burn them, trample them under, and so on. Consider what it would be like in practice. Suppose you have saved money to buy a house for yourself and your family. Now suppose that the principle, "everybody owns everything," becomes adopted. Well then, why shouldn't every itinerant hippie just come in and take over, sleeping in your beds and eating in your kitchen and not bothering to replace the food supply or clean up the mess? After all, it belongs to all of us, doesn't it? So we have just as much right to it as you, the buyer, have. What happens if we *all* want to sleep in the bedroom and there's not room for all of us? Is it the strongest who wins?

What would be the result? Since no one would be responsible for anything, the property would soon be destroyed, the food used up, the facilities nonfunctional. Beginning as a house that *one* family could use, it would end up as a house that *no one* could use. And if the principle continued to be adopted, no one would build houses any more—or anything else. What for? They would only be occupied and used by others, without remuneration.

Suppose two men are cast ashore on an island, and they agree that each will cultivate half of it. The first man is industrious and grows crops and builds a shelter, making the most of the situation with which he is confronted.

The second man, perhaps thinking that the warm days will last forever, lies in the sun, picks coconuts while they last, and does a minimum of work to sustain himself. At the time of harvest, the second man has nothing to harvest, nor does he assist the first man in his labors. But later when there is a dearth of food on the island, the second man comes to the first man and demands half of the harvest as his right. But of course he has no right to the product of the first man's labors. The first man may freely choose to give part of his harvest to the second out of charity rather than see him starve; but that is just what it is—charity, not the second man's right.

How can any of man's rights be violated? Ultimately, only by the use of force. I can make suggestions to you, I can reason with you, entreat you (if you are willing to listen), but I cannot force you without violating your rights; only by forcing you do I cut the cord between your free decisions and your actions. Voluntary relations between individuals involve no deprivation of rights, but murder, assault, and rape do, because in doing these things I make you the unwilling victim of my actions. A man is beating his wife involves no violation of rights if she *wanted* to be beaten. *Force is behavior that requires the unwilling involvement of other persons.*

Thus the use of force need not involve the use of physical violence. If I trespass on your property or dump garbage on it, I am violating your property rights, as indeed I am when I steal your watch; although this is not force in the sense of violence, it *is* a case of your being an unwilling victim of my action. Similarly, if you shout at me so that I cannot be heard when I try to speak, or blow a siren in my ear, or start a factory next door which pollutes my land, you are again violating my rights (to free speech, to property); I am, again, an unwilling victim of your actions. Similarly, if you steal a manuscript of mine and publish it as your own, you are confiscating a piece of my property and thus violating my right to keep what is the product of my labor. Of course, if I give you the manuscript with permission to sign your name to it and keep the proceeds, no violation of rights is involved—any more than if I give you permission to dump garbage on my yard.

According to libertarianism, the role of government should be limited to the retaliatory use of force against those who have initiated its use. It should not enter into any other areas, such as religion, social organization, and economics.

GOVERNMENT

Government is the most dangerous institution known to man. Throughout history it has violated the rights of men more than any individual or group of individuals could do: it has killed people, enslaved them, sent them to forced labor and concentration camps, and regularly robbed and pillaged them of the fruits of their expended labor. Unlike individual criminals, government has the power to arrest and try; unlike individual criminals, it can surround and encompass a person totally, dominating every aspect of one's life, so that one has no recourse from it but to leave the country (and in totalitarian nations even that is prohibited). Government throughout history has a much sorrier record than any individual, even that of a ruthless mass murderer. The signs we see on bumper stickers are chillingly accurate: "Beware: the Government is Armed and Dangerous."

The only proper role of government, according to libertarians, is that of the protector of the citizen against aggression by other individuals. The government, of course, should never initiate aggression; its proper role is as the embodiment of the *retaliatory* use of force against anyone who initiates its use.

If each individual had constantly to defend himself against possible aggressors, he would have to spend a considerable portion of his life in target practice, karate exercises, and other means of self-defenses, and even so he would probably be helpless against groups of individuals who might try to kill, maim, or rob him. He would have little time for cultivating those qualities which are essential to civilized life, nor would improvements in science, medicine, and the arts be likely to occur. The function of government is to take this responsibility off his shoulders: the government undertakes to defend him against aggressors and to punish them if they attack him. When the government is effective in doing this, it enables the citizen to go about his business unmolested and without constant fear for his life. To do this, of course, government must have physical power—the police, to protect the citizen from aggression within its borders, and the armed forces, to protect him from aggressors outside. Beyond that, the government should not intrude upon his life, either to run his business, or adjust his daily activities, or prescribe his personal moral code.

Government, then, undertakes to be the individual's protector; but historically governments have gone far beyond this function. Since they already have the physical power, they have not hesitated to use it for purposes far beyond that which was entrusted to them in the first place. Undertaking initially to protect its citizens against aggression, it has often itself become an aggressor—a far greater aggressor, indeed, than the criminals against whom it was supposed to protect its citizens. Governments have done what no private citizens can do: arrest and imprison individuals without a trial and send them to slave labor camps. Government must have power in order to be effective—and yet the very means by which alone it can be effective make it vulnerable to the abuse of power, leading to managing the lives of individuals and even inflicting terror upon them.

What then should be the function of government? In a word, the *protection of human rights.*

1. *The right to life:* libertarians support all such legislation as will protect human beings against the use of force by others, for example, laws against killing, attempted killing, maiming, beating, and all kinds of physical violence.

2. .*The right to liberty:* there should be no laws compromising in any way freedom of speech, of the press, and of peaceable assembly. There should be no censorship of ideas, books, films, or of anything else by government.
3. *The right to property:* libertarians support legislation that protects the property rights of individuals against confiscation, nationalization, eminent domain, robbery, trespass, fraud and misrepresentation, patent and copyright, libel and slander.

Someone has violently assaulted you. Should he be legally liable? Of course. He has violated one of your rights. He has knowingly injured you, and since he has initiated aggression against you he should be made to expiate.

Someone has negligently left his bicycle on the sidewalk where you trip over it in the dark and injure yourself. He didn't do it intentionally; he didn't mean you any harm. Should he be legally liable? Of course: he has, however unwittingly, injured you, and since the injury is caused by him and you are the victim, he should pay.

Someone across the street is unemployed. Should you be taxed extra to pay for his expenses? Not at all. You have not injured him, you are not responsible for the fact that he is unemployed (unless you are a senator or bureaucrat who agitated for further curtailing of business, which legislation passed, with the result that your neighbor was laid off by the curtailed business). You may voluntarily wish to help him out, or better still, try to get him a job to put him on his feet again; but since you have initiated no aggressive act against him, and neither purposely nor accidentally injured him in any way, you should not be legally penalized for the fact of his unemployment. (Actually, it is just such penalties that increase unemployment.)

One man, A, works hard for years and finally earns a high salary as a professional man. A second man, B, prefers not to work at all, and to spend wastefully what money he has (through inheritance), so that after a year or two he has nothing left. At the end of this time he has a long siege of illness and lots of medical bills to pay. He demands that the bills be paid by the government—that is, by the taxpayers of the land, including Mr. A.

But of course B has no such right. He chose to lead his life in a certain way—that was his voluntary decision. One consequence of that choice is that he must depend on charity in case of later need. Mr. A chose not to live that way. (And if everyone lived like Mr. B, on whom would he depend in case of later need?) Each has a right to live in the way he pleases, but each must live with the consequences of his own decision (which, as always, fall primarily on himself). He cannot, in time of need, claim A's beneficence as his right.

If a house-guest of yours starts to carve his initials in your walls and break up your furniture, you have a right to evict him, and call the police if he makes trouble. If someone starts to destroy the machinery in a factory, the factory owner is also entitled to evict him and call the police. In both cases, persons other than the owner are permitted on the property only under certain conditions, at the pleasure of the owner. If those conditions are violated, the owner is entitled to use force to set things straight. The case is exactly the same on a college or university campus: if a campus demonstrator starts breaking windows, occupying the president's office, and setting fire to a dean, the college authorities are certainly within their rights to evict him forcibly; one is permitted on the college grounds only under specific conditions, set by the administration: study, peaceful student activity, even political activity if those in charge choose to permit it. If they do not choose to permit peaceful political activity on campus, they may be unwise, since a campus is after all a place where all sides of every issue should get discussed, and the college that doesn't permit this may soon lose its reputation and its students. All the same, the college official who does not permit it is quite within his rights; the students do not own the campus, nor do the hired trouble-makers imported from elsewhere. In the case of a privately owned college, the owners, or whoever they have delegated to administer it, have the right to make the decisions as to who shall be permitted on the campus and under what conditions. In the case of a state university or college, the ownership problem is more complex: one could say that the "government" owns the campus or that "the people" do since they are the taxpayers who support it; but in either case, the university administration has the delegated task of keeping order, and until they are removed by the state administration or the taxpayers, it is theirs to decide who shall be permitted on campus, and what non-academic activities will be permitted to their students on the premises.

Property rights can be violated by physical trespass, of course, or by anyone entering on your property for any reason without your consent. (If you *do* consent to having your neighbor dump garbage on your yard there is no violation of your rights.) But the physical trespass of a person is only a special case of violation of property rights. Property rights can be violated by sound-waves, in the form of a loud noise, or the sounds of your neighbor's hi-fi set while you are trying to sleep. Such violations of property rights are of course the subject of action in the courts. . . .

What about property which you do not work to earn, but which you *inherit* from someone else? Do you have a right to that? You have no right to it until someone decides to give it to you. Consider the man who willed it to you; it was his, he had the right to use and dispose of it as *he* saw fit; and if he decided to give it to you, this is a windfall for you, but it was only the exercise of *his* right. Had the property been seized by the government at the man's death, or distributed among numerous other people designated by the government, it *would* have been a violation of his rights: for he, who worked to earn and sustain it, would not have been able to dispose of it according to his own judgment. If he doesn't have the right to determine who shall have it, who does? . . .

Laws may be classified into three types: (1) laws protecting individuals against themselves, such as laws against fornication and other sexual behavior, alcohol, and drugs; (2) laws protecting individuals against aggressions by other individuals, such as laws against murder, robbery, and fraud; (3) laws requiring people to help one another; for example, all laws which rob Peter to pay Paul, such as welfare.

Libertarians reject the first class of laws totally. Behavior which harms no one else is strictly the individual's own affair. Thus, there should be no laws against becoming intoxicated, since whether or not to become intoxicated is the individual's own decision; but there should be laws against driving while intoxicated, since the drunken driver is a threat to every other motorist on the highway (drunken driving falls into type 2). Similarly, there should be no laws against drugs (except the prohibition of sale of drugs to minors) as long as the taking of these drugs poses no threat to anyone else. Drug addiction is a psychological problem to which no present solution exists. Most of the social harm caused by addicts, other than to themselves, is the result of thefts which they perform in order to continue their habit—and then the *legal* crime is the theft, not the addiction. The actual cost of heroin is about ten cents a shot; if it were legalized, the enormous traffic in illegal sale and purchase of it would stop, as well as the accompanying proselytization to get new addicts (to make more money for the pusher) and the thefts performed by addicts who often require eighty dollars a day just to keep up the habit. Addiction would not stop, but the crimes would: it is estimated that 75 percent of the burglaries in New York City today are performed by addicts, and all these crimes could be wiped out at one stroke through the legalization of drugs. (Only when the taking of drugs could be shown to constitute a threat to *others* should it be prohibited by law. It is only laws protecting people against *themselves* that libertarians oppose.)

Laws should be limited to the second class only: aggression by individuals against other individuals. These are laws whose function is to protect human beings against encroachment by others; and this, as we have seen, is (according to libertarianism) the sole function of government.

Libertarians also reject the third class of laws totally: no one should be forced by law to help others, not even to tell them the time of day if requested, and certainly not to give them a portion of one's weekly paycheck. Governments, in the guise of humanitarianism, have given to some by taking from others (charging a "handling fee" in the process, which, because of the government's waste and inefficiency, sometimes is several hundred percent). And in so doing they have decreased incentive, violated the rights of individuals, and lowered the standard of living of almost everyone.

All such laws constitute what libertarians call *moral cannibalism*. A cannibal in the physical sense is a person who lives off the flesh of other human beings. A *moral* cannibal is one who believes he has a right to live off the "spirit" of other human beings—who believes that he has a moral claim on the productive capacity, time, and effort expended by others.

It has become fashionable to claim virtually everything that one needs or desires as one's *right*. Thus, many people claim that they have a right to a job, the right to free medical care, to free food and clothing, to a decent home, and so on. Now if one asks, apart from any specific context, whether it would be desirable if everyone had these things, one might well say yes. But there is a gimmick attached to each of them: *At whose expense?* Jobs, medical care, education, and so on, don't grow on trees. These are goods and services *produced only by men.* Who, then, is to provide them, and under what conditions?

If you have a right to a job, who is to supply it? Must an employer supply it even if he doesn't want to hire you? What if you are unemployable, or incurably lazy? (If you say "the government must supply it," does that mean that a job must be created for you which no employer needs done, and that you must be kept in it regardless of how much or little you work?) If the employer is forced to supply it at his expense even if he doesn't need you, then isn't *he* being enslaved to that extent? What ever happened to *his* right to conduct his life and his affairs in accordance with his choices?

If you have a right to free medical care, then, since medical care doesn't exist in nature as wild apples do, some people will have to supply it to you for free: that is, they will have to spend their time and money and energy taking care of you whether they want to or not. What ever happened to *their* right to conduct their lives as they see fit? Or do you have a right to violate theirs? Can there be a right to violate rights?

All those who demand this or that as a "free service" are consciously or unconsciously evading the fact that there is in reality no such thing as free services. All man-made goods and services are the result of human expenditure of time and effort. There is no such thing as "something for nothing" in this world. If you demand something free, you are demanding that other men give their time and effort to you without compensation. If they voluntarily choose to do this, there is no problem; but if you demand that they be *forced* to do it, you are interfering with their right not to do it if they so choose. "Swimming in this pool ought to be free!" says the indignant passerby. What he means is that others should build a pool, others should provide the materials, and still others should run it and keep it in functioning order, so that he can use it without fee. But what right has he to the expenditure of *their* time and effort? To expect something "for free" is to expect it *to be paid for by others* whether they choose to or not.

Many questions, particularly about economic matters, will be generated by the libertarian account of human rights and the role of government. Should government have no role in assisting the needy, in providing social security, in legislating minimum wages, in fixing prices and putting a ceiling on rents, in curbing monopolies, in erecting tariffs, in guaranteeing jobs, in managing the money supply? To these and all similar questions the libertarian answers with an unequivocal no.

"But then you'd let people go hungry!" comes the rejoinder. This, the libertarian insists, is precisely what would not happen; with the restrictions removed, the economy would flourish as never before. With the controls taken off business, existing enterprises would expand and new ones would spring into existence satisfying more and more consumer needs; millions more people would be gainfully employed instead of subsisting on welfare, and all kinds of research and production, released from the stranglehold of government, would proliferate, fulfilling man's needs and desires as never before. It has always been so whenever government has permitted men to be free traders on a free market. But *why* this is so, and how the free market is the best solution to all problems relating to the material aspect of man's life, is another and far longer story.

NOTE

1. William W. Bayes, "What Is Property?" *The Freeman,* July 1970, p. 348.

Egalitarianism
Thomas Nagel

Thomas Nagel is Professor of Philosophy and Law at New York University. Among his more important contributions to philosophy, especially moral and political philosophy, are *The Possibility of Altruism* (1970) and *The View from Nowhere* (1986).

In this selection from his more recent book, *Equality and Partiality*, Nagel explains and defends an egalitarian position concerning distributive justice, a position that is a part of Nagel's more general approach to philosophy. According to that more general approach, human beings perceive and interact with the world from both a personal and an impersonal standpoint. From the impersonal (or impartial) standpoint, each of us is able to view oneself in the third person, as simply one person among many, all of whom are equally real. It is this standpoint that makes it possible for us to detach ourselves from our personal standpoint and try to put ourselves in another's shoes, viewing the world from that person's point of view. The impartial standpoint, Nagel believes, gives rise to demands for equality. He argues that from this standpoint, the needs of those who are worst off will be seen as having priority over those who are better off, leading us to favor a society in which there is radically less inequality than currently exists in our own. An important aspect of Nagel's position is that the pressure toward more equal institutions does not come from some external source, but arises from an impersonal manner of viewing the world that he believes is a part of our very nature. The pressure for equality, then, arises from within us. At the end of the selection, Nagel suggests that inequalities, which demand attention, are only those for which the parties are not responsible.

It is the motive of impartiality which gives us a reason for wanting more equality than we have. If impartiality is not admitted as an important motive in determining the acceptability of a social system—if every such system is just a bargain struck among self-interested parties—then there will be no call for equality except to the extent needed to ensure stability. But I believe that impartiality emerges from an essential aspect of the human point of view, and that it naturally seeks expression through the institutions under which we live. . . .

We are so accustomed to great social and economic inequalities that it is easy to become dulled to them. But if everyone matters just as much as everyone else, it is appalling that the most effective social systems we have been able to devise permit so many people to be born into conditions of harsh deprivation which crush their prospects for leading a decent life, while many others are well provided for from birth, come to control substantial

From *Equality and Partiality*, by Thomas Nagel (New York: Oxford University Press, 1991), pp. 63–71.

resources, and are free to enjoy advantages vastly beyond the conditions of mere decency. The mutual perception of these material inequalities is part of a broader inequality of social status, personal freedom, and self-respect. Those with high income, extensive education, inherited wealth, family connections, and genteel employment are served and in many cultures treated deferentially by those who have none of these things. One cannot ignore the difficulties of escaping from this situation, but that is no reason not to dislike it.

The impartial attitude is, I believe, strongly egalitarian both in itself and in its implications. As I have said, it comes from our capacity to take up a point of view which abstracts from who we are, but which appreciates fully and takes to heart the value of every person's life and welfare. We put ourselves in each person's shoes and take as our preliminary guide to the value we assign to what happens to him the value which it has from his point of view. This gives to each person's well-being very great importance, and from the impersonal standpoint everyone's primary importance, leaving aside his effect on the welfare of others, is the same.

The result is an enormous set of values deriving from individual lives, without as yet any method of combining them or weighing them against one another when they conflict, as they inevitably will in the real world. The question whether impartiality is egalitarian in itself is the question whether the correct method of combination will include a built-in bias in favor of equality, over and above the equality of importance that everyone's life has in the initial set of values to be combined.

Even if impartiality were not in this sense egalitarian in itself, it would be egalitarian in its distributive consequences because of the familiar fact of diminishing marginal utility. Within any person's life, an additional thousand dollars added to fifty thousand will be spent on something less important than an additional thousand added to five hundred—since we satisfy more important needs before less important ones. And people are similar enough in their basic needs and desires so that something roughly comparable holds between one person and another: Transferable resources will usually benefit a person with less more than they will benefit a person with significantly more. So if everyone's benefit counts the same from the impersonal standpoint, and if there is a presumption in favor of greater benefit, there will be a reason to prefer a more equal to a less equal distribution of a given quantity of resources.

But I believe that impartiality is also egalitarian in itself, and that is a more controversial claim. What it means is that impartiality generates a greater interest in benefiting the worse off than in benefiting the better off—a kind of priority to the former over the latter. Of course impartiality means a concern for everyone's good, so added benefit is desirable, whoever gets it. But when it comes to a choice of whom to benefit, there is still the question of how to combine distinct and conflicting claims, and the pure idea of concern for everyone's good does not answer it.

The answer will depend on many things. We may be able to benefit more persons or fewer, and we may be able to benefit them to a greater or lesser extent. Both of these efficiency factors are certainly relevant, and impartiality will favor the first alternative over the second in each case, other things being equal. But in addition, I believe that the proper form of equal concern for all will sometimes favor benefit to the worse off even when numbers or quantity go the other way. Such a ranking of concern is internal to the attitude, correctly understood, giving the worst off a priority in their claim on our concern.[1]

The reason is that concern for everyone has to be particularized: It must contain a separate and equal concern for each person's good. When we occupy the impersonal standpoint, our impartial concern for each person exists side by side with our concern for every other person. These concerns should not be conglomerated. Even though we cannot contain all these separate lives together in our imagination, their separateness must be preserved somehow in the system of impersonal values which impartiality generates.

The point is famously made by Rawls in his charge that utilitarianism does not take seriously the distinction between persons.[2] Rawls's construal of the moral attitude that underlies the sense of justice, as modeled in the Original Position, includes this strongly individualized impartial concern as an essential element. Because we are asked to choose principles without knowing who we are, we must put ourselves fully into the position of each representative person in the society. While the results of this simultaneous multiple identification may be obscure, it is clearly one of the sources of the egalitarian character of his theory.

This is connected with its Kantian inspiration, even though Kant himself did not draw egalitarian conclusions from the condition of treating each individual as an end in himself. If we try to view things simultaneously from everyone's point of view, as Kant insisted, we are led, I think, in an egalitarian direction. I believe this egalitarian feature is present even in pure, detached benevolence, but it also takes us part of the way toward the conditions of universal acceptability demanded by Kantian universalization: Up to a point, more equality makes it harder for anyone to object.

The fundamental point about individualized impartial concern is that it generates a large set of separate values corresponding to separate lives, and we must then make a further judgment about how to decide the inevitable conflicts among them. We cannot simply assume that they are to be combined like vectors of force, which add together or cancel one another out. That is the utilitarian solution, but it seems in fact the wrong way to treat them. Instead they have to be compared with one another at least partly in accordance with some standard of relative priority.

The separateness of the concerns does not rule out all ranking of alternatives involving different persons, nor does it mean that benefiting more people is not in itself preferable to benefiting fewer. But it does introduce a significant element of nonaggregative, pairwise comparison between the persons affected by any choice or policy, whereby the situation of each and the potential gains of each are compared separately with those of every other. I believe that when this is done, on careful reflection, a ranking of urgency naturally emerges. The claims on our impartial concern of an individual who is badly off present themselves as having some priority over the claims of *each* individual who is better off: as being ahead in the queue, so to speak. And this means there is reason to try to satisfy them first, even at some loss in efficiency, and therefore even beyond the already significant preference that derives from the diminishing marginal utility of resources. . . . I do not suggest that impartiality imposes an absolute priority for benefit to the worse off. But it includes some priority of this kind as a significant element, and it should incline us to favor the alternative that is least unacceptable to the persons to whom it is most unacceptable.[3]

This is a direct consequence of what I take to be the proper form of imaginative identification with the points of view of others, when we recognize their importance from the impersonal standpoint. Instead of combining all their experiences into an undifferentiated whole, or choosing as if we had an equal chance of being any of them, we must try to think about it as if we were each of them separately—as if each of their lives were our only life. Even though this is a tall order and does not describe a logical possibility, I believe it means something imaginatively and morally: It belongs to the same moral outlook that requires unanimity as a condition of legitimacy.

Pure impartiality is intrinsically egalitarian, then, in the sense of favoring the worse off over the better off. It is not egalitarian in the sense of begrudging advantages to the better off which cost the worse off nothing, since impartial concern is universal. But for more than one reason the impersonal standpoint generates an attitude of impartiality which attracts us strongly to a social ideal in which large inequalities in the distribution of resources are avoided if possible, and in which development of this possibility is an important aim. And economic inequality is only part of the story. It may support stifling social stratification and class or communal oppression, inequality of political rights, and so forth. These are evils to which the equal concern of impartiality responds, favoring those at the bottom of the heap and those institutions which improve their status. All this comes from putting oneself in everyone's shoes, and even if we leave unspecified the strength of the egalitarian factor, measured by these standards the world is clearly a pretty terrible place. . . .

To embody egalitarian values in a political ideal would be an involved task. An essential part of that task would be to introduce an appropriate condition of non-responsibility into the specification of those goods and evils whose equal possession is desirable. What seems bad is not that people should be unequal in advantages or disadvantages generally, but that they should be unequal in the advantages or disadvantages for which they are not responsible. Only then must priority be given to the interests of the worse off. Two people born into a situation which gave them equal life chances can end up leading lives of very different quality as a result of their own free choices, and that should not be objectionable to an egalitarian. But to make sense of such a condition generates notorious problems.

. . . [T]here is wide disagreement over when an individual is responsible for what happens to him, ranging from disputes over freedom of the will in general to disputes over the conditions of knowledge and opportunity needed to confer responsibility for an outcome, to disputes over when the use of a natural ability or fortunate circumstance for which one is not responsible nevertheless makes one responsible for the results. These are large issues of moral philosophy into which I shall not enter here. They may themselves bring up considerations of equality in their treatment. Let me simply say that it seems to me clear that, whatever remotely plausible positive condition of responsibility one takes as correct, many of the important things in life—especially the advantages and disadvantages with which people are born or which form the basic framework within which they must lead their lives—cannot be regarded as goods or evils for which they are responsible, and so fall under the egalitarian principle.

NOTES

1. Derek Parfit, in *On Giving Priority to the Worse Off*, calls this form of egalitarianism the Pure Priority View, to distinguish it from an attachment to equality which is a pure aversion to inequality—even inequality which benefits the worst off—and which he calls Relational Egalitarianism. Later I shall discuss a further factor —a form of fairness—which lends support to this second, stronger type of egalitarianism under some conditions.
2. John Rawls, *A Theory of Justice* (Cambridge, MA: Harvard University Press, 1971), p. 27.
3. There is some discussion of this idea in the chapter called "Equality" in *Mortal Questions,* pp. 122–25. In that essay I also explore the connection between egalitarianism and the requirement of unanimity.

The Right to Eat and
the Duty to Work
Trudy Govier

Trudy Govier, a Canadian philosopher who was teaching at Trent University when this essay first appeared, distinguishes three positions that might be taken on the issue of welfare. They are: (1) individualism, a libertarian position that would condemn using tax funds to assist those facing economic hardship, (2) Puritanism, a position that would guarantee the resources sufficient to meet basic needs to those who are willing to work for those resources, and (3) permissivism, according to which each member of society would receive an unconditional guarantee of the resources necessary to meet basic needs.

The essay is divided into three parts. In the first, Govier describes each of the three positions. She then argues that some of the concepts that play a crucial role in the debate among advocates of the three positions, for example the concept of work, need to be clarified before either the individualist or Puritan system could be accepted. In the final section, she defends the permissive system, maintaining both that it would produce more desirable social consequences than the other two approaches to welfare and that it would more fully realize reasonable ideals of social justice.

———————

Although the topic of welfare is not one with which philosophers have often concerned themselves, it is a topic which gives rise to many complex and fascinating questions—some in the area of political philosophy, some in the area of ethics, and some of a more practical kind. The variety of issues related to the subject of welfare makes it particularly necessary to be clear just which issue one is examining in a discussion of welfare. In a recent book on the subject, Nicholas Rescher asks:

> In what respects and to what extent is society, working through the instrumentality of the state, responsible for the welfare of its members? What demands for the promotion of his welfare can an individual reasonably make upon his society? These are questions to which no answer can be given in terms of some *a priori* approach with reference to universal ultimates. Whatever answer can appropriately be given will depend, in the final analysis, on what the society decides it should be.[1]

Rescher raises this question only to avoid it. His response to his own question is that a society has all and only those responsibilities for its members that it thinks it has. Although this claim is trivially true as regards legal responsibilities, it is inadequate from a moral perspective. If one imagines the case of an affluent society which leaves the blind, the disabled, and the needy

From *Philosophy of the Social Sciences* 5 (1975), pp. 125–143.

to die of starvation, the incompleteness of Rescher's account becomes obvious. In this imagined case one is naturally led to raise the question as to whether those in power ought to supply those in need with the necessities of life. Though the needy have no legal right to welfare benefits of any kind, one might very well say that they ought to have such a right. It is this claim which I propose to discuss here.[2]

I shall approach this issue by examining three positions which may be adopted in response to it. These are:

1. *The Individualist Position:* Even in an affluent society, one ought not to have any legal right to state-supplied welfare benefits.
2. *The Permissive Position:* In a society with sufficient resources, one ought to have an unconditional legal right to receive state supplied welfare benefits. (That is, one's right to receive such benefits ought not to depend on one's behaviour; it should be guaranteed).
3. *The Puritan Position:* In a society with sufficient resources one ought to have a legal right to state-supplied welfare benefits; this right ought to be conditional, however, on one's willingness to work.

But before we examine these positions, some preliminary clarification must be attempted. . . . The present analysis of welfare is intended to apply to societies which (*a*) have the institution of private property, if not for means of production, at least for some basic good; and (*b*) possess sufficient resources so that it is at least possible for every member of the society to be supplied with the necessities of life.

1. THE INDIVIDUALIST VIEW

It might be maintained that a person in need has no legitimate moral claim on those around him and that the hypothetical inattentive society which left its blind citizens to beg or starve cannot rightly be censured for doing so. This view, which is dramatically at odds with most of contemporary social thinking, lives on in the writings of Ayn Rand and her followers.[3] The Individualist sets a high value on uncoerced personal choice. He sees each person as a responsible agent who is able to make his own decisions and to plan his own life. He insists that with the freedom to make decisions goes responsibility for the consequences of those decisions. A person has every right, for example, to spend ten years of his life studying Sanskrit—but if, as a result of this choice, he is unemployable, he ought not to expect others to labour on his behalf. No one has a proper claim on the labour of another, or on the income ensuing from that labour, unless he can repay the labourer in a way acceptable to that labourer himself. Government welfare schemes provide benefits from funds gained largely by taxing earned income. One cannot 'opt out' of such schemes. To the Individualist, this means that a person is forced to work part of his time for others.

Suppose that a man works forty hours and earns two hundred dollars. Under modern-day taxation, it may well be that he can spend only two-thirds of that money as he chooses. The rest is taken by government and goes to support programmes which the working individual may not himself endorse. The beneficiaries of such programmes—those beneficiaries who do not work themselves—are as though they have slaves working for them. Backed by the force which government authorities can command, they are able to exist on the earnings of others. Those who support them do not do so voluntarily, out of charity; they do so on government command.

> Someone across the street is unemployed. Should you be taxed extra to pay for his expenses? Not at all. You have not injured him, you are not responsible for the fact that he is unemployed (unless you are a senator or bureaucrat who agitated for further curtailing of business which legislation passed, with the result that your neighbour was laid off by the curtailed business). You may voluntarily wish to help him out, or better still, try to get him a job to put him on his feet again; but since you have initiated no aggressive act against him, and neither purposefully nor accidentally injured him in any way, you should not be legally penalized for the fact of his unemployment.[4]

The Individualist need not lack concern for those in need. He may give generously to charity; he might give more generously still, if his whole income were his to use, as he would like it to be. He may also believe that, as a matter of empirical fact, existing government programmes do not actually help the poor. They support a cumbersome bureaucracy and they use financial resources which, if untaxed, might be used by those with initiative to pursue job-creating endeavours. The thrust of the Individualist's position is that each person owns his own body and his own labour; thus each person is taken to have a virtually unconditional right to the income which that labour can earn him in a free market place.[5] For anyone to preempt part of a worker's earnings without that worker's voluntary consent is tantamount to robbery. And the fact that the government is the intermediary through which this deed is committed does not change its moral status one iota.

On an Individualist's view, those in need should be cared for by charities or through other schemes to which contributions are voluntary. Many people may wish to insure themselves against unforeseen calamities and they should be free to do so. But there is no justification for non-optional government schemes financed by taxpayers' money. . . .

2. THE PERMISSIVE VIEW

Directly contrary to the Individualist view of welfare is what I have termed the Permissive view. According to this view, in a society which has sufficient resources so that everyone could be supplied with the necessities of life, every individual ought to be given the legal right to social security, and this right ought not to be conditional in any way upon an individual's behaviour. *Ex hypothesi* the society which we are discussing has sufficient goods to provide everyone with food, clothing, shelter and other necessities. Someone who does without these basic goods is scarcely living at all, and a society which takes no steps to change this state of affairs implies by its inaction that the life of such a person is without value. It does not execute him; but it may allow him to die. It does not put him in prison; but it may leave him with a life of lower quality than that of some prison inmates. A society which can rectify these circumstances and does not can justly be accused of imposing upon the needy either death or lifelong deprivation. And those characteristics which make a person needy—whether they be illness, old age, insanity, feeblemindedness, inability to find paid work, or even poor moral character—are insufficient to make him deserve the fate to which an inactive society would in effect condemn him. One would not be executed for inability or failure to find paid work; neither should one be allowed to die for this misfortune or failing.

A person who cannot or does not find his own means of social security does not thereby forfeit his status as a human being. If other human beings, with physical, mental and moral qualities different from his, are regarded as having the right to life and to the means of life, then so too should he be regarded. A society which does not accept the responsibility for supplying such a person with the basic necessities of life is, in effect, endorsing a difference between its members which is without moral justification. . . .

The adoption of a Permissive view of welfare would have significant practical implications. If there were a legal right, unconditional upon behaviour, to a specified level of state-supplied benefits, then state investigation of the prospective welfare recipient could be kept to a minimum. Why he is in need, whether he can work, whether he is willing to work, and what he does while receiving welfare benefits are on this view quite irrelevant to his right to receive those benefits. A welfare recipient is a person who claims from his society that to which he is legally entitled under a morally based welfare scheme. The fact that he makes this claim licenses no special state or societal interference with his behaviour. If the Permissive view of welfare were widely believed, then there would be no social stigma attached to being on welfare. . . .

3. THE PURITAN VIEW

This view of welfare rather naturally emerges when we consider that no one can have a right to something without someone else's, or some group of other persons', having responsibilities correlative to this right. In the case in which the right in question is a legal right to social security, the correlative responsibilities may be rather extensive. They have been deemed responsibilities of 'the state'. The state will require resources and funds to meet these responsibilities, and these do not emerge from the sky miraculously, or zip into existence as a consequence of virtually effortless acts of will. They are taken by the state from its citizens, often in the form of taxation on earned income. The funds given to the welfare recipient and many of the goods which he purchases with these funds are produced by other members of society, many of whom give a considerable portion of their time and their energy to this end. If a state has the moral responsibility to ensure the social security of its citizens then all the citizens of that state have the responsibility to provide state agencies with the means to carry out their duties. This responsibility, in our present contingent circumstances, seems to generate an obligation to *work*.

A person who works helps to produce the goods which all use in daily living and, when paid, contributes through taxation to government endeavours. The person who does not work, even though able to work, does not make his contribution to social efforts towards obtaining the means of life. He is not entitled to a share of the goods produced by others if he chooses not to take part in their labours. Unless he can show that there is a moral justification for his not making the sacrifice of time and energy which others make, he has no legitimate claim to welfare benefits. If he is disabled or unable to obtain work, he cannot work; hence he has no need to justify his failure to work. But if he does choose not to work, he would have to justify his choice by saying 'others should sacrifice their time and energy for me; I have no need to sacrifice time and energy for them'. This principle, a version of what Rawls refers to as a free-rider's principle, simply will not stand up to criticism.[6] To deliberately avoid working and benefit from the labours of others is morally indefensible.

Within a welfare system erected on these principles, the right to welfare is conditional upon one's satisfactorily accounting for his failure to obtain the necessities of life by his own efforts. Someone who is severely disabled mentally or physically, or who for some other reason cannot work, is morally entitled to receive welfare benefits. Someone who chooses not to work is not. The Puritan view of welfare is a kind of compromise between the Individualist view and the Permissive view. . . .

The Puritan view of welfare, based as it is on the inter-relation between welfare and work, provides a rationale for two connected principles. . . . First of all, those on welfare should never receive a higher income than the working poor. Secondly, a welfare scheme should, in some way or other, incorporate incentives to work. These principles, which presuppose that it is better to work than not to work, emerge rather naturally from the contingency which is at the basis of the Puritan view: the goods essential for social security are products of the labour of some members of society. If we wish to have a continued supply of such goods, we must encourage those who work to produce them. . . .

Assessment of These Views

My assessment of the preceding doctrines falls into two main sections. Within each of these there are several subdivisions. The first section deals with difficulties pertaining to certain concepts which are central in the exposition of the Individualist and Puritan views—namely those of responsibility, of ownership of income, and of work. The second section consists of an attempt to appraise the views as social policies, on the basis of their probable consequences and their claims to satisfy the demands of social justice.

A. EXPOSITIONAL DIFFICULTIES

1. Responsibility

The Individualist holds that each person is responsible for the economic situation in which he finds himself, since he is in that situation as a result of previous freely taken decisions of his own. This line of reasoning is most unpromising. First of all, it is at best true of some people some of the time, that they find themselves in economic circumstances as a result of their own previous decisions. And even when this is, in a sense, true, the alternatives among which a person chooses are determined by social, economic and political factors which are by no means amenable to change on the basis of his individual actions. The Individualist wishes to argue from the 'fact' of voluntary choice to the claim that a person must take responsibility for the consequences ensuing from this choice. There does not seem to be any strict logical link here. However, the move has a certain plausibility if we restrict ourselves to considering foreseen or foreseeable consequences of choices. But if this restriction is incorporated into the Individualist's argument, his position loses its applicability to the current economic situation. Our best economists do not seem to be able to foresee what our economic situation will be in one year's time. An ordinary individual can scarcely be expected to foresee the consequences of those of his own decisions whose effects depend heavily upon the state of the economy. He may, for example, embark upon a programme of training for a type of job, only to find himself unemployable when he is trained, because the job has been mechanized or because of changing consumer demands. In this kind of case, the fact that a person chooses the training which he undertakes does not suffice to make him personally responsible for the situation in which he finds himself.

The Individualist bases his account on individual responsibility for individual decisions and his consequences. However people's social and economic fates are linked in many ways, most notably through the institution of the family. If A is married to B, and then this marriage ends, A's situation is a result not solely of prior decisions of his own, but of B's decisions as well. To insist that A and B must have shared all decisions while married is simply unrealistic. The difficulty in applying Individualist thinking to cases where there is family breakdown is more than incidental in the context of welfare benefits, since many of these go to women raising children alone after marital breakdown.

2. Ownership of Earned Income

The Individualist assumes that each person has a virtually unconditional moral right to spend all his earned income as he chooses. In this respect his view contrasts with both the Puritan and the Permissive views. The Puritan will allow taxation of earned income to provide benefits to others, provided the others are not 'free-riders'. The Permissivist sees no moral problem in taxing earned income.

There are many respects in which ownership is limited with reference to the needs and interests of persons other than the owner. If I own a car, this does not mean that I have the right (legal or moral) to do anything I choose with it; there are many limitations, and these are based on the dangers to other people which will result if I use my car in the proscribed ways. Furthermore, the range of what can be privately owned is restricted. I may own a house, or land, but I cannot own all the air above Toronto, so as to be able to charge people for breathing it. It seems unlikely that even a rigorous Individualist would want to dispense with these limitations on private ownership. So long as they are maintained ownership is understood in a way which does not necessarily entail total and unconditional control of property by individual owners. With this understanding of what ownership is, it is both tendentious and disingenuous to insist that taxation to support welfare schemes amounts to 'legalized robbery'.

3. Work

The Puritan view of welfare emphasized the interconnection between welfare and work. Legitimate entitlement to welfare benefits is seen as conditional upon willingness to work (if able), since these benefits come from the work of others. The Puritan places a high value on work and believes that those who do not work fail to make a contribution to society. This articulation of the Puritan view gives rise to many questions about the nature and value of work.

It is surprisingly difficult to give an adequate definition of the term 'work'. In the context of discussions of welfare, work seems to be anything you do which results in your being paid so that the government does not have to support you. But as any housewife will testify not all work is paid work. One Oxford dictionary definition goes as follows: To work is to do something involving effort of body or mind/to exert oneself for a definite purpose, especially in order to produce something or to effect a useful result, or to gain one's livelihood. This definition is so general that it is hard to see how anyone could *fail* to work, in this sense of 'work'.

It is true that most of those on welfare do not work, if by 'work' we mean 'putting forth efforts for pay, in order to gain one's livelihood'. This definition is adequate for the present discussion, but it is important to note that it does not permit the Puritan's conflation of *working* and *contributing to society*. A person who cares for children, who does volunteer work, or who is politically active may contribute to society without earning any money. In a society where there is not full employment, someone who chooses not to work might even be said to make a contribution by doing this. He is content to be

without a job and not all can work: the job he does not take is open to someone who wants it.

It must be admitted that a person can work and yet contribute nothing
to society. Some jobs are of negative social value. They are boring and frustrating to the worker, they use valuable resources, cause pollution, and produce
goods of either negative or neutral social value. (Manufacturing toy pistols out
of scarce petroleum products perhaps satisfies this description.) Anyone who
thinks that it is better for people to work at jobs of this description than for
them not to work at all must be putting a very high value on work as such.
This evaluation would have to be independent of the evaluation of the product, the consequences of doing the work as felt by the workers and the social
consequences of the manufacturing process. To value work *qua* work as highly
as the Puritan does, in cases where there are so many negative factors, seems
downright irrational.

The Puritan view of welfare is based upon the supposition that it is those
who work who contribute to society and that it is always better for an able-
bodied person to work than for him not to work. But, given valuable unpaid
efforts, unemployment and paid work which is of negative value overall, these
assumptions do not hold.

B. APPRAISAL OF POLICIES: SOCIAL
CONSEQUENCES AND SOCIAL JUSTICE

. . . In appraising social polices we have to weigh up considerations of total
well-being against considerations of justice. Just how this is to be done, precisely, I would not pretend to know. However, the absence of precise methods
does not mean that we should relinquish attempts at appraisal: some problems are already with us, and thought which is necessarily tentative and im-
precise is still preferable to no thought at all.

1. Consequences of Welfare Schemes

First, let us consider the consequences of the non-scheme advocated by the
Individualist. He would have us abolish all non-optional government
programmes which have as their goal the improvement of anyone's personal
welfare. This rejection extends to health schemes, pension plans and education, as well as to welfare and unemployment insurance. So following the
Individualist would lead to very sweeping changes.

The Individualist will claim (as do Hospers and Ayn Rand) that on the
whole his non-scheme will bring beneficial consequences. He will admit, as
he must, that there are people who would suffer tremendously if welfare and
other social security programmes were simply terminated. Some would even
die as a result. We cannot assume that spontaneously developing charities
would cover every case of dire need. Nevertheless the Individualist wants to
point to benefits which would accrue to businessmen and to working people

and their families if taxation were drastically cut. It is his claim that consumption would rise, hence production would rise, job opportunities would be extended, and there would be an economic boom, if people could only spend all their earned income as they wished. This boom would benefit both rich and poor.

There are significant omissions which are necessary in order to render the Individualist's optimism plausible. Either workers and businessmen would have insurance of various kinds, or they would be insecure in their prosperity. If they did have insurance to cover health problems, old age and possible job loss, then they would pay for it; hence they would not be spending their whole earned income on consumer goods. Those who run the insurance schemes could, of course, put this money back into the economy—but government schemes already do this. The economic boom under individualism would not be as loud as originally expected. Furthermore the goal of increased consumption-increased productivity must be questioned from an ecological viewpoint: many necessary materials are available only in limited quantities.

Finally, a word about charity. It is not to be expected that those who are at the mercy of charities will benefit from this state, either materially or psychologically. Those who prosper will be able to choose between giving a great deal to charity and suffering from the very real insecurity and guilt which would accompany the existence of starvation and grim poverty outside their padlocked doors. It is to be hoped that they would opt for the first alternative. But, if they did, this might be every bit as expensive for them as government-supported benefit schemes are now. If, they did not give generously to charity, violence might result. However one looks at it, the consequences of Individualism are unlikely to be good.

Welfare schemes operating in Canada today are almost without exception based upon the principles of the Puritan view. To see the consequences of that type of welfare scheme we have only to look at the results of our own welfare programmes. Taxation to support such schemes is high, though not so intolerably so as to have led to widescale resentment among taxpayers. Canadian welfare programmes are attended by complicated and often cumbersome bureaucracy, some of which results from the interlocking of municipal, provincial and federal governments in the administration and financing of welfare programmes. The cost of the programmes is no doubt increased by this bureaucracy; not all the tax money directed to welfare programmes goes to those in need. Puritan welfare schemes do not result in social catastrophe or in significant business stagnation—this much we know, because we already live with such schemes. Their adverse consequences, if any, are felt primarily not by society generally nor by businessmen and the working segment of the public, but rather by recipients of welfare.

. . . Welfare officials have the power to check on welfare recipients and cut off or limit their benefits under a large number of circumstances. The dangers to welfare recipients in terms of anxiety, threats to privacy and loss of dignity are obvious. . . . Concern that a welfare recipient either be unable to work or be willing to work (if unemployed) can easily turn into concern about how he spends the income supplied him, what his plans for the future are, where he lives, how many children he has. And the rationale underlying the Puritan scheme makes the degradation of welfare recipients a natural consequence of welfare institutions. Work is valued and only he who works is thought to contribute to society. Welfare recipients are regarded as parasites and spongers—so when they are treated as such, this is only what we should have expected. Being on welfare in a society which thinks and acts in this fashion can be psychologically debilitating. Welfare recipients who are demoralized by their downgraded status and relative lack of personal freedom can be expected to be made less capable of self-sufficiency. To the extent that this is so, welfare systems erected on Puritan principles may defeat their own purposes.

In fairness, it must be noted here that bureaucratic checks and controls are not a feature only of Puritan welfare systems. To a limited extent, Permissive systems would have to incorporate them too. Within those systems, welfare benefits would be given only to those whose income was inadequate to meet basic needs. However, there would be no checks on 'willingness to work', and there would be no need for welfare workers to evaluate the merits of the daily activities of recipients. If a Permissive guaranteed income system were administered through income tax returns, everyone receiving the basic income and those not needing it paying it back in taxes, then the special status of welfare recipients would fade. They would no longer be singled out as a special group within the population. It is to be expected that living solely on government-supplied benefits would be psychologically easier in that type of situation.

Thus it can be argued that for the recipients of welfare, a Permissive scheme has more advantages than a Puritan one. This is not a very surprising conclusion. The Puritan scheme is relatively disadvantageous to recipients, and Puritans would acknowledge this point; they will argue that the overall consequences of Permissive schemes are negative in that these schemes benefit some at too great a cost to others. (Remember, we are not yet concerned with the *justice* of welfare policies, but solely with their consequences as regards *total* human well-being within the society in question.) The concern which most people have regarding the Permissive scheme relates to its costs and its dangers to the 'work ethic'. It is commonly thought that people work only because they have to work to survive in a tolerable style. If a guaranteed income scheme were adopted by the government, this incentive to work would disappear. No one would be faced with the choice between a nasty and boring job and starvation. Who would do the nasty and boring jobs then? Many of them are not eliminable and they have to be done somehow, by someone. Puritans fear that a great many people—even some with relatively pleasant jobs—might simply cease to work if they could receive non-stigmatized government money to live on. If this were to happen, the permissive society would simply grind to a halt.

In addressing these anxieties about the consequences of Permissive welfare schemes, we must recall that welfare benefits are set to ensure only that those who do not work have a bearable existence, with an income sufficient for basic needs, and that they have this income regardless of why they fail to work. Welfare benefits will not finance luxury living for a family of five! If jobs are adequately paid so that workers receive more than the minimum welfare income in an earned salary, then there will still be a financial incentive to take jobs. What guaranteed income schemes will do is to raise the salary floor. This change will benefit the many non-unionized workers in service and clerical occupations.

Furthermore it is unlikely that people work solely due to (i) the desire for money and the things it can buy and (ii) belief in the Puritan work ethic. There are many other reasons for working, some of which would persist in a society which had adopted a Permissive welfare system. Most people are happier when their time is structured in some way, when they are active outside their own homes, when they feel themselves part of an endeavour whose purposes transcend their particular egoistic ones. Women often choose to work outside the home for these reasons as much as for financial ones. With these and other factors operating I cannot see that the adoption of a Permissive welfare scheme would be followed by a level of slothfulness which would jeopardize human well-being. . .

In summary, we can appraise Individualism, Puritanism and Permissivism with respect to their anticipated consequences, as follows: Individualism is unacceptable; Puritanism is tolerable, but has some undesirable consequences for welfare recipients; Permissivism appears to be the winner. Worries about bad effects which Permissive welfare schemes might have due to high costs and (alleged) reduced work-incentives appear to be without solid basis.

2. Social Justice under Proposed Welfare Schemes

We must now try to consider the merits of Individualism, Puritanism and Permissivism with regard to their impact on the distribution of the goods necessary for well-being. Nozick has argued against the whole conception of a distributive justice on the grounds that it presupposes that goods are like manna from heaven: we simply get them and then have a problem—to whom to give them. According to Nozick we know where things come from and we do not have the problem of to whom to give them. There is not really a problem of distributive justice, for there is no central distributor giving out manna from heaven! It is necessary to counter Nozick on this point since his reaction to the (purported) problems of distributive justice would undercut much of what follows.

There is a level at which Nozick's point is obviously valid. If A discovers a cure for cancer, then it is A and not B or C who is responsible for this discovery. On Nozick's view this is taken to imply that A should reap any monetary profits which are forthcoming; other people will benefit from the cure itself. Now although it cannot be doubted that A is a bright and hard-working person, neither can it be denied that A and his circumstances are the product of many co-operative endeavours: schools and laboratories, for instance. Because this is so, I find Nozick's claim that 'we know where things come from' unconvincing at a deeper level. Since achievements like A's presuppose extensive social co-operation, it is morally permissible to regard even the monetary profits accruing from them as shareable by the 'owner' and society at large.

Laws support existing income levels in many ways. Governments specify taxation so as to further determine net income. Property ownership is a legal matter. In all these ways people's incomes and possibilities for obtaining income are affected by deliberate state action. It is always possible to raise questions about the moral desirability of actual conventional arrangements. Should university professors earn less than lawyers? More than waitresses? Why? Why not? Anyone who gives an account of distributive justice is trying to specify principles which will make it possible to answer questions such as these, and nothing in Nozick's argument suffices to show that the questions are meaningless or unimportant.

Any human distribution of anything is unjust insofar as differences exist for no good reason. If goods did come like manna from heaven and the Central Distributor gave A ten times more than B, we should want to know why. The skewed distribution might be deemed a just one if A's needs were objectively ten times greater than B's, or if B refused to accept more than his small portion of goods. But if no reason at all could be given for it, or if only an irrelevant reason could be given (e.g., A is blue-eyed and B is not), then it is an unjust distribution. All the views we have expounded concerning welfare permit differences in income level. Some philosophers would say that such differences are never just, although they may be necessary, for historical or utilitarian reasons. Whether or not this is so, it is admittedly very difficult to say just what would constitute a good reason for giving A a higher income than B. Level of need, degree of responsibility, amount of training, unpleasant-ness of work—all these have been proposed and all have some plausibility. We do not need to tackle all this larger problem in order to consider justice under proposed welfare systems. For we can deal here solely with the question of whether everyone should receive a floor level of income; decisions on this matter are independent of decisions on overall equality or principles of variation among incomes above the floor. The Permissivist contends that all should receive at least the floor income; the Individualist and the Puritan deny this. All would claim justice for their side.

The Individualist attempts to justify extreme variations in income, with some people below the level where they can fulfil their basic needs, with reference to the fact of people's actual accomplishments. This approach to the question is open to the same objections as those which have already been raised against Nozick's non-manna-from-heaven argument, and I shall not repeat them here. Let us move on to the Puritan account. It is because goods emerge from human efforts that the Puritan advances his view of welfare. He stresses the unfairness of a system which would permit some people to take advantage of others. A Permissive welfare system would do this, as it makes no attempt to distinguish between those who choose not to work and those who cannot work. No one should be able to take advantage of another under the auspices of a government institution. The Puritan scheme seeks to eliminate this possibility, and for that reason, Puritans would allege, it is a more just scheme than the Permissive one.

Permissivists can best reply to this contention by acknowledging that any instance of free-riding would be an instance where those working were done an injustice, but by showing that any justice which the Puritan preserves by eliminating free-riding is outweighed by *injustice* perpetrated elsewhere. Consider the children of the Puritan's free-riders. They will suffer greatly for the 'sins' of their parents. Within the institution of the family, the Puritan cannot suitably hurt the guilty without cruelly depriving the innocent. There is a sense, too, in which Puritanism does injustice to the many people on welfare who are not free-riders. It perpetuates the opinion that they are non-contributors to society and this doctrine, which is over-simplified if not downright false, has a harmful effect upon welfare recipients.

Social justice is not simply a matter of the distribution of goods, or the income with which goods are to be purchased. It is also a matter of the protection of rights. Western societies claim to give their citizens equal rights in political and legal contexts; they also claim to endorse the larger conception of a right to life. Now it is possible to interpret these rights in a limited and formalistic way, so that the duties correlative to them are minimal. On the limited, or negative, interpretation, to say that A has a right to life is simply to say that others have a duty not to interfere with A's attempts to keep himself alive. This interpretation of the right to life is compatible with Individualism as well as with Puritanism. But it is an inadequate interpretation of the right to life and of other rights. A right to vote is meaningless if one is starving and unable to get to the polls; a right to equality before the law is meaningless if one cannot afford to hire a lawyer. And so on.

Even a Permissive welfare scheme will go only a very small way towards protecting people's rights. It will amount to a meaningful acknowledgement of a right to life, by ensuring income adequate to purchase food, clothing and shelter—at the very least. These minimum necessities are presupposed by all other rights a society may endorse in that their possession is a precondition of being able to exercise these other rights. Because it protects the rights of all within a society better than do Puritanism and Individualism, the Permissive view can rightly claim superiority over the others with regard to justice.

NOTES

1. Nicholas Rescher, *Welfare: Social Issues in Philosophical Perspective,* p. 114.

2. One might wish to discuss moral questions concerning welfare in the context of natural rights doctrines. Indeed, Article 22 of the United Nations Declaration of Human Rights states, 'Everyone, as a member of society, has the right to social security and is entitled, through national effort and international cooperation and in accordance with the organization and resources of each State, to the economic, social and cultural rights indispensable for his dignity and the free development of his personality'. I make no attempt to defend the right to welfare as a natural right. Granting that rights imply responsibilities or duties and that 'ought' implies 'can', it would only be intelligible to regard the right to social security as a natural right if all states were able to ensure the minimum well-being of their citizens. This is not the case. And a natural right is one which is by definition supposed to belong to all human beings simply in virtue of their status as human beings. The analysis given here in the permissive view is compatible with the claim that all human beings have a *prima facie* natural right to social security. It is not, however, compatible with the claim that all human beings have a natural right to social security if this right is regarded as one which is so absolute as to be inviolable under any and all conditions.

3. See, for example, Ayn Rand's *Atlas Shrugged, The Virtue of Selfishness,* and *Capitalism: the Unknown Ideal.*

4. John Hospers, *Libertarianism: A Political Philosophy for Tomorrow,* p. 67.

5. I say virtually unconditional, because an Individualist such as John Hospers sees a legitimate moral role for government in preventing the use of force by some citizens against others. Since this is the case, I presume that he would also regard as legitimate such taxation as was necessary to support this function. Presumably that taxation would be seen as consented to by all, on the grounds that all 'really want' government protection.

6. See *A Theory of Justice,* pp. 124, 136. Rawls defines the free-rider as one who relies on the principle 'everyone is to act justly except for myself, if I choose not to', and says that his position is a version of egoism which is eliminated as a morally acceptable principle by formal constraints. This conclusion regarding the tenability of egoism is one which I accept and which is taken for granted in the present context.

Women, Welfare, and the
Politics of Need Interpretation
Nancy Fraser

Nancy Fraser is a professor of political science at The New School for Social Research. In this essay, selected from her book *Unruly Practices: Power, Discourse, and Gender in Contemporary Social Theory*, Fraser develops an understanding of welfare from a feminist point of view. First she points out that the programs usually considered to be welfare programs (e.g., AFDC, food stamps, and Medicaid) serve women both directly and indirectly more than they do men. Hence, if welfare "reform" reduces the benefits provided by these programs, women will be the primary losers. Nonetheless, even retention of the current welfare programs would tend to oppress women because of the way in which they understand the needs of women. Of particular interest is Fraser's analysis of the differences between government programs, such as unemployment insurance, that traditionally have primarily assisted men and programs that traditionally have primarily assisted women. An important difference, she argues, is the way in which beneficiaries of "masculine" programs are portrayed as bearers of rights, while beneficiaries of "feminine" programs have been portrayed as recipients of public charity.

What some writers are calling "the coming welfare wars" will be largely wars about, even against, women. Because women constitute the overwhelming majority of social-welfare program recipients and employees, women and women's needs will be the principal stakes in the battles over social spending likely to dominate national politics in the coming period. Moreover, the welfare wars will not be limited to the tenure of Reagan or even of Reaganism. On the contrary, they will be protracted, both in time and in space. What James O'Connor theorized over fifteen years ago as "the fiscal crisis of the state" is a long-term, structural phenomenon of international proportions.[1] Not just the United States but every late capitalist welfare state in Western Europe and North America is facing some version of it. And the fiscal crisis of the welfare state coincides everywhere with a second long-term structural tendency: the feminization of poverty. This is Diana Pearce's term for the rapidly increasing proportion of women in the adult poverty population, an increase tied to, among other things, the rise in "female-headed households."[2] In the U.S. this increase is so pronounced and so steep that analysts project that should it continue, the poverty population will consist entirely of women and their children before the year 2000.[3]

This conjunction of the fiscal crisis of the state and the feminization of poverty suggests that struggles around social welfare will and should become

From *Unruly Practices: Power, Discourse, and Gender in Contemporary Social Theory* by Nancy Fraser (Minneapolis: University of Minnesota Press, 1989), pp. 144–160.

increasingly focal for feminists. But such struggles raise a great many problems, some of which can be thought of as structural. To take one example, increasing numbers of women depend directly for their livelihoods on social-welfare programs; and many other women benefit indirectly, since the existence of even a minimal and inadequate "safety net" increases the leverage of women who are economically dependent on individual men. Thus, feminists have no choice but to oppose social-welfare cuts. However, economists like Pearce, Nancy Barrett, and Steven Erie, Martin Rein, and Barbara Wiget have shown that programs like Aid to Families with Dependent Children actually institutionalize the feminization of poverty.[4] The benefits they provide are system-conforming ones that reinforce rather than challenge basic structural inequalities. Thus, feminists cannot simply support existing social-welfare programs. To use the suggestive but ultimately too simple terms popularized by Carol Brown: If to eliminate or to reduce welfare is to bolster "private patriarchy," then simply to defend it is to consolidate "public patriarchy."[5]

Feminists also face a second set of problems in the coming welfare wars. These problems, seemingly more ideological and less structural than the first set, arise from the typical way in which issues get framed, given the institutional dynamics of the political system.[6] Typically, social-welfare issues are posed like this: Shall the state undertake to satisfy the social needs of a given constituency, and if so, to what degree? Now, this way of framing issues permits only a relatively small number of answers, and it tends to cast debates in quantitative terms. More importantly, it takes for granted the definition of the needs in question, as if that were self-evident and beyond dispute. It therefore occludes the fact that the interpretation of people's needs is itself a political stake, indeed sometimes *the* political stake. Clearly, this way of framing issues poses obstacles for feminist politics, since at the heart of such politics lie questions about what various groups of women really need and whose interpretations of women's needs should be authoritative. Only in terms of a discourse oriented to the *politics of need interpretation*[7] can feminists meaningfully intervene in the coming welfare wars. But this requires a challenge to the dominant policy framework.

Both sets of problems, the structural and the ideological, are extremely important and difficult. In what follows, I shall not offer solutions to either of them. Rather, I want to attempt the much more modest and preliminary task of exploring how they might be thought about in relation to one another. Specifically, I want to propose a framework for inquiry that can shed light on both of them simultaneously.

Consider that in order to address the structural problem it will be necessary to clarify the phenomenon of "public patriarchy." One type of inquiry that is useful here is the familiar sort of economic analysis alluded to earlier, analysis that shows, for example, that "workfare" programs function to subsidize employers of low-wage "women's work" in the service sector and thus to reproduce the sex-segmented, dual labor market. Now, important as such inquiry is, it does not tell the whole story, since it leaves out of focus the discursive or ideological dimension of social-welfare programs. By the discursive or ideological dimension, I do not mean anything distinct from, or epiphenomenal to, welfare practices; I mean, rather, the tacit norms and implicit assumptions that are constitutive of those practices. To get at this dimension requires a meaning-oriented sort of inquiry, one that considers welfare programs as, among other things, institutionalized patterns of interpretation.[8] Such inquiry would make explicit the social meanings embedded within welfare programs, meanings that tend otherwise simply to go without saying.

In spelling out such meanings, the inquiry I am proposing could do two things simultaneously. First, it could tell us something important about the structure of the U.S. welfare system, since it might identify some underlying norms and assumptions that lend a measure of coherence to diverse programs and practices. Second, it could illuminate what I called "the politics of need interpretation," since it could expose the processes by which welfare practices construct women and women's needs according to certain specific—and, in principle, contestable—interpretations even as they lend those interpretations an aura of facticity that discourages contestation. Thus, this inquiry could shed light on both the structural and ideological problems identified earlier.

The principal aim of this paper is to provide an account of this sort for the present U.S. social-welfare system. The account is intended to help clarify some key structural aspects of male dominance in late capitalist welfare state societies. At the same time, it is meant to point the way to a broader, discourse-oriented focus that can address political conflicts over the interpretation of women's needs.

The paper proceeds from some relatively "hard," uncontroversial facts about the U.S. social-welfare system (section 1) through a series of increasingly interpreted accounts of that system (sections 2 and 3). These culminate (in section 4) in a highly theorized characterization of the welfare system as a "juridical-administrative-therapeutic state apparatus." Finally, (in section 5) the paper situates that apparatus as one force among others in a larger and highly contested political field of discourse about needs that also includes the feminist movement.

1

Long before the emergence of welfare states, governments have defined legally secured arenas of societal action. In so doing, they have at the same time codified corresponding patterns of agency or social roles. Thus, early modern states defined an economic arena and the corresponding role of an economic person capable of entering into contracts. More or less at the same time, they codified the "private sphere" of the household and the role of head of the household. Somewhat later, governments were led to secure a sphere of political participation and the corresponding role of citizen with (limited) political rights. In each of these cases, the original and paradigmatic subject of the newly codified social role was male. Only secondarily, and much later, was it conceded that women, too, could occupy these subject-positions, without, however, entirely dispelling the association with masculinity.

Matters are different, however, with the contemporary welfare state. When this type of government defined a new arena of activity—call it "the social"— and a new societal role—the welfare client—it included women among its original and paradigmatic subjects. Today, in fact, women have become the principal subjects of the welfare state. On the one hand, they make up the overwhelming majority both of program recipients and of paid social-service workers. On the other hand, they are the wives, mothers, and daughters whose unpaid activities and obligations are redefined as the welfare state increasingly oversees forms of caregiving. Since this beneficiary/social worker/caregiver nexus of roles is constitutive of the social-welfare arena, one might even call this arena a feminized terrain.

A brief statistical overview confirms women's greater involvement with and dependence on the U.S. social-welfare system. Consider, first, women's greater dependence as program clients and beneficiaries. In each of the major "means-tested" programs in the U.S., women and the children for whom they are responsible now comprise the overwhelming majority of clients. For example, more than 81 percent of households receiving Aid to Families with Dependent Children (AFDC) are headed by women, more than 60 percent of families receiving food stamps or Medicaid are headed by women, and 70 percent of all households in publicly owned or subsidized housing are headed by women.[9] High as they are, these figures actually underestimate the representation of women. As Barbara Nelson notes, in the androcentric reporting system, households counted as female-headed contain by definition no healthy adult men.[10] But healthy adult women live in most households counted as male-headed. Such women may directly or indirectly receive benefits going to "male-headed" households, but they are invisible in the statistics, even though they usually do the work of securing and maintaining program eligibility.

Women also predominate in the major U.S. "age-tested" programs. For example, 61.6 percent of all adult beneficiaries of Social Security are women, and 64 percent of those covered by Medicare are women.[11] In sum, because women as a group are significantly poorer than men—indeed, women now compose nearly two-thirds of all U.S. adults below the official poverty line— and because women tend to live longer than men, women depend more on the social-welfare system as clients and beneficiaries.

But this is not the whole story. Women also depend more on the social-welfare system as paid human-service workers—a category of employment that includes education and health as well as social work and services administration. In 1980, 70 percent of the 17.3 million paid jobs in this sector in the U.S. were held by women. This accounts for one-third of U.S. women's total paid employment and a full 80 percent of all professional jobs held by women. The figures for women of color are even higher than this average, since 37 percent of their total paid employment and 82.4 percent of their professional employment is in this sector.[12] It is a distinctive feature of the U.S. social-welfare system—as opposed to, say, the British and Scandinavian systems—that only 3 percent of these jobs are in the form of direct federal government employment. The rest are in state and local government, in the "private non-profit" sector, and in the "private" sector. However, the more decentralized and privatized character of the U.S. system does not make paid welfare workers any less vulnerable in the face of federal program cuts. On the contrary, the level of federal social-welfare spending affects the level of human-service employment in *all* sectors. State and local government jobs depend on federal and federally financed state and local government contracts, and private profit and nonprofit jobs depend on federally financed transfer payments to individuals and households for the purchase in the market of services like health care.[13] Thus, reductions in social spending mean the loss of jobs for women. Moreover, as Barbara Ehrenreich and Frances Fox Piven note, this loss is not compensated when spending is shifted to the military, since only one-half of 1 percent of the entire female paid workforce is employed in work on military contracts. In fact, one study they cite estimates that with each one-billion-dollar increase in military spending, ninety-five hundred jobs are lost to women.[14]

Finally, women are subjects of and subject to the social-welfare system in their traditional capacity as unpaid caregivers. It is well known that the sexual division of labor assigns women primary responsibility for the care of those who cannot care for themselves. (I leave aside women's traditional obligations to provide personal services to adult males—husbands, fathers, grown sons, lovers—who can very well care for themselves.) Such responsibility includes child care, of course, but also care for sick and/or elderly relatives, often parents. For example, a British study conducted in 1975 and cited by Hilary Land found that three times as many elderly people live with married daughters as with married sons and that those without a close female relative were more likely to be institutionalized, irrespective of degree of infirmity.[15] Thus, as unpaid caregivers, women are more directly affected than men by the level and character of government social services for children, the sick, and the elderly.

As clients, paid human-service workers and unpaid caregivers, then, women are the principal subjects of the social-welfare system. It is as if this branch of the state were in effect a Bureau of Women's Affairs.

2

Of course, the welfare system does not deal with women on women's terms. On the contrary, it has its own characteristic ways of interpreting women's needs and positioning women as subjects. In order to understand these, we need to examine how gender norms and meanings are encoded in the structure of the U.S. social-welfare system.

This issue is quite complicated. On the one hand, nearly all U.S. social-welfare programs are officially gender-neutral. Nevertheless, the system as a whole is a dual or two-tiered one, and it has an unmistakable gender subtext.[16] One set of programs is oriented to *individuals* and tied to participation in the paid work force—for example, unemployment insurance and Social Security. This set of programs is designed to supplement and compensate for the primary market in paid labor power. A second set of programs is oriented to *households* and tied to combined household income—for example, AFDC, food stamps, and Medicaid. This set of programs is designed to compensate for what are considered to be family failures, in particular the absence of a male breadwinner.

What integrates the two sets of programs is a common core of assumptions concerning the sexual division of labor, domestic and nondomestic. It is assumed that families do or should contain one primary breadwinner who is male and one unpaid domestic worker (homemaker and mother) who is female. It is further assumed that when a woman undertakes paid work outside the home, this is or should be in order to supplement the male breadwinner's wage and neither does nor should override her primary housewifely and maternal responsibilities. It is assumed, in other words, that society is divided into two separate spheres of home and outside work and that these are women's and men's spheres, respectively.[17]

These assumptions are increasingly counterfactual. At present, fewer than 15 percent of U.S. families conform to the normative ideal of a domicile shared by a husband who is the sole breadwinner, a wife who is a full-time homemaker, and their offspring. Nonetheless, the "separate spheres" norms determine the structure of the social-welfare system. They determine that it contain one subsystem related to the primary labor market and another subsystem related to the family or household. Moreover, they determine that these subsystems be gender-linked, that the primary-labor-market-related system be implicitly "masculine" and the family-related system be implicitly "feminine." Consequently, the normative, ideal-typical recipient of primary-labor-market-oriented programs is a (white) male, whereas the normative, ideal-typical adult client of household-based programs is a female.

This gender subtext of the U.S. welfare system is confirmed when we take a second look at participation figures. Consider again the figures just cited for the "feminine" or family-based programs, which I referred to earlier as "means tested" programs: more than 81 percent of households receiving AFDC are female-headed, as are more than 70 percent of those receiving housing assistance and more than 60 percent of those receiving Medicaid and food stamps. Now recall that these figures do not compare female *individuals* with male *individuals* but, rather, female-headed *households* with male-headed *households*. They therefore confirm four things: (1) these programs have a distinctive administrative identity in that their recipients are not individualized but *familialized;* (2) they serve what are considered to be defective families, overwhelmingly families without a male breadwinner; (3) the ideal-typical (adult) client is female; and (4) she makes her claim for benefits on the basis of her status as an unpaid domestic worker, a homemaker, and mother, not as a paid worker based in the labor market.

Now, contrast this with the case of a typical labor-market-based and thus "masculine" program, namely, unemployment insurance. Here the percentage of female claimants drops to 38 percent, a figure that contrasts female and male *individuals,* as opposed to female-headed and male-headed households. As Diana Pearce notes, this drop reflects at least two different circumstances.[18] First, and most straightforwardly, it reflects women's lower rate of participation in the paid work force. Second, it reflects the fact that many women wageworkers are not eligible to participate in this program, for example, paid household service workers, part-time workers, pregnant workers, and workers in the "irregular economy" such as prostitutes, baby-sitters, and home typists. The exclusion of these female wageworkers testifies to the existence of a gender-segmented labor market, divided into "primary" and "secondary" employment. It reflects the more general assumption that women's earnings are "merely supplementary," not on a par with those of the primary (male) breadwinner. Altogether, then, the figures tell us four things about programs like unemployment insurance: (1) they are administered in a way that *individualizes* rather than familializes recipients; (2) they are designed to compensate primary-labor-market effects, such as the temporary displacement of a primary breadwinner; (3) the ideal-typical recipient is male; and (4) he makes his claim on the basis of his identity as a paid worker, not as an unpaid domestic worker or parent. . . .

3

So far, I have established the dualistic structure of the U.S. social-welfare system and the gender subtext of that dualism. Now I can better tease out the system's implicit norms and tacit assumptions by examining its mode of operation. To see how welfare programs interpret women's needs, we must consider what benefits consist in. To see how programs position women as subjects, we need to examine administrative practices. In general, we shall see that the "masculine" and "feminine" subsystems are not only separate but also unequal.

Consider that the "masculine" social-welfare programs are social insurance schemes. They include unemployment insurance, Social Security (retirement insurance), Medicare (age-tested health insurance), and Supplemental Social Security Insurance (disability insurance for those with paid work records). These programs are contributory (wageworkers and their employers pay into trust funds), they are administered on a national basis, and benefit levels are uniform across the country. Though bureaucratically organized and administered, they require less, and less demeaning, effort on the part of beneficiaries in qualifying and maintaining eligibility than do "feminine" programs. They are far less subject to intrusive controls and in most cases lack the dimension of surveillance. They also tend to require less of beneficiaries in the way of actual efforts to collect their benefits, with the notable exception of unemployment insurance.

In sum, "masculine" social insurance schemes position recipients primarily as *rights-bearers*. The beneficiaries of these programs are in the main not stigmatized. Neither administrative practice nor popular discourse constitutes them as "on the dole." They are constituted rather as receiving what they deserve; what they, in "partnership" with their employers, have already "paid in" for; what they, therefore, have a *right* to. Moreover, these beneficiaries are also positioned as *purchasing consumers.* They often receive cash as opposed to "in kind" benefits and so are positioned as having "the liberty to strike the best bargain they can in purchasing services of their choice on the open market." In sum, these beneficiaries are what C. B. MacPherson calls "possessive individuals."[19] Proprietors of their own persons who have freely contracted to sell their labor power, they become participants in social insurance schemes and, thence, paying consumers of human services. They therefore qualify as *social citizens* in virtually the fullest sense that term can acquire within the framework of a male-dominated, capitalist society.

All this stands in stark contrast to the "feminine" sector of the U.S. social-welfare system. This sector consists in relief programs, such as AFDC, food stamps, Medicaid, and public-housing assistance. These programs are not contributory but are financed out of general tax revenues (usually with one-third of the funds coming from the federal government and two-thirds coming from the states); and they are not administered federally but rather by the states. As a result, benefit levels vary dramatically, though they are everywhere inadequate, deliberately pegged below the official poverty line. The relief programs are notorious for the varieties of administrative humiliation they inflict upon clients. They require considerable work in qualifying and maintaining eligibility, and they have a heavy component of surveillance.

These programs do not in any meaningful sense position their subjects as rights-bearers. Far from being considered as having a right to what they receive, recipients are defined as "beneficiaries of governmental largess" or "clients of public charity."[20] Moreover, their actual treatment fails to live up to even that definition, since they are treated as "chiselers," "deviants," and "human failures." In the androcentric administrative framework, "welfare mothers" are considered not to work and so are sometimes required—that is to say, coerced—to "work off" their benefits via "workfare." They thus become inmates of what Diana Pearce calls a "workhouse without walls."[21] Indeed, the only sense in which the category of rights is relevant to these clients' situation is the somewhat dubious one according to which they are entitled to treatment governed by the standards of formal bureaucratic procedural rationality. But if that right is construed as protection from administrative caprice, then even it is widely and routinely disregarded.

Moreover, recipients of public relief are generally not positioned as purchasing consumers. A significant portion of their benefits is "in kind," and what cash they receive comes already carved up and earmarked for specific, administratively designated purposes. These recipients are therefore essentially *clients,* a subject-position that carries far less power and dignity in capitalist societies than does the alternative position of purchaser. In these societies, to be a client (in the sense relevant to relief recipients) is to be an abject dependent. Indeed, this sense of the term carries connotations of a fall from autonomy, as when we speak, for example of "the client states of empires or superpowers." As clients, then, recipients of relief are *the negatives of possessive individuals.* Largely excluded from the market both as workers and as consumers, claiming benefits not as individuals but as members of "failed" families, these recipients are effectively denied the trappings of social citizenship as it is defined within male-dominated, capitalist societies.[22]

Clearly, this system creates a double bind for women raising children without a male breadwinner. By failing to offer these women day care for their children, job training, a job that pays a "family wage;" or some combination of these, it constructs them exclusively as mothers. As a consequence, it interprets their needs as maternal needs and their sphere of activity as that of "the family." Now, according to the ideology of separate spheres, this should be an honored social identity. Yet the system does not honor these women. On the contrary, instead of providing them a guaranteed income equivalent to a family wage as a matter of right, it stigmatizes, humiliates, and harasses them. In effect, it decrees simultaneously that these women must be and yet cannot be normative mothers.

Moreover, the way in which the U.S. social-welfare system interprets "maternity" and "the family" is both race-specific and culture-specific. The bias is made plain in Carol Stack's study, *All Our Kin.*[23] Stack analyzes domestic arrangements of very poor black welfare recipients in a midwestern city. Where conservative ideologues see the "disorganization of *the* black family," she finds complex, highly organized kinship structures. These include kin-based networks of resource pooling and exchange, which enable those in direst poverty to survive economically and communally. The networks organize delayed exchanges or "gifts," in Mauss's sense,[24] of prepared meals, food stamps, cooking, shopping, groceries, furniture, sleeping space, cash (including wages and AFDC allowances), transportation, clothing, child care, even children. They span several physically distinct households and so transcend the principal administrative category that organizes relief programs. It is significant that Stack took great pains to conceal the identities of her subjects, even going so far as to disguise the identity of their city. The reason, though unstated, is obvious: these people would lose their benefits if program administrators learned that they did not utilize them within the confines and boundaries of a "household."

We can summarize the separate and unequal character of the two-tiered, gender-linked, race- and culture-biased U.S. social-welfare system in the following formulas: Participants in the "masculine" subsystem are positioned as *rights-bearing beneficiaries* and *purchasing consumers of services,* thus as *possessive individuals.* Participants in the "feminine" subsystem, on the other hand, are positioned as *dependent clients,* or *the negatives of possessive individuals.*

4

Clearly, the identities and needs that the social-welfare system fashions for its recipients are *interpreted* identities and needs. Moreover, they are highly political interpretations and, as such, are in principle subject to dispute. Yet these needs and identities are not always recognized as interpretations. Too often, they simply go without saying and are rendered immune from analysis and critique. Doubtless one reason for this "reification effect" is the depth at which gender meanings and norms are embedded in our general culture. But there may also be another reason more specific to the welfare system.

Let me suggest yet another way of analyzing the U.S. social-welfare system, this time as a "juridical-administrative-therapeutic state apparatus" (JAT).[25] The point is to emphasize a distinctive style of operation. Qua JAT, the welfare system works by linking together a series of juridical, administrative, and therapeutic procedures. As a consequence, it tends to translate political issues concerning the interpretation of people's needs into legal, administrative, and/or therapeutic matters. Thus, the system executes political policy in a way that appears nonpolitical and tends to be depoliticizing.

Considered abstractly, the subject-positions constructed for beneficiaries of *both* the "masculine" and the "feminine" components of the system can be analyzed as combinations of three distinct elements. The first element is a *juridical* one, which positions recipients vis-à-vis the legal system by according or denying them various *rights.* Thus, the subject of the "masculine" sub-system has a right to benefits and is protected from some legally sanctioned forms of administrative caprice, whereas the subject of the "feminine" sub-system largely lacks rights.

This juridical element is then linked with a second one, an *administrative* element. In order to qualify to receive benefits, subjects must assume the stance of petitioners with respect to an administrative body; they must petition a bureaucratic institution empowered to decide their claims on the basis of administratively defined criteria. In the "masculine" subsystem, for example, claimants must prove their "cases" meet administratively defined criteria of entitlement; in the "feminine" subsystem, on the other hand, claimants must prove conformity to administratively defined criteria of need. The enormous qualitative differences between the two sets of procedures notwithstanding, both are variations on the same administrative moment. Both require claimants to translate their experienced situations and life problems into administrable needs, to present their predicaments as bona fide instances of specified generalized states of affairs that could in principle befall anyone.[26]

If and when they qualify, social-welfare claimants get positioned either as purchasing consumers or dependent clients. In either case, their needs are redefined as correlates of bureaucratically administered satisfactions. This means they are quantified, rendered as equivalents of a sum of money.[27] Thus, in the "feminine" subsystem, clients are positioned passively to receive monetarily measured, predefined, and prepackaged services; in the "masculine" subsystem, on the other hand, beneficiaries receive a specified, predetermined amount of cash.

In both subsystems, then, people's needs are subject to a sort of rewriting operation. Experienced situations and life problems are translated into administrable needs; and since the latter are not necessarily isomorphic to the former, the possibility of a gap between them arises. This possibility is especially likely in the "feminine" subsystem, for there, as we saw, clients are constructed as deviant, and service provision has the character of normalization—albeit normalization designed more to stigmatize than to "reform."

Here, then, is the opening for the third, *therapeutic,* moment of the JAT's modus operandi. Especially in the "feminine" subsystem, service provision often includes an implicit or explicit therapeutic or quasi-therapeutic dimension. In AFDC, for example, social workers concern themselves with the "mental health" aspects of their clients' lives, often construing these in terms of "character problems." More explicitly and less moralistically, municipal programs for poor unmarried pregnant teenage women include not only prenatal care, mothering instruction, and tutoring or schooling but also counseling sessions with psychiatric social workers. As observed by Prudence Rains, such sessions are intended to bring girls to acknowledge what are considered to be their true, deep, latent, emotional problems, on the assumption that this will enable them to avoid future pregnancies.[28] Ludicrous as this sounds, it is only an extreme example of a more pervasive phenomenon, namely, the tendency of especially "feminine" social-welfare programs to construct gender-political and political-economic problems as individual, psychological problems. In fact, some therapeutic or quasi-therapeutic welfare services can be regarded as second-order services to compensate for the debilitating effects of first-order services. In any case, the therapeutic dimension of the U.S. social-welfare system encourages clients to close gaps between their culturally shaped lived experience and their administratively defined situation by bringing the former into line with the latter.

Clearly, this analysis of the U.S. welfare system as a "juridical-administrative-therapeutic state apparatus" lets us see both "feminine" and "masculine" subsystems more critically. It suggests that the problem is not only that women are disempowered by the *denial* of social citizenship in the "feminine" subsystem—although they are—but also that women and men are disempowered by the *realization* of an androcentric, possessive individualist form of social citizenship in the "masculine" subsystem. In both subsystems, even the "masculine" one, the JAT positions its subjects in ways that do not empower them. It personalizes them as "cases" and so militates against their collective identification. It imposes monological, administrative definitions of situation and need and so preempts dialogically achieved self-definition and self-determination. It positions its subjects as passive clients or consumer recipients and not as active co-participants involved in shaping their life conditions. Lastly, it construes experienced discontent with these arrangements as material for adjustment-oriented, usually sexist therapy and not as material for empowering processes of consciousness-raising.

All told, then, the form of social citizenship constructed even in the *best* part of the U.S. social-welfare system is a degraded and depoliticized one. It is a form of passive citizenship in which the state preempts the power to define and satisfy people's needs. This form of passive citizenship arises in part as a result of the JAT's distinctive style of operation. The JAT treats the interpretation of people's needs as pregiven and unproblematic, while itself redefining them as amenable to system-conforming satisfactions. Thus, the JAT shifts attention away from the question, Who interprets social needs and how? It tends to substitute the *juridical, administrative, and therapeutic management of need satisfaction* for the *politics of need interpretation.* That is, it tends to substitute *monological, administrative processes of need definition* for *dialogical, participatory processes of need interpretation.*[29]

5

Usually, analyses of social complexes as "institutionalized patterns of interpretation" are implicitly or explicitly functionalist. They purport to show how culturally hegemonic systems of meaning are stabilized and reproduced over time. As a result, such analyses often screen out "dysfunctional" events like micro- and macro-political resistances and conflicts. More generally, they tend to obscure the active side of social processes, the ways in which even the most routinized practice of social agents involves the active construction, deconstruction, and reconstruction of social meanings. It is no wonder, then, that many feminist scholars have become suspicious of functionalist methodologies, for when applied to gender issues, these methods occult female agency and construe women as mere passive victims of male dominance.

In order to avoid any such suggestion here, I want to conclude by situating the foregoing analysis in a broader, nonfunctionalist perspective. I want to sketch a picture according to which the social-welfare apparatus is one force among others in a larger and highly contested political arena.

Consider that the ideological (as opposed to economic) effects of the JAT's mode of need interpretation operate within a specific and relatively new societal arena. I call this arena "the social" in order to mark its noncoincidence with the familiar institutionalized spaces of family and official economy. As I conceive it, the social is not exactly equivalent to the traditional public sphere of political discourse defined by Jürgen Habermas,[30] nor is it coextensive with the state. Rather, the social is a site of discourse about people's needs, specifically about those needs that have broken out of the domestic and/or official economic spheres that earlier contained them as "private matters." Thus, the social is a site of discourse about problematic needs, needs that have come to exceed the apparently (but not really) self-regulating domestic and official economic institutions of male-dominated, capitalist societies.[31]

As the site of this excess, the social is by definition a terrain of contestation. It is a space in which conflicts among rival interpretations of people's needs are played out. "In" the social, then, one would expect to find a plurality of competing ways of talking about needs. And, in fact, what we do find here are at least three major kinds: (1) "expert" needs discourses of, for example, social workers and therapists, on the one hand, and welfare administrators, planners, and policy makers, on the other, (2) oppositional movement needs discourses of, for example, feminists, lesbians and gays, people of color, workers, and welfare clients, and (3) "reprivatization" discourses of constituencies seeking to repatriate newly problematized needs to their former domestic or official economic enclaves. Such discourses, and others, compete with one another in addressing the fractured social identities of potential adherents.

Seen from this vantage point, the social has a twofold character. It is simultaneously a new arena of state activity and, equally important, a new terrain of wider political contestation. It is both the home turf of the JAT and a field of struggle on which the JAT acts as simply one contestant among others. It would be a mistake, then, to treat the JAT as the undisputed master of the terrain of the social. In fact, much of the growth and activity of the social branch of the state has come in response to the activities of social movements, especially the labor, black, feminist, and Progressive movements. Moreover, as Theda Skocpol has shown, the social state is not simply a unified, self-possessed political agent.[32] It is, rather, in significant respects a resultant, a complex and polyvalent nexus of compromise formations in which are sedimented the outcomes of past struggles as well as the conditions for present and future ones. In fact, even when the JAT does act as an agent, the results are often unintended. When it takes responsibility for matters previously left to the family and/or the official economy it tends to denaturalize those matters and thus risks fostering their further politicization.

In any case, social movements, too, act on the terrain of the social (as do, on a smaller scale, clients who engage the JAT in micropolitical resistances and negotiations). In fact, the JAT's monological, administrative approach to need definition can also be seen as a strategy to contain social movements. Such movements tend by their very nature to be dialogic and participatory. They represent the emergent capacities of newly politicized groups to cast off the apparently natural and prepolitical interpretations that enveloped their needs in the official economy and/or family. In social movements, people come to articulate alternative, politicized interpretations of their needs as they engage in processes of dialogue and collective struggle. Thus, the confrontation of such movements with the JAT on the terrain of the social is a confrontation between conflicting logics of need definition.

Feminists too, then, are actors on the terrain of the social. Indeed, from this perspective, we can distinguish several analytically distinct but practically intermingled kinds of feminist struggles worth engaging in the coming welfare wars. First, there are struggles to secure the political status of women's needs, that is, to legitimate women's needs as genuine political issues as opposed to "private" domestic or market matters. Here, feminists would engage especially antiwelfarist defenders of privatization. Second, there are struggles over the interpreted content of women's needs, struggles to challenge the apparently natural, traditional interpretations still enveloping needs only recently sprung from domestic and official economic enclaves of privacy. Here, feminists would engage all those forces in the culture that perpetuate androcentric and sexist interpretations of women's needs, including, but not only, the social state. Third, there are struggles over the who and how of need interpretation, struggles to empower women to interpret their own needs and to challenge the antiparticipatory, monological practices of the welfare system qua JAT. Fourth, there are struggles to elaborate and win support for policies based on feminist interpretations of women's needs, policies that avoid both the Scylla of private patriarchy and the Charybdis of public patriarchy.

In all these cases, the focus would be as much on need interpretation as on need satisfaction. This is as it should be, since any satisfactions we are able to win will be problematic to the degree we fail to fight and win the battle of interpretation.

NOTES

1. James O'Connor, *The Fiscal Crisis of the State* (New York, 1973).
2. Diana Pearce, "Women, Work, and Welfare: The Feminization of Poverty," in *Working Women and Families,* ed. Karen Wolk Feinstein (Beverly Hills, Calif., 1979).
3. Barbara Ehrenreich and Frances Fox Piven, "The Feminization of Poverty," *Dissent* 31, no. 2 (Spring 1984): 162–70.
4. Pearce, "Women, Work, and Welfare"; Nancy S. Barrett, "The Welfare Trap" (American Economic Association, Dallas, Texas, 1984); and Steven P Erie, Martin Rein, and Barbara Wiget, "Women and the Reagan Revolution: Thermidor for the Social Welfare Economy," in *Families, Politics, and Public Policies: A Feminist Dialogue on Women and the State,* ed. Irene Diamond (New York, 1983).
5. Carol Brown, "Mothers, Fathers, and Children: From Private to Public Patriarchy," in *Women and Revolution: A Discussion of the Unhappy Marriage of Marxism and Feminism,* ed. Lydia Sargent (Boston, 1981). I believe that Brown's terms are too simple on two counts. First, for reasons elaborated by Gayle Rubin ("The Traffic in Women: Notes on the 'Political Economy' of Sex," in *Towards an Anthropology of Women,* ed. Rayna R. Reiter [New York, 1975]), I prefer not to use 'patriarchy' as a generic term for male dominance but rather as the designation of a specific historical social formation. Second, Brown's public/private contrast oversimplifies the structure of both laissez-faire and welfare state capitalism, since it posits two major societal zones where there are actually four (family, official economy, state, and sphere of public political discourse) and conflates two distinct public/private divisions. These problems notwithstanding, it remains the case that Brown's terms are immensely suggestive and that we currently have no better terminology. Thus, in what follows I occasionally use 'public patriarchy' for want of an alternative.
6. For an analysis of the dynamics whereby late capitalist political systems tend to select certain types of interests while excluding others, see Claus Offe, "Political Authority and Class Structure: An Analysis of Late Capitalist Societies," *International Journal of Sociology* 2, no. 1 (Spring 1982): 73–108; "Structural Problems of the Capitalist State: Class Rule and the Political System—On the Selectiveness of Political Institutions," in *German Political Studies,* ed. Klaus von Beyme (London, 1974); and "The Separation of Form and Content in Liberal Democratic Politics," *Studies in Political Economy* 3 (Spring 1980): 5–16. For a feminist application of Offe's approach, see Drude Dahlerup, "Overcoming the Barriers: An Approach to the Study of How Women's Issues are Kept from the Political Agenda," in *Women's Views of the Political World of Men,* ed. Judith H. Stiehm (Dobbs Ferry, N.Y., 1984).

7. This phrase owes its inspiration to Jürgen Habermas, *Legitimation Crisis,* trans. Thomas McCarthy (Boston, 1975).

8. I owe this phrase to Thomas McCarthy (personal communication).

9. Erie, Rein, and Wiget, "Women and the Reagan Revolution"; and Barbara J. Nelson, "Women's Poverty and Women's Citizenship: Some Political Consequences of Economic Marginality." *Signs: Journal of Women in Culture and Society* 10, no. 2 (Winter 1984): 209-31.

10. Nelson, "Women's Poverty and Women's Citizenship."

11. Erie, Rein, and Wiget, "Women and the Reagan Revolution"; and Nelson, "Women's Poverty and Women's Citizenship."

12. Erie, Rein, and Wiget, "Women and the Reagan Revolution."

13. *Ibid.*

14. Ehrenreich and Piven, "The Feminization of Poverty."

15. Hilary Land, "Who Cares for the Family?" *Journal of Social Policy* 7, no. 3 (July 1978): 257-84.

16. I owe the phrase "gender subtext" to Dorothy Smith, "The Gender Subtext of Power" (Ontario Institute for Studies in Education, Toronto, 1984). A number of writers have noticed the two-tiered character of the U.S, social-welfare system. Andrew Hacker (" 'Welfare': The Future of an Illusion," *New York Review of Books,* 28 February 1985, 37–43) correlates the dualism with class but not with gender. Diana Pearce ("Women, Work, and Welfare") and Erie, Rein, and Wiget ("Women and the Reagan Revolution") correlate the dualism with gender and with the dual labor market, itself gender-correlated. Barbara Nelson ("Women's Poverty and Women's Citizenship") correlates the dualism with gender, the dual labor market, and the sexual division of paid *and unpaid* labor. My account owes a great deal to all of these writers, especially to Barbara Nelson.

17. Hilary Land ("Who Cares for the Family?") identifies similar assumptions at work in the British social-welfare system.

18. Pearce, "Women, Work, and Welfare."

19. C. B. MacPherson, *The Political Theory of Possessive Individualism: Hobbes to Locke* (New York, 1964).

20. I owe these formulations to Virginia Held (personal communication).

21. Pearce, "Women, Work, and Welfare."

22. It should be noted that I am here taking issue with the view of some left theorists that "decommodification" in the form of in kind social-welfare benefits represents an emancipatory or progressive development. In the context of a two-tiered welfare system like the one described here, this assumption is clearly false, since in kind benefits are qualitatively and quantitatively inferior to the corresponding commodities and since they function to stigmatize those who receive them.

23. Carol B. Stack, *All Our Kin: Strategies for Survival in a Black Community* (New York, 1974).

24. Marcel Mauss, *The Gift: Forms and Functions of Exchange in Archaic Societies,* trans. Ian Cunnison (New York, 1967).

25. This term echoes Louis Althusser's term, "ideological state apparatus." ("Ideology and Ideological State Apparatuses: Notes towards an Investigation," in *Essays on Ideology,* trans. Ben Brewster [London, 1984]). Certainly, the U.S. social-welfare system as described in the present section of this paper counts as "ISA" in Althusser's sense. However, I prefer the term 'juridical-administrative-therapeutic

state apparatus' as more concrete and descriptive of the specific ways in which welfare programs produce and reproduce ideology. In general, then, a JAT can be understood as a subclass of an ISA. On the other hand, Althusserian-like terminology aside, readers will find that the account in this section owes more to Michel Foucault (*Discipline and Punish: The Birth of the Prison*, trans. Alan Sheridan [New York, 1979]) and Jürgen Habermas (*Theorie des kommunikativen Handelns*, vol. 2, *Zur Kritik der funktionalistischen Vermunft* [Frankfurt on Main, 1981]) than to Althusser. Of course, neither Habermas nor Foucault is sensitive to the gendered character of social-welfare programs.

26. Habermas, *Theorie des kommunikativen Handelns*, vol. 2.

27. *Ibid.*

28. Prudence Mors Rains, *Becoming an Unwed Mother: A Sociological Account* (Chicago, 1971).

29. These formulations owe much to Jürgen Habermas, *Legitimation Crisis*, and *Theorie des Kommunikativen Handelns*, vol. 2.

30. Habermas, *Legitimation Crisis*, and *Theorie des Kommunikativen Handelns*, vol. 2.

31. I borrow the term 'social' from Hannah Arendt (*The Human Condition* [Chicago, 1958]). However, my use of it differs from hers in several important ways. First, Arendt and I both understand the social as a historically emergent societal space specific to modernity. And we both understand the emergence of the social as tending to undercut or blur an earlier, more distinct separation of public and private spheres. But she treats the emergence of the social as a fall or lapse, and she valorizes the earlier separation of public and private as a preferred state of affairs appropriate to "the human condition." I, on the other hand, make no assumptions about the human condition; nor do I regret the passing of the private/public separation; nor do I consider the emergence of the social a fall or lapse. Second, Arendt and I agree that one salient, defining feature of the social is the emergence of heretofore "private" needs into public view. Arendt, however, treats this as a violation of the proper order of things: she assumes that needs are wholly natural and are forever doomed to be things of brute compulsion. Thus, she supposes that needs can have no genuinely political dimension and that their emergence from the private sphere into the social spells the death of authentic politics. I, on the other hand, assume that needs are irreducibly interpretive and that need interpretations are in principle contestable. It follows from my view that the emergence of needs from the "private" into the social is a generally positive development, since such needs thereby lose their illusory aura of naturalness as their interpretations become subject to critique and contestation. I, therefore, suppose that this represents the (possible) flourishing of politics, rather than the (necessary) death of politics. Finally, Arendt assumes that the emergence of the social and of public concern with needs necessarily means the triumph of administration and instrumental reason. I, on the other hand, assume that instrumental reason represents only one possible way of defining and addressing social needs and that administration represents only one possible way of institutionalizing the social. Thus, I would argue for the existence of another possibility: an alternative socialist-feminist, dialogical mode of need interpretation and a participatory-democratic institutionalization of the social.

32. Theda Skocpol, "Political Response to Capitalist Crisis: Neo-Marxist Theories of the State and the Case of the New Deal," *Politics and Society* 10 (1980): 155–201.

Famine, Affluence, and Morality
Peter Singer

Peter Singer, a member of the Centre for Human Bioethics and a professor of philosophy at Monash University in Australia, has been a prominent contributor to debates in applied ethics for more than twenty years. Among his influential publications are *Animal Liberation* (1975) and *Practical Ethics* (1993).

In this essay, Singer argues that those of us who are relatively affluent have a moral duty to accept fairly radical changes in the way we live to prevent famine. One version of his argument maintains that if one can prevent something very bad from occurring without sacrificing anything of moral significance, then one would be wrong not to do so. Since starvation is very bad, Singer believes this simple principle, which he claims should not be controversial, implies that we have a duty to do much more than we do to prevent world hunger. Much of the essay is devoted to considering and answering objections to this argument.

As I write this, in November 1971, people are dying in East Bengal from lack of food, shelter, and medical care. The suffering and death that are occurring there now are not inevitable, not unavoidable in any fatalistic sense of the term. Constant poverty, a cyclone, and a civil war have turned at least nine million people into destitute refugees; nevertheless, it is not beyond the capacity of the richer nations to give enough assistance to reduce any further suffering to very small proportions. The decisions and actions of human beings can prevent this kind of suffering. Unfortunately, human beings have not made the necessary decisions. At the individual level, people have, with very few exceptions, not responded to the situation in any significant way. Generally speaking, people have not given large sums to relief funds; they have not written to their parliamentary representatives demanding increased government assistance; they have not demonstrated in the streets, held symbolic fasts, or done anything else directed toward providing the refugees with the means to satisfy their essential needs. At the government level, no government has given the sort of massive aid that would enable the refugees to survive for more than a few days. Britain, for instance, has given rather more than most countries. It has, to date, given £14,750,000. For comparative purposes, Britain's share of the nonrecoverable development costs of the Anglo-French Concorde project is already in excess of £275,000,000, and on present estimates will reach £440,000,000. The implication is that the British government values a supersonic transport more than thirty times as highly as it values the lives of the nine million refugees. Australia is another country which, on a per capita basis, is well up in the "aid to Bengal" table. Australia's aid,

From *Philosophy & Public Affairs* 1 (1972), 229–243.

however, amounts to less than one-twelfth of the cost of Sydney's new opera house. The total amount given, from all sources, now stands at about £65,000,000. The estimated cost of keeping the refugees alive for one year is £464,000,000. Most of the refugees have now been in the camps for more than six months. The World Bank has said that India needs a minimum of £300,000,000 in assistance from other countries before the end of the year. It seems obvious that assistance on this scale will not be forthcoming. India will be forced to choose between letting the refugees starve or diverting funds from her own development program, which will mean that more of her own people will starve in the future.[1]

These are the essential facts about the present situation in Bengal. So far as it concerns us here, there is nothing unique about this situation except its magnitude. The Bengal emergency is just the latest and most acute of a series of major emergencies in various parts of the world, arising both from natural and from man-made causes. There are also many parts of the world in which people die from malnutrition and lack of food independent of any special emergency. I take Bengal as my example only because it is the present concern, and because the size of the problem has ensured that it has been given adequate publicity. Neither individuals nor governments can claim to be unaware of what is happening there.

What are the moral implications of a situation like this? In what follows, I shall argue that the way people in relatively affluent countries react to a situation like that in Bengal cannot be justified; indeed the whole way we look at moral issues—our moral conceptual scheme—needs to be altered, and with it, the way of life that has come to be taken for granted in our society.

In arguing for this conclusion I will not, of course, claim to be morally neutral. I shall, however, try to argue for the moral position that I take, so that anyone who accepts certain assumptions, to be made explicit, will, I hope, accept my conclusion.

I begin with the assumption that suffering and death from lack of food, shelter, and medical care are bad. I think most people will agree about this, although one may reach the same view by different routes. I shall not argue for this view. People can hold all sorts of eccentric positions, and perhaps from some of them it would not follow that death by starvation is in itself bad. It is difficult, perhaps impossible, to refute such positions, and so for brevity I will henceforth take this assumption as accepted. Those who disagree need read no further.

My next point is this: if it is in our power to prevent something bad from happening, without thereby sacrificing anything of comparable moral importance, we ought, morally, to do it. By "without sacrificing anything of comparable moral importance" I mean without causing anything else comparably bad to happen, or doing something that is wrong in itself, or failing to promote some moral good, comparable in significance to the bad thing that we can prevent. This principle seems almost as uncontroversial as the last one. It requires us only to prevent what is bad, and not to promote what is good, and it requires this of us only when we can do it without sacrificing anything that is, from the moral point of view, comparably important. I could even, as far as the application of my argument to the Bengal emergency is concerned, qualify the point so as to make it: if it is in our power to prevent something very bad from happening, without thereby sacrificing anything morally significant, we ought, morally, to do it. An application of this principle would be as follows: if I am walking past a shallow pond and see a child drowning in it, I ought to wade in and pull the child out. This will mean getting my clothes muddy, but this is insignificant, while the death of the child would presumably be a very bad thing.

The uncontroversial appearance of the principle just stated is deceptive. If it were acted upon, even in its qualified form, our lives, our society, and our world would be fundamentally changed. For the principle takes, firstly, no account of proximity or distance. It makes no moral difference whether the person I can help is a neighbor's child ten yards from me or a Bengali whose name I shall never know, ten thousand miles away. Secondly, the principle makes no distinction between cases in which I am the only person who could possibly do anything and cases in which I am just one among millions in the same position.

I do not think I need to say much in defense of the refusal to take proximity and distance into account. The fact that a person is physically near to us, so that we have personal contact with him, may make it more likely that we *shall* assist him, but this does not show that we *ought* to help him rather than another who happens to be further away. If we accept any principle of impartiality, universalizability, equality, or whatever, we cannot discriminate against someone merely because he is far away from us (or we are far away from him). Admittedly, it is possible that we are in a better position to judge what needs to be done to help a person near to us than one far away, and perhaps also to provide the assistance we judge to be necessary. If this were the case, it would be a reason for helping those near to us first. This may once have been a justification for being more concerned with the poor in one's own town than with famine victims in India. Unfortunately for those who like to keep their moral responsibilities limited, instant communication and swift transportation have changed the situation. From the moral point of view, the development of the world into a "global village" has made an important, though still unrecognized, difference to our moral situation. Expert observers and supervisors, sent out by famine relief organizations or permanently stationed in famine-prone areas, can direct our aid to a refugee in Bengal almost as effectively as we could get it to someone in our own block. There would seem, therefore, to be no possible justification for discriminating on geographical grounds.

There may be a greater need to defend the second implication of my principle—that the fact that there are millions of other people in the same position, in respect to the Bengali refugees, as I am, does not make the situation significantly different from a situation in which I am the only person who can prevent something very bad from occurring. Again, of course, I admit that there is a psychological difference between the cases; one feels less guilty about doing nothing if one can point to others, similarly placed, who have also done nothing. Yet this can make no real difference to our moral obligations.[2] Should I consider that I am less obliged to pull the drowning child out of the pond if on looking around I see other people, no further away than I am, who have also noticed the child but are doing nothing? One has only to ask this question to see the absurdity of the view that numbers lessen obligation. It is a view that is an ideal excuse for inactivity; unfortunately most of the major evils—poverty, overpopulation, pollution—are problems in which everyone is almost equally involved.

The view that numbers do make a difference can be made plausible if stated in this way: if everyone in circumstances like mine gave £5 to the Bengal Relief Fund, there would be enough to provide food, shelter, and medical care for the refugees; there is no reason why I should give more than anyone else in the same circumstances as I am; therefore I have no obligation to give more than £5. Each premise in this argument is true, and the argument looks sound. It may convince us, unless we notice that it is based on a hypothetical premise, although the conclusion is not stated hypothetically. The argument would be sound if the conclusion were: if everyone in circumstances like mine were to give £5, I would have no obligation to give more than £5. If the conclusion were so stated, however, it would be obvious that the argument has no bearing on a situation in which it is not the case that everyone else gives £5. This, of course, is the actual situation. It is more or less certain that not everyone in circumstances like mine will give £5. So there will not be enough to provide the needed food, shelter, and medical care. Therefore by giving more than £5 I will prevent more suffering than I would if I gave just £5.

It might be thought that this argument has an absurd consequence. Since the situation appears to be that very few people are likely to give substantial amounts, it follows that I and everyone else in similar circumstances ought to give as much as possible, that is, at least up to the point at which by giving more one would begin to cause serious suffering for oneself and one's dependents—perhaps even beyond this point to the point of marginal utility, at which by giving more one would cause oneself and one's dependents as much suffering as one would prevent in Bengal. If everyone does this, however, there will be more than can be used for the benefit of the refugees, and some of the sacrifice will have been unnecessary. Thus, if everyone does what he ought to do, the result will not be as good as it would be if everyone did a little less than he ought to do, or if only some do all that they ought to do.

The paradox here arises only if we assume that the actions in question—sending money to the relief funds—are performed more or less simultaneously, and are also unexpected. For if it is to be expected that everyone is going to contribute something, then clearly each is not obliged to give as much as he would have been obliged to had others not been giving too. And if everyone is not acting more or less simultaneously, then those giving later will know how much more is needed, and will have no obligation to give more than is necessary to reach this amount. To say this is not to deny the principle that people in the same circumstances have the same obligations, but to point out that the fact that others have given, or may be expected to give, is a relevant circumstance: those giving after it has become known that many others are giving and those giving before are not in the same circumstances. So the seemingly absurd consequence of the principle I have put forward can occur only if people are in error about the actual circumstances—that is, if they think they are giving when others are not, but in fact they are giving when others are. The result of everyone doing what he really ought to do cannot be worse than the result of everyone doing less than he ought to do, although the result of everyone doing what he reasonably believes he ought to do could be.

If my argument so far has been sound, neither our distance from a preventable evil nor the number of other people who, in respect to that evil, are in the same situation as we are, lessens our obligation to mitigate or prevent that evil. I shall therefore take as established the principle I asserted earlier. As I have already said, I need to assert it only in its qualified form: if it is in our power to prevent something very bad from happening, without thereby sacrificing anything else morally significant, we ought, morally, to do it.

The outcome of this argument is that our traditional moral categories are upset. The traditional distinction between duty and charity cannot be drawn, or at least, not in the place we normally draw it. Giving money to the Bengal Relief Fund is regarded as an act of charity in our society. The bodies which collect money are known as "charities." These organizations see themselves in this way—if you send them a check, you will be thanked for your "generosity." Because giving money is regarded as an act of charity, it is not thought that there is anything wrong with not giving. The charitable man may be praised, but the man who is not charitable is not condemned. People do not feel in any way ashamed or guilty about spending money on new clothes or a new car instead of giving it to famine relief. (Indeed, the alternative does not occur to them.) This way of looking at the matter cannot be justified. When we buy new clothes not to keep ourselves warm but to look "well-dressed" we are not providing for any important need. We would not be sacrificing anything significant if we were to continue to wear our old clothes, and give the money to famine relief. By doing so, we would be preventing another person from starving. It follows from what I have said earlier that we ought to give money away, rather than spend it on clothes which we do not need to keep us warm. To do so is not charitable, or generous. Nor is it the kind of act which philosophers and theologians have called "supererogatory"—an act which it would be good to do, but not wrong not to do. On the contrary, we ought to give the money away, and it is wrong not to do so. . . .

Despite the limited nature of the revision in our moral conceptual scheme which I am proposing, the revision would, given the extent of both affluence and famine in the world today, have radical implications. These implications may lead to further objections, distinct from those I have already considered. I shall discuss two of these.

One objection to the position I have taken might be simply that it is too drastic a revision of our moral scheme. People do not ordinarily judge in the way I have suggested they should. Most people reserve their moral condemnation for those who violate some moral norm, such as the norm against taking another person's property. They do not condemn those who indulge in luxury instead of giving to famine relief. But given that I did not set out to present a morally neutral description of the way people make moral judgments, the way people do in fact judge has nothing to do with the validity of my conclusion. My conclusion follows from the principle which I advanced earlier, and unless that principle is rejected, or the arguments shown to be unsound, I think the conclusion must stand, however strange it appears.

It might, nevertheless, be interesting to consider why our society, and most other societies, do judge differently from the way I have suggested they should. In a well-known article, J. O. Urmson suggests that the imperatives of duty, which tell us what we must do, as distinct from what it would be good to do but not wrong not to do, function so as to prohibit behavior that is intolerable if men are to live together in society.[3] This may explain the origin and continued existence of the present division between acts of duty and acts of charity. Moral attitudes are shaped by the needs of society, and no doubt society needs people who will observe the rules that make social existence tolerable. From the point of view of a particular society, it is essential to prevent violations of norms against killing, stealing, and so on. It is quite inessential, however, to help people outside one's own society.

If this is an explanation of our common distinction between duty and supererogation, however, it is not a justification of it. The moral point of view requires us to look beyond the interests of our own society. Previously, as I have already mentioned, this may hardly have been feasible, but it is quite feasible now. From the moral point of view, the prevention of the starvation of millions of people outside our society must be considered at least as pressing as the upholding of property norms within our society.

It has been argued by some writers, among them Sidgwick and Urmson, that we need to have a basic moral code which is not too far beyond the capacities of the ordinary man, for otherwise there will be a general breakdown of compliance with the moral code. Crudely stated, this argument suggests that if we tell people that they ought to refrain from murder and give everything they do not really need to famine relief, they will do neither, whereas if we tell them that they ought to refrain from murder and that it is good to give to famine relief but not wrong not to do so, they will at least refrain from murder. The issue here is: Where should we drawn the line between conduct that is required and conduct that is good although not required, so as to get the best possible result? This would seem to be an empirical question, although a very difficult one. One objection to the Sidgwick-Urmson line of argument is that it takes insufficient account of the effect that moral standards can have on the decisions we make. Given a society in which a wealthy man who gives five percent of his income to famine relief is regarded as most generous, it is not surprising that a proposal that we all ought to give away half our incomes will be thought to be absurdly unrealistic. In a society which held that no man should have more than enough while others have less than they need, such a proposal might seem narrow-minded. What it is possible for a man to do and what he is likely to do are both, I think, very greatly influenced by what people around him are doing and expecting him to do. In any case, the possibility that by spreading the idea that we ought to be doing very much more than we are to relieve famine we shall bring about a general breakdown of moral behavior seems remote. If the stakes are an end to widespread starvation, it is worth the risk. Finally, it should be emphasized that these considerations are relevant only to the issue of what we should require from others, and not to what we ourselves ought to do.

The second objection to my attack on the present distinction between duty and charity is one which has from time to time been made against utilitarianism. It follows from some forms of utilitarian theory that we all ought, morally, to be working full time to increase the balance of happiness over misery. The position I have taken here would not lead to this conclusion in all circumstances, for if there were no bad occurrences that we could prevent without sacrificing something of comparable moral importance, my argument would have no application. Given the present conditions in many parts of the world, however, it does follow from my argument that we ought, morally, to be working full time to relieve great suffering of the sort that occurs as a result of famine or other disasters. Of course, mitigating circumstances can be adduced—for instance, that if we wear ourselves out through overwork, we shall be less effective than we would otherwise have been. Nevertheless, when all considerations of this sort have been taken into account, the conclusion remains: we ought to be preventing as much suffering as we can without sacrificing something else of comparable moral importance. This conclusion is one which we may be reluctant to face. I cannot see, though, why it should be regarded as a criticism of the position for which I have argued, rather than a criticism of our ordinary standards of behavior. Since most people are self-interested to some degree, very few of us are likely to do everything that we ought to do. It would, however, hardly be honest to take this as evidence that it is not the case that we ought to do it.

It may still be thought that my conclusions are so wildly out of line with what everyone else thinks and has always thought that there must be something wrong with the argument somewhere. In order to show that my conclusions, while certainly contrary to contemporary Western moral standards, would not have seemed so extraordinary at other times and in other places, I would like to quote a passage from a writer not normally thought of as a way-out radical, Thomas Aquinas.

> Now, according to the natural order instituted by divine providence, material goods are provided for the satisfaction of human needs. Therefore the division and appropriation of property, which proceeds from human law, must not hinder the satisfaction of man's necessity from such goods. Equally, whatever a man has in super-abundance is owed, of natural right, to the poor for their sustenance. So Ambrosius says, and it is also to be found in the *Decretum Gratiani*: "The bread which you withhold belongs to the hungry; the clothing you shut away, to the naked; and the money you bury in the earth is the redemption and freedom of the penniless."[4]

I now want to consider a number of points, more practical than philosophical, which are relevant to the application of the moral conclusion we have reached. These points challenge not the idea that we ought to be doing all we can to prevent starvation, but the idea that giving away a great deal of money is the best means to this end.

It is sometimes said that overseas aid should be a government responsibility, and that therefore one ought not to give to privately run charities. Giving privately, it is said, allows the government and the noncontributing members of society to escape their responsibilities.

This argument seems to assume that the more people there are who give to privately organized famine relief funds, the less likely it is that the government will take over full responsibility for such aid. This assumption is unsupported, and does not strike me as at all plausible. The opposite view—that if no one gives voluntarily, a government will assume that its citizens are uninterested in famine relief and would not wish to be forced into giving aid— seems more plausible. In any case, unless there were a definite probability that by refusing to give one would be helping to bring about massive government assistance, people who do refuse to make voluntary contributions are refusing to prevent a certain amount of suffering without being able to point to any tangible beneficial consequence of their refusal. So the onus of showing how their refusal will bring about government action is on those who refuse to give.

I do not, of course, want to dispute the contention that governments of affluent nations should be giving many times the amount of genuine, no-strings-attached aid that they are giving now. I agree, too, that giving privately is not enough, and that we ought to be campaigning actively for entirely new standards for both public and private contributions to famine relief. Indeed, I would sympathize with someone who thought that campaigning was more important than giving oneself, although I doubt whether preaching what one does not practice would be very effective. Unfortunately, for many people the idea that "it's the government's responsibility" is a reason for not giving which does not appear to entail any political action either.

Another, more serious reason for not giving to famine relief funds is that until there is effective population control, relieving famine merely postpones starvation. If we save the Bengal refugees now, others, perhaps the children of these refugees, will face starvation in a few years' time. In support of this, one may cite the now well-known facts about the population explosion and the relatively limited scope for expanded production.

This point, like the previous one, is an argument against relieving suffering that is happening now, because of a belief about what might happen in the future; it is unlike the previous point in that very good evidence can be adduced in support of this belief about the future. I will not go into the evidence here. I accept that the earth cannot support indefinitely a population rising at the present rate. This certainly poses a problem for anyone who thinks it important to prevent famine. Again, however, one could accept the argument without drawing the conclusion that it absolves one from any obligation to do anything to prevent famine. The conclusion that should be drawn is that the best means of preventing famine, in the long run, is population control. It would then follow from the position reached earlier that one ought to be doing all one can to promote population control (unless one held that all forms of population control were wrong in themselves, or would have significantly bad consequences). Since there are organizations working specifically for population control, one would then support them rather than more orthodox methods of preventing famine.

A third point raised by the conclusion reached earlier relates to the question of just how much we all ought to be giving away. One possibility, which has already been mentioned, is that we ought to give until we reach the level of marginal utility—that is, the level at which, by giving more, I would cause as much suffering to myself or my dependents as I would relieve by my gift. This would mean, of course, that one would reduce oneself to very near the material circumstances of a Bengali refugee. It will be recalled that earlier I put forward both a strong and a moderate version of the principle of preventing bad occurrences. The strong version, which required us to prevent bad things from happening unless in doing so we would be sacrificing something of comparable moral significance, does seem to require reducing ourselves to the level of marginal utility. I should also say that the strong version seems to me to be the correct one. I proposed the more moderate version—that we should prevent bad occurrences unless, to do so, we had to sacrifice something morally significant—only in order to show that even on this surely undeniable principle a great change in our way of life is required. On the more moderate principle, it may not follow that we ought to reduce ourselves to the level of marginal utility, for one might hold that to reduce oneself and one's family to this level is to cause something significantly bad to happen. Whether this is so I shall not discuss, since, as I have said, I can see no good reason for holding the moderate version of the principle rather than the strong version. Even if we accepted the principle only in its moderate form, however, it should be clear that we would have to give away enough to ensure that the consumer society, dependent as it is on people spending on trivia rather than giving to famine relief, would slow down and perhaps disappear entirely. There are several reasons why this would be desirable in itself. The value and necessity of economic growth are now being questioned not only by conservationists, but by economists as well.[5] There is no doubt, too, that the consumer society has had a distorting effect on the goals and purposes of its members. Yet looking at the matter purely from the point of view of overseas aid, there must be a limit to the extent to which we should deliberately slow down our economy; for it might be the case that if we gave away, say, forty percent of our Gross National Product, we would slow down the economy so much that in absolute terms we would be giving less than if we gave twenty-five percent of the much larger GNP that we would have if we limited our contribution to this smaller percentage.

I mention this only as an indication of the sort of factor that one would have to take into account in working out an ideal. Since Western societies generally consider one percent of the GNP an acceptable level for overseas aid, the matter is entirely academic. Nor does it affect the question of how much an individual should give in a society in which very few are giving substantial amounts.

It is sometimes said, though less often now than it used to be, that philosophers have no special role to play in public affairs, since most public issues depend primarily on an assessment of facts. On questions of fact, it is said, philosophers as such have no special expertise, and so it has been possible to engage in philosophy without committing oneself to any position on major public issues. No doubt there are some issues of social policy and foreign policy about which it can truly be said that a really expert assessment of the facts is required before taking sides or acting, but the issue of famine is surely not one of these. The facts about the existence of suffering are beyond dispute. Nor, I think, is it disputed that we can do something about it, either through orthodox methods of famine relief or through population control or both. This is therefore an issue on which philosophers are competent to take a position. The issue is one which faces everyone who has more money than he needs to support himself and his dependents, or who is in a position to take some sort of political action. These categories must include practically every teacher and student of philosophy in the universities of the Western world. If philosophy is to deal with matters that are relevant to both teachers and students, this is an issue that philosophers should discuss.

Discussion, though, is not enough. What is the point of relating philosophy to public (and personal) affairs if we do not take our conclusions seriously? In this instance, taking our conclusion seriously means acting upon it. The philosopher will not find it any easier than anyone else to alter his attitudes and way of life to the extent that, if I am right, is involved in doing everything that we ought to be doing. At the very least, though, one can make a start. The philosopher who does so will have to sacrifice some of the benefits of the consumer society, but he can find compensation in the satisfaction of a way life in which theory and practice, if not yet in harmony, are at least coming together.

NOTES

1. There was also a third possibility: that India would go to war to enable the refugees to return to their lands. Since I wrote this paper, India has taken this way out. The situation is no longer that described above, but this does not affect my argument, as the next paragraph indicates.

2. In view of the special sense philosophers often give to the term, I should say that I use "obligation" simply as the abstract noun derived from "ought," so that "I have an obligation to" means no more, and no less, than "I ought to." This usage is in accordance with the definition of "ought" given by the *Shorter Oxford English Dictionary*: "the general verb to express duty or obligation." I do not think any issue of substance hangs on the way the term is used; sentences in which I use "obligation" could all be rewritten, although somewhat clumsily, as sentences in which a clause containing "ought" replaces the term "obligation."

3. J. O. Urmson, "Saints and Heroes," in *Essays in Moral Philosophy*, ed. Abraham I. Melden (Seattle and London, 1958), p. 214. For a related but significantly different view see also Henry Sidgwick, *The Methods of Ethics,* 7th edn. (London, 1907), pp. 220-221, 492-493.

4. *Summa Theologica,* II–II, Question 66, Article 7, in *Aquinas, Selected Political Writings,* ed. A. P. d'Entreves, trans. J. G. Dawson (Oxford, 1948), p. 171.

5. See, for instance, John Kenneth Galbraith, *The New Industrial State* (Boston, 1967); and E. J. Mishan, *The Costs of Economic Growth* (London, 1967).

Living on a Lifeboat
Garrett Hardin

Garrett Hardin, a professor of biology at the University of California at Santa Barbara and the author of *Living Within Limits: Ecology, Economics, and Population Taboos* (1993), argues against giving food to prevent starvation in countries other than one's own. He believes that such aid would in the long run be harmful to both the nations providing the aid and those nations receiving it. As a metaphor he suggests that nations should employ lifeboat ethics. A lifeboat is capable of carrying only a limited number of passengers safely. Those who manage their lifeboat well keep the number of passengers below this "carrying capacity," leaving a safety margin for emergencies. When affluent nations provide food to nations unable to supply food for their own populations, they harm themselves by reducing their safety margin, and they harm the long term interests of the nations they help by allowing the population in those nations to further exceed the nations' carrying capacities, setting the stage for much more disastrous famines down the road. Hardin further argues that similar considerations show that rich nations should carefully control immigration.

No generation has viewed the problem of the survival of the human species as seriously as we have. Inevitably, we have entered this world of concern through the door of metaphor. Environmentalists have emphasized the image of the earth as a spaceship—Spaceship Earth. Kenneth Boulding (1966) is the principal architect of this metaphor. It is time, he says, that we replace the wasteful "cowboy economy" of the past with the frugal "spaceship economy" required for continued survival in the limited world we now see ours to be. The metaphor is notably useful in justifying pollution control measures.

Unfortunately, the image of a spaceship is also used to promote measures that are suicidal. One of these is a generous immigration policy, which is only a particular instance of a class of policies that are in error because they lead to the tragedy of the commons (Hardin 1968). These suicidal policies are attractive because they mesh with what we unthinkingly take to be the ideals of "the best people." What is missing in the idealistic view is an insistence that rights and responsibilities must go together. The "generous" attitude of all too many people results in asserting inalienable rights while ignoring or denying matching responsibilities.

For the metaphor of a spaceship to be correct the aggregate of people on board would have to be under unitary sovereign control (Ophuls 1974). A true ship always has a captain. It is conceivable that a ship could be run by a committee. But it could not possibly survive if its course were determined by bickering tribes that claimed rights without responsibilities. . . .

From *BioScience* 24 (1974), 561-568.

LIFEBOAT ETHICS

Before taking up certain substantive issues let us look at an alternative metaphor, that of a lifeboat. . . .

Approximately two-thirds of the world is desperately poor, and only one-third is comparatively rich. . . . Metaphorically, each rich nation amounts to a lifeboat full of comparatively rich people. The poor of the world are in other, much more crowded lifeboats. Continuously, so to speak, the poor fall out of their lifeboats and swim for a while in the water outside, hoping to be admitted to a rich lifeboat, or in some other way to benefit from the "goodies" on board. What should the passengers on a rich lifeboat do? This is the central problem of "the ethics of a lifeboat."

First we must acknowledge that each lifeboat is effectively limited in capacity. The land of every nation has a limited carrying capacity. The exact limit is a matter for argument, but the energy crunch is convincing more people every day that we have already exceeded the carrying capacity of the land. We have been living on "capital"—stored petroleum and coal—and soon we must live on income alone.

Let us look at only one lifeboat—ours. The ethical problem is the same for all, and is as follows. Here we sit, say 50 people in a lifeboat. To be generous, let us assume our boat has a capacity of 10 more, making 60. (This, however, is to violate the engineering principle of the "safety factor." A new plant disease or a bad change in the weather may decimate our population if we don't preserve some excess capacity as a safety factor.)

The 50 of us in the lifeboat see 100 others swimming in the water outside, asking for admission to the boat, or for handouts. How shall we respond to their calls? There are several possibilities.

1. We may be tempted to try to live by the Christian ideal of being "our brother's keeper," or by the Marxian ideal (Marx 1875) of "from each according to his abilities, to each according to his needs." Since the needs of all are the same, we take all the needy into our boat, making a total of 150 in a boat with a capacity of 60. The boat is swamped, and everyone drowns. Complete justice, complete catastrophe.

2. Since the boat has an unused excess capacity of 10, we admit just 10 more to it. This has the disadvantage of getting rid of the safety factor, for which action we will sooner or later pay dearly. Moreover, *which 10* do we let in? "First come, first served?" The best 10? The neediest 10? How do we *discriminate*? And what do we say to the 90 who are excluded?

3. Admit no more to the boat and preserve the small safety factor. Survival of the people in the lifeboat is then possible (though we shall have to be on our guard against boarding parties).

The last solution is abhorrent to many people. It is unjust, they say. Let us grant that it is.

"I feel guilty about my good luck," say some. The reply to this is simple: *Get out and yield your place to others.* Such a selfless action might satisfy the conscience of those who are addicted to guilt but it would not change the ethics of the lifeboat. The needy person to whom a guilt-addict yields his place will not himself feel guilty about his sudden good luck. (If he did he would not climb aboard.) The net result of conscience-stricken people relinquishing their unjustly held positions is the elimination of their kind of conscience from the lifeboat. The lifeboat, as it were, purifies itself of guilt. The ethics of the lifeboat persist, unchanged by such momentary aberrations.

This then is the basic metaphor within which we must work out our solutions. Let us enrich the image step by step with substantive additions from the real world.

REPRODUCTION

The harsh characteristics of lifeboat ethics are heightened by reproduction, particularly by reproductive differences. The people inside the lifeboats of the wealthy nations are doubling in numbers every 87 years; those outside are doubling every 35 years, on the average. And the relative difference in prosperity is becoming greater.

Let us, for a while, think primarily of the U.S. lifeboat. As of 1973 the United States had a population of 210 million people, who were increasing by 0.8% per year, that is, doubling in number every 87 years.

Although the citizens of rich nations are outnumbered two to one by the poor, let us imagine an equal number of poor people outside our lifeboat—a mere 210 million poor people reproducing at a quite different rate. If we imagine these to be the combined populations of Colombia, Venezuela, Ecuador, Morocco, Thailand, Pakistan, and the Philippines, the average rate of increase of the people "outside" is 3.3% per year. The doubling time of this population is 21 years.

Suppose that all these countries, and the United States, agreed to live by the Marxian ideal, "to each according to his needs," the ideal of most Christians as well. Needs, of course, are determined by population size, which is affected by reproduction. Every nation regards its rate of reproduction as a sovereign right. If our lifeboat were big enough in the beginning it might be possible to live *for a while* by Christian-Marxian ideals. *Might.*

Initially, in the model given, the ratio of non-Americans to Americans would be one to one. But consider what the ratio would be 87 years later. By this time Americans would have doubled to a population of 420 million. The other group (doubling every 21 years) would now have swollen to 3,540 million. Each American would have more than eight people to share with. How could the lifeboat possibly keep afloat?

All this involves extrapolation of current trends into the future, and is consequently suspect. Trends may change. Granted: but the change will not necessarily be favorable. If—as seems likely—the rate of population increase falls faster in the ethnic group presently inside the lifeboat than it does among those now outside, the future will turn out to be even worse than mathematics predicts, and sharing will be even more suicidal.

RUIN IN THE COMMONS

The fundamental error of the sharing ethics is that it leads to the tragedy of the commons. Under a system of private property the man (or group of men) who own property recognize their responsibility to care for it, for if they don't they will eventually suffer. A farmer, for instance, if he is intelligent will allow no more cattle in a pasture than its carrying capacity justifies. If he overloads the pasture, weeds take over, erosion sets in, and the owner loses in the long run.

But if a pasture is run as a common open to all, the right of each to use it is not matched by an operational responsibility to take care of it. It is no use asking independent herdsmen in a commons to act responsibly, for they dare not. The considerate herdsman who refrains from overloading the commons suffers more than a selfish one who says his needs are greater. (As Leo Duroche says, "Nice guys finish last.") Christian-Marxian idealism is counterproductive. That it *sounds* nice is no excuse. With distribution systems, as with individual morality, good intentions are no substitute for good performance.

A social system is stable only if it is insensitive to errors. To the Christian-Marxian idealist a selfish person is a sort of "error." Prosperity in the system of the commons cannot survive errors. If *everyone* would only restrain himself all would be well; but it takes *only one less than everyone* to ruin a system of voluntary restraint. In a crowded world of less than perfect human beings—and we will never know any other—mutual ruin is inevitable in the commons. This is the core of the tragedy of the commons.

One of the major tasks of education today is to create such an awareness of the dangers of the commons that people will be able to recognize its many varieties, however disguised. There is pollution of the air and water because these media are treated as commons. Further growth of population and growth in the per capita conversion of natural resources into pollutants require that the system of the commons be modified or abandoned in the disposal of "externalities."

The fish populations of the oceans are exploited as commons, and ruin lies ahead. No technological invention can prevent this fate: in fact, all improvements in the art of fishing merely hasten the day of complete ruin. Only the replacement of the system of the commons with a responsible system can save oceanic fisheries.

The management of western range lands, though nominally rational, is in fact (under the steady pressure of cattle ranchers) often merely a government-sanctioned system of the commons, drifting toward ultimate ruin for both the rangelands and the residual enterprisers.

WORLD FOOD BANKS

In the international arena we have recently heard a proposal to create a new commons, namely an international depository of food reserves to which nations will contribute according to their abilities, and from which nations may draw according to their needs. Nobel laureate Norman Borlaug has lent the prestige of his name to this proposal.

A world food bank appeals powerfully to our humanitarian impulses. We remember John Donne's celebrated line, "Any man's death diminishes me." But before we rush out to see for whom the bell tolls let us recognize where the greatest political push for international granaries comes from, lest we be disillusioned later. . . .

What happens if some organizations budget for emergencies and others do not? If each organization is solely responsible for its own well-being, poorly managed ones will suffer. But they should be able to learn from experience. They have a chance to mend their ways and learn to budget for infrequent but certain emergencies. The weather, for instance, always varies and periodic crop failures are certain. A wise and competent government saves out of the production of the good years in anticipation of bad years that are sure to come. This is not a new idea. The Bible tells us that Joseph taught this policy to Pharaoh in Egypt more than 2,000 years ago. Yet it is literally true that the vast majority of the governments of the world today have no such policy. They lack either the wisdom or the competence, or both. Far more difficult than the transfer of wealth from one country to another is the transfer of wisdom between sovereign powers or between generations.

"But it isn't their fault! How can we blame the poor people who are caught in an emergency? Why must we punish them?" The concepts of blame and punishment are irrelevant. The question is, what are the operational consequences of establishing a world food bank? If it is open to every country every time a need develops, slovenly rulers will not be motivated to take Joseph's advice. Why should they? Others will bail them out whenever they are in trouble.

Some countries will make deposits in the world food bank and others will withdraw from it: there will be almost no overlap. Calling such a depository-transfer unit a "bank" is stretching the metaphor of *bank* beyond its elastic limits. The proposers, of course, never call attention to the metaphorical nature of the word they use.

THE RATCHET EFFECT

An "international food bank" is really, then, not a true bank but a disguised one-way transfer device for moving wealth from rich countries to poor. In the absence of such a bank, in a world inhabited by individually responsible sovereign nations, the population of each nation would repeatedly go through a cycle. . . . A state of overpopulation [arises] which becomes obvious upon the appearance of an "accident," e.g., a crop failure. If the "emergency" is not met by outside help, the population drops back to the "normal" level—the "carrying capacity" of the environment—or even below. In the absence of population control by a sovereign, sooner or later the population grows . . . again and the cycle repeats. The long-term population curve (Hardin 1966) is an irregularly fluctuating one, equilibrating more or less about the carrying capacity.

A demographic cycle of this sort obviously involves great suffering in the restrictive phase, but such a cycle is normal to any independent country with inadequate population control. The third century theologian Tertullian (Hardin 1969a) expressed what must have been the recognition of many wise men when he wrote: "The scourges of pestilence, famine, wars, and earthquakes have come to be regarded as a blessing to overcrowded nations, since they serve to prune away the luxuriant growth of the human race."

Only under a strong and farsighted sovereign—which theoretically could be the people themselves, democratically organized—can a population equilibrate at some set point below the carrying capacity, thus avoiding the pains normally caused by periodic and unavoidable disasters. For this happy state to be achieved it is necessary that those in power be able to contemplate with equanimity the "waste" of surplus food in times of bountiful harvests. It is essential that those in power resist the temptation to convert extra food into extra babies. On the public relations level it is necessary that the phrase "surplus food" be replaced by "safety factor."

But wise sovereigns seem not to exist in the poor world today. The more anguishing problems are created by poor countries that are governed by rulers insufficiently wise and powerful. If such countries can draw on a world food bank in times of "emergency," the population *cycle* . . . [described] earlier will be replaced by the population *escalator.* The input of food from a food bank acts as the pawl of a ratchet, preventing the population from retracting its steps to a lower level. Reproduction pushes the population upward, inputs from the world bank prevent its moving downward. Population size escalates, as does the absolute magnitude of "accidents" and "emergencies." The process is brought to an end only by the total collapse of the whole system, producing a catastrophe of scarcely imaginable proportions.

Such are the implications of the well-meant sharing of food in a world of irresponsible reproduction.

ECO-DESTRUCTION VIA THE GREEN REVOLUTION

The demoralizing effect of charity on the recipient has long been known. "Give a man a fish and he will eat for a day: teach him how to fish and he will eat for the rest of his days." So runs an ancient Chinese proverb. Acting on this advice the Rockefeller and Ford Foundations have financed a multipronged program for improving agriculture in the hungry nations. The result, known as the "Green Revolution," has been quite remarkable. "Miracle wheat" and "miracle rice" are splendid technological achievements in the realm of plant genetics.

Whether or not the Green Revolution can increase food production is doubtful (Harris 1972, Paddock 1970, Wilkes 1972), but in any event not particularly important. What is missing in this great and well-meaning humanitarian effort is a firm grasp of fundamentals. Considering the importance of the Rockefeller Foundation in this effort it is ironic that the late Alan Gregg, a much-respected vice-president of the Foundation, strongly expressed his doubts of the wisdom of all attempts to increase food production some two decades ago. (This was before Borlaug's work—supported by Rockefeller—had resulted in the development of "miracle wheat.") Gregg (1955) likened the growth and spreading of humanity over the surface of the earth to the metastasis of cancer in the human body, wryly remarking that "Cancerous growths demand food; but, as far as I know, they have never been cured by getting it."

"Man does not live by bread alone"—the scriptural statement has a rich meaning even in the material realm. Every human being born constitutes a draft on all aspects of the environment—food, air, water, unspoiled scenery, occasional and optional solitude, beaches, contact with wild animals, fishing, hunting—the list is long and incompletely known. Food can, perhaps, be significantly increased: but what about clean beaches, unspoiled forests, and solitude? If we satisfy the need for food in a growing population we necessarily decrease the supply of other goods, and thereby increase the difficulty of equitably allocating scarce goods (Harding 1969b, 1972b).

The present population of India is 600 million, and it is increasing by 15 million per year. The environmental load of this population is already great. The forests of India are only a small fraction of what they were three centuries ago. Soil erosion, floods, and the psychological costs of crowding are serious. Every one of the net 15 million lives added each year stresses the Indian environment more severely. *Every life saved this year in a poor country diminishes the quality of life for subsequent generations.*

Observant critics have shown how much harm we wealthy nations have already done to poor nations through our well-intentioned but misguided attempts to help them (Paddock and Paddock 1973). Particularly reprehensible is our failure to carry out post-audits of these attempts (Farvar and Milton 1972). Thus have we shielded our tender consciences from knowledge of the harm we have done. Must we Americans continue to fail to monitor the consequences of our external "do-gooding?" If, for instance, we thoughtlessly make it possible for the present 600 million Indians to swell to 1,200 millions by the year 2001—as their present growth rate promises— will posterity in India thank *us* for facilitating an even greater destruction of *their* environment? Are good intentions ever a sufficient excuse for bad consequences?

IMMIGRATION CREATES A COMMONS

I come now to the final example of a commons in action, one for which the public is least prepared for rational discussion. The topic is at present enveloped by a great silence which reminds me of a comment made by Sherlock Holmes in A. Conan Doyle's story, "Silver Blaze." Inspector Gregory had asked, "Is there any point to which you would wish to draw my attention?" To this Holmes responded:

> "To the curious incident of the dog in the night-time."

> "The dog did nothing in the night-time," said the Inspector.

> "That was the curious incident," remarked Sherlock Holmes.

By asking himself what would repress the normal barking instinct of a watch dog Holmes realized that it must be the dog's recognition of his master as the criminal trespasser. In a similar way we should ask ourselves what repression keeps us from discussing something as important as immigration?

It cannot be that immigration is numerically of no consequence. Our government acknowledges a *net* inflow of 400,000 a year. Hard data are understandably lacking on the extent of illegal entries, but a not implausible figure is 600,000 per year (Buchanan 1973). The natural increase of the resident population is now about 1.7 million per year. This means that the yearly gain from immigration is at least 19%, and may be 37%, of the total increase. It is quite conceivable that educational campaigns like that of Zero Population Growth, Inc., coupled with adverse social and economic factors—inflation, housing shortage, depression, and loss of confidence in national leaders—may lower the fertility of American women to a point at which all of the yearly increase in population would be accounted for by immigration. Should we not at least ask if that is what we want? How curious it is that we so seldom discuss immigration these days!

Curious, but understandable—as one finds out the moment he publicly questions the wisdom of the status quo in immigration. He who does so is promptly charged with *isolationism, bigotry, prejudice, ethnocentrism, chauvinism,* and *selfishness.* These are hard accusations to bear. It is pleasanter to talk about other matters, leaving immigration policy to wallow in the crosscurrents of special interests that take no account of the good of the whole— *or of the interests of posterity.*

We Americans have a bad conscience because of things we said in the past about immigrants. Two generations ago the popular press was rife with references to *Dagos, Wops, Pollacks, Japs, Chinks*, and *Krauts*—all pejorative terms which failed to acknowledge our indebtedness to Goya, Leonardo, Copernicus, Hiroshige, Confucius, and Bach. Because the implied inferiority of foreigners was *then* the justification for keeping them out, it is *now* thoughtlessly assumed that restrictive policies can only be based on the assumption of immigrant inferiority. *This is not so. . . .*

From this point on, *it will be assumed that immigrants and native-born citizens are of exactly equal quality,* however quality may be defined. The focus is only on quantity. The conclusions reached depend on nothing else, so all charges of ethnocentrism are irrelevant.

World food banks move food to the people, thus facilitating the exhaustion of the environment of the poor. By contrast, unrestricted immigration moves people to the food, thus speeding up the destruction of the environment in rich countries. Why poor people should want to make this transfer is no mystery: but why should rich hosts encourage it? This transfer, like the reverse one, is supported by both selfish interests and humanitarian impulses.

The principal selfish interest in unimpeded immigration is easy to identify: it is the interest of the employer of cheap labor, particularly that needed for degrading jobs. We have been deceived about the forces of history by the lines of Emma Lazarus inscribed on the Statue of Liberty:

Give me your tired, your poor

Your huddled masses yearning to breathe free,

The wretched refuse of your teeming shore,

Send these, the homeless, tempest-tossed, to me:

I lift my lamp beside the golden door.

The image is one of an infinitely generous earth-mother, passively opening her arms to hordes of immigrants who come here on their own initiative. Such an image may have been adequate for the early days of colonization, but by the time these lines were written (1886) the force for immigration was largely manufactured inside our own borders by factory and mine owners who sought cheap labor not to be found among laborers already here. One group of foreigners after another was thus enticed into the United States to work at wretched jobs for wretched wages.

At present, it is largely the Mexicans who are being so exploited. It is particularly to the advantage of certain employers that there be many illegal immigrants. Illegal immigrant workers dare not complain about their working conditions for fear of being repatriated. Their presence reduces the bargaining power of all Mexican-American laborers. Cesar Chavez has repeatedly pleaded with congressional committees to close the doors to more Mexicans so that those here can negotiate effectively for higher wages and decent working conditions. Chavez understands the ethics of a lifeboat. . . .

THE ASYMMETRY OF DOOR-SHUTTING

We must now answer this telling point: "How can you justify slamming the door once you're inside? You say that immigrants should be kept out. But aren't we all immigrants, or the descendants of immigrants? Since we refuse to leave, must we not, as a matter of justice and symmetry, admit all others?"

It is literally true that we Americans of non-Indian ancestry are the descendants of thieves. Should we not, then, "give back" the land to the Indians; that is, give it to the now-living Americans of Indian ancestry? As an exercise in pure logic I see no way to reject this proposal. Yet I am unwilling to live by it; and I know no one who is. Our reluctance to embrace pure justice may spring from pure selfishness. On the other hand, it may arise from an unspoken recognition of consequences that have not yet been clearly spelled out.

Suppose, becoming intoxicated with pure justice, we "Anglos" should decide to turn our land over to the Indians. Since all our other wealth has also been derived from the land, we would have to give that to the Indians, too. Then what would we non-Indians do? Where would we go? There is no open land in the world on which men without capital can make their living (and not much unoccupied land on which men with capital can either). Where would 209 million putatively justice-loving, non-Indian, Americans go? Most of them—in the persons of their ancestors—came from Europe, but they wouldn't be welcomed back there. Anyway, Europeans have no better title to their land than we to ours. They also would have to give up their homes. (But to whom? And where would *they* go?)

Clearly, the concept of pure justice produces an infinite regress. The law long ago invented statutes of limitations to justify the rejection of pure justice, in the interest of preventing massive disorder. The law zealously defends property rights—but only *recent* property rights. It is as though the physical principle of exponential decay applies to property rights. Drawing a line in time may be unjust, but any other action is practically worse.

We are all the descendants of thieves, and the world's resources are inequitably distributed, but we must begin the journey to tomorrow from the point where we are today. We cannot remake the past. We cannot, without violent disorder and suffering, give land and resources back to the "original" owners—who are dead anyway.

We cannot safely divide the wealth equitably among all present peoples, so long as people reproduce at different rates, because to do so would guarantee that our grandchildren—everyone's grandchildren—would have only a ruined world to inhabit.

MUST EXCLUSION BE ABSOLUTE?

To show the logical structure of the immigration problem I have ignored many factors that would enter into real decisions made in a real world. No matter how convincing the logic may be it is probable that we would want, from time to time, to admit a few people from the outside to our lifeboat. Political refugees in particular are likely to cause us to make exceptions: We remember the Jewish refugees from Germany after 1933, and the Hungarian refugees after 1956. Moreover, the interests of national defense, broadly conceived, could justify admitting many men and women of unusual talents, whether refugees or not. (This raises the quality issue, which is not the subject of this essay.)

Such exceptions threaten to create runaway population growth inside the lifeboat, i.e., the receiving country. However, the threat can be neutralized by a population policy that includes immigration. An effective policy is one of flexible control.

Suppose, for example, that the nation has achieved a stable condition of ZPG, which (say) permits 1.5 million births yearly. We must suppose that an acceptable system of allocating birth-rights to potential parents is in effect. Now suppose that an inhumane regime in some other part of the world creates a horde of refugees, and that there is a widespread desire to admit some to our country. At the same time, we do not want to sabotage our population control system. Clearly, the rational path to pursue is the following. If we decide to admit 100,000 refugees this year we should compensate for this by reducing the allocation of birth-rights in the following year by a similar amount, that is downward to a total of 1.4 million. In that way we could achieve both humanitarian and population control goals. (And the refugees would have to accept the population controls of the society that admits them. It is not inconceivable that they might be given proportionately fewer rights than the native population.)

In a democracy, the admission of immigrants should properly be voted on. But by whom? It is not obvious. The usual rule of a democracy is votes for all. But it can be questioned whether a universal franchise is the most just one in a case of this sort. Whatever benefits there are in the admission of immigrants presumably accrue to everyone. But the costs would be seen as falling most heavily on potential parents, some of whom would have to postpone or forego having their (next) child because of the influx of immigrants. The double question *Who benefits? Who pays?* suggests that a restriction of the usual democratic franchise would be appropriate and just in this case. Would our particular quasi-democratic form of government be flexible enough to institute such a novelty? If not, the majority might, out of humanitarian motives, impose an unacceptable burden (the foregoing of parenthood) on a minority, thus producing political instability.

Plainly many new problems will arise when we consciously face the immigration question and seek rational answers. No workable answers can be found if we ignore population problems. And—if the argument of this essay is correct—so long as there is no true world government to control reproduction everywhere it is impossible to survive in dignity if we are to be guided by Spaceship ethics. Without a world government that is sovereign in reproductive matters mankind lives, in fact, on a number of sovereign lifeboats. For the foreseeable future survival demands that we govern our actions by the ethics of a lifeboat. Posterity will be ill served if we do not.

REFERENCES

Anonymous. 1974. *Wall Street Journal* 19 Feb.

Borlaug, N. 1973. Civilization's future: a call for international granaries. *Bull. At. Sci.* 29: 7–15.

Boulding, K. 1966. The economics of the coming Spaceship earth. *In* H. Jarrett, ed. Environmental Quality in a Growing Economy. Johns Hopkins Press, Baltimore.

Buchanan, W. 1973. Immigration statistics. *Equilibrium* 1(3): 16-19.

Davis, K. 1963. Population, *Sci. Amer.* 209(3): 62-71.

Farvar, M. T., and J. P. Milton. 1972. The Careless Technology. Natural History Press, Garden City, N.Y.

Gregg, A. 1955. A medical aspect of the population problem. *Science* 121: 681-682.

Hardin, G. 1966. Chap. 9 *in* Biology: Its Principles and Implications, 2nd ed. Freeman, San Francisco.

_____. 1968. The tragedy of the commons. *Science* 162: 1243-1248.

_____. 1969a Page 18 *in* Population, Evolution, and Birth Control, 2nd ed. Freeman. San Francisco.

_____. 1969b. The economics of wilderness. *Nat. Hist.* 78(6): 20-27.

_____. 1972a. Pages 81-82 *in* Exploring New Ethics for Survival: The Voyage of the Spaceship *Beagle.* Viking, N.Y.

_____. 1972b. Preserving quality on Spaceship Earth. *In* J. B. Trefethen, ed. Transactions of the Thirty-Seventh North American Wildlife and Natural Resources Conference, Wildlife Management Institute, Washington, D.C.

_____. 1973. Chap. 23 *in* Stalking the Wild Taboo. Kaufmann, Los Altos, Cal.

Harris, M. 1972. How green the revolution. *Nat. Hist.* 81(3): 28-30.

Langer, S. K. 1942. Philosophy in a New Key. Harvard University Press, Cambridge.

Lansner, K. 1974. Should foreign aid begin at home? *Newsweek,* 11 Feb., p. 32.

Marx. K. 1875. Critique of the Gotha program. Page 388 *in* R. C. Tucker, ed. The Marx-Engels Reader. Norton, N.Y., 1972.

Ophuls, W. 1974. The scarcity society. *Harpers* 248(1487): 47-52.

Paddock, W. C. 1970. How green is the green revolution? *BioScience* 20: 897-902.

Paddock, W., and E. Paddock. 1973. We Don't Know How. Iowa State University Press, Ames, Iowa.

Paddock, W. and P. Paddock. 1967. Famine—1975! Little, Brown, Boston.

Wilkes, H. G. 1972. The green revolution. *Environment* 14(8): 32-39.

Perspectives on World Hunger and the Extent of Our Positive Duties
Robert N. Van Wyk

Robert N. Van Wyk teaches philosophy at the University of Pittsburgh, Johnstown. He points out that both Singer and Hardin approach world hunger from a consequentialist perspective, but he argues that Kantians should believe that those of us in affluent nations have a duty to help. In many cases, the duty to help those who are hungry in other nations could be derived from our perfect duty not to harm others. If their condition was brought about by our harmful or negligent behavior, then we have harmed them and have a duty to make reparations. Such a duty would exist, according to Van Wyk, even if we have unintentionally benefited by the harmful behavior of others that has led to poverty in other nations. Even in those cases where the severe need is not the result of past injustice, Van Wyk believes that a duty to provide others with the resources to meet their basic needs is required by the Kantian demand that we treat other persons as ends in themselves.

Finally Van Wyk addresses a serious worry that many have about the claim that we should help those who are in serious need. The worry arises from the fact that there are so many people in need. Suppose I help one such person. Immediately, I would notice there is another. Can I refuse to help? If not, it would seem that the demands on my resources would be so great that I would be unable to pursue my own personal goals in life. Van Wyk suggests that Kantian considerations can be given for the conclusion that one's duty is met by giving one's fair share to help others, where one's fair share is understood in terms of what would be reasonably regarded as one's fair contribution to assistance if everyone in a position to help were doing so.

A moral problem that faces institutions—especially governments, as well as individuals, is the question of the extent of the duty to prevent harm to other people, and/or benefit them. This is not an academic problem but one that stares us in the face through the eyes of starving and malnourished people, and in particular, children. Estimates of the number of severely malnourished people in the world have ranged from seventy million[1], to 460 million,[2] to one billion.[3] What duties do individuals have to help?

II. UTILITARIAN/CONSEQUENTIALIST APPROACHES

A. The Views of Peter Singer and Garrett Hardin

According to some moral theories the very fact of widespread hunger imposes a duty on each person to do whatever he or she is capable of doing to

From *Public Affairs Quarterly* 2 (1988), 75–90.

accomplish whatever is necessary to see to it that all people have enough to eat. Peter Singer, a utilitarian, writes:

> I begin with the assumption that suffering and death from lack of food, shelter, and medical care are bad . . . My next point is this: if it is in our power to prevent something bad from happening without thereby sacrificing anything of comparable moral importance, we ought, morally, to do it.[4]

Does this mean that governments of prosperous countries ought to call upon their citizens to sacrifice enough of the luxuries of life to pay taxes that will be used to see to it that everyone in the world has the basic necessities of life? Suppose that governments do not do this. Suppose I give a considerable amount to famine relief but the need remains great because many others have not given. Is this case parallel to the following one to which Singer compares it? I have saved the life of one drowning person. There is still another person who needs to be saved. Other people could have saved the second person while I was saving the first but no one did. Even though I have saved one, and even though other people have failed in their duty to try to save the other, it would seem reasonable to claim that I have a duty to try to do so. Would I similarly have a duty to keep on giving more to aid the hungry regardless of the personal sacrifice involved? Many objections raised against giving sacrificially have to do with whether certain kinds of assistance really do much good. But such objections do not really affect the question of how much one should sacrifice to help others, but only have to do with the best way of using what is given (for example, for food assistance, development assistance, family planning, encouraging political change, supporting education, and so on). But if we reach the conclusion that we have a duty to do all we can, just as in the case of the drowning people, we are faced with the problem that James Fishkin has written about, of being overwhelmed with obligations in a way that expands the area of moral duty to the point of obliterating both the area of the morally indifferent and the area of the morally supererogatory.[5]

There are, however, other considerations. What are the long range consequences of keeping people alive? "Neo-malthusians" and "crisis environmentalists" argue that population growth is outstripping food production and also leading both to the depletion of the world's natural resources and the pollution of the environment, so that the more people who are saved the more misery there will be in the long run. Garrett Hardin compares rich nations to lifeboats and the poor of the world to drowning people trying to get into the lifeboats. To allow them in would be to risk sinking the lifeboats and so to risk bringing disaster on everyone. The high rate of population growth among the poor nations insures that even if there is enough room at the moment, eventually the lifeboats will be swamped.[6] The lifeboat ethic is an application of what Hardin calls the logic of the commons. If a pasture is held as common property each herdsman is tempted to overgraze it for the sake of short-term profits. Even the individual who wants to preserve the land for the future has no reason to stop as long as there are others who will continue to overgraze it. Similarly, if we regard the food production of the world as a "commons" to which everyone is entitled we undermine any incentive among the poor of the world to increase production and limit population growth. The increasing population will continually reduce the amount available for each individual while at the same time increasing pollution and putting other strains on the environment.[7] So Hardin writes that "for posterity's sake we should never send food to any population that is beyond the realistic carrying capacity of its land."[8] This view that certain countries should be left to have "massive diebacks of population,"[9] while others should perhaps be helped, has been called "triage."[10]

B. *Questions about These Approaches*

One way of responding to Hardin's argument is to raise questions about the choice of metaphors and their applicability.[11] Why speak of lifeboats rather than of luxury liners? Why should the Asian or African people be compared to the "sheep" who are the greatest threat to the commons when the average American uses up thirty times the amount of the earth's resources as does the average Asian or African,[12] and when the developed nations import more protein from the developing nations than they export to them?[13] How are the lifeboat metaphors applicable when apart from special famine conditions almost every country in the world has the resources necessary to feed its people if they were used primarily for that purpose?[14]

The focus here, however, will be on moral theory. In spite of their very different conclusions, Singer and Hardin both presuppose a utilitarian position that says that what we ought to do depends completely on the anticipated consequences of our choices.[15] A defender of Singer might say that all Hardin's observations do is to impose on all people a duty to redouble their efforts to find and support solutions that avoid both short range hunger and long range disaster. But that answer only increases the problem of overload that Fishkin is concerned with.

III. HUNGER, RESPECT FOR PERSONS AND NEGATIVE DUTIES

Many philosophers, especially those emphasizing the stringency of negative duties, subscribe to Kant's principle of respect for persons, whether or not they are supporters of Kant's moral philosophy taken as a whole. Robert Nozick uses the principle of respect for persons to defend absolute duties to do no harm while at the same time denying the existence of any duties to benefit others.[16] Kant himself, however, maintained that we have imperfect duties to help others.

Nozick's views can be attacked at many points. Even if they were correct, however, it would not follow that governments would have no right to tax citizens to aid people in distress. This is because individuals, corporations (to which individuals are related as stockholders and employees), and governments would still have duties not to harm, and thus also duties to take corrective action in response to past harms. So wealthy countries and their citizens could still have many responsibilities of compensatory justice with respect to the world's poor. Some countries face poverty because their economies are heavily dependent on a single export material or crop (for example, copper in Chile), the prices of which are subject to great fluctuations. If the original situation, or the subsequent fluctuations, were brought about by policies of wealthy nations or their corporations, then suffering does not just happen but is caused by the actions of people in developed nations. If corporations can strangle economies of developing nations and choose to do so if they do not get special tax advantages, or unfairly advantageous contracts, then poverty and hunger are harms caused by the decisions of the wealthy.[17] If, furthermore, government officials are bribed to keep taxes down, as was done in Honduras by the banana companies, then poverty is directly caused by human actions. If a developed nation overthrows the government of a poor nation which tries to correct some past injustice (as was done when the C.I.A. helped overthrow the democratically elected government of Guatamala in 1954 in order to protect the interests of the United Fruit Company), then poverty is a harm caused by human actions.[18] The decisions of the Soviet Union to import large amounts of grain from the United States during the Nixon administration led to a dramatic and unexpected rise in the price of grain on the world market, which in turn caused hunger. Americans' use of energy at twice the rate of Western Europeans must raise energy prices for the poor. Dramatic price increases by oil exporting nations no doubt meant that people went without petroleum-based fertilizers, or energy to transport food or pump water for irrigation, and so led to additional people dying of hunger.[19] When petroleum prices fall the poverty of people in some oil-exporting countries is aggravated because of the difficulty their governments have financing their debts—debts which were acquired partially due to the encouragement of the banks in the wealthy countries.

What duties do the wealthy countries have to the poor and hungry of the world? The first duty is not to harm them. While seldom are the hungry intentionally killed, they are often killed in the same way that someone is killed by a reckless driver who just does not take into consideration what his actions might do to other vulnerable human beings, and there is no doubt that reckless drivers are to be held accountable for what they do.[20] In some cases it may be morally justifiable to endanger the lives of people in order to work toward some desirable goal, as it may be morally justifiable to risk people's lives in order to rush a critically ill person to the hospital. But a person who is speeding for good reason, or who benefits from that speeding, is not thereby relieved of responsibility for someone who is thereby injured, for otherwise the endangered or harmed would be treated only as means to the ends of others. Similarly, those who make or benefit from economic and political decisions are not relieved of responsibility for those who are thereby harmed or endangered. So even if we were to accept the view that no individual or government has any duty to aid those in distress simply because they are in distress, there would still be few people of more than adequate means in the real world who would not have an obligation to aid those in need. As Onora Nell writes:

> Only if we knew that we were not part of any system of activities causing unjustifiable deaths could we have no duties to support policies which seek to avoid such deaths. Modern economic causal chains are so complex that it is likely that only those who are economically isolated and self-sufficient could know that they are part of no such system of activities.[21]

With respect to compensating those who have been harmed we do not have to be part of the causal chain that causes harm in order to have an obligation to those who still bear the effects of past harm. If *A* stole *B*'s money yesterday and gave the money to *C* today, *C* obviously has a duty to return it. While in some cases mentioned above decisions were made by companies, individuals and governments still were beneficiaries of such decisions through lower prices and increased tax revenue. Furthermore, it would not make any difference if *A* stole *B*'s money before *C* was born. Consider the following case:

> Bengal (today's Bangledesh and the West Bengal state of India), the first territory the British conquered in Asia, was a prosperous province with highly developed centers of manufacturing and trade, and an economy as advanced as any prior to the industrial revolution. The British reduced Bengal to poverty through plunder, heavy land taxes and trade restrictions that barred competitive Indian goods from England, but gave British goods free entry into India. India's late Prime Minister Nehru commented bitterly, "Bengal can take pride in the fact that she helped greatly in giving birth to the Industrial Revolution in England."[22]

Those who benefited from the Industrial Revolution in England, including those alive today, would still have duties to aid Bengal, just as those who inherited a fortune partially based on stolen money have a duty to return what was stolen, with interest, even though they themselves are in no way guilty of the theft. So it is with most citizens of the industrialized West with respect to the poor of some parts of the world. However, in the light of the complexity of both the causal chains of harm and the causal chains of benefit, we are again faced with a great deal of uncertainty as to the allocation of responsibility for correcting for past injustices.[23]

IV. HUNGER, POSITIVE DUTIES, AND THE IDEA OF A FAIR SHARE

So there is no doubt that a Kantian ethic would include duties of reparation for harms done to people in the past and that this would be a basis of obligations to aid many of the underdeveloped countries in the world today, even though it would be difficult to specify the extent of obligation. But is there a duty to help those in severe need even if the causes of the need are not due to any past injustice or are unknown, as may also be true about parts of the world today? Kant does not always treat duties to aid others as fully binding, but whether or not, as one Kantian argues, "it is impermissible not to promote the well-being of others,"[24] it can be argued that it is impermissible not to relieve others in distress and provide them with the basic necessities of life, for this is to fail to treat them as having any value as ends in themselves.[25] To put it another way, failing to help is to violate subsistence rights, and, as Henry Shue argues, whatever sorts of reasons can be given in favor of regarding human beings as having security rights can also be given in favor of regarding them as having subsistence rights.[26] Or, to put it another way, it is to fail to take into account the vulnerability of the world's poor toward the affluent (taken collectively), and it is the vulnerability of people to others (individually or collectively) that is the foundation of most (or all) of both our positive and negative duties to others.[27]

To what extent do individuals and nations have a duty to relieve those in distress? Is there a middle way between Singer and Nozick? Perhaps the following line of reasoning would provide a guideline. An estimate can be made of what resources would be needed to feed the hungry, bring about political and economic change, promote development, limit population growth, and to do whatever is necessary to see that all people have a minimally decent standard of living (or that their basic rights are met). Some formula based on ability to help could determine what a fair share would be for each citizen of a developed country to contribute to the needs of those in distress in that country and to that country's share of helping the people of other nations. To the extent that nations adopt this procedure and make it part of their tax structure a person could fulfill the duty of doing her share by paying her taxes.[28] The ideal would be for nations to do this so that the responsibilities would be carried out and the burden would be distributed fairly.[29] To the extent that nations have not done this (and it is unlikely that any have) what duties do citizens have to contribute through private or religious agencies? Henry Shue correctly observes that "How much sacrifice can reasonably be expected from one person for the sake of another, even for the sake of honoring the other's rights, is one of the most fundamental questions in morality."[30] Nozick, as we have seen, answers with "None." Many answer with "Some" without going on to give a more precise answer. In the absence of adequate government action each individual could still make some sort of estimate of what a fair share would be and give that amount (or what remains of that amount after taking into consideration that part of her taxes that are used for appropriate purposes) through private or religious agencies. I am claiming that it is a strict duty or duty of perfect obligation for an individual to give at least her fair share, according to some plausible formula,[31] toward seeing that all human beings are treated as ends in themselves, which involves seeing that they have the basic necessities of life in so far as that can depend on the actions of others.[32] . . .

On the other hand there is the problem of whether the failure of some people to fulfill their duties increases the duties of others. If many are not giving a fair share, does the individual who is already giving a fair share have a duty to give more? The example of the two drowning people suggests that the individual who has done his fair share does have a duty to do more. But there is a major difference between the two cases. Saving people from drowning, in so far as the chances of losing one's own life are not great, is something that takes a minimal amount of time out of the rescuer's life and does not threaten his ability to live a life of pursuing goals he sets for himself. A similar duty to keep on giving of one's resources, even after one has done his fair share, would threaten to eclipse everything else a person might choose to do with his life, for example, develop his talents, raise a family, send his children to college, and so on, so that person would become nothing but a means to meeting the needs of others.[33] The idea of a strict duty to do at least one's fair share seems to avoid the problem of overload (unless the total need is overwhelming) and draws a line at a plausible point somewhere between doing nothing and sacrificing one's whole life to the cause of relieving the distress of others.[34] . . . Of course a person might choose to make the rescuing of those in distress her special vocation, and it may be noble for her to do so, but to claim that if the needs of others are great enough she has a duty to surrender any choice about the direction of her own life is to claim that a person has a duty to be purely the means to meeting the needs of others, and so in fact a duty to love others not as oneself, but instead of oneself. On the other hand, not to recognize a duty to give a fair share is to indicate that one believes either that it is not important that the needs of those in distress should be met (perhaps because they do not have subsistence rights) or that others should do more than their fair share.[35] It might be said that the first is at least a sin against compassion (if not also against justice) and the second is a sin against fairness or justice. In either case one is treating the ends and purposes of others as having less validity than one's own, or from another point of view, one is not loving others as oneself.

NOTES

1. This is a projection made by Nick Eberstadt from the World Health Organization's estimate that there are ten million severely malnourished children under five in the world. ("Myths of the Food Crisis," *New York Review of Books,* vol. 23 Feb. 19, 1976,) pp. 32–37.
2. This is a figure prepared by the United Nations for the 1974 World Food Conference in Rome.
3. Lester Brown, *In the Human Interest* (New York: Norton, 1974), p. 98.
4. Peter Singer, "Famine, Affluence, and Morality," *Philosophy and Public Affairs,* vol. 1 (1972), p. 231.
5. James Fishkin, *The Limits of Obligation* (New Haven: Yale University Press, 1982), especially chapters 1–7, 9 and 18.
6. Garrett Hardin, "Lifeboat Ethics: "The Case Against Helping the Poor," *Psychology Today,* vol. 8 (1974), pp. 38–43, 123–126.
7. Garrett Hardin, "The Tragedy of the Commons," *Science,* vol. 102 (1968), pp. 1243–1248.

8. Garrett Hardin, "Carrying Capacity as an Ethical Concept," in George R. Lucas and Thomas W. Ogletree (eds.), *Lifeboat Ethics: The Moral Dilemmas of World Hunger,* (New York: Harper and Row, 1976), p. 131.

9. Part of the title of an article by Garrett Hardin, "Another Face of Bioethics: The Case for Massive 'Diebacks' of Population," *Modern Medicine,* vol. 65 (March 1, 1975).

10. The word originally had to do with the choice of giving medical help to those who could be expected to recover if and only if they were treated rather than to those who would likely recover without help or to those with little hope of survival. [See Stuart W. Hinds, 'Relations of Medical Triage to World Famine: A History," in Lucas and Ogletree, *op. cit.* pp. 29-51.] The term was first applied to problems of hunger and population in 1967 by Paul and William Paddock in *Famine—1975!* (Boston: Little, Brown & Co., 1967). The application of the term to world hunger and to nations rather than to individuals has been challenged. [See Hinds, "Relations," and Donald W. Schriver, Jr., "Lifeboaters and Mainliners," in Lucas and Ogletree, *op. cit.,* p. 144.]

11. Paul Verghese, "Muddled Metaphors," in Lucas and Ogletree, *op. cit.,* p. 152.

12. *Ibid.* While changes in cattle production and eating habits may have brought some changes, at one time it was estimated that the average American citizen consumed 1,850 pounds of grain a year directly and through meat production, compared to 400 pounds in poor countries. [Arthur Simon, *Bread for the World* (New York: Paulist Press; Grand Rapids, Michigan: Wm B. Eerdmans, 1975), p. 56.] It was also estimated that the United States used as much energy for its air-conditioners as the billion people of China used for all purposes and that the United States wasted as much energy as Japan used.

13. U.N.'s *Handbook of International Trade and Development Statistics,* 1972; and U.N.'s *Monthly Bulletin of Statistics,* July 1975 and Feb., 1976; both cited by Ronald J. Sidor, *Rich Christians in an Age of Hunger* (Downers Grove, Ill.: Inter-varsity Press, 1977), p. 154; U.S. Bureau of the Census, *Statistical Abstract of the U.S.,* 1976, pp. 818, 820, cited by Sidor, p. 156. Protein is imported in the form of oilseed, oilseed products, and fish meal while grain is exported.

14. Frances Moore Lappe and Joseph Collins, *Exploding the Hunger Myths* (San Francisco: Institute for Food and Development Policy, 1979), pp. 5-7.

15. John Plamenatz points out that Paley and Bentham also arrived at incompatible conclusions on almost all practical issues from very similar theoretical principles [*The English Utilitarians* (Oxford: Blackwell, 2nd ed., 1958), p. 56]. When Joseph Fletcher interprets the Christian ethic of loving one's neighbor in a way that makes it indistinguishable from such utilitarianism it faces the same difficulties. See Fletcher, "Feeding the Hungry, an Ethical Appraisal," in Lucas and Ogletree, *op. cit.,* pp. 52-79.

16. Robert Nozick, *Anarchy, State, and Utopia* (New York: Basic Books, Inc., 1974), pp. 30-35.

17. As occurred in Panama, Honduras, and Costa Rica at the hands of the fruit and banana imported companies, United Brands, Castle and Cooke, and Del Monte.

18. At that time the U.S. Secretary of State was John Foster Dulles, past president of United Fruit and a large shareholder. Allen Dulles, whose law firm had written agreements between Guatamala and United Fruit, was head of the CIA. See Carl Oglesby and Richard Shaull, *Containment and Change* (New York: Macmillan, 1967), p. 104.

19. This occurred after the developed nations introduced into Third World countries more productive types of grain which, unfortunately, need more water and fertilizer than other types.

20. There are, of course, still problems with the moral relevance of different sorts of causal relationships between past actions and harm to others. Have Western nations incurred special obligations to do something about poverty and hunger because they encouraged population growth by providing medicine and sanitation without dealing with the birth rate? If advantages to some countries and disadvantages to others are a byproduct of chance conditions and the operation of the free market system, do those who have benefited from these conditions have duties to those who were harmed? (For example, in 1968 it cost Brazil 45 bags of coffee to buy one U.S. jeep as compared to 14 in 1954) [Pierre Ghedo, *Why is the Third World Poor?* (Maryknoll, N.Y.: Orbis Books, 1973), p. 64.])

21. Onora Nell, "Lifeboat Earth," *Philosophy and Public Affairs,* vol. 4 (1975), p. 286.

22. Arthur Simon, *Bread for the World,* (New York: Paulist Press, 1975), p. 41.

23. For some of these problems see Goodin, *Protecting the Vulnerable* (Chicago: University of Chicago Press, 1986), pp. 159-160.

24. Alan Donagan, *Theory of Morality* (Chicago: University of Chicago Press, 1977), p. 85.

25. J. G. Murphy thinks that Kant gets into difficulty because he fails to distinguish the duty to relieve distress from the duty to benefit others (which he treats as not absolutely binding). [*Kant: The Philosophy of Right* (New York: St. Martin's Press, 1970), pp. 45-46.]

26. Henry Shue, *Basic Rights* (Princeton: Princeton University Press, 1980), Chapters 1 & 2.

27. This is the thesis of Goodin's book *(op. cit.)* with which I am in general agreement.

28. I would agree with Henry Shue's claim that the positive duties that a government has toward persons outside its jurisdiction are duties it has, not directly, but as an agent of its citizens as they employ it to carry out their duties. (Henry Shue, *op. cit.,* p. 151)

29. As is also argued for by Goodin *(op. cit.,* p. 164) and Shue *(op. cit.* p. 118).

30. Shue, *op. cit.,* p. 114.

31. Of course the idea of a fair share is rather inexact. Presumably one should think in terms of placing a graduated income tax on oneself. But with what sort of gradation?

32. Henry Shue places things that might be sacrificed on a scale. Each individual has a duty to sacrifice the first level and only the first level of goods, that is, the fulfillment of preferences, in order to meet the basic rights of others, unless everyone's making that level of sacrifice will not be sufficient to meet those rights. In that case he has a duty to sacrifice goods of the next level, those of cultural enrichment *(op. cit.,* pp. 114-115). Suppose, however, that the basic rights of others could be met if each affluent person sacrificed 25% of his or her preferences (assuming for the sake of the example that they have the same number of preferences) but that 75% fail to do so. Does this mean that the other 25% have a duty of perfect obligation to sacrifice 100% of their preferences? I would say that they do not.

33. Shue's views seem to be similar. He says that a person never has a duty to sacrifice a basic right and that, while doing so for the sake of the basic rights of others would always be super-erogatory, doing so for something other than the

basic rights of others should be forbidden (*op. cit.,* pp. 115–116). But what could be a more basic right than the right to have a life of one's own to live? Saving many people from drowning does not threaten that.

34. Again this is the "overload" problem that Fishkin devotes attention to. Some other formula could also avoid the overload problem, such as whatever is necessary up to one and a half times one's fair share. But I do not see any way to argue for one formula rather than another

35. See also Goodin, *op. cit.,* p. 165.

SUGGESTIONS FOR FURTHER READING

Aiken, William and Hugh LaFollette, eds. *World Hunger and Moral Obligation.* (Englewood Cliffs, NJ: Prentice-Hall, 1977).

This good anthology contains a postscript by Peter Singer to his "Famine, Affluence, and Morality."

Cullity, Garrett. "International Aid and the Scope of Kindness,"*Ethics* 105:1 (October 1994), 99–127.

This is a recent attempt to defend the conclusions reached by Peter Singer in "Famine, Affluence, and Morality" concerning the wrongness of failing to help those who are hungry.

Dworkin, Ronald. "What Is Equality? Part 1: Equality of Welfare,"*Philosophy & Public Affairs* 10:3 (Summer 1981), 185–246, and "What Is Equality? Part 2: Equality of Resources," *Philosophy & Public Affairs* 10:4 (Fall 1981), 283–45.

These are an attempt to define and defend an egalitarian ideal by a prominent legal philosopher.

Nozick, Robert. *Anarchy, State, and Utopia.* (New York: Basic Books, 1974).

This is a very sophisticated elaboration and defense of a libertarian position. This is probably the most influential statement of libertarianism, at least among academics who are not themselves libertarians.

O'Neill, Onora. "Ending World Hunger." In Tom Regan (ed.), *Matters of Life and Death*, 3rd edition (New York: McGraw-Hill, 1993), pp. 235–279.

An excellent summary of the problem of world hunger. It discusses how both utilitarians and Kantians would approach the problem.

Rawls, John. *A Theory of Justice.* (Cambridge, MA: Harvard University Press, 1971).

Already a "classic" in moral and political philosophy, in this work Rawls defends a liberal conception of justice according to which the justice of basic social institutions depends in part on the extent to which they work to the advantage of those members of society who are worst off. Short selections from this work are reprinted in Chapter 1.

Sterba, James P. "From Liberty to Welfare," *Ethics* 105:1 (October 1994), 64–98.

Sterba believes that all defensible contemporary conceptions of justice will have the same practical implications. In particular, all will support a right to welfare and a right to equal opportunity. In this paper Sterba argues that the proper construal of libertarianism will lead to support for these rights.

Chapter 6

DISCRIMINATION AND AFFIRMATIVE ACTION

With its 1954 decision in *Brown v. Board of Education*, the United States Supreme Court found that racial segregation in "separate but equal" educational institutions was unconstitutional. This significant public policy decision was followed in 1964 by the passage of the Civil Rights Act, which made it illegal for employers to discriminate against a prospective employee on the basis of such characteristics as race, color, religion, sex or national origin. Since most of you reading this chapter will have been born well after both of these events, you might be inclined to think that discrimination is a thing of the past. Many Americans, however, continue to experience some form of discrimination. From the stubbornness of the so-called "Glass Ceiling" in major corporations that discourages women from being promoted to senior management levels, to the recent lawsuit brought by four African-American federal law enforcement officials against a national restaurant chain for refusing to serve them breakfast, acts of discrimination continue to take place, and broader patterns of discrimination are still woven throughout society.

Because it is a present-day reality for many, the problem of discrimination demands careful study. Even if one were to claim that invidious forms of discrimination such as legally segregated schools or workplaces no longer exist, the negative *effects* of these forms of discrimination continue to linger. Racist attitudes, incidents of racial harassment, and a racial imbalance in the distribution of resources in society are problematic. How, though, should society correct the injustices of its past discriminatory practices so as to address these negative effects? This question, as linked to the continuing debate over affirmative action in this society, will form the focus of our attention in this chapter.

WHAT IS DISCRIMINATION?

Before we turn to consider this question, we need to clarify what discrimination is and why discrimination can be unjust.

Imagine the following situation: You show up for this course on the first day of class, hoping to add it to your schedule for the term. Five other students also show up with the same hope, and there is only one empty seat in the class. After talking with you and the other students, the professor decides to give you the available space on the basis of the fact that although all of you need to take this course to fulfill a requirement, you alone are a senior and the others first- and second-year students.

Have you been the beneficiary of discriminatory behavior on the part of the professor? One could argue that the professor has indeed *made a discrimination*, simply by virtue of making a choice that gives one person a recognized good (a seat in the class) by denying it to someone else. However, making a discrimination and discriminating against someone are not the same thing. What turns the one into the other has to do with the reasons for why the decision went one way and not another. In this case, the decision to admit you to the class was based on your status as a senior. If you could not add the class, your graduation date might have been affected; if the other students were turned away from the class, there would also be a negative impact on them, but it would not be as great. Since being a senior is generally a *relevant* consideration for adding a student to a course, the professor has not discriminated against the other students in excluding them from the class.

It has often been said that one of the principles of justice is the demand that equals be treated as equals; from this perspective, discrimination would occur when equals are treated in an unequal manner. In our example, though, those affected by the professor's action are all students and hence all equal members of a group. This suggests a need for a more complex definition of discrimination. Here is one possibility:

> Discrimination is the denial of a right or a good to someone on the basis of an *irrelevant* consideration related to that person's membership in a particular group.

Thus, if you were given the remaining seat in this class not because you were a senior but because you were Hispanic and the other students were Asian-American, or because you were Protestant and the others were Islamic, or because you were married and the other students were single, the professor's decision to give you the seat would count as discrimination in this sense.

Two points need to be made about this definition of discrimination:

1. Discrimination in the sense just defined is "unjust discrimination." Unless specifically indicated otherwise, the word "discrimination" in this chapter will mean "unjust discrimination."
2. Very often, discrimination is motivated by dislike, scorn, or even hatred for a particular group, and/or a belief that this group is inferior to the group to which one belongs oneself. While these factors play a key role in the problem of discrimination, they are not a part of the definition of discrimination itself.

On a broad scale, what makes discrimination unjust is its denial of a "level playing field" of opportunities for all members of society. In this society, blacks have been particularly disadvantaged by Jim Crow laws that followed in the aftermath of slavery and which denied them goods solely on the basis of the color of their skin, but women, Native Americans, and other racial and ethnic minorities have also been denied educational and job opportunities just because of their gender or group membership. Since our society demands that something be done to right the balance when acts of injustice are directed toward specific individuals, it makes sense that it has also sought a way to rectify the injustice done to many of this country's citizens who historically have been victims of discrimination. Hopes that such a level playing field could be brought about through government intervention led to the development of the policy of affirmative action, first proposed in close association with the Civil Rights Act of 1964.

THE DEBATE OVER AFFIRMATIVE ACTION

As Louis P. Pojman points out in one of this chapter's reading selections, Title VII of the Civil Rights Act expressly prohibits discrimination in employment on the basis of considerations such as race and sex. Title VII also makes it clear that the intent of this prohibition is to lead to equality of opportunity in employment, not to programs of preferential treatment. Such programs, though, quickly followed on the heels of the Civil Rights Act in order to speed up the process of achieving more equity in employment. In 1965 and 1967, President Lyndon Johnson issued two executive orders calling for "affirmative action" to supplement the provisions of Title VII. He also created a new office, the Office of Federal Contract Compliance, under the Department of Labor to administer affirmative action.

By the early 1970s, this office called for contractors (including universities with government contracts) to develop "goals and timetables" for the hiring of members of "under-utilized" groups, such as women and minorities, that had suffered under the discriminatory laws, practices and policies in our history. This language seemed to point toward a shift in the focus of affirmative action. Its original goal of creating equality of opportunity through such practices as actively recruiting applications for positions in the workforce and educational institutions from members of groups that were unfairly denied such positions in the past now appeared to be overshadowed by a stronger goal. Affirmative action now appeared focused on creating equality of results through practices of preferential treatment aimed at giving various degrees of preference to members of these disadvantaged groups in employment and admission to universities, and in awarding contracts.

Even though affirmative action has been controversial since its inception, it is under stronger attack as we write this introduction in 1996 than it has been at any point in the intervening thirty years. Currently, for example, sufficient signatures have been collected in the state of California to place before the voters an amendment to the state's constitution essentially ending all such programs. In March 1996, the United States Court of Appeals for the Fifth Circuit ruled that an affirmative action program at the University of Texas School of Law that took race into account in its admissions process was unconstitutional. This ruling represented a challenge to the precedent established in the 1978 Supreme Court *Bakke* decision, a portion of which is included in this chapter. Few, at this point, expect affirmative action to survive in its present state. Even President Bill Clinton, whose political affiliations are primarily with those who have supported affirmative action, has recently said that it is time to rethink the practice. Such a rethinking should include thought both about the purposes for which affirmative action was designed and about the features of it that many find objectionable.

Both considerations of justice, and more consequentialist considerations about policies needed to bring about a better society, play a role in the debate about affirmative action. Supporters of affirmative action frequently argue that it is demanded by justice, while those who are opposed often argue that justice condemns the practice. Similarly, supporters and opponents tend to disagree about the consequences of affirmative action. We shall turn now to sketch some of the frequently heard claims about the justice or injustice of affirmative action and then consider some of the disagreements about its consequences.

Justice Requires Affirmative Action

The most straightforward argument based on justice offered in support of the policy of affirmative action stresses the injustice of discrimination in our nation's history. Since those who were the objects of such discrimination were wronged, it is not morally sufficient merely to end that wrongdoing, as arguably was done by civil rights legislation and court decisions. Unjust discrimination has created economic and educational disadvantages for those who were its victims. Since those disadvantages were wrongly imposed, it can be argued that they must be removed (a matter of rectification) or that compensation for them must be paid by those who are guilty of the wrongdoing. Even if it is granted that rectification or compensation is required by justice, the defender of affirmative action policies needs to argue further that those policies are appropriate forms of rectification or compensation. Since at least part of the wrongness of discrimination lies in its creation of unjust economic and educational disadvantages, giving preference in hiring practices and educational admissions to those who suffered discrimination may seem to be a reasonable way to remove or compensate for some of those disadvantages.

Those opposed to affirmative action programs may grant that wrongful harms require compensation but respond that at least many such programs fail to provide compensation to those who deserve it and exact it from the wrong parties. Legally sanctioned discrimination, it is argued, has been absent from our society for decades. As a result, both those who suffered it and those who engaged in it are either no longer alive or beyond the age at which they could be affected directly by affirmative action, the impact of which is felt primarily by younger members of society who are seeking employment or admission to educational institutions. Affirmative action programs that give preference to members of groups who were targets of discrimination will do little to compensate a ninety-year-old black sharecropper who has lived his entire life in the Deep South who almost certainly was the target of discrimination, nor to the ninety-year-old woman who aspired to be a physician only to be told that nursing was the only role in medicine for which her sex suited her. Similarly, affirmative action exacts no direct compensation from the ninety-year-old Ku Klux Klan member nor the retired dean of a prestigious medical school who worked diligently during his service to exclude women from the student body. By the same token, consider the twenty-one-year-old white male who is denied admission to law school, even though he would have been admitted were there no preferential treatment in admissions. It is he who pays the compensation—even though he is unlikely to have been guilty of at least the most overt forms of discrimination and oppression from our past. Similarly, the beneficiaries of affirmative action tend to be younger, and hence less deserving of compensation. Even if those who pay and receive compensation under affirmative action programs deserve to do so, it can be argued that they are less deserving than those left untouched by them.

In response to this attack on the compensation justification of affirmative action, at least two strategies might be employed. First, one could claim that it is not necessarily the case that affirmative action programs compensate the wrong parties. A second approach would be to take the position that affirmative action programs do not necessarily exact compensation from the wrong parties.

The first strategy mentioned in the preceding paragraph derives from the perception that it is false to view discrimination as a horror largely confined to the past. Even though Jim Crow laws are behind us, and the professions are open to women, many women and members of minority groups face obstacles that white males largely do not. In discussions about this issue in classes at our university, nearly every Hispanic and African American male has stories to tell about being pulled over by police officers merely because he did not "look like" he should be where he was. While such experiences are not unknown to some white males, they are less a feature of daily life. The prevalence of sexual harassment in education and the workplace, the victims of which are primarily—though not exclusively—women, might also be regarded as a form of discrimination for which some remedy is needed. Thus, given the continuing social presence of discrimination, arguably even young members of traditionally discriminated-against groups may themselves be targets of discrimination.

The second strategy that might be used to respond to this attack on the compensation justification of affirmative action addresses the claim that young white males owe no compensation if they themselves are guiltless of discrimination. It is based on the idea that even those who are guiltless of wrongdoing can owe compensation to those who are victims of it when those who are guiltless have been innocent beneficiaries of injustice. Suppose, for instance, that you buy a used car without knowing the seller had stolen the vehicle and forged the registration and title. It may be thought that though you are innocent of any wrongdoing, you have no right to the car if its original owner claims it. Of course, you have a claim against the thief, but if the thief has disappeared, it can be argued that you must rectify the wrong by returning the car even though you are guiltless and will suffer economic loss by returning it. Given the way in which wealth is distributed in the United States, it may be argued that at least many whites are the beneficiaries of past unjust oppression and discrimination, and that at least many nonwhites are victims of the same injustice. If so, some defenders of affirmative action might argue that the programs are justifiable as compensation. However, it is worth asking whether current affirmative action programs which are based entirely on considerations of sex and ethnicity, without consideration of the particular histories of the individuals involved, could be justified by this line of argument.

Justice Condemns Affirmative Action

Many argue that affirmative action is incompatible with a demand of justice that society not discriminate against any of its members on grounds of race, ethnicity, or gender. Given this demand, opponents of affirmative action, such as Lisa Newton, sometimes argue that the policy constitutes "reverse discrimination" and is wrong in exactly the same way, and for the same reasons, as the policies of past discrimination to which it is a response. What justice demands, according to this line of thought, is a color- and gender-blind society. Some who propose this argument maintain that affirmative action programs discriminate against white males and are therefore just like the historical discrimination in our society against nonwhites and women.

While there are similarities between policies of affirmative action and, for example, segregationalist policies, there are dissimilarities as well. To evaluate carefully the argument that affirmative action is unjust in the same way as segregation, it would be necessary to consider both the similarities and differences, and ask which are more significant morally. Opponents of affirmative action are likely to point to considerations about desert, maintaining that those most qualified for positions in the workplace or educational institutions deserve those positions and that both affirmative action and historical discrimination fail to award such positions purely on the basis of qualifications, and hence fail to give to people what they deserve. To elaborate this line of argument, one would need to explain why being more qualified makes someone more deserving of a position, as well as what makes a person more qualified than another for a position. Defenders of some forms of affirmative action would argue that the policy is, in fact, required to ensure that the more qualified receive adequate consideration since some factors traditionally thought to be aspects of qualification are racially or gender biased.

Supporters of affirmative action are also likely to argue that some of the ways in which it differs from historical discrimination are of more moral significance than the similarities between the two. In particular, defenders point to the differences in motives and outcomes. The purpose behind historical discrimination was to exclude members of certain groups from opportunities, while affirmative action is intended to include members of groups who have been previously excluded. This difference in purpose leads also to a difference in outcome. During the period of "separate but equal," if one went to at least some southern state universities, one would see no blacks among the students and faculty. If one currently goes to a prestigious law school with a strong affirmative action program, one might see fewer white males than one would see in the absence of such a program, but one would still see many white males among the students and faculty. In other words, under affirmative action policies some individual white males may be excluded from opportunities they might have without those policies, but many white males will still have those opportunities. White males as a group are not excluded.

This difference in purpose and outcome, it would be argued by some defenders of affirmative action, is also significant because it makes a difference in the "message" sent to those who are excluded. With historical discrimination, those excluded from opportunities were stigmatized as being members of a group unworthy of full opportunity. As Edwin Hettinger points out in his defense of affirmative action included in this chapter, affirmative action does not stigmatize the individual white males who may not receive a position in the same way.

Those opposed to affirmative action might respond to the considerations raised above by arguing that they too quickly dismiss the complaint of the individual white males who are excluded from certain opportunities because of affirmative action. Indeed they might argue that this defense only further strengthens the claim that affirmative action is unjust in the same way as historical discrimination. Part of the injustice of discrimination of all types, according to this line of thought, is a failure to judge people as individuals with their own particular strengths and weaknesses and, instead, to judge them as members of some group. This view would be another way of claiming that a just society would be color and gender blind.

Considerations of the Social Good

A goal of many on both sides of the affirmative action issue is the promotion of a society in which individuals are in fact judged more as individuals, a society freer of discrimination of any sort. For some, the disagreement about affirmative action is about whether it furthers or hinders that goal. We would like now to look briefly at some of the hopes and concerns that have been raised about the social effects of affirmative action.

One social goal potentially served by affirmative action might be to reduce the economic inequality in America. Even if one is not opposed in principle to great disparities in wealth, one might believe that such inequality is particularly insidious when it falls largely along ethnic and gender lines. Men in our society do tend to control greater wealth and power than women, and whites more than nonwhites. This form of inequality might be thought to be unfortunate for more than one reason. It might be thought, for instance, that such distributions could only be brought about by unjust institutions; if everyone truly had equal opportunities, the distribution of wealth, prestige, and power resulting from competition for those opportunities would not be expected to be skewed along lines of gender and ethnicity. This line of argument, however, leads back to affirmative action as a means of providing compensation for past injustice, and here we are more concerned with more future-oriented considerations.

One concern about inequality, especially inequality that includes many living in poverty, is that poverty can lead to social instability. The desperately poor, for instance, may have an incentive to turn to crime. While these considerations may lend support to some form of preferential treatment for the poor, some would argue these considerations would not support current affirmative action policies which give preferential treatment on the basis of race and gender rather than on grounds of economic disadvantage. In fact, some who currently advocate the rethinking of affirmative action do support replacing current policies with ones based on economic disadvantage. Still, advocates of our current policies might claim that some race- and gender-conscious policies might be in order, because the destabilizing effects of poverty may be exacerbated when members of some ethnic groups are much more likely to suffer it than members of others.

In the 1978 Supreme Court *Bakke* decision, it was ruled that some forms of affirmative action in admission to educational institutions could be justified by the educational benefits derived from having a racially diverse student body. In large part because of that decision, many programs in colleges and universities that once would have been called "affirmative action" programs are now called "diversity" programs. At least some of the concerns about diversity are also concerns about the future good of society. One concern, different from the one endorsed by the Supreme Court, might be that we should want education to serve the needs of the entire society. Since our society is diverse, the entire society will be served only if the student body is diverse as well. What are the educational benefits of diversity accepted by the Supreme Court? They may include straightforward educational benefits in academic disciplines, but more important, perhaps, are possible aspects of what might be thought of as social education. In a diverse society, it is arguably important that one learn about people different from oneself. Such learning would include lessons both about how we are all the same and about ways in which we differ. Such learning is much more likely to occur in institutional and social environments that include people from diverse backgrounds than in ones that are *de facto* segregated. One possible benefit of this lesson would be the possible disintegration of negative stereotypes that many hold about ethnic groups different from their own.

Ironically, many of those who are most fervently opposed to affirmative action argue that these programs have had a result quite different from the beneficial one we have been considering. Instead of erasing negative stereotypes, they argue that affirmative action has reinforced them in those who already held them and, even much worse, created such stereotypes in some who would not have held them had there been no policies of affirmative action. They argue that since affirmative action gives preferential treatment in hiring and admissions to members of some groups, at least some members of those groups are hired or admitted who are less qualified for their positions than those who do not belong to groups receiving preferential treatment. The result, it is argued, is that there are generally lower levels of performance and higher rates of failure among the groups who are preferred. The inferior performance then enhances the negative stereotype that members of those groups are less able. As Shelby Steele argues in this chapter, not only are such stereotypes enhanced among members of groups who do not receive preferential treatment, but individuals from groups receiving preferential treatment may also either think of themselves as inferior or worry that they could not have "made it on their own" without such a preference. A further, though related, negative result might be that some white males who see themselves as being unfairly denied opportunities being given to those less qualified become bitter, and in at least some cases, develop racist and misogynist beliefs.

Even though affirmative action certainly has had some unfortunate effects on the attitudes that some people have on matters of gender and ethnicity, these bad effects need to be balanced against the good effects such programs have had. It is likely that for some the educational benefits of diversity have included a weakening of negative stereotypes. It is arguable that without the programs trying to create diversity in education and the workplace over the past decades, there would be much greater *de facto* gender and ethnic segregation in such environments, and that it is much easier to maintain false stereotypes in such homogeneous environments than in more heterogeneous ones. Someone arguing in this manner would claim that while affirmative action programs do have some bad effects, the effects of having no such programs would be worse. However, it is not enough to try to compare only our current affirmative action policies with having no such policies at all. It is also worth asking whether there are different programs that can effectively pursue those goals of affirmative action worthy of pursuit, while addressing the concerns of those critical of affirmative action in its present state. In this chapter's reading selections, both Leo Groarke and Thomas E. Hill Jr. take up this question, and thus contribute to the newly invigorated debate about affirmative action in our current society.

The Regents of the
University of California v. Allan Bakke

The *Bakke* decision was a major test of affirmative action as applied to higher education. When Allan Bakke, a white male, applied to medical school at the University of California at Davis in 1973 and 1974, the school had set aside a number of spaces in the entering class for which only members of minority groups could compete in a special admissions process. While Bakke was turned down for admission both times he applied, some of the spaces reserved for minority applicants did not get filled, and many who were accepted for those spaces had lesser qualifications than Bakke. Bakke filed a lawsuit charging reverse discrimination. In 1976, after Bakke won his lawsuit on appeal, the University of California asked the Supreme court to rule on the constitutionality of its special admissions program.

The *Bakke* case was decided by the Supreme court in 1978. In a split decision (5-4), the Court maintained that all but one of the reasons the university used to defend its special admissions program were suspect; and although it perceived that the state did have a valid interest in increasing diversity within the student body of the university, it declared the state had acted unconstitutionally in setting up a "quota" system in order to satisfy this interest. The university could, it declared, take race or ethnicity into account in making admissions decisions, but could not set up special admissions program that excluded some applicants on the basis of their racial or ethnic background.

438 U.S. 265 (1978)

MR. JUSTICE POWELL announced the judgment of the Court.

This case presents a challenge to the special admissions program of the petitioner, the Medical School of the University of California at Davis, which is designed to assure the admission of a specified number of students from certain minority groups. The Superior Court of California sustained respondent's challenge, holding that petitioner's program violated the California Constitution, Title VI of the Civil Rights Act of 1964, 42 U.S.C. §2000d *et. seq.*, and the Equal Protection Clause of the Fourteenth Amendment.

For the reasons stated in the following opinion, I believe that so much of the judgment of the California court as holds petitioner's special admissions program unlawful and directs that respondent be admitted to the Medical School must be affirmed. . . .

I also conclude for the reasons stated in the following opinion that the portion of the court's judgment enjoining petitioner from according any consideration to race in its admissions process must be reversed. . . .

Allan Bakke is a white male who applied to the Davis Medical School in both 1973 and 1974. In both years Bakke's application was considered under the general admissions program, and he received an interview. His 1973 interview was with Dr. Theodore C. West, who considered Bakke "a very desirable applicant to [the] medical school." Despite a strong benchmark score of 468 out of 500, Bakke was rejected. His application had come late in the year, and no applicants in the general admissions process with scores below 470 were accepted after Bakke's application was completed. There were four special admissions slots unfilled at that time, however, for which Bakke was not considered. After his 1973 rejection, Bakke wrote to Dr. George H. Lowrey, Associate Dean and Chairman of the Admissions Committee, protesting that the special admissions program operated as a racial and ethnic quota.

Bakke's 1974 application was completed early in the year. His student interviewer gave him an overall rating of 94, finding him "friendly, well tempered, conscientious and delightful to speak with." His faculty interviewer was, by coincidence, the same Dr. Lowrey to whom he had written in protest of the special admissions program. Dr. Lowrey found Bakke "rather limited in his approach" to the problems of the medical profession and found disturbing Bakke's "very definite opinions which were based more on his personal viewpoints than upon a study of the total problem." Dr. Lowrey gave Bakke the lowest of his six ratings, an 86; his total was 549 out of 600. Again, Bakke's application was rejected. In neither year did the chairman of the admissions committee, Dr. Lowrey, exercise his discretion to place Bakke on the waiting list. In both years, applicants were admitted under the special program with grade point averages, MCAT scores, and benchmark scores significantly lower than Bakke's. . . .

IV

We have held that in "order to justify the use of a suspect classification, a State must show that its purpose or interest is both constitutionally permissible and substantial, and that its use of the classification is 'necessary . . . to the accomplishment' of its purpose or the safeguarding of its interest." The special admissions program purports to serve the purposes of: (i) "reducing the historic deficit of traditionally disfavored minorities in medical schools and in the medical profession," (ii) countering the effects of societal discrimination; (iii) increasing the number of physicians who will practice in communities currently underserved; and (iv) obtaining the educational benefits that flow from an ethnically diverse student body. It is necessary to decide which, if any, of these purposes is substantial enough to support the use of a suspect classification.

A

If petitioner's purpose is to assure within its student body some specified percentage of a particular group merely because of its race or ethnic origin, such a preferential purpose must be rejected not as insubstantial but as facially invalid. Preferring members of any one group for no reason other than race or ethnic origin is discrimination for its own sake. This the Constitution forbids. *E. g., Loving v. Virginia, supra,* at 11; *McLaughlin v. Florida, supra,* at 196; *Brown v. Board of Education,* 347 U.S. 483 (1954).

B

The State certainly has a legitimate and substantial interest in ameliorating, or eliminating where feasible, the disabling effects of identified discrimination. The line of school desegregation cases, commencing with *Brown,* attests to the importance of this state goal and the commitment of the judiciary to affirm all lawful means toward its attainment. In the school cases, the States were required by court order to redress the wrongs worked by specific instances of racial discrimination. That goal was far more focused than the remedying of the effects of "societal discrimination," an amorphous concept of injury that may be ageless in its reach into the past.

We have never approved a classification that aids persons perceived as members of relatively victimized groups at the expense of other innocent individuals in the absence of judicial, legislative, or administrative findings of constitutional or statutory violations. After such findings have been made, the governmental interest in preferring members of the injured groups at the expense of others is substantial, since the legal rights of the victims must be vindicated. In such a case, the extent of the injury and the consequent remedy will have been judicially, legislatively, or administratively defined. Also, the remedial action usually remains subject to continuing oversight to assure that it will work the least harm possible to other innocent persons competing for the benefit. Without such findings of constitutional or statutory violations, it cannot be said that the government has any greater interest in helping one individual than in refraining from harming another. Thus, the government has no compelling justification for inflicting such harm.

Petitioner does not purport to have made, and is in no position to make, such findings. Its broad mission is education, not the formulation of any legislative policy or the adjudication of particular claims of illegality. For reasons similar to those stated in part III of this opinion, isolated segments of our vast governmental structures are not competent to make those decisions, at least in the absence of legislative mandates and legislatively determined criteria. Before relying upon these sorts of findings in establishing a racial classification, a governmental body must have the authority and capability to establish, in the record, that the classification is responsive to identified discrimination. Lacking this capability, petitioner has not carried its burden of justification on this issue.

Hence, the purpose of helping certain groups whom the faculty of the Davis Medical School perceived as victims of "societal discrimination" does not justify a classification that imposes disadvantages upon persons like respondent, who bear no responsibility for whatever harm the beneficiaries of the special admissions program are thought to have suffered. To hold otherwise would be to convert a remedy heretofore reserved for violations of legal rights into a privilege that all institutions throughout the Nation could grant at their pleasure to whatever groups are perceived as victims of societal discrimination. That is a step we have never approved.

C

Petitioner identifies, as another purpose of its program, improving the delivery of health-care services to communities currently underserved. It may be assumed that in some situations a State's interest in facilitating the health care of its citizens is sufficiently compelling to support the use of a suspect classification. But there is virtually no evidence in the record indicating that petitioner's special admissions program is either needed or geared to promote that goal. . . .

Petitioner has simply not carried its burden of demonstrating that it must prefer members of particular ethnic groups over all other individuals in order to promote better health-care delivery to deprived citizens. Indeed, petitioner has not shown that its preferential classification is likely to have any significant effect on the problem.

D

The fourth goal asserted by petitioner is the attainment of a diverse student body. This clearly is a constitutionally permissible goal for an institution of higher education. Academic freedom, though not a specifically enumerated constitutional right, long has been viewed as a special concern of the First Amendment. The freedom of a university to make its own judgments as to education includes the selection of its student body. . . . The, atmosphere of "speculation, experiment and creation"—so essential to the quality of higher education—is widely believed to be promoted by a diverse student body. . . . [I]t is not too much to say that the "nation's future depends upon leaders trained through wide exposure" to the ideas and mores of students as diverse as this Nation of many peoples.

Thus, in arguing that its universities must be accorded the right to select those students who will contribute the most to the "robust exchange of ideas," petitioner invokes a countervailing constitutional interest, that of the First Amendment. In this light, petitioner must be viewed as seeking to achieve a goal that is of paramount importance in the fulfillment of its mission.

It may be argued that there is greater force to these views at the undergraduate level than in a medical school where the training is centered primarily on professional competency. But even at the graduate level, our tradition and experience lend support to the view that the contribution of diversity is substantial. . . . Physicians serve a heterogenous population. An otherwise qualified medical student with a particular background—whether it be ethnic, geographic, culturally advantaged or disadvantaged—may bring to a professional school of medicine experiences, outlooks, and ideas that enrich the training of its student body and better equip its graduates to render with understanding their vital service to humanity.

Ethnic diversity, however, is only one element in a range of factors a university properly may consider in attaining the goal of a heterogenous student body. Although a university must have wide discretion in making the sensitive judgments as to who should be admitted, constitutional limitations protecting individual rights may not be disregarded. Respondent urges—and the courts below have held—that petitioner's dual admissions program is a racial classification that impermissibly infringes his rights under the Fourteenth Amendment. As the interest of diversity is compelling in the context of a university's admissions program, the question remains whether the program's racial classification is necessary to promote this interest. *In re Griffiths,* 413 U.S., at 721–722.

V

A

It may be assumed that the reservation of a specified number of seats in each class for individuals from the preferred ethnic groups would contribute to the attainment of considerable ethnic diversity in the student body. But petitioner's argument that this is the only effective means of serving the interest of diversity is seriously flawed. In a most fundamental sense the argument misconceives the nature of the state interest that would justify consideration of race or ethnic background. It is not an interest in simple ethnic diversity, in which a specified percentage of the student body is in effect guaranteed to be members of selected ethnic groups, with the remaining percentage an undifferentiated aggregation of students. The diversity that furthers a compelling state interest encompasses a far broader array of qualifications and characteristics of which racial or ethnic origin is but a single though important element. Petitioner's special admissions program, focused *solely* on ethnic diversity, would hinder rather than further attainment of genuine diversity.

Nor would the state interest in genuine diversity be served by expanding petitioner's two-track system into a multitrack program with a prescribed number of seats set aside for each identifiable category of applicants. Indeed, it is inconceivable that a university would thus pursue the logic of petitioner's two-track program to the illogical end of insulating each category of applicants with certain desired qualifications from competition with all other applicants.

The experience of other university admissions programs, which take race into account in achieving the educational diversity valued by the First Amendment, demonstrates that the assignment of a fixed number of places to a minority group is not a necessary means toward that end. An illuminating example is found in the Harvard college program:

> "In recent years Harvard College has expanded the concept of diversity to include students from disadvantaged economic, racial and ethnic groups.

Harvard College now recruits not only Californians or Louisianans but also blacks and Chicanos and other minority students. . . .

"In practice, this new definition of diversity has meant that race has been a factor in some admission decisions. When the Committee on Admissions reviews the large middle group of applicants who are 'admissible' and deemed capable of doing good work in their courses, the race of an applicant may tip the balance in his favor just as geographic origin or a life spent on a farm may tip the balance in other candidates' cases. A farm boy from Idaho can bring something to Harvard College that a Bostonian cannot offer. Similarly, a black student can usually bring something that a white person cannot offer. . . .

"In Harvard college admissions the Committee has not set target-quotas for the number of blacks, or of musicians, football players, physicists or Californians to be admitted in a given year. . . . But that awareness [of the necessity of including more than a token number of black students] does not mean that the Committee sets a minimum number of blacks or of people from west of the Mississippi who are to be admitted. It means only that in choosing among thousands of applicants who are not only 'admissible' academically but have other strong qualities, the Committee, with a number of criteria in mind, pays some attention to distribution among many types and categories of students." App. to Brief for Columbia University, Harvard University, Stanford University, and the University of Pennsylvania, as *Amici Curiae* 2-3.

In such an admissions program, race or ethnic background may be deemed a "plus" in a particular applicant's file, yet it does not insulate the individual from comparison with all other candidates for the available seats. The file of a particular black applicant may be examined for his potential contribution to diversity without the factor of race being decisive when compared, for example, with that of an applicant identified as an Italian-American if the latter is thought to exhibit qualities more likely to promote beneficial educational pluralism. Such qualities could include exceptional personal talents, unique work or service experience, leadership potential, maturity, demonstrated compassion, a history of overcoming disadvantage, ability to communicate with the poor, or other qualifications deemed important. In short, an admissions program operated in this way is flexible enough to consider all pertinent elements of diversity in light of the particular qualifications of each applicant, and to place them on the same footing for consideration, although not necessarily according them the same weight. Indeed, the weight attributed to a particular quality may vary from year to year depending upon the "mix" both of the student body and the applicants for the incoming class.

This kind of program treats each applicant as an individual in the admissions process. The applicant who loses out on the last available seat to another candidate receiving a "plus" on the basis of ethnic background will not have been foreclosed from all consideration for that seat simply because he was not the right color or had the wrong surname. It would mean only that his combined qualifications, which may have included similar nonobjective factors, did not outweigh those of the other applicant. His qualifications would have been weighed fairly and competitively, and he would have no basis to complain of unequal treatment under the Fourteenth Amendment.

It has been suggested that an admissions program which considers race only as one factor is simply a subtle and more sophisticated—but no less effective—means of according racial preference than the Davis program. A facial intent to discriminate, however, is evident in petitioner's preference program and not denied in this case. No such facial infirmity exists in an admissions program where race or ethnic background is simply one element—to be weighed fairly against other elements—in the selection process. . . . And a court would not assume that a university, professing to employ a facially nondiscriminatory admissions policy, would operate it as a cover for the functional equivalent of a quota system. In short, good faith would be presumed in the absence of a showing to the contrary in the manner permitted by our cases.

B

In summary, it is evident that the Davis special admissions program involves the use of an explicit racial classification never before countenanced by this Court. It tells applicants who are not Negro, Asian, or Chicano that they are totally excluded from a specific percentage of the seats in an entering class. No matter how strong their qualifications, quantitative and extracurricular, including their own potential for contribution to educational diversity, they are never afforded the chance to compete with applicants from the preferred groups for the special admissions seats. At the same time, the preferred applicants have the opportunity to compete for every seat in the class.

The fatal flaw in petitioner's preferential program is its disregard of individual rights as guaranteed by the Fourteenth Amendment. Such rights are not absolute. But when a State's distribution of benefits or imposition of burdens hinges on ancestry or the color of a person's skin or ancestry, that individual is entitled to a demonstration that the challenged classification is necessary to promote a substantial state interest. Petitioner has failed to carry this burden. For this reason, that portion of the California court's judgment holding petitioner's special admissions invalid under the Fourteenth Amendment must be affirmed.

C

In enjoining petitioner from ever considering the race of any applicant, however, the courts below failed to recognize that the State has a substantial interest that legitimately may be served by a properly devised admissions program involving the competitive consideration of race and ethnic origin. For this reason, so much of the California court's judgment as enjoins petitioner from any consideration of race of any applicant must be reversed. . . .

The Moral Status of
Affirmative Action
Louis P. Pojman

Louis P. Pojman is a professor of philosophy at the University of Mississippi and has published widely on topics in ethics. In this essay, Pojman surveys the historical development of affirmative action policies, as well as a number of arguments both in favor of and against such policies. He distinguishes between two forms of affirmative action: weak affirmative action—in which, for example, a woman might be hired over a white male if all other qualifications were equal—and strong affirmative action—in which, for example, a lesser-qualified female might be hired over a more-qualified male in order to increase the representation of women on a work force. The arguments against strong affirmative action, in Pojman's view, are more compelling than those in its favor. While recognizing that a slightly better case can be made for weak affirmative action, Pojman rejects it as well on the basis of his belief that it is all too likely to turn into its stronger relative.

Hardly a week goes by but that the subject of Affirmative Action does not come up. Whether in the guise of reverse discrimination, preferential hiring, non-traditional casting, quotas, goals and time tables, minority scholarships, or race-norming, the issue confronts us as a terribly perplexing problem. Last summer's Actor's Equity debacle over the casting of the British actor, Jonathan Pryce, as a Eurasian in Miss Saigon; Assistant Secretary of Education Michael Williams' judgement that Minority Scholarships are unconstitutional; the "Civil Rights Bill of 1991," reversing recent decisions of the Supreme Court which constrain preferential hiring practices; the demand that Harvard Law School hire a black female professor; grade stipends for black students at Pennsylvania State University and other schools; the revelations of race norming in state employment agencies; as well as debates over quotas, underutilization guidelines, and diversity in employment; all testify to the importance of this subject for contemporary society.

There is something salutary as well as terribly tragic inherent in this problem. The salutary aspect is the fact that our society has shown itself committed to eliminating unjust discrimination. Even in the heart of Dixie there is a recognition of the injustice of racial discrimination. Both sides of the affirmative action debate have good will and appeal to moral principles. Both sides are attempting to bring about a better society, one which is color blind, but they differ profoundly on the morally proper means to accomplish that goal.

And this is just the tragedy of the situation: good people on both sides of the issue are ready to tear each other to pieces over a problem that has no

From *Public Affairs Quarterly* 6 (April 1992), 181–206.

easy or obvious solution. And so the voices become shrill and the rhetoric hyperbolic. . . . I have seen family members and close friends who until recently fought on the same side of the barricades against racial injustice divide in enmity over this issue. . . .

In this paper I will confine myself to Affirmative Action policies with regard to race, but much of what I say can be applied to the areas of gender and ethnic minorities. . . .

A BRIEF HISTORY OF AFFIRMATIVE ACTION

1. After a long legacy of egregious racial discrimination the forces of civil justice came to a head during the decade of 1954–1964. In the 1954 U.S. Supreme Court decision, Brown *v.* Board of Education, racial segregation was declared inherently and unjustly discriminatory, a violation of the constitutional right to equal protection, and in 1964 Congress passed the Civil Rights Act which banned all forms of racial discrimination.

    During this time the goal of the Civil Rights Movement was Equal Opportunity. The thinking was that if only we could remove the hindrances to progress, invidious segregation, discriminatory laws, and irrational prejudice against blacks, we could free our country from the evils of past injustice and usher in a just society in which the grandchildren of the slave could play together and compete with the grandchildren of the slave owner. We were after a color-blind society in which every child had an equal chance to attain the highest positions based not on his skin color but on the quality of his credentials. In the early 60's when the idea of reverse discrimination was mentioned in Civil Rights groups, it was usually rejected as a new racism. The Executive Director of the NAACP, Roy Wilkins, stated this position unequivocally during congressional consideration of the 1964 civil rights law. "Our association has never been in favor of a quota system. We believe the quota system is unfair whether it is used for [blacks] or against [blacks]... [We] feel people ought to be hired because of their ability, irrespective of their color... We want equality, equality of opportunity and employment on the basis of ability."[1]

    So the Civil Rights Act of 1964 was passed outlawing discrimination on the basis of race or sex.

    > Title VII, Section 703(a) Civil Rights Act of 1964: It shall be an unlawful practice for an employer—(1) to fail or refuse to hire or to discharge any individual or otherwise to discriminate against any individual with respect to his compensation, terms, conditions, or privileges of employment, because of such individual's race, color, sex, or national origin; or
    >
    > (2) to limit, segregate, or classify his employees or applicants for employment in any way which would deprive or tend to deprive

any individual of employment opportunities or otherwise adversely affect his status as an employee because of such individual's race, color, religion, sex, or national origin. [42 U.S.C.2000e-2(j)]

...Nothing contained in this title shall be interpreted to require any employer...to grant preferential treatment to any individual or to any group...on account of an imbalance which may exist with respect to the total numbers or percentage of persons of any race...employed by any employer...in comparison with the total or percentage of persons of such race...in any community, State, section, or other areas, or in the available work force in any community, State, section, or other area. [42 U.S.C.2000e-2(j)]

The Civil Rights Act of 1964 espouses a meritocratic philosophy, calling for equal opportunity and prohibits reverse discrimination as just another form of prejudice. The Voting Rights Act (1965) was passed and Jim Crow laws throughout the South were overturned. Schools were integrated and public accommodations opened to all. Branch Rickey's promotion of Jackie Robinson from the minor leagues in 1947 to play for the Brooklyn Dodgers was seen as the paradigm case of this kind of equal opportunity—the successful recruiting of a deserving person.

2. But it was soon noticed that the elimination of discriminatory laws was not producing the fully integrated society that leaders of the civil rights movement had envisioned. Eager to improve the situation, in 1965 President Johnson went beyond equal opportunity to Affirmative Action. He issued the famous Executive Order 11246 in which the Department of Labor was enjoined to issue government contracts with construction companies on the basis of race. That is, it would engage in reverse discrimination in order to make up for the evils of the past. He explained the act in terms of the shackled runner analogy.

Imagine a hundred yard dash in which one of the two runners has his legs shackled together. He has progressed 10 yds., while the unshackled runner has gone 50 yds. How do they rectify the situation? Do they merely remove the shackles and allow the race to proceed? Then they could say that "equal opportunity" now prevailed. But one of the runners would still be forty yards ahead of the other. Would it not be the better part of justice to allow the previously shackled runner to make-up the forty yard gap; or to start the race all over again? That would be affirmative action towards equality. (President Lyndon Johnson 1965 inaugurating the Affirmative Action Policy of Executive Order 11246).

In 1967 President Johnson issued Executive Order 11375 extending Affirmative Action (henceforth "AA") to women. Note here that AA originates in the executive branch of government. Until the Kennedy-Hawkins Civil Rights Act of 1990, AA policy was never put to a vote or passed by Congress. Gradually, the benefits of AA were extended to Hispanics, native Americans, Asians, and handicapped people.[2]

The phrase "An Equal Opportunity/Affirmative Action Employer" ("AA/EO") began to appear as official public policy. But few noticed an ambiguity in the notion of "AA" which could lead to a contradiction in juxtaposing it with "EO," for there are two types of AA. At first AA was interpreted as, what I have called, "Weak Affirmative Action," in line with equal opportunity, signifying wider advertisement of positions, announcements that applications from blacks would be welcomed, active recruitment and hiring blacks (and women) over *equally* qualified men. While few liberals objected to these measures, some expressed fears of an impending slippery slope towards reverse discrimination.

However, except in professional sports—including those sponsored by universities—Weak Affirmative Action was not working, so in the late 60's and early 70's a stronger version of Affirmative Action was embarked upon—one aimed at equal results, quotas (or "goals"—a euphemism for "quotas"). In *Swann v. Charlotte-Mecklenburg* (1971), regarding the busing of children out of their neighborhood in order to promote integration, the Court, led by Justice Brennan, held that Affirmative Action was implied in *Brown* and was consistent with the Civil Rights Act of 1964. The NAACP now began to support reverse discrimination. . . .

3. In 1968 the Department of Labor ordered employers to engage in utilization studies as part of its policy of eliminating discrimination in the work place. The office of Federal Contract Compliance of the U.S. Department of Labor (Executive Order 11246) stated that employers with a history of *underutilization* of minorities and women were required to institute programs that went beyond passive nondiscrimination through deliberate efforts to identify people of "affected classes" for the purpose of advancing their employment. Many employers found it wise to adopt policies of preferential hiring in order to preempt expensive government suits.

Employers were to engage in "utilization analysis" of their present work force in order to develop "specific and result-oriented procedures" to which the employer commits *"every good-faith effort"* in order to provide "relief for members of an *'affected class,'* who by virtue of *past discrimination* continue to suffer the present effects of that discrimination." This self-analysis is supposed to discover areas in which such affected classes are underused, considering their availability and skills. *"Goals and timetables* are to be developed to guide efforts to correct deficiencies in the employment of affected classes [of] people in each level and segment of the work force." Affirmative Action also calls for "rigorous examination" of standards and criteria for job performance, not so as to "dilute necessary standards" but in order to ensure that "arbitrary and discriminatory employment practices are eliminated" and to eliminate unnecessary criteria which "have had the effect of eliminating women and minorities" either from selection or promotion.[3]

4. In 1969 two important events occurred. (a) The Philadelphia Plan—The Department of Labor called for "goals and time tables" for recruiting minority workers. In Philadelphia area construction industries, where these companies were all white, family run businesses, the contractor's union took the case to court on the grounds that Title VII of the Civil Rights Act prohibits quotas. The Third Circuit Court of Appeals upheld the Labor Department, and the Supreme Court refused to hear it. This case became the basis of the EEOC's aggressive pursuit of "goals and time tables" in other business situations.

   (b) In the Spring of 1969 James Forman disrupted the service of Riverside Church in New York City and issued the Black Manifesto to the American Churches, demanding that they pay blacks $500,000,000 in reparations. The argument of the Black Manifesto was that for three and a half centuries blacks in America have been "exploited and degraded, brutalized, killed and persecuted" by whites; that this was part of the persistent institutional patterns of first, legal slavery and then, legal discrimination and forced segregation; and that through slavery and discrimination whites had procured enormous wealth from black labor with little return to blacks. These facts were said to constitute grounds for reparations on a massive scale. The American churches were but the first institutions to be asked for reparations.[4]

5. The Department of Labor issued guidelines in 1970 calling for hiring representatives of *underutilized* groups. "*Nondiscrimination* requires the elimination of all existing discriminatory conditions, whether purposeful or inadvertent...*Affirmative action* requires...the employer to make additional efforts to recruit, employ and promote qualified members of groups formerly excluded" (HEW Executive Order 22346, 1972). In December of 1971 Guidelines were issued to eliminate underutilization of minorities, aiming at realignment of job force at every level of society.

6. In *Griggs v. Duke Power Company* (1971) the Supreme Court interpreted Title VII of the Civil Rights Act as forbidding use of aptitude tests and high school diplomas in hiring personnel. These tests were deemed presumptively discriminatory, employers having the burden of proving such tests relevant to performance. The notion of *sufficiency* replaced that of excellence or best qualified, as it was realized (though not explicitly stated) that the social goal of racial diversity required compromising the standards of competence.

7. In 1977, the EEOC called for and *expected* proportional representation of minorities in every area of work (including universities).

8. In 1978 the Supreme Court addressed the Bakke case. Allan Bakke had been denied admission to the University of California at Davis Medical School even though his test scores were higher than the 16 blacks who were admitted under the Affirmative Action quota program. He sued the University of California and the U.S. Supreme Court ruled (*University of California v Bakke*, July 28, 1978) in a 5 to 4 vote that reverse discrimination and quotas are illegal except (as Justice Powell put it) when engaged in for purposes of promoting diversity (interpreted as a means to extend free speech under the First Amendment) and restoring a situation where an institution has had a history of prejudicial discrimination. The decision was greeted with applause from anti-AA quarters and dismay from pro-AA quarters. Ken Tollett lamented, "The affirmance of Bakke would mean the reversal of affirmative action; it would be an officially sanctioned signal to turn against blacks in this country.... Opposition to special minority admissions programs and affirmative action is anti-black."[5]

   But Tollett was wrong. The Bakke case only shifted the rhetoric from "quota" language to "goals and time tables" and "diversity" language. In the 80's affirmative action was alive and well, with preferential hiring, minority scholarships, and "race norming" prevailing in all walks of life. No other white who has been excluded from admission to college because of his race has even won his case. In fact only a year later, Justice Brennan was to write in *U.S. Steel v. Weber* that prohibition of racial discrimination against "any individual" in Title VII of the Civil Rights Act did not apply to discrimination against whites.[6] . . .

9. In the *Ward Cove, Richmond,* and *Martin* decisions of the mid-80's the Supreme Court limited preferential hiring practices, placing a greater burden of proof on the plaintiff, now required to prove that employers have discriminated. The Kennedy-Hawkins Civil Rights Act of 1990, which was passed by Congress last year, sought to reverse these decisions by requiring employers to justify statistical imbalances not only in the employment of racial minorities but also that of ethnic and religious minorities. Wherever underrepresentation of an "identified" group exists, the employer bears the burden of proving he is innocent of prejudicial behavior. In other words, the bill would make it easier for minorities to sue employers. President Bush vetoed the bill, deeming it a subterfuge for quotas. . . .

   Affirmative Action in the guise of underutilized or "affected groups" now extends to American Indians, Hispanics—Spaniards (including Spanish nobles) but not Portuguese, Asians, the handicapped, and in some places Irish and Italians. Estimates are that 75% of Americans may obtain AA status as minorities: everyone except the white non-handicapped male. It is a strange policy that affords special treatment to the children of Spanish nobles and illegal immigrants but not the children of the survivors of Russian pogroms or Nazi concentration camps.

ARGUMENTS FOR AFFIRMATIVE ACTION

Let us now survey the main arguments typically cited in the debate over Affirmative Action. . . .

Need for Role Models

This argument is straightforward. We all have need of role models, and it helps to know that others like us can be successful. We learn and are encouraged to strive for excellence by emulating our heroes and role models.

However, it is doubtful whether role models of one's own racial or sexual type are necessary for success. One of my heroes was Gandhi, an Indian Hindu, another was my grade school science teacher, one Miss DeVoe, and another was Martin Luther King. More important than having role models of one's own type is having genuinely good people, of whatever race or gender, to emulate. . . .

The Need of Breaking the Stereotypes

Society may simply need to know that there are talented blacks and women, so that it does not automatically assign them lesser respect or status. We need to have unjustified stereotype beliefs replaced with more accurate ones about the talents of blacks and women. So we need to engage in preferential hiring of qualified minorities even when they are not the most qualified.

Again, the response is that hiring the less qualified is neither fair to those better qualified who are passed over nor an effective way of removing inaccurate stereotypes. If competence is accepted as the criterion for hiring, then it is unjust to override it for purposes of social engineering. Furthermore, if blacks or women are known to hold high positions simply because of reverse discrimination, then they will still lack the respect due to those of their rank. . . .

Equal Results Argument

Some philosophers and social scientists hold that human nature is roughly identical, so that on a fair playing field the same proportion from every race and gender and ethnic group would attain to the highest positions in every area of endeavor. It would follow that any inequality of results itself is evidence for inequality of opportunity. John Arthur, in discussing an intelligence test, Test 21, puts the case this way.

> History is important when considering governmental rules like Test 21 because low scores by blacks can be traced in large measure to the legacy of slavery and racism: segregation, poor schooling, exclusion from trade unions,

malnutrition, and poverty have all played their roles. Unless one assumes that blacks are naturally less able to pass the test, the conclusion must be that the results are themselves socially and legally constructed, not a mere given for which law and society can claim no responsibility.

The conclusion seems to be that genuine equality eventually requires equal results. Obviously blacks have been treated unequally throughout U.S. history, and just as obviously the economic and psychological effects of that inequality linger to this day, showing up in lower income and poorer performance in school and on tests than whites achieve. Since we have no reason to believe that differences in performance can be explained by factors other than history, equal results are a good benchmark by which to measure progress made toward genuine equality.[7]

The result of a just society should be equal numbers in proportion to each group in the work force.

However, Arthur fails even to consider studies that suggest that there are innate differences between races, sexes, and groups. If there are genetic differences in intelligence and temperament within families, why should we not expect such differences between racial groups and the two genders? Why should the evidence for this be completely discounted?

Furthermore, on Arthur's logic, we should take aggressive AA against Asians and Jews since they are over-represented in science, technology, and medicine. So that each group receives its fair share, we should ensure that 12% of the philosophers in the United States are Black, reduce the percentage of Jews from an estimated 15% to 2%—firing about 1,300 Jewish philosophers. The fact that Asians are producing 50% of Ph.D.'s in science and math and blacks less than 1% clearly shows, on this reasoning, that we are providing special secret advantages to Asians.

But why does society have to enter into this results game in the first place? Why do we have to decide whether all difference is environmental or genetic? Perhaps we should simply admit that we lack sufficient evidence to pronounce on these issues with any certainty—but if so, should we not be more modest in insisting on equal results? . . .

The Compensation Argument

The argument goes like this: blacks have been wronged and severely harmed by whites. Therefore white society should compensate blacks for the injury caused them. Reverse discrimination in terms of preferential hiring, contracts, and scholarships is a fitting way to compensate for the past wrongs.

This argument actually involves a distorted notion of compensation. Normally, we think of compensation as owed by a specific person A to another person B whom A has wronged in a specific way C. For example, if I have stolen your car and used it for a period of time to make business profits that would have gone to you, it is not enough that I return your car. I must pay you an amount reflecting your loss and my ability to pay. If I have only made $5,000 and only have $10,000 in assets, it would not be possible for you to collect $20,000 in damages—even though that is the amount of loss you have incurred.

Sometimes compensation is extended to groups of people who have been unjustly harmed by the greater society. For example, the United States government has compensated the Japanese-Americans who were interred during the Second World War, and the West German government has paid reparations to the survivors of Nazi concentration camps. But here a specific people have been identified who were wronged in an identifiable way by the government of the nation in question.

On the face of it the demand by blacks for compensation does not fit the usual pattern. Perhaps Southern States with Jim Crow laws could be accused of unjustly harming blacks, but it is hard to see that the United States government was involved in doing so. Furthermore, it is not clear that all blacks were harmed in the same way or whether some were *unjustly* harmed or harmed more than poor whites and others (e.g. short people). Finally, even if identifiable blacks were harmed by identifiable social practices, it is not clear that most forms of Affirmative Action are appropriate to restore the situation. The usual practice of a financial payment seems more appropriate than giving a high level job to someone unqualified or only minimally qualified, who, speculatively, might have been better qualified had he not been subject to racial discrimination. . . .

Still, there may be something intuitively compelling about compensating members of an oppressed group who are minimally qualified. Suppose that the Hatfields and the McCoys are enemy clans and some youths from the Hatfields go over and steal diamonds and gold from the McCoys, distributing it within the Hatfield economy. Even though we do not know which Hatfield youths did the stealing, we would want to restore the wealth, as far as possible, to the McCoys. One way might be to tax the Hatfields, but another might be to give preferential treatment in terms of scholarships and training programs and hiring to the McCoys.[8]

This is perhaps the strongest argument for Affirmative Action, and it may well justify some weak versions of AA, but it is doubtful whether it is sufficient to justify strong versions with quotas and goals and time tables in skilled positions. There are at least two reasons for this. First, we have no way of knowing how many people of group G would have been at competence level L had the world been different. Secondly, the normal criterion of competence is a strong prima facie consideration when the most important positions are at stake. There are two reasons for this: (1) society has given people expectations that if they attain certain levels of excellence they will be awarded appropriately and (2) filling the most important positions with the best qualified is the best way to insure efficiency in job-related areas and in society in general. These reasons are not absolutes. They can be overridden. But there is a strong presumption in their favor so that a burden of proof rests with those who would override them.

At this point we get into the problem of whether innocent non-blacks should have to pay a penalty in terms of preferential hiring of blacks. We turn to that argument.

Compensation from Those who Innocently Benefited from Past Injustice

White males as innocent beneficiaries of unjust discrimination of blacks and women have no grounds for complaint when society seeks to rectify the tilted field. White males may be innocent of oppressing blacks and minorities (and women), but they have unjustly benefited from that oppression or discrimination. So it is perfectly proper that less qualified women and blacks be hired before them.

The operative principle is: He who knowingly and willingly benefits from a wrong must help pay for the wrong. Judith Jarvis Thomson puts it this way. "Many [white males] have been direct beneficiaries of policies which have down-graded blacks and women...and even those who did not directly benefit...had, at any rate, the advantage in the competition which comes of the confidence in one's full membership [in the community], and of one's right being recognized as a matter of course."[9] That is, white males obtain advantages in self-respect and self-confidence deriving from a racist system which denies these to blacks and women.

Objection. As I noted in the previous section, compensation is normally individual and specific. If *A* harms *B* regarding *x, B* has a right to compensation from *A* in regards to *x*. If *A* steals *B*'s car and wrecks it, *A* has an obligation to compensate *B* for the stolen car, but *A*'s son has no obligation to compensate *B*. Furthermore, if *A* dies or disappears, *B* has no moral right to claim that society compensate him for the stolen car—though if he has insurance, he can make such a claim to the insurance company. Sometimes a wrong cannot be compensated, and we just have to make the best of an imperfect world. . . .

The Diversity Argument

It is important that we learn to live in a pluralistic world, learning to get along with those of other races and cultures, so we should have fully integrated schools and employment situations. Diversity is an important symbol and educative device. Thus preferential treatment is warranted to perform this role in society.

But, again, while we can admit the value of diversity, it hardly seems adequate to override considerations of merit and efficiency. . . . At least at the higher levels of business and the professions, competence far outweighs considerations of diversity. I do not care whether the group of surgeons operating on me reflect racial or gender balance, but I do care that they are highly qualified. And likewise with airplane pilots, military leaders, business executives, and, may I say it, teachers and professors. Moreover, there are other ways of learning about other cultures besides engaging in reverse discrimination.

Anti-Meritocratic (Desert) Argument to
Justify Reverse Discrimination: "No One Deserves His Talents"

According to this argument, the competent do not deserve their intelligence, their superior character, their industriousness, or their discipline; therefore they have no right to the best positions in society; therefore society is not unjust in giving these positions to less (but still minimally) qualified blacks and women. In one form this argument holds that since no one deserves anything, society may use any criteria it pleases to distribute goods. The criterion most often designated is social utility. Versions of this argument are found in the writings of John Arthur, John Rawls, Bernard Boxill, Michael Kinsley, Ronald Dworkin, and Richard Wasserstrom. Rawls writes, "No one deserves his place in the distribution of native endowments, any more than one deserves one's initial starting place in society. The assertion that a man deserves the superior character that enables him to make the effort to cultivate his abilities is equally problematic; for his character depends in large part upon fortunate family and social circumstances for which he can claim no credit. The notion of desert seems not to apply to these cases."[10] . . .

It will help to put the argument in outline form.

1. Society may award jobs and positions as it sees fit as long as individuals have no claim to these positions.
2. To have a claim to something means that one has earned it or deserves it.
3. But no one has earned or deserves his intelligence, talent, education or cultural values which produce superior qualifications.
4. If a person does not deserve what produces something, he does not deserve its products.
5. Therefore better qualified people do not deserve their qualifications.
6. Therefore, society may override their qualifications in awarding jobs and positions as it sees fit (for social utility or to compensate for previous wrongs).

So it is permissible if a minimally qualified black or woman is admitted to law or medical school ahead of a white male with excellent credentials or if a less qualified person from an "underutilized" group gets a professorship ahead of a far better qualified white male. Sufficiency and underutilization together outweigh excellence.

OBJECTION   Premise 4 is false. To see this, reflect that just because I do not deserve the money that I have been given as a gift (for instance) does not mean that I am not entitled to what I get with that money. If you and I both get a gift of $100 and I bury mine in the sand for 5 years while you invest yours wisely and double its value at the end of five years, I cannot complain that you should split the increase 50/50 since neither of us deserved the original gift. If we accept the notion of responsibility at all, we must hold that persons deserve the fruits of their labor and conscious choices. Of course, we might want to distinguish moral from legal desert and argue that, morally speaking, effort is more important than outcome, whereas, legally speaking, outcome may be more important. Nevertheless, there are good reasons in terms of efficiency, motivation, and rough justice for holding a strong prima facie principle of giving scarce high positions to those most competent.

The attack on moral desert is perhaps the most radical move that egalitarians like Rawls and company have made against meritocracy, but the ramifications of their attack are far reaching. The following are some of its implications. Since I do not deserve my two good eyes or two good kidneys, the social engineers may take one of each from me to give to those needing an eye or a kidney—even if they have damaged their organs by their own voluntary actions. Since no one deserves anything, we do not deserve pay for our labors or praise for a job well done or first prize in the race we win. The notion of moral responsibility vanishes in a system of levelling.

But there is no good reason to accept the argument against desert. We do act freely and, as such, we are responsible for our actions. We deserve the fruits of our labor, reward for our noble feats and punishment for our misbehavior. . . .

ARGUMENTS AGAINST AFFIRMATIVE ACTION

Affirmative Action Requires Discrimination Against a Different Group

Weak Affirmative Action weakly discriminates against new minorities, mostly innocent young white males, and Strong Affirmative Action strongly discriminates against these new minorities. As I argued [above], this discrimination is unwarranted, since, even if some compensation to blacks were indicated, it would be unfair to make innocent white males bear the whole brunt of the payments. In fact, it is poor white youth who become the new pariahs on the job market. The children of the wealthy have no trouble getting into the best private grammar schools and, on the basis of superior early education, into the best universities, graduate schools, managerial and professional positions. Affirmative Action simply shifts injustice, setting blacks and women against young white males, especially ethnic and poor white males. It does little to rectify the goal of providing equal opportunity to all. If the goal is a society where everyone has a fair chance, then it would be better to concentrate on support for families and early education and decide the matter of university admissions and job hiring on the basis of traditional standards of competence.

Affirmative Action Perpetuates the Victimization Syndrome

Shelby Steele admits that Affirmative Action may seem "the meagerest recompense for centuries of unrelieved oppression" and that it helps promote diversity. At the same time, though, notes Steele, Affirmative Action reinforces the spirit of victimization by telling blacks that they can gain more by emphasizing their suffering, degradation and helplessness than by discipline and work. This message holds the danger of blacks becoming permanently handicapped by a need for special treatment. It also sends to society at large the message that blacks cannot make it on their own. . . .

Affirmative Action Policies
Unjustly Shift the Burden of Proof

Affirmative Action legislation tends to place the burden of proof on the employer who does not have an "adequate" representation of "underutilized" groups in his work force. He is guilty until proven innocent. I have already recounted how in the mid-eighties the Supreme Court shifted the burden of proof back onto the plaintiff, while Congress is now attempting to shift the burden back to the employer. Those in favor of deeming disproportional representation "guilty until proven innocent" argue that it is easy for employers to discriminate against minorities by various subterfuges, and I agree that steps should be taken to monitor against prejudicial treatment. But being prejudiced against employers is not the way to attain a just solution to discrimination. The principle: innocent until proven guilty, applies to employers as well as criminals. Indeed, it is clearly special pleading to reject this basic principle of Anglo-American law in this case of discrimination while adhering to it everywhere else.

An Argument from Merit

Traditionally, we have believed that the highest positions in society should be awarded to those who are best qualified. . . . Rewarding excellence both seems just to the individuals in the competition and makes for efficiency. Note that one of the most successful acts of integration, the recruitment of Jackie Robinson in the late 40's, was done in just this way, according to merit. If Robinson had been brought into the major league as a mediocre player or had batted .200 he would have been scorned and sent back to the minors where he belonged.

Merit is not an absolute value. There are times when it may be overridden for social goals, but there is a strong prima facie reason for awarding positions on its basis, and it should enjoy a weighty presumption in our social practices.

In a celebrated article Ronald Dworkin says that "Bakke had no case" because society did not owe Bakke anything. That may be, but then why does it owe anyone anything? Dworkin puts the matter in Utility terms, but if that is the case, society may owe Bakke a place at the University of California/ Davis, for it seems a reasonable rule-utilitarian principle that achievement should be rewarded in society. We generally want the best to have the best positions, the best qualified candidate to win the political office, the most brilliant and competent scientist to be chosen for the most challenging research project, the best qualified pilots to become commercial pilots, only the best soldiers to become generals. Only when little is at stake do we weaken the standards and content ourselves with sufficiency (rather than excellence).

The Slippery Slope

Even if Strong AA or Reverse Discrimination could meet the other objections, it would face a tough question: once you embark on this project, how do you limit it? Who should be excluded from reverse discrimination? Asians and Jews are overrepresented, so if we give blacks positive quotas, should we place negative quotas to these other groups? Since white males, "WMs," are a minority which is suffering from reverse discrimination will we need a New Affirmative Action policy in the 21st century to compensate for the discrimination against WMs in the late 20th century?

Furthermore, Affirmative Action has stigmatized the *young* white male. Assuming that we accept reverse discrimination, the fair way to make sacrifices would be to retire *older* white males who are more likely to have benefited from a favored status. Probably the least guilty of any harm to minority groups is the young white male—usually a liberal who has been required to bear the brunt of ages of past injustice. Justice Brennan's announcement that the Civil Rights Act did not apply to discrimination against whites shows how the clearest language can be bent to serve the ideology of the moment.[11]

The Mounting Evidence Against the Success of Affirmative Action

Thomas Sowell of the Hoover Institute has shown in his book *Preferential Policies: An International Perspective* that preferential hiring almost never solves social problems. It generally builds in mediocrity or incompetence and causes deep resentment. It is a short term solution which lacks serious grounding in social realities.

For instance, Sowell cites some disturbing statistics on education. Although twice as many blacks as Asians students took the nationwide Scholastic Aptitude Test in 1983, approximately fifteen times as many Asian students scored above 700 (out of a possible 800) on the mathematics half of the SAT. The percentage of Asians who scored above 700 in math was also more than six times higher than the percentage of American Indians and more than ten times higher than that of Mexican Americans—as well as more than double the percentage of whites. As Sowell points out, in all countries studied, "intergroup performance disparities are huge" (108).

> There are dozens of American colleges and universities where the median combined verbal SAT score and mathematics SAT score total 1200 or above. As of 1983 there were less than 600 black students in the entire US with combined SAT scores of 1200. This meant that, despite widespread attempts to get a black student "representation" comparable to the black percentage of the population (about 11%), there were not enough black students in the entire country for the Ivy League alone to have such a "representation"

without going beyond this pool—even if the entire pool went to the eight Ivy League colleges.[12]

Often it is claimed that a cultural bias is the cause of the poor performance of blacks on SAT (or IQ tests), but Sowell shows that these test scores are actually a better predictor of college performance for blacks than for Asians and whites. He also shows the harmfulness of the effect on blacks of preferential acceptance. At the University of California, Berkeley, where the freshman class closely reflects the actual ethnic distribution of California high school students, more than 70% of blacks fail to graduate. All 312 black students entering Berkeley in 1987 were admitted under "Affirmative Action" criteria rather than by meeting standard academic criteria. So were 480 out of 507 Hispanic students. In 1986 the median SAT score for blacks at Berkeley was 952, for Mexican Americans 1014, for American Indians 1082 and for Asian Americans 1254. (The average SAT for all students was 1181.)

The result of this mismatching is that blacks who might do well if they went to a second tier or third tier school where their test scores would indicate they belong, actually are harmed by preferential treatment. They cannot compete in the institutions where high abilities are necessary. . . .

The tendency has been to focus at the high level end of education and employment rather than on the lower level of family structure and early education. But if we really want to help the worst off improve, we need to concentrate on the family and early education. It is foolish to expect equal results when we begin with grossly unequal starting points—and discriminating against young white males is no more just than discriminating against women, blacks or anyone else.

CONCLUSION

Let me sum up. The goal of the Civil Rights movement and of moral people everywhere has been equal opportunity. The question is: how best to get there. Civil Rights legislation removed the legal barriers to equal opportunity, but did not tackle the deeper causes that produced differential results. Weak Affirmative Action aims at encouraging minorities in striving for the highest positions without unduly jeopardizing the rights of majorities, but the problem of Weak Affirmative Action is that it easily slides into Strong Affirmative Action where quotas, "goals," and equal results are forced into groups, thus promoting mediocrity, inefficiency, and resentment. Furthermore, Affirmative Action aims at the higher levels of society—universities and skilled jobs—yet if we want to improve our society, the best way to do it is to concentrate on families, children, early education, and the like. Affirmative Action is, on the one hand, too much, too soon and on the other hand, too little, too late.

Martin Luther said that humanity is like a man mounting a horse who always tends to fall off on the other side of the horse. This seems to be the case with Affirmative Action. Attempting to redress the discriminatory iniquities of our history, our well-intentioned social engineers engage in new forms of discriminatory iniquity and thereby think that they have successfully mounted the horse of racial harmony. They have only fallen off on the other side of the issue.

NOTES

1. Quoted in William Bradford Reynolds, "Affirmative Action Is Unjust" in D. Bender and B. Leone (eds.), *Social Justice* (St. Paul, MN, 1984), p. 23.
2. Some of the material in this section is based on Nicholas Capaldi's *Out of Order: Affirmative Action and the Crisis of Doctrinaire Liberalism* (Buffalo, NY, 1985), chapters 1 and 2. Capaldi, using the shackled runner analogy, divides the history into three stages: a *platitude stage* "in which it is reaffirmed that the race is to be fair, and a fair race is one in which no one has either special disadvantages or special advantages (equal opportunity)"; a *remedial stage* in which victims of past discrimination are to be given special help in overcoming their disadvantages; and a *realignment stage* "in which all runners will be reassigned to those positions on the course that they would have had if the race had been fair from the beginning" (p. 18f).
3. Wanda Warren Berry, "Affirmative Action is Just" in D. Bender, *op. cit.,* p. 18.
4. Robert Fullinwider, *The Reverse Discrimination Controversy* (Totowa, NJ, 1970), p. 25.
5. Quoted in Fullinwider, *op. cit.,* p. 4f.
6. See Lino A. Graglia, "'Affirmative Action,' the Constitution, and the 1964 Civil Rights Act," *Measure,* no. 92 (1991).
7. John Arthur, *The Unfinished Constitution* (Belmont, CA, 1990), p. 238.
8. See Michael Levin, "Is Racial Discrimination Special?" *Policy Review,* Fall issue (1982).
9. Judith Jarvis Thomson, "Preferential Hiring" in Marshall Cohen, Thomas Nagel and Thomas Scanlon (eds.), *Equality and Preferential Treatment* (Princeton, 1977).
10. John Rawls, *A Theory of Justice* (Cambridge, 1971), p. 104; See Richard Wasserstrom "A Defense of Programs of Preferential Treatment," *National Forum* (Phi Kappa Phi Journal), vol. 58 (1978). See also Bernard Boxill, "The Morality of Preferential Hiring," *Philosophy and Public Affairs,* vol. 7 (1978).
11. The extreme form of this New Speak is incarnate in the Politically Correct Movement ("PC" ideology) where a new orthodoxy has emerged, condemning white, European culture and seeing African culture as the new savior of us all. Perhaps the clearest example of this is Paula Rothenberg's book *Racism and Sexism* (New York, 1987) which asserts that there is no such thing as black racism; only whites are capable of racism (p. 6). Ms. Rothenberg's book has been scheduled as required reading for all freshmen at the University of Texas. See Joseph Salemi, "Lone Star Academic Politics," no. 87 (1990).
12. Thomas Sowell, *Preferential Policies: An International Perspective* (New York, 1990), p. 108.

Reverse Discrimination as Unjustified
Lisa H. Newton

In this brief essay Lisa H. Newton, a professor of philosophy at Fairfield University, raises a number of questions about reverse discrimination. In her viewpoint, the concept of reverse discrimination is logically flawed. Given the meaning of political justice as equal treatment under the law, reverse discrimination, she claims, is as unjust as discrimination itself. Newton also fears that preferential treatment intended to benefit women and blacks could be the start of a slippery slope where all American minorities could claim a right to restitution for an indefinite period of time.

———

I have heard it argued that "simple justice" requires that we favor women and blacks in employment and educational opportunities, since women and blacks were "unjustly" excluded from such opportunities for so many years in the not so distant past. It is a strange argument, an example of a possible implication of a true proposition advanced to dispute the proposition itself, like an octopus absent-mindedly slicing off his head with a stray tentacle. A fatal confusion underlies this argument, a confusion fundamentally relevant to our understanding of the notion of the rule of law.

Two senses of justice and equality are involved in this confusion. The root notion of justice, progenitor of the other, is the one that Aristotle (*Nichomachean Ethics* 5.6; *Politics* 1.2; 3.1) assumes to be the foundation and proper virtue of the political association. It is the condition which free men establish among themselves when they "share a common life in order that their association bring them self-sufficiency"—the regulation of their relationship by law, and the establishment, by law, of equality before the law. Rule of law is the name and pattern of this justice; its equality stands against the inequalities—of wealth, talent, etc.—otherwise obtaining among its participants, who by virtue of that equality are called "citizens." It is an achievement— complete, or, more frequently, partial—of certain people in certain concrete situations. It is fragile and easily disrupted by powerful individuals who discover that the blind equality of rule of law is inconvenient for their interests. Despite its obvious instability, Aristotle assumed that the establishment of justice in this sense, the creation of citizenship, was a permanent possibility for men and that the resultant association of citizens was the natural home of the species. At levels below the political association, this rule-governed equality is easily found; it is exemplified by any group of children agreeing together to play a game. At the level of the political association, the attainment of this justice is more difficult, simply because the stakes are so much higher for each participant. The equality of citizenship is not something that happens of

From *Ethics* 83 (1973) 308-312

its own accord, and without the expenditure of a fair amount of effort it will collapse into the rule of a powerful few over an apathetic many. But at least it has been achieved, at some times in some places; it is always worth trying to achieve, and eminently worth trying to maintain, wherever and to whatever degree it has been brought into being.

Aristotle's parochialism is notorious; he really did not imagine that persons other than Greeks could associate freely in justice, and the only form of association he had in mind was the Greek *polis*. With the decline of the *polis* and the shift in the center of political thought, his notion of justice underwent a change. To be exact, it ceased to represent a political type and became a moral ideal: the ideal of equality as we know it. This ideal demands that all men be included in citizenship—that one Law govern all equally, that all men regard all other men as fellow citizens, with the same guarantees, rights, and protections. Briefly, it demands that the circle of citizenship achieved by any group be extended to include the entire human race. Properly understood, its effect on our associations can be excellent: it congratulates us on our achievement of rule of law as a process of government but refuses to let us remain complacent until we have expanded the associations to include others within the ambit of the rules, as often and as far as possible. While one man is a slave, none of us may feel truly free. We are constantly prodded by this ideal to look for possible unjustifiable discrimination, for inequalities not absolutely required for the functioning of the society and advantageous to all. And after twenty centuries of pressure, not at all constant, from this ideal, it might be said that some progress has been made. To take the cases in point for this problem, we are now prepared to assert, as Aristotle would never have been, the equality of sexes and of persons of different colors. The ambit of American citizenship, once restricted to white males of property, has been extended to include all adult free men, then all adult males including ex-slaves, then all women. The process of acquisition of full citizenship was for these groups a sporadic trail of half-measures, even now not complete; the steps on the road to full equality are marked by legislation and judicial decisions which are only recently concluded and still often not enforced. But the fact that we can now discuss the possibility of favoring such groups in hiring shows that over the area that concerns us, at least, full equality is presupposed as a basis for discussion. To that extent, they are full citizens, fully protected by the law of the land.

It is important for my argument that the moral ideal of equality be recognized as logically distinct from the condition (or virtue) of justice in the political sense. Justice in this sense exists *among* a citizenry, irrespective of the number of the populace included in that citizenry. Further, the moral ideal is parasitic upon the political virtue, for "equality" is unspecified—it means nothing until we are told in what respect that equality is to be realized. In a political context, "equality" is specified as "equal rights"—equal access to the public realm, public goods and offices, equal treatment under the law—in brief, the equality of citizenship. If citizenship is not a possibility, political equality is unintelligible. The ideal emerges as a generalization of the real condition and refers back to that condition for its content.

Now, if justice (Aristotle's justice in the political sense) is equal treatment under law for all citizens, what is injustice? Clearly, injustice is the violation of that equality, discriminating for or against a group of citizens, favoring them with special immunities and privileges or depriving them of those guaranteed to the others. When the southern employer refuses to hire blacks in white collar jobs, when Wall Street will only hire women as secretaries with new titles, when Mississippi high schools routinely flunk all black boys above ninth grade, we have examples of injustice, and we work to restore the equality of the public realm by ensuring that equal opportunity will be provided in such cases in the future. But of course, when the employers and the schools *favor* women and blacks, the same injustice is done. Just as the previous discrimination did, this reverse discrimination violates the public equality which defines citizenship and destroys the rule of law for the areas in which these favors are granted. To the extent that we adopt a program of discrimination, reverse or otherwise, justice in the political sense is destroyed, and none of us, specifically affected or not, is a citizen, a bearer of rights—we are all petitioners for favors. And to the same extent, the ideal of equality is undermined, for it has content only where justice obtains, and by destroying justice we render the ideal meaningless. It is, then, an ironic paradox, if not a contradiction in terms, to assert that the ideal of equality justifies the violation of justice; it is as if one should argue, with William Buckley, that an ideal of humanity can justify the destruction of the human race.

Logically, the conclusion is simple enough: all discrimination is wrong prima facie because it violates justice, and that goes for reverse discrimination too. No violation of justice among the citizens may be justified (may overcome the prima facie objection) by appeal to the ideal of equality, for that ideal is logically dependent upon the notion of justice. Reverse discrimination, then, which attempts no other justification than an appeal to equality, is wrong. But let us try to make the conclusion more plausible by suggesting some of the implications of the suggested practice of reverse discrimination in employment and education. My argument will be that the problems raised there are insoluble, not only in practice but in principle.

We may argue, if we like, about what "discrimination" consists of. Do I discriminate against blacks if I admit none to my school when none of the black applicants are qualified by the tests I always give? How far must I go to root out cultural bias from my application forms and tests before I can say that I have not discriminated against those of different cultures? Can I assume that women are not strong enough to be roughnecks on my oil rigs, or must I test them individually? But this controversy, the most popular and well-argued aspect of the issue, is not as fatal as two others which cannot be avoided: if we are regarding the blacks as a "minority" victimized by discrimination, what is a "minority"? And for any group—blacks, women, whatever—that has been discriminated against, what amount of reverse discrimination wipes out the initial discrimination? Let us grant as true that women and blacks were discriminated against, even where laws forbade such discrimination, and grant for the sake of argument that a history of discrimination must be wiped out by reverse discrimination. What follows?

First, are there other groups which have been discriminated against? For they should have the same right of restitution. What about American Indians, Chicanos, Appalachian Mountain whites, Puerto Ricans, Jews, Cajuns, and Orientals? And if these are to be included, the principle according to which we specify a "minority" is simply the criterion of "ethnic (sub) group," and we're stuck with every hyphenated American in the lower-middle class clamoring for special privileges for *his* group—and with equal justification. For be it noted, when we run down the Harvard roster, we find not only a scarcity of blacks (in comparison with the proportion in the population) but an even more striking scarcity of those second-, third-, and fourth-generation ethnics who make up the loudest voice of Middle America. Shouldn't they demand *their* share? And eventually, the WASPs will have to form their own lobby, for they too are a minority. The point is simply this: there is no "majority" in America who will not mind giving up just a bit of their rights to make room for a favored minority. There are only other minorities, each of which is discriminated against by the favoring. The initial injustice is then repeated dozens of times, and if each minority is granted the same right of restitution as the others, an entire area of rule governance is dissolved into a pushing and shoving match between self-interested groups. Each works to catch the public eye and political popularity by whatever means of advertising and power politics lend themselves to the effort, to capitalize as much as possible on temporary popularity until the restless mob picks another group to feel sorry for. Hardly an edifying spectacle, and in the long run no one can benefit: the pie is no larger—it's just that instead of setting up and enforcing rules for getting a piece, we've turned the contest into a free-for-all, requiring much more effort for no larger a reward. It would be in the interests of all the participants to reestablish an objective rule to govern the process, carefully enforced and the same for all.

Second, supposing that we do manage to agree in general that women and blacks (and all the others) have some right of restitution, some right to a privileged place in the structure of opportunities for a while, how will we know when that while is up? How much privilege is enough? When will the guilt be gone, the price paid, the balance restored? What recompense is right for centuries of exclusion? What criterion tells us when we are done? Our experience with the Civil Rights movement shows us that agreement on these terms cannot be presupposed: a process that appears to some to be going at a mad gallop into a black takeover appears to the rest of us to be at a standstill. Should a practice of reverse discrimination be adopted, we may safely predict that just as some of us begin to see "a satisfactory start toward righting the balance," others of us will see that we "have already gone too far in the other direction" and will suggest that the discrimination ought to be reversed again. And such disagreement is inevitable, for the point is that we could not *possibly* have any criteria for evaluating the kind of recompense we have in mind. The context presumed by any discussion of restitution is the context of rule of law: law sets the rights of men and simultaneously sets the method for remedying the violation of those rights. You may exact suffering from others and/or damage payments for yourself if and only if the others have violated your rights; the suffering you have endured is not sufficient reason for them to suffer. And remedial rights exist only where there is law: primary human rights are useful guides to legislation but cannot stand as reasons for awarding remedies for injuries sustained. But then, the context presupposed by any discussion of restitution is the context of preexistent full citizenship. No remedial rights could exist for the excluded; neither in law nor in logic does there exist a right to *sue* for a standing to sue.

From these two considerations, then, the difficulties with reverse discrimination become evident. Restitution for a disadvantaged group whose rights under the law have been violated is possible by legal means, but restitution for a disadvantaged group whose grievance is that there was no law to protect them simply is not. First, outside of the area of justice defined by the law, no sense can be made of "the group's rights," for no law recognizes that group or the individuals in it, qua members, as bearers of rights (hence *any* group can constitute itself as a disadvantaged minority in some sense and demand similar restitution). Second, outside of the area of protection of law, no sense can be made of the violation of rights (hence the amount of the recompense cannot be decided by any objective criterion). For both reasons, the practice of reverse discrimination undermines the foundation of the very ideal in whose name it is advocated; it destroys justice, law, equality, and citizenship itself, and replaces them with power struggles and popularity contests.

Affirmative Action:
The Price of Preference

Shelby Steele

Shelby Steele is an English professor at San Jose State University and the author of *The Content of Our Character*, from which the following selection was taken. Like Lisa Newton in the previous reading, Steele also has serious reservations about the policy of affirmative action, but his objections are more concerned with its actual practice than the principles behind it. Steele claims that affirmative action policies aimed at creating diversity lead to a "democracy of colors," but do little to close significant gaps between whites and nonwhites in areas such as college retention rates and earned income potential. He also believes affirmative action, as currently conceived, undermines its own goals by promoting a "victim mentality" in its beneficiaries and by causing further discrimination against blacks. For these reasons, Steele suspects blacks would be better served by a return to the original aims of affirmative action: enforcing equal opportunity for all in the university and the workplace.

In a few short years, when my two children will be applying to college, the affirmative action policies by which most universities offer black students some form of preferential treatment will present me with a dilemma. I am a middle-class black, a college professor, far from wealthy, but also well-removed from the kind of deprivation that would qualify my children for the label "disadvantaged." Both of them have endured racial insensitivity from whites. They have been called names, have suffered slights, and have experienced firsthand the peculiar malevolence that racism brings out in people. Yet, they have never experienced racial discrimination, have never been stopped by their race on any path they have chosen to follow. Still, their society now tells them that if they will only designate themselves as black on their college applications, they will likely do better in the college lottery than if they conceal this fact. I think there is something of a Faustian bargain in this.

Of course, many blacks and a considerable number of whites would say that I was sanctimoniously making affirmative action into a test of character. They would say that this small preference is the meagerest recompense for centuries of unrelieved oppression. And to these arguments other very obvious facts must be added. In America, many marginally competent or flatly incompetent whites are hired everyday—some because their white skin suits the conscious or unconscious racial preference of their employer. The white children of alumni are often grandfathered into elite universities in what can

From *The Content of Our Character,* by Shelby Steele (New York: St. Martin's Press, 1990), pp. 111–125.

only be seen as a residual benefit of historic white privilege. Worse, white incompetence is always an individual matter, while for blacks it is often confirmation of ugly stereotypes. The Peter Principle was not conceived with only blacks in mind. Given that unfairness cuts both ways, doesn't it only balance the scales of history that my children now receive a slight preference over whites? Doesn't this repay, in a small way, the systematic denial under which their grandfather lived out his days?

So, in theory, affirmative action certainly has all the moral symmetry that fairness requires—the injustice of historical and even contemporary white advantage is offset with black advantage; preference replaces prejudice, inclusion answers exclusion. It is reformist and corrective, even repentant and redemptive. And I would never sneer at these good intentions. Born in the late forties in Chicago, I started my education (a charitable term in this case) in a segregated school and suffered all the indignities that come to blacks in a segregated society. My father, born in the South, only made it to the third grade before the white man's fields took permanent priority over his formal education. And though he educated himself into an advanced reader with an almost professorial authority, he could only drive a truck for a living and never earned more than ninety dollars a week in his entire life. So yes, it is crucial to my sense of citizenship, to my ability to identify with the spirit and the interests of America, to know that this country, however imperfectly, recognizes its past sins and wishes to correct them.

Yet good intentions, because of the opportunity for innocence they offer us, are very seductive and can blind us to the effects they generate when implemented. In our society, affirmative action is, among other things, a testament to white goodwill and to black power, and in the midst of these heavy investments, its effects can be hard to see. But after twenty years of implementation, I think affirmative action has shown itself to be more bad than good and that blacks—whom I will focus on in this essay—now stand to lose more from it than they gain.

In talking with affirmative action administrators and with blacks and whites in general, it is clear that supporters of affirmative action focus on its good intentions while detractors emphasize its negative effects. Proponents talk about "diversity" and "pluralism"; opponents speak of "reverse discrimination," the unfairness of quotas and set-asides. It was virtually impossible to find people outside either camp. The closest I came was a white male manager at a large computer company who said, "I think it amounts to reverse discrimination, but I'll put up with a little of that for a little more diversity." I'll live with a little of the effect to gain a little of the intention, he seemed to be saying. But this only makes him a halfhearted supporter of affirmative action. I think many people who don't really like affirmative action support it to one degree or another anyway.

I believe they do this because of what happened to white and black Americans in the crucible of the sixties when whites were confronted with their racial guilt and blacks tasted their first real power. In this stormy time white absolution and black power coalesced into virtual mandates for society. Affirmative action became a meeting ground for these mandates in the law, and in the late sixties and early seventies it underwent a remarkable escalation of its mission from simple anti-discrimination enforcement to social engineering by means of quotas, goals, timetables, set-asides and other forms of preferential treatment.

Legally, this was achieved through a series of executive orders and EEOC guidelines that allowed racial imbalances in the workplace to stand as proof of racial discrimination. Once it could be assumed that discrimination explained racial imbalances, it became easy to justify group remedies to presumed discrimination, rather than the normal case-by-case redress for proven discrimination. Preferential treatment through quotas, goals, and so on is designed to correct imbalances based on the assumption that they always indicate discrimination. This expansion of what constitutes discrimination allowed affirmative action to escalate into the business of social engineering in the name of anti-discrimination, to push society toward statistically proportionate racial representation, without any obligation of proving actual discrimination.

What accounted for this shift, I believe, was the white mandate to achieve a new racial innocence and the black mandate to gain power. Even though blacks had made great advances during the sixties without quotas, these mandates, which came to a head in the very late sixties, could no longer be satisfied by anything less than racial preferences. I don't think these mandates in themselves were wrong, since whites clearly needed to do better by blacks and blacks needed more real power in society. But, as they came together in affirmative action, their effect was to distort our understanding of racial discrimination in a way that allowed us to offer the remediation of preference on the basis of mere color rather than actual injury. By making black the color of preference, these mandates have reburdened society with the very marriage of color and preference (in reverse) that we set out to eradicate. The old sin is reaffirmed in a new guise.

But the essential problem with this form of affirmative action is the way it leaps over the hard business of developing a formerly oppressed people to the point where they can achieve proportionate representation on their own (given equal opportunity) and goes straight for the proportionate representation. This may satisfy some whites of their innocence and some blacks of their power, but it does very little to truly uplift blacks.

A white female affirmative action officer at an Ivy League university told me what many supporters of affirmative action now say: "We're after diversity. We ideally want a student body where racial and ethnic groups are represented according to their proportion in society." When affirmative action escalated into social engineering, diversity became a golden word. It grants whites an egalitarian fairness (innocence) and blacks an entitlement to proportionate representation (power). *Diversity* is a term that applies democratic principles to races and cultures rather than to citizens, despite the fact that there is nothing to indicate that real diversity is the same thing as proportionate representation. Too often the result of this on campuses (for example) has been a democracy of colors rather than of people, an artificial diversity that gives the appearance of an educational parity between black and white students that has not yet been achieved in reality. Here again, racial preferences allow society to leapfrog over the difficult problem of developing blacks to parity with whites and into a cosmetic diversity that covers the blemish of disparity—a full six years after admission, only about 26 percent of black students graduate from college.

Racial representation is not the same thing as racial development, yet affirmative action fosters a confusion of these very different needs. Representation can be manufactured; development is always hard-earned. However, it is the music of innocence and power that we hear in affirmative action that causes us to cling to it and to its distracting emphasis on representation. The fact is that after twenty years of racial preferences, the gap between white and black median income is greater than it was in the seventies. None of this is to say that blacks don't need policies that ensure our right to equal opportunity, but what we need more is the development that will let us take advantage of society's efforts to include us.

I think that one of the most troubling effects of racial preferences for blacks is a kind of demoralization, or put another way, an enlargement of self-doubt. Under affirmative action the quality that earns us preferential treatment is an implied inferiority. However this inferiority is explained—and it is easily enough explained by the myriad deprivations that grew out of our oppression—it is still inferiority. There are explanations, and then there is the fact. And the fact must be borne by the individual as a condition apart from the explanation, apart even from the fact that others like himself also bear this condition. In integrated situations where blacks must compete with whites who may be better prepared, these explanations may quickly wear thin and expose the individual to racial as well as personal self-doubt.

All of this is compounded by the cultural myth of black inferiority that blacks have always lived with. What this means in practical terms is that when blacks deliver themselves into integrated situations, they encounter a nasty little reflex in whites, a mindless, atavistic reflex that responds to the color black with alarm. Attributions may follow this alarm if the white cares to indulge them, and if they do, they will most likely be negative—one such attribution is intellectual ineptness. I think this reflex and the attributions that may follow it embarrass most whites today, therefore, it is usually quickly repressed. Nevertheless, on an equally atavistic level, the black will be aware of the reflex his color triggers and will feel a stab of horror at seeing himself reflected in this way. He, too, will do a quick repression, but a lifetime of such stabbings is what constitutes his inner realm of racial doubt.

The effects of this may be a subject for another essay. The point here is that the implication of inferiority that racial preferences engender in both the white and black mind expands rather than contracts this doubt. Even when the black sees no implication of inferiority in racial preferences, he knows that whites do, so that—consciously or unconsciously—the result is virtually the same. The effect of preferential treatment—the lowering of normal standards to increase black representation—puts blacks at war with an expanded realm of debilitating doubt, so that the doubt itself becomes an unrecognized preoccupation that undermines their ability to perform, especially in integrated situations. On largely white campuses, blacks are five times more likely to drop out than whites. Preferential treatment, no matter how it is justified in the light of day, subjects blacks to a midnight of self-doubt, and so often transforms their advantage into a revolving door.

Another liability of affirmative action comes from the fact that it indirectly encourages blacks to exploit their own past victimization as a source of power and privilege. Victimization, like implied inferiority, is what justifies preference, so that to receive the benefits of preferential treatment one must, to some extent, become invested in the view of one's self as a victim. In this way, affirmative action nurtures a victim-focused identity in blacks. The obvious irony here is that we become inadvertently invested in the very condition we are trying to overcome. Racial preferences send us the message that there is more power in our past suffering than our present achievements—none of which could bring us a *preference* over others.

When power itself grows out of suffering, then blacks are encouraged to expand the boundaries of what qualifies as racial oppression, a situation that can lead us to paint our victimization in vivid colors, even as we receive the benefits of preference. The same corporations and institutions that give us preference are also seen as our oppressors. At Stanford University minority students—some of whom enjoy as much as $15,000 a year in financial aid—recently took over the president's office demanding, among other things, more financial aid. The power to be found in victimization, like any power, is intoxicating and can lend itself to the creation of a new class of super-victims who can feel the pea of victimization under twenty mattresses. Preferential treatment rewards us for being underdogs rather than for moving beyond that status—a misplacement of incentives that, along with its deepening of our doubt, is more a yoke than a spur.

But, I think, one of the worst prices that blacks pay for preference has to do with an illusion. I saw this illusion at work recently in the mother of a middle-class black student who was going off to his first semester of college. "They owe us this, so don't think for a minute that you don't belong there." This is the logic by which many blacks, and some whites, justify affirmative action—it is something "owed," a form of reparation. But this logic overlooks a much harder and less digestible reality, that it is impossible to repay blacks living today for the historic suffering of the race. If all blacks were given a million dollars tomorrow morning it would not amount to a dime on the dollar of three centuries of oppression, nor would it obviate the residues of that oppression that we still carry today. The concept of historic reparation grows out of man's need to impose a degree of justice on the world that simply does not exist. Suffering can be endured and overcome, it cannot be repaid. Blacks cannot be repaid for the injustice done to the race, but we can be corrupted by society's guilty gestures of repayment.

Affirmative action is such a gesture. It tells us that racial preferences can do for us what we cannot do for ourselves. The corruption here is in the hidden incentive *not* to do what we believe preferences will do. This is an incentive to be reliant on others just as we are struggling for self-reliance. And it keeps alive the illusion that we can find some deliverance in repayment. The hardest thing for any sufferer to accept is that his suffering excuses him from very little and never has enough currency to restore him. To think otherwise is to prolong the suffering.

Several blacks I spoke with said they were still in favor of affirmative action because of the "subtle" discrimination blacks were subject to once on the job. One photojournalist said, "They have ways of ignoring you." A black female television producer said, "You can't file a lawsuit when your boss doesn't invite you to the insider meetings without ruining your career. So we still need affirmative action." Others mentioned the infamous "glass ceiling" through which blacks can see the top positions of authority but never reach them. But I don't think racial preferences are a protection against this subtle discrimination; I think they contribute to it.

In any workplace, racial preferences will always create two-tiered populations composed of preferreds and unpreferreds. This division makes automatic a perception of enhanced competence for the unpreferreds and of questionable competence for the preferreds—the former earned his way, even though others were given preference, while the latter made it by color as much as by competence. Racial preferences implicitly mark whites with an exaggerated superiority just as they mark blacks with an exaggerated inferiority. They not only reinforce America's oldest racial myth but, for blacks, they have the effect of stigmatizing the already stigmatized.

I think that much of the "subtle" discrimination that blacks talk about is often (not always) discrimination against the stigma of questionable competence that affirmative action delivers to blacks. In this sense, preferences scapegoat the very people they seek to help. And it may be that at a certain level employers impose a glass ceiling, but this may not be against the race so much as against the race's reputation for having advanced by color as much as by competence. Affirmative action makes a glass ceiling virtually necessary as a protection against the corruptions of preferential treatment. This ceiling is the point at which corporations shift the emphasis from color to competency and stop playing the affirmative action game. Here preference backfires for blacks and becomes a taint that holds them back. Of course, one could argue that this taint, which is, after all, in the minds of whites, becomes nothing more than an excuse to discriminate against blacks. And certainly the result is the same in either case—blacks don't get past the glass ceiling. But this argument does not get around the fact that racial preferences now taint this color with a new theme of suspicion that makes it even more vulnerable to the impulse in others to discriminate. In this crucial yet gray area of perceived competence, preferences make whites look better than they are and blacks worse, while doing nothing whatever to stop the very real discrimination that blacks may encounter. I don't wish to justify the glass ceiling here, but only to suggest the very subtle ways that affirmative action revives rather than extinguishes the old rationalizations for racial discrimination.

In education, a revolving door; in employment, a glass ceiling.

I believe affirmative action is problematic in our society because it tries to function like a social program. Rather than ask it to ensure equal opportunity we have demanded that it create parity between the races. But preferential treatment does not teach skills, or educate, or instill motivation. It only passes out entitlement by color, a situation that in my profession has created an unrealistically high demand for black professors. The social engineer's assumption is that this high demand will inspire more blacks to earn Ph. D.'s and join the profession. In fact, the number of blacks earning Ph.D.'s has declined in recent years. A Ph.D. must be developed from preschool on. He requires family and community support. He must acquire an entire system of values that enables him to work hard while delaying gratification. There are social programs, I believe, that can (and should) help blacks *develop* in all these areas, but entitlement by color is not a social program; it is a dubious reward for being black.

It now seems clear that the Supreme Court, in a series of recent decisions, is moving away from racial preferences. It has disallowed preferences except in instances of "identified discrimination," eroded the precedent that statistical racial imbalances are *prima facie* evidence of discrimination, and in effect granted white males the right to challenge consent degrees that use preference to achieve racial balances in the workplace. One civil rights leader said, "Night has fallen on civil rights." But I am not so sure. The effect of these decisions is to protect the constitutional rights of everyone rather than take rights away from blacks. What they do take away from blacks is the special entitlement to more rights than others that preferences always grant. Night has fallen on racial preferences, not on the fundamental rights of black Americans. The reason for this shift, I believe, is that the white mandate for absolution from past racial sins has weakened considerably during the eighties. Whites are now less willing to endure unfairness to themselves in order to grant special entitlements to blacks, even when these entitlements are justified in the name of past suffering. Yet the black mandate for more power in society has remained unchanged. And I think part of the anxiety that many blacks feel over these decisions has to do with the loss of black power they may signal. We had won a certain specialness and now we are losing it.

But the power we've lost by these decisions is really only the power that grows out of our victimization—the power to claim special entitlements under the law because of past oppression. This is not a very substantial or reliable power, and it is important that we know this so we can focus more exclusively on the kind of development that will bring enduring power. There is talk now that Congress will pass new legislation to compensate for these new limits on affirmative action. If this happens, I hope that their focus will be on development and anti-discrimination rather than entitlement, on achieving racial parity rather than jerry-building racial diversity.

I would also like to see affirmative action go back to its original purpose of enforcing equal opportunity—a purpose that in itself disallows racial preferences. We cannot be sure that the discriminatory impulse in America has yet been shamed into extinction, and I believe affirmative action can make its greatest contribution by providing a rigorous vigilance in this area. It can guard constitutional rather than racial rights, and help institutions evolve standards of merit and selection that are appropriate to the institution's needs yet as free of racial bias as possible (again, with the understanding that racial imbalances are not always an indication of racial bias). One of the most important things affirmative action can do is to define exactly what racial discrimination is and how it might manifest itself within a specific institution. The impulse to discriminate is subtle and cannot be ferreted out unless its many guises are made clear to people. Along with this there should be monitoring of institutions and heavy sanctions brought to bear when actual discrimination is found. This is the sort of affirmative action that America owes to blacks and to itself. It goes after the evil of discrimination itself, while preferences only sidestep the evil and grant entitlement to its *presumed* victims.

But if not preferences, then what? I think we need social policies that are committed to two goals: the educational and economic development of disadvantaged people, regardless of race, and the eradication from our society—through close monitoring and severe sanctions—of racial, ethnic, or gender discrimination. Preferences will not deliver us to either of these goals, since they tend to benefit those who are not disadvantaged—middle-class white women and middle-class blacks—and attack one form of discrimination with another. Preferences are inexpensive and carry the glamour of good intentions—change the numbers and the good deed is done. To be against them is to be unkind. But I think the unkindest cut is to bestow on children like my own an undeserved advantage while neglecting the development of those disadvantaged children on the East Side of my city who will likely never be in a position to benefit from a preference. Give my children fairness; give disadvantaged children a better shot at development—better elementary and secondary schools, job training, safer neighborhoods, better financial assistance for college, and so on. Fewer blacks go to college today than ten years ago; more black males of college age are in prison or under the control of the criminal justice system than in college. This despite racial preferences.

The mandates of black power and white absolution out of which preferences emerged were not wrong in themselves. What was wrong was that both races focused more on the goals of these mandates than on the means to the goals. Blacks can have no real power without taking responsibility for their own educational and economic development. Whites can have no racial innocence without earning it by eradicating discrimination and helping the disadvantaged to develop. Because we ignored the means, the goals have not been reached, and the real work remains to be done.

What Is Wrong with
Reverse Discrimination?

Edwin C. Hettinger

Edwin C. Hettinger, a professor of philosophy at the College of Charleston, argues here
that even if affirmative action constitutes reverse discrimination, it can still be justified
on consequentialist grounds. In Hettinger's view, the point of affirmative action is to
bring an end to racial and sexual inequalities and thus create a more egalitarian society.
With this goal in mind, he addresses a number of objections to reverse discrimination
and argues that most of them can be easily met. For instance, he counters the idea that
reverse discrimination discriminates against white males by appealing to the fact that it
neither encourages negative stereotypes of white males nor contempt for them as a
group. He does, though, concede that the process of achieving the goal of affirmative
action puts extra burdens on white male job applicants, who are often denied
employment for affirmative-action related reasons. Given that these burdens are usually
temporary and spread evenly throughout society, Hettinger concludes that such injustice
is a small matter compared to the greater injustice of discrimination itself.

Many people think it obvious that reverse discrimination is unjust. Calling
affirmative action reverse discrimination itself suggests this. This discussion
evaluates numerous reasons given for this alleged injustice. Most of these accounts of what is wrong with reverse discrimination are found to be deficient. The explanations for why reverse discrimination is morally troubling
show only that it is unjust in a relatively weak sense. This result has an important consequence for the wider issue of the moral justifiability of affirmative
action. If social policies which involve minor injustice are permissible (and
perhaps required) when they are required in order to overcome much greater
injustice, then the mild injustice of reverse discrimination is easily overridden
by its contribution to the important social goal of dismantling our sexual and
racial caste system.[1]

By 'reverse discrimination' or 'affirmative action' I shall mean hiring or
admitting a slightly less well qualified woman or black, rather than a slightly
more qualified white male,[2] for the purpose of helping to eradicate sexual
and/or racial inequality, or for the purpose of compensating women and blacks
for the burdens and injustices they have suffered due to past and ongoing
sexism and racism.[3] There are weaker forms of affirmative action, such as
giving preference to minority candidates only when qualifications are equal,
or providing special educational opportunities for youths in disadvantaged
groups. This paper seeks to defend the more controversial sort of reverse

From *Business and Professional Ethics Journal* 6 (1987), 39–51.

discrimination defined above. I begin by considering several spurious objections to reverse discrimination. In the second part, I identity the ways in which this policy is morally troubling and then assess the significance of these negative features.

SPURIOUS OBJECTIONS

1. Reverse Discrimination as Equivalent to Racism and Sexism

In a discussion on national television, George Will, the conservative news analyst and political philosopher, articulated the most common objection to reverse discrimination. It is unjust, he said, because it is discrimination on the basis of race or sex. Reverse discrimination against white males is the same evil as traditional discrimination against women and blacks. The only difference is that in this case it is the white male who is being discriminated against. Thus if traditional racism and sexism are wrong and unjust, so is reverse discrimination, and for the very same reasons.

But reverse discrimination is not at all like traditional sexism and racism. The motives and intentions behind it are completely different, as are its consequences. Consider some of the motives underlying traditional racial discrimination.[4] Blacks were not hired or allowed into schools because it was felt that contact with them was degrading, and sullied whites. These policies were based on contempt and loathing for blacks, on a feeling that blacks were suitable only for subservient positions and that they should never have positions of authority over whites. Slightly better qualified white males are not being turned down under affirmative action for any of these reasons. No defenders or practitioners of affirmative action (and no significant segment of the general public) think that contact with white males is degrading or sullying, that white males are contemptible and loathsome, or that white males—by their nature—should be subservient to blacks or women.

The consequences of these two policies differ radically as well. Affirmative action does not stigmatize white males; it does not perpetuate unfortunate stereotypes about white males; it is not part of a pattern of discrimination that makes being a white male incredibly burdensome.[5] Nor does it add to a particular group's "already overabundant supply" of power, authority, wealth, and opportunity, as does traditional racial and sexual discrimination.[6] On the contrary, it results in a more egalitarian distribution of these social economic benefits. If the motives and consequences of reverse discrimination and of traditional racism and sexism are completely different, in what sense could they be morally equivalent acts? If acts are to be individuated (for moral purposes) by including the motives, intentions, and consequences in their description, then clearly these two acts are not identical.

It might be argued that although the motives and consequences are different, the act itself is the same: reverse discrimination is discrimination on the basis of race and sex, and this is wrong in itself independently of the motives or consequences. But discriminating (i.e., making distinctions in how one treats people) on the basis of race or sex is not always wrong, nor is it necessarily unjust. It is not wrong, for example, to discriminate against one's own sex when choosing a spouse. Nor is racial or sexual discrimination in hiring necessarily wrong. This is shown by Peter Singer's example in which a director of a play about ghetto conditions in New York City refuses to consider any white applicants for the actors because she wants the play to be authentic.[7] If I am looking for a representative of the black community, or doing a study about blacks and disease, it is perfectly legitimate to discriminate against all whites. Their whiteness makes them unsuitable for my (legitimate) purposes. Similarly, if I am hiring a wet-nurse, or a person to patrol the women's change rooms in my department store, discriminating against males is perfectly legitimate.

These examples show that racial and sexual discrimination are not wrong in themselves. This is not to say that they are never wrong; most often they clearly are. Whether or not they are wrong, however, depends on the purposes, consequences, and context of such discrimination.

2. Race and Sex as Morally Arbitrary and Irrelevant Characteristics

A typical reason given for the alleged injustice of all racial and sexual discrimination (including affirmative action) is that it is morally arbitrary to consider race or sex when hiring, since these characteristics are not relevant to the decision. But the above examples show that not all uses of race or sex as a criterion in hiring decisions are morally arbitrary or irrelevant. Similarly, when an affirmative action officer takes into account race and sex, use of these characteristics is not morally irrelevant or arbitrary. Since affirmative action aims to help end racial and sexual inequality by providing black and female role models for minorities (and non-minorities), the race and sex of the job candidates are clearly relevant to the decision. There is nothing arbitrary about the affirmative action officer focusing on race and sex. Hence, if reverse discrimination is wrong, it is not wrong for the reason that it uses morally irrelevant and arbitrary characteristics to distinguish between applicants.

3. Reverse Discrimination as Unjustified Stereotyping

It might be argued that reverse discrimination involves judging people by alleged average characteristics of a class to which they belong, instead of judging them on the basis of their individual characteristics, and that such judging on the basis of stereotypes is unjust. But the defense of affirmative action suggested in this paper does not rely on stereotyping. When an employer hires a slightly less well qualified woman or black over a slightly more qualified white male for the purpose of helping to overcome sexual and racial inequality, she judges the applicants on the basis of their individual characteristics.

She uses this person's sex or skin color as a mechanism to help achieve the goals of affirmative action. Individual characteristics of the white male (his skin color and sex) prevent him from serving one of the legitimate goals of employment policies, and he is turned down on this basis.

Notice that the objection does have some force against those who defend reverse discrimination on the grounds of compensatory justice. An affirmative action policy whose purpose is to compensate women and blacks for past and current injustices judges that women and blacks on the average are owed greater compensation than are white males. Although this is true, opponents of affirmative action argue that some white males have been more severely and unfairly disadvantaged than some women and blacks.[8] A poor white male from Appalachia may have suffered greater undeserved disadvantages than the upper-middle class woman or black with whom he competes. Although there is a high correlation between being female (or being black) and being especially owed compensation for unfair disadvantages suffered, the correlation is not universal.

Thus defending affirmative action on the grounds of compensatory justice, may lead to unjust treatment of white males in individual cases. Despite the fact that certain white males are owed greater compensation than are some women or blacks, it is the latter that receive compensation. This is the result of judging candidates for jobs on the basis of the average characteristics of their class, rather than on the basis of their individual characteristics. Thus compensatory justice defenses of reverse discrimination may involve potentially problematic stereotyping.[9] But this is not the defense of affirmative action considered here.

4. Failing to Hire the Most Qualified Person Is Unjust

One of the major reasons people think reverse discrimination is unjust is because they think that the most qualified person should get the job. But why should the most qualified person be hired?

A. EFFICIENCY   One obvious answer to this question is that one should hire the most qualified person because doing so promotes efficiency. If job qualifications are positively correlated with job performance, then the more qualified person will tend to do a better job. Although it is not always true that there is such a correlation, in general there is, and hence this point is well taken. There are short term efficiency costs of reverse discrimination as defined here.[10]

Note that a weaker version of affirmative action has no such efficiency costs. If one hires a black or woman over a white male only in cases where qualifications are roughly equal, job performance will not be affected. Furthermore, efficiency costs will be a function of the qualifications gap between the black or woman hired, and the white male rejected: the larger the gap, the greater the efficiency costs.[11] The existence of efficiency costs is also a function of the type of work performed. Many of the jobs in our society are ones which any normal person can do (e.g., assembly line worker, janitor, truck driver, etc.). Affirmative action hiring for these positions is unlikely to have significant efficiency costs (assuming whoever is hired is willing to work hard). In general, professional positions are the ones in which people's performance levels will vary significantly, and hence these are the jobs in which reverse discrimination could have significant efficiency costs.

While concern for efficiency gives us a reason for hiring the most qualified person, it in no way explains the alleged injustice suffered by the white male who is passed over due to reverse discrimination. If the affirmative action employer is treating the white male unjustly, it is not because the hiring policy is inefficient. Failing to maximize efficiency does not generally involve acting unjustly. For instance, a person who carries one bag of groceries at a time, rather than two, is acting inefficiently, though not unjustly.

It is arguable that the manager of a business who fails to hire the most qualified person (and thereby sacrifices some efficiency) treats the owners of the company unjustly, for their profits may suffer, and this violates one conception of the manager's fiduciary responsibility to the shareholders. Perhaps the administrator of a hospital who hires a slightly less well qualified black doctor (for the purposes of affirmative action) treats the future patients at that hospital unjustly, for doing so may reduce the level of health care they receive (and it is arguable that they have a legitimate expectation to receive the best health care possible for the money they spend). But neither of these examples of inefficiency leading to injustice concern the white male "victim" of affirmative action, and it is precisely this person who the opponents of reverse discrimination claim is being unfairly treated.

To many people, that a policy is inefficient is a sufficient reason for condemning it. This is especially true in the competitive and profit oriented world of business. However, profit maximization is not the only legitimate goal of business hiring policies (or other business decisions). Businesses have responsibilities to help heal society's ills, especially those (like racism and sexism) which they in large part helped to create and perpetuate. Unless one takes the implausible position that business' only legitimate goal is profit maximization, the efficiency costs of affirmative action are not an automatic reason for rejecting it. And as we have noted, affirmative action's efficiency costs are of no help in substantiating and explaining its alleged injustice to white males.

B. The Most Qualified Person Has a Right to the Job   One could argue that the most qualified person for the job has a right to be hired in virtue of superior qualifications. On this view, reverse discrimination violates the better qualified white male's right to be hired for the job. But the most qualified applicant holds no such right. If you are the best painter in town, and a person hires her brother to paint her house, instead of you, your rights have not been violated. People do not have rights to be hired for particular jobs (though I think a plausible case can be made for the claim that there is a fundamental human right to employment). If anyone has a right in this matter, it is the employer. This is not to say, of course, that the employer cannot do wrong in her hiring decision; she obviously can. If she hires a white because she loathes blacks, she does wrong. The point is that her wrong does not consist in violating the right some candidate has to her job (though this would violate other rights of the candidate).

C. The Most Qualified Person Deserves the Job   It could be argued that the most qualified person should get the job because she deserves it in virtue of her superior qualifications. But the assumption that the person most qualified for a job is the one who most deserves it is problematic. Very often people do not deserve their qualifications, and hence they do not deserve anything on the basis of those qualifications.[12] A person's qualifications are a function of at least the following factors: (a) innate abilities, (b) home environment, (c) socio-economic class of parents, (d) quality of the schools attended, (e) luck, and (f) effort or perseverance. A person is only responsible for the last factor on this list, and hence one only deserves one's qualifications to the extent that they are a function of effort.[13]

It is undoubtedly often the case that a person who is less well qualified for a job is more deserving of the job (because she worked harder to achieve those lower qualifications) than is someone with superior qualifications. This is frequently true of women and blacks in the job market: they worked harder to overcome disadvantages most (or all) white males never faced. Hence, affirmative action policies which permit the hiring of slightly less well qualified candidates may often be more in line with considerations of desert than are the standard meritocratic procedures.

The point is not that affirmative action is defensible because it helps insure that more deserving candidates get jobs. Nor is it that desert should be the only or even the most important consideration in hiring decisions. The claim is simply that hiring the most qualified person for a job need not (and quite often does not) involve hiring the most deserving candidate. Hence the intuition that morality requires one to hire the most qualified people cannot be justified on the grounds that these people deserve to be hired.[14]

D. The Most Qualified Person Is Entitled to the Job   One might think that although the most qualified person neither deserves the job nor has a right to the job, still this person is entitled to the job. By 'entitlement' in this context, I mean a natural and legitimate expectation based on a type of social promise. Society has implicitly encouraged the belief that the most qualified candidate will get the job. Society has set up a competition and the prize is a job which is awarded to those applying with the best qualifications. Society thus reneges on an implicit promise it has made to its members when it allows reverse discrimination to occur. It is dashing legitimate expectations it has encouraged. It is violating the very rules of a game it created.

Furthermore, the argument goes, by allowing reverse discrimination, society is breaking an explicit promise (contained in the Civil Rights Act of 1964) that it will not allow race or sex to be used against one of its citizens. Title VII of that Act prohibits discrimination in employment on the basis of race or sex (as well as color, religion, or national origin).

In response to this argument, it should first be noted that the above interpretation of the Civil Rights Act is misleading. In fact, the Supreme Court has interpreted the Act as allowing race and sex to be considered in hiring or admission decisions.[15] More importantly, since affirmative action has been an explicit national policy for the last twenty years (and has been supported in numerous court cases), it is implausible to argue that society has promised its members that it will not allow race or sex to outweigh superior qualifications in hiring decisions. In addition, the objection takes a naive and utopian view of actual hiring decisions. It presents a picture of our society as a pure meritocracy in which hiring decisions are based solely on qualifications. The only exception it sees to these meritocratic procedures is the unfortunate policy of affirmative action. But this picture is dramatically distorted. Elected government officials, political appointees, business managers, and many others clearly do not have their positions solely or even mostly because of their qualifications.[16] Given the widespread acceptance in our society of procedures which are far from meritocratic, claiming that the most qualified person has a socially endorsed entitlement to the job is not believable.

5. Undermining Equal
Opportunity for White Males

It has been claimed that the right of white males to an equal chance of employment is violated by affirmative action.[17] Reverse discrimination, it is said, undermines equality of opportunity for white males.

If equality of opportunity requires a social environment in which everyone at birth has roughly the same chance of succeeding through the use of his or her natural talents, then it could well be argued that given the cultural, and educational disadvantages placed on women and blacks, preferential treatment of these groups brings us closer to equality of opportunity. White males are full members of the community in a way in which women and blacks are not, and this advantage is diminished by affirmative action. Affirmative action takes away the greater than equal opportunity white males generally have, and thus it brings us closer to a situation in which all members of society have an equal chance of succeeding through the use of their talents.

It should be noted that the goal of affirmative action is to bring about a society in which there is equality of opportunity for women and blacks without preferential treatment of these groups. It is not the purpose of the sort of affirmative action defended here to disadvantage white males in order to take away the advantage a sexist and racist society gives to them. But noticing that this occurs is sufficient to dispel the illusion that affirmative action undermines the equality of opportunity for white males.[18]

LEGITIMATE OBJECTIONS

The following two considerations explain what is morally troubling about reverse discrimination.

1. Judging on the Basis of Involuntary Characteristics

In cases of reverse discrimination, white males are passed over on the basis of membership in a group they were born into. When an affirmative action employer hires a slightly less well qualified black (or woman), rather than a more highly qualified white male, skin color (or sex) is being used as one criterion for determining who gets a very important benefit. Making distinctions in how one treats people on the basis of characteristics they cannot help having (such as skin color or sex) is morally problematic because it reduces individual autonomy. Discriminating between people on the basis of features they can do something about is preferable, since it gives them some control over how others act towards them. They can develop the characteristics others use to give them favorable treatment and avoid those characteristics others use as grounds for unfavorable treatment.[19]

For example, if employers refuse to hire you because you are a member of the American Nazi Party, and if you do not like the fact that you are having a hard time finding a job, you can choose to leave the party. However, if a white male is having trouble finding employment because slightly less well qualified women and blacks are being given jobs to meet affirmative action requirements, there is nothing he can do about this disadvantage, and his autonomy is curtailed.[20]

Discriminating between people on the basis of their involuntary characteristics is morally undesirable, and thus reverse discrimination is also morally undesirable. Of course, that something is morally undesirable does not show that it is unjust, nor that it is morally unjustifiable.

How morally troubling is it to judge people on the basis of involuntary characteristics? Notice that our society frequently uses these sorts of features to distinguish between people. Height and good looks are characteristics one cannot do much about, and yet basketball players and models are ordinarily chosen and rejected on the basis of precisely these features. To a large extent our intelligence is also a feature beyond our control, and yet intelligence is clearly one of the major characteristics our society uses to determine what happens to people.

Of course there are good reasons why we distinguish between people on the basis of these sorts of involuntary characteristics. Given the goals of basketball teams, model agencies, and employers in general, hiring the taller, better looking or more intelligent person (respectively) makes good sense. It promotes efficiency, since all these people are likely to do a better job. Hiring policies based on these involuntary characteristics serve the legitimate purposes of these businesses (e.g. profit and serving the public), and hence they may be morally justified despite their tendency to reduce the control people have over their own lives.

This argument applies to reverse discrimination as well. The purpose of affirmative action is to help eradicate racial and sexual injustice. If affirmative action policies help bring about this goal, then they can be morally justified despite their tendency to reduce the control white males have over their lives.

In one respect this sort of consequentialist argument is more forceful in the case of affirmative action. Rather than merely promoting the goal of efficiency (which is the justification for businesses hiring naturally brighter, taller, or more attractive individuals), affirmative action promotes the non-utilitarian goal of an egalitarian society. In general, promoting a consideration of justice (such as equality) is more important than is promoting efficiency or utility.[21] Thus in terms of the importance of the objective, this consequentialist argument is stronger in the case of affirmative action. If one can justify reducing individual autonomy on the grounds that it promotes efficiency, one can certainly do so on the grounds that it reduces the injustice of racial and sexual inequality.

2. Burdening White Males Without Compensation

Perhaps the strongest moral intuition concerning the wrongness of reverse discrimination is that it is unfair to job seeking white males. It is unfair because they have been given an undeserved disadvantage in the competition for employment; they have been handicapped because of something that is not their fault. Why should white males be made to pay for the sins of others?

It would be a mistake to argue for reverse discrimination on the grounds that white males deserve to be burdened and that therefore we should hire women and blacks even when white males are better qualified.[22] Young white males who are now entering the job market are not more responsible for the evils of racial and sexual inequality than are other members of society. Thus, reverse discrimination is not properly viewed as punishment administered to white males.

The justification for affirmative action supported here claims that bringing about sexual and racial equality necessitates sacrifice on the part of white males who seek employment. An important step in bringing about the desired egalitarian society involves speeding up the process by which women and blacks get into positions of power and authority. This requires that white males find it harder to achieve these same positions. But this is not punishment for deeds done.

Thomas Nagel's helpful analogy is state condemnation of property under the right of eminent domain for the purpose of building a highway.[23] Forcing some in the community to move in order that the community as a whole may benefit is unfair. Why should these individuals suffer rather than others? The answer is: Because they happen to live in a place where it is important to build a road. A similar response should be given to the white male who objects to reverse discrimination with the same "Why me?" question. The answer is: Because job seeking white males happen to be in the way of an important road leading to the desired egalitarian society. Job-seeking white males are being made to bear the brunt of the burden of affirmative action because of accidental considerations, just as are homeowners whose property is condemned in order to build a highway.

This analogy is extremely illuminating and helpful in explaining the nature of reverse discrimination. There is, however, an important dissimilarity that Nagel does not mention. In cases of property condemnation, compensation is paid to the owner. Affirmative action policies, however, do not compensate white males for shouldering this burden of moving toward the desired egalitarian society. So affirmative action is unfair to job seeking white males because they are forced to bear an unduly large share of the burden of achieving racial and sexual equality without being compensated for this sacrifice. Since we have singled out job seeking white males from the larger pool of white males who should also help achieve this goal, it seems that some compensation from the latter to the former is appropriate.[24]

This is a serious objection to affirmative action policies only if the uncompensated burden is substantial. Usually it is not. Most white male "victims" of affirmative action easily find employment. It is highly unlikely that the same white male will repeatedly fail to get hired because of affirmative action.[25] The burdens of affirmative action should be spread as evenly as possible among all the job seeking white males. Furthermore, the burden job seeking white males face—of finding it somewhat more difficult to get employment—is inconsequential when compared to the burdens ongoing discrimination places on women and blacks.[26] Forcing job seeking white males to bear an extra burden is acceptable because this is a necessary step toward achieving a much greater reduction in the unfair burdens our society places on women and blacks. If affirmative action is a necessary mechanism for a timely dismantlement of our racial and sexual caste system, the extra burdens it places on job seeking white males are justified.

Still the question remains: Why isn't compensation paid? When members of society who do not deserve extra burdens are singled out to sacrifice for an important community goal, society owes them compensation. This objection loses some of its force when one realizes that society continually places undeserved burdens on its members without compensating them. For instance, the burden of seeking efficiency is placed on the shoulders of the least naturally talented and intelligent. That one is born less intelligent (or otherwise less talented) does not mean that one deserves to have reduced employment opportunities, and yet our society's meritocratic hiring procedures make it much harder for less naturally talented members to find meaningful employment. These people are not compensated for their sacrifices either.

Of course, pointing out that there are other examples of an allegedly problematic social policy does not justify that policy. Nonetheless, if this analogy is sound, failing to compensate job-seeking white males for the sacrifices placed on them by reverse discrimination is not without precedent. Furthermore, it is no more morally troublesome than is failing to compensate less talented members of society for their undeserved sacrifice of employment opportunities for the sake of efficiency.

CONCLUSION

This article has shown the difficulties in pinpointing what is morally troubling about reverse discrimination. The most commonly heard objections to reverse discrimination fail to make their case. Reverse discrimination is not morally equivalent to traditional racism and sexism since its goals and consequences are entirely different, and the act of treating people differently on the basis of race or sex is not necessarily morally wrong. The race and sex of the candidates are not morally irrelevant in all hiring decisions, and affirmative action hiring is an example where discriminating on the basis of race or sex is not morally arbitrary. Furthermore, affirmative action can be defended on grounds that do not involve stereotyping. Though affirmative action hiring of less well qualified applicants can lead to short run inefficiency, failing to hire the most qualified applicant does not violate this person's rights, entitlements, or deserts. Additionally, affirmative action hiring does not generally undermine equal opportunity for white males.

Reverse discrimination is morally troublesome in that it judges people on the basis of involuntary characteristics and thus reduces the control they have over their lives. It also places a larger than fair share of the burden of achieving an egalitarian society on the shoulders of job seeking white males without compensating them for this sacrifice. But these problems are relatively minor when compared to the grave injustice of racial and sexual inequality, and they are easily outweighed if affirmative action helps alleviate this far greater injustice.[27]

NOTES

1. Thomas Nagel uses the phrase "racial caste system" in his illuminating testimony before the Subcommittee on the Constitution of the Senate Judiciary Committee, on June 18, 1981. This testimony is reprinted as "A Defense of Affirmative Action" in *Ethical Theory and Business,* 2nd edition, ed. Tom Beauchamp and Norman Bowie (Englewood Cliffs, NJ: Prentice-Hall, 1983), pp. 483–487.

2. What should count as qualifications is controversial. By 'qualifications' I refer to such things as grades, test scores, prior experience, and letters of recommendation. I will not include black skin or female sex in my use of 'qualification,' though there are strong arguments for counting these as legitimate qualifications (in the sense of characteristics which would help the candidate achieve the legitimate goals of the hiring or admitting institution). For these arguments see Ronald Dworkin, "Why Bakke Has No Case," *The New York Review of Books,* November 10th, 1977.

3. This paper assumes the controversial premise that we live in a racist and sexist society. Statistics provide immediate and powerful support for this claim. The fact that blacks comprise 12% of the U.S. population, while comprising a minuscule percentage of those in positions of power and authority is sufficient evidence that our society continues to be significantly racist in results, if not in intent. Unless one assumes that blacks are innately less able to attain, or less desirous of

attaining these positions to a degree that would account for this huge under-representation, one must conclude that our social organizations significantly disadvantage blacks. This is (in part) the injustice that I call racism. The argument for the charge of sexism is analogous (and perhaps even more persuasive given that women comprise over 50% of the population). For more supporting evidence, see Tom Beauchamp's article "The Justification of Reverse Discrimination in Hiring" in *Ethical Theory and Business,* pp. 495-506.

4. Although the examples in this paper focus more on racism than on sexism, it is not clear that the former is a worse problem than is the latter. In many ways, sexism is a more subtle and pervasive form of discrimination. It is also less likely to be acknowledged.

5. This is Paul Woodruff's helpful definition of unjust discrimination. See Paul Woodruff, "What's Wrong With Discrimination," *Analysis,* vol. 36, no. 3, 1976, pp. 158-160.

6. This point is made by Richard Wasserstrom in his excellent article "A Defense of Programs of Preferential Treatment," *National Forum* (The Phi Kappa Phi Journal), vol. viii, no. 1 (Winter 1978), pp. 15-18. The article is reprinted in *Social Ethics,* 2nd edition, ed. Thomas Mappes and Jane Zembaty (New York: McGraw-Hill, 1982), pp. 187-191. The quoted phrase is Wasserstrom's.

7. Peter Singer, "Is Racial Discrimination Arbitrary?" *Philosophia,* vol. 8 (November 1978), pp. 185-203.

8. See, for example, Robert Simon, "Preferential Hiring: A Reply to Judith Jarvis Thomson," *Philosophy and Public Affairs,* vol. 3, no. 3 (Spring 1974).

9. If it is true (and it is certainly plausible) that every black or woman, no matter how fortunate, has suffered from racism and sexism in a way in which no white male has suffered from racism and sexism, then compensation for this injustice would be owed to all and only blacks and women. Given this, arguing for affirmative action on the grounds of compensatory justice would not involve judging individuals by average features of classes of which they are members. Still it might be argued that for certain blacks and women such injustices are not nearly as severe as the different type of injustice suffered by some white males. Thus one would have to provide a reason for why we should compensate (with affirmative action) any black or woman before any white male. Perhaps administrative convenience is such a reason. Being black or female (rather than white and male) correlates nicely with the property of being more greatly and unfairly disadvantaged, and thus race and sex are useful rough guidelines for determining who most needs compensation. This does, however, involve stereotyping.

10. In the long run, however, reverse discrimination may actually promote overall societal efficiency by breaking down the barriers to a vast reservoir of untapped potential in women and blacks.

11. See Thomas Nagel, "A Defense of Affirmative Action," p. 484.

12. This is Wasserstrom's point. See "A Defense of Programs of Preferential Treatment," in *Social Ethics,* p. 190.

13. By 'effort' I intend to include (1) how hard a person tries to achieve certain goals, (2) the amount of risk voluntarily incurred in seeking these goals, and (3) the degree to which moral considerations play a role in choosing these goals. The harder one tries, the more one is wiling to sacrifice, and the worthier the goal, the greater are one's deserts. For support of the claim that voluntary past action is the only valid basis for desert, see James Rachels, "What People Deserve," in

Justice and Economic Distribution, ed. John Arthur and William Shaw (Englewood Cliffs, NJ: Prentice-Hall, 1978), pp. 150–163.

14. It would be useful to know if there is a correlation between the candidate who is most deserving (because she worked the hardest) and the one with the best qualifications. In other words, are better qualified candidates in general those who worked harder to achieve their qualifications? Perhaps people who have the greatest natural abilities and the most fortunate social circumstances will be the ones who work the hardest to develop their talents. This raises the possibility, suggested by John Rawls, that the ability to put forward effort is itself a function of factors outside a person's control. See his *A Theory of Justice* (Cambridge, MA: Harvard University Press, 1971), pp. 103–104. But if anything is under a person's control, and hence is something a person is responsible for, it is how hard she tries. Thus if there is an appropriate criterion for desert, it will include how much effort a person exerts.

15. See Justice William Brennan's majority opinion in United Steel Workers and Kaiser Aluminum v. Weber, United States Supreme Court, *443 U.S. 193* (1979). See also Justice Lewis Powell's majority opinion in the University of California v. Bakke, United States Supreme Court, *438 U.S. 265* (1978).

16. This is Wasserstrom's point. See "A Defense of Programs of Preferential Treatment," p. 189.

17. This is Judith Thomson's way of characterizing the alleged injustice. See "Preferential Hiring," *Philosophy and Public Affairs,* vol. 2, no. 4 (Summer 1973).

18. If it is true that some white males are more severely disadvantaged in our society than are some women and blacks, affirmative action would increase the inequality of opportunity for these white males. But since these individuals are a small minority of white males, the overall result of affirmative action would be to move us closer toward equality of opportunity.

19. James Rachels makes this point in "What People Deserve," p. 159. Joel Feinberg has also discussed related points. See his *Social Philosophy* (Englewood Cliffs, NJ: Prentice-Hall, 1973), p. 108.

20. He could work harder to get better qualifications and hope that the qualifications gap between him and the best woman or black would become so great that the efficiency cost of pursuing affirmative action would be prohibitive. Still he can do nothing to get rid of the disadvantage (in affirmative action contexts) of being a white male.

21. For a discussion of how considerations of justice typically outweigh considerations of utility, see Manuel Velasquez, *Business Ethics* (Englewood, NJ: Prentice-Hall, 1982), Chapter Two.

22. On the average, however, white males have unfairly benefited from the holding back of blacks and women, and hence it is not altogether inappropriate that this unfair benefit be removed.

23. Nagel, "A Defense of Affirmative Action," p. 484.

24. It would be inappropriate to extract compensation from women or blacks since they are the ones who suffer the injustice affirmative action attempts to alleviate.

25. This is a potential worry, however, and so it is important to insure that the same white male does not repeatedly sacrifice for the goals of affirmative action.

26. Cheshire Calhoun reminded me of this point.

27. Of course one must argue that reverse discrimination is effective in bringing about an egalitarian society. There are complicated consequentialist arguments

both for and against this claim, and I have not discussed them here. Some of the questions to be addressed are: (1) How damaging is reverse discrimination to the self-esteem of blacks and women? (2) Does reverse discrimination promote racial and sexual strife more than it helps to alleviate them? (3) Does it perpetuate unfortunate stereotypes about blacks and women? (4) How long are we justified in waiting to pull blacks and women into the mainstream of our social life? (5) What sorts of alternative mechanisms are possible and politically practical for achieving affirmative action goals (for instance, massive early educational funding for children from impoverished backgrounds)?

Affirmative Action as a Form of Restitution
Leo Groarke

Leo Groarke is the author of *Nuclear War: Philosophical Perspectives* (1985) and an associate professor of philosophy at Wilfrid Laurier University in Ontario, Canada. In this reading, he presents a "common sense" defense of affirmative action based on the basic principle of compensatory justice: compensation needs to be made to those who have been the victims of discrimination by those who have been its unjust beneficiaries (primarily older white males). He also recognizes that in practice as well as in philosophical argument this principle is often ignored, as in general it is younger white males who are called upon to make compensation to those who have suffered indirectly from historical discrimination. Because affirmative action thus violates justice, it is vulnerable to criticism as a form of "reverse discrimination." Rather than calling for an end to affirmative action, Groarke suggests changes that could be made to affirmative action practices so that actual victims of discrimination could be compensated by those who are primarily responsible for their being wronged.

1. INTRODUCTION

Though it has not been clearly recognized by philosophers and other commentators, the common sense defense of affirmative action or "employment equity"[1] appeals to principles of restitution. It is because some groups have suffered, and other groups have benefited, from discrimination that it seems that we should compensate the former by awarding them preferential treatment paid for by the latter (in the sense that they must lose their right to equal treatment). Philosophers have nonetheless defended affirmative action in ways that reject this appeal to restitution. In contrast, I defend it, arguing (1) that alternative attempts to defend affirmative action fail; and (2) that ordinary affirmative action programs are not in keeping with the principles of restitution. Present programs should not, I argue, be rejected out of hand, though we are obliged to supplement and amend them in keeping with the proposals I suggest.

2. AFFIRMATIVE ACTION: A CRITIQUE

In some ways, the appeal to restitution which is the implicit basis of affirmative action is persuasive and compelling. In North America, women, natives, blacks and other groups have suffered, and white males have benefited, from discrimination in the past, and it seems reasonable to alleviate this injustice

From *Journal of Business Ethics* 9 (1990), 207–213.

by asking the latter to compensate the former. The appeal to restitution this implies (and the notion that affirmative action can be defended by obvious and intuitive principles of justice) is, however, problematic as soon as one considers the internal make up of the groups affected by affirmative action programs. As many commentators have pointed out, the costs of such pro-grams are borne by young white males (candidates for jobs and programs awarded to other groups), though it is *older* white males who have been the main perpetrators and beneficiaries of discrimination (cf. Carr, 1982). It fol-lows that standard affirmative action violates the principles of restitution, for they suggest that those who have gained unjust advantage (in this case, older white males) should compensate those who have been disadvantaged.

Though it has received less attention, an analogous problem arises when one considers the victims of discrimination, for they are, first and foremost, *older* individuals who belong to discriminated groups (e.g., older women who pursued jobs and careers when discrimination was accepted). The problem is that restitution requires that they be compensated for their losses, though they receive no compensation from standard affirmative action programs. In-stead, the benefits provided are made available to other, younger members of the groups that they belong to (cf. Wolf-Devine, 1988).

Looked at from the point of view of restitution, it seems to follow that ordinary affirmative action neither compensates nor taxes the appropriate individuals (the main victims, and the main beneficiaries, of discrimination). If analogous principles were used in dealing with individuals, they would not force John to return to Jacinth property he has wrongly acquired, but force Jack (i.e. someone else entirely) to provide benefits to Jill. Such sanctions would obviously be a travesty of justice and it needs to be explained why ordinary affirmative action should not be viewed in the same light.

Rather than meet this challenge, commentators who defend affirmative action usually ignore the problems it implies, employing categories that gloss over the distinction between older and younger members of the groups that they discuss. Judith Jarvis Thomson's oft quoted defense of preferential hiring is, for example, founded on the following analogy between affirmative action and the way a dining club might decide to allocate tables when there are not enough to go around.

> ...suppose that we have of late had reason to be especially grateful to one of the members, whom I'll call Smith: Smith has done a series of very great favors for the club. It seems to me we might, out of gratitude to Smith, adopt the following policy: for the next six months, if two members arrive at the same time, and there is only one available table, then Smith gets in first, if he's one of the two; whereas if he's not, then the headwaiter shall toss a coin....
>
> It seems to me that there would be no impropriety in our taking these actions—by which I mean to include that there would be no injustice in our taking them. Suppose another member, Jones, votes No. Suppose he says "Look. I admit we all benefited from what Smith did for us. But still, I'm a member and a member in as good standing as Smith is. So I have a right to an equal

chance (and equal share), and I demand what I have a right to." I think we may rightly feel that Jones merely shows insensitivity: he does not adequately appreciate what Smith did for us. Jones, like all of us, has a right to an equal chance at such benefits as the club has available for distribution to the members; but there is no injustice in a majority's refusing to grant the members this equal chance, in the name of a debt of gratitude to Smith. (Thomson, 1981, 297–8)

According to Thomson, justice, or at least common decency, similarly shows that society has a debt to blacks, women and others, and that it is reasonable to use preferential hiring as one way of repaying it.

The problem with Thomson's claim is her assumption that different members of society are equally responsible for the debt it owes to groups which have suffered from discrimination, and that members of these groups are equally entitled to be compensated. A better analogy would compare the situation that precipitates affirmative action to a dining club in which the older members of the club have treated its employees unfairly. In such circumstances, it hardly need be said that it would be wrong to rectify this injustice by forcing new members of the club who have not mistreated the employees (and who can ill afford to pay) to provide the necessary compensation. Such a proposal would be all the more objectionable if it forced them to make restitution, not to the employees who have been mistreated, but to new employees. If the new employees have suffered some discrimination, they deserve to be compensated to this extent (and the new members deserve to pay), but justice and common decency require that the major beneficiaries should be the old employees. In an analogous way restitution demands that the major costs of restitution be paid for by the club's older members.

Thomson's arguments make affirmative action plausible only by glossing the distinctions which seem to demonstrate its injustice (the distinctions between older and younger members of the groups in question). The same mistake characterizes many other thinkers (see, e.g., Martin, 1976; Dworkin, 1981: esp. pp. 326–7; and Boxill, 1984) who justify affirmative action by arguing that social goals must take precedence over the rights of young white males, ignoring the principle that society's debts should be paid by those who have incurred them. It is not that young white males have an explicit right to the jobs they lose because of affirmative action (the straw man position Boxill attributes to those who criticize it), but that they have a right not to have to pay for other people's debts. Analogously, older women, blacks and others have a right to enjoy the compensation that is paid to debts owed primarily to them. Granting that there are social goals that must be met (this is not in question), justice still requires that this be done in a way that respects the demands of restitution (as we shall see, this is not difficult to accomplish).

In answer to such arguments, one might try to justify affirmative action by appealing to present, rather than past discrimination. So construed, it need not be seen as an attempt to pay debts owed by (and to) older members of the groups it deals with, and is not so obviously unjust. It is in keeping with this that commentators like Thomson and Boxill have argued that discrimination persists in North American society, and that younger members of the relevant groups can, therefore, be reasonably compensated or asked to pay its cost. Thomson, for example writes that "Large-scale, blatant, overt wrongs have presumably disappeared; but it is only within the last twenty-five years (perhaps the last ten years in the case of women), that it has become at all widely agreed in this country that blacks and women must be recognized as having, not merely this or that particular right normally recognized as belonging to white males, but all of the rights and respect which go with full membership in the community." (Thomson, 1981: 299). The problem is that these very comments, especially as they were made in 1973, themselves suggest that the major victims and beneficiaries of discrimination are older individuals, and that they should, therefore, be the focus of attempts to make up for past discrimination. Thus morality, justice and restitution all demand that attempts to make up for past discrimination should be aimed, first and foremost, at its *major* victims, and that compensation should be provided by its *major* beneficiaries.

3. AFFIRMATIVE ACTION AS RESTITUTION

Given the various objections to affirmative action, many commentators have concluded that it should be rejected out of hand (see, for example, Newton, 1987). Such a move ignores rather than rectifies the enormous discrimination that has existed in the past, however, and it follows that justice demands some restitution, though it must be restitution that is not susceptible to the criticisms we have already noted. Despite an almost universal failure to consider how this might be achieved, it can be easily accomplished by designing affirmative action programs that make more of an attempt to abide by the principles of restitution. In particular, this requires more of an attempt to (1) compensate those individuals who are the main victims of discrimination, and (2) ensure that such compensation is provided by those who have been its main beneficiaries. The first objective requires programs that provide benefits to older women, blacks, etc. The second requires an arrangement that ensures that they are funded by older white males.

One way to satisfy these requirements is by instituting ordinary affirmative action in circumstances where it has the requisite effects. The experience needed for senior (as opposed to entry level) positions in universities, business, or government means, for example that it is older individuals who apply for such positions, and that affirmative action in this context benefits and burdens the appropriate groups (on the one hand, older blacks, women, natives, etc.; on the other, older white males, who are disadvantaged when other individuals are favoured). This being said, the possibilities for restitution such opportunities provide are extremely limited, both because there are few positions of this nature, and because those who have suffered from discrimination usually lack the qualifications they demand. Given that it is particularly important that qualified individuals occupy influential roles, it is, moreover, difficult to argue for strong affirmative action policies along these lines, though it can be said that preference should be given, all things being equal, to individuals from groups that have suffered from discrimination.[2] More comprehensive kinds of affirmative action are, however, needed if it is to compensate, in any serious way, for past discrimination.

The best way to overcome the shortcomings of such programs from the point of view of restitution is by compensating the victims of past discrimination in ways that go beyond job allocation. Given the enormous economic losses they have suffered,[3] this can be accomplished by instituting programs that provide financial benefits. Among other things, such programs should include pension reform, tax breaks and other economic benefits that are targeted at older members of those groups which have suffered from discrimination. Pension reform is, in particular, needed to alleviate the plight of many older women, blacks and others whose work has not been recognized by regular pension plans, and who have been denied careers that can provide them with adequate support in later life (women over sixty-five are said to occupy the lowest economic rung in North America). More generally, the details of such programs need to be determined by looking at the needs of these specific individuals. The principle that the costs of affirmative action should be borne by those who have most benefited from discrimination, can be satisfied by taxing older white males to pay for the programs this implies. As we have already noted, they have benefited from discrimination (by not having to compete with women, blacks and others for careers, and by enjoying laws and social programs that favour their interests) and it is in view of this that this burden is appropriate.

A third way to redress the debts owed to the victims of discrimination is by instituting affirmative action programs as we now know them. To see how they can be understood as restitution to the victims of past discrimination, we need note that the losses they have suffered are not restricted to the economic losses that attend the loss of well paid professional positions. On the contrary, they have also suffered because their exclusion from universities, governments, businesses, hospitals and other major institutions has meant that their interests have not been adequately represented in social goals and policies. It is in view of this that such losses can be alleviated by ordinary affirmative action that entails a more equitable distribution of positions to the groups that they belong to. The hiring of younger women can, for example, help rectify women's lack of social power, and thus protect women's interests. In some cases, such women may not have the same concerns as older women, but their interests are likely to be closer than those of men and there is no other way to ensure that women have a more significant share of the positions (and the influence) held by particular professions.

It may, however, seem that it is difficult to make ordinary affirmative action programs compatible with the principle that they be paid for by those who have benefited from discrimination, but this can be accomplished by tying them to retirement policies. Especially in circumstances where opportunities are scarce, such policies play an important role in dealing with discrimination, for a decision to allow individuals to keep their positions past normal retirement age prolongs the effects of past discrimination, perpetuating the inequities it produced (the lack of women faculty in universities, for example).[4] Such problems are exacerbated by the high salaries of individuals with a great deal of seniority, for it follows that the attempt to finance this decision greatly limits the ability of an institution to pursue other goals. Given such considerations, one way to make more opportunities available for groups which have suffered from discrimination is by restricting the ability of older white males to work past normal retirement age, thereby freeing the resources and positions that are needed for effective affirmative action programs. Adopting such a policy is one way to ensure that the costs of such programs are borne primarily by older white males who are denied the opportunity to continue in their positions.[5] Such policies are, it should be noted, possible even if one rejects mandatory retirement (the practice of requiring retirement of all individuals who reach normal retirement age), for one may make exceptions in the case of exceptional individuals (allowing them to continue past normal retirement), thus allowing exceptions to the rule. Though there are other alternatives, one way to institute such a policy is by requiring all individuals who reach the normal age of retirement to compete for their positions in an open competition (exceptionally qualified individuals will win such competitions, other individuals will not). In the present context, the important point is that the principles of restitution show that older individuals should pay the costs of affirmative action and such moves will, like the other policies we have already noted, help ensure this is the case.

4. AN OBJECTION:
REVERSE DISCRIMINATION

One way to assess the proposed affirmative action programs is in terms of their relationship to the standard criticism of affirmative action, reverse discrimination. It should in this regard be noted that, in addition to making affirmative action consistent with the principles of restitution, these proposals minimize the charges of reverse discrimination that can be raised against it. The standard claim is that affirmative action discriminates against young white males, but this is not a serious issue in the present case, for the proposed programs are designed so that their disadvantages are not borne by young white males. One might answer that they merely shift the burden to older white males, but this is justified by the principles of restitution. Indeed, the debt they owe to the victims of discrimination has been (especially in discussions of retirement policy—see, e.g., Brett, 1987) too long ignored and the proposed programs are important because they can rectify this oversight.

One might answer that the proposed affirmative action still implies unjust discrimination in individual cases where restitution cannot justify the penalties imposed on particular older white males. An older white male growing up in extreme poverty in an area where whites suffer discrimination may, for example, have been more disadvantaged than a successful upper class black who was insulated from discrimination, and one might therefore ask why he (the white) should be taxed to make, for example, financial benefits available to the latter (cf. Sher, 1987 and Simon, 1982). There is, it must be said, something to such concerns and it is in view of them that it makes sense to try to minimize such possibilities. In instituting economic benefits for older individuals (in terms of pension reform, e.g.), it thus makes sense to restrict them to those in need, especially as such obligations (in contrast to obligations to those better off) must rank high on our list of priorities and cannot be easily overridden by competing obligations to other groups in society (the need to support education, pollution control, and so on). Such a move will to some extent eliminate the specific case that we have noted (disqualifying the wealthy black from consideration), though it must simply be accepted that it is impossible to design social programs that ensure that no individual receives unwarranted benefits or taxes. On the contrary, some exceptions cannot be avoided when one works on such a grand scale and the limited reverse discrimination this implies must simply be accepted as the cost of rectifying past injustice (social programs must rely on generalizations which inevitably have exceptions). This does not show that the proposed affirmative action policies should be rejected, however, for such exceptions *are* exceptions and, therefore, the lesser evil when compared with the injustice of making no attempt to rectify past discrimination. Given the pervasiveness of the latter and a reasonable attempt to minimize reverse discrimination, any serious commitment to the eradication of discrimination must give priority to affirmative action and the discrimination it addresses, not to the much less serious reverse discrimination it may sometimes cause.

5. CONCLUSION

Given the kinds of affirmative action that are usually defended, some of the proposed alternatives may seem radical. This is because they are unfamiliar, however, and not because they are problematic from a moral point of view. On the contrary, they are a straightforward application of the principles of restitution and not open to the standard criticisms of affirmative action policies. It is not these proposals, but the failure of commentators to consider them which is difficult to understand.[6] The closest one appears to come is Thomson's remark that ". . . it isn't only the young male applicant for a university job who has benefited from the exclusion of blacks and women: the older white male, now comfortably tenured, also benefited . . . Well, presumably, we can't demand that he give up his job, or share it. But it seems to me in place to expect the occupants of comfortable professorial chairs to contribute in some way, to make some form of return to the young white male who bears the cost, and is turned away. . . . I find the outcry now heard against preferential hiring in the universities objectionable; it would also be objectionable that those of us who are now securely situated should placidly defend it, with no more than a sigh of regret for the young white male who pays for it." (Thomson, 1981, 301–2) There is something to these sentiments, though it should by now be clear that they greatly underestimate the obligations of older faculty who have benefited from discrimination (it isn't that they have *also* benefited, it is that they have been the *major* beneficiaries), completely ignore the debt owed to older members of discriminated groups, and fail to propose any concrete means of ensuring that older white males meet the obligations that they countenance. Contra Thomson, it is not difficult to design programs that achieve these ends.

NOTES

1. This new name highlights the fact that affirmative action allocates a more equitable number of jobs to women, natives, blacks and other groups, but it is unfortunately ambiguous (perhaps purposely so). Whatever label one applies, it must be accepted that affirmative action promotes inequity in the sense that it grants preference to individuals of a particular sex, race, etc. Rather than hide this fact, a defense of affirmative action must show that such inequity is the lesser of two evils, and justified as a way to dealing with the greater evils perpetrated by discrimination now or in the past. The term "affirmative action" might (like "employment equity") also be said to be a loaded term, but it can at least be said that it does not so blatantly assume that the standard objection to such policies (viz., the claim that they promote inequity) is mistaken.

2. This is, in effect, applying the kind of affirmative action Thomson proposes to these specific cases. Such programs are particularly important, for the individuals they benefit can act as important role models that help undermine the stereotypes that promote discrimination.

3. In the case of women, for example, the financial rewards from occupying one third, one half, or an even greater portion of the positions held by older male doctors, lawyers, judges, professors, etc. is difficult to exaggerate.

4. Especially as male faculty seem very reluctant to retire when they are given the opportunity to continue. The only survey I know of was conducted at the University of Manitoba when it adopted an open policy in response to the Manitoba Supreme Court's ruling against mandatory retirement. Of eighteen individuals scheduled to retire, fourteen indicated that they planned to continue teaching, two of them on a part time basis. As the university concludes, such prospects leave the university with "a pretty bleak picture in the area of staff renewal" (Weston, 1983).

5. Younger white males will still be disadvantaged by ordinary affirmative action, though this disadvantage will be much less onerous given the extra positions such policies would make available.

6. One can only point to the relative ability (and inability) of different social classes to protect their interests. Women and other groups have, for example, gained

enough of a hearing to demand the redress of inequities, while older white males have retained the power to see that such debts are not paid by them (in contrast, young white males occupy an almost powerless position in the present social ladder). I hasten to add that I am not suggesting that different groups have *intentionally* pursued their own interests and disregarded those of other groups. On the contrary, the moral is how difficult it is to see past one's own interests.

The Message of Affirmative Action
Thomas E. Hill, Jr.

A professor of philosophy at the University of North Carolina and the author of *Autonomy and Self-Respect* (1991), Thomas E. Hill, Jr. takes a different focus on affirmative action from other authors included in this chapter who argue in its favor. His concern is less with these arguments in themselves than with the messages they send to those who benefit from affirmative action, as well as to those who are denied benefits by it. Both consequentialist-based and justice-based arguments for affirmative action, he believes, send the wrong message to both groups of people. The first sends the message that "we care more about achieving the goals of affirmative action than you as a person." The second sends the message that "we are not sure you are someone we want with us, but we accept you have a right to be here." Drawing upon recent work in contemporary moral theory that stresses the importance of narrative connectedness and the value of community in human life, Hill proposes a different message for affirmative action that he hopes would better reflect its point. Among other objectives, such a message would recognize the history of racism and sexism involved in discrimination, and emphasize the Kantian value of respect for both affirmative action's beneficiaries and those it harms.

Affirmative action programs remain controversial, I suspect, partly because the familiar arguments for and against them start from significantly different moral perspectives. Thus I want to step back for a while from the details of debate about particular programs and give attention to the moral viewpoints presupposed in different *types* of argument. My aim, more specifically, is to compare the "messages" expressed when affirmative action is defended from different moral perspectives. Exclusively forward-looking (for example, utilitarian) arguments, I suggest, tend to express the wrong message, but this is also true of exclusively backward-looking (for example, reparation-based) arguments. However, a moral outlook that focuses on cross-temporal narrative values (such as mutually respectful social relations) suggests a more appropriate account of what affirmative action should try to express. Assessment of the message, admittedly, is only one aspect of a complex issue, but it is a relatively neglected one. My discussion takes for granted some common-sense ideas about the communicative function of action, and so I begin with these.

Actions, as the saying goes, often *speak* louder than words. There are times, too, when only actions can effectively communicate the message we

From *Social Philosophy & Policy* 8 (Spring 1991), 108–129

want to convey and times when giving a message is a central part of the purpose of action. What our actions say to others depends largely, though not entirely, upon our avowed reasons for acting; and this is a matter for reflective decision, not something we discover later by looking back at what we did and its effects. The decision is important because "the same act" can have very different consequences, depending upon how we choose to justify it. In a sense, acts done for different reasons are not "the same act" even if they are otherwise similar, and so not merely the consequences but also the moral nature of our acts depends in part on our decisions about the reasons for doing them.

Unfortunately, the message actually conveyed by our actions does not depend only on our intentions and reasons, for our acts may have a meaning for others quite at odds with what we hoped to express. Others may misunderstand our intentions, doubt our sincerity, or discern a subtext that undermines the primary message. Even if sincere, well-intended, and successfully conveyed, the message of an act or policy does not by itself justify the means by which it is conveyed; it is almost always a relevant factor, however, in the moral assessment of an act or policy. . . .

I shall focus attention for a while upon this relatively neglected issue of the message of affirmative action. In particular, I want to consider what message we *should try* to give with affirmative action programs and what messages we should try to avoid. What is the best way to convey the intended message, and indeed whether it is likely to be heard, are empirical questions that I cannot settle; but the question I propose to consider is nonetheless important, and it is a *prior* question. What do we want to say with our affirmative action programs, and why? Since the message that is received and its consequences are likely to depend to some extent on what we decide, in all sincerity, to be the rationale for such programs, it would be premature and foolish to try to infer or predict these outcomes without adequate reflection on what the message and rationale should be. Also, for those who accept the historical/narrative perspective described in [this essay], there is additional reason to focus first on the desired message; for that perspective treats the message of affirmative action not merely as a minor side effect to be weighed in, for or against, but rather as an important part of the legitimate purpose of affirmative action.

Much useful discussion has been devoted to the constitutionality of affirmative action programs, to the relative moral rights involved, and to the advantages and disadvantages of specific types of programs.[1] By deemphasizing these matters here, I do not mean to suggest that they are unimportant. Even more, my remarks are not meant to convey the message, "It doesn't matter what we do or achieve, all that matters is what we *say*." To the contrary, I believe that mere gestures are insufficient and that universities cannot even communicate what they should by affirmative action policies unless these are sincerely designed to result in increased opportunities for those disadvantaged and insulted by racism and sexism. . . .

STRATEGIES OF JUSTIFICATION:
CONSEQUENCES AND REPARATIONS

Some arguments for affirmative action look exclusively to its future benefits. The idea is that what has happened in the past is not in itself relevant to what we should do; at most, it provides clues as to what acts and policies are likely to bring about the best future. The philosophical tradition associated with this approach is utilitarianism, which declares that the morally right act is whatever produces the best consequences. Traditionally, utilitarianism evaluated consequences in terms of happiness and unhappiness, but the anticipated consequences of affirmative action are often described more specifically. For example, some argue that affirmative action will ease racial tensions, prevent riots, improve services in minority neighborhoods, reduce unemployment, remove inequities in income distribution, eliminate racial and sexual prejudice, and enhance the self-esteem of blacks and women. Some have called attention to the fact that women and minorities provide alternative perspectives on history, literature, philosophy, and politics, and that this has beneficial effects for both education and research.

These are important considerations, not irrelevant to the larger responsibilities of universities. For several reasons, however, I think it is a mistake for advocates of affirmative action to rest their case exclusively on such forward-looking arguments. First, critics raise reasonable doubts about whether affirmative action is necessary to achieve these admirable results. The economist Thomas Sowell argues that a free-market economy can achieve the same results more efficiently; his view is therefore that even if affirmative action has beneficial results (which he denies), it is not necessary for the purpose.[2] Though Sowell's position can be contested, the controversy itself tends to weaken confidence in the entirely forward-looking defense of affirmative action.

An even more obvious reason why affirmative action advocates should explore other avenues for its defense is that the exclusively forward-looking approach must give equal consideration to possible negative consequences of affirmative action. It may be, for example, that affirmative action will temporarily increase racial tensions, especially if its message is misunderstood. Even legitimate use of race and sex categories may encourage others to abuse the categories for unjust purposes. If applied without sensitive regard to the educational and research purposes of the university, affirmative action might severely undermine its efforts to fulfill these primary responsibilities. If affirmative action programs were to lower academic standards for blacks and women, they would run the risk of damaging the respect that highly qualified blacks and women have earned by leading others to suspect that these highly qualified people lack the merits of white males in the same positions. This could also be damaging to the self-respect of those who accept affirmative action positions. Even programs that disavow "lower standards" unfortunately arouse the suspicion that they don't really do so, and this by itself can cause problems. Although I believe that well-designed affirmative action programs can minimize these negative effects, the fact that they are a risk is a reason for not resting the case for affirmative action on a delicate balance of costs and benefits.

Reflection on the *message* of affirmative action also leads me to move beyond entirely forward-looking arguments. For if the sole purpose is to bring about a brighter future, then we give the wrong message to both the white males who are rejected and to the women and blacks who are benefited. To the latter what we say, in effect, is this: "Never mind how you have been treated. Forget about the fact that your race or sex has in the past been actively excluded and discouraged, and that you yourself may have had handicaps due to prejudice. Our sole concern is to bring about certain good results in the future, and giving you a break happens to be a useful means for doing this. Don't think this is a recognition of your rights as in individual or your disadvantages as a member of a group. Nor does it mean that we have confidence in your abilities. We would do the same for those who are privileged and academically inferior if it would have the same socially beneficial results."

To the white male who would have had a university position but for affirmative action, the exclusively forward-looking approach says: "We deny you the place you otherwise would have had simply as a means to produce certain socially desirable outcomes. We have not judged that others are more deserving, or have a right, to the place we are giving them instead of you. Past racism and sexism are irrelevant. The point is just that the sacrifice of your concerns is a useful means to the larger end of the future welfare of others."

This, I think, is the wrong message to give. It is also unnecessary. The proper alternative, however, is not to ignore the possible future benefits of affirmative action but rather to take them into account as a part of a larger picture.

A radically different strategy for justifying affirmative action is to rely on backward-looking arguments. Such arguments call our attention to certain events in the past and assert that *because* these past events occurred, we have certain duties now. The modern philosopher who most influentially endorsed such arguments was W.D. Ross.[3] He argued that there are duties of fidelity, justice, gratitude, and reparation that have a moral force independent of any tendency these may have to promote good consequences. The fact that you have made a promise, for example, gives you a strong moral reason to do what you promised, whether or not doing so will on balance have more beneficial consequences. The Rossian principle that is often invoked in affirmative action debates is a principle of reparation. This says that those who wrongfully injure others have a *(prima facie)* duty to apologize and make restitution. Those who have wronged others owe reparation.

James Forman dramatically expressed this idea in New York in 1969 when he presented "The Black Manifesto," which demanded five hundred million dollars in reparation to American blacks from white churches and synagogues.[4] Such organizations, the Manifesto contends, contributed to our history of slavery and racial injustice; as a result, they incurred a debt to the black community that still suffers from its effects. Objections were immediately raised: for example, both slaves and slave-owners are no longer alive; not every American white is guilty of racial oppression; and not every black in America was a victim of slavery and its aftermath.

Bernard Boxill, author of *Blacks and Social Justice,* developed a more sophisticated version of the backward-looking argument with a view to meeting these objections.[5] Let us admit, he says, that both the perpetrators and the primary victims of slavery are gone, and let us not insist that contemporary whites are guilty of perpetrating further injustices. Some do, and some do not, and public administrators cannot be expected to sort out the guilty from the non-guilty. However, reparation, or at least some "compensation,"[6] is still owed, because contemporary whites have reaped the profits of past injustice to blacks. He asks us to consider the analogy with a stolen bicycle. Suppose my parent stole your parent's bicycle some time ago, both have since died, and I "inherited" the bike from my parent, the thief. Though I may be innocent of any wrongdoing (so far), I am in possession of stolen goods rightfully belonging to you, the person who would have inherited the bike if it had not been stolen. For me to keep the bike and declare that I owe you nothing would be wrong, even if I was not the cause of your being deprived. By analogy, present-day whites owe reparations to contemporary blacks, not because they are themselves guilty of causing the disadvantages of blacks, but because they are in possession of advantages that fell to them as a result of the gross injustices of their ancestors. Special advantages continue to fall even to innocent whites because of the ongoing prejudice of their white neighbors.

Although it raises many questions, this line of argument acknowledges some important points missing in most exclusively forward-looking arguments: for example, it stresses the (intrinsic) relevance of past injustice and it calls attention to the rights and current disadvantages of blacks (in contrast with future benefits for others). When developed as an argument for affirmative action, it does not accuse all white males of prejudice and wrongdoing; at the same time, however, it sees the fundamental value as justice. As a result, it avoids giving the message to either rejected white males or reluctant affirmative action applicants that they are "mere means" to a social goal that is largely independent of their rights and interests as individuals.

There are, however, serious problems in trying to justify affirmative action by this backward-looking argument, especially if it is treated as the exclusive or central argument. Degrees of being advantaged and disadvantaged are notoriously hard to measure. New immigrants have not shared our history of past injustices, and so the argument may not apply to them in any straightforward way. The argument appeals to controversial ideas about property rights, inheritance, and group responsibilities. Some argue that affirmative action tends to benefit the least disadvantaged blacks and women; though this does not mean that they are owed nothing, their claims would seem to have lower priority than the needs of the most disadvantaged. Some highly qualified blacks and women object that affirmative action is damaging to their reputations and self-esteem, whereas the reparation argument seems to assume that it is a welcome benefit to all blacks and women.

If we focus on the message that the backward-looking argument sends, there are also some potential problems. Though rightly acknowledging past injustice, the argument (by itself) seems to convey the message that racial and sexual oppression consisted primarily in the loss of tangible goods, or the deprivation of specific rights and opportunities, that can be "paid back" in kind. The background idea, which goes back at least to Aristotle, is that persons wrongfully deprived of their "due" can justly demand an "equivalent" to what they have lost.[7] But, while specific deprivations were an important part of our racist and sexist past, they are far from the whole story. Among the worst wrongs then, as now, were humiliations and contemptuous treatment of a type that cannot, strictly, be "paid back." The problem was, and is, not just that specific rights and advantages were denied, but that prejudicial attitudes damaged self-esteem, undermined motivations, limited realistic options, and made even "officially open" opportunities seem undesirable. Racism and sexism were (and are) *insults,* not merely tangible *injuries.*[8] These are not the sort of thing that can be adequately measured and repaid with equivalents. The trouble with treating insulting racist and sexist practices on a pure reparation model is not merely the practical difficulty of identifying the offenders, determining the degree of guilt, assessing the amount of payment due, etc. It is also that penalty payments and compensation for lost benefits are not the only, or primary, moral responses that are called for. When affirmative action is defended exclusively by analogy with reparation, it tends to express the misleading message that the evils of racism and sexism are all tangible losses that can be "paid off"; by being silent on the insulting nature of racism and sexism, it tends to add insult to insult.

The message suggested by the reparation argument, by itself, also seems objectionable because it conveys the idea that higher education, teaching, and doing research are mainly benefits awarded in response to self-centered demands. The underlying picture too easily suggested is that applicants are a group of self-interested, bickering people, each grasping for limited "goodies" and insisting on a right to them. When a university grants an opportunity through affirmative action, its message would seem to be this. "We concede that you have a valid claim to this benefit and we yield to your demand, though this is not to suggest that we have confidence in your abilities or any desire to have you here." This invitation seems too concessive, the atmosphere too adversarial, and the emphasis too much on the benefits rather than the responsibilities of being a part of the university.

PHILOSOPHICAL INTERLUDE:
AN ALTERNATIVE PERSPECTIVE

Here I want to digress from the explicit consideration of affirmative action in order to consider more abstract philosophical questions about the ways we evaluate acts and policies. At the risk of oversimplifying, I want to contrast some assumptions that have, until recently, been dominant in ethical theory with alternatives suggested by contemporary philosophers who emphasize historical context, narrative unity, and community values.[9] Although these alternatives, in my opinion, have not yet been adequately developed, there seem to be at least four distinguishable themes worth considering.

First, when we reflect on what we deeply value, we find that we care not merely about the present moment and each future moment in isolation but also about how our past, present, and future cohere or fit together into a life and a piece of history. Some of our values, we might say, are cross-time wholes, with past, present, and future parts united in certain ways. Thus, for example, the commitments I have made, the projects I have begun, what I have shared with those I love, the injuries I have caused, and the hopes I have encouraged importantly affect both whether I am satisfied with my present and how I want the future to go.

Second, in reflecting on stretches of our lives and histories, we frequently use evaluative concepts drawn more from narrative literature than from accounting. Thus, for example, we think of our lives as having significant beginnings, crises, turning points, dramatic tension, character development, climaxes, resolutions, comic interludes, tragic disruptions, and eventually fitting (or unfitting) endings. The value of any moment often depends on what came before and what we anticipate to follow. And since our lives are intertwined with others in a common history, we also care about how our moments cohere with others' life stories. The past is seen as more than a time of accumulated debts and assets, and the future is valued as more than an opportunity for reinvesting and cashing in assets.

Third, evaluation must take into account one's particular historical context, including one's cultural, national, and ethnic traditions, and the actual individuals in one's life. Sometimes this point is exaggerated, I think, to suggest a dubious cultural relativism or "particularism" in ethics: for example, the thesis that what is valuable for a person is defined by the person's culture or that evaluations imply no general reasons beyond particular judgments, such as "That's *our* way" and "John is *my* son."[10] But, construed modestly as a practical or epistemological point, it seems obvious enough, on reflection, that we should take into account the historical context of our acts and that we are often in a better position to judge what is appropriate in particular cases than we are to articulate universally valid premises supporting the judgment. . . .

Fourth, when we evaluate particular acts and policies as parts of lives and histories, what is often most important is the value of the whole, which cannot always be determined by "summing up" the values of the parts. Lives, histories, and interpersonal relations over time are what G.E. Moore called "organic unities"—that is, wholes the value of which is not necessarily the sum of the values of the parts.[11] The point here is not merely the obvious practical limitation that we cannot measure and quantify values in this area. More fundamentally, the idea is that it would be a mistake even to try to evaluate certain unities by assessing different parts in isolation from one an-other, then adding up all their values. Suppose, for example, a woman with terminal cancer considered two quite different ways of spending her last days. One way, perhaps taking a world cruise, might seem best when evaluated in terms of the quality of each future moment, in isolation from her past and her present ties; but another way, perhaps seeking closure in projects and with estranged family members, might seem more valuable when seen as a part of her whole life.

Taken together, these ideas cast doubt on both the exclusively forward-looking method of assessment and the standard backward-looking alternative. Consequentialism, or the exclusively forward-looking method, attempts to de-termine what ought to be done at present by fixing attention entirely on future results. To be sure, any sensible consequentialist will consult the past for lessons and clues helpful in predicting future outcomes: for example, re-calling that you offended someone yesterday may enable you to predict that the person will be cool to you tomorrow unless you apologize. But beyond this, consequentialists have no concern with the past, for their "bottom line" is always "what happens from now on," evaluated independently of the earlier chapters of our lives and histories. For the consequentialist, assessing a life or history from a narrative perspective becomes impossible or at least bizarre, as what must be evaluated at each shifting moment is "the story from now on" independently of what has already been written.[12]

The standard Rossian alternative to this exclusively forward-looking per-spective is to introduce certain *(prima facie) duties* to respond to certain past events in specified ways—for example, pay debts, keep promises, pay reparation for injuries. These duties are supposed to be self-evident and uni-versal (though they are *prima facie*), and they do not hold because they tend to promote anything good or valuable. Apart from aspects of the acts mentioned in the principles (for example, fulfilling a promise, returning fa-vors, not injuring, etc.), details of historical and personal context are consid-ered irrelevant.

By contrast, the narrative perspective sketched above considers the past as an integral part of the valued unities that we aim to bring about, not merely as a source of duties. If one has negligently wronged another, Ross regards this past event as generating a duty to pay reparations even if doing so will result in nothing good. But from the narrative perspective, the past becomes relevant in a further way. One may say, for example, that the *whole* consisting of your life and your relationship with that person from the time of the injury into the future will be a better thing if you acknowledge the wrong and make efforts to restore what you have damaged. For Ross, the duty is generated by the past and unrelated to bringing about anything good; from the narrative perspective, however, the requirement is just what is required to bring about a valuable connected whole with past, present, and future parts—the best way to complete a chapter, so to speak, in two intersecting life-stories.

So far, neither the Rossian nor the narrative account has told us much about the ultimate reasons for their evaluations, but they reveal ways to consider the matter. The Rossian asks us to judge particular cases in the light of "self-evident" general principles asserting that certain past events tend to generate present (or future) duties. The alternative perspective calls for examining lives and relationships, over time, in context, as organic unities evaluated (partly) in narrative terms.

To illustrate, consider two persons, John and Mary. John values having Mary's trust and respect, and conversely Mary values having John's; moreover, John values the fact that Mary values being trusted and respected by him, and conversely Mary values the same about John.[13]

Now suppose that other people have been abusive and insulting to Mary, and that John is worried that Mary may take things he had said and done as similarly insulting, even though he does not think that he consciously meant them this way. Though he is worried, Mary does not seem to suspect him; he fears that he may only make matters worse if he raises the issue, creating suspicions she did not have or focusing on doubts that he cannot allay. Perhaps, he thinks, their future relationship would be better served if he just remained silent, hoping that the trouble, if any, will fade in time. If so, consequentialist thinking would recommend silence. Acknowledging this, he might nonetheless feel that duties of friendship and fidelity demand that he raise the issue, regardless of whether or not the result will be worse. Then he would be thinking as a Rossian.

But, instead, he might look at the problem from an alternative perspective, asking himself what response best affirms and contributes to the sort of ongoing relationship he has and wants to continue with Mary. Given their history together, it is important to him to do his part towards restoring the relationship if it indeed has been marred by perceived insults or suspicions. To be sure, he wants *future* relations of mutual trust and respect, but not at any price and not by just any means. Their history together is not irrelevant, for what he values is not merely a future of a certain kind, but that their relationship over time be of the sort he values. He values an ongoing history of mutual trust and respect that *calls for* an explicit response in this current situation, not merely as a means to a brighter future but as a present affirmation of what they value together. Even if unsure which course will be best for the future, he may be reasonably confident that the act that best expresses his respect and trust (and his valuing hers, etc.) is to confront the problem, express his regrets, reaffirm his respect, ask for her trust, be patient with her doubts, and welcome an open dialogue. If the insults were deep and it is not entirely clear whether or not he really associated himself with them, then mere words may not be enough to convey the message or even to assure himself of his own sincerity. Positive efforts, even at considerable cost, may be needed to express appropriately and convincingly what needs to be said. How the next chapter unfolds is not entirely up to him, and he would not be respectful if he presumed otherwise by trying to manipulate the best future unilaterally.

The example concerns only two persons and their personal values, but it illustrates a perspective that one can also take regarding moral problems involving many persons.

MUTUAL RESPECT, FAIR OPPORTUNITY, AND AFFIRMATIVE ACTION

Turning back to our main subject, I suggest that some of the values that give affirmative action its point are best seen as cross-time values that fall outside the exclusively forward-looking and backward-looking perspectives. They include having a history of racial and gender relations governed, so far as possible, by the ideals of mutual respect, trust, and fair opportunity for all.

Our national history provides a context of increasing recognition and broader interpretation of the democratic ideal of the equal dignity of all human beings—an ideal that has been flagrantly abused from the outset, partially affirmed in the bloody Civil War, and increasingly extended in the civil rights movement, but is still far from being fully respected. More specifically, blacks and women were systematically treated in an unfair and demeaning way by public institutions, including universities, until quite recently, and few could confidently claim to have rooted out racism and sexism even now.[14] The historical context is not what grounds or legitimates democratic values, but it is the background of the current problem, the sometimes admirable and often ugly way the chapters up until now have been written.

Consider the social ideal of mutual respect and trust among citizens. The problem of implementing this in the current context is different from the problem in the two-person example discussed above, for the history of our racial and gender relations is obviously not an idyllic story of mutual respect and trust momentarily interrupted by a crisis. Even so, the question to ask is not merely, "What will promote respectful and trusting racial and gender relations in future generations?", but rather, "Given our checkered past, how can we appropriately express the social value of mutual respect and trust that we want, so far as possible, to characterize our history?" We cannot change our racist and sexist past, but we also cannot express full respect for those present individuals who live in its aftermath if we ignore it. What is called for is not merely repayment of tangible debts incurred by past injuries, but also a message to counter the deep insult inherent in racism and sexism. . . .

CONCLUSION

The message is called for not just as a means to future good relations or a dutiful payment of a debt incurred by our past. It is called for by the ideal of being related to other human beings over time, so that our histories and biographies reflect the responses of those who deeply care about fair opportunity, mutual trust, and respect for all.

If so, what should public universities try to say to those offered opportunities through affirmative action? Perhaps something like this: "Whether we individually are among the guilty or not, we acknowledge that you have been wronged—if not by specific injuries which could be named and repaid, at least by the humiliating and debilitating attitudes prevalent in our country and our institutions. We deplore and denounce these attitudes and the wrongs that spring from them. We acknowledge that, so far, most of you have had your opportunities in life diminished by the effects of these attitudes, and we want no one's prospects to be diminished by injustice. We recognize your understandable grounds for suspicion and mistrust when we express these high-minded sentiments, and we want not only to ask respectfully for your trust but also to give concrete evidence of our sincerity. We welcome you respectfully into the university community and ask you to take a full share of the responsibilities as well as the benefits. By creating special opportunities, we recognize the disadvantages you have probably suffered; we show our respect for your talents and our commitment to the ideals of the university, however, by not faking grades and honors for you. Given current attitudes about affirmative action, accepting this position will probably have drawbacks as well as advantages.[15] It is an opportunity and a responsibility offered neither as charity nor as entitlement, but rather as part of a special effort to welcome and encourage minorities and women to participate more fully in the university at all levels. We believe that this program affirms some of the best ideals implicit in our history without violating the rights of any applicants. We hope that you will choose to accept the position in this spirit as well as for your own benefit."

The appropriate message is no doubt harder to communicate to those who stand to lose some traditional advantages under a legitimate affirmative action program. But if we set aside practical difficulties and suppose that the proper message could be sincerely given and accepted as such, what would it say? Ideally, it would convey an understanding of the moral reasoning for the program; perhaps, in conclusion, it would say something like the following.

"These are the concerns that we felt made necessary the policy under which the university is temporarily giving special attention to women and minorities. We respect your rights to formal justice and to a policy guided by the university's education and research mission as well as its social responsibilities. Our policy in no way implies the view that your opportunities are less important than others', but we estimate (roughly, as we must) that as a white male you have probably had advantages and encouragement that for a long time have been systematically, unfairly, insultingly unavailable to most women and minorities. We deplore invidious race and gender distinctions; we hope that no misunderstanding of our program will prolong them. Unfortunately, nearly all blacks and women have been disadvantaged to some degree by bias against their groups, and it is impractical for universities to undertake the detailed investigations that would be needed to assess how much particular individuals have suffered or gained from racism and sexism. We appeal to you to share the historical values of fair opportunity and mutual respect that underlie this policy; we hope that, even though its effects may be personally disappointing, you can see the policy as an appropriate response to the current situation."

Unfortunately, as interests conflict and tempers rise, it is difficult to convey this idea without giving an unintended message as well. White males unhappy about the immediate effects of affirmative action may read the policy as saying that "justice" is the official word for giving preferential treatment to whatever group one happens to favor. Some may see a subtext insinuating that blacks and women are naturally inferior and "cannot make it on their own." Such cynical readings reveal either misunderstanding or the willful refusal to take the moral reasoning underlying affirmative action seriously. They pose serious obstacles to the success of affirmative action—practical problems that may be more intractable than respectful moral disagreement and counter-argument. But some types of affirmative action invite misunderstanding and suspicion more than others. For this reason, anyone who accepts the general case for affirmative action suggested here would do well to reexamine in detail the means by which they hope to communicate its message.[16]

NOTES

1. See, for example, the following: John Arthur, ed., *Morality and Moral Controversies,* 2nd ed. (Englewood Cliffs: Prentice-Hall, Inc., 1986), ch. 11, pp. 305–47; William T. Blackstone and Robert D. Heslep, eds., *Social Justice and Preferential Treatment* (Athens: The University of Georgia Press, 1977); Bernard Boxill, *Blacks and Social Justice* (Totowa: Rowman and Allanheld, 1984); Marshall Cohen, Thomas Nagel, and Thomas Scanlon, eds., *Equality and Preferential Treatment* (Princeton: Princeton University Press, 1977); Robert K. Fullinwider, *The Reverse Discrimination Controversy* (Totowa: Rowman and Littlefield, 1980); Alan H. Goldman, *Justice and Reverse Discrimination* (Princeton: Princeton University Press, 1979); Kent Greenawalt, *Discrimination and Reverse Discrimination* (New York: Alfred A. Knopf, 1983), Barry R. Gross, ed., *Reverse Discrimination* (Buffalo: Prometheus Press, 1977); Thomas A. Mappes and Jane S. Zembaty, eds., *Social Ethics* (2nd ed.; New York: McGraw-Hill Book Company, 1982), ch. 5, pp. 159–98.
2. Thomas Sowell, *Race and Economics* (New York: David McKay Co., 1975), ch. 6; *Markets and Minorities* (New York: Basic Books, Inc., 1981), pp. 114–15.
3. W. D. Ross, *The Right and the Good* (Oxford: Clarendon Press, 1930).
4. James Forman was at the time director of international affairs for SNCC (Student Nonviolent Coordinating Committee). The "Black Manifesto" stems from an economic development conference sponsored by the Interreligious Foundation for Community Organizations, April 26, 1969, and presented by Forman at the New York Interdenominational Riverside Church on May 4, 1969. Later the demand was raised to three billion dollars. See Robert S. Lecky and H. Elliot Wright, *Black Manifesto* (New York: Sheed and Ward Publishers, 1969), pp. vii, 114–26.
5. Bernard Boxill, "The Morality of Reparation," *Social Theory and Practice,* vol. 2, no. 1 (1972), pp. 113–22, and *Blacks and Social Justice,* ch. 7.

6. In the article cited above, Boxill calls what is owed "reparation," but in the book (above) he calls it "compensation." The latter term, preferred by many, is used more broadly to cover not only restitution for wrongdoing but also "making up" for deficiencies and losses that are not anyone's fault (for example, naturally caused physical handicaps, or damages unavoidably resulting from legitimate and necessary activities). We could describe the backward-looking arguments presented here as demands for "compensation" rather than "reparation," so long as we keep in mind that the compensation is supposed to be due as the morally appropriate response to past wrongdoing.

7. Aristotle, *Nicomachean Ethics,* tr. A. K. Thomson (Baltimore: Penguin Books, Inc., 1955), bk. V, esp. pp. 143–55.

8. See Boxill, *Blacks and Social Justice,* pp. 132ff., and Ronald Dworkin, "Reverse Discrimination," in *Taking Rights Seriously* (Cambridge: Harvard University Press, 1978), pp. 231ff.

9. See, for example, Alasdair MacIntyre, *After Virtue* (Notre Dame: Notre Dame University Press, 1981). Similar themes are found in Carol Gilligan's *In A Different Voice* (Cambridge: Harvard University Press, 1982) and in Lawrence Blum, *Friendship, Altruism, and Morality* (Boston: Routledge and Kegan Paul, 1980).

10. Regarding cultural and moral relativism see, for example, David B. Wong, *Moral Relativity* (Berkeley and Los Angeles: University of California Press, 1984), with an excellent bibliography, and Richard B. Brandt, *Ethical Theory* (Englewood Cliffs: Prentice-Hall Inc., 1959), ch. 11, pp. 271–94. Versions of particularism are presented in Andrew Oldenquist, "Loyalties," *The Journal of Philosophy,* vol. 79 (1982), pp. 173–93; Lawrence Blum, *Friendship, Altruism, and Morality*; and Bernard Williams, "Persons, Character and Morality" in *Moral Luck* (New York: Cambridge University Press, 1981), pp. 1–19.

11. G. E. Moore, *Principia Ethica* (Cambridge University Press, 1912), pp. 27ff.

12. That is, the evaluation is independent of the past in the sense that the past makes no intrinsic difference to the final judgment and the future is not evaluated as a part of a temporal whole including the past. As noted, however, consequentialists will still look to the past for lessons and clues about how to bring about the best future.

13. For an interesting illustration of reciprocal desires (e.g., A wanting B, B wanting A, A wanting B to want A, B wanting A to want B, A wanting B to want A to want B, etc.), see Thomas Nagel, "Sexual Perversion," *The Journal of Philosophy,* vol. 66 (1969).

14. Racism and sexism present significantly different problems, but I shall not try to analyze the differences here. For the most part my primary focus is on racism, but the relevance of the general type of moral thinking considered here to the problems of sexism should nonetheless be evident.

15. How severe these drawbacks are will, of course, depend upon the particular means of affirmative action that are selected and how appropriate these are for the situation. For example, if, to meet mandated quotas, highly-ranked colleges and universities offer special admission to students not expected to succeed, then they may well be misleading those students into a wasteful and humiliating experience when those students could have thrived at lower-ranked educational institutions. This practice was explicitly rejected in the policies at Pomona College and at U.C.L.A., but William Allen suggested to me in discussion that, in his opinion, the practice is quite common. The practice, I think, is unconscionable, and my argument in no way supports it.

Geoffrey Miller described in discussion another possible affirmative action program that would be quite inappropriate to the circumstances but is again not supported by the line of argument I have suggested. He asks us to imagine a "permanent underclass" of immigrants who are "genetically or culturally deficient" and as a result fail to succeed. Since we do not share a common social and cultural history of injustice resulting in their condition, the historical dimension of my case for affirmative action is missing. And since they are a "permanent" underclass, and thus the "genetic or cultural deficiencies" that result in their failure cannot be altered, one cannot argue that universities can help them or even can sincerely give them an encouraging "message" through affirmative action. This does not mean, however, that there are not other reasons for society to extend appropriate help. Also, any suggestion that certain urban populations that are now *called* a "permanent underclass" are accurately and fairly described by the "fictional" example is politically charged and needs careful examination.

16. Although my aim in this paper has been to survey general types of arguments for thinking that some sort of affirmative action is needed, rather than to argue for any particular program, one cannot reasonably implement the general idea without considering many contextual factors that I have set aside here. Thus, the need for more detailed discussion is obvious.

SUGGESTIONS FOR FURTHER READING

Boxill, Bernard. *Blacks and Social Justice.* (Totowa, NJ: Rowman and Allenheld, 1984).

In Chapter 7, Boxill defends the soundness of affirmative action policies using a combination of consequentialist reasons and considerations of compensatory justice.

Cohen, Carl. *Naked Racial Preference: The Case Against Affirmative Action.* (Lanham, MD: Madison Books, 1995).

Addressing the issue of affirmative action through an analysis of a number of court decisions and their consequences, Cohen concludes that no grounds can be given to support the claim that affirmative action is either right or good.

Cohen, Marshall, et. al. *Equality and Preferential Treatment.* (Princeton, NJ: Princeton University Press, 1977).

Part One contains readings on the moral aspects of affirmative action. Part Two deals with its legal aspects. Almost all selections first appeared in *Philosophy and Public Affairs.*

Dworkin, Ronald. *A Matter of Principle.* (Cambridge, MA: Harvard University Press, 1985).

Part Five contains essays on affirmative action, including excellent analyses of the *Bakke* decision ("Bakke's Case: Are Quotas Unfair?"; "What Did *Bakke* Really Decide?"). A third essay, "How to Read the Civil Rights Act," looks at *United Steelworkers of America v. Weber,* a case that addressed the constitutionality of affirmative action plans developed by private employers.

Eastland, Terry and William J. Bennett. *Counting by Race*. (New York: Basic Books, 1979).

Eastland and Bennett look at both *Bakke* and *Weber* in the light of the history of the civil rights debate in America, and maintain that these decisions violated the principle that "all men are created equal."

Fullinwider, Robert K. "Affirmative Action and Fairness." *Report from the Institute for Philosophy and Public Policy* 11 (Winter 1991): 10-13.

In the light of a presidential veto in 1990 against the new Civil Rights Act, Fullinwider discusses conditions under which quotas might be an appropriate response to the continuing existence of discrimination.

Miller, David. "Deserving Jobs," *The Philosophical Quarterly* 42 (1992), 161-181.

Miller addresses the question of what it means to say that a person deserves a job. He offers an interpretation of the idea of desert that both a) explains why it is unjust to deny a job to the most qualified candidate and b) is compatible with the principle of affirmative action.

Rosenfeld, Michael. *Affirmative Action and Justice: A Philosophical and Constitutional Inquiry*. (New Haven, CT: Yale University Press, 1991).

This is an attempt to go beyond liberal theories of justice in providing a defense of affirmative action.

Shaw, Bill. "Affirmative Action: An Ethical Evaluation." *Journal of Business Ethics* 7 (1988), 763-770.

Shaw defends affirmative action against several objections, including the idea that it is wrong because hiring decisions ought to be "color-blind."

Sowell, Thomas. *Civil Rights: Rhetoric or Reality?* (New York: William Morrow and Co., 1984).

This is an attack on affirmative action. In Sowell's view, discrimination is not the primary cause of social inequities between whites and nonwhites, so affirmative action is not the solution.

Thomson, Judith Jarvis. "Preferential Hiring." *Philosophy & Public Affairs* 2 (Summer 1973), 364-384.

One of the first philosophical treatments of affirmative action, Thomson argues that preferential hiring is justifiable in public university settings.

Chapter 7

ANIMALS AND THE ENVIRONMENT

Anyone who visits a national park such as Yellowstone or Yosemite in the middle of the summer can hardly fail to notice how the earth is shared with a great many living creatures: not only other human beings, but also a large number of different types of animals and other sentient beings, along with a wide variety of other biological entities such as trees and plants. Up until this point, our focus in this book has been on particular ethical questions arising out of the relations of human beings to one another. In this chapter we will turn our attention in a different direction and consider some of the ethical issues involved in our relations to nonhuman others.

Without question, we are currently facing a number of problems deriving from these relations: the rapid depletion of our natural resources, particularly nonrenewable ones such as fossil fuels; the harm caused to Native American lands and other geographical regions by toxic waste sites and spills; the decrease in the diversity of the world's animal populations; the ongoing depletion of the ozone level brought about by the rise of chlorofluorocarbons in the earth's atmosphere; the pollution of our streams and rivers; and the list goes on. While these problems are by now familiar ones, they come to our attention with a particular sense of urgency. While issues related to abortion, capital punishment, and euthanasia involve questions about the life and death of single individuals, the issues related to animals and the environment involve questions about the survival of groups of individuals and biological species. To some people, these issues might seem to be purely economic in character: Given that it is less expensive to curb industrial pollution now than to clean up the effects of it later, they would argue that industries ought to take whatever steps are necessary in order to stop polluting the environment. However, are our obligations to animals and the environment only derivable from such a cost-benefit analysis? Just what *ethical* obligations do we have to the nonhuman living world?

While this question in itself is an old one—St. Francis of Assisi, for example, addressed it in his contemplations—it is a relatively new one to engage philosophical attention. Still, in the twenty-five years or so since philosophers have also begun to give it serious consideration, it has produced a lively and energetic debate, as well as a new philosophical field of inquiry called environmental ethics. In this chapter we will look at two major aspects of this question: What is the basis for saying that animals and the natural environment deserve moral consideration? If we gave animals and the environment moral consideration, how would our relations to them be different from what they are today? We will also examine the conflict arising between those who believe that animals deserve greater moral consideration than does the natural environment and those who believe the opposite is true.

WHY GIVE MORAL CONSIDERATION TO ANIMALS?

Historically, to the extent to which philosophers have dealt at all with the issue of why moral consideration should be given to animals, they have tended to focus on the benefits that the ethical treatment of animals brings to human beings. In other words, the interests of humans, not the interests of animals, have guided reflection on this issue. Since any view which singles out human interests as the most significant interests at stake in a matter can be called *anthropocentric*, it has often been said that this approach to thinking about our moral obligations toward animals is an anthropocentric one.

Immanuel Kant's approach to this issue is a case in point. For Kant, the matter of our duties toward animals was a trivial one, on the same order of importance as our duties toward invisible spirits.[1] Motivating Kant's view was his belief that human beings have intrinsic value or dignity, based on their nature as rational beings capable of acting in accordance with universal moral laws. Lacking the ability to reason, animals have no dignity or value in themselves. Thus no similarities exist between people and animals that could provide a basis for arguing that humans have ethical duties toward animals. From this, though, Kant did not draw the conclusion that people could treat animals any way they liked; that they were free, for instance, to dispose of their work animals once they had grown too old to be of any use. Abuse of animals opens the door to an ethical slippery slope: Start treating animals unkindly, Kant reasoned, and one will end up acting in a mean manner toward other people. In a similar vein, he also proposed that we have an indirect duty not to destroy the natural environment because we could potentially be depriving others of something that they could put to good use.

Does Kant give a satisfactory answer to the question of why we have ethical duties to animals? As Peter Singer points out in one of this chapter's reading selections, there was a time not all that long ago when the idea that animals possessed rights seemed as absurd as the idea that women possessed rights. Nowadays, however, the idea that women and men do not deserve equal moral consideration would strike the majority of Americans as absurd. In this society at least, it has now become a generally accepted idea that all human beings, no matter what their gender, cultural background or racial identity, have equal moral importance. Some would see this as a milestone of moral progress, the natural next step of which would be to recognize the inadequacy of the anthropocentric point of view by coming to see that animals have moral value independently of their relations to human beings. A further step would be to view animals as having equal moral importance to human beings. However, if Kant's judgment that animals have no independent moral standing is wrong, then what is the basis for taking these steps and rejecting the Kantian approach? In contrast to the anthropocentric point of view, the perspectives we turn now to discuss do not place special value on human interests. Rather, such approaches emphasize the equal moral value of animal and human life.

Animals Have Interests

One basis for claiming that animals have independent moral standing is to be found in the idea that animals just like humans have interests. In this chapter, Peter Singer defends the view that the specific interest that provides animals with moral standing, a standing equal to that of human beings, is their interest in avoiding suffering. His view is basically a utilitarian one, rooted in Jeremy Bentham's idea that any being with the capacity to suffer deserves moral consideration, no matter what its capacity for reason might be. Faced with the problem of what to do to treat animals ethically, according to Singer we should put their interest in avoiding pain on a scale against our competing interests in eating animals and using them for other purposes, and see which way the balance tips.

Animals Have Rights

A different view of why animals have independent moral standing is offered in this chapter by Tom Regan. The position he defends is basically a deontological one, based on the Kantian view that any being with inherent value has moral standing. Unlike Kant, however, Regan believes that the fact that both animals and human beings are the subjects of their own lives provides not only human beings but also animals with inherent value. Because animals have inherent value, they have not only an *interest* in not being harmed, but also a *right* not to be harmed. Because on Regan's model all beings with inherent value need to be given equal moral consideration, figuring out what our moral relations to animals ought to be is a matter of weighing the right not to be harmed belonging to individual animals against the interests human beings have in continuing to put them in harm's way.

Consequences of and Challenges to the Animal Equality View

Regan believes his position that animals have rights is a stronger justification for the belief that animals should not be harmed than the utilitarian position offered by Singer. As Regan indicates, it could turn out, for example, that our present treatment of animals is in harmony with the general utilitarian goal of maximizing good. Despite the philosophical differences between these views, however, the same practical consequences for human behavior are implied by both. On both of these views, many of our present practices concerning animals turn out to be immoral. These include raising animals under the confining conditions of "factory farming," using animals in scientific research and product testing, and eating meat as a part of one's diet. We are morally obligated to become vegetarians, Singer and Regan would agree, once we recognize that animals and humans have equal moral standing.

Is it true, however, that animals do have an equal moral standing to human beings? Do we have an obligation for this reason to put an end to the practices just mentioned? For example, suppose we admit that the pleasures of looking beautiful do not outweigh the harms caused by testing cosmetics on animals. What, though, about the pleasures of living long enough to reach the age associated with a normal life expectancy? There seems to be something odd about using the category of "causing suffering to living beings" alone to evaluate the moral status of using animals for the purposes of medical research.

This observation suggests grounds for a potential challenge to the idea that animals and humans have equal moral standing. This challenge could be expressed as follows: The fact that animals and humans have an interest in avoiding suffering is a *necessary* but not a *sufficient* reason for believing that animals and humans have equal moral standing. In other words, the fact that animals and humans have an interest in avoiding suffering is not the *only* morally relevant consideration that needs to be taken into account in determining what our moral obligations toward animals actually are.

With regard to Singer's essay, such a challenge would amount to a denial of his analogy between racism and sexism on the one hand, and "speciesism" on the other. A case could be made that while racism and sexism are unjust forms of discrimination, which make it morally wrong to be a racist or a sexist, speciesism is a just form of discrimination, and so being a "speciesist" is acceptable. As Singer points out, what makes it wrong to be a racist or a sexist is the fact that such a person mistakes a morally neutral difference between members of one group and members of another group, such as race or sex, to be a morally significant difference. Speciesism appears wrong, then, when a human being makes the same mistake in evaluating the differences between humans and animals. However, speciesism could be acceptable if morally significant differences can be found to exist between the two groups. Without falling back into anthropocentrism, one could appeal to these particular differences in order to defend the moral superiority of human beings over animals.

If there are morally significant differences between human beings and animals that support the view that humans are morally more important than animals, what might they be? It has been proposed, for instance, that the fact that human beings can be motivated by moral considerations to act responsibly while animals cannot is one such difference:

> If rats invade our houses, carrying disease and biting our children, we cannot reason with them, hoping to persuade them of the injustice they do us. We can only attempt to get rid of them. And it is this that makes it reasonable for us to accord them a separate and not equal moral status, even though their capacity to suffer provides us with some reason to kill them painlessly. . . .[2]

One could make a similar argument in support of the idea that while animals and human beings both have rights, the rights of human beings are stronger than the rights of animals, and thus deserve greater consideration. In opposition to Regan's idea that animals and humans possess equal inherent value, one could claim that our capacity for having moral interactions with others partially explains why the way in which we are the subjects of our own lives is more complex and of more interest to us than the way in which animals are subjects of their own lives. Such subjective richness could provide a basis for the idea that inherent value is not an all-or-nothing matter, but rather can be a matter of degree.

It is important to note that while these criticisms can lead to questioning the idea that it is morally necessary to radically alter our relations to animals, they do not directly challenge the fundamental principle of the animal equality view that animals have independent moral standing. For this reason, these criticisms can be interpreted as leading to the conclusion that although the animal equality view is flawed, we still ought to treat animals better than we do now.

WHY GIVE MORAL CONSIDERATION TO THE ENVIRONMENT?

The defenses presented in this chapter of the idea that the environment deserves moral consideration can also be taken (as we will show) as an additional criticism of the animal equality view. The animal equality view looks at animals in the abstract, rather than approaching them as they exist in a particular natural context. Arguably, though, it would be more appropriate to consider the question of our moral obligations to animals by reflecting on animals within their environmental context. Given that animals are not the only living creatures within the natural environment, once one changes perspective to think about what moral obligations humans might have toward animals in an environmental context, one is naturally led to wonder what sorts of moral obligation, if any, we have toward other natural entities—and even to nature as a whole (including oceans, rocks, and the soil itself). Because defenses of the idea that the environment deserves moral consideration often involve a rethinking of at least some fundamental assumptions of standard ethical theory, they can be said to compose a new, *environmental ethic*.

For Holmes Rolston III, a developer of environmental ethics and the author of one of this chapter's reading selections, a key element in understanding that the environment deserves moral consideration lies in recognizing the moral significance of the fact that in nature individual animals and plants are grouped together into species, a number of which at the moment appear headed toward extinction. As a contributor to the "biotic diversity" of nature, any single species can be seen to have inherent value, and thus count as an entity with moral standing. Rolston believes we thus have an obligation to prevent species from becoming extinct, even if fulfilling this obligation might involve killing individual animals or plants belonging to species that are not threatened with eradication.

In suggesting that species and even more complex natural organizations such as ecosystems should have moral standing, Rolston and other environmental ethicists (such as Aldo Leopold, the founder of what is known as the "land ethic") take the critique of anthropomorphism discussed earlier one step further. In their perception, the idea that the value of nature is dependent on human beings is one part of a larger ethical picture, all of which needs to be called into question. While supporters of the animal equality view reject anthropocentrism, their case for giving animals equal moral standing as humans is based on the similarities that animals, regarded as individual entities, have to human beings, regarded as individual entities. This emphasis on the individual entity is in accord with the basic assumptions of the modern deontological and consequentialist ethical theories discussed in the first chapter of this book, in which the notion of the individual as an independent, "stand-alone" self occupies a fundamental place. Thus supporters of the animal equality view are still committed to the *individualistic* emphasis of anthropomorphism. In the eyes of an environmental ethicist such as Rolston, the animal equality view appears as an incomplete critique of anthropocentrism. Because living creatures exist in nature not as "stand-alone" selves but as participants in the life of a species, and because modernist ethical theory focuses on how individuals can make ethical decisions about other individuals, a new ethics in Rolston's view is needed in order for persons to make moral decisions concerning the environment.

What, however, is a species? If it is seen simply as a biological collection of individual organisms, one might argue that the environment could have moral standing without generating a need for a new environmental ethic. Support for this argument could be found in the fact that a species is after all not extinct until the last living individual of that species dies. This objection, though, in Rolston's opinion would not carry much weight: What is morally relevant about a species or an ecosystem is the *order* that it forms. This order can be seen as a kind of community, where those who live within it cannot be reasonably considered apart from their connections and their interrelations to others.

Rolston's approach to ethics, in contrast to the individualistic approach of modern ethics, is often thought of as *holistic*. Rolston admits that taking such a holistic approach runs counter to our customary views of what sorts of things deserve ethical consideration, but he also says we need to adjust our perception to look for signs of community rather than individuality in making decisions about the environment:

> An ecosystem has no genome, no brain, no self-identification. It does not defend itself against injury or death as do blue jays, milkweeds, cougars. . . . But to find such characteristics missing and then to judge that ecosystems do not count morally is to make another category mistake. To look at one level for what is appropriate at another faults *communities* as though they ought to be organismic *individuals*.[3]

A second difference between holistic and individualistic approaches to ethics, which might also seem troublesome to anyone used to the latter approach has to do with the particular values that a holistic approach to the environment takes as morally significant. If species and ecosystems, not individuals, are the primary "units" with moral standing, then those values associated with the moral protection of individual interests and rights—such as freedom, dignity, and autonomy—are not the primary values that matter in ethical decision making about the environment. However, if these values are not primary, then which ones are? Taking as a clue to answering this question Rolston's idea that a species can be seen as being like a character in a story line, one could say that the values we need to uphold in order to treat the environment better are the same values that contribute to the making of a good story. Among them would be unity, stability, integrity or wholeness, complexity, and beauty. From the viewpoint of environmental ethics, the particular duties that we have toward orders of living things should reflect a concern with preserving these values; any actions that would serve to undermine them would be immoral. For Rolston, these duties include refraining from actions that would cause irreversible ecological harm, and taking positive steps to protect the diversity of natural environments through such means as including greenbelts within urban settings.

Another holistic approach to environmental ethics is *deep ecology*, represented in this chapter by George Sessions and Bill Devall. Derived in part, like the position just described, from the fact of the existence of biotic diversity, deep ecology recognizes that all living things form part of a larger community, or biosphere. From the existence of this biosphere, in which all living things are interrelated, deep ecology infers that all living things have intrinsic value, and thus moral standing. In other words, deep ecology moves away from the *anthropocentric* perspective discussed earlier toward a more inclusive perspective that, just like Rolston's theory, is *biocentric* or "life-centered" in its basic character.

While this view might appear to be virtually identical with Rolston's position, deep ecology develops even further his critique of anthropocentrism.

Not only does deep ecology deny that we have moral responsibilities toward other living things as individual entities, it also challenges the idea that we can best understand our responsibilities toward the ecosphere if we think of ourselves and other living creatures as belonging to individual species. Thinking of ourselves as divided from other living things because of our species boundaries implies placing ourselves over these other living things, rather than accepting our place within a community of living things where clear separations between the self and others cannot be drawn. Thus deep ecology appears not only as a new way of thinking about our ethical responsibilities toward nature, but also as a new way of conceptualizing the self. From its perspective, any action that lets nature "take its course" or that attempts to fit in human activity as gently as possible with natural processes would be morally right; any action that forces a large-scale change upon nature that disturbs its ecosystemic harmony, such as increasing the expansion in Southern California of human settlements into desert areas, would be judged to be wrong.

Challenges to Environmental Ethics

Challenges to the ideas presented by environmental ethics positions, such as those represented in this chapter, have arisen from a number of different perspectives. An especially significant challenge to environmental ethics comes from the views of animal equality discussed earlier in this introduction. While these views are similar to those held by environmental ethics in that they both extend the idea of moral consideration beyond the limits proposed by traditional ethical theories, they are at philosophical odds with one another. For instance, the animal rights organization PETA (People for the Ethical Treatment of Animals) began a protest in 1996 against fishing on the grounds that capturing fish by hooking them in the mouth, as well as causing them to die from asphyxiation, is immoral due to the pain and suffering it causes. From an environmental ethics point of view, however, the practice of fishing or any other deliberate killing of animals for food would not necessarily be wrong, since other factors besides the effect of such practices on particular sentient individuals would need to be taken into account before a moral judgment could be made about these practices.

If for example the practice of fishing in a particular locale is on an appropriate scale, that is, is not disruptive to the stability of the local ecosystem, then from an environmental ethics position there would be no moral objections to be made about it. Those who think from a perspective of animal equality would question this holistic approach on the grounds that it does not adequately address the interests and rights of individual animals within the communities it recognizes as deserving of moral consideration. In turn, an environmental ethicist might respond by pointing to the fact that, within the context of these natural communities, "animal equality" can legitimately be interpreted as meaning that members of any particular species are fair game for the members of the other species who prey upon them. With this in mind, the choice many people make to feed upon animals can be accepted as a reasonable means for human beings to satisfy basic needs. Killing animals for food in itself, then, would arguably not be immoral. What would rather be immoral for the environmental ethicist would be the unnecessary or senseless killing of animals, such as the accidental slaughter of dolphins from certain types of nets used by tuna fishermen.

A second objection is that biocentric approaches to the ethical problems arising in our relation to the environment overlook the interests of individual human beings in ways that seem to run counter to our moral intuitions. This objection does not deny that the values stressed by biocentric holism are important ethical values. Rather, it denies that environmental ethics can replace more traditional ethical theories on the basis that there are important ethical values that go unrecognized by environmental ethics. To take an example suggested by Tom Regan, cotton production in the American South after the Civil War did not violate any standards of environmental stability or harmony. While an environmental holist would therefore say that this practice was justified, other ethicists would condemn it as a violation of justice, given its dependency on exploiting the labor of former slaves.[4] Because justice towards individuals appears on the "back burner," so to speak, among the values affirmed by the holistic viewpoint, Regan scathingly criticizes this viewpoint by calling it an "environmental fascism."

In another reading included in this chapter, Ramachandra Guha raises a form of this objection against deep ecology. His worry is that deep ecology provides particularly inadequate protection of the interests of those living under conditions of poverty. In light of its fundamental ideas, such as the principle that human interference with nature should be kept to a minimum, deep ecology encourages actions and public policies directed towards the preservation of wilderness—which Guha argues are often not in the best interests of local populations who depend on the use of these natural lands for their very survival. While Guha's primary concerns lie with affected groups in the Third World, he would likely share similar concerns over whether indigenous Americans whose traditional ways of life involve hunting and gathering are actually harmed by the preservation of wilderness areas, which are primarily enjoyed by relatively affluent citizens on vacations. In reply, it could be claimed that although deep ecology does take the preservation of wilderness areas as a central aim of environmentalism, when conflicts arise between the survival needs of local human populations and the need to protect the inhabitants of the natural environment, the principles of deep ecology do not automatically point to resolving these conflicts in favor of protecting the environment at the expense of causing harm to humans.

A third objection to environmental ethics, found in the course of Guha's essay, can be expressed as follows: Even given the scope and the variety of the threats to the environment that now face us, to address these threats, it is not necessary to develop a new type of ethics that extends moral consideration to entities traditionally not seen as appropriate subjects for such consideration. Guha suggests that moving to biocentrism as an ethical perspective actually undermines the possibility of adequately dealing with environmental problems by obscuring their real source. In his eyes, this source lies in the overuse of resources and the consumer-oriented lifestyles found in industrialized society, not in the anthropocentric point of view.

Even if one disagrees with Guha's assessment that deep ecology is actually part of the problem rather than the solution, one might still want to side with his doubts over whether a new ethical theory is needed in order to deal with matters related to the environment. While some might propose that we can avoid environmental disaster only by evaluating environmental problems through the eyes of a new ethic, others would suggest that traditional ethics can provide adequate conceptual resources to address the new concerns arising from the human impact on and interaction with the natural world.

Looked at from a larger perspective, the debates among those whose perspectives are represented in this chapter show the complexity of the issues that are associated with moral concern over our treatment of animals and the environment. Because of this complexity, it has been suggested that since it bases "right" action on a single value or group of values, a single ethical perspective might not be sufficient to address them. Whether or not this is the case, it is certainly true that the further one extends the concept of moral consideration, the greater the number of needs and interests one has to take into account in making a moral decision. Finding an appropriate balance among these interests is the most critical demand facing anyone who would like to reflect further on the issues raised in this chapter.

NOTES

1. Immanuel Kant, *Lectures on Ethics*, Louis Infield, trans. (Indianapolis: Hackett, 1963), pp. 239–241.
2. Bonnie Steinbock, "Speciesism and the Idea of Equality," *Philosophy 53* (April 1978), pp. 247–256.
3. Holmes Rolston III, *Environmental Ethics* (Philadelphia: Temple University Press, 1988), p. 172.
4. Tom Regan, "Abolishing Animal Agriculture," In *The Thee Generation* (Philadelphia: Temple University Press, 1991), pp. 120–123.

Animal Liberation
Peter Singer

In his book *Animal Liberation*, Peter Singer, who was introduced in Chapter 5, first develops a moral basis for the ethical treatment of animals and then proceeds to argue that on this basis many current practices involving harm to animals, including factory farming and experimentation on animals, cannot be justified. The following selection is taken from the first chapter, "All Animals Are Equal."

Most people, Singer contends, take the fact that they are intellectually superior to animals to imply that they are morally superior to animals as well. In light of this generally accepted view, most people believe that animals deserve less ethical consideration than do other human beings. Drawing an analogy to racism and sexism, Singer calls this attitude "speciesism." Just as racists dismiss the interests of those with a different skin color, and sexists dismiss the interests of women, so speciesists dismiss the interests of animals as not being worthy of consideration. Singer argues that just as the interests of all humans deserve equal consideration, so the interests of all animals deserve equal consideration with human interests. To support his view, Singer turns to Jeremy Bentham's declaration that any creature with the capacity for suffering has a right to equal consideration with others with a similar capacity. In his opinion, overcoming speciesism does not involve accepting the idea that killing a dog is just as wrong as killing a human being. What it does mean is to extend the concept of a "right to life" to apply to animals as well as humans, and to stop treating animals as cheaply as we do now.

"Animal Liberation" may sound more like a parody of other liberation movements than a serious objective. The idea of "The Rights of Animals" actually was once used to parody the case for women's rights. When Mary Wollstonecraft, a forerunner of today's feminists, published her *Vindication of the Rights of Woman* in 1792, her views were widely regarded as absurd, and before long an anonymous publication appeared entitled *A Vindication of the Rights of Brutes*. The author of this satirical work (now known to have been Thomas Taylor, a distinguished Cambridge philosopher) tried to refute Mary Wollstonecraft's arguments by showing that they could be carried one stage further. If the argument for equality was sound when applied to women, why should it not be applied to dogs, cats, and horses? The reasoning seemed to hold for these "brutes" too; yet to hold that brutes had rights was manifestly absurd; therefore the reasoning by which this conclusion had been reached must be unsound, and if unsound when applied to brutes, it must also be unsound when applied to women, since the very same arguments had been used in each case.

From *Animal Liberation*, by Peter Singer (New York: Random House, 1975), pp. 1-27.

In order to explain the basis of the case for the equality of animals, it will be helpful to start with an examination of the case for the equality of women. Let us assume that we wish to defend the case for women's rights against the attack by Thomas Taylor. How should we reply?

One way in which we might reply is by saying that the case for equality between men and women cannot validly be extended to nonhuman animals. Women have a right to vote, for instance, because they are just as capable of making rational decisions about the future as men are; dogs, on the other hand, are incapable of understanding the significance of voting, so they cannot have the right to vote. There are many other obvious ways in which men and women resemble each other closely, while humans and animals differ greatly. So, it might be said, men and women are similar beings and should have similar rights, while humans and nonhumans are different and should not have equal rights.

The reasoning behind this reply to Taylor's analogy is correct up to a point, but it does not go far enough. There *are* important differences between humans and other animals, and these differences must give rise to *some* differences in the rights that each have. Recognizing this obvious fact, however, is no barrier to the case for extending the basic principle of equality to nonhuman animals. The differences that exist between men and women are equally undeniable, and the supporters of Women's Liberation are aware that these differences may give rise to different rights. Many feminists hold that women have the right to an abortion on request. It does not follow that since these same feminists are campaigning for equality between men and women they must support the right of men to have abortions too. Since a man cannot have an abortion, it is meaningless to talk of his right to have one. Since a dog can't vote, it is meaningless to talk of its right to vote. There is no reason why either Women's Liberation or Animal Liberation should get involved in such nonsense. The extension of the basic principle of equality from one group to another does not imply that we must treat both groups in exactly the same way, or grant exactly the same rights to both groups. Whether we should do so will depend on the nature of the members of the two groups. The basic principle of equality does not require equal or identical *treatment*; it requires equal *consideration*. Equal consideration for different beings may lead to different treatment and different rights.

So there is a different way of replying to Taylor's attempt to parody the case for women's rights, a way that does not deny the obvious differences between humans and nonhumans but goes more deeply into the question of equality and concludes by finding nothing absurd in the idea that the basic principle of equality applies to so-called "brutes." At this point such a conclusion may appear odd; but if we examine more deeply the basis on which our opposition to discrimination on grounds of race or sex ultimately rests, we will see that we would be on shaky ground if we were to demand equality for blacks, women, and other groups of oppressed humans while denying equal consideration to nonhumans. To make this clear we need to see, first, exactly why racism and sexism are wrong.

When we say that all human beings, whatever their race, creed, or sex, are equal, what is it that we are asserting? Those who wish to defend hierarchical, inegalitarian societies have often pointed out that by whatever test we choose it simply is not true that all humans are equal. Like it or not we must face the fact that humans come in different shapes and sizes; they come with different moral capacities, different intellectual abilities, different amounts of benevolent feeling and sensitivity to the needs of others, different abilities to communicate effectively, and different capacities to experience pleasure and pain. In short, if the demand for equality were based on the actual equality of all human beings, we would have to stop demanding equality.

Still, one might cling to the view that the demand for equality among human beings is based on the actual equality of the different races and sexes. Although, it may be said, humans differ as individuals there are no differences between the races and sexes *as such.* From the mere fact that a person is black or a woman we cannot infer anything about that person's intellectual or moral capacities. This, it may be said, is why racism and sexism are wrong. The white racist claims that whites are superior to blacks, but this is false— although there are differences among individuals, some blacks are superior to some whites in all of the capacities and abilities that could conceivably be relevant. The opponent of sexism would say the same: a person's sex is no guide to his or her abilities, and this is why it is unjustifiable to discriminate on the basis of sex.

The existence of individual variations that cut across the lines of race or sex, however, provides us with no defense at all against a more sophisticated opponent of equality, one who proposes that, say, the interests of all those with IQ scores below 100 be given less consideration than the interests of those with ratings over 100. Perhaps those scoring below the mark would, in this society, be made the slaves of those scoring higher. Would a hierarchical society of this sort really be so much better than one based on race or sex? I think not. But if we tie the moral principle of equality to the factual equality of the different races or sexes, taken as a whole, our opposition to racism and sexism does not provide us with any basis for objecting to this kind of inegalitarianism.

There is a second important reason why we ought not to base our opposition to racism and sexism on any kind of factual equality, even the limited kind that asserts that variations in capacities and abilities are spread evenly between the different races and sexes: we can have no absolute guarantee that these capacities and abilities really are distributed evenly, without regard to race or sex, among human beings. So far as actual abilities are concerned there do seem to be certain measurable differences between both races and sexes. These differences do not, of course, appear in each case, but only when averages are taken. More important still, we do not yet know how much of these differences is really due to the different genetic endowments of the different races and sexes, and how much is due to poor schools, poor housing, and other factors that are the result of past and continuing discrimination.

Perhaps all of the important differences will eventually prove to be environmental rather than genetic. Anyone opposed to racism and sexism will certainly hope that this will be so, for it will make the task of ending discrimination a lot easier; nevertheless it would be dangerous to rest the case against racism and sexism on the belief that all significant differences are environmental in origin. The opponent of, say, racism who takes this line will be unable to avoid conceding that *if* differences in ability do after all prove to have some genetic connection with race, racism would in some way be defensible.

Fortunately there is no need to pin the case for equality to one particular outcome of a scientific investigation. The appropriate response to those who claim to have found evidence of genetically based differences in ability between the races or sexes is not to stick to the belief that the genetic explanation must be wrong, whatever evidence to the contrary may turn up: instead we should make it quite clear that the claim to equality does not depend on intelligence, moral capacity, physical strength, or similar matters of fact. Equality is a moral idea, not an assertion of fact. There is no logically compelling reason for assuming that a factual difference in ability between two people justifies any difference in the amount of consideration we give to their needs and interests. *The principle of the equality of human beings is not a description of an alleged actual equality among humans: it is a prescription of how we should treat humans.*

Jeremy Bentham, the founder of the reforming utilitarian school of moral philosophy, incorporated the essential basis of moral equality into his system of ethics by means of the formula: "Each to count for one and none for more than one." In other words, the interests of every being affected by an action are to be taken into account and given the same weight as the like interests of any other being. A later utilitarian, Henry Sidgwick, put the point in this way: "The good of any one individual is of no more importance, from the point of view (if I may say so) of the Universe, than the good of any other." More recently the leading figures in contemporary moral philosophy have shown a great deal of agreement in specifying as a fundamental presupposition of their moral theories some similar requirement which operates so as to give everyone's interests equal consideration—although these writers generally cannot agree on how this requirement is best formulated.[1]

It is an implication of this principle of equality that our concern for others and our readiness to consider their interests ought not to depend on what they are like or on what abilities they may possess. Precisely what this concern or consideration requires us to do may vary according to the characteristics of those affected by what we do: concern for the well-being of a child growing up in America would require that we teach him to read; concern for the well-being of a pig may require no more than that we leave him alone with other pigs in a place where there is adequate food and room to run freely. But the basic element—the taking into account of the interests of the being, whatever those interests may be—must, according to the principle of equality, be extended to all beings, black or white, masculine or feminine, human or nonhuman.

Thomas Jefferson, who was responsible for writing the principle of the equality of men into the American Declaration of Independence, saw this point. It led him to oppose slavery even though he was unable to free himself fully from his slaveholding background. He wrote in a letter to the author of a book that emphasized the notable intellectual achievements of Negroes in order to refute the then common view that they had limited intellectual capacities:

> Be assured that no person living wishes more sincerely than I do, to see a complete refutation of the doubts I have myself entertained and expressed on the grade of understanding allotted to them by nature, and to find that they are on a par with ourselves . . . but whatever be their degree of talent it is no measure of their rights. Because Sir Isaac Newton was superior to others in understanding, he was not therefore lord of the property or person of others.[2]

Similarly when in the 1850s the call for women's rights was raised in the United States a remarkable black feminist named Sojourner Truth made the same point in more robust terms at a feminist convention:

> . . . they talk about this thing in the head; what do they call it? ["Intellect," whispered someone near by.] That's it. What's that got to do with women's rights or Negroes' rights? If my cup won't hold but a pint and yours holds a quart, wouldn't you be mean not to let me have my little half-measure full?[3]

It is on this basis that the case against racism and the case against sexism must both ultimately rest; and it is in accordance with this principle that the attitude that we may call "speciesism," by analogy with racism, must also be condemned. Speciesism—the word is not an attractive one, but I can think of no better term—is a prejudice or attitude of bias toward the interests of members of one's own species and against those of members of other species. It should be obvious that the fundamental objections to racism and sexism made by Thomas Jefferson and Sojourner Truth apply equally to speciesism. If possessing a higher degree of intelligence does not entitle one human to use another for his own ends, how can it entitle humans to exploit nonhumans for the same purpose?[4]

Many philosophers and other writers have proposed the principle of equal consideration of interests, in some form or other, as a basic moral principle; but not many of them have recognized that this principle applies to members of other species as well as to our own. Jeremy Bentham was one of the few who did realize this. In a forward-looking passage written at a time when black slaves had been freed by the French but in the British dominions were still being treated in the way we now treat animals, Bentham wrote:

> The day *may* come when the rest of the animal creation may acquire those rights which never could have been withholden from them but by the hand of tyranny. The French have already discovered that the blackness of the

skin is no reason why a human being should be abandoned without redress to the caprice of a tormentor. It may one day come to be recognized that the number of the legs, the villosity of the skin, or the termination of the *os sacrum* are reasons equally insufficient for abandoning a sensitive being to the same fate. What else is it that should trace the insuperable line? Is it the faculty of reason, or perhaps the faculty of discourse? But a full-grown horse or dog is beyond comparison a more rational, as well as a more conversable animal, than an infant of a day or a week or even a month, old. But suppose they were otherwise, what would it avail? The question is not, Can they *reason?* nor Can they *talk?* but, *Can they suffer?*[5]

In this passage Bentham points to the capacity for suffering as the vital characteristic that gives a being the right to equal consideration. The capacity for suffering—or more strictly, for suffering and/or enjoyment or happiness— is not just another characteristic like the capacity for language or higher mathematics. Bentham is not saying that those who try to mark "the insuperable line" that determines whether the interests of a being should be considered happen to have chosen the wrong characteristic. By saying that we must consider the interests of all beings with the capacity for suffering or enjoyment Bentham does not arbitrarily exclude from consideration any interests at all—as those who draw the line with reference to the possession of reason or language do. The capacity for suffering and enjoyment is a *prerequisite for having interests at all*, a condition that must be satisfied before we can speak of interests in a meaningful way. It would be nonsense to say that it was not in the interests of a stone to be kicked along the road by a schoolboy. A stone does not have interests because it cannot suffer. Nothing that we can do to it could possibly make any difference to its welfare. A mouse, on the other hand, does have an interest in not being kicked along the road, because it will suffer if it is.

If a being suffers there can be no moral justification for refusing to take that suffering into consideration. No matter what the nature of the being, the principle of equality requires that its suffering be counted equally with the like suffering—in so far as rough comparisons can be made—of any other being. If a being is not capable of suffering, or of experiencing enjoyment or happiness, there is nothing to be taken into account. So the limit of sentience (using the term as a convenient if not strictly accurate shorthand for the capacity to suffer and/or experience enjoyment) is the only defensible boundary of concern for the interests of others. To mark this boundary by some other characteristic like intelligence or rationality would be to mark it in an arbitrary manner. Why not choose some other characteristic, like skin color?

The racist violates the principle of equality by giving greater weight to the interests of members of his own race when there is a clash between their interests and the interests of those of another race. The sexist violates the principle of equality by favoring the interests of his own sex. Similarly the speciesist allows the interests of his own species to override the greater interests of members of other species. The pattern is identical in each case.

Most human beings are speciesists. . . .

Animals can feel pain. As we saw earlier, there can be no moral justifica-tion for regarding the pain (or pleasure) that animals feel as less important than the same amount of pain (or pleasure) felt by humans. But what exactly does this mean, in practical terms? To prevent misunderstanding I shall spell out what I mean a little more fully.

If I give a horse a hard slap across its rump with my open hand, the horse may start, but it presumably feels little pain. Its skin is thick enough to protect it against a mere slap. If I slap a baby in the same way, however, the baby will cry and presumably does feel pain, for its skin is more sensitive. So it is worse to slap a baby than a horse, if both slaps are administered with equal force. But there must be some kind of blow—I don't know exactly what it would be, but perhaps a blow with a heavy stick—that would cause the horse as much pain as we cause a baby by slapping it with our hand. That is what I mean by "the same amount of pain" and if we consider it wrong to inflict that much pain on a baby for no good reason then we must, unless we are speciesists, consider it equally wrong to inflict the same amount of pain on a horse for no good reason.

There are other differences between humans and animals that cause other complications. Normal adult human beings have mental capacities which will, in certain circumstances, lead them to suffer more than animals would in the same circumstances. If, for instance, we decided to perform extremely painful or lethal scientific experiments on normal adult humans, kidnaped at random from public parks for this purpose, every adult who entered a park would become fearful that he would be kidnaped. The resultant terror would be a form of suffering additional to the pain of the experiment. The same experi-ments performed on nonhuman animals would cause less suffering since the animals would not have the anticipatory dread of being kidnaped and experi-mented upon. This does not mean, of course, that it would be *right* to per-form the experiment on animals, but only that there is a reason, which is *not* speciesist, for preferring to use animals rather than normal adult humans, if the experiment is to be done at all. It should be noted, however, that this same argument gives us a reason for preferring to use human infants—or-phans perhaps—or retarded humans for experiments, rather than adults, since infants and retarded humans would also have no idea of what was going to happen to them. So far as this argument is concerned nonhuman animals and infants and retarded humans are in the same category; and if we use this argument to justify experiments on nonhuman animals we have to ask our-selves whether we are also prepared to allow experiments on human infants and retarded adults; and if we make a distinction between animals and these humans, on what basis can we do it, other than a bare-faced—and morally indefensible—preference for members of our own species?

There are many areas in which the superior mental powers of normal adult humans make a difference: anticipation, more detailed memory, greater knowledge of what is happening, and so on. Yet these differences do not all point to greater suffering on the part of the normal human being. Sometimes an animal may suffer more because of his more limited understanding. If, for instance, we are taking prisoners in wartime we can explain to them that while they must submit to capture, search, and confinement they will not otherwise be harmed and will be set free at the conclusion of hostilities. If we capture a wild animal, however, we cannot explain that we are not threatening its life. A wild animal cannot distinguish an attempt to overpower and confine from an attempt to kill; the one causes as much terror as the other.

It may be objected that comparisons of the sufferings of different species are impossible to make, and that for this reason when the interests of animals and humans clash the principle of equality gives no guidance. It is probably true that comparisons of suffering between members of different species cannot be made precisely, but precision is not essential. Even if we were to prevent the infliction of suffering on animals only when it is quite certain that the interests of humans will not be affected to anything like the extent that animals are affected, we would be forced to make radical changes in our treatment of animals that would involve our diet, the farming methods we use, experimental procedures in many fields of science, our approach to wildlife and to hunting, trapping and the wearing of furs, and areas of entertainment like circuses, rodeos, and zoos. As a result, a vast amount of suffering would be avoided.

So far I have said a lot about the infliction of suffering on animals, but nothing about killing them. This omission has been deliberate. The application of the principle of equality to the infliction of suffering is, in theory at least, fairly straight-forward. Pain and suffering are bad and should be prevented or minimized, irrespective of the race, sex, or species of the being that suffers. How bad a pain is depends on how intense it is and how long it lasts, but pains of the same intensity and duration are equally bad, whether felt by humans or animals.

The wrongness of killing a being is more complicated. I have kept, and shall continue to keep, the question of killing in the background because in the present state of human tyranny over other species the more simple, straightforward principle of equal consideration of pain or pleasure is a sufficient basis for identifying and protesting against all the major abuses of animals that humans practice. Nevertheless, it is necessary to say something about killing.

Just as most humans are speciesists in their readiness to cause pain to animals when they would not cause a similar pain to humans for the same reason, so most humans are speciesists in their readiness to kill other animals when they would not kill humans. We need to proceed more cautiously here, however, because people hold widely differing views about when it is legitimate to kill humans, as the continuing debates over abortion and euthanasia attest. Nor have moral philosophers been able to agree on exactly what it is that makes it wrong to kill humans, and under what circumstances killing a human being may be justifiable.

Let us consider first the view that it is always wrong to take an innocent human life. We may call this the "sanctity of life" view. People who take this view oppose abortion and euthanasia. They do not usually, however, oppose the killing of nonhumans—so perhaps it would be more accurate to describe this view as the "sanctity of *human* life" view.

The belief that human life, and only human life, is sacrosanct is a form of speciesism. To see this, consider the following example.

Assume that, as sometimes happens, an infant has been born with massive and irreparable brain damage. The damage is so severe that the infant can never be any more than a "human vegetable," unable to talk, recognize other people, act independently of others, or develop a sense of self-awareness. The parents of the infant, realizing that they cannot hope for any improvement in their child's condition and being in any case unwilling to spend, or ask the state to spend, the thousands of dollars that would be needed annually for proper care of the infant, ask the doctor to kill the infant painlessly.

Should the doctor do what the parents ask? Legally, he should not, and in this respect the law reflects the sanctity of life view. The life of every human being is sacred. Yet people who would say this about the infant do not object to the killing of nonhuman animals. How can they justify their different judgments? Adult chimpanzees, dogs, pigs, and many other species far surpass the brain-damaged infant in their ability to relate to others, act independently, be self-aware, and any other capacity that could reasonably be said to give value to life. With the most intensive care possible, there are retarded infants who can never achieve the intelligence level of a dog. Nor can we appeal to the concern of the infant's parents, since they themselves, in this imaginary example (and in some actual cases) do not want the infant kept alive.

The only thing that distinguishes the infant from the animal, in the eyes of those who claim it has a "right to life," is that it is, biologically, a member of the species Homo sapiens, whereas chimpanzees, dogs, and pigs are not. But to use *this* difference as the basis for granting a right to life to the infant and not to the other animals is, of course, pure speciesism.[6] It is exactly the kind of arbitrary difference that the most crude and overt kind of racist uses in attempting to justify racial discrimination.

This does not mean that to avoid speciesism we must hold that it is as wrong to kill a dog as it is to kill a normal human being. The only position that is irredeemably speciesist is the one that tries to make the boundary of the right to life run exactly parallel to the boundary of our own species. Those who hold the sanctity of life view do this, because while distinguishing sharply between humans and other animals they allow no distinctions to be made within our own species, objecting to the killing of the severely retarded and the hopelessly senile as strongly as they object to the killing of normal adults.

To avoid speciesism we must allow that beings which are similar in all relevant respects have a similar right to life—and mere membership in our own biological species cannot be a morally relevant criterion for this right. Within these limits we could still hold that, for instance, it is worse to kill a normal adult human, with a capacity for self-awareness, and the ability to plan for the future and have meaningful relations with others, than it is to kill a mouse, which presumably does not share all of these characteristics; or we might appeal to the close family and other personal ties which humans have but mice do not have to the same degree; or we might think that it is the consequences for other humans, who will be put in fear of their own lives, that makes the crucial difference; or we might think it is some combination of these factors, or other factors altogether.

Whatever criteria we choose, however, we will have to admit that they do not follow precisely the boundary of our own species. We may legitimately hold that there are some features of certain beings which make their lives more valuable than those of other beings; but there will surely be some nonhuman animals whose lives, by any standards, are more valuable than the lives of some humans. A chimpanzee, dog, or pig, for instance, will have a higher degree of self-awareness and a greater capacity for meaningful relations with others than a severely retarded infant or someone in a state of advanced senility. So if we base the right to life on these characteristics we must grant these animals a right to life as good as, or better than, such retarded or senile humans.

Now this argument cuts both ways. It could be taken as showing that chimpanzees, dogs, and pigs, along with some other species, have a right to life and we commit a grave moral offense whenever we kill them, even when they are old and suffering and our intention is to put them out of their misery. Alternatively one could take the argument as showing that the severely retarded and hopelessly senile have no right to life and may be killed for quite trivial reasons, as we now kill animals.

Since my focus is on ethical questions concerning animals and not on the morality of euthanasia I shall not attempt to settle this issue finally. I think it is reasonably clear, though, that while both of the positions just described avoid speciesism, neither is entirely satisfactory. What we need is some middle position which would avoid speciesism but would not make the lives of the retarded and senile as cheap as the lives of pigs and dogs now are, nor make the lives of pigs and dogs so sacrosanct that we think it wrong to put them out of hopeless misery. What we must do is bring nonhuman animals within our sphere of moral concern and cease to treat their lives as expendable for whatever trivial purposes we may have. At the same time, once we realize that the fact that a being is a member of our own species is not in itself enough to make it always wrong to kill that being, we may come to reconsider our policy of preserving human lives at all costs, even when there is no prospect of a meaningful life or of existence without terrible pain.

I conclude, then, that a rejection of speciesism does not imply that all lives are of equal worth. While self-awareness, intelligence, the capacity for meaningful relations with others, and so on are not relevant to the question of inflicting pain—since pain is pain, whatever other capacities, beyond the capacity to feel pain, the being may have—these capacities may be relevant to the question of taking life. It is not arbitrary to hold that the life of a self-aware being, capable of abstract thought, of planning for the future, of complex acts of communication, and so on, is more valuable than the life of a being without these capacities. To see the difference between the issues of inflicting pain and taking life, consider how we would choose within our own species. If we had to choose to save the life of a normal human or a mentally defective human, we would probably choose to save the life of the normal human; but if we had to choose between preventing pain in the normal human or the mental defective—imagine that both have received painful but superficial injuries, and we only have enough painkiller for one of them—it is not nearly so clear how we ought to choose. The same is true when we consider other species. The evil of pain is, in itself, unaffected by the other characteristics of the being that feels the pain; the value of life is affected by these other characteristics.

Normally this will mean that if we have to choose between the life of a human being and the life of another animal we should choose to save the life of the human; but there may be special cases in which the reverse holds true, because the human being in question does not have the capacities of a normal human being. So this view is not speciesist, although it may appear to be at first glance. The preference, in normal cases, for saving a human life over the life of an animal when a choice *has* to be made is a preference based on the characteristics that normal humans have, and not on the mere fact that they are members of our own species. This is why when we consider members of our own species who lack the characteristics of normal humans we can no longer say that their lives are always to be preferred to those of other animals. . . . In general, though, the question of when it is wrong to kill (painlessly) an animal is one to which we need give no precise answer. As long as we remember that we should give the same respect to the lives of animals as we give to the lives of those humans at a similar mental level, we shall not go far wrong.

Notes

1. For Bentham's moral philosophy, see his *Introduction to the Principles of Morals and Legislation*, and for Sidgwick's see *The Methods of Ethics* (the passage quoted is from the seventh edition, p. 382). As examples of leading contemporary moral philosophers who incorporate a requirement of equal consideration of interests, see R. M. Hare, *Freedom and Reason* (New York: Oxford University Press, 1963) and John Rawls, *A Theory of Justice* (Cambridge: Harvard University Press, 1972). For a brief account of the essential agreement on this issue between these and other positions, see R. M. Hare, "Rules of War and Moral Reasoning," *Philosophy and Public Affairs*, vol. 1, no. 2 (1972).

2. Letter to Henri Gregoire, February 25, 1809.

3. Reminiscences by Francis D. Gage, from Susan B. Anthony, *The History of Woman Suffrage*, vol. 1; the passage is to be found in the extract in Leslie Tanner, ed., *Voices from Women's Liberation* (New York: Signet, 1970).

4. I owe the term "speciesism" to Richard Ryder.

5. *Introduction to the Principles of Morals and Legislation*, chapter 17.
6. I am here putting aside religious views, for example the doctrine that all and only humans have immortal souls, or are made in the image of God. Historically these views have been very important, and no doubt are partly responsible for the idea that human life has a special sanctity. . . . Logically, however, these religious views are unsatisfactory, since a reasoned explanation of why it should be that all humans and no nonhumans have immortal souls is not offered. This belief too, therefore, comes under suspicion as a form of speciesism. In any case, defenders of the "sanctity of life" view are generally reluctant to base their position on purely religious doctrines, since these doctrines are no longer as widely accepted as they once were.

Animal Rights, Human Wrongs
Tom Regan

Tom Regan is a professor of philosophy at North Carolina State University and the author of numerous publications on animal rights and the environment, including *The Case for Animal Rights* (1984).

In this essay he examines the Kantian position on the moral treatment of animals and the utilitarian view defended by Peter Singer in the preceding article. Both views are found to be commendable but unconvincing. Like Singer, he argues that the Kantian view is unconvincing because it is based on the anthropomorphic premise that only *human* interests really matter. The utilitarian view is likewise unsatisfactory. While accepting its premise that animal interests ought to count equally with those of humans to be an improvement over the Kantian position, Regan worries that this is not enough to guarantee animals will be treated fairly. The key to the ethical treatment of animals, he contends, lies in seeing that just like humans, animals have inherent value. Because human beings have inherent value, they have rights to be treated in ways that respect this value. This means they have the right not to be harmed. The same can be said for animals. Because the rights of an individual can generally be said to outweigh the interests of a group, Regan concludes, the interests of those making a profit from the consumption of meat or the use of cosmetics whose development involves animal testing, as well as the interests of those who enjoy eating meat and wearing such cosmetics, do not outweigh the rights of individual animals not to be harmed.

INTRODUCTION

At this moment workers on board the mother ship of a whaling fleet are disassembling the carcass of a whale. Though the species is officially protected by agreement of the member nations of the International Whaling Commission, it is not too fanciful to imagine the crew butchering a great blue whale, the largest creature ever known to have lived on the Earth—larger than thirty elephants, larger even than three of the largest dinosaurs laid end to end. A good catch, this leviathan of the deep. And, increasingly, a rare one. For the great blue, like hundreds of other animal species, is endangered, may, in fact, already be beyond the point of recovery.

But the crew has other things on their mind. It will take hours of hard work to butcher the huge carcass, a process now carried out at sea. Nor is butchering at sea the only thing in whaling that has changed. The fabled days of a real hunt, of an individual Ahab pitted against a treacherous whale, must remain the work of fiction now. Whaling is applied technology, from the use of the most sophisticated sonar to on-board refrigeration, from tracking

From *Environmental Ethics* 2 (Summer 1980), pp. 99–120.

helicopters to explosive harpoons, the latter a technological advance that expedites a whale's death. Average time to die: less than an hour. . . .

For what? To what end? Why is this being done to the last remaining members of an irreplaceable species, certainly until recently, possibly at this very moment, by supposedly civilized men? For candle wax. For soap and oil. For pet food, margarine, fertilizer. For perfume. . . .

Not far from here, perhaps at this moment, a rabbit makes a futile effort to escape from a restraining device, called a stock, which holds the creature in place by clamping down around its neck. Immediately the reader thinks of trapping in the wild—that the stock must be a sort of trap, like the infamous leg-hold trap—but this is not so. The stock is a handmaiden of science, and the rabbit confined by it is not in the wild but in a research laboratory. If we look closely, we will see that one of the rabbit's eyes is ulcerated. It is badly inflamed, an open, running sore. After some hours the sore increases in size until barely half the eye is visible. In a few days the eye will become permanently blind. Sometimes the eye is literally burned out of its socket.

This rabbit is a research subject in what is known as the Draize test, named after its inventor. This rabbit, and hundreds like it, is being used because rabbits happen not to have tear ducts and so cannot flush irritants from their eyes. Nor can they dilute them. The Draize test procedes routinely as follows: concentrated solutions of a substance are made to drip into one of the rabbit's eyes; the other eye, a sort of control, is left untroubled. Swelling, redness, destruction of iris or cornea, loss of vision are measured and the substance's eye irritancy is thereby scientifically established.

What is this substance which in concentrated form invades the rabbit's eye? Probably a cosmetic, a new variety of toothpaste, shampoo, mouthwash, talcum, hand lotion, eye cosmetic, face cream, hair conditioner, perfume, cologne. Why? To what end? In the name of what purpose does this unanesthetized rabbit endure the slow burning destruction of its eye? So that a researcher might establish the eye-irritancy of mouthwash and talc, toothpaste and cologne.

A final individual bids for our attention at this moment. A bobbie calf is a male calf born in a dairy herd. Since the calf cannot give milk, something must be done with it. A common practice is to sell it as a source of veal, as in veal Parmigiana. To make this commercially profitable the calf must be raised in highly unnatural conditions. Otherwise the youngster would romp and play, as is its wont; equally bad, it would forage and consume roughage. From a businessman's point of view, this is detrimental to the product. The romping produces muscle, which makes for tough meat, and the roughage will contain natural sources of iron, which will turn the calf's flesh red. But studies show that consumers have a decided preference for pale veal. So the calf is kept permanently indoors, in a stall too narrow for it to turn around, frequently tethered to confine it further, its short life lived mostly in the dark on a floor of wood slats, its only contact with other living beings coming when it is fed and when, at the end, it is transported to the slaughterhouse.

Envision then the tethered calf, unable to turn around, unable to sit down without hunching up, devoid of companionship, its natural urges to romp and forage denied, fed a wholly liquid diet deliberately deficient in iron so as not to compromise its pale flesh but to keep it anemic. For what? To what end? In the name of what purpose does the calf live so? So that humans might have pale veal!

Multiply these cases by the hundreds, multiply them by the thousands, and we approach, perhaps, the magnitude of the death and suffering animals are enduring, at this moment, at the hands of human beings. The numbers are like distances in astronomy. We can write them down, compare them, add and subtract them, but, like light years stacked on light years, we lack the intellectual or imaginative wherewithal to hold them in steady focus. Item: two million whales killed in the last fifty years. Item: in the mid-nineteenth century there were upwards of two billion passenger pigeons in the United States; now there are none. Item: when white settlers set foot on North America, there were sixty million buffalo; now the largest wild herd numbers 600. Item: the bald eagle, the national symbol of the United States, and the kangaroo, Australia's national symbol, are both teetering on the edge of extinction. . . .

But numbers prove nothing. They neither establish that something is right nor that it is wrong. They merely confirm what we know already. The use of animals as a primary food source and as subjects in scientific research knows no geographical boundaries. The extinction of unique species is not perpetrated by only a few political ideologies. Aside from economic considerations, and excluding the privileged status which pet animals may have as honorary members of the family, few things are regarded so cheaply as an animal's life. Few things now call forth less collective compassion of humankind than the great suffering animals endure in the name of human interests.

But these numbers serve another function. They serve as an index of the complexity of any questioning of those activities which involve the pain or destruction of animals. Questions about morality here are not likely to have simple answers. They require patient examination, due attention to competing forces, an eye for subtlety and nuance. Difficult questions are like knots; they are not unraveled just by pulling hard on one idea. For example, there is no reason to believe that such ideas as "all life is sacred," or "we ought to reverence all life," or "all forms of life are good" will dissolve the complexity before us. For these ideas, simply stated, leave unanswered crucial questions that arise when the interests of one form of life come into conflict with those of another. What is needed is not a simple declaration that all life is sacred, etc. What is wanted is some rational way to resolve such conflicts. What is wanted are moral principles which resolve the conflict equitably.

Now, these moral principles will not tell us, for example, how the population of whales will be affected if whaling is stopped or how that will affect the population of tuna. By themselves, that is, moral principles will not tell us *the facts* about whaling practices, nor will they give us a means of predicting what the facts will be. What these principles *will* tell us is what sort of facts to look for. In other words, they will tell us what facts are *morally relevant* to reaching a rational decision. The task of identifying what these principles are is one of the distinctive tasks of moral philosophy. This task occupies most of my attention in what follows. But I also want to bring my results back to the [animals] with which we began.

THE KANTIAN ACCOUNT

It is a commonplace to say that morality places some limits on how animals may be treated. We are not to kick dogs, set fire to cats' tails, torment hamsters or parakeets. Philosophically, the issue is not so much *whether* but *why* these acts are wrong.

An answer favored by many philosophers, including Thomas Aquinas and Immanuel Kant, is that people who treat animals in these ways develop a habit which, in time, inclines them to treat humans similarly. People who torment animals will, or are likely to, torment people. It is this spillover effect that makes mistreating animals wrong. We are not concerned directly with the ill-treatment that the animals themselves receive. Rather, our concern is that this bodes ill for humankind. So, on this Kantian account, the moral principle runs something like this: don't treat animals in ways that will lead you to mistreat human beings.

One need have no quarrel with this principle itself. The real quarrel lies with the grounds on which this principle is allegedly based. Peter Singer argues that there is a close parallel between this view and those of the racist and sexist, a view which he denominates speciesism. The racist believes that the interests of others matter only if they happen to be members of his own race. The speciesist believes that the interests of others matter only if they happen to be members of his own species. Racism has been unmasked for the prejudice that it is. The color of one's skin cannot be used to determine the relevance of an individual's interests. Singer and Ryder both argue that neither can the number of one's legs, whether one walks upright or on all fours, lives in the trees, the sea or the suburbs. Here they recall Bentham. There is, they argue forcefully, no rational, unprejudiced way to exclude the interests of nonhuman animals just because they are not the interests of human beings. Because the Kantian account would have us think otherwise, we are right to reject it. . . .

THE UTILITARIAN ACCOUNT

Utilitarians give a different account of the constraints regarding how animals ought to be treated. The utilitarian account, or one version of it, involves two principles.[1] The first is a principle of equality. This principle declares that the desires, needs, hopes, etc. of different individuals, when these are of equal importance *to* these individuals, *are* of equal importance or value no matter who the individuals are, prince or pauper, genius or moron, white or black, male or female, *human or animal.* . . .

The second principle is that of utility itself. Roughly speaking, according to this principle, we are to act so as to bring about the greatest possible balance of good over evil, for example, the greatest possible balance of satisfaction over dissatisfaction, taking the interests of everyone affected into account *and* counting equal interests equally. Now, since animals have interests, *their* interests must be taken into account, and because their interests are frequently as important to them as comparable interests are to human beings, *their* interests must be given the same weight as comparable human interests. It is because kicking dogs and setting fire to cats' tails run counter to the principles of equality and utility that, on this utilitarian account, they are wrong.

The utilitarian account has much to recommend it. How far can it take us in challenging the way in which animals are routinely treated, for example, as subjects in scientific research? Peter Singer, a utilitarian whose work has well deserved influence, holds that utilitarianism leads to far-reaching consequences here. Singer argues that we become vegetarians *and* that we oppose much (even if not quite all) research involving animal subjects. Singer's main argument is that the intensive rearing of animals as well as their routine use in experimentation violates the equality of interests principle. The animals involved, we have reason to believe, have an interest in not being made to suffer, and this interest, we have further reason to believe, is as important to them as is the comparable interest in the case of human beings. This being so, Singer contends, it is wrong to do to animals what we would not do to humans. It cannot be right to raise animals intensively or use them in research if we would morally oppose doing these things to human beings. We do condemn cannibalism and the coerced use of humans in research and we must, Singer argues, morally condemn the comparable treatment of animals. We have a moral obligation to become vegetarians and oppose much, if not quite all, vivisection.

As clear and powerful as this argument is, I do not believe that Singer succeeds in making a fully convincing case. He shows that animals are treated differently than human beings, but not that this differential treatment violates either the equality of interests principle or the principle of utility. Consider the equality of interests principle first. We can count equal interests equally, no matter whose interests they are, and still treat individuals quite differently. For example, I might correctly regard my son's and my neighbor's son's interests in receiving a medical education as being equal and yet help only my son. I treat them differently but I do *not* necessarily count their equal interests differently, and neither do I thereby do anything that is in any obvious sense morally reprehensible. I have duties to my son which I do not have to the children of others.

The general point is this: the differential treatment of individuals with equal interests does not by itself violate the equality of interests principle. Singer has to give an *argument* which shows *more* than that they are treated differently. What argument does he give and how adequate is it? Singer proceeds by asking whether we would do to humans what we allow to be done to ani-mals.[2] For example, would a researcher use an orphaned, profoundly retarded human baby in the sort of painful experiment in which he is willing to use a more intellectually and emotionally developed animal? If the researcher says no, Singer charges him with speciesism, with violating the equality of interests principle. The animal's interest in avoiding pain is just as important to it as is the infant's interest to him/her.

This argument begs the question. It assumes that by treating the involved individuals differently, we count their equal interests differently. As I have ex-plained, however, this is not always true. Whether it is true in any particular case, therefore, is something which must be established, not simply assumed on the basis of differential treatment. Singer, I believe, assumes just this, and thus begs the question.

Singer's argument has a further deficiency, which involves the principle of utility. First, Singer does not show that the differential treatment of animals runs counter to the utilitarian objective of bringing about the greatest pos-sible balance of good over evil. To show this Singer would have to give an elaborate, detailed description, not only of how animals are treated, a part of the task which he does complete with great skill, but an analysis of what, all considered, are the consequences for everyone involved. He would have to inquire how the world's economy depends on present levels of productivity in the animal industry, how many people's lives are directly and indirectly involved with the maintenance or growth of this industry, etc. Even more, he would have to show in detail what would probably be the consequences of a collapse or slowdown of the animal industry's productivity.

Secondly, Singer needs to make a compelling case for the view that *not* raising animals intensively or *not* using them routinely in research leads to better consequences, all considered, than those which now result from treat-ing animals in these ways. Singer is required to show that better consequences *would* result, or at least that it is *very probable* that they would. Showing that it is possible or conceivable that they might is insufficient. It comes as a disappointment, therefore, that we do not find anything approaching this kind of required empirical data. . . .

This, then, is the first thing to note regarding Singer and the principle of utility: *he fails to show, with reference to this principle, that it is wrong* to treat animals as they are now being treated in modern farming and scientific research. The second thing to note is that, for all we know and so long as we rely on the principle of utility, the present treatment of animals might actually be justified. The grounds for thinking so are as follows.

On the face of it, utilitarianism seems to be the fairest, least prejudicial view available. Everyone's interests count, and no one's counts for more or less than the equal interests of anyone else. The trouble is, as we have seen, that there is no necessary connection, no preestablished harmony between respect for the equality of interests principle *and* promoting the utilitarian objective of maximizing the balance of good over bad. On the contrary, the principle of utility might be used to justify the most radical kinds of differential treatment between individuals or groups of individuals, and thus it might justify forms of racism and sexism, for these prejudices can take different forms and find expression in different ways. One form consists in not even taking the interests of a given race or sex into account at all; another takes these interests into account but does not count them equally with those of the equal interests of the favored group. Another does take their interests into account equally, but adopts laws and policies, engages in practices and customs which give greater opportunities to the members of the favored group, because doing so promotes the greatest balance of good over evil, all considered.

Thus, forms of racism or sexism, which seem to be eliminated by the utilitarian principle of equality of interests, could well be resurrected and justified by the principle of utility. . . .

Similarly with speciesism. . . .

ANIMAL RIGHTS

. . . Various analyses of the concept of a right have been proposed. We will bypass the nooks and crannies of these competing analyses so as to focus attention on the role that moral rights play in our thinking about the status of the individual, relative to the interests of the group. Here the truth seems to lie where Ronald Dworkin sees it: the rights of the individual trump the goals of the group.[3]

What does this mean? It means that the moral rights of the individual place a justifiable limit on what the group can do to the individual. Suppose a group of people stand to gain enjoyment by arranging for others to be harmed. Imagine, for example, the Romans enjoying how the Christians go up against lions. Such a group does wrong because they allow their interests to override the individual's moral rights. This does not mean that there are no circumstances in which an individual's rights must give way to the collective interest. Imagine that Bert has inadvertently swallowed the microfilmed code which we must have in order to prevent a massive nuclear explosion in New Zealand. Bert sits safely in Tuscon, Arizona. We explain the situation but Bert refuses to consent to our request that we operate, retrieve the code, and prevent the explosion. He cites his right to determine what is to be done to his body. In such a case it is not implausible to say that Bert's right must give way to the collective interests of others.

Individual rights then normally, but not always, trump collective interests. To give a precise statement of the conditions which determine which ought to prevail is very difficult indeed, but the following conditions, which deal only with the right not to be harmed, at least seem to incorporate necessary conditions for overriding this right.

An individual's right not to be harmed can justifiably be overridden only if—

a. we have very good reason to believe that overriding the individual's right by itself will prevent, and is the only realistic way to prevent, vastly greater harm to other innocent individuals; or

b. we have very good reason to believe that allowing the individual to be harmed is a necessary link in a chain of events which collectively will prevent vastly greater harm to innocent individuals, *and* we have very good reason to believe that this chain of events is the only realistic way to prevent this vastly greater harm; or

c. we have very good reason to believe that it is only if we override the individual's right that we can have a reasonable hope of preventing vastly greater harm to other innocent individuals. . . .

These conditions share an extremely important feature. Each specifies what we must know or have good reason to believe if we are justified in overriding an individual's right not to be harmed. Each requires anyone who would harm an individual to show that this does not involve violating the individual's right. Part of the importance of the question, whether animals have rights, specifically, the right not to be harmed, now comes into clear focus. *If* they have this right, then it will be violated whenever animals are harmed and condition (a), (b), (c) is not satisfied. Moreover, the onus of justification is always on those who harm animals to explain how they are not violating the right of animals not to be harmed, if animals have this right. So, the question continues to press itself upon us. Do animals have the right not to be harmed? . . .

We begin by asking about our reasons for thinking that human beings have the moral right not to be harmed; then we go on to ask whether, given these reasons, a case can be made for saying that animals have this right as well. Let us go back to the idea that individual human beings have this right and that, except in extreme cases, this right trumps collective interest. Why? What is there about being a human being to which we can point and say, "*That's* why you must not harm the individual even if the group benefits?"

The heart of the answer lies, I believe, in thinking that human beings have a certain kind of value, inherent value. By this I mean that each human being has value logically independently of whether he/she is valued by anyone else (or, what perhaps comes to the same thing, whether he/she is the object of anyone else's interest). The view that human beings have inherent value implies that the kind of value properly attributable to them is not exclusively instrumental. Humans have value not just because, and not just so long as, they are good for something. They have value distinct from their utility and skill.

If this is true, we can explain, in general terms reminiscent of Kant, what is involved in mistreating human beings. Humans are mistreated if they are treated as valuable only if they forward the interests of other beings. To treat a human being thus is to show a lack of proper respect for the sort of value humans have. In Kant's terms, what has value in itself must always be treated as an end, never merely as a means. However, this is precisely what we are doing if we harm an individual so that others might gain pleasure or profit;

we are treating the individual merely as a means, as valuable only to the extent he/she contributes to the collective interest.

Now, *if* we accept the postulate that human beings have inherent value, we can press on and ask how rights enter the picture. They enter in being grounded in inherent value. In other words, it is individuals who have inherent value who have moral rights, and it is *because* they have value of this kind that they have a moral right not to be treated in ways that deny their having this kind of value. Rather than rights being connected with the *value of consequences* which affect individuals for good or ill, rather than rights being justified by the utility of recognizing them, rights are based on *the value of individuals*. In the case of the right not to be harmed, then, what we can say is that individuals who have inherent value have the right not to be harmed, which precludes treating them merely as a means. This would fail to treat these individuals with that respect to which, because of the kind of value they have, they are entitled.

Now, certainly the foregoing is not a definitive account of the view that individuals having inherent value have basic moral rights, in particular the right not to be harmed. One omission is especially conspicuous. What is there about being a human being that underlies this inherent value? Any answer is controversial, and a sustained defense of the answer proposed here is not possible. But here is the answer I would give: human beings not only are alive; *they have a life*. What is more, we are the subjects of a life that is better or worse for us, logically independently of anyone else's valuing us or finding us useful.

I do not mean that others cannot contribute to or detract from the value of our lives. On the contrary, the great goods of life (love, friendship, and, in general, fellow feeling) and its great evils (hatred, enmity, loneliness, alienation) all involve our relationships with other persons. What I mean, rather, is that our being *the subject* of a life that is better or worse for us does not depend logically on what others do or do not do. This fact, I believe, provides the illumination we seek. Humans have inherent value because we are ourselves the subjects of a life that is more or less valuable to us. In sum:

> Human beings have inherent value because, logically independently of the interest of others, each individual is the subject of a life that is better or worse for that individual. Because of the type of value that human beings have, it is wrong (a sign of disrespect and a violation of rights) to treat humans as if they had value merely as a means (e.g., to use humans merely to advance the pleasures of the group). In particular, to harm human beings for the sake of the profit or pleasure of any group is to violate their right not to be harmed.

The question now arises whether this same line of argument can be developed in the case of animals? It can, at least in the case of those animals who are the subjects of a life that is better or worse for them, logically independently of whether they are valued by anyone else. And there can be no rational doubt that there *are* numerous species of animals of which this is true, including the great blue whale, gibbons, and the others with which we began. They too have a distinctive kind of value in their own right, if we do; therefore, they too have a right not to be treated in ways that fail to respect this value, if we do. And, like humans, this right of theirs will be overridden unjustifiably if they are harmed merely to advance the profits or pleasures of others.

* * *

Those who would harm [animals], therefore, must justify doing so. Thus, members of the whaling industry, the cosmetics industry, the farming industry, the network of hunters-exporters-importers must justify the harm they bring animals in a way that is consistent with recognizing the animals' right not to be harmed. To produce such a justification it is not enough to argue that people profit, satisfy their curiosity, or derive pleasure from allowing animals to be treated in these ways. These facts are not the morally relevant ones. Rather, what must be shown is that overriding the right of animals not to be harmed is justified because of further facts. For example, because we have very good reason to believe that overriding the individual's right prevents, and is the only realistic way to prevent, vastly greater harm to other innocent individuals.

Let us ask the whaling industry whether they have so justified their trade. Have they made their case in terms of the morally relevant facts? Our answer must be: no! And the cosmetic industry? No! The farmers who raise veal calves? No! . . . A thousand times we must say: no! I do not say that they cannot possibly justify what they do. The individual's right not to be harmed, we have argued, almost always trumps the interests of the group, but it is possible that such a right must sometimes give way. Possibly the rights of animals must sometimes give way to human interests. It would be a mistake to rule this possibility out. Nevertheless, the onus of justification must be borne by those who cause the harm to show that they do not violate the rights of the individuals involved.

We allow then that it is *possible* that harming animals might be justified; but we also maintain that those harming animals typically fail to show that the harm caused is *actually* justified. A further question we must ask ourselves is what, morally speaking, we ought to do in such a situation? Reflection on comparable situations involving human beings will help make the answer clear.

Consider racism and sexism. Imagine that slavery is an institution of the day and that it is built on racist or sexist lines. Blacks or women are assigned the rank of slave. Suppose we are told that in extreme circumstances even slavery might conceivably be justified, and that we ought not to object to it or try to bring it down, even though no one has shown that it is actually justified in the present case. Well, I do not believe for a moment that we would accept such an attempt to dissuade us from toppling the institution of slavery. Not for a moment would we accept the general principle involved here, that an institution actually is justified because it might conceivably be justified. We would accept the quite different principle that we are morally obligated to oppose any practice which appears to violate rights unless we are shown that it really does not do so. To be satisfied with anything less is to cheapen the value attributable to the victims of the practice.

Exactly the same line of reasoning applies in the case where animals are regarded as so many dispensable commodities, models, subjects, etc. We ought not to back away from bringing these industries and related practices to a halt just because it is *possible* that the harm caused to the animals *might* be justified. If we do, we fail to mean it when we say that animals are not mere things, that they are the subjects of a life that is better or worse for them, that they have inherent value. As in the comparable case involving harm to human beings, our duty is to act, to do all that we can to put an end to the harm animals are made to endure. The fact that the animals themselves cannot speak out on their own behalf, the fact that they cannot organize, petition, march, exert political pressure, or raise our level of consciousness—all this does not weaken our obligation to act on their behalf. If anything, their impotence makes our obligation the greater. . . .

Notes

1. The utilitarian position I consider is the one associated with Bentham and forcefully presented by Peter Singer. That Singer is a utilitarian is made unmistakably clear in his "The Fable of the Fox and the Unliberated Animals" *Ethics* 88 (1978): pp. 119-25.
2. See Peter Singer, *Animal Liberation* (New York: Avon Books, 1976), especially pp. 78-83.
3. Ronald Dworkin, *Taking Rights Seriously* (Cambridge: Harvard University Press, 1977).

Duties to Endangered Species
Holmes Rolston III

A professor in the philosophy department at Colorado State University, Holmes Rolston III is the author of *Environmental Ethics* (1988), a study of our responsibilities towards the natural world. The following excerpts are taken from Chapter 6. In these passages, Rolston looks at our duties toward animals within the context of an environmental ethics. In the course of his investigation he makes and defends two controversial claims: 1) Human beings have moral duties to species, not just toward particular members of a species, and 2) The moral duties we have toward endangered species outweigh the responsibilities we have to protect the rights of individual animals not to be harmed.

Taking a non-anthropomorphic approach similar to that taken by Singer and Regan, Rolston disagrees with their belief that we can have duties to individual members of a species, but not to a species itself. In his opinion, the fact that an animal species as an entity has no consciousness does not mean that we have no duties toward it. Because a species is a biological system that preserves its identity over time, it has a character, much like a character in a play. From this viewpoint, it is reasonable to see a species as being an "individual" in relation to other species. Because this "individuality" is more basic than the individual members of the species, Rolston concludes we not only have a duty to protect individual species but we also have more of a duty to protect individual species than individual organisms themselves.

In his view, whenever human interference with animal life results in the extinction of a species, one of the characters in the drama of life on earth is lost forever. Humans have no more right to engage in such "superkilling," as he calls it, than do members of a theater audience have to rise up and kill off a character in the play they are watching. Given that we have both the knowledge to see when our actions can lead to the extinction of a species and the power to stop this extinction from occuring, Rolston believes we are morally obligated to use this power, even if it means, as it did in the protection of the "Santa Barbara live-forever" plant, the sacrifice of individual members of nonendangered species.

———

"Certainly . . . the destruction of a whole species can be a great evil." John Rawls, however, advocating his most perceptive contemporary theory of justice, admits that in his theory "no account is given of right conduct in regard to animals and the rest of nature."[1] . . . One searches in vain through several thousand years of philosophy (back at least to Noah!) for any serious reference to endangered species. Previously, humans were seldom able to destroy species; this "great evil" did not threaten, so there are few resources in our heritage with which to confront it. Even the ethics we have so far developed

From *Environmental Ethics*, (Philadelphia: Temple University Press, 1988), pp. 126–159.

for sentient animals and other organisms has not yet directly addressed obligations concerning species.

But the *Global 2000 Report* projects a massive loss of Earth's species (up to 20 percent) within a few decades if present trends go unreversed.[2] These losses will be about evenly distributed through major groups of plants and animals in the United States and in the world. Congress has lamented, in the Endangered Species Act, the lack of "adequate concern (for) and conservation (of)" species.[3] The act was tougher than was realized by most of those who passed it. The Supreme Court, interpreting the law, said that species are to be conserved with "no exception" at "whatever the cost," their protection overriding even the "primary missions" of federal agencies.[4] That seemed extreme, and the act has been modified. Still, that many do not wish to weaken it much has been shown by its repeated renewal. Articulating an ethic here involves an unprecedented mix of science and conscience.

DUTIES TO PERSONS
CONCERNING SPECIES

Some say there are no duties to endangered species, only duties to persons. "The preservation of species," by the usual utilitarian account, reported by Stuart Hampshire, is "to be aimed at and commended only in so far as human beings are, or will be, emotionally and sentimentally interested."[5] Joel Feinberg says, "We do have duties to protect threatened species, not duties to the species themselves as such, but rather duties to future human beings, duties derived from our housekeeping role as temporary inhabitants of this planet."[6] The relation is three-place. Person A has a duty *to* person B which *concerns* species C, but is not *to* C. Using traditional ethics, we can reapply familiar duties to persons and see whether this exhausts our moral intuitions or leaves a residue of concern. Such a line of argument can be impressive but seems to leave deeper reasons untouched.

Species as Stabilizers and Resources

Persons have a strong duty of nonmaleficence not to harm others and a weaker, though important, duty of beneficence to help others. Arguing the threat of harm, Paul and Anne Ehrlich maintain, in a blunt metaphor, that the myriad species are rivets in the airplane in which humans are flying. Extinctions are maleficent rivet-popping. On the Earthship in which we ride there is considerable redundancy, but humans cannot safely lose 1.5 million species-rivets, and any loss of redundancy is to be deplored. Species, including endangered ones, are stabilizers.[7]

In this model, nonrivet species, if there are any, have no value. Nor is any particular species the object of care. Humans desire only the diversity that prevents a crash. No single thread, but the strength of the fabric is the issue. The care is not for species, not for a breeding population of each kind, but (in

Norman Myers's variant metaphor picturing the failing Earthship) for the "sinking ark."[8] To worry about a sinking ark seems a strange twist on the Noah story. Noah built the ark to preserve each species, brought on board carefully, two of each kind. In the Ehrlich/Myers account, the species-rivets are preserved to keep the ark from sinking! The reversed justification is revealing.

On the benefits side, species that are not rivets may have resource value. Wild species can have agricultural, medical, industrial, and scientific uses. Thomas Eisner testified to Congress that only about 2 percent of the flowering plants have been tested for alkaloids, which often have medical uses.[9] North Americans regularly eat almost nothing native to their ecosystem. Elsewhere in the world, loss of the wild stocks of the cultivars leaves Americans genetically vulnerable, so it is prudent to save the native materials. The International Union for the Conservation of Nature and Natural Resources (IUCN) says, "The ultimate protection of nature, . . . and all its endangered forms of life, demands . . . an enlightened exploitation of its wild resources."[10] Myers further urges "conserving our global stock."[11] At first that seems wise, yet later somewhat demeaning for humans to regard all other species as *stock*.

Ingenious biologists and ethicists can stretch the meaning of rivet and resource. On the harm side, the loss of a few species may have no evident results now, but this has destabilizing lag effects generations later. When an extremely cold winter hits, the ecosystem will be thrown into a degenerating spiral. Rare species do not now function significantly in the ecosystem, but they lie in wait as part of the backup resilience. The extinction of nonrivet and nonresource species will affect rivet and resource species. Getting by with a few extinctions lulls humans into thinking that they can get by with more, when in fact the danger increases exponentially with subtractions from the ecosystem. Humans will stumble over the disaster threshold because of bad habits formed when these extinctions were not yet harmful. Concern for all species puts up guard rails and provides a margin of safety on a slippery slope.

Species, Science, and Natural History

One should count as resources all those species that generate recreational, aesthetic, and scientific experiences. The rare species fascinate enthusiastic naturalists and are often key scientific study species. They provide entertainments and new knowledge of spaceship Earth, regardless of their stabilizing or economic benefits. One whooping crane in a flock of sandhills perks up a bird watcher's day. A National Science Foundation report advocated saving the Devil's Hole pupfish, *Cyprinodon diabolis,* in a case that went to the Supreme Court, because it and its relatives thrive in hot or salty water.

> Such extreme conditions tell us something about the creatures' extraordinary thermoregulatory system and kidney function—but not enough as yet. . . . They can serve as useful biological models for future research on the human kidney—and on survival in a seemingly hostile environment. . . . Man,

in the opinion of many ecologists, will need all the help he can get in understanding and adapting to the expansion of arid areas over the Earth.[12]

The Socorro isopod, *Exosphaeroma thermophilum*, has lost its natural habitat and lives only in the drain of an abandoned bath-house at a New Mexico hot springs site. Nevertheless the U.S. Fish and Wildlife Service claims that it "is of particular interest and importance. . . . How this species arrived at its present state of evolutionary adaptation is of concern to isopod specialists, and the concept of landlocked fauna is of concern to biologists as a whole."[13] *Eriogonum gypsophilum* is worth saving for a Ph.D. candidate to find out its adaptation to gypsum, even though this could restrict the proposed lake that would threaten its habitat and despite the fact that nothing practical may come from the dissertation. *Shortia galacifolia* is worth saving as a historical souvenir of the excitement of the early American botanists who traded specimens at $50 each.

Destroying species is like tearing pages out of an unread book, written in a language humans hardly know how to read, about the place where they live. We do not know, for instance, whether there are five or ten million species on Earth. We know little about the processes of *ecosystem* evolution as something more than organismic evolution. We do not know whether or how natural selection operates at that level. Biologists are divided over whether interspecific competition is a minimal or a major force in evolution, and sizable natural systems with all their species preserved intact are the likeliest places to settle this debate.

No sensible person would destroy the Rosetta Stone, and no self-respecting humans will destroy the mouse lemur, endangered in Madagascar and thought to be the modern animal nearest to the relatively unspecialized primates from which the human line evolved. Nor should we destroy *Zoonosaurus hazofotsi*, the Madagascar lizard with a third eye atop its head, the pineal eyespot, from which humans might learn about the parallel evolution of sight. Still, following this logic, humans have duties not to the book, the stone, or the species but to ourselves, duties both of prudence and education. Humans need insight into the full text of natural history. They need to understand the evolving world in which they are placed. It is not endangered species but an endangered human future that is of concern.

Such reasons are pragmatic and impressive. They are also moral, since persons are benefited or hurt. But are they exhaustive? Can all duties concerning species be analyzed as duties to persons? Do we simply want to protect these endangered forms of life *for* exploitation, or do we sometimes want to protect them *from* exploitation? . . .

Human Prudence and Moral Principles

The deeper problem with the anthropocentric rationale, beyond overstatement, is that its justifications are submoral and fundamentally exploitive and self-serving, even if subtly so. This is not true intraspecifically among humans, when out of a sense of duty an individual defers to the values of fellows. But it is true interspecifically, since *Homo sapiens* treats all other species as rivets, resources, study materials, or entertainments. Ethics has always been about partners with entwined destinies. But it has never been very convincing when pleaded as enlightened self-interest (that one ought always to do what is in one's intelligent self-interest), including class self-interest, even though in practice altruistic ethics often needs to be reinforced by self-interest. To value all other species only for human interests is rather like a nation's arguing all its foreign policy in terms of national self-interest. Neither seems fully moral. . . .

It is safe to say that in the decades ahead the quality of life will decline in proportion to the loss of biotic diversity, though it is usually thought that we are sacrificing biotic diversity in order to improve human life. So there is a sense in which humans will not be losers if we save endangered species. There is a sense in which those who do the right thing never lose, even when they respect values other than their own. Slaveowners do not really lose when they free their slaves, since the slaveowners become better persons by freeing their slaves, to whom they can thereafter relate person-to-person. Subsequently, human relationships will be richer. In morality, only the immoral lose—ultimately. Similarly, humans who protect endangered species will, if and when they change their value priorities, be better persons for their admiring respect for other forms of life.

But this should not obscure the fact that humans can be short-term losers. Sometimes we do have to make sacrifices, at least in terms of what we presently value, to preserve species. Moreover, the claim that we are better humans if we protect species is an empirical, statistical claim—true on average, true unless shown otherwise. There might be cases where the worth of a species, coupled with human benefits from respecting it, do not override the human benefits to be gained by sacrificing it. Then humans might be duty-bound to be losers in the sense that they sacrifice values, although they would still be winners for doing the right thing.

Dealing with a problem correctly requires an appropriate way of thinking about it. On the scale of evolutionary time, humans appear late and suddenly. Even more lately and suddenly, they dramatically increase the extinction rate. About 500 species, sub-species, and varieties have been lost in the United States since 1600; the natural rate of extinction would have resulted in about ten.[14] In Hawaii, a bellwether state, half the 2,200 native plants are endangered or threatened; of sixty-eight species of birds unique to the islands, forty-one are extinct or virtually so. In the near future, humans threaten to approach and even exceed the catastrophic rates of the geological past, if indeed we are not doing this already. What is offensive in such conduct is not merely senseless destabilizing, not merely the loss of resources and rivets, but the maelstrom of killing and insensitivity to forms of life and the sources producing them. What is required is not prudence but principled responsibility to the biospheric Earth. . . .

DUTIES TO SPECIES

Humans versus Endangered Species

. . . The obligation to protect humans trumps the obligation to protect *individual* animals and plants, short of extenuating circumstances and even if critical animal and plant goods sometimes outweigh nonbasic humans goods. But it does not follow that the obligation to protect one or even a group of humans trumps the obligation to protect whole *species*. Further, our obligation to protect *existing* lives can be greater than our obligation to bring into existence yet *unborn* lives, and this may offset the otherwise greater obligation to protect humans over animals and plants. It could be more important to protect one million existing species than to bring into existence an additional one million persons—a choice not as farfetched as it may first appear in view of the present pace of tropical deforestation. . . .

A Florida panther, one of about thirty surviving in an endangered subspecies, was mangled when hit by a car. Named Big Guy, he was flown by helicopter to the state university veterinary medical school. Steel plates were inserted in both legs, and the right foot rebuilt. Is this appropriate treatment? Is it something humans ought to do out of justice or benevolence? Because of concern for the individual animal or for the subspecies? Big Guy's story mostly served to bring to focus a bigger issue. He cannot be released into the wild but is being bred and his offspring will be used for experiments to protect his species.

Protecting the panther, Florida's state animal, could cost $112.5 million. The subspecies is peculiarly adapted to the Florida swamps, in contrast with the dry, mountainous areas inhabited by the West's cougars. The panther is nearly extinct because of dwindling habitat, and the last critical habitat—the Big Cypress Swamp, adjacent to the Everglades—is being cut in half by Interstate 75. Florida has argued for spending $27 million (about $1 million per panther) to build forty bridges that will allow the panthers to pass under the high-fenced interstate: both "animal crossings," bridges over dry land, and "extended bridges," bridges over water with spans over land at each end. Otherwise, as Big Guy illustrates, many will be killed by the fast, increasing traffic. Critics—including some federal authorities, who bear 90 percent of the costs—say this is too expensive and won't work. Wildlife biologists claim that it will (as the Alaska pipeline was redesigned to permit caribou migration); they have tracked radio-collared cats and located their routes. . . .

Again, though humans are superior to panthers, the human costs here (about $10 per Floridian, about fifty cents per U.S. citizen) hardly seem high enough to justify the extinction of a sub-species. The loss of limited recreation and sport hunting would be offset by renewed respect for life. Wildlands acquired or protected in an already overcrowded state are valuable with or without the panther. Corridors and crossings that connect otherwise isolated reserves are important for many mammals. The bridges may prove futile, but Americans regularly risk those amounts of money in lotteries. To be gained is the continued existence of an animal handsome enough to be chosen as the state symbol, highly evolved on the top trophic rung of a rare Everglades ecosystem, thought by many to be the most aesthetically exciting animal on the North American continent. In this case too, if in fact humans can be shown to lose, they ought to be the losers in favor of the cat.

Sentient Life versus Endangered Species

A concern for species is not just a way of protecting sentient lives or even individual organisms. The National Park Service allows hundreds of elk to starve in Yellowstone each year, but the starving of an equal number of grizzly bears, which would involve about the same loss in felt experience, would be of much greater concern. Only about 100 whooping cranes remain; to kill and eat them would result in jail sentences. But we kill and eat 100 turkeys without a thought. Something more is at stake ethically than a concern for individual lives. Humans have no duty to deny their ecology and thus do not interrupt spontaneous nature (assume no duty to feed the elk), and humans do sacrifice individual animals and plants to meet their needs. But humans have at least some duty not to cause ecological disruption, a duty not to waste species. . . .

On San Clemente Island, the U.S. Fish and Wildlife Service and the California Department of Fish and Game asked the Navy to shoot 2,000 feral goats to save three endangered plant species: *Malacothamnus clementinus, Castilleja grisea, Delphinium kinkiense.* That would mean killing several goats for each known surviving plant. Isolated from the mainland, the island had evolved a number of unique species. Goats, introduced in the early 1800s, thrived even after humans abandoned them but adversely affected the ecosystem. They have probably already eradicated several never-known species. Following renewed interest in endangered species, officials decided to eliminate the goats. By herding and trapping, 21,000 were removed, but the remaining goats were in inaccessible canyons, which required their being shot from helicopters.

The Fund for Animals filed suit to prevent this, and the court ordered all goats removed. After the shooting of 600 goats, the Fund put political pressure on the Department of the Navy to secure a moratorium on further shooting. Happily, workers for the Fund rescued most of the goats with novel trapping techniques; unhappily, neither they nor others have been able to live-trap them all. The goats reproduce rapidly during any delay, and there are still more than 1,000 on the island.[15]

Despite the Fund's objections, the Park Service did kill hundreds of rabbits on Santa Barbara Island to protect a few plants of *Dudleya traskiae*, once thought extinct and curiously called the Santa Barbara live-forever. This island endemic was once common. But New Zealand red rabbits, introduced about 1900, fed on it; by 1970 no *Dudleya* could be found. With the discovery in 1975 of five plants, a decision was made to eradicate the rabbits.

Does protecting endangered species justify causing suffering and death? Does the fact that the animals were exotic make a difference? An ethic based on animal rights will come to one answer, but a more broadly based environmental ethic will prefer plant species, especially species in their eco-systems, over sentient animals that are exotic misfits. . . .

Every extinction is a kind of superkilling. It kills forms (*species*), beyond individuals. It kills "essences" beyond "existences," the "soul" as well as the "body." It kills collectively, not just distributively. A duty to a species is more like being responsible to a cause than to a person. It is commitment to an *idea* (Greek, *idea*, "form," sometimes a synonym for the Latin *species*). This duty is a categori-cal imperative to living categories. It is not merely the loss of potential human information that we lament but the loss of biological information that is present independent of instrumental human uses of it. At stake is something vital, past something biological, and all this is something more than an anthropocentric concern. We are called on, again, objectively to evaluate (appraise the worth of) what we may or may not subjectively value (have a personal preference for).

Much is conserved in Earth's subroutines and cycles (matter, energy, mate-rials); much can be recycled and renewed (water, energy, nutrients); there are many equilibria (food chains, species turnover, natural extinctions with respeciation). But in human-caused extinctions there is the loss of unique bio-logical information, with no conservation by respeciation. A shutdown of the life stream is the most destructive event possible. "Ought species x to exist?" is a distributive increment in the collective question, "Ought life on Earth to ex-ist?" Life on Earth cannot exist without its individuals either, but a lost indi-vidual is always reproducible; a lost species is never reproducible. The answer to the species question is not always the same as the answer to the collective question, but since life on Earth is an aggregate of many species, the two are sufficiently related that the burden of proof lies with those who wish deliber-ately to extinguish a species and simultaneously to care for life on Earth.

Every species is a "display" or "show" (also a meaning of the Latin *species*) in the natural history book. These stories are plural, diverse, erratic, but they are not wholly fragmented episodes. The pressures of natural selection pull them into roles into their communities, fit them into niches, give continuity to the stories, and make more unified ecosystemic stories of the many stories. Always, there are themes in their settings, characters moving through space and time, problems and their resolutions, the plotting of life paths. Exceeding the births and deaths of individual members, a specific form of life unfolds an intergenerational narrative. What humans are bound to respect in natural his-tory is not one another's scientific, recreational, or reading material, not rivets in their Earthship, but the living drama, continuing with all its actors. To kill a species is to shut down a unique story, and although all specific stories must eventually end, we seldom want unnatural ends. Humans ought not to play the role of murderers. The duty to species can be overridden—for example, in the case of pests or disease organisms—but a prima facie duty stands never-theless.

One form of life has never endangered so many others. Never before has this level of question—superkilling by a superkiller—been deliberately faced.

Humans have more understanding than ever of the natural world they inhabit and of the speciating processes, more predictive power to foresee the intended and unintended results of their actions, and more power to reverse the undesirable consequences. The duties that such power and vision generate no longer attach simply to individuals or persons but are emerging duties to specific forms of life. If, in this world of uncertain moral convictions, it makes any sense to claim that one ought not to kill individuals without justification, it makes more sense to claim that one ought not to superkill the species without superjustification.

INDIVIDUALS AND SPECIES

Many will be uncomfortable with claims about duties to species because their ethical theory does not allow duty to a collection, only to individuals. Only individuals can inject preferences into the system. As Joel Feinberg writes, "A whole collection, as such, cannot have beliefs, expectations, wants, or desires.... Individual elephants can have interests, but the species elephant cannot."[16] That premise underlies Feinberg's conclusion, cited earlier, that duties cannot be to species but must be to future humans, who will have beliefs, desires, and so on. Singer asserts, "Species as such are not conscious entities and so do not have interests above and beyond the interests of the individual animals that are members of the species." That premise supports Singer's conclusion that all our duties must be to sentient beings.[17]

Tom Regan defines the "rights view" as "a view about the moral rights of individuals. Species are not individuals, and the rights view does not recognize the moral rights of species to anything, including survival."[18] Nicholas Rescher says, "Moral obligation is thus always interest-oriented. But only individuals can be said to have interests; one only has moral obligations to particular individuals or particular groups thereof. Accordingly, the duty to save a species is not a matter of moral duty toward it, because moral duties are only oriented to individuals. A species as such is the wrong sort of target for a moral obligation."[19] But beliefs, desires, conscious awareness, rights, individuality, and so forth, are not the only relevant criteria in an emerging environmental ethic. . . .

Value at the Species Level

There is no value without an evaluator. So runs a well-entrenched dogma in value theory. Humans clearly evaluate their world; sentient animals may do so also. Less clearly, any organism "evaluates" its environment, as when an *Escherichia coli* bacterium prefers glucose over lactose (even though it is programmed to do this genetically). But (some say) no species—whatever "species" exactly is—can evaluate anything, and therefore nothing called "species" can be the holder of intrinsic value, although a collection may be of instrumental value to ("valuable," able to be valued by) bona fide evaluators. Hence, any duties that humans have cannot be to species (though they may concern them) but must be to those evaluators (normally other humans) in whom sooner or later values come to birth.

But we need to revise this logic. Biologists and linguists have learned to accept the concept of information without any subject who speaks or understands. Can environmental ethicists learn to accept value in, and duty to, an informed process in which centered individuality or sentience is absent? Here events can be of value at the specific level, an additional consideration to whether they are beneficial to individuals. The species-in-environment is an interactive complex, a selective system where individuals are pawns on a chessboard. When human conduct endangers these specific games of life, destroying the habitats in which they are played, duties may appear.

The older ethic will say that duties attach to singular lives, most evidently those with a self or some analogue to a self. In an individual organism the organs report to a center; the good of a whole is defended. But the members of a species report to no center. A species has no self. It is not a bounded singular. Each individual has its own centeredness, but the species has no specific analogue to the nervous hookups or circulatory flows that characterize the organism. Like the market in economics, however, an organized system does not have to have a controlling center to have identity. Perhaps singularity, centeredness, selfhood, individuality are not the only processes to which duty attaches.

Having a biological identity reasserted genetically over time is as true of the species as of the individual. In fact, taxonomists can often distinguish two species more readily than two individuals within a species. Uniqueness attaches to the dynamic historical lineage, even if the members also are, in their own ways, idiographic. Individual organisms come and go; the marks of the individual species collectively remain much longer. Biological identity need not attach to the centered organism; it can persist as a discrete, vital pattern over time.

A consideration of species strains any ethic fixed on individual organisms, much less on sentience or persons. But the result can be biologically sounder, though it revises what was formerly thought logically permissible or ethically binding. When ethics is informed by this kind of biology, it is appropriate to attach duty dynamically to the specific form of life. The species line is the more fundamental living system, the whole of which individual organisms are the essential parts. The species too has its integrity, its individuality, its "right to life" (if we must use the rhetoric of rights), and it is more important to protect this than to protect individual integrity. Again and again, processes of value found first in an organic individual reappear at the specific level: defending a particular form of life, pursuing a pathway through the world, resisting death (extinction), regeneration maintaining a normative identity over time, storied achievements, creative resilience learning survival skills. If, at the specific level, these processes are just as evident or even more so, what prevents duties from arising at that level? The appropriate survival unit is the appropriate level of moral concern. . . .

NOTES

1. John Rawls, *A Theory of Justice* (Cambridge, Mass.: Harvard University Press, 1971), p. 512.

     A shorter version of this chapter appeared as "Duties to Endangered Species," *BioScience* 35 (1985): pp. 718-26, © AIBS 1985; reprinted in Rolston, *Philosophy Gone Wild* (Buffalo, N.Y.: Prometheus Books, 1986), pp. 206-20. For an introduction to these issues, see Bryan G. Norton, ed., *Preservation of Species* (Princeton, N.J.: Princeton University Press, 1986).

2. Council on Environmental Quality and the Department of State, *The Global 2000 Report to the President* (Washington, D.C.: U.S. Government Printing Office, 1980), vol. 1, p. 37; vol. 2, pp. 327-33.

3. Endangered Species Act of 1973, sec. 2 (a) (1) Public Law 93-205, 87 Stat. 884.

4. TVA v. Hill, 437 U.S. 153 (1978) at 173, 184, 185.

5. Stuart Hampshire, *Morality and Pessimism* (New York: Cambridge University Press, 1972), pp. 3-4.

6. Joel Feinberg, "The Rights of Animals and Unborn Generations," in W.T. Blackstone, ed., *Philosophy and Environmental Crisis* (Athens: University of Georgia Press, 1974), pp. 43-68, citation on p. 56. Feinberg holds that the duty to preserve species is more important than any rights of individual animals but is not a duty that can properly be attributed to species as a whole.

7. Paul Ehrlich and Anne Ehrlich, *Extinction* (New York: Random House, 1981), pp. xi-xiv.

8. Norman Myers, *The Sinking Ark* (Oxford: Pergamon Press, 1979).

9. "Statement of Thomas Eisner," *Endangered Species Act Oversight*, Hearings, 8 and 10 December 1981 (Washington, D.C.: U.S. Government Printing Office, 1982), pp. 295-97.

10. James Fisher, Noel Simon, Jack Vincent, and IUCN staff, *Wildlife in Danger* (New York: Viking Press, 1969), p. 19.

11. Norman Myers, "Conserving Our Global Stock," *Environment* 21, no.9 (November 1979): 25-33.

12. National Science Foundation, "The Biology of Aridity," *Mosaic* 8, no. 1 (January/February 1977): 28-35, citation on p. 28.

13. *Endangered Species Technical Bulletin* 3, no. 1 (January 1978): 5.

14. Paul A. Opler, "The Parade of Passing Species: A Survey of Extinctions in the U.S.," *Science Teacher* 43, no. 9 (December 1976): 30-34.

15. Details from Jan Larson, Natural Resources Manager, Naval Air Station, North Island, San Diego, California.

16. Feinberg, "Rights of Animals and Unborn Generations," pp. 55-56.

17. Peter Singer, "Not for Humans Only: The Place of Nonhumans in Environmental Issues," in K. E. Goodpaster and K. M. Sayre, eds., *Ethics and Problems of the 21st Century* (Notre Dame, Ind.: University of Notre Dame Press, 1979), pp. 191-206, citation on p. 203.

18. Tom Regan, *The Case for Animal Rights* (Berkeley: University of California Press, 1983), p. 359.

19. Nicholas Rescher, "Why Save Endangered Species?" in *Unpopular Essays on Technological Progress* (Pittsburgh, Pa.: University of Pittsburgh Press, 1980), pp. 79-92, citation on p. 83.

Deep Ecology
Bill Devall and George Sessions

In 1985 Bill Devall, a member of the sociology department at Humboldt State University, and George Sessions, who teaches philosophy at Sierra College, published a book called *Deep Ecology: Living As If Nature Mattered.* The following selections from that book are taken from the chapters on "Deep Ecology" and "Natural Resource Conservation."

"Deep ecology" describes a way of thinking about the natural environment that takes its basic starting point from the idea that every living being has intrinsic value and "a place in the Earth household." Thus nature does not matter because we matter; nature simply matters. While deep ecology was first developed by the Norwegian thinker Arne Naess, Bill Devall and George Sessions have been instrumental in clarifying its basic principles and showing its applications to particular environmental problems.

As understood from the viewpoint of deep ecology, all existence is interrelated. No firm boundaries exist between the human and the nonhuman world. For Devall and Sessions, this implies that human beings need to be able to take perspectives that go beyond the limits of the individual self in order to be able to treat nature in an ethical manner. In their view, anyone who adopts a deep ecological approach to resource conservation would not seek to find better techniques for resource management but would rather look to enhance ways for human life to interact more harmoniously with other life processes. Such "righteous management," as John Muir called it, could involve protecting the rights of native peoples to kill members of endangered species in order to protect the ways of life of their own communities.

The term *deep ecology* was coined by Arne Naess in his 1973 article, "The Shallow and the Deep, Long-Range Ecology Movements."[1] Naess was attempting to describe the deeper, more spiritual approach to Nature exemplified in the writings of Aldo Leopold and Rachel Carson. He thought that this deeper approach resulted from a more sensitive openness to ourselves and non-human life around us. The essence of deep ecology is to keep asking more searching questions about human life, society, and Nature as in the Western philosophical tradition of Socrates. As examples of this deep questioning, Naess points out "that we ask why and how, where others do not. For instance, ecology as a science does not ask what kind of a society would be the best for maintaining a particular ecosystem—that is considered a question for value theory, for politics, for ethics." Thus deep ecology goes beyond the so-called factual scientific level to the level of self and Earth wisdom.

From *Deep Ecology: Living as if Nature Mattered*, by Bill Devall and George Sessions (Salt Lake City, UT: Peregrine Smith Books, 1985).

Deep ecology goes beyond a limited piecemeal shallow approach to environmental problems and attempts to articulate a comprehensive religious and philosophical worldview. . . .

Many of [the] questions [it raises] are perennial philosophical and religious questions faced by humans in all cultures over the ages. What does it mean to be a unique human individual? How can the individual self maintain and increase its uniqueness while also being an inseparable aspect of the whole system wherein there are no sharp breaks between self and the *other?* An ecological perspective, in this deeper sense, results in what Theodore Roszak calls "an awakening of wholes greater than the sum of their parts. In spirit, the discipline is contemplative and therapeutic."[2]

Ecological consciousness and deep ecology are in sharp contrast with the dominant worldview of technocratic-industrial societies which regards humans as isolated and fundamentally separate from the rest of Nature, as superior to, and in charge of, the rest of creation. But the view of humans as separate and superior to the rest of Nature is only part of larger cultural patterns. For thousands of years, Western culture has become increasingly obsessed with the idea of *dominance*: with dominance of humans over nonhuman Nature, masculine over the feminine, wealthy and powerful over the poor, with the dominance of the West over non-Western cultures. Deep ecological consciousness allows us to see through these erroneous and dangerous illusions.

For deep ecology, the study of our place in the Earth household includes the study of ourselves as part of the organic whole. Going beyond a narrowly materialist scientific understanding of reality, the spiritual and the material aspects of reality fuse together. While the leading intellectuals of the dominant worldview have tended to view religion as "just superstition," and have looked upon ancient spiritual practice and enlightenment, such as found in Zen Buddhism, as essentially subjective, the search for deep ecological consciousness is the search for a more objective consciousness and state of being through an active deep questioning and meditative process and way of life.

Many people have asked these deeper questions and cultivated ecological consciousness within the context of different spiritual traditions—Christianity, Taoism, Buddhism, and Native American rituals, for example. While differing greatly in other regards, many in these traditions agree with the basic principles of deep ecology.

Warwick Fox, an Australian philosopher, has succinctly expressed the central intuition of deep ecology: "It is the idea that we can make no firm ontological divide in the field of existence: That there is no bifurcation in reality between the human and the non-human realms . . . to the extent that we perceive boundaries, we fall short of deep ecological consciousness."[3]

From this most basic insight or characteristic of deep ecological consciousness, Arne Naess has developed two *ultimate norms* or intuitions which are themselves not derivable from other principles or intuitions. They are arrived at by the deep questioning process and reveal the importance of moving to the philosophical and religious level of wisdom. They cannot be validated, of course, by the methodology of modern science based on its usual mechanistic assumptions and its very narrow definition of data. These ultimate norms are *self-realization* and *biocentric equality*.

I. SELF-REALIZATION

In keeping with the spiritual traditions of many of the world's religions, the deep ecology norm of self-realization goes beyond the modern Western *self* which is defined as an isolated ego striving primarily for hedonistic gratification or for a narrow sense of individual salvation in this life or the next. This socially programmed sense of the narrow self or social self dislocates us, and leaves us prey to whatever fad or fashion is prevalent in our society or social reference group. We are thus robbed of beginning the search for our unique spiritual/biological personhood. Spiritual growth, or unfolding, begins when we cease to understand or see ourselves as isolated and narrow competing egos and begin to identify with other humans from our family and friends to, eventually, our species. But the deep ecology sense of self requires a further maturity and growth, an identification which goes beyond humanity to include the nonhuman world. We must see beyond our narrow contemporary cultural assumptions and values, and the conventional wisdom of our time and place, and this is best achieved by the meditative deep questioning process. Only in this way can we hope to attain full mature personhood and uniqueness.

A nurturing nondominating society can help in the "real work" of becoming a whole person. The "real work" can be summarized symbolically as the realization of "self-in-Self" where "Self" stands for organic wholeness. This process of the full unfolding of the self can also be summarized by the phrase, "No one is saved until we are all saved," where the phrase "one" includes not only me, an individual human, but all humans, whales, grizzly bears, whole rain forest ecosystems, mountains and rivers, the tiniest microbes in the soil, and so on.

II. BIOCENTRIC EQUALITY

The intuition of biocentric equality is that all things in the biosphere have an equal right to live and blossom and to reach their own individual forms of unfolding and self-realization within the larger Self-realization. This basic intuition is that all organisms and entities in the ecosphere, as parts of the interrelated whole, are equal in intrinsic worth. Naess suggests that biocentric equality as an intuition is true in principle, although in the process of living, all species use each other as food, shelter, etc. Mutual predation is a biological fact of life, and many of the world's religions have struggled with the spiritual implications of this. Some animal liberationists who attempt to side-step this problem by advocating vegetarianism are forced to say that the entire plant kingdom including rain forests have no right to their own existence. This evasion flies in the face of the basic intuition of equality.[4] Aldo Leopold expressed this intuition when he said humans are "plain citizens" of the biotic community, not lord and master over all other species.

Biocentric equality is intimately related to the all-inclusive Self-realization in the sense that if we harm the rest of Nature then we are harming ourselves. There are no boundaries and everything is interrelated. But insofar as we perceive things as individual organisms or entities, the insight draws us to respect all human and non-human individuals in their own right as parts of the whole without feeling the need to set up hierarchies of species with humans at the top.

The practical implications of this intuition or norm suggest that we should live with minimum rather than maximum impact on other species and on the Earth in general. . . .

A fuller discussion of the biocentric norm as it unfolds itself in practice begins with the realization that we, as individual humans, and as communities of humans, have vital needs which go beyond such basics as food, water, and shelter to include love, play, creative expression, intimate relationships with a particular landscape (or Nature taken in its entirety) as well as intimate relationships with other humans, and the vital need for spiritual growth, for becoming a mature human being.

Our vital material needs are probably more simple than many realize. In technocratic-industrial societies there is overwhelming propaganda and advertising which encourages false needs and destructive desires designed to foster increased production and consumption of goods. Most of this actually diverts us from facing reality in an objective way and from beginning the "real work" of spiritual growth and maturity.

Many people who do not see themselves as supporters of deep ecology nevertheless recognize an overriding vital human need for a healthy and high-quality natural environment for humans, if not for all life, with minimum intrusion of toxic waste, nuclear radiation from human enterprises, minimum acid rain and smog, and enough free flowing wilderness so humans can get in touch with their sources, the natural rhythms and the flow of time and place. . . .

The ultimate [principles] of deep ecology suggest a view of the nature of reality and our place as an individual (many in the one) in the larger scheme of things. They cannot be fully grasped intellectually but are ultimately experiential. . . .

BASIC PRINCIPLES

1. The well-being and flourishing of human and nonhuman Life on Earth have value in themselves (synonyms: intrinsic value, inherent value). These values are independent of the usefulness of the nonhuman world for human purposes.
2. Richness and diversity of life forms contribute to the realization of these values and are also values in themselves.

3. Humans have no right to reduce this richness and diversity except to satisfy *vital* needs.

4. The flourishing of human life and cultures is compatible with a substantial decrease of the human population. The flourishing of nonhuman life requires such a decrease.

5. Present human interference with the nonhuman world is excessive, and the situation is rapidly worsening.

6. Policies must therefore be changed. These policies affect basic economic, technological, and ideological structures. The resulting state of affairs will be deeply different from the present.

7. The ideological change is mainly that of appreciating *life quality* (dwelling in situations of inherent value) rather than adhering to an increasingly higher standard of living. There will be a profound awareness of the difference between big and great.

8. Those who subscribe to the foregoing points have an obligation directly or indirectly to try to implement the necessary changes.

* * *

After spending three nights with President Theodore Roosevelt under the oaks and pine trees of Yosemite National Park in 1903, John Muir proclaimed in his journal, "Now Ho! for righteous management." Muir was hopeful at the beginning of the twentieth century that under the leadership of wise managers, the national parks and forests would be left essentially wild, preserved as watershed and wildlife habitat. The national parks would remain largely wilderness. Utilitarian uses of the national forests would respect the ongoing, healthy functioning of ecosystems. But his hopes for the wise management of the nation's forests and wild lands were soon to be destroyed.

It now seems obvious that we are in the midst of an environmental and spiritual crisis more severe than the one that sent Muir to his grave defending wild Nature in Yosemite. For now the whole planet is threatened by the possible holocaust of nuclear war and by the continued "peaceful" development of natural resources in the tropical rain forests and in the oceans. "Balanced use of resources," "wise use," "scientific management," and "genetic improvement" of forests are all central concepts of the management ideology based upon the assumption that humans are the central figures and actors in history, together with the idea that the whole of Nature is to be understood as resources for humans and thus is open for unlimited human manipulation.

Among resource managers there seems to be some awareness of the philosophical assumptions underlying the anthropocentric resource ideology. But generally the problems that arise in this kind of management are perceived to be technical, economic, or political issues. Many people trained in this ideology see themselves as being "value-free" and beyond politics in their decisions. In keeping with this ideology, when environmentalists try to discuss forestry management with public agencies such as the Forest Service, their positions and arguments are viewed from the subjective standpoint of a

"special interest" group. The generally nonreflective position of Resource Conservation and Development (RCD) managers makes it almost impossible to
discuss issues on a deeper philosophical level. The anthropocentric versus
biocentric worldviews of land use managers and environmentalists generally
mean that they share little common ground and, as a result, they talk past
each other. The basic philosophical differences tend to be obscured or de-
flected into discussions of technical issues. For example, those who oppose
aerial spraying of herbicides on forests are trapped into arguing over the research data of very technical studies of dispersion rates, the effects on pregnant women, and so on. But the chains of interrelationships in an ecosystem
are so complex that the results of such studies are usually tentative and inconclusive. And if the burden of proof is on those opposed to the spraying to
demonstrate its harmful effects, then the spraying will continue. Those with a
philosophically biocentric perspective that respects all of Nature and its processes would most likely arrive at a contrary conclusion.

The usual rhetoric of "conservation," "stewardship," and "wise use" in the
contemporary version of RCD now means in practice the development of
resources as quickly as is technically possible with the available capital to
serve human "needs." The whole of Nature and nonhuman species are not
seen as having value in themselves and the right to follow out their own
evolutionary destinies. In the ideology of RCD, humans are not understood
or experienced to be an integral part of natural processes, but rather as rightfully dominating and controlling the rest of Nature based on principles of
scientific management. This means altering Nature to produce more or "better" commodities for human consumption and directing Nature to do the
bidding of humans on the utilitarian principle of the "greatest good for the
greatest number" of humans.[5] . . .

1. Some General Suggestions

An alternative approach to that suggested by resource economists and current versions of the Resource Conservation ideology is suggested [here].

Our first principle is to encourage agencies, legislators, property owners
and managers to consider flowing with rather than forcing natural processes.
Second, in facing practical situations we favor working within the minority
tradition, in the local community, especially the bioregion.

One of the criticisms of scientific management as now practiced is the
attention to building "abstract models" which in our estimation have little
relevance to site-specific situations. For example, the U.S. Forest Service has
attempted to develop and implement decision-making by setting goals for each
forest. The goals are "commodity outputs" per time frame (usually every ten
years). A computer model (Forplan) takes data collected by sampling techniques, adds numerous questionable assumptions and yields output tables
telling the managers how many board feet or cubic feet of trees can be cut
to meet the goals. This abstracting of Nature is a dangerous and uncaring
approach and lulls the manager into thinking he has the relevant variables

under control. We need to take seriously the ecologists' principle that Nature is more complex than we now know and more complex than we possibly can know.

This is not to say we don't see some value to scientific data collection. But it should be specifically addressing a more local site, valley or bioregion. Many primal peoples were excellent observers of natural processes, knowing the weather, pattern of changes in the seasons, habits of wildlife and so forth. Science and technology can be an aid but they are no substitute for this kind of direct land wisdom.

This knowledge was used to serve vital needs for food collection, materials for building shelters, and so forth. Therefore, drawing upon the distinction in wildlife management between "hands-on" and "hands-off" techniques, Muir's righteous management (biocentric ecological management) would be essentially hands-off management.

Righteous management would also be consistent with Taoist philosophy and ways of life wherein human activities fit in and flow with the larger cycles of Nature rather than attempt to modify Nature on a large scale to fit grandiose human projects and whims. There is some indication that this is what Muir had in mind for the national forests when they were established in the 1880s and 1890s, and his concluding essay, "The Bee Pastures of California," in *The Mountains of California*, presents a vision of righteous management which has been long overlooked by planners and reform environmentalists.

Muir saw the national forests as places where the flow of wild Nature would be protected against the ravages of expanding industrial civilization. . . [and] national parks as places where wilderness would predominate. It is perhaps ironic that now in the United States nearly every national park is also being threatened by encroaching industrial civilization. And as ecologists such as Paul Erlich call for vast unmanaged wilderness ecosystems as essential for human survival, the Forest Service has launched a publicity campaign through its pamphlets and other means to condition the public to accept "tree farms" in place of natural forests. "Is Nature Always Right?" one pamphlet asks. "Nature often works in slow, ponderous rhythms which are not always efficient" and "natural growth results in a crowded haphazard mix." The forester can give Nature a helping hand to provide forest products for growing human needs.

There seems to be a general principle involved here that, in terms of hands-on, manipulative management, increasingly intensive management produces a host of unintended consequences which are perceived by the managers and the general public, and especially by the environmental/ecology movement, as real and severe problems. The usual approach, however, is to seek ever more intensive management, which spawns even more problems. And each of these problems is seen as separate, with separate experts and interest groups speaking to each other across a chasm of different technical vocabularies, hidden agendas and very narrow ideas of their own self-interest.

An extreme example of this situation, well documented by historians, ecologists and government agencies, is the situation in California's Central Valley, where the intensively managed agri-industry, which claims as its goal, "feeding the hungry of the world," is now creating an unhealthy, almost unfit environment for many human inhabitants of the Valley. Massive construction projects designed to bring more water to more acres of land have caused desertification, air and water pollution, failure of the underground water system and destruction of fisheries and estuaries in the San Francisco Bay and Sacramento River delta.

Alternatives can be derived from Aldo Leopold's land ethic, which he states as a general principle for maintaining the integrity of natural processes. The land—birds, plants, soil, etc.—is included in the community along with humans, and consideration of vital human needs is placed in the context of the needs of others for self-realization. Both individuals and collectives of organisms and ecosystems are considered when making decisions.

For example, when it is shown that a proposed project will threaten a rare or endangered species, much more careful consideration is given to the project. Mitigation by removing some individuals of the endangered species, such as California condors from their nests or eggs from their nests, breeding some of these in captivity or freezing their genes as genetic resources for future generations are *not* acceptable alternatives.

The killing of the remaining whales to "serve the food needs" or the "needs for jobs" of a few people for a few years in the whaling industry is not an acceptable alternative. Furthermore, ecologists and others interested in preserving wild species should not be required to solve all the problems of jobs, urbanization, and industries in order to advocate protection of other species. Environmentalists are never against jobs as some opponents charge, but are certainly proponents of jobs which are ecologically benign.

2. "Not Do"

Many of the specific goals of preservation of habitat of other species consistent with biocentric equality are summarized in the phrase "Let the river live," where the "river" includes a broader definition of living—not just human populations or even the trees along the river, but the ecosystem of flowing energy. Another perspective on management consistent with Naess's key slogan, "simple in means, rich in ends," is "not do."

It is well documented, for example, that huge areas of the American West have been overgrazed by domestic livestock during the last hundred years so that the carrying capacity, the ability of the range to support certain "head" of livestock over the long term, has diminished. But federal subsidies in the form of low grazing fees (in comparison to fees charged on private lands) and letting ranchers (because of their political pull) continue running livestock on overgrazed lands in herds which are too large for sustainability, increase the problem.

A simple "not do" solution is to end federal subsidies and restrict use of public lands for grazing to a level consistent with recovery of grasslands as estimated by professional ecologists.

3. Living in Mixed Communities of Humans and Nonhumans

While the bioregional, minority tradition seems appropriate to us for cultivating ecological consciousness, allowing for biological diversity and simplicity of means, there are tough, practical decisions to make. We cite several examples.

Consistent with our ultimate norms, it seems that one principle is protection of endangered species of plants and animals as part of the general norm of unity in diversity.

Another norm is bioregional responsibility. The local community is the place for decisions. However, what happens when a local community's needs conflict with the norm of protecting species diversity?

Such a situation occurred on the north slope of Alaska where native Eskimos were hunting bowhead whales in the 1970s. The International Whaling Commission ruled that this was an endangered species of whale and considered a total ban on the killing of bowheads. However, the native Eskimos pleaded that it was part of their tradition to kill whales. Their myths and lifestyle were dependent on it. If they didn't kill whales they would be more dependent on canned meat from the "lower forty-eight" given them by welfare departments.

This somewhat split the environmentalists. Many groups supported a total ban on the killing of bowheads until ecologists determined that their population had "sufficiently increased," but Friends of the Earth took the position that Eskimos be allowed to take a regulated number of bowheads using their traditional methods (no advanced technology for killing them was allowed). . . .

4. Recovery of Damaged Ecosystems

We have argued that Muir's righteous management is management based upon a worldview and a spiritual way of life similar to the outlook of Taoism, the American Indians, and other primal societies wherein the best management is, in principle, the least management. But we also realize that vast areas of the Earth have been seriously distressed and disrupted by careless and highly exploitive human activity. Strip mining and deforestation are only two obvious examples in the United States. Should these kinds of environmental degradation be left to heal naturally or should humans intervene to help the healing process? . . .

It would seem to be compatible with deep ecology principles and righteous management that, in general, if humans have distressed an ecosystem, they have an obligation to help heal that system. The recovery of human-damaged ecosystems is not strictly a scientific matter, for reasons mentioned earlier, but would involve a combination of art, science, and most importantly, a sense of place. That is, those humans involved in reinhabiting or restoring an ecosystem to health would need to be sensitive to the spiritual as well as the biological needs of that place. . . .

When the patient is in a state of crisis, the healers need both skills and luck to stabilize the condition. This was the case with Redwood Creek. Until the 1880s, this watershed was inhabited by old-growth redwoods, black bear, Roosevelt elk, oak trees, egrets, river otter, Pacific salmon, and a small tribe (two to four hundred) of Chilula Indians. The Chilula led lives filled with rituals and with a sense of place. Their "churches" were rocks and waterfalls and small lakes where they prayed, held puberty rites, communed with the spirits, and sought to understand. They ate salmon from Redwood Creek and engaged in some prescribed burning, allowing grasses to continue to grow which they used in making baskets. After 1880 the Indians were removed to the Hupa reservation and the lands of Redwood Creek passed to large timber corporations. As late as 1950, however, most of the old-growth redwood forests (which were considered the only commercially valuable wood in the forests) were still intact.

By 1978, only 9,500 acres of old-growth redwoods remained. Clear-cuts on steep slopes were eroding. Exotic species of trees had been planted in some areas by the timber corporations. In the Act establishing Redwood National Park, Congress directed the Park Service to undertake ". . . the rehabilitation of areas within and upstream from the park contributing significant sedimentation because of past logging disturbances and road conditions. . . ."[6] The land managers agreed that, "Successful management of erosion is as much a philosophical and political problem as a technical one."

In the first three years of rehabilitation, sites were selected on the basis of the seriousness of the "wounds," estimates of the potential for increasing sediment to the drainage, and "complications" such as gullying from the failure of culverts on logging roads. Each site had a "prescription" written for it.

An example of a site-specific prescription is found in the recommendations for the Tall Trees Grove, an alluvial flat of old-growth redwoods containing some of the tallest trees on Earth. This grove is surrounded on three sides by Redwood Creek, which is still carrying heavy quantities of man-induced erosion material, and by clear-cuts on the uphill slopes. The report claimed that: "Most likely the Tall Trees Grove has a long history of flooding and sedimentation, as with other similar groves on alluvial flats, and it is necessary to see that this continues with minimum adverse change. This will be difficult, because the past half-century has been one of major changes on the watershed related to human use." A whole series of subtle conditions relating to rates of sedimentation, fine sediment versus coarse bedloads, rates of tree growth, and seedling survival was found to be necessary for maintaining these groves. The long, slow, inexorable processes of Nature could not be circumvented by technological ingenuity if these groves were to continue to prosper. It was concluded that, "Management of these groves with the objective of their preservation must allow for such events and their maintenance."

The ecological and rehabilitation studies which resulted in the prescriptions for maintaining the redwood groves, together with other practices such as allowing forest fires to burn in uninhabited areas, further underscores Commoner's law that "Nature knows best." It is encouraging to see the U.S. Park Service begin to incorporate ecological wisdom in their management plans and as an ideal by which to guide management and rehabilitation policy. . . .

NOTES

1. Arne Naess, "The Shallow and The Deep, Long-Range Ecology Movements: A Summary," *Inquiry* 16 (Oslo, 1973), pp. 95–100.
2. Theodore Roszak, *Where the Wasteland Ends* (New York: Anchor, 1972).
3. Warwick Fox, "The Intuition of Deep Ecology" (Paper presented at the Ecology and Philosophy Conference, Australian National University, September, 1983). To appear in *The Ecologist* (England, Fall 1984).
4. Tom Regan, *The Case for Animal Rights* (New York: Random House, 1983). For excellent critiques of the animal rights movement, see John Rodman, "The Liberation of Nature?" *Inquiry* 20 (Oslo, 1977). J. Baird Callicott, "Animal Liberation," *Environmental Ethics* 2, 4, (1980); see also John Rodman, "Four Forms of Ecological Consciousness Reconsidered" in T. Attig and D. Scherer, eds., *Ethics and the Environment* (Englewood Cliffs, N.J.: Prentice-Hall, 1983).
5. John Rodman, "Resource Conservation: Economics and Beyond" (Unpublished paper, Claremont, Ca.: Pitzer College, 1976).
6. Public Law 95–250, Sec. 01 (a) (b).

Radical American Environmentalism and Wilderness Preservation: A Third World Critique

Ramachandra Guha

Ramachandra Guha, an Indian historian and sociologist on the faculty of Delhi University, is the author of *The Unquiet Woods: Ecological Change and Peasant Resistance in the Indian Himalaya* (1990). In this essay, Guha criticizes the position of American deep ecology, as represented by Bill Sessions and George Devall, from the perspective of an inhabitant of the Third World. The gist of his critique, which he develops from four different angles, is that deep ecology fails to be responsive to human needs, particularly the needs of those in society who are economically disadvantaged. Because it takes the preservation of wilderness to be the central concern of an environmental ethics, American deep ecology in Guha's view goes hand in hand with American consumer society. Deep ecology conceives of wilderness areas as places where one can enjoy time away from civilization, but it does not wonder about the deeper relations between civilization and the environment. As a result, he claims that deep ecologists are blind to the relationships between the overconsumption of resources in industrial society on the one hand and the degradation of the environment on the other. Because of these limitations, Guha doubts that deep ecology can serve as a viable model for a global environmental ethics. As a model for a Third World environmental ethics, he believes that deep ecology's focus on wilderness preservation is "positively harmful." From Guha's point of view, a better approach to solving the problems of the environment, not only for the Third World but for America as well, is one that would combine environmental concern with a less consumer-oriented and more peaceful way of life.

I. INTRODUCTION

The respected radical journalist Kirkpatrick Sale recently celebrated "the passion of a new and growing movement that has become disenchanted with the environmental establishment and has in recent years mounted a serious and sweeping attack on it—style, substance, systems, sensibilities and all."[1] The vision of those whom Sale calls the "New Ecologists"—and what I refer to in this article as deep ecology—is a compelling one. Decrying the narrowly economic goals of mainstream environmentalism, this new movement aims at nothing less than a philosophical and cultural revolution in human attitudes toward nature. In contrast to the conventional lobbying efforts of environmental professionals based in Washington, it proposes a militant defence of "Mother Earth," an unflinching opposition to human attacks on

From *Environmental Ethics* 11 (Spring 1989), 71–83.

undisturbed wilderness. With their goals ranging from the spiritual to the political, the adherents of deep ecology span a wide spectrum of the American environmental movement. . . .

In this article I develop a critique of deep ecology from the perspective of a sympathetic outsider. . . . I speak admittedly as a partisan, but of the environmental movement in India, a country with an ecological diversity comparable to the U.S., but with a radically dissimilar cultural and social history. . . . Specifically, I examine the cultural rootedness of a philosophy that likes to present itself in universalistic terms. I make two main arguments: first, that deep ecology is uniquely American, and despite superficial similarities in rhetorical style, the social and political goals of radical environmentalism in other cultural contexts (e.g., West Germany and India) are quite different; second, that the social consequences of putting deep ecology into practice on a worldwide basis (what its practitioners are aiming for) are very grave indeed.

II. THE TENETS OF DEEP ECOLOGY

. . . Adherents of the deep ecological perspective in [America], while arguing intensely among themselves over its political and philosophical implications, share some fundamental premises about human-nature interactions. As I see it, the defining characteristics of deep ecology are fourfold:

First, deep ecology argues, that the environmental movement must shift from an "anthropocentric" to a "biocentric" perspective. In many respects, an acceptance of the primacy of this distinction constitutes the litmus test of deep ecology. A considerable effort is expended by deep ecologists in showing that the dominant motif in Western philosophy has been anthropocentric— i.e., the belief that man and his works are the center of the universe—and conversely, in identifying those lonely thinkers (Leopold, Thoreau, Muir, Aldous Huxley, Santayana, etc.) who, in assigning man a more humble place in the natural order, anticipated deep ecological thinking. In the political realm, meanwhile, establishment environmentalism (shallow ecology) is chided for casting its arguments in human-centered terms. Preserving nature, the deep ecologists say, has an intrinsic worth quite apart from any benefits preservation may convey to future human generations. The anthropocentric-biocentric distinction is accepted as axiomatic by deep ecologists, it structures their discourse, and much of the present discussion remains mired within it.

The second characteristic of deep ecology is its focus on the preservation of unspoilt wilderness—and the restoration of degraded areas to a more pristine condition—to the relative (and sometimes absolute) neglect of other issues on the environmental agenda. . . . Morally, [this] is an imperative that follows from the biocentric perspective; other species of plants and animals, and nature itself, have an intrinsic right to exist. . . . The preservation of wilderness also turns on a scientific argument—viz., the value of biological diversity in stabilizing ecological regimes and in retaining a gene pool for future generations. Truly radical policy proposals have been put forward by deep ecologists on the basis of these arguments. The influential poet Gary Snyder, for example, would like to see a 90 percent reduction in human populations to allow a restoration of pristine environments, while others have argued forcefully that a large portion of the globe must be immediately cordoned off from human beings.

Third, there is a widespread invocation of Eastern spiritual traditions as forerunners of deep ecology. Deep ecology, it is suggested, was practiced both by major religious traditions and at a more popular level by "primal" peoples in non-Western settings. This complements the search for an authentic lineage in Western thought. At one level, the task is to recover those dissenting voices within the Judeo-Christian tradition; at another, to suggest that religious traditions in other cultures are, in contrast, dominantly if not exclusively "biocentric" in their orientation. This coupling of (ancient) Eastern and (modern) ecological wisdom seemingly helps consolidate the claim that deep ecology is a philosophy of universal significance.

Fourth, deep ecologists, whatever their internal differences, share the belief that they are the "leading edge" of the environmental movement. As the polarity of the shallow/deep and anthropocentric/biocentric distinctions makes clear, they see themselves as the spiritual, philosophical, and political vanguard of American and world environmentalism.

III. TOWARD A CRITIQUE

Although I analyze each of these tenets independently, it is important to recognize, as deep ecologists are fond of remarking in reference to nature, the interconnectedness and unity of these individual themes.

1. Insofar as it has begun to act as a check on man's arrogance and ecological hubris, the transition from an anthropocentric (human-centered) to a biocentric (humans as only one element in the ecosystem) view in both religious and scientific traditions is only to be welcomed. What is unacceptable are the radical conclusions drawn by deep ecology, in particular, that intervention in nature should be guided primarily by the need to preserve biotic integrity rather than by the needs of humans. The latter for deep ecologists is anthropocentric, the former biocentric. This dichotomy is, however, of very little use in understanding the dynamics of environmental degradation. The two fundamental ecological problems facing the globe are (i) over-consumption by the industrialized world and by urban elites in the Third World and (ii) growing militarization, both in a short-term sense (i.e., ongoing regional wars) and in a long-term sense (i.e., the arms race and the prospect of nuclear annihilation). Neither of these problems has any tangible connection to the anthropocentric-biocentric distinction. Indeed, the agents of these processes would barely comprehend this philosophical dichotomy. The proximate causes of the ecologically wasteful characteristics of industrial society and of militarization are far more mundane: at an aggregate level, the dialectic of economic and political structures, and at a micro-level, the lifestyle choices of individuals. These causes cannot be reduced, whatever the level of analysis, to

a deeper anthropocentric attitude toward nature; on the contrary, by constituting a grave threat to human survival, the ecological degradation they cause does not even serve the best interests of human beings! If my identification of the major dangers to the integrity of the natural world is correct, invoking the bogy of anthropocentricism is at best irrelevant and at worst a dangerous obfuscation.

2. If the above dichotomy is irrelevant, the emphasis on wilderness is positively harmful when applied to the Third World. If in the U.S. the preservationist/utilitarian division is seen as mirroring the conflict between "people" and "interests," in countries such as India the situation is very nearly the reverse. Because India is a long settled and densely populated country in which agrarian populations have a finely balanced relationship with nature, the setting aside of wilderness areas has resulted in a direct transfer of resources from the poor to the rich. Thus, Project Tiger, a network of parks hailed by the international conservation community as an outstanding success, sharply posits the interests of the tiger against those of poor peasants living in and around the reserve. The designation of tiger reserves was made possible only by the physical displacement of existing villages and their inhabitants; their management requires the continuing exclusion of peasants and livestock. The initial impetus for setting up parks for the tiger and other large mammals such as the rhinoceros and elephant came from two social groups, first, a class of ex-hunters turned conservationists belonging mostly to the declining Indian feudal elite and second, representatives of international agencies, such as the World Wildlife Fund (WWF) and the International Union for the Conservation of Nature and Natural Resources (IUCN), seeking to transplant the American system of national parks onto Indian soil. In no case have the needs of the local population been taken into account, and as in many parts of Africa, the designated wildlands are managed primarily for the benefit of rich tourists. Until very recently, wildlands preservation has been identified with environmentalism by the state and the conservation elite; in consequence, environmental problems that impinge far more directly on the lives of the poor—e.g., fuel, fodder, water shortages, soil erosion, and air and water pollution—have not been adequately addressed.

Deep ecology provides, perhaps unwittingly, a justification for the continuation of such narrow and inequitable conservation practices under a newly acquired radical guise. Increasingly, the international conservation elite is using the philosophical, moral, and scientific arguments used by deep ecologists in advancing their wilderness crusade. A striking but by no means atypical example is the recent plea by a prominent American biologist for the takeover of large portions of the globe by the author and his scientific colleagues. Writing in a prestigious scientific forum, the *Annual Review of Ecology and Systematics*, Daniel Janzen argues that only biologists have the competence to decide how the tropical landscape should be used. . . . Janzen exhorts his colleagues to advance their territorial claims on the tropical world more forcefully, warning that the very existence of these areas is at stake: "if biologists want a tropics in which to biologize, they are going to have to buy it with care, energy, effort, strategy, tactics, time, and cash."[2]

This frankly imperialist manifesto highlights the multiple dangers of the preoccupation with wilderness preservation that is characteristic of deep ecology. As I have suggested, it seriously compounds the neglect by the American movement of far more pressing environmental problems within the Third World. But perhaps more importantly, and in a more insidious fashion, it also provides an impetus to the imperialist yearning of Western biologists and their financial sponsors, organizations such as the WWF and IUCN. The wholesale transfer of a movement culturally rooted in American conservation history can only result in the social uprooting of human populations in other parts of the globe.

3. I come now to the persistent invocation of Eastern philosophies as antecedent in point of time but convergent in their structure with deep ecology. Complex and internally differentiated religious traditions—Hinduism, Buddhism, and Taoism—are lumped together as holding a view of nature believed to be quintessentially biocentric. Individual philosophers such as the Taoist Lao Tzu are identified as being forerunners of deep ecology. Even an intensely political, pragmatic and Christian influenced thinker such as Gandhi has been accorded a wholly undeserved place in the deep ecological pantheon. Thus the Zen teacher Robert Aitken Roshi makes the strange claim that Gandhi's thought was not human-centered and that he practiced an embryonic form of deep ecology which is "traditionally Eastern and is found with differing emphasis in Hinduism, Taoism and in Theravada and Mahayana Buddhism."[3] Moving away from the realm of high philosophy and scriptural religion, deep ecologists make the further claim that at the level of material and spiritual practice "primal" peoples subordinated themselves to the integrity of the biotic universe they inhabited.

I have indicated that this appropriation of Eastern traditions is in part dictated by the need to construct an authentic lineage and in part a desire to present deep ecology as a universalistic philosophy. . . . As it stands, [this reading] does considerable violence to the historical record. Throughout most recorded history the characteristic form of human activity in the "East" has been a finely tuned but nonetheless conscious and dynamic manipulation of nature. Although mystics such as Lao Tzu did reflect on the spiritual essence of human relations with nature, it must be recognized that such ascetics and their reflections were supported by a society of cultivators whose relationship with nature was a far more *active* one. Many agricultural communities do have a sophisticated knowledge of the natural environment that may equal (and sometimes surpass) codified "scientific" knowledge; yet, the elaboration of such traditional ecological knowledge (in both material and spiritual contexts) can hardly be said to rest on a mystical affinity with nature of a deep ecological kind. . .

In a brilliant article, the Chicago historian Ronald Inden points out that this romantic and essentially positive view of the East is a mirror image of the scientific and essentially pejorative view normally upheld by Western scholars of the Orient. In either case, the East constitutes the Other, a body wholly separate and alien from the West; it is defined by a uniquely spiritual and nonrational "essence," even if this essence is valorized quite differently by the two schools. Eastern man exhibits a spiritual dependence with respect to nature—on the one hand, this is symptomatic of his prescientific and backward self, on the other, of his ecological wisdom and deep ecological consciousness. Both views are monolithic, simplistic, and have the characteristic effect—intended in one case, perhaps unintended in the other—of denying agency and reason to the East and making it the privileged orbit of Western thinkers. . . .

4. How radical, finally, are the deep ecologists? . . . To my mind, deep ecology is best viewed as a radical trend within the wilderness preservation movement. Although advancing philosophical rather than aesthetic arguments and encouraging political militancy rather than negotiation, its practical emphasis—viz., preservation of unspoilt nature—is virtually identical. For the mainstream movement, the function of wilderness is to provide a temporary antidote to modern civilization. As a special institution within an industrialized society, the national park "provides an opportunity for respite, contrast, contemplation, and affirmation of values for those who live most of their lives in the workaday world."[4] Indeed, the rapid increase in visitations to the national parks in postwar America is a direct consequence of economic expansion. . . .

Here, the enjoyment of nature is an integral part of the consumer society. The private automobile (and the life style it has spawned) is in many respects the ultimate ecological villain, and an untouched wilderness the prototype of ecological harmony; yet, for most Americans it is perfectly consistent to drive a thousand miles to spend a holiday in a national park. They possess a vast, beautiful, and sparsely populated continent and are also able to draw upon the natural resources of large portions of the globe by virtue of their economic and political dominance. In consequence, America can simultaneously enjoy the material benefits of an expanding economy and the aesthetic benefits of unspoilt nature. The two poles of "wilderness" and "civilization" mutually coexist in an internally coherent whole, and philosophers of both poles are assigned a prominent place in this culture. Paradoxically as it may seem, it is no accident that Star Wars technology and deep ecology both find their fullest expression in that leading sector of Western civilization, California.

Deep ecology runs parallel to the consumer society without seriously questioning its ecological and socio-political basis. . . . The archetypal concerns of radical environmentalists in other cultural contexts are in fact quite different. The German Greens, for example, have elaborated a devastating critique of industrial society which turns on the acceptance of environmental limits to growth. Pointing to the intimate links between industrialization, militari-zation, and conquest, the Greens argue that economic growth in the West has historically rested on the economic and ecological exploitation of the Third World. . . .

[Hence,] the roots of global ecological problems lie in the disproportionate share of resources consumed by the industrialized countries as a whole *and* the urban elite within the Third World. Since it is impossible to reproduce an industrial monoculture worldwide, the ecological movement in the West must begin by cleaning up its own act. . . . The expansionist character of modern Western man will have to give way to an ethic of renunciation and self-limitation, in which spiritual and communal values play an increasing role in sustaining social life. . . .

Many elements of the Green program find a strong resonance in countries such as India, where a history of Western colonialism and industrial development has benefited only a tiny elite while exacting tremendous social and environmental costs. The ecological battles presently being fought in India have as their epicenter the conflict over nature between the subsistence and largely rural sector and the vastly more powerful commercial-industrial sector. Perhaps the most celebrated of these battles concerns the Chipko (Hug the Tree) movement, a peasant movement against deforestation in the Himalayan foothills. Chipko is only one of several movements that have sharply questioned the nonsustainable demand being placed on the land and vegetative base by urban centers and industry. These include opposition to large dams by displaced peasants, the conflict between small artisan fishing and large-scale trawler fishing for export, the countrywide movements against commercial forest operations, and opposition to industrial pollution among downstream agricultural and fishing communities.

Two features distinguish these environmental movements from their Western counterparts. First, for the sections of society most critically affected by environmental degradation—poor and landless peasants, women, and tribals— it is a question of sheer survival, not of enhancing the quality of life. Second, and as a consequence, the environmental solutions they articulate deeply involve questions of equity as well as economic and political redistribution. Highlighting these differences, a leading Indian environmentalist stresses that "environmental protection per se is of least concern to most of these groups. Their main concern is about the use of the environment and who should benefit from it." They seek to wrest control of nature away from the state and the industrial sector and place it in the hands of rural communities who live within that environment but are increasingly denied access to it. These communities have far more basic needs, their demands on the environment are far less intense, and they can draw upon a reservoir of cooperative social institutions and local ecological knowledge in managing the "commons"—forests, grasslands, and the waters—on a sustainable basis. If colonial and capitalist expansion has both accentuated social inequalities and signaled a precipitous fall in ecological wisdom, an alternate ecology must rest on an alternate society and polity as well.

This brief overview of German and Indian environmentalism has some major implications for deep ecology. Both German and Indian environmental traditions allow for a greater integration of ecological concerns with livelihood and work. They also place a greater emphasis on equity and social justice (both within individual countries and on a global scale) on the grounds that in the absence of social regeneration environmental regeneration has very little chance of succeeding. Finally, and perhaps most significantly, they have escaped the preoccupation with wilderness preservation so characteristic of American cultural and environmental history.

IV. A HOMILY

In 1958, the economist J. K. Galbraith referred to overconsumption as the unasked question of the American conservation movement. There is a marked selectivity, he wrote, "in the conservationist's approach to materials consumption. If we are concerned about our great appetite for materials, it is plausible to seek to increase the supply, to decrease waste, to make better use of the stocks available, and to develop substitutes. But what of the appetite itself. Surely this is the ultimate source of the problem. If it continues its geometric course, will it not one day have to be restrained? Yet in the literature of the resource problem this is the forbidden question. Over it hangs a nearly total silence."[5]

The consumer economy and society have expanded tremendously in the three decades since Galbraith penned these words; yet his criticisms are nearly as valid today. I have said "nearly," for there are some hopeful signs. Within the environmental movement several dispersed groups are working to develop ecologically benign technologies and to encourage less wasteful life styles. Moreover, outside the self-defined boundaries of American environmentalism, opposition to the permanent war economy is being carried on by a peace movement that has a distinguished history and impeccable moral and political credentials. . . . A truly radical ecology in the American context ought to work toward a synthesis of the appropriate technology, alternate life style, and peace movements. By making the (largely spurious) anthropocentric-biocentric distinction central to the debate, deep ecologists may have appropriated the moral high ground, but they are at the same time doing a serious disservice to American and global environmentalism.

NOTES

1. Kirkpatrick Sale, "The Forest for the Trees: Can Today's Environmentalists Tell the Difference," *Mother Jones* 11, no. 8 (November 1986): 26.
2. Daniel Janzen, "The Future of Tropical Ecology," *Annual Review of Ecology and Systematics* 17 (1986): 305–06; emphasis added.
3. Robert Aitken Roshi, "Gandhi, Dogen, and Deep Ecology," reprinted as appendix C in Bill Devall and George Sessions, *Deep Ecology: Living as if Nature Mattered* (Salt Lake City: Peregrine Smith Books, 1985).
4. Joseph Sax, *Mountains Without Handrails: Reflections on the National Parks* (Ann Arbor: University of Michigan Press, 1980), p. 42.

5. John Kenneth Galbraith, "How Much Should a Country Consume?" in Henry Jarrett, ed., *Perspectives on Conservation* (Baltimore: Johns Hopkins Press, 1958), pp. 91–92.

SUGGESTIONS FOR FURTHER READING

Callicott, J. Baird. "In Search of an Environmental Ethic." In Tom Regan, ed., *Matters of Life and Death*, 3rd ed. (New York, McGraw-Hill, 1993), pp. 322–380.

Callicott presents a thorough analysis of the development of philosophical concern about animals and the environment, from anthropomorphic responses to the environmental crisis of the 1960s through deep ecology and ecofeminism. Of particular interest are Callicott's criteria for evaluating differing views such as Singer's and Rolston's.

Elliot, Robert, ed. *Environmental Ethics.* (Oxford, England: Oxford University Press, 1995).

This is a collection of essays on a variety of topics in the field, including duties to future generations and the preservation of species and the wilderness.

Hargrove, Eugene C., ed. *The Animal Rights/Environmental Ethics Debate: The Environmental Perspective* (Albany, NY: State University of New York Press, 1992).

A variety of authors representing the environmental perspective explore the issues involved in the debate between animal rights and environmental ethics.

Leopold, Aldo. *A Sand County Almanac: And Sketches Here and There*, commemorative ed. (Oxford, England: Oxford University Press, 1977).

Originally released in 1949, this book lays out the foundations for what Leopold termed the "land ethic": an environmental ethics whose core premise is the idea that human beings are part of a "biotic team"—that is, members of a community that also includes animals, flowers and the soil.

List, Peter C. *Radical Environmentalism.* (Belmont, CA: Wadsworth, 1993).

The philosophical foundations of environmental activism are explored in this book, which includes articles on deep ecology, ecofeminism, and social ecology as well as essays dealing with Greenpeace and the Earth First! movement.

Merchant, Carolyn. *The Death of Nature.* (New York: Harper and Row, 1980).

In this important work for the development of ecofeminism, Merchant traces the history of the rise of the modern mechanistic view of nature, and shows how this view legitimated both the domination of nature and the oppression of women.

Naess, Arne. *Ecology, Community and Lifestyle: Outline of an Ecosophy.* David Rothenberg, trans. (Cambridge, England: Cambridge University Press, 1989).

This is the most complete statement of deep ecology, by the founder of this movement.

Regan, Tom. *The Case for Animal Rights* (Berkeley, CA: University of California Press, 1980).

This has become a classic defense of animal rights. Because animals have rights, Regan argues, it follows that vegetarianism is morally correct and that practices such as factory farming and the use of animals in biomedical research should be eliminated.

Singer, Peter. "Animal Liberation or Animal Rights?" *The Monist* 70 (1987), 3–13.

Singer replies here to the criticisms proffered by Regan. This issue of *The Monist* is devoted to the topic of animal rights.

_____. *Practical Ethics*, 2nd ed. (Cambridge, England: Cambridge University Press, 1993).

Chapter Three, ("Equality for Animals?,") is a follow-up to *Animal Liberation*, taking into account criticisms directed against that work. Chapter Ten, "The Environment," is a discussion of the fundamental values that go to make up an environmental ethic.

Steinbock, Bonnie. "Speciesism and the Idea of Equality," *Philosophy* 53 (April 1978), 247–256.

Steinbock argues that while animals certainly have an interest in avoiding suffering, and that while this interest provides humans with a reason for giving animals some moral consideration, it is not enough to justify giving animals and humans equal moral consideration.

Taylor, Paul W. *Respect for Nature: A Theory of Environmental Ethics* (Princeton, NJ: Princeton University Press, 1986).

Taylor argues that nonhuman organisms have equal moral standing with humans, not because they are sentient or have rights, but because each living organism has a good of its own to pursue; thus, an intrinsic value that one ought to respect.

Warren, Karen J. "The Power and the Promise of Ecological Feminism," *Environmental Ethics* 12 (Summer 1990), 125–146.

Going beyond Peter Singer's idea that the case for treating animals as the moral equals of humans can be modeled after the case for treating women as the moral equals of men, Warren argues there is an intrinsic connection between feminism and concern for the environment. She also lays out eight principles for a feminist environmental ethics, or ecofeminism.

Zimmerman, Michael E., et. al., *Environmental Philosophy: From Animal Rights to Radical Ecology* (Englewood Cliffs, NJ: Prentice-Hall, 1993).

This excellent anthology has selections from some of the most significant contributions to the field.

Chapter 8

FREEDOM OF EXPRESSION

The First Amendment to the U. S. Constitution protects the rights of citizens to make a wide variety of public statements, ranging all the way from claims that nearly everybody would agree with, to ideas and beliefs that many would find offensive, false, immoral, or demeaning and derogatory towards others. It is this latter group of controversial expressions of speech that arouse both individual passion and philosophical argumentation. Granted that a democratic society has a particular interest in preserving liberty, as well as in protecting individuals living in that society from being harmed, where should the limits to free speech be drawn? Should pornography, for example, be censored by a democratic society? Should universities restrict at least some forms of racist and other types of offensive speech? These are the questions that will form the focus of our consideration in this chapter.

THE MODERN FOUNDATION OF FREEDOM OF SPEECH

Possibly no advocate of the value of free speech is as well-known as the British philosopher John Stuart Mill, whose book *On Liberty* (1859) is a relatively brief but powerful justification for keeping social restrictions on individual liberty at a minimum. In his book, a selection from which is included in this chapter, Mill argues that the freedom to express oneself is such a fundamental condition of a democracy that it should be limited only if exercising this freedom causes harm to others. Mill's position is staunchly *antipaternalistic*: In other words, he thinks society should back off from attempts to promote the good of individuals by preventing them from exercising their freedom in ways that were harmful only to themselves. While it is not precisely certain what Mill means by "harm," it is fairly easy to identify his reasons for proposing a principle, commonly referred to as the *harm principle*, that severely limits society's right to restrict individual liberty in general, and thus, as a special case, to impose limits on freedom of expression.

One reason can be summarized as follows: *Increasing free speech increases the opportunity for discovering truth.* The clash of opinions created by open discussion and free exchange, whether live or in print, often leads to new truths in contentious areas of human life such as politics, ethics, and religion. In addition, Mill believes that often each side of an issue carried with it some insight; if one side were silenced, part of the truth would be lost. Thus, a responsible society would cultivate a "free marketplace" of opinions. Such a society would tolerate the expression of unpopular opinions as well as popular ones, not simply because it cares about promoting mutual respect among those with differing beliefs, but more importantly because it values getting at the truth.

A further danger of censorship, according to Mill, lies in the threat it poses to individual well-being. *Increasing free speech increases the opportunity for an individual to discover a way of life that best suits him or her.* Ideas and opinions open up possibilities of ways of living which one can choose to adopt for oneself in the pursuit of one's own well-being. New, non-conforming ideas can open up possibilities for new, non-conforming lifestyles that some might find more suitable to follow for their own well-being than a more established lifestyle. For example, the idea that "anything with a face deserves respect" might lead one to adopt a lifestyle centered around vegetarianism, pacifism, and other non-violent practices. Thus freedom of expression can provide a catalyst for the discovery of new ways of living whose adoption can in turn further human happiness.

Given Mill's belief that the only legitimate interest society has in curtailing what someone says is to prevent harm to others, the conditions under which speech can be censored are quite limited, and have more to do with the context of speech than with its content. Inflammatory speech or "fighting words" can be censored, because these often put a person at risk of getting harmed. Offensive forms of expression, such as expressions of religious or racial bigotry, or images that many find to be offensive, such as the artist Robert Mapplethorpe's photographs of the sexual practices of gay men, are another matter. While Mill personally found offensive speech to be contemptible, he believed that society had no authority to restrict it. One might disagree with Mill's view on this matter on the grounds that some offensive forms of expression need to be restricted because they endorse immoral personal conduct. (Some urged that exhibits of Mapplethorpe's photographs be censored for just this reason.) Here, though, Mill would contend that such restrictions would fall outside the sphere of justifiable social interference. Those who would restrict expression in the name of morality claim to know what is morally best for others, a claim Mill believes has no foundation. As long as an individual's conduct is not harming others, the judgment of whether this conduct is moral is, he thinks, best left up to that individual alone.

THE DEBATE OVER PORNOGRAPHY

Background Court Decisions

In 1956, a New York publisher and distributor of pornography named Samuel Roth appealed to the Supreme Court to overturn his conviction for violating a Federal ban on sending obscene materials through the mail. *Roth v. United States* (1957) turned out to be a landmark case in the history of Supreme Court decisions concerning pornography, with the Court going beyond the question of whether or not the particular materials sent by Roth were obscene to rule on a wider issue: Is obscenity a protected form of speech under the First Amendment? In its decision, the Court denied it was, and thus affirmed the constitutional validity of a federal statute against obscenity. Writing for the majority, Justice William Brennen defended the decision on the grounds that:

> All ideas having even the slightest redeeming social importance—unortho-dox ideas, controversial ideas, even ideas hateful to the prevailing climate of opinion—have the full protection of the guaranties [of the First Amendment]. . . . But implicit in the history of the First Amendment is the rejection of obscenity as utterly without redeeming social importance. . . . It is therefore vital that the standards for judging obscenity safeguard the protection of freedom of speech and press for material which does not treat sex in a manner appealing to prurient interest.[1]

Thus morally reprehensible ideas have social value and deserve First Amendment protection, but obscenity fails the "social value test" because it expresses no ideas whatsoever and thus is "utterly without redeeming social importance." Putting aside the issue of whether or not pornography causes social harm, Justice Brennen observed that failing this test was sufficient grounds for censorship. Interestingly enough, this decision opened up the way for the Supreme Court to later rule that the movie version of *Lady Chatterly's Lover* could not be banned on the charge that it portrayed adultery in a positive light. Likewise, bans on the book *Fanny Hill* and the Swedish film *I am Curious Yellow* were lifted when courts found these works to have "artistic merit" and thus social value.

Since the *Roth* decision, the legal concept of obscenity has undergone some modifications. The current standard for what is legally obscene comes from the case of *Miller v. California* (1973). In this case, the Supreme Court judged it was unrealistic to have a federal standard of obscenity in a country as large and diverse as the United States, where what might appear obscene, say, to residents of Utah might not appear obscene to residents of the neighboring state of Nevada. Accordingly, *Miller* recognized that obscenity was best determined at a state level. Under the standard developed in *Miller*, pornographic material can be prohibited if it meets the following criteria:

1. Taking community standards into account, the average person would find that it appeals to prurient interests.

2. As a whole, it represents sexual conduct in an obviously offensive manner.

3. As a whole, it lacks serious literary, artistic, political, or scientific value.

While this standard serves to define obscenity, it has not resolved the question of when restrictions on pornography may be legally enforced. As several of the readings in this chapter show, attention to this question in recent years has shifted away from a focus on the sexual content of pornography to the violence that is often associated with this content. In turn, this shift in focus has raised questions about the standard for restricting pornography developed in *Miller v. California.*

Pornography and Censorship: The Liberal View

The most typical argument in defense of pornography as a form of legally protected speech can be called the liberal view of pornography. In this chapter, the liberal view is defended in the selection by Barry Lynn. It is useful to distinguish between three versions of this view. The first two versions are both consequentialist in their approach and strongly influenced by the line of thought Mill pursued in *On Liberty*.

> Version One: The direct social benefits of pornography outweigh any harms it might cause to society; on this basis, pornography deserves First Amendment protection.
>
> Version Two: The potential harm caused to society by the suppression of speech, no matter how immoral or offensive such speech might be, outweighs any harm pornography might cause to society; on this basis, pornography deserves First Amendment protection.

At first glance there might not seem to be much of a difference between these two statements of the liberal view. The first version, though, makes stronger claims about the direct positive benefits of pornography than does the second version. For example, one of these claims is that pornography has a "cathartic" effect on the sexual drives of its consumers, so that a society where pornography is easily available would experience a lower rate of sexually related crimes than a society where pornography is more restricted. Another is that pornography has a "liberating" effect for some of its consumers in promoting a healthy view of human sexuality. A difficulty, though, with this line of reasoning is that it depends on inconclusive evidence. For instance, one might dispute the claim that increased access to pornography discourages rapes by pointing to the fact that many rapes often go unreported.

The second version of the liberal argument is more concerned with the potential harm caused by censorship than with the possible direct benefits of pornography. Adhering closely to Mill's defense of freedom of expression, supporters of this view take the position that censorship of pornography cannot be justified on the grounds that pornography is immoral or offensive. Supporters of this argument believe that censorship cannot be justified on the grounds that pornography poses a threat of harm to society, because they suspect that censorship itself poses a greater threat of harm to society. Even if, they might claim, pornography should in an ideal world be prohibited, prohibiting it in the real world requires giving the power to regulate speech to real, and hence less than ideal, people. The danger that the people given such power may misuse or abuse that power outweighs the potential harms that pornography might cause. Because much disagreement surrounds this particular point, anyone arguing from this version of the liberal position needs either to be prepared to show that a causal relationship between pornography and social harm cannot be definitely established or that its social harms are outweighed by the harms caused by censorship.

A third version of the liberal argument could be stated as follows:

> Version Three: The freedom to express oneself is an important component in personal autonomy. Because of this, pornography deserves First Amendment protection, as one ought to be able to choose to express oneself in an indecent or obscene manner, without interference from the state, if that is what one wishes to do.

Unlike the first two versions of the liberal view, this version provides non-consequentialist reasons for the state's not interfering with pornographic types of expression. In other words, it accepts freedom of expression as desirable in its own right, rather than because of the positive social outcomes to which freedom of expression could lead. At the heart of this version lies the moral importance of autonomy, the ability to decide a course of action for oneself, without the interference of others. One could also extend this argument to support the idea that the state should not interfere with one's access to pornographic materials, as the choice of whether or not to be a consumer of pornography is a choice that, on this line of reasoning, is best left up to each individual.

Arguments in Favor of Censorship

Arguments supporting the censorship of pornography in a democratic society generally involve one or more of the following claims:

1. The majority of people in society agree that pornography is morally distasteful.
2. If allowed to spread, pornography can cause grave damage to the moral fabric of society.
3. Pornography is directly harmful to particular members of society.

Taken by itself, the first claim would not provide a very persuasive basis for censorship, at least for followers of Mill. Why is that so? After all, some of one's most passionate commitments often lie behind one's beliefs that certain activities or attitudes are morally distasteful; and it might be supposed that if most members in a society express passionate opposition to pornography on the grounds that it is morally distasteful then pornography should be suppressed simply because a majority is against it. Still, no matter how high public opinion might ride against pornography, this alone does not imply that this majority should have a legal right to impose their beliefs on others who disagree with them. Again, the key principle here is the harm principle, which in this case calls for toleration of the moral beliefs of a minority group.

A more promising case against permitting pornography in democratic society can be made by looking at the first and second claims together. Suppose the majority of members in society find pornography to be morally distasteful, but in spite of this fact place very few controls on pornography other than to limit its availability to consenting adults and to make the production and distribution of child pornography illegal. Over time, the easy availability of pornography would cause the moral tone of society to deteriorate. It can be argued that pornography works much like advertising in its ability to affect behavior through its very presence. Images of consumer goods make people buy products; pornographic images of sex put sex on people's minds. As these images in a society proliferate, sexual images in general will proliferate. As such a society becomes increasingly preoccupied with sex, a shift occurs: Things such as the use of sexually explicit language, once thought improper in the course of ordinary conversation, will become the norm.[2] Since this society would not be one that a majority opposed to pornography would want to live in, so this argument goes, this majority could rightly control the spread of pornography.

This argument raises two questions that its defenders need to address. First of all, is public opinion really aligned against pornography in the way specified in claim 1? Does general opposition to pornography on moral grounds in fact exist? Secondly, even if a poll were to be taken that confirmed the existence of this opposition, one might still wonder about the basis of this opposition. What lies behind moral outrage against pornography? It has been argued that only if it can be shown that this outrage reflects not simply joint but also *rational* agreement, rather than emotions or prejudice, should pornography be restricted.

Another argument supporting the second claim above is offered in this chapter by Raymond Gastil. Gastil claims that the easy availability of pornographic materials in a society tilts the interest of members of that society toward obtaining pleasure. This disrupts social interest in other goods that are necessary to be cultivated if a society is not to suffer serious harm.

The third claim above states that particular persons, not the moral fabric of society, are the direct victims of pornography. Those who share this viewpoint, including many feminist philosophers, claim that pornography ought to be legally restricted because it causes a variety of harms, especially to women. Pornography in general is said to harm women through portraying them as mere sexual objects, a portrayal that promotes disrespect towards women and also reinforces women's place in society as "second-class citizens." Pornographic images showing women being violently degraded and abused are also said to harm women by leading to incidents of sexually-related crimes and domestic violence. In 1986, for instance, a commission formed by then–Attorney General Edwin Meese to investigate whether pornography causes harm concluded that clinical evidence overwhelmingly suggests that exposure to violent pornography has a causal connection to acts of aggression toward women. However, has the evidence for this connection been established beyond all question? Those favoring the liberal position would claim that it has not and would argue that many factors besides pornography play a more important causal role in violent behavior against women.

No matter where one stands on the question of pornography's role in causing social harm, it is clear that much of the debate over this issue in recent years has shifted in focus away from the obscenity considerations at stake in *Miller v. California*. In one of the readings in this chapter, Judith DeCew explores a question central to the new terms of the current debate: Ought pornography to be regulated not so much for the *sexual explicitness* of its images but for their *violent* sexual character? Even if it cannot be conclusively shown that violent pornography leads to physical harm against women, she maintains, it does not automatically follow that one ought to adopt the liberal view on pornography. Because it suggests the acceptability of treating human beings in an undignified manner, violent pornography is morally wrong and thus reasonably subject to social condemnation and appropriate action.

Pornography and Women's Civil Rights

In considering the question of what legal sanctions, if any, are appropriate for a democratic society to exert against pornography, some feminists have doubted whether it is reasonable to consider pornography as a free speech issue at all. Developing this doubt into an approach for the social control of pornography, such thinkers have not urged that regulations for pornography be pursued under the First Amendment. Rather they have proposed that pornography be best seen in the light of the Fourteenth Amendment, as an issue of civil rights. Law professor Catharine MacKinnon, for example, has argued that pornography is best seen not as obscene words or degrading images, but as acts that define what it is to be female in present-day society. In her view, the act of pornography defines women as being subjugated to men, and thus less than their equals. Pornography turns out to be a form of sexual discrimination against women.

Along with her colleague Andrea Dworkin, MacKinnon has worked to develop antipornography statutes reflective of the idea that pornography harms women by violating their civil rights. One such statute, proposed for the city of Indianapolis and tested in *American Booksellers Association, Inc. v. Hudnut*, selections of which are included in this chapter, was overturned on grounds that it sought to limit pornography for its content and thus was unconstitutional. Still, as Rae Langton shows in one of this chapter's essays, good philosophical reasons can be identified for taking pornography to be an act rather than an expression. Drawing upon the work of the British ordinary language philosopher J. L. Austin, Langton identifies pornography as a "speech act," an act which drowns out the less powerful voices of those who wish not only to represent women's sexuality in ways that question the representations offered by pornography, but who also wish to act with their speech by protesting pornography and violence against women. On this basis, pornography can be said to silence the voices of women, and thus legal restrictions on pornography, Langton argues, may be appropriate.

FREE SPEECH IN THE ENVIRONMENT OF HIGHER EDUCATION

In American society, one of the most controversial debates presently taking place regarding freedom of expression centers on the question: Do colleges and universities have a moral right to regulate offensive speech? At the beginning of this chapter, we pointed out that a democratic society has two interests that need to be considered in looking at the issue of freedom of expression: an interest in preserving liberty, and an interest in protecting its population from harm. As institutions within American society, colleges and universities share these two interests. It could also be argued that institutions of higher learning have *special* responsibilities in both these areas. Because of their commitments to the pursuit of truth and knowledge, universities need to guarantee a supportive environment for free and open discussion of ideas and issues, no matter how controversial these might be. In other words, universities have a duty to preserve academic freedom by promoting freedom of expression and the opportunity to debate differing points of view. Likewise, because they are also living and learning *communities*, universities need to make an effort to promote values, such as trust and respect for others, that help to create a sense of belonging to a larger whole. In addition to these considerations, universities by law need to guarantee all of their students the equal opportunity to an education.

Until fairly recently, the focus of free speech issues within the university has tended to be on the first of these responsibilities. During the period of the Vietnam War, for instance, many students defended their right to publicly express their opposition to this war and to openly criticize university administrators who were supportive of it. "Free speech zones" and "teach-ins" during this time provided students an opportunity to express controversial political opinions without fear of censorship by university administrators.

Today, the focus has shifted to involve *both* responsibilities mentioned in the preceding paragraph. Two factors largely account for this shift: the rise in gender, ethnic, and cultural diversity within student body populations, and an increase in incidents where individual students or groups of students are the real or perceived "targets" of offensive expression. Consider the following incidents, both actual and fictitious:

1. A fraternity at a large state university advertises a "South of the Border" party using T-shirts on which appear a caricature of a Hispanic male in an advanced state of intoxication.
2. A male professor, teaching a course in advanced thermodynamics, constantly tells his students that women are incapable of becoming good engineers.
3. The words "Jesus Saves" are scrawled in huge letters across posters placed around campus announcing a lecture and other events connected to the celebration of "Gay Pride Week."
4. Two African-American students move into a dorm room next to two Caucasian students. The next day, on the door to their room, the Caucasian students put up Confederate flag decals and a map of Africa on which they have written racial slurs.

How should a university deal with these incidents? Should any or all of them be tolerated, both in the specific name of academic freedom and in the broader name of freedom of expression? Or should a university take a stand against offensive expression? If it takes a stand, should it do so by developing a "speech code" that would rule some types of offensive expression off-limits? Earlier, in speaking about John Stuart Mill, we introduced the concept of "offensive" speech without specifying what *gives* speech the character of being offensive to begin with. To better understand the debate around the questions just mentioned, we need to take a closer look at what it means for something to be offensive, as well as the relation between offensive speech and harm.

What is "Offensiveness?"

"Offensiveness" is not that simple to define.[3] One reason for this is that the state of being offended can vary widely. One can be offended and experience a slight feeling of annoyance, but one can also be offended and experience feelings of extreme disgust and revulsion. Annoyance, disgust, and revulsion are, however, all unpleasant mental states. It also seems reasonable to say that there is nothing one can do to offend oneself. However, even though offense is caused by the actions of others, one's own beliefs are directly involved in the experience. Consider a person who is offended by the sight of an interracial couple holding hands. Without this person believing that interracial relationships are morally wrong, the experience of being offended could not occur.

A conflict, then, between one's own beliefs and the beliefs implied or expressed by another's conduct or speech is another important element of the experience of offense. In the second example mentioned earlier, a student might experience a feeling of disgust upon hearing the professor's remark, if it runs directly counter to his strongly held belief that women can be just as proficient engineers as men.

The direct involvement of a person's beliefs in the experience of being offended points to a way of distinguishing offense from harm. It is possible for you to be harmed without your beliefs playing any role in the matter.

Suppose you are riding in a car with a friend who decides to light up a cigarette. You might find this conduct offensive, if you believe it is important to maintain one's personal health. You might also be harmed by the second-hand smoke coming from the cigarette. Here, though, the possibility of your being harmed would have nothing to do with your beliefs concerning the importance of preserving one's health, the way that friends ought to treat other friends, or anything else.

In one of the readings in this chapter, Joel Feinberg recognizes that even if the evils caused by offensive acts are not as great as those caused by harmful ones, they are still evils nonetheless. This suggests that under some conditions society can legitimately limit conduct or expression that is offensive to others. Exactly what these conditions might be is the issue Feinberg wrestles with in this selection.

Offensive Speech and Verbal Harassment

Although it is true that nearly anything can be found to be offensive by someone, some expressions of speech, in certain contexts, tend to provoke a more intense feeling of offense than others. Of particular importance for the question of the regulation of speech on college campuses are expressions of speech that insult, indicate bias toward or devalue a group of people taken as a whole. If one is exposed to such speech *and* if one is a member of the particular group addressed by the speech, one might very well experience more than just a feeling of unpleasantness or even disgust. Because she believes that women can be good engineers and because she thinks of herself as a female pre-professional, a female student of the faculty member described above could experience a feeling of offense combined with anxiety and perhaps even fear. Instances where someone is called names that show contempt for that person's racial or ethnic background can produce a similar feeling.

In the light of this, a policy developed to regulate speech at Stanford University is worth considering. In this policy, included in this chapter's final reading selection by Charles R. Lawrence III, one of this policy's authors, a line was drawn between protected forms of offensive speech and offensive speech that is arguably discriminatory in character. A key to understanding how offensive speech can be discriminatory lies in reflecting on how feelings such as anxiety, fear, and anger are often associated with the experience of offense, and tend to be felt most vigorously when one is the direct object of a racial insult or slur. Behind Stanford's policy lies the idea that universities are justified in regulating such speech because of the injury it causes, but are not justified in regulating other forms of speech, including the expression of offensive points of view. So this policy would not provide a basis for action to be taken against the chauvinist engineering professor in our example. Use of the words "nigger," "fag," and the like directly to someone's face would, though, constitute appropriate cause for university intervention.

While we were putting this book together, a California court found Stanford's speech policy to be unconstitutional. At the moment, the future of policies regulating speech on college campuses is uncertain, although incidents of alleged offensive and harassing speech are on the rise. As this debate goes on, it is worth considering Charles Lawrence's suggestion that universities might have better success in dealing with this problem if they were to address the question of racist and harassing speech within the larger context of social attitudes about race and domination in general.

NOTES

1. In Edward De Grazia, *Censorship Landmarks*. (New York: R.R. Bowker Company: 1969), pp. 292-293.
2. See Ronald Dworkin's construction of an argument against pornography in his chapter on "Liberty and Moralism," in *Taking Rights Seriously*. (Cambridge, MA: Harvard University Press, 1978).
3. One of the most interesting pieces on the variety of offensive acts is Joel Feinberg's "A Ride on the Bus," in *Offense to Others*. (Oxford, England: Oxford University Press, 1985), pp. 10-13.

On Liberty

John Stuart Mill

The following selections are taken from *On Liberty*, by John Stuart Mill, who is introduced in Chapter 1. In the first selection, Mill offers three reasons for why society should guarantee a climate conducive to the free expression of opinion. All three reasons have as their foundation the idea that free expression supports society in its search for truth. First of all, without freedom of expression, opinions that are in fact true but not generally accepted as true might be stifled. Second, while freedom of expression does allow for false beliefs to circulate unrepressed, without the constant challenge of false beliefs, understanding why true beliefs are indeed true becomes more difficult. Third, freedom of expression promotes a diversity of opinions each with a partial insight into the truth of a particular issue. Such diversity is important to protect, Mill argues, as any one opinion seldom reflects a matter's entire truth.

In the second selection, Mill presents a defense of his harm principle. While recognizing that individuals have a right, if not a moral duty, to encourage others to act virtuously and to use their judgment wisely, Mill claims this right stops short of being a permission to criticize others for behaving as they think best, as long as their behavior does not negatively impact on the interests of others. Only when an individual's behavior harms others are members of a free society justified in stepping in to interfere.

––––––––––

The time, it is hoped, is gone by when any defense would be necessary of the "liberty of the press" as one of the securities against corrupt or tyrannical government. No argument, we may suppose, can now be needed against permitting a legislature or an executive, not identified in interest with the people, to prescribe opinions to them and determine what doctrines or what arguments they shall be allowed to hear. This aspect of the question, besides, has been so often and so triumphantly enforced by preceding writers that it needs not be specially insisted on in this place. Though the law of England, on the subject of the press, is as servile to this day as it was in the time of the Tudors, there is little danger of its being actually put in force against political discussion except during some temporary panic when fear of insurrection drives ministers and judges from their propriety; and, speaking generally, it is not, in constitutional countries, to be apprehended that the government, whether completely responsible to the people or not, will often attempt to control the expression of opinion, except when in doing so it makes itself the organ of the general intolerance of the public. Let us suppose, therefore, that the government is entirely at one with the people, and never thinks of exerting any power of coercion unless in agreement with what it conceives to be

From *On Liberty*, by John Stuart Mill (1859).

their voice. But I deny the right of the people to exercise such coercion, either by themselves or by their government. The power itself is illegitimate. The best government has no more title to it than the worst. It is as noxious, or more noxious, when exerted in accordance with public opinion than when in opposition to it. If all mankind minus one were of one opinion, mankind would be no more justified in silencing that one person than he, if he had the power, would be justified in silencing mankind. Were an opinion a personal possession of no value except to the owner, if to be obstructed in the enjoyment of it were simply a private injury, it would make some difference whether the injury was inflicted only on a few persons or on many. But the peculiar evil of silencing the expression of an opinion is that it is robbing the human race, posterity as well as the existing generation—those who dissent from the opinion, still more than those who hold it. If the opinion is right, they are deprived of the opportunity of exchanging error for truth; if wrong, they lose, what is almost as great a benefit, the clearer perception and livelier impression of truth produced by its collision with error.

It is necessary to consider separately these two hypotheses, each of which has a distinct branch of the argument corresponding to it. We can never be sure that the opinion we are endeavoring to stifle is a false opinion; and if we were sure, stifling it would be an evil still.

First, the opinion which it is attempted to suppress by authority may possibly be true. Those who desire to suppress it, of course, deny its truth; but they are not infallible. They have no authority to decide the question for all mankind and exclude every other person from the means of judging. To refuse a hearing to an opinion because they are sure that it is false is to assume that *their* certainty is the same thing as *absolute* certainty. All silencing of discussion is an assumption of infallibility. Its condemnation may be allowed to rest on this common argument, not the worse for being common.

Unfortunately for the good sense of mankind, the fact of their fallibility is far from carrying the weight in their practical judgment which is always allowed to it in theory; for while everyone well knows himself to be fallible, few think it necessary to take any precautions against their own fallibility, or admit the supposition that any opinion of which they feel very certain may be one of the examples of the error to which they acknowledge themselves to be liable. Absolute princes, or others who are accustomed to unlimited deference, usually feel this complete confidence in their own opinions on nearly all subjects. People more happily situated, who sometimes hear their opinions disputed and are not wholly unused to be set right when they are wrong, place the same unbounded reliance only on such of their opinions as are shared by all who surround them, or to whom they habitually defer; for in proportion to a man's want of confidence in his own solitary judgment does he usually repose, with implicit trust, on the infallibility of "the world" in general. And the world, to each individual, means the part of it with which he comes in contact: his party, his sect, his church, his class of society; the man may be called, by comparison, almost liberal and large-minded to whom it means anything so comprehensive as his own country or his own age. Nor is his faith in this collective authority at all shaken by his being aware that other ages, countries, sects, churches, classes, and parties have thought, and even now think, the exact reverse. He devolves upon his own world the responsibility of being in the right against the dissentient worlds of other people; and it never troubles him that mere accident has decided which of these numerous worlds is the object of his reliance, and that the same causes which make him a churchman in London would have made him a Buddhist or a Confucian in Peking. Yet it is as evident in itself, as any amount of argument can make it, that ages are no more infallible than individuals—every age having held many opinions which subsequent ages have deemed not only false but absurd; and it is as certain that many opinions, now general, will be rejected by future ages, as it is that many, once general, are rejected by the present. . . .

Let us now pass to the second division of the argument, and dismissing the supposition that any of the received opinions may be false, let us assume them to be true and examine into the worth of the manner in which they are likely to be held when their truth is not freely and openly canvassed. However unwillingly a person who has a strong opinion may admit the possibility that his opinion may be false, he ought to be moved by the consideration that, however true it may be, if it is not fully, frequently, and fearlessly discussed, it will be held as a dead dogma, not a living truth.

If the cultivation of the understanding consists in one thing more than in another, it is surely in learning the grounds of one's own opinions. Whatever people believe, on subjects on which it is of the first importance to believe rightly, they ought to be able to defend against at least the common objections. But, someone may say, "let them be *taught* the grounds of their opinions. It does not follow that opinions must be merely parroted because they are never heard controverted. Persons who learn geometry do not simply commit the theorems to memory, but understand and learn likewise the demonstrations; and it would be absurd to say that they remain ignorant of the grounds of geometrical truths because they never hear anyone deny and attempt to disprove them." Undoubtedly: and such teaching suffices on a subject like mathematics, where there is nothing at all to be said on the wrong side of the question. The peculiarity of the evidence of mathematical truths is that all the argument is on one side. There are no objections, and no answers to objections. But on every subject on which difference of opinion is possible, the truth depends on a balance to be struck between two sets of conflicting reasons. Even in natural philosophy, there is always some other explanation possible of the same facts; some geocentric theory instead of heliocentric, some phlogiston instead of oxygen; and it has to be shown why that other theory cannot be the true one; and until this is shown, and until we know how it is shown, we do not understand the grounds of our opinion. But when we turn to subjects infinitely more complicated, to morals, religion, politics, social relations, and the business of life, three-fourths of the arguments for every disputed opinion consist in dispelling the appearances which favor some opinion different from it. The greatest orator, save one, of antiquity, has left it on record that he always studied his adversary's case with as great if not still greater, intensity than even his own. What Cicero practiced as the means of forensic success requires to be imitated by all who study any subject in order to arrive at the truth. He who knows only his own side of the case knows little of that. His reasons may be good, and no one may have been able to refute them. But if he is equally unable to refute the reasons on the opposite side, if he does not so much as know what they are, he has no ground for preferring either opinion. The rational position for him would be suspension of judgment, and unless he contents himself with that, he is either led by authority or adopts, like the generality of the world, the side to which he feels most inclination. Nor is it enough that he should hear the arguments of adversaries from his own teachers, presented as they state them, and accompanied by what they offer as refutations. That is not the way to do justice to the arguments or bring them into real contact with his own mind. He must be able to hear them from persons who actually believe them, who defend them in earnest and do their very utmost for them. He must know them in their most plausible and persuasive form; he must feel the whole force of the difficulty which the true view of the subject has to encounter and dispose of, else he will never really possess himself of the portion of truth which meets and removes that difficulty. Ninety-nine in a hundred of what are called educated men are in this condition, even of those who can argue fluently for their opinions. Their conclusions may be true, but it might be false for anything they know; they have never thrown themselves into the mental position of those who think differently from them, and considered what such persons may have to say; and, consequently, they do not, in any proper sense of the word, know the doctrine which they themselves profess. They do not know those parts of it which explain and justify the remainder—the considerations which show that a fact which seemingly conflicts with another is reconcilable with it, or that, of two apparently strong reasons, one and not the other ought to be preferred. All that part of the truth which turns the scale and decides the judgment of a completely informed mind, they are strangers to; nor is it ever really known but to those who have attended equally and impartially to both sides and endeavored to see the reasons of both in the strongest light. So essential is this discipline to a real understanding of moral and human subjects that, if opponents of all-important truths do not exist, it is indispensable to imagine them and supply them with the strongest arguments which the most skillful devil's advocate can conjure up . . .

It still remains to speak of one of the principal causes which make diversity of opinion advantageous, and will continue to do so until mankind shall have entered a stage of intellectual advancement which at present seems at an incalculable distance. We have hitherto considered only two possibilities: that the received opinion may be false, and some other opinion, consequently, true; or that, the received opinion being true, a conflict with the opposite error is essential to a clear apprehension and deep feeling of its truth. But there is a commoner case than either of these: when the conflicting doctrines, instead of being one true and the other false, share the truth between them, and the nonconforming opinion is needed to supply the remainder of the truth of which the received doctrine embodies only a part. Popular opinions, on subjects not palpable to sense, are often true, but seldom or never the whole truth. They are a part of the truth, sometimes a greater, sometimes a smaller part, but exaggerated, distorted, and disjointed from the truths by which they ought to be accompanied and limited. Heretical opinions, on the other hand, are generally some of these suppressed and neglected truths, bursting the bonds which kept them down, and either seeking reconciliation with the truth contained in the common opinion, or fronting it as enemies, and setting themselves up, with similar exclusiveness, as the whole truth. The latter case is hitherto the most frequent, as, in the human mind, one-sidedness has always been the rule, and many-sidedness the exception. Hence, even in revolutions of opinion, one part of the truth usually sets while another rises. Even progress, which ought to superadd, for the most part only substitutes one partial and incomplete truth for another; improvement consisting chiefly in this, that the new fragment of truth is more wanted, more adapted to the needs of the time than that which it displaces. Such being the partial character of prevailing opinions, even when resting on a true foundation, every opinion which embodies somewhat of the portion of truth which the common opinion omits ought to be considered precious, with whatever amount of error and confusion that truth may be blended. No sober judge of human affairs will feel bound to be indignant because those who force on our notice truths which we should otherwise have overlooked, overlook some of those which we see. Rather, he will think that so long as popular truth is one-sided, it is more desirable than otherwise that unpopular truth should have one-sided assertors, too, such being usually the most energetic and the most likely to compel reluctant attention to the fragment of wisdom which they proclaim as if it were the whole. . . .

In politics, again, it is almost a commonplace that a party of order or stability and a party of progress or reform are both necessary elements of a healthy state of political life, until the one or the other shall have so enlarged its mental grasp as to be a party equally of order and of progress, knowing and distinguishing what is fit to be preserved from what ought to be swept away. Each of these modes of thinking derives its utility from the deficiencies of the other; but it is in a great measure the opposition of the other that keeps each within the limits of reason and sanity. Unless opinions favorable to democracy and to aristocracy, to property and to equality, to co-operation and to competition, to luxury and to abstinence, to sociality and individuality, to liberty and discipline, and all the other standing antagonisms of practical life, are expressed with equal freedom and enforced and defended with equal talent and energy, there is no chance of both elements obtaining their due; one scale is sure to go up, and the other down. Truth, in the great practical concerns of life, is so much a question of the reconciling and combining of opposites that very few have minds sufficiently capacious and impartial to make the adjustment with an approach to correctness, and it has to be made by the rough process of a struggle between combatants fighting under hostile banners. On any of the great open questions just enumerated, if either of the two opinions has a better claim than the other, not merely to be tolerated, but to be encouraged and countenanced, it is the one which happens at the particular time and place to be in a minority. That is the opinion which, for the time being, represents the neglected interests, the side of human well-being which is in danger of obtaining less than its share. I am aware that there is not, in this country, any intolerance of differences of opinion on most of these topics. They are adduced to show, by admitted and multiplied examples, the universality of the fact that only through diversity of opinion is there, in the existing state of human intellect, a chance of fair play to all sides of the truth. When there are persons to be found who form an exception to the apparent unanimity of the world on any subject, even if the world is in the right, it is always probable that dissentients have something worth hearing to say for themselves, and that truth would lose something by their silence.

* * *

What, then, is the rightful limit to the sovereignty of the individual over himself? Where does the authority of society begin? How much of human life should be assigned to individuality, and how much to society?

Each will receive its proper share if each has that which more particularly concerns it. To individuality should belong the part of life in which it is chiefly the individual that is interested; to society, the part which chiefly interests society.

Though society is not founded on a contract, and though no good purpose is answered by inventing a contract in order to deduce social obligations from it, everyone who receives the protection of society owes a return for the benefit, and the fact of living in society renders it indispensable that each should be bound to observe a certain line of conduct toward the rest. This conduct consists, first, in not injuring the interests of one another, or rather certain interests which, either by express legal provision or by tacit understanding, ought to be considered as rights; and secondly, in each person's bearing his share (to be fixed on some equitable principle) of the labors and sacrifices incurred for defending the society or its members from injury and molestation. These conditions society is justified in enforcing at all costs to those who endeavor to withhold fulfillment. Nor is this all that society may do. The acts of an individual may be hurtful to others or wanting in due consideration for their welfare, without going to the length of violating any of their constituted rights. The offender may then be justly punished by opinion, though not by law. As soon as any part of a person's conduct affects prejudicially the interests of others, society has jurisdiction over it, and the question whether the general welfare will or will not be promoted by interfering with it becomes open to discussion. But there is no room for entertaining any such question when a person's conduct affects the interests of no persons besides himself, or needs not affect them unless they like (all the persons concerned being of full age and the ordinary amount of understanding). In all such cases, there should be perfect freedom, legal and social, to do the action and stand the consequences.

It would be a great misunderstanding of this doctrine to suppose that it is one of selfish indifference which pretends that human beings have no business with each other's conduct in life, and that they should not concern themselves about the well-doing or well-being of one another, unless their own interest is involved. Instead of any diminution, there is need of a great increase of disinterested exertion to promote the good of others. But disinterested benevolence can find other instruments to persuade people to their good than whips and scourges, either of the literal or the metaphorical sort. I am the last person to undervalue the self-regarding virtues; they are only second in importance, if even second, to the social. It is equally the business of education to cultivate both. But even education works by conviction and persuasion as well as by compulsion, and it is by the former only that, when the period of education is past, the self-regarding virtues should be inculcated. Human beings owe to each other help to distinguish the better from the worse, and encouragement to choose the former and avoid the latter. They should be forever stimulating each other to increased exercise of their higher faculties and increased direction of their feelings and aims toward wise instead of foolish, elevating instead of degrading, objects and contemplations. But neither one person, nor any number of persons, is warranted in saying to another human creature of ripe years that he shall not do with his life for his own benefit what he chooses to do with it. He is the person most interested in his own well-being: the interest which any other person, except in cases of strong personal attachment, can have in it is trifling compared with that which he himself has; the interest which society has in him individually (except as to his conduct to others) is fractional and altogether indirect, while with respect to his own feelings and circumstances the most ordinary man or woman has means of knowledge immeasurably surpassing those that can be possessed by anyone else. The interference of society to overrule his judgment and purposes in what only regards himself must be grounded on general presumptions which may be altogether wrong and, even if right, are as likely as not to be misapplied to individual cases, by persons no better acquainted with the circumstances of such cases than those are who look at them merely from without. In this department, therefore, of human affairs, individuality has its proper field of action. In the conduct of human beings toward one another it is necessary that general rules should for the most part be observed in order that people may know what they have to expect; but in each person's own concerns his individual spontaneity is entitled to free exercise. Considerations to aid his judgment, exhortations to strengthen his will may be offered to him, even obtruded on him, by others; but he himself is the final judge. All errors which he is likely to commit against advice and warning are far out-weighed by the evil of allowing others to constrain him to what they deem his good.

We have a right, also, in various ways, to act upon our unfavorable opinion of anyone, not to the oppression of his individuality, but in the exercise of ours. We are not bound, for example, to seek his society; we have a right to avoid it (though not to parade the avoidance), for we have a right to choose the society most acceptable to us. We have a right, and it may be our duty, to caution others against him if we think his example or conversation likely to have a pernicious effect on those with whom he associates. We may give others a preference over him in optional good offices, except those which tend to his improvement. In these various modes a person may suffer very severe penalties at the hands of others for faults which directly concern only himself; but he suffers these penalties only in so far as they are the natural and, as it were, the spontaneous consequences of the faults themselves, not because they are purposely inflicted on him for the sake of punishment. A person who shows rashness, obstinacy, self-conceit—who cannot live within moderate means; who cannot restrain himself from hurtful indulgence; who pursues animal pleasures at the expense of those of feeling and intellect—must expect to be lowered in the opinion of others, and to have a less share of their favorable sentiments; but of this he has no right to complain unless he has merited their favor by special excellence in his social relations and has thus established a title to their good offices, which is not affected by his demerits toward himself. . . .

The distinction between the loss of consideration which a person may rightly incur by defect of prudence or of personal dignity, and the reprobation which is due to him for an offense against the rights of others, is not a merely nominal distinction. It makes a vast difference both in our feelings and in our conduct toward him whether he displeases us in things in which we think we have a right to control him or in things in which we know that we have not. If he displeases us, we may express our distaste, and we may stand aloof from a person as well as from a thing that displeases us; but we shall not therefore feel called on to make his life uncomfortable. We shall reflect that he already bears, or will bear, the whole penalty of his error; if he spoils his life by mismanagement, we shall not, for that reason, desire to spoil it still further; instead of wishing to punish him, we shall rather endeavor to allevi-ate his punishment by showing him how he may avoid or cure the evils his conduct tends to bring upon him. He may be to us an object of pity, perhaps of dislike, but not of anger or resentment; we shall not treat him like an enemy of society; the worst we shall think ourselves justified in doing is leaving him to himself, if we do not interfere benevolently by showing inter-est or concern for him. It is far otherwise if he has infringed the rules neces-sary for the protection of his fellow creatures, individually or collectively. The evil consequences of his acts do not then fall on himself, but on others; and society, as the protector of all its members, must retaliate on him, must inflict pain on him for the express purpose of punishment, and must take care that it be sufficiently severe. In the one case, he is an offender at our bar, and we are called on not only to sit in judgment on him, but, in one shape or another, to execute our own sentence; in the other case, it is not our part to inflict any suffering on him, except what may incidentally follow from our using the same liberty in the regulation of our own affairs which we allow to him in his.

Pornography and Free Speech:
The Civil Rights Approach
Barry Lynn

At the time this essay was written, Barry Lynn was a counsel to the American Civil Liberties Union in Washington, D.C. In this essay, he provides a defense of the liberal position regarding censorship of pornography against the civil rights approach to pornography also discussed in this chapter. From his viewpoint, pornography is simply *one* form of communicative material among others, and thus deserves the same constitutional protection as other forms of expression. While Lynn believes that the expression of any idea, no matter how intellectually suspect or morally disturbing, rightfully deserves First Amendment protection, he challenges the idea that pornography does in fact communicate messages that are intellectually suspect. The messages pornography sends, he maintains, can aid in the development of an improved social understanding of human sexuality, and also can have a positive value in aiding the imagination to envision different possibilities of human ways of life. In addition, Lynn denies that any causal relationship exists between pornography and sexual assault or other harms to women.

Most objections to pornography, Lynn contends, are really objections to the ideas it communicates. Even the recent argument that pornography violates the civil rights of women is, he claims, an attack on the moral ideas expressed in pornography, and so amounts to a pro-censorship argument in disguise. Lynn thus agrees with the position taken by some feminists that anti-pornography laws serve to endorse a "correct" view of human sexuality.

Many practitioners of "wicca," a pre-Christian nature religion, have engaged in a lengthy public relations campaign against the filming of John Updike's *The Witches of Eastwick* because of the film's allegedly negative stereotyping of "witches" as Devil-worshipping fanatics. Some Arab-Americans and Asian-Americans have orchestrated well-publicized protests against *The Delta Force* and *Year of the Dragon*, respectively, because of those films' depictions of ethnic groups in an allegedly derogatory fashion. Black Americans in some communities continue to object to the use of Mark Twain's *The Adventures of Huckleberry Finn* in public school classrooms because, notwithstanding its author's apparent sympathy with abolitionism, the work contains characters using racial epithets considered demeaning and objectionable. Even Christian fundamentalists have launched objections against television networks in the United States for their supposed systematically unfavorable portrayal of members of the clergy.

From *Civil Liberties in Conflict*, ed. Larry Gostin (New York: Routledge, 1988), pp. 170–184.

In each of these cases, the often rightly indignant group has essentially argued that the imagery in the objectionable books or films would be interpreted by readers or viewers to reflect the general, or perhaps even total, experience of the class: that all "witches" are evil or all Arab nationals are terrorists. In essence, the protesters argue that the depictions "lie" by suggesting universality for the worst attributes of a few members of the group or, even worse, misrepresent the group by fabricating erroneous attributes. All this is of concern because of the belief that speech, written or visual, has the power to alter (or at least reinforce) perceptions and thus to shape attitudes and, in the long run, actions.

Supporters of a free speech principle, guaranteed in the United States Constitution in the First Amendment which warrants that "Congress shall make no law . . . abridging the freedom of speech, or of the press," would resist any effort by any of these groups to use the coercive power of government to prohibit or "correct" the imagery and ideas contained in the offending productions. Nevertheless, few would argue that the chain of reasoning employed was wholly irrelevant, since free speech advocates recognize that one major significance of the principle is that speech may indeed persuade persons to view some issue differently, and perhaps to act in accordance with that worldview. If speech had no impact, there would be little but academic interest in protecting it. The communicative possibility of words and pictures is precisely why they must be so vigorously protected.

In a fashion akin to that of the ethnic and religious groups cited above, some feminist groups have picketed screenings of explicit "pornographic" films which "displayed" women, as well as helped shutter more "mainstream" horror films which depicted grotesque brutality against women.

Some feminists have taken their effort one step further, however. Although claiming to eschew "censorship," they have been promoting so-called "civil rights" laws which could make publishers, film-makers, distributors, and even retail merchants extremely cautious about creating or disseminating certain sexually oriented images and ideas. These laws are to replace existing regulation of sexual material under "obscenity" laws. . . .

In essence, this approach would permit civil lawsuits against those who create (and in most cases those who distribute) "pornographic" material in which women are coerced to appear, where the material is used to harass women in the workplace, or which is implicated in some act of sexual assault. Most also create liability for "trafficking" in certain forbidden material. The definition of "pornography" in recent county ordinances in Indianapolis, Indiana, and elsewhere, drafted by law professor Catharine MacKinnon and author Andrea Dworkin, was the "graphic sexually-explicit subordination of women, whether in pictures or words" which also include scenarios ranging from those in which women are "presented as sexual objects who enjoy pain or humiliation" to those which depict women in "postures or positions of servility or submission or display."[1]

Whether the rubric for analysis is "obscenity" law or newer "anti-pornography" approaches, the universe of material to be controlled is largely co-extensive. The definition of "pornography" is no more "objective" than that in "obscenity" law, and is therefore no less susceptible to abuse. In fact, the new definition is as subjective and fluid as that created by the *Miller* test, taking within its ambit vast amounts of popular culture, from the writings of Erica Jong and Ernest Hemingway to feminist health-care and sex-education materials. It poses the problems related to any vague statute, including inducing citizens to "steer far wider of the unlawful zone" than if the boundaries of the forbidden areas were clearly marked.[2] This is the so-called "chilling effect" which occurs where the fear of future sanction has the practical effect of influencing whether a product is created or distributed. Moreover, these new statutes generally reflect the mistaken view that the product called pornography is itself what "harms," when in fact it is the action of some who produce or consume it which is what should be regulated.

There is actually nothing which ought to distinguish pornography itself from other constitutionally protected speech. Although *Das Kapital* is indeed different in form from a centerfold in *Hustler* magazine, rational discourse should not be treated as a matter of law as superior to even the rawest of emotional appeals. Producers of communicative material should have the opportunity to speak through whatever medium they choose. If someone wishes to argue the merits of oral sex, he or she should not be accorded lesser constitutional protection if the "argument" is made in a XXX-rated video than in the prose of an academic psychology journal.

It is important to re-emphasize that pornography is indeed "communicative." Religious opponents of the material quite correctly note that it often represents a dazzling assault on the concepts of traditional morality, urging a "pornotopic" vision filled with lack of commitment, abandon, non-procreational goals, and a search for pleasure for its own sake. Feminist opponents also recognize much of it as a powerful advocate for the view that women affirmatively desire domination in sexual relationships. If it were not successful in transmitting these views, no one would bother to find ways to suppress it....

That pornography achieves its communication through primarily non-cognitive means should not distinguish it constitutionally, either. Even the Supreme Court, in a famous case in which it upheld the right of a war protestor to wear a jacket emblazoned with the words "Fuck the Draft," noted that

> We cannot sanction the view that the Constitution, while solicitous of the cognitive content of individual speech, has little or no regard for that emotive function which, practically speaking, may often be the more important element of the overall message sought to be communicated.[3]

The court also has upheld the claim that live nude dancing was "speech,"[4] and lower courts have accorded First Amendment protection to the "emotive" (and sometimes even "wordless") communication of rock and roll, jazz, bagpiping, and even mime.[5] ...

Of course, communication does not have value only if it has some role in a political debate. Pornography also has what may be characterized as a "self-actualization" function. Its "message" can be significant to the self-identity of some viewers, particularly to those in sexual minorities. Indeed, now that pornography has transcended its earlier nearly exclusive interest in the breasts of young women, there is a message that 50-year-old grandmothers, pregnant women, and other-abled persons may also be viewed as sexual beings. Perhaps the real tragedy is that it is only in sexually explicit materials that this message is likely to be found. Certainly, the acknowledgement of the sexual diversity of our society can be an important step in the direction of a healthier understanding of overall human sexuality.

Moreover, the material can simply legitimatize the exploration of fantasy, without any impact on conduct. The Feminist Anti-Censorship Taskforce has noted:

> Depictions of ways of living and acting that are radically different from our own can enlarge the range of human possibilities open to us and help us grasp the potentialities of human behavior, both good and bad. Rich fantasy imagery allows us to experience in imagination ways of being that we may not wish to experience in real life. Such an enlarged vision of possible realities enhances our human potential, and is highly relevant to our decision-making as citizens on a wide range of social and ethical issues.[6]

This "positive" value to sexually explicit material is yet another basis for rejecting the characterization as "low-value" speech.

Clearly, there is no serious basis for treating sexual speech differently than other speech. Moreover, the specific elements of these "civil rights" ordinances illustrate the dangerous fallacies generally utilized to justify the suppression of sexually oriented material.

The first component of such measures is a cause of action for assault "caused" by pornography. There is no question that there are "copycat" actions where people replicate in real life the things they see in a variety of pornographic and non-pornographic material. Children see stunts on television and attempt them with tragic results; Japanese teenagers commit suicide after they learn on the national news of the suicide of a pop music idol; a man who views the television movie *The Burning Bed* burns his sleeping wife to death that night, mirroring the action of the abused wife against her abusive husband in the film; and a boy dies of strangulation with a men's magazine containing an article (albeit critical) about autoerotic asphyxiation found open near his corpse. . . .

The argument of causation, of course, usually goes beyond the neat parallelism of anecdotal evidence. However, there is no general scientific evidence to support the view that pornography "causes" men to commit sexual assault. Even researchers whose work was cited in the recent Attorney General's Commission on Pornography *Final Report*, to buttress its conclusion that pornography was harmful, have now publicly repudiated any claim that their data demonstrate such causation.[7] Two commissioners, one a well-known sex offender therapist, writing in partial dissent, noted that "efforts to tease the current data into proof of a causal link between these acts simply cannot be accepted."[8] The most that scientific data can show is some short-term attitude change in some experimental subjects after significant exposure to certain kinds of pornography. That is, some viewers temporarily see women in a more "negative" light, or have a more "positive" attitude toward non-marital sexual activity, and indicate such opinions on attitudinal surveys.[9] This is hardly a surprising finding, since laboratory studies show short-term attitudinal alteration after exposing subjects to almost any "message," from those in anti-smoking films to those in movies portraying other-abled persons in a favorable light.[10] The longevity of these altered impressions is likely to be short, and even laboratory data on the effects of violent "anti-women" films demonstrate only brief alterations in opinions of subjects.[11]

The US Pornography Commission and other pornography critics allege that attitude changes obviously affect behavior. Although it is logically true that attitude change always precedes behavioral change, not every attitude shift results in behavior modification. There are literally thousands of passing thoughts which would get the average person in trouble, if not in jail, every day if governments were allowed to punish "bad thoughts." Luckily, however, this nation regulates acts, not thoughts. In fact, were a demonstration of attitude change itself sufficient to permit the regulation of speech, the First Amendment would lose all significance. Certainly the amendment at least means that persons shall have an unencumbered opportunity to alter the attitudes of others by presenting them with powerful ideas and images.

Measures of association between pornography circulation and rape incidents are also not viable as a justification for regulating this material. One widely publicized study, by Baron and Straus, has been interpreted as a demonstration that sexual assault rates correlate with circulation rates of adult magazines.[12] This study, however, has now been characterized by one of its authors as not indicating that pornography causes rape. Moreover, he has indicated that introducing new factors into the equation statistically invalidates the relationship between circulation and assault rates.[13] In other countries, there remain data supporting correlations between wide availability of "hardcore" material and low rape rates (Japan),[14] as well as decreased or stable rates of sexual assault and other "sex" crimes as material is decriminalized (West Germany and Denmark, respectively).[15]

In other words, there is nothing to demonstrate any measurable increase in the aggregate level of sexual violence in the nation due to the presence of pornography. One commentator argues that "it is highly plausible to believe that the general climate reinforced by pornography contributes to an increased level of sexual violence against women." Such a standard of "plausibility" is not only insufficient to regulate speech; such speculative conclusions would properly preclude even regulation of commodities like food products and medicine. If there was a clear connection between pornography and sexual violence it would be apparent, not "plausible." . . .

The civil rights approach also usually contains a remedy for the "forcing" of pornography on unwilling persons. Public display of this material is hardly a major problem for most Americans. Surveys show that a remarkably high percentage of persons have never seen it at all, as it remains invisible to most non-consumers.[16] Many who are bothered by the material actually see nothing more explicit than the covers of the monthly *Cosmopolitan* or the swimsuit issue of *Sports Illustrated* when they look at the cover of the pornographic item. They are really concerned about the internal contents, which they would view only were they to open the periodical or insert the video cassette into a player.

Unwanted presentation is not a trivial matter, but no tolerant society can impose legal sanctions on the basis of chance encounters with offensive images. The Supreme Court, in a decision regarding nudity occasionally spotted by drivers passing an outdoor movie theater, noted that, absent a showing that substantial privacy interests were being invaded in an "essentially intolerable manner, the burden normally falls upon the viewer to avoid further bombardment of [his] sensibilities by averting [his] eyes."[17] It is in fact possible to walk through the vast majority of streets in America without observing, even by happenstance, a single explicit sexual image.

Where there are truly occurrences of malicious harassment by forced exposure to pornography, tort laws in most states already provide an avenue for redress.[18] In addition, courts are increasingly allowing suits under Title VII of the 1964 Civil Rights Law where employers, for example, display graphic material in the workplace so that a specific woman worker is presented with an essentially intolerable work environment.[19] These legal remedies are often justified, but the mere presence of offensive material inside magazines or the black plastic cases of video cassettes must remain an uncompensated offense, a *damnum absque injuria*, that the law cannot be reasonably expected to redress. . . .

A final cause of action is the most amorphous of all, creating a remedy against those who "traffic" in pornography. This is an apparent effort to permit any woman who believes that pornography has led to discrimination against her to sue the publisher, distributor, or retailer. This is possibly the baldest effort in such laws simply to frighten people out of the business of sexually explicit material from fear of lawsuits, even by those who have never been coerced into performing, forced to observe it, or assaulted by a viewer. It is predicated, however, on the assumption that pornography plays some major role in sex discrimination, but this, like previous arguments, is untenable. The status of women in places like Saudi Arabia, where there is virtually no pornography, cannot be considered superior to the position of women in the United States, where there is possibly an $8 billion industry in the material. Likewise, measures of the economic status of women in various states correlate positively with the circulation rates of major pornographic magazines. The fact that there is statistical correlation between higher women's status and a large number of sexual magazines is certainly not the result of any causative relationship, but it also tends to disprove the significance of the material in causing social disparity between the sexes.[20]

One other facile argument which has been advanced to justify new restriction is that the First Amendment rights of anti-pornography activists (and, by extension, the women they purport to "represent" in their efforts) have somehow been abridged by the pornographers, and that the government therefore owed some affirmative duty to try to equalize the power of those competing voices.[21] In fact, a vast amount of public attention has been given to the feminist anti-pornography effort in every conceivable popular medium. The underlying critique of the "pornotopic" vision is also present in a large array of scholarly and mass-market books which are readily available. Feminism as a vital social critique can hardly be said to have generated equality, but it has certainly changed both the consciousness and culture of American society. It has always done so by a critique of existing patriarchal doctrine, and not by an effort to silence the patriarchs. There is no constitutional basis for demanding that government scrutinize speech about any subject in order to determine the relative volume expressing particular viewpoints, much less then to effect a balance by curtailing some expressions of the "majoritarian" speakers.

Another variation which infuses the "new" debate over pornography is that there is no "corrective" to the way in which women's sexuality is depicted in the material. However, responsible researchers like Edward Donnerstein have been careful to "debrief" their experimental subjects, who have been "taught" rape myths with certain visual material, by providing them with factual information about the nature of sexual assault. They consistently find significant improvement in the understanding of rape following the debriefings, a demonstration that erroneous viewpoints about sexuality can indeed be successfully combated through the presentation of alternative ideas.[22] "More speech" supplants even "pornographic" speech. There is no magical or mystical ability of this material to alter behavior, notwithstanding its general ability to cause erections. It is no better a conditioner than any other form of expression, and when its viewpoint is offensive it may be effectively rebutted in the same way one can challenge the views of witches, Arabs, Asians, blacks, or Christians with which this chapter began.

Regardless of the name given to the efforts to regulate pornographic images, it is hard to construe them as anything but efforts at governmental censorship. All require enlisting the state, directly or indirectly, in removing certain sexual views from the culture. It is the political or moral ideas expressed therein which are offensive, and therefore deemed dangerous. Although Catharine MacKinnon, the author of the Indianapolis ordinance, repeatedly claims that hers is not a "moral" crusade,[23] she is in fact enlisting the government's courts to support her view of correct sexuality. By frightening "incorrect" expressions from the scene for fear of civil sanction, she is attempting to hurt financially those who promote such attitudes. Ultimately, there is little difference between the goal of her ordinances and the goal of traditional obscenity law.

The treatment by the US Supreme Court of sexual materials as a unique content-circumscribed class clearly has a ripple effect of ominous proportions. The very existence of "obscenity" laws, predicated on the constitutional difference between explicit speech about sex and other speech, has helped legitimatize the premise of these new ordinances that some sexual material is entitled to no First Amendment protection. "Sexual speech" fuels local efforts of others to ban Judy Blume novels from the high-school shelves or to eliminate the feminist works on women's health care from the local library, because these materials too are "about" sex. Whether any individual effort succeeds or fails, censorship is no phantom danger. The goal of regulating or suppressing certain sexual viewpoints is, nearly, in turn, indistinguishable in purpose from that noted by Justice William Brennan in his dissent in *Paris Adult Theatres v. Slaton*:

> If a state may, in an effort to maintain or create a moral tone, prescribe what its citizens cannot read or cannot see, then it would seem to follow that in pursuit of that same objective a state could decree that its citizens must read certain books or must view certain films.[24]

If the courts may tell us what is wrong or incorrect, why not tell us precisely what is right and correct as well?

The ferocity of the debate among feminists is strong evidence of the complexity and danger of the effort to constrain a correct female sexuality. The Feminist Anti-Censorship Taskforce, in its *amicus* brief challenging the Indianapolis ordinance, notes with irony that the ordinance

> delegitimates and makes socially invisible women who find sexually explicit images of women "in positions of display" or "penetrated by objects" to be erotic, liberating, or educational. These women are told that their perceptions are a product of "false consciousness" and that such images are so inherently degrading that they may be suppressed by the state.[25]

The whole discussion of pornography and the law was substantially polluted in 1986 by the release of the *Final Report* of the Attorney General's Commission on Pornography, a curious mix of moralizing and pseudo-feminist musings which urged a nationwide crackdown on sexually oriented material. Since the commission's method of data-gathering was so intellectually irresponsible, it is regrettable that its data and conclusions have received any acceptance by responsible persons. Indeed, the conclusions of the commission were essentially embodied in the documents which created the body, most notably the serious problem posed by the material and the need for further regulation. When combined with a membership which had, for the most part, staked out an "anti-pornography" position before their appointment, the likelihood of serious inquiry was jeopardized.

Although the Pornography Commission's emphasis on enforcing existing (or slightly "improved") obscenity laws was rejected by feminist anti-pornography advocates, those groups generally endorsed the conclusions of the commission about the "harmfulness" of the material for women, including its implication in acts of sexual violence. Moreover, the commission's recurring conclusion that regulating much of this material had no serious free speech implications was also seen by some feminists as a boon to their analysis, particularly since the commission endorsed legislative examination of the new "civil rights" laws. . . .

The new approaches rest on unacceptable analytical principles and a legal philosophy that is antithetical to the civil liberties guarantee of free expression. It would hold speech about sexuality hostage to even the most unique and unintended response of the most susceptible viewer or reader.

NOTES

1. Indianapolis, Ind., City–County General Ordinance 35 Sec. 16–3 (q) (6) (11 June 1984).
2. *Grayned v. City of Rockford*, 408 US 104, 108–9, quoting *Baggett v. Bullitt*, 377 US 360, 372 (1964), quoting *Speiser v. Randall*, 357 US 513, 526 (1958).
3. *Cohen v. California*, 403 US 15, 26 (1970).
4. *Schad v. Borough of Mount Ephraim*, 452 US 61, 65 (1981).
5. See *Cinevision Corp. v. City of Burbank*, 745 F. 2d 560, 569 (9th Cir. 1984) (music); *Fact Concerts, Inc. v. City of Newport*, 626 F. 2d 1060 (1st Cir. 1980) (jazz); *Davenport v. City of Alexandria*, 710 F. 2d 148 (4th Cir. 1983) (bagpiping); *Birkenshaw v. Haley*, 409 F. Supp. 13 (E. D. Mich. 1974) (mime).
6. *Amicus* brief of the Feminist Anti-Censorship Taskforce at 29, *American Booksellers Assn v. Hudnut*, 771 F. 2d 323 (7th Cir. 1985).
7. *New York Times*, 17 May 1986, at A–1, col. 1.
8. *Attorney General's Commission on Pornography, US Department of Justice, Final Report* (1986) (statement of Ellen Levine and Judith Becker).
9. See e.g. N. Malamuth and J. V. P. Check, "The effects of mass media exposure on acceptance of violence against women: a field experiment," *Journal of Research in Personality* 15 (1981): 436 (acceptance of violence); *Transcript of Proceedings, US Dept of Justice, The Attorney General's Commission on Pornography*, public hearing, Houston, Texas (11 September 1985): 112 (statement of Dr. Dolf Zillman, summarizing his research in acceptance of non-marital sexual activity).
10. See e.g. Timothy R. Elliott and E. Keith Byrd, "Attitude change toward disability through television portrayal," *Journal of Applied Rehabilitation Counseling* 14 (1983): 35; "Smoker's luck: can a shocking programme change attitudes to smoking?" *Addictive Behavior* 8 (1983): 43.
11. J. Ceniti and N. Malamuth, "Effects of repeated exposure to sexually violent or sexually non-violent stimuli on sexual arousal to rape and non-rape depictions," *Research and Therapy* (1985).
12. L. Baron and M. Straus, "Sexual stratification, pornography, and rape in the United States," in N. Malamuth and E. Donnerstein (eds.) *Pornography and Sexual Aggression* (London, 1984): 185.
13. *Final Report* (*supra* note 8): 950.
14. P. Abramson and H. Hayashi, "Pornography in Japan: cross-cultural and theoretical considerations in pornography and sexual aggression," in Malamuth and Donnerstein (*supra* note 12): 173.

15. B. Kutchinsky, "Pornography and its effects in Denmark and the United States: a rejoinder and beyond," in R. F. Tomasson (ed.) *Comparative Social Research* (1985): 8.

16. See Pornography Commission, *Transcript*, Houston hearing (*supra* note 9): 310–E (author's calculations from testimony of Diana Russell indicate that 58 percent of women had never seen pornography, and 56 percent of those who did were not "upset" by it.)

17. *Erznoznik v. City of Jacksonville*, 422 US 205, 210 (1985), citing *Cohen v. California*, 403 US 15, 21 (1971).

18. See e.g. *Shaffer v. National Can Corp.*, 565 F. Supp. 909 (E. D. Pa. 1983) ("pornographic entertainment" offered to female employee by supervisor can be element of claim for intentional infliction of emotional distress).

19. See e.g. *Kyriazi v. Western Electric Co.*, 461 Supp. 894 (D. NJ 1978).

20. Baron and Straus (*supra* note 12).

21. See e.g. A. Dworkin, "Against the male flood: censorship, pornography and equality," *Harvard Women's Law Journal* 8 (1985): 1, 13.

22. See e.g. E. Donnerstein and L. Berkowitz, "Victim reactions in aggressive erotic films as a factor in violence against women," *Journal of Personality and Social Psychology* 41 (1981): 710.

23. See e.g. C. MacKinnon, "Not a moral issue," *Yale Law and Policy Review* 2 (1984): 321.

24. 413 US 110.

25. *Amicus* (*supra* note 6): 42.

The Moral Right of the Majority to Restrict Obscenity and Pornography Through Law
Raymond D. Gastil

Raymond Gastil, an independent consultant in public policy analysis, argues in the following essay that a plausible case for state regulation of pornography can be made on moral grounds. He suggests that three factors are relevant to making this case: a distinction between private and public realms of human activity, a distinction between political and non-political rights to expression, and a good argument that pornography actually creates harm for the majority of members in society.

It is this third consideration that Gastil takes as his primary point of focus. The key to understanding the moral grounds on which pornography can be justifiably censored, Gastil suggests, is in seeing how society is morally strengthened by the recognition that there are many ultimate goods, including significance, creativity and pleasure. A good society reflects an equitable balance of these three ultimate goods; in a morally corrupt society, these goods will not be valued equally. The more toleration society shows for pornography, argues Gastil, the more the value of pleasure comes to dominate over values of significance and creativity. Thus society has a moral right to enact legal sanctions against pornography in order to preserve within its bounds a balance of ultimate goods.

Obscenity and pornography may be defined as the use of language or images relating to the body, violence, or sex that exceed the bounds of propriety that a significant part of the public finds appropriate for the context and requirements of the situation in which they are used. Efforts to limit obscenity and pornography either legally or informally are frustrated by the lack of an acceptable intellectual basis in liberal societies for such limitations. Appeals to community standards or lack of redeeming social value are weakened by a widespread feeling, especially in academic circles and the media, that the majority has no right to impose its standards on individuals or to decide on social values unless clear physical harm is involved. Moreover, attempts to regulate obscenity are frequently criticized on the ground that the regulators are enforcing standards that neither they nor the majority observe in their own lives.

The recent controversy that has focused on the works of H. L. A. Hart and Lord Devlin on the one hand, and the reports of government commissions to look into the regulation of obscenity on the other, has summarized but not greatly advanced the argument.[1] In his defense of controls, Lord Devlin fails

From *Ethics* 86 (1976), 231–240.

to accept the intellectual weakness and thus ultimate unsatisfactoriness of controls defended largely by populism and conservatism, nor is he sufficiently aware of the dangers of an open-ended appeal to the popular will. On the other hand, in the Mill tradition, Hart fails to stake out the rights of the majority as firmly as he does those of the minority. He promotes a form of libertarian elitism that should be rejected because it represents an undue infringement on the freedom of potential majorities that they will not freely accept. Devlin's intuition that law and morality should reinforce one another cannot simply be ignored. Since inadequacies in the Hart position lead to an unacceptable libertarianism and those in Devlin's may lead to a purely instrumental view of freedom, both may lay the groundwork for a new "escape from freedom."[2]

In order to avoid this danger, I suggest that we build a case for the control of obscenity by establishing the following: (1) a distinction of private from public rights to expression, (2) a distinction of political from nonpolitical rights to expression, and (3) a plausible case that the majority can claim harm from public obscenity.

1. THE PRIVATE/PUBLIC DISTINCTION

In a free society, the majority is responsible for establishing the laws of the community, while at the same time this responsibility is limited by certain absolute privileges granted to minorities and individuals because of attachment to a concept of basic rights or freedoms. Aside from those rational political and civil freedoms that are necessary to guarantee a democratic structure, these include rights to that degree of freedom that is consonant with the freedom of others. Yet what are the rules for this consonance? For example, surely one freedom of those in the majority is to have the kind of social and aesthetic environment that they desire in the moral mode. It is with this in mind that nudists are asked to disrobe only in private or in camps segregated for that purpose. If the clash between the majority and minority over nudism meant that nudists could appear anywhere in public, then in this case majority rights would be nugatory while the minority rights would be guaranteed. To expect majorities to long accede to such situations is to imagine that people will give up being interested in determining many aspects of their social environment that have formerly been considered of importance.

The problem for the liberal, therefore, is to define basic civil rights in such a way that they preserve a meaningful area of freedom both to individuals who can form majorities capable of determining a way of life for themselves and to individuals who have not or cannot form a majority. The right to try to form new majorities is the basic right given to individuals in both the majority and the minority that makes meaningful the rights of either. Adding to this an absolute right to a private sphere of life guarantees the development of that degree of individuality that would seem consonant with human dignity in the liberal view. Once he has staked out a private realm for minority rights beyond the public political sphere, the liberal may go on to make the utilitarian case that the majority will also benefit from eschewing regulation of most social behavior. But this is an area appropriate for continual readjustment of interests and not for basic guarantees. . . .

The public or private value of an action may be an integral part of its "rightness" or "wrongness," for, physically and biologically, actions are generally neutral and their morality or immorality is in most cases judged with reference to the context of their occurrence. Opposition to sexual obscenity might be founded upon a desire to control the tone of sexual behavior by reinforcing one set of meanings associated with it rather than another. If so, the place and the participants in expression determine its relative desirability. Second, there are many continuums upon which we wish to start and do not desire to finish but where nevertheless the exact stopping point must be arbitrary and conventional. For example, everyone should have equal political and civil rights, but how we define "everyone" is necessarily conventional. It would be foolish to give one-year-olds voting rights, but whether the age at which one receives this right should be twelve, eighteen, twenty-one, or twenty-five can be discussed as a matter of reasoned argument. Therefore, as a basis of compromise between majority and minority rights, the private/public distinction remains the most salient available—a view supported by its acceptance in both of the reports cited above.

2. THE POLITICAL/NONPOLITICAL DISTINCTION

In the United States, the argument against controls on obscenity is frequently made in the context of the right of free speech under the First Amendment to the Constitution. Yet as Alexander Meiklejohn has pointed out: ". . . the principle of freedom of speech is derived . . . from the necessities of self-government by universal suffrage. . . . The guarantee by the First Amendment is . . . assured only to speech which bears, directly or indirectly upon issues with which voters have to deal—only, therefore, to a consideration of matters of public interest. Private speech, or private interest in speech . . . has no claim whatever to the protection of the First Amendment."[3] Therefore, it is wrong for the authors of the *Report of the Commission on Obscenity and Pornography* to assert that controls should not be imposed because of the American tradition of free speech.[4] American history has not been remarkable for libertarianism, except in regard to politically related speech and behavior. This is even more true of a democracy such as Switzerland.

There are borderline cases. Profanity and nudity are sometimes regarded as political expression, or random violence may carry a political message. However, if the courts were not confused by the claim that the First Amendment gave an unlimited right to all expression, they might plausibly determine what is an authentic political message.

But they have been so confused.[5] Although in the Roth case (1957) the Supreme Court exempted obscenity from coverage by the First Amendment, the stipulation that any redeeming social value would lift a work of art or literature into legality was based more on J. S. Mill than the writers of the Constitution. A more recent (1973) Supreme Court decision that a work must have serious literary, artistic, political, or scientific value to escape potential condemnation as obscene[6] gives more recognition to the fact that the majority has a right to intervene when it feels there is more social disvalue than value in a particular unity of expression. Yet the court signally fails to distinguish politically and nonpolitically relevant rights and by adding "scientific" appears to rest its justification on utilitarian arguments for freedom that may unfortunately wilt when calculations change. In a majoritarian state, freedom of speech must, instead, be protected by a more absolute but less all-inclusive principle that refers to rational political discourse as an ineluctable requirement of political democracy.

3. A PLAUSIBLE CASE THAT THE MAJORITY CAN CLAIM HARM FROM PUBLIC OBSCENITY

Since regulation of obscenity and pornography limits freedom, and since they bring pleasure to many, their legal restriction in a liberal society cannot be advocated unless a plausible case can be made that lack of restriction does substantial harm to potential majority interests.

Both Mill and Hart assert that only harm to individuals can be a basis of regulation, and primarily harm to individuals other than the actors. But this is hardly a confining limit if the concept of harm may be extended through psychic to social and spiritual harm to individuals or to the society of which they are a part. Three broad extensions of the principle of harm have been proposed.[7] The first is the conservative hypothesis that since received moral and legal codes are the tested results of trial and error, they are likely to meet social needs better than untested alternatives. The second is the disintegration hypothesis that lack of regulation of conduct offensive to the majority will result in the loss of a unified moral consensus in the community and thus undercut its whole moral structure, washing away finally even the limitations that the most libertarian would hate to lose. . . . The third majoritarian hypothesis[8] [is] that the people of any community have a right to legislate their way of life. If wearing clothes, for example, is a part of their way of life, they have a right to enforce this custom irrespective of lack of proof as to the harm of individual nudity to others.

These arguments are supportive of control, yet they are not enough for a plausible case. As to the majoritarian hypothesis, in a democracy, of course, a majority can force its will eventually, but this fact does not help us decide whether majorities or their leaders should be taught that they have a right to exert force in a particular sphere of life. Majorities are often wrong and frivolous, and this is one reason for constitutions and basic civil rights. The disintegration hypothesis may be correct—clashing views do lead to instability—but this is a weak case for enforcing old standards. It is true that attitudes about decency in the arts and on the streets have been changing rapidly, and the wide dissemination of pornography is speeding up the change. One result of any social change is instability, and instability has losses. Yet it might be possible in the future to achieve consensus that "anything goes" in obscene expression, and in these terms stability could be restructured. Conservatively, I would argue that those who launch confusion have the heavier burden of proof. Yet this does not alter the fact that the defender of the old assumptions of a society has the responsibility to give a rational case for those assumptions or to suggest revisions in those assumptions that accord with a rational case. A living conservative tradition must be a changing tradition, or else it will fail to preserve social integration, community identity, and cherished values.

In a recent review of the relevant theoretical and empirical evidence for potential harm that has been developed by the social sciences, James Q. Wilson compared two attempts to summarize such evidence for policy purposes in the United States.[9] He found that in both cases the supporting evidence for the conclusions was weak and often only tangentially related to real-world concerns. Nevertheless, the National Commission on the Causes and Prevention of Violence recommended that violence in the media should be controlled, or further investigated with an eye to control, because of the probability that fictional violence may make individuals behave violently. On the other hand, the Commission on Obscenity and Pornography recommended widespread decontrol of sexually explicit materials because no negative results of their general dissemination could be demonstrated. Wilson reasonably surmises that the reason for the disparity between the treatment of the relation between evidence and conclusion in the two reports is due to the bias of their authors against violence and in favor of sex.

Wilson, however, goes on to point out that almost all recent major American studies testing hypotheses that major long-term behavior changes result from particular social policy or educational inputs have provided inconclusive or negative findings. Thus, studies have in recent years shown that the type of school or educational method makes no difference (Coleman report), that Head Start accomplishes little, that prison correction systems produce little gain, and that psychiatry does little for the patient. He suggests, and it is probably true, that in real-life situations there is too much going on, too many cycles of reinforcement stretched over too many years, for particular interventions to get up out of the noise. Still this does not mean that there is not a great deal of change over time[10] and that the arts, the schools, and the media do not participate in positive or negative feedback relationships that eventuate in these changes. Because Head Start did not work very well does not mean early education is not important. As the violence commission report suggests, since advertisers feel that exposure to certain symbols and fictional experiences will influence buying behavior, it is reasonable to suppose that an increasing flow of violent pornography will influence other social behavior. The "no harmful effects" of sexual pornography reported by the pornography commission included an observation that exposure led to a more open attitude toward sex and, after initial increase in sexual interest, a general adaptation to pornography.[11]

But what is behavior? One of the curious aspects of the claim that obscenity and pornography are not significant influences on behavior is that both their production and consumption (direct and indirect) are forms of behavior. In this sense, there are then two significant but not unrelated results of uncontrolled pornography and obscenity. First, we are granted only so much time in our lives, and our minds have only so much capacity for attention at any one time. Therefore, if there is more of X there will be less of Y in our attention. And so if there is more obscenity there is less of something else. Our lives are changed (of course, some not at all, many to a degree, and few greatly changed). Second, the parts of our lives are unlikely to be either watertight compartments or tightly interconnected. The verbal and artistic forms and images we use are just that, and yet at the same time they carry meanings that habituate us to different qualities of behavior. With the generalization of violent and sexual pornography, our bodies become depersonalized emotive machines with many buttons to push. . . .

As an analogy, let us imagine an attractive but small square in a large city surrounded by medium-sized apartments. Among those who used the square, 25 percent were inclined to be disorderly and kept trash lying around their apartments for days, while 75 percent were neat. However, the square was always neat, for few people dropped trash in the square and a weekly cleaning by the city was quite enough for even its neatest users.

One year, however, 5 percent of the users began to drop their trash in the square. Those disturbed by the change in its appearance asked for the enforcement of antilittering laws, but the courts held that no one was being injured, for there was no danger to health because of the weekly municipal cleanup. Yet, toward the end of each week trash grew so thick that users who had not previously dropped their trash began to become less careful, and so the percentage of litterers grew to at least equal the percentage who were also disorderly inside their own apartments. By now many of those who had formerly enjoyed the square partially because of its appearance stayed away, so that finally more than 50 percent of the users were also litterers, and in the end dropping trash casually about became the social custom. For health reasons cleanup was now three times a week, but with the heavy population it was a rather trashy park most of the time. By now, many of those who formerly had kept clean apartments but had become litterers in public also kept littered apartments.

This is the course of events which those disturbed with pornography and obscenity believe they are witnessing today. I do not know if any court has ruled against littering laws in the way they have against blue laws. But if the question of the extra cost of cleanup were kept out of the legal calculation, I see no reason why in the name of individual freedom the courts should not equally do away with such laws. Why is the filling of the public arena with pornography and obscenity to be regarded as different from the delict of littering? When the movie marquee, newsstands, and popular songs all blare out *Deep Throat* and its equivalents, the city becomes a different place to walk in just as it does when everyone carelessly drops his lunch sack, candy wrapper, or pop bottle. Since everyone's likes and dislikes cannot be accommodated in the same square, the obvious basis of decision as to regulation becomes the desire of the majority of users.

Let me, then, somewhat formalize the case for restriction of obscenity in perfectionist terms. . .

First, I define the moral-action mode as one in which a person assumes that one of his interests will be to act in ways that accord with his highest image of how a man should act. He knows he will have other interests at other times and from other vantage points, but in the moral mode he wants to act in terms of this image, and he wants to advocate that others act in these terms. If we view all actions as basically self-interested, we will assume that the actor believes that his moral actions will improve the esteem in which he is held and thus his status, and that this gain is better than other possible gains. If we assume that an actor can internalize desires to achieve the good of others or of society, then he may act morally or support such action when projected gain to self-esteem balances other possible gains pursued by other means.

Since the moral mode is only one of several, there is no obvious hypocrisy in a society prohibiting obscenity or pornography that most of its members in fact enjoy. One may believe that it would be better for him to eat less ice cream; he will avoid ice-cream shops, but when faced with an ice-cream counter he will always order two scoops.

Let us, then, define morality as action that is guided in the moral-action mode by a reasoned balancing of the claims to consideration of a variety of ultimate goods for man or society, limited by a set of basic moral rules placed outside immediate consideration. A moral society is one that forms its customs and laws in terms of trade-offs within limits among the ultimate goods accepted by its members. The ultimate goods are many, and no two people will have the same list. But moral persons will, in fact, develop lists that have a great deal of overlap.

For the purposes of this discussion I will classify ultimate goods under three headings. First are the goods of pleasure in all of the manifold forms in which they occur. Second are the goods of creativity, the making and doing of something beyond the self. Creativity may be intellectual, technical, organizational, or artistic. Third are the goods of significance. Most people are concerned with their place in time, with their dignity as men and women, with their specialness. It is true of course that heroic generalization would allow us to reduce all goods to those of pleasure. Yet ancient Athens was not as remarkable for the pleasures of its inhabitants as for Athenian creativity and the significance that Athenian high culture gave to man as separate from nature. For many, satisfaction with life does not come from a quantum of fun but from the significance that they find in it. The rights and dignities afforded by policies that guarantee individual freedom offer one basis of individual significance, but not the only one.

In the moral society, limits are placed on the balancing of ultimate goods both because of a mistrust of rationalization and because of the hierarchical relation of ultimate goods. For example, if an analyst hypothesizes basic social rights such as those to food, respect, and life and basic civil rights such as those to freedoms that do not infringe on the freedom of others, he in effect sets limits that he will not recommend infringing except in such extreme circumstances as a danger of imminent destruction of the human race. On the other hand, less basic ultimate goods may in ordinary circumstances be traded off against other personal and social interest in deciding upon moral action.

In order to go beyond conservative, disintegration, and majoritarian hypotheses to build a case for limiting pornography and obscenity, it is necessary to show that it is not irrational for men to value the ultimate goods of creativity and significance equally with those of pleasure. For those who evaluate in these terms, actions that move society away from a balanced mix of the ultimate goods do moral harm to individuals both separately and collectively.

As I have pointed out, moral harm may come in a variety of forms. The *Brave New World* could offer most people manifold pleasures yet fall short in offering what the reader might consider sufficient significance to the average human life. Therefore, the controls of this society would harm its members. Similarly, lack of sufficient discipline may result in a person who is so unable to put off immediate gratification that he falls short of what others consider true humanity. Lack of discipline has harmed this person as surely as dropping a rock on his foot.

In perfectionist terms, the case against obscenity is either that it diminishes man or reduces his creativity. Since the second case depends on an analysis of extensive empirical evidence that I do not have, I shall limit the argument largely to the first. Historically, one way to achieve human significance has been to emphasize the specialness of man either as an individual or as a human group. This may be because many feel that there can be no meaning to a life except to itself if it is a replaceable part in a process that could do without it. And to have meaning only to oneself is ultimately to seem to have no meaning at all.

An obvious way to establish meaning is to sharply distinguish human from animal life. No civilization has placed human and prehuman life on a plane, even when, as in Hinduism and Buddhism, animal life is highly respected. Only in recent years has man come, by means of science, to concentrate on the similarities among existences—to flatten all differences, including those between animate and inanimate matter. This is one reason why the naive reaction to Darwin was so strong. If man is only part of a process and probably not a final stage, then his consciousness, ideals, and creativity are only epiphenomena. Since what is really important is his biology, beyond eugenics the reformer's goal can only be to make the progress of individuals through the stages of life as painless as possible for all. For a person to believe that he should really live up to a set of symbolic standards or should not try to get away with whatever he can seems to be to allow oneself to be brainwashed by a social machine justified as oiling the succession of the generations. Self-fulfillment becomes letting everything happen to oneself that can, enjoying all the possibilities before it is too late. From this perspective, even self-actu-alization is a mocking game.

Maintaining a system of symbolic restraints on language and the arts has historically been a means of underscoring the difference between man and the process from which he emerged. Let me pose as a critical difference between man and animal the development of symbolic systems that allow us to disvalue public viewing of biological processes such as defecation, urina-tion, or sexual intercourse. Why? There is nothing "wrong" with these actions. I suggest that what is wrong, just as what is "wrong" with the naked body, is that they remind us of our biology, of our presymbolic connections. This is why Duncan Williams attacks modern literature as the depiction of *The Trousered Ape*,[12] and this is why he sees pornography as both violent and sexual—the realm of the forbidden and animal in the popular mythology.

The spread of obscenity through the popular arts and up and down the streets can be interpreted as a reflection of the victory of science over reli-gious belief. The Marquis de Sade reasoned that since man was determined and essentially a machine, anything that he might do that he found pleasur-able he should do. As Francis Schaeffer has pointed out, as this view of man has come to be popularly accepted, it has been accompanied by an overrid-ing mood of despair in the arts.[13] But literary and artistic critics have gone further in note the resulting shattering of a sense of purpose and order and standards to the arts, with dependence on sex and violence as the most universal and easiest to understand common denominator.[14] It may be plau-sibly argued, then, that once casual sex and violence fill our viewing and creating lives, this feeds back to further reinforce and popularize a dimin-ished view of man.

The case, then, is that the presentation or acting out of sex or violence in public, or advertising such activities in public, will tend to popularize and familiarize a view of man and an attitude toward the self that will diminish the view that people have of the significance through specialness of human life and also divert creative artists from creative activity through the diversion of the time and money of the public toward an art world whose standards have been undermined, both directly (through taking up the space and time of the audience) and indirectly (through its feedback support of nihilism) by pornography. In the account of some people, the losses in significance and creativity are not made up for by gains in creativity and significance (free-dom) released by the decontrol of pornography, or by the gains in sensual pleasure. These judgments are contingent upon a time and place in which nihilism is already far advanced and in which culture as "adversary culture" is the accepted stance.[15] The relative gains and losses in a Victorian age such as that which Freud encountered might well be different.

4. CONCLUDING NOTE

In making these arguments, it is well to note that I have not tried to prove that contentions of those who would regulate obscenity but only to establish the extent of their moral right. The majority has a moral right to legislate, outside of the political realm, their not unreasonable conclusions as to what should be permitted in public in a moral society. In the case of pornography and obscenity, their representatives can make a plausible case for regulation. Beyond this, for any particular legislation or mode of enforcement, advocates must establish more detailed consequentialist arguments for particular definitions of public and private, political and nonpolitical, and obscenity and pornography before a framework for effective control can be preserved or constructed.

NOTES

1. See Patrick Devlin, *The Enforcement of Morals* (London: Oxford University Press, 1965); H. L. A. Hart, *Law, Liberty, and Morality* (Stanford, Calif.: Stanford University Press, 1963); Basil Mitchell, *Law, Morality and Religion in a Secular Society* (London: Oxford University Press, 1967); the *Wolfenden Report: Report of the Committee on Homosexual Offenses and Prostitution* (New York: Stein & Day, 1963); and *Report of the Commission on Obscenity and Pornography* (Washington, D.C., 1970), esp. p. 53.
2. On the undermining of freedom by liberalism see Thomas Molnar, "Zur Gesellschaft der Zukunft," *Schweizer Monatshefte* 54, no. 2 (1974): 97-104.
3. Alexander Meiklejohn, *Free Speech and Its Relation to Self-Government* (New York: Harper & Row, 1948), pp. 93-94.
4. *Report of the Commission on Obscenity and Pornography,* pp. 53-54.
5. See *Ibid.,* pp. 295-370.
6. *New York Times* (January 24, 1973).
7. In addition to Hart and Devlin, see C. L. Ten, "Enforcing a Shared Morality," *Ethics* 82, no. 4 (1972): 321-29; and Basil Mitchell, pp. 45-47.
8. Mislabeled "conservative" by Ten, *Ibid.*
9. James Q. Wilson, "Violence, Pornography, and Social Science," *Public Interest* 22 (Winter 1971): 45-61. Even a strong defender of the report of the pornography commission agrees with this analysis. See Weldon Johnson, "The Pornography Report," *Duquesne Law Review* 10 (Winter 1971): 190-219 (note p. 219).
10. For example, a Gallup poll shows a 20 percent drop in the percent opposing premarital sexual relations over the four years 1969-73 (*New York Times* [August 12, 1973]).
11. *Report of the Commission on Obscenity and Pornography,* pp. 139-264.
12. Duncan Williams, *Trousered Apes: A Study on the Influence of Literature on Modern Society* (London: Churchill Press, 1971).
13. Francis A. Schaeffer, *Escape from Reason* (Downer's Grove, Ill.: Intervarsity Press, 1968).
14. In addition to Williams, see Paul Horgan, "The Abdication of the Artist" *Proceedings of the American Philosophical Society* 109, no. 5 (1965); 267-71; Katherine

Ann Porter, "A Country and Some People I Love," *Harper's Magazine* 231 (September 1965): 58–68.

15. See Daniel Bell and Irving Kristol, *Capitalism Today* (New York: Basic Books, 1971), p. 22; and Irving Howe, *Decline of the New* (New York: Harcourt, Brace & World, 1963).

Violent Pornography: Censorship, Morality, and Social Alternatives
Judith W. DeCew

Judith W. DeCew is philosophy professor at Clark University and the author of a number of articles in applied ethics and philosophy of law. In this essay, her main concern is with the question of how a democratic society should respond to the increasing presence of violent pornography in its midst.

To censor violent pornography on the grounds that it leads to social violence would be, she maintains, unjustifiable. DeCew offers the following reasons in support of her belief: 1) no definitive causal connection between violent pornography and harm has been established, and 2) arguments both for and against censorship of pornography fail to be convincing. Still, she argues that society can reasonably condemn violent pornography as immoral, since it portrays human beings in ways that fail to respect their dignity and worth. Given this, DeCew next explores possible social responses to violent pornography other than censorship, and considers the issue of whether universities should allow violent pornographic films to be shown on campus.

CENSORSHIP AND FREE SPEECH

a. Moralism, Offence and Harm

A variety of arguments in favour of censoring pornography have been offered, most often based on three types of claims: that pornography is morally wrong, irrespective of whether or not it is harmful; that it is offensive; and that it causes harm to society, to individuals, or both. These claims have been general, not distinguishing pornographic materials depicting violence.

The worry that pornography is morally wrong takes at least two forms. Sometimes it is urged that we must protect individual morals and character from corruption. This justification for restraint by the state is clearly paternalistic. The more common version of the moralistic argument, epitomised by the Supreme Court's claim that obscenity tends to "injure the community as a whole" by polluting the "public environment",[1] urges that the state must protect society's moral standards from erosion, and censorship of pornography is required to accomplish that goal.

The second reason cited for censoring pornography is that it is offensive. According to this view we must protect the sensibilities of the public audience from shock, or the risk of shock, from exposure to pornographic materials. And the argument is often augmented to support repression rather than mere regulation by defending the claim that what others see, hear, and read, intrudes on us all, like it or not.

From *Journal of Applied Philosophy* 1 (1984), 79–94.

Finally, the most common argument given for banning pornography is that it does cause harm. On this view there is a causal link between pornographic material and socially harmful attitudes and acts, and the state must safeguard against dangerous behaviour, in this case by removing one cause of harm.

The ambiguities and difficulties with these arguments are not trivial. Clearly not every moral wrong or offence is, or should be, a legal wrong. One is not liable for every lie, broken promise or offensive remark. Apparently, even if we grant that pornography is morally wrong and offensive, more is needed to justify its censorship. In addition, it is troublesome to determine a test of moral wrong or offence. A community standard may seem initially plausible, but a majority or interest group opinion will not be sufficient. Before moral feelings become criminal law they must be subjected to sympathetic yet critical scrutiny to avoid prejudice, ignorance or misunderstanding.[2] Without clearly identifiable and justified standards of morality and offence, the first two arguments fail.

The most compelling argument for censorship of pornography is the third, that pornographic materials are harmful, because they promote antisocial attitudes and behaviour. It might seem that John Stuart Mill's classic view that restriction of individual liberty is only justified 'to prevent harm to others' can be marshalled in defense of this argument. But ambiguities associated with Mill's principle make its application difficult. Must there be direct harm to individuals or is general harm to society sufficient? Must the harm be physical, or is mental harm as worthy of protection?[3] And can any harm from pornography be established as existing?

Lawrence Tribe's position is that censorship is incompatible with the First Amendment premise that awareness alone is unharmful.[4] Yet even if we focus on less problematic physical harm to individuals, the sociological studies on the relationship between pornography and crime are notoriously contradictory and controversial. Despite the graphic illustration of the Hinckley case, it is extremely difficult to identify causal relations between particular books or films and individual acts. Moreover, it may be argued to the contrary that the availability of pornography serves as an outlet for psychosexual tensions or provides a release through fantasy of feelings which might otherwise lead to more harmful actions.

b. Pornography and the First Amendment

Those who advocate censorship of pornographic material generally have as their target of attack the 'liberal' view that consenting adults should be able to see or read anything they wish. This emphasises that pornography is deliberately displayed or published for a voluntary audience, and it is indisputable that there is a large American market for such material. Understandably, then, the major argument against censorship is that it violates human liberty, particularly free speech rights.

John Stuart Mill was perhaps the most articulate defender of these rights, advocating in *On Liberty* "absolute freedom of opinion and sentiment on all subjects" as well as the individual right to publish and have access to any expressions or opinions. However Joel Feinberg has claimed that "Mill did not consider public nudity, indecency, public displays of 'dirty pictures,' and the like, to be forms of 'symbolic speech,' or expression of opinion of any kind."[5] The judicial tendency to treat First Amendment rights, especially free speech, as weightier than other rights, is based on the historical concern to protect individuals voicing unpopular political or religious views. It is difficult to determine whether or not all purely pornographic material carries a 'message' which is protected by free speech rights, although some may be intended to do so by advocating certain sexual techniques, for example. In any case, freedom of speech has never meant the freedom to do or say whatever one pleases in front of a public audience.

Hence, if none of the arguments *for* censoring pornography are unproblematic, the free speech argument *against* censorship is not clear-cut either. It seems, then, that we either advocate no censorship, and no exceptions, or we take an alternate view and try to determine what is acceptable and what is repressive censorship. The latter option seems reasonable if, for example, we endorse the Supreme Court's 1982 decision that child pornography should be banned (and no libertarian has yet advocated such pornography). But it leaves us with a slippery slope problem. How do we draw the line between acceptable and unacceptable pornography? If we ban child pornography, why not ban pornography which portrays violent sex acts, or ban any depiction of violence?

Given the inconclusiveness of the various arguments for censoring pornography, concerns about the fairness and likelihood of legal enforcement of such laws, the existing market for pornography, and the priority given individual freedom in our society, it seems important to look beyond issues of censorship. I think it worthwhile to address the following questions: Is pornography morally wrong? If so, why? And if so, what are the social alternatives to censoring it? I believe answers to these questions may depend on our characterisation of pornography and distinctions not always made in discussions of pornography.

c. Erotica and Violent Pornography

Millions of people read Erica Jong's *Fear of Flying*, fantasising with the heroine over the 'zipless fuck'. Many others who normally would not see pornographic movies went to see 'popular' pornographic films such as *Deep Throat* and *The Devil in Miss Jones*. But a disturbing phenomenon has been the rise in what might be called violent pornography, allegedly appearing in an advertisement in as popular a magazine as *Vogue*. It is difficult to distinguish clearly between what could be classified as erotica or 'softcore' pornography and violent pornography. Erotica, emphasising the sensual or physical aspects of sex, attempts to be appealing to the audience, and need not be incompatible with the values of mutual pleasure, care and concern for others. While Berger claims that "even sadistic pornography . . . depicts people as having enjoyment",[6] violent pornography does not merely show pleasure in its subjects, not does it merely portray people having sex. Depictions of gagging, whipping, bondage, torture, rape, beating, mutilation, or other abuse in a sexual context, sometimes compounded with racist stereotypes, and most often (though not exclusively) by men against women,[7] form a very distinct class, even if the material also attempts to attract and arouse some audience.

It will not do to characterise violent pornography merely as depiction of sex with violence, however, since rape, for example, need not be violent. It is important to focus as well on domination and force. Thus we might characterise violent pornography as sexual material portraying violent, coercive, abusive, or non-consensual acts, where 'abusive' covers instances in which models appear to abuse themselves. But, according to this definition, materials which describe or represent a rape in order to analyse the consequences of the assault on the victim, as well as the film *Not a Love Story*—made as a pornographic exposé depicting pornographically violent materials to educate the public about their production, their deleterious impact, and how morally degrading they are—would be classified as violent pornography. In order to distinguish these, it is preferable to add that violent pornography not only tolerates, but even encourages, the behavior shown, implicitly or explicitly. Thus I shall mean by violent pornography sexual material which depicts violent, coercive, abusive or non-consensual acts, and which endorses or recommends such behavior.[8] Given my descriptions, erotica and violent pornography do not exhaust all sexually explicit materials. Nevertheless, without further differentiation, I shall assume we have a general idea of the difference between them. For the rest of this paper I shall focus on the moral status of, and social responses to, violent pornography.

IS VIOLENT PORNOGRAPHY MORALLY WRONG?

a. Rights Violations

There appear to be a wealth of arguments that violent pornography is morally wrong, derived by applying traditional ethical principles. First, it would be wrong if it involved a serious violation of individual rights. If actors or actresses are abused in any way that fails to protect their rights to privacy or bodily security, for example, then it is difficult to see how the rights of others to have access to the material, or any benefit to consumers, could outweigh such a violation.

However, it is not easy to defend the view that any rights have been violated if the material is written or if the participants are consenting adults. The major problem with the latter is determining the extent to which participants genuinely and knowingly consent or are pressured by other individuals or social forces. It seems clear that in some cases there is virtually no consent, or that consent is not genuine, so individual rights are violated. For example, Linda Lovelace of *Deep Throat* and other pornography models indicate that some participants are sold or coerced by spouses or parents to perform, that physical violence and forced drugs are sometimes used to gain 'consent', and that models who do agree to participate, even in written contracts, often feel trapped when they discover that what happens after signing is beyond their control.[9] Nevertheless, this fails as a general moral argument against *all* violent pornography, for in literary work as well as films, photographs, or plays done by consenting sadists, it is hard to identify any individual rights that are being transgressed. (Note, however, that sado-masochistic pornography may *portray* consensual pleasure, without using sadistic models.)

b. Treatment of Human Beings

One might rely on the more general statement that violent pornography portrays actions which fail to respect the integrity, worth and dignity of human beings. The claim could be made to show that individual rights are violated, but as such the argument is extremely vague.[10] The claim might be used more successfully as a general moral indictment of violent pornography because it approvingly depicts treatment of human beings in a violent, nonconsensual manner which thus fails to respect their worth. As such, it would apply as well to other violent literature, movies, and television shows which portray human life as expendable, violence toward others without cause as acceptable, etc. While some may believe this could adequately justify legal censorship, it is worthwhile to note that it is not and never has been a criminal offence to publish accounts or photographs of harmful or illegal actions. Thus, unless we radically change our views on criminal law, portrayal of violence alone provides no argument for repression of what is displayed or written. Still, it may be plausible to say that such material, including violent pornography, is morally objectionable due to its content: approving depiction of violent, nonconsensual treatment of human beings.[11]

c. Harm to Participants

A third way of arguing that violent pornography is morally wrong involves appealing to the harm (apart from violation of rights) it causes either (a) to the participants, or (b) to others. It is extremely difficult for those of us not part of the pornographic industry to have a clear idea of the extent models in films or photographs, for example, actually suffer pain, or merely act as though they do. However, the pornographic thriller, *Snuff,* banned six years ago, has recently resurfaced on videotape. This film depicts the dismemberment and murder of a woman for the sexual stimulation of male characters and viewers, and it is rumoured that at least one actress actually died during the filming. Pornographic models also relate stories of women having to endure hot candle wax dripped on their breasts, cigarette burns on their bodies, and other pain.[12] Furthermore, it is not difficult to imagine that many participants are exploited in much the same way that prostitutes are exploited by pimps. The exploitation might be physical or psychological. I suspect the analogy is a fair one, and it is substantiated by personal reports.[13] But virtually no research has corroborated the extent and pervasiveness of harm caused to participants to make this a firm moral argument against violent pornography.

d. Harm to Others

The argument that violent pornography harms others is more diffuse but at least as important and troubling. It is worrisome because it relies on the premise that there is a causal relationship between violent pornography and violence produced in society at large. Yet, as already noted, the studies on the extent to which exposure to pornography leads to crime yield conflicting results. Moreover, most of the empirical studies have not aimed at gaining the type of information necessary for the argument. For example, the Congressional Committee on Obscenity concluded in 1970 that exposure to erotica had "little or no effect" on attitudes toward sexuality or sexual morality, that patterns of sexual behavior were "not altered substantially by exposure to erotica", and that their data did not show "erotic material as a significant cause of sex crime".[14] But concluding that there is no evidence relating *erotica* to violent attitudes or behaviour does not even address the effects of *violent pornography.* If violent pornography depicts and recommends sexual relations with someone getting hurt involuntarily, and through its approval of such behaviour encourages emulation, then it may well have effects on others.

Given that the President's Commission on the Causes and Prevention of Violence concluded in 1969 that media violence can induce viewers to act aggressively, it is reasonable to infer that analogous results follow for viewers of sexual violence. Some studies done in the last ten years do show that violent pornography is closely linked to violent behaviour. But to have a moral argument against violent pornography based on the harm it inflicts on others, we need studies verifying not merely a *correlation,* but also a *causal relationship* between portrayals of violent pornography and crime. Such information would also provide a strong, though not unproblematic, argument for censorship of violent pornography. However, we still await solid confirming data. And research establishing effects in the world is always difficult because of discrepancies between what people say and what they really believe, and between what they think they will do and what they actually do.[15]

e. Sexism and Violence

Although there are exceptions, violent pornography is overwhelmingly intended for the gratification of males, and is acknowledged by many to be sexist in the sense that it exploits sexual inequality and enhances a degrading view of women. Women's groups view most violent pornography as bloody, woman-as-victim, horror shows. Irving Kristol says, of pornography in general, that

.... there can be no question that pornography is a form of "sexism," as the Women's Liberation Movement calls it, and the instinct of Women's Lib has been unerring in perceiving that, when pornography is perpetrated, it is perpetrated against them, as part of a conspiracy to deprive them of their full humanity.[16]

Others believe that pornography often reflects the worse social conceptions of sexual relations in that many of the scenes depict male dominance over women, females as sexual servants or toys, and male aggression and violence toward women.

It would be ideal if we could argue separately for the immorality of violence and the immorality of sexism. They clearly can be different. Dismemberment is distinguishable from debasement of women. With respect to violence, depictions which encourage it, especially those that lead to violent acts against innocents, must surely be morally wrong. The difficulty arises in establishing a causal relationship between portrayal and physical harm. For sexism, the concern is perhaps more controversial. It is not merely that there is harm to an image of women (whatever that may mean), nor is it easy to identify direct harm to women. The claim is that sexism is morally wrong because it condones, recommends, and perpetuates an immoral view about how women should act and be treated. To the extent that pornography expresses that view or affects behaviour, it is also morally wrong.

Unfortunately it is especially difficult to separate arguments about violent and sexist pornography. Robert Baker and Frederick Elliston have pointed out, for example, strong linguistic evidence that our society connects the concept of sex with the concept of harm, traditionally using male subjects and female objects.[17] Feminist Julia Robbins worries that part of pornography's hateful message is that a "steady diet of [pornographic] images suggests that females will never say no or, at least, never mean it. Men . . . buy the idea that women are there for the taking".[18] The concern is that violence depicted in a sexual context conveys the message that women *desire* and *enjoy* being treated in an abusive way, or *want* and *need* to be forced to submit. While pornography which is sexist may be wrong independently of any violence, violent pornography which portrays sexism in a dramatic way by condoning and encouraging such acts as rape and battering of women, is worse for intertwined reasons. We cannot usually separate what sexually excites, what is sexist, and what is violent.

f. Summary

Each of the arguments discussed give some ground for moral complaint against violent pornography. It is noteworthy and initially surprising, however, that the conclusions that violent pornography is morally wrong are generally conditional ones. That is, violent pornography is immoral *when* it depicts sexist attitudes, or *if* it fosters sexist behaviour, or *if* it leads to violent crime, or *if* it exploits or abuses participants psychologically or physically, or *if* it violates an individual's right by involving participation without genuine consent. In each case, concluding that violent pornography is morally wrong depends on accepting one of these conditions which may not always be true.

The only unconditional conclusion that all violent pornography is wrong is based on the claim that every portrayal endorsing and recommending treatment of human beings in a way disregarding their dignity and worth, is immoral. Then, given that violent, coercive, abusive or non-consensual treatment of human beings disregards their dignity and worth, all violent pornography is morally wrong.

I think it is reasonable to accept this argument. More generally, I believe it is reasonable to judge violent pornography on its content: it is morally wrong when it enhances a degrading view of women (and men) through an unworthy portrayal of violent, hurtful treatment of human beings, even if it leads to no sexist or violent behaviour in the world. But it has been suggested that more support may be needed to argue that morally objectionable content is sufficient to judge material itself unethical.[19] Anyone who finds such a portrayal misguided or ignorant, but not properly judged morally wrong, or any consequentialist who believes moral right and wrong are determined solely by effects, will be unpersuaded by this argument.

SOCIAL ALTERNATIVES TO CENSORSHIP OF VIOLENT PORNOGRAPHY: TWO APPROACHES

At the very least the arguments above show we must continue to gather the empirical evidence necessary to make informed legal and ethical recommendations. But even given uncontroversial confirming data on harm caused by violent pornography, for example, it not clear how best to respond to it.

a. Reasonable Avoidability

Joel Feinberg has recently claimed that "obscenity should be treated more as a nuisance than as a menace. . . ."[20] According to Feinberg, obscenity (in its ordinary and non-technical sense, meaning "material dealing with nudity, sex, or excretion in an offensive manner"[21] is one example of what might be called a 'harmless offence'. Although material that offends someone might be said for that reason to be harmful, on Feinberg's view it is harmless in a narrower sense if it does not lead to further harm or violations of interests.

Nuisance law protects individuals from loud noises, stenches, and other direct and inescapable irritants to the senses. Similarly, Feinberg believes we should be protected from certain 'harmless offenses', including obscenity, which can cause embarrassment, shame or some other uncomfortable psychic jolt to many normal people. Feinberg thinks that instances of what is a harmless offence, such as a billboard in Times Square displaying sodomy techniques,[22] or what becomes offensive because of inappropriate circumstances, such as nudity on a public bus, cannot be prohibited unless we endorse some version of an offence principle.

Specifically, Feinberg advocates restriction of one's personal liberty by the state to prevent offence to others.[23] Because people take genuine offence at socially useful, or what many would find innocent, activities, Feinberg sets limitations on the principle he defends:

1. *the standard of universality:* for the offence to justify coercion it should cause a reaction (not inspired merely by knowledge of private behavior) that could be expected from virtually any person,

and

2. *the standard of reasonable avoidability:* no one has a right to protection from the state against offensiveness if (s)he can effectively avoid those experiences with no unreasonable effort of inconvenience.

Furthermore,

3. no attention should be paid to "abnormal susceptibilities,"

and

4. anyone restricted from being offensive to others must be granted an allowable alternative mode of expression,

and

5. the penalty for a "harmless offence" ought always to be less than for conduct harming or threatening harm.[24]

Feinberg insists that he would permit public *advocacy* of any 'values' whatever on sex, religion, and politics,[25] so his principle is compatible with Mill's defense of free speech. Nevertheless, he is defending legal enforcement of a carefully restricted offence principle which he says would justify the "prohibition of public conduct and publicly pictured conduct that is in its inherent character repellent (e.g. buggery, bestiality, sexual sado-masochism)".[26] Clearly Feinberg is not advocating censorship of either written material or pornographic movies or shows; he is arguing for legal regulations, not bans.

If we apply Feinberg's position to violent pornography by assuming that all instances of violent pornography satisfy his condition (1), we could argue that:

(P_1) The state must protect an individual's right to avoid violent pornography without unreasonable effort.

Assuming (1), that violent pornography is 'universally' offensive, makes (3) unnecessary. And we need not add (4) and (5) if violent pornography is not 'harmless' in the narrow sense of not leading to further harm or violations of interests.

The fundamental advantage of (P_1) is that it allows us to protect all those who want and need protection—especially children—from publicly flaunted and imposed violent pornography without depriving the rights of those who wish to have access to such books, magazines, and movies (at least those discreetly marketed and not on obvious drive-in screens). (P_1) also avoids many of the troublesome consequences of censorship, such as the chilling effect, discussed in the first section. Furthermore, depending on how 'without unreasonable effort' is interpreted, it might be possible to use (P_1) to defend zoning of bookstores, shows, etc., which sell, distribute or display violent pornographic material, enhancing individuals' rights to create and maintain the sort of community in which they wish to live while allowing others' rights to patronise zoned areas.

It is important to note that legal enforcement of Feinberg's right of reasonable avoidability for violent pornography would be *more* restrictive than current legal treatment of non-harmful, non-dangerous offenses. As the Supreme Court said in *Cohen v. California,* "the Constitution leaves matters of taste and style . . . largely to the individual", so mere "intolerance or animosity cannot be the basis for abridgement". Rather, the Constitution requires those offended simply to "avert their eyes".[27] The basic principle underlying these statements is that being forced to conform is more intrusive than being forced by the unusual to avert one's eyes. But by protecting a right of reasonable avoidability we require not merely that one avert one's eyes from violent pornography, but also that it not be allowed in public displays where those who do not want to view it even have to go so far as averting their eyes. Anyone who wishes access to violent pornography must make a positive effort to gain it. And a right of sanctuary is provided for those who want to avoid it.

Feinberg's standard of reasonable avoidability seems more plausible for violent pornography than for non-harmful, non-dangerous offenses. This is because on Feinberg's view the *Cohen* case was decided wrongly, and Cohen should have been convicted for wearing a jacket bearing the words 'Fuck the Draft' in a public courthouse. Feinberg's intuitions on the *Cohen* case are jarring, and if that type of result is mandated by his restricted offence principle, it provides good reason to reject it for harmless offenses. Alternatively, Feinberg might better have argued that (1), his standard of universality, was not satisfied in the *Cohen* case. Although displayed in public, the word which potentially could have caused offence did not do so on that particular occasion (according to the facts reported in the case). There was no 'universal' offence.

While I remain concerned that, depending on how 'universal offensiveness' is determined, Feinberg's restricted offence principle is too strong for non-harmful, non-dangerous offenses, protection of a right of reasonable avoidability provides an attractive legal alternative to censorship of violent pornography. Nevertheless, it is not an ideal solution. Those who want all violent pornography banned will be unhappy with the proposal as too weak a remedy. And enforcing it may be too strong if it has the consequence of increasing private supply, demand, and proliferation of violent pornography, a major problem according to supporters as well as foes of censorship.

Additionally, by applying Feinberg's reasonable avoidability standard to violent pornography as I have suggested, we may avoid a subjective determination of how embarrassed or repulsed the public must be before material is considered offensive. But the weight of that judgment falls on two other assumptions: (i) that we can adequately distinguish violent pornography and erotica, so that only violent, coercive, non-consensual material is restricted, and (ii) that we can clarify the standard of 'reasonable avoidability'. While these may be less problematic than producing a clearly identifiable and justified standard of offence, they are not trivial assumptions. The latter, especially, raises difficult questions such as "how blatant, brazen, or blaring a . . . display must be before it constitutes an unavoidable assault on an unwilling spectator's sense".[28]

Finally, even if we could clarify what effort is reasonably required to say that a viewer has not voluntarily assumed the risk of offence, it might still seem that although (P_1) encompasses the maximum acceptable legal restriction, it is ultimately too weak as a social response to violent pornography. Imagine that a student group on a university campus shows a film which we assume is clearly an instance of violent pornography. Students flock to see it and so such films are shown on a regular basis for the audience and as a fundraiser for other activities. While we may assume the advertisements are innocuous and that the films are clearly avoidable without unreasonable effort, they may have been purchased with funds from students who would not want to attend. Or even if students' funds are not used, each film showing is subsidised by the university as long as it is shown on university property.

b. Refusing Support and Subsidy

Assuming that violent pornography is morally objectionable, it might be that as an alternative or supplement to (P_1) we should endorse:

> (P_2) It is morally wrong for any individual or institution to do anything which supports or subsidises the industry that produces violent pornography.[29]

This principle defends a position much stronger than one advocating avoidance or even boycotting. In the above example, according to (P_2) the individual students are morally wrong to show the movie, even if there is an audience for it and it provides a hefty income, and the university is morally wrong to allow its property to be used to show the film. But as described, neither is restricted by (P_1).

However, there are major difficulties with (P_2). First, other examples lead to the worry that (P_2) is too strong. Consider the following: suppose someone subscribes to a cable television channel to get news and weather information and movies unavailable on commercial television. The station then begins to add pornographic films, including violent ones, late at night to increase its subscriber audience. Imagine also that alternative cable channels with similar benefits (but without the pornographic films) are not available in the geographical areas. Furthermore, the subscriber has no interest in the pornographic films, and never watches them. Nevertheless, aware that they are part of the parcel, is it morally wrong for one to continue subscribing to the channel?

The case can be altered a bit, and become even more puzzling. Suppose on a trip one stays in a hotel with a television which one discovers shows, among other things, violent pornographic films. Even if one does not watch the films, is one morally required to get another room without a television? Or a room without a television showing the pornography? Or move to another hotel to avoid any action which subsidises violent pornography in any way?

Our examples lead us to a second slippery slope problem. How much is morally required of one who finds violent pornography morally wrong for any or all of the reasons discussed above? Must one give up the benefits of cablevision because the station in one's area shows the objectionable films? Must one leave one's hotel room even if it is late at night, one has an early business meeting the next day, and it is a great inconvenience? Must one check out even in the extreme case when no alternative lodging is available? Apparently we must answer yes if we accept (P$_2$), according to which it is morally wrong to do *anything* which supports or subsidises the industry producing violent pornography.

Second, (P$_2$), is ambiguous. How are we to interpret it? Is the implicit assumption that the multi-million dollar industry, allegedly linked with organised crime, illicit drugs, and prostitution, is immoral and should not be supported? If so, it seems analogous support and subsidy for the industry producing erotica is also wrong, and thus accepting (P$_2$) requires defending a position stronger than many are willing to endorse.

Or is the assumption that the industry exploits and violates the rights of models in the production of violently pornographic material? On this reading, (P$_2$) may again be too broad because it very likely implies acceptance of an analogous principle applying to erotica as well. Also, on this interpretation, the principle appears too weak since it may apply to the production of films, peep shows, posters, etc., but not to books or other written material.

Or is the basis of the objection the only unconditional one, that the content of violent pornography generally portrays, endorses and recommends immoral attitudes and behavior? If so, then (P$_2$) is too strong as formulated. Even if the content is unethical, it does not follow that producing, distributing and perceiving it are.[30]

Or is the objection implicit in (P$_2$) the most worrisome one, that violent pornography has dangerous effects, assuming that this is true and that it can be shown that such pornography is causally related to increases in violent crime, particularly against women? If so, then (P$_2$) focuses on the effects of the material, which are independent of objections to the industry.

Determining the best response to violent pornography requires getting clearer on what is most objectionable about it. If our objections focus on the *content* of most violent pornography because of the attitudes it portrays and recommends or on the *effects* it has due to the behaviour it incites, rather than its *source* in the industry, then we must reformulate (P$_2$) to reflect the basis of our moral protest. But then it is less obvious what the moral responsibilities of institutions and individuals are.

Consider again the student film example. If the university decides to ban violent pornographic films on campus on the grounds that it is morally wrong to allow university property to be used to display materials whose *content* is morally objectionable, then we may ask what standard of morality is being used for the judgment. Moreover, if the university does ban the film on campus, then it is clearly making a decision that affects what students may or may not see or hear on campus. Even if the reason for the ban is a moral objection to the content of the film, the effect of the university's action is control over availability of what may be seen or heard. This of course is the essence of censorship, considered contrary to a free society and antithetical to the concept of a university. If there is no harm to others, Mill defended the liberty of tastes and pursuits, even though others think them foolish, perverse or wrong.

Universities have used similar reasoning for permitting speakers such as Professor William Shockley, the Stanford physicist whose theories concerning the genetic transmission of intelligence are considered by many to be false as well as racist. On this view, there should be no restraints on the availability of information or expression, even if it fosters objectionable opinions and attitudes. A public invitation to a speaker does not acknowledge the acceptability of the views. Indeed, heckling and protest are allowed. Furthermore, it is claimed that banning such speakers from campus carries the implicit assumption that students cannot distinguish true from false, or worthy from unworthy, and such banning is thus presumptuous and insulting to the intellectual maturity of the university community. Analogously, allowing violent pornographic films on university property neither condones nor acknowledges their acceptability. A contrary decision to ban the films from campus, if made by the institution and not, for example, by a referendum of the student body, can be viewed as a paternalistic decision in its *least* justifiable form.[31] The university is interfering with a person's liberty, not because the person is physically or psychologically unable to make a thoughtful choice about whether or not to attend, but because the content is thought inappropriate.

In reply, it might be argued that violent pornographic films do not in any identifiable way further the quest for truth. Not all 'expression' is information. Moreover, it can be claimed that the university decision is not a paternalistic one. It is not one that restricts an individual's liberty for his or her *own* good, but does so to take a strong moral stand on the part of the university. The Constitution provides against governmental repression, but a university need not provide a forum for such films. Most compellingly, if the university cannot proscribe use of its property in the case of violent pornography, when can it assert moral leadership, a role often viewed as an essential function of a university?

Limitations on free speech can be justified based on either (a) the content of, or (b) the effect of, the expression. Historically, the courts have found non-content features, such as time, place, volume, and 'clear risk' of danger, to be admissible justifications. But what has consistently been viewed as an illegitimate ground for curbing expression is any reason based on the content or message. Unfortunately, the line between these two types of justification is not easy to draw.[32] With respect to violent pornography it is especially troublesome to distinguish material which endorses and invites objectionable attitudes and behaviour, from that which poses a 'clear risk' of violent actions. Nor is it at all clear how great a threat generates a 'clear risk' of violence.

If a university administration has good reason to fear dangerous effects from allowing violent pornographic films on campus (effects such as increased violence in the dorms), then I believe it has no choice but to refuse to allow the films.[33] However not all deleterious effects are sufficient to justify campus bans. The problem, of course, is determining whether violent and non-violent effects ever exist independently. In my view, barring clear risk of violent behaviour, a university may allow students to show violent pornographic films. While it is difficult to justify violent pornography at a serious workplace, a university can take a strong moral stand on it by issuing public disclaimers, for example, without resorting to campus bans based on arguments normally found unacceptable as grounds for state censorship. Of course a university need not always take a moral stand by issuing public statements rather than taking action. A university can and should refuse funding from racist countries, and limit recruitment of campus by groups that do not admit minorities. But in the case of violent pornography, if the major concern is the *content* of the material, not dangerous *effects,* then the issue is what others may or may not see and hear. It is thus distinguishable from other instances where a university might want to assert moral leadership.

CONCLUSION

I have shown that there is only one argument for the conclusion that *all* violent pornography is immoral—an argument based on the premise that violent pornography approvingly depicts and recommends attitudes and behaviour that fail to respect the dignity and worth of human beings. To the extent the production and availability of it violates individual rights, exploits participants emotionally or physically, fosters sexist attitudes and behaviour, and causes violent crime, we have further moral claims against it.

In response to violent pornography, enforcing Feinberg's right of reasonable avoidability as described in (P_1) may be the strongest legal action we can justify. But even if the notion of 'reasonable avoidability' can be clarified, (P_1) is too weak as a social reaction. It makes it too easy and morally permissible to ignore the existence of violent pornography, and it does not prescribe any action to minimise, criticise, or educate others about it. Alternatively, to defend (P_2) and argue that *any* action which supports or subsidises violent pornography is morally wrong, is too strong.

It is difficult to draw the line in between, because the issues raised are complex and controversial. However, it is by exercising justified power to make an economic impact as individuals or institutions, even at some inconvenience or cost to ourselves, that we can be most effective exposing the immorality of, and reducing the prevalence of, violent pornography.

NOTES

1. *Paris Adult Theatre 1,* 413 U.S. 68-69.

2. See Wasserstrom, Richard (Ed.) (1971) *Morality and the Law,* (Belmont, CA, Wadsworth) especially H. L. A. Hart's 'Immorality and treason', and Ronald Dworkin's 'Lord Devlin and the enforcement of morals'. The former is reprinted in Dworkin (Ed.) *The Philosophy of Law,* (Oxford University Press, 1977), and the latter is in *Yale Law Journal,* 75 (1966), pp. 986-1005, and is reprinted in Dworkin's *Taking Rights Seriously,* chapter 10 (Harvard University Press, 1977).

3. Feinberg, Joel (1973) *Social Philosophy,* especially chapters 2 and 3 (London, Prentice-Hall).

4. Tribe, Lawrence (1978) *American Constitutional Law,* p. 669 (The Foundation Press Inc.).

5. Feinberg, Joel (1980) 'Harmless immoralities' and offensive nuisances, in: Feinberg, J. (Ed.) *Rights, Justice, and the Bounds of Liberty,* p. 71 (Princeton University Press).

6. Berger, Fred (1977) Pornography, sex, and censorship, *Social Theory and Practice,* vol. 4, no. 2, spring. Reprinted in Wasserstrom, Richard, (Ed.) *Today's Moral Problems* (2nd ed., Macmillan, 1979), p. 353.

7. An explicit film described to me shows a man drilling a jack hammer up a woman's vagina. For other graphic examples, including a description of the *Vogue* advertisement, and disturbing statistics on the prevalence of such materials, see Lederer, Laura (Ed.) *Take Back the Night* (Bantam Books, 1982).

8. This is similar to the definition of pornography in the National Lawyer's Guild Resolution on Pornography, passed by the Convention on August 9, 1980, except that I have added 'abusive' as explained. I am grateful to Gail Hanton of Women Against Violence Against Women in Boston for the NLG material and for suggesting the addition, although WAVAW uses 'degrading' instead of 'abusive' for portrayals of self-abuse. Like the NLG, others have used 'pornography' non-neutrally. Gloria Steinem distinguishes erotica and pornography, where the latter involves violence, dominance, and conquest, but she fails to make clear the difference between material which *endorses* the power portrayed and that which does not. Erotica and pornography: a clear and present difference, *Ms.,* 1978. Helen Longino proposes a definition of pornography emphasising the approving quality of the material, but which may be broader than my definition, depending on how one interprets 'degrading' and 'abusive'. She says, "Pornography, then, is verbal or pictorial material which represents or describes sexual behavior that is degrading or abusive to one or more of the participants *in such a way as to endorse the degradation*". Pornography, oppression, and freedom: a closer look, in Lederer, *op. cit.,* pp. 36-41.

9. Lovelace, Linda (1980) *Ordeal* (Seacaucus, New Jersey, Citadel Press). Lederer, Laura, Then and now: an interview with a former pornography model, in Lederer, *op. cit.,* pp. 45-59.

10. This appears to be one type of argument defended by Helen Longino. On her view, portrayals in pornography violate women's rights to respect and against defamation and libel. Longino, *op. cit.*

11. But see below p. 13 and note 25.

12. Laura Lederer, *op. cit.,* (note 16).

13. *Ibid.*

14. *The Report of the Commission on Obscenity and Pornography* (Bantam Books, 1970). Excerpts reprinted in Gunther, Gerals (1980) *Constitutional Law,* pp. 1355-1356 (The Foundation Press). The Commission was given a $2 million appropriation, but chose to focus on 'erotic' or 'explicit sexual materials'. It is not clear whether the Commission used 'erotica' in the sense I have, but it *is* clear that few materials used in their studies would qualify as violent pornography as I have defined it. Several members of the Commission protested about this and argued that other available studies wore ignored or underrated. The minority also accused the majority of being biased, of suppressing evidence, of misrepresentation and misinterpretation of research statistics and conclusions, underscoring how controversial the report was. Feminist critiques describing biases and inadequacies of the Commission's majority report are in Lederer, *op. cit.,* section IV.

15. Because much of the research on pornography was done before violence pervaded it, studies focusing on violent pornography are still rare. Perhaps the best thus far are by Malamuth and his colleagues, but even these show *correlations* and are not uncontroversial. See Lederer, *op. cit.,* section IV, especially pp. 228-236.

16. Kristol, Irving (1971) Pornography, obscenity, and the case for censorship, *New York Times Magazine,* March 28, reprinted in Feinberg & Gross (Eds.) *Philosophy of Law,* 2nd ed., p. 222 (New York, Wadsworth, 1980).

17. Baker, Robert & Elliston, Frederick (1975) 'Pricks' and 'chicks': a plea for persons, *Philosophy and Sex,* (Buffalo, New York, Prometheus Books). For example, the active male screws, fucks, bangs, the passive female.

18. Robbins, Julia (1983) Pornography's hateful message, Letter to the Editor, *Boston Globe,* February 4. Robbins' critique is directed against all pornography, and to that extent is surely an overgeneralisation.

19. Garry, Ann (1978) Pornography and respect for women, *Social Theory and Practice 4,* pp. 395-421. Reprinted in Bayles & Henley (Eds.) *Right Conduct: Theories and Applications* (Random House, Inc., 1983).

20. Feinberg, Joel (1980) Reply to 'Harmless immoralities' and offensive nuisances, *Rights, Justice, and the Bounds of Liberty, op. cit.,* expanded from Feinberg's *Social Philosophy, op. cit.,* p. 85.

21. Feinberg, 'Harmless immoralities' and offensive nuisances, *op. cit.,* p. 85.

22. Feinberg, Reply to 'Harmless immoralities' and offensive nuisances, *op. cit.,* p. 86. The example is from Schwartz, Louis B. (1963) Morals offenses and the model penal code, *Columbia Law Review,* 63, p. 670.

23. [The limitations on the offense principle discussed in this essay represent an earlier version of the limitations defended by Joel Feinberg in his essay included in this chapter.]

24. Ibid., pp. 88-89. Feinberg further qualifies the universality standard so that mocking, abusive language aimed at minorities but which might not offend *most* people would be ruled out as well.

25. *Ibid.,* p. 86.

26. *Ibid.,* p. 86.

27. 403 U.S. 15.

28. Tong, Rosemarie (1983) Feminism, pornography, and censorship, read at Violent Pornography: Legal Censorship or Alternative Community Responses?, a conference at Clark University, April 9, 1983, p. 12.

29. S. J. Keyser first suggested this alternative to me. For those like myself, who agree all violent pornography is morally wrong because of its content—portrayal and endorsement of coercive, abusive, non-consensual actions which fail to respect human dignity—it is clear we can recommend moral or legal action against all violent pornography.

    Those who do not accept this unconditional argument recognise that conclusions from empirical studies will be generalisations and will not apply to every instance. It is surely possible, however rare, for a violently pornographic book, for example, not to violate any individual rights, promote sexism, or lead to violence. Thus they must determine whether to recommend action against all violent pornography, even if not all produces harmful consequences.

    It is likely that they will not know of a particular instance, however, whether it has the morally objectionable features or effects. They may have subjective opinions about the material, and certain cases may seem obviously wrong, but they may yet have no general standard for judging instances of violent pornography and its effects. If this is correct, they may also be justified in recommending action against all violent pornography, recognising that they cannot adequately distinguish that which is unobjectionable. 'Innocent' materials will be sacrificed in order to deal with the rest.

30. In *Stanley v. Georgia*, 394 U.S. 577 (1969), the Supreme Court argued that individual freedom and a right to privacy protect an individual's right to view obscene material in the privacy of his or her home. And it is not at all clear, although it is a serious and important question, that this individual freedom and privacy should be overridden if the material is violent pornography. Thus, criticism of the content does not suffice as criticism of the industry, especially where there is a voluntary audience.

31. See Dworkin, Gerald (1971) Paternalism, in: Wasserstrom (Ed.) *Morality and the Law, op. cit.,* for a view on when paternalism might be justified, namely when it "enhances for the individual his ability to rationally consider and carry out his own decisions", p. 125.

32. For interesting examples and discussion see Scanlan, T. M. 'A theory of freedom of expression', in: Dworkin, *Philosophy of Law, op. cit.*

33. For example, a striking study by Feshbach and Malamuth found that of 53 male students who voluntarily read a passage describing a male student raping a female student after holding a knife to her throat when she refused his offer to walk her to her car, an astounding 51% responded they might act as the rapist did if they were assured they would not be caught! Feshbach, Shymour & Malamuth, Neal (1978) Sex and aggression: proving the link, *Psychology Today,* 12, 6, November, pp. 116–117. Donald Mosher claims that these high percentages are misleading because of the methods used for calculating subjects' agreement with various sentences, in 'Social and psychological effects of violent pornography', presented at Violent Pornography: Legal Censorship or Alternative Community Responses?, a conference at Clark University, April 9 1883. For a summary of other recent results similar to Malamuth's, see 'Sex and violence: pornography hurts', *Science News,* 118, September 13 1980.

American Booksellers Association, Inc. v. Hudnut

In this case an Indianapolis antipornography ordinance developed by Catharine MacKinnon and Andrea Dworkin was found by a Federal Court of Appeals to be unconstitutional. The ordinance, which treated pornography as a form of sex discrimination against women, would have allowed civil suits to be brought against those who produced or sold pornography and who forced others to participate in its production. While the Court was sympathetic to the view that pornography influences behavior, and in particular helps to maintain the social conditions of women's exploitation and subordination to men, it did not find any reason to support the legality of the ordinance. Many opinions and ideas influence action and shape culture, Judge Frank Easterbrook noted in writing the opinion of the court. To protect some of these ideas through public policies while not protecting others on the basis of their content is, he indicates, to engage in a form of "thought control" in which the state has no right to engage.

EASTERBROOK, Circuit Judge

Indianapolis enacted an ordinance defining "pornography" as a practice that discriminates against women. "Pornography" is to be redressed through the administrative and judicial methods used for other discrimination. The City's definition of "pornography" is considerably different from "obscenity," which the Supreme Court has held is not protected by the First Amendment.

[1] To be "obscene" under *Miller v. California* "a publication must, taken as a whole, appeal to the prurient interest, must contain patently offensive depictions or descriptions of specified sexual conduct, and on the whole have no serious literary, artistic, political, or scientific value." Offensiveness must be assessed under the standards of the community. Both offensiveness and an appeal to something other than "normal, healthy sexual desires" are essential elements of "obscenity."

"Pornography" under the ordinance is "the graphic sexually explicit subordination of women, whether in pictures or in words, that also includes one or more of the following:

1. Women are presented as sexual objects who enjoy pain or humiliation; or
2. Women are presented as sexual objects who experience sexual pleasure in being raped; or
3. Women are presented as sexual objects tied up or cut up or mutilated or bruised or physically hurt, or as dismembered or truncated or fragmented or severed into body parts; or

---

771 F.2d. 323 (7th Cir. 1985)   [Citations omitted.]

4. Women are presented as being penetrated by objects or animals; or

5. Women are presented in scenarios of degradation, injury, abasement, torture, shown as filthy or inferior, bleeding, bruised, or hurt in a context that makes these conditions sexual; or

6. Women are presented as sexual objects for domination, conquest, violation, exploitation, possession, or use, or through postures or positions of servility or submission or display." . . .

The Indianapolis ordinance does not refer to the prurient interest, to offensiveness, or to the standards of the community. It demands attention to particular depictions, not to the work judged as a whole. It is irrelevant under the ordinance whether the work has literary, artistic, political, or scientific value. The City and many amici point to these omissions as virtues. They maintain that pornography influences attitudes, and the statute is a way to alter the socialization of men and women rather than to vindicate community standards of offensiveness. And as one of the principal drafters of the ordinance has asserted, "if a woman is subjected, why should it matter that the work has other value?"

Civil rights groups and feminists have entered this case as amici on both sides. Those supporting the ordinance say that it will play an important role in reducing the tendency of men to view women as sexual objects, a tendency that leads to both unacceptable attitudes and discrimination in the workplace and violence away from it. Those opposing the ordinance point out that much radical feminist literature is explicit and depicts women in ways forbidden by the ordinance and that the ordinance would reopen old battles. It is unclear how Indianapolis would treat works from James Joyce's *Ulysses* to Homer's *Iliad;* both depict women as submissive objects for conquest and domination.

We do not try to balance the arguments for and against an ordinance such as this. The ordinance discriminates on the ground of the content of the speech. Speech treating women in the approved way—in sexual encounters "premised on equality"—is lawful no matter how sexually explicit. Speech treating women in the disapproved way—as submissive in matters sexual or as enjoying humiliation—is unlawful no matter how significant the literary, artistic, or political qualities of the work taken as a whole. The state may not ordain preferred viewpoints in this way. The Constitution forbids the state to declare one perspective right and silence opponents.

* * *

"If there is any fixed star in our constitutional constellation, it is that no official, high or petty, can prescribe what shall be orthodox in politics, nationalism, religion, or other matters of opinion or force citizens to confess by word or act their faith therein." Under the First Amendment the government must leave to the people the evaluation of ideas. Bald or subtle, an idea is as powerful as the audience allows it to be. A belief may be pernicious—the beliefs of Nazis led to the death of millions, those of the Klan to the repression of millions. A pernicious belief may prevail. Totalitarian governments today rule much of the planet, practicing suppression of billions and spreading dogma that may enslave others. One of the things that separates our society from theirs is our absolute right to propagate opinions that the government finds wrong or even hateful. . . . People may criticize the President by misrepresenting his positions, and they have a right to post their misrepresentations on public property. People may teach religions that others despise. People may seek to repeal laws guaranteeing equal opportunity in employment or to revoke the constitutional amendments granting the vote to blacks and women. They may do this because "above all else, the First Amendment means that government has no power to restrict expression because of its message [or] its ideas. . . ."

Under the ordinance graphic sexually explicit speech is "pornography" or not depending on the perspective the author adopts. Speech that "subordinates" women and also, for example, presents women as enjoying pain, humiliation, or rape, or even simply presents women in "positions of servility or submission or display" is forbidden, no matter how great the literary or political value of the work taken as a whole. Speech that portrays women in positions of equality is lawful, no matter how graphic the sexual content. This is thought control. It establishes an "approved" view of women, of how they may react to sexual encounters, of how the sexes may relate to each other. Those who espouse the approved view may use sexual images; those who do not, may not.

Indianapolis justifies the ordinance on the ground that pornography affects thoughts. Men who see women depicted as subordinate are more likely to treat them so. Pornography is an aspect of dominance. It does not persuade people so much as change them. It works by socializing, by establishing the expected and the permissible. In this view pornography is not an idea; pornography is the injury.

There is much to this perspective. Beliefs are also facts. People often act in accordance with the images and patterns they find around them. People raised in a religion tend to accept the tenets of that religion, often without independent examination. People taught from birth that black people are fit only for slavery rarely rebelled against that creed; beliefs coupled with the self-interest of the masters established a social structure that inflicted great harm while enduring for centuries. Words and images act at the level of the subconscious before they persuade at the level of the conscious.

Therefore we accept the premises of this legislation. Depictions of subordination tend to perpetuate subordination. The subordinate status of women in turn leads to affront and lower pay at work, insult and injury at home, battery and rape on the streets. In the language of the legislature, "[p]ornography is central in creating and maintaining sex as a basis of discrimination. Pornography is a systematic practice of exploitation and subordination based on sex which differentially harms women. The bigotry and contempt it produces, with the acts of aggression it fosters, harm women's opportunities for equality and rights [of all kinds]."

Yet this simply demonstrates the power of pornography as speech. . . . Pornography affects how people see the world, their fellows, and social relations. If pornography is what pornography does, so is other speech. Hitler's orations affected how some Germans saw Jews. Communism is a world view, not simply a *Manifesto* by Marx and Engels or a set of speeches. Efforts to suppress communist speech in the United States were based on the belief that the public acceptability of such ideas would increase the likelihood of totalitarian government. Religions affect socialization in the most pervasive way. . . . Many people believe that the existence of television, apart from the content of specific programs, leads to intellectual laziness, to a penchant for violence, to many other ills. . . .

Racial bigotry, anti-semitism, violence on television, reporters' biases—these and many more influence the culture and shape our socialization. None is directly answerable by more speech, unless that speech too finds its place in the popular culture. Yet all is protected as speech, however insidious. Any other answer leaves the government in control of all of the institutions of culture, the great censor and director of which thoughts are good for us. . . .

It is possible to interpret the claim that the pornography is the harm in a different way. Indianapolis emphasizes the injury that models in pornographic films and pictures may suffer. The record contains materials depicting sexual torture, penetration of women by red-hot irons and the like. These concerns have nothing to do with written materials subject to the statute, and physical injury can occur with or without the "subordination" of women. . . .

The more immediate point, however, is that the image of pain is not necessarily pain. In *Body Double,* a suspense film directed by Brian DePalma, a woman who has disrobed and presented a sexually explicit display is murdered by an intruder with a drill. The drill runs through the woman's body. The film is sexually explicit and a murder occurs—yet no one believes that the actress suffered pain or died. In *Barbarella* a character played by Jane Fonda is at times displayed in sexually explicit ways and at times shown "bleeding, bruised, [and] hurt in a context that makes these conditions sexual"—and again no one believes that Fonda was actually tortured to make the film. In *Carnal Knowledge* a woman grovels to please the sexual whims of a character played by Jack Nicholson; no one believes that there was a real sexual submission, and the Supreme Court held the film protected by the First Amendment. . . .

We come, finally, to the argument that pornography is "low value" speech, that it is enough like obscenity that Indianapolis may prohibit it. Some cases hold that speech far removed from politics and other subjects at the core of the Framers' concerns may be subjected to special regulation. These cases do not sustain statutes that select among viewpoints, however. In *Pacifica* the FCC sought to keep vile language off the air during certain times. The Court held that it may; but the Court would not have sustained a regulation prohibiting scatological descriptions of Republicans but not scatological descriptions of Democrats, or any other form of selection among viewpoints. . . .

Any rationale we could imagine in support of this ordinance could not be limited to sex discrimination. Free speech has been on balance an ally of those seeking change. Governments that want stasis start by restricting speech. Culture is a powerful force of continuity; Indianapolis paints pornography as part of the culture of power. Change in any complex system ultimately depends on the ability of outsiders to challenge accepted views and the reigning institutions. Without a strong guarantee of freedom of speech, there is no effective right to challenge what is.

The definition of "pornography" is unconstitutional. . . . No amount of struggle with particular words and phrases in this ordinance can leave anything in effect. The district court came to the same conclusion. Its judgment is therefore

AFFIRMED.

Speech Acts and Unspeakable Acts
Rae Langton

Rae Langton, who teaches philosophy at Monash University in Australia, provides a
partial defense of the claims that pornography subordinates and silences women. These
claims that have been advocated by the feminist lawyer Catharine MacKinnon have
been attacked as being philosophically indefensible and as resting on dangerous
confusion. By appealing to ideas from the British philosopher J. L. Austin, Langton
attempts to show that whether or not these claims are true, they can at least be shown
to be ones that make sense. No one has doubted that it makes sense to claim that
pornography can *depict* women as being subordinated and that such depictions may
lead to the subordination of women, but doubt has been expressed concerning the
coherence of the claim that pornographic works can themselves be understood as
constituting acts of subordinating women.

J. L. Austin, in his book *How to Do Things with Words*, argues that philosophers
have concerned themselves with the ways in which our words can be used to express
ideas and the ways in which those expressions can have causal effects, but that they
have failed to focus on the ways in which we use words to do things other than
express ideas and bring about causal effects. To use a common example, under certain
circumstances the words "I promise" not only express some intention on the part of the
speaker and create expectations on the part of the listener, they also constitute the act
of promising. By elaborating and extending such Austinian ideas, Langton hopes to show
that a plausible case can be made for the claim that pornographic expressions
constitute acts of subordination and silencing. If this plausible case can be adequately
defended, Langton believes it would serve as the basis for a strong argument that
pornography should be banned.

Pornography is speech. So the courts declared in judging it protected by the
First Amendment. Pornography is a kind of act. So Catharine MacKinnon declared in arguing for laws against it.[1] Put these together and we have: pornography is a kind of speech act. In what follows I take this suggestion seriously.

If pornography is speech, what does it say? If pornography is a kind of
act, what does it do? Judge Frank Easterbrook, accepting the premises of anti-
pornography legislation, gave an answer. Pornography is speech that depicts
subordination. In the words of the feminist ordinance passed in Indianapolis,
pornography depicts women

> dehumanized as sexual objects, things or commodities; enjoying pain or hu-
> miliation or rape; being tied up, cut up, mutilated, bruised, or physically hurt;
> in postures of sexual submission or servility or display; reduced to body

---

From *Philosophy & Public Affairs* 22 (1993), pp. 293–330.

parts, penetrated by objects or animals, or presented in scenarios of degradation, injury, torture; shown as filthy or inferior; bleeding, bruised or hurt in a context which makes these conditions sexual.[2]

Pornography is a kind of act that has certain effects. Depictions of subordination, said Easterbrook, "tend to perpetuate subordination. The subordinate status of women in turn leads to affront and lower pay at work, insult and injury at home, battery and rape on the streets." His conclusion was that the ordinance was unconstitutional: for, he said, "this simply demonstrates the power of pornography as speech."[3]

Pornography, on this view, depicts subordination and causes it. A closer look at the words of the ordinance shows us that MacKinnon is saying something more. Before describing what pornography depicts, the ordinance begins: "We define pornography as the graphic sexually explicit subordination of women in pictures or words." Besides depicting and causing subordination, as Easterbrook allowed, pornography *is*, in and of itself, a form of subordination.[4]

This latter aspect of the legislation provoked the ire of judges and philosophers alike. In proposing that pornography actually is subordination, the drafters of the ordinance were tricksters, guilty of "a certain sleight of hand," said Judge Barker, in the district court.[5] They were guilty of conceptual confusion, and their claim was "philosophically indefensible," said William Parent in the *Journal of Philosophy*.[6] It is all very well to talk about what pornography depicts; and it is all very well to talk about the effects it has on the lives of women. It is all very well to say, with Easterbrook, that pornography depicts subordination and causes it. Such claims may be unnerving, and they may be empirically false, but they are not, at least, incoherent. MacKinnon wants to say something more: she wants to attend not simply to the content of pornography speech, nor simply to its effects, but to the actions constituted by it.

What she says may strike a chord of recognition among those who recall an older, more tranquil debate in the philosophy of language, and a philosopher who took as his starting point the slogan that "to say something is to *do* something." In *How to Do Things with Words*, J. L. Austin complained of a "constant tendency in philosophy" to overlook something of great importance: a tendency to consider the content of a linguistic utterance, and its effects on hearers, but to overlook the action constituted by it.[7] . . . Words, he said, were used to perform all kinds of actions—warning, promising, marrying, and the like—that philosophy had blithely ignored.

To say something is usually to do a number of different things. An example (from Austin):[8] Two men stand beside a woman. The first man turns to the second, and says "Shoot her." The second man looks shocked, then raises a gun and shoots the woman. You witness the scene and describe it later. The first man said to the second, "Shoot her," meaning by "shoot" to shoot with a gun, and referring by "her" to the woman nearby. That description roughly captures the content of what was said: it captures what Austin called the *locutionary* act. To perform a locutionary act is to utter a sentence that has a particular meaning, as traditionally conceived.[9] However, there is more to what you witnessed, so you describe the scene again. *By* saying "shoot her," the first man *shocked* the second; by saying "shoot her," the first man *persuaded* the second to shoot the woman. That description captures some of the effects of what was said: it captures what Austin called the *perlocutionary* act. But if you stop there you will still have left something out. You will have ignored what the first man did in saying what he said. So you go on. *In* saying "shoot her," the first man *urged* the second to shoot the woman. That description captures the action constituted by the utterance itself: it captures what Austin called the *illocutionary* act. The actions listed earlier—warning, promising, marrying—are illocutionary acts. Austin's complaint was that this latter dimension to speech was often ignored, that there was "a tendency in philosophy to elide [illocutions] in favour of the other two."[10]

Pornography is not always done with words. Yet Easterbrook's description exemplifies the tendency of which Austin complained. Pornography depicts subordination and causes it. That—in Austin's terms—is to describe its locutionary and perlocutionary dimensions. What is missing is a description of the actions constituted by pornographic utterances: in Austin's terms, pornography's *illocutionary* force. MacKinnon supplies such a description when she says that pornography is an act of subordination. . . .

Austin and MacKinnon are emerging as close, if unlikely, cousins. In this article I exploit the work of the former to illuminate and defend the latter. I shall be concerned with two central claims. First is the claim already encountered, that pornography *subordinates* women. . . . Second is the claim that pornography *silences* women.[11] This idea is sometimes offered in reply to the traditional "free speech" defense of pornography. "The free speech of men silences the free speech of women. It is the same social goal, just other *people*," says MacKinnon, arguing that feminist antipornography legislation is motivated by the very values enshrined in the First Amendment.[12] This claim too has been regarded as problematic: its detractors describe it as "dangerous confusion," while even sympathizers have reservations, conceding that the silence in question is "figurative," "metaphorical."[13] Drawing on Austin, we can show that the silence is not metaphorical, but literal, and that the second feminist claim is as defensible as the first.

The claim that pornography subordinates women, however interpreted, is a claim that pornography determines women's inferior civil status. Viewed thus, the ordinance poses an apparent conflict between liberty and equality: the liberty of men to produce and consume pornography, and the rights of women to equal civil status. That is how the case was viewed by the courts. It posed a conflict between the right to free speech guaranteed by the First Amendment, and the right to equality guaranteed by the Fourteenth Amendment. The claim that pornography silences women expresses a different conflict, one within liberty itself. Viewed thus, the ordinance poses an apparent conflict between the liberty of men to produce and consume pornography, and the liberty of women to speak. . . .

My paper divides into two parts, addressing the two ideas one at a time. Once we consider pornographic images and texts as speech acts, we are in a position to apply to them Austin's distinctions between locutionary, illocutionary, and perlocutionary acts. We can make good sense of some central feminist claims when we focus on the illocutionary aspect of pornographic speech. In the first section I develop and defend the claim about subordinating. In the second section I develop and defend the claim about silencing, drawing again on Austin. The relationship between speech and power is a large and daunting topic, but without getting into deep theoretical water we can begin with the following simple observation. The ability to perform speech acts of certain kinds can be a mark of political power. To put the point crudely: powerful people can generally do more, say more, and have their speech count for more than can the powerless. If you are powerful, there are more things you can do with your words.

This bears on the question about silence. If you are powerful, you sometimes have the ability to silence the speech of the powerless. One way might be to stop the powerless from speaking at all. Gag them, threaten them, condemn them to solitary confinement. But there is another, less dramatic but equally effective, way. Let them speak. Let them say whatever they like to whomever they like, but stop that speech from counting as an *action*. More precisely, stop it from counting as the action it was intended to be. That is the kind of silencing I will consider, and it is a kind of silencing about which Austin had something to say, without commenting on its political significance. Some speech acts are *unspeakable* for women in some contexts: although the appropriate words can be uttered, those utterances fail to count as the actions they were intended to be. If it can be shown that pornography contributes to this kind of silencing, then we will have a new way of understanding the second feminist claim. . . .

I. "PORNOGRAPHY SUBORDINATES"

Speech Acts

Before considering whether pornographic speech acts may subordinate, we will first look at speech acts in closer detail, and then ask whether in principle speech acts may subordinate.

Austin's chief concern was with illocutionary speech acts, and much labor in *How to Do Things with Words* is devoted to discovering what is distinctive about them. An illocutionary act is the action performed simply *in* saying something. A perlocutionary act is the action performed *by* saying something. A perlocutionary act is an utterance considered in terms of its consequences, such as the effects it has on its hearers. Austin took pains to distinguish illocutions from perlocutions, and he thought that the phrases "in saying" and "by saying" were typical—though by no means infallible—markers of the two.

"In saying 'I do' I was marrying; by saying 'I do' I greatly distressed my mother." Saying "I do" in the right context counts as—constitutes—marrying: that is the illocutionary act performed. It does not count as distressing my mother, even if it has that effect: that is the perlocutionary act performed.

Austin's belief that there is something distinctive about illocutionary acts seems right. What we have here are utterances whose force is something more than the semantic content of the sentence uttered—the locution—and something other than the effects achieved by the utterance—the perlocution. What is responsible for this important third dimension? Austin's answer was that an utterance has illocutionary force of a certain kind when it satisfied certain felicity conditions. These are typically set by conventions, written or unwritten, and typically require that the speaker is intending to do something with his words. . . . Whether in saying "I do" the speaker is marrying depends on the felicity conditions of marriage, which require that the speaker intends to marry, and that the utterance takes place in the course of a particular conventional procedure, with appropriate participants (adult heterosexual couple, unmarried, plus priest or registrar). The speaker will also need to secure "uptake": that is to say, the hearer must recognize that an illocution of a certain kind is being performed. So, at any rate, the typical cases run.

Subordinating Speech Acts

We turn now to the second preliminary task: the question of whether speech acts can, in principle, subordinate. Austin placed his theory of speech and action firmly in the arena of social activity, and there is a political dimension to this arena. People manage to do all kinds of things with words. Besides advising, warning, and marrying one another, people also manage to hurt and oppress one another. A child may chant that "sticks and stones may break my bones, but names will never hurt." Names do hurt, though. That is just why she chants. And that is why the law regards some speech as injury. Words can break bones. "Shoot her!" might break a few, as a perlocutionary act at any rate. ("By saying 'shoot her' he caused her skull to be fractured.") Speech can do more than break bones. It can determine civil status, as Easterbrook agreed, interpreting the idea in perlocutionary terms: by depicting subordination, pornographers perpetuate subordination.

When MacKinnon says that speech can subordinate, she means something more: that pornography can have the illocutionary force of subordination, and not simply have subordination as its locutionary content, or as its perlocutionary effect: *in* depicting subordination, pornographers subordinate. This is the alleged "sleight of hand."[14]

We need to evaluate this charge. Can a speech act be an illocutionary act of subordination? The answer, I think, is yes. Consider this utterance: "Blacks are not permitted to vote." Imagine that it is uttered by a legislator in Pretoria in the context of enacting legislation that underpins apartheid. It is a locutionary act: by "Blacks" it refers to blacks. It is a perlocutionary act: it will have the effect, among others, that blacks stay away from polling booths. But it is, first and foremost, an illocutionary act: it makes it the case that blacks are not permitted to vote. It—plausibly—subordinates blacks. So does this utterance: "Whites only."[15] It too is a locutionary act: by "Whites" it refers to whites. It has some important perlocutionary effects: it keeps blacks away from white areas, ensures that only whites go there, and perpetuates racism. It is—one might say—a perlocutionary act of subordination. But it is also an illocutionary act: it orders blacks away, welcomes whites, permits whites to act in a discriminatory way towards blacks. It subordinates blacks.[16] If this is correct, then there is no sleight of hand, no philosophical impropriety, about the claim that a certain kind of speech can be an illocutionary act of subordination.

In virtue of what do the speech acts of apartheid subordinate? In virtue of what are they illocutionary acts of subordination? In virtue of at least the following three features, I suggest. They *rank* blacks as having inferior worth. They *legitimate* discriminatory behavior on the part of whites. And finally, they *deprive* blacks of some important powers: for example, the power to go to certain areas and the power to vote. Here I am in broad agreement with MacKinnon, who says that to subordinate someone is to put them in a position of inferiority or loss of power, or to demean or denigrate them.[17] . . .

Speech acts of this kind belong to an important class of illocutions discussed by Austin towards the end of his work. Some illocutions involve the authoritative delivery of a finding about some matters of fact or value. Actions of ranking, valuing, and placing are illocutions of this kind, labeled *verdictive* by Austin. For example: An umpire calls "Fault" at a tennis match. He expresses his opinion. He describes the world as he sees it. But he does much more than that: he gives his verdict. . . . The authoritative role of the speaker imbues the utterance with a force that would be absent were it made by someone who did not occupy that role.

Close relatives of verdictives are illocutions that confer powers and rights on people, or deprive people of powers and rights. Actions of ordering, permitting, prohibiting, authorizing, enacting law, and dismissing an employee are illocutions of this kind, labelled *exercitive* by Austin.[18] The speech acts of apartheid that legitimate discriminatory behavior and unjustly deprive blacks of certain rights have an exercitive force that would be absent if they were made by speakers who did not have the appropriate authority.

It is in virtue of these particular verdictive and exercitive dimensions, then, that the speech acts of apartheid subordinate. This already tells us something important about any claim that a certain kind of speech subordinates. For the crucial feature of verdictive and exercitive illocutions is their sensitivity to the speaker's authority, and we can accordingly group them together under the label *authoritative* illocutions: actions whose felicity conditions require that the speaker occupy a position of authority in a relevant domain. . . . Subordinating speech acts are authoritative speech acts, so if we are ever to count some class of speech acts as subordinating speech, the speakers in question must have authority. This is something to bear in mind in what follows.

Pornography

MacKinnon thinks that pornography in particular subordinates. The courts sometimes view this claim as a description of pornography's content. "Those words and pictures which *depict women in sexually subordinate roles* are banned by the Ordinance," said Judge Barker in the district court, giving this as grounds for the Indianapolis Ordinance's unconstitutionality.[19] Barker is mistaken: the ordinance does not ban material simply by virtue of its content, for at this locutionary level there is nothing particularly distinctive about pornography. Not all sexually explicit depictions of subordination are pornography, as MacKinnon herself points out.[20] Utterances whose locutions depict subordination do not always subordinate. Locutions that depict subordination could in principle be used to perform speech acts that are a far cry from pornography: documentaries, for example, or police reports, or government studies, or books that protest against sexual violence, or perhaps even legal definitions of pornography. It all depends, as Austin might have said, on the *use* to which the locution is put. If we are to find what is distinctive about pornography, it seems that we must look elsewhere.

The perlocutionary aspect of pornographic utterances has rightly attracted much attention. This, as we saw, is how Easterbrook interpreted MacKinnon's claim when he said that pornography "perpetuates" subordination. At the perlocutionary level, pornographic speech can be variously described. Some hearers are entertained and sexually aroused by it. At this level a difference between pornography and documentaries that depict subordination does emerge. Although similar locutions may be used in both cases, different effects are achieved in the hearers: sexual arousal in the one case, indignation, perhaps, in the other. Pornography does more than arouse. Some of its hearers are distressed by it, as was made evident at the 1983 Minneapolis hearings. Some, it seems, have their attitudes and behavior altered by it in ways that ultimately hurt women: they can become more likely to view women as inferior, more disposed to accept rape myths (for example, that women enjoy rape), more likely to view rape victims as deserving of their treatment, and more likely to say that they themselves would rape if they could get away with it.[21] This in turn means that some women are hurt by it. In Easterbrook's words, pornography perpetuates the cycle of "insult and injury at home, battery and rape on the streets."

The claim that pornography harms women is not yet the perlocutionary claim conceded by the court that pornography perpetuates women's subordination. Plenty of people are harmed by cigarettes, but they are not thereby subordinated. A link between harm and subordination is made, though, when we shift our perspective on the asymmetric pattern of sexual violence and view it afresh, not simply as harm or as crime, but as an aspect of women's subordinate status.[22] To view it otherwise would be to obscure its systematically discriminatory nature, and to obscure the fact that the perpetrators are nearly always members of one class of citizens, the victims nearly always members of another. This shift in perspective is an important feature of feminist political analysis, and it affects how we are to characterize pornography in perlocutionary (and, we shall see shortly, illocutionary) terms. If pornography has sexual violence as its effect and sexual violence is an aspect of women's subordination, then pornography is a *perlocutionary* act of subordination. That is how we reach the claim conceded by Easterbrook: pornography perpetuates women's subordination.

However, the claim that pornography subordinates women is an illocutionary claim that goes beyond these locutionary and perlocutionary dimensions, and it is related to other illocutionary claims that feminists have made about pornography. Pornography is said to *rank* women as sex objects, "defined on the basis of [their] looks . . . [their] availability for sexual pleasure."[23] Pornography represents degrading and abusive sexual behavior "in such a way as to *endorse* the degradation."[24] MacKinnon has a striking list of illocutionary verbs: "Pornography sexualizes rape, battery, sexual harassment . . . and child sexual abuse; it . . . *celebrates, promotes, authorizes* and *legitimates* them."[25] These descriptions bear on the claim that pornography subordinates. Recall that we found three features in virtue of which the speech acts of apartheid were plausibly described as illocutionary acts of subordination. They rank certain people as inferior; they legitimate discriminatory behavior towards them; and they deprive them of powers and rights. The feminist claims we have just considered ascribe to pornography the first two of the three features. Pornography is, first, verdictive speech that ranks women as sex objects, and, second, exercitive speech that legitimates sexual violence. Since sexual violence is not simply harm, not simply crime, but discriminatory behavior, pornography subordinates because it legitimates this behavior. (Now we see how the feminist shift of perspective on violence affects our characterization of pornography at the illocutionary level as well.) For these two reasons, then, pornography is an *illocutionary* act of subordination. That, at any rate, is the claim. . . .

We are now in a position to consider the disputed question: does pornography subordinate? Since there is a dispute, it may be that pornography fails to match exactly the illocutionary paradigm. I have not tried to say exactly what the paradigm for subordination is, but I have suggested that the speech acts of apartheid offer a clear example. They have verdictive and exercitive force: they rank a class of people, legitimate discrimination against them, and deprive them of rights and powers. Their felicity conditions include the condition that the speakers occupy a position of authority. They are speech acts that achieve a certain uptake: they are taken to be verdictive and exercitive acts (though not all hearers will take them to be subordinating acts). They are illocutions that have a pattern of perlocutionary effects on the beliefs and behavior of the population: whites believe blacks to be inferior, believe discrimination against them to be legitimate, and believe them to have fewer rights; whites discriminate against blacks, and blacks stay away from polling booths. Such speech acts are clearly acts of subordination.

Pornography falls short of this devastating paradigm in a number of important respects, but it may nonetheless be subordination. . . . We might find *explanations* for pornography's perlocutionary effects in terms of its illocutionary force. If the earlier claims are right, then pornography has a certain pattern of perlocutionary effects. It can affect attitudes and behavior, making its hearers more likely to view women as inferior, more disposed to accept rape myths, more likely to view rape victims as deserving of their treatment, and more likely to say that they themselves would rape if they could get away with it. Part of the explanation for this pattern might be that pornography has a particular illocutionary force: it ranks women as sex objects, and legitimates that kind of behavior. If pornography has the perlocutionary effects MacKinnon claims, then there is some reason for thinking it has the illocutionary force she and other feminist writers have ascribed to it. . . .

What *uptake* does pornography secure in its hearers? What act do its hearers take it to be? The answer is mixed. Some hearers take it to be entertainment, escapist storytelling. Other hearers take it to be subordination. They take pornography to be something that ranks them, judges them, denigrates them, and legitimates ways of behaving that hurt women. Here we find vivid disagreement among the hearers as to just what the speech act is. Austin said that in such cases utterances are liable to have "a construction put upon them by judges," but who is in a position to judge? We might say that those women who take pornography to be subordination are in a better position to judge, that they can tell better than some other hearers what ranks them, what demeans and denigrates them, and what seems to legitimate ways of acting that are violent. But unless we privilege one group of hearers in this way, our result with this way of arguing will be inconclusive, though it may give some support to the claim that pornography subordinates.

The task of discovering whether some important *felicity conditions* are met looks more hopeful, for at least we know one felicity condition for subordination, and could in principle know whether pornography satisfies it. Since verdictives and exercitives are both *authoritative* illocutions, we know that the ability to perform them depends on the speaker's authority. The umpire, and not the bystander, can call a fault. The government, and not the private citizen, can enact law that ranks and legitimates. The authority in question need not be as formally recognized as in those cases, but it needs to be there. This means that in order to answer the question, "Does pornography subordinate?" one must first answer another: "Do its speakers have authority?" If they do, then a crucial felicity condition is satisfied: pornographers' speech acts may be illocutions that authoritatively rank women, legitimate violence, and thus subordinate.

This question is, I think, at the heart of the controversy. If you believe that pornographic utterances are made by a powerless minority, a fringe group especially vulnerable to moralistic persecution, then you will answer negatively.

Not so if you believe, with MacKinnon, that pornography's voice is the voice of the ruling power. Liberal debate about pornography has typically been premised on the former belief, and part of MacKinnon's task is to persuade us that it is false. Just as the speech of the umpire is authoritative within a certain domain—the game of tennis—so pornographic speech is authoritative within a certain domain—the game of sex. The authors of pornographic speech are not mere bystanders to the game; they are speakers whose verdict counts. Pornography tells its hearers what women are worth: it ranks women as things, as objects, as prey. Pornography tells its hearers which moves are appropriate and permissible: if it tells them that certain moves are appropriate because women want to be raped, it legitimates violence. If pornography is authoritative speech it may subordinate.

Does pornographic speech have the authority required to substantiate MacKinnon's claim? Is this crucial felicity condition satisfied? These are not really questions to be settled from the philosopher's armchair. To answer them one needs to know about the role pornographers occupy as authoritative speakers about the facts, or supposed facts, of sex. What is important here is not whether the speech of pornographers is universally held in high esteem: it is not—hence the common assumption among liberals that in defending pornographers they are defending the underdog. What is important is whether it is authoritative in the domain that counts—the domain of speech about sex—and whether it is authoritative for the hearers that count: people, men, boys, who in addition to wanting "entertainment," want to discover the right way to do things, want to know which moves in the sexual game are legitimate. What is important is whether it is authoritative for those hearers who—one way or another—do seem to learn that violence is sexy and coercion legitimate: the fifty percent of boys who "think it is okay for a man to rape a woman if he is sexually aroused by her," the fifteen percent of male college undergraduates who say they have raped a woman on a date, the eighty-six percent who say that they enjoy the conquest part of sex, the thirty percent who rank faces of women displaying pain and fear to be more sexually attractive than faces showing pleasure.[26] In this domain, and for these hearers, it may be that pornography has all the authority of a monopoly.[27] . . .

The claim that pornography subordinates has good philosophical credentials: it is not trickery, or "sleight of hand": it is by no means "philosophically indefensible." Moreover, considerations about explanation, uptake, and the felicity conditions for subordination give us reasons—though not conclusive ones—for thinking that the claim may be true. Pornography's effects may be best explained by supposing that it has the illocutionary force of subordination. An important group of pornography's hearers—even if not its intended hearers—take it to be subordination. And if the empirical premise about pornography's authority turns out to be true, then pornography satisfies a crucial felicity condition for subordination.

What we have not yet considered, however, is whether speech that subordinates should be restricted by law. As we noted at the outset, it does not immediately follow from the claim that pornography subordinates women that censorship is the best answer. What follows is that there is a conflict between liberty and equality, just as the courts declared. One possible response to this conflict might be to fight for equality in ways compatible with respecting the liberty of pornographers. What I have said leaves open that possibility. If pornography subordinates women, then it is not in virtue of its content but of its authority that it does so. It need not have that authority. There are imaginable circumstances where material just like pornography in other respects would have no authority, and in such circumstances such speech would not subordinate. MacKinnon's claim is that those circumstances are not ours, though one can hope that someday they will be.

This way of understanding the subordination claim thus has implications for policy. There may be ways of undermining pornography's authority that fall short of outright censorship, ways that would eventually relegate pornographers to the status of mere bystanders to the game, whose speech does not count. Perhaps pornographic speech could be fought with more speech: the speech of education to counter pornography's falsehoods, where women tell the world what women are really like,[28] or with the speech of competition to counter pornography's monopoly, where women themselves become authors of erotica that is arousing and explicit but does not subordinate.[29]

All this may be possible if women can indeed fight speech with more speech. But if pornography not only subordinates but *silences* women, it is not easy to see how there can be any such fight. At this point the second feminist claim demands our attention. Whether women can fight speech with more speech depends on whether, and to what extent, women can speak.

II. "PORNOGRAPHY SILENCES"

Silenced Speech Acts

If speech is action, then silence is failure to act. If pornography silences women, then it prevents women from doing things with their words. Before considering whether pornography silences women, I will look at how speech acts, in general, may be silenced, and then ask whether in principle speech acts can silence.

The ability to perform speech acts can be a measure of political power. Those who are able to use the utterance "Blacks are not permitted to vote" with the illocutionary force of prohibition are, as we saw, the ones with authority. Conversely, one mark of powerlessness is an inability to perform speech acts that one might otherwise like to perform. Corresponding to Austin's threefold distinction, we can distinguish three kinds of silence, for there are three kinds of acts one may fail to perform. All three have their political significance, I think, but my chief interest will be in the third.

At the first and most basic level, members of a powerless group may be silent because they are intimidated, or because they believe that no one will listen. They do not protest at all, because they think that protest is futile. They do not vote at all, because they fear the guns. In such cases no words are uttered at all. In Austin's terms, speakers fail to perform even a *locutionary* act.

Sometimes, however, people will speak, but what they say will fail to achieve the effects that they intend: such speakers fail to perform their intended perlocutionary act. Silencing of this second kind, which we can call *perlocutionary frustration*, is a common enough fact of life: one argues, but no one is persuaded; one invites, but nobody attends the party; one votes, hoping to oust the government, but one is outnumbered. Such frustration can have a political dimension when the effects achieved depend on the speaker's membership in a particular social class.

But there is a third kind of silencing that happens when one speaks, one utters words, and fails not simply to achieve the effect one aims at, but fails to perform the very action one intends. Here speech misfires, and the act is unhappy in the way that Austin described: although the appropriate words are uttered, with the appropriate intention, the speaker fails to perform the intended illocutionary act. Silencing of this third kind we can call *illocutionary disablement*, and it is that to which we now turn our attention.[30]

In the previous section we considered how certain illocutions include among their felicity conditions the requirement that the speaker have authority in a relevant domain. Having authority can thus enable a speaker to perform illocutionary acts not otherwise available. Illocutionary disablement presents us with the other side of the same phenomenon: not having authority in the relevant domain can disable a speaker from performing illocutionary acts. That is why the ability to perform illocutionary acts can be viewed as a measure of authority, a measure of political power. . . .

Example (1): Warning. This example is from Donald Davidson.

> Imagine this: the actor is acting a scene in which there is supposed to be a fire. . . . It is his role to imitate as persuasively as he can a man who is trying to warn others of a fire. "Fire!" he screams. And perhaps he adds, at the behest of the author, "I mean it! Look at the smoke!" etc. And now a real fire breaks out, and the actor tries vainly to warn the real audience. "Fire!" he screams. "I mean it! Look at the smoke!" etc.[31]

The actor says words that are appropriate for the action he wants to perform. He gets the locutionary act exactly right. He intends to warn; if appropriate intention is among warning's felicity conditions, then that is a condition he satisfies. But he does not warn. Uptake is not secured. Something about the role he occupies prevents his utterance from counting as a warning. Something, perhaps, about the conventions of theatre constrains the speech acts he can make. The same words said with the same intentions by an audience member would count as a warning. The actor, though, has been silenced. The act of warning has been made unspeakable for him.

Example (2): Marriage. To say, "I do" is, given the right circumstances, to marry, given that the felicity conditions of marriage are satisfied. Suppose now that both parties intending to marry are male. They sincerely intend to marry. The speaker uses the right locution. The priest is no mere actor. The ceremony is performed by the book. The speaker satisfies all the felicity conditions but one. Something about who he is, and who his partner is, prevents him from satisfying one crucial felicity condition. The act of marrying misfires. The felicity conditions of marriage are such that two male participants cannot succeed. The act of marriage is not speakable for homosexual couples. The power to marry, an important power available to other citizens, is not available to them.

Example (3): Voting. A white South African makes marks on a piece of paper in a polling booth. A black South African makes marks that look just the same, and in similar conditions. Their intentions, we can imagine, are just the same. But the former has succeeded in doing something significant. He has voted. The latter has not. Something about who he is prevents him from satisfying a crucial felicity condition. South African law prevents his utterance from counting as a vote: voting is not speakable for him. He too lacks an important political power available to other citizens.

Example (4): Divorce. To utter the words "*mutallaqa, mutallaqa, mutallaqa*" (literally "divorced, divorced, divorced") is to perform the illocutionary act of divorce in a country where Islamic law is in force, provided certain felicity conditions are met. Pronounced by a husband to his wife, it is an act of divorce. Not so if it is pronounced by the wife to her husband. No matter how hard she tries, a woman cannot succeed in divorcing her spouse by making that or any relevantly similar utterance. Divorce of that kind is an act that is unspeakable for women.[32]

Silencing Speech Acts

We have just considered briefly some ways in which speech can be silenced: simple silence, where nothing is said at all; perlocutionary frustration, where a speaker says words, succeeds in performing the intended illocution, but fails to achieve the intended effect; and the special silence of illocutionary disablement, singled out and illustrated in the above examples. The next task is to address the question of whether and how speech can actively silence. This question has been addressed by many other writers, and there are all kinds of subtle ways that speech can silence that I shall not consider. But we will see that each of the three kinds of silence to which I drew attention in the last section can be brought about by speech. This means we can usefully distinguish three kinds of silencing speech, in line with Austin's categories. My chief interest is in the question of whether speech can bring about the third silence of illocutionary disablement. . . .

Is it possible for speech to silence in this latter way? Is it possible to silence someone, not by ordering or threatening them into simple silence, not by frustrating their perlocutionary goals, but by making their speech acts unspeakable? This is a question about the role speech may play in disabling speakers, preventing them from satisfying the felicity conditions for some illocutions they might want to perform. So far we have noted the phenomenon of illocutionary disablement, but not yet asked how it comes about. Austin offers little explicit guidance here, but there is an implicit answer.

Felicity conditions, he says, are fixed by conventions. In examples (2)-(4) they are formal laws spelling out the conditions that must be met for marriage, voting, and divorce. Felicity conditions are not always (not even usually) spelled out in laws though, and for promising, warning, urging, protesting, and so forth, it will not always be clear just what the felicity conditions are, what the conventions are, or whether there are really conventions at all. Suppose we go with Austin and use "convention" as a loose label for whatever sets felicity conditions. How do these come into being? When we consider some of Austin's paradigm cases, we see that one way that conventions are brought into being, one way that felicity conditions are set, is indeed by means of other speech acts. These are "*words that set conditions*" in MacKinnon's phrase.[33] In examples (2)-(4), laws are *enacted* that set felicity conditions for marriage, voting, and divorce. Some illocutionary acts fix the range and scope of other illocutionary acts. Some speech acts build a space, as it were, for other speech acts, making it possible for some people to marry, vote, and divorce. Some speech acts, in contrast, set limits to that space, making it impossible for other people to marry, vote, divorce. Some speech determines the kind of speech there can be. This shows that it is indeed possible to silence someone, not just by frustrating their perlocutionary goals, but by making their speech acts unspeakable. It is possible to use speech to disable speakers, and possible to prevent them from satisfying the felicity conditions for some illocutions they might want to perform.

Felicity conditions for illocutions in general are rarely spelled out in the words of legal enactments. What then of the conventions that set conditions for other illocutions, warning, protesting, urging, and the rest? If it is hard to say just what the conditions are, it will be harder still to say what sets them. But again, the answer may be that, by analogy with the legal cases, they can be set by what is said, this time by informal practices of speech and communication that gradually establish precedents and informal rules about what counts as, for example, a warning. As in the legal examples, felicity conditions can be set by words. The space for potential speech acts can be built by speakers, as can the limits on that space, the constraints responsible for the silence of illocutionary disablement. Let us at least take this as our working hypothesis.

Pornography

We have seen how speech can be silenced, and we have seen how speech can silence. MacKinnon's claim is that pornographic speech, in particular, silences the speech of women. It is time now to address that claim. But I approach it indirectly, with some more examples.

Example (5): Refusal. Consider the utterance "no." We all know how to do things with this word. We use it, typically, to disagree, to refuse, or to prohibit. In sexual contexts a woman sometimes uses it to refuse sex, to prohibit further sexual advances. However, in sexual contexts something odd happens. Sometimes a woman tries to use the "no" locution to refuse sex, and it does not work. It does not work for the twenty percent of undergraduate women who report that they have been date raped. It does not work for the twenty-five percent of final-year schoolgirls who report that they have been sexually forced.[34] Saying "no" sometimes doesn't work, but there are two ways in which it can fail to work. Sometimes the woman's hearer recognizes the action she performs: i.e., he recognizes that she is refusing. Uptake is secured. In saying "no," she really does refuse. By saying "no," she intends to prevent her hearer from continuing his advances. But the hearer goes ahead and forces sex on the woman. She prohibits, but he fails to obey. She fails to achieve the goal of her refusal. Her refusal is frustrated. "Perlocutionary frustration" is too meek and academic a label for what is simple rape.

Sometimes, though, there is the different phenomenon of illocutionary disablement. Sometimes "no," when spoken by a woman, does not *count* as the act of refusal. The hearer fails to recognize the utterance as a refusal; uptake is not secured. In saying "no" she may well intend to refuse. By saying "no" she intends to prevent sex, but she is far from doing as she intends. Since illocutionary force depends, in part, on uptake being secured, the woman fails to refuse. She is in the position of the actor in Davidson's story, silenced as surely as the actor is silenced. He shouts "Fire!" He performs the appropriate locutionary act. He means what he says. He intends to warn. He tries to warn. But what he says misfires. Something about him, something about the role he occupies, prevents him from warning the audience. She says "no." She performs the appropriate locutionary act. She means what she says. She intends to refuse. She tries to refuse. But what she says misfires. Something about her, something about the role she occupies, prevents her from voicing refusal. Refusal—in that context—has become unspeakable for her. In this case refusal is not simply frustrated but disabled.

Example (6): Protest. The following appeared in a mail-order catalog advertising "adult reading," flanked by such titles as *426. Forbidden Sexual Fantasies* and *428. Orgy: an Erotic Experience.*

> *No. 427 ORDEAL: an autobiography by Linda Lovelace.* With M. McGrady. The star of *Deep Throat* tells the shocking story of her enslavement in the pornographic underworld, a nightmarish ordeal of savage violence and unspeakable perversion, of thrill seeking celebrities and sadistic criminals. For Sale to Adults Over 21 Only.

Ordeal is a book that has been much cited by feminists who oppose pornography.[35] The testimony of Linda Lovelace, or Linda Marchiano, to use her real name, features in evidence about pornography presented at the 1983

Minneapolis hearings.[36] In the book Marchiano tells the story of her involvement with the making of the film *Deep Throat*, describing how she was beaten, hypnotized, and tortured in order to perform her starring role.... *Ordeal* is an act of protest, a resounding denunciation of the industry in which Marchiano says she was forced to perform. One can see why it was used in the antipornography hearings. As a locutionary act *Ordeal* depicts the subordination of a woman: it depicts a woman "in scenarios of degradation, injury and torture." But it does not invite fantasy and arousal. It invites indignation. It does not "endorse the degradation"; it does not "celebrate, promote, authorize and legitimate" the sexual violence. It does not have pornography's illocutionary force.

Why then is *Ordeal* in a mail-order catalog for adult reading? The answer is simple. It is there because it is pornography after all: here, in this context, for these intended hearers, the uptake secured is bound to be that of pornography. Marchiano says the words appropriate for an act of protest. She uses the right locutions, words that graphically depict her own subordination. She intends to protest. But her speech misfires. Something about who she is, something about the role she occupies, prevents her from satisfying protest's felicity conditions, at least here. Though the threats and gags are gone, there is silence of another kind. She too is in the plight of Davidson's actor. Warning was unspeakable for him. Protest is unspeakable for her.[37] What he tries to say comes out as "merely acted." What she tries to say comes out as pornography. Her protest has been disabled.

MacKinnon claims that pornography silences the speech of women. But how? We noted that one way that speech can silence is in virtue of being an order or a threat that induces simple silence in its hearers. That is the first kind of silencing. MacKinnon cites cases where pornography itself is used to threaten: children coerced into pornography are blackmailed into silence by pornographers who threaten to show the pornography to their parents and teachers. Pornographic depictions of their subordination are used to threaten and thereby perpetuate that same subordination.[38] The silence here is simple: the children say nothing because they are afraid.

Pornography may silence in the second way: by preventing women, not from speaking, but from achieving the effects they want to achieve. If, as was argued above, pornography legitimates sexual violence, then it follows that one of pornography's effects may be to prevent a woman's refusal of sex from achieving its intended purpose. If pornography legitimates rape, then it may silence refusal by frustrating its perlocutionary goal. For many cases of rape, and probably all that reach the courts, match the first pattern described in (5) above: the woman whose hearer recognized that she refused, and persisted in spite of it, or perhaps because of it; the woman whose hearer recognized the prohibition and disobeyed. If pornography legitimates rape of this kind, it does so by sexualizing the use of force in response to refusal that is recognized as refusal. Such pornography eroticizes refusal itself, presenting the overpowering of a woman's will as exciting. Someone learning the rules of the sexual game from that kind of pornography would recognize a woman's refusal and disobey it. This would be one way in which pornography frustrates the goals of women's speech.

But we have seen that there is the possibility of a different kind of silence: the silence not just of frustration but of illocutionary disablement, manifested by the would-be warnings, marriages, votes, and divorces of examples (1)–(4). And this silencing is manifested in examples (5) and (6): the illocutionary disablement of the second rape victim, whose attempted refusal is not even recognized as a refusal; the disablement of an author whose attempted protest is not recognized as protest. These misfires betray the presence of structural constraints on women's speech. If Austin is right, the explanation for the unhappiness here is that the felicity conditions for refusal, for protest, are not being met. Something is robbing the speech of its intended force. Whatever the conventions governing sexual interactions may be, they can mean that intending to refuse, intending to protest, is not enough. The rules fixing possible moves in the language games of sex are such that saying "no" can fail to count as making a refusal move, and telling the story of one's own subordination can fail to count as a move of protest. These are illocutions whose felicity conditions, it seems, cannot be satisfied by women, at least in these contexts.

What, if anything, has pornography to do with this third kind of silence, this disablement of women's speech that can make rape so hard to prevent and hard to protest about? If the felicity conditions for such illocutions constrain women in these contexts, we need to ask how those conditions came into being. This question was asked about the conditions that constrain illocutions of marriage, divorce, and the like, and the answer was that they were set by the speech of the legislator. How then are these other felicity conditions set? We know that felicity conditions for illocutions in general can be set by other speech acts. MacKinnon's claim that pornography silences women can be interpreted in just this way. *The felicity conditions for women's speech acts are set by the speech acts of pornography.* The words of the pornographer, like the words of the legislator, are "words that set conditions." They are words that constrain, that make certain actions—refusal, protest—unspeakable for women in some contexts. This is speech that determines the kind of speech there can be. . . .

How common is silencing of this kind and the rape that accompanies it? It is hard to tell because so tiny a fraction of rapes are reported and these would be least reported of all. But the study that found that one in four final-year schoolgirls had been sexually forced also found that one in seven boys of the same age reported having refused to take no for an answer. One reading of this is that the boys in question recognized the refusal and persisted in spite of it. Naomi Wolf's comment suggests something further: that

> boys rape and girls get raped *as a normal course of events.* The boys may even be unaware that what they are doing is wrong; violent sexual imagery may well have raised a generation of young men who can rape women without even knowing it.[39]

If young men can rape without knowing it, then women sometimes fail to secure uptake for their attempted refusals. This is the silence, not simply of frustration, but of disablement.

Refusal, here, is a kind of prohibition, and it is an exercitive illocution, in Austin's terms. To satisfy its felicity conditions, the speaker must have authority in a relevant domain. A government that prohibits has authority over a large domain; a parent who prohibits has authority within the smaller domain of the family; a patient who prohibits treatment has authority within the local domain of his own life, his own body. A woman who prohibits sexual advances also has authority within the local domain of her own life, her own body. If she cannot prohibit, cannot refuse, the authority is absent. If she is disabled from speaking refusal, it is a sign that her body is, in a sense, not her own. If pornography prevents her from refusing, then pornography destroys her authority as it twists her words.

Part of the concern about whether pornography silences women is a concern that pornography may prevent women from fighting speech with more speech. In considering the feminist ordinance, the courts had to consider whether pornographic speech "operates self-entrenchingly, disabling its natural enemies —its victims—from countering it with effective speech of their own."[40] . . .

The story about *Ordeal* in (5) is anecdotal, but it illustrates the way that pornography can operate self-entrenchingly. Marchiano tries to protest, but she only succeeds in making more pornography. The pornographers know how to do things with her words: stories of "savage violence" and "enslavement in the pornographic underworld" are simply pornography to readers for whom violence has been legitimated as sex. And there is ironic truth in what the pornographers say: the violence is indeed "unspeakable" for Marchiano, for they have made it so. If you are a woman using sexually explicit speech, describing in some detail the savage sexual violence you have suffered, and especially if you are already a famous pornography star, what you say simply counts as pornography. It is an effective way to silence, not simply by depriving speech of its intended illocutionary force, but by replacing it with a force that is its antithesis.

The story is not, I think, an isolated anecdote. If MacKinnon is right, it has something in common with a phenomenon that is widespread and pernicious, a phenomenon that deserves more attention than I give it here: namely, the analogous disablement encountered by women who give testimony in court about rape and about sexual harassment, and whose testimony, and descriptions of their experience, achieve the uptake appropriate to a description of normal sex.[41] If pornography legitimates violence as sex, then it can silence the intended actions of those who want to testify about violence. This too is an aspect of its self-entrenching character.

If pornography sets up the rules in the language games of sex—if pornography is speech that determines the kind of speech there can be—then it is exercitive speech in Austin's sense, for it is in the class of speech that confers and removes rights and powers. We saw that the claim that pornography subordinates requires the premise that pornography is authoritative speech, otherwise it could not rank and legitimate. We can now see that the claim that pornography silences requires the same premise: pornographic speech must be authoritative if it is to engender the silence of illocutionary disablement.

The claim that pornography silences women, like the claim about subordination, has been taken to be philosophically problematic. It is at best "metaphorical," and at worst a "dangerous confusion." I have tried to show that it is neither.

The claim that pornography silences is one that can be taken literally. One might object that the silencing I have described is not literal silencing because pornography does not—except in rare circumstances when it is used to threaten—literally prevent women from uttering words.[42] It does not—in Austin's terms—usually prevent women from performing locutionary acts. But to think that way is to exhibit just the tendency of which Austin complained, to be preoccupied with the content of what is said, at the expense of the action performed. One way of being silent is to make no noise. Another way of being silent—literally silent—is to perform no speech act. On Austin's view, locutions on their own are nothing. Locutions are there to be used. Words are tools. Words are for doing things with. There is little point in giving someone tools if they cannot do things with them. And there is little point in allowing women words if we cannot do things with them. That, at any rate, is not free speech.

The claim is not metaphor; it is not confusion either. Dworkin says that it is a confusion to suppose that pornography silences women, because it is a confusion to "characterize certain ideas as silencing ideas."[43] Dworkin misconstrues the argument. The feminist claim is not that ideas are silencing ideas, but that acts can be silencing acts. That, as we have seen, is no confusion. People do all kinds of things with words: besides advising, warning, and hurting one another, they also silence one another. They silence by preventing speakers from doing things with words. They can silence simply, by ordering or by threatening; they can silence by frustrating a speaker's perlocutionary acts; they can silence by disabling a speaker's illocutionary acts. We have seen that pornography can silence in all three ways.

The silencing claim is not really about ideas at all, but about people and what they do. It is not uncommon, in discussions about free speech, to cast ideas as the heroes of the story. Free speech is a good thing, because it provides a free marketplace for ideas where the best and truest ideas can win out in the end.[44] To say that some speech silences is to describe a kind of shopping problem: some ideas that could be on the market are not. Censorship may or may not be needed as a means of improving the marketplace, a little local regulation to improve things overall. Perhaps some ideas must be censored so that others can find space on the shelves. Here again we have the tendency of which Austin complained: a focus on content, while ignoring the speech act performed. The claim that pornography silences women is not about ideas, but about people.

Free speech is a good thing because it *enables people to act,* enables people to do things with words: argue, protest, question, answer. Speech that silences is bad, not just because it restricts the ideas available on the shelves, but because it constrains people's actions. It is true that women have problems developing and expressing new ideas about themselves, about sexuality, about life, when pornography has a market monopoly. The marketplace is certainly missing out on some valuable ideas. But that is not the point. The point is that a woman's liberty to speak the *actions* she wants to speak has been curtailed: her liberty to protest against pornography and rape, to refuse sex when she wants to, to argue about violence in court, or to celebrate and promote new ways of thinking about sexuality. The point is that women cannot *do things* with words, even when we think we know how.

III. CONCLUDING REMARKS

The claims that pornography subordinates and silences women make perfect sense; they are not sleight of hand, not philosophically indefensible, not confused. Moreover, if pornographic speech is indeed authoritative, the claims may well be true. The premise about pornography's authority is an empirical one. If you think it is false, you will disagree with the conclusion about the truth of the claims, but not, I hope, with the conclusion about their coherence.

If pornography subordinates women, it presents a conflict between pornographers' right to liberty and women's right to equality. If pornography silences women, it presents a conflict within liberty itself, between pornographers' right to speak and women's. If pornography silences women, women will have difficulty fighting subordinating speech with speech of their own. Does this give us reason for thinking that MacKinnon may be right, not only in the two claims considered, but in her view that pornography should be restricted by law? Perhaps. Or perhaps we need independent argument to bridge the gap. Such an argument is beyond my project here, but it may not be too hard to find. For an influential liberal view has it that it is wrong for a government to allow private citizens to violate the liberty of other citizens by preventing them from saying what they wish. . . . If that is correct, it may be wrong to permit some speakers to silence others by preventing them from speaking the actions they wish to speak. Women wish to be able to speak some important actions: to be able to refuse, to protest, or to give testimony. The speech of pornographers may prevent them from doing so. If it does, then it may be wrong for a government to allow pornographers to speak.

NOTES

1. In, e.g., Catharine MacKinnon, "Linda's Life and Andrea's Work," *Feminism Unmodified* (Cambridge, Mass.: Harvard University Press, 1987), p. 130. Pornography, as defined by MacKinnon, and as discussed in this paper, is not the same as

obscenity. See MacKinnon, "Not a Moral Issue," ibid.; and Frank Michelman, "Conceptions of Democracy in American Constitutional Argument: The Case of Pornography Regulation," *Tennessee Law Review* 56 (1989): 294n.8. MacKinnon drafted an ordinance that was passed in Indianapolis in 1984, but was then challenged and defeated. See American Booksellers, Inc. v. Hudnut, 598 F. Supp. 1327 (S.D. Ind. 1984). The ordinance made trafficking in pornography civilly actionable, rather than simply prohibiting it. I do not address this admittedly important feature of the legislation here.

2. MacKinnon, "Francis Biddle's Sister," *Feminism Unmodified*, p. 176.

3. American Booksellers, Inc. v. Hudnut, 771 F.2d 329 (7th Cir. 1985).

4. Easterbrook's omission has been commented upon by Melinda Vadas in "A First Look at the Pornography/Civil Rights Ordinance: Could Pornography Be the Subordination of Women?" *Journal of Philosophy* 84 (1987): 487–511. Vadas is interested, as I am, in saving the "subordinating" claim from charges of conceptual confusion, and she develops an interesting analysis which differs from that offered here. She says that some predicates can apply to a representational depiction because they apply to the scene depicted. "Subordinates" is such a predicate, in her view, so pornographic depictions of subordination can themselves subordinate. My view is that the link is not as close as she sees it: an utterance's depicting subordination is neither necessary nor sufficient for its having the force of subordination. The reasons for this will emerge shortly.

5. Hudnut, 598 F. Supp. 1316 (1984).

6. W. A. Parent, "A Second Look at Pornography and the Subordination of Women," *Journal of Philosophy* 87 (1990): 205–11. Parent's article is a response to Vadas's. He argues, by means of the following remarkable non sequitur, for the different conclusion that pornography is morally evil (p. 211). "Evil" means "depraved." "To deprave" means "to debase." "To debase" means "to bring into contempt." Pornography brings women into contempt, ergo pornography is evil. What actually follows from Parent's lexicographical premises is of course that *women* are evil. Women are brought into contempt (by pornography), therefore debased, therefore depraved, therefore evil.

7. J. L. Austin, *How to Do Things with Words* (London: Oxford University Press, 1962).

8. *Ibid.*, p. 101 (my version is a slight elaboration).

9. *Ibid.*, p. 109.

10. *Ibid.*, p. 103.

11. This idea is developed by MacKinnon and others in many places, but see, e.g., MacKinnon, "Sexual Politics of the First Amendment," *Feminism Unmodified*, p. 209.

12. MacKinnon, "Not a Moral Issue," ibid., p. 156. (I don't think much hinges here on MacKinnon's talk of free speech being a social goal, rather than a right.)

13. Defending censorship in the name of liberty is "a dangerous confusion"; the idea that pornography silences is "confusion"; see Ronald Dworkin, "Two Concepts of Liberty," in *Isaiah Berlin: A Celebration*, ed. Edna and Avishai Margalit (London: Hogarth Press, 1991), pp. 103, 108. The claim that pornography silences is "somewhat figurative," and "metaphorical," according to Frank Michelman, "Conceptions of Democracy," p. 294n.8. (This figurativeness is not a handicap to the silencing argument in his view, however.) Dworkin's argument is criticized in more detail by Jennifer Hornsby, "Language, Power, and 'Silencing'," and by myself in "Pornography and Liberty: Reply to Dworkin," both in progress.

14. Judge Barker's accusation, see 598 F. Supp 1316 (1984).

15. MacKinnon uses this example to make the point that words can be "an integral act in a system of segregation, which is a system of force" (MacKinnon, "On Collaboration," *Feminism Unmodified*, p. 202).

16. Here I depart from Vadas ("A First Look"), for it is not in virtue of depicting subordination that the "whites only" sign subordinates, if it does. That utterance does not depict subordination, any more than "I do" depicts a marriage. So something can subordinate without depicting subordination. The converse is also true. Something can depict subordination without subordinating (a documentary, for example). Some examples of this will be considered shortly.

17. MacKinnon, "Francis Biddle's Sister," *Feminism Unmodified*, p. 176.

18. Austin's discussion of verdictives and exercitives is in lecture 11, especially sections 1 and 2, pp. 152-56. The description I give of exercitives is used by him for what is strictly a proper subset of that class (p. 155).

19. 598 F. Supp. 1316 (1984), my italics.

20. MacKinnon, "Francis Biddle's Sister," p. 176.

21. So I interpret the available evidence. See Edward Donnerstein, Daniel Linz, and Steven Penrod, *The Question of Pornography: Research Findings and Policy Implications* (New York: Free Press; London: Collier Macmillan, 1987). Note that material that is sexually arousing and violent but *not* sexually explicit may also have these effects. See also *Public Hearings on Ordinances to Add Pornography as Discrimination Against Women*, Committee on Government Operations, City Council, Minneapolis, Minn. (Dec. 12-13, 1983); transcript of hearings published as *Pornography and Sexual Violence: Evidence of the Links* (London: Everywoman, 1988); and the *Report of the Attorney General's Commission on Pornography* (Washington, D.C.: United States Government Printing Office, 1986).

22. MacKinnon argues for this change of perspective in "Francis Biddle's Sister" and elsewhere.

23. MacKinnon, "Francis Biddle's Sister," p. 173.

24. Helen E. Longino, "Pornography, Oppression and Freedom: A Closer Look," in *Take Back the Night: Women in Pornography*, ed. Laura Lederer (New York: William Morrow, 1980), p. 29. (Longino has the entire phrase in italics.)

25. MacKinnon, "Francis Biddle's Sister," p. 171, emphasis mine. I do not italicize "sexualizes" because I think it may be a perlocutionary rather than an illocutionary verb, meaning something like "makes viewers find the thought of rape, etc., sexually arousing." But perhaps it is an illocutionary verb meaning something like "legitimates rape, etc., in describing it as if it were normal sex."

26. The first statistic comes from a UCLA study, Jacqueline Goodchild et al. cited in Robin Warshaw, *I Never Called It Rape* (New York: Harper and Row, 1988), p. 120; the second and third from studies by Alfred B. Heilbrun, Emory University, and Maura P. Loftus, Auburn University, cited in Naomi Wolf, *The Beauty Myth* (New York: Vintage, 1990), p. 166; the fourth from research done by Virginia Greenlinger, Williams College, and Donna Byrne, SUNY-Albany, cited in Warshaw, p. 93.

27. For a good discussion of the effect of this monopoly on the fantasy lives of these hearers and women as well, see Wolf, *The Beauty Myth*, esp. pp. 162-68.

28. In the final chapter of *The Question of Pornography*, Edward Donnerstein advocates education to counteract pornography's harmful effects.

29. This is advocated by the Women Against Censorship group, who, as *amici curiae*, protested against the MacKinnon ordinance; see also *Pleasure and Danger: Exploring Female Sexuality*, ed Carol Vance (London: Routledge and Kegan Paul, 1984); and the collection *Sex Exposed: Sexuality and the Pornography Debate*, ed. Lynne Segal and Mary MacIntosh (New Brunswick, N.J.: Rutgers University Press, 1993).

30. Habermas too is interested in the connection between the social power of speakers and the opportunities those speakers have to select and employ speech acts. But the constraints on speech acts that interest him (e.g., economic, psychological) are different from the structural constraints that interest me here. Insofar as illocutionary acts are identified by Habermas with *communicative* speech acts, which are to be found in the utopian "ideal speech situation," his version of speech-act theory would in fact make the analysis I give here impossible. See Jürgen Habermas, *The Theory of Communicative Action* (Boston: Beacon Press, 1984), esp. vol. 1, pp. 288–91. I am interested in precisely those illocutions that he leaves aside, those that are made against a backdrop of social inequality and sometimes help to bring that inequality about.

31. Donald Davidson, "Communication and Convention" in *Inquiries into Truth and Interpretation* (Oxford: Oxford University Press, 1984), p. 269. Davidson does not, of course, take this example to illustrate the power of convention, as I do. On the contrary, he infers from this example that convention can do far less than it is commonly supposed to do; in particular, convention could never succeed in making an utterance count as an assertion. I am not sure that I have any quarrel with the latter, but I am interested here in a different question: whether conventions of a different kind, those of theatre, can sometimes be sufficient to block an utterance's having the intended illocutionary force.

32. As far as *talak* divorce is concerned, "a woman [has] no power of divorce"; see Honorable Moulvi Mahomed Yusoof Khan Bahadur, *Mahomedan Law*, vol. 3 (Calcutta: Thacker, Spink & Co., 1898), p. 47. However, there are some qualifications. The husband may delegate the right of *talaq* to his wife; see Keith Hodkinson, *Muslim Family Law* (London: Croom Helm, 1984), p. 222. Although *talaq* is the commonest kind of divorce, there are other means of achieving divorce, some of which are available to women in certain special circumstances (ibid., pp. 219–306).

33. MacKinnon, *Feminism Unmodified*, p. 228, my italics. She is referring here to the words of legal enactments, but it is not quite—or rather, not just—*felicity* conditions she has in mind.

34. The first statistic comes from a study of students at the University of South Dakota. There are comparable and worse figures for other universities: St. Cloud State University (twenty-nine percent of the women students reported having been raped), Auburn University (twenty-five percent reported having been raped at least once), and Brown University (sixteen percent reported having been date raped), cited in Wolf, *The Beauty Myth*, pp. 166, 167. The second statistic comes from J. Caputi, *The Age of Sex Crime* (London: The Women's Press, Ltd., 1987), p. 119.

35. Linda Lovelace, with Mike McGrady, *Ordeal* (Secaucus, N.J.: Citadel Press, 1980).

36. See *Hearings*.

37. *Ordeal* has not misfired *tout court*; in many contexts it has succeeded as an illocutionary act of protest. A similar sexually explicit depiction of subordination

that aims to be protest rather than pornography is Andrea Dworkin's *Mercy* (London: Secker and Warburg, 1990), and it may provoke similar paradoxes. Harriet Gilbert argues that Dworkin's *Mercy* and Sade's *Justine* have much in common, and that the former could arguably count as pornography by the ordinance definition, showing, in her view, the futility of attempts at legal definition ("So Long as It's Not Sex and Violence," in *Sex Exposed*).

38. MacKinnon, "Francis Biddle's Sister," p. 180, citing evidence from the Minneapolis hearings.
39. Wolf, *Beauty Myth*, p. 167. "Refusing to take no for an answer" might be ambiguous between failing to recognize a woman's refusal and failing to obey it. The study of Toronto schoolchildren is discussed in Caputi, *The Age of Sex Crime*.
40. See Michelman, "Conceptions of Democracy," p. 299.
41. It is estimated that only one in ten rapes are reported to the police and far fewer make it to court. See MacKinnon, *Feminism Unmodified*, pp. 110-15.
42. Michelman says this in "Conceptions of Democracy," p. 296 n. 13.
43. Dworkin, "Two Concepts," p. 108.
44. "The best test of truth is the power of the thought to get itself accepted in the competition of the market," said Justice Holmes in *Abrams*, quoted in Tribe, *Constitutional Law*, p. 686.

Mediating the Offense Principle
Joel Feinberg

These reflections on the legitimacy of social interference with offensive conduct and expression are taken from *Offense to Others*, the second volume of Joel Feinberg's work, *The Moral Limits of the Criminal Law*. Feinberg is introduced in Chapter 3.

Feinberg claims that although offense to others is not as great an evil as harm to others, it is still an evil that under some conditions society is justified in preventing, through the application of what he calls the "offense principle." In this discussion, Feinberg attempts to spell out in a very general way what these conditions might be. In order to determine whether a restriction on offensive conduct or speech is justified, he argues that society needs to weigh the "reasonableness" of the offending behavior against the seriousness of the offense. He also offers standards against which both reasonableness and seriousness can be judged. While agreeing with John Stuart Mill that restraints on the free expression of viewpoints are antithetical to a free society, he recognizes a difference between the content of an offensive opinion and its manner of presentation. When the latter is offensive, Feinberg suggests, society might be justified in preventing its expression.

1. ON THE SCALES:
THE SERIOUSNESS OF THE OFFENSE

. . . Offensiveness produces unpleasant experiences and causes annoying inconveniences, both of which are surely evils, though not as great evils as actual harms. Unlike certain other evils, however, offenses and harms are done to persons. They have determinate victims with genuine grievances and a right to complain against determinate wrongdoers about the way in which they have been treated. . . . Those facts, it seems to me, constitute as good reasons as one could expect to find for the legitimacy in principle of legal interference, even though in a given case, or even in all given cases, there are stronger countervailing reasons of a practical kind.

There are abundant reasons, however, for being extremely cautious in applying the offense principle. People take offense—perfectly genuine offense—at many socially useful or even necessary activities, from commercial advertisement to inane chatter. Moreover, bigoted prejudices of a very widespread kind (e.g., against interracial couples strolling hand in hand down the main street of a town in the deep South) can lead onlookers to be disgusted and shocked, even "morally" repelled, by perfectly innocent activities, and we should be loath to permit their groundless repugnance to outweigh the innocence of the offending conduct. For these and similar reasons, the offense principle

From *Offense to Others*, by Joel Feinberg (Oxford, England: Oxford University Press, 1985), pp. 25–49.

must be formulated in a very precise way, and supplemented by appropriate standards or mediating maxims, so as not to open the door to wholesale and intuitively unwarranted legal interference.

As formulated so far, the offense principle commits us only to the view that when public conduct causes offense to someone, the fact of that offense is relevant to the permissibility of the conduct in question. A relevant consideration, of course, can be outweighed by relevant reasons on the other side, and there always is another side, namely that of the offending actor's own interests. Hence conscientious legislators can no more escape the necessity of balancing conflicting considerations when they consider prohibiting offensive conduct than they can escape interest-balancing in the application of the harm principle. Following the model of nuisance law, they will have to weigh, in each main category and context of offensiveness, the seriousness of the offense caused to unwilling witnesses against the reasonableness of the offender's conduct. The seriousness of the offensiveness would be determined by (1) the intensity and durability of the repugnance produced, and the extent to which repugnance could be anticipated to be the general reaction of strangers to the conduct displayed or represented (conduct offensive only to persons with an abnormal suspectibility to offense would not count as *very* offensive); (2) the ease with which unwilling witnesses can avoid the offensive displays; and (3) whether or not the witnesses have willingly assumed the risk of being offended either through curiosity or the anticipation of pleasure. (The maxim *Volenti non fit injuria* applies to offense as well as to harm.) We can refer to these norms, in order, as "the extent of offense standard," "the reasonable avoidability standard," and "the *Volenti* standard."

These factors would be weighed as a group against the reasonableness of the offending party's conduct as determined by (1) its personal importance to the actors themselves and its social value generally, remembering always the enormous social utility of unhampered expression (in those cases where expression is involved); (2) the availability of alternative times and places where the conduct in question would cause less offense; (3) the extent, if any, to which the offense is caused with spiteful motives. In addition, the legislature would examine the prior established character of various neighborhoods, and consider establishing licensed zones in areas where the conduct in question is known to be already prevalent, so that people inclined to be offended are not likely to stumble on it to their surprise. . . .

Consider the plight of the innocent black . . . who is deeply offended by racist banners, or the Jew who is insulted by swastikas that mock the memory of his murdered kinsmen. Even though the interpersonal *extent* of the offense caused might not be great (not as great as that caused by public defecation, eating vomit, etc., etc.), the other weighable factors could make up for that. The sharply pointed, threatening edge of the offense could make up in intensity, for example, for what is lacking in extent. Indeed, the intensity of the offense, within certain limits, may tend to vary inversely with the number of those likely to share it. Thus, a banner saying that "All Americans are Pigs" would tend to offend most Americans to some extent, but few very intensely, whereas "All American blacks are pigs" might offend fewer but those much more intensely. If John Smith, . . . [a] black [man], . . . sees it, he will be shocked and outraged. If the sign says simply "John Smith is a pig," or "John Smith's wife [or mother] is a pig," Smith may be no more offended on balance than he would be by the insult to his race, but the sign will be even more ominously personal and threatening, and his evoked feelings appropriately more intense. Clearly, the pointed and personal character of the offense tends to make up in "weight" for its lack of widespreadedness. . . .

When the offense caused by a contemplated action is predictably likely to offend virtually any person who might happen to behold it (or would offend nearly any person who found himself the target of a similar affront, when the offense is aimed more narrowly), then there is a very powerful case for forbidding it, even though the universality of the response is neither necessary nor, taken by itself, sufficient for legitimate prohibition. . . . When conduct is so extremely offensive that it is likely to offend nearly everyone, there is hardly anyone who would be willing to engage in it! Seriously offending everyone is no normal person's idea of a good time. It is a tautology to say that people don't like to be offended. They have a tendency to strike back and one way or another make life miserable for the people they find revolting, disgusting, embarrassing, and annoying. . . . Our social taboos, enforced by the powerful sanction of "public opinion," are more than powerful enough to protect us from . . . [seriously offending] conduct without the assistance of the law. We hardly need specific legislation directed at evils that are so rare that they occur only once a decade in a country of two hundred million citizens. And so there is a benign sort of paradox pointed up by the "extent of offense" standard: the more universal and severe a form of offensiveness, the less danger there is that it will occur, and the less we need rely on criminal sanctions to deter it.

The second mediating maxim for the application of the offense principle is the *standard of reasonable avoidability*. The easier it is to avoid a particular offense, or to terminate it once it occurs, without inconvenience to oneself, the less serious the offense is. . . . Obscene remarks over a loudspeaker, pornographic handbills thrust into the hands of passing pedestrians, and lurid billboards in Times Square graphically advertising the joys of pederasty would all fail to be reasonably avoidable.[1]

On the other hand, no one has a right to protection from the state against offensive experiences if he can easily and effectively avoid them without unreasonable effort or inconvenience. In particular, the offense principle, properly qualified, can give no warrant to the suppression of *books* on the grounds of obscenity. When printed words hide decorously behind covers of books sitting passively on the shelves of a bookstore, their offensiveness is easily avoided. The opposite position is no doubt encouraged by the common comparison of obscenity with "smut," "filth," or "dirt." This in turn suggests an analogy to nuisance law, which governs cases where certain activities create ugly messes and terrible odors offensive to neighbors. There is, however, one vitiating difference. In the case of "dirty books," the offense is easily avoidable. Nothing comparable to the smell of rancid garbage oozes out through the covers of a book whether one looks at it or not. When an "obscene" book sits on a shelf, who is there to be offended? Those who want to read it for the sake of erotic stimulation presumably will not be offended (else they wouldn't read it), and those who choose not to read it will have no experience of it to be offended by. If its covers are too decorous, some unsuspecting readers might browse through it by mistake and then be offended by what they find, but they need only close the book again to escape the offense.

Still another mediating maxim for the application of the offense principle is our old friend, *Volenti non fit injuria*. One can in fact be offended by conduct to which one has consented. A businessman Doe may know that Roe is filthy, smelly, and vulgar, yet quite deliberately choose to put up with his offensive presence at a business luncheon for the sake of future profits. On another occasion Doe may quite voluntarily enter a pornographic cinema quite confident that the film he is about to see will disgust, embarrass, and annoy him, yet he will be willing to suffer that offense for the sake of curiosity, or for some other good reason of his own. The offended states induced by such voluntarily undertaken experiences are perfectly real, just as the broken bones incurred by the stunt motorcyclist are perfectly real harms, but in neither case can the victim complain of a grievance. Insofar as they undertook the dangerous activity or the offensive experience voluntarily, they were not *wronged* by anyone. For the purpose of a plausible offense principle, voluntarily suffered offenses are not to count as offenses at all, and voluntarily assumed risks of offense render inadmissible subsequent complaints that the risked offense has materialized.

One further restriction on the offense principle is necessary. This qualification, though implicit in the extent of offense standard, is important enough to be made fully explicit and emphatic. This is the requirement, parallel to a mediating maxim for the harm principle, that the seriousness of the offense be discounted to the extent that it is the product of abnormal susceptibilities. As we have already seen, the law of nuisance has for centuries downgraded the inconveniences that stem from rare and special susceptibilities in unfortunate plaintiffs; a criminal law of nuisance, protecting the senses and sensibilities of the general public, would have no choice but to do the same.[2] "The standard," writes Prosser, "must necessarily be that of definite offensiveness, inconvenience, or annoyance to the normal person in the community."[3] It is not a public nuisance to ring church bells . . . or to "run a factory where the smoke aggravates the plaintiff's bronchitis [provided it would not affect the health of a normal person] . . . Neither is a keg of spikes by the side of the road a public nuisance because it frightens an unduly skittish horse."[4]

Human beings who take offense at remarkably little provocation should have the same standing in law courts as the owners of skittish horses. The most "skittish" imaginable person is he who suffers acute disgust and revulsion, shock to sensibilities, shameful embarrassment, annoyance, frustration, resentment or humiliation *not* from something he sees, feels, smells, or hears, but rather from unseen activities he knows or fears may be happening beyond his ken. If the law permits some form of harmless activity that he regards as odious and disgusting, but permits it only when done discreetly between consenting adults behind locked doors and drawn blinds, he fears as he walks down the street that such activities may be going on in any of the darkened houses he passes, and the "bare knowledge" fills him with dread, anxiety, and shame. It will be even worse if he has strong evidence that the revolting activities are occurring in a given house on the street, for the "bare thought" in this case is more likely to get an obsessive grip on his consciousness. . . .

It seems clear, however, that the more fragile our sensitive sufferer's psyche, the less protection he can expect from the criminal law. Provided that the conduct the very thought of which upsets him has any redeeming value at all, personal or social, his own claim to protection is likely to be overridden. If a mere sneeze causes a glass window to break, we should blame the weakness or brittleness of the glass and not the sneeze. Similarly, if "bare knowledge" that discreet and harmless "immoralities" are occurring in private leads to severe mental distress, we should attribute the distress to abnormal suspectibilities rather than to the precipitating cause. We don't punish persons when their normally harmless and independently valuable (at least to themselves) activities happen to startle a skittish horse whose presence was unsuspected. Rather we expect the owners of skittish horses to keep them away from "startling" activities and to take steps to cure them of their skittishness. . . .

In summary, the seriousness of an offense is determined by the following standards:

1. *The magnitude of the offense*, which is a function of its intensity, duration, and extent.
   a. *Intensity.* The more intense a typical offense taken at the type of conduct in question, the more serious is an actual instance of such an offense.
   b. *Duration.* The more durable a typical offense taken at the type of conduct in question, the more serious is an actual instance of such offense.
   c. *Extent.* The more widespread the susceptibility to a given kind of offense, the more serious is a given instance of that kind of offense.
2. *The standard of reasonable avoidability.* The more difficult it is to avoid a given offense without serious inconvenience to oneself the more serious is that offense.
3. *The Volenti maxim.* Offended states that were voluntarily incurred, or the risk of which was voluntarily assumed by the person who experienced them, are not to count as "offenses" at all in the application of a legislative "offense principle."

4. *The discounting of abnormal susceptibilities.* (This can be thought of as a kind of corollary of 1.) Insofar as offended states occur because of a person's abnormal susceptibility to offense, their seriousness is to be discounted in the application of a legislative "offense principle."...

2. ON THE SCALES: THE REASONABLENESS OF THE OFFENDING CONDUCT

Having determined the seriousness of a given category of offense by the application of four standards to it, the careful legislator will proceed to balance that seriousness against the reasonableness of the various kinds of conduct that can produce it. For the reasons already cited he will not concern himself with whether or not the offense is taken reasonably, but the reasonableness of the conduct to which the offense is taken is quite another matter. Conduct that is ordinary, useful, or necessary cannot properly be interfered with except for the most urgent reasons; whereas conduct that is trivial or frivolous will have less weight on the balancing scales.

The "reasonableness" of a type of conduct that may cause offense is determined first of all by its importance to the actor himself. If the conduct in question is part of the activity by which the actor earns his living so that its curtailment would harm his economic interest, then obviously it is important to him, whatever others may think of it. Similarly, it will be a matter of great personal importance if it contributes significantly to his health, talent, knowledge, or virtue, and even more so if it is necessary for the promotion of those goals. Similarly, the conduct has importance to its actor if it contributes to his pleasure, or is an integral part of a pattern of activities central to his love life, family life, or social life. Even if the conduct is not necessary to the promotion of any of his interests, it may have some value to him in that alternatives to it, while equally effective means to his goals, would be inconvenient. After all, if the convenience of offended parties has weight on the legislative scales, there is no reason to discount the convenience of the persons whose conduct offends. On the other hand, utterly frivolous, wanton, perverse, or gratuitous behavior; easily avoidable actions done impulsively on a passing whim; self-defeating actions that have no more value for the actor than for those he offends; and trivial, mindless, arbitrary actions, all fail to satisfy the standard of personal importance and can be discounted accordingly.

A second standard for judging the "reasonableness" of the offending conduct is its social utility, or as Prosser puts it, "the social value which the law attaches to its ultimate purpose."[5] If the conduct that annoys or inconveniences others is part of the activity of moving or demolishing buildings, repairing ruptured gas or water lines, investigating a crime, pursuing an escaped felon, or reporting a news story, it has a great deal of public value, as part of a kind of activity that is socially useful, but if it is valuable only to the person who engages in it, as for example, hawking a product for sale, loitering in or near a public place for the purpose of soliciting deviate sexual relations, purveying offensive materials for the purpose of making a personal profit, and so on, then it contributes little but nuisance to the rest of the community. Playing a portable radio on a public bus may have some value to the person who does it and to that extent at least deserves a legislator's respect, but it is hardly the sort of activity that contributes to the public good. Conversing freely, easily, and naturally with an acquaintance, on the other hand, whether in a public bus . . . or elsewhere, is a type of activity that is not only vitally important to individuals, but also productive of far more good than harm to the community on the whole. Unregulated impromptu communication between individuals is in general a necessary condition for efficient social functioning.

It is at least partly by virtue of the high social value attached to it that unfettered *expression of opinion* has such a privileged position in American law.[6] To be sure, expressing opinions openly in spontaneous conversation, writing, or through more powerful media of communication is also of great importance to private individuals themselves, since self-expression is valued both as an end in itself and as a means of effecting desired changes. But it is also a necessary condition for the satisfactory functioning of any government that relies heavily on enlightened public opinion in its decision making. It is important to each individual to voice his own opinion about matters of public policy, but it is also important to him that he have fair access to the opinions and arguments of all his fellows, and important to the whole community that all possible roads to truth be left open lest our leaders become committed to insufficiently examined policies, with disastrous social consequences. It is necessary to emphasize here, as Mill did in *On Liberty*,[7] that unpopular, unorthodox, and extreme opinions, no less than any others, need their spokesmen, in order that our chances of discovering truths and making wise decisions be increased. There is a social gain then from constantly reexamining public policies, probing for difficulties and soft spots, bringing to light new and relevant facts, and subjecting to doubt hitherto unquestioned first premises. Without these challenges, nations have a natural tendency to drift complacently into dead ends and quagmires. For that reason, no amount of offensiveness in an expressed opinion can counterbalance the vital social value of allowing unfettered personal expression.

There are two ways, however, in which an expression of opinion can be offensive. An audience can be offended by the opinion expressed or implied in an utterance, as, for example, a devout Christian might be offended by the bare assertion of atheism; or the audience might be offended instead by the manner in which the opinion itself is expressed, for example as a caption to an obscene poster of Jesus and Mary. . . . Something other than an opinion itself offends when offending conduct does not involve language or symbolism, or when it offends by means of an utterance with no clear propositional content at all (for example, obscene epithets), or when an opinion is expressed but is only incidental to the cause of offense, which is the manner or context of expression.[8] Utterances that give offense in the latter ways may have some value to the person who makes them, and have some weight for that reason, but they derive very little weight from the standard of social utility, and consequently can be rightly restricted by law when the offense they cause is sufficiently serious. In contrast, the offensiveness of the opinion itself is never serious enough to outweigh the heavy public interest in open discussion and free expression of opinion. One should be free to shout to a crowd, or carry a sign or words on one's back, to the effect that we should abandon democracy for Nazism or Communism, that our troops should invade Cuba or bomb China, that churches should be nationalized, that homosexual intercourse in public should be encouraged—offensive as these opinions may be to many people. A non-offensive utterance of an opinion, even of an offensive opinion, is a kind of trump card in the application of the offense principle. The standards of personal importance and social utility confer on it an absolute immunity; no amount of offensiveness can enable it to be overridden.

It should be clear then how the qualified offense principle would apply to so-called "thematic obscenity." It would permit public *advocacy*, whether in hand bills or magazines, on billboards, or from soap boxes, of *any* policies or values whatever, pertaining to sex, religion, politics, or anything else; but it would not necessarily permit graphic portrayals of seriously offensive scenes to unwilling captive audiences, for example lurid paintings of sexual couplings on billboards in a crowded urban center. So precious is free speech on questions of public policy, however, that public *advocacy* of laws permitting graphically obscene billboards should be permitted. Indeed, public advocacy even of the legalization of homicide should be permitted provided the manner of advocacy itself is not offensive in one of the ways recognized by the qualified offense principle.

Another factor to be considered in any determination of the reasonableness of conduct that causes offense to others is the degree to which non-offensive alternatives that are equally satisfactory to the actor are available. If the offending person, by doing his thing at another place or time, can avoid causing offense to a captive audience without loss or unreasonable inconvenience to himself, then his offending conduct is unreasonable if done in circumstances that permit offense. Very often offensive conduct is quite unobjectionable in itself and could be performed quite legally in the privacy of the actor's own abode or some other private place, in which case he can have no complaint if the law prevents him from doing it right under the noses of unwilling observers. . . .

This brings us to the next maxim for determining the reasonableness of offensive conduct. By and large the offending person's motives are his own business, and the law should respect them whatever they are. But when the motive is merely malicious or spiteful it deserves no respect at all. Offending the senses or sensibilities of others simply for the sake of doing so is hardly less unreasonable than harming the interests of others simply for the sake of doing so. Conduct cannot be reasonable in the eyes of the law (or on the scales of the legislator) if its entire motive is malice or spite. Even abnormal vulnerabilities and super-sensitive, "skittish" sensibilities, which, as we have seen, have little claim to protection against even minimally reasonable behavior, can make some claim at least to protection against persecuting harassment and wholly spiteful flaunting that has no purpose whatever except to cause offense. Unlike special vulnerabilities to harm, however, abnormal susceptibilities to offense find more appropriate legal protection against malicious exploitation through means other than the criminal law, for example, through injunctions, civil suits, or permitted private "abatement."

In practice, however, malice and spite may be very hard to distinguish from another motive that is surely more reasonable, however it must be treated by the law. The nude housewife in the supermarket may fancy herself a kind of moral reformer, trying to exercise a modifying influence on prevailing attitudes that she regards as benighted. She may be trying to do her share (her *duty* as she conceives it) to habituate the public to the sight of nude bodies so that what she takes to be the unreasonable susceptibility to offense at the sight of nudity may diminish and eventually disappear along with various unwholesome attitudes towards sex to which it may be connected. She may be aware that her nudity will cause some observers to experience painful embarrassment, but she acts despite that awareness, not because of it. Her case is surely to be distinguished from that of the mischievous troublemaker and the spiteful misanthrope. One would hope that she would not be seriously punished by a court. The question of whether her conduct could pass the tests of reasonableness required by an enlightened application of the offense principle, however, is more difficult.

Donald VanDeVeer argues persuasively that it is possible in principle to distinguish malicious from what he calls "conscientious" offensive conduct. As an example of the former, he has us consider the following: "Smith, an eccentric liberal Democrat, paints a swastika on his roof to irritate his Jewish neighbor, but not with the intention of winning converts to Neo-Nazism or achieving any further purpose."[9] VanDeVeer also points out that political dissidents often cannot "get a hearing" without media attention, and "cannot achieve that without offensive behavior" like guerilla theatre performances and shocking symbolic acts. VanDeVeer would discount purely spiteful motivation, as we too have suggested, while permitting offensive conduct when conscientious. I am sympathetic with his view, although I draw back from an absolutist principle that would make conscientiousness an automatically sufficient condition for permissibility. What conscientiousness in VanDeVeer's sense shows is that the conduct is genuine political expression and not mere malicious insult without advocacy, or some use of symbolism other than defending a thesis or making a point. It therefore brings the full weight of free expression as an important social value down on the side of the scale weighing the reasonableness of the offending conduct. There would be considerably less political value in using a symbol simply to shock a neighbor, or exposing oneself in the supermarket for sexual self-stimulation, or to solicit sexual relations, or simply to upset the excessively prudish as an end in itself.

The final consideration relevant to the reasonableness of conduct that tends to offend has to do with the nature of the neighborhood in which the offending conduct takes place. The maxim that offensive conduct performed in *de facto* restricted areas where it is known to be common is more reasonable than it would be were it performed in locales where it is uncommon is a corollary of the "available alternatives" standard that deserves some separate discussion. Homosexual lovers petting and kissing on a public bus are unreasonably offensive, by the present standard, if there is an area of their city, not unreasonably distant, that is known to be frequented regularly and primarily by homosexuals who commonly engage in the same sort of activity on the street corners, in the taverns and night clubs, even in the local buses. Similarly, sex shops, pornographic cinemas, and dirty book stores, all with neon identifying signs and lurid advertising posters, create an irritating and unwanted ambience in residential and most commercial areas of a city, but can cause very little offense in neighborhoods already abandoned to them, like 42nd Street and Charing Cross Road. . . .

In summary, the reasonableness of conduct that happens to cause offense to others is determined by the following standards, each of which can be understood to be a kind of mediating maxim governing the application of the offense principle to legislative or judicial deliberations:

1. *Personal importance.* The more important the offending conduct is to the actor, as measured by his own preferences and the vitality of those of the actor's own interests it is meant to advance, the more reasonable that conduct is.

2. *Social value.* The greater the social utility of the kind of conduct of which the actor's is an instance, the more reasonable is the actor's conduct.

3. *Free expression.* (A corollary of 1 and 2.) Expressions of opinion, especially about matters of public policy, but also about matters of empirical fact, and about historical, scientific, theological, philosophical, political, and moral questions, must be presumed to have the highest social importance in virtue of the great social utility of free expression and discussion generally, as well as the vital personal interest most people have in being able to speak their minds fearlessly. No degree of offensiveness in the expressed opinion itself is sufficient to override the case for free expression, although the offensiveness of the manner of expression, as opposed to its substance, may have sufficient weight in some contexts.

4. *Alternative opportunities.* The greater the availability of alternative times or places that would be equally satisfactory to the actor and his partners (if any) but inoffensive to others, the less reasonable is conduct done in circumstances that render it offensive to others.

5. *Malice and spite*. Offensive conduct is unreasonable to the extent that its impelling motive is spiteful or malicious. Wholly spiteful conduct, done with the intention of offending and for no other reason, is wholly unreasonable. Especial care is required in the application of this standard, for spiteful motives are easily confused with conscientious ones.

6. *Nature of the locality*. (A corollary of 4.) Offensive conduct performed in neighborhoods where it is common, and widely known to be common, is less unreasonable than it would be in neighborhoods where it is rare and unexpected.

3. READING THE BALANCE

Having assessed the reasonableness of the offender's conduct by the application of the above standards, the legislator or judge (when the legislature has permitted him discretion) must "balance" it against the seriousness of the offense caused, as determined by the four standards mentioned earlier. A legislature does not, of course, concern itself with specific actions and specific offended states. Rather it must weigh against one another generalized *types* of conduct and offense. In hard cases this balancing procedure can be very complex and uncertain, but there are some cases that fall clearly under one or another standard in such a way as to leave no doubt how they must be decided. Thus, for example, the *Volenti* standard preempts all the rest when it clearly applies. Film exhibitors, for example, cannot reasonably be charged with criminally offensive conduct when the only people who witness their films are those who voluntarily purchased tickets to do so, knowing full well what sort of film they were about to see.[10] One cannot be *wrongly* offended by that to which one fully consents. Similarly, *books* cannot be legitimately banned on the grounds of offensiveness, by virtue of the standard of reasonable avoidability, nor can inoffensive expressions of offensive political or theological opinions, by virtue of their personal and social importance. On the other side, purely spiteful motives in the offender can be a preemptive consideration weighting the balance scale decisively on the side of unreasonableness.

In some cases, no one standard is preemptive, but nevertheless all applicable standards pull together towards one inevitable decision. . . . In hard cases, however, when standards conflict and none apply in a preemptive way, where for example a given kind of conduct is offensive to a moderate degree, and only moderately unreasonable, there will be no automatic mathematical way of coming to a clearly correct decision. The theorist can identify the factors that must be considered and compared, but, in the end, there is no substitute for *judgment*. When the facts are all in, and the standards all duly applied to them, there is no more need for a philosopher; the judge or legislator is entirely on his own. The scales used in the legislative and judicial balancing act have no dials and pointing arrows like those on ordinary bathroom scales (which suggests another interpretation of the saying that justice is blind). When the case is close, and all the relevant principles have been applied to it by means of all the proper standards, the legislative or judicial decision may yet be unwise, or properly criticized as "wrong," but it cannot be "illegitimate," in the sense of applying an inadmissible kind of reason. . . .

NOTES

1. In respect to the billboard example, Michael Bayles points out that it would be unnecessary and uneconomical to prevent such evils by making it a crime to put up lurid billboards. Instead, the legislature could give statutory authority to officials to require that the picture be taken down, reserving punishment and abatement only for disobedience to the order. As Bayles ruefully notes, however, the Model Penal Code would permit imprisonment for up to one year for displaying an obscene billboard! See Michael D. Bayles, "Comments," in *Issues in Law and Morality*, ed. Norman Care and Thomas Trelogan (Cleveland: Case Western Reserve University Press, 1973), pp. 122, 124.

2. It is easy to overstate this point, as I have in the past. It is an overstatement to say that "No respect should be shown for abnormal susceptibilities." Rather one should say that the more "abnormal" the susceptibility, the less weight it has on the scales, so that an excessive sensitivity is easily outweighed by a socially valuable activity. On the other hand, one must not neglect to discount the "social value" of the offending activity when it can be done in such a way as to avoid the offensive. Donald VanDeVeer ("Coercive Restraint of Offensive Actions," *Philosophy and Public Affairs*, vol. 8 (1979), pp. 184–85) gives examples of the numerous ways the law has already found to respect abnormal vulnerabilities without compromising valuable activities: ". . . laws prohibiting blowing automobile horns or otherwise disrupting quiet in hospital zones, as well as requirements that motorists give right of way to blind persons . . . or proper access to public institutions for those in wheelchairs."

3. William L. Prosser, *Handbook of the Law of Torts*, 4th ed. (St. Paul: West Publishing Co., 1971), p. 578. For the bronchitis example, Prosser cites *Judd v. Granite State Brick Co.*, 68 N.H. 185, 37A, 1041 (1804). For the skittish horse example, he cites *Rozell v. Northern Pacific R.R. Co.*, 39 N.D. 475, 167 N.W. 489 (1918).

4. Prosser, *loc. cit.*

5. Prosser, *op. cit.* (footnote 9), p. 597.

6. For classic statements of the value of free expression, see Zechariah Chaffe, *Free Speech in the United States* (Cambridge, Mass.: Harvard University Press, 1964) and Thomas I. Emerson, *The System of Free Expression* (New York: Random House, 1970). For penetrating discussions of the derivation of the right of free expression, see Thomas M. Scanlon's two articles, "A Theory of Free Expression," *Philosophy and Public Affairs*, vol. 1 (1972), and "Freedom of Expression and Categories of Expression," *University of Pittsburgh Law Review* 40 (1979).

7. John Stuart Mill, *On Liberty*, chap. 2.

8. Sometimes linguistic obscenities in the manner of expression are to be classified as essential to what is being expressed, and not merely extra "nose-thumbing"

for its own sake. See *Cohen v. California*, 91 S. Ct. (1971). On this point my earlier view was mistaken (*Rights, Justice, and the Bounds of Liberty*. Princeton, N.J.: Princeton University Press, 1980, pp. 100–102).

9. VanDeVeer, *op. cit.* (footnote 1), p. 186.

10. *Pace* Chief Justice Warren Burger and the United States Supreme Court majority in *Paris Adult Theatre I v. Slaton*, 413 U.S. (1973).

If He Hollers Let Him Go:
Regulating Racist Speech on Campus

Charles R. Lawrence III

A professor of law at Georgetown University and one of the authors of Stanford University's verbal harassment policy, Charles R. Lawrence III here takes up the question of whether the best cure for racist speech is more speech—that is, whether it is in the best interests of racial minorities to side with those opposed to regulation of speech on the grounds that freedom of expression is the "lifeblood of our democratic system." In Lawrence's view, such a claim is based on an inadequate understanding of the nature of the harms to which racist speech can lead. He suggests that listening to the accounts of those who have been the targets of hate speech can lead to a better understanding of the serious harms that such speech can cause. To say that racial minorities need to swallow such harm in order not to undermine the social benefits of free speech is, Lawrence insists, an unjust burden to bear. In addition, Lawrence questions the idea that a society without some restraints on hate speech can truly think of itself as an environment that promotes the free debate and circulation of ideas.

In recent years, university campuses have seen a resurgence of racial violence and a corresponding rise in the incidence of verbal and symbolic assault and harassment to which blacks and other traditionally subjugated groups are subjected. There is a heated debate in the civil liberties community concerning the proper response to incidents of racist speech on campus. Strong disagreements have arisen between those individuals who believe that racist speech such as that described above should be regulated by the university or some public body and those individuals who believe that racist expression should be protected from all public regulation. At the center of the controversy is a tension between the constitutional values of free speech and equality. Like the debate over affirmative action in university admissions, this issue has divided old allies and revealed unrecognized or unacknowledged differences in the experience, perceptions, and values of members of longstanding alliances. It also has caused considerable soul searching by individuals with longtime commitments to both the cause of political expression and the cause of racial equality.

I write this from within the cauldron of this controversy. I make no pretense of dispassion or objectivity, but I do claim a deep commitment to the values that motivate both sides of the debate. I have spent the better part of my life as a dissenter. As a high school student I was threatened with suspension for my refusal to participate in a civil defense drill, and I have been a

From *Duke Law Journal* vol. 1990, no. 2, 431ff.   [Endnotes omitted.]

conspicuous consumer of my first amendment liberties ever since. I also have experienced the injury of the historical, ubiquitous, and continuous defamation of American racism. I grew up with Little Black Sambo and Amos and Andy, and I continue to receive racist tracts in the mail and shoved under my door. As I struggle with the tension between these constitutional values, I particularly appreciate the experience of both belonging and not belonging that gives to African Americans and other outsider groups a sense of duality. W.E.B. DuBois—scholar and founder of the National Association for the Advancement of Colored People (NAACP)—called the gift and burden inherent in the dual, conflicting heritage of all African Americans their "second-sight."

The double consciousness of groups outside the ethnic mainstream is particularly apparent in the context of this controversy. Blacks know and value the protection the first amendment affords those of us who must rely upon our voices to petition both government and our neighbors for redress of grievances. Our political tradition has looked to "the word," to the moral power of ideas, to change the system when neither the power of the vote nor that of the gun were available. This part of us has known the experience of belonging and recognizes our common and inseparable interest in preserving the right of free speech for all. But we also know the experience of the outsider. The framers excluded us from the protection of the first amendment. The same Constitution that established rights for others endorsed a story that proclaimed our inferiority. It is a story that remains deeply ingrained in the American psyche. We see a different world than that seen by Americans who do not share this historical experience. We often hear racist speech when our white neighbors are not aware of its presence.

It is not my purpose to belittle or trivialize the importance of defending unpopular speech against the tyranny of the majority. There are very strong reasons for protecting even racist speech. Perhaps the most important reasons are that it reinforces our society's commitment to the value of tolerance, and that by shielding racist speech from government regulation, we are forced to combat it as a community. These reasons for protecting racist speech should not be set aside hastily, and I will not argue that we should be less vigilant in protecting the speech and associational rights of speakers with whom most of us would disagree.

But I am deeply concerned about the role that many civil libertarians have played, or the roles we have failed to play, in the continuing, real-life struggle through which we define the community in which we live. I fear that by framing the debate as we have—as one in which the liberty of free speech is in conflict with the elimination of racism—we have advanced the cause of racial oppression and placed the bigot on the moral high ground, fanning the rising flames of racism. Above all, I am troubled that we have not listened to the real victims, that we have shown so little empathy or understanding for their injury, and that we have abandoned those individuals whose race, gender, or sexual orientation provokes others to regard them as second-class citizens. These individuals' civil liberties are most directly at stake in the debate. In this [essay] I focus on racism. Although I will not address violent pornography and homophobic hate speech directly, I will draw on the experience of women and gays as victims of hate speech where they operate as instructive analogues.

I have set two goals in constructing this [essay]. The first goal is limited and perhaps overly modest, but it is nonetheless extremely important: I will demonstrate that much of the argument for protecting racist speech is based on the distinction that many civil libertarians draw between direct, face-to-face insults, which they think deserve first amendment protection, and all other fighting words, which they find unprotected by the first amendment. I argue that the distinction is false, that it advances none of the purposes of the first amendment, and that the time has come to put an end to the ringing rhetoric that condemns all efforts to regulate racist speech, even narrowly drafted provisions aimed at racist speech that results in direct, immediate, and substantial injury.

I also urge the regulation of racial epithets and vilification that do not involve face-to-face encounters—situations in which the victim is part of a captive audience and the injury is experienced by all members of a racial group who are forced to hear or see these words. In such cases, the insulting words are aimed at an entire group with the effect of causing significant harm to individual group members.

My second goal is more ambitious and more indeterminate. I propose several ways in which the traditional civil liberties position on free speech does not take into account important values expressed elsewhere in the Constitution. Further, I argue that even those values the first amendment itself is intended to promote are frustrated by an interpretation that is acontextual and idealized, by presupposing a world characterized by equal opportunity and the absence of societally created and culturally ingrained racism. . . .

BROWN V. BOARD OF EDUCATION: A CASE ABOUT REGULATING RACIST SPEECH

The landmark case of *Brown v. Board of Education* is not one we normally think of as concerning speech. As read most narrowly, the case is about the rights of Black children to equal educational opportunity. But *Brown* can also be read more broadly to articulate a principle central to any substantive understanding of the equal protection clause, the foundation on which all antidiscrimination law rests. This is the principle of equal citizenship. Under that principle, "Every individual is presumptively entitled to be treated by the organized society as a respected, responsible, and participating member." The principle further requires the affirmative disestablishment of societal practices that treat people as members of an inferior or dependent caste, as unworthy to participate in the larger community. The holding in *Brown*—that racially segregated schools violate the equal protection clause—reflects the fact that segregation amounts to a demeaning, caste-creating practice. The prevention of stigma was at the core of the Supreme Court's unanimous decision in *Brown* that segregated public schools are inherently unequal. Observing that the segregation of Black pupils "generates a feeling of inferiority as to their status in the community," Chief Justice Earl Warren recognized what a majority of the Court had ignored almost sixty years earlier in *Plessy v. Ferguson*. The social meaning of racial segregation in the United States is the designation of a superior and an inferior caste, and segregation proceeds "on the ground that colored citizens are . . . inferior and degraded."

The key to this understanding of *Brown* is that the practice of segregation, the practice the Court held inherently unconstitutional, was *speech*. *Brown* held that segregation is unconstitutional not simply because the physical separation of Black and white children is bad or because resources were distributed unequally among Black and white schools. *Brown* held that segregated schools were unconstitutional primarily because of the *message* segregation conveys—the message that Black children are an untouchable caste, unfit to be educated with white children. Segregation serves its purpose by conveying an idea. It stamps a badge of inferiority upon Blacks, and this badge communicates a message to others in the community, as well as to Blacks wearing the badge, that is injurious to Blacks. Therefore, *Brown* may be read as regulating the content of racist speech. As a regulation of racist speech, the decision is an exception to the usual rule that regulation of speech content is presumed unconstitutional. . . .

Some civil libertarians argue that my analysis of *Brown* conflates speech and conduct. They maintain that the segregation outlawed in *Brown* was discriminatory conduct, not speech, and the defamatory message conveyed by segregation simply was an incidental by-product of that conduct. This position is often stated as follows: "Of course segregation conveys a message, but this could be said of almost all conduct. To take an extreme example, a murderer conveys a message of hatred for his victim. But we would not argue that we cannot punish the murder—the primary conduct—merely because of this message, which is its secondary by-product." The Court has been reluctant to concede that the first amendment has any relevance whatsoever in examples like this one, because the law would not be directed at anything resembling speech or at the views expressed. In such a case the regulation of speech is truly incidental to the regulation of the conduct.

These same civil libertarians assert that I suggest that all conduct with an expressive component should be treated alike—namely, as unprotected speech. This reading of my position clearly misperceives the central point of my argument. I do not contend that *all* conduct with an expressive component should be treated as unprotected speech. To the contrary, my suggestion that *racist* conduct amounts to speech is premised upon a unique characteristic of racism—namely its reliance upon the defamatory message of white supremacy to achieve its injurious purpose. . . . I ask the question of whether there is a purpose to outlawing segregation that is unrelated to its message and conclude that the answer is no. . . .

The public accommodations provisions of the Civil Rights Act of 1964 illuminate why laws against discrimination also regulate racist speech. The legislative history and the Supreme Court's opinions upholding the act establish that Congress was concerned that Blacks have access to public accommodations to eliminate impediments to the free flow of interstate commerce, but this purpose could have been achieved through a regime of separate but equal accommodations. Title II of the Civil Rights Act goes farther; it incorporates the principle of the inherent inequality of segregation and prohibits restaurant owners from providing separate places at the lunch counter for "whites" and "coloreds." Even if the same food and the same service are provided, separate but equal facilities are unlawful. If the signs indicating separate facilities remain in place, then the statute is violated despite proof that restaurant patrons are free to disregard the signs. Outlawing these signs graphically illustrates my point that antidiscrimination laws are primarily regulations of the content of racist speech.

In the summer of 1966, Robert Cover and I were working as summer interns with C. B. King in Albany, Georgia. One day we stopped for lunch at a take-out chicken joint. The establishment was housed in a long diner-like structure with an awning extending from each of two doors in the side of the building. A sign was painted at the end of each awning. One said White, the other Colored. Bob and I entered the "white" side together, knowing we were not welcome to do so. When the proprietor took my order, I asked if he knew that the signs on his awnings were illegal under Title II of the Civil Rights Act of 1964. He responded, "People can come in this place through any door they want to." What this story makes apparent is that the signs themselves violate the antidiscrimination principle even when the conduct of denial of access is not present. . . .

It is difficult to recognize the institutional significance of white supremacy or how it *acts* to harm, partially because of its ubiquity. We simply do not see most racist conduct because we experience a world in which whites are supreme as simply "the world." Much racist conduct is considered unrelated to race or regarded as neutral because racist conduct maintains the status quo, the status quo of the world as we have known it. . . .

Racism is both 100 percent speech and 100 percent conduct. Discriminatory conduct is not racist unless it also conveys the message of white supremacy—unless it is interpreted within the culture to advance the structure and ideology of white supremacy. Likewise, all racist speech constructs the social reality that constrains the liberty of nonwhites because of their race. By limiting the life opportunities of others, this act of constructing meaning also makes racist speech conduct. . . .

RACIST SPEECH AS THE FUNCTIONAL
EQUIVALENT OF FIGHTING WORDS

Much recent debate over the efficacy of regulating racist speech has focused on the efforts by colleges and universities to respond to the burgeoning incidents of racial harassment on their campuses. At Stanford . . . there has been considerable controversy over whether racist and other discriminatory verbal harassment should be regulated and what form any regulation should take. Proponents of regulation have been sensitive to the danger of inhibiting expression, and the current regulation (which was drafted by my colleague Tom Grey) manifests that sensitivity. It is drafted somewhat more narrowly than I would have preferred, leaving unregulated hate speech that occurs in settings where there is a captive audience, but I largely agree with this regulation's substance and approach. I include it here as one example of a regulation of racist speech that I would argue violates neither first amendment precedent nor principle. The regulation reads as follows:

Fundamental Standard Interpretation: Free Expression and Discriminatory Harassment

1. Stanford is committed to the principles of free inquiry and free expression. Students have the right to hold and vigorously defend and promote their opinions, thus entering them into the life of the University, there to flourish or wither according to their merits. Respect for this right requires that students tolerate even expression of opinions which they find abhorrent. Intimidation of students by other students in their exercise of this right, by violence or threat of violence, is therefore considered to be a violation of the Fundamental Standard.

2. Stanford is also committed to principles of equal opportunity and non-discrimination. Each student has the right to equal access to a Stanford education, without discrimination on the basis of sex, race, color, handicap, religion, sexual orientation, or national and ethnic origin. Harassment of students on the basis of any of these characteristics tends to create a hostile environment that makes access to education for those subjected to it less than equal. Such discriminatory harassment is therefore considered to be a violation of the Fundamental Standard.

3. This interpretation of the Fundamental Standard is intended to clarify the point at which protected free expression ends and prohibited discriminatory harassment begins. Prohibited harassment includes discriminatory intimidation by threats of violence, and also includes personal vilification of students on the basis of their sex, race, color, handicap, religion, sexual orientation, or national and ethnic origin.

4. Speech or other expression constitutes harassment by vilification if it:
   a) is intended to insult or stigmatize an individual or a small number of individuals on the basis of their sex, race, color, handicap, religion, sexual orientation, or national and ethnic origin; and
   b) is addressed directly to the individual or individuals whom it insults or stigmatizes; and
   c) makes use of "fighting" words or non-verbal symbols.
   In the context of discriminatory harassment, "fighting" words or nonverbal symbols are words, pictures or symbols that, by virtue

of their form, are commonly understood to convey direct and visceral hatred or contempt for human beings on the basis of their sex, race, color, handicap, religion, sexual orientation, and national and ethnic origin.

This regulation and others like it have been characterized in the press as the work of "thought police," but the rule does nothing more than prohibit intentional face-to-face insults, a form of speech that is unprotected by the first amendment. When racist speech takes the form of face-to-face insults, catcalls, or other assaultive speech aimed at an individual or a small group of persons, then it falls within the "fighting words" exception to first amendment protection. The Supreme Court has held that words that "by their very utterance inflict injury or tend to incite an immediate breach of the peace" are not constitutionally protected.

Face-to-face racial insults, like fighting words, are undeserving of first amendment protection for two reasons. The first reason is the immediacy of the injurious impact of racial insults. The experience of being called "nigger," "spic," "Jap," or "kike" is like receiving a slap in the face. The injury is instantaneous. There is neither an opportunity for intermediary reflection on the idea conveyed nor an opportunity for responsive speech. The harm to be avoided is both clear and present. The second reason that racial insults should not fall under protected speech relates to the purpose underlying the first amendment. The purpose of the first amendment is to foster the greatest amount of speech. Racial insults disserve that purpose. Assaultive racist speech functions as a preemptive strike. The racial invective is experienced as a blow, not a proffered idea, and once the blow is struck, it is unlikely that dialogue will follow. Racial insults are undeserving of first amendment protection because the perpetrator's intention is not to discover truth or initiate dialogue, but to injure the victim.

The fighting words doctrine anticipates that the verbal slap in the face of insulting words will provoke a violent response, resulting in a breach of the peace. When racial insults are hurled at minorities, the response may be silence or flight rather than a fight, but the preemptive effect on further speech is the same. Women and minorities often report that they find themselves speechless in the face of discriminatory verbal attacks. This inability to respond is not the result of oversensitivity among these groups, as some individuals who oppose protective regulation have argued. Rather it is the product of several factors, all of which evidence the nonspeech character of the initial preemptive verbal assault. The first factor is that the visceral emotional response to personal attack precludes speech. Attack produces an instinctive, defensive psychological reaction. Fear, rage, shock, and flight all interfere with any reasoned response. Words like "nigger," "kike," and "faggot" produce physical symptoms that temporarily disable the victim, and the perpetrators often use these words with the intention of producing this effect. Many victims do not find words of response until well after the assault, when the cowardly assaulter has departed.

A second factor that distinguishes racial insults from protected speech is the preemptive nature of such insults—words of response to such verbal attacks may never be forthcoming because speech is usually an inadequate response. When one is personally attacked with words that denote one's subhuman status and untouchability, there is little, if anything, that can be said to redress either the emotional or reputational injury. This is particularly true when the message and meaning of the epithet resonates with beliefs widely held in society. This preservation of widespread beliefs is what makes the face-to-face racial attack more likely to preempt speech than other fighting words do. The racist name caller is accompanied by a cultural chorus of equally demeaning speech and symbols. Segregation and other forms of racist speech injure victims because of their dehumanizing and excluding message. Each individual message gains its power because of the cumulative and reinforcing effect of countless similar messages that are conveyed in a society where racism is ubiquitous.

The subordinated victims of fighting words also are silenced by their relatively powerless position in society. Because of the significance of power and position, the categorization of racial epithets as fighting words provides an inadequate paradigm; instead one must speak of their functional equivalent. The fighting words doctrine presupposes an encounter between two persons of relatively equal power who have been acculturated to respond to face-to-face insults with violence: The fighting words doctrine is a paradigm based on a white male point of view. It captures the "macho" quality of male discourse. It is accepted, justifiable, and even praiseworthy when "real men" respond to personal insult with violence. (Presidential candidate George Bush effectively emulated the most macho—and not coincidentally most violent—of movie stars, Clint Eastwood, when he repeatedly used the phrase, "Read my lips!" Any teenage boy will tell you the subtext of this message: "I've got nothing else to say about this and if you don't like what I'm saying we can step outside.") The fighting words doctrine's responsiveness to this male stance in the world and its blindness to the cultural experience of women is another example of how neutral principles of law reflect the values of those who are dominant.

Black men also are well aware of the double standard that our culture applies in responding to insult. Part of the culture of racial domination through violence—a culture of dominance manifested historically in thousands of lynchings in the South and more recently in the racial violence at Howard Beach and Bensonhurst—is the paradoxical expectation on the part of whites that Black males will accept insult from whites without protest, yet will become violent without provocation. These expectations combine two assumptions: First, that Blacks as a group—and especially Black men—are more violent; and second, that as inferior persons, Blacks have no right to feel insulted. One can imagine the response of universities if Black men started to respond to racist fighting words by beating up white students.

In most situations, minorities correctly perceive that a violent response to fighting words will result in a risk to their own life and limb. This risk forces targets to remain silent and submissive. This response is most obvious when women submit to sexually assaultive speech or when the racist name caller is in a more powerful position—the boss on the job or a member of a violent racist group. . . . Less obvious, but just as significant, is the effect of pervasive racial and sexual violence and coercion on individual members of subordinated groups, who must learn the survival techniques of suppressing and disguising rage and anger at an early age. . . .

KNOWING THE INJURY AND STRIKING THE BALANCE: UNDERSTANDING WHAT IS AT STAKE IN RACIST SPEECH CASES

. . . The arguments most commonly advanced against the regulation of racist speech go something like this: We recognize that minority groups suffer pain and injury as the result of racist speech, but we must allow this hate mongering for the benefit of society as a whole. Freedom of speech is the lifeblood of our democratic system. It is a freedom that enables us to persuade others to our point of view. Free speech is especially important for minorities because often it is their only vehicle for rallying support for redress of their grievances. Even though we do not wish anyone to be persuaded that racist lies are true, we cannot allow the public regulation of racist invective and vilification because any prohibition broad enough to prevent racist speech would catch in the same net forms of speech that are central to a democratic society.

Whenever we argue that racist epithets and vilification must be allowed, not because we would condone them ourselves but because of the potential danger the precedent of regulation would pose for the speech of all dissenters, we are balancing our concern for the free flow of ideas and the democratic process with our desire for equality. This kind of categorical balance is struck whenever we frame any rule—even an absolute rule. It is important to be conscious of the nature and extent of injury to both concerns when we engage in this kind of balancing. In this case, we must place on one side of the balance the nature and extent of the injury caused by racism. We must also consider whether the racist speech we propose to regulate is advancing or retarding the values of the first amendment. . . .

There can be no meaningful discussion about how to reconcile our commitment to equality and our commitment to free speech until we acknowledge that racist speech inflicts real harm and that this harm is far from trivial. I should state that more strongly: To engage in a debate about the first amendment and racist speech without a full understanding of the nature and extent of the harm of racist speech risks making the first amendment an instrument of domination rather than a vehicle of liberation. Not everyone has known the experience of being victimized by racist, misogynist, or homophobic speech, and we do not share equally the burden of the societal harm it inflicts. Often we are too quick to say we have heard the victims' cries when we have not; we are too eager to assure ourselves we have experienced the same injury and therefore can make the constitutional balance without danger of mismeasurement. For many of us who have fought for the rights of oppressed minorities, it is difficult to accept that by underestimating the injury from racist speech we too might be implicated in the vicious words we would never utter. Until we have eradicated racism and sexism and no longer share in the fruits of those forms of domination, we cannot legitimately strike the balance without hearing the protest of those who are dominated. . . .

Again, *Brown v. Board of Education* is a useful case for our analysis. *Brown* is helpful because it articulates the nature of the injury inflicted by the racist message of segregation. When one considers the injuries identified in the *Brown* decision, it is clear that racist speech causes tangible injury, and it is the kind of injury for which the law commonly provides, and even requires, redress.

Psychic injury is no less an injury than being struck in the face, and it often is far more severe. *Brown* speaks directly to the psychic injury inflicted by racist speech in noting that the symbolic message of segregation affected "the hearts and minds" of Negro children "in a way unlikely ever to be undone." Racial epithets and harassment often cause deep emotional scarring and feelings of anxiety and fear that pervade every aspect of a victim's life. Many victims of hate propaganda have experienced physiological and emotional symptoms, such as rapid pulse rate and difficulty in breathing.

A second injury identified in *Brown* . . . is reputational injury. . . . *Brown* is a case about group defamation. The message of segregation was stigmatizing to Black children. To be labeled unfit to attend school with white children injured the reputation of Black children, thereby foreclosing employment opportunities and the right to be regarded as respected members of the body politic. . . . *Brown* reflects the understanding that racism is a form of subordination that achieves its purposes through group defamation.

The third injury identified in *Brown* is the denial of equal educational opportunity. *Brown* recognized that even where segregated facilities are materially equal, Black children did not have an equal opportunity to learn and participate in the school community if they bore the additional burden of being subjected to the humiliation and psychic assault that accompanies the message of segregation. University students bear an analogous burden when they are forced to live and work in an environment where at any moment they may be subjected to denigrating verbal harassment and assault. The testimony of nonwhite students about the detrimental effect of racial harassment on their academic performance and social integration in the college community is overwhelming. A similar injury is recognized and addressed in the requirement of Title VII of the Civil Rights Act that employers maintain a nondiscriminatory, nonhostile work environment and in federal and state regulations prohibiting sexual harassment on campuses as well as in the workplace.

All three of these very tangible, continuing, and often irreparable forms of injury—psychic, reputational, and the denial of equal educational opportunity —must be recognized, accounted for, and balanced against the claim that a regulation aimed at the prevention of these injuries may lead to restrictions on important first amendment liberties. . . .

In striking a balance, we also must think about what we are weighing on the side of speech. Most Blacks—unlike many white civil libertarians—do not have faith in free speech as the most important vehicle for liberation. The first amendment coexisted with slavery, and we still are not sure it will protect us to the same extent that it protects whites. It often is argued that minorities have benefited greatly from first amendment protection and therefore should guard it jealously. We are aware that the struggle for racial equality has relied heavily on the persuasion of peaceful protest protected by the first amendment, but experience also teaches us that our petitions often go unanswered until protests disrupt business as usual and require the self-interested attention of those persons in power. . . .

Blacks and other people of color are equally skeptical about the absolutist argument that even the most injurious speech must remain unregulated because in an unregulated marketplace of ideas the best ideas will rise to the top and gain acceptance. Our experience tells us the opposite. We have seen too many demagogues elected by appealing to U.S. racism. We have seen too many good, liberal politicians shy away from the issues that might brand them as too closely allied with us. The American marketplace of ideas was founded with the idea of the racial inferiority of nonwhites as one of its chief commodities, and ever since the market opened, racism has remained its most active item in trade.

But it is not just the prevalence and strength of the idea of racism that make the unregulated marketplace of ideas an untenable paradigm for those individuals who seek full and equal personhood for all. The real problem is that the idea of the racial inferiority of nonwhites infects, skews, and disables the operation of a market (like a computer virus, sick cattle, or diseased wheat). It trumps good ideas that contend with it in the market. It is an epidemic that distorts the marketplace of ideas and renders it dysfunctional.

Racism is irrational. Individuals do not embrace or reject racist beliefs as the result of reasoned deliberation. For the most part, we do not even recognize the myriad ways in which the racism that pervades our history and culture influences our beliefs. But racism is ubiquitous. We are all racists. Often we fail to see it because racism is so woven into our culture that it seems normal. In other words, most of our racism is unconscious. So it must have been with the middle-aged, white, male lawyer who thought he was complimenting a Mexican-American law student of mine who had applied for a job with his firm. "You speak very good English," he said. But she was a fourth-generation Californian, not the stereotypical poor immigrant he unconsciously imagined she must be.

The disruptive and disabling effect on the market of an idea that is ubiquitous and irrational, but seldom seen or acknowledged, should be apparent. If the community is considering competing ideas about providing food for children, shelter for the homeless, or abortions for pregnant women, and the choices made among the proposed solutions are influenced by the idea that some children, families, or women are less deserving of our sympathy because they are racially inferior, then the market is not functioning as either John Stuart Mill or Oliver Wendell Holmes envisioned it. . . .

Prejudice that is unconscious or unacknowledged causes the most significant distortions in the market. When racism operates at a conscious level, opposing ideas may prevail in open competition for the rational or moral sensibilities of the market participant. But when individuals are unaware of their prejudice, neither reason nor moral persuasion will likely succeed.

Racist speech also distorts the marketplace of ideas by muting or devaluing the speech of Blacks and other despised minorities. Regardless of intrinsic value, their words and ideas become less salable in the marketplace of ideas. An idea that would be embraced by large numbers of individuals if it were offered by a white individual will be rejected or given less credence if its author belongs to a group demeaned and stigmatized by racist beliefs.

An obvious example of this type of devaluation is the Black political candidate whose ideas go unheard or are rejected by white voters, although voters would embrace the same ideas if they were championed by a white candidate. . . . [T]he experience of one of my gay students provides a paradigmatic example of how ideas are less acceptable when their authors are members of a group that has been victimized by hatred and vilification. Bob had not "come out" when he first came to law school. During his first year, when issues relating to heterosexism came up in class or in discussions with other students, he spoke to these issues as a sympathetic "straight" white male student. His arguments were listened to and taken seriously. In his second year, when he had come out and his classmates knew that he was gay, he found that he was not nearly as persuasive an advocate for his position as when he was identified as straight. He was the same person saying the same things, but his identity gave him less authority. . . .

Finally, racist speech decreases the total amount of speech that reaches the market by coercively silencing members of those groups who are its targets. I noted earlier in this chapter the ways in which racist speech is inextricably linked with racist conduct. The primary purpose and effect of the speech/conduct that constitutes white supremacy is the exclusion of nonwhites from full participation in the body politic. Sometimes the speech/conduct of racism is direct and obvious. When the Klan burns a cross on the lawn of a Black person who joined the NAACP or exercised the right to move to a formerly all-white neighborhood, the effect of this speech does not result from the persuasive power of an idea operating freely in the market. It is a threat; a threat made in the context of a history of lynchings, beatings, and economic reprisals that made good on earlier threats; a threat that silences a potential speaker. Such a threat may be difficult to recognize because the tie between the speech and the threatened act is unstated. The tie does not need to be explicit because the promised violence is systemic. The threat is effective because racially motivated violence is a well-known historical and contemporary reality.

The threat may be even more effective than a phone call that takes responsibility for a terrorist bomb attack and promises another, a situation in which we easily recognize the inextricable link between the speech and the threatened act. The Black student who is subjected to racial epithets, like the Black person on whose lawn the Klan has burned a cross, is threatened and silenced by a credible connection between racist hate speech and racist violence. Certainly the recipients of hate speech may be uncommonly brave or foolhardy and ignore the system of violence in which this abusive speech is only a bit player. But it is more likely that we, as a community, will be denied the benefit of many of their thoughts and ideas. . . .

[T]he regulation of certain face-to-face racial vilification on university campuses may be justified under current first amendment doctrine as an analogy to the protection of certain classes of captive audiences. Most important, we must continue this discussion. It must be a discussion in which the victims of racist speech are heard. We must be as attentive to the achievement of the constitutional ideal of equality as we are to the ideal of untrammeled expression. There can be no true free speech where there are still masters and slaves.

EPILOGUE

"Eeny, meeny, miney, mo."

It is recess time at the South Main Street School. It is 1952, and I am nine. Eddie Becker, Muck Makowski, John Thomas, Terry Flynn, Howie Martin, and I are standing in a circle, each with our right foot thrust forward. The toes of our black, high-top Keds sneakers touch, forming a tight hub of white rubber at the center, our skinny blue-jeaned legs extending like spokes from the hub. Heads bowed, we are intently watching Muck, who is hunkered down on one knee so that he can touch our toes as he calls out the rhyme. We are enthralled and entranced by the drama of this boyhood ritual, this customary pregame incantation. It is no less important than the game itself.

But my mind is not on the ritual. I have lost track of the count that will determine whose foot must be removed from the hub, who will no longer have a chance to be a captain in this game. I hardly feel Muck's index finger as it presses through the rubber to my toes. My mind is on the rhyme. I am the only Black boy in this circle of towheaded prepubescent males. Time stands still for me. My palms are sweaty and I feel a prickly heat at the back of my neck. I know that Muck will not say the word.

"Catch a tiger by the toe."

The heads stay down. No one looks at me. But I know that none of them is picturing the capture of a large striped animal. They are thinking of me, imagining my toe beneath the white rubber of my Keds sneaker—my toe attached to a large, dark, thick-lipped, burr-headed American fantasy nightmare.

"If he hollers let him go."

Tigers don't holler. I wish I could right now.

My parents have told me to ignore this word that is ringing unuttered in my ears. "You must not allow those who speak it to make you feel small or ugly," they say. They are proud, Mississippi-bred Black professionals and long-time political activists. Oft-wounded veterans of the war against the racist speech/conduct of Jim Crow and his many relations, they have, on countless occasions, answered the bad speech/conduct of racism with the good speech/conduct of their lives—representing the race; being smarter, cleaner, and more morally upright than white folk to prove that Black folk are equal, are fully human—refuting the lies of the cultural myth that is American racism. "You must know that it is their smallness, their ugliness of which this word speaks," they say.

I am struggling to heed their words, to follow their example, but I feel powerless before this word and its minions. In a moment's time it has made me an other. In an instant it has rebuilt the wall between my friends' humanity and my own, the wall that I have so painstakingly disassembled.

I was good at games, not just a good athlete, but a strategist, a leader. I knew how to make my teammates feel good about themselves so that they played better. It just came naturally to me. I could choose up a team and make the members feel like family. When other folks felt good, I felt good too. Being good at games was the main tool I used to knock down the wall I'd found when I came to this white school in this white town. I looked forward to recess because that was when I could do the most damage to the wall. But now this rhyme, this word, had undone all my labors.

"Eeny, meeny, miney, mo."

I have no memory of who got to be captain that day or what game we played. I just wished Muck had used "One potato, two potato . . ." We always used that at home.

SUGGESTIONS FOR
FURTHER READING

Cohen, Joshua. "Freedom of Expression." *Philosophy and Public Affairs* 22 (Summer 1993), 207–263.

Drawing on the recent debate over pornography to address concerns about hate speech on campuses, Cohen defends policies that would regulate "fighting words" against a number of objections.

DeCew, Judith Wagner. "Free Speech on Campus." In Steven M. Cahn, ed., *Morality, Responsibility and the University*. (Philadelphia: Temple University Press, 1990), pp. 32–55.

DeCew considers a variety of cases involving free speech issues on campuses and explores how universities might take a stand against hate speech without resorting to censorship.

Duggan, Lisa, Nan Hunter, and Carole Vance. "False Promises: Feminist Antipornography Legislation." In Varda Burstyn, ed. *Women Against Censorship*. (Toronto: Douglas and McIntyre, 1985), pp. 130–151.

Duggan and her associates take a feminist stand against Catharine MacKinnon's attempt to develop antipornography ordinances. Their basis is the idea that such ordinances could actually work against women's efforts to produce beneficial social change.

Dworkin, Ronald. *Taking Rights Seriously*. (Cambridge, MA: Harvard University Press, 1978).

Chapter 10, "Liberty and Moralism," is in part concerned with the question of regulating pornography on moral grounds. Dworkin argues that even if a society's moral beliefs were stacked against pornography, this would not provide society with justification for restricting it.

Dyzenhaus, David. "John Stuart Mill and the Harm of Pornography," *Ethics* 102 (April 1992), 534–551.

Dyzenhaus raises the question of what John Stuart Mill might have said about pornography. In analyzing Mill's *The Subjection of Women* to find the answer, Dyzenhaus suggests that liberals do have grounds for recommending that pornography be censored.

Easton, Susan M. *The Problem of Pornography: Regulation and the Right to Free Speech*. (New York: Routledge, 1994).

This book attempts to bridge the differences between feminist and liberal approaches to pornography. Easton argues that the law might be used to regulate pornography without abridging the right of free speech.

Final Report of the Attorney General's Commission on Pornography. (Washington, DC: U.S. Department of Justice, 1986).

In its findings, this most recent federal commission on pornography determined that some types of pornography caused social harm and called for more enforcement of existing obscenity laws.

Gould, James A. "Why Pornography is Valuable." *The International Journal of Applied Philosophy* 6 (1991), 53–55.

Gould presents a summary defense of the benefits of pornography in the face of its multiple critics.

Greenawalt, Kent. *Fighting Words: Individuals, Communities and Liberties of Speech.* (Princeton, NJ: Princeton University Press, 1995).

In this examination of recent free speech controversies, Greenawalt considers whether the use of racial epithets and other forms of insulting speech should be criminalized, and also looks at speech codes on college campuses.

Longino, Helen. "Pornography, Freedom and Oppression: A Closer Look." In Laura Lederer, ed., *Take Back the Night.* (New York: William Morrow, 1980), pp. 26–39.

In one of the first feminist critiques of pornography, Longino claims that pornography harms women by portraying them in a dehumanizing manner, and thus should not be socially tolerated.

MacKinnon, Catharine. *Toward a Feminist Theory of the State.* (Cambridge, MA: Harvard University Press, 1989).

In Chapter 11, "Pornography: On Morality and Politics," MacKinnon defends the idea that pornography does not simply present degrading images of female sexuality but more significantly creates and defines what it is to be female as being subordinate to men.

Schauer, Frederick. *Free Speech: A Philosophical Enquiry.* (Cambridge, England: Cambridge University Press, 1982).

Schauer argues that since the point of pornography is to stimulate sexual arousal, it does not communicate any ideas and thus ought not to be viewed as a form of speech.

Skipper, Robert. "Mill and Pornography," *Ethics* 103 (July 1993), 726–730.

In this response to David Dyzenhaus, Skipper defends the idea that Mill would not have been in favor of censoring pornography.

Soble, Alan. *Pornography.* (New Haven, CT: Yale University Press, 1986).

Soble provides an analysis and defense of pornography from a Marxist point of view. Chapter 6 addresses feminists' concern that pornography is dehumanizing to women.

Tucker, D.F.B. *Law, Liberalism and Free Speech.* (Totowa, NJ: Rowman and Littlefield, 1985).

Tucker looks at a number of free speech concerns, including the problem of offensive speech (Chapter 7), from within a deontological framework strongly influenced by John Rawls and Ronald Dworkin.

Chapter 9

GAY RIGHTS AND
SEXUAL HARASSMENT

Considerations of the ethical issues related to human sexual activity and sexual relationships can be said to fall under the category of sexual morality. This category covers a wide range of issues, from questions concerning the moral status of extramarital sex, or sexual relations between partners of the same sex, to debates over what ought to count as legitimate state intervention in sexually-related matters. In this chapter, our focus will be on two of these debates engaging American society today: the controversy over gay rights and the problem of sexual harassment.

By focusing on these two issues, we do not mean to deny the ways in which sexual harassment can be understood as an issue of power rather than sexual conduct, or the social importance of other ethical issues related to sexual conduct. One of the concerns of applied ethics is to examine those moral issues about which public policies can be developed. Many discussions concerning sexual morality—those dealing with the morality of extramarital sex, for example—tend to take place outside of a context of concern with public policy. Nonetheless, the moral attitudes regarding sexual conduct that can often be found in these discussions also play a role in the two debates addressed in this chapter. For that reason, we will begin by briefly surveying these attitudes, and then go on to consider the primary questions and general lines of argument that help to shape philosophical reflection about gay rights and sexual harassment.

POPULAR VIEWS OF SEXUAL MORALITY

A very popular attitude concerning sexual morality can be summed up as follows: All sexual activity outside of the scope of marriage is immoral; within marriage, not all sexual activity is necessarily moral. While a person might hold this view of sexual morality independently of her or his religious beliefs, because this view has its central source in the Judeo-Christian religious tradition, we can refer to it as the *theological* view of sexual morality. The cornerstone of the theological view lies in its affirmation of a "natural" purpose of human sexual activity and the identification of this purpose with the procreation of children. As defined within the Roman Catholic tradition, these ideas can be traced back to a central belief of the theory of natural law developed by St. Thomas Aquinas in the thirteenth century: Any activity is moral only when it is directed towards its natural (and therefore good) purpose. Following natural law theory, numerous sexual practices, such as sex between homosexual partners, masturbation—as well as the use of artificial means of birth control even within the context of marriage—would be condemned on moral grounds.

While most other Judeo-Christian religions would accept the use of artificial means of birth control, they would join the Roman Catholic tradition in affirming the value of the institution of marriage for its ability to provide the most stable framework within which to raise children. This outlook yields another important element of the theological view: Sexual activity is moral only when it occurs between a married couple. Both sexual activity between unmarried partners (even between partners intending to get married) and extramarital sex are considered immoral from this perspective.

While the theological view of sexual morality recognizes a relatively narrow range of sexual activity as being morally permissible, the opposite is true of what we could call the *liberal* view of sexual morality. The key concept for understanding this viewpoint is not "natural" but "consensual." Someone who takes this point of view would believe it is false to claim that sexual activity has a natural purpose or even one single purpose. According to this view, sexual morality is not directly linked to particular forms of sexual activity but rather to the human context within which sexual activity and sexual relationships are able to have a meaningful place. Echoing the ideas of John Stuart Mill (see Chapter 8), someone holding this position would argue that sexual activity is moral if it is perceived to contribute to one's well being as an individual, and if whoever is involved has freely consented to such activity. The absence of consent poses a moral limit to personal sexual conduct, since sexual activity that is in any way forced upon a person can pose significant harm to that individual, and following Mill's harm principle, it is morally wrong to cause harm to others.

While a few forms of sexual conduct would always be immoral from this particular viewpoint, including rape and sex with a noncompetent person, most would not. In general, whenever two adults of the same or opposite sex freely give their consent to have sexual relations with each other, in the belief that such activity would be worthwhile, such activity would be seen as morally permissible.

A different version of this position, also based on the importance of consent, could be represented as the *moderate* view of sexual morality. A person who adopts this view would reject the idea that sexual activity has a natural purpose, but would think that sexual activity within the context of mutual consent as well as marriage or a similar long-term relationship is to be morally preferred over sexual activity within other contexts. In support of this view, he or she might point out that what one consents to in marriage is not simply a sexual relationship with another person but also a promise of sexual fidelity; to break this promise (or to betray a similar commitment of trust) would be morally wrong. A consequentialist argument could also be made in favor of sexual exclusivity on the basis of the idea that building one's life around another person can produce more jointly shared personal satisfaction than can a sexual relationship free of any commitment to exclusivity. Given these preferences, a person guided by the moderate view of sexual morality would not have moral objections to a gay couple living in a marriage-like relationship, but would object to a heterosexual who was sexually promiscuous. By the same token, such a person would condone premarital sex, although not in all instances, and would disagree with a representative of the liberal viewpoint over the moral permissibility of extramarital sex.

The three distinctions just described are far from reflecting all of the attitudes that members of society have regarding the morality of sexual conduct. They do, though, represent the main considerations to be found in many of these attitudes, and they have a significant influence over the shape of public discussions concerning the formation of social policies in matters dealing with sexual conduct.

GAY RIGHTS

One of the places where this influence can clearly be seen is in the continuing controversy within American society over the issue of gay and lesbian rights. Unrecognizable by the color of their skin or other physical characteristics, gays and lesbians constitute an invisible, and by many counts, sizable American minority. Like many members of visible minority groups such as paraplegics or African Americans, gays as a group have historically suffered prejudice and personal discrimination; with the rise of AIDS, fear has added to the causes of anti-gay bias. Given this social context, many gays prefer to be invisible and to remain "closeted" rather than reveal their sexual identity. The state has also been an important contributor to this preference for invisibility. As recently as 1961, sexual activity between homosexual partners was illegal in each one of the United States. In *Bowers v. Hardwick* (1988), a significant Supreme Court decision involving gay rights, the court denied that any constitutional basis could be found to grant homosexuals the same right that could be claimed by heterosexuals to engage in sexual relations in the privacy of their homes.

While this ruling upheld a Georgia law making sodomy a criminal offense, many states have by now overturned their sodomy laws. As a result, the current "gay rights" movement is less focused on guaranteeing the right to privacy for homosexuals. Generally speaking, concern with discrimination has taken the place of concern about decriminalization. The most current issue at stake in the gay rights debate is whether discrimination in the areas of employment, housing, and other social services should be prohibited on the basis of sexual orientation, as it is at present on the basis of gender, race, religion, age, national origin, and disability. At the point of writing this introduction, only nine states have approved such legislation. Additionally, in a 1996 ruling striking down a Colorado initiative that would have permitted gays to be excluded from employment and housing opportunities on the basis of sexual orientation, the U.S. Supreme Court did not go so far as to claim that all discrimination on the basis of sexual orientation should be prohibited. Those who see homosexuality as morally permissible tend to support such antidiscrimination legislation, while those adopting the theological view of sexual morality tend to take the opposite stand.

One of the primary reasons supporters of gay rights legislation use to justify their view is that such legislation is necessary in order to bring about a more equitable society, one in which gays and lesbians would have the same opportunities and rights as their non-gay fellow citizens. As Morris Kaplan points out in his essay included in this chapter, these opportunities are not insured by the extension of privacy rights to gays and lesbians; the right of an adult homosexual to engage in consensual sex in the privacy of his home does not protect him from being turned down for a job simply because his prospective employer harbors a bias against gays. Because only a few states currently include sexual orientation as a protected category in civil rights statutes, gays and lesbians who do not keep their sexual identities hidden are often left vulnerable to loss of income or housing. Consequently, it is argued, gay civil rights are needed in order to insure equal justice for gays in these areas and thus contribute to a more just society.

In American society, considerable opposition exists, however, to the idea of gay civil rights. Many people who disagree with the idea of gay rights accept what we earlier called the theological view of sexual morality. They would agree with the idea defended by Michael Levin in one of the selections in this chapter that the practice of homosexuality is unnatural, and further accept (unlike Levin) the idea that it is immoral. Still, the belief that homosexuality is immoral cannot automatically provide a justification for opposition to gay rights. Because there is a difference between a moral and a legal wrong, those against gay rights must appeal to other considerations besides the rule that what is unnatural is immoral to defend their point of view.

One possible appeal is to the perceived negative effects of gay rights legislation on the stability of society. The introduction of such legislation, according to this line of argument, would provide public sanction for homosexuality. Giving homosexuals protection from discrimination in housing would allow homosexual couples to be able to live together more openly than they can at present. In turn, this would help to erode the most fundamental unit of a strong society: the institution of the family. Since the family as a social institution is made up of a heterosexual couple plus their children, an increase in the number of gay families—created by making gay marriages legal and making it easier for gay couples to adopt children—would, on this view, only serve to make such erosion worse.

Another popular argument against legitimating gay rights rests on a denial of the analogy between gays and lesbians as a group, and other groups, such as blacks and women, that are already protected by civil rights law. Guarantees of equal opportunity in employment are necessary to protect the latter groups, this line of reasoning goes, because these groups were and continue to be economically disadvantaged by acts of discrimination. While there is evidence that gays are discriminated against, there is little evidence that they as a group have suffered economic injustice as a result of discrimination. Therefore there is no reason why gays need special civil rights to protect them any more than, say, do atheists, who have also admittedly been victims of discrimination but not economic injustice.

In one of this chapter's readings, Michael Levin extends another and admittedly controversial argument against gay rights. His argument is based on the premises that homosexual behavior involves a "misuse of body parts" and that because of human genetic makeup, we are happier when we use body parts correctly than when we use them incorrectly. Since on this account homosexual behavior leads to unhappiness, Levin contends the state has a moral duty not to enact gay rights legislation. Agreeing with the first objection described above that such legislation would amount to official public approval of homosexuality, Levin suspects this approval would result in an increase in the number of homosexuals and thus an increase in unhappiness.

Can these arguments against gay rights be met? One possible strategy would be to point out that the mere fact that discrimination on the basis of sexual orientation persists against gays as a group in employment and housing is a necessary and sufficient condition for creating legal protection for gays and lesbians. Groups do not have to demonstrate they have suffered economically in order to be considered as the possible subject of civil rights legislation. Their task is a simpler one: to show that they have been the victims of unfair grounds for discrimination. In this respect, a person's sexual orientation is no different from his religious beliefs or her gender. These characteristics all represent unfair grounds for discrimination in employment and housing, since they bear no relation to a person's ability to do a job well or to pay the costs of housing.

In general, supporters of gay rights legislation would agree with Levin's point that the passage of such legislation would amount to a public "speech act" pronouncing homosexuality to be a legitimate form of sexual orientation. What could be questioned, however, is whether this is the only or most important message such legislation would send. In this regard, a comparison could be made to other legislation which permits things many regard as immoral. Laws protecting freedom of expression send the message that pornography is tolerable, but they also, and arguably more fundamentally, send the message that the right of an individual to freedom of expression is a basic right deserving recognition within a democratic society.

In this light, one could take the position that the most important message sent by gay–civil rights legislation is not a message about homosexuality but about democracy. As Richard Mohr shows in another of this chapter's readings, an argument can be made for gay civil rights on the basis of the idea that a just democratic society is one in which everyone has equal civic and political rights, including freedom of speech and public association. Without legal safeguards against housing or employment discrimination, gays and heterosexuals hold these rights differently (and unequally), since in general gays are much less free to exercise them. Mohr, then, would take the basic message of gay rights legislation to be a reaffirmation of the principle that every citizen of a democratic society deserves equal access to partipation in the political process.

In his essay, Morris Kaplan finds public endorsement of gay rights to deliver a different but just as fundamental message concerning the right to intimate association. The freedom at stake in the efforts of gays and lesbians to attain rights such as the right to marry is, in Kaplan's opinion, nothing less than the freedom to form close, meaningful relationships on the basis of mutual consent. Were society to legalize this right, it would not be declaring itself "anti-family," but would rather be reaffirming that a society committed to a liberal democracy needs to respect a variety of concepts of the good life, and thus a variety of types of intimate association.

Whatever the outcome of the public debate over gay civil rights turns out to be, these considerations demonstrate that it is not only a disagreement over sexual morality. At a deeper level, it is also a conflict about how to read the messages that are sent when public policies are changed.

SEXUAL HARASSMENT

Debates over the problem of sexual harassment have a much different focus than disagreements over gay rights. In part, this is due to the national attention brought to this problem by the 1991 Senate confirmation hearings for current U.S. Supreme Court Judge Clarence Thomas. In these hearings, attorney Anita Hill testified that during the time she had worked for Thomas, they had had conversations during which he made obscene remarks and otherwise sexually harassed her. Attention to this issue also came with Robert Packwood's resignation in 1995 from the U.S. Senate prompted by numerous sexual harassment charges against him. Like Packwood, who has publically claimed he now "gets it" that his behavior toward the women raising these charges was morally wrong, many Americans have come to understand that sexual harassment does not simply consist in annoying or unprofessional conduct, but more importantly in conduct that is morally wrong. Even F. M. Christensen, who takes the position in an essay included in this chapter that the concept of sexual harassment does not represent a real phenomenon, agrees that some behavior now associated with this concept is condemnable on moral grounds.

But while there is general agreement that sexual harassment is morally wrong, there is less agreement over what makes it so. Questions also exist concerning what counts as sexual harassment and what the appropriate penalties for sexual harassment ought to be.

One way of looking at sexual harassment is to see it as a form of coercive behavior. Imagine you have a part-time job. You always show up on time to work and perform your duties as required; in short, you are a model employee. One day your supervisor unexpectedly asks you to perform a sexual act and indicates you will be fired unless you comply. This threat forces you into a situation where you are faced with the choice of doing something against your will in order to avoid the undesirable consequence of losing your job. Because you cannot make this choice freely, and you will be harmed if you do not make it, you are being coerced. Such coercion is morally wrong.

The view that the coercive character of sexual harassment is what makes sexual harassment morally wrong is taken by Larry May and John Hughes in their essay included in this chapter. This view appears to account particuarly well for what makes a *quid pro quo* (literally, "this for that") incident of sexual harassment like the one described in the preceding paragraph immoral. *Quid pro quo* acts of sexual harassment are also illegal. In the language of the Equal Employment Opportunity Commission:

> Harassment on the basis of sex is a violation of Sec. 703 of Title VII [of the 1964 Civil Rights Act]. Unwelcome sexual advances, requests for sexual favors, and other verbal or physical conduct of a sexual nature constitute sexual harassment when (1) submission to such conduct is made either explicitly or implicitly a term or condition of an individual's employment, (2) submission to or rejection of such conduct by an individual is used as the basis for employment decisions affecting such individual.[1]

While *quid pro quo* incidents of sexual harassment often involve *sexual threats*, they can also take the form of what May and Hughes call *sexual offers*. For example, rather than threatening to fire you, your boss could have offered to give you a raise in exchange for performing a sexual act. Is such an offer morally wrong? After all, you would benefit from the extra income if you accepted it. As May, Hughes, and others have shown, however, one could argue that a sexual offer is just as coercive as a sexual threat. If you accept the offer, you are exposed to the harm of starting something you do not want to start; if you decline it, you also expose yourself to harm by running the risk your employer will retaliate, possibly to the point of making a sexual threat.

The EEOC also recognizes that sexual harassment can occur even when no explicit sexual threats or offers have been made. If sexually related behavior

> ... has the purpose or effect of unreasonably interfering with an individual's work performance or creating an intimidating, hostile, or offensive working environment. . .[2]

it is also sexual harassment. For example, *sexual communications*—dirty jokes, put-downs or compliments about someone's physical makeup, and other remarks with a sexual content—may be considered as sexual harassment under this "*hostile working environment*" category.

Is sexual harassment falling under this category coercive? It is difficult to see how this could be the case. While you might be offended if your supervisor or coworker makes comments of a sexual nature to you or in your presence, there is no particular choice or decision being imposed upon you to make. Still, there seems to be something morally wrong about such behavior, particularly when it is repetitive in nature. Just what that is, though, is not immediately obvious.

One possible explanation of what makes this type of behavior morally wrong is that it discriminates against women. This explanation, often suggested by feminist thinkers, seems arguably to offer a more promising account of what makes sexual harassment wrong in general, since it applies to all three categories defined by the EEOC. On this view, behavior associated with sexual harassment sends the message that women exist primarily to satisfy male sexual desires: In other words, it is right to regard women as basically being sexual objects. Although acts of sexual harassment are directed toward individual women, they are understood on the terms of this position to be harmful to women as a whole. They are harmful to women as a whole because they help perpetuate a view of women that in its turn helps perpetuate the inferior status of women within society. This perspective on sexual harassment is defended in this chapter in the selection by Anita Superson.

If sexual harassment is morally wrong because it furthers sexual discrimination against women, then what about women who sexually harass men? *Can* women sexually harass men? If yes, then that would represent a fairly obvious objection to the view just described. Those who claim that sexual harassment discriminates against women need to respond to this objection. One possible response, given by Superson in her article, is that women cannot by definition sexually harass men. This requires her to first redefine sexual harassment in order to emphasize that conduct which counts as sexual harassment can only be shown by a member of the dominant social class—that is, by men.

Superson's position calls attention to another question associated with the problem of sexual harassment: how to identify particular incidents of sexually related behavior as incidents of sexual harassment. The debate here focuses on the place of intentions and other mental states in determining sexual harassment, particularly in cases in which sexual communications play a major role. Consider these two brief scenarios.

1. A male professor has several framed drawings of nude women hanging on his office wall. Some of his female students are offended by these drawings and feel uncomfortable visiting this professor during office hours.
2. During his office hours, a male professor takes a concerned interest in the sex life of one of his female students. When she gets up to

leave, he gives her a big hug. She believes he is acting fatherly and is not offended.

Given that legal protection from sexual harassment on university campuses was extended to students in 1972, do either of these examples illustrate sexual harassment? If one believes that sexual harassment is more a matter of one's actions than one's intent, then the answer to the above question would be yes. Those who favor such a behaviorial definition of sexual harrassment see its main advantage as lying in its objectivity. Without an objective basis in behavior to determine what counts as sexual harassment, it is left up to "the eye of the beholder." They worry that if what counts as sexual harassment depends on states of mind, the interests of women will be adversely affected. Men can escape sexual harassment charges by claiming benign intentions; they can also escape them when, as in the second example above, the recipient simply does not recognize what is going on and thus is not offended.

On the other side are those who believe that intentions are important in determining sexual harassment. They would single out the behaviorial view as being inadequate for several reasons. First of all, they would question this view's ability to account for the "one-on-one" character of sexual harassment. If a person does not intend for a particular act to be harassing, and it is not experienced as harassing then, they would argue, no harassment has occured. Secondly, they would question the ability of this view to distinguish between innocent acts to initiate a date or other social relationship, and sexual harassment. Finally, they would argue that if intentions are not permitted to play a significant role in determinining what counts as sexual harassment, the interests of men would be adversely affected, since all a woman would have to do to claim she *was* sexually harassed is to make a claim that she *felt* herself to be a victim of sexual harassment.

Finally, given that acts of sexual harassment are immoral, what should be done about them? Whether or not one sides with Christensen in his view that the legal concept of sexual harassment should be eliminated, one would have to agree with him that as the term is currently used it refers to a wide variety of forms of behavior. The complex character of sexual harassment makes the question of what penalties should go with specific acts of sexual harassment a difficult one. Christensen's position appears to be that only acts where individuals are specifically singled out and made a target of serious harassment should be penalized; acts falling outside of this context should not be. Falling under this second category would be many acts involving sexual communications, including ones that are obviously sexist and annoying.

Those who agree with this division might say that the right approach to take to those individuals whose behavior falls under this second category is to confront them in an informal manner. Others, however, would disagree with this position, although they might accept the idea that whether or not the individual's behavior in question was intentional should be taken into account when sanctions are imposed. Under this view the professor in the first example above would be subject to milder penalties than the professor in the second example if both were found to have committed an act of sexual harassment. Such considerations represent some, but not all, of the issues involved in determining where to draw the line between forms of sexual harrassment that demand official sanctions and those that do not.

NOTES

1. Equal Employment Opportunity Commission, *Guidelines on Discrimination Because of Sex.* 29 C. F. R. Sec. 1604.11(a), 1980.
2. *Ibid.*

Invisible Minorities, Civic Rights, Democracy: Three Arguments for Gay Rights

Richard D. Mohr

The 1964 Civil Rights Act protects American citizens from discrimination on the basis of sex (among other factors), but not on the basis of sexual orientation. According to Richard D. Mohr, a professor of philosophy at the University of Illinois at Urbana and the author of a number of books on gay rights including *Gays/Justice: A Study of Ethics, Society, and Law* (1988), without a guarantee of protection against discrimination on the basis of sexual orientation, civil rights legislation fails gays and lesbians. Notice that Mohr is not primarily interested in this essay in backing gay rights for the reason that gays ought to have the same opportunities for equal employment and housing as non-gays. His suggestion is that to deny gays and lesbians equal rights in these areas amounts to effectively denying them additional rights, rights that are essential to their full and equal participation in democratic society.

Mohr's first argument focuses on civic rights, such as the right to use the judicial system. Without gay civil rights, he believes, gays are effectively excluded from participation in this system, since often they do not wish to risk losing their jobs or housing by making their sexual orientation public, and as a result often refrain from using the courts to rectify injustices against them. As Mohr shows in his second argument, a similar case can be made for gay rights as a condition for gays to fully have the right of free speech and other political rights. In his third argument, Mohr proposes that democracy depends on citizens representing their own interests to the makers of legislation; granting rights to gays, on this view, would be a necessary step in insuring the democratic process.

―――――――

In what follows I give three related arguments for the inclusion of sexual orientation in such legislation as the U.S. 1964 Civil Rights Act as a characteristic for which a person may not be discriminated against in employment, housing and public services. I will be arguing that such protections from discrimination are necessary enabling conditions for gays having reasonably guaranteed access to an array of fundamental rights—both civic and political—which almost everyone would agree are supposed to pertain equally to all persons. For gays, these rights are eclipsed, I will argue, in consequence of the *indirect* results which widespread discrimination has when it affects members of invisible minorities.

The arguments here are not, then, general arguments for civil rights legislation based on the *direct* or immediate deleterious effects which discrimination

From *The Philosophical Forum* 27 (Fall 1985), 1–24.

in employment, housing and public services would have on *any* person or even on society as a whole and which might on their own be sufficiently grave to justify a government ban on all but good faith discriminations in these areas —a ban which *per accidens* would catch gays within its broad protective reach. Such direct deleterious effects might include affronts to personal dignity, self-reliance, general prosperity and individual flourishing. . . .

The arguments only presuppose the acceptability of a governmental system which is a constitutionally regulated representative democracy with a developed body of civic law. Such, in broad outline, is the government of the United States and its various states. The arguments, then, hold that gay civil rights are a necessary precondition for the proper functioning of this system. Specifically, they hold: 1) that gay rights are necessary for gays having reasonably guaranteed access to judicial or civic rights; 2) that gay rights are necessary for gays having reasonably guaranteed access to the political rights of the sort found in the First Amendment of the U.S. Constitution; and 3) that gay rights are necessary if democracy is consistently and coherently to be given a preference-utilitarian rationale.

I

I wish to argue that civil rights for gays can be ethically grounded as being necessary preconditions for gays having equitable access to civic rights. By civic rights I mean rights to the impartial administration of civil and criminal law in defense of property and person. In the absence of such rights there is no rule of law. An invisible minority historically subjected to widespread social discrimination has reasonably guaranteed access to these rights only when the minority is guaranteed non-discrimination in employment, housing, and public services.

For an invisible minority possessing civil rights has the same ethical justification as everyone's having the right when on criminal trial to have a lawyer at government expense. A lawyer through his special knowledge and skills provides his client with *access* to the substantive and procedural rights of the courts—rights to which a layman left to his own devices would not have reasonably guaranteed access. Without the guarantee of a lawyer, judicial rights are not equal rights but are rights of the well-to-do.

Imagine the following scenario. Steven, who teaches math in a suburban high school and coaches the swim team, on a weekend night heads to the city to try his luck at Up and Coming, a popular gay cruise bar. There he meets Tom, a self-employed contractor, who in his former life sired two sons by a woman who now hates him, but who is ignorant of his new life. Tom and Steve decide to walk to Tom's near-by flat, which he rents from a bigot who bemoans the fact that the community is going gay and refuses to rent to people he supposes to be gay; Tom's weekend visitations from his sons are his cover.

Meanwhile, at a near-by Children's Aid Home for teenagers, the leader of the Anglo gang is taunting Tony, the leader of the Latino gang, with the accusation of being a faggot. After much protestation to the contrary, Tony claims he will prove to the Anglos once and for all that he is not a faggot and hits the streets with his gang members, who tote with them the blunt and not so blunt instruments of the queer-basher's trade. They descend on Tom and Steve, downing their victims in a blizzard of strokes and blows. Local residents coming home from parties and others walking their dogs witness the whole event.

Imagine that two miracles occur. One, a squad car happens by, and two, the police actually do their job. Tony and another of the fleeing queer-bashers are caught and arrested on the felony charges of aggravated assault and battery, and attempted murder. Other squad cars arrive and while witnesses' reports are gathered, Steve and Tom are taken to the nearest emergency room. Once Steve and Tom are in wards the police arrive to take statements of complaint from them, complaints which will engage the wheels of justice in what appears to be an open and shut case. But Steve knows the exposure of a trial will terminate his employment. And Tom knows the exposure of a trial would give his ex-wife the legal excuse she desires to deny his visitation rights, and he knows he will eventually lose his apartment. So neither man can reasonably risk pressing charges. Tony is, therefore, released, and within twelve hours of attempting murder, he returns to the Children's Aid Home hailed by all as a conquering hero. Gay rights are a necessary material condition for judicial access.

Any reader of gay urban tabloids . . . knows that the events which I have sketched—miracles excepted—are typical of daily occurrences. . . .

It is unreasonable to expect anyone to give up that by which he lives, his employment, his shelter, his access to goods and services and to loved ones in order for judicial procedures to be carried out equitably, in order to demand legal protections. Even if one were tempted to follow the libertarian and say that these are in fact reasonable expenses to pay for making the choice of living an open lifestyle, that a person always makes trade-offs among his necessarily limited options, and that this condition does not warrant the state coercing *others* on his behalf—even if one believed all that, one would not, I think, go on and say that these costs are a reasonable price to pay to see one's assailants dealt justice or to enter a court of equity. . . . If the judicial system is to be open and fair, it is necessary that gays be granted civil rights. Otherwise judicial access becomes a right only for the dominant culture.[1]

In being *de facto* cast beyond the pale of civic procedures, gays, when faced with assaults on property and person, are left with only the equally unjust alternatives of the resignation of the impotent or the rage of man in a state of nature. Societies may remain orderly even when some of their members are denied civic procedures. Many tyrannies do. But such societies cannot be said to be civil societies which respect the rule of law.[2]

II

In the absence of gay civil rights legislation, gays are—over the range of issues which most centrally affect their minority status—effectively denied access to the political rights of the First Amendment, that is, freedom of speech, freedom of press, freedom of assembly, and freedom to petition for the redress of grievances. Further, gays are especially denied the emergent Constitutional right of association—an amalgam of the freedoms of speech and assembly— which establishes the right to join and be identified with other persons for common (political) goals.[3]

This eclipse of political access is most evident if we look at gays severally. Put concretely, does a gay man who has to laugh at and manufacture fag jokes in work-place elevators and around work-place coffee urns, in order to deflect suspicion from himself in an office which routinely fires gay employees, have freedom to express his views on gay issues? Is it likely that such a person could reasonably risk appearing in public at a gay rights rally? Would such a person be able to participate in a march celebrating the Stonewall Riots and the start of gay activism? Would such a man be able to sign, let alone circulate, a petition protesting the firing of a gay worker? Would such a man likely try to persuade workmates to vote for a gay-positive city-councilman? Would such a man sign a letter to the editor protesting abusive reportage of gay issues and events, or advocating the discussion of gay issues in high schools? Such a man is usually so transfixed by fear that it is highly unlikely that he could even be persuaded to write out a check to a gay rights organization.[4]

In the absence of 1964 Civil Rights Act protections, the vast majority of gays is effectively denied the ability to participate equally in First Amendment rights, which are supposed to pertain equally to every citizen *qua* individual. First Amendment rights, like other such rights, apply directly to citizens or persons as individuals. They do not apply directly to groups and only derivatively to individuals.[5] It will not do then to suggest that even if some, or even most, gays cannot reasonably participate in politics, this is unproblematic on the alleged ground that other gays—those who are open about their minority status—may voice the interests of those who are not. This position simply confuses individual rights, like First Amendment rights, with group "rights." The position further naively assumes that gays uniformly have the same interests and espouse the same views on any given gay issue, so that one simply needs to know one sociological fact—percent of gays in the general population—to know the extent to which some publicly espoused gay interest is held.

If First Amendment rights are not to be demoted to privileges, to which only the dominant culture has access, then invisible minorities that are subject to widespread social discrimination will have to be guaranteed protection from those forces which maintain them in their position of invisibility. Civil rights protections are a very long step in that direction.

Now, it might be argued that First Amendment rights are to be construed as mere immunities, that they merely prevent the government from interfering with certain types of actions, so that as long as the government and its agents do not, say, refuse parade permits to gays, smash up the gay press, deny the formation of gay student groups on state university campuses, and the like, then in fact gays do have First Amendment rights just like everyone else. In these circumstances, it would be reasonable to say that gays are *free from* active government interference in their political designs. Nevertheless, gays would still remain effectively denied the *freedom to act* politically.

Whatever else First Amendment rights might be, they have as one of their chief rationales and purposes not merely *not making impossible* the procedures of democracy, but also actually promoting, enhancing, and making likely the proper working of democratic processes. To this end, then, First Amendment rights need somehow to be construed not merely as immunities, as the mere absences of government interference, but as somewhat stronger rights. Indeed, they need to be realized as powers which place the government under a certain liability. . . .

Only when the government protects gays against discrimination in housing, employment, and public accommodation will they have First Amendment rights as powers. For all potentially effective political strategies involve *public* actions. More specifically, all the actions protected by the First Amendment are public actions (speaking, publishing, petitioning, assembling, associating). Now, a person who is a member of an invisible minority and who must remain invisible, hidden, and secreted in respect to his minority status as a condition for maintaining his livelihood, this person is not free to be public about his minority status or to incur suspicion by publicly associating with others who are open about their similar status. And so he is effectively denied all political power—except the right to vote. But, voting aside, he will be denied the freedom to express his views in a public forum and to unite with or organize other like-minded individuals in an attempt to elect persons who will support the policies advocated by his group. He is denied all effective use of legally available means of influencing public opinion prior to voting and all effective means of lobbying after elections are held.

Such denials to minorities of First Amendment rights as powers differ in kind depending upon the minority affected; and remedies vary accordingly. Blacks, for instance, though constituting a visible minority, nevertheless, as the result of being in general poorer than whites, are effectively denied First Amendment rights as powers, since blacks are, for financial reasons, effectively denied the political use of such expensive mass media tools as purchasing television time and newspaper space.[6]

For gays, it is not poverty *per se* which effectively denies gays First Amendment rights. Indeed gays are, as Kinsey showed, dispersed nearly homogeneously throughout all social and economic classes. Rather it is the recriminations that descend upon gays who are publicly gay that effectively deny them First Amendment rights and might even more effectively deny to them these rights than poverty denies them to blacks, since the poor but visible at least have available to them such inexpensive but limited methods of public communication as sit-ins, marches, and demonstrations. Gays—as long as job discrimination is widespread—are effectively denied even these limited modes of public access.

On the one hand, the closeted condition of most gays has meant that nothing remotely approaching the widespread dissemination of views on gay issues necessary for any potentially effective political strategy has occurred in this country or any other. The condition has caused gay political organizations to be small, weak, inbred, ill-financed, impermanent, and subterranean.

On the other hand, local dissemination of views is also impeded. Indeed, the closeted condition of gays blocks the most effective sort of political communication in which gays in particular might engage with others—personal conversation. Social reality is such that many people do not know or think they do not know any gay people firsthand. Such widespread ignorance is a breeding ground for vicious stereotypes. Problems compound when misunderstanding is added to ignorance. Many people *sort of* think they know that someone, say, a workmate is gay. But given the way the workmate acts, especially in avoiding certain topics, in being selectively "absent" from social intercourse or in confusingly broadcasting mixed messages, others think the gay person is embarrassed about his status and so do not initiate any discussion of it, and so further they are left with the impression that there is something wrong with gays because gays themselves seem to act as though there is. The non-gay person oddly fails to realize that the gay person may have or—what comes to the same—may *suppose* he has solid prudential reasons for his skittish behavior.

When this widespread ignorance and misunderstanding combines with gut reactions to gays of fear and loathing or even just queasiness and discomfort, mere reportage (even accurate reportage) about gays or mere abstract discussion (even insightful discussion) of gay issues has little chance of success in changing the attitudes by which people conduct their lives. When people's attitudes are informed by deeply held emotional responses—ones perhaps central to their conceptions of themselves—reason's hope is slight. The most effective way of changing non-gays' views about gays is for non-gays to interact personally with some openly gay people.[7] . . . And yet such personal outreach of gays to the non-gay person is not likely to occur, however willing the non-gay person, as long as a gay person has to put his job and other major interests on the line to make the contact. It is after all at the job site and in certain public accommodations that people tend to have the sorts of contacts with others, initially strangers, which might lead to personal conversations. And yet it is exactly in these locations that a gay person is most likely to encounter discrimination if he is open about his status. And so the most effective avenue of communication for gays about the issues of importance to them as gays is effectively blocked in the absence of civil rights protections. . . .

III

I have suggested that the absence of civil rights protections for gays casts doubt on the fairness of current political *procedures* surrounding democratic voting. I now wish to suggest that the same absence also casts doubt on the adequacy of certain *justifications* for democracy.

Perhaps the strongest argument for democracy is that democracy is justified on utilitarian grounds. Those who try to justify democracy deontologically as the institution which most directly gives expression to individual dignity simply overestimate the significance of political activity and voting in people's lives. The *consequences* of a democratically enacted statute may be great for an individual, but for the vast majority of people, an individual's *contribution* to the democratic system—unless he is political by profession—is slight in his overall pattern of life. Campaigning and voting are sporadic activities. They are neither activities by which individuals sustain their day-to-day lives nor those in which everyday activities culminate. At least one never hears anyone say "I work that I might vote" or "I live that I might vote." And so politics and voting are not integrative principles nor even integral parts of day-to-.day life. They are not activities in terms of which any but a few do or should define their lives. The childless curmudgeon who religiously votes against school levies is no more dignified than the social worker who, caught up in a flurry of commitments, fails to vote. The resident alien is not deprived of essential dignity by his inability to participate fully in the mechanisms of democracy.[8]

This is not to deny that many, even most, of the things that individuals do in their day-to-day lives have political overtones. As nearly all of everyday discourse is devoted to persuading people of this or that, or asserting to others the value of this or that, an individual's day-to-day activities will tend to shape other people's views in ways that may well register at the ballot box, but this registration is usually an entirely incidental and unconscious spin-off effect of day-to-day activities and not what motivates them or gives them importance in individuals' lives.

To make democratic politics the paradigmatically human activity is also to place it uncomfortably at odds with soundly held beliefs that voting should be restricted in what it may achieve. If one views voting as the paramount human value and if voting is not to be made a hollow activity, a mere formal ritual, in virtue of having its effects voided, then one will be committed to a pure, direct democracy operating without substantive constitutional restraints and holding out the prospect that law can be the mere amassing of prejudice—a position virtually everyone would reject. . . .

In sum, democracy is a better registrar of desire than of dignity. And as such, democracy is best justified in utilitarian terms.

It is reasonable to suppose that the policies that represent the wishes of the most people will be the policies which will most likely maximize utility. For given the complexity of *predicting* precise consequences of social policies for large and complex populations relying on the *preferences* of the people in general rather than on the *predictions* of social engineers as likely indicators of future utility seems eminently reasonable. . . .[9]

However, if preferences pure and simple were the whole rationale for establishing social policy, social policies could be determined simply by direct democracy, as manifest in referenda and plebiscites.

For democracy coherently to have a preference-utilitarian justification, though, requires that a distinction be drawn between an individual's internal and external preferences. His internal preferences are preferences for goods and services *for himself.* His external preferences are preferences that he has for things *for persons other than himself.* To be *coherent,* preference-justified democracy must discount and disregard a person's external preferences. For the man who has external preferences and who would have society act upon them is assuming for himself the role of social engineer—a role discredited by the very premises of the argument justifying democracy in terms of preferences. . . .[10]

If, in consequence, external preferences are to be disregarded in the calculus of preferences, then direct democracy can not be the instrument for this measurement. For referenda and plebiscites give equal weight to internal and external preferences; they give equal weight to the views of bigots and nonbigots. The remedy—where the distribution of powers rather than immunities is concerned—is a form of representative democracy in which the elected official, it is hoped, is rational enough and impartial enough to rise above popular prejudices taking into account only the internal preferences of his constituents. . . .

The rational legislator will sift through his mail, public debates, editorials, letter columns, and all the other modes of public discussion of social policies and will winnow out external preferences. The legislator in this scheme is as justified in disregarding the altruistic opinions of the well-intended heterosexual (or would-be heterosexual) do-gooder who writes him supporting gay-positive legislation, as he is in disregarding the opinion of the religious zealot who desires state persecution of gays.

If this system of justifications for democratic procedures is to work, it presupposes that people can present publicly their opinions on social policy as desires for things for themselves. They must be able to present themselves publicly as members of classes of which they in fact are members, so that they can promote legislation which benefits them as members of their classes.

For preference-utilitarianism to be a coherent rationale for democracy, everyone must be permitted to present himself in public debate as what he is. For preference democracy to be coherent, gays must be free to present themselves publicly as gays; and gays are effectively precluded this option, if the means by which they live can be removed from them at whim for being publicly gay. Civil rights protections for invisible minorities are a necessary prerequisite for coherent democratic processes. . . .

IV

Current society puts gays in the queer position of not being able to fight for gay rights unless gays are already "out" and gays cannot be "out" unless gays already have gay rights. Paradoxically, gays can not get gay rights, unless they already have them. This "particularly vicious circle" was noted over thirty years ago by an author himself closeted. Little has changed:

On the one hand . . . the social punishment of acknowledgment [of one's homosexuality is] so great that pretense is almost universal; on the other hand, only a leadership that would acknowledge [its homosexuality] would be able to break down the barriers . . . of discrimination. Until the world is able to accept us on an equal basis as human beings entitled to the full rights of life, we are unlikely to have any great numbers willing to become martyrs . . . But until we are willing to speak out openly and frankly in defense of our activities and to identify ourselves with the millions pursuing these activities, we are unlikely to find the attitudes of the world undergoing any significant change.[11]

The author perhaps overestimates the potential effectiveness of martyrs,[12] but his main point is sound. As an invisible minority, gays cannot fight for the right to be open about being gay, unless gays are already open about it, and gays cannot reasonably be open about being gay, until gays have the right to be openly gay. One would hope that once society was made aware of this paradox, if society had any sense of decency and fair play, it would on its own move to establish civil rights for gays.

NOTES

1. Inequitable procedures and results tend to characterize those criminal cases with gay victims which do go to trial. In this regard, gay experience parallels that of blacks. The life and liberty of gays and blacks simply count for less than the life and liberty of members of the dominant culture. This devaluation of gays and blacks registers in the sentencing of their assailants to punishments which are disproportionally weak when compared to similar cases with non-gay and white victims.

2. In this section, I have not intended to address a complementary problem of criminal justice for gays: whether, when gays stand accused of crime or pursue civil litigation, they get fair treatment from police, bench, and jury. For some eye-opening examples of patently prejudicial and abusive treatment of gays from the bench, see Rhonda R. Rivera's magisterial "Our Straight-Laced Judges: The Legal Position of Homosexual Persons in the U.S.", 30 *Hastings Law Review,* (1979), 799-955.

3. See Lawrence Wilson and Raphael Shannon, "Homosexual Organizations and the Right of Association," *Hastings Law Journal,* 30 (1979), 1029-1074, and Donald Solomon, "The Emergence of Associational Rights for Homosexual Persons," *Journal of Homosexuality,* 5 (1979-80), 147-155.

4. Some organizations, like National Gay Rights Advocates, desperately aware of this last problem's magnitude, set up fundraising account "fronts" with innocuous sounding names, like "Legal Foundation for Personal Liberties," in an attempt to ease money, if not persons, out of the closet. Many organizations simply dissimulate, lying by omission or vagueness in assuming for themselves closeted names; thus the national gay political action committee baptizes itself "The Human Rights Campaign Fund."

5. "It is true that in *Griswold* the right to privacy in question inhered in the marital relationship. Yet the marital couple is not an independent entity with a mind and heart of its own, but an association of two individuals each with a

separate intellectual and emotional makeup. If the right to privacy means anything, it is the right of the *individual,* married or single, to be free from unwarranted governmental intrusion into matters so fundamentally affecting a person
as the decision whether to bear or beget a child" *Eisenstadt v. Baird,* 405 U.S.
438, 453, emphasis in original.

6. For a general defense of First Amendment rights as powers and for an application
   of the view to blacks, see Alan Gewirth, *Human Rights* (Chicago: Univ. Chicago
   Press, 1982), pp. 310–328.

7. The State of Oregon conducted a study of gay employment discrimination and
   found that positive attitudes towards gays in the workplace index closely to the
   degree of workers' firsthand acquaintance with gays (State of Oregon, Department
   of Human Resources, *Final Report of the Task Force on Sexual Preference,* Portland: State of Oregon, Department of Human Resources, 1978, pp. 73–87). For a
   review of the empirical literature on stereotyping of gays, see Alan Taylor, "Conceptions of Masculinity and Femininity as a Basis for Stereotypes of Male and Female
   Homosexuals," *Journal of Homosexuality* 9:1 (1983), 37–53, especially 37–44.

8. For a critique of the view that politics represents the central medium for dignity
   and human value, see Gerald Doppelt, "Rawls' System of Justice: A Critique from
   the Left" *Nous,* 15 (1981), 259–307.

9. For a related argument to this end, see Ronald Dworkin, *Taking Rights Seriously*
   (Cambridge, MA: Harvard Univ. Press, 1977), p. 233.

10. This argument is similar to an argument that Dworkin makes only in passing to
    the effect that in many cases counting a person's external political preferences
    (say, for some group not to get some scarce resource, when the person does not
    want or need the resource for himself) will simply be self-defeating from a utili-
    tarian standpoint (p. 235 middle). I do not wish to commit my argument to
    Dworkin's assumptions that the right to treatment as an equal is the most funda-
    mental of rights (p. 273) and that taking external preferences into account in
    social policy is wrong as violating that right (pp. 234–235, 275–276).

    Even the necessary proviso in any utilitarian justification for democracy that
    each person's preferences are to count for one can be justified in purely utilitar-
    ian terms without appeals to general principles of equality. For, given the pre-
    sumption that we are only considering conscious homo sapiens as voters and are
    not including in the franchise, say, comatose individuals or especially sensitive crea-
    tures from space, and given that people are more equal than unequal in their
    sensitivity and in the volume of their desires, then it seems likely that assigning
    one non-weighted vote to each will be a more accurate gauge in general of over-
    all preference than if we try to establish some (unimaginable) mechanism to weight
    votes for small variations in either sensitivities or intensities of preferences.

11. Donald Webster Cory [pseud.], *The Homosexual in America* (New York: Greenberg,
    1951), p. 14.

12. Thus during the 1985 nationally televised Academy Awards, a seemingly ingenuous
    presenter could describe a documentary of the assassination of an activist gay
    elected-official (see n. 9 *supra*) merely as "a film about American values in con-
    flict," *GayLife,* 10:39, March 28, 1985, X, p. 1. Had the film not won the award, no
    one in the audience of millions not already in the know would have learned that
    the film even had a gay content. As it was, the award recipients made mention
    only of their subject's pride, not his death, while those in the know were left with
    the suspicion that the Academy supposes that killing gays is an "American value."

Why Homosexuality Is Abnormal
Michael Levin

Michael Levin, a professor of philosophy at City College of the City University of New York, makes a case that homosexual behavior is abnormal because it involves a "misuse of body parts." Although one might imagine him to go on from this point to claim that because homosexuality is unnatural it is also immoral, his argument turns out to be more complex. Accepting the sociobiological belief that human evolution shapes behavior, Levin points out that human beings are genetically inclined to get greater happiness when they use their body parts correctly than when they do not. An example of the correct use of one's body is physical exercise; because an active person stands a better chance of survival than an inactive person, human beings are naturally disposed to enjoy running, working out, and the like. Still, a person who does not exercise is not acting immorally but rather imprudently, ignoring what is most conducive to his or her own happiness. A similar judgment, Levin asserts, can be made regarding homosexual behavior. Given its likelihood of leading to unhappiness, it is best understood not as morally wrong but rather as undesirable. Levin concludes his essay by looking at the implications of his view for the development of public policies that address issues of gay rights. Because such policies could increase the chances of individuals becoming gay and thus unhappy, he claims society is better off without them.

This paper defends the view that homosexuality is abnormal and hence undesirable—not because it is immoral or sinful, or because it weakens society or hampers evolutionary development, but for a purely mechanical reason. It is a misuse of bodily parts. Clear empirical sense attaches to the idea of *the use* of such bodily parts as genitals, the idea that they are *for* something, and consequently to the idea of their misuse. I argue on grounds involving natural selection that misuse of bodily parts can with high probability be connected to unhappiness. I regard these matters as prolegomena to such policy issues as the rights of homosexuals, the rights of those desiring not to associate with homosexuals, and legislation concerning homosexuality, issues which I shall not discuss systematically here. However, I do in the last section draw a seemingly evident corollary from my view that homosexuality is abnormal and likely to lead to unhappiness. . . .

Despite the publicity currently enjoyed by the claim that one's "sexual preference" is nobody's business but one's own, the intuition that there is something unnatural about homosexuality remains vital. The erect penis fits the vagina, and fits it better than any other natural orifice; penis and vagina seem made for each other. This intuition ultimately derives from, or is another way of capturing, the idea that the penis is not *for* inserting into the anus of

From *The Monist* 67 (1984), 251–281.

another man—that so using the penis is not the way it is *supposed,* even *intended,* to be used. . . . Furthermore, when we understand the sense in which homosexual acts involve a misuse of genitalia, we will see why such misuse is bad and not to be encouraged.

* * *

To bring into relief the point of the idea that homosexuality involves a misuse of bodily parts, I will begin with an uncontroversial case of misuse, a case in which the clarity of our intuitions is not obscured by the conviction that they are untrustworthy. Mr. Jones pulls all his teeth and strings them around his neck because he thinks his teeth look nice as a necklace. He takes puréed liquids supplemented by intravenous solutions for nourishment. It is surely natural to say that Jones is misusing his teeth, that he is not using them for what they are for, that indeed the way he is using them is incompatible with what they are for. Pedants might argue that Jones's teeth are no longer part of him and hence that he is not misusing any bodily parts. To them I offer Mr. Smith, who likes to play "Old MacDonald" on his teeth. So devoted is he to this amusement, in fact, that he never uses his teeth for chewing—like Jones, he takes nourishment intravenously. Now, not only do we find it perfectly plain that Smith and Jones are misusing their teeth, we predict a dim future for them on purely physiological grounds; we expect the muscles of Jones's jaw that are used for—that *are* for—chewing to lose their tone, and we expect this to affect Jones's gums. Those parts of Jones's digestive tract that are for processing solids will also suffer from disuse. The net result will be deteriorating health and perhaps a shortened life. Nor is this all. Human beings enjoy chewing. Not only has natural selection selected in muscles for chewing and favored creatures with such muscles, it has selected in a tendency to find the use of those muscles reinforcing. Creatures who do not enjoy using such parts of their bodies as deteriorate with disuse, will tend to be selected out. Jones, product of natural selection that he is, descended from creatures who at least tended to enjoy the use of such parts. Competitors who didn't simply had fewer descendants. So we expect Jones sooner or later to experience vague yearnings to chew something, just as we find people who take no exercise to experience a general listlessness. Even waiving for now my apparent reification of the evolutionary process, let me emphasize how little anyone is tempted to say "each to his own" about Jones or to regard Jones's disposition of his teeth as simply a deviation from a statistical norm. This sort of case is my paradigm when discussing homosexuality. . . .

Nature is interested in making its creatures like what is (inclusively) good for them. A creature that does not enjoy using its teeth for chewing uses them less than does a toothed competitor who enjoys chewing. Since the use of teeth for chewing favors the survival of an individual with teeth, and, other things being equal, traits favorable to the survival of individuals favor survival of the relevant cohort, toothed creatures who do not enjoy chewing tend to get selected out. We today are the filtrate of this process, descendants of creatures who like to chew. . . .

And here—to return to the main strand of the argument—is why it is advisable to use your organs for what they are for: you will enjoy it. Jones's behavior is ill-advised not only because of the avertible objective consequences of his defanging himself, but because he will feel that something is missing. Similarly, this is why you should exercise. It is not just that muscles are for running. We have already heard the skeptic's reply to that: "So what? Suppose I don't mind being flabby? Suppose I don't give a hang about what will propagate my genetic cohort?" Rather, running is good because nature made sure people like to run. This is, of course, the prudential "good," not the moral "good"—but I disavowed at the outset the doctrine that misuse of bodily parts is *morally* bad at least in any narrow sense. You ought to run because running was once necessary for catching food: creatures who did not enjoy running, if there ever were any, caught less food and reproduced less frequently than competitors who enjoyed running. These competitors passed on their appetites along with their muscles *to you.* This is not to say that those who suffer the affective consequences of laziness must recognize them as such, or even be able to identify them against their general background feeling-tone. They may not realize they would feel better if they exercised. They may even doubt it. They may have allowed their muscles to deteriorate beyond the point at which satisfying exercise is possible. For all that, evolution has decreed that a life involving regular exercise is on the whole more enjoyable than a life without. The same holds for every activity that is the purpose of an organ.

* * *

The application of this general picture to homosexuality should be obvious. There can be no reasonable doubt that one of the functions of the penis is to introduce semen into the vagina. It does this, and it has been selected in because it does this. Nature has consequently made this use of the penis rewarding. It is clear enough that any proto-human males who found unrewarding the insertion of penis into vagina have left no descendants. In particular, proto-human males who enjoyed inserting their penises into each other's anuses have left no descendants. This is why homosexuality is abnormal, and why its abnormality counts prudentially against it. Homosexuality is likely to cause unhappiness because it leaves unfulfilled an innate and innately rewarding desire. And should the reader's environmentalism threaten to get the upper hand, let me remind him again of an unproblematic case. Lack of exercise is bad and even abnormal not only because it is unhealthy but also because one feels poorly without regular exercise. Nature made exercise rewarding because, until recently, we had to exercise to survive. Creatures who found running after game unrewarding were eliminated. Laziness leaves unreaped the rewards nature has planted in exercise, even if the lazy man cannot tell this introspectively. If this is a correct description of the place of exercise in human life, it is by the same token a correct description of the place of heterosexuality.

It hardly needs saying, but perhaps I should say it anyway, that this argument concerns tendencies and probabilities. Generalizations about human affairs being notoriously "true by and large and for the most part" only, saying that homosexuals are bound to be less happy than heterosexuals must be understood as short for "Not coincidentally, a larger proportion of homosexuals will be unhappy than a corresponding selection of the heterosexual population." There are, after all, genuinely jolly fat men. To say that laziness leads to adverse affective consequences means that, because of our evolutionary history, the odds are relatively good that a man who takes no exercise will suffer adverse affective consequences. Obviously, some people will get away with misusing their bodily parts. Thus, when evaluating the empirical evidence that bears on this account, it will be pointless to cite cases of well-adjusted homosexuals. I do not say they are non-existent; my claim is that, of biological necessity, they are rare. . . .

Talk of what is "in the genes" inevitably provokes the observation that we should not blame homosexuals for their homosexuality if it is "in their genes." True enough. Indeed, since nobody decides what he is going to find sexually arousing, the moral appraisal of sexual object "choice" is entirely absurd. However, so saying is quite consistent with regarding homosexuality as a misfortune, and taking steps—this being within the realm of the will—to minimize its incidence, especially among children. Calling homosexuality involuntary does not place it outside the scope of evaluation. Victims of sickle-cell anemia are not blameworthy, but it is absurd to pretend that there is nothing wrong with them. Homosexual activists are partial to genetic explanations and hostile to Freudian environmentalism in part because they see a genetic cause as exempting homosexuals from blame. But surely people are equally blameless for indelible traits acquired in early childhood. And anyway, a blameless condition may still be worth trying to prevent.

* * *

I have argued that homosexuality is "abnormal" in both a descriptive and a normative sense because—for evolutionary reasons—homosexuals are bound to be unhappy. . . . What is the evidence for my view? For one thing, by emphasizing homosexual unhappiness, my view explains a ubiquitous fact in a simple way. The fact is the universally acknowledged unhappiness of homosexuals. Even the staunchest defenders of homosexuality admit that, as of now, homosexuals are not happy. . . .

The usual environmentalist explanation for homosexuals' unhappiness is the misunderstanding, contempt and abuse that society heaps on them. But this not only leaves unexplained why society has this attitude, it sins against parsimony by explaining a nearly universal phenomenon in terms of variable circumstances that have, by coincidence, the same upshot. Parsimony urges that we seek the explanation of homosexual unhappiness in the nature of homosexuality itself, as my explanation does. Having to "stay in the closet" may be a great strain, but it does not account for all the miseries that writers on homosexuality say is the homosexual's lot. . . .

But does not my position also predict—contrary to fact—that any sexual activity not aimed at procreation or at least sexual intercourse leads to unhappiness? First, I am not sure this conclusion is contrary to the facts properly understood. It is universally recognized that, for humans and the higher animals, sex is more than the insertion of the penis into the vagina. Foreplay is necessary to prepare the female and, to a lesser extent, the male. Ethologists have studied the elaborate mating rituals of even relatively simple animals. Sexual intercourse must therefore be understood to include the kisses and caresses that necessarily precede copulation, behaviors that nature has made rewarding. What my view does predict is that exclusive preoccupation with behaviors normally preparatory for intercourse is highly correlated with unhappiness. . . . In this sense, sexual intercourse really is virtually necessary for well-being. . . .

Nor does my position predict, again contrary to fact, that celibate priests will be unhappy. My view is compatible with the existence of happy celibates who deny themselves as part of a higher calling which yields compensating satisfactions. Indeed, the very fact that one needs to explain how the priesthood can compensate for the lack of family means that people do regard heterosexual mating as the natural or "inertial" state of human relations. The comparison between priests and homosexuals is in any case inapt. Priests do not simply give up sexual activity without ill-effect; they give it up for a reason. Homosexuals have hardly given up the use of their sexual organs, for a higher calling or anything else. Homosexuals continue to use them, but, unlike priests, they use them for what they are not for. . . .

* * *

Homosexuality is intrinsically bad only in a prudential sense. It makes for unhappiness. However, this does not exempt homosexuality from the larger categories of ethics—rights, duties, liabilities. . . .

If homosexuality is unnatural, legislation which raises the odds that a given child will become homosexual raises the odds that he will be unhappy. The only gap in the syllogism is whether legislation which legitimates, endorses or protects homosexuality does increase the chances that a child will become homosexual. If so, such legislation is *prima facie* objectionable. The question is not whether homosexual elementary school teachers will molest their charges. Pro-homosexual legislation might increase the incidence of homosexuality in subtler ways. If it does, and if the protection of children is a fundamental obligation of society, legislation which legitimates homosexuality is a dereliction of duty. I am reluctant to deploy the language of "children's rights," which usually serves as one more excuse to interfere with the prerogatives of parents. But we do have obligations to our children and one of them is to protect them from harm. If, as some have suggested, children have a right to protection from a religious education, they surely have a right to protection from homosexuality. So protecting them limits somebody else's freedom, but we are often willing to protect quite obscure children's rights at the expense of the freedom of others. There is a movement to ban TV commercials for sugar-coated cereals, to protect children from the relatively trivial harm of tooth decay. Such a ban would restrict the freedom of advertisers, and restrict it even though the last clear chance of avoiding the harm, and thus the responsibility, lies with the parents who control the TV set. I cannot see how one can consistently support such legislation and also urge homosexual rights, which risk much graver damage to children in exchange for increased freedom for homosexuals. (If homosexual behavior is largely compulsive, it is falsifying the issue to present it as balancing risks to children against the freedom of homosexuals.) The right of a homosexual to work for the Fire Department is not a negligible good. Neither is fostering a legal atmosphere in which as many people as possible grow up heterosexual.

It is commonly asserted that legislation granting homosexuals the privilege or right to be firemen endorses not homosexuality, but an expanded conception of human liberation. It is conjectural how sincerely this can be said in a legal order that forbids employers to hire whom they please and demands hours of paperwork for an interstate shipment of hamburger. But in any case legislation "legalizing homosexuality" cannot be neutral because passing it would have an inexpungeable speech-act dimension. Society cannot grant unaccustomed rights and privileges to homosexuals while remaining neutral about the value of homosexuality. Working from the assumption that society rests on the family and its consequences, the Judaeo-Christian tradition has deemed homosexuality a sin and withheld many privileges from homosexuals. Whether or not such denial was right, for our society to grant these privileges to homosexuals *now* would amount to declaring that it has rethought the matter and decided that homosexuality is not as bad as it had previously supposed. And unless such rethinking is a direct response to new empirical findings about homosexuality, it can only be a revaluing. . . . A society that grants privileges to homosexuals while recognizing that, in the light of generally known history, this act can be interpreted as a positive re-evaluation of homosexuality, is signalling that it now thinks homosexuality is all right. Many commentators in the popular press have observed that homosexuals, unlike members of racial minorities, can always "stay in the closet" when applying for jobs. What homosexual rights activists really want, therefore, is not access to jobs but legitimation of their homosexuality. Since this is known, giving them what they want will be seen as conceding their claim to legitimacy. . . . [The] symbolic meaning of passing antidiscrimination ordinances is to declare homosexuality legitimate. . . .

Intimacy and Equality: The Question of Lesbian and Gay Marriage
Morris B. Kaplan

Morris B. Kaplan is a philosophy professor at the State University of New York at Purchase and the author of *Sexual Justice* (1995). In this essay, he argues that gays and lesbians should be granted the same rights as heterosexuals to marry or form domestic parnerships. No matter what their sexual orientation, Kaplan claims, all human beings have a need to share their lives with others. Because one's sense of oneself as an individual grows out of the relations one has with others, if this need for intimacy is not met, one's life can appear empty and meaningless.

Drawing upon the dissenting opinion of Justice Harry Blackmun in the case of *Bowers v. Hardwick* for support, Kaplan points out that in a democratic society such as ours, where many different conceptions of the good life flourish, the state has a responsibility to protect the freedom of its citizens to form a variety of intimate relationships in order to pursue these differing conceptions of the good life. While he recognizes an objection to this view could be made on the grounds that marriage is an inherently flawed institution, Kaplan believes that the legal recognition of gay and lesbian domestic relationships could help to undermine traditional gender roles within marriage, and thus benefit men and women in general by leading to greater equality.

———————

"Intimacy and Equality," like *Sexual Justice,* the larger project of which it is a part, juxtaposes terms which do not sit easily together in the terms of liberal political discourse; the sense of incongruity is heightened by the proximity to "lesbian and gay marriage." If not quite oxymorons, these phrases suggest a conflation of categories of private and public, at the very least, a blurring of boundaries, which many modern thinkers have been concerned clearly to delineate and protect.

This paper begins with an interrogation of the increasing demand by lesbian and gay citizens for a right to marry or otherwise to establish legally- and socially-recognized domestic partnerships. In modern democratic societies marriage provides one of the few instrumentalities by which individuals may join together to form associations that impose obligations on third parties. The desire to establish institutions to sustain shared lives and to have one's intimate commitments socially recognized expresses the extent of human needs for affiliation and domesticity. The critical point, I will argue, is that the need for intimate human connection runs very deep and across differing modes of sexuality and that social recognition and legal support is needed to maintain the always precarious associations through which such

———————

From *The Philosophical Forum* 25 (Summer 1994), 333–360.

needs are met. No doubt under the anomic conditions of modernity, couples and families are under enormous strain; these fragile relations are often made to bear the full weight of individual needs for community. The emergence of claims for the recognition of lesbian and gay families is itself inconceivable without the background of an increasingly visible queer community within which such social choices become feasible. In this sense the political overcoming of the closet has provided the historical and social conditions for reconstructing lesbian and gay intimate associations. Whether these aspirations may best be fulfilled through securing access on equal terms to the already troubled institution of marriage or through the creation of new forms of socially-recognized intimate relations and family life remains an open and contested question. . . .

WHY LESBIAN AND GAY MARRIAGE?

Historically, claims of lesbian and gay rights have focused primarily on two distinct areas defining the relations between queer citizens and the state: 1) decriminalization of homosexual activities between consenting adults; and 2) the prohibition of discrimination against lesbians and gays in employment, housing, and public accommodations. In recent years there has emerged an increasing insistence on the legal and social recognition of lesbian and gay relationships and community institutions. The emphasis on lesbian and gay associations and families foregrounds a more complex conception of the relations among sexuality, citizenship and domesticity than that implied by arguments for decriminalization or for protection against discrimination. Moral and political opposition to the criminalization of intimate sexual behavior has been generally articulated in terms of the principles of John Stuart Mill's classic essay *On Liberty*. These arguments define privacy rights in terms of negative liberty, an individual "right to be let alone," limiting the state's authority over private behavior between consenting adults in which no one is harmed.[1] A different range of concerns has informed opposition to discrimination against lesbians and gays. The movement for lesbian and gay rights joins African-Americans, women, religious and ethnic minorities, and the disabled in seeking the protections of the civil rights laws. When couched in constitutional terms, these claims invoke the "equal protection clause" of the 14th Amendment, whereas privacy claims depend upon the "due process" clause.[2] Anti-discrimination claims envision a more positive role for the state than do arguments supporting decriminalization: civil rights laws prohibit private citizens from exercising their prejudices against designated groups in specified areas of commercial life. Richard Mohr has described this role of the state as that of "a civil shield;" he has argued importantly that such protections are necessary if lesbians and gays are not to be penalized for exercising their full rights of political participation.[3]

A related but distinct class of claims emerges when we turn to the growing demand for recognition of lesbian and gay relationships, families and

institutions. Among the practical issues addressed here are: the right of lesbians and gays to marry or otherwise establish "domestic partnerships;" the
demands of lesbian and gay organizations for official status in public schools,
universities, or professional associations; the status of lesbian and gay institutions in the AIDS crisis; the claims of lesbian mothers and gay fathers to the
custody of their own children and of lesbians and gays more generally to be
considered as foster or adoptive parents; the demand to end the ban on openly
gay and lesbian participation in the military.[4] The state functions in these
claims not only as a "civil shield" protecting lesbian and gay citizens against
discrimination, but also as a positive agency for realizing their aspirations to
lead full lives. Although these claims appeal to fundamental conceptions of
political equality, they go beyond anti-discrimination arguments by asserting
the positive status of lesbian and gay citizenship. This development emphasizes human interdependence and situates individual efforts to attain a good
life within a context of personal, familial and civic relations and responsibilities. Moreover, the rights at issue pertain not only to individuals, but to couples,
families, and voluntary associations. The personal contexts from which such
claims emerge matter enormously to the people affected; they are at the heart
of the efforts of many to find meaning and satisfaction in their lives. At the
same time, many citizens not otherwise unfriendly to lesbian and gay rights
stop short of endorsing the demands of queer families to enjoy equal social
and legal status with their straight counterparts. Ultimately what is at stake is
acceptance of the moral legitimacy and ethical validity of the shared ways of
life of lesbian and gay citizens.[5]

What are we to make of the attention given to these issues in recent
months? Especially when we remember that half of the states continue to
outlaw same-sex activities in some form or another and that only eight states
protect lesbian and gay citizens against discrimination. Certainly, for those affected, the status of marriage or domestic partnership brings concrete financial and material benefits. In addition, recognition of a couple's status acts to
legitimate them in the eyes of the community, their families, and even themselves. The conjunction of material and symbolic gains associated with marital
or partnership status requires some untangling here to clarify the political
and ethical issues involved.[6] Let me emphasize again: the institution of marriage in modern societies provides a distinctive opportunity for individuals to
create by their own decision a new association that institutionalizes mutual
obligations and imposes duties on third parties. Both legally and socially, spouses
are entitled to consideration not available to those not so recognized. Coverage under employee-benefit plans is only one of the most obvious of these
entitlements, which range from shared invitations to social events to rights
under a lease or rent-control law to access to hospital rooms and nursing
homes and participation in life-or-death decisions concerning one's partner.
Generally, two persons may adopt a child together only if they are married to
each other. The experience of many gay men during the AIDS epidemic has
forcefully and painfully brought home the extent to which involvement in the

fate of another may be reserved to spouses and members of a "natural family." In late modern liberal societies, access to the status of marriage remains an important mode of personal empowerment.

Perhaps even more importantly, the assertion of lesbian and gay demands for recognition of the forms of our shared lives, with particular emphasis on intimacy and family, signals the emergence of queer politics from a defensive fight for mere survival towards an effort to secure the social conditions of human flourishing on equal terms with straight citizens. Lesbians and gays have been able to survive at all on the margins of society only through the creation of informal networks of sustenance and support. Individuals have struggled to maintain intimate personal ties against considerable odds, and they have been supported in their efforts by relations of friendship and community. In fact, queer social life has become the site of processes of redefining kinship in modern society with implications for all sorts of folk whose needs are not met by prevailing models. As communitarian thinkers have especially emphasized, human life is a social enterprise. We are born needy and dependent; our emergence as individuals results from interaction with others in the contexts of family and community. Our needs for recognition by and exchange with others are transformed as we mature, but we do not outgrow a fundamentally social condition. In modern liberal societies, the claims of community depend on individual choices to create and sustain common institutions. By turning to marriage, partnership and family rights, the movement for lesbian and gay rights and liberation affirms deeply felt human needs to establish intimate relationships as part of the ongoing conduct of life, culminating for many in the desire to bear and raise children of their own or otherwise to share in the care of others. . . .

THE ETHICS AND POLITICS OF INTIMATE ASSOCIATION

. . . The most comprehensive argument in support of the constitutional right of privacy appears in Justice Blackmun's dissent in *Bowers v. Hardwick.* . . . In his *Hardwick* dissent, Blackmun summarizes the constitutional jurisprudence of privacy rights as providing protection for both certain decisions that are taken to belong primarily to the individuals affected and certain places that are insulated against social and legal intrusions. In responding to the Court's limitation of these protections to matters regarding marriage and the family, Blackmun warns against "closing our eyes to the basic reasons why certain rights associated with the family have been accorded shelter under the Fourteenth Amendment's Due Process Clause."[7] Blackmun concludes that these reasons have less to do with some calculus of social benefits to be derived from family institutions than "because they form so central a part of an individual's life." His argument focuses on the underlying ethical concerns expressed in claims to fundamental rights. . . . Critically, he de-naturalizes family values by interpreting them as various ways in which people come together to construct shared lives:

. . . a necessary corollary of giving individuals freedom to choose how to conduct their lives is acceptance of the fact that different persons will make different choices. [The] fact that different individuals define themselves in a significant way through their intimate sexual relationships with others suggests, in a Nation as diverse as ours, that there may be many "right" ways of conducting those relationships, and that much of the richness of a relationship will come from the freedom an individual has to choose the form and nature of these intensely personal bonds. . . . the Court really has refused to recognize . . . the fundamental interest all individuals have in controlling the nature of their intimate associations with others.[8]

This argument concentrates a number of important insights into both sexual freedom and the character of domestic institutions. For Justice Blackmun, individual freedom must be socially situated and expressed through affiliation with others. A society that truly values individual freedom must eventually recognize a diversity of shared forms of life, especially in the context of intimate association. Although voluntary choice is a necessary component in legitimizing common institutions within democratic societies, freedom requires embodiment in social practices and institutions if individuals are to flourish.[9]

Blackmun's point, central to any understanding of modern intimacy, is that consensual relations among adults are both expressions of the voluntary choices of individual participants and necessary elements in the construction of intersubjectively-constituted personal identities. Freedom in the choice of partners and modes of relationship is one component of the good of intimate association that produces socially-recognized shared forms of life. Intimate associations often find expression in sexual activity. Blackmun suggests that a plurality of forms of intimate association may itself be a good in a nation so large and diverse as the United States.[10] Thus, diversity of personal and sexual expression has an irreducibly political dimension requiring the social recognition of "experiments in living": the existence of different sexualities with their own modes of intimacy is itself a contribution to human flourishing. The critical importance of intimacy as a constituent in most persons' conceptions of themselves and of a good life leads to its protection as a fundamental right: "[It] is precisely because the issue raised in this case touches the heart of what makes individuals what they are that we should be especially sensitive to the rights of those whose choices upset the majority."[11]

Finally, Justice Blackmun's analysis of the freedom of intimate association reframes the question of marriage and the family in the privacy jurisprudence. The freedom of intimate association requires not just a negative right to be left alone, but the positive capacity to create intimate spaces and the social support of personal choices that enable individuals to establish and develop their relationships.[12] These intimate spaces are often figured as home. Domesticity is the metaphorical and actual space of intimacy: the privacy cases demonstrate the dependence of such a sphere on its recognition by legal and social authorities. These decisions have constructed a domain of intimacy through which mutual personal decisions are not only insulated against interference from government or society but also given a place in the world. In part, this construction results from recognition of tradition and established social practice; in part, it has required the Court to apply fundamental principles of liberty and equality to domains previously governed by majoritarian morality. Blackmun's analysis points toward the need for recognizing a plurality of intimate associations through which individuals may pursue their goals and within which they may establish their homes and together shape their personal identities.

Within the normative framework of democratic constitutionalism, the recognition of intimate associations requires their conformity to ideals of freedom and reciprocity. In the earlier privacy cases, traditional marriage and family arrangements were emphasized without acknowledging that they may conflict with overriding concerns for individual autonomy and civic equality. These intimate associations are entitled to constitutional protection as fundamental rights only when they comport with the requirements of equal liberty for all. Justice Blackmun's argument for a constitutional right of privacy grounded in a positive freedom of intimate association recognizes deep human needs for intimacy and the extent to which even the most personal relations require social and legal support. But why marriage? To what extent may the valorization of marriage implicit in demands for lesbian and gay equality of access be at odds with feminist theory and the aspirations of the women's movement to overcome gender subordination and the institutionalized abuse of women? Feminists have eloquently and persuasively demonstrated the ways in which the institution of marriage has historically reinforced male privilege and implemented the subordination of women. Recent scholarship has demonstrated that many of the recent reforms in divorce law, sometimes in the name of gender equality, have also functioned to disadvantage women both economically and socially. In ongoing relationships, marital privacy has been invoked to shield abusive men and perpetuate the vulnerability of women to sexual and physical abuse.

The decision of the Supreme Court of the State of Hawaii in *Baehr v. Lewin* . . . has called attention to a different feminist analysis of same-sex marriage. In deciding that the denial of marital status to same-sex couples must be scrutinized in light of state constitutional prohibitions on sex discrimination, that Court has given legal authority and political impetus to an argument that has been advanced by a number of scholars in recent years.[13] Before concluding my own argument, I want to consider briefly the argument about gender equality and heterosexual marriage; I will discuss its formulation by Cass Sunstein.[14] The argument develops the analogy between miscegenation laws that banned interracial marriage and the denial of marital status to same-sex couples. In terms of constitutional equality, both cases present instances of formal legal equality established against a background of social hierarchy. Bans on miscegenation applied equally to whites and blacks; current restrictions on marriage equally affect women who want to marry women and men who want to marry men. How then is the denial of marital status to same-sex couples a case of sex discrimination? In *Loving v. Virginia,* the Supreme Court held that the prohibition of interracial marriages was part of a system that maintained white supremacy. Sunstein argues that the institution of marriage works to maintain a caste system based on gender through its restriction to heterosexual couples. Drawing on feminist legal and social analysis, he argues that gender hierarchy is supported by a definition of roles in which heterosexuality is employed to subordinate women to the men they love and marry. For women or men to refuse their place in this heterosexual matrix is to be cast out of central social institutions. Heterosexual marriage has perpetuated a gendered division of labor within the household and social divisions between private and public that maintain women's subordination. Sunstein concludes that constitutional norms of sexual equality require access to marriage for lesbians and gays as part of an assault on the gender caste system. If Sunstein's view is correct, the establishment of lesbian and gay marriages should have transformative, or at least subversive, effects on the organization of gender relations.

This argument is not easily evaluated in part because it requires complex historical judgments and predictions concerning the effects of legal and social innovation. At one level, the institution of same-sex marriages and households must pose a challenge and provide alternatives to the gendered divisions of labor still prevalent in so many places. Of course, lesbians and gays may replicate these patterns through the assumption of gender-stereotyped roles. But the evident disarticulation between social role and biological sex within such same-sex couples subverts social assumptions about the naturalness of gender. Moreover, to the extent that gender remains at work, even in same-sex relationships, it is hard to see that securing the legal recognition of lesbian and gay marriage will necessarily increase its power. Justice Blackmun's dissent points toward the desirability of legal and social recognition for a diversity of forms of intimate association and family life. However, focusing on a "right to marry" that has been denied to lesbian and gay citizens has distinct proximal advantages. As directed at a status currently available to heterosexual citizens, marriage claims can be formulated in terms of the denial of constitutionally-protected "equal protection of the laws." The argument that this exclusion is a form of sex discrimination in particular strengthens that case given the current status of homosexuals in constitutional law. If Justice Blackmun provides ethical grounds for recognizing fundamental rights of intimate association, then political ideals of equal citizenship and legal norms of "equal protection" complete a constitutional case for recognizing lesbian and gay marriage. The ethical and social question remains: whether the identification of rights to intimate association with access to marriage might foreclose the diversity of forms of life that Blackmun so eloquently evokes.

I have several concerns about the argument for lesbian and gay marriage based on gender equality. First, the legal strategy must not be permitted to obscure the specificity of lesbian and gay oppression nor subordinate the claims of queer citizens to tactical moves in the struggle for gender equality.

The equality of the sexes and equal citizenship for sexual minorities are related but distinct goals. In the United States today, pervasive legal disabilities define homosexuals as second-class citizens. Consider the following: the criminalization of same-sex activities in one-half-of the states and the denial to homosexuals of constitutional privacy rights that are well established for heterosexual citizens; the failure of most states and the federal government to protect lesbian and gay citizens from retaliation for the exercise of political freedom in their efforts to attain full equality; the stigmatization as demands for "special rights" of efforts to attain constitutional equality; and the systematic denial of legal recognition to same-sex couples and queer families who want to establish lasting relationships. The legal status of homosexuals in the contemporary United States effectively relegates queer citizens to a second-class citizenship fundamentally at odds with the egalitarian aspirations of modern democracy. The claim of a right to marry derives ethical and political force by appealing to ideals of equal citizenship. In terms of other inequalities, tied to class difference and income, marital status makes available "off the rack" a package of rights otherwise available only through expensive "custom-made" legal arrangements. While continuing to hope for and celebrate a plurality of "experiments in living," I am reluctant to accept a legal condition where lesbian and gay citizens must find alternatives to marriage whether they wish to or not, whether they can afford it or not. Thus, the demand for recognition of lesbian and gay marriage or domestic partnership appears as a necessary corollary of equal citizenship in the domestic sphere. Although some advocates worry that success on this front would result in the assimilation of lesbian and gay ethos to the imitation of heterosexist models, this objection strikes me as both understating and exaggerating the importance of formal legal rights. It underestimates the practical consequences of legal recognition as a form of empowerment by which individuals may create institutions that third parties must acknowledge. On the other hand, it overstates the extent to which such recognition deprives individuals of the capacity to shape and revise the institutions they voluntarily create. To the extent that opposition to lesbian and gay domesticity invokes an image of sexual outlaws inventing radically alternative forms of life, it underestimates the extent to which even our most intimate activities are implicated in forms of social life, even through their interdiction. After all, outlaws, especially, are defined by the law.

No one can deny that marriage is already a troubled institution in modern liberal societies. The rate of divorce, the number of single-parent households with children, the increasing incidence of single-person or unmarried-combination living arrangements, the number of children growing up with connections to multiple families through remarriage—all these facts emphasize the extent to which the model of a nuclear family composed of husband, wife and the children they have conceived together is already a fiction. The need to re-think the legal arrangements by which we secure our common lives and the rearing of our children seems obvious. I find it hard to believe that pressure for lesbian and gay marriages and parental rights will actually operate to entrench further and more fully legitimate these institutions as we know them. One of the merits of focusing on queer families as a political issue is its small-scale and associational character. In fact, lesbians and gays are "marrying," sharing commitment ceremonies, bearing and raising children, establishing households and families, in unprecedented numbers. What they seek from the state is the additional empowerment that derives from legal recognition. Moreover, this shifting pattern of homosexual intimacy is itself the product of decades of concerted activities through which more and more queer citizens have rejected the closet to create a movement of personal and political transformation. The proliferation of queer couples and families may help to redefine the social and legal conditions available to sustain intimate and domestic relationships more generally. In the meantime, the energies mobilized around the demands for recognition of lesbian and gay families already extend the discourse of "family values" beyond the terms of conservative lament and the scapegoating of single mothers. Lesbian and gay marriages, domestic partnerships, the reconceiving of family institutions as modes of intimate association among free and equal citizens, are all efforts to appropriate, extend, and transform the available possibilities.

NOTES

1. Approximately one-half of the states still prohibit sodomy in some form, either between any "persons" or between persons of the same sex.
2. According to a survey published in the *Harvard Law Review* in 1989, over sixty jurisdictions included sexual orientation as a protected class under their civil rights laws. That list included only two states; subsequently, six other states have amended their civil rights laws to include sexual orientation, as have numerous other jurisdictions. However, some localities have rescinded the inclusion of lesbians and gays. This matter has been the subject of highly-publicized state-wide referenda in Oregon and Colorado. Cf. Developments in the law—sexual orientation and the law. 62 *Harv. L. Rev.* 617 Jan. 1989.
3. Richard Mohr has effectively marshaled the arguments favoring the inclusion of sexual orientation in civil rights legislation, emphasizing the importance of such legislation as a guarantee that lesbian and gay citizens exercising their fundamental political rights may not be subjected to certain kinds of retaliation. Mohr described the role of the state in this contest as that of a "civil shield." Richard Mohr, *Gays/Justice* (New York: Columbia University Press, 1990), especially chapters 5-7.
4. Although in part an argument against discrimination by the state, this claim depends importantly on the notion that lesbians and gays are entitled to equal citizenship *as lesbian and gay,* that is, without having to conceal or deny their sexual orientation.
5. Cf. Mark Blasius, "An Ethos of Lesbian and Gay Existence," *Political Theory,* vol. 20 no. 3, 642-72 (Nov. 1992).
6. In late December 1992, *The New York Times* reported that Stanford and Chicago Universities had extended health benefits to the unmarried domestic partners of

their employees. Stanford restricted such coverage to same-sex couples on the ground that they are denied the choice of marriage. In January 1993, Mayor David Dinkins announced the creation of a registry for unmarried domestic partnerships in New York City and the extension of some limited benefits to city employees in such partnerships. Although the movement to recognize domestic partnerships is an important trend, most such efforts fall far short of conveying the range of rights and benefits associated with marital status.

7. 478 U.S. 186 at 204 (Blackmun, J., dissenting).

8. 478 U.S. 186 at 205-06 (Blackmun, J., dissenting).

9. Michael Sandel has argued that the invocation of privacy on behalf of lesbian and gay rights in the *Hardwick* dissents shares a generic liberal proceduralism which avoids substantive ethical argumentation with its necessary reference to conceptions of a good life. Sandel's claim seriously mistakes the force and direction of Justice Blackmun's argument. The redefinition of privacy rights as protecting freedom of intimate association does more than trigger the protections of the due process clause. Michael Sandel, "Moral Argument and Liberal Toleration: Abortion and Homosexuality," 77 *Cal. L. Rev.* 521 (1989).

10. The notion that a plurality of forms of shared life represents a positive good rather than simply a political retreat from substantive ethics has been an important component of liberal thought from the Federalist papers through J. S. Mill to Isaiah Berlin.

11. 478 U.S. 186 at 211 (Blackmun, J., dissenting).

12. Although the right to marry belongs to individuals and requires state action for its fulfillment, it distinctively depends on mutual and joint decision making for its realization. At the same time, the married couple enjoy special status vis-a-vis both state and society. The family unit created by marriage comes to have independent status even in relation to those individuals who created it. Until the wave of reform in state's divorce laws since the 1960s, and even today in some jurisdictions, state authority has made it quite difficult to dissolve a marriage once formed. Indeed, nowhere is it as easy to end as to initiate a marriage, and this remains true even where there are no children whose welfare may be at issue. One reader of this paper insisted that he would go along with the argument for lesbian and gay marriage so long as it was clear that there would also be a right of lesbian and gay divorce.

13. Andrew Koppelman, "The Miscegenation Analogy: Sodomy Law as Sex Discrimination," *Yale L. J. 98* (Nov. 1988) 145-164; Sylvia Law, "Homosexuality and the Social Meaning of Gender," 1988 *Wis. L. Rev.* 187.

14. "Homosexuality and the Constitution," *Metaphilosophy*, October 1994.

Is Sexual Harassment Coercive?

Larry May and John C. Hughes

Larry May, a philosopher at Washington University, and John C. Hughes, a political scientist at St. Michael's College, wrote the following essay shortly after the Equal Employment Opportunity Commission defined sexual harassment as a form of discrimination prohibited under Title VII of the 1964 Civil Rights Act. In it they seek to explain why sexual harassment is a moral wrong as well as a matter of public concern. Focusing on the two types of *quid pro quo* sexual harassment recognized by the EEOC, sexual threats and sexual offers, they argue that sexual harassment is morally wrong primarily because of its coercive character. Sexual threats are clearly coercive, since they have a constraining effect on the freedom of action of the person who has been threatened, and they force a change for the worse in that person's work environment. Sexual offers are less clearly coercive, since the person to whom a sexual offer has been made would benefit from accepting it. Still, many women feel they have no choice but to take such offers, and in that sense, in the authors' view, sexual offers are coercive. They are also coercive because, once made, the work environment is worsened for the recipient of the offer, who now is forced to contend with the implication that she is valued more as a sexual object than as an employee.

In their discussion, May and Hughes also support the position of the EEOC that sexual harassment is a form of sex discrimination. Sexual harassment, they write, harms not only individual women but women as a whole by reinforcing sexual stereotypes and thus adding to women's second-class status within society. This is why legal penalties are needed for the moral wrong of sexual harassment.

A number of recent lawsuits filed under Title VII of the 1964 Civil Rights Act have brought the problem of sexual harassment into the footlights of contemporary political and moral discussion. Is sexual harassment a purely private matter between two individuals, or is it a social problem? If sexual harassment is to be treated as something more than a purely personal dispute, how do we distinguish the social problem from benevolent forms of social interaction between members of a work hierarchy? We will argue here that sexual harassment of women workers is a public issue because it is inherently coercive, regardless of whether it takes the form of a threat for noncompliance, or of a reward for compliance. We will further argue that the harm of harassment is felt beyond the individuals immediately involved because it contributes to a pervasive pattern of discrimination and exploitation based on sex.

The term *sexual harassment* refers to the intimidation of persons in subordinate positions by those holding power and authority over them in order

From *Moral Rights in the Workplace*, ed. Gertrude Ezorsky (Albany, NY: State University of New York Press, 1987), pp. 115–122. [Citations omitted.]

to exact sexual favors that would ordinarily not have been granted. Sexual harassment of male subordinates by female superiors is conceivable, and probably occurs, albeit infrequently. Positions of authority are more likely to be occupied by males, while women are predominantly relegated to positions of subservience and dependency. Furthermore, strong cultural patterns induce female sexual passivity and acquiescence to male initiative. These factors combine to produce a dominant pattern of male harassment of females. However, it might bear reflecting that the poisoning of the work environment that may result from sexual intimidation may affect members of both sexes, so that sexual harassment should be viewed as more than merely a women's issue. . . .

I

Like most interpersonal transactions, sexual advances may take many forms. There is of course the sincere proposal, motivated by genuine feeling for another, made in a context of mutual respect for the other's autonomy and dignity. Such offers are possible between members of a work hierarchy, but are of no concern here. Rather, we are interested in advances that take the following forms: (1) Sexual threat: "If you don't provide a sexual benefit, I will punish you by withholding a promotion or a raise that would otherwise be due, or ultimately fire you." (2) Sexual offer: "If you provide a sexual benefit, I will reward you with a promotion or a raise that would otherwise not be due." There are also sexual harassment situations that are merely annoying, but without demonstrable sanction or reward. It is worth noting at the outset that all three forms of sexual harassment have been proscribed under . . . Equal Employment Opportunity Commission guidelines implementing Title VII.

Sexual harassment in the form of threats is coercive behavior that forces the employee to accept a course of conduct she wouldn't otherwise accept. What is wrong with this? Why can't she simply resist the threats and remain as before? Viewed in the abstract, one can seemingly resist threats, for unlike physical restraint, threatening does not completely deny individual choice over her alternatives. A person who is physically restrained is literally no longer in control of her own life. The victim is no longer reaching decisions of her own and autonomously carrying them out. Threats do not have this dramatic effect on a person's autonomy. Rather, the effect of the threat is that the recipient of a threat is much less inclined to act as she would have absent the threat— generally out of fear. Fear is the calculation of expected harm and the decision to avoid it. Reasonably prudent individuals will not, without a sufficiently expected possibility of gain, risk harm. The first thing wrong with sexual threats then is that, for the reasonable person, it now takes a very good reason to resist the threat, whereas no such strength of reasoning was required before to resist a sexual advance.

Sexual threats are coercive because they worsen the objective situation the employee finds herself in. To examine this claim, consider her situation before and after the threat has been made (preproposition stage and postproposition stage). In the preproposition stage, a secretary, for example, is judged by standards of efficiency to determine whether she should be allowed to retain her job. She would naturally view her employer as having power over her, but only in the rather limited domain concerning the job-related functions she performs. Her personal life would be her own. She could choose her own social relationships, without fear that these decisions might adversely affect her job. In the postproposition stage, she can no longer remain employed under the same conditions while not choosing to have relations with her employer. Further, the efficient performance of job-related functions is no longer sufficient for the retention of her job. She can no longer look to her supervisor as one who exercises power merely over the performance of her office duties. He now wields power over a part of her personal life . . . [M]any women leave their jobs after such a proposition has been tendered. They cannot simply go on as before, for their new situation is correctly perceived as worse than the old situation.

It is the worsening of the woman's situation after the threat has been made that contributes to the likelihood of her acquiescence to the threat. The perception of job insecurity created by the threat can only be alleviated by her acceptance of the sexual proposition. But what of the woman who prefers to have a sexual relationship with her employer than not to do so? Has this woman also been made objectively worse off than she was before the threat occurred? We contend that she has, for before the threat was made she could pursue her preference without feeling forced to do so. If the liaison developed and then turned sour, she could quit the relationship and not so clearly risk a worsening of her employment situation. Now, however, her continued job success might be held ransom to the continued sexual demands of her employer. This also may adversely affect other women in the business organization. What the employer has done is to establish a precedent for employment decisions based upon the stereotype that values women for their sexuality rather than for their job skills. This has a discriminatory impact on women individually and as a group. Focusing on this effect will shed some light on the harm of both sexual threats and sexual offers.

II

Consider the following case. Barnes was hired as an administrative assistant by the director of a federal agency. In a preemployment interview, the director, a male, promised to promote Barnes, a female, within ninety days. Shortly after beginning her job, (1) the director repeatedly asked her for a date after work hours, even though she consistently refused; (2) made repeated remarks to her that were sexual in nature; and (3) repeatedly told her that if she did not cooperate with him by engaging in sexual relations, her employment status would be affected. After consistently rebuffing him, she finally told him she wished for their relationship to remain a strictly professional one. Thereafter the director, sometimes in concert with others, began a campaign to belittle and demean her within the office. Subsequently she was stripped of most of her job duties, culminating in the eventual abolition of her job. Barnes filed suit, claiming that these actions would not have occurred but for the fact that she was a woman.

Under Title VII, it is now widely accepted that the kind of sexual threat illustrated by this case is an instance of sex discrimination in employment. Such threats treat women differently than men in employment contexts even though gender is not a relevantly applicable category for making employment-related decisions. The underlying principle here is that like persons should be treated alike. Unless there are relevant differences among persons, it is harmful to disadvantage one particular class of persons. In the normal course of events, male employees are not threatened sexually by employers or supervisors. The threats disadvantage a woman in that an additional requirement is placed in her path for successful job retention, one not placed in the path of male employees. When persons who are otherwise similarly situated are distinguished on the basis of their sex, and rewards or burdens are apportioned according to these gender-based classifications, illegal sex discrimination has occurred. Applying this theory of discrimination to Barnes' complaint, the federal appellate court ruled:

> So it was, by her version, that retention of her job was conditioned upon submission to sexual relations—an exaction which the supervisor would not have made of any male. It is much too late in the day to contend that Title VII does not outlaw terms of employment for women which differ appreciably from those set for men and which are not genuinely and reasonably related to the performance on the job. . . . Put another way, she became the target of her superior's sexual desires because she was a woman and was asked to bow to demands as the price for holding her job.

There is a second way in which this behavior might be viewed as discriminatory. Sexual threats also contribute to a pervasive pattern of disadvantaged treatment of women as a group. Under this approach, the harm is not viewed as resulting from the arbitrary and unfair use of gender as a criterion for employment decisions. Rather, emphasis is on the effect the classification has of continuing the subordination of women as a group. The harm results regardless of whether the specific incident could be given an employment rationale or not. Sexual harassment perpetuates sex discrimination, and illustrates the harm that occurs for members of a group that have historically been disadvantaged. This theory was applied to sexual harassment in another federal lawsuit, *Tomkins* v. *Public Service Gas and Electric Co.* The plaintiff's lawyers argued that employer tolerance of sexual harassment and its pattern of reprisals had a disparate impact upon women as an already disadvantaged group and was inherently degrading to all women.

Sexual threats are harmful to the individual woman because she is coerced and treated unfairly by her employer, disadvantaging her for no good reason. Beyond this, such practices further contribute to a pervasive pattern of disadvantaged status for her and all women in society. The sexual stereo-typing makes it less likely, and sometimes impossible, that women will be treated on the basis of job efficiency, intelligence, or administrative skill. These women must now compete on a very different level, and in the case where sexual threats are common or at least accepted, this level is clearly inferior to that occupied by men. The few male employees who are harassed in the workplace suffer the first harm but not the second. We shall next show that there are also two harms of sexual offers in employment, only one of which can also be said to befall men.

III

The harm of sexual offers is much more difficult to identify and analyze. Indeed, some may even see sexual offers as contributing to a differentiation based on sex that advantages rather than disadvantages women, individually and as a group. After all, males cannot normally gain promotions by engaging in sexual relations with their employers. We shall argue, on the contrary, that a sexual offer disadvantages the woman employee by changing the work environment so that she is viewed by others, and may come to view herself, less in terms of her work productivity and more in terms of her sexual allure. This change, like the threat, makes it unlikely that she can return to the preproposition stage even though she might prefer to do so. Furthermore, to offset her diminished status and to protect against later retaliation, a prudent woman would feel that she must accept the offer. Here, sexual offers resemble the coercive threat. The specific harm to women becomes clearer when one looks at the group impact of sexual offers in employment. Women are already more economically vulnerable and socially passive than men. When sexual offers are tendered, exploitation of a woman employee is accomplished by taking advantage of a preexisting vulnerability males generally do not share.

Seduction accomplished through sexual offers and coercive threats blend together most clearly in the mixed case of the sexual offer of a promotion with the lurking threat of retaliation if the offer is turned down. Both combine together to compel the woman to engage in sexual relations with her employer. Gifts are so rare in economic matters that it is best to be suspicious of all offers and to look for their hidden costs. . . [S]exual offers often contain veiled threats and are for that reason coercive.

Why are the clearly mixed cases, where there is both an offer and a (sometimes only implied) threat, coercive rather than noncoercive? To return to our initial discussion, why is it that one is made worse off by the existence of these proposals? In one sense they enable women to do things they couldn't otherwise do, namely, get a promotion that they did not deserve, thus seeming to be noncoercive. On the other hand, if the woman prefers not having sexual relations with her employer (while retaining her job) to having sexual relations with him (with ensuing promotion), then it is predominantly a threat and more clearly coercive. The best reason for not preferring the postproposition stage is that she is then made worse off if she rejects the proposition, and if she accepts, she nonetheless risks future harm or retaliation. This latter condition is also true for more straightforward offers, as we shall now show.

A number of contemporary philosophers have argued that offers place people in truly advantageous positions, for they can always be turned down with the ensuing return to the preoffer stage. In the case of sexual offers, however, the mere proposal of a promotion in exchange for sexual relations changes the work environment. Once sexual relations are seriously proposed as a sufficient condition for employment success, the woman realizes that this male employer sees her (and will probably continue to see her) as a sex object as well as an employee. A prudent woman will henceforth worry that she is not being regarded as an employee who simply happens to be a woman, but rather as a woman made more vulnerable by the fact that she happens to be an employee. If she accepts the offer, she lends credence to the stereotype, and because of this, it is more likely that she may experience future offers or even threats. She would thus worry about her ability to achieve on the basis of her work-related merits. If she rejects the offer, she would still worry about her employer's attitude toward her status as a worker. Furthermore, because of the volatility of sexual feelings, these offers cannot be turned down without the risk of offending or alienating one's employer, something any employee would wish to avoid. She may reasonably conclude from these two considerations that neither postoffer alternative is desirable. This is one of the hidden costs of sexual offers in the workplace.

It may be claimed that such environmental changes are no different for men who can also be the objects of sexual offers in the workplace. One needs to show that the changed environment is worse for those who are women. Sexual employment offers take advantage of unequal power relations that exist between employer and employee so as to force a particular outcome further benefitting those who are already in advantageous positions. But beyond this, sexual offers are doubly exploitative for female employees, because women already enter the employment arena from a position of vulnerability. As we have indicated, this is true because of the history of their economic powerlessness and because of their culturally ingrained passivity and acquiescence in the face of male initiatives. Women enter the employment arena much more ripe for coercion than their male colleagues. Thus, women are more likely to be harmed by these offers.

Men are not similarly harmed by sexual offers because they do not have the same history of sexual exploitation. Men are likely to regard such seductive offers either humorously or as insults to be aggressively combatted, while women have been socialized to be passive rather than combative in such situations. The woman to whom the offer is made becomes less sure of her real abilities by virtue of the proposal itself. This self-denigrating response to an unwelcomed proposal is a vestige of women's history of subordination. Even without the veiled threat, sexual offers can cause women to act in ways they would not choose to act otherwise. To this extent, these sexual offers are coercive.

Most offers are not coercive because one would prefer to have the offer made. This is because one of the postoffer alternatives (rejecting the offer) is equivalent to the preoffer alternative (having no offer at all). Sexual offers made by male employers to female employees are different, however, because they more closely resemble threats than ordinary offers. As we have shown, the preoffer alternative—being employed, unpromoted, yet able to obtain promotion according to one's merits—is different from, and preferable to, either of the postoffer alternatives—accepting the promotion, and having sexual relations with her employer, with all of its negative consequences, or rejecting the offer of promotion, but with the risk that the promotion may now prove unobtainable on the basis of merit. By blocking a return to the more preferable preoffer alternative, the male employer has acted similarly to the employer who uses sexual threats. The woman is forced to choose between two undesirable alternatives because she cannot have what she would have chosen before the proposal was made. Stressing these hidden costs, which are much greater for women than for men, exposes the coercive element inherent in sexual offers as well as in sexual threats. We are thus led to conclude that both of these employment practices are harmful to women and . . . were properly proscribed by the U.S. Equal Employment Opportunity Commission.

A Feminist Definition of
Sexual Harassment

Anita M. Superson

In this essay Anita M. Superson, a member of the philosophy department at the University of Kentucky at Lexington, presents and defends a new definition of sexual harassment, which she believes better fits the problem of sexual harassment than the definitions currently used in the American judicial system. She believes her definition is an improvement for two reasons: First, it identifies sexual harassment on the basis of behavior alone, not by the impact of the behavior on the victim or the intentions of the perpetrator. This makes it a more objective definition than the ones currently recognized under the law. It also shifts the burden of proof away from the victim, thus making it more fair to women. Secondly, this definition clearly accounts for why sexual harassment is morally wrong. Sexual harassment is morally wrong because it brings about both individual and social harm. Any particular act of sexual harassment, Superson emphasizes, actually harms all women by reinforcing the sexist belief that women ought to occupy a subordinate role in society.

According to Superson's definition, behavior only constitutes sexual harassment if the behavior is caused by a member of the dominant social class. Thus, women cannot by definition sexually harass men. While Superson recognizes that this is a controversial claim, she supports it on the grounds that women are powerless to cause harm to men as a group.

INTRODUCTION

By far the most pervasive form of discrimination against women is sexual harassment (SH). Women in every walk of life are subject to it, and I would venture to say, on a daily basis.[1] Even though the law is changing to the benefit of victims of SH, the fact that SH is still so pervasive shows that there is too much tolerance of it, and that victims do not have sufficient legal recourse to be protected.

The main source for this problem is that the way SH is defined by various Titles and other sources does not adequately reflect the social nature of SH, or the harm it causes all women. As a result, SH comes to be defined in subjective ways. One upshot is that when subjective definitions infuse the case law on SH, the more subtle but equally harmful forms of SH do not get counted as SH and thus not afforded legal protection.

My primary aim in this paper is to offer an objective definition of SH that accounts for the group harm all forms of SH have in common. Though my aim is to offer a moral definition of SH, I offer it in hopes that it will effect

From *Journal of Social Philosophy* 24 (1993), 46–64.

changes in the law. It is only by defining SH in a way that covers all of its forms and gets at the heart of the problem that legal protection can be given to all victims in all circumstances. . . .

I define SH in the following way:

> any behavior (verbal or physical) caused by a person, A, in the dominant class directed at another, B, in the subjugated class, that expresses and perpetuates the attitude that B or members of B's sex is/are inferior because of their sex, thereby causing harm to either B and/or members of B's sex.

THE SOCIAL NATURE OF SEXUAL HARASSMENT

Sexual harassment, a form of sexism, is about domination, in particular, the domination of the group of men over the group of women. Domination involves control or power which can be seen in the economic, political, and social spheres of society. Sexual harassment is not simply an assertion of power, for power can be used in beneficial ways. The power men have over women has been wielded in ways that oppress women. The power expressed in SH is oppression, power used wrongly.

Sexual harassment is integrally related to sex roles. It reveals the belief that a person is to be relegated to certain roles on the basis of her sex, including not only women's being sex objects, but also their being caretakers, motherers, nurturers, sympathizers, etc. In general, the sex roles women are relegated to are associated with the body (v. mind) and emotions (v. reason).

When A sexually harasses B, the comment or behavior is really directed at the group of all women, not just a particular woman, a point often missed by the courts. After all, many derogatory behaviors are issued at women the harasser does not even know (e.g., scanning a stranger's body). Even when the harasser knows his victim, the behavior is directed at the particular woman because she happens to be "available" at the time, though its message is for all women. For instance, a catcall says not (merely) that the perpetrator likes a woman's body but that he thinks women are at least primarily sex objects and he—because of the power he holds by being in the dominant group— gets to rate them according to how much pleasure they give him. The professor who refers to his female students as "chicks" makes a statement that women are intellectually inferior to men as they can be likened to non-rational animals, perhaps even soft, cuddly ones that are to serve as the objects of (men's) pleasure. Physicians' using Playboy centerfolds in medical schools to "spice up their lectures" sends the message that women lack the competence to make it in a "man's world" and should perform the "softer tasks" associated with bearing and raising children.[2]

These and other examples make it clear that SH is not about dislike for a certain person; instead, it expresses a person's beliefs about women as a group on the basis of their sex, namely, that they are primarily emotional and bodily beings. Some theorists—Catharine MacKinnon, John Hughes and Larry May— have recognized the social nature of SH. Hughes and May claim that women are a disadvantaged group because (1) they are a social group having a distinct identity and existence apart from their individual identities, (2) they occupy a subordinate position in American society, and (3) their political power is severely circumscribed.[3] They continue:

> Once it is established that women qualify for special disadvantaged group status, all practices tending to stigmatize women as a group, or which contribute to the maintenance of their subordinate social status, would become legally suspect.[4]

This last point, I believe, should be central to the definition of SH.

Because SH has as its target the group of all women, this *group* suffers harm as a result of the behavior. Indeed, when any one woman is in any way sexually harassed, all women are harmed. The group harm SH causes is different from the harm suffered by particular women as individuals: it is often more vague in nature as it is not easily causally tied to any particular incident of harassment. The group harm has to do primarily with the fact that the behavior reflects and reinforces sexist attitudes that women are inferior to men and that they do and ought to occupy certain sex roles. For example, comments and behavior that relegate women to the role of sex objects reinforce the belief that women *are* sex objects and that they *ought to* occupy this sex role. Similarly, when a female professor's cogent comments at department colloquia are met with frowns and rolled eyes from her colleagues, this behavior reflects and reinforces the view that women are not fit to occupy positions men arrogate to themselves.

The harm women suffer as a group from any single instance of SH is significant. It takes many forms. A Kantian analysis would show what is wrong with being solely a sex object. Though there is nothing wrong with being a caretaker or nurturer, etc., *per se,* it is sexist—and so wrong—to assign such roles to women. In addition, it is wrong to assign a person to a role she may not want to occupy. Basically women are not allowed to decide for themselves which roles they are to occupy, but this gets decided for them, no matter what they do. Even if some women occupy important positions in society that men traditionally occupy, they are still viewed as being sex objects, caretakers, etc., since all women are thought to be more "bodily" and emotional than men. This is a denial of women's autonomy, and degrading to them. It also contributes to women's oppression. The belief that women must occupy certain sex roles is both a cause and an effect of their oppression. It is a cause because women are believed to be more suited for certain roles given their association with body and emotions. It is an effect because once they occupy these roles and are victims of oppression, the belief that they *must* occupy these sex roles is reinforced.

Women are harmed by SH in yet another way. The belief that they are sex objects, caretakers, etc., gets reflected in social and political practices in ways that are unfair to women. It has undoubtedly meant many lost opportunities that are readily available to men. Women are not likely to be hired for jobs that require them to act in ways other than the ways the sex roles dictate, and if they are, what is expected of them is different from what is expected of men. Mothers are not paid for their work, and caretakers are not paid well in comparison to jobs traditionally held by men. Lack of economic reward is paralleled by lack of respect and appreciation for those occupying such roles. Certain rights granted men are likely not to be granted women (e.g., the right to bodily self-determination, and marriage rights).

Another harm SH causes all women is that the particular form sex stereotyping takes promotes two myths: (1) that male behavior is normally and naturally predatory, and (2) that females naturally (because they are taken to be primarily bodily and emotional) and even willingly acquiesce despite the appearance of protest. Because the behavior perpetuated by these myths is taken to be normal, it is not seen as sexist, and in turn is not counted as SH. . . .

Last, but certainly not least, women suffer group harm from SH because they come to be stereotyped as victims. Many men see SH as something they can do to women, and in many cases, get away with. Women come to see themselves as victims, and come to believe that the roles they *can* occupy are only the sex roles men have designated for them. Obviously these harms are quite serious for women, so the elimination of all forms of SH is warranted.

I have spoken so far as if it is only men who can sexually harass women, and I am now in a position to defend this controversial view. When a woman engages in the very same behavior harassing men engage in, the underlying message implicit in male-to-female harassment is missing. For example, when a woman scans a man's body, she might be considering him to be a sex object, but all the views about domination and being relegated to certain sex roles are absent. She cannot remind the man that he is inferior because of his sex, since given the way things are in society, he is not. In general, women cannot harm or degrade or dominate men *as a group,* for it is impossible to send the message that one dominates (and so cause group harm) if one does not dominate. Of course, if the sexist roles predominant in our society were reversed, women *could* sexually harass men. The way things are, any bothersome behavior a woman engages in, even though it may be of a sexual nature, does not constitute SH because it lacks the social impact present in male-to-female harassment. Tort law would be sufficient to protect against this behavior, since it is unproblematic in these cases that tort law fails to recognize group harm.

SUBJECTIVE V. OBJECTIVE DEFINITIONS
OF SEXUAL HARASSMENT

Most definitions of 'sexual harassment' make reference to the behavior's being "unwelcome", or "annoying" to the victim. *Black's Law Dictionary* defines 'harassment' as a term used "to describe words, gestures and actions which tend to annoy, alarm and abuse (verbally) another person." The *American Heritage Dictionary* defines 'harass' as "to disturb or irritate persistently," and states further that [h]arass implies systematic persecution by besetting with annoyances, threats, or demands." The EEOC *Guidelines* state that behavior constituting SH is identified as "unwelcome sexual advances, requests for sexual favors, and other verbal or physical conduct of a sexual nature." In their philosophical account of SH, Hughes and May define 'harassment' as "a class of annoying or unwelcome acts undertaken by one person (or group of persons) against another person (or group of persons)." And Rosemarie Tong takes the feminists' definition of noncoercive SH to be that which "denotes sexual misconduct that merely annoys or offends the person to whom it is directed. . . ."

Though it is true that many women are bothered by the behavior at issue, I think it is seriously mistaken to say that whether the victim is bothered determines whether the behavior constitutes SH. This is so for several reasons.

First, we would have to establish that the victim was bothered by it, either by the victim's complaints, or by examining the victim's response to the behavior. The fact of the matter is that many women are quite hesitant to report being harassed, for a number of reasons. Primary among them is that they fear negative consequences from reporting the conduct. As is often the case, harassment comes from a person in a position of institutional power, whether he be a supervisor, a company president, a member of a dissertation committee, the chair of the department, and so on. Unfortunately for many women, as a review of the case law reveals, their fears are warranted. Women have been fired, their jobs have been made miserable forcing them to quit, professors have handed out unfair low grades, and so on. Worries about such consequences mean that complaints are not filed, or are filed years after the incident, as in the Anita Hill v. Clarence Thomas case. But this should not be taken to imply that the victim was not harassed.

Moreover, women are hesitant to report harassment because they do not want anything to happen to the perpetrator, but just want the behavior to stop. Women do not complain because they do not want to deal with the perpetrator's reaction when faced with the charge. He might claim that he was "only trying to be friendly." Women are fully aware that perpetrators can often clear themselves quite easily, especially in tort law cases where the perpetrator's intentions are directly relevant to whether he is guilty. And most incidents of SH occur without any witnesses—many perpetrators plan it this way. It then becomes the harasser's word against the victim's. To complicate matters, many women are insecure and doubt themselves. Women's insecurity is capitalized upon by harassers whose behavior is in the least bit ambiguous. Clever harassers who fear they might get caught or be reported often attempt to get on the good side of their victim in order to confuse her about the behavior, as well as to have a defense ready in case a charge is made. Harassers might offer special teaching assignments to their graduate students, special help with exams and publications, promotions, generous raises, and the like. Of course, this is all irrelevant to whether he harasses, but the point is that it makes the victim less likely to complain. On top of all this, women's credibility is very often questioned (unfairly) when they bring forth a charge. They are taken to be "hypersensitive." There is an attitude among judges and others that women must "develop a thick skin." Thus, the blame is shifted off the perpetrator and onto the victim. Given this, if a woman thinks she will get no positive response—or, indeed, will get a negative one—from complaining, she is unlikely to do so. . . .

An *objective* view of SH avoids the problems inherent in a subjective view. According to the objective view defended here, what is decisive in determining whether behavior constitutes SH is not whether the victim is bothered, but whether the behavior is an instance of a practice that expresses and perpetuates the attitude that the victim and members of her sex are inferior because of their sex. . . .

[A related topic] is the issue of the harasser's intentions. In subjective definitions this is the counterpart to the victim's being bothered. Tort law makes reference to the injuror's intentions: in battery tort, the harasser's intent to contact, in assault tort, the harasser's intent to arouse psychic apprehension in the victim, and in the tort of intentional emotional distress, the harasser's intent or recklessness, must be established in order for the victim to win her case.

But like the victim's feelings, the harasser's intentions are irrelevant to whether his behavior is harassment. As I just pointed out, many men do not take their behavior to be bothersome, and sometimes even mistakenly believe that women enjoy crude compliments about their bodies, ogling, pinching, etc. From perusing cases brought before the courts, I have come to believe that many men have psychological feelings of power over women, feelings of being in control of their world, and the like, when they harass. These feelings might be subconscious, but this should not be admitted as a defense of the harasser. Also, as I have said, many men believe women encourage SH either by their dress or language, or simply by the fact that they tolerate the abuse without protest (usually out of fear of repercussion). In light of these facts, it would be wrongheaded to allow the harasser's intentions to count in assessing harassment, though they might become relevant in determining punishment. I am arguing for an objective definition of SH: it is the attitudes embedded and reflected *in the practice* the behavior is an instance of, not the attitudes or intentions *of the perpetrator,* that make the behavior SH.

Yet the idea that the behavior must be directed at a certain person in order for it to count as harassment, seems to suggest that intentions *do* count in assessing harassment. This feature is evident both in my definition, as well as in that found in *Black's Law Dictionary,* which takes harassment to be conduct directed against a specific person causing substantial emotional distress. If conduct is directed at a particular individual, it seems that the person expressing himself must be intentionally singling out that individual, wanting to cause her harm.

I think this is mistaken. Since the harasser can subconsciously enjoy the feeling of power harassing gives him, or might even consider his behavior to be flattering, his behavior can be directed at a specific person (or group of persons) without implying any ill intention on his part. By 'directed at a particular individual,' I mean that the behavior is in some way observed by a particular person (or persons). This includes, for example, sexist comments a student hears her professor say, pornographic pictures a worker sees, etc. . . .

IMPLICATIONS OF THE OBJECTIVE DEFINITION

One implication of my objective definition is that it reflects the correct way power comes into play in SH. Traditionally, SH has been taken to exist only between persons of unequal power, usually in the workplace or an educational institution. It is believed that SH in universities occurs only when a professor harasses a student, but not *vice versa.* It is said that students can cause "sexual hassle," because they cannot "destroy [the professor's] self-esteem or endanger his intellectual self-confidence," and professors "seldom suffer the complex psychological effects of sexual harassment victims." MacKinnon, in her earlier book, defines SH as "the unwanted imposition of sexual requirements in the context of a relationship of unequal power."[5]

Though it is true that a lot of harassment occurs between unequals, it is false that harassment occurs *only* between unequals: equals and subordinates can harass. Indeed, power is irrelevant to tort law, and the courts now recognize harassment among coworkers under Title VII.

The one sense in which it is true that the harasser must have power over his victim is that men have power—social, political, and economic—over women as a group. This cannot be understood by singling out individual men and showing that they have power over women or any particular woman for that matter. It is power that all men have, in virtue of being men. Defining SH in the objective way I do allows us to see that *this* is the sense in which power exists in SH, in *all* of its forms. The benefit of not restricting SH to cases of unequal institutional power is that *all* victims are afforded protection.

A second implication of my definition is that it gives the courts a way of distinguishing SH from sexual attraction. It can be difficult to make this distinction, since "traditional courtship activities" are often quite sexist and frequently involve behavior that is harassment. The key is to examine the practice the behavior is an instance of. If the behavior reflects the attitude that the victim is inferior because of her sex, then it is SH. Sexual harassment is not about a man's attempting to date a woman who is not interested, as the courts have tended to believe; it is about domination, which might be reflected, of course, in the way a man goes about trying to get a date. My definition allows us to separate cases of SH from genuine sexual attraction by forcing the courts to focus on the social nature of SH.

Moreover, defining SH in the objective way I do shifts the burden and the blame off the victim. On the subjective view, the burden is on the victim to prove that she is bothered significantly enough to win a tort case, or under Title VII, to show that the behavior unreasonably interfered with her work. In tort law, where the perpetrator's intentions are allowed to figure in, the blame could easily shift to the victim by showing that she in some way welcomed or even encouraged the behavior, thereby relinquishing the perpetrator from responsibility. By focusing on the practice the behavior is an instance of, my definition has nothing to do with proving that the victim responds a certain way to the behavior, nor does it in any way blame the victim for the behavior.

Finally, defining SH in a subjective way means that the victim herself must come forward and complain, as it is her response that must be assessed. But given that most judges, law enforcement officers, and even superiors are men, it is difficult for women to do so. They are embarrassed, afraid to confront someone of the same sex as the harasser who is likely not to see the problem. They do not feel their voices will be heard. Working with my definition will I hope assuage this. Recognizing SH as a group harm will allow women to come to each other's aid as co-complainers, thereby alleviating the problem of reticence. Even if the person the behavior is directed at does not feel bothered, other women can complain, as they suffer the group harm associated with SH. . . .

NOTES

1. Rosemarie Tong, "Sexual Harassment," in *Women and Values,* Marilyn Pearsall, ed., (Belmont, CA: Wadsworth Publishing Company, 1986), pp. 148–166. Tong cites a *Redbook* study that reported 88 percent of 9,000 readers sampled experienced some sort of sexual harassment (p. 149).

2. Frances Conley, a 50-year-old distinguished neurophysician at Stanford University, recently came forward with this story. Conley resigned after years of putting up with sexual harassment from her colleagues. Not only did they use Playboy spreads during their lectures, but they routinely called her 'hon,' invited her to bed, and fondled her legs under the operating table. *Chicago Tribune,* Sunday, June 9, 1991, Section 1, p. 22.

3. John C. Hughes and Larry May, "Sexual Harassment," *Social Theory and Practice,* Vol. 6, No. 3 (Fall, 1980), pp. 264–265.

4. *Ibid.,* p. 265.

5. Catharine MacKinnon, *Sexual Harassment of Working Women: A Case of Sex Discrimination* (New Haven: Yale University Press, 1979), p. 1. It is actually not clear that MacKinnon endorses this definition throughout this book, as what she says seems to suggest that harassment can occur at least between equals. In her most recent book, she recognizes that harassment "also happens among coworkers, from third parties, even by subordinates in the workplace, men who are women's hierarchical inferiors or peers." Catharine A. Mackinnon, *Feminism Unmodified: Discourses on Life and Law.* (Cambridge: Harvard University Press, 1987), p. 107.

"Sexual Harassment" Must Be Eliminated

F. M. Christensen

A professor in the Department of Philosophy at the University of Alberta at Edmonton, F. M. Christensen presents a philosophical challenge in the following essay to the very concept of sexual harassment itself. Disagreeing with Anita Superson's position that improvements in the law need to be made to increase women's opportunities for pursuing sexual harassment charges, Christensen suggests that the term "sexual harassment" groups together a number of unrelated behaviors, and is thus incoherent. As he sees it, because North American society has traditionally been uncomfortable with sexual frankness, the idea of sexual harassment became popularly accepted despite its incoherence. Christensen additionally objects to the concept of sexual harassment on two counts of sexism. It is sexist toward women because it reflects the patronizing attitude that due to their special sensibilities women need to be sheltered from sexual conversation. Given that men and women have differing ways of making sexual advances to each other, the concept of sexual harassment is sexist toward men because only those ways of making sexual advances that are characteristic of male behavior are recognized as being potentially harassing. Christensen recommends that universities end "politically correct" sexual harassment investigatory boards and grow more concernful about non-sexually related conflicts in the workplace. He also recommends that more victims of serious offenses now covered under the umbrella of sexual harassment should file appropriate criminal or civil charges.

Please read the title of this article again. It is not about sexual harassment, but "sexual harassment"—the phrase and its associated concept. Ironically, charges standardly leveled against sexual harassment actually fit the concept itself instead. . . .

    In fact, "sexual harassment" is better described as a *pseudo*-concept; there is something fundamentally illegitimate about it. Suppose someone were to introduce the notion of "automobile harassment," meant to include shooting at someone from a car, speeding dangerously past in or running someone down with a car, insulting someone from a car, and waving at someone who doesn't want to be waved at from a car. Such a category would be very suspicious: (1) It lumps together serious crimes, minor offenses, and actions that are arguably not wrong at all. (2) What the actions do have in common—the fact that they all involve a car—is irrelevant to what it is about each action that makes it wrong. Confronted with such an artificial concept, one would wonder what irrationality or hidden agenda had led to that lumping together.

From *Public Affairs Quarterly* 8 (January 1994), 1-17.

So it is with the notion of "sexual harassment." (For convenience, often abbreviated hereafter as "SH.") Though its details take highly various forms, "SH" is standardly meant to include attempted or actual extortion of sexual favors, bodily contact of a sexual nature, and sexual expressions of any kind: jokes, insults, propositions, passing comments, visual displays, facial expressions, etc., etc. When we attempt to state explicitly what "sexual harassment" consists in, the only possible answer is, "Something or other to do with sex that someone or other may find objectionable." As in the automotive analogy, then, the range of offenses commonly included in this heterogeneous category is immense— some "sexual harassment" policies even list rape under its rubric. Also as in the analogy, the fact that sex is involved has nothing to do with why or whether any of the proscribed actions is wrong. Sexual extortion is heinous because it is extortion, not because it is sexual; unwanted sexual touching is wrong because it is an invasion of personal space, not specifically because it is sexual; sexual insults are objectionable because they are an attempt to hurt, not because they are sexual. And simple sexual frankness is not wrong at all.

Language can be very seductive. For example, many will assume that if a *term* exists, there must be a corresponding *category* that is both significant (morally significant, in this instance) and well defined. Because of that power to deceive, the manipulative use of language—sophistry, it is standardly called— is a very effective way to illegitimately influence beliefs and actions. In the case at hand, (1) the indiscriminate lumping of "dirty words" together with assault and extortion is a clear example of the sophistry of guilt by association: organically linking serious felonies with things that are at worst obnoxious causes the latter to partake of some of the horror of the former. Similarly, (2) the fact that sexuality is the only unifying element in an otherwise catch-all category makes sex the focus of attention—and hence turns a morally incidental feature into the core evil involved. Indeed, the only plausible motive for creating the pseudo-concept of "sexual harassment" was precisely to have these effects.

Further evidence for such a motive lies in the following fact: virtually none of the institutions that have created "sexual harassment" policies have adopted explicit rules to penalize all the major and minor *non*-sexual ways one person can harm or offend another. The author knows of cases in which co-workers or supervisors have deliberately made life miserable for someone, forcing the person to quit; also of cases of non-sexual extortion by supervisors—e.g., a professor and his wife arm-twisting a graduate student into granny-sitting for a summer. In most institutions, except for ethnic and gender discrimination, the larger portion of the many ways in which one person can mistreat or upset another are not in any specific way prohibited. Why single out the sexual ones?

Indeed, why not simply adopt *general* policies of "worksite harassment" (or the like), which would automatically cover the sexual variety *as well as* all the other kinds of extortion, assault and offensive expressions? Again, the obvious answer is that certain people are much more interested in forging a special association between sex and harmful behavior than they are in providing protection from harmful behavior to all who need it. They are especially anxious to make a crime out of things that otherwise might be seen only as bad taste or bad judgment, or as not objectionable at all. For it is pretty unlikely that any *non*-sexual "harassment" rules that might be implemented would see people pilloried or even fired over non-hostile (or even hostile) comments, invitations, and facial expressions *in general*—the Big-Brother violation of the rights of freedom of expression would in that case be obvious to everyone.

Then why would this pseudo-concept have been invented in the first place? After all, sexual assault and extortion were already regarded as crimes before the introduction of "SH" in the 1970's; attention could easily have been called to their unrecognized degree of incidence or unacknowledged degree of seriousness without inventing such an all-inclusive category. Manifestly, creating a new and serious offense of uttering sexual speech was the goal.

* * *

Why would the illegitimate concept have been so readily acquiesced in by the general public? One of two main reasons is this culture's long-entrenched antisexualism: sex is debased and debasing unless "redeemed" by something noble (love, art, etc.). Even today, this attitude is still so thoroughly internalized that most cannot really comprehend the contrary view—though different people "draw the line" between acceptable and unacceptable degrees of sexual frankness in very different places. For even today, most people have little concrete appreciation of the great power of mindless conditioning and indoctrination over their emotions—they just assume their aversive gut-response to sexual frankness represents genuine moral knowledge. Because of the intensity of that reaction in many, even those not sharing it are apt to go along with it.

A better illustration of this taboo at work could hardly be asked than the Anita Hill-Clarence Thomas incident. There were basically only two sides: "He didn't do that terrible thing," and "He *did* do that terrible thing." The issue of whether it *was* a terrible thing to speak frankly about sex to her was almost never raised. (At least not in public. But perhaps most of the large majority who initially supported Thomas over Hill did so because they didn't see it as a serious matter even if she was telling the truth.) The question of whether Ms. Hill was *justified* in taking offence at "dirty words" was not seriously raised —a fact that, objectively speaking, is as astounding as it is revealing of the power of antisexualism. The fact that a type of behavior as harmless and as natural for human beings as talking about sex would be treated as a crime reveals something deeply perverted in this culture.

Imagine a culture in which people were socialized with feelings of aversion toward emotional closeness, or one in which anti-religious feelings ran high. Merely making an offer to share companionship, or wearing a crucifix or a yarmulke in someone else's presence, would by analogy elicit a charge of "friendship harassment" or "religious harassment." Rather than the person with the unnatural feelings of aversion being advised to get some serious counseling, the "harasser" would be publicly reviled and punished or sent to re-education sessions and forced to confess to thought-crimes. It has been only a few short years since interracial marriage was a felony in many U.S. states, and portrayal of interracial couples was banned from movies; to this day—though now they can't say so openly—some people feel great offense at being involuntarily exposed to biracial couples. Is such exposure "biracial harassment" of those offended? As a matter of objective morality, there is not an iota of difference between these other sorts of "harassment" and frank sexual talk: there is nothing intrinsic to their nature, or to human nature, to cause harm or feelings of degradation. On the contrary, in all these cases the real moral evil lies in the well-conditioned intolerance of those who *take* the offense, and in the harm to others they feel that gut-response justifies them in committing.

The foregoing remarks are in defense of sexual frankness per se; they do not, of course, apply to *every* variety of sexual (*or* non-sexual) communication. Again, extortion is a serious evil; and reckless or malicious speech can hurt—often, more than a physical attack. There certainly are, moreover, borderline cases in which no harm is intended or foreseen but arguably should be foreseen, notably, making sexual requests to someone over whom one has supervisory authority: for all the recipient knows, the person having that authority might use it to retaliate for being rejected. Even here, however, the degree of punitiveness displayed by "SH" proponents and policies is grotesquely disproportionate, revealing a serious unconcern for the subtleties of human interaction. And even when the supervised person is the one who makes the first advance—clearly signalling a lack of fear of retaliation—the supervisor is likely to be accused of "harassing" the other person if it is made known. Even more revealingly, there are no special regulations to restrain a superior from making *non*-sexual requests—involving anything from religion to politics to friendship to money—even though in all those cases as well, the other person might fear retaliation over the wrong response.

Another genuinely objectionable case is the use of sexual talk to insult another person. Once again, it is the intent to cause distress that is the wrong here, not the mere vehicle of that intent. Note also that the reason why sexual words are available for this use in the first place is that they are taboo—they already have shock-value. Consequently, having special rules against even the non-hostile use of sexual words can only reinforce the taboo, thereby *increasing* the tendency to employ them as weapons. Indeed, in some incidents sexual frankness has been employed to insult certain persons as retaliation, precisely because the latter had complained about some non-hostile sexual frankness. Why would the proponents of "SH" support such manifestly counterproductive policies?

Finally, unjustifiably hounding someone—over sex or anything else whatever—is certainly objectionable, and those who engage in such behavior must be restrained. Notice once again, however, that cases not involving sex are

dealt with in a manner much more appropriate to the offense, or even ignored altogether, by institutions with "SH" policies. Notice also that this is a
case of real harassment: dictionaries define that word in terms of ongoing
efforts that vex someone else. Yet from the very beginning, it has been insisted that single acts should count as "sexual harassment." This is yet another
example of misuse of words to make the behavior in question seem worse
than it is. . . . The consequences of this are serious. Individuals given no fair
warning that certain behavior is "unwanted" are being severely punished for
honestly failing to foresee the response. Indeed, one cannot safely ask first
whether a certain kind of sexual communication will be found offensive, since
even doing that "involves sex" and may be "unwanted." Hence the effect of
such a policy is *not* merely to restrict sexual speech around those who find
it offensive; it is to restrict sexual speech, period.

* * *

Like the claim that sexual frankness is degrading, a second belief passes
with little public challenge these days: that it is discriminatory toward women.
Well before the introduction of the notion of "sexual harassment," sexual openness by a male around a female was being labeled "sexist" and "male chauvinist" by certain feminists. Now, real sexism is a serious matter. This culture's
awakening, over the last 25 years or so, to the harms women have suffered
under societal structures around the world has been a moral advance of the
first magnitude. Also like the claim that sexual frankness is degrading, however, the allegation that it constitutes discrimination against women is a serious falsehood; it is a parasite upon the ideal of gender equality. That this
second view has become so widely accepted—even endorsed by the Supreme
Courts of the U.S and Canada—reveals once again the power of certain irrational influences to subvert intellectual honesty.

In its general sense, to discriminate is simply to differentiate in some
manner: to treat, in attitude or in behavior, one person or thing differently than
another. To discriminate in the common *negative* sense of the word ("*invidious* discrimination") is to treat some person or persons *unfairly or unjustly*
vis-à-vis someone else: to treat him or her or them worse or less well without
having adequate grounds for doing so. Racial discrimination ("racism," for short)
consists in treating someone unfairly because of her/his race; similarly for
"sexism." There is also the useful concept of de facto racial or sexual discrimination: treatment on unfair grounds *other than* race or sex, but in circumstances such that members of one race or sex are disproportionately harmed
by it. At least, such are the official meanings of these terms; again, one can
unwittingly or deliberately misuse words—and that has happened wholesale
with the word "sexism. . . ."

[One] reason why some may allege [sexual frankness] constitutes sexism
toward women begins with a genuine and very serious type of sexism. Traditionally, women in this culture were limited to the roles of sex partner and
mother, hence they were not valued as much as men for all the other things

they could do. What seems to have happened since the rise of feminism is that the roles women were traditionally *allowed* have been aversively associated, in the minds of some, with those they were *denied.* Consequently, calling attention to sexuality seems to these individuals to devalue women's other roles—notably, that of productive worker. As legitimate as the underlying concern is, the fact remains that guilt by association is a fallacy, and can only lead to new problems rather than solving old ones. The appropriate response to the old role imbalance is not a new imbalance in which women are seen as asexual ("comrade wife, heroically working for the production quota") but one that recognizes the *full* humanity—including the sexuality—of everyone; the embargo on sex-talk that "SH" advocates promote treats people as less than fully human.

The illegitimacy of this antisexual response is especially clear when we realize that sexual expression generally calls attention to the erotic potential of *both* genders, not just that of women. It is further revealed by the fact that no similar reaction has occurred regarding that other role to which women were historically limited: no prohibitions against talk about parenting have been created to assure that women are thought of as paid workers and not just as mothers. Finally, notice that *genuine* (overt) stereotyping and sex-role affirmation are legally protected on grounds of freedom of speech, whereas sexual harassment is not; clearly, the reasons for punishing sexual openness as sexist discrimination do *not* include its alleged tendency to reinforce roles and stereotypes. The fallacious reasoning about women's societal roles is at best a minor motivation for the "SH" movement. . . .

The most plausible reason why sexual openness is considered "sexist" is a special aspect of our culture's entrenched anti-eroticism. Sexual openness has long been seen not just as offensive, but specifically as offensive to women. In times when the general notion of sexism toward females was virtually unheard of and woman's "place" viewed as God-given, for a male to speak openly of sex around a female was considered grossly disrespectful—"Please! There are ladies present!" Women were viewed as too morally pure and too delicate in their sensitivities to be exposed to anything so crass and degrading. We might call this attitude the "double standard of sexual offense;" though attenuated since the "sexual revolution," it is still very much with us today. Relative to that double standard, then, treating women *the same* as men in regard to sexual frankness is seen as treating them *worse*—i.e., discriminating against them. Yesterday's charge of "disrespect for women" has simply become today's "sexism against women. . . ."

Yet is the differential treatment justified? After all, being raised in a society already having that double standard results in women being more conditioned to find sexual frankness distressing. On the contrary, this fact no more justifies "SH" penalties than the fact that some people have been conditioned to have racist feelings justifies punitive regulations to protect *their* sensitivities. That the two genders feel different degrees of aversion to sexual openness argues for changing their differential conditioning, not reinforcing it. . . .

In conclusion, the ubiquitous charge that sexual frankness is "sexist" toward women is utterly false. The claim is based either upon confusion and mindless conditioning or upon sophistical distortion.

* * *

Ironically, in fact, the double standard of offense is itself sexist. First of all, it is discriminatory toward women themselves. It is not sexually frank males who are sexist, but those of both genders who promote the "SH" concept, with its differential treatment of men and women. This was called forcefully to the author's attention by a recent experience as the lone male in a meeting of young women engineers and students. I had suggested that perhaps men *should* be cautious in their language around women, given the latter's more sheltered background. Unanimously and politely but firmly, they told me that was a sexist (their term) idea, the sort of stance that would keep women and men from being full equals. . . .

To see the truth of their point, one need only reflect on the fact that the double standard of sexual *offense* is tightly bound up with the double standard of sexual *behavior,* which has been so central to discrimination against women. Its worst victims were the "fallen women" of years past, forced into lives of abject misery; even today the attitude claims many lesser victims. Beyond that, the double standard has been a powerful source of control over women, as is revealed by the right-wing dictum, "Women are better than men and we aim to keep them that way." In part, at least, the special solicitousness shown to women lest they be traumatized by sexual frankness has been a cover for a special desire to keep them in their place.

Sheltering women from crass things like sex is part of a broader traditional pattern. It was hinted earlier that a second major reason, besides culturally engrained anxiety over sex, explains why an illegitimate concept like "sexual harassment" would be so readily accepted in this society. That second reason is another powerfully trained societal attitude, one we might call the "double standard of *concern*:" a greater degree of solicitude over harm or potential harm to women and girls. It goes well beyond the legitimate concern felt for any individual—of *either* sex—who is more vulnerable, involving as it does stereotypes and sweeping value-attitudes based on gender rather than on individual circumstances.

This mindframe is reflected in a multitude of ways in our culture: in such traditional dicta as "Save the women and children first" and "You can't hit your sister back, she's a girl!" in opinion-surveys showing that suffering by a woman is regarded much more seriously than exactly equal suffering by a man, and so on. . . . Consciously and unconsciously, the double standard of concern continues to exert a powerful influence over all of our thinking about gender.

The results of such societal protectiveness have not all been advantageous to women, however. In many ways, the consequences for them have been disastrous, notably a trained helplessness in girls and women that feminists have so rightly decried. The moderate biological difference between the sexes in regard to average physical strength has been culturally exaggerated into a much larger one, and a difference between them in *emotional* toughness has been created where there is evidently no biological difference to begin with. Women's greater fears and vulnerabilities are largely the result of having been overly sheltered, in those early childhood years when boys are taught to "take it like a man" and all through life. . . .

There is yet more sexism inherent in "SH," however; the concept and its enforcement constitute sexist discrimination toward men. At a minimum, this is true in the de facto sense: they constantly produce serious injustices against individuals, the great majority of whom are male. (This fact is unlikely to garner much sympathy in public, given the pervasiveness of the double standard of concern and other current political influences.) Though usually written in gender-neutral language, "sexual harassment" regulations are as objectionable as they would be if they penalized intrinsically harmless behavior that is more typically female. There are several important facts, however, that make their discriminatory nature particularly clear.

One of these is the social tradition requiring males to do the initiating, if any romantic or sexual contact is to be made at all. . . . In spite of 25 years of talk about gender equality, women in general and feminists in particular have done little to alter this pattern regarding who must initiate—even though they alone *can* change it. Hence he is the one at risk, in case his approach should turn out to be "unwanted." "*You* must make any overtures that are to be made, and we will judge whether they are acceptable or criminal," is the message of women supporters of "SH" to men. If women had to worry that their approaches would be not only rejected but prosecuted, the "unwanted remarks and invitations" section of the category would be swiftly jettisoned. . . .

This leads us to a more overt way in which "SH" policies discriminate against men. In general, those who have crafted or interpreted the details of the policies have not allowed the wearing of revealing clothing to count as a form of sexual harassment. In other words, the methods generally used by men to express sexual interest are considered punishable, those used mostly by women are not. Suggestive dress is as much a way of "calling attention to sex" as is suggestive speech (or display of pin-ups, etc.)—indeed, once again, sexual display antedates spoken language as a way to send a sexual message—but the powers that be refuse to recognize the fact. (Instead, paradoxically, responding to that sort of visual statement with a verbal one—even to complain that such dress is inappropriate to the work place—is itself apt to be penalized as sexual harassment!) . . .

Similarly, the use of one's sexual attractiveness to get special treatment is not explicitly listed in "SH" regulations. And when sex is exchanged for employment favors, it is the person who got the sex, not the one who got the perk or promotion, who is apt to be blamed for "harassing" the other. . . . Nor are you likely to see sexual teasing listed on an index prohibitorum for "SH"— even if it is done to exert power or to humiliate. After all, holding out false promises of sex is a *female* behavior that *males* object to. Or at least, males perceive females as doing it, and in the standard ideology of "sexual harassment," what a female "perceives" a situation to be, not a male's perception or his actual intent, is what determines whether it is objectionable. Clearly, what underlies all this discrimination against men in "SH" rules is sexist attitudes. Indeed, outside of the policies themselves, even the pretense of gender inclusiveness is generally dropped. Again and again, in the literature of "sexual harassment" policy advocates, the frankly stated purpose is to punish a man for whatever a woman finds offensive.

* * *

The basic point of the foregoing paragraphs is that the double standard of offense has been very harmful to both men and women. And efforts to promote it—in the form of "SH" regulations or any other—constitute unjust treatment, in different ways, of both. "Sexual harassment" is indeed sexist discrimination.

Of course, efforts to resist the "SH" juggernaut are met with accusations of bad faith and callousness. In the familiar words of its proponents, "men just don't get it." It is certainly true that many men, traditionally, have failed to realize the anguish women have suffered as the result of sexual extortion and assault, and out of fear of those evils. That must continue to change. However, such insensitivity is largely the result of men's and women's experiences in life being so different. It is difficult—for a member of *either* sex—to be cognizant of tribulations that one does not have to face oneself. (Note well that this is a case of not *realizing,* not one of not *caring;* again, once the degree of suffering *is* known, both men and women care more about the pain of others who are women.) It is thus likewise true that many women do not appreciate the special sorts of trauma men have to face—from growing up in a society that may force them to go off and die in battle to having their children ripped away as a matter of course in divorce court to being the primary recipients of *non-*sexual violence from the day they are born. Or, to the point here, the trauma of having vicious charges thrown at them for their sexual feelings, and the fear of being deprived of their careers over a few inadvertent words. Yet the "SH" proponents never raise the issue of whether women understand men's special vulnerabilities; in their eyes, "getting it" is a one-way street. . . .

Men and women *must* come to understand each other better. And in general, the best way to do that is by decreasing the differences in their life-experiences—not increasing them by reinforcing the old double standards. The other way to promote such understanding is by increasing the communication between them over their differing feelings—*not de*creasing communication by promoting blame and punishment for expressing the "wrong" feelings. The illegitimate concept of "sexual harassment" is part of the disease of sexism, not part of the cure. . . .

What should be done instead, then? Given the fact that protection from some of the offenses included in "sexual harassment" codes is genuinely warranted, what is the just response? The answer is very clear. First, those codes and their tribunals should be replaced by mediators—men and women trained to deal with delicate human conflicts without the inquisitorial face and victim-victimizer mentality of the "SH" machinery. And they should deal with conflicts of *all* kinds, not just those over sex, thus eliminating their antisexual implications. The abuse of civil rights codes and tribunals in this arena should also be ended, leaving them to deal with real racial and gender discrimination. Finally the genuine crimes and harmful behavior that have been lumped together with dirty words and pictures should be handled by the criminal and civil law—and those systems should be suitably sensitized to harms they may have ignored in the past. "Sexual harassment" must be eliminated.

SUGGESTIONS FOR FURTHER READING

Dodds, Susan M., Lucy Frost, Robert Pargetter, and Elizabeth W. Prior. "Sexual Harassment." *Social Theory and Practice* 14 (Summer 1988), 111–130.

The authors question the view that sexual harassment is a form of sex discrimination. In its place they offer a behaviorial account of sexual harassment, suggesting this is a more promising foundation for social policy.

Kaplan, Morris. "Autonomy, Equality, Community: The Question of Lesbian and Gay Rights." *Praxis International* 11 (July 1991), 195–213.

Moving beyond defenses of lesbian and gay rights based on an individual's right to privacy or protection of his or her civil rights, Kaplan draws upon John Rawls's idea of justice as fairness in claiming these rights are group rights needing state recognition for gay and lesbian communities to flourish.

MacKinnon, Catharine. *Sexual Harassment of Working Women.* (London: Yale University Press, 1979).

In this influential treatment of the issue, MacKinnon argues that sexual harassment is a form of sex discrimination against women.

Magnuson, Roger J. *Are Gay Rights Right?* (Portland, OR: Multnomah Press, 1990).

Magnuson answers the question raised by his title in the negative, largely on the basis of the idea that gays do not make up a minority group deserving of civil rights protection.

Mohr, Richard. *Gays/Justice: A Study of Ethics, Society and Law.* (New York: Columbia University Press, 1988).

A thorough-going defense of the need for civil rights legislation to protect gays and lesbians from discrimination.

Murphy, Timothy F. "Homosexuality and Nature: Happiness and the Law at Stake," *Journal of Applied Philosophy* 4 (1987), 195–204.

This essay is a reply to the article by Michael Levin included in this chapter. Murphy criticizes a number of aspects of Levin's argument, including his claim that homosexuality leads to unhappiness.

Tong, Rosemarie. *Women, Sex and the Law.* (Totowa, NJ: Rowman and Allanheld, 1984).

Chapter Three, "Sexual Harassment," includes an analysis of coercive and noncoercive forms of sexual harassment as well as a wider category of sexual harassment Tong calls "gender harassment," and of the avenues available to fight sexual harassment both in and out of the courts.

Wall, Edmund. "The Definition of Sexual Harassment." *Public Affairs Quarterly* 5 (October 1991), 371–385.

Wall takes issue with both the view that sexual harassment is morally wrong because it is coercive and with the view that it is wrong because it is discriminatory. Focusing on its interpersonal aspects, he takes sexual harassment to be wrong because it violates an individual's right to privacy.

Chapter 10

PRIVACY ISSUES

Is privacy a value at risk in American society today? Those who would argue that it is could draw on different types of evidence to back up their claim. They might cite just how often we are asked to reveal Social Security numbers or other pieces of information about ourselves in various processes, such as checking books out of the library or confirming one's identity in order to complete some routine transaction. They could also draw attention to the ever-increasing ease for someone armed with one piece of information about another person—be it a Social Security number, credit card number, or even the license plate number of that person's car—to access enough stored computerized information about that person to construct a fairly accurate picture of his or her habits and preferences, all without that person's knowledge.

While not all would agree with the idea that American society is currently facing a crisis of privacy, even those suspicious of the idea would agree that it is a value that ought to be protected. But just why should privacy be protected? Answering this question requires reflection on the concept and value of privacy. In this chapter we will look at some of the moral and legal aspects of privacy, as well as some of the ways it has traditionally been understood. We will also consider a few of the debates arising out of conflicts between privacy and other human values. The particular issues we will examine here are ones emerging from changing conditions in society, including questions relating to confidentiality in the treatment of patients with AIDS and to the impact of data-gathering technology on an individual's ability to keep personal information from entering the public domain.

PRIVACY AS A MORAL VALUE

Why does privacy matter to us? Why do so many of us make an effort to preserve our privacy? Questions such as these ask about the value of privacy in general. Our interest in this section concerns one aspect of the general value of privacy that makes privacy significant to us: its moral value. Since understanding what privacy is can inform us about why it is meaningful, we will consider the moral values associated with privacy by starting with some of the ways in which privacy has been defined.

One very popular view maintains that we have a moral right to privacy as one aspect of a more general right not to be bothered or interfered with. Statements such as "I just want to have my own space" or "I just want to be left alone" rely on this concept of privacy in order to make their point. What can be learned about the value of privacy from this understanding of the importance of privacy? On the face of it, this understanding appears to miss a good part of what is essentially important about privacy. To see this, consider the following example. Suppose that someone routinely videotapes you through your kitchen window while you are making dinner. This person acts discretely enough that you do not realize there is anyone monitoring your activities. What she does, does not interfere with what you are doing in any way; in some sense at least, she can be said to be leaving you alone. However, surely most of us would rightly object to such videotaping as constituting an unfair invasion of privacy.

This example suggests that the understanding of privacy as a right not to be bothered or interfered with is less than adequate. Another, related under-standing of privacy—privacy as a right not to be interfered with when mak-ing decisions about matters connected to how one wishes to lead one's own life—would also be inadequate to explain why privacy has been invaded in the example just given. Still, this understanding of privacy can account for many instances in which one feels one's privacy has been invaded, and clearly demonstrates one reason why we take privacy to be important. For example, it is true that in American society, but not in all societies, one is free to name one's child virtually anything one wants. If our government were to mandate that children's first names be chosen from an approved list, no doubt most would find this to be an unfair invasion of privacy. It has also been suggested that in order to improve race relations in this country, only interracial mar-riages ought to be legal. Again, if this suggestion were put into law, most would probably react in a similar way. The moral aspect of privacy that can be seen from these examples is the value of autonomy. One reason we value privacy as much as we do is because having it allows us to act in an autono-mous way when making decisions that relate to the personal aspects of our lives. Were others, particularly the government, to become involved in deter-mining how these decisions ought to be made, we would be robbed of our freedom to make these choices, which are often ones that provide the most meaning for our lives. Thus the primary moral value connected to privacy—seen as the right to be left alone in personal decision making—can be taken to be the value of autonomy. (For more concerning the value of autonomy, see the selection from Immanuel Kant in Chapter 1.)

Another familiar expression related to privacy is: "That really isn't any of your business." Behind this statement lies a related but conceptually different aspect of privacy from the one just described. Privacy in this sense, as dis-cussed by W. A. Parent in his contribution to this chapter, relates not to the right to exclude others from control over aspects of decision making, but the right to exclude them from possessing information that one considers to be of a personal nature.

On the basis of this understanding of privacy, there are several reasons why privacy can be said to be valuable. As James Rachels points out in another of this chapter's readings, sometimes we want to protect our privacy in order to prevent information about ourselves from being known to others, if we perceive that information as being potentially damaging or embarrassing to ourselves if reported to others or if it fell into the wrong hands. For example, if someone has a laboratory for making illegal drugs inside his house, it would be reasonable for him to want to keep this a secret; if someone else worries about being located by a person intending to do her harm, it makes sense to get an unlisted phone number. By a similar token, if one enjoys reading the morning newspaper while standing on one's head, it is conceivable that one would not want anyone else to know about this habit, out of concern about how this knowledge would affect one's image in the eyes of others. On this way of looking at privacy, its value arises chiefly out of its usefulness in guarding our own interests against the potentially competing interests of others.

How important is this value to the significance of privacy? Rachels's view is that while this value can be thought of as one aspect of why privacy matters, it cannot be the most important or even one of the most important reasons for why we care about privacy as much as we do. To back up his view, Rachels points to the desires that people have to keep their privacy intact even when they are engaged in activities that they have no reason to hide and which would not be embarrassing or pose a danger to themselves were word about them to get out to others. Alone, the value of privacy in guarding the interests mentioned above seems unable to account for why many of us would like to preserve privacy even in contexts where no reasonable person could have an interest in what we are doing.

In another analysis of privacy found in this chapter, also based on the idea that privacy is primarily the right to control who has access to information about oneself, Richard Wasserstrom proposes that we have an interest in keeping some activities private or free from observation because otherwise we would experience an unpleasant feeling of vulnerability. This might provide an explanation of why we want to preserve privacy in both a variety of innocuous situations as well as those of a less innocent kind. While it could be said that privacy matters to us because we do not enjoy the feeling of vulnerability that we experience in its absence, such an understanding of why privacy matters points more to the psychological value than to the moral value of privacy. On the basis of this understanding, however, a moral value connected to privacy defined as the right to determine who has access to personal information does appear to suggest itself. Again, this moral value appears to be that of autonomy. Having privacy allows oneself the freedom to make decisions regarding just to whom if anyone to reveal information concerning oneself. Again, as we saw earlier in considering how privacy is related to the freedom of making personal decisions for oneself, what we view as personal information often turns out to be those facts about ourselves that relate to the areas of our lives from which we derive the most meaning. However, Larry Hunter, another author represented in this chapter, raises the interesting point that there is a good reason to retain control over who has access to personal information about oneself that one might consider to be relatively meaningless or trivial in nature—for instance, what brand of potato chips one regularly buys at the grocery store. His concern is that many innocuous pieces of personal information could be used by others to form a picture of oneself that is quite misleading. (To see how easily this could happen, suppose you are a nondrinker but enjoy entertaining your friends on a weekly basis. If frequent and substantial purchases of liquor appear on your credit card bills, anyone who has access to this information might well draw the conclusion that you are an alcoholic.)

While privacy is needed to protect the moral value of autonomy, autonomy is not the only significant moral value associated with privacy. As both Rachels and Wasserstrom suggest in this chapter, privacy is also necessary in order to protect the variety of our personal relationships. Their thinking is based on the idea that one's ability to have a number of different kinds of personal relationships in large part depends on being able to decide with whom to share just what items of personal information. For example, the information that one shares with one's close friends is not the same as what one shares with one's tennis partners or with one's parents. Without the ability to give some people but not others access to personal information, the specific character and thus the very existence of these unique relationships would be jeopardized. Because our personal relationships hold such significance for us, Rachels and Wasserstrom contend it is worth our while to insure that our lives have a private dimension to them.

PRIVACY AS A LEGAL RIGHT

Along with arguments based on moral grounds that privacy is an important feature of a good human life, there are other reasons to protect privacy that stem from a legal standpoint. Currently American law recognizes a constitutionally guaranteed right to privacy. It is generally agreed that the first important defense of the idea of a legal right to privacy stems from an 1890 *Harvard Law Review* article ("The Right to Privacy") written by Samuel Warren and Louis Brandeis. The existence of the legal right to privacy, however, is not without controversy. At the heart of the controversy lies the issue of whether or not the basis for recognizing a legal right to privacy is a legitimate one.

Just what is the basis for recognizing a legal right to privacy? The controversy concerning a legal right to privacy arises from the fact that the Constitution does not explicitly guarantee a right to privacy in the same way as it guarantees the right to freedom of speech and freedom of religion. In other words, looking through the Bill of Rights one would not find a right to privacy mentioned as such. The case for a legal right to privacy, then, is built around an interpretation of the Constitution. This interpretation was first defended by the U. S. Supreme Court in 1965 in its decision in *Griswold v. Connecticut*, which can be found among this chapter's readings. (A brief description of this defense can be found in the introduction to the reading.) Other decisions made by the Supreme Court in the light of the establishment of the right to privacy have generally been consistent with the idea that this right guards the individual against the government becoming involved in at least some aspects of personal decision making. For example, in *Loving v. Virginia*, a law forbidding interracial marriage was declared unconstitutional on the basis of the right to privacy. The idea behind this ruling was that such decisions ought to be left up to the particular parties involved in the relationship rather than to the government. *Roe v. Wade*, still the most controversial case decided by the Supreme Court in the context of the right to privacy, overturned a state law permitting abortions only when the mother's life was in danger on the grounds that a decision to terminate a pregnancy ought to be left up to the particular woman involved and not to the state.

Some who question a legal right to privacy do so on the basis of considerations involving the concept of a right to privacy itself. Their argument is that such a right is actually superfluous, given that anything which could be protected under it is already protected on the basis of some other right, such as the right to private property. Another objection to the notion of a legal right to privacy is directly related to the Supreme Court decision in *Griswold v. Connecticut*. It takes the form of denying that the interpretation of the Constitution which seemingly admits a right to privacy is a reasonable interpretation. One of the supporters of this view is Robert S. Bork, whose Senate confirmation hearings in 1987 for a position on the Supreme Court drew nationwide attention. Following the belief that courts should look to the "original meaning" of the Constitution in making its decisions, Bork has claimed that the decision in *Griswold v. Connecticut* represents an illegitimate extension of judicial power: Given that there is no mention of a right to privacy in the Constitution, to claim there is a constitutional basis for one, in Bork's view, is tantamount to creating rather than interpreting the law. Because in his view the right to privacy amounts to an invention, he is also concerned that it has the potential to become a "loose canon" in the law, conceivably allowing for activities such as drug use, prostitution, and spousal abuse to become legitimated under its protective umbrella.[1]

Finally, what is the relation between the moral right and the legal right to privacy? As the court decisions described above show, the legal right to privacy could be viewed as affirming the chief value that we earlier saw was associated with the moral right to privacy: the value of autonomy. Having a right to privacy in the sense we have been talking about gives one legal protection from government interference when it comes to making many personal decisions. What seems less obviously protected by this right is one's privacy to control who has access to personal information in the first place. Following the passage of the Privacy Act by the U.S. Congress in 1974, it became illegal for an agency of the federal government to share data collected on a particular person with another federal agency. So this act, in principle, protects an individual reporting personal information to the Internal Revenue Service, for example, from having that information in turn reported to the Federal Bureau of Investigation. Nothing in the Privacy Act, however, allows an individual to take control over the information that federal agencies can compile on him; nor does it protect an individual against private corporations who wish to collect personal data for marketing or other purposes.

WHEN ARE INVASIONS OF PRIVACY JUSTIFIED?

As the discussion above shows, the legal right to privacy in American society is connected to protecting individuals from undue government interference in personal aspects of their lives. Those who consider privacy to be at risk in this society today, however, would claim that many current threats to personal privacy do not so much involve the political power of government as they do other forms of power, including the power of different types of sophisticated technology. In this section, we will briefly consider three general situations where the value of privacy, threatened by nonstate sources, appears in direct conflict with other important values. Are any of these conflicts resolvable? If so, on what grounds? When are invasions of privacy justified? We will take up these questions in conjunction with a look at three privacy issues of social concern: genetic testing in employment, physician-patient confidentiality in regard to AIDS testing, and large-scale computerized collection of personal information.

Genetic Testing in Employment

In recent years, the development of ever more sophisticated screening techniques for genetic traits and abnormalities have brought the promise of being able to know in advance whether or not one is at risk for a particular disease. Along with this promise comes a fear that these techniques will be misused if information is given to anyone other than the person who is screened. Because such screening is generally voluntary, anyone who is concerned that her genetic information might fall into the wrong hands (an insurance company, for example) might simply decide not to be tested, even if she suspects she might be a likely candidate to come down with a particular disease. What, though, about cases where an employer mandates such testing of his employees as a condition for future or continuing employment? When, if ever, does an employer's interest in knowing about the genetic makeup of employees override one's moral right to privacy of genetic information?

Anyone who would take the position on this issue that the interests of the employer ought in most cases to override the interests of the employee would likely contend that just as employers have a right to require physical examinations of those within their workforce, they also have a right to require genetic screening if they see fit. For example, it would not be controversial if an employer required a physical exam for a job involving heavy lifting; to hire someone with a bad back for such a position would not make economic sense. Along the same lines, it could be argued for the same reasons that an employer has a right to know if a particular candidate for a position carries, for instance, the gene for long QT syndrome, a cardiac tendency that can sometimes result in death, before a hiring decision is made.

Those who would argue the opposite point of view could offer at least two reasons for their opposition. One reason that could be offered against mandatory genetic screening in employment has to do with the lack of a direct causal relationship between a person's carrying a particular gene for a trait or condition and actually developing this trait or condition. For example, some scientists now claim they have isolated a particular "personality" gene whose carriers are predisposed towards thrill-seeking. Because studies of those who possess the gene show that such persons are also inclined to be quick-tempered, an employer might very well be interested in testing for this gene, since someone who angers easily could cause conflict in the workplace and reduce productivity. However, it could be argued that the thrill-seeking gene is just one influence in an individual's personal makeup; simply carrying the gene does not necessarily mean one will turn out to be a disruptive employee. Another reason to support an employee's moral right to privacy with respect to genetic screening is connected to the value of privacy in protecting democratic principles. Given that genes for medical conditions, such as sickle-cell anemia or Tay-Sach's disease, are not distributed equally across the general population, it could be claimed that mandatory genetic screening could open up the possibility that employers could use the results of such screening as a reason to discriminate against members of a particular racial or ethnic group.

David Resnik, writing on this issue in one of this chapter's readings, argues that although many employers have an economic interest in pursuing such mandatory testing, in most cases an employee's right to privacy should prevail over this interest. Exceptions ought to occur, he claims, only in order to make sure an employee can do the job at the moment, not at some future date. In other words, Resnik believes genetic screening is justified in order to reveal if a particular employee possesses a genetic condition that has a good chance of interfering with that employee's immediate job performance. Although he does not explicitly make this comparison, this use of mandatory genetic screening would be comparable to the use of mandatory drug testing in employment. While Resnik bases part of his argument on the facts about what genetic information can and cannot prove, he also makes use of five general criteria suggested by W. A. Parent for judging whether a particular invasion of privacy is justified in a particular situation. These criteria are worth keeping in mind in reflecting on the two other issues of privacy considered in this chapter.

Confidentiality and the AIDS Virus

While medical technology is obviously involved in testing individuals for the presence of the AIDS virus, the privacy issue in this context is not directly connected to this technology but rather to the relationship between the physician and the patient who tests positively for the virus. Traditionally, medical ethics has held that the center of medical practice, the physician-patient relationship, should be a relationship of confidentiality. This traditional principle of confidentiality has been questioned recently by those who believe that in certain situations a physician's moral obligations to others outweigh her obligation to the patient she is treating to keep that patient's medical condition confidential. Such questioning is largely directed at the relationship of confidentiality between a physician and a patient suffering from AIDS. One reason that those who support the view that guarantees of confidentiality should be dropped from this relationship has to do with the fact that physicians (according to the Hippocratic Oath) are supposed to "do no harm." By maintaining confidentiality in the case of AIDS patients, this argument goes, physicians are actually causing harm by not communicating to the sexual partners of AIDS patients the fact that they could be at risk for the disease, information which in turn could prompt these individuals to be tested and receive medical attention if necessary. "Doing no harm" on this view implies physicians have a social responsibility to break confidentiality. One could also take a more general position on this issue and claim that considerations of public health dictate that the principle of confidentiality be suspended in this particular context.

On the opposite side, those who would support the idea of maintaining confidentiality in this context often claim it plays a positive role in actually reducing the public health risks associated with AIDS. For a person considering being tested for HIV infection, the knowledge that a positive result would not necessarily be kept confidential could be sufficient to tip the balance of his deliberations against being tested. Thus, the argument goes, many more people who are HIV positive might infect others if physician-patient confidentiality were no longer to hold in this situation than if it were to continue to remain intact.

In this chapter, Grant Gillett, himself a physician, presents the view that physicians do have a moral obligation to inform others who might have possibly been infected by their patients with AIDS, even if such patients explicitly do not wish their condition to become known. While Gillett is primarily concerned with addressing the consequentialist argument given in the preceding paragraph for keeping confidentiality, he is also interested in providing deontological reasons to back up his view. On this line of reasoning, persons who insist on keeping their medical condition a secret from others and who understand that such secrecy could conceivably result in the death of others are, in Gillett's opinion, showing such a lack of respect for others that they have in essence placed themselves outside the moral community. The unconscionability of their behavior creates an obligation for the physician to in essence act as a "whistle blower" and inform others who have been sexually involved with the patient of the possibility that they might be infected with the AIDS virus.

Gillett argues that because the physician is obligated to inform only these particular others, and not employers or others who might have non-medically related interests in knowing whether or not a particular person has AIDS, those who are concerned that a loss of confidentiality would add to rather than detract from the public health risk of AIDS have nothing to worry about. One could, though, respond to Gillett's argument for a limited suspension of confidentiality in the case of physicians treating AIDS patients by questioning whether in practice such suspension would turn out to be as limited as Gillett thinks it could be. Because the past sexual partners who would be informed under Gillett's proposal are not restricted by constraints of confidentiality, they are under no obligation to keep to themselves the information given to them by the physician. Thus, arguably the concerns put forward by those who wish to maintain physician-patient confidentiality would not be addressed at this level. Other policy questions related to AIDS, such as the debate over whether or not screening for the presence of the HIV virus should be mandatory for selected groups of pregnant women, also involve issues of privacy and similar arguments on both sides of the matter as to whether or not such mandatory testing would act to reduce or worsen the public health risks associated with this particular disease.

Computers, Privacy, and Personal Information

Just as the development of genetic screening technologies has brought with it both benefits with respect to improved health and threats with respect to personal privacy, so the growth of computerized databases in American society has had both positive and negative impacts. On the positive side, it is now a relatively quick and simple matter for anyone with the appropriate technology to access vast quantities of information about whatever she might take an interest in. On the negative side, it continues to get easier every year for an organization with an interest in collecting information about a particular individual and with the computerized means to collect this information to do so, and thus potentially unjustly invade that individual's privacy. Such technology assists both government agencies and corporations in learning what an individual is like, including her likes and preferences, through storing and reviewing the "trail" she leaves behind her every time she makes a computerized transaction.

Those who would defend the right for these institutions to maintain large data banks of personal information base their claim on the fact that this information is valuable to these organizations in their decision making. For example, if a corporation is able to rely on stored computerized personal information in order to determine that individuals of a particular age, gender, and economic status are more likely to purchase a particular product than individuals falling outside that category, they would then be able to carry out new product research and development more efficiently and economically. Given that this is a free society, such organizations arguably have a right to collect and use personal information for these kinds of purposes. In other words, those who would defend these practices would say that although they do result in invasions of personal privacy, such invasions cannot be objected to on moral or legal grounds.

Defenders of this line of argument run up against a number of objections. At the heart of these objections rests the idea that many if not most of these invasions are morally unjustifiable. However, what would be the grounds for separating ones that are justifiable from ones that are not? Following Larry Hunter's account in his essay included among this chapter's selections, the line needs to be drawn at a point not connected to the gathering of information but rather to its use: Some uses of gathered personal information are legitimate whereas others are not. For Hunter, it appears as though the more traditional the use, the more its chances are of being legitimate. When a store uses computers to compile personal information on what shoppers are buying in order to keep inventory, they are using this information according to Hunter in a legitimate manner. The information being gathered is not being used to construct a profile on a particular consumer, but rather to get a picture of general trends associated with a body of consumers. They would, though, be crossing the line were they to use the information to try to influence what a person buys, say by putting particular consumers on particular mailing lists based on their understanding of those consumers' preferences.

Although he does not say so explicitly, the moral perspective behind this view appears to be a deontological one. The practice of computerized data-gathering that creates individual profiles which are then used without an individual's knowledge is in general wrong because the practice is being carried out in the absence of consent. Certain uses of electronically stored personal information constitute unjustifiable invasions of privacy because they do not treat individuals with the respect these individuals deserve. In other words, they do not treat individuals as autonomous beings.

Another perspective on the use of technology to create "personal profiles" is offered in this chapter by Richard Wasserstrom. Wasserstrom's concern about these profiles is more consequentialist in its orientation, as he sees in the ability of technology to "shadow" our lives by making detailed records of our actions a threat to the quality of our lives, in particular a threat to our ability to live our lives as we now do with an element of spontaneity and lack of deliberation. Interestingly enough, however, Wasserstrom does not immediately draw the conclusion from these concerns that we need to take stronger steps than we are presently taking in order to protect information about ourselves from becoming stored In data banks. A possible alternative to exerting more control over personal information, he suggests, is to take the opposite approach and become less concerned with trying to keep a line drawn in one's own life between what is private and what is not. Privacy, as he points out, is not always a good thing; it can be used to hide one's real (and perhaps morally deficient) self from the eyes of others. This response to the problem of technologically-aided invasions of privacy can be contrasted with more conventional views, such as those represented by Hunter, who proposes that in order to protect privacy in this context individuals should have the ability to treat personal information as if it were private property and be able to choose whether or not to make it available to those who have an interest in obtaining it. While both approaches can be found appealing for different reasons and also have different problems associated with them, they both serve to point out the significant problem caused to personal privacy associated with the rapid expansion of electronic means of data storage.

NOTE

1. Robert S. Bork discusses the right of privacy in *The Tempting of America: The Political Seduction of the Law*. (New York: Macmillan, 1990). See especially pp. 95-100.

Griswold v. Connecticut

Estelle T. Griswold, the executive director of the Planned Parenthood League of Connecticut, was arrested in 1961 on charges of providing information about contraception to married couples. Both using contraceptive devices and providing instructions on their use were offenses at that time under Connecticut state law. After being found guilty on these charges, Griswold appealed the decision to a higher court, which upheld her conviction. Griswold then appealed to the U.S. Supreme Court.

In reversing the lower court's decision in 1965, the Supreme Court delivered a landmark ruling. It interpreted the Constitution as guaranteeing a right of privacy, despite the fact that nowhere in this document is such a right explicitly mentioned. In expressing the opinion of the Court, Justice William O. Douglas pointed out that several amendments to the Constitution—such as the Fourth Amendment's protection against unreasonable searches and seizures—cast a "penumbra" of implied rights, without which the rights it does guarantee would be less efficacious. He identified the right to privacy as lying within this penumbra. In further support of this decision, Douglas drew upon the Ninth Amendment's recognition that the rights citizens actually have might exceed those specifically granted by the Constitution. Not all the justices accepted Douglas's opinion. In writing for the dissent, Justice Potter Stewart argued that it was a misinterpretation of the Constitution to read it as suggesting a right to privacy. Although he personally found little to be said in favor of the Connecticut law, it was not in his view unconstitutional.

Following *Griswold v. Connecticut*, other Supreme Court decisions extended the legal right to privacy beyond the limits of the marriage relationship. Of these decisions, the most controversial is still *Roe v. Wade*, which legalized abortion on the basis of a woman's right to privacy in choosing whether or not to terminate her pregnancy. (See Chapter 2, "The Abortion Struggle in America.")

Mr. Justice DOUGLAS Delivered
the Opinion of the Court

Appellant Griswold is Executive Director of the Planned Parenthood League of Connecticut. Appellant Buxton is a licensed physician and a professor at the Yale Medical School who served as Medical Director for the League at its Center in New Haven—a center open and operating from November 1 to November 10, 1961, when appellants were arrested.

They gave information, instruction, and medical advice to *married persons* as to the means of preventing conception. They examined the wife and prescribed the best contraceptive device or material for her use. Fees were usually charged, although some couples were serviced free.

---

381 U.S. 479 (1965). [Most citations omitted.]

The statutes whose constitutionality is involved in this appeal are §§53-32 and 54-196 of the General Statutes of Connecticut (1958 rev.). The former provides:

"Any person who uses any drug, medicinal article or instrument for the purpose of preventing conception shall be fined not less than fifty dollars or imprisoned not less than sixty days nor more than one year or be both fined and imprisoned."

Section 54-196 provides:

"Any person who assists, abets, counsels, causes, hires or commands another to commit any offense may be prosecuted and punished as if he were the principal offender."

The appellants were found guilty as accessories and fined $100 each, against the claim that the accessory statute as so applied violated the Fourteenth Amendment. The Appellate Division of the Circuit Court affirmed. The Supreme Court of Errors affirmed that judgment. We noted probable jurisdiction. . . .

The association of people is not mentioned in the Constitution nor in the Bill of Rights. The right to educate a child in a school of the parents' choice—whether public or private or parochial—is also not mentioned. Nor is the right to study any particular subject or any foreign language. Yet the First Amendment has been construed to include certain of those rights.

By Pierce v. Society of Sisters, the right to educate one's children as one chooses is made applicable to the States by the force of the First and Fourteenth Amendments. By Meyer v. State of Nebraska the same dignity is given the right to study the German language in a private school. In other words, the State may not, consistently with the spirit of the First Amendment, contract the spectrum of available knowledge. The right of freedom of speech and press includes not only the right to utter or to print, but the right to distribute, the right to receive, the right to read and freedom of inquiry, freedom of thought, and freedom to teach—indeed the freedom of the entire university community. Without those peripheral rights the specific rights would be less secure. And so we reaffirm the principle of the Pierce and the Meyer cases.

In NAACP v. State of Alabama, we protected the "freedom to associate and privacy in one's associations," noting that freedom of association was a peripheral First Amendment right. Disclosure of membership lists of a constitutionally valid association, we held, was invalid "as entailing the likelihood of a substantial restraint upon the exercise by petitioner's members of their right to freedom of association." In other words, the First Amendment has a penumbra where privacy is protected from governmental intrusion. In like context, we have protected forms of "association" that are not political in the customary sense but pertain to the social, legal, and economic benefit of the members. In Schware v. Board of Bar Examiners, we held it not permissible to bar a lawyer from practice, because he had once been a member of the Communist Party. The man's "association with that Party" was not shown to be "anything more than a political faith in a political party" and was not action of a kind proving bad moral character.

Those cases involved more than the "right of assembly"—a right that extends to all irrespective of their race or ideology. The right of "association," like the right of belief is more than the right to attend a meeting; it includes the right to express one's attitudes or philosophies by membership in a group or by affiliation with it or by other lawful means. Association in that context is a form of expression of opinion; and while it is not expressly included in the First Amendment its existence is necessary in making the express guarantees fully meaningful.

The foregoing cases suggest that specific guarantees in the Bill of Rights have penumbras, formed by emanations from those guarantees that help give them life and substance. Various guarantees create zones of privacy. The right of association contained in the penumbra of the First Amendment is one, as we have seen. The Third Amendment in its prohibition against the quartering of soldiers "in any house" in time of peace without the consent of the owner is another facet of that privacy. The Fourth Amendment explicitly affirms the "right of the people to be secure in their persons, houses, papers, and effects, against unreasonable searches and seizures." The Fifth Amendment in its Self-Incrimination Clause enables the citizen to create a zone of privacy which government may not force him to surrender to his detriment. The Ninth Amendment provides: "The enumeration in the Constitution, of certain rights, shall not be construed to deny or disparage others retained by the people."

The Fourth and Fifth Amendments were described in Boyd v. United States, 116 U.S. 616, 630, 6 S.Ct. 524, 532, 29 L.Ed. 746, as protection against all governmental invasions "of the sanctity of a man's home and the privacies of life. . . ."

The present case, then, concerns a relationship lying within the zone of privacy created by several fundamental constitutional guarantees. And it concerns a law which, in forbidding the *use* of contraceptives rather than regulating their manufacture or sale, seeks to achieve its goals by means having a maximum destructive impact upon that relationship. Such a law cannot stand in light of the familiar principle, so often applied by this Court, that a "governmental purpose to control or prevent activities constitutionally subject to state regulation may not be achieved by means which sweep unnecessarily broadly and thereby invade the area of protected freedoms." Would we allow the police to search the sacred precincts of marital bedrooms for telltale signs of the use of contraceptives? The very idea is repulsive to the notions of privacy surrounding the marriage relationship.

We deal with a right of privacy older than the Bill of Rights—older than our political parties, older than our school system. Marriage is a coming together for better or for worse, hopefully enduring, and intimate to the degree of being sacred. It is an association that promotes a way of life, not causes; a harmony in living, not political faiths; a bilateral loyalty, not commercial or social projects. Yet it is an association for as noble a purpose as any involved in our prior decisions.

Reversed. . . .

Mr. Justice STEWART,
Whom Mr. Justice BLACK Joins, Dissenting

Since 1879 Connecticut has had on its books a law which forbids the use of contraceptives by anyone. I think this is an uncommonly silly law. As a practical matter, the law is obviously unenforceable, except in the oblique context of the present case. As a philosophical matter, I believe the use of contraceptives in the relationship of marriage should be left to personal and private choice, based upon each individual's moral, ethical, and religious beliefs. As a matter of social policy, I think professional counsel about methods of birth control should be available to all, so that each individual's choice can be meaningfully made. But we are not asked in this case to say whether we think this law is unwise, or even asinine. We are asked to hold that it violates the United States Constitution. And that I cannot do.

In the course of its opinion the Court refers to no less than six Amendments to the Constitution: the First, the Third, the Fourth, the Fifth, the Ninth, and the Fourteenth. But the Court does not say which of these Amendments, if any, it thinks is infringed by this Connecticut law.

We *are* told that the Due Process Clause of the Fourteenth Amendment is not, as such, the "guide" in this case. With that much I agree. There is no claim that this law, duly enacted by the Connecticut Legislature, is unconstitutionally vague. There is not claim that the appellants were denied any of the elements of procedural due process at their trial, so as to make their convictions constitutionally invalid. And, as the Court says, the day has long passed since the Due Process Clause was regarded as a proper instrument for determining "the wisdom, need, and propriety" of state laws. . . .

As to the First, Third, Fourth, and Fifth Amendments, I can find nothing in any of them to invalidate this Connecticut law, even assuming that all those Amendments are fully applicable against the States.[1] It has not even been argued that this is a law "respecting an establishment of religion, or prohibiting the free exercise thereof."[2] And surely, unless the solemn process of constitutional adjudication is to descend to the level of a play on words, there is not involved here any abridgment of "the freedom of speech, or of the press; or the right of the people peaceably to assemble, and to petition the Government for a redress of grievances."[3] No soldier has been quartered in any house.[4] There has been no search, and no seizure.[5] Nobody has been compelled to be a witness against himself.[6]

The Court also quotes the Ninth Amendment. . . . But to say that the Ninth Amendment has anything to do with this case is to turn somersaults with history. The Ninth Amendment. . . was framed by James Madison and adopted by the States simply to make clear that the adoption of the Bill of Rights did not alter the plan that the *Federal* Government was to be a government of express and limited powers, and that all rights and powers not delegated to it were retained by the people and the individual States. Until today no member of this Court has ever suggested that the Ninth Amendment meant anything else, and the idea that a federal court could ever use the Ninth Amendment to annul a law passed by the elected representatives of the people of the State of Connecticut would have caused James Madison no little wonder.

What provision of the Constitution, then, does make this state law invalid? The Court says it is the right of privacy "created by several fundamental constitutional guarantees." With all deference, I can find no such general right of privacy in the Bill of Rights, in any other part of the Constitution, or in any case ever before decided by this Court.

At the oral argument in this case we were told that the Connecticut law does not "conform to current community standards." But it is not the function of this Court to decide cases on the basis of community standards. We are here to decide cases "agreeably to the Constitution and laws of the United States." It is the essence of judicial duty to subordinate our own personal views, our own ideas of what legislation is wise and what is not. If, as I should surely hope, the law before us does not reflect the standards of the people of Connecticut, the people of Connecticut can freely exercise their true Ninth and Tenth Amendment rights to persuade their elected representatives to repeal it. That is the constitutional way to take this law off the books.

NOTES

1. The Amendments in question were, as everyone knows, originally adopted as limitations upon the power of the newly created Federal Government, not as limitations upon the powers of the individual States. But the Court has held that many of the provisions of the first eight amendments are fully embraced by the Fourteenth Amendment as limitations upon state action, and some members of the Court have held the view that the adoption of the Fourteenth Amendment made every provision of the first eight amendments fully applicable against the States. See Adamson v. People of State of California, 332 U.S. 46, 68, 67 S.Ct. 1672, 1684 (dissenting opinion of Mr. Justice Black).

2. U.S. Constitution, Amendment I. To be sure, the injunction contained in the Connecticut statute coincides with the doctrine of certain religious faiths. But if that were enough to invalidate a law under the provisions of the First Amendment relating to religion, then most criminal laws would be invalidated. See, e.g., the Ten Commandments, The Bible, Exodus 20:2-17 (King James).

3. U.S. Constitution, Amendment I.

4. U.S. Constitution, Amendment III.

5. U.S. Constitution, Amendment IV.

6. U.S. Constitution, Amendment V.

Why Privacy Is Important
James Rachels

In this essay James Rachels, who was introduced in Chapter 3, focuses on the question, "Why does privacy matter?" Rachels first dismisses one popular response to this question: Privacy matters so that others will not get information about us that could be embarrassing or damaging to our own interests. As plausible as this view sounds, Rachels believes there is a deeper and more positive value to privacy than this, since privacy matters to persons even when they are not in a position of having anything to hide. Without the capability of controlling who has what information about us, he explains, we would suffer a significant loss. Most human beings are involved in a number of different social relationships: One might work with a number of different people, have a set of close friends who are not one's colleagues, and additionally have a spouse and children. In Rachels's view each type of social relationship brings with it a different type of behavior, and a different evaluation on one's part of what type of personal information it is appropriate to share. These differences in behavior and information sharing make the variety of these social relations possible. Thus, Rachels concludes, if there were no boundaries on the access that others can have to our personal information, we could not have the different types of relations that we enjoy having today.

I

Why, exactly, is privacy important to us? There is no one simple answer to this question, since people have a number of interests that may be harmed by invasions of their privacy.

> a. Privacy is sometimes necessary to protect people's interests in competitive situations. For example, it obviously would be a disadvantage to Bobby Fischer if he could not analyze the adjourned position in a chess game in private, without his opponent learning his results.
>
> b. In other cases someone may want to keep some aspect of his life or behavior private simply because it would be embarrassing for other people to know about it. There is a splendid example of this in John Barth's novel *End of the Road*. The narrator of the story, Jake Horner, is with Joe Morgan's wife, Rennie, and they are approaching the Morgan house where Joe is at home alone:
>
> > "Want to eavesdrop?" I whispered impulsively to Rennie. "Come on, it's great! See the animals in their natural habitat."
> > Rennie looked shocked. "What for?"

From *Philosophy & Public Affairs* 4 (Summer 1975), 323–333.

"You mean you never spy on people when they're alone? It's wonderful! Come on, be a sneak! It's the most unfair thing you can do to a person."

"You disgust me, Jake!" Rennie hissed. "He's just reading. You don't know Joe at all, do you?"

"What does that mean?"

"Real people aren't any different when they're alone. No masks. What you see of them is authentic."

. . . . Quite reluctantly, she came over to the window and peeped in beside me.

It is indeed the grossest of injustices to observe a person who believes himself to be alone. Joe Morgan, back from his Boy Scout meeting, had evidently intended to do some reading, for there were books lying open on the writing table and on the floor beside the bookcase. But Joe wasn't reading. He was standing in the exact center of the bare room, fully dressed, smartly executing military commands. About *face!* Right *dress!* 'Ten-*shun!* Parade *Rest!* He saluted briskly, his cheeks blown out and his tongue extended, and then proceeded to cavort about the room—spinning, pirouetting, bowing, leaping, kicking. I watched entranced by his performance, for I cannot say that in my strangest moments (and a bachelor has strange ones) I have surpassed him. Rennie trembled from head to foot.[1]

The scene continues even more embarrassingly.

c. There are several reasons why medical records should be kept private, having to do with the consequences to individuals of facts about them becoming public knowledge. "The average patient doesn't realize the importance of the confidentiality of medical records. Passing out information on venereal disease can wreck a marriage. Revealing a pattern of alcoholism or drug abuse can result in a man's losing his job or make it impossible for him to obtain insurance protection."[2]

d. When people apply for credit (or for large amounts of insurance or for jobs of certain types) they are often investigated, and the result is a fat file of information about them. Now there is something to be said in favor of such investigations, for business people surely do have the right to know whether credit-applicants are financially reliable. The trouble is that all sorts of other information goes into such files, for example, information about the applicant's sex-life, his political views, and so forth. Clearly it is unfair for one's application for credit to be influenced by such irrelevant matters.

These examples illustrate the variety of interests that may be protected by guaranteeing people's privacy, and it would be easy to give further examples of the same general sort. However, I do not think that examining such cases will provide a complete understanding of the importance of privacy, for two reasons.

First, these cases all involve relatively unusual sorts of situations, in which someone has something to hide or in which information about a person might provide someone with a reason for mistreating him in some way. Thus, reflection on these cases gives us little help in understanding the value which privacy has in *normal* or *ordinary* situations. By this I mean situations in which there is nothing embarrassing or shameful or unpopular in what we are doing, and nothing ominous or threatening connected with its possible disclosure. For example, even married couples whose sex-lives are normal (whatever that is), and so who have nothing to be ashamed of, by even the most conventional standards, and certainly nothing to be blackmailed about, do not want their bedrooms bugged. We need an account of the value which privacy has for us, not only in the few special cases but in the many common and unremarkable cases as well.

Second, even those invasions of privacy that *do* result in embarrassment or in some specific harm to our other interests are objectionable on other grounds. A woman may rightly be upset if her credit-rating is adversely affected by a report about her sexual behavior because the use of such information is unfair; however, she may also object to the report simply because she feels—as most of us do—that her sex-life is *nobody else's business*. This, I think, is an extremely important point. We have a "sense of privacy" which is violated in such affairs, and this sense of privacy cannot adequately be explained merely in terms of our fear of being embarrassed or disadvantaged in one of these obvious ways. An adequate account of privacy should help us to understand what makes something "someone's business" and why intrusions into things that are "none of your business" are, as such, offensive.

These considerations lead me to suspect that there is something important about privacy which we shall miss if we confine our attention to examples such as (a), (b), (c), and (d). In what follows I will try to bring out what this something is.

I want now to give an account of the value of privacy based on the idea that there is a close connection between our ability to control who has access to us and to information about us, and our ability to create and maintain different sorts of social relationships with different people. According to this account, privacy is necessary if we are to maintain the variety of social relationships with other people that we want to have, and that is why it is important to us. By a "social relationship" I do not mean anything especially unusual or technical; I mean the sort of thing which we usually have in mind when we say of two people that they are friends or that they are husband and wife or that one is the other's employer.

The first point I want to make about these relationships is that, often, there are fairly definite patterns of behavior associated with them. Our relationships with other people determine, in large part, how we act toward them and how they behave toward us. Moreover, there are *different* patterns of behavior associated with different relationships. Thus a man may be playful and affectionate with his children (although sometimes firm), businesslike with his employees, and respectful and polite with his mother-in-law. And to his close friends he may show a side of his personality that others never see—perhaps he is secretly a poet, and rather shy about it, and shows his verse only to his best friends.

It is sometimes suggested that there is something deceitful or hypocritical about such differences in behavior. It is suggested that underneath all the role-playing there is the "real" person, and that the various "masks" that we wear in dealing with some people are some sort of phony disguise that we use to conceal our "true" selves from them. I take it that this is what is behind Rennie's remark, in the passage from Barth, that, "*Real* people aren't any different when they're alone. No masks. What you see of them is authentic." According to this way of looking at things, the fact that we observe different standards of conduct with different people is merely a sign of dishonesty. Thus the cold-hearted businessman who reads poetry to his friends is "really" a gentle poetic soul whose businesslike demeanor in front of his employees is only a false front; and the man who curses and swears when talking to his friends, but who would never use such language around his mother-in-law, is just putting on an act for her.

This, I think, is quite wrong. Of course the man who does not swear in front of his mother-in-law may be just putting on an act so that, for example, she will not disinherit him, when otherwise he would curse freely in front of her without caring what she thinks. But it may be that his conception of how he ought to behave with his mother-in-law is very different from his conception of how he may behave with his friends. Or it may not be appropriate for him to swear around *her* because "she is not that sort of person." Similarly, the businessman may be putting up a false front for his employees, perhaps because he dislikes his work and has to make a continual, disagreeable effort to maintain the role. But on the other hand he may be, quite comfortably and naturally, a businessman with a certain conception of how it is appropriate for a businessman to behave; and this conception is compatible with his also being a husband, a father, and a friend, with different conceptions of how it is appropriate to behave with his wife, his children, and his friends. There need be nothing dishonest or hypocritical in any of this, and neither side of his personality need be the "real" him, any more than any of the others.

It is not merely accidental that we vary our behavior with different people according to the different social relationships that we have with them. Rather, the different patterns of behavior are (partly) what define the different relationships; they are an important part of what makes the different relationships what they are. The relation of friendship, for example, involves bonds of affection and special obligations, such as the duty of loyalty, which friends owe to one another; but it is also an important part of what it means to have a friend that we welcome his company, that we confide in him, that we tell him things about ourselves, and that we show him sides of our personalities which we would not tell or show to just anyone. Suppose I believe that someone is my close friend, and then I discover that he is worried about his job and is afraid of being fired. But, while he has discussed this situation with several other people, he has not mentioned it at all to me. And then I learn that he writes poetry, and that this is an important part of his life; but while he has shown his poems to many other people, he has not shown them to me. Moreover, I learn that he behaves with his other friends in a much more informal way than he behaves with me, that he makes a point of seeing them socially much more than he sees me, and so on. In the absence of some special explanation of his behavior, I would have to conclude that we are not as close as I had thought.

The same general point can be made about other sorts of human relationships: businessman to employee, minister to congregant, doctor to patient, husband to wife, parent to child, and so on. In each case, the sort of relationship that people have to one another involves a conception of how it is appropriate for them to behave with each other, and what is more, a conception of the kind and degree of knowledge concerning one another which it is appropriate for them to have. (I will say more about this later.) I do not mean to imply that such relationships are, or ought to be, structured in exactly the same way for everyone. Some parents are casual and easy-going with their children, while others are more formal and reserved. Some doctors want to be friends with at least some of their patients; others are businesslike with all. Moreover, the requirements of social roles may vary from community to community—for example, the role of wife may not require exactly the same sort of behavior in rural Alabama as it does in New York or New Guinea. And, the requirements of social roles may change: the women's liberation movement is making an attempt to redefine the husband-wife relationship. The examples that I have been giving are drawn, loosely speaking, from contemporary American society; but this is mainly a matter of convenience. The only point that I want to insist on is that *however* one conceives one's relations with other people, there is inseparable from that conception an idea of how it is appropriate to behave with and around them, and what information about oneself it is appropriate for them to have.

The point may be underscored by observing that new types of social institutions and practices sometimes make possible new sorts of human relationships, which in turn make it appropriate to behave around people, and to say things in their presence, that would have been inappropriate before. "Group therapy" is a case in point. Many psychological patients find the prospect of group therapy unsettling, because they will have to speak openly to the group about intimate matters. They sense that there is something inappropriate about this: one simply does not reveal one's deepest feelings to strangers. Our aspirations, our problems, our frustrations and disappointments are things that we may confide to our husbands and wives, our friends, and perhaps to some others—but it is out of the question to speak of such matters to people that we do not even know. Resistance to this aspect of group therapy is overcome when the patients begin to think of each other not as strangers but as *fellow members of the group*. The definition of a kind of relation between them

makes possible frank and intimate conversation which would have been totally out of place when they were merely strangers.

All of this has to do with the way that a crucial part of our lives—our
relations with other people—is organized, and as such its importance to us
can hardly be exaggerated. Thus we have good reason to object to anything
that interferes with these relationships and makes it difficult or impossible for
us to maintain them in the way that we want to. Conversely, because our
ability to control who has access to us, and who knows what about us, allows
us to maintain the variety of relationships with other people that we want to
have, it is, I think, one of the most important reasons why we value privacy.

First, consider what happens when two close friends are joined by a casual acquaintance. The character of the group changes; and one of the changes
is that conversation about intimate matters is now out of order. Then suppose these friends could *never* be alone; suppose there were always third
parties (let us say casual acquaintances or strangers) intruding. Then they could
do either of two things. They could carry on as close friends do, sharing
confidences, freely expressing their feelings about things, and so on. But this
would mean violating their sense of how it is appropriate to behave around
casual acquaintances or strangers. Or they could avoid doing or saying anything which they think inappropriate to do or say around a third party. But
this would mean that they could no longer behave with one another in the
way that friends do and further that, eventually, they would no longer *be*
close friends.

Again, consider the differences between the way that a husband and wife
behave when they are alone and the way they behave in the company of
third parties. Alone, they may be affectionate, sexually intimate, have their
fights and quarrels, and so on; but with others, a more "public" face is in order.
If they could never be alone together, they would either have to abandon the
relationship that they would otherwise have as husband and wife or else
behave in front of others in ways they now deem inappropriate.

These considerations suggest that we need to separate our associations, at
least to some extent, if we are to maintain a system of different relationships
with different people. Separation allows us to behave with certain people in
the way that is appropriate to the sort of relationship we have with them,
without at the same time violating our sense of how it is appropriate to behave with, and in the presence of, others with whom we have a different kind
of relationship. Thus, if we are to be able to control the relationships that we
have with other people, we must have control over who has access to us.

We now have an explanation of the value of privacy in ordinary situations in which we have nothing to hide. The explanation is that, even in the
most common and unremarkable circumstances, we regulate our behavior
according to the kinds of relationships we have with the people around us. If
we cannot control who has access to us, sometimes including and sometimes
excluding various people, then we cannot control the patterns of behavior
we need to adopt (this is one reason why privacy is an aspect of liberty) or

the kinds of relations with other people that we will have. But what about our feeling that certain facts about us are "simply nobody else's business"? Here, too, I think the answer requires reference to our relationships with people. If someone is our doctor, then it literally is his business to keep track of our health; if someone is our employer, then it literally is his business to know what salary we are paid; our financial dealings literally are the business of the people who extend us credit; and so on. In general, a fact about ourselves is someone's business if there is a specific social relationship between us which entitles them to know. We are often free to choose whether or not to enter into such relationships, and those who want to maintain as much privacy as possible will enter them only reluctantly. What we cannot do is accept such a social role with respect to another person and then expect to retain the same degree of privacy relative to him that we had before. Thus, if we are asked how much money we have in the bank, we cannot say, "It's none of your business," to our banker, to prospective creditors, or to our spouses, because their relationships with us do entitle them to know. But, at the risk of being boorish, we could say that to others with whom we have no such relationship. . . .

NOTES

1. John Barth, *End of the Road* (New York, 1960), pp. 57–58.
2. Dr. Malcolm Todd, President of the A.M.A., quoted in the *Miami Herald*, 26 October, 1973, p. 18–A.

Privacy, Morality, and the Law
W. A. Parent

W. A. Parent is a professor of philosophy at Santa Clara University and the co-editor of *The Constitution of Rights: Human Dignity and American Values* (1992).

In the following essay, Parent first criticizes several popular definitions of privacy on the grounds that they do not adequately reflect what privacy really is. He proposes an alternative definition of privacy as the "condition of not having undocumented personal knowledge about one possessed by others." Using his definition of privacy as a starting point, Parent next suggests why privacy is worth defending as a basic and important moral value. Unless society protects the value of privacy, he warns, its members could become vulnerable to exploitation by others, or become objects of unwarranted derision. Perhaps most importantly, society needs to protect individual privacy out of respect for individual autonomy: Most people simply do not want others to have access to the details of their lives without their permission. In the final part of this essay, Parent turns to the question of how to determine whether a particular act counts as a wrongful invasion of privacy, and offers some general guidelines for how this question might be answered.

I. THE DEFINITION OF PRIVACY

Privacy is the condition of not having undocumented personal knowledge about one possessed by others. A person's privacy is diminished exactly to the degree that others possess this kind of knowledge about him. I want to stress that what I am defining is the condition of privacy, not the right to privacy. My definition is new, and I believe it to be superior to all of the other conceptions that have been proposed. . . .

A full explication of the personal knowledge definition requires that we clarify the concept of personal information. My suggestion is that it be understood to consist of *facts* about a person which most individuals in a given society at a given time do not want widely known about themselves. They may not be concerned that a few close friends, relatives, or professional associates know these facts, but they would be very much concerned if the information passed beyond this limited circle. In contemporary America facts about a person's sexual preferences, drinking or drug habits, income, the state of his or her marriage and health belong to the class of personal information. Ten years from now some of these facts may be a part of everyday conversation; if so their disclosure would not diminish individual privacy.

This account of personal information, which makes it a function of existing cultural norms and social practices, needs to be broadened a bit to accommodate a particular and unusual class of cases of the following sort. Most of

From *Philosophy & Public Affairs* 12 (Fall 1983), 269-288.

us don't care if our height, say, is widely known. But there are a few persons who are extremely sensitive about their height (or weight or voice pitch). They might take extreme measures to ensure that other people not find it out. For such individuals height is a very personal matter. Were someone to find it out by ingenious snooping we should not hesitate to talk about an invasion of privacy.

Let us, then, say that personal information consists of facts which most persons in a given society choose not to reveal about themselves (except to close friends, family, . . .) or of facts about which a particular individual is acutely sensitive and which he therefore does not choose to reveal about himself, even though most people don't care if these same facts are widely known about themselves. . . .

I believe the personal knowledge definition isolates the conceptual one of privacy, its distinctive and unique meaning. It does not appropriate ideas which properly belong to other concepts. Unfortunately the three most popular definitions do just this, confusing privacy with quite different values.

1. *Privacy consists of being let alone.* Warren and Brandeis were the first to advocate this broad definition.[1] Brandeis movingly appealed to it again in his celebrated dissent to the U.S. Supreme Court's majority ruling in *Olmstead v. U.S.*[2] Objecting to the Court's view that telephone wiretapping does not constitute a search and seizure, Brandeis delivered an impassioned defense of every citizens' right to be let alone, which he called our most cherished entitlement. . . .

What proponents of the Brandeis definition fail to see is that there are innumerable ways of failing to let a person alone which have nothing to do with his privacy. Suppose, for instance, that A clubs B on the head or repeatedly insults him. We should describe and evaluate such actions by appeal to concepts like force, violence, and harassment. Nothing in the way of analytical clarity and justificatory power is lost if the concept of privacy is limited, as I have suggested that it be, to cases involving the acquisition of undocumented personal knowledge. Inflationary conceptions of privacy invite muddled reasoning.

2. *Privacy consists of a form of autonomy or control over significant personal matters.* "If the right to privacy means anything, it is the right of the individual, married or single, to be free from unwarranted government invasion into matters so fundamentally affecting a person as the decision whether to bear or beget a child."[3] With these words, from the Supreme Court case of *Eisenstadt v. Baird*, Mr. Justice Brennan expresses a second influential theory of privacy.

Indeed, definitions of privacy in terms of control dominate the literature. Perhaps the most favored among them equates privacy with the control over personal information about oneself. . . .

All of these definitions should be jettisoned. To see why, consider the example of a person who voluntarily divulges all sorts of intimate, personal, and undocumented information about himself to a friend. She is doubtless exercising control, in a paradigm sense of the term, over personal information about herself as well as over (cognitive) access to herself. But we would not and should not say that in doing so she is preserving or protecting her privacy. On the contrary, she is voluntarily relinquishing much of her privacy. People can and do choose to give up privacy for many reasons. An adequate conception of privacy must allow for this fact. Control definitions do not. . . .

3. *Privacy is the limitation on access to the self.* This definition, defended by Garrett and Gavison[4] among others, has the virtue of separating privacy from liberty. But it still is unsatisfactory. If we understand "access" to mean something like "physical proximity," then the difficulty becomes that there are other viable concepts which much more precisely describe what is at stake by limiting such access. Among these concepts I would include personal property, solitude, and peace. If, on the other hand, "access" is interpreted as referring to the acquisition of personal knowledge, we're still faced with a seemingly intractable counterexample. A taps B's phone and overhears many of her conversations, including some of a very intimate nature. Official restraints have been imposed on A's snooping, though. He must obtain permission from a judge before listening in on B. This case shows that limitation of cognitive access does not imply privacy. . . .

II. THE VALUE OF PRIVACY

. . . [There] are very good reasons why people in societies like ours desire privacy as I have defined it. First of all, if others manage to obtain sensitive personal knowledge about us they will by that very fact acquire power over us. Their power could then be used to our disadvantage. The possibilities for exploitation become very real. The definite connection between harm and the invasion of privacy explains why we place a value on not having undocumented personal information about ourselves widely known.

Second, as long as we live in a society where individuals are generally intolerant of life styles, habits, and ways of thinking that differ significantly from their own, and where human foibles tend to become the object of scorn and ridicule, our desire for privacy will continue unabated. No one wants to be laughed at and made to feel ashamed of himself. And we all have things about us which, if known, might very well trigger these kinds of unfeeling and wholly unwarranted responses.

Third, we desire privacy out of a sincere conviction that there are certain facts about us which other people, particularly strangers and casual acquaintances, are not entitled to know. This conviction is constitutive of "the liberal ethic," a conviction centering on the basic thesis that individuals are not to be treated as mere property of the state but instead are to be respected as autonomous, independent beings with unique aims to fulfill. These aims, in turn, will perforce lead people down life's separate paths. Those of us educated under this liberal ideology feel that our lives are our own business (hence the importance of personal liberty) and that personal facts about our lives are for the most part ours alone to know. The suggestion that all personal facts should be made available for public inspection is contrary to this view. Thus, our desire for privacy is to a large extent a matter of principle.

For most people, this desire is perfectly innocent. We are not seeking to hurt or disadvantage anyone by exercising it. Unquestionably some people at times demand privacy for fraudulent purposes, for example, to hide discreditable facts about themselves from future employers who are entitled to this information. . . . But not everyone values privacy for this reason, and, even for those who do, misrepresentation is most often not the only or the overriding motive.

So there are several good reasons why we hold privacy to be an important value, one worth arguing for, and defending from unwarranted invasion. Now I want to suggest that anyone who deliberately and without justification frustrates or contravenes our desire for privacy violates the distinctively liberal, moral principle of respect for persons. Let us say that A frustrates B's desire for privacy if he invades B's privacy and B knows it. A acts in contravention of B's desire for privacy if he invades B's privacy without B's knowing it. Assuming that A has no justification for doing either, we can and should accuse him of acting in disregard of B's own desires and interests. A's action displays contempt for B in the sense that it is undertaken with no effort to identify with her life purposes or to appreciate what the fulfillment of these purposes might mean to her. Specifically by gratuitously or indiscriminately invading B's privacy (I will explain these terms shortly), A manifests disrespect for B in the sense that he ignores or counts as having no significance B's desire, spawned and nurtured by the liberal values of her society, not to have personal facts about herself known by ingenious or persistent snooping.[5]

The above argument establishes that privacy is indeed a moral value for persons who also prize freedom and individuality. That we should seek to protect it against unwarranted invasion should come, then, as no surprise. Advocating a moral right to privacy comprises an integral part of this effort. It expresses our conviction that privacy should only be infringed under exigent circumstances and for the most compelling reasons, for example, law enforcement and health care provision. . . .

III. CRITERIA OF WRONGFUL INVASION

Which invasions of privacy are justifiable and which are not? A complete conception of the right to privacy must address this question, providing general criteria of wrongful invasion, which will then have to be applied to specific cases. . . .

The following questions are central to assessing alleged violations of the right to privacy:

1. For what purpose(s) is the undocumented personal knowledge sought?
2. Is this purpose a legitimate and important one?
3. Is the knowledge sought through invasion of privacy relevant to its justifying purpose?
4. Is invasion of privacy the only or the least offensive means of obtaining the knowledge?
5. What restrictions or procedural restraints have been placed on the privacy-invading techniques?
6. What protection is to be afforded the personal knowledge once it has been acquired?

The first four questions all have to do with the rationale for invading privacy. We can say that the right to privacy is violated by *gratuitous* invasions and that these occur when: there is no purpose at all to them; when the purpose is less than compelling; when the personal facts sought have nothing to do with the justifying purposes; when the personal information could have been obtained by less intrusive measures. Among the legitimate purposes for acquiring undocumented personal information are efficient law enforcement, confirmation of eligibility criteria set forth in various government welfare programs, and the compilation of statistical data concerning important behavioral trends.

Question 5 pertains to the actual invasion of privacy itself. We can say that the right to privacy is violated by *indiscriminate* invasions and that these occur when insufficient procedural safeguards have been imposed on the techniques employed so that either: all sorts of personal information, some germane to the investigation but some totally irrelevant thereto, is obtained; or persons with no business knowing the personal facts acquired are allowed to gain cognitive access to them. One can argue against a proposed invasion of privacy on the grounds that it is too likely to be indiscriminate in either of these two senses.

Question 6 pertains to postinvasion safeguards. We can say that the right to privacy is violated when the undocumented personal information acquired is not adequately protected against unwarranted cognitive intrusion or unauthorized uses. It is also violated, of course, by actual instances of such intrusions and uses.

Let us look at a concrete example. Suppose a large city is faced with the growing problem of welfare fraud. It decides that to combat this problem an elaborate system of surveillance must be initiated. Personal information regarding welfare recipients' income, family status, sexual habits, and spending habits is to be obtained. Search warrants are obtained permitting unlimited surveillance and specifying the kind of information being sought. Once obtained the information is to be stored on magnetic tapes and kept in the welfare department.

Any person who takes the right to privacy seriously will raise the following questions and make the following observations about this city's (C's) action:

i. C presents no arguments or evidence in support of its belief that the problem of welfare fraud can be solved by resorting to large-scale surveillance. We should demand that C do so.

ii. C presents no arguments or evidence showing that surveillance is the only way to acquire the relevant personal information. Did it first try to obtain knowledge of welfare recipients' life styles by asking them about it or sending them questionnaires? Were there other, less intensive measures available for acquiring this knowledge?

iii. Search warrants permitting unlimited surveillance are insufficiently discriminating. So are warrants which do not particularly describe the places to be observed and the facts to be gathered. C should have insisted that the warrants place restrictions on the time periods of surveillance as well as on its scope.

iv. Why is it necessary to acquire information about welfare recipients' sexual habits? How is this knowledge relevant to the objective of eradicating fraud?

v. What kind of security does C intend to provide for the magnetic tapes containing the acquired information? Who will enjoy access to these tapes? Will they eventually be erased or destroyed? C has the duty to guard against the potential abuse of the stored facts.

I hope this brief analysis is helpful in isolating some of the crucial issues and difficult questions that must be confronted when applying the right of privacy to particular cases. Often there will be strong disagreement over whether proposed programs of physical, psychological, and data surveillance are gratuitous or indiscriminate. This is to be expected. The results of these disputes will determine the contours of the privacy right. . . .

NOTES

1. Samuel Warren and Louis Brandeis, "The Right to Privacy," *The Harvard Law Review*, 4 (1890): 205-07.
2. *Olmstead v. U.S.*, 277 U.S. 438 (1928): 475-76.
3. *Eisenstadt v. Baird*, 405 U.S. 438 (1972): 453.
4. Roland Garrett, "The Nature of Privacy," *Philosophy Today* 18 (1974): 264; and Ruth Gavison, "Privacy and the Limits of the Law," *Yale Law Journal* 89 (1980): 428.
5. I don't mean to identify the liberal principle of respect for persons with Kant's conception of respect for humanity. Kant does not formulate his conception in terms of what persons desire. Instead he focuses on the property of rationality that all persons possess and that, in his view, confers intrinsic worth upon them.

Genetic Privacy in Employment
David B. Resnik

Employers have historically always had an interest in the physical condition of their potential and prospective employees, due to their desire to have a healthy and productive workforce and to keep down their costs of providing health care. As genetic screening techniques continue to improve, one can expect more and more employers to take an interest in screening employees to see if they are carrying the "genetic markers" for disabling conditions such as alcoholism or degenerative diseases such as Parkinson's disease or Alzheimer's, which could conceivably interfere with work performance at great expense to the companies involved. When, though, does an employer have a right to such personal information, and when does asking for it constitute an unjust invasion of privacy?

David B. Resnik, a philosopher at the University of Wyoming, offers an answer to this question in the following selection. Taking into account both W. A. Parent's guidelines for wrongful invasion of privacy described in the previous essay, as well as the facts about what can be learned from genetic information, Resnik concludes that employers can legitimately invade the "genetic privacy" of employees only for the purposes of determining if an employee's immediate work performance might be hampered by a particular medical condition or disease. Collecting genetic information for other reasons, such as to cut down on the costs of health care, would for Resnik constitute a wrongful invasion of privacy.

I. INTRODUCTION

Recent and projected advances in molecular genetics and in genetic screening technology will bring us a wealth of information regarding genetic diseases, abnormalities, and predispositions. This new knowledge will most certainly have positive effects on medicine and health care, but it could also have detrimental consequences for privacy. Employers, insurance companies, governments, and other agencies will try to gain access to genetic information in order to increase profits and efficiency and decrease liabilities and risks. In order to insure that these advances in genetics do not compromise privacy, it is important to formulate a policy regarding the use of genetic information before our brave new science and technology get out of control. In this paper, I shall take some steps toward that goal by proposing some guidelines for the disclosure of genetic information in employment. I shall argue that the moral right to privacy allows employees to restrict their employers' access to genetic information in most situations, but that employers may invade an employee's genetic privacy *only if* such an invasion meets criteria for a legitimate (or justified) invasion.

From *Public Affairs Quarterly* 7 (January 1993), 47–56.

II. THE RIGHT TO PRIVACY

It is not my aim in this paper to defend a definition of privacy or explore the moral basis of privacy.... According to Parent, the right to privacy depends on a prior conception of privacy. Privacy, for Parent, "is the condition of not having undocumented personal knowledge about one possessed by others."[1]...

Given this conception of privacy, Parent defines the moral right to privacy as a "right not to become the victim of wrongful invasions [of privacy]."[2] The moral right to privacy is not the right to not have privacy invaded, since there are legitimate invasions of privacy; it is a right not to have privacy *wrongly* invaded.... So what counts as a wrongful invasion of privacy? For the purposes of this paper, I shall define a wrongful invasion as one that is not legitimate (or justified). A legitimate invasion is an invasion of privacy which meets *all* of the following criteria (or necessary conditions); a wrongful one does not:[3]

A. *Justification.* Good reasons or purposes justify the invasion.
B. *Relevancy.* The information obtained by the invasion is relevant to the reasons or purposes of the invasion.
C. *Intrusiveness.* The invasion uses the least intrusive means of obtaining the information.
D. *Specificity.* The invasion is discriminate and has procedural restraints and safeguards.
E. *Secrecy.* The invasion has post-invasion safeguards to prevent the unwarranted disclosure of information.

III. PRIVACY IN EMPLOYMENT

Given that we have a right to privacy, how does employment affect this right? This question raises a number issues concerning employee rights and the employee-employer relationship. . . . [I]n order to posit a conceptual framework for addressing the question of genetic privacy in employment, . . . [I] shall utilize a contractarian model of the employee-employer relationship and employee rights.[4] . . .

According to the contractarian model, the employee-employer relationship is a business contract between consenting adults. In the contract, the employee agrees to provide the employer with goods and services in return for money, goods, or other forms of compensation. In addition, the employer may entrust the employee with tools, property, information, and various goods in order to enable her to do her job. This contract will be valid only if a) both parties are responsible and autonomous; and b) both parties respect the rights claims of other contractees. People do not lose their right to privacy when they gain or seek employment; on the contrary, people cannot become employees unless they have rights and these rights are respected.

Employers can legitimately gain access to personal information about their employees (or prospective employees), according to the contractarian approach, in order to insure the validity of the employee-employer contract. Employers need to have this information in order to determine whether their employees will be able to satisfactorily fulfill the duties and responsibilities outlined by the employee's job description in the contract. Employers can legitimately gain access to certain kinds of information about their employees, provided that they continue to respect their employees' privacy rights. In other words, employers can invade employee privacy only when this invasion would qualify as a legitimate invasion of privacy according to the criteria listed above. On the other hand, if an employee (or prospective employee) refuses to disclose certain kinds of information to her employer (or prospective employer), and this disclosure would qualify as a legitimate invasion, then her employer is justified in refusing to hire her (or in firing her).

Having established a conceptual framework for discussing privacy in employment, I am in a better position to answer the central question of this paper: what are the conditions for an employer's legitimate invasion of an employee's genetic privacy? Before answering this question, I need to discuss some facts about genetic information and how it is acquired, since these facts will help us determine what constitutes a legitimate invasion of genetic privacy.

IV. GENETIC INFORMATION

Nature vs. Nurture

Some traits, such as sex, are determined entirely by our genes, but most traits are determined by both genetic and environmental factors. Although one might claim that possession of a certain gene gives individuals a predisposition for developing a disease (or trait) whether this predisposition is realized depends on environmental factors.

Causal vs. Statistical Connections

The causal pathway from genetic information, encoded in DNA, to an adult human being is incredibly complex, involving thousands of different genes and millions of different chemical reactions. Most traits are not determined by one gene or one environmental factor, but by many different genes and environmental factors. Given this complex interplay of genes and the environment, we can rarely establish a strong causal connection between possessing a genetic characteristic and developing a phenotypic trait; more often than not we must settle for a statistical connection. We may be able to show that possessing a gene gives one a high probability or risk of developing a trait, but it is very difficult to show that a gene causes or determines a trait.

Timing

Although many genes produce their effects throughout a person's entire life, other genes produce their effects during specific times in a person's life span. The important consequence of this fact is that a piece of genetic information might indicate that a person is likely to develop a disease at some time in their life, but this period may not coincide with their period of employment.

Treatment

We can use genetic information to cure or help people, rather than to stigmatize them or seal their fate. As we learn more about human genetics, we also learn how to treat (or prevent) genetic diseases. In the future, we may be able to diagnose and treat a wide variety of genetically based illnesses, such as heart disease, diabetes, and cancer.

Testing

In the past, the only way to acquire genetic information about a person would be to do a pedigree analysis of their family tree. However, pedigree analysis is unreliable and limited because it is an indirect method of detecting the presence of genes. Due to advances in biotechnology, we now have a more reliable and powerful method for determining an individual's genetic constitution, genetic screening. Genetic screening is more reliable and powerful than pedigree analysis because it allows scientists to directly examine an individual's genetic material through microscopy or biochemical analysis. In principle, one can give genetic screening tests during any stage of an individual's development, including the fetal stage. Genetic screening is still in its infancy, and it is not perfectly reliable or accurate, but in the foreseeable future it should be possible to use this technology to produce an entire genetic blueprint for any individual—the total gene screen.

V. LEGITIMATE INVASIONS
OF GENETIC PRIVACY

Given this brief discussion of genetic information, I am in a position to apply my conceptual framework to the issue of genetic privacy in employment. My main thesis in this section is that invasions of genetic privacy are legitimate *only if* they meet all five of the criteria for invasion discussed in section II. If an invasion of genetic privacy fails to meet any one of these criteria, then it is a wrongful invasion. In order to defend my main thesis, I shall discuss each criterion in the context of human genetics.

1. *Justification.* The first criterion that an invasion needs to meet is that it must be done for good reasons or purposes. An employer's primary reason for invading genetic privacy is to validate the employee-employer contract. An employer may need to acquire information about an employee's genetic constitution in order to insure that she is able to satisfactorily fulfill her duties and obligations outlined in the job description. Since this reason already justifies the disclosure of many types of information to employers, such as education, work

record, and so on, it could also be used to justify the disclosure of
genetic information, provided that other conditions are met. . . .

2. *Relevancy.* Assuming that the primary justification for invading genetic privacy is validation of the employee-employer contract, then
   the information sought must be relevant to this purpose. In other
   words, invasions of genetic privacy are legitimate provided that the
   information sought is job-relevant. Can genetic information ever be
   job-relevant? My preliminary answer to this question is "sometimes
   yes," although I hasten to add that the concept of "job-relevancy"is
   extremely context-dependent: it varies according to the job-description and the type of information sought.

Despite these misgivings, I do not think we must settle for a case-by-case
approach to relevancy. My earlier discussion of genetic information should be
useful in formulating some general guidelines for determining whether a piece
of genetic information is job-relevant. Genetic information is job-relevant if
and only if the following conditions are met:

1. Possessing the genetic characteristic in question gives one a statistically significant risk of not satisfactorily performing duties outlined by the job-description.
2. The characteristic is likely to produce its phenotypic effects during the employee's period of employment.
3. The characteristic's effects cannot be satisfactorily altered, modified, or treated through medicine or therapy. . . .

3. *Intrusiveness.* This condition for a legitimate invasion can be easily
   satisfied, since employers can use genetic screening, a technique which
   is the least intrusive (available) means of gaining genetic information.
4. *Specificity.* Although this condition is not as easily satisfied as condition (3), it can be met provided that appropriate safeguards are in
   place. In performing a genetic screening test on an individual, the
   screener will have access to a wealth of genetic information. Employers can make their genetic screening discriminate by instructing testers
   to ignore the excess information and focus on the information in
   question.
5. *Secrecy.* This condition, like condition (4), can also be met, provided
   that appropriate safeguards are in place. While no one can prevent all
   information leaks, employers can minimize leaks by enacting policies
   to protect the secrecy of genetic information. Information from genetic tests should be distributed on a need to know basis, and those
   who do not need the information should not have access to it. The
   people who should have access to the genetic information include
   people who make personnel decisions, and especially the person who
   has been tested. If you submit to a genetic test, then you have the
   right to know the results of the test, since these results may provide
   you with important health information.

VI. DISCUSSION OF
HYPOTHETICAL CASES

The following hypothetical cases serve to illustrate my views on genetic privacy and allow me to address some pertinent objections.

Case 1: The Narcolepsy Gene

Suppose it is discovered that a small percentage of the population possess a gene, gene X, that makes them highly susceptible to narcolepsy. People with gene X have a significant risk of falling asleep during normal waking hours, and there is no effective treatment for this disorder. A major airline company, Safe Air, has had some trouble with pilots falling asleep, and narcolepsy has become an important safety concern. The company decides to require its pilots (and prospective pilots) to submit to a genetic screening test for gene X. The test will focus only on gene X, and the company will provide safeguards to protect the secrecy of the results.

In this case, Safe Air's invasion of privacy is legitimate since the invasion meets all the criteria for legitimacy. The airline has a strong justification for genetic screening: it wants to validate the employee contract and insure the safety of its employees and customers. The information sought is relevant to the purpose of the invasion: people with gene X run a high risk of succumbing to narcolepsy, and narcoleptics cannot satisfactorily pilot airplanes.

Case 2: The Cancer Gene

In the second case, suppose that a chemical company, Acme Industries, exposes its workers to a small amount of a carcinogenic substance, carconine, during the production of plastics. Most people run a very small risk (0.1% chance) of contracting lung cancer when exposed to a small amount of carconine, but a small percentage of the population possesses a gene, gene Y, which gives them a significant risk (33% chance) of developing lung cancer after being exposed to carconine. Also suppose that Acme Industries has taken all reasonable steps to avoid exposing its employees to carconine; in order to further reduce carconine exposure it would have to stop producing plastic, its most profitable operation. Acme Industries decides to institute a genetic screening program for gene Y in order to protect its employees and reduce health care costs. The program focuses only on gene Y, and steps are taken to maintain secrecy.

Although this case is not as clear-cut as the first one, it still meets the criteria for a legitimate invasion of privacy. Relevancy, intrusiveness, specificity, and secrecy would not seem to be at issue in the case, but the justification would appear to be controversial. The problem with the justification is that the invasion is not done for the purpose of validating the employee-employer contract, assuming that lung cancer does not affect one's job performance until it reaches its final stages. The two stated reasons for invading genetic privacy are to protect employees and to reduce health care costs. Although neither of these reasons, by itself, could justify an invasion of privacy, taken together, they form a good justification for invading privacy in this case. . . .

Case 3: The Heart Attack Gene

Suppose we discover that individuals with gene Z run a high risk of having a heart attack by the time they are 40 years old, but their risk is not significantly greater than the risk run by individuals without gene Z who lead an unhealthy lifestyle (smoke, drink, eat meat, etc...) Nevertheless, a toy manufacturer, Fun Industries, decides to screen potential employees for gene Z for the purpose of avoiding health care costs and maximizing its investment in training costs. It will make sure that its screening program is discriminate and protects secrecy.

Can Fun Industries legitimately request individuals to take a test for gene Z? My answer is a definite "no." Fun Industries' main reason for invading privacy in this case is to minimize health care and training costs. Information about gene Z could not be considered necessary to validate the employment contract or protect employees. Employees with gene Z should be able to do their work as well as people without gene Z, and they will impose no significant risks or hardships on others.

One might object that health can be part of a person's job description and that the purpose of invasion is to validate the employment contract. However, allowing health to be a part of a person's job description would create a slippery slope that would eventually lead to discrimination and bias against the unhealthy. Allowing genetic screening in this case opens the door to a broad range of cases in which employers seek to discriminate against individuals deemed "health risks." Allowing genetic screening in cases 1 and 2, on the other hand would not result in such disastrous consequences. In cases 1 and 2 the screening is done for highly specific reasons directly related to job performance or genuine health concerns, while in cases the screening is done for more general reasons relating to cost minimization and profit. Screening in cases 1 and 2 is not based on reasons which could also justify screening in a wide range of cases, while screening in case 3 is based on reasons which could justify screening in a wide range of cases. Hence, allowing screening in cases 1 and 2 would probably not lead us down a "slippery slope" toward unjust discrimination and stigmatization. . . .

NOTES

1. W. A. Parent, "Privacy, Morality, and the Law," *Philosophy and Public Affairs,* vol. 12 (1983), p. 269.
2. Parent, *op. cit.,* p. 273.
3. I have derived these criteria from Parent's position; these are not his exact words.
4. See Norman E. Bowie, "The Moral Contract Between Employer and Employee," in Tom Beauchamp and Norman Bowie (eds.), *Ethical Theory and Business* (Englewood Cliffs, NJ: Prentice-Hall, 1983), pp. 150–161.

AIDS and Confidentiality
Grant Gillett

Whenever we make a visit to a physician, we assume that the facts of our medical diagnosis will not be passed on by that physician to others. Such confidentiality within the doctor-patient relationship is an important and long-standing tradition within the ethics of medical practice. The spread of AIDS, however, has caused some to question whether this principle of confidentiality ought to be maintained, given the potential harms to the lives of those that AIDS patients have put at risk.

In this selection Grant Gillett, a medical ethicist at the University of Otago Medical School in New Zealand, defends the view that a physician treating a patient with AIDS ought to inform those whom the patient has directly put at risk of his condition, even if that means going against the express wish of the patient that such information not be disclosed. Doctor-patient confidentiality, he argues, ought not to be treated as an absolute rule but rather as a *prima facie* duty that needs to be balanced against a physician's other duties, one of which is to see that others not suffer harm. In Gillett's view, an AIDS patient who wants confidentiality maintained even at the expense of harm to others has in effect excluded himself from the moral community by acting in an untrustworthy manner. In such a situation, the physician's duty to protect others from harm outweighs the duty to respect confidentiality. Given that the conditions under which a physician could violate confidentiality are extremely limited, Gillett believes that the consequentialist objection to his position—that society will be harmed since fewer persons will seek AIDS testing knowing the results might be disclosed—is unwarranted.

I

Does a doctor confronted by a patient with AIDS have a duty to maintain absolute confidentiality or could that doctor be considered to have some overriding duty to the sexual contacts of the AIDS sufferer? AIDS or Acquired Immune Deficiency Disease is a viral disease transmitted for the most part by sexual contact. It is fatal in the short or long term (i.e. nine months to six years) in those infected people who go on to develop the full-blown form of the disease.

Let us say that a 39 year old man goes to his family doctor with a dry persistent cough which has lasted three or four weeks and a 10 day history of night sweats. He admits that he is bisexually active. He is tested and found to have antibodies to HIV virus (indicating that he is infected with the virus that causes AIDS). In the setting of this clinical picture he must be considered to have the disease. He is told of his condition and also, in the course of a prolonged interview, of the risk to his wife and of the distinct possibility of

From *Journal of Applied Philosophy* 4 (1987), 15–20.

his children aged one and three years old being left without parents should she contract the disease. He refuses to allow her to be told of his condition. The doctor finally accedes to his demand for absolute confidentiality. After one or two initial illnesses which are successfully combatted he dies some 18 months later. Over the last few weeks of his life he relents on his former demands and allows his wife to be informed of his problem. She is tested and, though asymptomatic, is found to be antibody positive. A year later she goes to the doctor with fever, dry cough and loss of appetite. Distraught on behalf of her children, she bitterly accuses the doctor of having failed her and them by allowing her husband to infect her when steps could have been taken to diminish the risk had she only known the truth.

In this case there is a powerful inclination to say that the wife is justified in her grievance. It seems just plain wrong for her doctor to sit back and allow her to fall victim to a fatal disease because of the wish of her husband. Against this intuition we can mobilise two powerful arguments—one deontological and the other utilitarian (of a rule or restricted utilitarian type.)[1]

    i. On a deontological view the practice of medicine will be guided by certain inviolate or absolute rules (not to harm, not to neglect the welfare of one's patients, etc.). Among these will be respect for confidentiality. Faced with this inviolable principle the deontologically inclined physician will not disclose what he has been told in confidence—he will regard the tacit agreement not to disclose his patient's affairs to others as tantamount to a substantive promise which he cannot break. Against this, in the present case, we might urge his *prima facie* duty not to neglect the welfare of his other patient, the young man's wife. His inaction has contributed to her death. In response to this he could both defend the absolute duty to respect confidentiality in general and urge some version of the doctrine of double effect,[2] claiming that his clear duty was to honour his implicit vow of confidentiality but it had the unfortunate effect, which he had foreseen as possible but not intended, that it caused the death of his other patient. One is inclined to offer an intuitive response such as 'No moral duty is so binding that you can hazard another person's life in this manner'. It is a notorious feature of deontological systems that they involve conflicts of duties for which there exists no principled method of resolution.

    ii. A rule-utilitarian doctor can mount a more convincing case. He can observe that confidentiality is a cornerstone of a successful AIDS practice. Lack of confidentiality can cause the irrational victimisation of sufferers by a poorly educated public who are prone to witch-hunts of all kinds. The detection and treatment of AIDS, and the consequent protection of that large group of people who have contacts with the patients being treated depends on the patients who seek medical advice believing that medical confidentiality is inviolate. If confidentiality were seen as a relative duty only, suspended or breached at the discretion of the doctor, then far fewer cases would present for detection and crucial guidance about diminishing risks of spread would not be obtained. This would lead to more people suffering and dying. It may be hard on a few, unfortunate enough to be involved with people like the recalcitrant young husband, but the general welfare can only be served by a compassionate but resolute refusal to abandon sound principles in the face of such cases. Many find this a convincing argument but I will argue that it is superficial in the understanding of moral issues that it espouses.

II

Imagine, in order to soften the way for a rather less neatly argued position, a doctor confronted by a young man who has a scratched face and blood on his shirt and who wants to be checked for VD. In the course of the doctor's taking his history it emerges that he has forcibly raped two women and is worried that the second was a prostitute. He says to the doctor "Of course, I am telling you this in confidence, doc, because I know that you won't rat on me." Producing a knife, he then says, "See, this is the blade that I get them going with." Rather troubled, the doctor takes samples and tells the young man that there is no evidence of VD. He tries to talk his patient into giving himself up for some kind of psychiatric treatment but the young man is adamant. It becomes clear that he has certain delusional and persecutional ideas. Two days later the doctor reads that his patient has been arrested because after leaving the surgery he raped and savagely mutilated a young woman who, as a result, required emergency surgery for multiple wounds and remains in a critical condition.

Here we might well feel that any principle which dictates that it is the moral duty of the doctor to keep silent is wrong—but as yet no principles conflicting with or supplementing those above have been introduced. A possible loophole is introduced by the rapist's sadomasochism and probable psychosis. . . . In such a case we suspend our normal moral obligations to respect the avowed interests of the patient and claim that he is incompetent to make a responsible and informed assessment of his own interests and so we assume the right to make certain decisions on his behalf. In this case it would probably mean arranging for him to be given psychiatric help and society to be protected from him in the meantime. . . . Such weight as one claims for one's own personal privileges and moral principles—such as the demand for confidentiality—is derived from a 'form of life' where the interpersonal transactions which define trust, respect, harm, and so on, are in play. . . . Of the insane rapist we can say that he has excluded himself from that moral community by the very fact of his violation of certain of its most basic tenets and assumptions. He has no right to demand a full place in that structure where morally significant human exchanges are operative because his behaviour and attitudes do not fit the place to which he pretends. We are, of course, not released from a *prima facie* duty to try and help him in his odious predicament but we cannot be expected to accord him the full privileges of a member of the moral community as he persists, for whatever reason, in callously turning his back on the constraints normally operative there (albeit, perhaps, without reflective malevolence in its more usual forms). So, in this case, confidentiality can be suspended for legitimate moral reasons. The mad rapist has moved beyond the pale in terms of normal moral interactions and though we may have a duty to try and restore him to full participation within that order we are also entitled to protect ourselves in the interim at the expense of those considerations that would apply to a normal person. Notice again that the boundaries of our attitudes are not arbitrary or merely conventional but involve our most basic human feelings and reactions to one another.

III

We can now move from a case where insanity weights the decision in a certain direction to a case where the issues are more purely moral. Imagine that a 45-year-old man goes to see his family doctor and is also worried about a sexually transmitted disease. On being questioned he admits, in confidence, not only to intercourse with a series of prostitutes but also to forced sexual intercourse with his daughter. He is confident that she will not tell anyone what is happening because she is too ashamed and scared. After counselling he gives no sign of a wish to change his ways but rather continues to justify himself because of his wife's behaviour. The doctor later hears from a school psychological service that the daughter is showing some potentially serious emotional problems.

Here, it seems to me, we have few compunctions about setting in motion that machinery to deal with child abuse, even though the sole source of our information is what was said, in medical confidence, by the father. The justification we might give for the doctor's actions is illuminating. We are concerned for the actual harm being done to the child, both physical and psychological, and we overturn the father's injunction to confidence in order to prevent further harm being done. In so doing we class the situation as one in which a *prima facie* moral claim can be suspended because of the actions and attitudes involved. I believe that we do so because we implicitly realise that here also the agent has acted in such a way as to put himself beyond the full play of moral consideration and to justify our withholding certain of his moral 'dues'. Confidentiality functions to allow the patient to be honest with the doctor and to put trust in him. Trust is (at least in part) a two-way thing and can only exist between morally sensitive human beings (this, of course, blurs a vast range of distinctions between degrees of sensitivity). A basic element of such moral attitudes is the responsiveness of the agents concerned to the moral features of human interactions. The legitimate expectation that a doctor be trustworthy and faithful to his patient's wishes regardless of the behaviour of that patient is undermined when the patient abuses the relationship so formed in ways which show a lack of these basic human reactions because it is just these reactions which ground the importance of confidentiality in general. Therefore, if the father in this example refuses to accept the enormity of what he is doing to his daughter, he thereby casts doubt upon his standing as a moral agent. Stated baldly, that sounds like an open warrant for moralistic medical paternalism, but I do not think it need be. In asking that his affairs be concealed from others, a person is demanding *either* the right to preserve himself from the harms that might befall him if the facts about his life were generally known, or that his sensitivity as an individual be respected and protected. On either count it is inconsistent for him to claim some moral justification for that demand when it is made solely with the aim of allowing him to inflict comparable disregard or harm upon another. By his implicit intention to use a position, which only remains tenable with the collusion of the doctor, callously to harm another individual, the father undermines the moral force of his own appeal. His case is only worsened by the fact that from any moral perspective he would be considered to have a special and protective obligation toward his own offspring.

IV

Implicit within what I have said is a reappraisal of the nature of medical confidentiality. I have argued that it is not to be treated as an absolute duty but is rather to rank among other *prima facie* duties and responsibilities of the doctor-patient relationship. Just as the performance of a life-saving procedure can be vetoed by the patient's choice to forego treatment, even though it is a doctor's duty to strive for his patient's life, so each of these duties can be negated by certain considerations. One generally attempts to prevent a fatal illness overtaking a patient but in the case of a deformed neonate or an elderly and demented patient often the attempt is not made. In the case of confidentiality, I have claimed that we recognise the right of a patient to preserve his own personal life as inviolate. We accept that patients can and should share with a doctor details which it would not be right to disclose to other people. But we must also recognise that implicit within this recognition is the assumption that the patient is one of us, morally speaking. Our attitude to him and his rights assumes that he is one of or a participant in a community of beings who matter (or are morally interacting individuals like himself to whom the same considerations apply). We could offer a superficial and rather gross systematisation of this assumption in the universalisability test.[3] The patient in the last two cases applies a standard to his own human concerns which he is not prepared to extend to others involved with him in relevant situations. We must therefore regard his moral demands as spurious; we are not at liberty to harm him but we are bound to see that his cynical abuse of the moral code within which he lives does not harm others. . . .

Now we can return to the AIDS patient. From what I have said it becomes clear that it is only the moral intransigent who forces us to breach confidentiality. In most cases it will be possible to guide the patient into telling those who need to know or allowing them to be told (and where it is possible to so guide him it will be mandatory to involve him in an informed way). In the face of an expressed disregard for the harm being caused to those others concerned, we will be morally correct in abandoning what would otherwise be a binding obligation. We should and do feel the need to preserve and protect the already affected life of the potential victim of his deception and in this feeling we exhibit a sensitivity to moral rectitude. Of course, it is only the active sexual partners of the patient who are at risk and thus it is only to them that we and the patient have a moral duty (in this respect talk of 'society at large' is just rhetoric). . . .

The doctor's obligation to inform, in the face of an enjoinder to keep his confidence can, even if I am right, be seen to be restricted to those in actual danger and would in no wise extend to employers, friends or non-sexual interacting relatives of the patient or any other person with an even more peripheral interest. His duty extends only so far as to avert the actual harm that he can reasonably expect to arise from his keeping confidence.

Given the intransigent case, one further desideratum presents itself. I believe that doctors should be open with their patients and that therefore the doctor is bound to share his moral dilemma with the patient and inform him of his intention to breach confidentiality. I think he can legitimately claim a preemptive duty to prevent harm befalling his patients and should do so in the case of the abuse of others which the patient intends. It may be the case, with the insane rapist for instance, that the doctor will need to deceive in order to carry out his prevailing duty but this will hardly ever be so, and should, I believe, be regarded as unacceptable in general.

One thorny problem remains—the possible deleterious effect on the detection and treatment of AIDS if confidentiality is seen as only a relative principle in medical practice. Clearly, if the attitude were ever to take root that the medical profession could not be trusted to 'keep their mouths shut' then the feared effect would occur. I believe that where agencies and informal groups were told of the *only* grounds on which confidentiality would be breached and the *only* people who would be informed then this effect would not occur.

It seems to me that the remarkable intensification of one's sensitivity to personal and ethical values that is produced by contact with life-threatening or 'abyss' situations means that the cynical abuse of confidentiality by the patient which I have sought to address is likely to be both rare and transient. The greatest resource available to any of us in 'the valley of the shadow' is the closeness of those who will walk alongside us, and for many that will be a close spiritual and sexual partner. Confidentiality within the mutuality of that relationship rather than interpersonal dishonesty would thus seem to be vital to the welfare not only of the co-respondent but also of the patient himself as he struggles to cope with the disease that has him in its grip. To foster that welfare seems to me to be as close as a doctor can ever come to an absolute duty.

NOTES

1. J. Rawls, "Two concepts of rules," *Philosophical Review,* 64 (1955), pp. 3–32.
2. J. Glover, *Causing Death and Saving Lives* (London: Penguin, 1977).
3. R. M. Hare, *Freedom and Reason* (New York: Oxford University Press, 1965).

Privacy: Some Arguments
and Assumptions
Richard A. Wasserstrom

Richard A. Wasserstrom is a professor of philosophy at the University of California at Santa Cruz. He has published widely in the area of contemporary moral problems.

While in the following essay Wasserstrom ties the definition of privacy to the desire to have control over personal information, his main concern is not with defending a particular meaning of privacy but rather with exploring what makes privacy meaningful for us. Imagining a society where everyone's thoughts and behavior were under continued surveillance, he describes several reasons why we would find such a society undesirable, even if the information obtained by such monitoring would not be put to any official use: (a) If someone else could have access to all our thoughts, we would not feel a distinct sense of ourselves as "persons"; (b) We would feel the pain of embarrassment if some of the private things we now do would be observed by others; (c) The spontaneity of our behavior would be extremely curtailed if we knew we were being observed; and (d) Because an important element of what makes close personal relationships possible—the intimacy created by mutual sharing of personal information—would be missing, the possibility of forming these relationships would be put in jeopardy.

Is our society, with its increasing technological potential for storing huge quantities of data about its members, anything like this imagined society? Wasserstrom worries it might be similar, and consequently might produce undesirable effects similar to those described above. In an interesting response to this worry, he suggests rather than increasing our efforts to protect our privacy in the Information Age, we should seriously consider the possibility that being less concerned about privacy than we are at present could actually lead to greater individual and social well-being.

In this paper I examine some issues involving privacy—issues with which the legal system of the United States has had and continues to have a good deal of concern. What I am interested in is the nature of privacy and the reasons why it might be thought important. The issues I consider have been of particular interest in recent years as changes in technology have made new ways to interfere with privacy possible. For this reason, too, I am primarily concerned with the ways in which government and other powerful institutions can and do interfere with privacy, for it is these institutions that tend to have the sophisticated instruments most at their disposal.

I consider first some distinctions that I think it important to make among different kinds of cases that involve privacy. I then consider in some detail

From *Philosophical Law*, ed. Richard Bronaugh (Westport, CT: Greenwood Press, 1978), pp. 148–167.

one plausible set of arguments for the value of privacy. These arguments help to explain why the law protects privacy in some of the ways it does and to provide a possible justification for continuing to do so. Some of the arguments are not without their problems, however. And in the final section of the article I raise certain questions about them and indicate the key issues that require additional exploration before any satisfactory justification can be developed.

It is apparent that there are a number of different claims that can be made in the name of privacy. A number—and perhaps all—of them involve the question of the kind and degree of control that a person ought to be able to exercise in respect to knowledge or the disclosure of information about himself or herself. This is not all there is to privacy, but it is surely one central theme.

It is also true that information about oneself is not all of the same type. As a result control over some kinds may be much more important than control over others. For this reason, I want to start by trying to identify some of the different types of information about oneself over which persons might desire to retain control, and I will describe the situations in which this information comes into being. To do this, I will consider four rather ordinary situations and look at the ways they resemble one another and differ from one another.

I

The cases I have in mind are these.

1. It is midafternoon and I am sitting in a chair resting. As I close my eyes and look inward, I become aware of numerous ideas running through my mind, of various emotions and feelings, and of a variety of bodily sensations—an itch on my scalp, a slight pain in my side, and so on.

2. I am in a closed telephone booth, no one is standing near the booth, and I am talking in a normal voice into the telephone. I have called my travel agent to find out what time there are flights to Chicago so that I can make a reservation for a trip.

3. I am in the bedroom of my home with my wife. We are both undressed, lying on the bed, having sexual intercourse.

4. I am considering hiring a research assistant for the summer. If I wish to, I dial a special number on the telephone and a few days later receive in the mail a computer printout consisting of a profile of the prospective assistant—her age, marital status, arrest record, if any, grades at school, income, as well as a summary of how she has spent her time over the past few years.

The first kind of case is that of the things that are going on within a person's head or body—especially, though, a person's head: his or her mental state. One thing that is significant about my dreams, my conscious thoughts, hopes, fears, and desires is that the most direct, the best, and often the only evidence for you of what they are consists in my deliberately revealing them to you. . . . The only way to obtain very detailed and accurate information about what I am thinking, fearing, imagining, desiring, or hating and how I am experiencing it is for me to tell you or show you. If I do not, the ideas and feeling remain within me and in some sense, at least, known only to me. Because people cannot read other people's minds, these things about me are known only to me in a way in which other things are not unless I decide to disclose them to you. . . .

The second kind of case was illustrated by an imagined telephone conversation from a phone booth with my travel agent to make the reservations for a trip. Another case of the same type is this: I am in the dining room of my house, the curtains are drawn, and I am eating dinner with my wife. In both of these cases it is the setting that makes the behavior distinctive and relevant for our purposes. In the example of the reservations over the telephone, the substance of my conversation with my travel agent is within my control if it is the case that no one is in a position to overhear (at my end) what I am saying to him, that no one is listening in along the way, and that only one person, the travel agent, is in a position to hear what I am telling him. It is less within my control, of course, than is information about my mental state, not yet revealed to anyone, because the agent can choose to reveal what I have told him.

In the second case—that of eating dinner in my dining room—knowledge of what I am eating and how I am eating is in the control of my wife and me if it is correct that no one else is in a position to observe us as we are eating. We might want to describe both of these cases as cases of things being done *in private* (although this is a very weak sense of private)—meaning that they were done in a setting in which there did not appear to be anyone other than the person to whom I was talking or with whom I was eating who was in a position to hear what was being said or to see what was being eaten at the time the behavior was taking place. Both of these are to be contrasted with the third example given earlier.

Instead of eating dinner with my wife in the dining room, we are having sexual intercourse in the bedroom. Or, instead of talking to my travel agent, imagine that I call my lawyer to discuss the terms of my will with her. Both of these things are being done in private in the same sense in which the discussion with the travel agent and the dinner with my wife were private. But these have an additional quality not possessed by the earlier two examples. While I expect that what I tell my lawyer is not being overheard by anyone else while I am telling her, I also reasonably expect that she will keep in confidence what I tell her. The conversation is private in the additional respect that the understanding is that it will not be subsequently disclosed to anyone without my consent. It is a private kind of communication. That is not the case with my phone reservations for Chicago. Absent special or unusual circumstances (for example, telling the agent that I do not want anyone to know when I am going to Chicago), I have no particular interest in retaining control over disclosure of this fact.

Similarly, having intercourse with my wife is private in the additional respect that it is the sort of intimate thing that is not appropriately observed by others or discussed with them—again, absent special or unusual circumstances. In addition to being done in private, it, too, is a private kind of thing. It is in this respect unlike the dinner we had together. There is no expectation on my part that what I ate or how I ate it will not be discussed with others by my wife.

The most obvious and the important connection between the idea of doing something in private and doing a private kind of thing is that we typically do private things only in situations where we reasonably believe that we are doing them in private. That we believe we are doing something in private is often a condition that has to be satisfied before we are willing to disclose an intimate fact about ourselves or to perform an intimate act. I would probably make my airplane reservations even in a crowded travel agency where there were lots of people who could overhear what I was saying. The telephone was a convenient way to make the reservations. But the fact that I was making them in a setting that appeared to be private was not important to me. It did not affect what I disclosed to the agent. Thus even if I had suspected that my agent's telephone was tapped so that someone unknown to us both overheard our conversation, I would probably have made the reservation. In the case of my conversation with my lawyer, however, it was the belief that the conversation was in a private setting that made me willing to reveal a private kind of information. If someone taped my discussion with my lawyer, he injured me in a way that is distinguishable on this basis alone from the injury, if any, done to me by taping my conversation with the travel agent. That is to say, he got me to do or to reveal something that I would not have done or revealed if they had not hidden his presence from me.

It should be evident, too, that there are important similarities, as well as some differences, between the first and third cases—between my knowledge of my own mental state and my disclosure of intimate or otherwise confidential information to those to whom I choose to disclose it. These can be brought out by considering what it would be like to live in a society whose technology permitted an observer to gain access to the information in question.

II

Suppose existing technology made it possible for an outsider in some way to look into or monitor another's mind. What, if anything, would be especially disturbing or objectionable about that?

To begin with, there is a real sense in which we have far less control over when we shall have certain thoughts and what their content will be than we have over, for example, to whom we shall reveal them and to what degree.

Because our inner thoughts, feelings, and bodily sensations are so largely be-yond our control, I think we would feel appreciably more insecure in our social environment than we do at present were it possible for another to "look in" without our consent to see what was going on in our heads.

This is so at least in part because many, although by no means all, of our uncommunicated thoughts and feelings are about very intimate matters. Our fantasies and our fears often concern just those matters that in our culture we would least choose to reveal to anyone else. At a minimum we might suffer great anxiety and feelings of shame were the decisions as to where, when, and to whom we disclose not to be wholly ours. Were access to our thoughts possible in this way, we would see ourselves as creatures who are far more vulnerable than we are now.

In addition, there is a more straightforward worry about accountability for our thoughts and feelings. As I mentioned, they are often not within our control. For all of the reasons that we ought not hold people accountable for behavior not within their control, we would not want the possibility of ac-countability to extend to uncommunicated thoughts and feelings.

Finally, one rather plausible conception of what it is to be a person car-ries with it the idea of the existence of a core of thoughts and feelings that are the person's alone. If anyone else could know all that I am thinking or perceive all that I am feeling except in the form I choose to filter and reveal what I am and how I see myself—if anyone could be aware of all this at will—I would cease to have as complete a sense of myself as a distinct and separate person as I have now. A fundamental part of what it is to be an individual is to be an entity that is capable of being exclusively aware of its own thoughts and feelings.

Considerations such as these—and particularly the last one—help us to understand some of the puzzles concerning the privilege against self-incrimi-nation. Because of the significance of exclusive control over our own thoughts and feelings, the privilege against self-incrimination can be seen to rest, ulti-mately, upon a concern that confessions never be coerced or required by the state. The point of the privilege is not primarily that the state must be in-duced not to torture individuals in order to extract information from them. Nor is the point even essentially that the topics of confession will necessarily (or even typically) be of the type that we are most unwilling to disclose because of the unfavorable nature of what this would reveal about us. Rather, the fundamental point is that required disclosure of one's thoughts by itself diminishes the concept of individual personhood within the society. For this reason, all immunity statutes that require persons to reveal what they think and believe—provided only that they will not be subsequently prosecuted for what they disclose—are beside the point and properly subject to criticism. For this reason, too, cases that permit the taking of a blood sample (to deter-mine alcohol content) from an unconscious or unwilling person—despite the existence of the privilege—are also defensible. Since a person is not in a privileged position in respect to the alcohol content of his or her own blood, the claim to exclusivity in respect to knowledge of this fact is not particularly persuasive.

In a society in which intrusion into the domain of one's uncommunicated thoughts and feelings was not possible, but in which communications between persons about private things could be intercepted, some of the problems would remain the same. To begin with, because of our social attitudes toward the disclosure of intimate facts and behavior, most of us would be extremely pained were we to learn that these had become known to persons other than those to whom we chose to disclose them. The pain can come about in several different ways. If I do something private with somebody and I believe that we are doing it in private, I may very well be hurt or embarrassed if I learn subsequently that we were observed but did not know it. Thus if I learn after the fact that someone had used a special kind of telescope to observe my wife and me while we were having intercourse, the knowledge that we were observed will cause us distress both because our expectations of privacy were incorrect and because we do not like the idea that we were observed during this kind of intimate act. People have the right to have the world be what it appears to be precisely in those cases in which they regard privacy as essential to the diminution of their own vulnerability.

Reasoning such as this lies behind, I think, a case that arose some years ago in California. A department store had complained to the police that homosexuals were using its men's room as a meeting place. The police responded by drilling a small hole in the ceiling over the enclosed stalls. A policeman then stationed himself on the floor above and peered down through the hole observing the persons using the stall for eliminatory purposes. Eventually the policeman discovered and apprehended two homosexuals who used the stall as a place to engage in forbidden sexual behavior. The California Supreme Court held the observations of the policeman to have been the result of an illegal search and ordered the conviction reversed. What made the search illegal, I believe, was that it occurred in the course of this practice, which deceived all of the persons who used the stall and who believed that they were doing in private something that was socially regarded as a private kind of thing. They were entitled, especially for this kind of activity, both to be free from observation and to have their expectations of privacy honored by the state.

There is an additional reason why the observation of certain sorts of activity is objectionable. That is because the kind of spontaneity and openness that is essential to them disappears with the presence of an observer. To see that this is so, consider a different case. Suppose I know in advance that we will be observed during intercourse. Here there is no problem of defeated reasonable expectations. But there may be injury nonetheless. For one thing, I may be unwilling or unable to communicate an intimate fact or engage in intimate behavior in the presence of an observer. In this sense I will be quite directly prevented from going forward. In addition, even if I do go ahead, the character of the experience may very well be altered. Knowing that someone is watching or listening may render what would have been an enjoyable experience unenjoyable. Or, having someone watch or listen may so alter the character of the relationship that it is simply not the same kind of relationship it was before. The presence of the observer may make spontaneity impossible. Aware of the observer, I am engaged in part in viewing or imagining what is going on from his or her perspective. I thus cannot lose myself as completely in the activity. . . .

There is still an additional reason why control over intimate facts and behavior might be of appreciable importance to individuals: our social universe would be altered in fundamental and deleterious ways were that control to be surrendered or lost. This is so because one way in which we mark off and distinguish certain interpersonal relationships from other ones is in terms of the kind of intimate information and behavior that we are willing to share with other persons. One way in which we make someone a friend rather than an acquaintance is by revealing things about ourselves to that person that we do not reveal to the world at large. On this view some degree of privacy is a logically necessary condition for the existence of many of our most meaningful social relationships.

III

The fourth kind of case that I want to consider is different from the previous three. It is suggested by the example I gave earlier of all of the information that might be made routinely available to me concerning possible appointees to the job of teaching assistant. It concerns the consequences of possessing the technological capability to store an enormous amount of information about each of the individual members of a society in such a way that the information can be retrieved and presented in a rapid, efficient, and relatively inexpensive fashion. This topic—the character, uses, and dangers of data banks—is one that has received a lot of attention in recent years. I think the worries are legitimate and that the reasons for concern have been too narrowly focused.

Consider a society in which the kinds of data collected about an individual are not very different from the kinds of quantity already collected in some fashion or other in our own society. It is surprising what a large number of interactions are deemed sufficiently important to record in some way. Thus, there are, for example, records of the traffic accidents I have been in, the applications I have made for life insurance, the purchases that I have made with my Mastercharge card, the COD packages I have signed for, the schools my children are enrolled in, the telephone numbers that have been called from my telephone, and so on. Now suppose that all of this information, which is presently recorded in some written fashion, were to be stored in some way so that it could be extracted on demand. What would result?

It is apparent that at least two different kinds of pictures of me would emerge. First, some sort of a qualitative picture of the kind of person I am would emerge. A whole lot of nontemporal facts would be made available—

what kind of driver I am, how many children I have, what sorts of purchases I have made, how often my telephone is used, how many times I have been arrested and for what offenses, what diseases I have had, how much life insurance I have, and so on.

Second, it would also be possible to reconstruct a rough, temporal picture of how I had been living and what I had been doing with my time. Thus, there might be evidence that I visited two or three stores a day and made purchases, that I cashed a check at the bank (and hence was there between the hours of 10 A.M. and 3 P.M.), that I ate lunch at a particular restaurant (and hence was probably there between noon and 2 P.M.), and so on. There might well be whole days for which there were no entries, and there might be many days for which the entries would give a very sketchy and incomplete picture of how I was spending my time. Still, it would be a picture that is fantastically more detailed, accurate, and complete than the one I could supply from my own memory or from my own memory as it is augmented by that of my friends. I would have to spend a substantial amount of time each day writing in my diary in order to begin to produce as complete and accurate a picture as the one that might be rendered by the storage and retrieval system I am envisaging—and even then I am doubtful that my own diary would be as accurate or as complete, unless I made it one of my major life tasks to keep accurate and detailed records for myself of everything that I did.

If we ask whether there would be anything troublesome about living in such a society, the first thing to recognize is that there are several different things that might be objectionable. First, such a scheme might make communications that were about intimate kinds of things less confidential. In order to receive welfare, life insurance, or psychiatric counseling, I may be required to supply information of a personal or confidential nature. If so, I reasonably expect that the material revealed will be known only to the recipient. If, however, the information is stored in a data bank, it now becomes possible for the information to be disclosed to persons other than those to whom disclosure was intended. Even if access to the data is controlled so as to avoid the risks of improper access, storage of the confidential information in the data bank necessarily makes the information less confidential than it was before it was so stored.

Second, information that does not concern intimate things can get distorted in one way or another through storage. The clearest contemporary case of this kind of information is a person's arrest record. The fact that someone has been arrested is not, I think, the kind of fact that the arrestee can insist ought to be kept secret. But he or she can legitimately make two other demands about it. The person can insist that incorrect inferences not be drawn from the information; that is, the person can legitimately point out that many individuals who are arrested are never prosecuted for the alleged offense nor are they guilty of the offense for which they were arrested. He or she can, therefore, quite appropriately complain about any practice that routinely and without more being known denies employment to persons with arrest records. And if such a practice exists, then a person can legitimately complain about the increased dissemination and availability of arrest records just because of the systematic misuse of that information. The storage of arrest records in a data bank becomes objectionable not because the arrest record is intrinsically private but because the information is so regularly misused that the unavailability of the information is less of an evil than its general availability. . . .

In addition, and related to some of the points I made earlier, there are independent worries about the storage of vast quantities of ostensibly innocuous material about the individual in the data bank. Suppose nothing intrinsically private is stored in the data bank; suppose nothing potentially or improperly derogatory is included; and suppose what does get stored is an enormous quantity of information about the individual—information about the person and the public, largely commercial, transactions that were entered into. There are many useful, efficient uses to which such a data bank might be put. Can there be any serious objections?

One thing is apparent. With such a data bank it would be possible to reconstruct a person's movements and activities more accurately and completely than the individual—or any group of individuals—could do simply from memory. As I have indicated, there would still be gaps in the picture. No one would be able to tell in detail what the individual had been doing a lot of the time, but the sketch would be a surprisingly rich and comprehensive one that is exceeded in detail in our society only by the keeping of a careful, thorough personal diary or by having someone under the surveillance of a corps of private detectives.

What distinguishes this scheme is the fact that it would make it possible to render an account of the movements and habits of every member of the society and in so doing it might transform the society in several notable respects.

In part what is involved is the fact that every transaction in which one engages would now take on additional significance. In such a society one would be both buying a tank of gas and leaving a part of a systematic record of where one was on that particular date. One would not just be applying for life insurance; one would also be recording in a permanent way one's health on that date and a variety of other facts about oneself. No matter how innocent one's intentions and actions at any given moment, I think that an inevitable consequence of such a practice of data collection would be that persons would think more carefully before they did things that would become part of the record. Life would to this degree become less spontaneous and more measured.

More significant are the consequences of such a practice upon attitudes toward privacy in the society. If it became routine to record and have readily accessible vast quantities of information about every individual, we might come to hold the belief that the detailed inspection of any individual's behavior is a perfectly appropriate societal undertaking. We might tend to take less seriously than we do at present the idea that there are occasions upon which an individual can plausibly claim to be left alone and unobserved. We might in addition become so used to being objects of public scrutiny that we would cease to deem privacy important in any of our social relationships. As observers we might become insensitive to the legitimate claims of an individual to a sphere of life in which the individual is at present autonomous and around which he or she can erect whatever shield is wished. As the subjects of continual observation we might become forgetful of the degree to which many of the most important relationships within which we now enter depend for their existence upon the possibility of privacy.

On the other hand, if we do continue to have a high regard for privacy, both because of what it permits us to be as individuals and because of the kinds of relationships and activities it makes possible and promotes, the maintenance of a scheme of systematic data collection would necessarily get in the way. This is so for the same reason discussed earlier. Much of the value and significance of being able to do intimate things in private is impaired whenever there is a serious lack of confidence about the privacy of the situation. No one could rationally believe that the establishment of data banks—no matter how pure the motives of those who maintain and have access to them—is calculated to enhance the confidentiality of much that is now known about each one of us. And even if only apparently innocuous material is to be stored, we could never be sure that it all was as innocuous as it seemed at the time. It is very likely, therefore, that we would go through life alert to these new, indelible consequences of everyday interactions and transactions. Just as our lives would be different from what they are now if we believed that every telephone conversation was being overheard, so our lives would be similarly affected if we believed that every transaction and application was being stored. In both cases we would go through life encumbered by a wariness and deliberateness that would make it less easy to live what we take to be the life of a free person.

IV

The foregoing constitute, I believe, a connected set of arguments for the distinctive value of privacy. While I find them persuasive, I also believe that some of them are persuasive only within the context of certain fundamental assumptions and presuppositions. And these assumptions and these presuppositions seem to be a good deal more problematic than is often supposed. What remains to be done, therefore, is to try to make them explicit so that they can then be subjected to analysis and assessment. One way to do this is to ask whether there is an alternative perspective through which a number of these issues might be considered. I believe that there is. I call it the perspective of the counterculture because it captures at least some of the significant ingredients of that point of view or way of life. In calling this alternative view the perspective of the counterculture, I do not mean to be explicating a view that was in fact held by any person or group. However, this view does provide a rationale for a number of the practices and ideals of one strain of the counterculture movement in the United States in the 1960s.

I have argued for the importance of reposing control over the disclosure or observation of intimate facts with the actor. One argument for doing so was that intimate facts about oneself—one's fears, fantasies, jealousies, and desires—are often embarrassing if disclosed to others than those to whom we choose to disclose them. Similarly there are acts of various sorts that cause us pain or are rendered unenjoyable unless they are done alone or in the company only of those we choose to have with us.

This is a significant feature of our culture—or at least of the culture in which I grew up. What I am less sure about is the question of whether it is necessarily a desirable feature of a culture. Indeed disagreement about just this issue seems to me to be one of the major sources of tension between the counterculture and the dominant older culture of my country. The disagreement concerns both a general theory of interpersonal relationships and a view about the significance of intimate thoughts and actions. The alternative view goes something like this.

We have made ourselves vulnerable—or at least far more vulnerable than we need be—by accepting the notion that there are thoughts and actions concerning which we ought to feel ashamed or embarrassed. When we realize that everyone has fantasies, desires, worries about all sorts of supposedly terrible, wicked, and shameful things, we ought to see that they really are not things to be ashamed of at all. We regard ourselves as vulnerable because in part we think we are different, if not unique. We have sexual feelings toward our parents, and no one else has ever had such wicked feelings. But if everyone does, then the fact that others know of this fantasy is less threatening. One is less vulnerable to their disapproval and contempt.

We have made ourselves excessively vulnerable, so this alternative point of view continues, because we have accepted the idea that many things are shameful unless done in private. And there is no reason to accept that convention. Of course we are embarrassed if others watch us having sexual intercourse—just as we are embarrassed if others see us unclothed. But that is because the culture has taught us to have these attitudes and not because they are intrinsically fitting. Indeed our culture would be healthier and happier if we diminished substantially the kinds of actions that we now feel comfortable doing only in private, or the kind of thoughts we now feel comfortable disclosing only to those with whom we have special relationships. This is so for at least three reasons. In the first place, there is simply no good reason why privacy is essential to these things. Sexual intercourse could be just as pleasurable in public (if we grew up unashamed) as is eating a good dinner in a good restaurant. Sexual intercourse is better in private only because society has told us so.

In the second place, it is clear that a change in our attitudes will make us more secure and at ease in the world. If we would be as indifferent to whether we are being watched when we have intercourse as we are to when we eat a meal, then we cannot be injured by the fact that we know others are watching us, and we cannot be injured nearly as much by even unknown observations.

In the third place, interpersonal relationships will in fact be better if there is less of a concern for privacy. After all, forthrightness, honesty, and candor are, for the most part, virtues, while hypocrisy and deceit are not. Yet this emphasis upon the maintenance of a private side to life tends to encourage hypocritical and deceitful ways of behavior. Individuals see themselves as leading dual lives—public ones and private ones. They present one view of themselves to the public—to casual friends, acquaintances, and strangers—and a different view of themselves to themselves and a few intimate associates. This way of living is hypocritical because it is, in essence, a life devoted to camouflaging the real, private self from public scrutiny. It is a dualistic, unintegrated life that renders the individuals who live it needlessly vulnerable, shame ridden, and lacking in a clear sense of self. It is to be contrasted with the more open, less guarded life of the person who has so little to fear from disclosures of self because he or she has nothing that requires hiding.

I think that this is an alternative view that deserves to be taken seriously. Any attempt to do so, moreover, should begin by considering more precisely the respects in which it departs from the more conventional view of the role of privacy maintained in the body of this essay, and the respects in which it does not. I have in mind three issues in particular that must be examined in detail before an intelligent decision can be made. The first is the question of the value that the counterculture ideal attaches to those characteristics of spontaneity and individuality that play such an important role in the more traditional view as I have described it. On at least one interpretation both views prize spontaneity and individuality equally highly, with the counterculture seeing openness in interpersonal relationships as a better way of achieving just those ends. On another interpretation, however, autonomy, spontaneity, and individuality are replaced as values by the satisfactions that attend the recognition of the likeness of all human experience and the sameness that characterizes all interpersonal relationships. Which way of living gives one more options concerning the kind of life that one will fashion for oneself is one of the central issues to be settled.

Still another issue that would have to be explored is the question of what would be gained and what would be lost in respect to the character of interpersonal relationships. One of the main arguments for the conventional view put forward earlier is that the sharing of one's intimate thoughts and behavior is one of the primary media through which close, meaningful interpersonal relationships are created, nourished, and confirmed. One thing that goes to define a relationship of close friendship is that the friends are willing to share truths about themselves with each other that they are unprepared to reveal to the world at large. One thing that helps to define and sustain a sexual love relationship is the willingness of the parties to share sexual intimacies with each other that they are unprepared to share with the world at large. If this makes sense, either as a conceptual or as an empirical truth, then perhaps acceptance of the counterculture ideal would mean that these kinds of relationships were either no longer possible or less likely. Or perhaps the conventional view is equally unsatisfactory here, too. Perhaps friendship and love both can and ought to depend upon some less proprietary, commercial conception of the exchange of commodities. Perhaps this view of intimate interpersonal relationships is as badly in need of alteration as is the attendant conception of the self.

Finally, we would want to examine more closely some other features of the counterculture ideal. Even if we no longer thought it important to mark off and distinguish our close friends from strangers (or even if we could still do that, but in some other way), might not the counterculture ideal of openness and honesty in all interpersonal relationships make ordinary social interaction vastly more complex and time-consuming than it now is—so much so, in fact, that these interactions, rather than the other tasks of living, would become the focus of our waking hours?

These are among the central issues that require continued exploration. They are certainly among the issues that the fully developed theory of privacy, its value and its place within the law, must confront and not settle by way of assumption and presupposition.

Public Image
Larry Hunter

Larry Hunter shares the belief expressed by Richard A. Wasserstrom in the preceding essay that a serious danger created by ever-expanding data banks containing personal information is the ability of strangers to construct and have access to profiles on each one of us. Unlike Wasserstrom, however, Hunter believes we need to take greater control of our "public image," as he calls the information profile that computers make available about ourselves. He recognizes that in our democratic society, the freedom to gather information that can be used to form these images is protected by guarantees under the First Amendment. As he points out, though, there is reason to be concerned about the uses to which this information can be put. Companies can use it to discriminate against traditionally underrepresented groups in ways that are difficult to track, and one could be harmed in cases where one's computerized public image distorts the facts of one's own life. To lessen the chances for the misuse of computer-gathered information, Hunter recommends that the law be changed in order to recognize personal information as private property. If we could own our public images, Hunter claims, we could have more control over the privacy of our own lives.

I live in your future. As a graduate student in Artificial Intelligence at Yale University, I am now using computer equipment that will be commonplace five years from now. I have a powerful workstation on my desk, connected in a high-speed network to more than one hundred other such machines, and, through other networks, to thousands of other computers and their users. I use these machines not only for research, but to keep my schedule, to write letters and articles, to read nationwide electronic "bulletin boards," to send electronic mail, and sometimes just to play games. I make constant use of fancy graphics, text formatters, laser printers—you name it. My gadgets are both my desk and my window on the world. I'm quite lucky to have access to all these machines.

But with this privilege comes a certain sobriety: I've begun to contemplate some of the effects the computer will have on society. It is impossible to predict what our interconnected, information-oriented society will look like in detail, but some of the outlines are becoming clearer. The ubiquity and power of the computer blur the distinction between public and private information. Our revolution will not be in gathering data—don't look for TV cameras in your bedroom—but in analyzing the information that is already willingly shared. Without any conspiratorial snooping or Big Brother antics, we may find our actions, our lifestyles, and even our beliefs under increasing public scrutiny as we move into the information age.

From *Whole Earth Review* (January 1985), 32–37.

. . . You've been giving out clues about yourself for years. Buying, working, socializing, and travelling are acts you do in public. Your lifestyle, income, education, home, and family are all deducible from existing records. The information that can be extracted from mundane records like your VISA or MasterCard receipts, phone bill, and credit record is all that's needed to put together a remarkably complete picture of who you are, what you do, and even what you think.

BLOC MODELLING

A powerful technique used by managers of large amounts of data is called *bloc modelling.* The goal of bloc modelling is to evaluate how people fit into an organization or group, based on their relations with other members of the group. The primary use of this practice which was developed more than a decade ago, has been to examine how employees fit into the firm where they work. Bell Labs, ABC, the Wharton School, and even the Institute for Social Management in Bulgaria are among those who have used the technique.

The mathematics and computations behind the process are complicated, but the underlying idea is simple: While the relationship between two people in an organization is rarely very informative by itself, when many pairs of relationships are connected, patterns can be detected. The people being modelled are broken up into groups, or *blocs.* The assumption made by modellers is that people in similar positions behave similarly. Blocs aren't tightly knit groups. You may never have heard of someone in your bloc, but because you both share a similar relationship with some third party you are lumped together. Your membership in a bloc might become the basis of a wide variety of judgements, from who gets job perks to who gets investigated by the FBI.

Where does the initial data come from? In the office, it may be who you talk to on the intercom, whose phone calls you return (or don't return), who you eat lunch with, who you send your memos to, even who you play softball with. Fancy telephone systems, electronic mail, and bulletin boards make gathering this relational data even easier. When personal computers are on every desk, routine information about who says what to whom is automatically generated and easily collected. Employers and others can keep track of that mundane information, and save it in a database that can be bloc modelled later.

Bloc modelling is used to separate people, cliques, and whole organizations into categories which determine the way the modeller may ultimately treat the groups. While conceptually similar to the more familiar "redlining," it is unlike other kinds of discrimination, since the blocs found are generally inconspicuous, and the members may easily fail to recognize their common fate. Furthermore, the existing laws protecting privacy, such as those that guarantee individuals access to their own files, do not address bloc modelling. It is difficult to imagine what remedies might be devised for this new form of guilt by association.

WHEN IS PRIVATE INFORMATION PUBLIC?

We live in a world of private and public acts. We consider what we do in our own bedrooms to be our own business; what we do on the street or in the supermarket is open for everyone to see. In the information age, our public acts disclose our private dispositions, even more than a camera in the bedroom would. This doesn't necessarily mean we should bring a veil of secrecy over public acts. The vast amount of public information both serves and endangers us.

To make this idea clear, I'd like to use an example invented by Jerry Samet, Professor of Philosophy at Bentley College. He suggests that, although we consider it a violation of privacy to look in somebody's window and notice what they are doing, we have no problem with the reverse: someone sitting in his living room looking out his window. If I'm looking out my window and I notice you walking down my street, I may notice that you are wearing a red sweater, holding hands with someone else, or heading towards the local bar. If I wanted to, I might write down what I saw out my window. Consider what happens if I write down everything I see out my window, and all my neighbors do, too. Suppose we shared notes and compiled the data we got just by looking out our own windows. When we sorted it all out, we would have detailed personal profiles of everyone we saw. If every move anyone made in public were recorded, correlated, and analyzed, the veil of anonymity protecting us from constant scrutiny would be torn away. Even if that record were never used, its very existence would certainly change the way we act in public. The idea that someone is always watching is no less threatening when the watching goes on in the supermarket, in the department store, and in the workplace than when it goes on in our homes.

The harmful consequences of just keeping personal profiles pale in comparison with the problems associated with their use. We don't have to look far into the future to imagine how such files could be used. There is a pressing example already apparent in two proposed additions to the National Crime Information Computer. The computer, or NCIC as it is commonly called, was set up to track wanted criminals and stolen property across state lines. When a policeman makes a routine traffic stop or otherwise confronts a stranger, the first thing he does is check the name through NCIC. If his name is in NCIC, the officer can search or arrest him, or take other discretionary action. The FBI now wants to add people to the database who have been accused of nothing, but are *suspected,* of organized crime connections, terrorism, or narcotics possession, or are "known associates" of drug traffickers. Their avowed goal is to keep track of the whereabouts of such people. The FBI claims that this represents a "logical progression" of the crime center's efforts. The idea that associating with someone who gets arrested could get your name into the national crime database is scary enough. Worse yet, the Secret Service wants to get into the act. They want to sidestep the judicial process by directly entering the names of people they consider to be dangerous to the President or other high officials into NCIC without obtaining warrants. If the

FBI and the Secret Service get their way, having the wrong friends or being on the wrong side of the Executive Branch could get your name into the computer, subjecting you to police harassment, surveillance, even detention. Since just adding a name to NCIC doesn't legally deprive anyone of liberty or property, constitutional due process constraints do not apply.

Why not make gathering this information against the law? Think of Samet's metaphor: do we really want to ban looking out the window? The information about groups and individuals that *is* public is public for a reason. Being able to write down what I see is fundamental to freedom of expression and belief, the freedoms we are trying to protect. Furthermore, public records serve us in very specific, important ways. We can have and use credit because credit records are kept. We can prevent the sale of handguns to convicted felons because criminal records are kept. Supermarkets must keep track of their inventories, and since their customers prefer that they accept checks, they keep information on the financial status of people who shop in their stores. In short, keeping and using the kind of data that can be turned into personal profiles is fundamental to our way of life—we cannot stop *gathering* this information.

What we have to do is find a way to control its *use*. We need to make it possible to draw distinctions between the kinds of information processing, dissemination, and use we want to allow and the kinds we want to prohibit. Some uses of personal information are quite reasonable. Using conviction records to avoid selling guns to criminals is a legitimate use of personal data. Keeping track of who I call on the telephone and for how long is legitimate if the purpose is to bill me for those calls. Writing down what books I buy is fine, so long as the intent is to maintain the inventory at my local bookstore. There are a variety of traditional, necessary, and non-threatening uses of personal information. Ideally, any use of information outside the scope of these traditional ones should require the knowledge and consent of the person the information is about. Marketing and direct advertising are not traditional uses of personal information, and should not be thought of as such. I should be able to choose whether or not I want my local bookstore to keep a list of the books I buy, even if they just want to mail me ads for new books they think I'd like. I should be able to prevent a company from selling my name and address to someone else without my permission. I don't want the FBI to be able to look at my consumer records and decide that my lifestyle fits their model of a subversive or a drug user. I certainly do not want employers to use bloc modelling to fire people on the basis of who they associate with, or politicians to use it to identify their "enemies."

INFORMATION AS PROPERTY

People under scrutiny ought to be able to exert some control over what other people do with that personal information. Our society grants individuals control over the activities of others primarily through the idea of property. A reasonable way to give individuals control over information about them is to vest them with a *property interest* in that information. Information about me is, in part, my property. Other people may, of course, also have an interest in that information. Citibank has some legitimate interests in the information about me that it has gathered. When my neighbor writes down that I was wearing a red sweater, both of us should share in the ownership of that information.

What does it mean to own information? To share in such ownership? How can existing laws about property be interpreted to make judgements about the use and control of information? These questions must ultimately be answered by the legislators who draft laws giving information property status, and the courts who interpret those laws. We can begin to imagine some of the implications of such an approach. What makes information different from other kinds of property is that it is intangible: it cannot be touched, held, or seen directly. The same information can be in two places at once. Other than that, information is like other kinds of property: it can have monetary value, it can be produced, improved, or degraded, and one can share, withhold, or transfer it to others.

Is information enough like property to be successfully integrated into property law? The process has already begun in many legislatures. Across the country laws are being passed that make unauthorized access, duplication, or tampering with information stored in computers a crime. These laws are deemed necessary because existing burglary statutes don't apply to copying information, or looking at it, especially if the access was by remote computer. When computer data is copied by an unauthorized outsider that action resembles burglary, and it is treated as such in these new laws. If it is like burglary, then something is being stolen. In this context, information is already being implicitly treated as if it were property.

If we are to treat information as property *explicitly,* some of our ideas about property will have to be changed. Information can be stolen by copying it, leaving the original behind. If information is merely what is known, how can it be taken away? How can vesting the individual with the rights associated with property, particularly the right of excluding others from that property, be specifically translated into control over analysis of data? How can we define information so that knowledge in a computer is property that can be controlled, but knowledge inside someone's head is not? Enforcement presents another problem: how can we tell if someone is using personal information illicitly? The example of copyright law suggests that, while finding small abuses of intangible property is difficult, finding major violations is no harder than other law enforcement tasks.

SEARCH AND SEIZURE OF INFORMATION

Treating information as property has an additional benefit. As the law currently stands, information isn't property, but computers are. The owner of the computer has been held to control everything "inside" his computer. That means that if I write a personal note on my office workstation, my employer has the right to read it. By contrast, he has no right to read a note I write on company stationery with a company pen and put in my (company owned) desk. More importantly, my employer can give permission to law enforcement agencies to go on a fishing expedition through my files in his computer, which, metaphorically, gives the police the right to rummage at random through any employee's "desk." This is not hypothetical, a case of just such abuse was reported by Larry Layton, a government employee.

Layton worked in a Defense Department office (DARCOM) which was fully electronic. Most employees had computers and all used electronic mail to communicate with each other. There were over 3000 users with access to the system, and 500 in-house users of internal workplace computers. All writing and interoffice communication, as well as other office support, was done on a computer. At least three times, the Army Criminal Investigation Division, in conjunction with the FBI, obtained complete dumps of all the workplace automation computers without any type of court order or specification of what they were looking for, other than "wrongful use of government property." A "complete dump" means that every bit of information was printed out and examined. Using the analogy to desks, it is as if the FBI went through every employee's desk looking at every piece of paper, through every address book, reading every memo and every piece of mail. After finding one person who had a recipe in an electronic mail message, and another who had a baby sitter's phone number in a telephone number file, the FBI read each his rights and threatened retribution. The legal staff of the operation advised the managers that the searches were legal since computer files don't fall under any of the same protections that, say, telephone usage does. The searches have resulted in the employees refraining from using the system for communication, electronic mail, filing, and many other applications.

This sort of witch-hunt is only the beginning. Electronic mail typically goes through several computers before reaching its final destination. The owner of each of those computers apparently has the full legal right to read, copy, and disseminate anything contained in his computer, including that mail. Since the U.S. Postal Service, MCI, and a host of other similar entities are operating electronic mail services, one might think that electronic mail had the same protection and privacy as a paper letter or a phone call. It does not. It is, for the time being, completely open to anyone through whose computer it passes. We must extend the special status of the letter and the phone call to all forms of electronic communication. The idea of *information as property* will protect that information with the rules of search and seizure that apply to other kinds of property. It will provide the connection between sending a letter and sending electronic mail necessary to protect the content of our communication.

PUBLIC IMAGES, LIMITED

It is time our legal technicians turned their attention to framing answers in the language of the law. We will need to define many gray areas, and insure that we tread carefully in these sensitive areas of personal information. I think we can specify the uses we consider traditional, and separate those we consider new or threatening. Lawyers, computer scientists, businessmen, and an informed public must work together to bring our legal system a carefully crafted new framework for thinking about information.

Computers and electronic communication are ushering in a new age. We will be able to talk to more people in more ways than ever before. The dramatic increase in our ability to communicate may be the glue that we need to hold our fragile world together. Computers also help us analyze all the information we can gather and exchange, helping us to understand the world around us. It is precisely those abilities which make computers threatening, too. Soon celebrities and politicians will not be the only ones who have public images but no private lives—it will be all of us. We must take control of the information about ourselves. We should own our personal profiles, not be bought and sold by them.

SUGGESTIONS FOR FURTHER READING

Beauchamp, Tom L. and James F. Childress. *Principles of Biomedical Ethics,* 4th ed. (Oxford, England: Oxford University Press, 1994).

Chapter 7 of this now-classic work, "Professional-Patient Relationships," addresses issues of privacy and confidentiality connected to the medical treatment of persons with the HIV-virus.

Bork, Robert. *The Tempting of America: The Political Seduction of the Law.* (New York: The Free Press, 1990).

This book contains a discussion of the *Griswold* decision. Bork claims there is no constitutional basis for a right to privacy, and he raises concerns over just how far the right recognized in *Griswold* can be taken.

Johnson, Deborah G. and Helen Nissenbaum. *Computers, Ethics and Social Values.* (Englewood Cliffs, N.J.: Prentice-Hall, 1995).

Chapter 4, "Privacy and Databases," contains twelve articles, some focusing on general philosophical questions about privacy, some on the legal dimensions of privacy, and others emphasizing privacy issues brought about by the computerized storage of information.

Johnson, Jeffrey. "Constitutional Privacy," *Law and Philosophy* 13 (May 1994), 161–193.

Johnson presents a thoughtful defense of the idea that interpreting the Constitution as containing a right to privacy is a legitimate act of interpretation.

Machamer, Peter and Barbara Boylan. "Freedom, Information and Privacy," *Business and Professional Ethics* 12 (Fall 1993), 47–68.

The authors discuss the conflicts that can arise between an individual's right to privacy and the media's claim for freedom of information, and the criteria that might be used to resolve them.

MacKinnon, Catharine A. *Toward a Feminist Theory of the State.* (Cambridge, MA: Harvard University Press, 1989).

Chapter 10, "Abortion: On Public and Private," is concerned that the legal right to privacy, which formed the basis for the decision in *Roe v. Wade,* is a right that ultimately serves to benefit men more than it does women.

Reamer, Frederic G. *AIDS and Ethics*. (New York: Columbia University Press, 1993).

Reamer provides perspectives from a variety of disciplines, including philosophy, on the question of privacy and other ethical issues involved with AIDS.

Schoeman, Ferdinand D., ed. *Philosophical Dimensions of Privacy: An Anthology* (Cambridge, England: Cambridge University Press, 1984).

This book offers a number of significant articles on privacy. Chapter 1, "Privacy: Philosophical Dimensions of the Literature," is a good analysis by Schoeman of the philosophical issues at stake in discussions of privacy and of the approaches to these issues taken by the contributors to this volume.

Simms, Michele. "Defining Privacy in Employee Health Screening Cases: Ethical Ramifications Concerning the Employee/Employer Relationship," *Journal of Business Ethics* 13 (May 1994), 315–325.

Simms looks at two court decisions involving employer drug and HIV testing and considers the impact of how the definition of privacy used by the courts impacts on the employee's interest in protecting privacy.

Spinello, Richard. *Ethical Aspects of Information Technology*. (Englewood Cliffs, NJ: Prentice-Hall, 1995).

Among other topics, this book addresses privacy issues created by the rise of information technology.

Wellman, Carl. "The Right to Privacy and Personal Autonomy." In Diana T. Meyers and Kenneth Kipnis, eds., *Philosophical Dimensions of the Constitution*. (Boulder, CO: Westview Press, 1988).

In this chapter Wellman seeks a core concept of privacy that would tie together various meanings of privacy that are involved in speaking about privacy as a right.

CREDITS

Charles R. Lawrence, III, "If He Hollers Let Him Go: Regulating Racist Speech on Campus," Duke Law Journal No. 2, 1990. Reprinted by permission.

Chapter 9

Richard D. Mohr, Invisible Minorities, Civic Rights, Democracy: Three Arguments for Gay Rights, The Philosophical Forum 17: 1-24. © 1985. Reprinted with permission.

Copyright © 1984, THE MONIST, La Salle, Illinois 61301. Reprinted by permission.

Morris B. Kaplan, Intimacy and Equality: The Question of Lesbian and Gay Marriage, The Philosophical Forum 25: 333-60. © 1994. Reprinted with permission.

Reprinted from Moral Rights in the Workplace by Gertrude Ezorsky by permission of the State University of New York Press.

Reprinted by permission of the Journal of Social Philosophy.

F.M. Christensen, "Sexual Harassment" Must Be Eliminated, Public Affairs Quarterly 8: 1-17. © 1994. Reprinted by permission.

Chapter 10

Public Domain

Rachels, James; WHY PRIVACY IS IMPORTANT, Philosophy and Public Affairs. Copyright © 1975 by Princeton University Press. Reprinted by permission of Princeton University Press.

Parent, W.A.; PRIVACY, MORALITY AND THE LAW, Philosophy and Public Affairs. Copyright © 1983 by Princeton University Press. Reprinted by permission of Princeton University Press.

David B. Resnik, Genetic Privacy in Employment, Public Affairs Quarterly 7: 47-56. © 1993. Reprinted with permission.

Grant Gillett, AIDS and Confidentiality, Journal of Applied Philosophy 4: 15-20. © 1987. Reprinted by permission of Blackwell Publishers.

Richard Bronaugh, ed. Philosophical Law Reprinted with permission of Greenwood Publishing Group, Inc., Westport, CT. © 1978.

Reprinted from Whole Earth Review, January 1985; subscriptions to WER are $20/year (4 issues) from FULCO, 30 Broad Street, Denville, NJ 07834, (800) 783-4903.